THEODORE ROOSEVELT
CYCLOPEDIA

PUBLICATIONS OF THE
ROOSEVELT MEMORIAL ASSOCIATION

The Works of Theodore Roosevelt. Memorial Edition. 24 volumes. (New York, Charles Scribner's Sons, 1923–26.)

The Works of Theodore Roosevelt. National Edition. 20 volumes. (New York, Charles Scribner's Sons, 1926.)

Hermann Hagedorn, *Roosevelt in the Bad Lands.* (Boston and New York, Houghton Mifflin Co., 1921.)

Ralph Stout (editor), *Roosevelt in the Kansas City Star; war-time editorials by Theodore Roosevelt.* (Boston and New York, Houghton Mifflin Co., 1921.)

Hermann Hagedorn (editor), *The Americanism of Theodore Roosevelt; selections from his writings and speeches.* (Boston and New York, Houghton Mifflin Co., 1923.) Edited for school use by John A. Lester.

Albert Bushnell Hart and Herbert Ronald Ferleger (editors), *Theodore Roosevelt Cyclopedia.*

IN PREPARATION

Herbert Ronald Ferleger (editor), *The Letters of Theodore Roosevelt.* (Approximately 10 volumes.)

M. Haley

Underwood

Theodore Roosevelt

THEODORE ROOSEVELT CYCLOPEDIA

Edited by
ALBERT BUSHNELL HART
Professor Emeritus, Harvard University

and

HERBERT RONALD FERLEGER
Roosevelt Memorial Association

Foreword by
WILLIAM ALLEN WHITE

ROOSEVELT MEMORIAL ASSOCIATION
ROOSEVELT HOUSE
NEW YORK CITY

COPYRIGHT, 1941, BY ROOSEVELT MEMORIAL ASSOCIATION

The selections reprinted in this book are used by permission of and special arrangement with the proprietors of their respective copyrights.

PRINTED IN THE UNITED STATES OF AMERICA
AMERICAN BOOK—STRATFORD PRESS, INC., NEW YORK

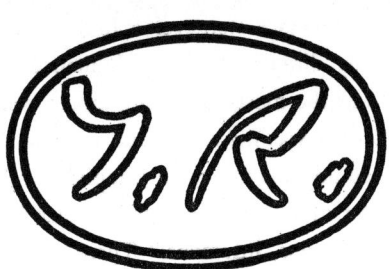

The glory of Theodore Roosevelt is that he personified the American Nation. From his earliest youth he was an American nationalist. In this faith he lived; in this faith he died; and the deeds he wrought and the words he spoke for the advancement of that faith are the unshakable foundations of his undying fame. More than any other man of his period, his character and his life typified the character and the life of the American people as a whole.—*Albert J. Beveridge.*

Roosevelt was a many-sided man and every side was like an electric battery. Such versatility, such vitality, such thoroughness, such copiousness, have rarely been united in one man. He was not only a full man, he was also a ready man and an exact man. He could bring all his vast resources of power and knowledge to bear upon a given subject instantly.—*John Burroughs.*

I met in him a man of such extraordinary power that to find a second at the same time on this globe would have been an impossibility; a man whom to associate with was a liberal education, and who could be in every way likened to radium, for warmth, force and light emanated from him and no spending of it could ever diminish his store. A man of immense interests, there was nothing in which he did not feel that there was something worthy of study; people of today, people of yesterday, animals, minerals, stones, stars, the past, the future—everything was of interest for him. He studied each thing, knew something about every subject.—*Jean J. Jusserand.*

His power to hold his own was the fruit of his omnivorous reading and almost uncanny memory. Whether the subject of the moment was political economy, the Greek drama, tropical fauna or flora, the Irish sagas, protective coloration in nature, metaphysics, the technique of football, or post-futurist painting, he was equally at home with the experts. . . . To appraise him coolly and impartially is a difficult task for those who loved him, but I have come definitely to the conclusion that of all the public men that I have known, on both sides of the Atlantic (and there are few that I have not known in the past thirty years), he stands out the greatest, and as the most potent influence for good upon the life of his generation. That influence extended far beyond the borders of his own country.—*Viscount Lee of Fareham.*

[v]

The more closely we scrutinize Theodore Roosevelt's life and the more carefully we consider his many ventures in many totally different fields of human activity, the less likely we are to challenge the assertion that his was the most interesting career ever vouchsafed to any American. . . . His style was tinglingly alive; it was masculine and vascular; and it was always the style of a gentleman and a scholar. He could puncture with a rapier and he could smash with a sledge-hammer; and if he used the latter more often than the former it was because of his consuming hatred of things "unmanly, ignominious, infamous." There was no mistaking the full intent of his words. He knew what he meant to say, and he knew how to say it with simple sincerity and with vigorous vivacity. His straightforwardness prevented his ever employing phrases that faced both ways.—*Brander Matthews.*

He did not originate great new truths, but he drove old fundamental truths into the minds and the hearts of his people so that they stuck and dominated. Old truths he insisted upon, enlarged upon, repeated over and over in many ways with quaint and interesting and attractive forms of expression, never straining for novelty or originality, but always driving, driving home the deep fundamental truths of public life, of a great self-governing democracy, the eternal truths upon which justice and liberty must depend among men. Savonarola originated no truths, nor Luther, nor Wesley, nor any of these flaming swords that cut into the consciousness of mankind with the old truths, that had been overlooked by indifference and error, wrong-heartedness and wrong-headedness. Review the roster of the few great men of history, our own history, the history of the world; and when you have finished the review, you will find that Theodore Roosevelt was the greatest teacher of the essentials of popular self-government the world has ever known. . . .

The future of our country will depend upon having men, real men of sincerity and truth, of unshakable conviction, of power, of personality, with the spirit of Justice and the fighting spirit through all the generations; and the mightiest service that can be seen today to accomplish that for our country is to make it impossible that Theodore Roosevelt, his teaching and his personality shall be forgotten. Oh, that we might have him with us now!—*Elihu Root.*

FOREWORD

HERE IN THESE PAGES is Theodore Roosevelt in his miraculous abundance, talking of labor and industry, swatting the malefactors of great wealth, laying down the principles of American foreign policy (and no one in his time did it with a sharper eye for the realities of a tough game), and trumpeting the program for a generation of progressive legislation, tossing in, incidentally, comments on adventurous living, the ancient Irish sagas and protective coloration of animals, with a side-swipe at nature-fakers and lyric tributes to landscapes in three continents which to him spelled enchantment.

Here he is again, the man who, for twenty years, made the front page a morning thriller for the readers all over the world. He wasn't always right. He could be—and was—occasionally dead wrong. Now and then he wasn't fair to an opponent, but he thought he was! At times his wide side-swipes and punches hit the wrong fellow, or hit the right fellow too hard or in the wrong place. But, by and large, generally he hit the man who ought to have been hit and defended the man who ought to have been defended; and the America that he wanted to see built was the kind of America that plain folks in Bangor or Los Angeles or Emporia would want to rear their children in.

The fact was that Theodore Roosevelt understood his time. It was a complex time that could be understood in all its aspects and its contradictions only by a man who could see around the corner —into the past through knowledge, into the future through imagination. Much has been written about the difference between a politician and a statesman, but the main difference hinges around the question of imagination. It takes imagination to see what is under your nose. For months the Wright brothers flew their contraption over the housetops of Dayton, but no one was more astonished than the good people of Dayton when the wires buzzed with the news of the flights at Kitty Hawk. They had seen but they hadn't believed, because their imaginations had been unable to conceive of human flight. A citizen will walk through a slum every day on his way to the office and it will mean nothing to him except squalor and a stench; but a statesman will see it once and make it the cradle of a social philosophy.

Theodore Roosevelt had that kind of imagination and it clarified issues which to others remained obscure, and made him able to act while others in high places were confused or paralyzed. We are beginning now to see him in perspective. He was the first American statesman of major proportions who saw and dramatized a new phase of the truth about freedom, its economic implications. For a thousand years the evolutionary path to freedom had led to a democratic ideal, realized in the Bill of Rights, in universal suffrage, in the secret ballot, in the struggle against political corruption. Theodore Roosevelt coined and gave world-wide circulation to the phrase "social and industrial justice." Here was a new turn in the path to freedom. Men began to see vaguely that political freedom, with all the significance implied in political equality, is not enough. They began to realize that in a machine age which creates vast economic surplus, the surplus creates a new problem endangering our ancient liberties.

If we allow that surplus to create in our republic permanent social classes based solely on wealth, if we permit a small group to pass down the generations an unearned, unwieldy portion of the surplus, political equality will pass. Political liberty will no longer protect men against the old tyrannies which broke the spirit of man in other days and times. All this Theodore Roosevelt saw and saw clearly. He lived for, fought for, and yearned passionately for this new vision of economic democracy. As Jefferson, a century and a quarter before, fought for the ideal of political democracy, Theodore Roosevelt, in his day, battled for economic freedom. Theodore Roosevelt did not solve the problem, but he, of all the long line of major statesmen in the millennial fight for freedom, stated the new problem, stood at the turn of the course, pointed to the present battleground. He was not all-wise. He could not chart the combat of today nor could he foresee tomorrow's victory with its blessings and its duties. But he, first of all the world's great leaders, realized and eagerly strove for the ideals of the new day.

The struggle was confused and side-tracked by the Great War. He was among the first to see that the German invasion of Belgium, which turned Europe upside down, had completely shifted the political issues in the United States also. Before we could talk about political or economic progress, he told us, we must look to our basic security. We must be ready to defend ourselves. He thundered that doctrine for two years and a half before the American people finally accepted it. In his lifetime they never did accept it more than partially. He believed in compulsory military service as a permanent policy so that we might never again be caught unarmed. We thought we knew better, and today we are back where we were in 1914.

I am glad that this *Cyclopedia* has been compiled and that the Roosevelt Memorial Association is publishing it. In the conflicts and confusions of this time we need the beacon of Theodore Roosevelt's life, of his wisdom, of his gorgeous, solid American optimism, to shine upon the struggle in which we are engaged, the very ancient struggle of men to be and to remain free from alien domination. As I turn the pages and listen again to the Colonel's thunders, I am reminded of the Old Testament prophets. He had the kind of concern for America that they had for Israel. They wanted their people to go right because, if they didn't, Jehovah would get them with various kinds of grief and ruin. Theodore Roosevelt was like that, a moral leader and a prophet above everything else, expounding the will of God and imploring his countrymen to obey it. So this book has a biblical quality. It might, in fact, without exaggeration, be called a Bible of Democracy.

Elihu Root—with whom some of us Bull Moosers were sometimes in painful disagreement—seems to me to have been right beyond dispute when, seven years after the fatal Republican convention of 1912, he wrote: "Review the roster of the few great men of history, our own history, the history of the world; and when you have finished the review, you will find that Theodore Roosevelt was the greatest teacher of the essentials of popular self-government the world has ever known." Well, here is his teaching from A to Izzard. We can't go wrong if we follow it. We are likely to go badly astray if once more we think we know better.

WILLIAM ALLEN WHITE.

Emporia, Kansas.
December 1940.

EDITORS' NOTE

WITHIN THE COVERS OF THIS BOOK is contained the essence of Theodore Roosevelt—the ideals, principles, and convictions for which he lived; the thoughts, views, and opinions he expressed on a multitude of issues. The variety of subjects represented lends added testimony to the breadth of Mr. Roosevelt's knowledge and the scope of his interests. No attempt has been made to include selections on every aspect of every topic; rather the emphasis has been placed on obtaining the most important and revealing quotations. With but two or three exceptions, in which the information is not available, each selection is dated and fully identified—whether taken from letter, speech, state paper, magazine article, or book by Theodore Roosevelt. In a like number of instances, parts of quotations have been duplicated for emphasis and to clarify other selections. The quotations have not been edited with a view toward introducing uniformity of style, form, or spelling; they were written over a period of almost half a century and since the divergences were Mr. Roosevelt's, they have been retained. However, certain obvious errors have been corrected when they interfered with the presentation of ideas.

The majority of selections have been secured from the following sources:

The Works of Theodore Roosevelt. Memorial Edition. 24 volumes. (New York, Charles Scribner's Sons, 1923–26.) Cited as *Mem. Ed.*

The Works of Theodore Roosevelt. National Edition. 20 volumes. (New York, Charles Scribner's Sons, 1926.) Cited as *Nat. Ed.*

Presidential Addresses and State Papers; European Addresses. Homeward Bound Edition. 8 volumes. (New York, The Review of Reviews Co., 1910.)

Selections from the Correspondence of Theodore Roosevelt and Henry Cabot Lodge, 1884–1918. 2 volumes. (New York, Charles Scribner's Sons, 1925.) Cited as Lodge *Letters.*

Letters from Theodore Roosevelt to Anna Roosevelt Cowles, 1870–1918. (New York, Charles Scribner's Sons, 1924.) Cited as Cowles *Letters.*

Theodore Roosevelt and His Time, shown in his own letters. By Joseph B. Bishop. 2 volumes. (New York, Charles Scribner's Sons, 1920.) Cited as Bishop.

Roosevelt in the Kansas City Star; war-time editorials by Theodore Roosevelt. Edited by Ralph Stout. (Boston and New York, Houghton Mifflin Co., 1921.)

Corinne Roosevelt Robinson, *My Brother, Theodore Roosevelt.* (New York, Charles Scribner's Sons, 1921.)

The Outlook.

An analysis of the contents of the *Memorial Edition* and the *National Edition* is presented in order to facilitate further reading and reference by those who may not have access to either of these collections but would like to consult other printings.

Memorial Edition

I. *Hunting Trips of a Ranchman.* (1885.)
"Game-Shooting in the West," Outing, 1886.
Good Hunting. (1907.)

II. *The Wilderness Hunter.* (1893.)

III. *Outdoor Pastimes of an American Hunter.* (1905.)

IV. *A Book-Lover's Holidays in the Open.* (1916.)
Ranch Life and the Hunting Trail. (1888.)

V. *African Game Trails.* (1910.)

VI. *Through the Brazilian Wilderness.* (1914.)
Papers on Natural History. (Speeches and articles in periodicals.)

VII. *The Naval War of 1812.* (1882.)

VIII. *Thomas Hart Benton.* (1887.)
Gouverneur Morris. (1888.)

IX. *Hero Tales from American History.* (1895.)
New York. (1891.)

X. *The Winning of the West.* (1889–1896.)

XI. *The Winning of the West.*

XII. *The Winning of the West.*
Men of Action. (Speeches, articles on contemporary and historical figures and events.)

XIII. *The Rough Riders.* (1899.)
Oliver Cromwell. (1900.)

XIV. Literary Essays. (Addresses, magazine articles, reviews on literature, history, books and authors.)

XV. *American Ideals.* (1897.)
The Strenuous Life. (1900.)
Realizable Ideals. (1912; lectures delivered spring 1911.)

XVI. Campaigns and Controversies. (Speeches and articles, 1882–1900.)

National Edition

I. *Hunting Trips of a Ranchman.*
Ranch Life and the Hunting Trail.

II. *The Wilderness Hunter.*
Outdoor Pastimes of an American Hunter.

III. *Outdoor Pastimes of an American Hunter.* (Concluded.)
A Book-Lover's Holidays in the Open.

IV. *African Game Trails.*

V. *Through the Brazilian Wilderness.*
Papers on Natural History.

VI. *The Naval War of 1812.*

VII. *Thomas Hart Benton.*
Gouverneur Morris.

VIII. *The Winning of the West.*

IX. *The Winning of the West.*

X. *Hero Tales from American History.*
Oliver Cromwell.
New York.

XI. *The Rough Riders.*
Men of Action.

XII. Literary Essays.

XIII. *American Ideals.*
The Strenuous Life.
Realizable Ideals.

XIV. Campaigns and Controversies.

XV. State Papers as Governor and President.

XVI. American Problems.

XVII. Social Justice and Popular Rule.

XVIII. America and the World War.
Fear God and Take Your Own Part.

Memorial Edition	National Edition
XVII. State Papers as Governor and President.	XIX. *The Foes of Our Own Household. The Great Adventure. Letters to His Children.*
XVIII. American Problems. (Miscellaneous addresses, etc.)	XX. *Autobiography.*
XIX. Social Justice and Popular Rule. (The Progressive Movement, 1910–1916.)	
XX. *America and the World War.* (1915.) *Fear God and Take Your Own Part.* (1916.)	
XXI. *The Foes of Our Own Household.* (1917.) *The Great Adventure.* (1918.) *Letters to His Children.*	
XXII. *Autobiography.* (1913.)	
XXIII–XXIV. *Theodore Roosevelt and His Time,* by Joseph B. Bishop.	

More than five hundred other works dealing with Theodore Roosevelt, his time and his contemporaries were consulted and quotations taken from about one-third of that number. In each case the excerpt is identified and the source indicated. The editors wish to acknowledge their indebtedness to the Roosevelt Estate; Charles Scribner's Sons; Doubleday, Doran and Company; D. Appleton-Century Company; G. P. Putnam's Sons; The Macmillan Company; Longmans, Green and Company; Harper and Brothers; Dodd, Mead and Company; Little, Brown and Company; Harcourt, Brace and Company; Farrar and Rinehart; Houghton Mifflin Company, as well as to the other publishers noted in the text.

A. B. H.
H. R. F.

November 1940.

CHRONOLOGY

1858	*October 27.* Born at 28 East Twentieth Street, New York City.	1904	*November 8.* Elected President over Alton B. Parker, the Democratic nominee.
1880	*June 30.* Graduates from Harvard University. *October 27.* Marries Alice Hathaway Lee.	1905	*March 4.* Inaugurated as President.
		1909	*March 4.* Roosevelt retires from the Presidency, being succeeded by William Howard Taft. *March 23.* Sails for Africa.
1882–84	Member of the New York State Assembly.		
1883	*September.* Establishes himself as a ranchman in western Dakota.	1909–10	Hunting in Central Africa.
		1910	*March 14.* Arrives at Khartum. *April-June.* Travels in Europe. *June 18.* Returns to New York. Publishes *The New Nationalism*.
1884	*February 14.* Death of his mother and his wife. *June.* Delegate to the Republican National Convention.		
		1912	*February 25.* Announces candidacy for the Republican nomination for President. *June.* Defeated at the Republican National Convention. *August 7.* Nominated for President by the Progressive Party. *October 14.* Shot at Milwaukee. *November 5.* Defeated by Woodrow Wilson.
1884–86	Ranchman in the Bad Lands of Dakota.		
1886	*November.* Candidate for Mayor of New York. Defeated by Abram S. Hewitt. *December 2.* Marries Edith Kermit Carow, in London.		
1889–95	United States Civil Service Commissioner.	1913–14	*Winter.* In the Brazilian wilderness; explores the River of Doubt.
1895–97	President of the Police Commission of the City of New York.	1915	*May.* Libel suit, William Barnes vs. Theodore Roosevelt; decided in favor of Roosevelt.
1897–98	Assistant Secretary of the Navy.		
1898	*May.* Resigns as Assistant Secretary to become Lieutenant-Colonel of the First United States Volunteer Cavalry (the Rough Riders). *November 8.* Elected Governor of New York.	1916	*June.* Nominated for President by the Progressive Party; refuses the nomination and gives his support to the Republican candidate, Charles E. Hughes.
1899	*January 2.* Takes office as Governor.	1917	*February.* Requests permission of President Wilson to raise and equip a division of volunteers for service in France. *May.* Request finally refused.
1900	*June 21.* Nominated for Vice-President by the Republican Party.		
1901	*March 4.* Takes office as Vice-President. *September 14.* President McKinley dies as the result of an assassin's bullet; Roosevelt becomes twenty-sixth President of the United States.	1918	*July.* Death of Quentin Roosevelt in France. Roosevelt refuses Republican nomination for Governor of New York.
		1919	*January 6.* Death of Theodore Roosevelt at Oyster Bay, N. Y.

THEODORE ROOSEVELT
CYCLOPEDIA

THEODORE ROOSEVELT CYCLOPEDIA

A

ABBEY THEATRE. In the Abbey Theatre Lady Gregory and those associated with her . . . have not only made an extraordinary contribution to the sum of Irish literary and artistic achievement, but have done more for the drama than has been accomplished in any other nation of recent years. England, Australia, South Africa, Hungary, and Germany are all now seeking to profit by this unique achievement. The Abbey Theatre is one of the healthiest signs of the revival of the ancient Irish spirit which has been so marked a feature of the world's progress during the present generation; and, like every healthy movement of the kind, it has been thoroughly national and has developed on its own lines, refusing merely to copy what has been outworn. It is especially noteworthy, and is a proof of the general Irish awakening, that this vigorous expression of Irish life, so honorable to the Irish people, should represent the combined work of so many different persons, and not that of only one person, whose activity might be merely sporadic and fortuitous. (*Outlook,* December 16, 1911.) *Mem. Ed.* XIV, 402; *Nat. Ed.* XII, 317.

ABBOTT, LYMAN. Dr. Abbott is one of those men whose work and life give strength to all who believe in this country, and hearten them in the effort to strive after better things. He has known how to combine to a very unusual degree a series of qualities, all of them necessary but by no means all often developed in the same individual. Exactly as in his writings he stands fearlessly for the rights of the laboring man and yet is equally fearless in his denunciation of any kind of mob violence or of attack on property; exactly as he unsparingly assails every corrupt politician and yet avoids the pit of mere slanderous accusation against all men in public life; so in his private character he combines a good-natured evenness of temper with the power of flaming wrath against unrighteousness, insistence upon adherence to a high ideal with ready recognition of the need of practical methods in the achievement of that ideal, and a serene and lofty hopefulness and belief in the future with a keen appreciation of all that is low, base, cruel, evil, and therefore mercilessly to be warred against in the present. (To Hamilton Wright Mabie, December 6, 1905.) *Outlook,* December 18, 1905, p. 16.

ABOLITIONISTS. Owing to a variety of causes, the Abolitionists have received an immense amount of hysterical praise, which they do not deserve, and have been credited with deeds done by other men, whom they in reality hampered and opposed rather than aided. After 1840 the professed Abolitionists formed but a small and comparatively unimportant portion of the forces that were working towards the restriction and ultimate destruction of slavery; and much of what they did was positively harmful to the cause for which they were fighting. Those of their number who considered the Constitution as a league with death and hell, and who therefore advocated a dissolution of the Union, acted as rationally as would anti-polygamists nowadays if, to show their disapproval of Mormonism, they should advocate that Utah should be allowed to form a separate nation. The only hope of ultimately suppressing slavery lay in the preservation of the Union, and every Abolitionist who argued or signed a petition for its dissolution was doing as much to perpetuate the evil he complained of as if he had been a slave-holder. (1887.) *Mem. Ed.* VIII, 216; *Nat. Ed.* VII, 187.

ABOLITIONISTS — CHARACTER AND INFLUENCE OF. Their courage, and for the most part their sincerity, cannot be too highly spoken of, but their share in abolishing slavery was far less than has commonly been represented; any single non-abolitionist politician, like Lincoln or Seward, did more than all the professional Abolitionists combined really to bring about its destruction. . . . Many of their leaders possessed no good qualities beyond their fearlessness and truth—qualities that were also possessed by the Southern fire-eaters. They belonged to that class of men that is always engaged in some agitation or other; only it happened that in this particular agitation they were right. (1887.) *Mem. Ed.* VIII, 118; *Nat. Ed.* VII, 103.

ABOLITIONISTS. *See also* SLAVERY.

ACCIDENT INSURANCE. *See* SOCIAL INSURANCE; WORKMEN'S COMPENSATION.

ACHIEVEMENT. *See* REWARDS.

ACTION. It is true of the Nation, as of the individual, that the greatest doer must also be a great dreamer. Of course, if the dream is not followed by action, then it is a bubble; it has merely served to divert the man from doing something. But great action, action that is really great, can not take place if the man has it not in his brain to think great thoughts, to dream great dreams. (At Clark University, Worcester, Mass., June 21, 1905.) *Presidential Addresses and State Papers* IV, 392.

———. I hate a man who never does anything. Why, I'd rather do something and get it wrong, and then apologize, than to do nothing. (In conversation with Joseph De Camp, autumn 1908.) Bradley Gilman, *Roosevelt: the Happy Warrior*. (Little, Brown, & Co., Boston, 1921), p. 265.

ACTION AND CRITICISM. The man who really counts in the world is the doer, not the mere critic—the man who actually does the work, even if roughly and imperfectly, not the man who only talks or writes about how it ought to be done. (1891.) *Mem. Ed.* IX, 420; *Nat. Ed.* X, 534.

———. [A man] can accomplish a certain amount by criticism if his criticism is intelligent and honest, but he can of course accomplish infinitely more by action. *Harvard Graduates' Magazine,* October 1892, p. 4.

———. Criticism is necessary and useful; it is often indispensable; but it can never take the place of action, or be even a poor substitute for it. . . . It is the doer of deeds who actually counts in the battle for life, and not the man who looks on and says how the fight ought to be fought, without himself sharing the stress and the danger. (*Atlantic Monthly,* August 1894.) *Mem. Ed.* XV, 53; *Nat. Ed.* XIII, 39.

———. It is not the critic who counts; not the man who points out how the strong man stumbles, or where the doer of deeds could have done them better. The credit belongs to the man who is actually in the arena, whose face is marred by dust and sweat and blood; who strives valiantly; who errs, and comes short again and again, because there is no effort without error and shortcoming; but who does actually strive to do the deeds; who knows the great enthusiasms, the great devotions; who spends himself in a worthy cause; who at the best knows in the end the triumph of high achievement, and who at the worst, if he fails, at least fails while daring greatly, so that his place shall never be with those cold and timid souls who know neither victory nor defeat. (At the Sorbonne, Paris, April 23, 1910.) *Mem. Ed.* XV, 354; *Nat. Ed.* XIII, 510.

ACTION AND RHETORIC. Rhetoric is a poor substitute for action, and we have trusted only to rhetoric. If we are really to be a great nation, we must not merely talk big; we must act big. And our actions have been very, very small! (*Metropolitan,* September 1917.) *Mem. Ed.* XXI, 21; *Nat. Ed.* XIX, 18.

ACTION. *See also* BOASTING; CRITICISM; DEEDS; ORATORY; PRACTICALITY.

ADDAMS, JANE. *See* MARRIAGE.

ADMINISTRATION. Good legislation does not secure good government, which can come only through a good administration. (At Merchants' Association Dinner, New York City, May 25, 1900.) *Mem. Ed.* XVI, 506.

———.Wise legislation is vitally important, but honest administration is even more important. (Before Republican National Convention, Phila., June 21, 1900.) *Mem. Ed.* XVI, 527; *Nat. Ed.* XIV, 344.

ADMINISTRATION. *See also* GOVERNMENT; LAWS; LEGISLATION.

ADULTERATION OF FOODS. *See* PURE FOOD LAW.

ADVENTURE—QUALIFICATIONS FOR. The man should have youth and strength who seeks adventure in the wide, waste spaces of the earth, in the marshes, and among the vast mountain masses, in the northern forests, amid the steaming jungles of the tropics, or on the deserts of sand or of snow. He must long greatly for the lonely winds that blow across the wilderness, and for sunrise and sunset over the rim of the empty world. His heart must thrill for the saddle and not for the hearthstone. He must be helmsman and chief, the cragsman, the rifleman, the boat steerer. He must be the wielder of axe and of paddle, the rider of fiery horses, the master of the craft that leaps through white water. His eye must be true and quick, his hand steady and strong. His heart must never fail nor his head grow bewildered, whether he face brute and human foes, or the frowning strength of hostile nature, or the awful fear that grips those who are lost in trackless lands. (1916.) *Mem. Ed.* IV, xxi; *Nat. Ed.* III, 181.

ADVENTURER—DELIGHTS OF THE. The grandest scenery of the world is his to look at if he chooses; and he can witness the strange ways of tribes who have survived into an alien age from an immemorial past, tribes whose priests dance in honor of the serpent and worship the spirits of the wolf and the bear. Far and wide, all the continents are open to him as they never were to any of his forefathers; the Nile and the Paraguay are easy of access, and the border-land between savagery and civilization; and the veil of the past has been lifted so that he can dimly see how, in time immeasurably remote, his ancestors—no less remote—led furtive lives among uncouth and terrible beasts, whose kind has perished utterly from the face of the earth. He will take books with him as he journeys; for the keenest enjoyment of the wilderness is reserved for him who enjoys also the garnered wisdom of the present and the past. He will take pleasure in the companionship of the men of the open. . . .

The beauty and charm of the wilderness are his for the asking, for the edges of the wilderness lie close beside the beaten roads of the present travel. He can see the red splendor of desert sunsets, and the unearthly glory of the afterglow on the battlements of desolate mountains. In sapphire gulfs of ocean he can visit islets, above which the wings of myriads of seafowl make a kind of shifting cuneiform script in the air. He can ride along the brink of the stupendous cliff-walled canyon, where eagles soar below him, and the cougars make their lairs on the ledges and harry the big-horned sheep. He can journey through the northern forests, the home of the giant moose, the forests of fragrant and murmuring life in summer, the iron-bound and melancholy forests of winter.

The joy of living is his who has the heart to demand it. (1916.) *Mem. Ed.* IV, xxii; *Nat. Ed.* III, 182.

ADVENTURE; ADVENTURER. *See also* EXPLORATION; HUNTER; HUNTING; MOUNTAIN CLIMBING; SPORTS.

AFRICA. "I speak of Africa and golden joys"; the joy of wandering through lonely lands; the joy of hunting the mighty and terrible lords of the wilderness, the cunning, the wary, and the grim.

There are mountain peaks whose snows are dazzling under the equatorial sun; swamps where the slime oozes and bubbles and festers in the steaming heat; lakes like seas; skies that burn above deserts where the iron desolation is shrouded from view by the wavering mockery of the mirage; vast grassy plains where palms and thorn-trees fringe the dwindling streams; mighty rivers rushing out of the heart of the continent through the sadness of endless marshes; forests of gorgeous beauty, where death broods in the dark and silent depths.

There are regions as healthy as the northland; and other regions, radiant with bright-hued flowers, birds, and butterflies, odorous with sweet and heavy scents, but treacherous in their beauty, and sinister to human life. . . .

The dark-skinned races that live in the land vary widely. Some are warlike, cattle-owning nomads; some till the soil and live in thatched huts shaped like bee-hives; some are fisherfolk; some are ape-like, naked savages, who dwell in the woods and prey on creatures not much wilder or lower than themselves. (1910.) *Mem. Ed.* V, xxv; *Nat. Ed.* IV, xxiii.

——————. Equatorial Africa is in most places none too healthy a place for the white man, and he must care for himself as he would scorn to do in the lands of pine and birch and frosty weather. Camping in the Rockies or the North woods can with advantage be combined with "roughing it"; and the early pioneers of the West, the explorers, prospectors, and hunters, who always roughed it, were as hardy as bears, and lived to a hale old age, if Indians and accidents permitted. But in tropic Africa a lamentable proportion of the early explorers paid in health or life for the hardships they endured; and throughout most of the country no man can long rough it, in the Western and Northern sense, with impunity. (1910.) *Mem. Ed.* V, 20; *Nat. Ed.* IV, 17.

——————. The widely spread rule of a strong European race in lands like Africa gives, as one incident thereof, the chance for nascent cultures, nascent semicivilizations, to develop without fear of being overwhelmed in the surrounding gulfs of savagery; and this aside from the direct stimulus to development conferred by the consciously and unconsciously exercised influence of the white man, wherein there is much of evil, but much more of ultimate good. In any region of wide-spread savagery, the chances for the growth of each self-produced civilization are necessarily small, because each little centre of effort toward this end is always exposed to destruction from the neighboring masses of pure savagery; and therefore progress is often immensely accelerated by outside invasion and control. In Africa the control and guidance is needed as much in the things of the spirit as in the things of the body. (1910.) *Mem. Ed.* V, 362-363; *Nat. Ed.* IV, 312.

──────────. As a field sure to yield valuable results to the student of early or primitive man, Africa holds a rank second to no other. Its vast extent, its amazing diversity, and the wide physical and cultural differences among its countless inhabitants, all conspire to make this great continent an inexhaustible source of archaeological and ethnographic interest. The need for scientific research in Africa is in proportion to the complexity and numbers of the problems presented by so great a field. . . .

All kinds of problems await the archaeological explorer and investigator in Africa. They range from the existence of a blond element in the Berber stock, and the existence of a possible similar element among the ancient Libyan invaders of Egypt, to the questions raised by the strange architecture of the cities southwest of the Sahara, such as Timbuktû. They include the ethnic changes due to infiltration, among the agricultural East African and Middle African negroes, of a northern pastoral type with very distinct physical and cultural characteristics. Isolated finds of stone implements in Somaliland, on the Upper Nile, in the Congo basin, and along the Zambesi, suggest still other archaeological questions regarding the early history of man in Africa. The tasks which await the ethnologist are of no less importance. The problems which at the present day are presented by the primitive tribes still existing in Africa are legion, be they those concerning low savages such as the Pigmies of the great central forests, or those concerning the relatively advanced Berbers and Abyssinians. They include the difficult but important problems of ethnic drift and change, of the small linguistic "islands" with which Africa abounds, and of great racial migrations. (Introduction, dated August 10, 1916.) *Harvard African Studies I, Varia Africana I.* (Peabody Museum, Cambridge, Mass., 1917.)

AFRICA—CONQUEST OF. There have been very dark spots in the European conquest and control of Africa; but on the whole the African regions which during the past century have seen the greatest cruelty, degradation, and suffering, the greatest diminution of population, are those where native control has been unchecked. The advance has been made in the regions that have been under European control or influence; that have been profoundly influenced by European administrators, and by European and American missionaries. Of course the best that can happen to any people that has not already a high civilization of its own is to assimilate and profit by American or European ideas, the ideas of civilization and Christianity, without submitting to alien control; but such control, in spite of all its defects, is in a very large number of cases the prerequisite condition to the moral and material advance of the peoples who dwell in the darker corners of the earth. Where the control is exercised brutally; where it is made use of merely to exploit the natives, without regard to their physical or moral well-being; it should be unsparingly criticised, and there should be resolute insistence on amendment and reform. But we must not, because of occasional wrong-doing, blind ourselves to the fact that on the whole the white administrator and the Christian missionary have exercised a profound and wholesome influence for good in savage regions. (At celebration of Methodist Episcopal Church, Washington, January 18, 1909.) *Mem. Ed.* XVIII, 343-344; *Nat. Ed.* XVI, 260-261.

AFRICA—FUTURE OF. The twentieth century will see and is now seeing the transformation of Africa into a new world. Within a few years its vast domain has been partitioned among various European nations. These nations are expending enormous sums of money and utilizing their best statesmanship and colonizing abilities in the development of colonial empires of wide extent and extraordinary material possibilities. Steamship-lines encircle the continent. A continental system of railways and of lake and river steamboats will soon extend northward from Cape Town six thousand miles to Cairo, while branch lines will unite the east and west coasts at several points. The latest results of science are being utilized in mining and agriculture, while scholarly experts in different centres of Europe are studying the questions of native languages and religions, as well as the best methods of advancing civilization among the many millions of native peoples. The wealth of the commerce which will be developed cannot be estimated. The white man rules; but there is only one white man on the continent to one hundred others, who are either barbaric black heathen or fanatical Mohammedans.

Self-interest and competition will, I believe, unite in making the governments fair to the people, and the indomitable energy of the adventurous settlers and the wealth of the nations behind them will result in exploiting the vast commercial resources of the continents. (At celebration of Methodist Episcopal Church, Washington, January 18, 1909.) *Mem. Ed.* XVIII, 351-352; *Nat. Ed.* XVI, 267.

AFRICA, EAST. In the highlands of British East Africa it is utterly impossible for a stranger to realize that he is under the equator; the climate is delightful and healthy. It is a white man's country, a country which should be filled with white settlers; and no place could be more attractive for visitors. There is no more danger to health incident to an ordinary trip to East Africa than there is to an ordinary trip to the Riviera. Of course, if one goes on a hunting trip there is always a certain amount of risk, including the risk of fever, just as there would be if a man camped out in some of the Italian marshes. But the ordinary visitor need have no more fear of his health than if he were travelling in Italy, and it is hard to imagine a trip better worth making than the trip from Mombasa to Nairobi and on to the Victoria Nyanza. (1910.) *Mem. Ed.* V, 123; *Nat. Ed.* IV, 106-107.

AFRICA, EAST—FRONTIER CONDITIONS IN. No new country is a place for weaklings; but the right kind of man, the settler who makes a success in similar parts of our own West, can do well in East Africa; while a man with money can undoubtedly do very well indeed; and incidentally both men will be leading their lives under conditions peculiarly attractive to a certain kind of spirit. It means hard work, of course; but success generally does imply hard work. (1910.) *Mem. Ed.* V, 32; *Nat. Ed.* IV, 28.

AFRICA. *See also* HUNTING; IMPERIALISM; UGANDA; WILDERNESS.

AFRICAN NATIVES. The porters are strong, patient, good-humored savages, with something childlike about them that makes one really fond of them. Of course, like all savages and most children, they have their limitations, and in dealing with them firmness is even more necessary than kindness; but the man is a poor creature who does not treat them with kindness also, and I am rather sorry for him if he does not grow to feel for them, and to make them in return feel for him, a real and friendly liking. They are subject to gusts of passion, and they are now and then guilty of grave misdeeds and shortcomings; sometimes for no conceivable reason, at least from the white man's standpoint. But they are generally cheerful, and when cheerful are always amusing; and they work hard, if the white man is able to combine tact and consideration with that insistence on the performance of duty and lack of which they despise as weakness. (1910.) *Mem. Ed.* V, 81; *Nat. Ed.* IV, 70.

AGRICULTURE — BROADER PROBLEMS OF. Our attention has been concentrated almost exclusively on getting better farming. In the beginning this was unquestionably the right thing to do. The farmer must first of all grow good crops in order to support himself and his family. But when this has been secured, the effort for better farming should cease to stand alone, and should be accompanied by the effort for better business and better living on the farm. It is at least as important that the farmer should get the largest possible return in money, comfort, and social advantages from the crops he grows, as that he should get the largest possible return in crops from land he farms. Agriculture is not the whole of country life. The great rural interests are human interests, and good crops are of little value to the farmer unless they open the door to a good kind of life on the farm. (Letter of appointment to Country Life Commission, August 1908.) *Mem. Ed.* XXII, 471; *Nat. Ed.* XX, 405.

AGRICULTURE — DEPARTMENT OF. The Department of Agriculture devotes its whole energy to working for the welfare of farmers and stock growers. In every section of our country it aids them in their constantly increasing search for a better agricultural education. It helps not only them, but all the nation, in seeing that our exports of meats have clean bills of health, and that there is rigid inspection of all meats that enter into interstate commerce. . . .

The Department of Agriculture has been helping our fruit men to establish markets abroad by studying methods of fruit preservation through refrigeration and through methods of handling and packing. . . .

Moreover, the Department has taken the lead in the effort to prevent the deforestation of the country. Where there are forests we seek to preserve them; and on the once treeless plains and the prairies we are doing our best to foster the habit of tree planting among our people. (At Sioux Falls, S. D., April 6, 1903.) *Presidential Addresses and State Papers* I, 303-305.

AGRICULTURE — GOVERNMENT AID TO. I am glad to say that in many sections of our country there has been an extraordinary

[5]

revival of recent years in intelligent interest in and work for those who live in the open country. In this movement the lead must be taken by the farmers themselves; but our people as a whole, through their governmental agencies, should back the farmers. . . .

The government must co-operate with the farmer to make the farm more productive. There must be no skinning of the soil. The farm should be left to the farmer's son in better, and not worse, condition because of its cultivation. Moreover, every invention and improvement, every discovery and economy, should be at the service of the farmer in the work of production. (Before Progressive National Convention, Chicago, August 6, 1912.) *Mem. Ed.* XIX, 377; *Nat. Ed.* XVII, 270.

AGRICULTURE—IMPORTANCE OF. We cannot permanently shape our course right on any international issue unless we are sound on the domestic issues; and this farm movement is the fundamental social issue—the one issue which is even more basic than the relations of capitalist and working man. The farm industry cannot stop; the world is never more than a year from starvation; this great war has immensely increased the cost of living without commensurately improving the condition of the men who produce the things on which we live. (1917.) *Mem. Ed.* XXI, 111; *Nat. Ed.* XIX, 113.

──────────. To improve our system of agriculture seems to me the most urgent of the tasks which lie before us. But it can not, in my judgment, be effected by measures which touch only the material and technical side of the subject; the whole business and life of the farmer must also be taken into account. . . .

I warn my countrymen that the great recent progress made in city life is not a full measure of our civilization; for our civilization rests at bottom on the wholesomeness, the attractiveness, and the completeness, as well as the prosperity, of life in the country. The men and women on the farms stand for what is fundamentally best and most needed in our American life. Upon the development of country life rests ultimately our ability, by methods of farming requiring the highest intelligence, to continue to feed and clothe the hungry nations; to supply the city with fresh blood, clean bodies, and clear brains that can endure the terrific strain of modern life; we need the development of men in the open country, who will be in the future, as in the past, the stay and strength of the nation in time of war, and its guiding and controlling spirit in time of peace. *Special Message from the President of the United States transmitting the report of the Country Life Commission, February 9, 1909.* (Washington, 1909), pp. 8-9.

AGRICULTURE—NEEDS OF. The elimination of the middleman by agricultural exchanges and by the use of improved business methods generally, the development of good roads, the reclamation of arid lands and swamplands, the improvement in the productivity of farms, the encouragement of all agencies which tend to bring people back to the soil and to make country life more interesting as well as more profitable—all these movements will help not only the farmer but the man who consumes the farmer's products. (Before Progressive National Convention, Chicago, August 6, 1912.) *Mem. Ed.* XIX, 399; *Nat. Ed.* XVII, 289.

AGRICULTURE, SCIENTIFIC. Nothing in the way of scientific work can ever take the place of business management on a farm. We ought all of us to teach ourselves as much as possible; but we can also all of us learn from others; and the farmer can best learn how to manage his farm even better than he now does by practice, under intelligent supervision, on his own soil in such way as to increase his income. . . . But much has been accomplished by the growth of what is broadly designated as agricultural science. . . . Much more can be accomplished in the future. . . . It is probably one of our faults as a nation that we are too impatient to wait a sufficient length of time to accomplish the best results; and in agriculture effective research often, although not always, involves slow and long-continued effort if the results are to be trustworthy. While applied science in agriculture as elsewhere must be judged largely from the standpoint of its actual return in dollars, yet the farmers, no more than anyone else, can afford to ignore the large results that can be enjoyed because of broader knowledge. The farmer must prepare for using the knowledge that can be obtained through agricultural colleges by insisting upon a constantly more practical curriculum in the schools in which his children are taught. He must not lose his independence, his initiative, his rugged self-sufficiency; and yet he must learn to work in the heartiest cooperation with his fellows. (At semicentennial celebration, founding of agricultural colleges; Lansing, Mich., May 31, 1907.) *Mem. Ed.* XVIII, 179; *Nat. Ed.* XVI, 135.

AGRICULTURE AND THE TARIFF. Agriculture is now, as it always has been, the basis of civilization. The six million farms of the United States, operated by men who, as a class, are steadfast, singleminded, and industrious, form the basis of all the other achievements of the American people and are more fruitful than all their other resources. The men on those six million farms receive from the protective tariff what they most need, and that is the best of all possible markets. All other classes depend upon the farmer, but the farmer in turn depends upon the market they furnish him for his produce. . . . American farmers have prospered because the growth of their market has kept pace with the growth of their farms. The additional market continually furnished for agricultural products by domestic manufacturers has been far in excess of the outlet to other lands. An export trade in farm products is necessary to dispose of our surplus; and the export trade of our farmers, both in animal products and in plant products, has very largely increased. Without the enlarged home market to keep this surplus down, we should have to reduce production or else feed the world at less than the cost of production. (Letter accepting Republican nomination for President, September 12, 1904.) *Mem. Ed.* XVIII, 522-523; *Nat. Ed.* XVI, 392-393.

AGRICULTURE. *See also* COUNTRY LIFE COMMISSION; FARM; FARMING.

AGUINALDO. *See* IMPERIALISM; PHILIPPINES.

AIRPLANES. *See* AVIATION.

ALASKA. Some form of local self-government should be provided, as simple and inexpensive as possible; it is impossible for the Congress to devote the necessary time to all the little details of necessary Alaskan legislation. Road-building and railway-building should be encouraged. The governor of Alaska should be given an ample appropriation wherewith to organize a force to preserve the public peace. Whiskey-selling to the natives should be made a felony. The coal-land laws should be changed so as to meet the peculiar needs of the Territory. . . . There should be another judicial division established. As early as possible lighthouses and buoys should be established as aids to navigation. (Seventh Annual Message, Washington, December 3, 1907.) *Mem. Ed.* XVII, 535-536; *Nat. Ed.* XV, 456.

―――――. Alaska should be developed at once, but in the interest of the actual settler. In Alaska the government has an opportunity of starting in what is almost a fresh field to work out various problems by actual experiment. The government should at once construct, own, and operate the railways in Alaska. The government should keep the fee of all the coal-fields and allow them to be operated by lessees with the conditions in the lease that non-use shall operate as a forfeit. Telegraph-lines should be operated as the railways are. Moreover, it would be well in Alaska to try a system of land taxation which will, so far as possible, remove all the burdens from those who actually use the land, whether for building or for agricultural purposes, and will operate against any man who holds the land for speculation, or derives an income from it based, not on his own exertions, but on the increase in value due to activities not his own. There is very real need that this nation shall seriously prepare itself for the task of remedying social injustice and meeting social problems by well-considered governmental effort; and the best preparation for such wise action is to test by actual experiment under favorable conditions the devices which we have reason to believe will work well, but which it is difficult to apply in old settled communities without preliminary experiment. (Before Progressive National Convention, Chicago, August 6, 1912.) *Mem. Ed.* XIX, 406; *Nat. Ed.* XVII, 294.

ALASKA―FUTURE OF. Alaska has interests of vital importance not merely to her but to the entire Union. Alaska contains a territory which will within this century support as large a population as the combined Scandinavian countries of Europe; those countries from which has sprung as wonderful a race as ever imprinted its characteristics upon the history of civilization. Exactly as the Scandinavian peoples have left their mark upon the entire history of Europe, so we shall see Alaska with its mines, its lumber, its fisheries, with its possibilities in agriculture and stock-raising, with its possibilities of commercial command, with the tremendous development that is going on within it even now, produce as hard and vigorous a people as any portion of North America. (At Seattle, Wash., May 23, 1903.) *Presidential Addresses and State Papers* II, 428-429.

ALASKAN BOUNDARY DISPUTE. The treaty of 1825 between Russia and England was undoubtedly intended to cut off England, which owned the Hinterland, from access to the sea. The word *lisière* used in the treaty means the strip of territory bordering all the navigable water of that portion of the Alaskan coast affected by the treaty, and this strip of territory is American of course. Equally of course in interpreting the treaty a prime consideration is the way in which all authorities interpreted it for the sixty years immediately succeeding its adoption. There is entire room for discussion and judicial and impartial agreement as to the exact boundary in any given locality—that is as to whether in such locality the boundary is to be pushed back ten marine leagues, or whether there is in actual fact nearer the coast a mountain chain which can be considered as running parallel to it.

In the principle involved there will of course be no compromise. The question is not in my judgment one in which it is possible for a moment to consider a reconciling of conflicting claims by mutual concessions. It is to determine whether the theory upon which Russia uniformly treated the boundary during her entire period of possession, upon which the United States has uniformly treated it ever since it acquired the territory, and upon which England uniformly treated it for over sixty years after the treaty was adopted, and according to which all the English as distinguished from the Canadian cartographers have since continued to treat it, is right in its entirety or wrong in its entirety. (To Elihu Root, Henry Cabot Lodge and George Turner, members of the Alaskan Boundary Tribunal, March 25, 1903.) Lodge *Letters* II, 5.

ALASKAN BOUNDARY DISPUTE—SETTLEMENT OF. The result is satisfactory in every way. It is of great material advantage to our people in the far Northwest. It has removed from the field of discussion and possible danger a question liable to become more acutely accentuated with each passing year. Finally, it has furnished a signal proof of the fairness and good-will with which two friendly nations can approach and determine issues involving national sovereignty and by their nature incapable of submission to a third power for adjudication.

The award is self-executing on the vital points. To make it effective as regards the others it only remains for the two governments to appoint, each on its own behalf, one or more scientific experts, who shall, with all convenient speed, proceed together to lay down the boundary-line in accordance with the decision of the majority of the tribunal. (Third Annual Message, Washington, December 7, 1903.) *Mem. Ed.* XVII, 212-213; *Nat. Ed.* XV, 182-183.

ALDRICH BILL. *See* BANKING.

ALGECIRAS CONFERENCE. [One] important achievement of my administration at least so far as foreign affairs were concerned, was the decisive part played by the United States at the Algeciras Conference of 1906. This was held against the wishes of France, on the insistence of the Kaiser, who was pursuing a dog-in-the-manger policy by supporting the Sultan of Morocco in his resistance to French aggressions. The Conference was faced with the delicate task of reconciling French claims to paramountcy in the Shereefian Empire with the German demand for the open door. The conflicting interests of the two countries soon created an impasse which promised to end in war. Henry White, my representative at the Conference, communicated the situation to me by cable. I sent for the French and German ambassadors and on a couple of those little White House cards jotted down the terms on which I believed that an amicable understanding could be arrived at. The ambassadors immediately communicated my suggestions to their governments and the Conference finally worked out a settlement of the dangerous Moroccan question based on the formula I had outlined.

The Kaiser, for all his blustering, did not want war with France at that time, and when he found himself on the verge of it he became frightened. He realized that he had gone too far and he was mighty glad to have me show him a way in which he could extricate himself without losing face. He was so pleased with my formula that he wrote me he should keep it by him, just as I had written it, and always use it in settling any difficulty with France in the future. (In conversation with Mr. Powell aboard *Hamburg*, March 1909.) E. Alexander Powell, *Yonder Lies Adventure!* (Macmillan Co., N. Y., 1932), pp. 315-316.

ALGECIRAS CONFERENCE. *See also* JUSSERAND, J. J.

ALIENS—TREATMENT OF. Special legislation should deal with the aliens who do not come here to be made citizens. But the alien who comes here intending to become a citizen should be helped in every way to advance himself, should be removed from every possible disadvantage, and in return should be required, under penalty of being sent back to the country from which he came, to prove that he is in good faith fitting himself to be an American citizen. We should set a high standard, and insist on men reaching it; but if they do reach it we should treat them as on a full equality with ourselves. (Before Knights of Columbus, New York City, October 12, 1915.) *Mem. Ed.* XX, 465; *Nat. Ed.* XVIII, 399.

ALIENS IN KEY POSITIONS. We cannot afford to leave American mines, munition plants, and general resources in the hands of alien workmen, alien to America and even likely to be made hostile to America by machinations such as have recently been provided in the case of . . . foreign embassies in Washington. We cannot afford to run the risk of having in time of war men working on our railways or working in our munition plants who would in the name of duty to their own foreign countries bring destruction to us. (Before Knights of Columbus, New York City, October 12, 1915.) *Mem. Ed.* XX, 469; *Nat. Ed.* XVIII, 403.

ALIENS. *See also* AMERICAN PEOPLE; AMERICANIZATION; CITIZENSHIP; IMMIGRANTS.

ALLEGIANCE. We can have no "fifty-fifty" allegiance in this country. Either a man is an American and nothing else, or he is not an American at all. We are akin by blood and descent to most of the nations of Europe; but we are separate from all of them; we are a new and distinct nation, and we are bound always to give our whole-hearted and undivided loyalty to our own flag, and in any international crisis to treat each and every foreign nation purely according to its conduct in that crisis. (New York *Times*, September 10, 1917.) *Mem. Ed.* XXI, 38; *Nat. Ed.* XIX, 33.

ALLEGIANCE, UNDIVIDED. There are two demands upon the spirit of Americanism, of nationalism. Each must be met. Each is essential. Each is vital, if we are to be a great and proud nation.

The first is that we shall tolerate no kind of divided allegiance in this country. There is no place for the hyphen in our citizenship. . . .

The other is equally important. We must treat every good American of German or of any other origin, without regard to his creed, as on a full and exact equality with every other good American, and set our faces like flint against the creatures who seek to discriminate against such an American, or to hold against him the birthplace of himself or his parents. . . . To discriminate in any way, . . . is a base infamy from the personal standpoint, and from the public standpoint is utterly un-American and profoundly unpatriotic. (1918.) *Mem. Ed.* XXI, 329, 331; *Nat. Ed.* XIX, 301, 303.

————. We are a different people from any people of Europe. It is our boast that we admit the immigrant to full fellowship and equality with the native-born. In return we demand that he shall share our undivided allegiance to the one flag which floats over all of us. (At Lincoln, Neb., June 14, 1917.) *Mem. Ed.* XXI, 192; *Nat. Ed.* XIX, 183.

ALLEGIANCE. *See also* AMERICANISM; AMERICANS, HYPHENATED; CITIZENSHIP; FLAG; GERMAN-AMERICANS; LOVE OF COUNTRY; LOYALTY; NATIONALISM; PATRIOTISM.

ALLIANCES—INSTABILITY OF. It is idle to trust to alliances. Alliances change. Russia and Japan are now fighting side by side, although nine years ago they were fighting against one another. Twenty years ago Russia and Germany stood side by side. Fifteen years ago England was more hostile to Russia, and even to France, than she was to Germany. It is perfectly possible that after the close of this war the present allies will fall out, or that Germany and Japan will turn up in close alliance. (*Everybody's*, January 1915.) *Mem. Ed.* XX, 167; *Nat. Ed.* XVIII, 143.

ALLIANCES. *See also* FOREIGN RELATIONS; LEAGUE FOR PEACE; NATIONAL SELF-RELIANCE; PREPAREDNESS.

ALLIES. *See* WORLD WAR.

ALTGELD, JOHN PETER. The attitude of many of our public men at the time of the great strike in July, 1894, was such as to call down on their heads the hearty condemnation of every American who wishes well to his country. It would be difficult to over-estimate the damage done by the example and action of a man like Governor Altgeld of Illinois. Whether he is honest or not in his beliefs is not of the slightest consequence. He is as emphatically the foe of decent government as Tweed himself, and is capable of doing far more damage than Tweed. The Governor, who began his career by pardoning anarchists, and whose most noteworthy feat since was his bitter and undignified, but fortunately futile, campaign against the election of the upright judge who sentenced the anarchists, is the foe of every true American and is the foe particularly of every honest workingman. With such a man it was to be expected that he should in time of civic commotion act as the foe of the law-abiding and the friend of the lawless classes, and endeavor, in company with the lowest and most abandoned office-seeking politicians, to prevent proper measures being taken to prevent riot and to punish the rioters. Had it not been for the admirable action of the Federal Government, Chicago would have seen a repetition of what occurred during the Paris Commune, while Illinois would have been torn by a fierce social war; and for all the horrible waste of life that this would have entailed Governor Altgeld would have been primarily responsible. It was a most fortunate thing that the action at Washington was so quick and so emphatic. (*Forum,* February 1895.) Mem. Ed. XV, 8-9; Nat. Ed. XIII, 7-8.

ALTGELD, JOHN PETER. See also BRYAN, W. J.; ELECTION OF 1896.

AMBASSADORS AS PUBLIC SERVANTS. There are a large number of well-meaning ambassadors and ministers, and even consuls and secretaries, who belong to what I call the pink-tea type, who merely reside in the service instead of working in the service, and these I intend to change whenever the need arises. . . .

I shall not make a fetish of keeping a man in, but if a man is a *really* good man he will be kept in. A pink-tea man shall stay in or go out, just as I find convenient. Of course, most places at embassies and legations are pink-tea places. A few are not, and in these we need real men, and these real men shall be rewarded. (To Richard Harding Davis, January 3, 1905.) Mem. Ed. XXIII, 410; Bishop I, 356.

———. You come in the category of public servants who desire to do public work, as distinguished from those whose desire is merely to occupy public place—a class for whom I have no particular respect. . . . The trouble with our ambassadors in stations of real importance is that they totally fail to give us real help and real information, and seem to think that the life work of an ambassador is a kind of glorified pink tea party. (To George von L. Meyer, December 26, 1904.) Mem. Ed. XXIII, 409; Bishop I, 356.

AMBASSADORS. See also DIPLOMATIC SERVICE; HAY, JOHN.

AMERICAN, THE AVERAGE. I hold that the average American is a decent, self-respecting man, with large capacities for good service to himself, his country and the world if a right appeal can be made to him and the right response evoked. Therefore, I hold that it is not best that he and his kind should perish from the earth. The great problem of civilization is to secure a relative increase of the valuable as compared with the less valuable or noxious elements in the population. (*Metropolitan,* October 1917.) Mem. Ed. XXI, 163; Nat. Ed. XIX, 157.

AMERICAN, THE BEST. That man is the best American who has in him the American spirit, the American soul. Such a man fears not the strong and harms not the weak. He scorns what is base or cruel or dishonest. He looks beyond the accidents of occupation or social condition and hails each of his fellow citizens as his brother, asking nothing save that each shall treat the other on his worth as a man, and that they shall all join together to do what in them lies for the uplifting of this mighty and vigorous people. (Before Society of Friendly Sons of St. Patrick, New York City, March 17, 1905.) Mem. Ed. XVIII, 50; Nat. Ed. XVI, 44.

AMERICAN, THE BLATANT AND THE SERVILE. The raw conceit of the vulgar "spread-eagle" American, screaming foolish defiance at Europe, and boasting with vainglorious ignorance of everything, good and bad, in this country, is distasteful to others and harmful to himself and to those who believe him; but it is on the whole rather preferable to the attitude of self-depreciation and apologetic servility habitually adopted in relation to their own land by some of our people, who though they dwell here are in reality by education and instinct entirely un-American. (*Cosmopolitan,* December 1892.) Mem. Ed. XIV, 368; Nat. Ed. XII, 302.

———. The screaming vulgarity of the foolish spread-eagle orator who is continually yelling defiance at Europe, praising everything American, good and bad, and resenting the introduction of any reform because it has previously been tried successfully abroad, is offensive and contemptible to the last degree; but after all it is scarcely as harmful as the peevish, fretful, sneering, and continual fault-finding of the refined, well-educated man, who is always attacking good and bad alike, who genuinely distrusts America, and in the true spirit of servile colonialism considers us inferior to the people across the water. (Before the Liberal Club, Buffalo, N. Y., January 26, 1893.) Mem. Ed. XV, 73; Nat. Ed. XIII, 290.

AMERICAN HISTORY. See HISTORY.

AMERICAN LITERATURE. See LITERATURE.

AMERICAN PEOPLE. We Americans are the children of the crucible. The crucible does not do its work unless it turns out those cast into it in one national mould; and that must be the mould established by Washington and his fellows when they made us into a nation. We must be Americans; and nothing else. Yet the events of the past three years bring us face to face with the question whether in the present century we are to continue as a separate nation at all or whether we are to become merely a huge polyglot boarding-house and counting-house, in which dollar-hunters of twenty different nationalities scramble for gain, while each really pays his soul-allegiance to some foreign power. (New York *Times,* September 10, 1917.) *Mem. Ed.* XXI, 35; *Nat. Ed.* XIX, 30.

——————. We are a nation coming from many different race strains, a new nation growing up in this new continent; closer akin to some of the nations of the Old World than others, but somewhat different from each and all. The worst deed that any man can do here, so far as the national life is concerned, is to try to keep himself apart from his fellow Americans, and to perpetuate Old World differences, whether of race, of speech, of religion, or of religious hatred, or on the other hand to try to discriminate against his fellow Americans because they may come of a different race stock from his. (Address, October 11, 1897.) *Two Hundredth Anniversary of the Old Dutch Church of Sleepy Hollow,* (First Reformed Church, Tarrytown, N. Y., 1898), p. 104.

——————. We are a new people; we differ from all other peoples; we are neither English nor Irish, neither German nor French; we are Americans, and only Americans. We are bound to treat all other nations on their conduct, and only on their conduct, in each crisis as it arises. (1918.) *Mem. Ed.* XXI, 342; *Nat. Ed.* XIX, 312.

——————. Some latter-day writers deplore the enormous immigration to our shores as making us a heterogeneous instead of a homogeneous people; but as a matter of fact we are less heterogeneous at the present day than we were at the outbreak of the Revolution. Our blood was as much mixed a century ago as it is now. (1889.) *Mem. Ed.* X, 20; *Nat. Ed.* VIII, 17-18.

——————. Recent English writers, and some of our own as well, have foretold woe to our nation, because the blood of the Cavalier and the Roundhead is being diluted with that of "German boors and Irish cotters." The alarm is needless. As a matter of fact the majority of the people of the middle colonies at the time of the Revolution were the descendants of Dutch and German boors and Scotch and Irish cotters; and in less degree the same was true of Georgia and the Carolinas. Even in New England, where the English stock was purest, there was plenty of other admixture, and two of her most distinguished Revolutionary families bore, one the Huguenot name of Bowdoin, and the other the Irish name of Sullivan. Indeed, from the very outset, from the days of Cromwell, there has been a large Irish admixture in New England. When our people began their existence as a nation, they already differed in blood from their ancestral relatives across the Atlantic much as the latter did from their forebears beyond the German Ocean; and on the whole, the immigration since has not materially changed the race strains in our nationality; a century back we were even less homogeneous than we are now. It is no doubt true that we are in the main an offshoot of the English stem; and cousins to our kinsfolk of Britain, we perhaps may be; but brothers we certainly are not. (1888.) *Mem. Ed.* VIII, 286-287; *Nat. Ed.* VII, 247.

——————. Before the outbreak of the Revolution the American people, not only because of their surroundings, physical and spiritual, but because of the mixture of blood that had already begun to take place, represented a new and distinct ethnic type. This type has never been fixed in blood. All through the colonial days new waves of immigration from time to time swept hither across the ocean, now from one country, now from another. The same thing has gone on ever since our birth as a nation; and for the last sixty years the tide of immigration has been at the full. The newcomers are soon absorbed into our eager national life, and are radically and profoundly changed thereby, the rapidity of their assimilation being marvellous. But each group of newcomers, as it adds its blood to the life, also changes it somewhat, and this change and growth and development have gone on steadily, generation by generation, throughout three centuries. (At Jamestown Exposition, April 26, 1907.) *Mem. Ed.* XII, 587-588; *Nat. Ed.* XI, 307.

——————. The American people are good-natured to the point of lax indifference; but once roused, they act with the most straightforward and practical resolution. (1891.) *Mem. Ed.* IX, 415; *Nat. Ed.* X, 530.

——————. If any man is thrown into close contact with any large body of our fellow citizens it is apt to be the man's own fault if he does not grow to feel for them a very hearty regard and, moreover, grow to understand that,

AMERICAN PEOPLE

on the great questions that lie at the root of human well-being, he and they feel alike. (At Labor Day Picnic, Chicago, September 3, 1900.) *Mem. Ed.* XVI, 512; *Nat. Ed.* XIII, 483.

———————. We Americans are a separate people. We are separated from, although akin to, many European peoples. The old Revolutionary stock was predominantly English, but by no means exclusively so; for many of the descendants of the Revolutionary New Yorkers, Pennsylvanians, and Georgians have, like myself, strains of Dutch, French, Scotch, Irish, Welsh, and German blood in their veins. During the century and a quarter that has elapsed since we became a nation, there has been far more immigration from Germany and Ireland and probably from Scandinavia than there has been from England. We have a right to ask all of these immigrants and the sons of these immigrants that they become Americans and nothing else; but we have no right to ask that they become transplanted or second-rate Englishmen. (*Metropolitan,* October 1915.) *Mem. Ed.* XX, 328; *Nat. Ed.* XVIII, 282.

AMERICAN PEOPLE—ADVANCE OF THE. I am inclined to think that on the whole our people are, spiritually as well as materially, on the average better and not worse off than they were a hundred years ago. (To Sir George Otto Trevelyan, March 9, 1905.) *Mem. Ed.* XXIV, 172; Bishop II, 147.

AMERICAN PEOPLE—FAITH IN. I have immense faith ultimately in the sober judgment of the American people. I believe that they are a law-abiding and an upright people, and I know that Republican government is worth preserving only on the supposition that in the long run the mass of the voters will stand for honesty and decency. (Before Liberal Club of Buffalo, N. Y., September 10, 1895.) *Mem. Ed.* XVI, 287; *Nat. Ed.* XIV, 206.

AMERICAN PEOPLE—HERITAGE OF THE. To us as a people it has been granted to lay the foundations of our national life in a new continent. We are the heirs of the ages, and yet we have had to pay few of the penalties which in old countries are exacted by the dead hand of a bygone civilization. We have not been obliged to fight for our existence against any alien race; and yet our life has called for the vigor and effort without which the manlier and hardier virtues wither away. Under such conditions it would be our own fault if we failed; and the success which we have had in the past, the success which we confidently believe the future will bring, should cause in us no feeling of vainglory, but rather a deep and abiding realization of all which life has offered us; a full acknowledgment of the responsibility which is ours; and a fixed determination to show that under a free government a mighty people can thrive best, alike as regards the things of the body and the things of the soul. (Inaugural Address as President, Washington, March 4, 1905.) *Mem. Ed.* XVII, 311; *Nat. Ed.* XV, 267.

AMERICAN PEOPLE—OBLIGATION OF THE. We, here in America, hold in our hands the hope of the world, the fate of the coming years; and shame and disgrace will be ours if in our eyes the light of high resolve is dimmed, if we trail in the dust the golden hopes of men. If on this continent we merely build another country of great but unjustly divided material prosperity, we shall have done nothing; and we shall do as little if we merely set the greed of envy against the greed of arrogance, and thereby destroy the material well-being of all of us. . . . The worth of our great experiment depends upon its being in good faith an experiment—the first that has ever been tried—in true democracy on the scale of a continent, on a scale as vast as that of the mightiest empires of the Old World. Surely this is a noble ideal, an ideal for which it is worth while to strive, an ideal for which at need it is worth while to sacrifice much; for our ideal is the rule of all the people in a spirit of friendliest brotherhood toward each and every one of the people. (At Carnegie Hall, New York City, March 20, 1912.) *Mem. Ed.* XIX, 223; *Nat. Ed.* XVII, 170.

AMERICAN PEOPLE—QUALITIES OF THE. From the very beginning our people have markedly combined practical capacity for affairs with power of devotion to an ideal. The lack of either quality would have rendered the possession of the other of small value. Mere ability to achieve success in things concerning the body would not have atoned for the failure to live the life of high endeavor; and, on the other hand, without a foundation of those qualities which bring material prosperity there would be nothing on which the higher life could be built. (At Union League, Phila., November 22, 1902.) *Mem. Ed.* XVIII, 479; *Nat. Ed.* XVI, 356.

AMERICAN PEOPLE—UNITY OF THE. In this country we must all stand together absolutely without regard to our several lines of descent, as Americans and nothing else; and, above all, we must do this as regards moral issues. The great issues with which we must now deal are moral even more than material; and on these issues every good American should be with us, without the slightest regard to the land from which his forefathers came. (1916.) *Mem. Ed.* XX, 250; *Nat. Ed.* XVIII, 216.

───────────. We are all of us Americans, and nothing else; we all have equal rights and equal obligations; we form part of one people, in the face of all other nations, paying allegiance only to one flag; and a wrong to any one of us is a wrong to all the rest of us. (New York *Times,* September 10, 1917.) *Mem. Ed.* XXI, 43; *Nat. Ed.* XIX, 37.

AMERICAN POSSESSIONS. *See also* ALASKA; HAWAII, INSULAR POSSESSIONS; PHILIPPINES; PORTO RICO.

AMERICAN PROTECTIVE ASSOCIATION. *See* RELIGIOUS DISCRIMINATION.

AMERICAN SYSTEM. *See* DEMOCRACY.

AMERICANISM. There is no room in this country for fifty-fifty Americanism. (March 2, 1918.) *Roosevelt in the Kansas City Star,* 111.

───────────. I cannot be with you, and so all I can do is to wish you Godspeed. There must be no sagging back in the fight for Americanism merely because the war is over. There are plenty of persons who have already made the assertion that they believe the American people have a short memory and that they intend to revive all the foreign associations which most directly interfere with the complete Americanization of our people. . . .

Any man who says he is an American, but something else also, isn't an American at all. We have room for but one flag, the American flag, and this excludes the red flag, which symbolizes all wars against liberty and civilization just as much as it excludes any foreign flag of a nation to which we are hostile. (To President of the American Defense Society, January 3, 1919; last message, read at meeting in New York, January 5, 1919.) *Mem. Ed.* XXIV, 554-555; Bishop II, 474.

───────────. Americanism is a question of principle, of purpose, of idealism, of character; . . . not a matter of birthplace, or creed, or line of descent. (At unveiling of monument to Gen. Phil Sheridan, Washington, November 25, 1908.) *Mem. Ed.* XII, 478; *Nat. Ed.* XI, 222.

───────────. There is one point upon which I wish to lay especial stress; that is, the necessity for a feeling of broad, radical, and intense Americanism, if good work is to be done in any direction. Above all, the one essential for success in every political movement which is to do lasting good, is that our citizens should act as Americans. . . . It is an outrage for a man to drag foreign politics into our contests, and vote as an Irishman or German or other foreigner, as the case may be. . . . But it is no less an outrage to discriminate against one who has become an American in good faith, merely because of his creed or birthplace. Every man who has gone into practical politics knows well enough that if he joins good men and fights those who are evil, he can pay no heed to lines of division drawn according to race and religion. (1890.) *Mem. Ed.* IX, 217; *Nat. Ed.* X, 360.

───────────. Americanism means many things. It means equality of rights and, therefore, equality of duty and of obligation. It means service to our common country. It means loyalty to one flag, to our flag, the flag of all of us. It means on the part of each of us respect for the rights of the rest of us. It means that all of us guarantee the rights of each of us. It means free education, genuinely representative government, freedom of speech and thought, equality before the law for all men, genuine political and religious freedom and the democratizing of industry so as to give at least a measurable equality of opportunity for all, and so as to place before us as our ideal in all industries where this ideal is possible of attainment, the system of co-operative ownership and management, in order that the tool users may, so far as possible, become the tool owners. Everything is un-American that tends either to government by a plutocracy or government by a mob. To divide along the lines of section or caste or creed is un-American. All privileges based on wealth, and all enmity to honest men merely because they are wealthy, are un-American —both of them equally so. Americanism means the virtues of courage, honor, justice, truth, sincerity, and hardihood—the virtues that made America. The things that will destroy America are prosperity-at-any-price, peace-at-any-price, safety-first instead of duty-first, the love of soft living and the get-rich-quick theory of life. (To S. S. Menken, January 10, 1917; read before National Security League, Washington, January 26, 1917.) *Proceedings of the Congress of Constructive Patriotism.* (New York, 1917), p. 172.

[13]

AMERICANISM AND INTERNATIONALISM. I believe in nationalism as the absolute prerequisite to internationalism. I believe in patriotism as the absolute prerequisite to the larger Americanism. I believe in Americanism because unless our people are good Americans first, America can accomplish little or nothing worth accomplishing for the good of the world as a whole. (1916.) *Mem. Ed.* XX, 529; *Nat. Ed.* XVIII, 454.

AMERICANISM AND PEACE. Let ours be true Americanism, the greater Americanism, and let us tolerate no other. Let us prepare ourselves for justice and efficiency within our own border during peace, for justice in international relations, and for efficiency in war. Only thus shall we have the peace worth having. (1916.) *Mem. Ed.* XX, 260; *Nat. Ed.* XVIII, 224.

AMERICANISM AS A CLOAK. There are plenty of scoundrels always ready to try to belittle reform movements or to bolster up existing iniquities in the name of Americanism; but this does not alter the fact that the man who can do most in this country is and must be the man whose Americanism is most sincere and intense. Outrageous though it is to use a noble idea as the cloak for evil, it is still worse to assail the noble idea itself because it can thus be used. The men who do iniquity in the name of patriotism, of reform, of Americanism, are merely one small division of the class that has always existed and will always exist—the class of hypocrites and demagogues, the class that is always prompt to steal the watchwords of righteousness and use them in the interests of evil-doing. (*Forum,* April 1894.) *Mem. Ed.* XV, 15; *Nat. Ed.* XIII, 13.

AMERICANISM VERSUS COSMOPOLITANISM. Whatever may be the case in an infinitely remote future, at present no people can render any service to humanity unless as a people they feel an intense sense of national cohesion and solidarity. . . . The United States can accomplish little for mankind, save in so far as within its borders it develops an intense spirit of Americanism. A flabby cosmopolitanism, especially if it expresses itself through a flabby pacifism, is not only silly, but degrading. It represents national emasculation. (1916.) *Mem. Ed.* XX, 233; *Nat. Ed.* XVIII, 201.

AMERICANISM VERSUS SECTIONALISM. The great lesson that all of us need to learn and to keep is the lesson that it is unimportant whether a man lives North or South, East or West, provided that he is genuinely and in good faith an American; that he feels every part of the United States as his own, and that he is honestly desirous to uphold the interests of all other Americans in whatever sections of the country they may dwell. (*Outlook,* September 10, 1910.) *Mem. Ed.* XVIII, 28; *Nat. Ed.* XVI, 25.

AMERICANISM. See also ALLEGIANCE; FLAG; FOURTH OF JULY; KNOW NOTHING MOVEMENT; LOYALTY; NATIONALISM; PATRIOTISM.

AMERICANIZATION. The process of assimilating, or as we should now say, of Americanizing, all foreign and non-English elements was going on almost as rapidly a hundred years ago as it is at present. A young Dutchman or Huguenot felt it necessary, then, to learn English, precisely as a young Scandinavian or German does now; and the churches of the former at the end of the last century were obliged to adopt English as the language for their ritual exactly as the churches of the latter do at the end of this. The most stirring, energetic, and progressive life of the colony was English; and all the young fellows of push and ambition gradually adopted this as their native language, and then refused to belong to congregations where the service was carried on in a less familiar speech. (1888.) *Mem. Ed.* VIII, 287; *Nat. Ed.* VII, 248.

———. The one overshadowing fact in this process of complete Americanization, the one side of the question that should be always borne in mind, is the enormous benefit it confers upon the person who is Americanized. The gain to the country is real, but the gain to the individual himself is everything. Immigrants who remain aliens, whether in language or in political thought, are of comparatively little benefit to the country; but they themselves are the individuals most damaged. The man who becomes completely Americanized—who celebrates our Constitutional Centennial instead of the Queen's Jubilee, or the Fourth of July rather than Saint Patrick's Day, and who "talks United States" instead of the dialect of the country which he has of his own free will abandoned—is not only doing his plain duty by his adopted land, but is also rendering to himself a service of immeasurable value.

This last point is one that cannot be too often insisted on. The chief interest served by Americanization is that of the individual himself. A man who speaks only German or Swedish may nevertheless be a most useful American citizen; but it is impossible for him to derive the full

AMERICANIZATION

benefit he should from American citizenship. And, on the other hand, it is impossible for him, under any circumstances, to retain the benefits incident to being a member of the nation of which he has left. It would be hard to imagine another alternative where the advantage was so wholly on one side. The case stands thus: by becoming completely Americanized the immigrant gains every right conferred upon citizenship in the country to which he has come; but, if he fails to become Americanized, he nevertheless loses all share and part in the nation which he has left, and gains nothing in return. He cannot possibly remain an Englishman, a German, or a Scandinavian; all he can do is to refuse to become an American, and thereby make himself a kind of mongrel waif, of no importance anywhere. *America,* April 14, 1888, p. 2.

——————. It is our duty from the standpoint of self-defense to secure the complete Americanization of our people; to make of the many peoples of this country a united nation, one in speech and feeling, and all, so far as possible, sharers in the best that each has brought to our shores.

The foreign-born population of this country must be an Americanized population. . . . It must possess American citizenship and American ideals—and therefore we native-born citizens must ourselves practise a high and fine idealism, and shun as we would the plague the sordid materialism which treats pecuniary profit and gross bodily comfort as the only evidences of success. (Before Knights of Columbus, New York City, October 12, 1915.) *Mem. Ed.* XX, 468; *Nat. Ed.* XVIII, 401.

——————. What we should have done, what we must do, is see to it that the immigrant is taken in hand and given a square deal. We must see to it that a real effort is made to Americanize him—he should have the opportunity to become Americanized. He should be given an opportunity, should be compelled to learn the English language, and if at the end of a stated period he has failed to do so, he should be sent back to the place from which he came. He must not be left to the agitator and the demagogue to exploit.

It is foolish to imagine that the immigrant will automatically and of his own will be converted into an American by his mere presence among us, so long as he comes here in masses, and settles down among his own kind, as ignorant of our ways, our customs, and our institutions as he is. (Fall 1917; reported by Leary.) *Talk with T. R. From the diaries of John J. Leary, Jr.* (Houghton Mifflin Co., Boston, 1920), p. 148.

AMERICANS

AMERICANIZATION — ESSENTIALS FOR. I ask you to make a special effort to deal with Americanization, the fusing into one nation, a nation necessarily different from all other nations, of all who come to our shores. Pay heed to the three principal essentials: (1) The need of a common language, English, with a minimum amount of illiteracy; (2) the need of a common civil standard, similar ideals, beliefs, and customs symbolized by the oath of allegiance to America; and (3) the need of a high standard of living, of reasonable equality of opportunity, and of social and industrial justice. (Before Knights of Columbus, New York City, October 12, 1915.) *Mem. Ed.* XX, 470; *Nat. Ed.* XVIII, 403.

AMERICANIZATION AND LANGUAGE. America is a Nation and not a mosaic of nationalities. The various nationalities that come here are not to remain separate, but to blend into the one American nationality—the nationality of Washington and Lincoln, of Muhlenberg and Sheridan. Therefore, we must have but one language, the English language. Every immigrant who comes here should be required within five years to learn English or to leave the country, for hereafter every immigrant should be treated as a future fellow citizen and not merely as a labor unit. English should be the only language taught or used in the primary schools. We should provide by law so that after a reasonable interval every newspaper in this country should be published in English. (April 27, 1918.) *Roosevelt in the Kansas City Star,* 143.

AMERICANIZATION. See also IMMIGRANTS; LANGUAGE; PUBLIC SCHOOLS.

AMERICANS, HYPHENATED. We welcome the German or the Irishman who becomes an American. We have no use for the German or Irishman who remains such. We do not wish German-Americans and Irish-Americans who figure as such in our social and political life; we want only Americans, and, provided they are such, we do not care whether they are of native or of Irish or of German ancestry. We have no room in any healthy American community for a German-American vote or an Irish-American vote, and it is contemptible demagogy to put planks into any party platform with the purpose of catching such a vote. We have no room for any people who do not act and vote simply as Americans and nothing else. (*Forum,* April 1894.) *Mem. Ed.* XV. 24; *Nat. Ed.* XIII, 21.

——————. The one being abhorrent to the powers above the earth and under them is the hyphenated American—the "German-American," the "Irish-American," or the "native-American." Be Americans, pure and simple! If you don't act on the theory that every man who in good faith assumes the duties and responsibilities of an American citizen in a spirit of true Americanism is an American, and is to be treated as such, . . . you are yourselves unfit to take part in managing our government and you are bound to make a failure if you try to better the condition of our cities. (Before Liberal Club, Buffalo, N. Y., September 10, 1895.) *Mem. Ed.* XVI, 276; *Nat. Ed.* XIV, 196.

——————. I am among those Americans whose ancestors include men and women from many different European countries. The proportion of Americans of this type will steadily increase. I do not believe in hyphenated Americans. I do not believe in German-Americans or Irish-Americans; and I believe just as little in English-Americans. I do not approve of American citizens of German descent forming organizations to force the United States into practical alliance with Germany because their ancestors came from Germany. Just as little do I believe in American citizens of English descent forming leagues to force the United States into an alliance with England because their ancestors came from England. (*Metropolitan,* October 1915.) *Mem. Ed.* XX, 328; *Nat. Ed.* XVIII, 281.

——————. There is no room in this country for hyphenated Americanism. When I refer to hyphenated Americans, I do not refer to naturalized Americans. Some of the very best Americans I have ever known were naturalized Americans, Americans born abroad. But a hyphenated American is not an American at all. This is just as true of the man who puts "native" before the hyphen as of the man who puts German or Irish or English or French before the hyphen. Americanism is a matter of the spirit and of the soul. Our allegiance must be purely to the United States. We must unsparingly condemn any man who holds any other allegiance. But if he is heartily and singly loyal to this Republic, then no matter where he was born, he is just as good an American as any one else.

The one absolutely certain way of bringing this nation to ruin, of preventing all possibility of its continuing to be a nation at all, would be to permit it to become a tangle of squabbling nationalities, an intricate knot of German-Americans, Irish-Americans, English-Americans, French-Americans, Scandinavian-Americans, or Italian-Americans, each preserving its separate nationality, each at heart feeling more sympathy with Europeans of that nationality than with the other citizens of the American Republic. The men who do not become Americans and nothing else are hyphenated Americans; and there ought to be no room for them in this country. The man who calls himself an American citizen and who yet shows by his actions that he is primarily the citizen of a foreign land, plays a thoroughly mischievous part in the life of our body politic. He has no place here; and the sooner he returns to the land to which he feels his real heart-allegiance, the better it will be for every good American. (Before Knights of Columbus, New York City, October 12, 1915.) *Mem. Ed.* XX, 456; *Nat. Ed.* XVIII, 392.

——————. Among the very many lessons taught by the last year has been the lesson that the effort to combine fealty to the flag of an immigrant's natal land with fealty to the flag of his adopted land, in practice means not merely disregard of, but hostility to, the flag of the United States. When two flags are hoisted on the same pole, one is always hoisted undermost. The hyphenated American always hoists the American flag undermost. (*Metropolitan,* October 1915.) *Mem. Ed.* XX, 324; *Nat. Ed.* XVIII, 278.

AMERICANS, HYPHENATED. *See also* ALLEGIANCE; GERMAN-AMERICANS; IRISH-AMERICANS; LOYALTY; NATIONALISM; PATRIOTISM.

AMERICANS IN POLITICS. We have a right to demand that every man, native born or foreign born, shall in American public life act merely as an American. (Speech at Boston, November 1893.) *Mem. Ed.* XV, 34; *Nat. Ed.* XIII, 275.

——————. It is exceedingly unlikely that I shall ever again be a candidate for office, but, if I am, no man will be wise who votes for me under the idea that I am anything but a straight-cut American. I care nothing for a man's creed, or his birthplace, or descent! but I regard him as an unworthy citizen unless he is an American and nothing else. (To Rev. Gustavus E. Hiller, February 4, 1916.) *Mem. Ed.* XXIV, 472; Bishop II, 401.

AMERICANS

———————. Americans should organize politically as Americans and not as bankers, or lawyers, or farmers, or wage-workers. (September 12, 1918.) *Roosevelt in the Kansas City Star*, 215.

AMERICANS IN POLITICS. See also POLITICAL ASSOCIATES.

AMUSEMENTS. The average individual will not spend the hours in which he is not working in doing something that is unpleasant, and absolutely the only way permanently to draw average men or women from occupations and amusements that are unhealthy for soul or body is to furnish an alternative which they will accept. To forbid all amusements, or to treat innocent and vicious amusements as on the same plane, simply insures recruits for the vicious amusements. (*Century*, October 1900.) *Mem. Ed.* XV, 428; *Nat. Ed.* XIII, 375.

AMUSEMENTS. See also LEISURE; SPORTS.

ANARCHISTS. The anarchist, and especially the anarchist in the United States, is merely one type of criminal, more dangerous than any other because he represents the same depravity in a greater degree. The man who advocates anarchy directly or indirectly, in any shape or fashion, or the man who apologizes for anarchists and their deeds, makes himself morally accessory to murder before the fact. The anarchist is a criminal whose perverted instincts lead him to prefer confusion and chaos to the most beneficent form of social order. His protest of concern for working men is outrageous in its impudent falsity; for if the political institutions of this country do not afford opportunity to every honest and intelligent son of toil, then the door of hope is forever closed against him. The anarchist is everywhere not merely the enemy of system and of progress, but the deadly foe of liberty. If ever anarchy is triumphant, its triumph will last for but one red moment, to be succeeded for ages by the gloomy night of despotism. (First Annual Message, Washington, December 3, 1901.) *Mem. Ed.* XVII, 97; *Nat. Ed.* XV, 84-85.

ANARCHISTS — TREATMENT OF. I treated anarchists and the bomb-throwing and dynamiting gentry precisely as I treated other criminals. Murder is murder. It is not rendered one whit better by the allegation that it is committed on behalf of "a cause." It is true that law and order are not all-sufficient; but they are essential; lawlessness and murderous violence must be quelled before any permanence of reform can be obtained. (1913.) *Mem. Ed.* XXII, 561; *Nat. Ed.* XX, 482.

ANIMALS

ANARCHISTS. See also BOLSHEVISM; IMMIGRATION; INDUSTRIAL WORKERS OF THE WORLD.

ANARCHY. Anarchy is always and everywhere the handmaiden of Tyranny and Liberty's deadliest foe. No people can permanently remain free unless it possesses the stern self-control and resolution necessary to put down anarchy. Order without liberty and liberty without order are equally destructive. (1918.) *Mem. Ed.* XXI, 377; *Nat. Ed.* XIX, 342.

ANARCHY. See also LIBERTY; ORDER; REVOLUTION; VIOLENCE.

ANDRE, JOHN, AND NATHAN HALE. Poor André! His tragedy was like that of Nathan Hale; and the tragedy was the same in the case of the brilliant young patrician, brilliant, fearless, devoted, and the plain, straightforward yeoman who just as bravely gave up his life in performing the same kind of duty. It was not a pleasant kind of duty; and the penalty was rightly the same in each case; and the countrymen of each man are also right to hold him in honor and to commemorate his memory by a monument. (To Sir George Otto Trevelyan, January 1, 1908.) *Mem. Ed.* XXIV, 198; Bishop II, 169.

ANDREWS, AVERY D. See POLICE COMMISSIONER.

ANGLO-SAXONS. See AMERICAN PEOPLE.

ANGLOMANIA AND ANGLOPHOBIA. I am sure you will agree with me that in our political life, very unlike what is the case in our social life, the temptation is toward Anglophobia, not toward Anglomania. . . . If an Anglomaniac in social life goes into political life he usually becomes politically an Anglophobiac, and the occasional political Anglophobiac whose curious ambition it is to associate socially with 'vacuity trimmed with lace' is equally sure to become an Anglomaniac in his new surroundings. (To Finley Peter Dunne, November 1904.) *Mem. Ed.* XXIII, 400; Bishop I, 348.

ANIMALS—ADAPTATION OF. With all wild animals it is a noticable fact that a course of contact with man continuing over many generations of animal life causes a species so to

[17]

adapt itself to its new surroundings that it can hold its own far better than formerly. When white men take up a new country, the game, and especially the big game, being entirely unused to contend with the new foe, succumb easily, and are almost completely killed out. If any individuals survive at all, however, the succeeding generations are far more difficult to exterminate than were their ancestors, and they cling much more tenaciously to their old homes. (1905.) *Mem. Ed.* III, 115; *Nat. Ed.* II, 489.

ANIMALS—DISAPPEARANCE OF. All species of animals of course ultimately disappear, some because their kind entirely dies out, and some because the species is transformed into a wholly different species, degenerate or not; but in our nomenclature we make no distinction between the two utterly different kinds of "disappearance." (To A. J. Balfour, March 5, 1908.) *Mem. Ed.* XXIV, 127; Bishop II, 109.

ANIMALS—NOMENCLATURE OF. The nomenclature and exact specific relationships of American sheep, deer, and antelope offer difficulties not only to the hunter but to the naturalist. As regards the nomenclature, we share the trouble encountered by all peoples of European descent who have gone into strange lands. The incomers are almost invariably men who are not accustomed to scientific precision of expression. Like other people, they do not like to invent names if they can by any possibility make use of those already in existence, and so in a large number of cases they call the new birds and animals by names applied to entirely different birds and animals of the Old World to which, in the eyes of the settlers, they bear some resemblance. In South America the Spaniards, for instance, christened "lion" and "tiger" the great cats which are properly known as cougar and jaguar. In South Africa the Dutch settlers, who came from a land where all big game had long been exterminated, gave fairly grotesque names to the great antelopes, calling them after the European elk, stag, and chamois. . . . Our own pioneers behaved in the same way. Hence it is that we have no distinctive name at all for the group of peculiarly American game-birds of which the bob-white is the typical representative; and that, when we could not use the words quail, partridge, or pheasant, we went for our terminology to the barnyard, and called our fine grouse, fool-hens, sage-hens, and prairie-chickens. The bear and wolf our people recognized at once. The bison they called a buffalo, which was no worse than the way in which in Europe the Old World bison was called an aurochs. The American true elk and reindeer were rechristened moose and caribou—excellent names, by the way, derived from the Indian. (1905.) *Mem. Ed.* III, 171, 172; *Nat. Ed.* III, 6, 7.

ANIMALS—PROTECTIVE COLORATION OF. Very much of what is commonly said about "protective coloration" has no basis whatever in fact. Black and white are normally the most conspicuous colors in nature (and yet are borne by numerous creatures who have succeeded well in the struggle for life); but almost any tint, or combination of tints, among the grays, browns and duns, harmonizes fairly well with at least some surroundings, in most landscapes; and in but a few instances among the larger mammals, and in almost none among those frequenting the open plains, is there the slightest reason for supposing that the creature gains any benefit whatever from what is loosely called its "protective coloration." Giraffes, leopards, and zebras, for instance, have actually been held up as instances of creatures that are "protectingly" colored and are benefited thereby. The giraffe is one of the most conspicuous objects in nature, and never makes the slightest effort to hide; near by its mottled hide is very noticeable, but as a matter of fact, under any ordinary circumstances any possible foe trusting to eyesight would discover the giraffe so far away that its coloring would seem uniform, that is, would because of the distance be indistinguishable from a general tint which really might have a slight protective value. In other words, while it is possible that the giraffe's beautifully waved coloring may under certain circumstances, and in an infinitesimally small number of cases, put it at a slight disadvantage in the struggle for life, in the enormous majority of cases—a majority so great as to make the remaining cases negligible—it has no effect whatever, one way or the other; and it is safe to say that under no conditions is its coloring of the slightest value to it as affording it "protection" from foes trusting to their eyesight. (1910.) *Mem. Ed.* V, 44-45; *Nat. Ed.* IV, 38-39.

———————. The truth is that no game of the plains is helped in any way by its coloration in evading its foes, and none seeks to escape the vision of its foes. The larger game animals of the plains are always walking and standing in conspicuous places, and never seek to hide or take advantage of cover; while, on the contrary, the little grass and bush antelopes, like the duiker and steinbuck, trust very much to their power of hiding, and endeavor to escape the sight of their foes by lying absolutely still, in

——————. I have no question whatever ... that concealing coloration is of real value in the struggle for existence to certain mammals and certain birds, not to mention invertebrates. The night-hawk, certain partridges and grouse, and numerous other birds which seek to escape observation by squatting motionless, do unquestionably owe an immense amount to the way in which their colors harmonize with the surrounding colors, thus enabling them to lie undetected while they keep still, and probably even protecting them somewhat if they try to skulk off. In these cases, where the theory really applies, the creature benefited by the coloration secures the benefit by acting in a way which enables the coloration to further its concealment. ... But it is wholly different when the theory is pushed to fantastic extremes, as by those who seek to make the coloration of big-game animals such as zebras, giraffes, hartbeests, and the like, protective. (1910; Appendix of *African Game Trails*.) *Mem. Ed.* VI, 377-378; *Nat. Ed.* V, 325.

——————. I have studied the facts as regards big game and certain other animals, and I am convinced that as regards these animals the protective-coloration theory either does not apply at all or applies so little as to render it necessary to accept with the utmost reserve the sweeping generalizations of Mr. Thayer and the protective-coloration extremists. It is an exceedingly interesting subject. It certainly seems that the theory must apply as regards many animals, but it is even more certain that it does not, as its advocates claim, apply universally; and careful study and cautious generalizations are imperatively necessary in striving to apply it extensively, while fanciful and impossible efforts to apply it where it certainly does not apply can do no real good. It is necessary to remember that some totally different principle, in addition to or in substitution for protective coloration, must have been at work where totally different colorations and color patterns seem to bring the same results to the wearers. The bear and the skunk are both catchers of small rodents, and when the color patterns of the back, nose, and breast, for instance, are directly opposite in the two animals, there is at least need of very great caution in deciding that either represents obliterative coloration of a sort that benefits the creature in catching its prey. (1910; Appendix of *African Game Trails*.) *Mem. Ed.* VI, 399-400; *Nat. Ed.* V, 344.

——————. Scientific men are no more immune from hysteria and suggestion than other mortals, and every now and then there arises among them some fad which for quite a time carries even sane men off their feet. This has been the case with the latter-day development of the theories of protective coloration and of warning and recognition marks—but especially the first. Because some animals are undoubtedly protectively colored and take advantage of their coloration and are served by it, a number of naturalists have carried the theory to fantastic extremes. They have applied it where it does not exist at all, and have endeavored to extend it to a degree that has tended to make the whole theory ridiculous. Most good observers are now agreed that in the higher vertebrates, that is, in mammals and birds, the coloration of probably the majority of the species has little or nothing to do with any protective or concealing quality. There are some hundreds of species which we can say with certainty are protectively colored; there are a great number which we can say with certainty are not protectively colored. As regards others we are still in doubt. There have not been sufficiently extensive observations made of wild animals under natural conditions to enable us to speak with certainty as to just the part played by protective coloration among large numbers of the smaller mammals and birds. We are, however, able to speak with certainty as regards most big birds and especially most big mammals. (Introduction to C. H. Stigand's *Hunting the Elephant in Africa;* 1913.) *Mem. Ed.* XIV, 495; *Nat. Ed.* XII, 364-365.

——————. My discussion of revealing and concealing coloration among birds and mammals covers but a tiny corner even of the question of animal coloration; but I do not think that it is possible to controvert my main thesis, which is, that as regards these higher vertebrates, concealing coloration (with or without counter-shading as a basis), as a survival factor working through natural selection, has been of trivial consequence in producing the special color patterns on the great majority of birds and mammals; that it has in an immense number of cases been wholly inactive, so that in very many of these cases the animals are extraordinarily conspicuous in nature at almost all times, including the vital moments of their lives; and that in most of the large number of cases where it has actually been a factor it has merely set limits of conspicuousness, sometimes very narrow, sometimes very broad, which must not be exceeded, but within which innumerable tints and patterns are developed, owing to some entirely different slant of causation. (*American*

Museum Journal, March 1918.) *Mem. Ed.* **VI**, 416; *Nat. Ed.* V, 359.

ANIMALS—SURVIVAL OF. Other things being equal, the length of an animal's stay in the land, when the arch-foe of all lower forms of animal life has made his appearance therein, depends upon the difficulty with which he is hunted and slain. But other influences have to be taken into account. The bighorn is shy and retiring; very few, compared to the whole number, will be killed; and yet the others vanish completely. Apparently, they will not remain where they are hunted and disturbed. With antelope and whitetail this does not hold; they will cling to a place far more tenaciously, even if often harassed. The former, being the more conspicuous and living in such open ground, is apt to be more persecuted; while the whitetail, longer than any other animal, keeps its place in the land in spite of the swinish game-butchers, who hunt for hides and not for sport or actual food. . . .

All game animals rely upon both eyes, ears, and nose to warn them of the approach of danger; but the amount of reliance placed on each sense varies greatly in different species. Those found out on the plains pay very little attention to what they hear; indeed, in the open they can hardly be approached near enough to make of much account any ordinary amount of noise caused by the stalker, especially as the latter is walking over little but grass and soft earth. (1885.) *Mem. Ed.* I, 130-131; *Nat. Ed.* I, 107.

———————. Among the higher vertebrates there are many known factors which have influence, some in one set of cases, some in another set of cases, in the development and preservation of species. Courage, intelligence, adaptability, prowess, bodily vigor, speed, alertness, ability to hide, ability to build structures which will protect the young while they are helpless, fecundity—all, and many more like them, have their several places; and behind all these visible causes there are at work other and often more potent causes of which as yet science can say nothing. Some species owe much to a given attribute which may be wholly lacking in influence on other species; and every one of the attributes above enumerated is a survival factor in some species, while in others it has no survival value whatever, and in yet others, although of benefit, it is not of sufficient benefit to offset the benefit conferred on foes or rivals by totally different attributes. Intelligence, for instance, is of course a survival factor; but to-day there exist multitudes of animals with very little intelligence which have persisted through immense periods of geologic time either unchanged or else without any change in the direction of increased intelligence; and during their species life they have witnessed the death of countless other species of far greater intelligence but in other ways less adapted to succeed in the environmental complex. (1914.) *Mem. Ed.* **VI**, 36-37; *Nat. Ed.* V, 31-32.

ANIMALS. *See also* BIRDS; GAME; HUNTING; NATURE STUDY; WILD LIFE.

ANNAPOLIS. Annapolis is, with the sole exception of its sister academy at West Point, the most typically democratic and American school of learning and preparation that there is in the entire country. Men go there from every State, from every walk of life, professing every creed —the chance of entry being open to all who perfect themselves in the necessary studies and who possess the necessary moral and physical qualities. There each man enters on his merits, stands on his merits, and graduates into a service where only his merit will enable him to be of value. (At Haverhill, Mass., August 26, 1902.) *Presidential Addresses and State Papers* I, 120.

ANNAPOLIS. *See also* HAZING; JONES, JOHN PAUL; WEST POINT.

ANTELOPE HUNTING. Of all kinds of hunting, the chase of the antelope is pre-eminently that requiring skill in the use of the rifle at long range. The distance at which shots have to be taken in antelope hunting is at last double the ordinary distance at which deer are fired at. . . . I have myself done but little hunting after antelopes, and have not, as a rule, been very successful in the pursuit.

Ordinary hounds are rarely, or never, used to chase this game; but coursing it with greyhounds is as manly and exhilarating a form of sport as can be imagined. (1885.) *Mem. Ed.* I, 180; *Nat. Ed.* I, 149.

ANTELOPE. *See also* PRONGBUCK.

ANTHRACITE COAL STRIKE. *See* COAL STRIKE.

ANTHROPOLOGY. *See* PRIMITIVE SOCIETY.

ANTI-SEMITISM. While I was police commissioner an anti-Semitic preacher from Berlin, Rector Ahlwardt, came over to New York to preach a crusade against the Jews. Many of the New York Jews were much excited and asked me to prevent him from speaking and not to give him police protection. This, I told them, was impossible; and if possible would have been undesirable because it would have made him a martyr. The proper thing to do was to make him ridiculous. Accordingly I detailed for his protection a Jew sergeant and a score or two of Jew policemen. He made his harangue against the Jews under the active protection of some forty policemen, every one of them a Jew! It was the most effective possible answer; and incidentally it was an object-lesson to our people, whose greatest need it is to learn that there must be no division by class hatred, whether this hatred be that of creed against creed, nationality against nationality, section against section, or men of one social or industrial condition against men of another social or industrial condition. (1913.) *Mem. Ed.* XXII, 224; *Nat. Ed.* XX, 192.

ANTI-SEMITISM. See also CHAMBERLAIN, HOUSTON S.; DREYFUS, ALFRED; JEWS; KISHINEFF MASSACRE; RELIGIOUS FREEDOM.

ANTLERS. See WAPITI.

APPOINTMENTS—BASIS OF. In the appointments I shall go on exactly as I did while I was Governor of New York. The Senators and Congressmen shall ordinarily name the men, but I shall name the standard, and the men have got to come up to it. (To Henry Cabot Lodge, October 11, 1901.) *Mem. Ed.* XXIII, 183; Bishop I, 157.

APPOINTMENTS — RESPONSIBILITY FOR. In appointing his successor, and in appointing all other officers to these places, I must keep in mind that it is I who am primarily responsible for the appointment, not the Senators. If I appoint a man who is unfit, then of course you must refuse to confirm him; and as a matter of fact, if you will give me a man of whom I can approve, I will gladly appoint him. There is no one whom I am personally desirous of putting in any of these positions. But I do not merely desire, but am firmly determined to have, a thoroughly good type of man in the position; and I cannot surrender to any one the right to decide for me whether or not I believe the man to be a good one. I cannot permit any one to say to me that such and such a man shall be appointed and no one else; nor if I believe a man to be unfit can I accept any one else's judgment that he is fit. In return, I have of course no right to insist that the Senate shall accept my judgment as to a man's fitness. They can reject any nominee of mine; and if they do so I will try to find some thoroughly good man whom they will accept. (To Senators from Oregon, August 25, 1903.) *Mem. Ed.* XXIII, 286; Bishop I, 248.

APPOINTMENTS AND PARTY ORGANIZATION. I want to stand well with the organization, and all that, but I wish it distinctly understood that I will appoint no man to office, even if recommended by the organization, unless he is wholly qualified for the position he seeks and is a man of integrity. (To a Senator from Illinois; conversation, October 1901.) *Mem. Ed.* XXIII, 181; Bishop I, 156.

APPOINTMENTS AND SENATORIAL COURTESY. I am not yet prepared to announce my decision about Mr. H., but I must emphatically dissent from your statement that "it ought to suffice for me to simply say that I prefer Y. to H."; and furthermore, that the appointment would "be recognized as an affront to the Senior Senator from the State of New York." ... I do not understand how you can make such a statement. It is my business to nominate or refuse to nominate, and yours, together with your colleagues, to confirm or refuse to confirm. Of course the common-sense way is to confer together and try to come to an agreement. (To Senator T. C. Platt, June 17, 1906.) *Mem. Ed.* XXIV, 18; Bishop II, 14.

——————. About appointments I was obliged by the Constitution to consult the Senate; and the long-established custom of the Senate meant that in practice this consultation was with individual senators and even with big politicians who stood behind the senators. I was only one-half the appointing power; I nominated; but the Senate confirmed. In practice, by what was called "the courtesy of the Senate," the Senate normally refused to confirm any appointment if the senator from the State objected to it. In exceptional cases, where I could arouse public attention, I could force through the appointment in spite of the opposition of the senators; in all ordinary cases this was impossible. On the other hand, the senator could of course do nothing for any man unless I chose to nominate him. In consequence the Constitution itself forced the President and the senators from each State to come to a working agreement on the appointments in and from that State. (1913.) *Mem. Ed.* XXII, 406; *Nat. Ed.* XX, 348.

APPOINTMENTS. See also CIVIL SERVICE; NEGRO APPOINTMENTS; OFFICE; PATRONAGE; SPOILS SYSTEM.

ARBITRATION. I do not believe that all matters between nations should be arbitrated, and I do not regard even good general arbitration treaties as of really prime importance, simply because they are not, and never can be self-acting, self-fulfilling. . . . But in good faith actually to arbitrate an existing arbitral question *is* action, and action of the most practical kind. *Outlook,* October 14, 1911, p. 365.

ARBITRATION—ISSUES NOT PERMITTING OF. It would be not merely foolish but wicked for us as a nation to agree to arbitrate any dispute that affects our vital interest or our independence or our honor; because such an agreement would amount on our part to a covenant to abandon our duty, to an agreement to surrender the rights of the American people about unknown matters at unknown times in the future. Such an agreement would be wicked if kept, and yet to break it—as it undoubtedly would be broken if the occasion arose—would be only less shameful than keeping it. *Outlook,* November 4, 1911, p. 566.

————. Of course as regards England, now that the Alaska Boundary is out of the way, there is not any question that we could not arbitrate, for neither England nor America would ever do anything adverse to the honor or vital interest of the other. But with either Germany or Japan it is perfectly conceivable that questions might arise which we could not submit to arbitration. If either one of them asked us to arbitrate the question of fortifying the Isthmus; or asked us to arbitrate the Monroe Doctrine, or the fortification or retention of Hawaii; or Germany's right to purchase the Danish Islands in the West Indies; or Japan's right to insist upon unlimited Japanese immigration—why! we would not and could not arbitrate. Of course mushy philanthropists, and short-sighted and greedy creatures in Boards of Trade, and the large idiot class generally, will howl about the treaty. (To H. C. Lodge, June 12, 1911.) Lodge *Letters* II, 404.

ARBITRATION AND PREPAREDNESS. Arbitration is an excellent thing, but ultimately those who wish to see this country at peace with foreign nations will be wise if they place reliance upon a first-class fleet of first-class battleships rather than on any arbitration treaty which the wit of man can devise. (Address as Assistant Secretary of the Navy, Naval War College, June 1897.) *Mem. Ed.* XV, 241; *Nat. Ed.* XIII, 183.

ARBITRATION TREATIES. Just at this moment . . . we have negotiated certain arbitration treaties with the great foreign Powers. I most earnestly hope that those arbitration treaties will become part of the supreme law of the land. Every friend of peace will join heartily in seeing that those arbitration treaties do become part of the supreme law of the land. By adopting them we will have taken a step, not a very long step, but undoubtedly a step in the direction of minimizing the chance for any trouble that might result in war; we will have in measurable degree provided for a method of substituting international disputes other than that of war as regards certain subjects, and as regards the particular nations with whom those treaties are negotiated. We can test the sincerity of those people devoted to peace largely by seeing whether this people does in effective fashion desire to have those treaties ratified, to have those treaties adopted. I have proceeded upon the assumption that this Nation was sincere when it said that it desired peace, that all proper steps to provide against the likelihood of war ought to be taken; and these arbitration treaties represent precisely those steps. (At Annapolis, Md., January 30, 1905.) *Presidential Addresses and State Papers* III, 212-213.

ARBITRATION TREATIES—SANCTITY OF. It is dishonorable for a nation as for an individual to break promises; and the most dishonorable way is both to break them and at the same time to make mere promises which cannot and ought not to be kept. This especially applies to international questions such as arbitration treaties. At this moment we are not living up to the treaties we have made, and yet are indulging in magniloquent talk about making new treaties, which in their turn would be promptly repudiated if ever the time came to reduce them to practice. Such a course justly exposes us to derision. It is as if in the business world a merchant repudiated his just debts, and at the same moment announced that he would like to incur new debts which there was no possibility of his paying. Only very silly people would be taken in by or approve such conduct. So it is with our nation and the question of arbitration treaties. We already have arbitration treaties. Let us continue them and live up to them, and until we have done so let us remember that it is idle folly to talk of making new treaties—that is, new promises—especially when these promises are themselves foolish. It is a mean morality which breaks a promise, and then as a substitute for keeping it proposes to make a new one which would certainly in its turn be broken. (At New York City, October 3, 1913.) *Mem. Ed.* XVIII, 397; *Nat. Ed.* XVI, 297.

ARBITRATION TREATIES — SINCERITY IN. I think that this amendment makes the treaties shams, and my present impression is that we had better abandon the whole business rather than give the impression of trickiness and insincerity which would be produced by solemnly promulgating a sham. The amendment, in effect, is to make any one of these so-called arbitration treaties solemnly enact that there shall be another arbitration treaty whenever the two governments decide that there shall be one. . . .

My present feeling is that I should like to have a clear-cut issue as to whether we are or are not to take this very short but real step toward settling international difficulties by arbitration, and that if we are not to take it I should prefer to withdraw the treaties and simply say that the temper of the Senate is hostile to arbitration.

In any event I think we should avoid above everything the suspicion that we are acting insincerely or trickily, or only with an eye for political effect and making believe to pass an arbitration treaty which in reality amounts to nothing. (To H. C. Lodge, January 6, 1905.) Lodge *Letters* II, 111, 112.

ARBITRATION TREATIES, GENERAL. A general arbitration treaty is nothing whatever but a promise, and surely every man in private life understands that the whole worth of a promise consists in its being kept, and that it is deeply discreditable for any man to make a promise when there is reasonable doubt whether he can keep it. A merchant who loosely promises all kinds of things without serious thought as to whether he will be able to keep his promises is in grave jeopardy of losing both his fortune and his good name. The same thing is true of a nation. We should understand that the time to weigh, and to weigh well and thoroughly, the full import of a promise is the time when it is desired to make that promise, and not the time when it is desired to break that promise. *Outlook,* January 18, 1913, p. 112.

——————. The all-inclusive arbitration treaties negotiated by the present administration amount to almost nothing. They are utterly worthless for good. They are however slightly mischievous because:

1. There is no provision for their enforcement, and,
2. They would be in some cases not only impossible but improper to enforce.

A treaty is a promise. It is like a promise to pay in the commercial world. Its value lies in the means provided for redeeming the promise. To make it, and not redeem it, is vicious. . . . The Wilson-Bryan all-inclusive arbitration treaties represent nothing whatever but international fiat money. To make them is no more honest than it is to issue fiat money. Mr. Bryan would not make a good secretary of the treasury, but he would do better in that position than as secretary of state. For his type of fiat obligations is a little worse in international than in internal affairs. The all-inclusive arbitration treaties, in whose free and unlimited negotiation Mr. Bryan takes such pleasure, are of less value than the thirty-cent dollars, whose free and unlimited coinage he formerly advocated. (*Everybody's,* January 1915.) *Mem. Ed.* XX, 157; *Nat. Ed.* XVIII, 135.

——————. I am not willing to admit that this nation has no duty to other nations. Yet the action of this government during the past year can only be defended on the assumption that we have no such duty to others.

Of course, it is a defensible, although not a lofty, position to deny that there is such a duty. But it is wholly indefensible to proclaim that there is such a duty and then in practice to abandon it. It is a base thing to propose to pass all-inclusive arbitration treaties, and to pass the thirty-odd all-inclusive commission peace treaties that actually have been passed during the last two years, and yet not to dare to say one word when The Hague conventions which we have already signed are violated by the strong at the expense of the weak. I agree with the abstract theory of the men responsible for all these various treaties; for this theory is to the effect that America owes a duty to the world, to humanity at large. I disagree with their practice, because I believe that we should in fact perform this duty, instead of merely talking about it in the abstract and then shamefully abandoning it the moment it becomes concrete. (*Metropolitan,* October 1915.) *Mem. Ed.* XX, 331; *Nat. Ed.* XVIII, 284.

ARBITRATION TREATIES, GENERAL —EFFECTS OF. A few weeks ago . . . people were stirred to a moment's belief that something had been accomplished by the enactment at Washington of a score or two of all-inclusive arbitration treaties; being not unnaturally misled by the fact that those responsible for the passage of the treaties indulged in some not wholly harmless bleating as to the good effects they would produce. As a matter of fact, they *probably* will not produce the smallest effect of any kind or sort. Yet it is *possible* they may have a mischievous effect, inasmuch as under certain circumstances to fulfil them would cause frightful disaster to the United States, while to break them, even although under compulsion and because it was absolutely necessary, would be fruitful of keen humiliation to every right-thinking man who is jealous of our international good name. (New York *Times*, November 1, 1914.) *Mem. Ed.* XX, 74; *Nat. Ed.* XVIII, 64.

ARBITRATION TREATIES, GENERAL—VALUE OF. Under existing conditions universal and all-inclusive arbitration treaties have been utterly worthless, because where there is no power to compel nations to arbitrate, and where it is perfectly certain that some nations will pay no respect to such agreements unless they can be forced to do so, it is mere folly for others to trust to promises impossible of performance; and it is an act of positive bad faith to make these promises when it is certain that the nation making them would violate them. But this does not in the least mean that we must abandon hope of taking action which will lessen the chance of war and make it more possible to circumscribe the limits of war's devastation. (*Outlook,* September 23, 1914.) *Mem. Ed.* XX, 33; *Nat. Ed.* XVIII, 28.

————————. Recently, there have been negotiated in Washington thirty or forty little all-inclusive arbitration or so-called "peace" treaties, which represent as high a degree of fatuity as is often achieved in these matters. There is no likelihood that they will do us any great material harm because it is absolutely certain that we would not pay the smallest attention to them in the event of their being invoked in any matter where our interests were seriously involved; but it would do us moral harm to break them, even although this were the least evil of two evil alternatives. It is a discreditable thing that at this very moment, with before our eyes such proof of the worthlessness of the neutrality treaties affecting Belgium and Luxembourg, our nation should be negotiating treaties which convince every sensible and well-informed observer abroad that we are either utterly heedless in making promises which cannot be kept or else willing to make promises which we have no intention of keeping. What has just happened shows that such treaties are worthless except to the degree that force can and will be used in backing them. (New York *Times,* October 4, 1914.) *Mem. Ed.* XX, 41; *Nat. Ed.* XVIII, 35.

ARBITRATION TREATIES, GENERAL VERSUS SPECIFIC. *General* arbitration treaties under the best circumstances can only be promises; they appeal especially to sentimentalists, who are never safe advisers, and their importance is usually exaggerated to a ludicrous degree; the really important thing is the practical application of the principle to *specific* instances. (*Outlook,* September 9, 1911.) *Mem. Ed.* XVIII, 421; *Nat. Ed.* XVI, 314.

ARBITRATION TREATIES, LIMITED. Genuine good can even now be accomplished by narrowly limited and defined arbitration treaties which are not all-inclusive, if they deal with subjects on which arbitration can be accepted. This nation has repeatedly acted in obedience to such treaties; and great good has come from arbitrations in such cases as, for example, the Dogger Bank incident, when the Russian fleet fired on British trawlers during the Russo-Japanese War. (New York *Times,* October 4, 1914.) *Mem. Ed.* XX, 36; *Nat. Ed.* XVIII, 31.

ARBITRATION TREATY WITH BRITISH EMPIRE. The time has now come when it would be perfectly safe to enter into universal arbitration treaties with the British Empire, for example, reserving such rights only as Australia and Canada themselves would reserve inside the British Empire; but there are a number of outside peoples with whom it would not be safe to go much further than above outlined. If we only made this one kind of agreement, we could keep it, and we should make no agreement that we would not and could not keep. More essential than anything else is it for us to remember that in matters of this kind an ounce of practical performance is worth a ton of windy rhetorical promises. (Kansas City *Star,* November 17, 1918.) *Mem. Ed.* XXI, 447; *Nat. Ed.* XIX, 403.

ARBITRATION TREATY WITH GERMANY. I hope you can see your way clear to have your Government enter into a treaty of arbitration with the United States. In the form in which the treaty now is I freely admit that it is not as effective as I could wish. Nevertheless good will result from the expression of goodwill implied in the treaty; and it would have a certain binding effect upon the Senate, making it morally obligatory to accept any reasonable agreement which might subsequently be made. Moreover it would confer a real benefit in the event of any sudden flurry both by providing the executives of the two countries with an excellent reason for demanding cool consideration of any question by their respective peoples, and also by enabling them to make a strong appeal under the sanction of a solemn treaty to both the peoples and their legislatures to accept an honorable arbitration. (To Emperor William II,

May 6, 1908.) *Mem. Ed.* XXIV, 333; Bishop II, 283.

ARBITRATION. *See also* HAGUE CONVENTIONS; HAGUE TREATIES; INTERNATIONAL DISPUTES; LEAGUE FOR PEACE; LEAGUE OF NATIONS; NEUTRALITY; PEACE; TREATIES.

ARBITRATION, INDUSTRIAL. *See* INDUSTRIAL ARBITRATION.

ARBOR DAY. Arbor Day (which means simply "Tree Day") is now observed in every State in our Union—and mainly in the schools. At various times from January to December, but chiefly in this month of April, you give a day or part of a day to special exercises and perhaps to actual tree-planting, in recognition of the importance of trees to us as a nation, and of what they yield in adornment, comfort, and useful products to the communities in which you live.

It is well that you should celebrate your Arbor Day thoughtfully, for within your lifetime the nation's need of trees will become serious. We of an older generation can get along with what we have, though with growing hardship; but in your full manhood and womanhood you will want what nature once so bountifully supplied and man so thoughtlessly destroyed; and because of that want you will reproach us, not for what we have used, but for what we have wasted....

A true forest is not merely a storehouse full of wood, but, as it were, a factory of wood, and at the same time a reservoir of water. When you help to preserve our forests or to plant new ones, you are acting the part of good citizens. The value of forestry deserves, therefore, to be taught in the schools, which aim to make good citizens of you. If your Arbor Day exercises help you to realize what benefits each one of you receives from the forests, and how by your assistance these benefits may continue, they will serve a good end. (Arbor Day message to school-children, Washington, April 15, 1907.) *Mem. Ed.* XVIII, 166-167; *Nat. Ed.* XVI, 127-128.

ARBOR DAY. *See also* CONSERVATION; FOREST; TREES.

ARCHAEOLOGY. Archaeologists, in order to reach the highest point in their profession, should be not merely antiquarians but out-of-door men, and above all, gifted with that supreme quality of the best type of historian, the quality of seeing the living body through the dry bones, and then making others see it also. In fact, this is just what the archaeologist is: a historian. The best archaeologist ought to be a man whose books would be as fascinating as Thucydides or Tacitus, Gibbon or Macaulay; as fascinating and as fundamentally truthful as Herodotus himself. (*Outlook,* September 30, 1911.) *Mem. Ed.* XIV, 55; *Nat. Ed.* XII, 174-175.

ARCHAEOLOGY. *See also* HISTORICAL KNOWLEDGE; INSCRIPTIONS; PRIMITIVE SOCIETY.

ARCHITECTURE. Mere copying, mere imitation is as thoroughly unworthy in architecture as in every other branch of art and life. We need to profit by everything which has been done in the past, or is now being done, in other countries. We need always to adopt and develop what we adopt, and, if possible, ourselves to develop what is new and original or else what is indigenous to our soil. California and the Southwest generally have been particularly successful in thus developing the old colonial Spanish architecture to our own uses; and in places the southwestern people are now doing the same thing with the far older architecture of the Pueblo Indians. The need of avoiding the aberrations of false or artificial originality must not blind us to the fact that unless there is real originality there will be no greatness.

To follow conventions merely because they are conventions is silly.... Let me give one small instance; the lion, because of the way in which his mane lends itself to use in stone, has always been a favorite for decorative purposes in architecture. He has in architecture become universally acclimatized and there is no objection to his use anywhere. But we happen to have here on this continent, in the bison with its shaggy frontlet and mane and short curved horns, a beast which equally lends itself to decorative use and which possesses the advantage of being our own. I earnestly wish that the conventions of architecture here in America would be so shaped as to include a widespread use of the bison's head; and in a case like that of the New York Public Library there would be advantage from every standpoint in substituting two complete bisons' figures for the preposterous lions, apparently in the preliminary stages of epilepsy, which now front on and disgrace Fifth Avenue.

There is good architecture, public and private, here in the United States, good architecture of all types from the loftiest to the humblest, but it is over-slaughed by the mass of poor architecture. If houses are built simply and comfortably, and if each feature possesses a definite and wholesome purpose, then, although they may lack distinction, they are never ridiculous or discreditable. But there are avenues in at least some of our big cities, and in at least some residential countrysides, which run between houses, mostly small houses, two-thirds of which represent painted and pretentious gimcrackery of the most odious type. There are districts crowded with domiciles of the very wealthy which are mere jumbles of unrelated copies of what is good abroad and of sporadic types of native ugliness. Yet there are also plenty of houses in the city and the country where wealth and taste have combined to give to the house distinction, while yet amplifying all that is useful and comfortable. These houses show love of beauty for its own sake, and also the power to heighten comfort and usefulness while making them beautiful. (Letter to American Institute of Architects, read December 7, 1916.) *Proceedings of the Fiftieth Annual Convention of the American Institute of Architects, Minneapolis, Minn.*, p. 45.

ARCHITECTURE. *See also* PUBLIC BUILDINGS.

ARCTIC AND ANTARCTIC REGIONS. The contrast in life between the arctic and antarctic regions is very striking. The antarctic continent is a vast snow-covered mass of land, absolutely lifeless except for the life of whale and seal, penguin and gull, on the fringes. This is a most interesting life for the naturalists. . . . But this life, though interesting, is limited. There are no mammals, and no man has ever dwelt there nor visited it save as explorers visit it. There has never been any permanent human habitation even on the fringe of the antarctic.

All this is reversed in the arctic region. There is an abundant life stretching very far toward the pole, and probably there are some representatives of this life which occasionally stray to the pole. Both in the water and on the ice when it is solid over the water, and on the land, in the brief arctic summer when the sun never sets, the arctic regions teem with life as do few other portions of the globe. Save where killed out by men, whales, seals, walruses, and innumerable fish literally swarm in the waters; myriads not only of water-birds but of land-birds fairly darken the air in their flights; and there are many strange mammals, some of which abound with a plenty which one would associate rather with the tropics. (*Outlook*, March 1, 1913.) *Mem. Ed.* XIV, 586; *Nat. Ed.* XII, 442.

ARCTIC EXPLORERS. *See* PEARY, ROBERT E.

ARGENTINA. *See* MONROE DOCTRINE.

ARISTOCRACY AND PLUTOCRACY. There is something to be said for government by a great aristocracy which has furnished leaders to the nation in peace and war for generations; even a democrat like myself must admit this. But there is absolutely nothing to be said for government by a plutocracy, for government by men very powerful in certain lines and gifted with the "money touch," but with ideals which in their essence are merely those of so many glorified pawnbrokers. (To Sir Edward Grey, November 15, 1913.) *Mem. Ed.* XXIV, 409; Bishop II, 347.

ARISTOCRACY AND PLUTOCRACY. *See also* MATERIALIST; MILLIONAIRES; WEALTH.

ARMAGEDDON. The present contest is but a phase of the larger struggle. Assuredly the fight will go on whether we win or lose; but it will be a sore disaster to lose. What happens to me is not of the slightest consequence; I am to be used, as in a doubtful battle any man is used, to his hurt or not, so long as he is useful, and is then cast aside or left to die. I wish you to feel this. I mean it; and I shall need no sympathy when you are through with me, for this fight is far too great to permit us to concern ourselves about any one man's welfare. If we are true to ourselves by putting far above our own interests the triumph of the high cause for which we battle we shall not lose. It would be far better to fail honorably for the cause we champion than it would be to win by foul methods the foul victory for which our opponents hope. But the victory shall be ours, and it shall be won as we have already won so many victories, by clean and honest fighting for the loftiest of causes. We fight in honorable fashion for the good of mankind; fearless of the future; unheeding of our individual fates; with unflinching hearts and undimmed eyes; we stand at Armageddon, and we battle for the Lord. (At Chicago, June 17, 1912.) *Mem. Ed.* XIX, 317; *Nat. Ed.* XVII, 231.

ARMAMENTS—LIMITATION OF. Something should be done as soon as possible to check the growth of armaments, especially vital armaments, by international agreement. No one power could or should act by itself; for it is eminently undesirable, from the standpoint of the peace of righteousness, that a power which really does believe in peace should place itself at the mercy of some rival which may at bottom have no such belief and no intention of acting on it. But, granted sincerity of purpose, the great powers of the world should find no insurmountable difficulty in reaching an agreement which would put an end to the present costly and growing extravagance of expenditure on naval armaments. An agreement merely to limit the size of ships would have been very useful a few years ago, and would still be of use; but the agreement should go much further. (Before Nobel Prize Committee, Christiania, Norway; May 5, 1910.) *Mem. Ed.* XVIII, 414; *Nat. Ed.* XVI, 308.

ARMAMENTS—NEED FOR. There is every reason why we should try to limit the cost of armaments, as these tend to grow excessive, but there is also every reason to remember that in the present stage of civilization a proper armament is the surest guarantee of peace—and is the only guarantee that war, if it does come, will not mean irreparable and overwhelming disaster. (1913.) *Mem. Ed.* XXII, 245; *Nat. Ed.* XX, 210.

ARMAMENTS. *See also* DISARMAMENT; MUNITIONS; NAVAL ARMAMENTS; PREPAREDNESS.

ARMENIAN MASSACRES. The news of the terrible fate that has befallen the Armenians must give a fresh shock of sympathy and indignation. Let me emphatically point out that the sympathy is useless unless it is accompanied with indignation, and that the indignation is useless if it exhausts itself in words instead of taking shape in deeds. (To Samuel T. Dutton, chairman, Committee on Armenian Outrages. November 24, 1915.) *Mem. Ed.* XX, 445; *Nat. Ed.* XVIII, 382.

ARMENIANS—SACRIFICE OF. Thanks largely to the very unhealthy influence of the men whose business it is to speculate in the money market, and who approach every subject from the financial standpoint, purely; and thanks quite as much to the cold-blooded brutality and calculating timidity of many European rulers and statesmen, the peace of Europe has been preserved, while the Turk has been allowed to butcher the Armenians with hideous and unmentionable barbarity, and has actually been helped to keep Crete in slavery. War has been averted at the cost of more bloodshed and infinitely more suffering and degradation to wretched women and children than have occured in any European struggle since the days of Waterloo. No war of recent years, no matter how wanton, has been so productive of horrible misery as the peace which the powers have maintained during the continuance of the Armenian butcheries. (Address as Assistant Secretary of the Navy, Naval War College; June, 1897.) *Mem. Ed.* XV, 242; *Nat. Ed.* XIII, 184.

ARMY—EFFICIENCY OF THE. As a nation we have always been short-sighted in providing for the efficiency of the army in time of peace. (Seventh Annual Message, Washington, December 3, 1907.) *Mem. Ed.* XVII, 547; *Nat. Ed.* XV, 466.

——————. In no country with an army worth calling such is there a chance for a man physically unfit to stay in the service. Our countrymen should understand that every army officer—and every marine officer—ought to be summarily removed from the service unless he is able to undergo far severer tests than those which, as a beginning, I imposed. To follow any other course is to put a premium on slothful incapacity, and to do the gravest wrong to the nation. (1913.) *Mem. Ed.* XXII, 59; *Nat. Ed.* XX, 51.

ARMY—PROMOTIONS IN THE. General X. has been in several times to see me, more often than any other candidate for promotion. He has an excellent record but seems unable to understand the utter impropriety of doing what he asks, which is, not to promote him to a vacancy but to punish some man now in the service by forcing him to retire in order to do a favor to General X. It is barely possible that some case would arise of so extreme a character as to justify such a proceeding, but I can hardly imagine it. There is no warrant whatever for doing it in General X.'s case as an exception, and it surely cannot be advocated as a general policy. It is not a question of giving General X. a promotion. It is a question of doing him a favor to which he has no more claim than hundreds of other officers, by doing a serious wrong and injustice to a man now in office. (To a Congressman from Maine, November 9, 1901.) *Mem. Ed.* XXIII, 182; Bishop I, 156.

——————. When I uphold the hands of the General Staff by taking their recommendations for promotion as against those of any outsider, no matter how influential, no matter how powerful, I am doing my best to prevent our little army from being reduced to a condition which would be only one degree above that to which it would be reduced if I tolerated actual corruption. In so acting, it seems to me that I am entitled to the support of every good American who feels that the Army is the property of the Nation, and not of one party, still less of any individual in that party. I can no more allow it to be run in the interest of politicians than I could allow it to be run in the interests of contractors or patentees. It is to be run in the interest of the entire American people, and with an eye single to making it the best that it can possibly be made. (To a Senator from Vermont, June 3, 1905.) *Mem. Ed.* XXIII, 510; Bishop I, 444.

──────────. I like what you say about the fact that 90 per cent of the officers in the division have risen from the ranks. . . . This represents the true American spirit; and when we get our universal service every officer in the army and the navy will have served for a year as an enlisted man before he is eligible for appointment as an officer. (To enlisted men, Twenty-seventh N. Y. Volunteer Division, April 6, 1918.) *Mem. Ed.* XXIV, 519; Bishop II, 443.

ARMY—RATIONS IN THE. It is all right to have differences in food and the like in times of peace and plenty, when everybody is comfortable. But in really hard times officers and men must share alike if the best work is to be done. (1913.) *Mem. Ed.* XXII, 302; *Nat. Ed.* XX, 258.

ARMY—REORGANIZATION OF THE. Our army needs complete reorganization,—not merely enlarging,—and the reorganization can only come as the result of legislation. A proper general staff should be established, and the positions of ordnance, commissary, and quartermaster officers should be filled by detail from the line. Above all, the army must be given the chance to exercise in large bodies. Never again should we see, as we saw in the Spanish war, major-generals in command of divisions who had never before commanded three companies together in the field. Yet, incredible to relate, Congress has shown a queer inability to learn some of the lessons of the war. There were large bodies of men in both branches who opposed the declaration of war, who opposed the ratification of peace, who opposed the upbuilding of the army, and who even opposed the purchase of armor at a reasonable price for the battleships and cruisers, thereby putting an absolute stop to the building of any new fighting-ships for the navy. If, during the years to come, any disaster should befall our arms, afloat or ashore, and thereby any shame come to the United States, remember that the blame will lie upon the men whose names appear upon the roll-calls of Congress on the wrong side of these great questions. On them will lie the burden of any loss of our soldiers and sailors, of any dishonor to the flag; and upon you and the people of this country will lie the blame if you do not repudiate, in no unmistakable way, what these men have done. (Before the Hamilton Club, Chicago, April 10, 1899.) *Mem. Ed.* XV, 276-277; *Nat. Ed.* XIII, 327.

ARMY, REGULAR. Provide a Regular Army of a quarter of a million men. Relatively to the nation this army would be no larger than the New York police force is relatively to the city of New York. On paper our present strength is one hundred thousand, and we have in the United States a mobile army of only thirty thousand men. We need ten thousand more men adequately to man our coast defenses at home, and five thousand additional adequately to man those abroad. We need twenty thousand additional men to provide an adequate mobile army for meeting a raid on our overseas possessions. At home we should have a mobile army of one hundred and fifty thousand men, in order to guarantee us against having New York or San Francisco at once seized by any big military nation which went to war with us. A quarter of a million in the Regular Army is the minimum that will insure the nation's safety from sudden attack. (*Metropolitan,* February 1916.) *Mem. Ed.* XX, 290; *Nat. Ed.* XVIII, 249.

ARMY, REGULAR—COST OF. In a country like ours a professional army will always be costly, for as regards such an army the government has to go into the labor market for its soldiers, and compete against industrialism. (*Metropolitan,* February 1916.) *Mem. Ed.* XX, 294; *Nat. Ed.* XVIII, 252.

ARMY, STANDING. I do not believe in a large standing army. Most emphatically I do not believe in militarism. Most emphatically I do not believe in any policy of aggression by us. But I do believe that no man is really fit to be the free citizen of a free republic unless he is able to bear arms and at need to serve with efficiency in the efficient army of the republic. (New York *Times,* November 15, 1914.) *Mem. Ed.* XX, 107; *Nat. Ed.* XVIII, 92.

ARMY IN A DEMOCRACY. If we are a true democracy, if we really believe in government of the people by the people and for the people, if we believe in social and industrial justice to be achieved through the people, and therefore in the right of the people to demand the service of all the people, let us make the army fundamentally an army of the whole people. (*Metropolitan,* November 1915.) *Mem. Ed.* XX, 391; *Nat. Ed.* XVIII, 335.

ARMY OFFICERS—TRAINING OF. The careful training in body and mind, and especially in character, gained in an academy like West Point, and the subsequent experience in the field, endow the regular officer with such advantages that, in any but a long war, he cannot be overtaken even by the best natural fighter. In the American Civil War, for instance, the greatest leaders were all West Pointers. Yet even there, by the end of the contest both armies had produced regimental, brigade, and division commanders, who though originally from civil life, had learned to know their business exactly as well as the best regular officers; and there was at least one such commander—Forrest—who, in his own class, was unequalled. If in a war the regular officers prove to have been trained merely to the pedantry of their profession, and do not happen to number men of exceptional ability in their ranks, then sooner or later the men who are born soldiers will come to the front, even though they have been civilians until late in life. (1900.) *Mem. Ed.* XIII, 335; *Nat. Ed.* X, 228.

ARMY. See also Chaplains; Desertion; Military Forces; Military History; Military Service; Military Training; National Guard; Rough Riders; West Point; Westward Movement.

ARNOLD, BENEDICT. How well you have done Benedict Arnold! How will you deal with his fall; with the money-paid treason of the rider of the war storm! What a base web was shot through the woof of his wild daring! He was at heart a Lucifer, that child of thunder and lover of the battle's hottest heat; and dreadful it is to think that when he fell his fall should have been, not that of the lightning-blasted Son of the Morning, but that of a mere Mammon or Belial. (To Sir George Otto Trevelyan, January 1, 1908.) *Mem. Ed.* XXIV, 197; Bishop II, 168.

ARNOLD, MATTHEW. Mr. Matthew Arnold's sudden death was felt almost as much in the American as in the English world of letters. We on this side of the water feel that we owe him as much as you do. We are far from agreeing with all his views; there are many of them which we do not believe could be held by a healthy and rudely vigorous nation; but we know that we get from his writings much of which our own civilization stands in especial need. Moreover, he is entitled to a most respectful hearing when he points out what he deems the shortcomings of our civilization; and were his remarks malicious, which they are not, and unjust, which they are only in part, it would not diminish in the least the debt due from us to him.

Mr. Arnold undoubtedly tried to write about us in the only way that can possibly produce good, either to the people criticized or to the other people who are to profit by the example portrayed. He wrote his last two articles only after some observation, and he evidently honestly endeavored to discriminate between the good and the bad. Where he failed to be fair, the failure was probably entirely unintentional; it was wholly out of his power to do full justice to a rough, pushing, vigorous people. The roseate-hued after-dinner account of an already prejudiced friend, produced after three months' travel, practically from one entertainment to another, however pleasant reading, is but a shade less useless than the bitter diatribe written by some one resolutely determined to see all things through a gloomy fog of dislike. Every people, as well as every system, has its faults and virtues; if the former overbalance the latter, the observer should say so, but he should be sure of his scales first. We honestly believe that our system has on the whole worked better than any other; but plenty of defects can be pointed out even by its friends; and if any foreigner who has studied it believes it to be bad, and fears that its influence both on our own people and on European races will be detrimental, then it is not only his right, but his duty, to say so and give his reasons. *Eclectic Magazine,* November 1888, p. 583.

ART. Art, or at least the art for which I care, must present the ideal through the temperament and the interpretation of the painter. I do not greatly care for the reproduction of landscapes which, in effect, I see whenever I ride or walk. I wish 'the light that never was on land or sea' in the pictures that I am to live with. (To P. Marcius Simons, March 19, 1904.) *Mem. Ed.* XXIII, 377; Bishop I, 327.

———. Of course an over-self-conscious straining after a nationalistic form of expression may defeat itself. But this is merely because self-consciousness is almost always a drawback. The self-conscious striving after originality also tends to defeat itself. Yet the fact remains that the greatest work must bear the stamp of originality. In exactly the same way the greatest work must bear the stamp of nationalism. American work must smack of our own soil, mental and moral, no less than physical, or it will have little of permanent value.

Let us profit by the scholarship, art, and literature of every other country and every other time; let us adapt to our own use whatever is of value in any other language, in any other literature, in any other art; but let us keep steadily in mind that in every field of endeavor the work best worth doing for Americans must in some degree express the distinctive characteristics of our own national soul. (Before Amer. Academy and Nat. Inst. of Arts and Letters, New York City, November 16, 1916.) *Mem. Ed.* XIV, 461-462; *Nat. Ed.* XII, 336.

ART—NATIONAL GALLERY OF. There should be a national gallery of art established in the capital city of this country. This is important not merely to the artistic but to the material welfare of the country; and the people are to be congratulated on the fact that the movement to establish such a gallery is taking definite form under the guidance of the Smithsonian Institution. So far from there being a tariff on works of art brought into the country, their importation should be encouraged in every way. There have been no sufficient collections of objects of art by the government, and what collections have been acquired are scattered and are generally placed in unsuitable and imperfectly lighted galleries. (Seventh Annual Message, Washington, December 3, 1907.) *Mem. Ed.* XVII, 541-542; *Nat. Ed.* XV, 461.

ART AND NATIONAL LIFE. Normally there must be some relation between art and the national life if the art is to represent a real contribution to the sum of artistic world development. Nations have achieved greatness without this greatness representing any artistic side; other great nations have developed an artistic side only after a preliminary adoption of what has been supplied by the creative genius of some wholly alien people. But the national greatness which is wholly divorced from every form of artistic production, whether in literature, painting, sculpture, or architecture, unless it is marked by extraordinary achievements in war and government, is not merely a one-sided, but a malformed, greatness, as witness Tyre, Sidon, and Carthage.

It behooves us in the United States not to be content with repeating on a larger scale the history of commercial materialism of the great Phœnician commonwealths. This means that here in America, if we do not develop a serious art and literature of our own, we shall have a warped national life. (Before Amer. Academy and Nat. Inst. of Arts and Letters, New York City, November 16, 1916.) *Mem. Ed.* XIV, 452; *Nat. Ed.* XII, 329.

ART. See also ARCHITECTURE; PAINTING; PUBLIC BUILDINGS.

ARTISTS. See REMINGTON, F.; SAINT-GAUDENS, AUGUSTUS.

ARYAN SUPREMACY. See CHAMBERLAIN, HOUSTON STEWART.

ASIA. See CHINA; INDIA; JAPAN; MONGOL INVASIONS; ORIENT; PHILIPPINES.

ASIATIC IMMIGRATION. See CHINESE IMMIGRATION; IMMIGRATION; JAPANESE EXCLUSION.

ASSASSINATION—RISK OF. The secret service men are a very small but very necessary thorn in the flesh. Of course they would not be the least use in preventing any assault upon my life. I do not believe there is any danger of such an assault, and if there were it would be simple nonsense to try to prevent it, for as Lincoln said, though it would be safer for a President to live in a cage, it would interfere with his business. (To H. C. Lodge, August 6, 1906.) Lodge *Letters* II, 224.

ASSASSINATION, ATTEMPTED. Prominence in public life inevitably means that creatures of morbid and semi-criminal type are incited thereby to murderous assault. But . . . I must say I have never understood public men who get nervous about assassination. For the last eleven years I have of course thoroughly understood that I might at any time be shot, and probably would be shot some time. I think I have come off uncommonly well. But what I cannot understand is any serious-minded public man not being so absorbed in the great and vital questions with which he has to deal as to exclude thoughts of assassination. I do not think this is a question of courage at all. I think it is a question of the major interest driving out the minor interest. (To Sir George Otto Trevelyan, October 29, 1912.) *Mem. Ed.* XXIV, 205; Bishop II, 176.

——————. Modern civilization is undoubtedly somewhat soft, and the average political orator or party leader, the average broker, or banker, or factory-owner, at least when he is past middle age, is apt to be soft—I mean both

[30]

mentally and physically—and such a man accepts being shot as a frightful and unheard-of calamity, and feels very sorry for himself and thinks only of himself and not of the work on which he is engaged or of his duty to others, or indeed of his real self-respect. But a good soldier or sailor, or for the matter of that even a civilian accustomed to hard and hazardous pursuits, a deep-sea fisherman, or railwayman, or cowboy, or lumber-jack, or miner, would normally act as I acted without thinking anything about it. . . .

There was then a perfectly obvious duty, which was to go on and make my speech. In the very unlikely event of the wound being mortal I wished to die with my boots on, so to speak. . . .

Moreover, I felt that under such circumstances it would be very difficult for people to disbelieve in my sincerity, and that therefore they would be apt to accept at the face value the speech I wished to make. (To Sir Edward Grey, November 15, 1912.) *Mem. Ed.* XXIV, 401, 403; Bishop II, 342, 343.

————. I have not the slightest feeling against him [the assassin]; I have a very strong feeling against the people who, by their ceaseless and intemperate abuse, excited him to the action, and against the mushy people who would excuse him and all other criminals once the crime has been committed. (To J. St. Loe Strachey, December 16, 1912.) *Mem. Ed.* XXIV, 404; Bishop II, 344.

————. I did not care a rap for being shot. It is a trade risk, which every prominent public man ought to accept as a matter of course. For eleven years I have been prepared any day to be shot; and if any one of the officers of my regiment had abandoned the battle merely because he received a wound that did nothing worse than break a rib, I should never have trusted that officer again. I would have expected him to keep on in the fight as long as he could stand; and what I expect lieutenants to do I expect *a fortiori*, a leader to do. (To Sir Cecil Arthur Spring-Rice, December 31, 1912.) *Mem. Ed.* XXIV, 404; Bishop II, 344.

ASSASSINATION, ATTEMPTED. *See also* BULL MOOSE.

ASSESSMENTS. *See* POLITICAL ASSESSMENTS.

ASSIMILATION. *See* AMERICAN PEOPLE; AMERICANIZATION; IMMIGRATION; LANGUAGE.

ATHLETICS. It is of far more importance that a man shall play something himself, even if he plays it badly, than that he shall go with hundreds of companions to see some one else play well. . . . We can not afford to turn out of college men who shrink from physical effort or from a little physical pain. In any republic courage is a prime necessity for the average citizen if he is to be a good citizen; and he needs physical courage no less than moral courage, the courage that dares as well as the courage that endures, the courage that will fight valiantly alike against the foes of the soul and the foes of the body. Athletics are good, especially in their rougher forms, because they tend to develop such courage. They are good also because they encourage a true democratic spirit; for in the athletic field the man must be judged not with reference to outside and accidental attributes, but to that combination of bodily vigor and moral quality which go to make up prowess. (At the Harvard Union, Cambridge, February 23, 1907.) *Mem. Ed.* XV, 483, 484; *Nat. Ed.* XIII, 560, 561.

————. I believe in athletics; but I believe in them chiefly because of the moral qualities that they display. I am glad to see the boy able to keep his nerve in a close baseball game, able to keep his courage under the punishment of a football game or in a four-mile boat race; because if the boy really amounts to anything and has got the right stuff in him, this means that he is going to keep his nerve and courage in more important things in after life. If your prowess is due simply to the possession of big muscles, it does not amount to much. What counts is the ability to back up the muscles with the right spirit. If you have the pluck, the grit, in you to count in sports, just as if you have the pluck and grit in you to count in your studies, so in both cases it will help you to count in after life. (At Georgetown College, Washington, D. C., June 14, 1906.) *Presidential Addresses and State Papers,* V, 789.

ATHLETICS — PROPER PLACE OF. Every vigorous game, from football to polo, if allowed to become more than a game, and if serious work is sacrificed to its enjoyment, is of course noxious. From the days when Trajan in his letters to Pliny spoke with such hearty contempt of the Greek overdevotion to athletics, every keen thinker has realized that vigorous sports are only good in their proper place. But in their proper place they are very good indeed. (Foreword to *The Master of Game* by Edward,

——————. The amateur athlete who thinks of nothing but athletics, and makes it the serious business of his life, becomes a bore, if nothing worse. A young man who has broken a running or jumping record, who has stroked a winning club crew, or played on his college nine or eleven, has a distinct claim to our respect; but if, when middle-aged, he has still done nothing more in the world, he forfeits even this claim which he originally had. (*North American Review,* August 1890.) *Mem. Ed.* XV, 520; *Nat. Ed.* XIII, 586-587.

——————. Athletic sports are excellent when treated as what they should be, that is as healthy pastimes; they become harmful if indulged in to excess, and if their importance in relation to the serious work of life is misestimated; and still more harmful when twisted into adjuncts of brutality or gambling. (Annual Message as Governor, Albany, January 3, 1900.) *Mem. Ed.* XVII, 66; *Nat. Ed.* XV, 57.

——————. I am delighted to have you play football. I believe in rough, manly sports. But I do not believe in them if they degenerate into the sole end of any one's existence. I don't want you to sacrifice standing well in your studies to any over-athleticism; and I need not tell you that character counts for a great deal more than either intellect or body in winning success in life. Athletic proficiency is a mighty good servant, and like so many other good servants, a mighty bad master. (To Theodore Roosevelt, Jr., October 4, 1903.) *Mem. Ed.* XXI, 502; *Nat. Ed.* XIX, 445.

ATHLETICS. See also BOXING; FOOTBALL; GYMNASTICS; JIU JITSU; PLAYGROUNDS; SPORTS.

ATTICS. How entirely I sympathize with your feelings in the attic! I know just what it is to get up into such a place and find the delightful, winding passages where one lay hidden with thrills of criminal delight, when the grown-ups were vainly demanding one's appearance at some legitimate and abhorred function; and then the once-beloved and half-forgotten treasures, and the emotions of peace and war, with reference to former companions, which they recall. (To Ethel Roosevelt, June 17, 1906.) *Mem. Ed.* XXI, 566; *Nat. Ed.* XIX, 508.

AUDUBON SOCIETIES. The Audubon Society and kindred organizations have done much for the proper protection of birds and of wild creatures generally; they have taken the lead in putting a stop to wanton or short-sighted destruction, and in giving effective utterance to the desires of those who wish to cultivate a spirit as far removed as possible from that which brings about such destruction. Sometimes, however, in endeavoring to impress upon a not easily aroused public the need for action, they in their zeal overstate this need. This is a very venial error compared to the good they have done, but in the interest of scientific accuracy it is to be desired that their cause should not be buttressed in such manner. (1905.) *Mem. Ed.* III, 313; *Nat. Ed.* III, 124.

——————. The Audubon societies and all similar organizations are doing a great work for the future of our country. Birds should be saved because of utilitarian reasons; and, moreover, they should be saved because of reasons unconnected with any return in dollars and cents. . . . And to lose the chance to see frigate-birds soaring in circles above the storm, or a file of pelicans winging their way homeward across the crimson afterglow of the sunset, or a myriad terns flashing in the bright light of midday as they hover in a shifting maze above the beach—why, the loss is like the loss of a gallery of the masterpieces of the artists of old time. (1916.) *Mem. Ed.* IV, 226-227; *Nat. Ed.* III, 376-377.

——————. I need hardly say how heartily I sympathize with the purposes of the Audubon Society. I would like to see all harmless wild things, but especially all birds, protected in every way. I do not understand how any man or woman who really loves nature can fail to try to exert all influence in support of such objects as those of the Audubon Society.

Spring would not be spring without bird songs, any more than it would be spring without buds and flowers, and I only wish that besides protecting the songsters, the birds of the grove, the orchard, the garden and the meadow, we could also protect the birds of the sea-shore and of the wildnerness. (To Chapman, March 22, 1899.) Frank M. Chapman, *Autobiography of a Bird-Lover.* (D. Appleton-Century Co., N. Y., 1933), pp. 180-181.

AUDUBON SOCIETIES. See also BIRDS; WILD LIFE.

AUSTRALIA — ADMIRATION FOR. I have, as every American ought to have, a hearty admiration for, and fellow feeling with, Australia, and I believe that America should be ready to stand back of Australia in any serious emergency. (1913.) *Mem. Ed.* XXII, 628; *Nat. Ed.* XX, 540.

AUTHORITY — CONDITIONS OF. No man is fit for control who does not possess intelligence, self-respect, and respect for the just rights of others. (1917.) *Mem. Ed.* XXI, 70; *Nat. Ed.* XIX, 59.

AUTHORITY. See also POWER.

AUTHORS. See ARNOLD, MATTHEW; BEEBE, WILLIAM; BEVERIDGE, ALBERT J.; BROWNING, ROBERT; BRYCE, LORD; BURROUGHS, JOHN; CARLYLE, THOMAS; CHAMBERLAIN, HOUSTON S.; COOPER, JAMES F.; DANTE; DAVIS, RICHARD H.; DICKENS, CHARLES; GARLAND, HAMLIN; GORKY, MAXIM; HARRIS, JOEL CHANDLER; LODGE, GEORGE CABOT; LOWELL, JAMES RUSSELL; MACAULAY, LORD; MAHAN, A. T.; MILTON, JOHN; MORRIS, WILLIAM; MUIR, JOHN; PARKMAN, FRANCIS; ROBINSON, E. A.; SELOUS, F. C.; SIMMS, W. G.; TOLSTOY, LEO; TREVELYAN, SIR GEORGE O.; WISTER, OWEN.

AVIATION IN WAR-TIME. We must also remember that while we are still only beginning to build the twenty thousand airplanes, and beginning to train the future twenty thousand aviators to fly, we have not yet even begun to train the few hundred aviators we already have, to fight. After the best type of airplane has been produced in vast numbers, and after the tens of thousands of men necessary have been trained to handle them in the air, it will still be necessary to train them how to do the actual shooting against the war-hawks on the other side, and the actual bombing at the same time that they dodge the anti-aircraft guns of the enemy. We have waited to learn all this and to do all this until war actually came, although for over two years and a half we were vouchsafed such warning as no other nation in recent times has had in advance of war. (Stafford Little Lecture at Princeton University, November 1917.) Theodore Roosevelt, *National Strength and International Duty.* (Princeton, N. J., 1917), pp. 50-51.

B

BACKWOODSMEN. See FRONTIERSMEN.

BACON, ROBERT. See ROOSEVELT DIVISION.

BAD LANDS. This broken country extends back from the river for many miles, and has been called always, by Indians, French voyageurs, and American trappers alike, the "Bad Lands," partly from its dreary and forbidding aspect and partly from the difficulty experienced in travelling through it. Every few miles it is crossed by creeks which open into the Little Missouri, of which they are simply repetitions in miniature, except that during most of the year they are almost dry, some of them having in their beds here and there a never-failing spring or muddy alkaline-water hole. From these creeks run coulées, or narrow, winding valleys, through which water flows when the snow melts; their bottoms contain patches of brush, and they lead back into the heart of the Bad Lands. Some of the buttes spread out into level plateaus, many miles in extent; others form chains, or rise as steep, isolated masses. Some are of volcanic origin, being composed of masses of scoria; the others, of sandstone or clay, are worn by water into the most fantastic shapes. In coloring they are as bizarre as in form. Among the level, parallel strata which make up the land are some of coal. When a coal vein gets on fire it makes what is called a burning mine, and the clay above it is turned into brick; so that where water wears away the side of a hill sharp streaks of black and red are seen across it, mingled with the grays, purples, and browns. Some of the buttes are overgrown with gnarled, stunted cedars, or small pines, and they are all cleft through and riven in every direction by deep narrow ravines, or by canyons with perpendicular sides.

In spite of their look of savage desolation, the Bad Lands make a good cattle country, for there is plenty of nourishing grass and excellent shelter from the winter storms. The cattle keep close to them in the cold months, while in the summertime they wander out on the broad prairies stretching back of them, or come down the river-bottoms. (1885.) *Mem. Ed.* I, 11-12; *Nat. Ed.* I, 9-10.

———————. The Bad Lands grade all the way from those that are almost rolling in character to those that are so fantastically broken in form and so bizarre in color as to seem hardly properly to belong to this earth. If the weathering forces have not been very active, the ground will look, from a little distance, almost like a level plain, but on approaching nearer, it will be seen to be crossed by straight-sided gullies and canyons, miles in length, cutting across the land in every direction and rendering it almost impassable for horsemen or wagon teams. If the

[33]

forces at work have been more intense, the walls between the different gullies have been cut down to thin edges, or broken through, leaving isolated peaks of strange shape, while the hollows have been channelled out deeper and deeper; such places show the extreme and most characteristic Bad Lands formation. When the weathering has gone on farther, the angles are rounded off, grass begins to grow, bushes and patches of small trees sprout up, [and] water is found in places. (1885.) *Mem. Ed.* I, 135; *Nat. Ed.* I, 111-112.

BAD LANDS—LIFE IN THE. I heartily enjoy this life, with its perfect freedom, for I am very fond of hunting, and there are few sensations I prefer to that of galloping over these rolling, limitless prairies, rifle in hand, or winding my way among the barren, fantastic and grimly picturesque deserts of the so-called Bad Lands. (To H. C. Lodge, August 24, 1884.) Lodge *Letters* I, 7.

BAD LANDS. *See also* CHIMNEY BUTTE RANCH; ELKHORN RANCH; RANCH LIFE.

BAKER, NEWTON D. Secretary Baker did not set himself to meet our greatest military need of to-day, which is a thorough mobilization of our whole man-power for service in our armies and in our war industries. He set himself to prevent the meeting of this need. Congress last spring made ready to go ahead with the "fight or work" plan. But Mr. Baker, acting for the President, intervened. He asked for delay, for procrastination, and of course thereby paralyzed congressional action. He protested against the enlargement of the draft-age limits. He protested against planning more than a few months in advance. He said that we were "many months ahead of our original hope in regard to the transportation of men" overseas; but he omitted to add that this was because the original plans were hopelessly inadequate. (*Metropolitan,* September 1918.) *Mem. Ed.* XXI, 307; *Nat. Ed.* XIX, 281.

BAKER, NEWTON D. *See also* ROOSEVELT DIVISION.

BALLOT, SHORT. I believe in the short ballot. You cannot get good service from the public servant if you cannot see him, and there is no more effective way of hiding him than by mixing him up with a multitude of others so that they are none of them important enough to catch the eye of the average, workaday citizen. (Before Ohio Constitutional Convention, Columbus, February 21, 1912.) *Mem. Ed.* XIX, 179; *Nat. Ed.* XVII, 132.

——————. The public servants for whom you vote should be so few in number that the people may know whom it is they are choosing to administer any particular office. A long ballot, cumbered with many names, is of all possible devices the one best adapted to give professional politicians, bread-and-butter politicians, the utmost possible advantage over ordinary citizens in the choice of public officers. The professional bread-and-butter man, whose business it is, can and will take the time to know about every man on such a ballot. It is his business, but you and I will not normally take the time. I will put it stronger than that. You and I cannot normally take the time; we cannot remember and we cannot be expected to remember the identity of a great number of individuals, no one of whom has to do a very important piece of work. (At Los Angeles, Cal., March 21, 1911.) *Mem. Ed.* XVIII, 605; *Nat. Ed.* XVI, 437.

BALLOT REFORM LAW. *See* ELECTION REFORMS.

BANKING. Our fiscal system is not good from the purely fiscal side. I am inclined to think that from this side, a central bank would be a good thing. Certainly I believe that at least a central bank, with branch banks in each of the States (I mean national banks, of course) would be good; but I doubt whether our people would support either scheme at present; and there is this grave objection, at least to the first, that the inevitable popular distrust of big financial men might result very dangerously if it were concentrated upon the officials of one huge bank. Sooner or later there would be in that bank some insolent man whose head would be turned by his own power and ability, who would fail to realize other types of ability and the limitations upon his power, and would by his actions awaken the slumbering popular distrust and cause a storm in which he would be as helpless as a child, and which would overwhelm not only him but other men and other things of far more importance. (To White, November 27, 1907.) Allan Nevins, *Henry White. Thirty Years of American Diplomacy.* (Harper & Bros., N. Y., 1930), p. 293.

BANKING AND CURRENCY SYSTEM. Now about the banking and currency system: I agree with you in your main contentions. I would like to see a thoroughly good system of banking and currency; but apparently you think little of the Aldrich bill, and yet this is the only measure that has been proposed that we can seriously consider. The trouble is that the minute

I try to get action all the financiers and business men differ so that nobody can advise me, nobody can give me any aid, and only Senator Aldrich has proposed a bill. (To Henry L. Higginson, February 19, 1908.) *Mem. Ed.* XXIV, 97; Bishop II, 83.

BANKING. *See also* CURRENCY; FINANCIERS; PANIC OF 1907.

BANKS—FUNCTION OF. Banks are the natural servants of commerce, and upon them should be placed, as far as practicable, the burden of furnishing and maintaining a circulation adequate to supply the needs of our diversified industries and of our domestic and foreign commerce; and the issue of this should be so regulated that a sufficient supply should be always available for the business interests of the country. (Second Annual Message, Washington, December 2, 1902.) *Mem. Ed.* XVII, 170; *Nat. Ed.* XV, 147.

BARBARIANS. *See* EXPANSION; IMPERIALISM; MISSIONARIES; PRIMITIVE SOCIETY; WARS OF CONQUEST; "YELLOW PERIL."

BARNES, WILLIAM. *See* LIBEL SUIT.

BATTLE FLEET—WORLD CRUISE OF. As regards the fleet going to the Pacific, there has been no change save that the naval board decided sooner than I had expected. I could not entertain any proposition to divide the fleet and send some vessels there, which has been the fool proposition of our own jingoes; but this winter we shall have reached the period when it is advisable to send the whole fleet on a practice cruise around the world. It became evident to me, from talking with the naval authorities, that in the event of war they would have a good deal to find out in the way of sending the fleet to the Pacific. Now, the one thing that I won't run the risk of is to experiment for the first time in a matter which would be of vital importance in time of war. Accordingly I concluded that it was imperative that we should send the fleet on what would practically be a practice voyage. I do not intend to keep it in the Pacific for any length of time; but I want all failures, blunders, and shortcomings to be made apparent in time of peace and not in time of war. Moreover, I think that before matters become more strained we had better make it evident that when it comes to visiting our own coasts on the Pacific or Atlantic and assembling the fleet in our own waters, we can not submit to any outside protests or interference. Curiously enough, the Japs have seen this more quickly than our own people. (To H. C. Lodge, July 10, 1907.) Lodge *Letters* II, 274.

———. I am more concerned over the Japanese situation than almost any other. Thank Heaven we have the navy in good shape. It is high time, however, that it should go on a cruise around the world. In the first place I think it will have a pacific effect to show that it can be done; and in the next place, after talking thoroughly over the situation with the naval board I became convinced that it was absolutely necessary for us to try in time of peace to see just what we could do in the way of putting a big battle fleet in the Pacific, and not make the experiment in time of war. (To Elihu Root, July 13, 1907.) *Mem. Ed.* XXIV, 74; Bishop II, 64.

———. This demonstration of combined courtesy and strength nowhere received a heartier response than in Japan, which is itself both strong and courteous. No English, German, or other battle fleet had ever gone to the Pacific. I regarded the Pacific as home waters just as much as the Atlantic, and regarded it as essential to find out in time of peace whether or not the fleet could be put there bodily. I determined on the move without consulting the Cabinet precisely as I took Panama without consulting the Cabinet. A council of war never fights, and in a crisis the duty of a leader is to lead and not to take refuge behind the generally timid wisdom of a multitude of counsellors. Except the digging of the Panama Canal this voyage of the battle fleet impressed Europe with a feeling of friendly respect for the United States more than anything else that had occurred since the Civil War. (In conversation with Joseph B. Bishop.) *Mem. Ed.* XXIV, 76; Bishop II, 65.

———. I am sure you would be delighted if you could see the accounts that have come from our battle fleet, which is now returning from its trip around the world. In gunnery and in battle tactics no less than in the ordinary voyage manœuvres, there has been a steady gain; and the fleet is far more efficient, collectively and individually, now than when it left these waters over a year ago. (To Emperor William II, January 2, 1909.) *Mem. Ed.* XXIV, 338; Bishop II, 287.

———. No nation regarded the cruise as fraught with any menace of hostility to itself; and yet every nation accepted it as a proof that we were not only desirous ourselves to keep the peace, but able to prevent the peace being broken at our expense. No cruise in any way approaching it has even been made by any fleet of any other power; and the best naval opinion abroad had been that no such feat was possible; that is, that no such cruise as that we actually made could be undertaken by a fleet of such size without innumerable breakdowns and accidents. The success of the cruise, performed as it was without a single accident, immeasurably raised the prestige, not only of our fleet, but of our nation; and was a distinct help to the cause of international peace. (*Outlook,* September 10, 1910.) *Mem. Ed.* XVIII, 24; *Nat. Ed.* XVI, 21.

——————. My point of view at the time the fleet sailed, was that if the Japanese attacked it, it was a certain sign that they were intending to attack us at the first favorable opportunity. I had been doing my best to be polite to the Japanese, and had finally become uncomfortably conscious of a very, very slight undertone of veiled truculence in their communications in connection with things that happened on the Pacific Slope; and I finally made up my mind that they thought I was afraid of them. . . .

I had great confidence in the fleet; I went over everything connected with it and found that the administrative officers on shore were calmly confident that they could keep everything in first-class shape, while the officers afloat, from the battleship commanders to the lieutenants in charge of the torpedo-boats, were straining like hounds in a leash, and the enlisted men were at least as eager, all desertions stopping and the ships becoming for the first time overmanned as soon as there was a rumor that we might have trouble with Japan, and that the fleet might move round to the Pacific. I felt that, in any event, if the fleet was not able to get to the Pacific in first-class shape, we had better find it out; and if Japan intended to have war it was infinitely better that we should gain two or three months necessary to prepare our fleet to start to the Pacific, instead of having to take those two or three months after war began. (To Sir George Otto Trevelyan, October 1, 1911.) *Mem. Ed.* XXIV, 291, 292; Bishop II, 249, 250.

BATTLE FLEET. *See also* BIG STICK; PEACE.

BATTLESHIPS—IMPORTANCE OF. Nothing that has yet occurred warrants us in feeling that we can afford to ease up in our programme of building battleships and cruisers, especially the former. The German submarines have done wonderfully in this war; their cruisers have done gallantly. But so far as Great Britain is concerned the vital and essential feature has been the fact that her great battle-fleet has kept the German fleet immured in its own home ports, has protected Britain from invasion, and has enabled her land strength to be used to its utmost capacity beside the armies of France and Belgium. (New York *Times,* November 22, 1914.) *Mem. Ed.* XX, 129; *Nat. Ed.* XVIII, 111.

BATTLESHIPS. *See also* NAVY.

BEAR HUNTING. Doubtless the grizzly could be hunted to advantage with dogs, which would not, of course, be expected to seize him, but simply to find and bay him, and distract his attention by barking and nipping. Occasionally, a bear can be caught in the open and killed with the aid of horses. But nine times out of ten the only way to get one is to put on moccasins and still-hunt it in its own haunts, shooting it at close quarters. Either its tracks should be followed until the bed wherein it lies during the day is found, or a given locality in which it is known to exist should be carefully beaten through, or else a bait should be left out, and a watch kept on it to catch the bear when he has come to visit it. (1885.) *Mem. Ed.* I, 281; *Nat. Ed.* I, 234.

BEARS. Bears are interesting creatures, and their habits are always worth watching. When I used to hunt grizzlies my experience tended to make me lay special emphasis on their variation in temper. There are savage and cowardly bears, just as there are big and little ones; and sometimes these variations are very marked among bears of the same district, and at other times all the bears of one district will seem to have a common code of behavior, which differs utterly from that of the bears of another district. (1905.) *Mem. Ed.* III, 68; *Nat. Ed.* II, 449.

BEARS, BLACK. Black bear are not, under normal conditions, formidable brutes. If they do charge and get home they may maul a man severely, and there are a number of instances on record in which they have killed men. Ordinarily, however, a black bear will not charge home, though he may bluster a good deal. I once shot one very close up, which made a most lamentable outcry and seemed to lose its head, its efforts to escape resulting in its bouncing about among the trees with such heedless hurry that I was easily able to kill it. Another black bear, which I also shot at close quarters, came straight for my companions and myself, and almost ran over the white hunter who was with me. This bear made no sound whatever when I first hit it, and I do not think it was charging.

I believe it was simply dazed, and by accident ran the wrong way and so almost came into collision with us. However, when it found itself face to face with the white hunter, and only four or five feet away, it prepared for hostilities, and I think would have mauled him if I had not brained it with another bullet. . . . None of the bears shot on this Colorado trip made a sound when hit; they all died silently, like so many wolves. (1905.) *Mem. Ed.* III, 71; *Nat. Ed.* II, 451.

BEARS, GRIZZLY. The grizzly is now chiefly a beast of the high hills and heavy timber; but this is merely because he has learned that he must rely on cover to guard him from man, and has forsaken the open ground accordingly. In old days, and in one or two very out-of-the-way places almost to the present time, he wandered at will over the plains. It is only the wariness born of fear which nowadays causes him to cling to the thick brush of the large river-bottoms throughout the plains country. When there were no rifle-bearing hunters in the land, to harass him and make him afraid, he roved hither and thither at will, in burly self-confidence. Then he cared little for cover, unless as a weather-break, or because it happened to contain food he liked. . . .

The grizzly is a shrewd beast and shows the usual bear-like capacity for adapting himself to changed conditions. He has in most places become a cover-haunting animal, sly in his ways, wary to a degree, and clinging to the shelter of the deepest forests in the mountains and of the most tangled thickets in the plains. (1893.) *Mem. Ed.* II, 247-248; *Nat. Ed.* II, 213-215.

BEEBE, WILLIAM. Nothing of this kind could have been done by the man who was only a good writer, only a trained scientific observer, or only an enterprising and adventurous traveller. Mr. Beebe is not merely one of these, but all three; and he is very much more in addition. He possesses a wide field of interest; he is in the truest sense of the word a man of broad and deep cultivation. He cares greatly for noble architecture and noble poetry; for beautiful pictures and statues and finely written books. Nor are his interests only concerned with nature apart from man and from the works of man. He possesses an extraordinary sympathy with and understanding of mankind itself, in all its myriad types and varieties. In this book, and in his other recent writing (for I wish to draw a sharp line in favor of what he has recently written as compared with his earlier and more commonplace work), some of his most interesting descriptions are of the wild folk he meets in the wilderness—black or yellow, brown or red— and of some nominally tamer folk with whom he has foregathered in civilization. (Review of *Jungle Peace;* N. Y. *Times Review of Books,* October 13, 1918.) *Mem. Ed.* XIV, 551; *Nat. Ed.* XII, 410-411.

BELGIAN REFUGEES—AID TO. At the outset of this war I said that hideous though the atrocities had been and dreadful though the suffering, yet we must not believe that these atrocities and this suffering paralleled the dreadful condition that had obtained in European warfare during, for example, the seventeenth century. It is lamentable to have to confess that I was probably in error. The fate that has befallen Belgium is as terrible as any that befell the countries of Middle Europe during the Thirty Years' War and the wars of the following half-century. There is no higher duty than to care for the refugees and above all the child refugees who have fled from Belgium. . . .

I appeal to the American people to picture to themselves the plight of these poor creatures and to endeavor in practical fashion to secure that they shall be saved from further avoidable suffering. Nothing that our people can do will remedy the frightful wrong that has been committed on these families. Nothing that can now be done by the civilized world, even if the neutral nations of the civilized world should at last wake up to the performance of the duty they have so shamefully failed to perform, can undo the dreadful wrong of which these unhappy children, these old men and women, have been the victims. All that can be done surely should be done to ease their suffering. The part that America has played in this great tragedy is not an exalted part; and there is all the more reason why Americans should hold up the hands of those of their number who, like Mrs. Wharton, are endeavoring to some extent to remedy the national shortcomings. We owe to Mrs. Wharton all the assistance we can give. We owe this assistance to the good name of America, and above all for the cause of humanity we owe it to the children, the women and the old men who have suffered such dreadful wrong for absolutely no fault of theirs. Introduction to *The Book of the Homeless,* edited by Edith Wharton. (Scribner's, N. Y., 1916), pp. ix-x.

BELGIANS—REGARD FOR. The Belgian officials and leading men whom I met impressed me very favorably, and their women seemed to me to have the domestic qualities developed much more like our women in England and America than was the case in France, and yet to have the charm and attractiveness of the

Frenchwomen. The king was a huge fair young man, evidently a thoroughly good fellow, with excellent manners, and not a touch of pretension. (To Sir George Otto Trevelyan, October 1, 1911.) *Mem. Ed.* XXIV, 274; Bishop II, 235.

BELGIUM — AMERICA'S DUTY TOWARD. If I had been President, I should have acted on the thirtieth or thirty-first of July, as head of a signatory power of The Hague treaties, calling attention to the guaranty of Belgium's neutrality and saying that I accepted the treaties as imposing a serious obligation which I expected not only the United States but all other neutral nations to join in enforcing. Of course I would not have made such a statement unless I was willing to back it up. I believe that if I had been President the American people would have followed me. (To Sir Cecil Spring-Rice, October 3, 1914.) *Mem. Ed.* XXIV, 437; Bishop II, 372.

———————. I am not concerned with the charges of individual atrocity. The prime fact is that Belgium committed no offense whatever, and yet that her territory has been invaded and her people subjugated. This prime fact cannot be left out of consideration in dealing with any matter that has occurred in connection with it. Her neutrality has certainly been violated, and this is in clear violation of the fundamental principles of The Hague conventions. It appears clear that undefended towns have been bombarded, and that towns which were defended have been attacked with bombs at a time when no attack was made upon the defenses. This is certainly in contravention of The Hague agreement forbidding the bombardment of undefended towns....

Now, it may be that there is an explanation and justification for a portion of what has been done. But if The Hague conventions mean anything, and if bad faith in the observation of treaties is not to be treated with cynical indifference, then the United States Government should inform itself as to the facts, and should take whatever action is necessary in reference thereto. The extent to which the action should go may properly be a subject for discussion. But that there should be some action is beyond discussion; unless, indeed, we ourselves are content to take the view that treaties, conventions, and international engagements and agreements of all kinds are to be treated by us and by everybody else as what they have been authoritatively declared to be, "scraps of paper," the writing on which is intended for no better purpose than temporarily to amuse the feeble-minded. (New York *Times,* November 8, 1914.) *Mem. Ed.* XX, 89; *Nat. Ed.* XVIII, 77.

———————. The assertion that our neutrality carries with it the obligation to be silent when our own Hague conventions are destroyed represents an active step against the peace of righteousness. The only way to show that our faith in public law was real was to protest against the assault on international morality implied in the invasion of Belgium. (New York *Times,* November 29, 1914.) *Mem. Ed.* XX, 201; *Nat. Ed.* XVIII, 172.

———————. When we sit idly by while Belgium is being overwhelmed, and rolling up our eyes prattle with unctuous self-righteousness about "the duty of neutrality," we show that we do not really fear God; on the contrary, we show an odious fear of the devil, and a mean readiness to serve him. (1916.) *Mem. Ed.* XX, 232; *Nat. Ed.* XVIII, 200.

———————. The United States Government has signally failed to take action on behalf of Belgium when The Hague conventions, to which the United States was a signatory power, were violated at Belgium's expense. During the last century no civilized power guiltless of wrong has suffered such a dreadful fate as has befallen Belgium. Belgium had not the smallest responsibility for the disaster that has overwhelmed it. The United States has been derelict to its duty, has signally failed to stand for international righteousness and international peace in the course it has pursued with reference to the wrongs of Belgium. (*Metropolitan,* February 1915.) *Mem. Ed.* XX, 512; *Nat. Ed.* XVIII, 440.

BELGIUM — FUTURE GUARANTEES TO. Little or nothing would be gained by a peace which merely stopped this war for the moment and left untouched all the causes that have brought it about. A peace which left the wrongs of Belgium unredressed, which did not leave her independent and secured against further wrong-doing, and which did not provide measures hereafter to safeguard all peaceful nations against suffering the fate that Belgium has suffered, would be mischievous rather than beneficial in its ultimate effects. If the United States had any part in bringing about such a peace it would be deeply to our discredit as a nation. Belgium has been terribly wronged, and the civilized world owes it to itself to see that this wrong is redressed and that steps are taken which will guarantee that hereafter conditions shall not be permitted to become such as either to require or to permit such action as that of Germany against Belgium. (New York *Times,* October 11, 1914.) *Mem. Ed.* XX, 52; *Nat. Ed.* XVIII, 44.

———————. At this moment any peace which leaves unredressed the wrongs of Belgium, and which does not effectively guarantee Belgium and all other small nations that behave themselves, against the repetition of such wrongs would be a well-nigh unmixed evil. As far as we personally are concerned, such a peace would inevitably mean that we should at once and in haste have to begin to arm ourselves or be exposed in our turn to the most frightful risk of disaster. Let our people take thought for the future. What Germany did to Belgium because her need was great and because she possessed the ruthless force with which to meet her need she would, of course, do to us if her need demanded it; and in such event what her representatives now say as to her intentions toward America would trouble her as little as her signature to the neutrality treaties troubled her when she subjugated Belgium. Nor does she stand alone in her views of international morality. More than one of the great powers engaged in this war has shown by her conduct in the past that if it profited her she would without the smallest scruple treat any land in the two Americas as Belgium has been treated. (New York *Times,* November 1, 1914.) *Mem. Ed.* XX, 78; *Nat. Ed.* XVIII, 67.

BELGIUM—INVASION OF. Of all the lessons hitherto taught by the war, the most essential for us to take to heart is that taught by the catastrophe that has befallen Belgium. One side of this catastrophe, one lesson taught by Belgium's case, is the immense gain in the self-respect of a people that has dared to fight heroically in the face of certain disaster and possible defeat. Every Belgian throughout the world carries his head higher now than he has ever carried it before, because of the proof of virile strength that his people have given. (New York *Times,* October 11, 1914.) *Mem. Ed.* XX, 49; *Nat. Ed.* XVIII, 42.

———————. There has been no more abhorrent spectacle in history than the revenge visited upon Belgium for her dauntless defense of national rights and international obligations. In all the grim record of the last year this is the overshadowing accomplishment of evil. . . . Deep though the hurts are which have been inflicted upon civilization by the sacrifice of millions of lives among the bravest and best of the men of Europe, yet deeper and more lasting is the wound given by the blow struck at international law and international righteousness in the destruction of Belgium. (*Metropolitan,* October 1915.) *Mem. Ed.* XX, 333; *Nat. Ed.* XVIII, 285.

———————. To me the crux of the situation has been Belgium. If England or France had acted toward Belgium as Germany has acted I should have opposed them, exactly as I now oppose Germany. I have emphatically approved your action as a model for what should be done by those who believe that treaties should be observed in good faith and that there is such a thing as international morality. I take this position as an American who is no more an Englishman than he is a German, who endeavors loyally to serve the interests of his own country, but who also endeavors to do what he can for justice and decency as regards mankind at large, and who therefore feels obliged to judge all other nations by their conduct on any given occasion. (To Sir Edward Grey, January 22, 1915.) *Mem. Ed.* XXIV, 439; Bishop II, 373.

BELGIUM—RELIEF FOR. The much advertised sending of food and supplies to Belgium has been of most benefit to the German conquerors of Belgium. They have taken the money and food of the Belgians and permitted the Belgians to be supported by outsiders. Of course, it was far better to send them food, even under such conditions, than to let them starve. (New York *Times,* November 15, 1914.) *Mem. Ed.* XX, 115; *Nat. Ed.* XVIII, 99.

BELGIUM AND THE ORIGINS OF THE WAR. I am very sad over this war. I believe that, in a way, it was fatally inevitable as regards the continental nations, and that each was right, from its own standpoint, under conditions as they actually were. But, to my mind, as regards Belgium, there is absolutely no question that all the right was on her side and all the wrong was committed against her, and she will have to receive full redress and assurance against the repetition of the wrongs, or else our civilization is to that extent broken down. England could not have done other than she did, in interfering for her. (To Elbert Francis Baldwin, October 5, 1914.) *Mem. Ed.* XXIV, 438; Bishop II, 372.

BELGIUM. *See also* HAGUE CONVENTIONS; HOOVER, HERBERT; NEUTRALITY; WORLD WAR.

BENTON, THOMAS HART. Benton's long political career can never be thoroughly understood unless it is kept in mind that he was primarily a Western and not a Southern statesman; and it owes its especial interest to the fact that during its continuance the West first rose to power, acting as a unit, and to the further fact that it was brought to a close by the same causes which soon afterward broke up the West exactly as the East was already broken. Benton was not one of the few statesmen who have left the indelible marks of their own individuality upon our history; but he was, perhaps, the most typical representative of the statesmanship of the Middle West at the time when the latter gave the tone to the political thought of the entire Mississippi valley. The political school which he represented came to its fullest development in the so-called Border States. . . . Benton was one of those public men who formulate and express, rather than shape, the thought of the people who stand behind them and whom they represent. A man of strong intellect and keen energy, he was for many years the foremost representative of at least one phase of that thought; being, also, a man of high principle and determined courage, when a younger generation had grown up and the bent of the thought had changed, he declined to change with it, bravely accepting political defeat as the alternative, and going down without flinching a hair's breadth from the ground on which he had always stood. (1887.) *Mem. Ed.* VIII, 11-12; *Nat. Ed.* VII, 10-11.

——————. Benton, in his mental training, came much nearer to the statesmen of the seaboard, and was far better bred and better educated, than the rest of the men around him. But he was, and was felt by them to be, thoroughly one of their number, and the most able expounder of their views; and it is just because he is so completely the type of a great and important class, rather than because even of his undoubted and commanding ability as a statesman, that his life and public services will always repay study. His vanity and boastfulness were faults which he shared with almost all his people; and, after all, if they overrated the consequence of their own deeds, the deeds, nevertheless, did possess great importance, and their fault was slight compared to that committed by some of us at the present day, who have gone to the opposite extreme and try to belittle the actions of our fathers. Benton was deeply imbued with the masterful, overbearing spirit of the West—a spirit whose manifestations are not always agreeable, but the possession of which is certainly a most healthy sign of the virile strength of a young community. (1887.) *Mem. Ed.* VIII, 27; *Nat. Ed.* VII, 24.

——————. Benton's capacity for work was at all times immense; he delighted in it for its own sake, and took a most justifiable pride in his wide reading, and especially in his full acquaintance with history, both ancient and modern. He was very fond of illustrating his speeches on American affairs with continual allusions and references to events in foreign countries or in old times, which he considered to be more or less parallel to those he was discussing; and indeed he often dragged in these comparisons when there was no particular need for such a display of his knowledge. He could fairly be called a learned man, for he had studied very many subjects deeply and thoroughly; and though he was too self-conscious and pompous in his utterances not to incur more than the suspicion of pedantry, yet the fact remains that hardly any other man has ever sat in the Senate whose range of information was as wide as his. (1887.) *Mem. Ed.* VIII, 151-152; *Nat. Ed.* VII, 131-132.

BENTON, THOMAS HART, AND THE OREGON QUESTION. One of the first subjects that attracted Benton's attention in the Senate was the Oregon question, and on this he showed himself at once in his true character as a Western man, proud alike of every part of his country, and as desirous of seeing the West extended in a northerly as in a southerly direction. Himself a slaveholder, from a slave State, he was one of the earliest and most vehement advocates of the extension of our free territory northward along the Pacific coast. . . . Benton's intense Americanism, and his pride and confidence in his country and in her unlimited capacity for growth of every sort, gifted him with the power to look much farther into the future, as regarded the expansion of the United States, than did his colleagues; and moreover caused him to consider the question from a much more far-seeing and statesmanlike standpoint. The land belonged to no man, and yet was sure to become very valuable; our title to it was not very good, but was probably better than that of any one else. Sooner or later it would be filled with the overflow of our population, and would border on our dominion, and on our dominion alone. It was therefore just, and moreover in the highest degree desirable, that it should be made a part of that dominion at the earliest possible moment. (1887.) *Mem. Ed.* VIII, 39-40; *Nat. Ed.* VII, 34-35.

BENTON, THOMAS HART, AND THE SLAVERY QUESTION. From this time the slavery question dwarfed all others, and was the one with which Benton, as well as other statesmen, had mainly to deal. He had been very loath to acknowledge that it was ever to become of such overshadowing importance; until late in his life he had not realized that, interwoven with the disunionist movement, it had grown so as to become in reality the one and only question before the people; but, this once thoroughly understood, he henceforth devoted his tremendous energies to the struggle with it. . . .

He had now entered on what may fairly be called the heroic part of his career; for it would be difficult to chose any other word to express our admiration for the unflinching and defiant courage with which, supported only by conscience and by his loving loyalty to the Union, he battled for the losing side, although by so doing he jeopardized and eventually ruined his political prospects. . . . His was one of those natures that show better in defeat than in victory. In his career there were many actions that must command our unqualified admiration; such were his hostility to the Nullifiers, wherein, taking into account his geographical location and his refusal to compromise, he did better than any other public man, not even excepting Jackson and Webster; his belief in honest money; and his attitude towards all questions involving the honor or the maintenance and extension of the Union. But in all these matters he was backed more or less heartily by his State. . . . When, however, the slavery question began to enter upon its final stage, Benton soon found himself opposed to a large and growing faction of the Missouri Democracy, which increased so rapidly that it soon became dominant. But he never for an instant yielded his convictions, even when he saw the ground being thus cut from under his feet, fighting for the right as sturdily as ever, facing his fate, fearlessly, and going down without a murmur. (1887.) *Mem. Ed.* VIII, 236, 237; *Nat. Ed.* VII, 204.

BENTON, THOMAS HART, AS EXPANSIONIST. Benton, greatly to the credit of his foresight, and largely in consequence of his strong nationalist feeling, thoroughly appreciated the importance of our geographical extensions. He was the great champion of the West and of western development, and a furious partisan of every movement in the direction of the enlargement of our western boundaries. . . . Without clearly formulating his opinions, even to himself, and while sometimes prone to attribute to his country at the moment a greatness she was not to possess for two or three generations to come, he, nevertheless, had engrained in his very marrow and fibre the knowledge that inevitably, and beyond all doubt, the coming years were to be hers. He knew that, while other nations held the past, and shared with his own the present, yet that to her belonged the still formless and unshaped future. More clearly than almost any other statesman he beheld the grandeur of the nation loom up, vast and shadowy, through the advancing years. (1887.) *Mem. Ed.* VIII, 195, 196; *Nat. Ed.* VII, 169.

BERRY SCHOOLS, THE. I have been intending, ever since I first saw Miss Martha Berry, to come down and see this school, not only for the sake of the school itself, not only for what is being done with you boys and girls here, but because I think that this school is an example that must be widely followed—I will put it a little stronger than that—that must in its essentials, be universally followed in the South and in the North also. . . .

As soon as I had seen her and heard what she had done, I saw in the first place that she was trying to do the right thing; and in the next place, that she knew how to do it. There is another thing that I was much struck by at once. Miss Berry said that this school was being made a Christian Industrial School. You are going to raise a mighty poor quality of Christians if you can't have decent houses and have the men and women lead decent lives in them. So you must have the school industrial. And, on the other hand, I think that the greatest industrial efficiency is a curse to a nation if those able to practice it fail to have and to live up to the ordinary Christian morality. This school does both. What this school aims to do is to train mind and body, and what is more than mind and body—character.

Again, one prime feature of this school is that it seeks to help each man in the only way in which any man can be permanently helped, by helping him to help himself. It trains the boy to go back to the farm, and to do his part in making farming a skilled profession; making it a profession like the law, like any other profession. It trains the girl so that she can go back to the farm and, as wife and mother, do her part—and it is a part even greater than the man's—in elevating the home. That is the industrial side of the school. You must have the Christian side as well. In addition to helping yourselves, you must steadily try to help others. (At Mount Berry, Ga., October 8, 1910.) *The Southern Highlander,* March 1919, pp. 6-7.

BEVERIDGE, ALBERT J. He has . . . played a distinguished part in our political life, and during his brilliant service of twelve years

[41]

in the United States Senate he championed with fidelity all the honorable causes for which Marshall and his fellow Federalists stood a century before; he emulated their devoted nationalism, their advocacy of military preparedness, their insistence upon a wide application of the powers of the government under the national Constitution, and their refusal to worship shams instead of facts; and he followed Abraham Lincoln in refusing to follow the Federalists where they were wrong—that is, in their distrust of and high-spirited impatience with the people. (*Outlook,* July 18, 1917.) *Mem. Ed.* XII, 427-428; *Nat. Ed.* XI, 189-190.

BIBLE AS A GUIDE. It would be a great misfortune for our people if they ever lost the Bible as one of their habitual standards and guides in morality. (*Outlook,* May 27, 1911), p. 223.

BIBLE READING IN PUBLIC SCHOOLS. I believe in absolutely non-sectarian public schools. It is not our business to have the Protestant Bible or the Catholic Vulgate or the Talmud read in those schools. There is no objection whatever, where the local sentiment favors it, for the teacher to read a few verses of the ethical or moral parts of the Bible, so long as this causes no offense to any one. But it is entirely wrong for the law to make this reading compulsory; and the Protestant fanatics who attempt to force this through are playing into the hands of the Catholic fanatics who want to break down the Public School system and introduce a system of sectarian schools. (To Michael Schaap, February 22, 1915.) *Mem. Ed.* XXIV, 422; Bishop II, 358.

BIBLE STUDY—DESIRABILITY OF. I enter a most earnest plea that in our hurried and rather bustling life of to-day we do not lose the hold that our forefathers had on the Bible. I wish to see Bible study as much a matter of course in the secular college as in the seminary. . . .

I ask that the Bible be studied for the sake of the breadth it must give to every man who studies it. (At Pacific Theological Seminary, Spring 1911.) *Mem. Ed.* XV, 607, 608; *Nat. Ed.* XIII, 643, 644.

BIBLE. See also CHRISTIANITY; RELIGION; SUNDAY SCHOOL; TEN COMMANDMENTS.

BIG BUSINESS. See BUSINESS.

BIG STICK, THE. Boasting and blustering are as objectionable among nations as among individuals, and the public men of a great nation owe it to their sense of national self-respect to speak courteously of foreign powers, just as a brave and self-respecting man treats all around him courteously. But though to boast is bad, and causelessly to insult another, worse, yet worse than all is it to be guilty of boasting, even without insult, and when called to the proof to be unable to make such boasting good. There is a homely old adge which runs: "Speak softly and carry a big stick; you will go far." If the American Nation will speak softly, and yet build, and keep at a pitch of the highest training, a thoroughly efficient navy, the Monroe Doctrine will go far. (At Chicago, Ill., April 2, 1903.) *Presidential Addresses and State Papers* I, 265-266.

———————. "Speak softly and carry a big stick—you will go far." If a man continually blusters, if he lacks civility, a big stick will not save him from trouble; and neither will speaking softly avail, if back of the softness there does not lie strength, power. In private life there are few things more obnoxious than the man who is always loudly boasting; and if the boaster is not prepared to back up his words his position becomes absolutely contemptible. So it is with the nation. It is both foolish and undignified to indulge in undue self-glorification, and, above all, in loose-tongued denunciation of other peoples. (At Minnesota State Fair, September 2, 1901.) *Mem. Ed.* XV, 334; *Nat. Ed.* XIII, 474.

———————. The only safe rule is to promise little, and faithfully to keep every promise; to "speak softly and carry a big stick." (1913.) *Mem. Ed.* XXII, 610; *Nat. Ed.* XX, 524.

———————. The recent voyage of the fleet around the world was not the first occasion in which I have used it to bring about prompt resumption of peaceful relations between this country and a foreign Power. But of course one of the conditions of such use is that it should be accompanied with every manifestation of politeness and friendship—manifestations which are sincere, by the way, for the foreign policy in which I believe is in very fact the policy of speaking softly and carrying a big stick. I want to make it evident to every foreign nation that I intend to do justice; and neither to wrong them nor to hurt their self-respect; but that on the other, I am both entirely ready and entirely able to see that our rights are maintained in their turn. (To Whitelaw Reid, December 4, 1908.) Thomas A.

Bailey, *Theodore Roosevelt and the Japanese-American Crisis.* (Stanford University Press, 1934), pp. 301-302.

BIG STICK, THE, AND THE WORLD WAR. One of the main lessons to learn from this war is embodied in the homely proverb: "Speak softly and carry a big stick." Persistently only half of this proverb has been quoted in deriding the men who wish to safeguard our national interest and honor. Persistently the effort has been made to insist that those who advocate keeping our country able to defend its rights are merely adopting "the policy of the big stick." In reality, we lay equal emphasis on the fact that it is necessary to speak softly; in other words, that it is necessary to be respectful toward all people and scrupulously to refrain from wronging them, while at the same time keeping ourselves in condition to prevent wrong being done to us. If a nation does not in this sense speak softly, then sooner or later the policy of the big stick is certain to result in war. But what befell Luxembourg five months ago, what has befallen China again and again during the past quarter of a century, shows that no amount of speaking softly will save any people which does not carry a big stick. (*Outlook,* September 23, 1914.) Mem. Ed. XX, 28; Nat. Ed. XVIII, 24.

BIGOTRY. Prejudice and bigotry never discriminate. If the bigot ever paused to discriminate, he would cease to be a bigot. (Fall 1917; reported by Leary.) *Talks with T. R.* From the diaries of John J. Leary, Jr. (Houghton Mifflin Co., Boston, 1920), p. 146.

BIGOTRY. *See also* ANTI-SEMITISM; CATHOLICS; RELIGIOUS DISCRIMINATION; TOLERANCE.

BIMETALLISM. *See* SILVER.

BIOGRAPHY. *See* MAHAN, A. T.

BIOLOGY. *See* SCIENCE.

BIRD COLLECTING. Three days ago I shot a yellow-throated or Dominican warbler here—the first I had ever seen. I was able to identify it with absolute certainty, but as the record might be deemed of importance I reluctantly shot the bird, a male, and gave the mutilated skin to the American Museum of Natural History people so that they might be sure of the identification. The breeding-season was past, and no damage came to the species from shooting the specimen; but I must say that I care less and less for the mere "collecting" as I grow older. (To John Burroughs, July 11, 1907.) Mem. Ed. XXIV, 87; Bishop II, 75.

BIRD STUDY WITH JOHN BURROUGHS. John Burroughs and I had a very pleasant time during our three days at Pine Knot. I was much pleased to be able to show him all the birds I had said I would, including the Bewick's wren, the blue grosbeak, the gnatcatcher, the summer redbird, etc. The one bird about which we were doubtful was the Henslow's bunting. I think he found the place almost too primitive, for a family of flying squirrels had made their abode inside the house. This tended to keep *him* awake at nights, whereas *we* have become rather attached to them. In one ploughed field I found a nighthawk sitting. If I had chosen to knock it down with my hat I could have done so, but I wanted not to hurt it; and as I endeavored softly to seize it, it got away just as my fingers touched it. It did not go far, but sat lengthwise along the limb of a small tree and let me come within two feet of it before flying. When I see you again I am going to point out one or two minor matters in connection with the song of the Bewick's wren and the looks of the blue grosbeak, where we were a little puzzled by your accounts. I suppose that there is a good deal of individual variation among the birds themselves as well as among the observers. (To Frank M. Chapman, May 10, 1908.) Mem. Ed. XXIV, 131; Bishop II, 113.

BIRDS—LEGAL PROTECTION OF. Laws to protect small and harmless wild life, especially birds, are indispensable. Such laws cannot be enacted or enforced until public opinion is back of them; and associations like the Audubon Societies do work of incalculable good in stirring, rousing, and giving effect to this opinion. (*Outlook,* January 20, 1915.) Mem. Ed. XIV, 568; Nat. Ed. XII, 426.

BIRDS—PRESERVATION OF. Birds that are useless for the table and not harmful to the farm should always be preserved; and the more beautiful they are, the more carefully they should be preserved. They look a great deal better in the swamps and on the beaches and among the trees than they do on hats. There are certain species in certain localities which it is still necessary to collect; but no really rare bird ought to be shot save in altogether exceptional circumstances and for public museums, and the common birds (which of course should also be placed in public museums) are entirely out of place in private collections; and this applies as much to their eggs and nests as to their skins. (*Outlook,* September 16, 1911.) *Mem. Ed.* XIV, 506; *Nat. Ed.* XII, 374.

―――――――――. The State should not permit within its limits factories to make bird-skins or bird-feathers into articles of ornament or wearing-apparel. Ordinarily birds, and especially song-birds, should be rigidly protected. Game-birds should never be shot to a greater extent than will offset the natural rate of increase. All spring shooting should be prohibited and efforts made by correspondence with the neighboring States to secure its prohibition within their borders. Care should be taken not to encourage the use of cold storage or other market systems which are a benefit to no one but the wealthy epicure who can afford to pay a heavy price for luxuries. (Annual Message as Governor, Albany, January 3, 1900.) *Mem. Ed.* XVII, 63; *Nat. Ed.* XV, 54-55.

―――――――――. As yet with the great majority of our most interesting and important wild birds and beasts the prime need is to protect them, not only by laws limiting the open season and the size of the individual bag, but especially by the creation of sanctuaries and refuges. And, while the work of the collector is still necessary, the work of the trained faunal naturalist, who is primarily an observer of the life histories of the wild things, is even more necessary. The progress made in the United States, of recent years, in creating and policing bird refuges, has been of capital importance. (1916.) *Mem. Ed.* IV, 224; *Nat. Ed.* III, 374-375.

BIRDS—PROTECTIVE COLORATION OF. There is probably no such thing among mammals and birds as a coloration which under all the conditions of the wearer's life is always either completely revealing or completely concealing; but it may be one or the other, nine hundred and ninety-nine times out of the thousand. Out in the Bad Lands of the Little Missouri I once saw a raven against a coal-seam in a cliff, and its color for the moment was concealing; and once at dusk a poorwill lit on the bare veranda beside me, and its coloration was for the moment revealing. Yet under all ordinary circumstances, the direct reverse is true in each case; and it is just as absurd to deny that a raven (or a crow, or a grackle, or a cowbunting, or a white egret, or a full-grown black-and-white skimmer on its nest) is revealingly colored and conspicuous, as to deny that a whippoorwill (or a nesting grouse, or a desert lark, or a fledgling skimmer) is concealingly colored and inconspicuous. (*American Museum Journal,* March 1918.) *Mem. Ed.* VI, 413-414; *Nat. Ed.* V, 356-357.

―――――――――. These common Argentine birds, most of them of the open country, and all of them with a strikingly advertising coloration, are interesting because of their beauty and their habits. They are also interesting because they offer such illuminating examples of the truth that many of the most common and successful birds not merely lack a concealing coloration, but possess a coloration which is in the highest degree revealing. The coloration and the habits of most of these birds are such that every hawk or other foe that can see at all must have its attention attracted to them. Evidently in their cases neither the coloration nor any habit of concealment based on the coloration is a survival factor, and this although they live in a land teeming with bird-eating hawks. (1914.) *Mem. Ed.* VI, 36; *Nat. Ed.* V, 31.

―――――――――. Certainly many of the markings of mammals, just as is the case with birds, must be wholly independent of any benefit they give to their possessors in the way of concealment. . . . An instant's reflection is sufficient to show that if the gaudily colored males of these two birds are really protectively colored, then the females are not, and vice versa; for the males and females inhabit similar places. (1910; Appendix of *African Game Trails.*) *Mem. Ed.* VI, 385-386; *Nat. Ed.* V, 332.

BIRDS. *See also* AUDUBON SOCIETIES; GREY, SIR EDWARD; LARK; MEADOW-LARK; MOCKING BIRD; OUSEL; WILD LIFE.

BIRTH CONTROL. Voluntary sterility among married men and women of good life is, even more than military or physical cowardice in the ordinary man, the capital sin of civilization, whether in France or Scandinavia, New England or New Zealand. If the best classes do not reproduce themselves the nation will of course go down; for the real question is encouraging the fit, and discouraging the unfit, to survive. (1916.) *Mem. Ed.* IV, 77; *Nat. Ed.* III, 249.

―――――――――. Thrift and hard work will avail no more than a cultivated taste and an amiable philanthropy if there is wilful sterility in marriage, if men and women forget the great primal and elemental law of racial well-being, and this whether the fault be due to vice in its crude and repulsive forms, or to timidity and unwillingness to run risk, or to cold and selfish shrinking from the trouble and labor which are inseparable from every kind of life that is really worth living. (*Outlook,* March 25, 1911.) *Mem. Ed.* XIX, 149; *Nat. Ed.* XVII, 107.

——————————. Criminals should not have children. Shiftless and worthless people should not marry and have families which they are unable to bring up properly. Such marriages are a curse to the community. But this is only the negative side of the matter; and the positive is always more important than the negative. In our civilization to-day the great danger is that there will be failure to have enough children of the marriages that ought to take place. What we most need is insistence upon the duty of decent people to have enough children, and the sternest condemnation of the practices commonly resorted to in order to secure sterility. (*Outlook,* April 8, 1911.) *Mem. Ed.* XIV, 164; *Nat. Ed.* XII, 195.

BIRTH CONTROL—EVILS OF. The loss of a healthy, vigorous, natural sexual instinct is fatal; and just as much so if the loss is by disuse and atrophy as if it is by abuse and perversion. Whether the man, in the exercise of one form of selfishness, leads a life of easy self-indulgence and celibate profligacy; or whether in the exercise of a colder but no less repulsive selfishness, he sacrifices what is highest to some form of mere material achievement in accord with the base proverb that "he travels farthest who travels alone"; or whether the sacrifice is made in the name of the warped and diseased conscience of asceticism; the result is equally evil. So, likewise, with the woman. In many modern novels there is portrayed a type of cold, selfish, sexless woman who plumes herself on being "respectable," but who is really a rather less desirable member of society than a prostitute. Unfortunately the portrayal is true to life. The woman who shrinks from motherhood is as low a creature as a man of the professional pacificist, or poltroon type, who shirks his duty as a soldier. (1916.) *Mem. Ed.* IV, 78; *Nat. Ed.* III, 250.

BIRTH CONTROL—FALSITY OF ARGUMENTS FOR. To quiet their uneasy consciences, cheap and shallow men and women, when confronted with these facts, answer that "quality is better than quantity," and that decrease of numbers will mean increase in individual prosperity. It is false. When quantity falls off, thanks to wilful sterility, the quality will go down too. During the half-century in which France has remained nearly stationary, while Germany has nearly doubled in population, the average of individual prosperity has grown much faster in Germany than in France; and social and industrial unrest and discontent have grown faster in France than in Germany. (*Outlook,* April 8, 1911.) *Mem. Ed.* XIV, 157; *Nat. Ed.* XII, 189.

BIRTH CONTROL—PENALTY FOR. If the national legislators were wise, they would place the heaviest burden of taxation on the unmarried; they would relieve every mother or father of a substantial sum of taxes for each child that they have; and they would so arrange the law that there would be *no relief from taxes for a married couple without children* and a very substantial additional and cumulative relief from taxes for the third child and the fourth child. I should personally favor continuing the relief in marked form for all subsequent children. *Outlook,* September 27, 1913, p. 163.

BIRTH CONTROL — REMEDIES FOR. There are many remedies, all of them partial. The State can do something, as the State is now doing in France. Legislation must be for the average, for the common good. Therefore legislation should at once abandon the noxious sentimentality of thinking that in America at this time the "only son" is entitled to preferential consideration, either for the sake of himself or of his mother. The preference, as regards all obligations to the State, should be given to the family having the third and fourth children. In all public offices in every grade the lowest salaries should be paid the man or woman with no children, or only one or two children, and a marked discrimination made in favor of the man or woman with a family of *over* three children. In taxation, the rate should be immensely heavier on the childless and on the families with one or two children, while an equally heavy discrimination should lie in favor of the family with *over* three children. This should apply to the income tax and inheritance tax, and as far as possible to other taxes. I speak, as usual, of the average, not the exception. Only the father and mother of over three children have done their full duty by the State; and the State should emphasize this fact. (*Metropolitan,* October 1917.) *Mem. Ed.* XXI, 168. *Nat. Ed.* XIX, 161.

BIRTH CONTROL—SELFISHNESS OF. I do not believe in reckless marriages, where the man is unable to support a wife, nor in couples who recklessly and thoughtlessly have multitudes of children whom they are unable to bring up properly, nor in the man who forces upon an unfit wife excessive and unlimited

[45]

child-bearing. But this form of reckless and brutal selfishness is not as wicked as the cold, calculating, and most unmanly and unwomanly selfishness which makes so many men and women shirk the most important of all their duties to the State. *Outlook,* September 27, 1913, p. 164.

BIRTH CONTROL—SPREAD OF. It is due to moral, and not physiological, shortcomings. It is due to coldness, to selfishness, to love of ease, to shrinking from risk, to an utter and pitiful failure in sense of perspective and in power of weighing what really makes the highest joy, and to a rooting out of the sense of duty or a twisting of that sense into improper channels. Moreover, this same racial crime is spreading almost as rapidly among the sons and daughters of immigrants as among the descendants of the native-born. If it were confined to Americans of old stock, while it would be a matter of shame to us who are of the old stock, we could at least feel that the traditions and principles and purposes of the founders of the Republic would find their believers and exponents among their descendants by adoption; and in such case I, for one, would heartily throw in my fate with the men of alien stock who were true to the old American principles rather than with the men of the old American stock who were traitors to the old American principles. But the children of the immigrants show the same wilful sterility that is shown by the people of the old stock. (*Outlook,* April 8, 1911.) *Mem. Ed.* XIV, 154; *Nat. Ed.* XII, 187.

BIRTH CONTROL VERSUS BIRTH ENCOURAGEMENT. What this nation vitally needs is not the negative preaching of birth control to the submerged tenth, and the tenth immediately adjoining, but the positive preaching of birth encouragement to the eight-tenths who make up the capable, self-respecting American stock which we wish to see perpetuate itself. (*Metropilitan,* October 1917.) *Mem. Ed.* XXI, 158; *Nat. Ed.* XIX, 153.

BIRTH RATE. Taking into account the women who for good reasons do not marry, or who when married are childless or are able to have but one or two children, it is evident that the married woman able to have children must on an average have four or the race will not perpetuate itself. This is the mere statement of a self-evident truth. (1913.) *Mem. Ed.* XXII, 194; *Nat. Ed.* XX, 166.

————. A caste or a race or a nation, where the average family consists of one child, faces immediate extinction, and therefore it matters not one particle how this child is brought up. But if there are plenty of children then there is always hope. Even if they have not been very well brought up, they *have been brought up,* and so there is something to work on. (*Metropolitan,* May 1916.) *Mem. Ed.* XXI, 146; *Nat. Ed.* XIX, 143.

BIRTH RATE—CHARACTER OF THE. Two-thirds of our increase now comes from the immigrants and not from the babies born here, not from young Americans who are to perpetuate the blood and traditions of the old stock. It surely ought to be so obvious as to be unnecessary to point out that all thought of the next generation, all thought of its vocational, artistic, or ethical training is wasted thought if there is not to be a next generation to train. The first duty of any nation that is worth considering at all is to perpetuate its own life, its own blood. That duty will not be performed unless we have not merely a high but a sober ideal of duty and devotion in family life, unless our men and women realize what true happiness is, realize and act on the belief that no other form of pleasure, no other form of enjoyment, in any way takes the place of that highest of all pleasures which comes only in the home, which comes from the love of the one man and the one woman for each other, and for their children. (At Pacific Theological Seminary, Spring 1911.) *Mem. Ed.* XV, 599; *Nat. Ed.* XIII, 636.

BIRTH RATE AND RACE PERPETUATION. If the average woman does not marry and become the mother of enough healthy children to permit the increase of the race; and if the average man does not, above all other things, wish to marry in time of peace, and to do his full duty in war if the need arises, then the race is decadent, and should be swept aside to make room for one that is better. Only that nation has a future whose sons and daughters recognize and obey the primary laws of their racial being. (1916.) *Mem. Ed.* IV, 79; *Nat. Ed.* III, 251.

————. The fundamental point to remember is that if there are not in the average family four children, the race goes back, and that the element which has three children is stationary, and that the group where the average family has two children or less represents a dying element in the race. I am of course speaking of averages, and not of exceptional cases. . . .

It is not a good thing to see a poor and shiftless couple have a very large number of chil-

[46]

dren, but it is a great deal better thing than seeing a prosperous capable family with but one or two. After all, while there is life there is hope, whereas nothing can be done with the dead. If a race, or an element in a race, dies out, then that is the end of it. But if a race or an element of a race continues to exist, even though under unfavorable conditions and with results that are not what they ought to be, there is always the chance that something can be made out of it in the future. The evil or shiftless man who leaves children behind him represents a bad element in the community. But the worst element in the community is that furnished by the men and women who ought to be good fathers and mothers of many healthy children, but who deliberately shirk their duty. (*Outlook*, January 3, 1914.) *Mem. Ed.* XIV, 173; *Nat. Ed.* XII, 202.

BIRTH RATE. See also CHILDREN; EUGENICS; MARRIAGE; RACE SUICIDE; SEX INSTINCT; WOMEN.

BISHOP, JOSEPH B. See GOETHALS, GEORGE W.

BISON. See BUFFALO.

BLACKMAIL. Law-abiding citizens are rarely blackmailed. The chief chance for blackmail, with all its frightful attendant demoralization, arises from having a law which is not strictly enforced, which certain people are allowed to violate with impunity for corrupt reasons, while other offenders who lack their political influence are mercilessly harassed. (New York *Sun*, June 20, 1895.) *Mem. Ed.* XVI, 260; *Nat. Ed.* XIV, 182.

BLAINE, JAMES G. Mr. Blaine was nominated much against the wishes of many of us, against my wishes and against my efforts. He was nominated fairly and honorably because the delegates at the Chicago convention fairly represented the sentiment of the great Republican States. He was nominated because those whom Abraham Lincoln, in one of his quaint, homely phrases that meant so much, called "the plain people," wished to see him as their President. He was nominated against the wishes of the most intellectual and the most virtuous and honorable men of the great seaboard cities, but he was nominated fairly and honorably, because those who represent the bone and sinew of the Republican party, those who have constituted the main strength of that party wished it, and I for one am quite content to abide by the decision of the plain people. (Before Republican meeting, Malden, Mass., October 20, 1884.) *Mem. Ed.* XVI, 81; *Nat. Ed.* XIV, 46.

——————. For my good fortune I knew Mr. Blaine quite well when he was Secretary of State, and I have thought again and again during the past few years how pleased he would have been to see so many of the principles for which he had stood approach fruition.

One secret, perhaps I might say the chief secret, of Mr. Blaine's extraordinary hold upon the affections of his countrymen was his entirely genuine and unaffected Americanism. . . . Mr. Blaine possessed to an eminent degree the confident hope in the nation's future which made him feel that she must ever strive to fit herself for a great destiny. He felt that this Republic must in every way take the lead in the Western Hemisphere. He felt that this Republic must play a great part among the nations of the earth. The last four years have shown how true that feeling of his was. (At Augusta, Me., August 26, 1902.) *Presidential Addresses and State Papers* I, 124-125.

BLAINE, JAMES G. See also ELECTION OF 1884.

BLOCKADE. See CONTRABAND.

BLOOD-AND-IRON. See FOREIGN POLICY; STATESMANSHIP.

BLUFF. I think I hate nothing more than a bluff where the bluffer does not intend to make it good. (To H. C. Lodge, May 2, 1896.) Lodge *Letters* I, 219.

——————. Neither in national nor in private affairs is it ordinarily advisable to make a bluff which cannot be put through—personally, I never believe in doing it under any circumstances. (1913.) *Mem. Ed.* XXII, 616; *Nat. Ed.* XX, 529.

BOASTING. There is a good deal about the system of censorship that we have established which has an unpleasant suggestion of being applicable only to out-patients of an idiot asylum. Much of it has been exceedingly foolish. But there is one line along which I wish the censorship could be extended. I wish it were possible to censor all boasting, and devote ourselves to achievement,—not to improper exaggeration of what we have done, and above all not to grandiloquent statements of what we are going to do. Censor the boasting! Remember that every great speech that has come down through history has obtained and kept its place only because it represented either achievement in the past, or a resolute purpose for achievement in the future. (At Trinity College, Hartford, June 16, 1918.) *Commencement at Trinity College.* (Hartford, Conn., 1918), p. 4.

BOASTING. *See also* DEEDS.

BOER AND BRITON. It was pleasant to see the good terms on which Boer and Briton met. Many of the English settlers whose guest I was, or with whom I hunted . . . had fought through the South African war; and so had all the Boers I met. The latter had been for the most part members of various particularly hard-fighting commandos; when the war closed they felt very bitterly, and wished to avoid living under the British flag. Some moved West and some East; those I met were among the many hundreds, indeed thousands, who travelled northward—a few overland, most of them by water—to German East Africa. But in the part in which they happened to settle they were decimated by fever, and their stock perished of cattle sickness; and most of them had again moved northward, and once more found themselves under the British flag. They were being treated precisely on an equality with the British settlers; and every well-wisher to his kind, and above all every well-wisher to Africa, must hope that the men who in South Africa fought so valiantly against one another, each for the right as he saw it, will speedily grow into a companionship of mutual respect, regard, and consideration such as that which, for our inestimable good fortune, now knits closely together in our own land the men who wore the blue and the men who wore the gray and their descendants. There could be no better and manlier people than those, both English and Dutch, who are at this moment engaged in the great and difficult task of adding East Africa to the domain of civilization; their work is bound to be hard enough anyhow; and it would be a lamentable calamity to render it more difficult by keeping alive a bitterness which has lost all point and justification, or by failing to recognize the fundamental virtues, the fundamental characteristics, in which the men of the two stocks are in reality so much alike. (1910.) *Mem. Ed.* V, 39-40; *Nat. Ed.* IV, 34-35.

BOER WAR. The South African business makes me really sad. I have a genuine admiration for the Boers; but the downfall of the British Empire, I should regard as a calamity to the race, and especially to this country. (To Anna Roosevelt Cowles, December 17, 1899.) Cowles *Letters,* 226.

———————. The trouble with the war is not that both sides are wrong, but that from their different standpoints both sides are right. The Boers feel themselves to be fighting for the same principle for which their ancestors and ours fought three centuries back against the Spaniards; whereas the English fight just as we should fight if, in Mexico for instance, the Americans were treated as the Uitlanders were treated in the Transvaal. (To Anna Roosevelt Cowles, February 2, 1900.) Cowles *Letters,* 234.

———————. I have a very warm feeling of regard for England, and have felt that though the Boers were perfectly right from their standpoint and also had the technical right in the case, yet that England was really fighting the battle of civilization. (To Anna Roosevelt Cowles, February 5, 1900.) Cowles *Letters,* 235.

———————. The British behaved so well to us during the Spanish War that I have no patience with these people who keep howling against them. I was mighty glad to see them conquer the Mahdi for the same reason that I think we should conquer Aguinaldo. The Sudan and Matabeleland will be better off under England's rule, just as the Philippines will be under our rule. But as against the Boers, I think the policy of Rhodes and Chamberlain has been one huge blunder, and exactly as you say, the British have won only by crushing superiority in numbers where they have won at all. Generally they have been completely outfought, while some of their blunders have been simply stupendous. Now of course I think it would be a great deal better if all the white people of South Africa spoke English, and if my Dutch kinsfolk over there grew to accept English as their language just as my people and I here have done, they would be a great deal better off. The more I have looked into this Boer War the more uncomfortable I have felt about it. Of course, this is for your eyes only. I do not want to mix in things which do not concern me, and I have no patience with the Senators and Representatives that attend anti-British meetings and howl about England. I notice that they are generally men that sympathized with Spain two years ago. (To Sewall, April 24, 1900.) William W. Sewall, *Bill Sewall's Story of T. R.* (Harper & Bros., N. Y., 1919), p. 105.

BOERS. The Boers are belated Cromwellians, with many fine traits. They deeply and earnestly believe in their cause, and they attract the sympathy which always goes to the small nation, even though the physical obstacles in the way may be such as to put the two contestants far more nearly on a par than at first sight seems to be the case. But it would be for the advantage of mankind to have English spoken south of the Zambesi just as in New York; and as I told one of my fellow Knickerbockers the other day, as we let the Uitlanders of old in here, I do not see why the same rule is not good enough in the Transvaal. The Boers are marvellous fighters, and the change in the conditions of warfare during the past forty years has been such as to give peculiar play to their qualities. Mere pluck in advancing shoulder to shoulder no longer counts for as much as skill in open order fighting, in taking cover and in the use of the rifle, or as power of acting on individual initiative. (To Spring Rice. December 2, 1899.) *The Letters and Friendships of Sir Cecil Spring Rice.* (Houghton Mifflin & Co., Boston, 1929), I, 305.

BOLSHEVISM. Every Bolshevist movement always contains crack-brained fanatics and foolish, simple people cheek by jowl with the sinister advocates of "direct action." It is folly to show these "direct action" people any consideration. Their purpose is to inspire terror by murder. They use the term "direct action," but they mean murder. Blatant anarchists of this type are miscreants and criminals. We ought to stamp them out by exerting the full power of the law in the sternest and most vigorous fashion against them and their sympathizers before, and not merely after, murder is committed. (*Outlook*, September 18, 1918.) *Mem. Ed.* XXI, 393; *Nat. Ed.* XIX, 356.

BOLSHEVISTS. These Russian exiles were not asked to come here. They came here so as to be free from persecution and to better themselves. They owe this country everything. But the only emotions aroused in the Bolshevist type are mean hatred, mean desire to slander, and a self-pity both mean and morbid. The moral and mental attitude it introduces into this country is much more permanently mischievous than the bubonic plague, and against it we should erect a far more rigorous quarantine. The oppressed of other lands who have developed this kind of character should be kept out of this land at all hazards; and our immigration laws should promptly be changed accordingly. There are plenty of sordid and arrogant capitalists in this land; but their most harmful and unlovely traits are no worse and no more dangerous than those of this particular type of professional proletarian. (*Metropolitan*, June 1918.) *Mem. Ed.* XXI, 387; *Nat. Ed.* XIX, 350.

BOLSHEVISM; BOLSHEVISTS. *See also* RUSSIA; SOCIALISM.

BONAPARTE, CHARLES J. *See* JUSTICE—DEPARTMENT OF.

BOOK LOVERS AND NATURE LOVERS. There are men who love out-of-doors who yet never open a book; and other men who love books but to whom the great book of nature is a sealed volume, and the lines written therein blurred and illegible. Nevertheless among those men whom I have known the love of books and the love of outdoors, in their highest expressions, have usually gone hand in hand. It is an affectation for the man who is praising outdoors to sneer at books. Usually the keenest appreciation of what is seen in nature is to be found in those who have also profited by the hoarded and recorded wisdom of their fellow men. (1913.) *Mem. Ed.* XXII, 359; *Nat. Ed.* XX, 308.

BOOKS. Books are almost as individual as friends. There is no earthly use in laying down general laws about them. Some meet the needs of one person, and some of another; and each person should beware of the booklover's besetting sin, of what Mr. Edgar Allan Poe calls "the mad pride of intellectuality," taking the shape of arrogant pity for the man who does not like the same kind of books. Of course there are books which a man or woman uses as instruments of a profession—law books, medical books, cookery books, and the like. I am not speaking of these, for they are not properly "books" at all; they come in the category of time-tables, telephone directories, and other useful agencies of civilized life. I am speaking of books that are meant to be read. (1913.) *Mem. Ed.* XXII, 375; *Nat. Ed.* XX, 322.

————. A thoroughly good book for young people is almost invariably one of the best books that grown people can read. Similarly, an introduction to any study, if done as it should be by a man capable of writing not merely the introduction, but also the study itself, is certain to be of interest to the most advanced student. (*Bookman*, February 1896.) *Mem. Ed.* XIV, 355; *Nat. Ed.* XII, 292.

————. To me the heading employed by some reviewers when they speak of "books of the week" comprehensively damns both the books themselves and the reviewer who is willing to notice them. I would much rather see the heading "books of the year before last." A book of the year before last which is still worth noticing would probably be worth reading; but one only entitled to be called a book of the week had better be tossed into the wastebasket at once. Still, there are plenty of new books which are not of permanent value but which nevertheless are worth more or less careful reading; partly because it is well to know something of what especially interests the mass of our fellows, and partly because these books, although of ephemeral worth, may really set forth something genuine in a fashion which for the moment stirs the hearts of all of us. (1916.) *Mem. Ed.* IV, 195; *Nat. Ed.* III, 350.

───────────. Fortunately I had enough good sense, or obstinacy, or something, to retain a subconscious belief that inasmuch as books were meant to be read, good books ought to be interesting, and the best books capable in addition of giving one a lift upward in some direction. (To Sir George Otto Trevelyan, January 23, 1904.) *Mem. Ed.* XXIV, 163; Bishop II, 140.

───────────. It seems rather odd that it should be necessary to insist upon the fact that the essence of a book is to be readable; but most certainly the average scientific or historical writer needs to have this elementary proposition drilled into his brain. Perhaps if this drilling were once accomplished, we Americans would stand a greater chance of producing an occasional Darwin or Gibbon; though there would necessarily be some havoc in the ranks of those small pedants who with laborious industry produce works which are never read excepting by other small pedants, or else by the rare master who can take the myriad bricks of these myriad little workers and out of them erect one of the great buildings of thought. (*Bookman*, February 1896.) *Mem. Ed.* XIV, 355-356; *Nat. Ed.* XII, 292-293.

───────────. Personally, granted that these books are decent and healthy, the one test to which I demand that they all submit is that of being interesting. If the book is not interesting to the reader, then in all but an infinitesimal number of cases it gives scant benefit to the reader. Of course any reader ought to cultivate his or her taste so that good books will appeal to it, and that trash won't. But after this point has once been reached, the needs of each reader must be met in a fashion that will appeal to those needs. Personally the books by which I have profited infinitely more than by any others have been those in which profit was a by-product of the pleasure; that is, I read them because I enjoyed them, because I liked reading them, and the profit came in as part of the enjoyment. (1913.) *Mem. Ed.* XXII, 376; *Nat. Ed.* XX, 322.

BOOKS—LISTS OF. Edith sent me ex-President Eliot's list of books. It is all right as *a* list of books which a cultivated man would like to read; but as *the* list it strikes me as slightly absurd. I have never head of Woolman's Journal, but to include it and Penn's "Fruits of Solitude," while leaving out Cervantes and Montaigne, seems odd. To put in Emerson's "English Traits," and leave out Herodotus, Tacitus and Thucydides; to put in Tennyson's "Becket," Middleton's "Changeling" and Dryden's "All for Love" and entirely leave out Æschylus, Sophocles, Molière and Calderon; to put in a translation of the Aeneid and to leave out Homer; in short to put in half the books he has put in, while leaving out scores of really great masters, of every description, from Aristotle to Chaucer and Pascal and Gibbon, not to speak of all poetry and novels —why I think that such things done and left undone make the list ridiculous as *the* list of books to "give a man the essentials of a liberal education"; although excellent if avowedly only one of a hundred possible lists of excellent books, any one of which lists would furnish good reading. (To H. C. Lodge, September 10, 1909.) Lodge *Letters* II, 347.

───────────. If President Eliot's "List of Best Books" is complete, will you send it to me? If I am able I'd like to write something on it; I don't believe in a list of "100" or "25" "best" books, because there are many thousands which may be "best" according to the country, the time, the condition, the reader; but I do believe in "a" 25 to 100 or any other number of "good" books, each such list being merely complementary to and not a substitute for many other similar lists. The books in my pigskin library on this hunt are good; they are no better than any one of the totally different sets I took on each of my last three hunting trips, except that I have a longer list for the longer trip. (To L. F. Abbott, October 21, 1909.) Lawrence F. Abbott, *Impressions of Theodore Roosevelt*. (Doubleday, Page & Co., Garden City, N. Y., 1919), p. 188.

───────────. As regards Mr. Eliot's list, I think it slightly absurd to compare any list of good books with any other list of good books in the sense of saying that one list is "better" or "worse" than another. Of course a list may be made up of worthless or noxious books; but there are so many thousands of good books that no list of small size is worth considering if it purports to give the "best" books. There is no such thing as *the* hundred best books, or *the* best five-foot library; but there can be drawn up a very large number of lists, each of which shall contain *a* hundred good books or fill *a* good five-foot library. This is, I am sure, all that Mr. Eliot has tried to do. (*Outlook,* April 30, 1910.) *Mem. Ed.* XIV, 470; *Nat. Ed.* XII, 343.

——————. The room for choice is so limitless that to my mind it seems absurd to try to make catalogues which shall be supposed to appeal to all the best thinkers. This is why I have no sympathy whatever with writing lists of *the* One Hundred Best Books or *the* Five-Foot Library. It is all right for a man to amuse himself by composing *a* list of a hundred very good books; and if he is to go off for a year or so where he cannot get many books, it is an excellent thing to choose a five-foot library of particular books which in that particular year and on that particular trip he would like to read. But there is no such thing as a hundred books that are best for all men, or for the majority of men, or for one man at all times; and there is no such thing as a five-foot library which will satisfy the needs of even one particular man on different occasions extending over a number of years. (1913.) *Mem. Ed.* XXII, 378; *Nat. Ed.* XX, 324.

——————. There is no such thing as a list of "the hundred best books," or the "best five-foot library."

Dozens of series of excellent books, one hundred to each series, can be named, all of reasonably equal merit and each better for many readers than any of the others. (1916.) *Mem. Ed.* IV, 189; *Nat. Ed.* III, 345.

BOOKS FOR CHILDREN. I think there ought to be children's books. I think that the child will like grown-up books also, and I do not believe a child's book is really good unless grown-ups get something out of it. (1913.) *Mem. Ed.* XXII, 20; *Nat. Ed.* XX, 17.

BOOKS FOR STATESMEN. Now and then I am asked as to "what books a statesman should read," and my answer is, poetry and novels—including short stories under the head of novels. I don't mean that he should read only novels and modern poetry. If he cannot also enjoy the Hebrew prophets and the Greek dramatists, he should be sorry. He ought to read interesting books on history and government, and books of science and philosophy; and really good books on these subjects are as enthralling as any fiction ever written in prose or verse. Gibbon and Macaulay, Herodotus, Thucydides and Tacitus, the Heimskringla, Froissart, Joinville and Villehardouin, Parkman and Mahan, Mommsen and Ranke—why! there are scores and scores of solid histories, the best in the world, which are as absorbing as the best of all the novels, and of as permanent value. The same thing is true of Darwin and Huxley and Carlyle and Emerson, and parts of Kant, and of volumes like Sutherland's "Growth of the Moral Instinct," or Acton's Essays and Lounsbury's studies—here again I am not trying to class books together, or measure one by another, or enumerate one in a thousand of those worth reading, but just to indicate that any man or woman of some intelligence and some cultivation can in some line or other of serious thought, scientific, or historical or philosophical or economic or governmental, find any number of books which are charming to read, and which in addition give that for which his or her soul hungers. I do not for a minute mean that the statesman ought not to read a great many different books of this character, just as every one else should read them. But, in the final event, the statesman, and the publicist, and the reformer, and the agitator for new things, and the upholder of what is good in old things, all need more than anything else to know human nature, to know the needs of the human soul; and they will find this nature and these needs set forth as nowhere else by the great imaginative writers, whether of prose or of poetry. (1913.) *Mem. Ed.* XXII, 377; *Nat. Ed.* XX, 323.

BOOKS. *See also* DRAMA; LITERATURE; PIGSKIN LIBRARY; POETRY; READING.

BOONE, DANIEL. Daniel Boone will always occupy a unique place in our history as the archetype of the hunter and wilderness wanderer. He was a true pioneer, and stood at the head of that class of Indian fighters, game-hunters, forest-fellers, and backwoods farmers who, generation after generation, pushed westward the border of civilization from the Alleghanies to the Pacific. (1895.) *Mem. Ed.* IX, 13-14; *Nat. Ed.* X, 12-13.

——————. Boone's claim to distinction rests not so much on his wide wanderings in unknown lands, for in this respect he did little more than was done by a hundred other backwoods hunters of his generation, but on the fact that he was able to turn his daring woodcraft to the advantage of his fellows. As he himself said, he was an instrument "ordained of God to settle the wilderness." He inspired confidence in all who met him, so that the men of means and influence were willing to trust adventurous enterprises to his care; and his success as an explorer, his skill as a hunter, and his prowess as an Indian fighter, enabled him to bring these enterprises to a successful conclusion, and in some degree to control the wild spirits associated with him. (1889.) *Mem. Ed.* X, 130; *Nat. Ed.* VIII, 115.

BORDER WARS. See FRONTIER WARFARE.

BOSS—MENACE OF THE. I will tell you who is the real menace in American political life—not the king; he does not exist and never will; not the dictator, but the boss; the man who does by manipulation, by intrigue, by alliance with crooked judges, by crooked business men, by the assessment of judges, in every way that is contrary to the principles of good citizenship, the man who by doing all that gets enormous political power and exercises it as he chooses, that man is a menace. (Speech at Troy, N. Y., October 17, 1910.) *Mem. Ed.* XIX, 47.

BOSS—POWER OF THE. A boss . . . can pull wires in conventions, can manipulate members of the legislature, can control the giving or withholding of office, and serves as the intermediary for bringing together the powers of corrupt politics and corrupt business. If he is at one end of the social scale, he may through his agents traffic in the most brutal forms of vice and give protection to the purveyors of shame and sin in return for money bribes. If at the other end of the scale, he may be the means of securing favors from high public officials, legislative or executive, to great industrial interests; the transaction being sometimes a naked matter of bargain and sale, and sometimes being carried on in such manner that both parties thereto can more or less successfully disguise it to their consciences as in the public interest. (1913.) *Mem. Ed.* XXII, 179; *Nat. Ed.* XX, 153.

———. You can have public influence in two ways; indeed, all of us who are practical politicians know that the "boss" is often far more powerful than is he who is the figurehead. The man who pulls the wires for definite purposes (generally for distinctly bad purposes) is the man of real power, and is often the man who does not hold public office at all. For our great good fortune it is true also that many of the men who do the best work publicly are men who are in private life. (At memorial meeting to George William Curtis, New York City, November 14, 1892.) *Mem. Ed.* XII, 483; *Nat. Ed.* XI, 227.

BOSS RULE. The present conditions in the two old parties, and the platforms put forth by both of them and judged by the standards outlined above, show that it is hopeless to get anything good out of them. To endeavor to punish each alternately by voting for the other is to follow the course most gratefully appreciated by the corrupt bosses of both. There is nothing that the bosses of the two parties more heartily approve than the action of the man who does not attempt to wrest control of either party away from the boss or to establish a new party, but contents himself with action which results in keeping the bosses in control of each party and merely forcing these bosses to alternate with one another in control of the government. Mr. Taft's election means the perpetuation of the control of the Cranes, Barneses, Penroses, and Guggenheims. Doctor Wilson's election means the perpetuation of the control of the Murphys, Taggarts, Sullivans, the Evans-Hughes people, and their like. The bosses are just as powerful in one party as in the other. (*Outlook*, July 27, 1912.) *Mem. Ed.* XIX, 349; *Nat. Ed.* XVII, 246.

BOSS RULE VERSUS POPULAR RULE. The main issue is that we stand against bossism, big or little, and in favor of genuine popular rule, not only at the election but within the party organization, and above all, that our war is ruthless against every species of corruption, big and little, and against the alliance between corrupt business and corrupt politics, as to which it has been found that too often in the past the boss system has offered a peculiarly efficient and objectionable means of communication. We are against the domination of the party and the public by special interests, whether these special interests are political, business, or a compound of the two. (New York *Times*, August 27, 1910.) *Mem. Ed.* XIX, 9; *Nat. Ed.* XVII, 4.

———. Democracy means nothing unless the people rule. The rule of the boss is the negation of democracy. It is absolutely essential that the people should exercise self-control and self-mastery, and he is a foe to popular government who in any way causes them to lose such self-control and self-mastery whether from without or within. But it must be literally self-control and not control by outsiders. (Before New York Republican State Convention, Saratoga, September 27, 1910.) *Mem. Ed.* XIX, 36; *Nat. Ed.* XVII, 28.

BOSSES—COOPERATION WITH. Even the boss who really is evil, like the business man who really is evil, may on certain points be sound, and be doing good work. It may be the highest duty of the patriotic public servant to work with the big boss or the big business man on these points, while refusing to work with him on others. . . . I have known in my life many big business men and many big political bosses who often or even generally did evil, but who on some occasions and on certain issues were right. I never hesitated to do battle against these men when they were wrong; and, on the other hand, as long as they were going my way I was glad to have them do so. To have repudiated their aid when they were right and were striving for a right end, and for what was of benefit to the people—no matter what their motives may have been—would have been childish, and moreover would have itself been misconduct against the people. (1913.) *Mem. Ed.* XXII, 182; *Nat. Ed.* XX, 156.

BOSSES—SUPPORTERS OF. The big bosses who control the national committee represent not merely the led captains of mercenary politics but the great crooked financiers who stand behind these led captains. These political bosses are obnoxious in themselves, but they are even more obnoxious because they represent privilege in its most sordid and dangerous form. (Address at Chicago, June 17, 1912.) *Mem. Ed.* XIX, 291; *Nat. Ed.* XVII, 209.

BOSSES—TACTICS OF SUCCESSFUL. A successful boss is very apt to be a man who, in addition to committing wickedness in his own interest, also does look after the interests of others, even if not from good motives. There are some communities so fortunate that there are very few men who have private interests to be served, and in these the power of the boss is at a minimum. There are many country communities of this type. But in communities where there is poverty and ignorance, the conditions are ripe for the growth of a boss. . . . He uses his influence to get jobs for young men who need them. He goes into court for a wild young fellow who has gotten into trouble. He helps out with cash or credit the widow who is in straits, or the breadwinner who is crippled or for some other cause temporarily out of work. He organizes clambakes and chowder parties and picnics, and is consulted by the local labor leaders when a cut in wages is threatened. For some of his constituents he does proper favors, and for others wholly improper favors; but he preserves human relations with all. (1913.) *Mem. Ed.* XXII, 180; *Nat. Ed.* XX, 154.

BOSSES AND LEADERS. People ask the difference between a leader and a boss. I will tell you. The leader holds his position, purely because he is able to appeal to the conscience and to the reason of those who support him, and the boss holds his position because he appeals to fear of punishment and hope of reward. The leader works in the open, and the boss in covert. The leader leads, and the boss drives. (At Binghamton, N. Y., October 24, 1910.) *Mem. Ed.* XIX, 58; *Nat. Ed.* XVII, 38.

BOSSES AND REFORMERS. One of the reasons why the boss so often keeps his hold, especially in municipal matters, is, or at least has been in the past, because so many of the men who claim to be reformers have been blind to the need of working in human fashion for social and industrial betterment. (1913.) *Mem. Ed.* XXII, 178; *Nat. Ed.* XX, 152.

BOSS; BOSSES. *See also* BRIBERY; CORRUPTION; INDEPENDENT; MACHINE; ORGANIZATION; PARTY ALLEGIANCE; PARTY SYSTEM; PLATT, T. C.; POLITICIANS; PRIMARIES; SALOON; TAMMANY HALL.

BOURGEOISIE, THE. The wealthier, or, as they would prefer to style themselves, the "upper" classes, tend distinctly towards the bougeois type; and an individual in the bourgeois stage of development, while honest, industrious, and virtuous, is also not unapt to be a miracle of timid and short-sighted selfishness. The commercial classes are only too likely to regard everything merely from the standpoint of "Does it pay?" and many a merchant does not take any part in politics because he is shortsighted enough to think that it will pay him better to attend purely to making money, and too selfish to be willing to undergo any trouble for the sake of abstract duty; while the younger men of this type are too much engrossed in their various social pleasures to be willing to give their time to anything else. It is also unfortunately true, especially throughout New England and the Middle States, that the general tendency among people of culture and high education has been to neglect and even to look down upon the rougher and manlier virtues, so that an advanced state of intellectual development is too often associated with a certain effeminacy of character. (*Century,* November 1886.) *Mem. Ed.* XV, 120; *Nat. Ed.* XIII, 81.

BOURGEOISIE. See also MATERIALIST; MIDDLE CLASS; MILLIONAIRES; MONEY; WEALTH.

BOXER REBELLION. See CHINA; CHINESE INDEMNITY.

BOXING. Boxing is a thoroughly good and manly sport. There are very few sports as good for strong young men who require an outlet for their vigor. *Outlook,* October 21, 1911, p. 409.

BOXING. See also PRIZE-FIGHTING.

BOY, THE AMERICAN. Of course what we have a right to expect of the American boy is that he shall turn out to be a good American man. Now, the chances are strong that he won't be much of a man unless he is a good deal of a boy. He must not be a coward or a weakling, a bully, a shirk, or a prig. He must work hard and play hard. He must be clean-minded and clean-lived, and able to hold his own under all circumstances and against all comers. It is only on these conditions that he will grow into the kind of American man of whom America can be really proud. (*St. Nicholas,* May 1900.) *Mem. Ed.* XV, 468; *Nat. Ed.* XIII, 401.

BOY SCOUTS. [The Boy Scout movement] has already done much good, and it will do far more, for it is in its essence a practical scheme through which to impart a proper standard of ethical conduct, proper standards of fair play and consideration for others, and courage and decency, to boys who have never been reached and never will be reached by the ordinary type of preaching, lay or clerical. . . .

The movement is one for efficiency and patriotism. It does not try to make soldiers of boy scouts, but to make boys who will turn out as men to be fine citizens, and who will, if their country needs them, make better soldiers for having been scouts. No one can be a good American unless he is a good citizen, and every boy ought to train himself so that as a man he will be able to do his full duty to the community. (To James E. West, July 20, 1911.) *Boy Scouts of America. The Official Handbook for Boys.* (New York, 1914), pp. 389-390.

——————. I wish to greet the Boy Scouts and to express my hearty belief in and admiration of the work they are doing. . . .

I believe in work and I believe in play; I believe in drudgery when drudgery is necessary; and in love of adventure also. Above all, I believe that the American citizen of the future should be brave and hardy, that he should possess also the personal prowess, and that he should also possess the spirit which puts personal prowess at the service of the Commonwealth; which is another way of saying that he must be law-abiding, and have consideration for the rights and the feelings of others. The Boy Scout Movement is pre-eminently successful along all of these different lines. (To J. W. Patton, April 12, 1913.) Murray, W. D. *History of the Boy Scouts of America.* (Boys Scouts of America, New York, 1937), p. 243.

BOYHOOD, ROOSEVELT'S. I was a rather sickly, rather timid little boy, very fond of desultory reading and of natural history, and not excelling in any form of sport. Owing to my asthma I was not able to go to school, and I was nervous and self-conscious, so that as far as I can remember my belief is that I was rather below than above my average playmate in point of leadership; though as I had an imaginative temperament this sometimes made up for my other shortcomings. Altogether, while, thanks to my father and mother, I had a very happy childhood I am inclined to look back at it with some wonder that I should have come out of it as well as I have! It was not until after I was sixteen that I began to show any prowess, or even ordinary capacity; up to that time, except making collections of natural history, reading a good deal in certain narrowly limited fields and indulging in the usual scribbling of the small boy who does not excel in sport, I cannot remember that I did anything that even lifted me up to the average. (To Richard Watson Gilder, August 20, 1903.) *Mem. Ed.* XXIII, 4; Bishop I, 2.

BOYS. I would rather have a boy of mine stand high in his studies than high in athletics, but I would a great deal rather have him show true manliness of character than show either intellectual or physical prowess. (To Kermit Roosevelt, October 2, 1903.) *Mem. Ed.* XXI, 500; *Nat. Ed.* XIX, 444.

BRAZIL. Brazil has been blessed beyond the average of her Spanish-American sisters because she won her way to republicanism by evolution rather than revolution. They plunged into the extremely difficult experiment of democratic, of popular, self-government, after enduring the atrophy of every quality of self-control, self-reliance, and initiative throughout three withering centuries of existence under the worst and most foolish form of colonial government, both from the civil and the religious standpoint, that has ever existed. The marvel is not that some of them failed, but that some of them have eventually succeeded in such striking fashion. Brazil, on the contrary, when she achieved independence, first exercised it under the form of an authoritative empire, then under the form of a liberal empire. When the republic came, the people were reasonably ripe for it. The great progress of Brazil—and it has been an astonishing progress—has been made under the republic. (1914.) *Mem. Ed.* VI, 326; *Nat. Ed.* V, 277-278.

——————. Brazil offers remarkable openings for settlers who have the toughness of the born pioneer, and for certain business men and engineers who have the mixture of daring enterprise and sound common sense needed by those who push the industrial development of new countries. Both classes have great opportunities, and both need to be perpetually on their guard against the swindlers and the crack-brained enthusiasts who are always sure to turn up in connection with any country of large developmental possibilities. On the frontier more than anywhere else, a man needs to be able to rely on himself and to remember that on every frontier there are innumerable failures. (1916.) *Mem. Ed.* IV, 81-82; *Nat. Ed.* III, 253.

BRAZIL. *See also* MONROE DOCTRINE.

BRAZILIAN EXPEDITION. The official and proper title of the expedition is that given it by the Brazilian Government: Expedicão Scientifica Roosevelt-Rondon. When I started from the United States, it was to make an expedition, primarily concerned with mammalogy and ornithology, for the American Museum of Natural History of New York. This was undertaken under the auspices of Messrs. Osborn and Chapman, acting on behalf of the Museum. The scope of the expedition was enlarged, and . . . was given a geographic as well as a zoological character, in consequence of the kind proposal of the Brazilian Secretary of State for Foreign Affairs, General Lauro Müller. In its altered and enlarged form the expedition was rendered possible only by the generous assistance of the Brazilian Government. (1914.) *Mem. Ed.* VI, xxxiii; *Nat. Ed.* V, xxxi.

BRIBERY. Any form of bribery is not only criminal but is also, unless done by an old hand, useless; what is known as a "bar room" canvass is, for a gentleman, especially ineffective; the loafers and vagabonds will take anyone's money, or drink with him, but will vote against him just the same. . . . Hiring wagons for voters, paying great numbers of men to work, etc., are generally, although not always, merely thinly disguised forms of bribery. In districts where crooked work is feared detectives must be hired. Some districts are so rotten that it is almost impossible to win without bribery; in such cases a gentleman should go in simply with the expectation of defeat; no form of bribery is ever admissible. (To Corinne Roosevelt Robinson, April 15, 1886.) Cowles *Letters,* 76.

——————. There can be no crime more serious than bribery. Other offenses violate one law while corruption strikes at the foundation of all law. Under our form of government all authority is vested in the people and by them delegated to those who represent them in official capacity. There can be no offense heavier than that of him in whom such a sacred trust has been reposed, who sells it for his own gain and enrichment; and no less heavy is the offense of the bribe-giver. He is worse than the thief, for the thief robs the individual, while the corrupt official plunders an entire city or State. He is as wicked as the murderer, for the murderer may only take one life against the law, while the corrupt official and the man who corrupts the official alike aim at the assassination of the Commonwealth itself. Government of the people, by the people, for the people, will perish from the face of the earth if bribery is tolerated. The givers and takers of bribes stand on an evil pre-eminence of infamy. The exposure and punishment of public corruption is an honor to a nation, not a disgrace. The shame lies in toleration, not in correction. (Third Annual Message, Washington, December 7, 1903.) *Mem. Ed.* XVII, 208-209; *Nat. Ed.* XV, 179-180.

BRIBERY—PREVENTION OF. I do not see how bribe-taking among legislators can be stopped until the public conscience becomes awake to the matter. Then it will stop fast enough; for just as soon as politicians realize that the people are in earnest in wanting a thing done, they make haste to do it. (*Century,* January 1885.) *Mem. Ed.* XV, 86; *Nat. Ed.* XIII, 52.

BRIBERY. *See also* BOSS; CORRUPTION; ELECTIONS.

BRITISH. *See* BOER WAR; ENGLAND.

"BROOMSTICK PREPAREDNESS." *See* PREPAREDNESS.

BROTHERHOOD. It seems to me that the great lesson to be taught our people is the lesson both of brotherhood and of self-help. In our several ways each of us must work hard to do his duty, each must preserve his sturdy independence; and yet each must realize his duty to others. And to each who performs his duty, in whatever way, must be given the full measure of respect. (Campaign Speech, New York City, October 5, 1898.) *Mem. Ed.* XVI, 449; *Nat. Ed.* XIV, 297.

BROTHERHOOD—THE RULE OF. When all is said and done, the rule of brotherhood remains as the indispensable prerequisite to success in the kind of national life for which we strive. Each man must work for himself, and unless he so works no outside help can avail him; but each man must remember also that he is indeed his brother's keeper, and that while no man who refuses to walk can be carried with advantage to himself or any one else, yet that each at times stumbles or halts, that each at times needs to have the helping hand outstretched to him. To be permanently effective, aid must always take the form of helping a man to help himself; and we can all best help ourselves by joining together in the work that is of common interest to all. (First Annual Message, Washington, December 3, 1901.) *Mem. Ed.* XVII, 110; *Nat. Ed.* XV, 95.

BROTHERHOOD—THE SPIRIT OF. Each group of men has its special interests; and yet the higher, the broader, and deeper interests are those which apply to all men alike; for the spirit of brotherhood in American citizenship, when rightly understood and rightly applied, is more important than aught else. (At Labor Day Picnic, Chicago, September 3, 1900.) *Mem. Ed.* XVI, 510; *Nat. Ed.* XIII, 481.

————. This spirit of brotherhood recognizes of necessity both the need of self-help and also the need of helping others in the only way which ever ultimately does great good, that is, of helping them to help themselves. Every man of us needs such help at some time or other, and each of us should be glad to stretch out his hand to a brother who stumbles. (Before Young Men's Christian Association, New York City, December 30, 1900.) *Mem. Ed.* XV, 528; *Nat. Ed.* XIII, 492.

BROTHERHOOD. *See also* CHARITY; FELLOWSHIP; PHILANTHROPY; YOUNG MEN'S CHRISTIAN ASSOCIATION.

BROWN, JOHN. John Brown rendered a great service to the cause of liberty in the earlier Kansas days; but his notion that the evils of slavery could be cured by a slave insurrection was a delusion. *Outlook*, September 3, 1910, p. 20.

BROWNING, ROBERT. Robert Browning was a real philosopher, and his writings have had a hundredfold the circulation and the effect of those of any similar philosopher who wrote in prose, just because, and only because, what he wrote was not merely philosophy but literature. The form in which he wrote challenged attention and provoked admiration. That part of his work which some of us—which I myself, for instance—most care for is merely poetry. But in that part of his work which has exercised most attraction and has given him the widest reputation, the poetry, the form of expression, bears to the thought expressed much the same relation that the expression of Lucretius bears to the thought of Lucretius. As regards this, the great mass of his product, he is primarily a philosopher, whose writings surpass in value those of other similar philosophers precisely because they are not only philosophy but literature. (Presidential Address, American Historical Association, Boston, December 27, 1912.) *Mem. Ed.* XIV, 4-5; *Nat. Ed.* XII, 4-5.

BROWNSVILLE, TEX., RIOT. I have been amazed and indignant at the attitude of the negroes and of short-sighted white sentimentalists as to my action. It has been shown conclusively that some of these troops made a midnight murderous and entirely unprovoked assault upon the citizens of Brownsville—for the fact that some of their number had been slighted by some of the citizens of Brownsville, though warranting criticism upon Brownsville, is not to be considered for a moment as provocation for such a murderous assault. All the men of the companies concerned, including their veteran non-commissioned officers, instantly banded together to shield the criminals. In other words, they took action which cannot be tolerated in any soldiers, black or white, in any policeman, black or white, and which, if taken generally in the army would mean not merely that the usefulness of the army was at an end but that it had better be disbanded in its entirety at once. Under no conceivable circumstances would I submit to such a condition of things. (To Silas McBee, November 27, 1906.) *Mem. Ed.* XXIV, 33; Bishop II, 28.

————. When I took the stand I did on these negro troops I of course realized that trouble would come of it politically because of the attitude certain to be taken, I regret to say, by unwise sentimentalists and self-seeking demagogues in our Northern States, especially in those where the negro vote is an important factor. But it was just one of those vital matters where I did not feel that I had any right to consider questions of political expediency and still less of personal expediency. (To B. Lawton Wiggins, late 1906.) *Mem. Ed.* XXIV, 34; Bishop II, 29.

BRYAN, WILLIAM J. Bryan is a personally honest and rather attractive man, a real orator and a born demagogue, who has every crank, fool and putative criminal in the country behind him, and a large proportion of the ignorant honest class; and in the middle west, where the decisive battle will be waged, we shall beat him only after a very hard struggle. (To Anna Roosevelt Cowles, July 19, 1896.) Cowles Letters, 187.

———————. Poor Bryan! I do not know whether I feel more irritated or sympathetic with him. I never saw a bubble pricked so quickly. No private citizen in my time, neither General Grant nor Mr. Blaine, for instance, has been received with such wild enthusiasm on his return from a foreign trip; and in twenty-four hours he made his speech and became an object of indignation and laughter. He has retained his good nature and kindliness; but he has still further lost credit since he made his speech and found out that his panacea of government ownership was unpopular, by attempting to crawfish on it, and thereby has added an appearance of insincerity to an appearance of folly and recklessness. (To Whitelaw Reid, September 25, 1906.) *Mem. Ed.* XXIV, 37; Bishop II, 31.

———————. Of course I do not dare in public to express my real opinion of Bryan. He is a kindly man and well-meaning in a weak way; always provided that to mean well must not be translated by him into doing well if it would interfere with his personal prospects. But he is the cheapest faker we have ever had proposed for President. (To William Kent, September 28, 1908.) *Mem. Ed.* XXIV, 115; Bishop II, 99.

BRYAN AND ALTGELD. For Mr. Bryan we can feel the contemptuous pity always felt for the small man unexpectedly thrust into a big place. He does not look well in a lion's skin, but that is chiefly the fault of those who put the skin on him. But in Mr. Altgeld's case we see all too clearly the jaws and hide of the wolf through the fleecy covering. Mr. Altgeld is a much more dangerous man than Mr. Bryan. He is much slyer, much more intelligent, much less silly, much more free from all the restraints of some public morality. The one is unscrupulous from vanity, the other from calculation. The one plans wholesale repudiation with a light heart and bubbling eloquence, because he lacks intelligence and is intoxicated by hope of power; the other would connive at wholesale murder and would justify it by elaborate and cunning sophistry for reasons known only to his own tortuous soul. (Before American Republican College League, Chicago, October 15, 1896.) *Mem. Ed.* XVI, 394-395; *Nat Ed.* XIV, 258-259.

BRYAN, WILLIAM J. *See also* ARBITRATION; ELECTION OF 1896; HAGUE CONVENTIONS; HYSTERICS; NATIONAL HONOR; WILSON, WOODROW; WORLD WAR.

BRYCE'S AMERICAN COMMONWEALTH. You must by this time be tired of hearing your book compared to De Tocqueville's; yet you must allow me one brief allusion to the two together. When I looked over the proofs you sent me I ranked your book and his together; now that I see your book as a whole I feel that the comparison did it great injustice. It has all of Tocqueville's really great merits; and has not got, as his book has, two or three serious and damaging faults. No one can help admiring the depth of your insight into our peculiar conditions, and the absolute fairness of your criticisms. Of course there are one or two minor points on which I disagree with you; but I think the fact that you give a good view of all sides is rather funnily shown by the way in which each man who refuses to see any but one side quotes your book as supporting his. (To Bryce, January 6, 1889.) H. A. L. Fisher, *James Bryce*. (Macmillan Co., N. Y., 1927), I, 235.

BUCHANAN, JAMES. *See* DEMOCRATIC PARTY; WILSON ADMINISTRATION.

BUFFALO—EXTERMINATION OF THE. While the slaughter of the buffalo has been in places needless and brutal, and while it is greatly to be regretted that the species is likely to become extinct, and while, moreover, from a purely selfish standpoint, many, including myself, would rather see it continue to exist as the chief feature in the unchanged life of the Western wilderness; yet, on the other hand, it must be remembered that its continued existence in any numbers was absolutely incompatible with anything but a very sparse settlement of the country; and that its destruction was the condition precedent upon the advance of white civilization in the West, and was a positive boon to the more thrifty and industrious frontiersmen. . . . Above all, the extermination of the buffalo was the only way of solving the

Indian question. (1885.) *Mem. Ed.* I, 229; *Nat. Ed.* I, 191.

───────────. The extermination of the buffalo has been a veritable tragedy of the animal world. Other races of animals have been destroyed within historic times, but these have been species of small size, local distribution, and limited numbers, usually found in some particular island or group of islands; while the huge buffalo, in countless myriads, ranged over the greater part of a continent. Its nearest relative, the Old World aurochs, formerly found all through the forests of Europe, is almost as near the verge of extinction, but with the latter the process has been slow and has extended over a period of a thousand years, instead of being compressed into a dozen. The destruction of the various larger species of South African game is much more local, and is proceeding at a much slower rate. It may truthfully be said that the sudden and complete extermination of the vast herds of buffalo is without a parallel in historic times.

No sight is more common on the plains than that of a bleached buffalo skull; and their countless numbers attest the abundance of the animal at a time not so very long past. On those portions where the herds made their last stand, the carcasses, dried in the clear, high air, or the mouldering skeletons, abound. (1885.) *Mem. Ed.* I, 223-224; *Nat. Ed.* I, 186.

BUFFALO HUNTING. The buffalo is more easily killed than any other kind of plains game; but its chase is very far from being the tame amusement it has lately been represented. It is genuine sport; it needs skill, marksmanship, and hardihood in the man who follows it, and if he hunts on horseback, it needs also pluck and good riding. It is in no way akin to various forms of so-called sport in vogue in parts of the East, such as killing deer in a lake or by fire-hunting, or even by watching at a runway. No man who is not of an adventurous temper, and able to stand rough food and living, will penetrate to the haunts of the buffalo. The animal is so tough and tenacious of life that it must be hit in the right spot; and care must be used in approaching it, for its nose is very keen, and though its sight is dull, yet, on the other hand, the plains it frequents are singularly bare of cover; while, finally, there is just a faint spice of danger in the pursuit, for the bison, though the least dangerous of all bovine animals, will, on occasions, turn upon the hunter, and though its attack is, as a rule, easily avoided, yet in rare cases it manages to charge home. (1885.) *Mem. Ed.* I, 230; *Nat. Ed.* I, 191-192.

BULL MOOSE. I wish in this campaign to do whatever you think wise—whatever is likely to produce the best results for the Republican ticket. I am as strong as a bull moose and you can use me to the limit. One side of the problem is the fact that I must not seem to neglect my duties as Governor of New York. (To Mark Hanna, June 27, 1900.) *Mem. Ed.* XXIII, 162; Bishop I, 139.

───────────. [On October 14, 1912 at Milwaukee, an attempt was made on Colonel Roosevelt's life; though wounded he insisted upon delivering his scheduled speech before being treated. His opening words to the great audience were:] Friends, I shall ask you to be as quiet as possible. I don't know whether you fully understand that I have just been shot; but it takes more than that to kill a Bull Moose. *Mem. Ed.* XIX, 441; *Nat. Ed.* XVII, 320.

BULL MOOSE CAMPAIGN. See ELECTION OF 1912; PROGRESSIVE MOVEMENT.

BULLYING. I abhor injustice and bullying by the strong at the expense of the weak, whether among nations or individuals. (1913.) *Mem. Ed.* XXII, 248; *Nat. Ed.* XX, 212.

BULLYING. See also FIGHTING MAN; FIGHTING QUALITIES; MANLY VIRTUES; "MOLLYCODDLE."

BUREAU OF CORPORATIONS. See CORPORATIONS.

BUREAUCRACY—TYRANY OF. The tyranny of politicians with a bureaucracy behind them and a mass of ignorant people supporting them would be just as insufferable as the tyranny of big corporations. *Outlook*, June 19, 1909, p. 392.

BUREAUCRACY. See also GOVERNMENT; POLITICIANS; PUBLIC OFFICIALS.

BURNS, JOHN. See LLOYD GEORGE, DAVID.

BURROUGHS, JOHN. Foremost of all American writers on outdoor life is John Burroughs; and I can scarcely suppose that any man who cares for existence outside the cities would willingly be without anything that he has ever written. To the naturalist, to the observer and lover of nature, he is of course worth many times more than any closet systematist; and though he has not been very much in really wild regions, his pages so thrill with the sights and sounds of outdoor life that nothing by any writer who is a mere professional scientist or a mere professional hunter can take their place or do more than supplement them—for scientist and hunter alike would do well to remember that before a book can take the highest rank in any particular line it must also rank high in literature proper. Of course for us Americans Burroughs has a peculiar charm that he cannot have for others, no matter how much they too may like him; for what he writes of is our own, and he calls to our minds memories and associations that are very dear. His books make us homesick when we read them in foreign lands; for they spring from our soil as truly as "Snowbound" or "The Biglow Papers." (1893.) *Mem. Ed.* II, 416; *Nat. Ed.* II, 356-357.

BURROUGHS, JOHN. *See also* Birds; Muir, John; Nature Fakers.

BUSINESS — COMPLEXITY OF MODERN. The machinery of modern business is so vast and complicated that great caution must be exercised in introducing radical changes for fear the unforeseen effects may take the shape of wide-spread disaster. Moreover, much that is complained about is not really the abuse so much as the inevitable development of our modern industrial life. We have moved far away from the old simple days when each community transacted almost all its work for itself and relied upon outsiders for but a fraction of the necessaries, and for not a very large portion even of the luxuries, of life. (Annual Message, Albany, January 3, 1900.) *Mem. Ed.* XVII, 49; *Nat. Ed.* XV, 43.

――――――. There has been an immense relative growth of urban population, and, in consequence, an immense growth of the body of wage-workers, together with an accumulation of enormous fortunes which more and more tend to express their power through great corporations that are themselves guided by some master mind of the business world. As a result, we are confronted by a formidable series of perplexing problems, with which it is absolutely necessary to deal, and yet with which it is not merely useless, but in the highest degree unwise and dangerous to deal, save with wisdom, insight, and self-restraint. (At Pan-American Exposition, Buffalo, N. Y., May 20, 1901.) *Mem. Ed.* XV, 314; *Nat. Ed.* XIII, 448.

BUSINESS—GOVERNMENT AID TO. It is our aim to help legitimate business. We wish to see the business man prosper and make money, for unless he does prosper and make money he can neither permanently pay good wages to his employees nor permanently render good service to the public. Therefore, on grounds not only of abstract morality but of self-interest, we wish to favor the business man and see him succeed. We wish to give him laws under which there will be a reasonable administrative governmental body to which he can appeal to find out just what he can and what he cannot do; laws which will encourage him in the use of the great modern business principles of combination and co-operation, and which by the creation of a proper administrative body will exercise such supervision and control over him as will guarantee that there will be no stock-watering or other devices of overcapitalization for which the honest investors and wage-workers alike have to pay, that there will be no unfair and discriminatory practices against rivals, no swindling of the general public, and no exploitation of wage-workers. (Before National Conference of Progressive Service, Portsmouth, R. I., July 2, 1913.) *Mem. Ed.* XIX, 526; *Nat. Ed.* XVII, 386.

BUSINESS — PROGRESSIVE POLICY TOWARD. The Progressive proposal is definite. It is practicable. We promise nothing that we cannot carry out. We promise nothing which will jeopardize honest business. We promise adequate control of all big business and the stern suppression of the evils connected with big business, and this promise we can absolutely keep.

Our proposal is to help honest business activity, however extensive, and to see that it is rewarded with fair returns so that there may be no oppression either of business men or of the common people. We propose to make it worth while for our business men to develop the most efficient business agencies for use in international trade; for it is to the interest of our whole people that we should do well in international business. But we propose to make those business agencies do complete justice to our own people. . . . We favor co-operation in business, and ask only that it be carried on in a spirit of honesty and fairness. We are against crooked business, big or little. We are in favor of honest business, big or little. We propose to penalize conduct and not size. (Before Progressive National Convention, Chicago, August 6, 1912.) *Mem. Ed.* XIX, 390, 391; *Nat. Ed.* XVII, 281, 282.

BUSINESS—REGULATION OF. It is absurd and wicked to treat the deliberate lawbreaker as on an exact par with the man eager to obey the law, whose only desire is to find out from some competent governmental authority what the law is and then live up to it. It is absurd to endeavor to regulate business in the interest of the public by means of long-drawn lawsuits without any accompaniment of administrative control and regulation, and without any attempt to discriminate between the honest man who has succeeded in business because of rendering a service to the public and the dishonest man who has succeeded in business by cheating the public. (Before Ohio Constitutional Convention, Columbus, February 21, 1912.) *Mem. Ed.* XIX, 171; *Nat. Ed.* XVII, 126.

——————. Our proposal is to put the government, acting for the general public, in such shape that it will not ask justice as a favor but demand it as a right which it is ready and able to enforce. We propose to use the power of the government to help the business community prosper by helping the honest business man in all honest and proper ways to make his business successful. We also propose to use it to protect the whole public against dishonest business men and to save the wage-worker from such cruel exploitation. (Before National Conference of Progressive Service, Portsmouth, R. I., July 2, 1913.) *Mem. Ed.* XIX, 526; *Nat. Ed.* XVII, 386.

BUSINESS, BIG. We must face the fact that big business has come to stay, and that it cannot be abolished in any great nation under penalty of that nation's slipping out of the front place in international industrialism. (1917.) *Mem. Ed.* XXI, 90; *Nat. Ed.* XIX, 78.

——————. There should be no penalizing of a business merely because of its size; although of course there is peculiar need of supervision of big business. (Before Republican State Convention, Saratoga Springs, N. Y., July 18, 1918.) *Mem. Ed.* XXI, 400; *Nat. Ed.* XIX, 363.

——————. This is an era of combination. Big business has come to stay. It cannot be put an end to; and if it could be put an end to, it would mean the most wide-spread disaster to the community. The proper thing to do is to socialize it, to moralize it, to make it more an agent for social good, and to do away with everything in it that tends toward social evil. . . . No great industrial well-being can come unless big business prospers. China is the home of the small industrial unit, and the Chinese laborer is badly off. (1917.) *Mem. Ed.* XXI, 84; *Nat. Ed.* XIX, 72.

BUSINESS, BIG—CONTROL OF. I stand for the adequate control, the real control, of all big business, and especially of all monopolistic big business where it proves unwise or impossible to break up the monopoly. (At Louisville, Ky., April 3, 1912.) *Mem. Ed.* XIX, 250; *Nat. Ed.* XVII, 185.

——————. What is needed is, first, the recognition that modern business conditions have come to stay, in so far at least as these conditions mean that business must be done in larger units, and then the cool-headed and resolute determination to introduce an effective method of regulating big corporations so as to help legitimate business as an incident to thoroughly and completely safeguarding the interests of the people as a whole. (Before Ohio Constitutional Convention, Columbus, February 21, 1912.) *Mem. Ed.* XIX, 170; *Nat. Ed.* XVII, 125.

——————. All very big business, even though honestly conducted, is fraught with such potentiality of menace that there should be thoroughgoing governmental control over it, so that its efficiency in promoting prosperity at home and increasing the power of the nation in international commerce may be maintained, and at the same time fair play insured to the wage-workers, the small business competitors, the investors, and the general public. (Before Progressive National Convention, Chicago, August 6, 1912.) *Mem. Ed.* XIX, 391; *Nat. Ed.* XVII, 282.

——————. It is imperative to exercise over big business a control and supervision which is unnecessary as regards small business. All business must be conducted under the law, and all business men, big or little, must act justly. But a wicked big interest is necessarily more dangerous to the community than a wicked little interest. "Big business" in the past has been responsible for much of the special privilege which must be unsparingly cut out of our national life. I do not believe in making mere size of and by itself criminal. The mere fact of size, however, does unquestionably carry the potentiality of such grave wrong-doing that there should be by law provision made for the strict supervision and regulation of these great industrial concerns doing an interstate business, much as we now regulate the transportation agencies which are engaged in interstate business. The antitrust law does good in so far as it can be invoked against combinations which really are monopolies or which restrict production or which artificially raise prices. But in so far as its workings are uncertain, or as it threatens corporations which have not been guilty of antisocial conduct, it does harm. Moreover, it cannot by itself accomplish more than a trifling part of the governmental regulation of big business which is needed. The nation and the States must co-operate in this matter. (Before Ohio Constitutional Convention, Columbus, February 21, 1912.) *Mem. Ed.* XIX, 172; *Nat. Ed.* XVII, 126.

BUSINESS, BIG—PRIVILEGE AND. The big business which depends for success upon special privilege, that is, upon having to secure that to which it is not entitled and to which other people are entitled, that kind of big business desires to own politicians, desires to own newspapers. (Speech at Elmira, N. Y., October 14, 1910.) *Mem. Ed.* XIX, 42; *Nat. Ed.* XVII, 33.

BUSINESS, BIG—ROLE OF. In the world of international industry the future belongs to the nation which develops either the big-scale businesses; or else the ability among small-scale business men, working men, and farmers, to co-operate, to work together and pool their resources for production, distribution, and the full use of scientific research; or else, what is most desirable, develops both types of business. The small individualistic business cannot compete in any field in which either of the other types flourishes. Therefore, whether we like it or not, we must either permit and encourage the development of these two types or fall behind other nations, as Spain once fell behind England and France. (1917.) *Mem. Ed.* XXI, 91; *Nat. Ed.* XIX, 78.

BUSINESS, BIG—THE SQUARE DEAL AND. We demand that big business give the people a square deal; in return we must insist that when any one engaged in big business honestly endeavors to do right he shall himself be given a square deal; and the first, and most elementary kind of square deal is to give him in advance full information as to just what he can, and what he cannot, legally and properly do. It is absurd and much worse than absurd to treat the deliberate lawbreaker as on an exact par with the man eager to obey the law, whose only desire is to find out from some competent governmental authority what the law is and then to live up to it. *Outlook,* November 18, 1911, p. 654.

BUSINESS, LEGITIMATE. I very much wish that legitimate business would no longer permit itself to be frightened by the outcries of illegitimate business into believing that they have any community of interest. Legitimate business ought to understand that its interests are jeopardized when they are confounded with those of illegitimate business; and the latter, whenever threatened with just control, always tries to persuade the former that it also is endangered. (Before Progressive National Convention, Chicago, August 6, 1912.) *Mem. Ed.* XIX, 392; *Nat. Ed.* XVII, 283.

BUSINESS, LEGITIMATE—TEST OF. If a business man cannot run a given business except by bribing or by submitting to blackmail let him get out of it and into some other business. If he cannot run his business save on condition of doing things which can only be done in the darkness, then let him enter into some totally different field of activity. The test is easy. Let him ask whether he is afraid anything will be found out or not. If he is not, he is all right; if he is, he is all wrong. (At Pacific Theological Seminary, Spring 1911.) *Mem. Ed.* XV, 622; *Nat. Ed.* XIII, 656.

BUSINESS AND GOVERNMENT. First and foremost we must stand firmly on a basis of good, sound ethics. We intend to do what is right for the ample and sufficient reason that it is right. If business is hurt by the stern exposure of crookedness and the result of efforts to punish the crooked man, then business must be hurt, even though good men are involved in the hurting, until it so adjusts itself that it is possible to prosecute wrong-doing without stampeding the business community into a terror-struck defense of the wrong doers and an angry assault upon those who have exposed them. *Outlook,* June 19, 1909, p. 392.

———————. We must quit the effort to meet modern conditions by flint-lock legislation. We must recognize, as modern Germany has recognized, that it is folly either to try to cripple business by making it ineffective, or to fail to insist that the wage-worker and consumer must be given their full share of the prosperity that comes from the successful application and use of modern industrial instrumentalities. (At Cooper Union, New York City, November 3, 1916.) *Mem. Ed.* XX, 517; *Nat. Ed.* XVIII, 444.

BUSINESS AND LABOR. Business and labor are different sides of the same problem.

It is impossible wisely to treat either without reference to the interests and duties of the other—and without reference to the fact that the interests of the general public, the commonwealth, are paramount to both. (1917.) *Mem. Ed.* XXI, 89; *Nat. Ed.* XIX, 77.

BUSINESS CLASS, THE. We are a business people. The tillers of the soil, the wage-workers, the business men—these are the three big and vitally important divisions of our population. The welfare of each division is vitally necessary to the welfare of the people as a whole. The great mass of business is of course done by men whose business is either small or of moderate size. The middle-sized business men form an element of strength which is of literally incalculable value to the nation. Taken as a class, they are among our best citizens. . . . The average business man of this type is, as a rule, a leading citizen of his community, foremost in everything that tells for its betterment, a man whom his neighbors look up to and respect. (Before Ohio Constitutional Convention, Columbus, February 21, 1912.) *Mem. Ed.* XIX, 170; *Nat. Ed.* XVII, 125.

BUSINESS IN WAR-TIME. In this present crisis the right course to follow is to guarantee the business man who works for the government a good profit; then to put a heavy progressive tax on all the excess profits above this. (1917.) *Mem. Ed.* XXI, 82; *Nat. Ed.* XIX, 71.

BUSINESS SUCCESS. Business success, whether for the individual or for the nation, is a good thing only so far as it is accompanied by and develops a high standard of conduct—honor, integrity, civic courage. The kind of business prosperity that blunts the standard of honor, that puts an inordinate value on mere wealth, that makes a man ruthless and conscienceless in trade, and weak and cowardly in citizenship, is not a good thing at all, but a very bad thing for the nation. (Fifth Annual Message, Washington, December 5, 1905.) *Mem. Ed.* XVII, 327; *Nat. Ed.* XV, 280.

BUSINESS. *See also* CAPITAL; COMBINATIONS; COMPETITION; CORPORATIONS; CORRUPTION; EMPLOYER; FINANCIERS; GOVERNMENT CONTROL; INDUSTRIAL REVOLUTION; LABOR; LAISSEZ-FAIRE; MONOPOLIES; PROFITS; SHERMAN ANTI-TRUST ACT; SPECULATION; TRUSTS; WALL STREET.

BYRNE, WILLIAM M. *See* OFFICE—CONDUCT IN.

C

CABINET, ROOSEVELT'S. I have been criticized for shifting and changing my cabinet so often, but I do it with a purpose. Just as soon as a Secretary of the Navy or Interior or any other department gets rusty or else settles down to ease and comfort I transfer him so that he will use the energy, which made him valuable in the first place, in some other department which needs bolstering up. I have not hesitated to drop cabinet officers when I found them inefficient, even though my affections for them urged me to retain them. It is so easy to put one's personal affections for men above the public service.

Meyer, Garfield, and Straus are ideal cabinet officers for me. They keep up the routine, and when it is a matter of national or international policy they promptly bring it up to me for a decision with a clear-cut recommendation. (Recorded by Butt in letter of January 27, 1909.) *The Letters of Archie Butt. Personal Aide to President Roosevelt.* (Doubleday, Page & Co., Garden City, N. Y., 1924), p. 311.

———. Before we take up any business, as this is our last meeting, I want to say to you that no President ever received more loyal support from his official family than I have received. The work that you have done I have received the credit for, which is the same in the Army—credit must go to the general in command. The only reward you receive is having the knowledge of doing your work well. (At Cabinet meeting, March 2, 1909; from Meyer's diary.) M. A. De Wolfe Howe, *George von Lengerke Meyer.* (Dodd, Mead & Co., N. Y., 1919), p. 420.

CALHOUN, JOHN C. *See* NULLIFICATION.

CALLISTHENICS. *See* GYMNASTICS.

CAMERA. *See* HUNTING; NATURE STUDY.

CAMPAIGN CONTRIBUTIONS. In political campaigns in a country as large and populous as ours it is inevitable that there should be much expense of an entirely legitimate kind. This, of course, means that many contributions, and some of them of large size, must be made, and, as a matter of fact, in any big political contest such contributions are always made to both sides. It is entirely proper both to give and receive them, unless there is an improper motive connected with either gift or reception. If they are extorted by any kind of pressure or promise, express or implied, direct or indirect, in the way of favor or immunity, then the giving or receiving becomes not only improper but criminal. . . . All contributions by corporations to any political committee or for any political purpose should be forbidden by law; directors should not be permitted to use stockholders money for such purposes; and, moreover, a prohibition of this kind would be, as far as it went, an effective method of stopping the evils aimed at in corrupt practices acts. Not only should both the national and the several State legislatures forbid any officer of a corporation from using the money of the corporation in or about any election, but they should also forbid such use of money in connection with any legislation save by the employment of counsel in public manner for distinctly legal services. (Fifth Annual Message, Washington, December 5, 1905.) *Mem. Ed.* XVII, 344-345; *Nat. Ed.* XV, 294-295.

―――――――. I have just been informed that the Standard Oil people have contributed $100,000 to our campaign fund. This may be entirely untrue. But if true I must ask you to direct that the money be returned to them forthwith. I appreciate to the full the need of funds to pay the legitimate and necessarily great expenses of the campaign. I appreciate to the full the fact that under no circumstances will we receive half as much as was received by the National Committee in 1900 and 1896. Moreover, it is entirely legitimate to accept contributions, no matter how large they are, from individuals and corporations on the terms on which I happen to know that you have accepted them, that is, with the explicit understanding that they were given and received with no thought of any more obligation on the part of the National Committee or of the national administration than is implied in the statement that every man shall receive a square deal, no more and no less, and that this I shall guarantee him in any event to the best of my ability. . . .

But we cannot under any circumstances afford to take a contribution which can be even improperly construed as putting us under an improper obligation, and in view of my past relations with the Standard Oil Company I fear that such a construction will be put upon receiving any aid from them. In returning the money to them I wish it made clear to them that there is not the slightest personal feeling against them, and that they can count upon being treated exactly as well by the administration, exactly as fairly, as if we had accepted the contribution. They shall not suffer in any way because we refused it, just as they would not have gained in any way if we had accepted it. (To George B. Courtelyou, October 26, 1904.) *Mem. Ed.* XXIII, 379, 380; Bishop I, 329.

―――――――. I have been informed that you, or some one on behalf of the National Committee, have requested contributions both from Mr. Archbold and Mr. Harriman. If this is true I wish to enter a most earnest protest, and to say that in my judgment not only should such contributions not be solicited, but if tendered they should be refused; and if they have been accepted they should immediately be returned. I am not the candidate, but I am the head of the Republican Administration, which is an issue in this campaign, and I protest most earnestly against men whom we are prosecuting being asked to contribute to elect a President who will appoint an Attorney-General to continue these prosecutions. (To George R. Sheldon, Treasurer of the Republican National Committee, September 21, 1908.) *Mem. Ed.* XXIV, 113; Bishop II, 97.

―――――――. I believe that usually the contributors, and the recipient, sincerely felt that the transaction was proper and subserved the cause of good politics and good business; and, indeed, as regards the major part of the contributions, it is probable that this was the fact, and that the only criticism that could properly be made about the contributions was that they were not made with publicity. . . . Many, probably most, of the contributors of this type never wished anything personal in exchange for their contributions. . . .

There was but one kind of money contribution as to which it seemed to me absolutely impossible for either the contributor or the recipient to disguise to themselves the evil meaning of the contribution. This was where a big corporation contributed to both political parties. (1913.) *Mem. Ed.* XXII, 314; *Nat. Ed.* XX, 269.

CAMPAIGN CONTRIBUTIONS. *See also* POLITICAL ASSESSMENTS.

CAMPAIGN EXPENSES. If a campaign is honestly carried on the expenses, though heavy, are less than is commonly supposed. There is some indispensable work to be done which has to be paid for. Tens of thousands of ballots have to be printed, folded and sent out to every voter in the district; no light labor. At every polling place there ought to be at least one man especially charged with the interest of the candidate singly and provided with his ballots, so as to give members of the opposite party a chance, if they wish it, to vote for him without the rest of the ticket. This man has to have a booth, ballots, posters, etc., which again costs money. Then there must be some advertisement in the papers, and some pasting of placards. If there are political processions a candidate will bear his share in defraying the expenses; also, if for an important position he must have rooms hired for headquarters, and if he speaks will have to pay for the hall, etc.

But whenever possible volunteers should be chosen instead of paid workers; they are much more effective. (To Corinne Roosevelt Robinson, April 15, 1886.) Cowles *Letters*, 75.

———————. So far from its being true that there is any lavish and unusual expenditure of money at an American election, such as the National Election of 1904, the reverse is the fact. I was interested in comparing the figures which show that the expenditures in the presidential election of 1904 were less than the expenditures at the last preceding election for members for Parliament in the British Isles, although there is a very stringent corrupt practices act, and although the voting constituency in the British Isles is so much smaller. (Letter to Cornelius N. Bliss, 1906.) James K. Pollock, Jr., *Party Campaign Funds*. (Alfred A. Knopf, N. Y., 1926), pp. 177-178.

———————. It is particularly important that all moneys received or expended for campaign purposes should be publicly accounted for, not only after election, but before election as well. Political action must be made simpler, easier, and freer from confusion for every citizen. (At Osawatomie, Kan., August 31, 1910.) *Mem. Ed.* XIX, 28; *Nat. Ed.* XVII, 20.

———————. I am with you on the question of the State paying the election expenses right away now. I have always stood for that course as the only one to give the poor man a fair chance in politics. (To William R. Nelson, July 1912.) *Roosevelt in the Kansas City Star*, xxii.

CAMPAIGN FUNDS. The need for collecting large campaign funds would vanish if Congress provided an appropriation for the proper and legitimate expenses of each of the great national parties, an appropriation ample enough to meet the necessity for thorough organization and machinery, which requires a large expenditure of money. Then the stipulation should be made that no party receiving campaign funds from the Treasury should accept more than a fixed amount from any individual subscriber or donor; and the necessary publicity for receipts and expenditures could without difficulty be provided. (Seventh Annual Message, Washington, December 3, 1907.) *Mem. Ed.* XVII, 541; *Nat. Ed.* XV, 461.

———————. I believe that political parties should be controlled by, and be paid for, as far as possible, by the actual men and women who vote at elections, in other words by the people. I do not insist upon any absolute equality in campaign gifts, and I am willing that the party should take the large campaign contribution, if honestly offered without condition or reservation, on exactly the same terms and in exactly the same spirit, as the small contribution. The real test of such gifts to a political party is the motive, not the size. (At Chicago, December 10, 1912.) *Mem. Ed.* XIX, 475; *Nat. Ed.* XVII, 351.

CANADIAN NORTHWEST — ANNEXATION OF. It would have been well for all America if we had insisted even more than we did upon the extension northward of our boundaries. Not only the Columbia but also the Red River of the North—and the Saskatchewan and Frazer as well—should lie wholly within our limits, less for our own sake than for the sake of the men who dwell along their banks. Columbia, Saskatchewan, and Manitoba would, as States of the American Union, hold positions incomparably more important, grander, and more dignified than they can ever hope to reach either as independent communities or as provincial dependencies of a foreign power that regards them with a kindly tolerance somewhat akin to contemptuous indifference. Of course no one would wish to see these, or any other settled communities, now added to our domain by force; we want no unwilling citizens to enter our Union; the time to have taken the lands was before settlers came into them. (1887.) *Mem. Ed.* VIII, 197; *Nat. Ed.* VII, 170-171.

CANAL ZONE. See PANAMA CANAL.

CANDIDATES FOR OFFICE. The most important thing for you . . . to know [is] how the man you choose will conduct himself in the office to which he is elected. Now, to know this you must not only understand his views and principles, but you must also know how well his practice corresponds with his principles. This is the all-important fact, and yet it is not a fact which needs much elaboration. No amount of argument can prove it or is necessary to prove it. Far more important than the candidate's words is the estimate you are able to put upon the closeness with which his deeds will correspond to his words.

No self-respecting man who is a candidate can state with exact minuteness what his line of conduct will be, because, while he must remain firm throughout in his adherence to the immovable principles of right, yet he must be prepared to meet the constantly shifting conditions of governmental life. It may, perhaps, be said without irreverence that a man should in his public as well as private life strive to conform his conduct to the principles laid down in those two ancient guides to conduct, the Decalogue and the Golden Rule. (Campaign speech, New York City, October 19, 1898.) *Mem. Ed.* XVI, 451-452; *Nat. Ed.* XIV, 298-299.

———. Politicians proverbially like a colorless candidate, and the very success of what I have done, the number of things I have accomplished, and the extent of my record, may prove to be against me. (To Henry White, April 4, 1904.) *Mem. Ed.* XXIII, 364; Bishop I, 316.

CAPITAL. See BUSINESS; COMBINATIONS; STOCK-WATERING; WEALTH.

CAPITAL AND LABOR. I represent neither capital nor labor; I represent every American citizen, be he laborer or be he capitalist. (In New York Assembly, April 18, 1883.) *Mem. Ed.* XVI, 33; *Nat. Ed.* XIV, 25.

———. In our complex industrial civilization of today the peace of righteousness and justice, the only kind of peace worth having, is at least as necessary in the industrial world as it is among nations. There is at least as much need to curb the cruel greed and arrogance of part of the world of capital, to curb the cruel greed and violence of part of the world of labor, as to check a cruel and unhealthy militarism in international relationships. *Outlook,* May 7, 1910, p. 19.

CAPITAL AND LABOR — ATTITUDE TOWARD. In my judgment, the only safe attitude for a private citizen, and still more for a public servant, to assume, is that he will draw the line on conduct, discriminating against neither corporation nor union as such, nor in favor of either as such, but endeavoring to make the decent member of the union and the upright capitalists alike feel that they are bound, not only by self-interest, but by every consideration of principle and duty to stand together on the matters of most moment to the nation. (Letter of November 26, 1903.) *Mem. Ed.* XXII, 566; *Nat. Ed.* XX, 487.

———. Sweeping attacks upon all property, upon all men of means, without regard to whether they do well or ill, would sound the death-knell of the Republic; and such attacks become inevitable if decent citizens permit rich men whose lives are corrupt and evil to domineer in swollen pride, unchecked and unhindered, over the destinies of this country. We act in no vindictive spirit, and we are no respecters of persons. If a labor union does what is wrong, we oppose it as fearlessly as we oppose a corporation that does wrong; and we stand with equal stoutness for the rights of the man of wealth and for the rights of the wage-workers; just as much so for one as for the other. We seek to stop wrong-doing; and we desire to punish the wrong-doer only so far as is necessary in order to achieve this end. We are the stanch upholders of every honest man, whether business man or wage-worker. (To Charles J. Bonaparte, January 2, 1908.) *Mem. Ed.* XXII, 523; *Nat. Ed.* XX, 450.

CAPITAL AND LABOR — ORGANIZATION OF. We recognize the organization of capital and the organization of labor as natural outcomes of our industrial system. Each kind of organization is to be favored so long as it acts in a spirit of justice and of regard for the rights of others. Each is to be granted the full protection of the law, and each in turn is to be held to a strict obedience to the law; for no man is above it and no man below it. The humblest individual is to have his rights safeguarded as scrupulously as those of the strongest organization, for each is to receive justice, no more and no less. The problems with which we have to deal in our modern industrial and social life are manifold; but the spirit in which it is necessary to approach their solution is simply the spirit of honesty, of courage, and of common sense. (Speech accepting nomination, July 27, 1904.) *Mem. Ed.* XXIII, 372; Bishop I, 323.

CAPITAL AND LABOR—PROBLEM OF. How to secure fair treatment alike for labor and for capital, how to hold in check the unscrupulous man, whether employer or employee, without weakening individual initiative, without hampering and cramping the industrial development of the country, is a problem fraught with great difficulties and one which it is of the highest importance to solve on lines of sanity and far-sighted common sense as well as of devotion to the right. (Second Annual

Message, Washington, December 2, 1902.) *Mem. Ed.* XVII, 171; *Nat. Ed.* XV, 148.

CAPITAL AND LABOR — RELATIONS BETWEEN. It is essential that capitalist and wage-worker should consult freely one with the other, should each strive to bring closer the day when both shall realize that they are properly partners and not enemies. To approach the questions which inevitably arise between them solely from the standpoint which treats each side in the mass as the enemy of the other side in the mass is both wicked and foolish. (Fifth Annual Message, Washington, December 5, 1905.) *Mem. Ed.* XVII, 335; *Nat. Ed.* XV, 287.

CAPITAL AND LABOR. *See also* COLLECTIVE BARGAINING; EMPLOYER; INDUSTRIAL REVOLUTION; LABOR; SQUARE DEAL; WORKERS.

CAPITAL PUNISHMENT. I have always felt impatient contempt for the effort to abolish the death penalty on account of sympathy with criminals. I am willing to listen to arguments in favor of abolishing the death penalty so far as they are based purely on grounds of public expediency.... But inasmuch as, without hesitation, in the performance of duty, I have again and again sent good and gallant and upright men to die, it seems to me the height of a folly both mischievous and mawkish to contend that criminals who have deserved death should nevertheless be allowed to shirk it. (1913.) *Mem. Ed.* XXII, 298; *Nat. Ed.* XX, 254, 255.

————. My experience of the way in which pardons are often granted is one of the reasons why I do not believe that life imprisonment for murder and rape is a proper substitute for the death penalty. The average term of so-called life imprisonment in this country is only about fourteen years. (1913.) *Mem. Ed.* XXII, 351; *Nat. Ed.* XX, 301.

CAPITAL PUNISHMENT. *See also* CRIMINALS; LYNCHING.

CAPITALISM. *See* CLASS; CORRUPTION; PROFITS; PROPERTY; SOCIALISM.

CAPITALIST AND LABOR LEADER. We can no more and no less afford to condone evil in the man of capital than evil in the man of no capital. The wealthy man who exults because there is a failure of justice in the effort to bring some trust magnate to an account for his misdeeds is as bad as, and no worse than, the so-called labor leader who clamorously strives to excite a foul class feeling on behalf of some other labor leader who is implicated in murder. One attitude is as bad as the other, and no worse; in each case the accused is entitled to exact justice; and in neither case is there need of action by others which can be construed into an expression of sympathy for crime. (Letter of April 26, 1906.) *Mem. Ed.* XXII, 563; *Nat. Ed.* XX, 484.

————. Capitalist and labor leader alike should be held to the same course of conduct. Both must obey the law; and, on the other hand, each has the right temperately and truthfully to point out where a given interpretation of the law by a given man works injustice. (*Outlook,* February 25, 1911.) *Mem. Ed.* XIX, 114; *Nat. Ed.* XVII, 77.

CAPITALISTS. A good capitalist, who employs his money and his leisure aright, is the most useful man we have. There are in this country but a very small number of great capitalists. I am not concerned for them, I am concerned for the great body of the people; because I know that the people cannot afford to go wrong or to do wrong. (At Utica, N. Y., September 29, 1896.) *Mem. Ed.* XVI, 393.

CAPITALISTS—REWARDS TO. It is not necessary that the Van Hornes and the Jim Hills of the future shall receive the enormous financial reward they have had in the past; but it must be substantial, or they will not lead to success the business in which the brakemen, switchmen, engineers, firemen will, we hope, ultimately become part owners as well as workers. Such leadership is absolutely needed by the men below, and it must be handsomely paid for—there is no more mischievous form of privilege than giving equal rewards for unequal service, and denying the great reward to the great service. But it need not be a reward fantastically out of proportion to the reward of the men beneath. (1917.) *Mem. Ed.* XXI, 93; *Nat. Ed.* XIX, 80.

CAPITALISTS AND GOVERNMENT. From the railroad rate law to the pure food law, every measure for honesty in business that has been pressed during the last six years has been opposed by these men, on its passage and in its administration, with every resource that bitter and unscrupulous craft could suggest, and the command of almost unlimited money secure. These men do not themselves speak or write; they hire others to do their bidding. Their spirit and purpose are made clear alike by the editorials of the papers owned in, or whose policy is dictated by, Wall Street, and by the speeches of public men who, as senators, governors, or mayors, have served these their masters to the cost of the plain people. (To Charles J. Bonaparte, January 2, 1908.) *Mem. Ed.* XXII, 516; *Nat. Ed.* XX, 443.

———————. It is essential that we should wrest the control of the Government out of the hands of rich men who use it for unhealthy purposes, and should keep it out of their hands; and to this end the first requisite is to provide means adequately to deal with corporations, which are essential to modern business, but which, under the decisions of the courts, and because of the shortsightedness of the public, have become the chief factors in political and business debasement. *Outlook,* June 19, 1909, p. 392.

CAPITALISTS. *See also* FINANCIERS; MILLIONAIRES; RIGHTS; WALL STREET; WEALTH.

CAPRON, ALLYN. There was Allyn Capron, who was, on the whole, the best soldier in the [Rough Rider] regiment. In fact, I think he was the ideal of what an American regular army officer should be. He was the fifth in descent from father to son who had served in the army of the United States, and in body and mind alike he was fitted to play his part to perfection. Tall and lithe, a remarkable boxer and walker, a first-class rider and shot, with yellow hair and piercing blue eyes, he looked what he was, the archetype of the fighting man. He had under him one of the two companies from the Indian Territory; and he so soon impressed himself upon the wild spirit of his followers, that he got them ahead in discipline faster than any other troop in the regiment, while at the same time taking care of their bodily wants. His ceaseless effort was so to train them, care for them, and inspire them as to bring their fighting efficiency to the highest possible pitch. He required instant obedience, and tolerated not the slightest evasion of duty; but his mastery of his art was so thorough and his performance of his own duty so rigid that he won at once not merely their admiration, but that soldierly affection so readily given by the man in the ranks to the superior who cares for his men and leads them fearlessly in battle. (1899.) *Mem. Ed.* XIII, 15; *Nat. Ed.* XI, 13.

CARIBBEAN AREA. *See* MONROE DOCTRINE.

CARLYLE, THOMAS. Carlyle's singular incapacity to "see veracity," as he would himself have phrased it, made him at times not merely tell half-truths, but deliberately invert the truth. He was of that not uncommon cloistered type which shrinks shuddering from actual contact with whatever it, in theory, most admires, and which, therefore, is reduced in self-justification to misjudge and misrepresent those facts of past history which form precedents for what is going on before the author's own eyes. (1900.) *Mem. Ed.* XIII, 287; *Nat. Ed.* X, 187.

———————. I have also been reading Carlyle; and the more I read him the more hearty grows my contempt for his profound untruthfulness and for his shrieking deification of shams. . . . If only Carlyle were alive how I would like to review his Frederick the Great with the same freedom of epithet which he practised! and with all the sincerity and truthfulness to which he paid such lip service, and in the practice of which he so wholly failed. Some of his writing is really fine; his battles for instance. . . . What I can't stand is his hypocrisy; his everlasting praise of veracity, accompanying the constant practise of every species of mendacity in order to give a false color to history and a false twist to ethics. . . . When he speaks of his hero—indeed of any of his heroes—he always uses morality as a synonym for ruthless efficiency, and sincerity as a synonym for shameless lack of scruple; but in dealing with people whom he does not like, the words at once revert to their ordinary uses, and he himself appears as the sternest rebuker of evil and treachery. (To Sir George Otto Trevelyan, September 10, 1909.) *Mem. Ed.* XXIV, 202-203; Bishop II, 173-174.

CARRANZA, VENUSTIANO. *See* MEXICO.

"CARRY YOUR OWN WEIGHT." *See* CHARITY.

CATASTROPHIES. *See* EXPERIENCE.

CATHOLIC CHURCH. *See* JESUITS; ROME.

CATHOLICS IN PUBLIC LIFE. You say that "the mass of the voters that are not Catholics will not support a man for any office, especially for President of the United States, who is a Roman Catholic." I believe that when you say this you foully slander your fellow countrymen. I do not for one moment believe that the mass of our fellow citizens, or that any considerable number of our fellow citizens, can be influenced by such narrow bigotry as to refuse to vote for any thoroughly upright and fit man because he happens to have a particular religious creed. Such a consideration should never be treated as a reason for either supporting or opposing a candidate for a political office. Are you aware that there are several States in this Union where the majority of the people are now Catholics? I should reprobate in the severest terms the Catholics who in those States (or in any other States) refused to vote for the most fit man because he happened to be a Protestant; and my condemnation would be exactly as severe for Protestants who, under reversed circumstances, refused to vote for a Catholic. In public life I am happy to say that I have known many men who were elected, and constantly re-elected, to office in districts where the great majority of their constituents were of a different religious belief. (To J. C. Martin, November 6, 1908.) *Mem. Ed.* XVIII, 54; *Nat. Ed.* XVI, 47.

CATTLE INDUSTRY. The best days of ranching are over; and though there are many ranchmen who still make money, yet during the past two or three years the majority have certainly lost. .... Stock-raising as now carried on is characteristic of a young and wild land. As the country grows older it will in some places die out, and in others entirely change its character; the ranches will be broken up, will be gradually modified into stock-farms, or if on good soil, may even fall under the sway of the husbandman.

In its present form stock-raising on the plains is doomed, and can hardly outlast the century. The great free ranches, with their barbarous, picturesque, and curiously fascinating surroundings, mark a primitive stage of existence as surely as do the great tracts of primeval forests and, like the latter, must pass away before the onward march of our people; and we who have felt the charm of the life, and have exulted in its abounding vigor and its bold, restless freedom, will not only regret its passing for our own sakes, but must also feel real sorrow that those who come after us are not to see as we have seen, what is perhaps the pleasantest, healthiest, and most exciting phase of American existence. (1888.) *Mem. Ed.* IV, 388-389; *Nat. Ed.* I, 292-293.

CATTLEMAN—PASSING OF THE. For we ourselves and the life that we lead will shortly pass away from the plains as completely as the red and white hunters who have vanished from before our herds. The free, open-air life of the ranchman, the pleasantest and healthiest life in America, is from its very nature ephemeral. The broad and boundless prairies have already been bounded and will soon be made narrow. It is scarcely a figure of speech to say that the tide of white settlement during the last few years has risen over the West like a flood; and the cattlemen are but the spray from the crest of the wave, thrown far in advance, but soon to be overtaken. As the settlers throng into the lands and seize the good ground, especially that near the streams, the great fenceless ranches, where the cattle and their mounted herdsmen wandered unchecked over hundreds of thousands of acres, will be broken up and divided into corn land, or else into small grazing farms where a few hundred head of stock are closely watched and taken care of. Of course the most powerful ranches, owned by wealthy corporations or individuals, and already firmly rooted in the soil, will long resist this crowding; in places, where the ground is not suited to agriculture, or where, through the old Spanish land-grants, the title has been acquired to a great tract of territory, cattle ranching will continue for a long time, though in a greatly modified form; elsewhere, I doubt if it lasts out the present century. (1885.) *Mem. Ed.* I, 20-21; *Nat. Ed.* I, 17.

CATTLE; CATTLEMAN. *See also* COWBOYS; RANCH LIFE; ROUND-UP.

CELTIC LITERATURE. I hope that an earnest effort will be made to endow chairs in American universities for the study of Celtic literature and for research in Celtic antiquities. It is only of recent years that the extraordinary wealth and beauty of the old Celtic Sagas have been fully appreciated, and we of America, who have so large a Celtic strain in our blood, cannot afford to be behindhand in the work of adding to modern scholarship by bringing within its ken the great Celtic literature of the past. (Before Society of Friendly Sons of St. Patrick, New York, March 17, 1905.) *Mem. Ed.* XVIII, 50; *Nat. Ed.* XVI, 43.

CELTIC LITERATURE. *See also* LITERATURE.

CENSORSHIP. *See* BOASTING; CRITICISM.

CHAMBERLAIN, HOUSTON STEWART. Mr. Chamberlain's thesis is that the nineteenth century, and therefore the twentieth and all future centuries, depend for everything in them worth mentioning and preserving upon the Teutonic branch of the Aryan race. He holds that there is no such thing as a general progress of mankind, that progress is only for those whom he calls the Teutons, and that when they mix with or are intruded upon by alien and, as he regards them, lower races, the result is fatal. Much that he says regarding the prevalent loose and sloppy talk about the general progress of humanity, the equality and identity of races, and the like, is not only perfectly true, but is emphatically worth considering by a generation accustomed, as its forefathers for the preceding generations were accustomed, to accept as true and useful thoroughly pernicious doctrines taught by well-meaning and feeble-minded sentimentalists; but Mr. Chamberlain himself is quite as fantastic an extremist as any of those whom he derides, and an extremist whose doctrines are based upon foolish hatred is even more unlovely than an extremist whose doctrines are based upon foolish benevolence. Mr. Chamberlain's hatreds cover a wide gamut. They include Jews, Darwinists, the Roman Catholic Church, the people of southern Europe, Peruvians, Semites, and an odd variety of literary men and historians. (*Outlook,* July 29, 1911.) *Mem. Ed.* XIV, 196; *Nat. Ed.* XII, 107.

CHAPLAINS—SELECTION OF. I want to see that hereafter no chaplain is appointed in the Army (and Navy) who is not a first-class man—a man who by education and training will be fitted to associate with his fellow officers, and yet who has in him the zeal and the practical sense which will enable him to do genuine work for the enlisted men. Above all, I want chaplains who will go in to do this work just as the best officers of the line or staff or the medical profession go in to do their work. I want to see that if possible we never appoint a man who desires the position as a soft job. How would it do to have the applicants of the different creeds pass some kind of examination before really high-grade clergymen of their own creeds? (To Secretaries of War and the Navy, June 10, 1902.) *Mem. Ed.* XXIII, 218; Bishop I, 190.

CHARACTER. Alike for the nation and the individual, the one indispensable requisite is character—character that does and dares as well as endures, character that is active in the performance of virtue no less than firm in the refusal to do aught that is vicious or degraded. (*Outlook,* March 31, 1900.) *Mem. Ed.* XV, 502; *Nat. Ed.* XIII, 386.

——————. The foundation-stone of national life is, and ever must be, the high individual character of the average citizen. (At Washington, April 14, 1906.) *Mem. Ed.* XVIII, 581; *Nat. Ed.* XVI, 424.

——————. Bodily vigor is good, and vigor of intellect is even better, but far above both is character. . . . In the long run, in the great battle of life, no brilliancy of intellect, no perfection of bodily development, will count when weighed in the balance against that assemblage of virtues, active and passive, of moral qualities, which we group together under the name of character. (*Outlook,* March 31, 1900.) *Mem. Ed.* XV, 496; *Nat. Ed.* XIII, 381.

CHARACTER—COMPONENTS OF. Character has two sides. It is composed of two sets of traits; in the first place the set of traits which we group together under such names as clean living, decency, morality, virtue, the desire and power to deal fairly each by his neighbor, each by his friends, each toward the State; that we have to have as fundamental. The abler, the more powerful any man is the worse he is if he has not got the root of righteousness in him. . . . In addition to decency, morality, virtue, clean living, you must have hardihood, resolution, courage, the power to do, the power to dare, the power to endure, and when you have that combination, then you get the proper type of American citizenship. (At Claremont, Cal., May 8, 1903.) Theodore Roosevelt, *California Addresses.* (San Francisco, 1903), pp. 22-23.

——————. By character I mean the sum of those qualities, distinct from the purely intellectual qualities, which are essential to moral efficiency. Among them are resolution, courage, energy, power of self-control combined with fearlessness in taking the initiative and assuming responsibility, and a just regard for the rights of others together with unflinching determination to one's self to succeed no matter what obstacles and barriers have to be beaten down—these qualities, and qualities such as these, are what rise to our minds when we speak of a man or a woman as having character, in contradistinction to one who possesses only intellect. . . . If the ordinary men and women of the republic have character, the future of the republic is assured; and if in its citizenship rugged strength and fealty to the common welfare are lacking, then no brilliancy of intellect and no piled-up material prosperity will avail to save the nation from destruction. *Outlook,* November 8, 1913, pp. 527, 528.

CHARACTER, PRIVATE, AND PUBLIC LIFE. A man can of course hold public office, and many a man does hold public office, and lead a public career of a sort, even if there are other men who possess secrets about him which he cannot afford to have divulged. But no man can lead a public career really worth leading, no man can act with rugged independence in serious crises, nor strike at great abuses, nor afford to make powerful and unscrupulous foes, if he is himself vulnerable in his private character.... He must be clean of life, so that he can laugh when his public or his private record is searched; and yet being clean of life will not avail him if he is either foolish or timid. He must walk warily and fearlessly, and while he should never brawl if he can avoid it, he must be ready to hit hard if the need arises. (1913.) *Mem. Ed.* XXII, 102; *Nat. Ed.* XX, 87.

CHARACTER AND INTELLIGENCE. Character is far more important than intellect to the race as to the individual. We need intellect, and there is no reason why we should not have it together with character; but if we must choose between the two we choose character without a moment's hesitation. (*North American Review*, July 1895.) *Mem. Ed.* XIV, 128; *Nat. Ed.* XIII, 241.

───────────. No man can reach the front rank if he is not intelligent and if he is not trained with intelligence; but mere intelligence by itself is worse than useless unless it is guided by an upright heart, unless there are also strength and courage behind it. Morality, decency, clean living, courage, manliness, self-respect—these qualities are more important in the make-up of a people than any mental subtlety. *Outlook*, April 23, 1910, p. 880.

───────────. I am far from decrying intellect. I join with the world in admiring it and paying homage to it. Without it—above all, without its highest expression, genius—the world would move forward but slowly, and the purple patches in the gray garment of our actual lives would be sadly shorn of their glory. Nevertheless exactly as strength comes before beauty, so character must ever stand above intellect, above genius. Intellect is fit to be the most useful of servants; but it is an evil master, unless itself mastered by character. This is true of the individual man. It is far more true of the nation, of the aggregate of individuals.... From the standpoint of national greatness, neither the intellect which finds its expression in commercialism nor the intellect which finds its expression in artistic achievement can permanently avail unless based on a foundation of character. *Outlook*, November 8, 1913, p. 527.

CHARACTER AND LAW. In the last analysis, the most important elements in any man's career must be the sum of those qualities which, in the aggregate, we speak of as character. If he has not got it, then no law that the wit of man can devise, no administration of the law by the boldest and strongest executive, will avail to help him. We must have the right kind of character—character that makes a man, first of all, a good man in the home, a good father, a good husband—that makes a man a good neighbor. You must have that, and, then, in addition, you must have the kind of law and the kind of administration of the law which will give to those qualities in the private citizen the best possible chance for development. (At Osawatomie, Kan., August 31, 1910.) *Mem. Ed.* XIX, 30; *Nat. Ed.* XVII, 22.

───────────. We are not proposing to substitute law for character. We are merely proposing to buttress character by law. We fully recognize that, as has been true in the past, so it is true now, and ever will be true, the prime factor in each man's or woman's success must normally be that man's or that woman's own character.... Nothing will avail a nation if there is not the right type of character among the average men and women, the plain people, the hard-working, decent-living, right-thinking people, who make up the great bulk of our citizenship.... In civil life, in the every-day life of our nation, it is individual character which counts most; and yet the individual character cannot avail unless in addition thereto there lie ready to hand the social weapons which can be forged only by law and by public opinion operating through and operated upon by law. (At Madison Square Garden, New York City, October 30, 1912.) *Mem. Ed.* XIX, 457; *Nat. Ed.* XVII, 335.

CHARACTER. *See also* CITIZENSHIP; COURAGE; EDUCATION; IDEALS; INTELLECTUAL ACUTENESS; MANHOOD; MANLINESS; MORAL SENSE; MORALITY; NATIONAL CHARACTER; SELF-MASTERY; SUCCESS; VIRTUES.

CHARITY. In charity the one thing always to be remembered is that, while any man may slip and should at once be helped to rise to his feet, yet no man can be carried with advantage either to him or to the community. The greatest possible good can be done by the extension of a helping hand at the right moment, but the attempt to carry any one permanently can end in nothing but harm. (*Century*, October 1900.) *Mem. Ed.* XV, 434; *Nat. Ed.* XIII, 380.

───────────. We must all learn the two lessons—the lesson of self-help and the lesson of giving help to and receiving help from our brother. . . . Yet, though each man can and ought thus to be helped at times, he is lost beyond redemption if he becomes so dependent upon outside help that he feels that his own exertions are secondary. Any man at times will stumble, and it is then our duty to lift him up and set him on his feet again; but no man can be permanently carried, for if he expects to be carried he shows that he is not worth carrying. (At Labor Day Picnic, September 3, 1900.) *Mem. Ed.* XVI, 517; *Nat. Ed.* XIII, 488.

——————. The first duty of each one of you here is to carry your own weight—to carry yourselves. You are not going to be able to do anything for any one else until you can support yourselves and those dependent upon you. I do not want to see you develop that kind of idealism which makes you filled with vague thoughts of beneficence for mankind and an awful drawback to your immediate families. (At Clark University, Worcester, Mass., June 21, 1905.) *Mem. Ed.* XV, 578; *Nat. Ed.* XIII, 618.

——————. While every man needs at times to be lifted up when he stumbles, no man can afford to let himself be carried, and it is worth no man's while to try thus to carry some one else. The man who lies down, who will not try to walk, has become a mere cumberer of the earth's surface. (Before Young Men's Christian Association, New York City, December 30, 1900.) *Mem. Ed.* XV, 528; *Nat. Ed.* XIII, 493.

——————. I think that the men and women who have made the subject of charities their special study in this State are to be congratulated for the steadiness with which they have refused to be led aside into that dangerous path which ends in the soup kitchen and pauperism. They ought to be congratulated for having kept steadily aloof from that kind of hysteric charity which is chiefly useful for purposes of advertisement, and it certainly is worse than useless from the standpoint of doing good. I think more and more we are realizing that in the long run the only way efficiently to help a man is to help him to help himself. There is no man who does not stumble. That includes not only those we are working for but all of us just as well: there is not one of us who does not stumble. There is not one of us who does not need to have a helping hand stretched to him at some time, and woe to the man who refuses to stretch that helping hand. Every man who stumbles needs to be helped on his feet. But you cannot carry him. If you try you hurt yourself and you hurt him more. If you teach him always to rely upon some one else you have ruined him for all time. It is the end of a man's being of use to himself or of use to any one else. (At Albany, N. Y., November 20, 1900.) *Proceedings of the New York State Conference of Charities and Correction at the First Annual Session.* (Albany, N. Y., 1901), pp. 6-7.

CHARITY. See also BROTHERHOOD; PHILANTHROPY; SELF-HELP.

CHAUVINISM. See NATIONALISM; PATRIOTISM.

CHAUVINISTS. See AMERICAN, THE BLATANT.

CHECKS AND BALANCES. See DIVISION OF POWERS.

CHEMING—SINKING OF THE. See GERMANY.

CHILD LABOR. You cannot have good citizens, good men and women of the next generation, if the boys and girls are worked in factories to the stunting of their moral, mental and physical growth. Wherever the National Government can reach, it should do away with the evils of child-labor, and I trust this will be done; but much must be done by the actions of the several State Legislatures; and do, each of you, in your several States, all that you can to secure the enactment and then the enforcement, of laws that shall put a stop to the employment of children of tender age in doing what only grown up people should do. (Before International Congress on the Welfare of the Child, White House, March 10, 1908.) *Presidential Addresses and State Papers* VII, 1675.

——————. I make an appeal for limiting by law the age under which children shall not be allowed to work, an appeal for limiting by law the hours that they shall be allowed to work in the daytime, and an appeal absolutely to prohibit by law working them at night.

I do not ask you to pay heed to anything I say, excepting as you judge it right in thinking of your own children. Are you content, would you be content to have your own children of tender age work even as much as sixty hours a week? Would you be content to have them work at night? Would you be content to have them work under a certain age? I only ask that you women and men, you mothers and fathers think of your own children, and see to it that the children of others, the children of the people of this generation who cannot help themselves, receive the protection by law that you are fortunate enough to be able to give in your own families to your own children.

You are able to protect your children yourselves. You are able to see that they have the chance to go to school, that they do not waste the best—"waste" is not the term—that they do not abuse and use up their young lives in labor when they are too young to work. You here can protect your children, and you do not need the state to step in to help you protect them. I ask you to see that the state, that the government that represents all of you, steps in to protect the other children who have not parents able and willing to protect them. (At Birmingham, Ala., March 10, 1911.) *Uniform Child Labor Laws. Proceedings of the Seventh Annual Conference of the National Child Labor Committee.* (Amer. Acad. of Pol. and Soc. Science, Phila., 1911), pp. 8-9.

CHILD LABOR—CONTROL OF. New York State is behind in its child-labor laws; but there are some other States even farther behind. For seven years the National Child Labor Committee and other agencies have attempted to raise the age limit to fourteen years throughout the Union. Surely, that is low enough. Surely, no girl or boy should be allowed to work under the age of fourteen! . . . The employment of children of twelve or ten years in the cotton-mill industry is not only a disgrace to the employers and the community permitting it, but a reproach to the American public. Nor are cotton-mills the only offenders. Children as young as five and six years work all winter in oyster and shrimp canneries on the Gulf coast, in Florida and elsewhere. Thousands of them work all summer in Maryland and Delaware vegetable-gardens and canneries, and all winter in Southern packing-houses. No law protects them, yet the work in which they are engaged is often ruinous to their health. This is a democracy; the spring cannot rise higher than its source. What kind of government, what kind of social conditions will you have from an electorate where the grown men and women have spent their childhood in such fashion?

I lack power to paint for you the hideous misery and hopelessness of some of these children's lives. (At New York City, October 20, 1911.) *Mem. Ed.* XVIII, 257-258; *Nat. Ed.* XVI, 192-193.

————. The National Government has an ultimate resort for control of child labor the use of the interstate commerce clause to prevent the products of child labor from entering into interstate commerce. But before using this it ought certainly to enact model laws on the subject for the Territories under its own immediate control. (Seventh Annual Message, Washington, December 3, 1907.) *Mem. Ed.* XVII, 514; *Nat. Ed.* XV, 438.

CHILD TRAINING. The way to give a child a fair chance in life is not to bring it up in luxury, but to see that it has the kind of training that will give it strength of character. (Before National Congress of Mothers, Washington, March 13, 1905.) *Mem. Ed.* XVIII, 231; *Nat. Ed.* XVI, 169.

CHILD TRAINING. *See also* BOYS; EDUCATION; TEACHERS.

CHILD WELFARE. As regards children, it is as essential to look after their physical as their mental training. We cannot afford to let children grow up ignorant; and if they are sent to school they cannot, while young, also work hard outside without detriment, physical, mental, and moral. There is urgent need for the health authorities to increase their care over the hygienic conditions and surroundings of children of tender years, and especially to supervise those in the schools. It is a good thing to try to reform bad children, to try to build up degenerate children; but it is an even better thing to try to keep healthy in soul, body, and mind those children who are now sound, but who may easily grow up unsound if no care is taken of them. . . . I am glad that there has been founded a national society of public-school hygiene, and I wish it, and all its branches, well in every way.

There is increasing need that the welfare of the children should be effectively safeguarded by governmental action; with the proviso, however, that this action shall be taken with knowledge and in a spirit of robust common sense; for philanthropy, whether governmental or individual, is a curse and not a blessing when marked by a spirit of foolish sentimentality and ignorance. (At Jamestown Exposition, Va., June 10, 1907.) *Mem. Ed.* XVIII, 238-239; *Nat. Ed.* XVI, 176.

CHILD WELFARE. *See also* PLAYGROUNDS.

CHILDREN. No quality in a race atones for the failure to produce an abundance of healthy children. (*Forum*, January 1897.) *Mem. Ed.* XIV, 146; *Nat. Ed.* XIII, 256.

———. The nation's most valuable asset is the children; for the children are the nation of the future. All people alive to the nation's need should join together to work for the moral, spiritual, and physical welfare of the children in all parts of our land. (At Jamestown Exposition, Va., June 10, 1907.) *Mem. Ed.* XVIII, 239; *Nat. Ed.* XVI, 176.

CHILDREN—DUTY TOWARD. We Americans are only on the threshold of the campaign for a better national life. We have only begun to consider our duty toward the child; to realize that the child-drudge is apt to turn into the shiftless grown-up; to realize that the child growing up in the streets has first-class opportunities for tending toward criminality; and, therefore, that playgrounds may be as necessary as schools. We have only begun to realize that the child's mother, if wise and duty-performing, is the only citizen who deserves even more from the state than does the soldier; and that, if in need, she is entitled to help from the state, so that she may rear and care for her children at home. (*Metropolitan,* May 1917.) *Mem. Ed.* XXI, 97; *Nat. Ed.* XIX, 84.

CHILDREN—LIFE WITH. There are many kinds of success in life worth having. It is exceedingly interesting and attractive to be a successful business man, or railroad man, or farmer, or a successful lawyer or doctor; or a writer, or a President, or a ranchman, or the colonel of a fighting regiment, or to kill grizzly bears and lions. But for unflagging interest and enjoyment, a household of children, if things go reasonably well, certainly makes all other forms of success and achievement lose their importance by comparison. . . .

The country is the place for children, and if not the country, a city small enough so that one can get out into the country. (1913.) *Mem. Ed.* XXII, 381; *Nat. Ed.* XX, 327.

CHILDREN. See also BIRTH CONTROL; BOOKS; FAMILY; HOME; INFANT MORTALITY; JUVENILE COURTS; MARRIAGE; PLAYGROUNDS.

"CHILDREN OF THE CRUCIBLE." See AMERICAN PEOPLE.

CHILDREN'S BUREAU. The first thing that should be done at Washington is to pass the legislation for the establishment in the Department of Commerce and Labor of a bureau, the purpose of which shall be to gather full information, official information, as to the condition of children and of child legislation in all the States of the Union, a bureau to be known as the Children's Bureau. It is difficult to act in one State when you can't find out what is being done in other States, and it is a spur to action in each State if there is a means of effectively publishing at the national capital the shortcomings in that State. Five years ago, when I was President, I recommended on several different occasions to Congress, the enactment of such a law. But I was not always able to persuade Congress to look at things like that as I did! For five years the passage of that law has been successfully resisted, and, friends, the reason why, I firmly believe, is to be found in the fact that that law appeals to no great special interest. We can not make any selfish appeal for the passage of that law, and, on the other hand, every man who has a selfish interest in the exploitation of child labor is against the passage of that law. Therefore, I ask you to make the general interest of the community your special interest, and to see that there is pressure brought to bear for the passage of that law. (Before Civic Forum and the Child Welfare League, Carnegie Hall, N. Y. C., October 20, 1911.) Theodore Roosevelt, *The Conservation of Womanhood and Childhood.* (Funk & Wagnalls Co., N. Y., 1912), 15-17.

CHILE. See MONROE DOCTRINE.

CHIMNEY BUTTE RANCH. I first reached the Little Missouri on a Northern Pacific train about three in the morning of a cool September day in 1883. Aside from the station, the only building was a ramshackle structure called the Pyramid Park Hotel. I dragged my duffle-bag thither, and hammered at the door until the frowsy proprietor appeared, muttering oaths. He ushered me up-stairs, where I was given one of the fourteen beds in the room which by itself constituted the entire upper floor. Next day I walked over to the abandoned army post, and, after some hours among the gray log shacks, a ranchman who had driven into the station agreed to take me out to his ranch, the Chimney Butte ranch, where he was living with his brother and their partner.

The ranch was a log structure with a dirt roof, a corral for the horses near by, and a chicken-house jabbed against the rear of the ranch-house. Inside there was only one room, with a table, three or four chairs, a cooking-stove, and three bunks. . . .

After a buffalo-hunt with my original friend, Joe Ferris, I entered into partnership with Merrifield and Sylvane Ferris, and we started a cow-ranch, with the maltese-cross brand—always known as "maltee cross" by the way, as the general impression along the Little Missouri was that "maltese" must be a plural. (1913.) *Mem. Ed.* XXII, 113-114; *Nat. Ed.* XX, 97-98.

CHIMNEY BUTTE RANCH. See also BAD LANDS; ELKHORN RANCH; RANCH LIFE.

CHINA. Our government has unswervingly advocated moderation and has materially aided in bringing about an adjustment which tends to enhance the welfare of China and to lead to a more beneficial intercourse between the empire and the modern world; while in the critical period of revolt and massacre we did our full share in safeguarding life and property, restoring order, and vindicating the national interest and honor. It behooves us to continue in these paths, doing what lies in our power to foster feelings of good-will, and leaving no effort untried to work out the great policy of full and fair intercourse between China and the nations, on a footing of equal rights and advantages to all. (First Annual Message, Washington, December 3, 1901.) *Mem. Ed.* XVII, 158-159; *Nat. Ed.* XV, 136-137.

CHINA—AWAKENING OF. China is awakening. There is increasing contact with foreigners, increasing foreign trade, and a growing adoption of modern methods of communication and transportation, while some progress is being made in the introduction of labor-saving devices, with consequent industrial evolution. In over a hundred cities there is now a more or less successful effort to introduce a Western police system, and what this means for the preservation of order it is hardly necessary to point out. Much admirable evangelistic, educational, and medical missionary work is being done by the missionaries; and a part of this consists in the introduction and broadcast circulation of translations of the Bible and of Western literature. The attitude of the Chinese toward learning from the West has been utterly changed ever since August, 1901, when, by an imperial edict, the old-style literary examinations were abolished, and it was directed that future candidates, for degrees as well as for office, should write their essays on such modern topics as Western science, government, and laws. (*Outlook,* November 28, 1908.) *Mem. Ed.* XVIII, 378-379; *Nat. Ed.* XVI, 284-285.

CHINA—EDUCATION IN. Americans are doing much for securing Christian education among the Chinese. They are training many of the future leaders and thousands of the rank and file. In 1907 there were nearly thirty thousand Chinese students among the eleven hundred and fifty-three American educational institutions in China, which embraced kindergartens, primary schools, high schools, colleges, universities, normal, divinity, and trade schools. Many men who have received their early training at some one of the American schools or colleges in China are now mightily influencing the industrial, political, and moral life of their land. One of the most important fuctions of these schools has been to supply good native teachers for China, and their graduates are in constantly increasing demand. (*Outlook,* November 28, 1908.) *Mem. Ed.* XVIII, 379-380; *Nat. Ed.* XVI, 285.

CHINA. See also OPEN DOOR; ORIENT.

CHINESE BOYCOTT. The boycott of our goods in China during the past year was especially injurious to the cotton manufacturers. This Government is doing, and will continue to do, all it can to put a stop to the boycott. But there is one measure to be taken toward this end in which I shall need the assistance of the Congress. We must insist firmly on our rights; and China must beware of persisting in a course of conduct to which we can not honorably submit. But we in our turn must recognize our duties exactly as we insist upon our rights. We can not go into the international court of equity unless we go in with clean hands. We can not expect China to do us justice unless we do China justice. The chief cause in bringing about the boycott of our goods in China was undoubtedly our attitude toward the Chinese who come to this country. This attitude of ours does not justify the action of the Chinese in the boycott, and especially some of the forms which that action has taken. But the fact remains that in the past we have come short of our duty toward the people of China. . . . I am convinced that the well-being of our wage-workers demands the exclusion of the Chinese coolies, and it is therefore our duty to exclude them, just as it would be the duty of China to exclude American laboring men if they became in any way a menace to China by entering into her country. The right is reciprocal, and in our last treaty with China it was explicitly recognized as inhering in both nations. But we should not only operate the law with as little harshness as possible, but we should show every courtesy and consideration and every encouragement to all Chinese who are not of the laboring class to come to this country. (At Atlanta, Ga., October 20, 1905.) *Presidential Addresses and State Papers* IV, 498-499.

CHINESE IMMIGRATION. The conditions in China are such that the entire coolie class, that is, the class of Chinese laborers, skilled and unskilled, legitimately come under the head of undesirable immigrants to this country, because of their numbers, the low wages for which they work, and their low standard of living. Not only is it to the interest of this country to keep them out, but the Chinese authorities do not desire that they should be admitted. At present their entrance is prohibited by laws amply adequate to accomplish this purpose. These laws have been, are being, and will be, thoroughly enforced. The violations of them are so few in number as to be infinitesimal and can be entirely disregarded. . . .

But in the effort to carry out the policy of excluding Chinese laborers, Chinese coolies, grave injustice and wrong have been done by this nation to the people of China, and therefore ultimately to this nation itself. Chinese students, business and professional men of all kinds—not only merchants, but bankers, doctors, manufacturers, professors, travellers, and the like—should be encouraged to come here, and treated on precisely the same footing that we treat students, business men, travellers, and the like of other nations. Our laws and treaties should be framed, not so as to put these people in the excepted classes, but to state that we will admit all Chinsee, except Chinese of the coolie class, Chinese skilled or unskilled laborers. (Fifth Annual Message, Washington, December 5, 1905.) *Mem. Ed.* XVII, 375-376; *Nat. Ed.* XV, 320-321.

CHINESE INDEMNITY. I ask for authority to reform the agreement with China under which the indemnity of 1900 was fixed, by remitting and cancelling the obligation of China for the payment of all that part of the stipulated indemnity which is in excess of the sum of $11,665,492.69, and interest at four per cent. After the rescue of the foreign legations in Peking during the Boxer troubles in 1900 the powers required from China the payment of equitable indemnities to the several nations, and the final protocol under which the troops were withdrawn, signed at Peking, September 7, 1901, fixed the amount of this indemnity allotted to the United States at over $20,000,000, and China paid, up to and including the 1st day of June last, a little over $6,000,000. It was the first intention of this government at the proper time, when all claims had been presented and all expenses ascertained as fully as possible, to revise the estimates and account, and as a proof of sincere friendship for China voluntarily to release that country from its legal liability for all payments in excess of the sum which should prove to be necessary for actual indemnity to the United States and its citizens.

This nation should help in every practicable way in the education of the Chinese people, so that the vast and populous empire of China may gradually adapt itself to modern conditions. One way of doing this is by promoting the coming of Chinese students to this country and making it attractive to them to take courses at our universities and higher educational institutions. Our educators should, so far as possible, take concerted action toward this end. (Seventh Annual Message, Washington, December 3, 1907.) *Mem. Ed.* XVII, 571; *Nat. Ed.* XV, 486.

CHIVALRY. We came down the Rhine in a steamboat. The scenery was lovely, but no more so than the Hudson except for the castles. These "robber knight" castles are so close together that I always wonder where there was room for the other people whom the Robber Knights robbed. The Age of Chivalry was lovely for the knights; but it must have at times been inexpressibly gloomy for the gentlemen who had to occasionally act in the capacity of daily bread for their betters. It is like the purely traditional "Merry England" of the Stuarts, where the merriment existed only for the Stuarts, who were about the worst dynasty that ever sat on a throne. (To Anna Roosevelt, August 21, 1881.) Cowles *Letters,* 48.

CHOATE, JOSEPH H. Mr. Choate was pre-eminently the good citizen, pre-eminently the man of stainless integrity, of a high-mindedness such that everyone who was in any shape or way associated with him took it for granted. It was a pleasure to be in the room with him; it was a pleasure to be associated with him in any way. . . .

Choate, like Hay, was one of those very, very rare men who actually say the things that ordinarily we only read about in writings that tell of the sayings of the contemporaries of Horace Walpole. Both Choate and Hay actually said the things that the rest of us only think of afterwards and then wish we had said them at the time. (At memorial exercises for Joseph H. Choate, New York City, January 19, 1918.) *Mem. Ed.* XII, 542; *Nat. Ed.* XI, 268, 269.

CHOATE, JOSEPH H. *See also* PANAMA CANAL.

CHRISTIAN, THE TRUE. The true Christian is the true citizen, lofty of purpose, resolute in endeavor, ready for a hero's deeds, but never looking down on his task because it is cast in the day of small things; scornful of baseness, awake to his own duties as well as to his rights, following the higher law with reverence, and in this world doing all that in him lies, so that when death comes he may feel that mankind is in some degree better because he has lived. (Before Young Men's Christian Association, New York City, December 30, 1900.) *Mem. Ed.* XV, 535; *Nat. Ed.* XIII, 499.

CHRISTIANITY. We must be doers—not hearers only. I am sure every one who tries to be a good Christian must feel a peculiar shame when he sees a hypocrite, or one who so conducts himself as to bring reproach upon Christianity. The man who observes all the ceremonials of the laws of the church but who does not carry them out in his daily life, is not a true Christian. To be doers of the Word it is necessary that we must be first hearers of the Word. Yet attendance at church is not enough. We must learn the lessons. We must study the Bible, but we must not let it end there. We must apply it in active life. The first duty of a man is to his own house. The necessity of heroic action on a great scale arises but seldom, but the humdrum of life is with us every day.

In business and in work, if you let Christianity stop as you go out of the church door, there is little righteousness in you. You must behave to your fellowmen as you would have them behave to you. You must have pride in your work if you would succeed. A man should get justice for himself, but he should also do justice to others. Help a man to help himself, but do not expend all your efforts in helping a man who will not help himself. (At Trinity Reformed Church, Chicago, early September 1901.) C. E. Banks and L. Armstrong, *Theodore Roosevelt, Twenty-Sixth President of the United States. A Typical American.* (Chicago, 1901), p. 163.

——————. Civilization can only be permanent and continue a blessing to any people if, in addition to promoting their material well-being, it also stands for an orderly individual liberty, for the growth of intelligence, and for equal justice in the administration of law. Christianity alone meets these fundamental requirements. (At celebration of Methodist Episcopal Church, Washington, January 18, 1909.) *Mem. Ed.* XVIII, 352; *Nat. Ed.* XVI, 267.

——————. In the wreck of the Old World, Christianity was all that the survivors had to cling to; and the Latin version of the Bible put it at their disposal. (At Pacific Theological Seminary, Spring 1911.) *Mem. Ed.* XV, 606; *Nat. Ed.* XIII, 642.

——————. We need to have our Christianity made what it originally was, a religion primarily for the people as a whole; and, while it should meet the religious needs of every class, yet most of all should it keep in view the needs and hopes and desires and lives of those whom Abraham Lincoln called "the plain people." *Outlook,* January 27, 1912, p. 161.

CHRISTIANITY AS A GUIDE. Our success in striving to help our fellow-men, and therefore to help ourselves, depends largely upon our success as we strive, with whatever shortcomings, with whatever failures, to lead our lives in accordance with the great ethical principles laid down in the life of Christ, and in the New Testament writings which seek to expound and apply his teachings. *Outlook,* May 27, 1911, p. 224.

CHRISTIANITY. *See also* BIBLE; CHURCH; JESUITS; MISSIONARIES; PIONEER PREACHERS; RELIGION; RELIGIOUS TEACHERS.

CHRISTMAS — RECOLLECTIONS OF. Christmas was an occasion of literally delirious joy. In the evening we hung up our stockings—or rather the biggest stockings we could borrow from the grown-ups—and before dawn we trooped in to open them while sitting on father's and mother's bed; and the bigger presents were arranged, those for each child on its own table, in the drawing-room, the doors to which were thrown open after breakfast. I never knew any one else have what seemed to me such attractive Christmases, and in the next generation I tried to reproduce them exactly for my own children. (1913.) *Mem. Ed.* XXII, 10; *Nat. Ed.* XX, 9.

CHRISTMAS CELEBRATIONS. I wonder whether there ever can come in life a thrill of greater exaltation and rapture than that which comes to one between the ages of say six and fourteen, when the library door is thrown open and you walk in to see all the gifts, like a materialized fairyland, arrayed on your special table? (To Corinne Roosevelt Robinson, December 26, 1903.) *Mem. Ed.* XXI, 514; *Nat. Ed.* XIX, 456.

CHURCH—FUNCTION OF THE. A living church organization should, more than any other, be a potent force in social uplifting. Churches are needed for all sorts and conditions of men under every kind of circumstances; but surely the largest field of usefulness is open to that church in which the spirit of brotherhood is a living and vital force, and not a cold formula;

in which the rich and poor gather together to aid one another in work for a common end. Brother can best help brother, not by almsgiving, but by joining with him in an intelligent and resolute effort for the uplifting of all. (*McClure's,* March 1901.) *Mem. Ed.* XV, 205; *Nat. Ed.* XIII, 267.

———————. The Church must be a living, breathing, vital force or it is no real Church. . . . Every serious student of our social and industrial conditions has learned to look with discomfort and alarm upon the diminishing part which churches play in the life of our great cities—for I need hardly say that no increase in the number of fashionable churches and of wealthy congregations in any shape or way atones for the diminution in the number of the churches in the very localities where there is most need for them. If ever the Christian Church ceases to be the Church of the plain people, it will cease to be the Christian Church. (Introduction dated April 7, 1906.) George Hodges and John Reichert, *The Administration of an Institutional Church.* (Harper & Bros., N. Y., 1906), p. ix.

———————. The church must fit itself for the practical betterment of mankind if it is to attract and retain the fealty of the men best worth holding and using. (1917.) *Mem. Ed.* XXI, 136; *Nat. Ed.* XIX, 135.

CHURCH ACTIVITIES — PARTICIPATION IN. The church is, of all places, that in which men should meet on the basis of their common humanity under conditions of sympathy and mutual self-respect. All must work alike in the church in order to get the full benefit from it; but it is not the less true that we have a peculiar right to expect systematic effort from men and women of education and leisure. Such people should justify by their work the conditions of society which have rendered possible their leisure, their education, and their wealth. Money can never take the place of service, and though here and there it is absolutely necessary to have the paid worker, yet normally he is not an adequate substitute for the volunteer. (*McClure's,* March 1901.) *Mem. Ed.* XV, 206-207; *Nat. Ed.* XIII, 268.

CHURCH AND STATE. Washington and his associates believed that it was essential to the existence of this Republic that there should never be any union of Church and State; and such union is partially accomplished wherever a given creed is aided by the State or when any public servant is elected or defeated because of his creed. (Before Knights of Columbus, New York City, October 12, 1915.) *Mem. Ed.* XX, 454; *Nat. Ed.* XVIII, 389.

CHURCH ATTENDANCE. In this actual world a churchless community, a community where men have abandoned and scoffed at or ignored their religious needs, is a community on the rapid down grade.

It is perfectly true that occasional individuals or families may have nothing to do with church or with religious practices and observances and yet maintain the highest standard of spirituality and of ethical obligation.

But this does not affect the case in the world as it now is, any more than that exceptional men and women under exceptional conditions have disregarded the marriage tie without moral harm to themselves interferes with the larger fact that such disregard if at all common means the complete moral disintegration of the body politic. . . .

On Sunday go to church. Yes—I know all the excuses. I know that one can worship the Creator and dedicate oneself to good living in a grove of trees, or by a running brook, or in one's own house, just as well as in church. But I also know that as a matter of cold fact the average man does not thus worship or thus dedicate himself. If he stays away from church he does not spend his time in good works or in lofty meditation. He looks over the colored supplement of the newspaper; he yawns; and he finally seeks relief from the mental vacuity of isolation by going where the combined mental vacuity of many partially relieves the mental vacuity of each particular individual. *Ladies' Home Journal,* October 1917, p. 12.

CHURCH IN A DEMOCRACY. Under the tense activity of modern social and industrial conditions the church, if it is to give real leadership, must grapple zealously, fearlessly and cool-headedly with these problems. Unless it is the poor man's church it is not a Christian church at all in any real sense. The rich man needs it, heaven knows, and is needed by it. But unless in the church he can work with all his toiling brothers for a common end, for their mutual benefit and for the benefit of those without its walls, the church has come short of its mission and its possibilities. Unless the church in a mining town or factory town or railway center is a leading force in the effort to secure cleaner and more wholesome surroundings, moral and physical, for the people, unless it concerns itself with the people's living and working conditions, with their workshops and houses and playgrounds, it has forfeited its right to the foremost place in the regard of men.

By their fruits shall ye know them! We judge a man nowadays by his conduct rather than by his dogma. And, to keep its hold on mankind, the church must, as in its early days, obey the great law of service; for the church shall not live by ceremonial and by dogmatic theology alone.

There are plenty of clergymen of all denominations who do obey this law; they render inestimable service. Yet these men can do but little unless keen, able, zealous laymen give them aid; and this aid is beyond comparison most effective when rendered by men who are themselves active participants in the work of the church. *Ladies' Home Journal,* October 1917, pp. 12, 119.

CHURCH. See also AMERICANIZATION; BIBLE; CATHOLICS; CHRISTIANITY; PIONEER PREACHERS; SUNDAY SCHOOL.

CHURCHES. See EPISCOPAL CHURCH; LUTHERAN CHURCH; METHODIST CHURCH; MORMONS.

CHURCHILL, WINSTON. I have never liked Winston Churchill, but, in view of what you tell me about his admirable conduct and nerve in mobilizing the Fleet, I do wish that if it comes your way you would extend to him my congratulations on his action. (To Arthur Lee, August 22, 1914.) From proof sheets of Viscount Lee of Fareham, *Autobiography.*

CITIZEN—DUTY OF THE. The first lesson to be learned by every citizen who desires to bring about a higher life in our American cities is that he must take an active part in managing the affairs of his own city. He has got to take some little trouble to do this, but if he is worth his salt, and possesses that healthy combativeness which ought to be aroused in every decent man by the insolence of evil, he will soon find municipal politics extremely interesting. (*Outlook,* December 21, 1895.) Mem. Ed. XV, 141; Nat. Ed. XIII, 297.

————. To take part in the work of government does not in the least mean of necessity to hold office. It means to take an intelligent, disinterested, and practical part in the every-day duties of the average citizen, of the citizen who is not a faddist or a doctrinaire, but who abhors corruption and dislikes inefficiency; who wishes to see decent government prevail at home, with genuine equality of opportunity for all men so far as it can be brought about; and who wishes, as far as foreign matters are concerned, to see this nation treat all other nations, great and small, with respect, and if need be with generosity, and at the same time show herself able to protect herself by her own might from any wrong at the hands of any outside power. (At the Harvard Union, Cambridge, February 23, 1907.) Mem. Ed. XV, 486; Nat. Ed. XIII, 562.

CITIZEN—TRAINING OF THE. In such a Republic as ours the one thing that we cannot afford to neglect is the problem of turning out decent citizens. The future of the nation depends upon the citizenship of the generations to come; the children of to-day are those who to-morrow will shape the destiny of our land, and we cannot afford to neglect them. (Fifth Annual Message, Washington, December 5, 1905.) Mem. Ed. XVII, 333; Nat. Ed. XV, 285.

CITIZEN, THE GOOD. The first requisite of a good citizen in this Republic of ours is that he shall be able and willing to pull his weight —that he shall not be a mere passenger, but shall do his share in the work that each generation of us finds ready to hand; and, furthermore, that in doing his work he shall show not only the capacity for sturdy self-help but also self-respecting regard for the rights of others. (At banquet of Chamber of Commerce of the State of New York, New York City, November 11, 1902.) *Presidential Addresses and State Papers* I, 200.

————. Back of the laws, back of the Administration, back of the system of government, lies the man, lies the average manhood of our people, and in the long run we shall go up or go down according as the average standard of our citizenship does or does not wax in growth and grace.

Now, when we come to the question of good citizenship, the first requisite is that the man shall do the homely, every-day humdrum duties well. A man is not a good citizen, I do not care how lofty his thoughts are about citizenship in the abstract, if in the concrete his actions do not bear them out. It does not make much difference how high his aspirations for mankind at large may be; if he does not behave well in his own family, those aspirations do not bear visible fruit. He has got to be a good breadwinner. He has got to take care of his wife and his children. He has got to be a neighbor whom his neighbors can trust. He has got to act squarely in his business relations. He has got to do those everyday, ordinary things first, or he is not a good citizen.

But he has got to do more than that. In this country of ours the average citizen must devote a good deal of thought and time to the affairs of the State as a whole, or those affairs will go backward; and he must devote that thought and that time steadily and intelligently. *Outlook,* September 13, 1902, p. 117.

———————. The good citizen is the man who, whatever his wealth or his poverty, strives manfully to do his duty to himself, to his family, to his neighbor, to the State; who is incapable of the baseness which manifests itself either in arrogance or in envy, but who while demanding justice for himself is no less scrupulous to do justice to others. It is because the average American citizen, rich or poor, is of just this type that we have cause for our profound faith in the future of the Republic. (At State Fair, Syracuse, N. Y., September 7, 1903.) *Mem. Ed.* XVIII, 63; *Nat. Ed.* XVI, 54.

———————. There are unfortunately a certain number of our fellow countrymen who seem to accept the view that unless a man can be proved guilty of some particular crime he shall be counted a good citizen, no matter how infamous the life he has led, no matter how pernicious his doctrines or his practices. This is the view announced from time to time with clamorous insistence, now by a group of predatory capitalists, now by a group of sinister anarchistic leaders and agitators, whenever a special champion of either class, no matter how evil his general life, is acquitted of one specific crime. (At Pilgrim Memorial Monument, Provincetown, Mass., August 20, 1907.) *Mem. Ed.* XVIII, 96; *Nat. Ed.* XVI, 81.

———————. Each people can do justice to itself only if it does justice to others; but each people can do its part in the world movement for all only if it first does its duty within its own household. The good citizen must be a good citizen of his own country first before he can with advantage be a citizen of the world at large. (At the University of Berlin, May 12, 1910.) *Mem. Ed.* XIV, 285; *Nat. Ed.* XII, 84.

CITIZEN AND NATION. A man must first care for his own household before he can be of use to the state. But no matter how well he cares for his household, he is not a good citizen unless he also takes thought of the state. In the same way, a great nation must think first of its own internal affairs; and yet it cannot substantiate its claim to be a great nation unless it also thinks of its position in the world at large. (*Outlook,* April 1, 1911.) *Mem. Ed.* XIX, 151; *Nat. Ed.* XVII, 108.

CITIZENSHIP. Good citizenship does not necessarily imply genius. Genius has been defined as an infinite capacity for taking pains, and good citizenship consists in the practice of ordinary, hum-drum, common virtues, which we all take for granted, and which, in practice, sad to say, all of us do not carry out.

Jefferson said that the whole art of government consists in being honest. That is not the whole art, but it is the foundation of all government. The foundation is not enough; but, if you do not have that, you cannot erect upon it any superstructure that is worth building. You must have honesty as the first requisite of good citizenship. We have too much of a tendency in this country to deify mere smartness, mere intellectual acumen, unaccompanied by morality. There is no attitude that speaks worse for a commonwealth than this of admiring, or failing to condemn, the man who is unconscientious, unscrupulous, and immoral, but who succeeds. If a man has not the root of honesty in him—has not, at the foundation of his character, righteousness and decency—then, the abler and the braver he is, the more dangerous he is. It is an additional shame to a man that he should be evil, when he has in him the power to do much good. (At Trinity Methodist Church, Newburgh, N. Y., Feb. 28, 1900.) Ferdinand C. Iglehart, *Theodore Roosevelt, The Man As I Knew Him.* (The Christian Herald, N. Y., 1919), p. 144.

———————. We citizens of these peaceful days need first and foremost the moral quality; and next, back of that moral quality, the courage, moral and physical as well, that makes the moral quality count. Yet these qualities by themselves are not enough. The greatest patriotism and the greatest courage can be hopelessly marred by folly. None of you are worth anything as citizens, none of you can be worth anything as citizens, if you have not the fund of moral qualities which find expression in love of country, love of neighbors, love of home, which make you honest, decent, clean-living, right-thinking. None of you will be worth anything if in addition to those qualities you haven't the courage, physical and moral, without which no American citizen can do his full duty as a citizen. And yet, back of them and in addition to them we must have the sanity, the common sense, the just judgment, which neither hysterically overemphasizes nor blindly refuses to acknowledge the wrongs that exist and the ways in which those wrongs must be cured. (At

Oyster Bay, N. Y., July, 4, 1906.) *Mem. Ed.* XVIII, 6; *Nat. Ed.* XVI, 5.

———————. I ask in our civic life that we . . . pay heed only to the man's quality of citizenship, to repudiate as the worst enemy that we can have whoever tries to get us to discriminate for or against any man because of his creed or his birthplace. (At Milwaukee, Wis., October 14, 1912.) *Mem. Ed.* XIX, 446; *Nat. Ed.* XVII, 324.

CITIZENSHIP—MEASURE OF. I ask that we see to it in our country that the line of division in the deeper matters of our citizenship be drawn, never between section and section, never between creed and creed, never, thrice never, between class and class; but that the line be drawn on the line of conduct, cutting through sections, cutting through creeds, cutting through classes; the line that divides the honest from the dishonest, the line that divides good citizenship from bad citizenship, the line that declares a man a good citizen only if, and always if, he acts in accordance with the immutable law of righteousness, which has been the same from the beginning of history to the present moment, and which will be the same from now until the end of recorded time. (At Spokane, Wash., May 26, 1903.) *Mem. Ed.* XVIII, 21; *Nat. Ed.* XVI, 19.

CITIZENSHIP — RESPONSIBILITY OF. Our public life depends primarily not upon the men who occupy public positions for the moment, because they are but an infinitesimal fraction of the whole. Our public life depends upon men who take an active interest in that public life; who are bound to see public affairs honestly and competently managed; but who have the good sense to know what honesty and competency actually mean. (At Groton School, Groton, Mass., May 24, 1904.) *Mem. Ed.* XV, 481; *Nat. Ed.* XIII, 558.

———————. In the long run, success or failure will be conditioned upon the way in which the average man, the average woman, does his or her duty, first in the ordinary, everyday affairs of life, and next in those great occasional crises which call for the heroic virtues. The average citizen must be a good citizen if our republics are to succeed. (At the Sorbonne, Paris, April 23, 1910.) *Mem. Ed.* XV, 352; *Nat. Ed.* XIII, 509.

———————. The fundamental evil in this country is the lack of sufficiently general appreciation of the responsibility of citizenship. Unfair business methods, the misused power of capital, the unjustified activities of labor, pork-barrel legislation, and graft among powerful politicians have all been made possible by, and have been manifestations of, this fundamental evil. (*Metropolitan*, February 1916.) *Mem. Ed.* XX, 298; *Nat. Ed.* XVIII, 255.

CITIZENSHIP, DUAL. Two or three years ago it was announced that Germany had passed a law by which she provided for her citizens, who became naturalized in the United States or elsewhere, the means of also retaining their German citizenship, so that these men would preserve a dual citizenship, what the Department of State . . . calls "a dual nationality." I hold that it was the business of our government as soon as this statement was published to investigate the facts, to require would-be citizens to repudiate this law, and to notify the German Government that we protested against and would refuse to recognize its action; that we declined to recognize or acquiesce in the principle of such a dual citizenship or a dual nationality; that we would hold naturalized citizens to the full performance of the duties of American citizenship, which were necessarily exclusive of and inconsistent with the profession of citizenship in or allegiance to any other nation, and that in return we would extend the same protection to these citizens that is extended to native-born citizens. Such action was not taken. It is a reproach to us as a nation that it was not taken. (*Metropolitan*, June 1915.) *Mem. Ed.* XX, 436; *Nat. Ed.* XVIII, 373.

CITIZENSHIP AND CHARACTER. The division between the worthy and the unworthy citizen must be drawn on conduct and character and not on wealth or poverty. (*Outlook*, March 25, 1911.) *Mem. Ed.* XIX, 141; *Nat. Ed.* XVII, 100.

———————. The first essential toward the achievement of good citizenship is, of course, the building up of the kind of character which will make the man a good husband, a good father, a good son; which will make the woman a good daughter when she is young, a good wife and mother as she grows older. (At Pacific Theological Seminary, Spring 1911.) *Mem. Ed.* XV, 593; *Nat. Ed.* XIII, 630.

CITIZENSHIP. *See also* ALIENS; ALLEGIANCE; AMERICANISM; AMERICANIZATION; CIVIC DUTY; COSMOPOLITANS; EDUCATION; GOVERNMENT; NATIONALISM; NATIONALITY; PARTISANSHIP; PARTY ALLEGIANCE; PARTY SYSTEM.

CITY AND COUNTRY. It is unhealthy and undesirable for the cities to grow at the expense of the country. (Third Annual Message, Washington, December 7, 1903.) *Mem. Ed.* XVII, 220; *Nat. Ed.* XV, 189.

———————. In one sense this problem with which we have to deal is very, very old. . . . No nation can develop a real civilization without cities. Up to a certain point the city movement is thoroughly healthy; yet it is a strange and lamentable fact that always hitherto after this point has been reached the city has tended to develop at the expense of the country by draining the country of what is best in it, and making an insignificant return for this best. . . . The problem does not consist merely in the growth of the city. Such a growth in itself is a good thing and not a bad thing for the country. The problem consists in the growth of the city at the expense of the country. (*Outlook,* August 27, 1910.) *Mem. Ed.* XVIII, 191; *Nat. Ed.* XVI, 146.

CITY AND COUNTRY. *See also* COUNTRY LIFE COMMISSION; FARM LIFE; ROADS.

CITY LIFE. The most serious disadvantage in city life is the tendency of each man to keep isolated in his own little set, and to look upon the vast majority of his fellow citizens indifferently, so that he soon comes to forget that they have the same red blood, the same loves and hates, the same likes and dislikes, the same desire for good, and the same perpetual tendency, ever needing to be checked and corrected, to lapse from good into evil. (At Labor Day Picnic, Chicago, September 3, 1900.) *Mem. Ed.* XVI, 510; *Nat. Ed.* XIII, 482.

CITY LIFE—IMPROVEMENT OF. There are many different ways in which a man or a woman can work for the higher life of American cities, and it would be worse than folly to expect the one who can do most in a certain line to devote an equal amount of attention to another line. . . . The published studies of Mr. Jacob Riis show what almost infinite labor could be expended with profit by those willing to devote a portion of their time to bettering the material conditions of life for the bulk of the populations of our large cities. The improvement of tenement-houses; the establishment of many small parks, of free libraries, baths, concerts, and picture shows; the larger development of the noble work now done by the social, college and university settlements; in short, all movements in the interest of making the life of the day-laborer in our cities less onerous and more wholesome—these are subjects which may well claim the attention of all those who would advance the higher life of American cities. (*Outlook,* December 21, 1895.) *Mem. Ed.* XV, 142-143; *Nat. Ed.* XIII, 298-299.

CITY LIFE. *See also* HOUSING; MUNICIPAL ADMINISTRATION.

CIVIC DUTY. It is a good thing to appeal to citizens to work for good government because it will better their estate materially, but it is a far better thing to appeal to them to work for good government because it is right in itself to do so. Doubtless, if we can have clean, honest politics, we shall be better off in material matters. . . . It is sometimes difficult to show the individual citizen that he will be individually better off in his business and in his home affairs for taking part in politics. I do not think it is always worth while to show that this will always be the case. The citizen should be appealed to primarily on the ground that it is plain duty, if he wishes to deserve the name of freeman, to do his full share in the hard and difficult work of self-government. He must do his share unless he is willing to prove himself unfit for free institutions, fit only to live under a government where he will be plundered and bullied because he deserves to be plundered and bullied on account of his selfish timidity and shortsightedness.

A clean and decent government is sure in the end to benefit our citizens in the material circumstances of their lives; but each citizen should be appealed to, to take part in bettering our politics, not for the sake of any possible improvement it may bring to his affairs, but on the ground that it is his plain duty to do so, and that this is a duty which it is cowardly and dishonorable in him to shirk. (*Forum,* July 1894.) *Mem. Ed.* XV, 48; *Nat. Ed.* XIII, 34.

———————. Each of us has not only his duty to himself, his family, and his neighbors, but his duty to the State and to the nation. We are in honor bound each to strive according to his or her strength to bring ever nearer the day when justice and wisdom shall obtain in public life as in private life. We cannot retain the full measure of our self-respect if we cannot retain pride in our citizenship. For the sake not only of ourselves but of our children and our children's children we must see that this nation stands for strength and honesty both at home and abroad. (At Colorado Springs, Col., August 2, 1901.) *Mem. Ed.* XV, 327; *Nat. Ed.* XIII, 458.

──────────. There is no truth more important than the truth that it is the performance of duty toward the Commonwealth, and not the enjoyment of unearned privilege from the Commonwealth, that breeds loyalty, devotion, patriotism. In a family, the father and mother who fail to rear their sons and daughters to recognize and perform their duties neither receive nor deserve the loyal devotion felt for the heads of the household where the whole household is trained to put duty ahead of pleasure. It is exactly the same with a nation. (New York *Times*, September 10, 1917.) *Mem. Ed.* XXI, 54; *Nat. Ed.* XIX, 46.

──────────. If there is an equality of rights, there is an inequality of duties. It is proper to demand more from the man with exceptional advantages than from the man without them. A heavy moral obligation rests upon the man of means and upon the man of education to do their full duty by their country. (*Atlantic Monthly*, August 1894.) *Mem. Ed.* XV, 50; *Nat. Ed.* XIII, 36.

CIVIC DUTY AND RIGHTS. I believe it is even more important for men to pay heed to their duties and to the rights of others than it is for them to pay heed to their own rights. But I believe also that they can only do their full duty when they enjoy fully their rights. (At St. Louis, Mo., March 28, 1912.) *Mem. Ed.* XIX, 239; *Nat. Ed.* XVII, 176.

CIVIC DUTY. *See also* CITIZEN; CITIZENSHIP; DUTY; FREEDOM; GOVERNMENT; MUNICIPAL GOVERNMENT; PARTY ALLEGIANCE; PARTY SYSTEM; POLITICAL DUTIES; POLITICS; RIGHTS; SELF-GOVERNMENT; SUFFRAGE; VOTING.

CIVIC PLANNING. *See* PUBLIC BUILDINGS.

CIVIC RIGHTEOUSNESS. The State will be saved, if the Lord puts it into the heart of the average man so to shape his life that the State shall be worth saving, and only on those terms. We need civic righteousness. The best constitution that the wit of man has ever devised, the best institutions that the ablest statesmen in the world have ever reduced to practice by law or by custom, all these shall be of no avail if they are not vivified by the spirit which makes a State great by making its citizens honest, just, and brave. (At Washington, October 25, 1903.) *Mem. Ed.* XV, 465; *Nat. Ed.* XIII, 551.

CIVIL SERVICE. The Federal Government can rarely act with the directness that the State governments act. It can, however, do a good deal. My purpose was to make the National Government itself a model employer of labor, the effort being to make the per diem employee just as much as the Cabinet officer regard himself as one of the partners employed in the service of the public, proud of his work, eager to do it in the best possible manner, and confident of just treatment. (1913.) *Mem. Ed.* XXII, 526; *Nat. Ed.* XX, 452.

CIVIL SERVICE. *See also* EIGHT HOUR DAY; GOVERNMENT EMPLOYEES; OPEN SHOP; POLITICAL ASSESSMENTS; VETERANS.

CIVIL SERVICE COMMISSION. The purpose of the Civil Service Commission is to secure an absolutely non-partisan public service; to have men appointed to and retained in office wholly without reference to their politics. In other words, we desire to make a man's honesty and capacity to do the work to which he is assigned the sole tests of his appointment and retention. In the departmental service at Washington we have succeeded in putting a nearly complete stop to removals for political purposes. Men are retained in the departments almost wholly without regard to politics. But it has been a matter of more difficulty to get them to come forward and enter the examinations without regard to politics.

The task set us is very difficult. We have to face the intense and interested hostility of the great mass of self-seeking politicians, and of the much larger mass of officeseekers, whose only hope of acquiring office rests in political influence, and is immediately cut off by the application of any, even the most modest, merit test. We have to overcome popular indifference or ignorance, and we have to do constant battle with that spirit of mean and vicious cynicism which so many men, respectable enough in their private life, assume as their attitude in public affairs. (*Atlantic Monthly*, July 1892.) *Mem. Ed.* XVI, 177-178; *Nat. Ed.* XIV, 115-116.

──────────. You say that there is a growing contempt for the Civil Service Law. My experience is directly the opposite, and I am positive that the contempt of which you speak exists only in the minds of the very ignorant, and that these very ignorant are less numerous, so far as this subject is concerned, than they were only a few years ago, and grow less numerous year by year. . . .

There is no "shell separating the commission from the outer world." All that we do is perfectly open. The registers for the ordinary posi-

[82]

tions are made public as soon as the papers are marked. In the case of special examinations, where there would be a chance of exercising political pressure or personal favoritism, the registers are not made public until after the appointments have been made. (To Judson Grenell, April 29, 1895.) Clemens, W. M., *Theodore Roosevelt, The American*. (F. T. Neely, N. Y., 1899), p. 90.

———. The public should exercise a most careful scrutiny over the appointment and over the acts of Civil Service Commissioners, for there is no office the effectiveness of which depends so much upon the way in which the man himself chooses to construe his duties. A Commissioner can keep within the letter of the law and do his routine work and yet accomplish absolutely nothing in the way of securing the observance of the law. The Commission, to do useful work, must be fearless and vigilant. It must actively interfere whenever wrong is done, and must take all the steps that can be taken to secure the punishment of the wrong-doer and to protect the employee threatened with molestation. (*Scribner's*, August 1895.) *Mem. Ed.* XV, 178-179; *Nat. Ed.* XIII, 101.

CIVIL SERVICE COMMISSIONER—ROOSEVELT AS. I am having a hard row to hoe. I have made this Commission a living force, and in consequence the outcry among the spoilsmen has become furious; it has evidently frightened both the President and Halford [President Harrison's Secretary] a little. They have shown symptoms of telling me that the law should be rigidly enforced where people will stand it, and *gingerly* handled elsewhere. But I answered militantly: that as long as I was responsible the law should be enforced up to the handle *every where;* fearlessly and honestly. I am a great believer in practical politics; but when my duty is to enforce a law, that law is surely going to be enforced, without fear or favor. I am perfectly willing to be turned out—or legislated out—but while in I mean business. (To H. C. Lodge, June 29, 1889.) Lodge *Letters* I, 80.

———. I am very glad to have been in this position; I think I have done good work, and a man ought to show that he can go out into the world and hold his own with other men. (To Anna Roosevelt, February 1, 1891.) Cowles *Letters*, 113.

———. My task for the past two years has been simple. I have only had to battle for a good law; and though this meant drawing down on me the bitter animosities of the men who in New York, at least, control politics, it was easy to perform creditably, and offered no obstacles in the way of being misunderstood or misrepresented by men of standing and intelligence. (To H. C. Lodge, June 29, 1891.) Lodge *Letters* I, 113.

CIVIL SERVICE REFORM. Civil service reform is designed primarily to give the average American citizen a fair chance in politics, to give to this citizen the same weight in politics that the "ward heeler" has. (1913.) *Mem. Ed.* XXII, 158; *Nat. Ed.* XX, 136.

———. People often speak of Civil Service Reform as if it were a matter of mere administration detail. People speak of it as "a good thing, of course." "We believe in it, of course; not practical, but still, it is a good thing." They say that "doubtless it would be a little better to have it so." They admit that it "might make an improvement in the public service." They do not appreciate that it is not merely a question of changing the methods of administration, but that it is a question of substituting a system of equity and justice for a system of brutal wrong. It is a question of working a great benefit, not merely to the public service, but to our public life; it is a question of making politics purer; of making a man hold his head higher because he is an American citizen. I do not think—I know—that the American people, which is true at the bottom, although with many oddities on top, nevertheless at the bottom an honest people, believing in fair play—do not realize the meaning of "To the victors belong the spoils," for if they did, they would not tolerate the system for one moment. (At memorial meeting for G. W. Curtis, New York City, November 14, 1892.) *Mem. Ed.* XII, 486-487; *Nat. Ed.* XI, 230.

———. The civil service reform movement was one from above downward, and the men who took the lead in it were not men who as a rule possessed a very profound sympathy with or understanding of the ways of thought and life of their average fellow citizen. They were not men who themselves desired to be letter-carriers or clerks or policemen, or to have their friends appointed to these positions. Having no temptation themselves in this direction, they were eagerly anxious to prevent other people getting such appointments as a reward for political services. In this they were quite right. It would be impossible to run any big public office to advantage save along the lines of the strictest application of civil service reform principles; and the system should be extended throughout our governmental service far more widely than is now the case. (1913.) *Mem. Ed.* XXII, 175; *Nat. Ed.* XX, 150.

CIVIL SERVICE REFORM—PURPOSE OF. My object . . . is less to raise the standard of the civil service than it is to take the office-holders out of politics. It is a good thing to raise the character of our public employees but it is better still to take out of politics the vast band of hired mercenaries whose very existence depends on their success, and who can almost always in the end overcome the efforts of men whose only care is to secure a pure and honest government, for in such a contest the discipline of regulars, fighting literally for their means of livelihood, is sure in the end to overcome the spasmodic ardor of volunteers. (In New York Assembly, April 9, 1883.) *Mem. Ed.* XVI, 31; *Nat. Ed.* XIV, 23.

———. It must always be remembered that the prime object of the reform under consideration is to take the Civil Service out of politics. To increase the efficiency and honesty of its management is of secondary importance, for the public service is already, for the most part, conducted with integrity and efficiency, and with reasonable economy. In all these respects it would probably compare favorably with the public service of almost any foreign nation; and at the time when the Pendleton Bill passed the Civil Service of the nation certainly stood uniformly higher, especially as regards honesty, than had been the case in time past. . . .

What made the reform vitally necessary to the well-being of the nation was the fact that the public service had by degrees been turned into a vast political engine; and thus even good public servants had become in many cases formidable instruments for thwarting the will of the people, and for debauching political life. In old times, when the law of the sword prevailed, rulers soon learned the value of a standing army of hirelings; and in turn the rulers of to-day, accommodating themselves to the changed conditions, relied for the perpetuation of their power largely upon the vast, well-organized horde of political mercenaries that were furnished ready to their hands by the system of appointing men to office under the State, not on the ground of merit, but for factional or personal reasons. *Princeton Review,* May 1886, pp. 363-364.

———. Civil-service reform is not merely a movement to better the public service. It achieves this end too; but its main purpose is to raise the tone of public life, and it is in this direction that its effects have been of incalculable good to the whole community. (*Scribner's* August 1895.) *Mem. Ed.* XV, 177; *Nat. Ed.* XIII, 100.

CIVIL SERVICE REFORM. See also Appointments; Boss; Cleveland, Grover; Machine; Merit System; Patronage; Political Assessments; Politics; Spoils System.

CIVIL WAR. The Civil War was a great war for righteousness, a war waged for the noblest ideals, but waged also in thorough-going, practical fashion. That is why you won then—because you had the ideals, because you had the lift of soul in you, and because also you had the right stuff in you to make those ideals count in actual life. You had to have the ideals, but if you had not been able to march and shoot you could not have put them into practice. It was one of the few wars which mean, in their successful outcome, a lift toward better things for the nations of mankind. Some wars have meant the triumph of order over anarchy and licentiousness masquerading as liberty; some wars have meant the triumph of liberty over tyranny masquerading as order; but this victorious war of ours meant the triumph of both liberty and order, the triumph of orderly liberty, the bestowal of civil rights upon the freed slaves, and at the same time the stern insistence on the supremacy of the national law throughout the length and breadth of the land. Moreover, this was one of those rare contests in which it was to the immeasurable interest of the vanquished that they should lose, while at the same time the victors acquired the precious privilege of transmitting to those who came after them, as a heritage of honor forever, not only the memory of their own valiant deeds, but the memory of the deeds of those who, no less valiantly and with equal sincerity of purpose, fought against the stars in their courses. (At Gettysburg, Pa., May 30, 1904.) *Mem. Ed.* XII, 607-608; *Nat. Ed.* XI, 324-325.

———. The great Civil War was remarkable in many ways, but in no way more remarkable than for the extraordinary mixture of inventive mechanical genius and of resolute daring shown by the combatants. After the first year, when the contestants had settled down to real fighting, and the preliminary mob work was over, the battles were marked by their extraordinary obstinacy and heavy loss. In no European conflict since the close of the Napoleonic wars has the fighting been anything like as obstinate and as bloody as was the fighting in our own Civil War. In addition to the fierce and dogged courage, this splendid fighting capacity, the contest also brought out the skilled inventive power of engineer and mechanician in a way that few other contests have ever done. . . .

The Civil War marks the break between the old style and the new. Terrible encounters took place when the terrible new engines of war were brought into action for the first time. (1895.) *Mem. Ed.* IX, 162; *Nat. Ed.* X, 142.

CIVIL WAR—CAUSE OF. You say that in no quarrel is the right all on one side, and the wrong all on the other. As regards the actual act of secession, the actual opening of the Civil War, I think the right was exclusively with the Union people and the wrong exclusively with the Secessionists; and indeed I do not know of another struggle in history in which this sharp division between right and wrong can be made in quite so clear-cut a manner (To James Ford Rhodes, November 29, 1904.) *Mem. Ed.* XXIII, 402; Bishop I, 349.

CIVIL WAR—HERITAGE OF. Dreadful was the suffering, dreadful the loss, of the Civil War. Yet it stands alone among wars in this, that now that the wounds are healed, the memory of the mighty deeds of valor performed on one side no less than on the other has become the common heritage of all our people in every quarter of this country. (At unveiling of monument to Gen. Philip H. Sheridan, Washington, D. C., November 25, 1908.) *Mem. Ed.* XII, 477; *Nat. Ed.* XI, 221.

——————. The Civil War has left, as all wars of brother against brother must leave, terrible and heartrending memories; but there remains as an offset the glory which has accrued to the nation by the countless deeds of heroism performed by both sides in the struggle. The captains and the armies that, after long years of dreary campaigning and bloody, stubborn fighting, brought the war to a close, have left us more than a reunited realm. North and South, all Americans, now have a common fund of glorious memories. We are richer for each grim campaign, for each hard-fought battle. We are the richer for valor displayed alike by those who fought so valiantly for the right, and by those who, no less valiantly, fought for what they deemed the right. We have in us nobler capacities for what is great and good because of the infinite woe and suffering, and because of the splendid ultimate triumph. We hold that it was vital to the welfare, not only of our people on this continent, but of the whole human race, that the Union should be preserved and slavery abolished; that one flag should fly from the Great Lakes to the Rio Grande; that we should all be free in fact as well as in name, and that the United States should stand as one nation—the greatest nation on the earth. But we recognize gladly that, South as well as North, when the fight was once on, the leaders of the armies, and the soldiers whom they led, displayed the same qualities of daring and steadfast courage, of disinterested loyalty and enthusiasm, and of high devotion to an ideal. (1895.) *Mem. Ed.* IX, 117-118; *Nat. Ed.* X, 103-104.

——————. The wounds left by the great Civil War, incomparably the greatest war of modern times, have healed; and its memories are now priceless heritage of honor alike to the North and to the South. The devotion, the self-sacrifice, the steadfast resolution and lofty daring, the high devotion to the right as each man saw it, whether Northerner or Southerner—all these qualities of the men and women of the early sixties now shine luminous and brilliant before our eyes, while the mists of anger and hatred that once dimmed them have passed away forever.

All of us, North and South, can glory alike in the valor of the men who wore the blue and of the men who wore the gray. Those were iron times, and only iron men could fight to its terrible finish the giant struggle between the hosts of Grant and Lee, the struggle that came to an end thirty-seven years ago this very day. To us of the present day, and to our children and children's children, the valiant deeds, the high endeavor, and abnegation of self shown in that struggle by those who took part therein will remain for evermore to mark the level to which we in our turn must rise whenever the hour of the nation's need may come. (At Charleston Exposition, S. C., April 9, 1902.) *Mem. Ed.* XVIII, 31-32; *Nat. Ed.* XVI, 26-27.

——————. Rich and prosperous though we are as a people, the proudest heritage that each of us has, no matter where he may dwell, North or South, East or West, is the immaterial heritage of feeling the right to claim as his own all the valor and all the steadfast devotion to duty shown by the men of both the great armies, of the soldiers whose leader was Grant and the soldiers whose leader was Lee. The men and the women of the Civil War did their duty bravely and well in the days that were dark and terrible and splendid. We, their de-

CIVIL WAR — CLASS CONSCIOUSNESS

scendants, who pay proud homage to their memories, and glory in the feats of might of one side no less than of the other, need to keep steadily in mind that the homage which counts is the homage of heart and of hand, and not of the lips, the homage of deeds and not of words only. We, too, in our turn, must prove our truth by our endeavor. We must show ourselves worthy sons of the men of the mighty days by the way in which we meet the problems of our own time. We carry our heads high because our fathers did well in the years that tried men's souls; and we must in our turn so bear ourselves that the children who come after us may feel that we too have done our duty. (At Jamestown Exposition, April 26, 1907.) *Mem. Ed.* XII, 592; *Nat. Ed.* XI, 311.

CIVIL WAR. *See also* ARMY OFFICERS; CONFEDERATES; COPPERHEADS; GRAND ARMY OF THE REPUBLIC; GRANT, U. S.; LEE, R. E.; LINCOLN, A.; PATRIOTIC SONGS; REVOLUTIONARY WAR; SECTIONALISM; SHERIDAN, P. H.; SLAVERY; SOUTH; VETERANS.

CIVILIZATION. Material prosperity without the moral lift toward righteousness means a diminished capacity for happiness and a debased character. The worth of a civilization is the worth of the man at its center. When this man lacks moral rectitude, material progress only makes bad worse, and social problems still darker and more complex. *Outlook*, September 13, 1902, p. 121.

————. No nation facing the unhealthy softening and relaxation of fibre which tend to accompany civilization can afford to neglect anything that will develop hardihood, resolution, and the scorn of discomfort and danger. (1905.) *Mem. Ed.* III, 311; *Nat. Ed.* III, 122.

CIVILIZATION, AMERICAN. We of the United States need above all things to remember that, while we are by blood and culture kin to each of the nations of Europe, we are also separate from each of them. We are a new and distinct nationality. We are developing our own distinctive culture and civilization, and the worth of this civilization will largely depend upon our determination to keep it distinctively our own. (Before Knights of Columbus, New York City, October 12, 1915.) *Mem. Ed.* XX, 452; *Nat. Ed.* XVIII, 388.

CIVILIZATIONS—CONFLICT OF. The intrusion of an alien race into another civilization, its growth and supremacy and dying away, is of course curiously paralleled by what we see in the animal world, and the parallel is complete in at least one point—that is, in the fact that in such case the causes may be shrouded in absolute darkness. (To A. J. Balfour, March 5, 1908.) *Mem. Ed.* XXIV, 125; Bishop II, 108.

CIVILIZATION. *See also* CITY; EDUCATION; EXPANSION; HISTORY; IMPERIALISM; LAW; MISSIONARIES; PRIMITIVE SOCIETY; PROGRESS; RACIAL DECAY; WARS OF CONQUEST; "YELLOW PERIL."

CLARK, GEORGE ROGERS. He was the sole originator of the plan for the conquest of the northwestern lands, and, almost unaided, he had executed his own scheme. For a year he had been wholly cut off from all communication with the home authorities, and had received no help of any kind. Alone, and with the very slenderest means, he had conquered and held a vast and beautiful region, which but for him would have formed part of a foreign and hostile empire; he had clothed and paid his soldiers with the spoils of his enemies; he had spent his own fortune as carelessly as he had risked his life, and the only reward that he was destined for many years to receive was the sword voted him by the legislature of Virginia. (1889.) *Mem. Ed.* X, 393-394; *Nat. Ed.* VIII, 343-344.

CLASS CONSCIOUSNESS. Any movement based on that class hatred which at times assumes the name of "class consciousness" is certain ultimately to fail, and if it temporarily succeeds, to do far-reaching damage. "Class consciousness," where it is merely another name for the odious vice of class selfishness, is equally noxious whether in an employer's association or in a working man's association. (Eighth Annual Message, Washington, December 8, 1908.) *Mem. Ed.* XVII, 595; *Nat. Ed.* XV, 506.

CLASS CONSCIOUSNESS OF CAPITALISTS. Too often we see the business community in a spirit of unhealthy class consciousness deplore the effort to hold to account under the law the wealthy men who in their management of great corporations, whether railroads, street-railways, or other industrial enterprises, have behaved in a way that revolts the conscience of the plain, decent people. Such an attitude cannot be condemned too severely, for men of property should recognize that they jeopardize the rights of property when they fail heartily to join in the effort to do away with the abuses of wealth. (Eighth Annual

Message, Washington, December 8, 1908.) *Mem. Ed.* XVII, 581; *Nat. Ed.* XV, 494.

———. Apparently these men are influenced by a class consciousness which I had not supposed existed in any such strength. They live softly. Circumstances for which they are not responsible have removed their lives from the fears and anxieties of the ordinary men who toil. When a movement is undertaken to make life a little easier, a little better, for the ordinary man, to give him a better chance, these men of soft life seem cast into panic lest something that is not rightly theirs may be taken from them. In unmanly fear they stand against all change, no matter how urgent such change may be. They not only come far short of their duty when they thus act, but they show a lamentable short-sightedness. (At Chicago, June 17, 1912.) *Mem. Ed.* XIX, 310; *Nat. Ed.* XVII, 225.

CLASS HATRED. Above all, we need to remember that any kind of class animosity in the political world is, if possible, even more wicked, even more destructive to national welfare, than sectional, race, or religious animosity. (Second Annual Message, Washington, December 2, 1902.) *Mem. Ed.* XVII, 172; *Nat. Ed.* XV, 149.

———. There have been a great many republics before our time, and again and again these republics have split upon the rock of disaster. The greatest and most dangerous rock in the course of any republic is the rock of class hatred. Sometimes in the past the republic became a republic in which one class grew to dominate over another class, so that for loyalty to the republic was substituted loyalty to a class. The result was in such case inevitable. It meant disaster and ultimately the downfall of the republic, and it mattered not one whit which class became dominant; it mattered not one whit whether the poor plundered the rich or the rich exploited the poor. In either case, just as soon as the republic became one in which one class substituted loyalty to that class for loyalty to the republic, the end of the republic was at hand. No true patriot will fail to do everything in his power to prevent the growth of any such spirit in this country. (At banquet of Iroquois Club, Chicago, Ill., May 10, 1905.) *Presidential Addresses and State Papers* IV, 372.

———. [Our] greatest need . . . is to learn that there must be no division by class hatred, whether this hatred be that of creed against creed, nationality against nationality, section against section, or men of one social or industrial condition against men of another social and industrial condition. We must ever judge each individual on his own conduct and merits, and not on his membership in any class, whether that class be based on theological, social, or industrial considerations. (1913.) *Mem. Ed.* XXII, 224; *Nat. Ed.* XX, 192.

CLASS JEALOUSY. Distrust above all other men the man who seeks to make you pass judgment upon your fellow citizens upon any ground of artificial distinction between you and them. Distrust the man who seeks to get you to favor them or discriminate against them either because they are well off or not well off, because they occupy one social position or another, because they live in one part of the country or another, or because they profess one creed or another. (At unveiling of monument to dead of 1st U. S. Volunteer Cavalry, Arlington, April 12, 1907.) *Mem. Ed.* XII, 628; *Nat. Ed.* XI, 342.

CLASS LINES. The gravest wrong upon his country is inflicted by that man, whatever his station, who seeks to make his countrymen divide primarily on the line that separates class from class, occupation from occupation, men of more wealth from men of less wealth, instead of remembering that the only safe standard is that which judges each man on his worth as a man, whether he be rich or poor, without regard to his profession or to his station in life. . . . There is no greater need to-day than the need to keep ever in mind the fact that the cleavage between right and wrong, between good citizenship and bad citizenship, runs at right angles to, and not parallel with, the lines of cleavage between class and class, between occupation and occupation. Ruin looks us in the face if we judge a man by his position instead of judging him by his conduct in that position. (At the Sorbonne, Paris, April 23, 1910.) *Mem. Ed.* XV, 370; *Nat. Ed.* XIII, 524.

CLASS LINES—DANGER OF. We can keep our government on a sane and healthy basis, we can make and keep our social system what it should be, only on condition of judging each man, not as a member of a class, but on his worth as a man. It is an infamous thing in our American life, and fundamentally treacherous to our institutions, to apply to any man any test save that of his personal worth, or to draw between two sets of men any distinction save the distinction of conduct, the distinction that marks off those who do well and wisely from those who do ill and foolishly. There are good citizens and bad citizens in every class as in every locality, and the attitude of decent people toward great public and social questions should be determined, not by the accidental questions of employment or locality, but by those deep-set principles which represent the innermost souls of men.

The failure in public and in private life thus to treat each man on his own merits, the recognition of this government as being either for the poor as such or for the rich as such, would prove fatal to our Republic, as such failure and such recognition have always proved fatal in the past to other republics. (At State Fair, Syracuse, N. Y., September 7, 1903.) *Mem. Ed.* XVIII, 59; *Nat. Ed.* XVI, 51.

——————. We must now see that there never comes any spirit of class antagonism in this country, any spirit of hostility between capitalist and wage-worker, between employer and employed; and we can avoid the upgrowth of any such feeling by remembering always to treat each man on his worth as a man. Do not hold it for him or against him that he is either rich or poor. If he is a crooked man and rich, hold it against him, not because he is rich, but because he is crooked. If he is not a rich man and crooked, hold it against him, still because he is crooked. If he is a square man, no matter how much or how little money he has, stand by him because he is a square man. Distrust more than any other man in this Republic the man who would try to teach Americans to substitute loyalty to any class for loyalty to the whole American people. Republics have flourished before now, and have fallen; and they have usually fallen because there arose within them parties that represented either the unscrupulous rich or the unscrupulous poor, and that persuaded the majority of the people to substitute loyalty to the one class for loyalty to the people as a whole. (At City Park, Little Rock, Ark., October 25, 1905.) *Presidential Addresses and State Papers* IV, 533-534.

CLASS LINES IN POLITICS. Any organization which tries to work along the line of caste or creed, which fails to treat all American citizens on their merits as men, will fail, and will deserve to fail. Where our political life is healthy, there is and can be no room for any movement organized to help or to antagonize men because they do or do not profess a certain religion, or because they were or were not born here or abroad. . . . There must be no discrimination for or against any man because of his social standing.

On the one side, there is nothing to be made out of a political organization which draws an exclusive social line, and on the other it must be remembered that it is just as un-American to vote against a man because he is rich as to vote against him because he is poor. The one has just as much right as the other to claim to be treated purely on his merits as a man. In short, to do good work in politics, the men who organize must organize wholly without regard to whether their associates were born here or abroad, whether they are Protestants or Catholics, Jews or Gentiles, whether they are bankers or butchers, professors or day-laborers. (*Forum*, July 1894.) *Mem. Ed.* XV, 45; *Nat. Ed.* XIII, 31.

——————. The prime lesson to be taught is the lesson of treating each man on his worth as a man. . . . In the long run our safety lies in recognizing the individual's worth or lack of worth as the chief basis of action, and in shaping our whole conduct, and especially our political conduct, accordingly. It is impossible for a democracy to endure if the political lines are drawn to coincide with class lines. (*Century*, January 1900.) *Mem. Ed.* XV, 410; *Nat. Ed.* XIII, 360.

——————. The real trouble with us is that some classes have had too much voice. One of the most important of all the lessons to be taught and to be learned is that a man should vote, not as a representative of a class, but merely as a good citizen, whose prime interests are the same as those of all other good citizens. The belief in different classes, each having a voice in the government, has given rise to much of our present difficulty; for whosoever believes in these separate classes, each with a voice, inevitably, even although unconsciously, tends to work, not for the good of the whole people, but for the protection of some special class—usually that to which he himself belongs. (At Carnegie Hall, New York City, March 20, 1912.) *Mem. Ed.* XIX, 210; *Nat. Ed.* XVII, 159.

CLASSES IN A REPUBLIC. No republic can permanently exist when it becomes a republic of classes, where the man feels not the interest of the whole people, but the interest of the particular class to which he belongs, or fancies that he belongs, as being of prime importance. (At Lafayette Opera House, Washington, November 22, 1904.) *Mem. Ed.* XV, 436; *Nat. Ed.* XIII, 531.

CLASSES IN AMERICA AND EUROPE. There are really no classes in our American life in the sense in which the word "class" is used in Europe. Our social and political systems do not admit of them in theory, and in practice they exist only in a very fluid state. In most European countries classes are separated by rigid boundaries, which can be crossed but rarely, and with the utmost difficulty and peril. Here the boundaries cannot properly be said to exist, and are certainly so fluctuating and evasive, so indistinctly marked, that they cannot be appreciated when seen near by. Any American family which lasts a few generations will be apt to have representatives in all the different classes. The great business men, even the great professional men, and especially the great statesmen and sailors and soldiers, are very apt to spring from among the farmers or wage-workers, and their kinsfolk remain near the old home or at the old trade. If ever there existed in the world a community where the identity of interest, of habit, of principle, and of ideals should be felt as a living force, ours is the one. (*Century,* January 1900.) *Mem. Ed.* XV, 407; *Nat. Ed.* XIII, 357.

CLASSES. *See also* CAPITALISTS; EQUALITY; FELLOW-FEELING; GOVERNING CLASS; LABOR; LEGISLATION; LOYALTY; MIDDLE CLASS; WORKERS.

CLAYTON-BULWER TREATY. *See* PANAMA CANAL.

CLEVELAND, GROVER. I do not think he is a demagogue; I do think he is a Democratic politician. Now, in the first place, it is necessary for me to say that in his personal relations with me he has always been most courteous and most considerate. He has been a good governor for a Democrat, but there has been nothing whatever in his past career to warrant us in saying that he will be able to resist the pressure of his party, that he will have the power to resist the almost incalculable pressure that will be brought to bear upon him if he is elected. He came in upon an enormous wave of popular approval in New York; or to speak more accurately, I should say, an enormous wave of popular disapproval of the Republican candidacy. . . .

His career can be roughly divided into two parts—first of all, his actions prior to the 1st of last March, when he was not talked about as the Democratic candidate; secondly, his actions after the 1st of March, and his actions after that were widely different from his actions before. He has done some very good things during the career as governor. For instance he recommended to the first legislature, which was Democratic, that it should take in hand and execute certain reforms. That legislature failed to adopt those reforms, but the next legislature —which was Republican—took them up and put them through. Then the governor approved part of them—those that did not bear too harshly on the Democratic organization. (Before Republican meeting, Malden, Mass., October 20, 1884.) *Mem. Ed.* XVI, 82-83; *Nat. Ed.* XIV, 47.

————————. Like all others who were thrown closely with him, I was much impressed by his high standard of official conduct and his rugged strength of character. Not only did I become intimately acquainted with the manner in which he upheld and enforced the civil service law, but I also saw at close quarters his successful fight against free silver, and the courage with which he, aided by men like the late Senator Cushman K. Davis of Minnesota, supported the judiciary at the time of the Chicago riot; and, finally, I happened to be in a position in which I knew intimately how he acted and the reasons why he acted in the Venezuelan matter. This knowledge gained at first hand enables me to bear testimony, which I am more than glad to bear, to the late President's earnest purpose to serve the whole country, and the high courage with which he encountered every species of opposition and attack. . . .

All Americans should pay honor to the memory of Mr. Cleveland because of the simplicity and dignity with which as ex-President he led his life in the beautiful college town wherein he elected to live. He had been true to the honorable tradition which has kept our Presidents from making money while in office. His life was therefore of necessity very simple; but it was the kind of life which it is a good thing to see led by any man who has held a position such as he held. (Letter to F. L. Stetson, November 16, 1908; read at Carnegie Hall, March 18, 1909.) *The Grover Cleveland Memorial.* (New York, 1910), pp. 38-40.

CLEVELAND AND THE CIVIL SERVICE. Doubtless, President Cleveland meant to make good his original pledges concerning the civil service; doubtless no one regrets more than himself his inability to stand up against the pressure of the spoilsmen within his own party; but the fact remains that he has signally failed thus to make good his pledges; that his acts have been absolutely at variance with his words; that hardly ever has an Administration been more false to its promises on any subject than this Administration has shown itself to be on the question of civil-service reform. (Before Union League Club, New York City, January

[89]

CLEVELAND AND THE SILVER QUESTION. During the last campaign I grew more and more to realize the very great service you had rendered to the whole country by what you did about free silver. As I said to a Republican audience in South Dakota, I think your letter on free silver prior to your second nomination was as bold a bit of honest writing as I have ever seen in American public life. And more than anything else it put you in the position of doing for the American public in this matter of free silver what at that time no other man could have done. I think now we have definitely won out on the free-silver business and, therefore, I think you are entitled to thanks and congratulations. (To Grover Cleveland, November 22, 1900.) *Mem. Ed.* XXIII, 169; Bishop I, 145.

CLEVELAND, GROVER. *See also* ALTGELD, JOHN PETER; ELECTION OF 1884.

COAL CONSERVATION. *See* MINERAL FUELS; OIL.

COAL STRIKE. The coal operators are not combined so as to enable us legally to call them a trust; and if they were, all that we could do would be to proceed against them under the law against trusts, and whatever might be the effect as between them and the consumers in ordinary times, such a proceeding would damage, slightly at least, both them and the working miners, and would therefore have no possible effect of a favorable nature upon the present strike even if it were not improper to take it. There is literally nothing, so far as I have yet been able to find out, which the national government has any power to do in the matter. Nor can I even imagine any remedial measure of immediate benefit that could be taken in Congress. That it would be a good thing to have national control, or at least supervision, over these big coal corporations, I am sure; but that would simply have to come as an incident of the general movement to exercise control over such corporations. (To H. C. Lodge, September 27, 1902.) *Lodge Letters* I, 533.

————————. What gives me the greatest concern at the moment is the coal famine. Of course, we have nothing whatever to do with this coal strike and no earthly responsibility for it. But the public at large will tend to visit upon our heads responsibility for the shortage in coal precisely as Kansas and Nebraska visited upon our heads their failure to raise good crops in the arid belt, eight, ten, or a dozen years ago. I do not see what I can do, and I know the coal operators are especially distrustful of anything which they regard as in the nature of political interference. But I do most earnestly feel that from every consideration of public policy and of good morals they should make some slight concession. (To Mark Hanna, September 27, 1902.) *Mem. Ed.* XXIII, 230; Bishop I, 200.

————————. I disclaim any right or duty to intervene in this way upon legal grounds or upon any official relation that I bear to the situation; but the urgency and the terrible nature of the catastrophe impending over a large portion of our people in the shape of a winter fuel famine impel me, after much anxious thought, to believe that my duty requires me to use whatever influence I personally can to bring to an end a situation which has become literally intolerable. With all the earnestness there is in me I ask that there be an immediate resumption of operations in the coal-mines in some such way as will, without a day's unnecessary delay, meet the crying needs of the people. I do not invite a discussion of your respective claims and positions. I appeal to your patriotism, to the spirit that sinks personal consideration and makes individual sacrifices for the general good. (Address to representatives of miners and operators, Washington, October 3, 1902.) *Mem. Ed.* XXIII, 232; Bishop I, 202.

————————. Well, I have tried and failed. I feel downhearted over the result, both because of the great misery made for the mass of our people, and because the attitude of the operators will beyond a doubt double the burden on us while standing between them and socialistic action. But I am glad I tried anyhow. I should have hated to feel that I had failed to make any effort. What my next move will be I cannot yet say. I feel most strongly that the attitude of the operators is one which accentuates the need of the Government having some power of supervision and regulation over such corporations. I should like to make a fairly radical experiment on the anthracite-coal companies to start with! At the meeting to-day the operators assumed a fairly hopeless attitude. None of them appeared to such advantage as Mitchell, whom most of them denounced with such violence and rancor that I felt he did very well to keep his temper. Between times they insulted me for not preserving order (and they evidently ignored such a trifling detail as the United States Constitution) and attacked Knox for not having brought suit against the Miners' Union as violating the Sherman Antitrust Law. (To Mark Hanna, October 3, 1902.) *Mem. Ed.* XXIII, 233; Bishop I, 203.

―――――――. I am very reluctant in view of the operators' attitude toward me to propose any plan to them at all. Curiously enough, if they had given me an opportunity I should have proposed just the plan you outlined, that is, that there should be a resumption of operations until April first, up to which time the two parties might seek to reach an agreement; and then, when the distress of the public would not be so terrible on account of the approach of warm weather, there would be less damage from their going on with their quarrel. . . . I think I shall now tell Mitchell that if the miners will go back to work I will appoint a commission to investigate the whole situation and will do whatever in my power lies to have the findings of such commission favorably acted upon. This seems to be the only step I can now take, or at least the best step at the moment to take. I feel the gravest apprehension concerning the misery pending over so many people this winter and the consequent rioting which may and probably will ensue. (To Grover Cleveland October 5, 1902.) *Mem. Ed.* XXIII, 237; Bishop I, 207.

―――――――. The situation is bad, especially because it is possible it may grow infinitely worse. If when the severe weather comes on there is a coal famine I dread to think of the suffering, in parts of our great cities especially, and I fear there will be fuel riots of as bad a type as any bread riots we have ever seen. *Of course, once the rioting has begun, once there is a resort to mob violence, the only thing to do is to maintain order.* It is a dreadful thing to be brought face to face with the necessity of taking measures, however unavoidable, which will mean the death of men who have been maddened by want and suffering. (To Robert Bacon, October 5, 1902.) *Mem. Ed.* XXIII, 238; Bishop I, 208.

―――――――. I am feeling my way step by step trying to get a solution of the coal matter. Most of my correspondents wish me to try something violent or impossible. A minor but very influential part desire that I send troops at once without a shadow of warrant into the coal districts, or that I bring suit against the labor organization. The others demand that I bring suit against the operators, or that under the law of eminent domain, or for the purpose of protecting the public health, I seize their property, or appoint a receiver, or do something else that is wholly impossible. My great concern is, of course, to break the famine; but I must not be drawn into any violent step which would bring reaction and disaster afterward. (To Henry Cabot Lodge, October 7, 1902.) *Mem. Ed.* XXIII, 239; Bishop I, 208.

―――――――. The situation in the coal strike has been as difficult as it well could be. I do not know that I have ever had a more puzzling or a more important problem to deal with. One great trouble was that the little world in which the operators moved was absolutely out of touch with the big world that included practically all the rest of the country. . . .

The trouble with the excellent gentlemen who said that they would far rather die of cold than yield on such a high principle as recognizing arbitration with these striking miners, was, that *they* were not in danger of dying of cold. They would pay extra for their coal and would get insufficient quantities and would suffer discomfort; but the poorer people around about them would and could get no coal and with them it would not be discomfort but acute misery and loss of life. In other words, these people really meant that they would rather somebody else should die of cold than that they should yield. Such a position was impossible.

Now the operators have acceded (and parenthetically, may Heaven preserve me from ever again dealing with so wooden-headed a set, when I wish to preserve their interests); and Mitchell has yielded. If the miners do not back him up, we have at any rate made an enormous stride in advance, for we have the issue of right and wrong clearly defined, and I think that the strike will practically be broken. But I earnestly hope that the miners will back him up and that in a day or two the strike will be over. (To Anna Roosevelt Cowles, October 16, 1902.) *Cowles Letters,* 252-254.

―――――――. I am being very much overpraised by everybody, and although I suppose I like it, it makes me feel uncomfortable too. Mind you, I speak the literal truth when I say I know perfectly well I do not deserve what is said of me. It really seems to me that any man of average courage and common-sense, who felt as deeply as I did the terrible calamity impending over our people, would have done just what I did. (To J. B. Bishop, October 18, 1902.) *Mem. Ed.* XXIII, 249; Bishop I, 217.

―――――――. I believe what I did in settling the anthracite-coal strike was a matter of very real moment from the standpoint not only of industrial but of social reform and progress. (To Sidney Brooks, December 28, 1908.) *Mem. Ed.* XXIV, 151; Bishop II, 129.

───────. First and foremost, my concern was to avert a frightful calamity to the United States. In the next place I was anxious to save the great coal operators and all of the class of big propertied men, of which they were members, from the dreadful punishment which their own folly would have brought on them if I had not acted; and one of the exasperating things was that they were so blinded that they could not see that I was trying to save them from themselves and to avert, not only for their sakes, but for the sake of the country, the excesses which would have been indulged in at their expense if they had longer persisted in their conduct. (1913.) *Mem. Ed.* XXII, 536; *Nat. Ed.* XX, 461.

COAST DEFENSE. See Navy.

COINAGE. I want to make a suggestion. It seems to me worth while to try for a really good coinage; though I suppose there will be a revolt about it! I was looking at some gold coins of Alexander the Great to-day, and I was struck by their high relief. Would it not be well to have our coins in high relief, and also to have the rims raised? The point of having the rims raised would be, of course, to protect the figure on the coin; and if we have the figures in high relief, like the figures on the old Greek coins, they will surely last longer. (To Augustus Saint-Gaudens, November 6, 1905.) *Mem. Ed.* XXIII, 413; Bishop I, 359.

───────. I am so glad you like the head of Liberty with the feather head-dress. Really, the feather head-dress can be treated as being the conventional cap of Liberty quite as much as if it was the Phrygian cap; and, after all, it is *our* Liberty—not what the ancient Greeks and Romans miscalled by that title—and we are entitled to a typically American head-dress for the lady. (To Augustus Saint-Gaudens, March 14, 1907.) *Mem. Ed.* XXIII, 416; Bishop I, 361.

COINAGE. See also "In God We Trust."

COLLECTIVE ACTION. There must . . . be collective action. This need of collective action is in part supplied by the unions, which, although they have on certain points been guilty of grave shortcomings, have nevertheless on the whole rendered inestimable service to the working man. In addition, there must be collective action through the government, the agent of all of us. (*Outlook*, February 4, 1911.) *Mem. Ed.* XIX, 104; *Nat. Ed.* XVII, 69.

COLLECTIVE ACTION. See also Contract; Individualism; Laissez-Faire.

COLLECTIVE BARGAINING. Wages and other most important conditions of employment must remain largely outside of governmental control and be left for adjustment by free contract between employer and employee, with the important proviso that there should be legislation to prevent the conditions that compel men and women to accept wages that represent less than will insure a decent living. But the question of contract between employer and employee should not be left to individual action, for under modern industrial conditions the individual is often too weak to guard his own rights as against a strongly organized body or a great capitalist. In the present state of society, and until we advance much farther than at present along lines of genuine altruism, there must be effective and organized collective action by the wage-workers in great industrial enterprises. They must act jointly through the process of collective bargaining. Only thus can they be put upon a plane of economic equality with their corporate employers. Capital is organized, and the laborer can secure proper liberty and proper treatment only if labor organizes also. (*Outlook*, February 4, 1911.) *Mem. Ed.* XIX, 108; *Nat. Ed.* XVII, 72.

───────. Labor likewise should have full right to co-operate and combine and full right to collective bargaining and collective action, subject always, as in the case of capital, to the paramount general interest of the public, of the Commonwealth; and the prime feature of this paramount general interest is that each man shall do justice and shall receive justice. (Before Republican State Convention, Saratoga Springs, N. Y., July 18, 1918.) *Mem. Ed.* XXI, 401; *Nat. Ed.* XIX, 364.

COLLECTIVE BARGAINING. See also Capital and Labor; Coal Strike; Contract; Industrial Arbitration; Labor Unions; Strikes.

COLLECTIVISM. In order to raise the status, not of the exceptional people, but of the great mass of those who work with their hands under modern industrial conditions, it is imperative that there should be more than merely individual action. The old plea that collective action by all the people through the State, or by some of them through a union or other association, is necessarily hostile to individual growth has been demonstrated to be false. On the contrary, in the world of labor as in the world of business, the advent of the giant corporation and the very wealthy employer has meant that the absence of all governmental supervision implies the emergence of a very few exceptionally powerful men at the head and the stamping out of all individual initiative and power lower down. Unrestricted individualism in violence during the dark ages merely produced a class of brutal and competent individual fighters at the top, resting on a broad foundation of abject serfs below. Unrestricted individualism in the modern industrial world produces results very little better, and in the end means the complete atrophy of all power of real individual initiative, real individual capacity for self-help, in the great mass of the workers. (*Outlook,* February 4, 1911.) *Mem. Ed.* XIX, 103; *Nat. Ed.* XVII, 68.

COLLECTIVISM AND INDIVIDUALISM. Every civilized government which contains the least possibility of progress, or in which life would be supportable, is administered on a system of mixed individualism and collectivism; and whether we increase or decrease the power of the state, and limit or enlarge the scope of individual activity, is a matter not for theory at all, but for decision upon grounds of mere practical expediency. A paid police department or paid fire department is in itself a manifestation of state socialism. The fact that such departments are absolutely necessary is sufficient to show that we need not be frightened from further experiments by any fear of the dangers of collectivism in the abstract; and on the other hand, their success does not afford the least justification for impairing the power of the individual where that power can be properly exercised. No hard-and-fast rule in the matter can be laid down. All that can be said is that, where possible, the individual must be left free; that he must always be left so free as to have a right to enjoy himself in his own way where he can do it without infringing on the rights of others; and that the reward for his efforts should be made, so far as may be, proportional to his efforts and abilities, so as to encourage enterprise, thrift, industry, and sobriety, and to discourage their opposites. But wherever it is found by actual practice and experiment, or by the failure of all other methods, that collectivism and state interference are wise and necessary, we should not be deterred from advocating them by any considerations of pure theory. (*Atlantic Monthly,* April 1895.) *Mem. Ed.* XIV, 207; *Nat. Ed.* XII, 226.

―――――――――. The growth in the complexity of community life means the partial substitution of collectivism for individualism, not to destroy, but to save individualism. . . . The government has been forced to take the place of the individual in a hundred different ways; in, for instance, such matters as the prevention of fires, the construction of drainage systems, the supply of water, light, and transportation. In a primitive community every man or family looks after his or its interest in all these matters. In a city it would be an absurdity either to expect every man to continue to do this, or to say that he had lost the power of individual initiative because he relegated any or all of these matters to the province of those public officers whose usefulness consists in expressing the collective activities of all the people. (*Century,* October 1913.) *Mem. Ed.* XIX, 535; *Nat. Ed.* XVII, 393.

COLLECTIVISM. *See also* FARMER COOPERATIVES; INDIVIDUALISM; SOCIALISM.

COLLEGE EDUCATION. A heavy moral obligation rests upon the man of means and upon the man of education to do their full duty by their country. On no class does this obligation rest more heavily than upon the men with a collegiate education, the men who are graduates of our universities. Their education gives them no right to feel the least superiority over any of their fellow citizens; but it certainly ought to make them feel that they should stand foremost in the honorable effort to serve the whole public by doing their duty as Americans in the body politic. (*Atlantic Monthly,* August 1894.) *Mem. Ed.* XV, 50; *Nat. Ed.* XIII, 36.

―――――――――. If the man is of such a character that he regards the college education as all-sufficient in itself, then I quite agree that he is far better off without one. But if he has the right stuff in him, if he regards the college education as supplying him with qualities which are invaluable additions to the other qualities that he has, then its good effects can hardly be overestimated. I want to lay particular stress upon that, because I have not the smallest sympathy with the people who insist upon regarding education as of no value whatever unless it has an important practical result. Besides that value, it has the very great value of the mere cultivation that it gives, of the broader outlook upon life, of the infinitely greater capacity for real enjoyment with which it endows the man or woman fortunate enough to receive it; of the infinitely greater capacity it gives to that man or woman to add to the enjoyment of those with whom he or she is thrown in contact, and especially in intimate contact, later on. (Before Iowa State Teachers' Association, Des Moines, November 4, 1910.) *Mem. Ed.* XVIII, 446; *Nat. Ed.* XVI, 332.

COLLEGE EDUCATION — FUNCTION OF. Only a small proportion of college boys are going to become real students and do original work in literature, science, or art; and these are certain to study their best in any event. The others are going into business or law or some kindred occupation; and these, of course, can study but little that will be directly of use to them in after-life. The college education of such men should be largely devoted to making them good citizens, and able to hold their own in the world. (*North American Review,* August 1890.) *Mem. Ed.* XV, 518; *Nat. Ed.* XIII, 585.

――――――. The greatest special function of a college, as distinguished from its general function of producing good citizenship, should be so to shape conditions as to put a premium upon the development of productive scholarship, of the creative mind, in any form of intellectual work. The men whose chief concern lies with the work of the student in study should bear this fact ever before them. (At the Harvard Union, Cambridge, February 23, 1907.) *Mem. Ed.* XV, 486; *Nat. Ed.* XIII, 562.

COLLEGE EDUCATION — RESPONSIBILITIES OF. The man with a university education is in honor bound to take an active part in our political life, and to do his full duty as a citizen by helping his fellow citizens to the extent of his power in the exercise of the rights of self-government. He is bound to rank action far above criticism, and to understand that the man deserving of credit is the man who actually does the things, even though imperfectly, and not the man who confines himself to talking about how they ought to be done. He is bound to have a high ideal and to strive to realize it, and yet he must make up his mind that he will never be able to get the highest good, and that he must devote himself with all his energy to getting the best that he can. Finally, his work must be disinterested and honest, and it must be given without regard to his own success or failure, and without regard to the effect it has upon his own fortunes; and while he must show the virtues of uprightness and tolerance and gentleness, he must also show the sterner virtues of courage, resolution, and hardihood, and the desire to war with merciless effectiveness against the existence of wrong. (*Atlantic Monthly,* August 1894.) *Mem. Ed.* XV, 62; *Nat. Ed.* XIII, 46.

――――――. With us in America the college man acquires by virtue of his education not special privileges but special duties, and this is as it should be. Every man who has been able to get better mental training than his fellows should feel an always increasing burden of responsibility for his actions, and should be ever ready to do more than even his full duty by the State. In time of war we have a right to expect that the men from our colleges will shed their blood, without thought, for the honor of their land. (Before American Republican College League, Chicago, October 15, 1896.) *Mem. Ed.* XVI, 395; *Nat. Ed.* XIV, 259.

――――――. If a college education means anything, it means fitting a man to do better service than he could do without it; if it does not mean that it means nothing, and if a man does not get that out of it, he gets less than nothing out of it. No man has a right to arrogate to himself one particle of superiority or consideration because he has had a college education, but he is bound, if he is in truth a man, to feel that the fact of his having had a college education imposes upon him a heavier burden of responsibility, that it makes it doubly incumbent upon him to do well and nobly in his life, private and public. (At Harvard Commencement Dinner, Cambridge, Mass., June 25, 1902.) *Presidential Addresses and State Papers* I, 79.

COLLEGE MEN—APPEAL TO. If we cannot look to our college trained men for leadership in our national life, then there is something radically wrong either in the colleges or in the national life. I am not willing to admit that either is the case. Therefore, I confidently appeal to the college men of the United States for practical translation into policy of what in books of advanced theology would be called a proper national ethic and a proper world-ethic. In other words, I ask the men to whom special cultural opportunities have been granted both to teach our people that no nation can help others unless it can defend itself by its own prepared strength, and also to teach them that this strength, the only safe foundation for national greatness, must in international matters be used with high regard for the rights of others. (Stafford Little Lecture at Princeton University, November 1917.) Theodore Roosevelt, *National Strength and International Duty*. (Princeton, N. J., 1917), pp. 30-31.

COLLEGE. *See also* EDUCATION, LIBERAL; UNIVERSITY.

COLLEGIATE SPORTS. *See* SPORTS.

COLOMBIA. To talk of Colombia as a responsible Power to be dealt with as we would deal with Holland or Belgium or Switzerland or Denmark is a mere absurdity. The analogy is with a group of Sicilian or Calabrian bandits; with Villa and Carranza at this moment. You could no more make an agreement with the Colombian rulers than you could nail currant jelly to a wall—and the failure to nail currant jelly to a wall is not due to the nail; it is due to the currant jelly. I did my best to get them to act straight. Then I determined that I would do what ought to be done without regard to them. The people of Panama were a unit in desiring the Canal and in wishing to overthrow the rule of Colombia. If they had not revolted, I should have recommended Congress to take possession of the Isthmus by force of arms; and, as you will see, I had actually written the first draft of my Message to this effect. When they revolted, I promptly used the Navy to prevent the bandits, who had tried to hold us up, from spending months of futile bloodshed in conquering or endeavoring to conquer the Isthmus, to the lasting damage of the Isthmus, of us, and of the world. I did not consult Hay, or Root, or any one else as to what I did, because a council of war does not fight; and I intended to do the job once for all. (To Thayer, July 2, 1915.) William R. Thayer, *The Life and Letters of John Hay*. (Houghton Mifflin Co., Boston, 1915), II, 327-328.

COLOMBIA. *See also* HAY-HERRAN TREATY; PANAMA CANAL; PANAMA REVOLUTION.

COLONIAL ADMINISTRATION. *See* INSULAR POSSESSIONS; WOOD, LEONARD.

COLONIAL SYSTEM, THE OLD. The European theory of a colony was that it was planted by the home government for the benefit of the home government and home people, not for the benefit of the colonists themselves. Hardly any one grasped the grandeur of the movement by which the English-speaking race was to spread over the world's waste spaces, until a fourth of the habitable globe was in its hands, and until it became the mightiest race on which the sun has ever shone. Those in power did not think of the spread of a mighty people, and of its growth by leaps and bounds, but of the planting of new trading-posts; they did not realize the elementary fact that if the men who stretch abroad the race limits by settlement and conquest are to be kept one with those who stay at home they must be granted an equal share with the latter in administering the common government. The colony was held to be the property of the mother country—property to be protected and well treated as a whole, but property nevertheless. Naturally the colonist himself was likewise held to occupy a similar position compared to the citizen of the home country. The Englishman felt himself to be the ruler and superior of the American; and even though he tried to rule wisely, and meant to act well toward the colonists, the fact remained that he considered them his inferiors, and that his scheme of government distinctly recognized them as such. The mere existence of such a feeling, and its embodiment in the governmental system, warranted a high-spirited people in revolting against it. (1891.) *Mem. Ed.* IX, 321-322; *Nat. Ed.* X, 450.

COLONIES—TREATMENT OF. England's treatment of her American subjects was thoroughly selfish; but that her conduct toward them was a wonder of tyranny will not now be seriously asserted; on the contrary, she stood decidedly above the general European standard in such matters, and certainly treated her colonies far better than France and Spain did theirs; and she herself had undoubted grounds for complaint in, for example, the readiness of the Americans to claim military help in time of danger, together with their frank reluctance to pay for it. It was impossible that she should be so far in advance of the age as to treat her colonists as equals; they themselves were sometimes quite as intolerant in their behavior toward men of a different race, creed, or color. (1888.) *Mem. Ed.* VIII, 281-282; *Nat. Ed.* VII, 243.

COLONIES. *See also* EXPANSION; IMPERIALISM; NORTHWEST ORDINANCE; REVOLUTIONARY WAR.

COMBINATIONS. Modern industrial conditions are such that combination is not only necessary but inevitable. It is so in the world of business just as it is so in the world of labor, and it is as idle to desire to put an end to all corporations, to all big combinations of capital, as to desire to put an end to combinations of labor. Corporation and labor-union alike have come to stay. Each if properly managed is a source of good and not evil. (Seventh Annual Message, Washington, December 3, 1907.) *Mem. Ed.* XVII, 488; *Nat. Ed.* XV, 416.

———————. The people of the United States have but one instrument which they can efficiently use against the colossal combinations of business—and that instrument is the government of the United States (and of course in the several States the governments of the States where they can be utilized). (At San Francisco, September 14, 1912.) *Mem. Ed.* XIX, 426; *Nat. Ed.* XVII, 312.

———————. It is practically impossible, and, if possible, it would be mischievous and undesirable, to try to break up all combinations merely because they are large and successful, and to put the business of the country back into the middle of the eighteenth century conditions of intense and unregulated competition between small and weak business concerns. Such an effort represents not progressiveness but an unintelligent though doubtless entirely well-meaning toryism. Moreover the effort to administer a law merely by lawsuits and court decisions is bound to end in signal failure, and meanwhile to be attended with delays and uncertainties, and to put a premium upon legal sharp practice. Such an effort does not adequately punish the guilty, and yet works great harm to the innocent. Moreover, it entirely fails to give the publicity which is one of the best by-products of the system of control by administrative officials; publicity, which is not only good in itself but furnishes the data for whatever further action may be necessary. *Outlook,* November 18, 1911, p. 656.

COMBINATIONS—CONTROL OF. Much of the legislation aimed to prevent the evils connected with the enormous development of these great corporations has been ineffective, partly because it aimed at doing too much, and partly because it did not confer on the Government a really efficient method of holding any guilty corporation to account. The effort to prevent all restraint of competition, whether harmful or beneficial, has been ill-judged; what is needed is not so much the effort to prevent combination as a vigilant and effective control of the combinations formed, so as to secure just and equitable dealing on their part alike toward the public generally, toward their smaller competitors, and toward the wage-workers in their employ. (At Chautauqua, N. Y., August 11, 1905.) *Presidential Addresses and State Papers* IV, 448.

———————. Combination of capital like combination of labor is a necessary element of our present industrial system. It is not possible completely to prevent it; and if it were possible, such complete prevention would do damage to the body politic. What we need is not vainly to try to prevent all combination, but to secure such rigorous and adequate control and supervision of the combinations as to prevent their injuring the public, or existing in such form as inevitably to threaten injury—for the mere fact that a combination has secured practically complete control of a necessary of life would under any circumstances show that such combination was to be presumed to be adverse to the public interest. (Sixth Annual Message, Washington, December 3, 1906.) *Mem. Ed.* XVII, 430; *Nat. Ed.* XV, 366.

———————. Our interests are at bottom common; in the long run we go up or go down together. Yet more and more it is evident that the State, and if necessary the nation, has got to possess the right of supervision and control as regards the great corporations which are its creatures; particularly as regards the great business combinations which derive a portion of their importance from the existence of some monopolistic tendency. The right should be exercised with caution and self-restraint; but it should exist, so that it may be invoked if the need arises. (At Minnesota State Fair, September 2, 1901.) *Mem. Ed.* XV, 332; *Nat. Ed.* XIII, 472.

———————. It is my personal belief that the same kind and degree of control and supervision which should be exercised over public-service corporations should be extended also to combinations which control necessaries of life, such as meat, oil, and coal, or which deal in them on an important scale. I have no doubt that the ordinary man who has control of them is much like ourselves. I have no doubt he would like to do well, but I want to have enough supervision to help him realize that desire to do well....

Combinations in industry are the result of an imperative economic law which cannot be repealed by political legislation. The effort at prohibiting all combination has substantially failed. The way out lies, not in attempting to prevent such combinations, but in completely controlling them in the interest of the public welfare. (At Osawatomie, Kan., August 31, 1910.) *Mem. Ed.* XIX, 18; *Nat. Ed.* XVII, 12.

COMBINATIONS — TREATMENT OF. My effort was to secure the creation of a Fed-

COMBINATIONS

eral Commission which should neither excuse nor tolerate monopoly, but prevent it when possible and uproot it when discovered; and which should in addition effectively control and regulate all big combinations, and should give honest business certainty as to what the law was and security as long as the law was obeyed. Such a commission would furnish a steady expert control, a control adapted to the problem; and dissolution is neither control nor regulation, but is purely negative; and negative remedies are of little permanent avail. (1913.) *Mem. Ed.* XXII, 492; *Nat. Ed.* XX, 423.

COMBINATIONS OF CAPITAL AND LABOR. Arrogant selfishness by a combination of capitalists, met by arrogant selfishness by a combination of working men, may be better than the reign of unchecked selfishness by either side alone; but it can never be satisfactory, and must always be fraught with grave danger to the whole social fabric. (1917.) *Mem. Ed.* XXI, 87; *Nat. Ed.* XIX, 75.

COMBINATIONS. *See also* BUSINESS; CAPITAL AND LABOR; COMPETITION; CORPORATIONS; GOVERNMENT CONTROL; INDUSTRIAL COMMISSION; LABOR; MONOPOLIES; SHERMAN ANTI-TRUST ACT; TRUSTS.

COMMERCE, FOREIGN. It is imperative to the welfare of our people that we enlarge and extend our foreign commerce. We are preeminently fitted to do this because as a people we have developed high skill in the art of manufacturing; our business men are strong executives, strong organizers. In every way possible our Federal Government should co-operate in this important matter. Any one who has had opportunity to study and observe first-hand Germany's course in this respect must realize that their policy of co-operation between government and business has in comparatively few years made them a leading competitor for the commerce of the world. It should be remembered that they are doing this on a national scale and with large units of business, while the Democrats would have us believe that we should do it with small units of business, which would be controlled not by the National Government but by forty-nine conflicting State sovereignties. Such a policy is utterly out of keeping with the progress of the times and gives our great commercial rivals in Europe—hungry for international markets—golden opportunities of which they are rapidly taking advantage. (Before Progressive National Convention, Chicago, August 6, 1912.) *Mem. Ed.* XIX, 392; *Nat. Ed.* XVII, 282.

COMPETITION

COMMERCE. *See also* BUSINESS; CONTRABAND; FREE TRADE; MUNITIONS; NEUTRAL TRADE; SOUTH AMERICA; TARIFF.

COMMERCE COMMISSION. *See* INTERSTATE COMMERCE.

COMMERCIAL IDEALS. *See* FORTUNES; MATERIALIST; MONEY; WEALTH.

COMMON SENSE. When we come to dealing with our social and industrial needs, remedies, rights and wrongs, a ton of oratory is not worth an ounce of hard-headed, kindly common sense. (At Labor Day Picnic, Chicago, September 3, 1900.) *Mem. Ed.* XVI, 509; *Nat. Ed.* XIII, 481.

———. There is . . . one quality which perhaps, strictly speaking, is as much intellectual as moral, but which is too often wholly lacking in men of high intellectual ability and without which real character cannot exist—namely, the fundamental gift of common sense. *Outlook,* November 8, 1913, p. 527.

COMMON SENSE. *See also* VIRTUES.

COMMONWEALTH OF ENGLAND. *See* ENGLAND.

COMMUNISM. *See* BOLSHEVISM; RUSSIA; SOCIALISM.

COMPETITION. It has been a misfortune that the national laws . . . have hitherto been of a negative or prohibitive rather than an affirmative kind, and still more that they have in part sought to prohibit what could not be effectively prohibited, and have in part in their prohibitions confounded what should be allowed and what should not be allowed. It is generally useless to try to prohibit all restraint on competition, whether this restraint be reasonable or unreasonable; and where it is not useless it is generally hurtful. . . .

What is needed is not sweeping prohibition of every arrangement, good or bad, which may tend to restrict competition, but such adequate supervision and regulation as will prevent any restriction of competition from being to the detriment of the public—as well as such supervision and regulation as will prevent other abuses in no way connected with restriction of competition. (Fifth Annual Message, Washington, December 5, 1905.) *Mem. Ed.* XVII, 319; *Nat. Ed.* XV, 273, 274.

———. Competition will remain as a very important factor when once we have destroyed the unfair business methods, the criminal interference with the rights of others, which alone enable certain swollen combinations to crush out their competitors—and incidentally, the "conservatives" will do well to remember that these unfair and iniquitous methods by great masters of corporate capital have done more to cause popular discontent with the propertied classes than all the orations of all the Socialist orators in the country put together. *Outlook,* November 18, 1911, p. 656.

—————————. Wherever it is practicable we propose to preserve competition; but where under modern conditions competition has been eliminated and cannot be successfully restored, then the government must step in and itself supply the needed control on behalf of the people as a whole. (Before Progressive National Convention, Chicago, August 6, 1912.) *Mem. Ed.* XIX, 391; *Nat. Ed.* XVII, 282.

COMPETITION. *See also* BUSINESS; COMBINATIONS; INDIVIDUALISM; LAISSEZ-FAIRE; MONOPOLIES; POLITICAL ISSUES; SHERMAN ANTI-TRUST ACT; TRUSTS.

COMPROMISE. It is not possible to lay down an inflexible rule as to when compromise is right and when wrong; when it is a sign of the highest statesmanship to temporize, and when it is merely a proof of weakness. Now and then one can stand uncompromisingly for a naked principle and force people up to it. This is always the attractive course; but in certain great crises it may be a very wrong course. Compromise, in the proper sense, merely means agreement; in the proper sense opportunism should merely mean doing the best possible with actual conditions as they exist. A compromise which results in a half-step toward evil is all wrong, just as the opportunist who saves himself for the moment by adopting a policy which is fraught with future disaster is all wrong; but no less wrong is the attitude of those who will not come to an agreement through which, or will not follow the course by which, it is alone possible to accomplish practical results for good. (*Century,* June 1900.) *Mem. Ed.* XV, 379-380; *Nat. Ed.* XIII, 343.

—————————. In politics, there has to be one continual compromise. Of course now and then questions arise upon which a compromise is inadmissible. There could be no compromise with secession, and there was none. There should be no avoidable compromise about any great moral question. But only a very few great reforms or great measures of any kind can be carried through without concession. No student of American history needs to be reminded that the Constitution itself is a bundle of compromises, and was adopted only because of this fact, and that the same thing is true of the Emancipation Proclamation. (*Atlantic Monthly,* August 1894.) *Mem. Ed.* XV, 61; *Nat. Ed.* XIII, 46.

—————————. When any public man says that he "will never compromise under any conditions," he is certain to receive the applause of a few emotional people who do not think correctly, and the one fact about him that can be instantly asserted as true beyond peradventure is that, if he is a serious personage at all, he is deliberately lying, while it is only less certain that he will be guilty of base and dishonorable compromise when the opportunity arises. "Compromise" is so often used in a bad sense that it is difficult to remember that properly it merely describes the process of reaching an agreement. Naturally there are certain subjects on which no man can compromise. For instance, there must be no compromise under any circumstances with official corruption, and of course no man should hesitate to say as much. Again, an honest politician is entirely justified in promising on the stump that he will make no compromise on any question of right and wrong. This promise he can and ought to make good. But when questions of policy arise—and most questions, from the tariff to municipal ownership of public utilities and the franchise tax, are primarily questions of policy—he will have to come to some kind of working agreement with his fellows, and if he says that he will not, he either deliberately utters what he knows to be false, or else he insures for himself the humiliation of being forced to break his word. (*Outlook,* July 28, 1900.) *Mem. Ed.* XV, 399; *Nat. Ed.* XIII, 397.

CONCEALING COLORATION. *See* ANIMALS; BIRDS.

CONDUCT. *See* CHARACTER; CONSCIENCE; COURAGE; COURTESY; CRIME; DISHONESTY; HONESTY; IDEALS; JUSTICE; MORALITY; TEN COMMANDMENTS; TRUTH; VICE; VIRTUES.

CONFEDERATES. The position of honor in your parade to-day is held by the Confederate veterans. They by their deeds reflect credit upon their descendants and upon all Americans, both because they did their duty in war and because they did their duty in peace. Now if the young men, their sons, will not only prove that they possess the same power of fealty to an ideal, but will also show the efficiency in the ranks of industrial life that their fathers, the Confederate veterans, showed that they possessed in the ranks of war, the industrial future of this great and typically American Commonwealth is assured. (At Raleigh, N. C., October 19, 1905.) *Presidential Addresses and State Papers* IV, 471.

———————. Let me say just one word to the men of the great Civil War, to the men who fought from '61 to '65. I am sure that you would be pleased if you could hear the applause that greets, in any audience in the North, any allusion to the valor, the self-devotion, the fealty to right as God gave them to see the right, of the men who wore the gray in the great contest forty years ago. We are indeed thrice fortunate as a people; because to us it has been given alone among peoples in modern times to pass through one of the most terrible contests of history; and, now that the bitterness has died away, to cherish as our most precious heritage the memories bequeathed to us alike by the men in blue and the men in gray, alike by those who followed Grant and those who followed Lee, because each man showed his readiness to sacrifice all, to sacrifice life itself, upon the altar of duty as he saw it. (At Atlanta, Ga., October 20, 1905.) *Presidential Addresses and State Papers* IV, 489-490.

———————. My father's people were all Union men. My mother's brothers fought in the Confederate navy, one being an admiral therein, and the other firing the last gun fired by the *Alabama* before she sank. When I recently visited Vicksburg in Mississippi, the State of Jefferson Davis, I was greeted with just as much enthusiasm as if it had been Massachusetts or Ohio. . . . After for many years talking about the fact that the deeds of valor shown by the men in gray and the men in blue are now the common heritage of all our people, those who talked and those who listened have now gradually grown first to believe with their minds, and then to feel with their hearts, the truth of what they have spoken. (To Sir George Otto Trevelyan, January 1, 1908.) *Mem. Ed.* XXIV, 199; Bishop II, 170.

CONFEDERATES. *See also* CIVIL WAR; VETERANS.

CONGRESS—SERVICE IN. Often much of the best service that is rendered in Congress must be done without any hope of approbation or reward. The measures that attract most attention are frequently not those of most lasting importance; and even where they are of such importance that attention is fixed upon them, the interested public may not appreciate the difference between the man who merely records his vote for a bill and the other who throws his whole strength into the contest to secure its passage. A man must have in him a strong and earnest sense of duty and the desire to accomplish good for the commonwealth, without regard to the effect upon himself, to be useful in Congress. *Harvard Graduates' Magazine,* October 1892, pp. 4-5.

CONGRESS AND THE ROOSEVELT POLICIES. I am criticized for interference with Congress. There really is not any answer I can make to this except to say that if I had not interfered we would not have had any rate bill, or any beef-packers' bill, or any pure-food bill, or any consular reform bill, or the Panama Canal, or the Empoyers' Liability Bill, or in short, any of the legislation which we have obtained during the last year. (To Jacob Riis, June 26, 1906.) *Mem. Ed.* XXIV, 24; Bishop II, 19.

———————. Congress is ending, but by no means in a blaze of glory. The leaders in the House and Senate felt a relief that they did not try to conceal at the fact that I was not to remain as President, and need not be too implicitly followed; and they forget that the discipline that they have been able to keep for the last six years over their followers was primarily due to the fact that we had a compact and aggressive organization, kept together by my leadership, due to my hold, and the hold the policies I championed had upon the people. Accordingly they have seen their own power crumble away under their hands and both the House and Senate are now in chaos. (To Whitelaw Reid, May 25, 1908.) *Mem. Ed.* XXIV, 98; Bishop II, 84.

CONGRESS. *See also* DEBATE; DIVISION OF POWERS; EXECUTIVE; FILIBUSTERING; INTERSTATE COMMERCE; LAW; LEGISLATION; LEGISLATURE; PRESIDENT; SENATE; TREATIES.

CONGRESSIONAL LEADERS. With every one of these men I at times differ radically on important questions; but they are the leaders, and their great intelligence and power and their desire in the last resort to do what is best for the government, make them not only essential to work with, but desirable to work with. Several of the leaders have special friends whom they desire to favor, or special interests with which they are connected and which they hope to serve. But, taken as a body, they are broad-minded and patriotic, as well as sagacious, skilful and resolute. (To William H. Taft, March 13, 1903.) *Mem. Ed.* XXIII, 273; Bishop I, 237.

CONGRESSMEN. From a pretty intimate acquaintance with several Congresses I am entirely satisfied that there is among the members a very small proportion indeed who are corruptible, in the sense that they will let their action be influenced by money or its equivalent. Congressmen are very often demagogues; they are very often blind partisans; they are often exceedingly short-sighted, narrow-minded, and bigoted; but they are not usually corrupt; and to accuse a narrow-minded demagogue of corruption when he is perfectly honest, is merely to set him more firmly in his evil course and to help him with his constituents, who recognize that the charge is entirely unjust, and in repelling it lose sight of the man's real shortcomings. (Before the Liberal Club, Buffalo, N. Y., January 26, 1893.) *Mem. Ed.* XV, 75; *Nat. Ed.* XIII, 291-292.

CONGRESSMEN. *See also* LEGISLATORS; REPRESENTATIVES; SENATORS.

CONQUEST. *See* WARS OF CONQUEST.

CONSCIENCE. It is a very bad thing to be morally callous, for moral callousness is disease. But inflammation of the conscience may be just as unhealthy so far as the public is concerned; and if a man's conscience is always telling him to do something foolish he will do well to mistrust its workings. (At the Harvard Union, Cambridge, February 23, 1907.) *Mem. Ed.* XV, 490; *Nat. Ed.* XIII, 565.

——————. The longer I have lived the more strongly I have felt the harm done by the practice among so many men of keeping their consciences in separate compartments; sometimes a Sunday conscience and a week-day conscience; sometimes a conscience as to what they say or what they like other people to say, and another conscience as to what they do and like other people to do; sometimes a conscience for their private affairs and a totally different conscience for their business relations. Or again, there may be one compartment in which the man keeps his conscience not only for his domestic affairs but for his business affairs, and a totally different compartment in which he keeps his conscience when he deals with public men and public measures. (At Pacific Theological Seminary, Spring 1911.) *Mem. Ed.* XV, 576; *Nat. Ed.* XIII, 616.

CONSCIENCE IN PUBLIC LIFE. I tried my best to lead the people, to advise them, to tell them what I thought was right; if necessary, I never hesitated to tell them what I thought they ought to hear, even though I thought it would be unpleasant for them to hear it; but I recognized that my task was to try to lead them and not to drive them, to take them into my confidence, to try to show them that I was right, and then loyally and in good faith to accept their decision. I will do anything for the people except what my conscience tells me is wrong, and that I can do for no man and no set of men; I hold that a man cannot serve the people well unless he serves his conscience; but I hold also that where his conscience bids him refuse to do what the people desire, he should not try to continue in office against their will. Our government system should be so shaped that the public servant, when he cannot conscientiously carry out the wishes of the people, shall at their desire leave his office and not misrepresent them in office; and I hold that the public servant can by so doing, better than in any other way, serve both them and his conscience. (Before Progressive National Convention, Chicago, August 6, 1912.) *Mem. Ed.* XIX, 410; *Nat. Ed.* XVII, 298.

CONSCIENCE. *See also* MORAL SENSE; MORALITY; RELIGIOUS FREEDOM; SELF-MASTERY; TOLERANCE.

CONSCIENTIOUS OBJECTORS. We have heard much of the conscientious objectors to military service, the outcry having been loudest among those objectors who are not conscientious at all but who are paid or unpaid agents of the German Government.

It is certain that only a small fraction of the men who call themselves conscientious objectors in this matter are actuated in any way by conscience. The bulk are slackers, pure and simple, or else traitorous pro-Germans. Some are actuated by lazy desire to avoid any duty that interferes with their ease and enjoyment, some by the evil desire to damage the United States and help Germany, some by sheer, simple, physical timidity. In the aggregate, the men of this type constitute the great majority of the men who claim to be conscientious objectors, and this fact must be remembered in endeavoring to deal with the class. (At Minneapolis, Minn., September 28, 1917.) *Mem. Ed.* XXI, 181; *Nat. Ed.* XIX, 173.

———————. The conscientious objector who won't serve as a soldier or won't pay his taxes has no place in a republic like ours, and should be expelled from it, for no man who won't pull his weight in the boat has a right in the boat. The Society of Friends have come forward in this war just as gallantly as they came forward in the Civil War, and all true believers in peace will do well to follow their example. (*Metropolitan,* November 1918.) *Mem. Ed.* XXI, 276; *Nat. Ed.* XIX, 255.

CONSCIENTIOUS OBJECTORS—INSINCERITY OF. The peace people . . . include the men who conscientiously object to all participation in any war however brutal the opponents, and however vital triumph may be to us and to mankind. These persons are entitled to precisely the respect we give any other persons whose conscience makes them do what is bad. We have had in this country some conscientious polygamists. We now have some conscientious objectors to taking part in this war. Where both are equally conscientious, the former are, on the whole, not as bad as the latter. Of course, if these conscientious objectors are sincere they decline in private life to oppose violence or brutality or to take advantage of the courage and strength of those who do oppose violence and brutality. . . . They are utterly insincere unless they decline to take advantage of police protection from burglary or highway-robbery. Of course, if such a man is really conscientious he cannot profit or allow his family to profit in any way by the safety secured to him and them by others, by soldiers in time of war, by judges and policemen in time of peace; for the receiver is as bad as the thief. I hold that such an attitude is infamous; and it is just as infamous to refuse to serve the country in arms during this war. If a man's conscience bids him so to act, then his conscience is a fit subject for the student of morbid pathology. (At Minneapolis, Minn., September 28, 1917.) *Mem. Ed.* XXI, 183; *Nat. Ed.* XIX, 175.

CONSCIENTIOUS OBJECTORS — TREATMENT OF. No American has the right to hold up his head if he has not sought with all his strength and ingenuity to get into this war. If a man is conscientious in not wanting to fight, I am equally conscientious in not wanting him to vote. The man who is not willing to fight for his country is not fit to work. I'd take him to the front anyway. I would not interfere with his conscience. If it does not permit him to shoot at the enemy, I would not make him shoot, but I would place him in a position where he would be shot at. I would put him at work digging kitchen sinks and doing other labor which would set other men of better fibre free for service which the unworthy manhood of the conscientious objector does not permit him to perform. (Speech of May 28, 1917.) *Mem. Ed.* XXIV, 502; Bishop II, 428.

———————. It is all wrong to permit conscientious objectors to remain in camp or military posts or to go back to their homes. They should be treated in one of three ways: First, demand of them military service, except the actual use of weapons with intent to kill, and if they refuse to render this service treat them as criminals and imprison them at hard labor; second, put them in labor battalions and send them to France behind the lines, where association with soldiers might have a missionary effect on them and cause them to forget their present base creed and rise to worthy levels in an atmosphere of self-sacrifice and of service and struggle for great ideals; third, if both of the above procedures are regarded as too drastic, intern them with alien enemies and send them permanently out of the country as soon as possible. (September 24, 1918.) *Roosevelt in the Kansas City Star,* 221.

CONSCIENTIOUS OBJECTORS. See also DRAFT; PACIFISM; PACIFIST; PREPAREDNESS.

CONSCRIPTION. See DRAFT; MILITARY SERVICE; MILITARY TRAINING.

CONSERVATION. When, at the beginning of my term of service as President, under the influence of Mr. Pinchot and Mr. Newell, I took up the cause of conservation, I was already fairly well awake to the need of social and industrial justice; and from the outset we had in view, not only the preservation of natural resources, but the prevention of monopoly in natural resources, so that they should inhere in the people as a whole. (*Outlook,* October 12, 1912.) *Mem. Ed.* XIX, 437; *Nat. Ed.* XVII, 317.

———————. In utilizing and conserving the natural resources of the Nation, the one characteristic more essential than any other is foresight. Unfortunately, foresight is not usually characteristic of a young and vigorous people, and it is obviously not a marked characteristic of us in the United States. Yet assuredly it should be the growing nation with a future which takes the long look ahead; and no other nation is growing so rapidly as ours or has a future so full of promise. No other nation enjoys so wonderful a measure of present prosperity which can of right be treated as an earnest of future success, and for no other are the rewards of foresight so great, so certain, and so easily foretold. Yet hitherto as a Nation we have tended to live with an eye single to the present, and have permitted the reckless waste and destruction of much of our natural wealth.

The conservation of our natural resources and their proper use constitute the fundamental problem which underlies almost every other problem of our national life. Unless we maintain an adequate material basis for our civilization, we can not maintain the institutions in which we take so great and so just a pride; and to waste and destroy our natural resources means to undermine this material basis. (Before National Editorial Association, Jamestown, Va., June 10, 1907.) *Presidential Addresses and State Papers* VI, 1310-1311.

————. Optimism is a good characteristic, but if carried to an excess it becomes foolishness. We are prone to speak of the resources of this country as inexhaustible; this is not so. The mineral wealth of the country, the coal, iron, oil, gas, and the like, does not reproduce itself, and therefore is certain to be exhausted ultimately; and wastefulness in dealing with it to-day means that our descendants will feel the exhaustion a generation or two before they otherwise would. But there are certain other forms of waste which could be entirely stopped—the waste of soil by washing, for instance, which is among the most dangerous of all wastes now in progress in the United States, is easily preventable, so that this present enormous loss of fertility is entirely unnecessary. The preservation or replacement of the forests is one of the most important means of preventing this loss. (Seventh Annual Message, Washington, December 3, 1907.) *Mem. Ed.* XVII, 526; *Nat. Ed.* XV, 448.

————. There must be a sound moral standard on public matters; our public men must represent and respond to the aroused conscience of the people. . . . All the great natural resources which are vital to the welfare of the whole people should be kept either in the hands or under the full control of the whole people. This applies to coal, oil, timber, water power, natural gas. Either natural resources of the land should be kept in the hands of the people and their development and use allowed under leasing arrangements (or otherwise); or, where this is not possible, there should be strict governmental control over their use. *Outlook,* April 20, 1912, p. 853.

————. Conservation means development as much as it does protection. I recognize the right and duty of this generation to develop and use the natural resources of our land; but I do not recognize the right to waste them, or to rob, by wasteful use, the generations that come after us. I ask nothing of the nation except that it so behave as each farmer here behaves with reference to his own children. That farmer is a poor creature who skins the land and leaves it worthless to his children. The farmer is a good farmer who, having enabled the land to support himself and to provide for the education of his children, leaves it to them a little better than he found it himself. I believe the same thing of a nation.

Moreover, I believe that the natural resources must be used for the benefit of all our people, and not monopolized for the benefit of the few, and here again is another case in which I am accused of taking a revolutionary attitude. People forget now that one hundred years ago there were public men of good character who advocated the nation selling its public lands in great quantities, so that the nation could get the most money out of it, and giving it to the men who could cultivate it for their own uses. We took the proper democratic ground that the land should be granted in small sections to the men who were actually to till it and live on it. Now, with the water-power, with the forests, with the mines, we are brought face to face with the fact that there are many people who will go with us in conserving the resources only if they are to be allowed to exploit them for their benefit. That is one of the fundamental reasons why the special interests should be driven out of politics. Of all the questions which can come before this nation, short of the actual preservation of its existence in a great war, there is none which compares in importance with the great central task of leaving this land even a better land for our descendants than it is for us, and training them into a better race to inhabit the land and pass it on. Conservation is a great moral issue, for it involves the patriotic duty of insuring the safety and continuance of the nation. (At Osawatomie, Kan., August 31, 1910.) *Mem. Ed.* XIX, 22; *Nat. Ed.* XVII, 15.

CONSERVATION—BASIS OF. We have become great because of the lavish use of our resources and we have just reason to be proud of our growth. But the time has come to inquire seriously what will happen when our forests are gone, when the coal, the iron, the oil, and the gas are exhausted, when the soils have been still further impoverished and washed into the streams, polluting the rivers, denuding the fields, and obstructing navigation. These questions do not relate only to the next century or to the next generation. It is time for us now as a nation to exercise the same reasonable foresight in dealing with our great natural resources that would be shown by any prudent man in conserving and widely using the property which contains the assurance of well-being for himself and his children. (At Conference on the Conservation of Natural Resources, Washington, May 13, 1908.) *Mem. Ed.* XVIII, 163; *Nat. Ed.* XVI, 124.

————————. Conservation and rural-life policies are really two sides of the same policy; and down at bottom this policy rests upon the fundamental law that neither man nor nation can prosper unless, in dealing with the present, thought is steadily taken for the future. (*Outlook*, August 27, 1910.) *Mem. Ed.* XVIII, 191; *Nat. Ed.* XVI, 146.

CONSERVATION — BEGINNINGS OF. The conservation movement was a direct outgrowth of the forest movement. It was nothing more than the application to our natural resources of the principles which had been worked out in connection with the forests. Without the basis of public sentiment which had been built up for the protection of the forests, and without the example of public foresight in the protection of this, one of the great natural resources, the conservation movement would have been impossible. (1913.) *Mem. Ed.* XXII, 463; *Nat. Ed.* XX, 398.

CONSERVATION — IMPORTANCE OF. There can be no greater issue than that of conservation in this country. Just as we must conserve our men, women, and children, so we must conserve the resources of the land on which they live. We must conserve the soil so that our children shall have a land that is more and not less fertile than that our fathers dwelt in. We must conserve the forests, not by disuse but by use, making them more valuable at the same time that we use them. We must conserve the mines. Moreover, we must insure so far as possible the use of certain types of great natural resources for the benefit of the people as a whole. The public should not alienate its fee in the water-power which will be of incalculable consequence as a source of power in the immediate future. The nation and the States within their several spheres should by immediate legislation keep the fee of the water-power, leasing its use only for a reasonable length of time on terms that will secure the interests of the public. Just as the nation has gone into the work of irrigation in the West, so it should go into the work of helping to reclaim the swamp-lands of the South. . . .

In the West, the forests, the grazing-lands, the reserves of every kind, should be so handled as to be in the interests of the actual settler, the actual home-maker. He should be encouraged to use them at once, but in such a way as to preserve and not exhaust them. (Before Progressive National Convention, Chicago, August 6, 1912.) *Mem. Ed.* XIX, 404; *Nat. Ed.* XVII, 293.

————————. I desire to make grateful acknowledgment to the men, both in and out of the Government service, who have prepared the first inventory of our natural resources. They have made it possible for this Nation to take a great step forward. Their work is helping us to see that the greatest questions before us are not partisan questions, but questions upon which men of all parties and all shades of opinion may be united for the common good. Among such questions, on the material side, the conservation of natural resources stands first. It is the bottom round of the ladder on our upward progress toward a condition in which the Nation as a whole, and its citizens as individuals, will set national efficiency and the public welfare before personal profit.

The policy of conservation is perhaps the most typical example of the general policies which this Government has made peculiarly its own during the opening years of the present century. The function of our Government is to insure to all its citizens, now and hereafter, their rights to life, liberty and the pursuit of happiness. If we of this generation destroy the resources from which our children would otherwise derive their livelihood, we reduce the capacity of our land to support a population, and so either degrade the standard of living or deprive the coming generations of their right to life on this continent. If we allow great industrial organizations to exercise unregulated control of the means of production and the necessaries of life, we deprive the Americans of today and of the future of industrial liberty, a right no less precious and vital than political freedom. Industrial liberty was a fruit of political liberty, and in turn has become one of its chief supports, and exactly as we stand for political democracy so we must stand for industrial democracy. (Message to Congress, January 22, 1909.) *Presidential Addresses and State Papers* VIII, 2093-2094.

CONSERVATION — LEADERS IN. Far and away the best work that has been done for the cause of conservation has been done by two men, James Garfield and Gifford Pinchot. I saw them work while I was President, and I can speak with the fullest knowledge of what they did. They took the policy of conservation when it was still nebulous and they applied it and made it work. They actually did the job that I and the others talked about. I know what they did because it was something in which I intensely believed, and yet it was something about which I did not have enough practical knowledge to enable me to work except through them and largely as the result of following out on my part their initiative. They did not confine themselves only to speaking. . . . They translated their words into actions; they actually did what we were all saying ought to be done; and our profound respect and appreciation is due them for their work. (At Harvard University, Cambridge, December 14, 1910.) *Mem. Ed.* XV, 558; *Nat. Ed.* XIII, 603-604.

CONSERVATION — PRINCIPLES OF. Now there is a considerable body of public opinion in favor of keeping for our children's children, as a priceless heritage, all the delicate beauty of the lesser and all the burly majesty of the mightier forms of wild life. We are fast learning that trees must not be cut down more rapidly than they are replaced; we have taken forward steps in learning that wild beasts and birds are by right not the property merely of the people alive to-day, but the property of the unborn generations, whose belongings we have no right to squander; and there are even faint signs of our growing to understand that wild flowers should be enjoyed unplucked where they grow, and that it is barbarism to ravage the woods and fields, rooting out the mayflower and breaking branches of dogwood as ornaments for automobiles filled with jovial but ignorant picnickers from cities. (*Outlook*, January 20, 1915.) *Mem. Ed.* XIV, 567; *Nat. Ed.* XII, 425.

CONSERVATION—PURPOSE OF. Surely our people do not understand even yet the rich heritage that is theirs. There can be nothing in the world more beautiful than the Yosemite, the groves of giant sequoias and redwoods, the Canyon of the Colorado, the Canyon of the Yellowstone, the Three Tetons; and our people should see to it that they are preserved for their children and their children's children forever, with their majestic beauty all unmarred. (1905.) *Mem. Ed.* III, 293; *Nat. Ed.*, III, 107.

——————. We do not intend that our natural resources shall be exploited by the few against the interests of the many, nor do we intend to turn them over to any man who will wastefully use them by destruction, and leave to those who come after us a heritage damaged by just so much. The man in whose interests we are working is the small farmer and settler, the man who works with his own hands, who is working not only for himself but for his children, and who wishes to leave to them the fruits of his labor. His permanent welfare is the prime factor for consideration in developing the policy of conservation; for our aim is to preserve our natural resources for the public as a whole, for the average man and the average woman who make up the body of the American people. (Before Progressive National Convention, Chicago, August 6, 1912.) *Mem. Ed.* XIX, 405; *Nat. Ed.* XVII, 294.

CONSERVATION—ROOSEVELT'S POLICY ON. I acted on the theory that the President could at any time in his discretion withdraw from entry any of the public lands of the United States and reserve the same for forestry, for water-power sites, for irrigation, and other public purposes. Without such action it would have been impossible to stop the activity of the land thieves. No one ventured to test its legality by lawsuit. (1913.) *Mem. Ed.* XXII, 412; *Nat. Ed.* XX, 353.

CONSERVATION AND PUBLIC RIGHTS. The rights of the public to the natural resources outweigh private rights, and must be given its first consideration. Until that time, in dealing with the national forests, and the public lands generally, private rights had almost uniformly been allowed to overbalance public rights. The change we made was right, and was vitally necessary; but, of course, it created bitter opposition from private interests. (1913.) *Mem. Ed.* XXII, 456; *Nat. Ed.* XX, 393.

CONSERVATION OF HUMAN LIFE. Let us remember, also, that conservation does not stop with the natural resources, but that the principle of making the best use of all we have requires with equal or greater insistence that we shall stop the waste of human life in industry and prevent the waste of human welfare which flows from the unfair use of concentrated power and wealth in the hands of men whose eagerness for profit blinds them to the cost of what they do. (Before Ohio Constitutional Convention, Columbus, February 21, 1912.) *Mem. Ed.* XIX, 165; *Nat. Ed.* XVII, 120.

CONSERVATION. *See also* ARBOR DAY; AUDUBON SOCIETIES; ELECTRIC POWER; FLOOD

Prevention; Forest; Game Preserves; Grand Canyon; Inland Waterways; Irrigation; Mineral Fuels; Mississippi River; Natural Resources; Oil; Pinchot, Gifford; Public Lands; Reclamation; Soil Conservation; Taft Administration; Trees; Water Power; Wild Life; Yellowstone Park.

CONSERVATIVES. I prefer to work with moderate, with rational, conservatives, provided only that they do in good faith strive forward toward the light. But when they halt and turn their backs to the light, and sit with the scorners on the seats of reaction, then I must part company with them. (At Carnegie Hall, New York City, March 20, 1912.) *Mem. Ed.* XIX, 221; *Nat. Ed.* XVII, 169.

CONSERVATIVES. *See also* Reactionaries.

CONSTITUTION. The Constitution belongs to the people and not the people to the Constitution. (Before National Conference of Progressive Service, Portsmouth, R. I., July 2, 1913.) *Mem. Ed.* XIX, 527; *Nat. Ed.* XVII, 387.

─────────. The Constitution that the members assembled in convention finally produced was not only the best possible one for America at that time, but it was also, in spite of its shortcomings, and taking into account its fitness for our own people and conditions, as well as its accordance with the principles of abstract right, probably the best that any nation has ever had, while it was beyond question a very much better one than any single member could have prepared. The particularist statesmen would have practically denied us any real union or efficient executive power; while there was hardly a Federalist member who would not, in his anxiety to avoid the evils from which we were suffering, have given us a government so centralized and aristocratic that it would have been utterly unsuited to a proud, liberty-loving, and essentially democratic race, and would have infallibly provoked a tremendous reactionary revolt. (1888.) *Mem. Ed.* VIII, 377; *Nat. Ed.* VII, 326.

─────────. It worked, primarily, because it was drawn up by practical politicians—by practical politicians who believed in decency, as well as in common sense. If they had been a set of excellent theorists, they would have drawn up a constitution which would have commended itself to other excellent theorists, but which would not have worked. If they had been base, corrupt men, mere opportunists, men who lacked elevating ideals, dishonest, cowardly, they would not have drawn up a document that would have worked at all. On the great scale the only practical politics is honest politics. The makers of our constitution were practical politicians, who were also sincere reformers, and as brave and upright as they were sensible. (At Trinity Methodist Church, Newburgh, N. Y., February 28, 1900.) Ferdinand C. Iglehart, *Theodore Roosevelt, The Man As I Knew Him.* (The Christian Herald, N. Y., 1919), p. 146.

CONSTITUTION — INTERPRETATION OF THE. It is the people, and not the judges, who are entitled to say what their constitution means, for the constitution is theirs, it belongs to them and not to their servants in office—any other theory is incompatible with the foundation principles of our government. If we, the people, choose to protect tenement-house dwellers in their homes, or women in sweat-shops and factories, or wage-earners in dangerous and unhealthy trades, or if we, the people, choose to define and regulate the conditions of corporate activity, it is for us, and not for our servants, to decide on the course we deem wise to follow. (Introduction dated July 1, 1912.) William L. Ransom, *Majority Rule and the Judiciary.* (Scribner's, N. Y., 1912), p. 6.

─────────. In the United States, where the courts are supreme over the legislature, it is vital that the people should keep in their own hands the right of interpreting their own Constitution when their public servants differ as to the interpretation.

I am well aware that every upholder of privilege, every hired agent or beneficiary of the special interests, including many well-meaning parlor reformers, will denounce all this as "Socialism" or "anarchy"—the same terms they used in the past in denouncing the movements to control the railways and to control public utilities. As a matter of fact, the propositions I make constitute neither anarchy nor Socialism, but, on the contrary, a corrective to Socialism and an antidote to anarchy. (Before Progressive National Convention, Chicago, August 6, 1912.) *Mem. Ed.* XIX, 370; *Nat. Ed.* XVII, 264.

─────────. I am not pleading for an extension of constitutional power. I am pleading that constitutional power which already exists shall be applied to new conditions which did not exist when the Constitution went into being. I ask that the national powers already conferred upon the National Government by the Constitution shall be so used as to bring national commerce and industry effectively under the authority of the Federal Government and thereby avert industrial chaos. My plea is not to bring about a condition of centralization. It is that the Government shall recognize a condition of centralization in a field where it already exists. When the national banking law was passed it represented in reality not centralization, but recognition of the fact that the country had so far advanced that the currency was already a matter of national concern and must be dealt with by the central authority at Washington. So it is with interstate industrialism and especially with the matter of interstate railroad operation to-day. Centralization has already taken place in the world of commerce and industry. All I ask is that the National Government look this fact in the face, accept it as a fact, and fit itself accordingly for a policy of supervision and control over this centralized commerce and industry. (At St. Louis, Mo., October 2, 1907.) *Presidential Addresses and State Papers* VI, 1404-1405.

CONSTITUTION — PERVERSION OF THE. We wish to see the people the masters of the court not to overthrow the Constitution but to overthrow those who have perverted the Constitution into an antisocial fetich, used to prevent our securing laws to protect the ordinary working man and working woman in their rights. (At New York City, February 12, 1913.) *Mem. Ed.* XIX, 495; *Nat. Ed.* XVII, 367.

CONSTITUTION — PROGRESSIVE STAND ON THE. We care for facts and not for formulas. We care for deeds and not for words. We recognize no sacred right of oppression. We recognize no divine right to work injustice. We stand for the Constitution. We recognize that one of its most useful functions is the protection of property. But we will not consent to make of the Constitution a fetich for the protection of fossilized wrong. We call the attention of those who thus interpret it to the fact that, in that great instrument of justice, life and liberty are put on a full level with property, indeed, are enumerated ahead of it in the order of their importance. (At Madison Square Garden, New York City, October 30, 1912.) *Mem. Ed.* XIX, 459; *Nat. Ed.* XVII, 337.

CONSTITUTION AS A CLOAK. These business men and lawyers were very adroit in using a word with fine and noble associations to cloak their opposition to vitally necessary movements for industrial fair play and decency. They made it evident that they valued the Constitution, not as a help to righteousness, but as a means for thwarting movements against unrighteousness. After my experience with them I became more set than ever in my distrust of those men, whether business men or lawyers, judges, legislators, or executive officers, who seek to make of the Constitution a fetich for the prevention of the work of social reform, for the prevention of work in the interest of those men, women, and children on whose behalf we should be at liberty to employ freely every governmental agency. (1913.) *Mem. Ed.* XXII, 241; *Nat. Ed.* XX, 206.

CONSTITUTION AS A STRAIT-JACKET. The men who disbelieve in the rule of the people, and who think that the people should be ruled by a part of them (for to call such a part "a representative part" is entirely meaningless), treat the Constitution as a strait-jacket for restraining an unruly patient—the people. We, on the contrary, treat the Constitution as an instrument designed to secure justice through giving full expression to the deliberate and well-thought-out judgment of the people. They are false friends of the people, and enemies of true constitutional government, who endeavor to twist the Constitution aside from this purpose. (At St. Louis, Mo., March 28, 1912.) *Mem. Ed.* XIX, 238; *Nat. Ed.* XVII, 175.

CONSTITUTION. *See also* COURTS; *Federalist, The;* FRANCHISE TAX; INTERSTATE COMMERCE; JUDGES; JUDICIARY; JUSTICE; LAW; LEGALISM; MARSHALL, JOHN; PARLIAMENTARY GOVERNMENT; RECALL; STATES' RIGHTS; SUPREME COURT; TARIFF; WILSON, JAMES.

CONSTITUTIONAL AMENDMENT. Judicial amendment of the Constitution is fatally easy. Popular amendment is so difficult that at best it needs ten or fifteen years to put it through. The theory of the Constitution against which we protest takes away from the people as a whole their sovereign right to govern themselves. It deposits this right to govern the people in the hands of well-meaning men who either are not elected by the people, or at least are not elected for any such purpose, who cannot be removed by the people, and who too often perversely pride themselves on having no direct responsibility to the people. We propose to make the process of Constitutional amendment far easier, speedier and simpler than at present. *Outlook,* November 15, 1913, p. 595.

CONSTITUTIONAL AMENDMENT — DIFFICULTY OF. The present process of constitutional amendment is too long, too cumbrous, and too uncertain to afford an adequate remedy, and, moreover, after the amendment has been carried, the law must once more be submitted to the same court which was, perhaps, originally at fault, in order to decide whether the new law comes within the amendment. (*Century,* October 1913.) Mem. Ed. XIX, 551; Nat. Ed. XVII, 406.

CONSTITUTIONAL AMENDMENT —NEED FOR.
The people themselves must be the ultimate makers of their own Constitution, and where their agents differ in their interpretations of the Constitution the people themselves should be given the chance, after full and deliberate judgment, authoritatively to settle what interpretation it is that their representatives shall thereafter adopt as binding.

Whenever in our constitutional system of government there exist general prohibitions that, as interpreted by the courts, nullify, or may be used to nullify, specific laws passed, and admittedly passed, in the interest of social justice, we are for such immediate law, or amendment to the Constitution, if that be necessary, as will thereafter permit a reference to the people of the public effect of such decision under forms securing full deliberation, to the end that the specific act of the legislative branch of the government thus judicially nullified, and such amendments thereof as come within its scope and purpose, may constitutionally be excepted by vote of the people from the general prohibitions, the same as if that particular act had been expressly excepted when the prohibition was adopted. This will necessitate the establishment of machinery for making much easier of amendment both the National and the several State Constitutions, especially with the view of prompt action on certain judicial decisions—action as specific and limited as that taken by the passage of the Eleventh Amendment to the National Constitution. (Before Progressive National Convention, Chicago, August 6, 1912.) Mem. Ed. XIX, 368; Nat. Ed. XVII, 263.

—————. We believe in the Constitution, and for that very reason we contemptuously thrust aside the efforts of the reactionaries to turn it into a fetich for the obstruction of justice. The Constitution was created to secure justice; and we refuse to allow it to be so perverted as to become a barrier between the people and justice. Every proposal we have made for applying and adapting the Constitution to our present needs is a proposal to save the Constitution by making it a more efficient instrument for securing justice for all the people. The so-called conservatives who object to our methods of applying the Constitution stand on an exact level with their predecessors, the so-called "conservatives" of fifty years ago, the men who opposed the Thirteenth Amendment on the ground that the "old Constitution" was good enough for them. Fifty years ago the "conservatives" championed a view of the Constitution which perpetuated chattel slavery for black men; the corresponding "conservatives" of to-day champion an interpretation of the Constitution which perpetuates industrial slavery for white women and children. (At Chicago, December 10, 1912.) Mem. Ed. XIX, 480; Nat. Ed. XVII, 355.

CONSTITUTIONAL AMENDMENT. See also FOURTEENTH AMENDMENT; INCOME TAX; NEGRO SUFFRAGE.

CONSTITUTIONAL CONVENTION — LEADERS OF.
They were great men; but it was less the greatness of mere genius than that springing from the union of strong, virile qualities with steadfast devotion to a high ideal. In certain respects they were ahead of all their European compeers; yet they preserved virtues forgotten or sneered at by the contemporaneous generation of transatlantic leaders. . . . The statesmen who met in 1787 were earnestly patriotic. They unselfishly desired the welfare of their countrymen. They were cool, resolute men, of strong convictions, with clear insight into the future. They were thoroughly acquainted with the needs of the community for which they were to act. Above all, they possessed that inestimable quality, so characteristic of their race, hard-headed common sense. Their theory of government was a very high one; but they understood perfectly that it had to be accommodated to the shortcomings of the average citizen. (1888.) Mem. Ed. VIII, 376-377; Nat Ed. VII, 325.

CONSTITUTIONAL CONVENTION. See also MADISON, JAMES; MORRIS, GOUVERNEUR.

CONSTITUTIONAL GOVERNMENT. See CROMWELL, OLIVER.

CONSTITUTIONALISM.
I am emphatically a believer in constitutionalism, and because of this fact I no less emphatically protest against any theory that would make of the constitution a means of thwarting instead of securing the absolute right of the people to rule themselves and to provide for their social and industrial well-being. . . .

It is a false constitutionalism, a false statesmanship, to endeavor by the exercise of a perverted ingenuity to seem to give the people full power and at the same time to trick them out of it. Yet this is precisely what is done in every case where the State permits its representatives, whether on the bench or in the legislature or in executive office, to declare that it has not the power to right grave social wrongs, or that any of the officers created by the people, and rightfully the servants of the people, can set themselves up to be the masters of the people. Constitution-makers should make it clear beyond shadow of doubt that the people in their legislative capacity have the power to enact into law any measure they deem necessary for the betterment of social and industrial conditions. The wisdom of framing any particular law of this kind is a proper subject of debate; but the power of the people to enact the law should not be subject to debate. To hold the contrary view is to be false to the cause of the people, to the cause of American democracy. (Before Ohio Constitutional Convention, Columbus, February 21, 1912.) *Mem. Ed.* XIX, 165, 167; *Nat. Ed.* XVII, 121, 123.

CONSTITUTIONS—OBJECT OF. All constitutions, those of the States no less than that of the nation, are designed, and must be interpreted and administered so as to fit human rights. . . .

The object of every American constitution worth calling such must be what it is set forth to be in the preamble to the National Constitution, "to establish justice," that is, to secure justice as between man and man by means of genuine popular self-government. If the constitution is successfully invoked to nullify the effort to remedy injustice, it is proof positive either that the constitution needs immediate amendment or else that it is being wrongfully and improperly construed. (Before Ohio Constitutional Convention, Columbus, February 21, 1912.) *Mem. Ed.* XIX, 165; *Nat Ed.* XVII, 121.

CONSULAR SERVICE. I feel most strongly that in the consular service, which stands entirely apart from the diplomatic service proper, entrance should be made by law into the lower grades and that the higher grades should be filled by a gradual process of weeding out and promotion; remembering, gentlemen, that the weeding-out process must not be interfered with. It is not any too easy, at best, to get rid of a kindly-natured elderly incompetent, and if you add to the difficulty by law, he then stays permanently. Make the entrance to the service as far as possible non-partisan and make it at the lower grades, so that desirable positions shall come to those who have rendered good and faithful service in the lower grades, so that those entering the lower grades shall feel that if they do well they have a long and worthy career ahead of them. (Before Consular Reform Association, White House, March 14, 1906.) *Presidential Addresses and State Papers* IV, 693.

CONSUMER. See FARMER AND CONSUMER.

CONTRABAND—TRADE IN. I think Great Britain is now showing great courtesy and forbearance. I believe that she has done things to our ships that ought not to have been done, but I am not aware that she is now doing them. I am not discussing this question from the standpoint of right. I am discussing it from the standpoint of expediency, in the interest of Great Britain. Our trade, under existing circumstances, is of vastly more service to you and France than to Germany. I think I under-estimate the case when I say it is ten times as valuable to the Allies as to Germany. There are circumstances, under which it might become not merely valuable but vital. I am not a naval man, I do not know what the possibilities of the submarine are. But they have accomplished some notable feats; and if they should now begin to destroy ships carrying foodstuffs to Great Britain, the effect might be not merely serious but appalling. Under such conditions, it would be of the utmost consequence to England to have accepted the most extreme view the United States could advance as to her right to ship cargoes unmolested. Even although this possibility, which I do not regard as more than a very remote possibility, is in reality wholly impossible, it yet remains true that the trade in contraband is overwhelmingly to the advantage of England, France, and Russia, because of your command of the seas. You assume that this command gives you the right to make the advantage still more overwhelming. I ask you merely to take careful thought, so that you shall not excite our Government, even wrongfully, to act in such a way that it would diminish or altogether abolish the great advantage you now have. (To Sir Edward Grey, January 22, 1915.) *Twenty-Five Years,* by Viscount Grey of Fallodon. (Hodder & Stoughton, London, 1925), II, 147.

CONTRABAND AND BLOCKADE. It is utterly impossible, in view of the immense rapidity of the change in modern war conditions, to formulate abstract policies about such matters as contraband and blockades. These policies must be actually tested in order to see how they work. Both England and the United States have reversed themselves in this matter on several different occasions. This is interesting as a matter of history, but from no other standpoint. If we are honorable and intelligent we will follow the course in this matter which, under existing conditions at this time, seems most likely to work justice in the immediate future. (Kansas City *Star,* November 22, 1918.) *Mem. Ed.* XXI, 428; *Nat. Ed.* XIX, 387.

CONTRABAND. *See also* MUNITIONS; NEUTRAL RIGHTS; NEUTRAL TRADE.

CONTRACT—LIBERTY OF. Probably the chief obstacle in the way of taking . . . wise collective action lies in the mental attitude of those who still adhere to the doctrinaire theory of eighteenth-century individualism, and treat as a cardinal virtue the right to absolute liberty of contract—and of course, carried out logically, the theory of absolute liberty of contract simply means the legalization of all kinds of slavery. It is essential that the nation and the State should be able to forbid the exercise of that kind of pseudo-liberty which means the abridgment of real liberty. (*Outlook,* February 4, 1911.) *Mem. Ed.* XIX, 104; *Nat. Ed.* XVII, 69.

CONTRACT—RIGHT OF PRIVATE. I am not an empiricist; I would no more deny that sometimes human affairs can be much bettered by legislation than I would affirm that they can always be so bettered. I would no more make a fetich of unrestricted individualism than I would admit the power of the State offhand and radically to reconstruct society. It may become necessary to interfere even more than we have done with the right of private contract, and to shackle cunning as we have shackled force. All I insist upon is that we must be sure of our ground before trying to get any legislation at all, and that we must not expect too much from this legislation, nor refuse to better ourselves a little because we cannot accomplish everything at a jump. (*Review of Reviews,* January 1897.) *Mem. Ed.* XVI, 377; *Nat. Ed.* XIII, 161.

CONTRACT. *See also* COLLECTIVE BARGAINING; INDUSTRIAL ARBITRATION; LABOR.

CONVICT LABOR. The State must get away from the theory that financial profit from its prisoners is its first consideration. The protection of society is the primary purpose of imprisonment and the next purpose is reformation. The penalty must be wise and humane and the prisoner must be made, as far as possible, to be self-supporting while in prison or under imprisonment. (*Annals* of American Academy of Pol. and Soc. Science, March 1913.) *Mem. Ed.* XVIII, 610; *Nat. Ed.* XVI, 441.

COOPER, JAMES F. After all, there are none to whom we so readily come back as to our own old favorites. Cooper, of course, is a writer to be read and reread again and again. His land fights are good; but his sea fights are unapproached. There is nothing else in naval fiction like some of his boat attacks and single-ship actions, such as the frigate's running fight and hair-breadth escape in "The Pilot"; while the vividly dramatic description of the cruising, the manoeuvring, and the final grapple between the rival fleets in the "Two Admirals," commemorates, as no other description in either history or novel begins to commemorate, a typical pitched battle at sea, in the days of the white-winged ships of the line. (*Cosmopolitan,* December 1892.) *Mem. Ed.* XIV, 374; *Nat. Ed.* XII, 308.

COOPERATION IN LIFE. To be patronized is as offensive as to be insulted. No one of us cares permanently to have some one else conscientiously striving to do him good; what we want is to work with that some one else for the good of both of us—any man will speedily find that other people can benefit him just as much as he can benefit them. (1913.) *Mem. Ed.* XXII, 75; *Nat. Ed.* XX, 65.

COOPERATION IN NATIONAL LIFE. We cannot possibly do our best work as a nation unless all of us know how to act in combination as well as how to act each individually for himself. (At Minnesota State Fair, September 2, 1901.) *Mem. Ed.* XV, 331; *Nat. Ed.* XIII, 471.

COOPERATION IN POLITICS. Of course, in a government like ours, a man can accomplish anything only by acting in combination with others, and equally, of course, a number of people can act together only by each sacrificing certain of his beliefs or prejudices. (*Forum,* July 1894.) *Mem. Ed.* XV, 43; *Nat. Ed.* XIII, 30.

COOPERATION. *See also* COLLECTIVE ACTION; COLLECTIVISM; FARMER COOPERATION; FELLOWSHIP; INDUSTRIAL COOPERATION; POLITICS.

COOPERATIVES. *See* FARMER COOPERATIVES.

COPPERHEADS. We cannot but admire at least the courage of those gallant soldiers of the South, who, from a terribly mistaken sense of duty, fought us so grimly and so stubbornly for four long years, but we feel nothing but contempt for their cowardly allies of the North, the dough-face and the copperhead, who had

COPYRIGHT LAW. Every reading man, every man interested in the growth of American literature, and finally, every man who cares for the honor of the American name and is keenly desirous that no reproach shall be rightly cast upon it, must rejoice that we have the present Copyright Law. It was won in the teeth of a violent and ignorant opposition, and in spite of the fact that many who had been supposed to be its friends turned against it at the last moment, on the shallow pretense that it did not go as far as they desired. It certainly should be a matter of congratulation for Harvard that her representatives were among the leaders in the fight on its behalf.

In the copyright struggle, as in all other Congressional contests, there were many different kinds of difficulties to be encountered. In the first place, there was undoubtedly a kernel of dishonest opposition to the bill, due to the presence of an active lobby, subsidized by certain third-rate newspaper and book concerns. In the next place, there was a mass of inert indifference to be overcome. Thirdly, the friends of the bill had to meet the bitter opposition of perfectly honest and very able, though, as we believe, entirely misguided, opponents of the measure,—men like Roger Q. Mills, for instance, whose character and capacity rightly gave them great weight in Congress. Finally, there was the need of guarding against the crankiness of certain friends of the measure, which actually threatened to defeat the whole bill merely because it contained some features to propitiate the printers,—features which were absolutely essential to its passage, and which were entirely non-essential when viewed from the standpoint either of abstract right or of expediency. . . . No one who was not himself present in the Capitol during these final, vital hours of the fight can appreciate the tact, resolution, energy, and downright hard work of the men who were prominent in passing the bill. This had to be done with absolute disinterestedness. No man did anything for the Copyright Bill from selfish motives. It was pressed by a body of men without political influence, and it was passed solely as a measure of justice, and from the highest motives. The men who were instrumental in passing it deserve to receive the credit always attaching to effective and disinterested work for a worthy ideal. *Harvard Graduates' Magazine,* October 1892, pp. 5-6.

CORPORATIONS—BRIBERY BY. If . . . you for a generation permit big corporations to purchase favors to which they are not entitled you will breed up a race of public men and business men who accept that condition of things as normal. And then, my friends, when you finally wake up, I wish you would remember that, great though their blame may be, your blame is even greater for having permitted such a condition of things to arise.

When the awakening comes, you will undoubtedly have to change the machinery of the law in order to meet the conditions that have become so bad. (At Pacific Theological Seminary, Spring 1911.) *Mem. Ed.* XV, 626; *Nat. Ed.* XIII, 659.

CORPORATIONS—BUREAU OF. The preliminary work of the Bureau of Corporations in the department has shown the wisdom of its creation. Publicity in corporate affairs will tend to do away with ignorance, and will afford facts upon which intelligent action may be taken. Systematic, intelligent investigation is already developing facts the knowledge of which is essential to a right understanding of the needs and duties of the business world. The corporation which is honestly and fairly organized, whose managers in the conduct of its business recognize their obligation to deal squarely with their stockholders, their competitors, and the public, has nothing to fear from such supervision. The purpose of this bureau is not to embarrass or assail legitimate business, but to aid in bringing about a better industrial condition—a condition under which there shall be obedience to law and recognition of public obligation by all corporations, great or small. (Third Annual Message, Washington, December 7, 1903.) *Mem. Ed.* XVII, 197-198; *Nat. Ed.* XV, 170.

——————. The policy of the bureau is to accomplish the purpose of its creation by co-operation, not antagonism; by making constructive legislation, not destructive prosecution, the immediate object of its inquiries; by conservative investigation of law and fact, and by refusal to issue incomplete and hence necessarily inaccurate reports. Its policy being thus one of open inquiry into, and not attack upon, business, the bureau has been able to gain not only the confidence, but, better still, the co-operation of men engaged in legitimate business.

The bureau offers to the Congress the means of getting at the cost of production of our various great staples of commerce. (Fourth Annual Message, Washington, December 6,

1904.) *Mem. Ed.* XVII, 261; *Nat. Ed.* XV, 224.

———————. The Federal Bureau of Corporations is an agency of first importance. Its powers, and, therefore, its efficiency, as well as that of the Interstate Commerce Commission, should be largely increased. We have a right to expect from the Bureau of Corporations and from the Interstate Commerce Commission a very high grade of public service. We should be as sure of the proper conduct of the interstate railways and the proper management of interstate business as we are now sure of the conduct and management of the national banks, and we should have as effective supervision in one case as in the other. (At Osawatomie, Kan., August 31, 1910.) *Mem. Ed.* XIX, 18; *Nat. Ed.* XVII, 12.

CORPORATIONS — COMMISSION CONTROL OF. Such a commission, with the power I advocate, would put a stop to abuses of big corporations and small corporations alike; it would draw the line on conduct and not on size; it would destroy monopoly, and make the biggest business man in the country conform squarely to the principles laid down by the American people, while at the same time giving fair play to the little man and certainty of knowledge as to what was wrong and what was right both to big man and little man. (1913.) *Mem. Ed.* XXII, 493; *Nat. Ed.* XX, 424.

CORPORATIONS — CONTROL OF. Undoubtedly there is need of regulation by the Government, in the interest of the public, of these great corporations which in modern life have shown themselves to be the most efficient business implements, and which are, therefore, the implements commonly employed by the owners of large fortunes. The corporation is the creature of the State. It should always be held accountable to some sovereign, and this accountability should be real and not sham. Therefore, in my judgment, all corporations doing an interstate business, and this means the great majority of the largest corporations, should be held accountable to the Federal Government, because their accountability should be co-extensive with their field of action. But most certainly we should not strive to prevent or limit corporate activity. We should strive to secure such effective supervision over it, such power of regulation over it, as to enable us to guarantee that its activity will be exercised only in ways beneficial to the public. (At Atlanta, Ga., October 20, 1905.) *Presidential Addresses and State Papers* IV, 492-493.

———————. The movement for Government control of the great business corporations is no more a move against liberty than a movement to put a stop to violence is a movement against liberty. . . . The huge irresponsible corporation which demands liberty from the supervision of Government agents stands on the same ground as the less dangerous criminal of the streets who wishes liberty from police interference. *Outlook,* June 19, 1909, p. 394.

———————. I wish to see the great corporations regulated. I wish to see the hand of the State, the hand of the nation, put on to the great corporations doing business on a gigantic scale, and I wish to see the movement for securing such collective supervision and control of the great corporations take place under the lead of sober, responsible men who shall be anxious to conserve the just rights of property and at the same time to remember that the rights of man must be paramount in any republic such as ours. (Before Chamber of Commerce, New Haven, Conn., December 13, 1910.) *Mem. Ed.* XVIII, 105; *Nat. Ed.* XVI, 88.

———————. The American people demand that efficient and genuine control over great corporations be exercised by the government. They will not permanently tolerate the failure to meet this rightful and proper demand. If the National Government, through the national judiciary, confines itself to mere negation, and by one series of decisions denies the National Government power to interfere in the matter, while at the same time by another series of decisions it tries to prevent the States from interfering, the result can only be to cause damage from every standpoint; for confidence in the National Government will be shaken, it will prove well-nigh impossible to prevent States from acting when they have a furiously indignant public opinion behind them, and there will be a real popular loss of confidence in the courts, a loss of confidence by the people at large, which is in no way permanently offset by exaggerated and hysterical praise of the courts by the organs of the capitalistic classes. . . . The power over these great corporations must be exercised. The people will not permit these enormous corporations to be free from governmental control, for the simple reason that they instinctively recognize the fact that unless the great corporations are controlled by the government they will themselves completely control the government. All that the national authorities, legislative, judicial, and executive alike, can determine is whether they shall give effect to the plain intent of the Constitution, and really and efficiently and not with academic ineptitude exercise this power, or whether they shall shelter themselves behind quibbles and technicalities and fail to exercise the power, with the certainty of seeing in a few years the effort to exercise it made by the several States, and chaos and disaster follow. (*Outlook,* March 11, 1911.) *Mem. Ed.* XIX, 138, 139; *Nat. Ed.* XVII, 97, 99.

———————. It may well be that in the end Government control of these great inter-State corporations may have to go much further than is indicated by the present Government control over the railways; but, in any event, the only possible satisfactory method of dealing with these great corporations of a monopolistic trend which are not railways is to follow the lines along which the Nation has gone in dealing with those of them which are railways, altering and developing the policy as conditions and events shall justify. Our prime object must be to have the regulation accomplished by continuous administrative action, and not by necessarily intermittent lawsuits. *Outlook,* June 3, 1911, p. 240.

———————. All the wise friends of the effort to secure governmental control of corporations know that this government control must be exercised through administrative and not judicial officers if it is to be effective. Everything possible should be done to minimize the chance of appealing from the decisions of the administrative officer to the courts. But it is not possible constitutionally, and probably would not be desirable anyhow, completely to abolish the appeal. (1913.) *Mem. Ed.* XXII, 496; *Nat. Ed.* XX, 427.

CORPORATIONS—MANAGEMENT OF. Great corporations are necessary, and only men of great and singular mental power can manage such corporations successfully, and such men must have great rewards. But these corporations should be managed with due regard to the interests of the public as a whole. Where this can be done under the present laws it must be done. Where these laws come short others should be enacted to supplement them. (Fourth Annual Message, Washington, December 6, 1904.) *Mem. Ed.* XVII, 258; *Nat. Ed.* XV, 222.

CORPORATIONS — POLITICAL ACTIVITY OF. There can be no effective control of corporations while their political activity remains. To put an end to it will be neither a short nor an easy task, but it can be done. . . . It is necessary that laws should be passed to prohibit the use of corporate funds directly or indirectly for political purposes; it is still more necessary that such laws should be thoroughly enforced. Corporate expenditures for political purposes, and especially such expenditures by public-service corporations, have supplied one of the principal sources of corruption in our political affairs. (At Osawatomie, Kan., August 31, 1910.) *Mem. Ed.* XIX, 17; *Nat. Ed.* XVII, 11.

CORPORATIONS—PROCEEDINGS AGAINST. I do not believe in a system of law in which the object of Governmental proceeding requires the dissolution of the corporation or the confiscation of its property, which may be ruinous to the public as well as to the corporation. The proceeding should be, in substance, to declare any corporation an injurious monopoly, and when that declaration should be definitely affirmed by the proper body, whatever it might be, to subject the corporation to thoroughgoing Governmental control as to rates, prices and general conduct. The present penalties for misbehavior—fines, the occasional imprisonment of men (usually subordinates), or the usual ineffectual dissolution of the corporation—are never wholly adequate, and are apt to be entirely inadequate. What is necessary is to permit the Government, when there is a definite proof that a given corporation is acting as a monopoly and is behaving in an actually potentially injurious manner, to assume thoroughgoing supervision over it—such supervision and control as that which is, and still more as that which will be, exercised by the Inter-State Commerce Commission over our railways. *Outlook,* January 28, 1911, p. 147.

———————. Any corporation, big or little, which has gained its position by unfair methods and by interference with the rights of others, which has raised prices or limited output in improper fashion and been guilty of demoralizing and corrupt practices, should not only be broken up, but it should be made the business of some competent governmental body by constant supervision to see that it does not come together again, save under such strict control as to insure the community against all danger of a repetition of the bad conduct. (Before Ohio Constitutional Convention, Columbus, February 21, 1912.) *Mem. Ed.* XIX, 174; *Nat. Ed.* XVII, 128.

CORPORATIONS — PROTECTION AGAINST. We do not propose to do injustice to any man, but we do propose adequately to guarantee the people against injustice by the mighty corporations which make up the predominant and characteristic feature of modern industrial life. (At Louisville, Ky., April 3, 1912.) *Mem. Ed.* XIX, 249; *Nat. Ed.* XVII, 184.

CORPORATIONS — PUBLICITY AND THE. Publicity can do no harm to the honest corporation. The only corporation that has cause to dread it is the corporation which shrinks from the light, and about the welfare of such corporations we need not be oversensitive. (Third Annual Message, Washington, December 7, 1903.) *Mem. Ed.* XVII, 199; *Nat. Ed.* XV, 171.

CORPORATIONS — RESPONSIBILITY OF. In order to insure a healthy social and industrial life, every big corporation should be held responsible by, and be accountable to, some sovereign strong enough to control its conduct. I am in no sense hostile to corporations. This is an age of combination, and any effort to prevent all combination will be not only useless, but in the end vicious, because of the contempt for law which the failure to enforce law inevitably produces. (Fifth Annual Message, Washington, December 5, 1905.) *Mem. Ed.* XVII, 317; *Nat. Ed.* XV, 271.

CORPORATIONS—ROLE OF. Our aim is not to do away with corporations; on the contrary, these big aggregations are an inevitable development of modern industrialism, and the effort to destroy them would be futile unless accomplished in ways that would work the utmost mischief to the entire body politic. We can do nothing of good in the way of regulating and supervising these corporations until we fix clearly in our minds that we are not attacking the corporations, but endeavoring to do away with any evil in them. We are not hostile to them; we are merely determined that they shall be so handled as to subserve the public good. We draw the line against misconduct, not against wealth. (Second Annual Message, Washington, December 2, 1902.) *Mem. Ed.* XVII, 164; *Nat. Ed.* XV, 141.

CORPORATIONS—SIZE OF. Size may, and in my opinion does, make a corporation fraught with potential menace to the community; and may, and in my opinion should, therefore make it incumbent upon the community to exercise through its administrative (not merely through its judicial) officers a strict supervision over the corporation in order to see that it does not go wrong; but the size in itself does not signify wrong-doing, and should not be held to signify wrong-doing. *Outlook*, November 18, 1911, p. 654.

CORPORATIONS — TAXATION OF. There is no reason whatever for refusing to tax a corporation because by its own acts it has created a burden of charges under which it staggers. The extravagant man who builds a needlessly large house nevertheless pays taxes on the house; and the corporation which has to pay great sums of interest owing to juggling transactions in the issue of stocks and bonds has just as little right to consideration. (Annual Message as Governor, Albany, January 3, 1900.) *Mem. Ed.* XVII, 53; *Nat. Ed.* XV, 46.

————. Offhand, it would seem to me that a tax on the net receipts of corporations would be the best way out on the Income Tax business. (To H. C. Lodge, July 26, 1909.) Lodge *Letters* II, 342.

CORPORATIONS — TREATMENT OF. The corporation must be protected, must be given its rights, but it must be prevented from doing wrong; and its managers must be held in strict accountability when it does wrong; and it must be deprived of all secret influence in our public life. (Before New York Republican State Convention, Saratoga, September 27, 1910.) *Mem. Ed.* XIX, 35; *Nat. Ed.* XVII, 27.

————. When you finally revolt, as revolt you will and must against being ruled by corporations, and when you assume the power over them, then is the time to remember that it is your duty to be honest to them just as much as to exact honesty from them; and that if you are guilty of the folly and iniquity of doing wrong at their expense, you have not made a step in advance, even though you have stopped them from doing wrong at your expense. (At Pacific Theological Seminary, Spring 1911.) *Mem. Ed.* XV, 626; *Nat. Ed.* XIII, 660.

————. Experience has proved that we cannot afford to leave the great corporations to determine for themselves without governmental supervision how they shall treat their employees, their rivals, their customers, and the general public. But experience has no less shown that it is as fatal for the agents of government to be unjust to the corporation as to fail to secure justice from them. In dealing with railways, for example, it is just as important that rates should not be too low as that they should not be too high. (*Century Magazine,* October 1913.) *Mem. Ed.* XIX, 548; *Nat. Ed.* XVII, 404.

CORPORATIONS AND THE LAW. The man who by swindling or wrong-doing acquires great wealth for himself at the expense of his fellow, stands as low morally as any predatory mediæval nobleman and is a more dangerous member of society. Any law, and any method of construing the law which will enable the community to punish him, either by taking away his wealth or by imprisonment, should be welcomed. Of course, such laws are even more needed in dealing with great corporations or trusts than with individuals. They are needed quite as much for the sake of honest corporations as for the sake of the public. The corporation that manages its affairs honestly has a right to demand protection against the dishonest corporation. We do not wish to put any burden on honest corporations. Neither do we wish to put an unnecessary burden of responsibility on enterprising men for acts which are immaterial; they should be relieved from such burdens, but held to a rigid financial accountability for acts that mislead the upright investor or stockholder, or defraud the public. (Annual Message as Governor, Albany, January 3, 1900.) *Mem. Ed.* XVII, 52; *Nat. Ed.* XV, 45.

CORPORATIONS AND THEIR STOCKHOLDERS. Nothing is sillier than this outcry on behalf of the "innocent stockholders" in the corporations. We are besought to pity the Standard Oil Company for a fine relatively far less great than the fines every day inflicted in the police courts upon multitudes of push-cart peddlers and other petty offenders, whose woes never extort one word from the men whose withers are wrung by the woes of the mighty. The stockholders have the control of the corporation in their own hands. The corporation officials are elected by those holding the majority of the stock and can keep office only by having behind them the good-will of these majority stockholders. They are not entitled to the slightest pity if they deliberately choose to resign into the hands of great wrong-doers the control of the corporations in which they own the stock. Of course innocent people have become involved in these big corporations and suffer because of the misdeeds of their criminal associates. Let these innocent people be careful not to invest in corporations where those in control are not men of probity, men who respect the laws; above all let them avoid the men who make it their one effort to evade or defy the laws. But if these honest, innocent people are in the majority in any corporation they can immediately resume control and throw out of the directory the men who misrepresent them. (To Charles J. Bonaparte, January 2, 1908.) *Mem. Ed.* XXII, 517; *Nat. Ed.* XX, 445.

CORPORATIONS. *See also* BUSINESS; COMBINATIONS; DIVIDENDS; FRANCHISE TAX; GOVERNMENT CONTROL; INDUSTRIAL COMMISSION; INSURANCE COMPANIES; INTERSTATE COMMERCE COMMISSION; KNIGHT CASE; MONOPOLIES; NORTHERN SECURITIES CASE; RAILROADS; SHERMAN ANTI-TRUST ACT; SQUARE DEAL; STOCK-WATERING; TRUSTS.

CORRUPTION. It is an even graver offense to sin against the commonwealth than to sin against an individual. The man who debauches our public life, whether by malversation of funds in office, by the actual bribery of voters or of legislators, or by the corrupt use of the offices as spoils wherewith to reward the unworthy and the vicious for their noxious and interested activity in the baser walks of political life—this man is a greater foe to our well-being as a nation than is even the defaulting cashier of a bank, or the betrayer of a private trust. (*Forum,* July 1894.) *Mem. Ed.* XV, 40; *Nat. Ed.* XIII, 27.

―――――――. Corruption in every form is the arch-enemy of this Republic, the arch-enemy of free institutions and of government by the people, an even more dangerous enemy than the open lawlessness of violence, because it works in hidden and furtive fashion. We are against corruption in politics; we are against corruption in business; and, above all, and with all our strength, we are against the degrading alliance of crooked business and crooked politics, the alliance which adds strength to the already powerful corrupt boss and to the already powerful corrupt head of big business, and which makes them in their dual capacity enemies against whom every patriotic man should stand with unwavering firmness. (Before New York Republican State Convention, Saratoga, September 27, 1910.) *Mem. Ed.* XIX, 34; *Nat. Ed.* XVII, 26.

―――――――. There is no greater duty than to war on the corrupt and unprincipled boss, and on the corrupt and unprincipled business man; and for the matter of that, on the corrupt and unprincipled labor leader also, and on the corrupt and unprincipled editor, and on any one else who is corrupt and unprincipled. (1913.) *Mem. Ed.* XXII, 189; *Nat. Ed.* XX, 162.

CORRUPTION—CAUSE OF. I do not believe that you have struck the right cause, nor come near striking the right cause of our corruption, and I think you are trying to cure a symptom and not a cause. I am heartily with you in the campaign for the abolition of privilege. Curiously enough, events have forced me to make my chief fights in public life against privilege, but I know from actual experience—from experience of the most intimate kind in the little village of Oyster Bay and out in the West at Medora, when there was not a special privilege of any kind in either place—that what is needed is the fundamental fight for morality. (To Steffens, June 12, 1908.) *The Letters of Lincoln Steffens.* (Harcourt, Brace & Co., N. Y., 1938), I, 198-199.

CORRUPTION—DANGER OF. No republic can last if corruption is allowed to eat into its public life. No republic can last if the private citizens sit supinely by and either encourage or tolerate corruption among their representatives. (Before the Hamilton Club, Chicago, September 8, 1910.) *Mem. Ed.* XV, 449; *Nat. Ed.* XIII, 538.

CORRUPTION AND CAPITALISM. The capitalist who thinks it is to the interest of his class to have in high office a corrupt man who will serve his class interest, is laying up for himself and for his children a day of terrible retribution; for if that type of capitalist has his way long enough he will persuade the whole community that the interest of the community is bound up in overthrowing every man in public office who serves property, even though he serves it honestly. The corrupt capitalist may help himself for the moment, and he may be defended by others of his own class on grounds of expediency; but in the end he works fearful damage to his fellow. (At Pacific Theological Seminary, Spring 1911.) *Mem. Ed.* XV, 621; *Nat. Ed.* XIII, 656.

————. There are localities, and many of them, where capitalists are in very fact the prime offenders; and a prime need of our political, social, and economic life is to suppress corrupt, and control overgrown, capitalism. But no war for decency will ever avail for permanent good unless we attack the scoundrel simply *because he is a scoundrel*, without regard to whether he is rich or poor. *Outlook*, November 11, 1911, p. 611.

CORRUPTION IN BUSINESS AND POLITICS. Just as the blackmailer and the bribe-giver stand on the same evil eminence of infamy, so the man who makes an enormous fortune by corrupting legislators and municipalities and fleecing his stockholders and the public stands on a level with the creature who fattens on the blood money of the gambling house, the saloon, and the brothel. . . . Corrupt business and corrupt politics act and react, with ever-increasing debasement, one on the other; the rebate-taker, the franchise-trafficker, the manipulator of securities, the purveyor and protector of vice, the blackmailing ward boss, the ballot-box stuffer, the demagogue, the mob leader, the hired bully and mankiller, all alike work at the same web of corruption, and all alike should be abhorred by honest men. (To Charles J. Bonaparte, January 2, 1908.) *Mem. Ed.* XXII, 520; *Nat. Ed.* XX, 447.

————. Corruption in any form, whether in the world of politics or in the world of business, represents an offense against the community of so grave a character that the offender should be hunted down as a criminal; and the greater his ability and success, the greater is the wrong he has committed, and the heavier should be his punishment. The sneering indifference to, or connivance at, corruption is almost as bad as corruption itself. Honesty, rigid honesty, is a root virtue; and if not present no other virtue can atone for its lack. But we cannot afford to be satisfied with the negative virtue of not being corrupt. We need the virile, positive virtues. *Outlook*, November 8, 1913, p. 528.

CORRUPTION. *See also* Boss; Bribery; Civil Service Reform; Dante; Demagogue; Elections; Honesty; Machine; Municipal Ownership; Politics; Social Conditions; Spoils System.

CORTELYOU, GEORGE B. *See* Campaign Contributions.

COSMOPOLITANISM. *See* Americanism; Citizenship; Internationalism; Morris, Gouverneur; Nationalism; Patriotism.

COSMOPOLITANS. There is no more hopeless creature from the point of view of humanity than the person who calls himself a cosmopolitan, who spreads himself out over the whole world, with the result that he spreads himself out so thin that he comes through in large spots. (Before American Academy and National Institute of Arts and Letters, New York,

[115]

November 16, 1916.) *Mem. Ed.* XIV, 451; *Nat. Ed.* XII, 327.

——————. One may fall very far short of treason and yet be an undesirable citizen in the community. The man who becomes Europeanized, who loses his power of doing good work on this side of the water, and who loses his love for his native land, is not a traitor; but he is a silly and undesirable citizen. He is as emphatically a noxious element in our body politic as is the man who comes here from abroad and remains a foreigner. Nothing will more quickly or more surely disqualify a man from doing good work in the world than the acquirement of that flaccid habit of mind which its possessors style cosmopolitanism. (*Forum*, April 1894.) *Mem. Ed.* XV, 20; *Nat. Ed.* XIII, 17.

COSMOPOLITANS. See also EXPATRIATES; FOREIGN WAYS.

COST OF LIVING. See TARIFF; TRUSTS.

COUGAR. No American beast has been the subject of so much loose writing or of such wild fables as the cougar. Even its name is unsettled. In the Eastern States it is usually called panther or painter; in the Western States, mountain-lion, or, toward the South, Mexican lion. The Spanish-speaking people usually call it simply lion. It is, however, sometimes called cougar in the West and Southwest of our country, and in South America, puma. As it is desirable, where possible, not to use a name that is misleading and is already appropriated to some entirely different animal, it is best to call it cougar.

The cougar is a very singular beast, shy and elusive to an extraordinary degree, very cowardly and yet blood-thirsty and ferocious, varying wonderfully in size, and subject, like many other beasts, to queer freaks of character in occasional individuals. This fact of individual variation in size and temper is almost always ignored in treating of the animal; whereas it ought never to be left out of sight. (1905.) *Mem. Ed.* III, 17; *Nat. Ed.* II, 405.

——————. The cougar sometimes stalks its prey, and sometimes lies in wait for it beside a game trail or drinking-pool—very rarely indeed does it crouch on the limb of a tree. When excited by the presence of game it is sometimes very bold. . . . The cougar roams over long distances, and often changes its hunting-ground, perhaps remaining in one place two or three months until the game is exhausted, and then shifting to another. When it does not lie in wait it usually spends most of the night, winter and summer, in prowling restlessly around the places where it thinks it may come across prey, and it will patiently follow an animal's trail. There is no kind of game, save the full-grown grizzly and buffalo, which it does not at times assail and master. (1893.) *Mem. Ed.* II, 313; *Nat. Ed.* II, 269.

——————. Fables aside, the cougar is a very interesting creature. It is found from the cold, desolate plains of Patagonia to north of the Canadian line, and lives alike among the snow-clad peaks of the Andes and in the steaming forests of the Amazon. Doubtless careful investigation will disclose several varying forms in an animal found over such immense tracts of country and living under such utterly diverse conditions. But in its essential habits and traits, the big, slinking, nearly unicolored cat seems to be much the same everywhere, whether living in mountain, open plain, or forest, under arctic cold or tropic heat. When the settlements become thick, it retires to dense forest, dark swamp, or inaccessible mountain gorge, and moves about only at night. In wilder regions it not infrequently roams during the day and ventures freely into the open. Deer are its customary prey where they are plentiful, bucks, does, and fawns being killed indifferently. Usually the deer is killed almost instantaneously, but occasionally there is quite a scuffle, in which the cougar may get bruised, though, as far as I know, never seriously. It is also a dreaded enemy of sheep, pigs, calves, and especially colts, and when pressed by hunger a big male cougar will kill a full-grown horse or cow, moose or wapiti. It is the special enemy of mountain-sheep. (1905.) *Mem. Ed.* III, 20; *Nat. Ed.* II, 408.

COUNTERFEITING. See STOCK-WATERING.

COUNTRY LIFE—IMPROVEMENT OF. I think that the country school should be made a social centre. I think that the time has come when our people must consider very seriously the question of trying to help the men of the country districts in building up their country life so as to make it not only equally attractive with city life, but equally full of opportunity. It can certainly be done, and while it must be done primarily by the farmers themselves—by the men who live in the open country, yet they must be stimulated to feel the need of doing it, and it is our duty to help them in every way in the effort to do it. (Before Iowa State Teachers' Association, Des Moines, November

4, 1910.) *Mem. Ed.* XVIII, 451; *Nat. Ed.* XVI, 336.

COUNTRY LIFE. *See also* AGRICULTURE; CITY; FARM LIFE; TAFT ADMINISTRATION.

COUNTRY LIFE COMMISSION. The first step ever taken toward the solution of these problems [of rural life] was taken by the Country Life Commission appointed by me, opposed with venomous hostility by the foolish reactionaries in Congress, and abandoned by my successor. Congress would not even print the report of this commission, and it was the public-spirited, far-sighted action of the Spokane Chamber of Commerce which alone secured the publication of the report. (*Century Magazine*, October 1913.) *Mem. Ed.* XIX, 546; *Nat. Ed.* XVII, 402.

─────────────. The object of the Commission on Country Life . . . is not to help the farmer raise better crops, but to call his attention to the opportunities for better business and better living on the farm. If country life is to become what it should be, and what I believe it ultimately will be—one of the most dignified, desirable, and sought-after ways of earning a living—the farmer must take advantage not only of the agricultural knowledge which is at his disposal, but of the methods which have raised and continue to raise the standards of living and of intelligence in other callings.

Those engaged in all other industrial and commercial callings have found it necessary, under modern economic conditions, to organize themselves for mutual advantage and for the protection of their own particular interests in relation to other interests. The farmers of every progressive European country have realized this essential fact and have found in the cooperative system exactly the form of business combination they need.

Now whatever the State may do toward improving the practice of agriculture, it is not within the sphere of any government to reorganize the farmers' business or reconstruct the social life of farming communities. It is, however, quite within its power to use its influence and the machinery of publicity which it can control for calling public attention to the needs and the facts. *Special Message from the President of the United States transmitting the report of the Country Life Commission, February 9, 1909.* (Washington, 1909), p. 4.

COURAGE. Every feat of heroism makes us forever indebted to the man who performed it. All daring and courage, all iron endurance of misfortune, all devotion to the ideal of honor and of the glory of the flag, make for a finer and nobler type of manhood. (Address as Assistant Secretary of the Navy, Naval War College, June 1897.) *Mem. Ed.* XV, 258; *Nat. Ed.* XIII, 197.

─────────────. In any republic courage is a prime necessity for the average citizen if he is to be a good citizen; and he needs physical courage no less than moral courage, the courage that dares as well as the courage that endures, the courage that will fight valiantly alike against the foes of the soul and the foes of the body. (At the Harvard Union, Cambridge, February 23, 1907.) *Mem. Ed.* XV, 484; *Nat. Ed.* XIII, 561.

COURAGE—DEVELOPMENT OF. He [a character in one of Marryat's books] says that at the outset almost every man is frightened when he goes into action, but that the course to follow is for the man to keep such a grip on himself that he can act just as if he was not frightened. After this is kept up long enough it changes from pretense to reality, and the man does in very fact become fearless by sheer dint of practising fearlessness when he does not feel it. . . . This was the theory upon which I went. There were all kinds of things of which I was afraid at first, ranging from grizzly bears to "mean" horses and gun-fighters; but by acting as if I was not afraid I gradually ceased to be afraid. Most men can have the same experience if they choose. They will first learn to bear themselves well in trials which they anticipate and which they school themselves in advance to meet. After a while the habit will grow on them, and they will behave well in sudden and unexpected emergencies which come upon them unawares.

It is of course much pleasanter if one is naturally fearless, and I envy and respect the men who are naturally fearless. But it is a good thing to remember that the man who does not enjoy this advantage can nevertheless stand beside the man who does, and can do his duty with the like efficiency, *if he chooses to.* Of course he must not let his desire take the form merely of a day-dream. Let him dream about being a fearless man, and the more he dreams the better he will be, always provided he does his best to realize the dream in practice. He can do his part honorably and well provided only he sets fearlessness before himself as an ideal, schools himself to think of danger merely as something to be faced and overcome, and regards life itself as he should regard it, not as something to be thrown away, but as a pawn to be promptly hazarded whenever the hazard is warranted by the larger interests of the great game in which we are all engaged. (1913.) *Mem. Ed.* XXII, 64; *Nat. Ed.* XX, 55.

COURAGE—INSISTENCE ON. Another quality on which to insist is courage. Be a man ever so honest, if he be cursed with a sufficient quantity of timidity he is a mere nuisance in any emergency. I think I am more apt to lose my temper with the timid good man than I am with the sharp, resolute, clever scoundrel whom I am going to fight anyway. (Before Liberal Club of Buffalo, N. Y., September 10, 1895.) *Mem. Ed.* XVI, 274; *Nat. Ed.* XIV, 195.

COURAGE—PLACE OF. Courage and hardihood are indispensable virtues in a people; but the people which possesses no others can never rise high in the scale either of power or of culture. Great peoples must have in addition the governmental capacity which comes only when individuals fully recognize their duties to one another and to the whole body politic, and are able to join together in feats of constructive statesmanship and of honest and effective administration. (At Louisiana Purchase Exposition, St. Louis, April 30, 1903.) *Mem. Ed.* XII, 604; *Nat. Ed.* XI, 321.

COURAGE IN WAR-TIME. Popular sentiment is just when it selects as popular heroes the men who have led in the struggle against malice domestic or foreign levy. No triumph of peace is quite so great as the supreme triumphs of war. The courage of the soldier, the courage of the statesman who has to meet storms which can be quelled only by soldierly qualities—this stands higher than any quality called out merely in time of peace. (Address as Assistant Secretary of the Navy, Naval War College, June 1897.) *Mem. Ed.* XV, 243; *Nat. Ed.* XIII, 185.

COURAGE. *See also* CHARACTER; COWARDICE; EXPLORATION; FIGHTING QUALITIES; FIGHTING VIRTUES; HEROIC VIRTUES; HONESTY; MANLINESS; MANLY VIRTUES; STRIFE.

COURTESY. Courtesy is as much the mark of a gentleman as courage. If we respect ourselves, we individually show both qualities; and, in our collective capacity, we should demand of our representatives that the nation show both qualities in its dealings with other nations. (*Outlook,* April 1, 1911.) *Mem. Ed.* XIX, 152; *Nat. Ed.* XVII, 109.

COURTESY. *See also* INTERNATIONAL COURTESY.

COURTS—DUTY OF. The courts to-day owe the country no greater or clearer duty than to keep their hands off such statutes when they have any reasonably permissible relation to the public good. In the past the courts have often failed to perform this duty, and their failure is the chief cause of whatever dissatisfaction there is with the working of our judicial system. One who seeks to prevent the irrevocable commission of such mistakes in the future may justly claim to be regarded as aiming to preserve and not to destroy the independence and power of the judiciary.

My remedy is not the result of a library study of constitutional law, but of actual and long-continued experience in the use of governmental power to redress social and industrial evils. Again and again earnest workers for social justice have said to me that the most serious obstacles that they have encountered during the many years that they have been trying to save American women and children from destruction in American industry have been the courts. That is the judgment of almost all the social workers I know, and of dozens of parish priests and clergymen, and of every executive and legislator who has been seriously attempting to use government as an agency for social and industrial betterment. What is the result of this system of judicial nullification? It was accurately stated by the court of appeals of New York in the employers' liability case, where it was calmly and judicially declared that the people under our Republican government are less free to correct the evils that oppress them than are the people of the monarchies of Europe.

To any man with vision, to any man with broad and real social sympathies, to any man who believes with all his heart in this great democratic Republic of ours, such a condition is intolerable. It is not government by the people, but mere sham government in which the will of the people is constantly defeated. It is out of this experience that my remedy has come; and let it be tried in this field. When, as the result of years of education and debate, a majority of the people have decided upon a remedy for an evil from which they suffer, and have chosen a legislature and executive pledged to embody that remedy in law, and the law has been finally passed and approved, I regard it as monstrous that a bench of judges shall then say to the people: "You must begin all over again." (At Carnegie Hall, N. Y. C., March 20, 1912.) *Mem. Ed.* XIX, 216; *Nat. Ed.* XVII, 164.

COURTS—INDEPENDENCE OF. I wish to keep the courts independent. But at present the independence of the courts is far more frequently menaced by special privilege than by any popular tyranny. I wish to protect them against both. The safe way to prevent popular discontent with the courts from becoming acute and chronic, is to provide the people with the simple, direct, effective, and yet limited power to secure the interpretation of their own constitution in accordance with their own deliberate judgment. (Introduction dated July 1, 1912.) William L. Ransom, *Majority Rule and the Judiciary*. (Scribner's, N. Y., 1912), pp. 23-24.

COURTS—POSITION OF. We in America have peculiar need thus to make the acts of the courts subject to the people, because, owing to causes which I need not now discuss, the courts have here grown to occupy a position unknown in any other country, a position of superiority over both the legislature and the Executive. Just at this time, when we have begun in this country to move toward social and industrial betterment and true industrial democracy, this attitude on the part of the courts is of grave portent, because privilege has intrenched itself in many courts just as it formerly intrenched itself in many legislative bodies and in many executive offices. (Before Progressive National Convention, Chicago, August 6, 1912.) *Mem. Ed.* XIX, 370; *Nat. Ed.* XVII, 264.

———. My plea is for rational growth; my plea is that the Court act with ordinary statesmanship, ordinary regard for the Constitution, as a living aid to growth, not as a straight jacket; ordinary regard for the laws, the rights of humanity, and the growth of civilization. I wish to state with all emphasis that no man who takes the opposite ground to that which I have taken in the article in question has any right to be on the bench; and it is a misfortune to have him there. (To Betts, June 2, 1911.) Charles H. Betts, *Betts-Roosevelt Letters*. (Lyons, N. Y., 1912), p. 10.

COURTS—RESPECT FOR. In no way can respect for the courts be so quickly undermined as by teaching the public through the action of a judge himself that there is reason for the loss of such respect. (To Charles J. Bonaparte, January 2, 1908.) *Mem. Ed.* XXII, 522; *Nat. Ed.* XX, 449.

COURTS—SANCTITY OF. I have said again and again that I do not advocate the recall of judges in all States and in all communities. In my own State I do not advocate it or believe it to be needed, for in this State our trouble lies not with corruption on the bench, but with the effort by the honest but wrong-headed judges to thwart the people in their struggle for social justice and fair dealing. . . .

But—I say it soberly—democracy has a right to approach the sanctuary of the courts when a special interest has corruptly found sanctuary there; and this is exactly what has happened in some of the States where the recall of the judges is a living issue. I would far more willingly trust the whole people to judge such a case than some special tribunal—perhaps appointed by the same power that chose the judge—if that tribunal is not itself really responsible to the people and is hampered and clogged by the technicalities of impeachment proceedings. (At Carnegie Hall, N. Y. C., March 20, 1912.) *Mem. Ed.* XIX, 204; *Nat. Ed.* XVII, 154.

———. Certain big men who, alas, have sometimes perverted the courts to their own uses now tell us that it is impious to speak of the people's insisting upon justice being done by the courts. We answer that with all our might we will uphold the courts against lawlessness; and that we also intend to see that in their turn the courts give justice to all. (At Louisville, Ky., April 3, 1912.) *Mem. Ed.* XIX, 252; *Nat. Ed.* XVII, 187.

COURTS—THE PEOPLE AND THE. I do not say that the people are infallible. But I do say that our whole history shows that the American people are more often sound in their decisions than is the case with any of the governmental bodies to whom, for their convenience, they have delegated portions of their power.

If this is not so, then there is no justification for the existence of our government; and if it is so, then there is no justification for refusing to give the people the real, and not merely the nominal, ultimate decision on questions of constitutional law.

Just as the people, and not the Supreme Court under Chief Justice Taney, were wise in their decision of the vital questions of their day, so I hold that now the American people as a whole have shown themselves wiser than the courts in the way they have approached and dealt with such vital questions of our day as those concerning the proper control of big corporations and of securing their rights to industrial workers. (Before Ohio Constitutional Convention, Columbus, February 21, 1912.) *Mem. Ed.* XIX, 190; *Nat. Ed.* XVII, 142.

———. My proposal is merely that we shall give to the people the power, to be used not wantonly but only in exceptional cases, themselves to see to it that the governmental action taken in their name is really the action that they desire.

The American people, and not the courts, are to determine their own fundamental policies. The people should have power to deal with the effect of the acts of all their governmental agencies. This must be extended to include the effects of judicial acts as well as the acts of the executive and legislative representatives of the people. Where the judge merely does justice as between man and man, not dealing with constitutional questions, then the interest of the public is only to see that he is a wise and upright judge. Means should be devised for making it easier than at present to get rid of an incompetent judge; means should be devised by the bar and the bench acting in conjunction with the various legislative bodies to make justice far more expeditious and more certain than at present. The stick-in-the-bark legalism, the legalism that subordinates equity to technicalities, should be recognized as a potent enemy of justice. But this is not the matter of most concern at the moment. Our prime concern is that in dealing with the fundamental law of the land, in assuming finally to interpret it, and therefore finally to make it, the acts of the courts should be subject to and not above the final control of the people as a whole. (Before Progressive National Convention, Chicago, August 6, 1912.) *Mem. Ed.* XIX, 367; *Nat. Ed.* XVII, 262.

——————. We hold with Abraham Lincoln that the people, acting deliberately and through the forms of law, are master over the courts as they are master over legislature and Senate, over governor and President. (At Chicago, December 10, 1912.) *Mem. Ed.* XIX, 480; *Nat. Ed.* XVII, 355.

——————. The courts are the servants of the people precisely as is true of all other public servants, legislative and executive alike. (Before National Conference of Progressive Service, Portsmouth, R. I., July 2, 1913.) *Mem. Ed.* XIX, 527; *Nat. Ed.* XVII, 387.

——————. I do not believe in sham. I do not believe in asserting that the people rule unless we make the actual fact correspond with the assertion. . . . The people must not surrender to the judiciary, any more than to the executive or legislative branches of the government, the final decision as to what laws they are to be permitted to have. . . . It often happens that vitally necessary and important laws, demanded in the interest of the people are declared unconstitutional by a reactionary court. In such a case what really happens is that one agent of the people, the legislature, passes the law and another agent of the people, the court, declares that it has not the power to pass it. The remedy in such a case is obvious. When two agents differ the principal must decide between them. The people are the masters of all their governmental agents if there is any sincerity in our belief in democracy. Where their servants, their agents, disagree, the people themselves should have the right to step in and say which of their two servants, the court or the legislature, represents their deliberate and well-thought-out conviction. *Outlook,* November 15, 1913, p. 591.

COURTS—USURPATION BY. I deny that the American people have surrendered to any set of men, no matter what their position or their character, the final right to determine those fundamental questions upon which free self-government ultimately depends. The people themselves must be the ultimate makers of their own Constitution. *Outlook,* August 17, 1912, p. 856.

——————. In the United States the courts have gradually assumed certain powers which are purely political. These powers are in no sense judicial. . . . In consequence it is necessary to provide for popular control over the exercise of these powers by the courts. . . . In the United States the courts have assumed to be the special interpreters of the Constitution. They have assumed the right to say what the people are, and what they are not, to be allowed to do in providing social and industrial justice. . . . The people must be in fact, and not merely nominally, the masters of their own destiny. . . .

The right to annul the law or to change it—as by judicial decision the fourteenth amendment to the United States Constitution has been vitally and, as I hold, lamentably changed—is the right to govern. The authority that is able to say by what laws the people shall be governed is the sovereign authority in the State. . . . For a third of a century it has now been exercised with what I am forced to say, speaking gravely and deliberately, has been inexcusable and reckless wantonness, on behalf of privilege, and against the interests of the people for whom it is most needful that the power of the Government should be invoked. . . . I am speaking of the exercise by the judges of the United States of the political or legislative right to annul laws, and to declare that the people have no power to enact those laws which the judges do not think they ought to enact. *Outlook,* November 15, 1913, pp. 592-594.

COURTS AND JUDGES. Our opponents say that we attack the courts. We do not. We attack judges when they go wrong, just exactly as we attack other people when they do wrong—Presidents, senators, congressmen. (At New York City, February 12, 1913.) *Mem. Ed.* XIX, 497; *Nat. Ed.* XVII, 369.

COURTS. *See also* CONSTITUTION; DIVISION OF POWERS; FRANCHISE TAX; HAGUE COURT; INTERNATIONAL COURT; JUDGES; JUDICIARY; JUSTICE; JUVENILE COURTS; LAWS; LEGALISM; MARSHALL, JOHN; MINORITY; RECALL; STATES' RIGHTS; SUPREME COURT.

COWARDICE. Cowardice in a race, as in an individual, is the unpardonable sin, and a wilful failure to prepare for danger may in its effects be as bad as cowardice. The timid man who cannot fight, and the selfish, short-sighted, or foolish man who will not take the steps that will enable him to fight, stand on almost the same plane. (Address as Assistant Secretary of the Navy, Naval War College, June 1897.) *Mem. Ed.* XV, 242; *Nat. Ed.* XIII, 184.

―――――――. A coward who appreciates that cowardice is a sin, an unpardonable sin if persevered in, may train himself so as, first to *act* like a brave man, and then finally to *feel* like and therefore to *be* a brave man. But the coward who excuses his cowardice, who tries to cloak it behind lofty words, who perseveres in it, and does not appreciate his own infamy, is beyond all hope. (*Metropolitan,* August 1915.) *Mem. Ed.* XX, 363; *Nat. Ed.* XVIII, 311.

COWARDICE. *See also* COURAGE; FIGHTING QUALITIES; FIGHTING VIRTUES; MANLY VIRTUES; "MOLLYCODDLE."

COWBOY RIDERS. Cowboys are certainly extremely good riders. As a class they have no superiors. Of course, they would at first be at a disadvantage in steeplechasing or fox-hunting, but their average of horsemanship is without doubt higher than that of the men who take part in these latter amusements. A cowboy would learn to ride across country in a quarter of the time it would take a cross-country rider to learn to handle a vicious bronco or to do good cow-work round and in a herd. (1888.) *Mem. Ed.* IV, 426; *Nat. Ed.* I, 324.

COWBOYS. The cowboys form a class by themselves, and are now quite as typical representatives of the wilder side of Western life as were a few years ago the skin-clad hunters and trappers. They are mostly of native birth, and although there are among them wild spirits from every land, yet the latter soon become undistinguishable from their American companions, for these plainsmen are far from being so heterogeneous as is commonly supposed. On the contrary, all have a curious similarity to each other; existence in the West seems to put the same stamp upon each and every one of them. Sinewy, hardy, self-reliant, their life forces them to be both daring and adventurous, and the passing over their heads of a few years leaves printed on their faces certain lines which tell of dangers quietly fronted and hardships uncomplainingly endured. They are far from being as lawless as they are described; though they sometimes cut queer antics when, after many months of lonely life, they come into a frontier town in which drinking and gambling are the only recognized forms of amusement, and where pleasure and vice are considered synonymous terms. On the round-ups, or when a number get together, there is much boisterous, often foul-mouthed, mirth; but they are rather silent, self-contained men when with strangers, and are frank and hospitable to a degree. The Texans are perhaps the best at the actual cowboy work. They are absolutely fearless riders and understand well the habits of the half-wild cattle, being unequalled in those most trying times when, for instance, the cattle are stampeded by a thunder-storm at night, while in the use of the rope they are only excelled by the Mexicans. On the other hand, they are prone to drink, and, when drunk, to shoot. (1885.) *Mem. Ed.* I, 8-9; *Nat. Ed.* I, 7-8.

―――――――. The cowboys, who have supplanted these old hunters and trappers as the typical men of the plains, themselves lead lives that are almost as full of hardship and adventure. The unbearable cold of winter sometimes makes the small outlying camps fairly uninhabitable if fuel runs short; and if the line-riders are caught in a blizzard while making their way to the home-ranch, they are lucky if they get off with nothing worse than frozen feet and faces.

They are, in the main, hard-working, faithful fellows, but of course are frequently obliged to get into scrapes through no fault of their own. (1888.) *Mem. Ed.* IV, 463-464; *Nat. Ed.* I, 356.

―――――――. It is utterly unfair to judge the whole class by what a few individuals do in the course of two or three days spent in town, instead of by the long months of weary, honest toil common to all alike. To appreciate properly his fine, manly qualities, the wild roughrider of the plains should be seen in his own home. There he passes his days, there he does his life-work, there, when he meets death, he faces it as he has faced many other evils, with quiet, uncomplaining fortitude. Brave, hospitable, hardy, and adventurous, he is the grim pioneer of our race; he prepares the way for the civilization from before whose face he must himself disappear. Hard and dangerous though his existence is, it has yet a wild attraction that strongly draws to it his bold, free spirit. (1888.) *Mem. Ed.* IV, 479; *Nat. Ed.* I, 369.

───────────. The cowboys resemble one another much more and outsiders much less than is the case even with their employers, the ranchmen. A town in the cattle country, when for some cause it is thronged with men from the neighborhood, always presents a picturesque sight. On the wooden sidewalks of the broad, dusty streets the men who ply the various industries known only to frontier existence jostle one another as they saunter to and fro or lounge lazily in front of the straggling, cheap-looking board houses. . . .

Everywhere among these plainsmen and mountain men, and more important than any are the cowboys—the men who follow the calling that has brought such towns into being. . . . They are smaller and less muscular than the wielders of axe and pick; but they are as hardy and self-reliant as any men who ever breathed—with bronzed, set faces, and keen eyes that look all the world straight in the face without flinching as they flash out from under the broad-brimmed hats. Peril and hardship, and years of long toil broken by weeks of brutal dissipation, draw haggard lines across their eager faces, but never dim their reckless eyes nor break their bearing of defiant self-confidence. . . . Although prompt to resent an injury, they are not at all apt to be rude to outsiders, treating them with what can almost be called a grave courtesy. They are much better fellows and pleasanter companions than small farmers or agricultural laborers; nor are the mechanics and workmen of a great city to be mentioned in the same breath. (1888.) *Mem. Ed.* IV, 369-372; *Nat. Ed.* I, 276-278.

───────────. The moral tone of a cow camp, indeed, is rather high than otherwise. Meanness, cowardice, and dishonesty are not tolerated. There is a high regard for truthfulness and keeping one's word, intense contempt for any kind of hypocrisy, and a hearty dislike for a man who shirks his work. Many of the men gamble and drink, but many do neither; and the conversation is not worse than in most bodies composed wholly of male human beings.

A cowboy will not submit tamely to an insult, and is ever ready to avenge his own wrongs; nor has he an overwrought fear of shedding blood. He possesses, in fact, few of the emasculated, milk-and-water moralities admired by the pseudophilanthropists; but he does possess, to a very high degree, the stern qualities that are invaluable to a nation. (1888.) *Mem. Ed.* IV, 427-428; *Nat. Ed.* I, 325-326.

COWBOYS. *See also* CATTLEMAN; RANCH LIFE; ROUND-UP.

COYOTES. Southern coyotes or prairie-wolves are only about one-third the size of the big gray timber-wolves of the Northern Rockies. They are too small to meddle with full-grown horses and cattle, but pick up young calves and kill sheep, as well as any small domesticated animal that they can get at. The big wolves flee from the neighborhood of anything like close settlements, but coyotes hang around the neighborhood of man much more persistently. They show a fox-like cunning in catching rabbits, prairie-dogs, gophers and the like. After nightfall they are noisy, and their melancholy wailing and yelling are familiar sounds to all who pass over the plains. . . .

Coyotes are sharp, wary, knowing creatures, and on most occasions take care to keep out of harm's way. (1905.) *Mem. Ed.* III, 96, 97; *Nat. Ed.* II, 473, 474.

CRAFTINESS. Craft unaccompanied by conscience makes the crafty man a social wild beast who preys on the community and must be hunted out of it. (Before Young Men's Christian Association, New York City, December 30, 1900.) *Mem. Ed.* XV, 535; *Nat. Ed.* XIII, 498.

CRAFTINESS. *See also* CONSCIENCE.

CRIME. The public and the representatives of the public, the high officials, whether on the bench or in executive or legislative positions, need to remember that often the most dangerous criminals, so far as the life of the nation is concerned, are not those who commit the crimes known to and condemned by the popular conscience for centuries, but those who commit crimes only rendered possible by the complex conditions of our modern industrial life. It makes not a particle of difference whether these crimes are committed by a capitalist or by a laborer, by a leading banker or manufacturer or railroad man, or by a leading representative of a labor-union. Swindling in stocks, corrupting legislatures, making fortunes by the infla-

[122]

tion of securities, by wrecking railroads, by destroying competitors through rebates—these forms of wrong-doing in the capitalist are far more infamous than any ordinary form of embezzlement or forgery; yet it is a matter of extreme difficulty to secure the punishment of the man most guilty of them, most responsible for them. (Seventh Annual Message, Washington, December 3, 1907.) *Mem. Ed.* XVII, 515; *Nat. Ed.* XV, 439.

——————. The most effective way to reduce crime is for the judges and magistrates to impose heavier sentences on criminals. The police do their duty well; but if the courts let the criminals go with inadequate sentences, the effect of the labor of the police is largely wasted. (Before N. Y. Preachers' Meeting, January 20, 1896.) *Mem. Ed.* XVI, 310-311; *Nat. Ed.* XIV, 217.

CRIME AND PUNISHMENT. I have not a particle of sympathy with the sentimentality—as I deem it, the mawkishness—which overflows with foolish pity for the criminal and cares not at all for the victim of the criminal. I am glad to see wrongdoers punished. The punishment is an absolute necessity from the standpoint of society; and I put the reformation of the criminal second to the welfare of society. But I do desire to see the man or woman who has paid the penalty and who wishes to reform given a helping hand—surely every one of us who knows his own heart must know that he too may stumble, and should be anxious to help his brother or sister who has stumbled. When the criminal has been punished, if he then shows a sincere desire to lead a decent and upright life, he should be given the chance, he should be helped and not hindered; and if he makes good, he should receive that respect from others which so often aids in creating self-respect—the most invaluable of all possessions. (1913.) *Mem. Ed.* XXII, 154; *Nat. Ed.* XX, 131.

CRIME. *See also* ASSASSINATION; BRIBERY; CAPITAL PUNISHMENT; CORRUPTION; INSANITY PLEA; JUVENILE COURTS; LYNCHING; STOCK-WATERING; VICE; WHITE SLAVE TRAFFIC.

CRIMINALS—PARDON OF. One of the painful duties of the chief executive in States like New York, as well as in the nation, is the refusing of pardons. Yet I can imagine nothing more necessary from the standpoint of good citizenship than the ability to steel one's heart in this matter of granting pardons. The pressure is always greatest in two classes of cases: first, that where capital punishment is inflicted; second, that where the man is prominent socially and in the business world, and where in consequence his crime is apt to have been one concerned in some way with finance. (1913.) *Mem. Ed.* XXII, 348; *Nat. Ed.* XX, 298.

——————. Every time that rape or criminal assault on a woman is pardoned, and anything less than the full penalty of the law exacted, a premium is put on the practice of lynching such offenders. Every time a big moneyed offender, who naturally excites interest and sympathy, and who has many friends, is excused from serving a sentence which a man of less prominence and fewer friends would have to serve, justice is discredited in the eyes of plain people—and to undermine faith in justice is to strike at the foundation of the Republic. As for ill health, it must be remembered that few people are as healthy in prison as they would be outside; and there should be no discrimination among criminals on this score; either all criminals who grow unhealthy should be let out, or none. Pardons must sometimes be given in order that the cause of justice may be served; but in cases such as these I am considering, while I know that many amiable people differ from me, I am obliged to say that in my judgment the pardons work far-reaching harm to the cause of justice. (1913.) *Mem. Ed.* XXII, 512; *Nat. Ed.* XX, 440.

CRIMINALS — SYMPATHY FOR. You don't want any mushy sentimentality when you are dealing with criminals. One of the things that many of our good reformers should learn is that fellow-feeling for the criminal is out of place. (Before Liberal Club of Buffalo, N. Y., September 10, 1895.) *Mem. Ed.* XVI, 282; *Nat. Ed.* XIV, 202.

——————. Any man who has ever had anything to do with the infliction of the death-penalty, or indeed with any form of punishment, knows that there are sentimental beings so constituted that their sympathies are always most keenly aroused on behalf of the offender who pays the penalty for a deed of peculiar atrocity. The explanation probably is that the more conspicuous the crime, the more their attention is arrested, and the more acute their manifestations of sympathy become. (1900.) *Mem. Ed.* XIII, 386; *Nat. Ed.* X, 272.

——————. It is criminal to permit sympathy for criminals to weaken our hands in upholding the law. (Sixth Annual Message,

Washington, December 3, 1906.) *Mem. Ed.* XVII, 407; *Nat. Ed.* XV, 347.

CRIMINALS — TREATMENT OF. There was one bit of frontier philosophy which I should like to see imitated in more advanced communities. Certain crimes of revolting baseness and cruelty were never forgiven. But in the case of ordinary offenses, the man who had served his term and who then tried to make good was given a fair chance; and of course this was equally true of the women. Every one who has studied the subject at all is only too well aware that the world offsets the readiness with which it condones a crime for which a man escapes punishment by its unforgiving relentlessness to the often far less guilty man who *is* punished, and who therefore has made his atonement. On the frontier, if the man honestly tried to behave himself there was generally a disposition to give him fair play and a decent show. (1913.) *Mem. Ed.* XXII, 153; *Nat. Ed.* XX, 131.

CRIMINALS. See also ANARCHISTS; LAW; MALEFACTORS OF GREAT WEALTH.

CRITICISM. I would not for one moment be understood as objecting to criticism or failing to appreciate its importance. . . . But it behooves every man to remember that the work of the critic, important though it is, is of altogether secondary importance, and that, in the end, progress is accomplished by the man who does the things, and not by the man who talks about how they ought or ought not to be done. (*Forum,* July 1894.) *Mem. Ed.* XV, 43; *Nat. Ed.* XIII, 29.

——————. There is but one thing that can hurt more surely than indiscriminate praise of everything American, good and bad, and that is, interminable and indiscriminate sneering and faultfinding. (At memorial meeting for G. W. Curtis, New York City, November 14, 1892.) *Mem. Ed.* XII, 485; *Nat. Ed.* XI, 229.

CRITICISM—FACULTY OF. An age in which the critical faculty is greatly developed often tends to develop a certain querulous inability to understand the fundamental truths which less critical ages accept as a matter of course. (*Outlook,* August 26, 1911.) *Mem. Ed.* XIV, 441; *Nat. Ed.* XII, 99.

CRITICISM—FUNCTION OF. There is . . . a need for proper critical work. Wrongs should be strenuously and fearlessly denounced; evil principles and evil men should be condemned.

The politician who cheats or swindles, or the newspaper man who lies in any form, should be made to feel that he is an object of scorn for all honest men. We need fearless criticism; but we need that it should also be intelligent. . . . Criticism which is ignorant or prejudiced is a source of great harm to the nation; and where ignorant or prejudiced critics are themselves educated men, their attitude does real harm also to the class to which they belong. (*Atlantic Monthly,* August 1894.) *Mem. Ed.* XV, 53; *Nat. Ed.* XIII, 39.

——————. There is much in our political life to censure as well as much to praise; but both censure and praise must be bestowed intelligently to be effective. Criticism is undoubtedly necessary, though less so than many other things—the men who criticise most severely are rarely those who work effectively to destroy the evils complained of—but excessive and indiscriminate scolding, fretting, and faultfinding are even more injurious than excessive and indiscriminate laudation. (*Cosmopolitan,* December 1892.) *Mem. Ed.* XIV, 371; *Nat. Ed.* XII, 315.

CRITICISM OF PUBLIC OFFICIALS. Undoubtedly good men in public life should be freely criticised whenever they do wrong; but all should be judged by one standard in making comparisons. It is folly to strengthen our foes by assailing our friends; and indiscriminate and unintelligent blame is quite as harmful as indiscriminate and unintelligent praise. We do not, as a people, suffer from the lack of criticism, but we do suffer from the lack of impartial and intelligent criticism. (*Century,* February 1890.) *Mem. Ed.* XVI, 166; *Nat. Ed.* XIV, 106.

——————. No servant of the people has a right to expect to be free from just and honest criticism. It is the newspapers, and the public men whose thoughts and deeds show them to be most alien to honesty and truth who themselves loudly object to truthful and honest criticism of their fellow servants of the great moneyed interests. (To Charles J. Bonaparte, January 2, 1908.) *Mem. Ed.* XXII, 523; *Nat. Ed.* XX, 450.

——————. I very seriously question whether, on the whole, we do not suffer in our public life quite as much from unjust assault upon upright public servants as from failure effectively to assault corruption and its exponents. Many newspapers and many magazines, sometimes because they are controlled by the special interests, and quite as often because they are seeking to capitalize sensationalism and to turn to commercial advantage the literature of exposure, have done, and are doing, all they can to degrade public life by practising every species of reckless sensational and hysterical mendacity at the cost of reputable public servants. (*Outlook,* March 4, 1911.) *Mem. Ed.* XIX, 117; *Nat. Ed.* XVII, 80.

CRITICISM OF THE GOVERNMENT. It is the duty of every American citizen fearlessly, but truthfully, to criticize not only his Government but his people, for wrongdoing, or for failure to do what is right. It is his duty to obey the injunction of President Wilson by insisting upon pitiless publicity of inefficiency, of subordination of public to private considerations, or of any other form of governmental failure to perform duty. Such criticism is absolutely indispensable if we are to do our duty in this war, and if we are to adopt a permanent policy of preparedness which will make this Nation safe. (October 1, 1917.) *Roosevelt in the Kansas City Star,* 7.

——————. In the United States the people are all citizens, including its President. The rest of them are fellow citizens of the President. In Germany the people are all subjects of the Kaiser. They are not his fellow citizens, they are his subjects. This is the essential difference between the United States and Germany, but the difference would vanish if we now submitted to the foolish or traitorous persons who endeavor to make it a crime to tell the truth about the administration when the administration is guilty of incompetence or other shortcomings. Such endeavor is itself a crime against the nation. Those who take such an attitude are guilty of moral treason of a kind both abject and dangerous. (1918.) *Mem. Ed.* XXI, 324; *Nat. Ed.* XIX, 296.

CRITICISM. *See also* ACTION; FREE SPEECH; INTERNATIONAL CRITICISM; LESE-MAJESTY; PRESIDENT; TRUTH.

CROMWELL, OLIVER. All his qualities, both good and bad, tended to render the forms and the narrowly limited powers of constitutional government irksome to him. His strength, his intensity of conviction, his delight in exercising powers for what he conceived to be good ends; his dislike of speculative reforms and his inability to appreciate the necessity of theories to a practical man who wishes to do good work; his hatred of both king and oligarchy, while he utterly distrusted a popular majority; his tendency to insist upon the superiority of the moral law, as he saw it, to the laws of mankind roundabout him—all these tendencies worked together to unfit him for the task of helping a liberty loving people on the road toward freedom. (1900.) *Mem. Ed.* XIII, 428-429; *Nat. Ed.* X, 308-309.

——————. Cromwell was far more concerned in righting specific cases of oppression than in advancing the great principles of constitutional government which alone make possible that orderly liberty which is the bar to such individual acts of wrong-doing. From the standpoint of the private man this is a distinctly better failing than is its opposite; but from the standpont of the statesman the reverse is true. Cromwell, like many a so-called "practical" man, would have done better work had he followed a more clearly defined theory; for though the practical man is better than the mere theorist, he cannot do the highest work unless he is a theorist also. (1900.) *Mem. Ed.* XIII, 319; *Nat. Ed.* X, 215.

——————. He had no great understanding of constitutional government, no full appreciation of the vital importance of the reign of law to the proper development of orderly liberty. His fervent religious ardor made all questions affecting faith and doctrine close to him; and his hatred of corruption and oppression inclined him to take the lead whenever any question arose of dealing, either with the wrongs done by Laud in the course of his religious persecutions, or with the irresponsible tyranny of the star-chamber, and the sufferings of its victims. The bent of Cromwell's mind was thus shown right in the beginning of his parliamentary career. His desire was to remedy specific evils. He was too impatient to found the kind of legal and constitutional system which could alone prevent the recurrence of such evils. This tendency, thus early shown, explains, at least in part, why it was that later he deviated from the path trod by Hampden, and afterward by Washington and Washington's colleagues: showing himself unable to build up free government or to establish the reign of law, until he was finally driven to substitute his own personal government for the personal government of the king whom he had helped to dethrone, and put to death. (1900.) *Mem. Ed.* XIII, 324-325; *Nat. Ed.* X, 219.

——————. Cromwell's government was a tyranny because it was based on his own personal rule, his personal decision as to what taxes should be levied, what ordinances issued, what police measures decreed and carried out, what foreign policy adopted or rejected. He was influenced very much by public opinion, when public opinion found definite expression in the action of a body of legislators or of an assembly of officers; but even in such cases he was only influenced, not controlled. In other words, he had gone back to the theory of government professed by the man he had executed, and by that man's predecessors. There was, however, the tremendous and far-reaching difference, that, whereas the Stuart kings clung to absolute power for the sake of rewarding favorites and of carrying out policies that were hostile to the honor and interest of England, Cromwell seized it with the sincere purpose of exalting the moral law at home and increasing the honor of England's name abroad. (1900.) *Mem. Ed.* XIII, 439-440; *Nat. Ed.* X, 318-319.

CROMWELL, OLIVER. See also SELF-GOVERNMENT; WASHINGTON, GEORGE.

CROWDER, GENERAL E. H. See DRAFT.

CUBA—INTERVENTION IN. I am a quietly rampant "Cuba Libre" man. I doubt whether the Cubans would do very well in the line of self-government, but anything would be better than continuance of Spanish rule. I believe that Cleveland ought now to recognize Cuba's independence and interfere; sending our fleet promptly to Havana. There would not, in my opinion, be very serious fighting, and what loss we encountered would be thrice over repaid by the ultimate results of our action. (To Anna Roosevelt Cowles, January 2, 1897.) *Cowles Letters*, 201.

―――――. I doubt if those Spaniards can really pacify Cuba, and if the insurrection goes on much longer I don't see how we can help interfering. *Germany is the power with whom I look foward to serious difficulty;* but oh, how bitterly angry I get at the attitude of some of our public men and some of our publicists! (To W. W. Kimball, December 17, 1897.) *Mem. Ed.* XXIII, 98; Bishop I, 84.

―――――. Personally, I feel that it is not too late to intervene in Cuba. What the Administration will do I know not. In some points it has followed too closely in Cleveland's footsteps to please me, excellently though it has done on the whole. In the name of humanity and of national interest alike, we should have interfered in Cuba two years ago, a year and a half ago last April, and again last December. The blood of the Cubans, the blood of women and children who have perished by the hundred thousand in hideous misery, lies at our door; and the blood of the murdered men of the *Maine* calls not for indemnity but for the full measure of atonement which can only come by driving the Spaniard from the New World. I have said this to the President before his Cabinet; I have said it to Judge Day, the real head of the State Department; and to my own Chief. I cannot say it publicly, for I am of course merely a minor official in the Administration. At least, however, I have borne testimony where I thought it would do good. (To Brooks Adams, March 21, 1898.) *Mem. Ed.* XXIII, 101; Bishop I, 87.

―――――. I have advised the President in the presence of his Cabinet, as well as Judge Day and Senator Hanna, as strongly as I knew how, to settle this matter instantly by armed intervention; and I told the President in the plainest language that no other course was compatible with our national honor, or with the claims of humanity on behalf of the wretched women and children of Cuba. I am more grieved and indignant than I can say at there being any delay on our part in a matter like this. A great crisis is upon us, and if we do not rise level to it, we shall have spotted the pages of our history with a dark blot of shame. (To W. S. Cowles, March 30, 1898.) *Mem. Ed.* XXIII, 103; Bishop I, 89.

CUBA—ROOSEVELT'S POLICY IN. Just at the moment I am so angry with that infernal little Cuban republic that I would like to wipe its people off the face of the earth. All that we have wanted from them was that they should behave themselves and be prosperous, and happy so that we would not have to interfere. And now, lo and behold, they have started an utterly unjustifiable and pointless revolution and may get things into such a snarl that we have no alternative save to intervene—which will at once convince the suspicious idiots in South America that we do wish to interfere after all, and perhaps have some land-hunger! (To White, September 13, 1906.) Allan Nevins, *Henry White. Thirty Years of American Diplomacy.* (Harper & Bros., N. Y., 1930), p. 255.

―――――. I did not send Taft and Bacon to Havana until Palma had repeatedly telegraphed us that his unalterable purpose was to resign forthwith; that the Vice-President and the members of his Cabinet would decline to take or remain in office, and that he was entirely unable to quell the insurrection. I have, I need hardly say, a horror of putting what is in effect a premium upon insurrection by letting the insurrectionists receive benefit from their action; but Palma's utter weakness—or, to speak with literal exactness, his impotence—to do anything effective toward quelling the revolt (for I treat as of less moment the undoubted and gross misbehavior of the party in power at the last election) made it absolutely imperative that I should take some step unless I wished to see chaos come in the Island. . . . Of course our permanent policy toward the Island must depend absolutely upon the action of Congress. No matter what construction is given the Platt Amendment, Congress has nothing to do but to refuse appropriations to put it into effect, and the Platt Amendment vanishes into air, and any stay of marines and troops in the Island becomes impossible. . . . I hope that . . . we shall not have to intervene in any permanent form at present, and that we can simply make temporary arrangements to keep order until an election can be held and a new government or modified government started. I am inclined to think that, thanks to the fact that I have shown that I was ready to intervene by force of arms if necessary, the necessity will be for the present avoided; but I am greatly disheartened at what has occurred and doubt very much whether in the end we shall not have to exercise a more immediate control over Cuba; and of course it is possible that we shall be unable to make a working scheme even now, and that we shall have to take possession of the Island temporarily this fall. But I shall do all that I can to avoid this and I hope to be successful. (To H. C. Lodge, September 27, 1906.) Lodge *Letters* II, 234-235.

——————. I got Congress to approve of my action in interfering in Cuba—and here, by the way, let me interject that I think we have given a pretty fair example of international good faith of the kind I preach, for after having our army for the second time for several years in Cuba, we are now about to leave the island prosperous and thriving and with a reasonable hope that it can achieve self-government for itself; at least, if it cannot, it is evident that we have done our best to put it on the road of stable and orderly independence. (To Sydney Brooks, December 28, 1908.) *Mem. Ed.* XXIV, 151; Bishop II, 130.

CUBA AND THE UNITED STATES. After having delivered the island from its oppressors, we refused to turn it loose offhand, with the certainty that it would sink back into chaos and savagery. For over three years we administered it on a plane higher than it had ever reached before during the four hundred years that had elapsed since the Spaniards first landed upon its shores. We brought moral and physical cleanliness into the government. We cleaned the cities for the first time in their existence. We stamped out yellow fever—an inestimable boon not merely to Cuba, but to the people of the Southern States as well. We established a school system. We made life and property secure, so that industry could again begin to thrive. Then when we had laid deep and broad the foundations upon which civil liberty and national independence must rest, we turned the island over to the hands of those whom its people had chosen as the founders of the new republic. It is a republic with which our own great Republic must ever be closely knit by the ties of common interests and common inspirations. Cuba must always be peculiarly related to us in international politics. She must in international affairs be to a degree a part of our political system. In return she must have peculiar relations with us economically. She must be in a sense part of our economic system. We expect her to accept a political attitude toward us which we think wisest both for her and for us. In return we must be prepared to put her in an economic position as regards our tariff system which will give her some measure of the prosperity which we enjoy. We cannot, in my judgment, avoid taking this attitude if we are to persevere in the course which we have outlined for ourselves as a nation during the past four years. (At Hartford, Conn., August 22, 1902.) *Mem. Ed.* XVIII, 358-359; *Nat. Ed.* XVI, 272-273.

CUBAN INDEPENDENCE. Cuba is, in my judgment, entitled ultimately to settle for itself whether it shall be an independent state or an integral portion of the mightiest of republics. But until order and stable liberty are secured, we must remain in the island to insure them, and infinite tact, judgment, moderation, and courage must be shown by our military and civil representatives in keeping the island pacified, in relentlessly stamping out brigandage, in protecting all alike, and yet in showing proper recognition to the men who have fought for Cuban liberty. (Before the Hamilton Club, Chicago, April 10, 1899.) *Mem. Ed.* XV, 279; *Nat. Ed.* XIII, 329.

——————. As a nation we have especial right to take honest pride in what we have done for Cuba. Our critics abroad and at home have insisted that we never intended to leave the island. But on the 20th of next month Cuba becomes a free republic, and we turn over to the islanders the control of their own government. It would be very difficult to find a parallel in the conduct of any other great State that has occupied such a position as ours. We have kept our word and done our duty, just as an honest individual in private life keeps his word and does his duty. (At Charleston Exposition, S. C., April 9, 1902.) *Mem. Ed.* XVIII, 35; *Nat. Ed.* XVI, 29.

─────────. It would have been a betrayal of our duty to have given Cuba independence out of hand. President McKinley, with his usual singular sagacity in the choice of agents, selected in General Leonard Wood the man of all others best fit to bring the island through its uncertain period of preparation for independence, and the result of his wisdom was shown when last May the island became in name and in fact a free Republic, for it started with a better equipment and under more favorable conditions than had ever previously been the case with any Spanish-American commonwealth. (At banquet in honor of birthday of William McKinley, Canton, O., January 27, 1903.) *Mem. Ed.* XII, 498; *Nat. Ed.* XI, 240-241.

CUBA; CUBAN. See also Intervention; *Maine;* Monroe Doctrine; Platt Amendment; Spanish American War; Wood, Leonard.

CUBISTS. See Painting.

CULTURAL EDUCATION. See Education, Liberal.

CUNNING. See Craftiness.

CURRENCY. The one element more essential than any other to the prosperity of a great civilized nation is a sound and stable currency. (Speech at Grand Rapids, Mich., September 7, 1900.) *Mem. Ed.* XVI, 531; *Nat. Ed.* XIV, 347.

─────────. Probably the most important aid which can be contributed by the National Government to the material well-being of the country is to ensure its financial stability. An honest currency is the strongest symbol and expression of honest business life. The business world must exist largely on credit, and to credit confidence is essential. Any tampering with the currency, no matter with what purpose, if fraught with the suspicion of dishonesty, in result is fatal in its effects on business prosperity. Very ignorant and primitive communities are continually obliged to learn the elementary truth that the repudiation of debts is in the end ruinous to the debtors as a class; and when communities have moved somewhat higher in the scale of civilization they also learn that anything in the nature of a debased currency works similar damage. A financial system of assured honesty is the first essential. (At Logansport, Ind., September 23, 1902.) *Presidential Addresses and State Papers* I, 189-190.

─────────. A metallic currency is always surer and safer than a paper currency; where it exists a laboring man dependent on his wages need fear less than any other member of the community the evils of bad banking. . . . A craze for "soft," or dishonest, money—a greenback movement, or one for short-weight silver dollars—works more to the disadvantage of the whole mass of the people than even to that of the capitalists; it is a move directly in the interests of "the money power," which its loud-mouthed advocates are ostensibly opposing in the interests of democracy. (1887.) *Mem. Ed.* VIII, 103; *Nat. Ed.* VII, 89.

CURRENCY—ELASTICITY OF. Our currency laws have been recently improved by specific declarations intended to secure permanency of values; but this does not imply that these laws may not be further improved and strengthened. It is wellnigh universally admitted, certainly in any business community such as this, that our currency system is wanting in elasticity; that is, the volume does not respond to the varying needs of the country as a whole, nor to the varying needs of the different localities as well as of different times. Our people scarcely need to be reminded that grain-raising communities require a larger volume of currency at harvest time than during the summer months; and the same principle in greater or less extent applies to every community. Our currency laws need such modification as will ensure definitely the parity of every dollar coined or issued by the government, and such expansion or contraction of the currency as will promptly and automatically respond to the varying needs of commerce. Permanent increase would be dangerous, permanent contraction ruinous, but the needed elasticity must be brought about by provisions which will permit both contraction and expansion as the varying needs of the several communities and business interests at different times and in different localities require. (At Quincy, Ill., April 29, 1903.) *Presidential Addresses and State Papers* I, 335.

─────────. Every consideration of prudence demands the addition of the element of elasticity to our currency system. The evil does not consist in an inadequate volume of money, but in the rigidity of this volume, which does not respond as it should to the varying needs of communities and of seasons. Inflation must be avoided; but some provision should be made that will insure a larger volume of money during the fall and winter months than in the less active seasons of the year; so that the currency will contract against speculation, and will expand for the needs of legitimate business. (Fifth Annual Message, Washington, December 5, 1905.) *Mem. Ed.* XVII, 342-343; *Nat. Ed.* XV, 293.

——————. We need a greater elasticity in our currency; provided, of course, that we recognize the even greater need of a safe and secure currency. There must always be the most rigid examination by the national authorities. Provision should be made for an emergency currency. The emergency issue should, of course, be made with an effective guarantee, and upon conditions carefully prescribed by the government. Such emergency issue must be based on adequate securities approved by the government, and must be issued under a heavy tax. This would permit currency being issued when the demand for it was urgent, while securing its requirement as the demand fell off. (Seventh Annual Message, Washington, December 3, 1907.) *Mem. Ed.* XVII, 500; *Nat. Ed.* XV, 426.

CURRENCY AND NATIONAL DEVELOPMENT. There is no doubt whatever that a nation is profoundly affected by the character of its currency; but there seems to be equally little doubt that the currency is only one, and by no means the most important, among a hundred causes which profoundly affect it. The United States has been on a gold basis, and on a silver basis; it has been on a paper basis, and on a basis of what might be called the scraps and odds and ends of the currencies of a dozen other nations; but it has kept on developing along the same lines no matter what its currency has been. If a change of currency were so enacted as to amount to dishonesty, that is, to the repudiation of debts, it would be a very bad thing morally; or, if a change took place in a manner that would temporarily reduce the purchasing power of the wage-earner, it would be a very bad thing materially; but the current of the national life would not be wholly diverted or arrested, it would merely be checked, even by such a radical change. The forces that most profoundly shape the course of a nation's life lie far deeper than the mere use of gold or of silver, the mere question of the appreciation or depreciation of one metal when compared with the other, or when compared with commodities generally. (*Forum*, January 1897.) *Mem. Ed.* XIV, 136; *Nat. Ed.* XIII, 248.

——————. In different stages of development, different countries face varying economic conditions, but at every stage and under all circumstances the most important element in securing their economic well-being is sound finance, honest money. So intimate is the connection between industrial prosperity and a sound currency that the former is jeopardized, not merely by unsound finance, but by the very threat of unsound finance. The business man and the farmer are vitally interested in this question; but no man's interest is so great as that of the wage-worker. A depreciated currency means loss and disaster to the business man; but it means grim suffering to the wage-worker. The capitalist will lose much of his capital and will suffer wearing anxiety and the loss of many comforts; but the wage-worker who loses his wages must suffer, and see his wife and children suffer, for the actual necessities of life. The one absolutely vital need of our whole industrial system is sound money. (Letter accepting nomination for Vice-Presidency, September 15, 1900.) *Mem. Ed.* XVI, 549-550; *Nat. Ed.* XIV, 363.

CURRENCY AND PANIC OF 1903. Most emphatically we need to have preached the fact that our currency system is on the whole a good one; that we need merely some simple remedial legislation, and above all nothing revolutionary. The only effect this administration has had as regards the panic has been that the action in the Northern Securities suit undoubtedly stopped a movement for the wildest speculation in railroad and similar combinations—a speculation which would have resulted probably by this time in a real panic—not such a stringency as we have seen this summer but a time of disaster like 1873 and 1893. (To Anna Roosevelt Cowles, August 26, 1903.) Cowles *Letters*, 258.

CURRENCY LEGISLATION—NEED OF. I earnestly and cordially agree with you on the need of currency legislation, and have been doing all I can for it; but the big financial men of the country, instead of trying to get sound currency legislation, seem to pass their time in lamenting, as Wall Street laments, our action about the railroads. (To Henry L. Higginson, February 11, 1907.) *Mem. Ed.* XXIV, 45-46; Bishop II, 39.

CURRENCY REFORM. The people of the United States suffer from periodical financial panics to a degree substantially unknown among the other nations which approach us in financial strength. There is no reason why we should suffer what they escape. It is of profound importance that our financial system should be promptly investigated, and so thoroughly and effectively revised as to make it certain that hereafter our currency will no longer fail at critical times to meet our needs. (At Osawatomie, Kan., August 31, 1910.) *Mem. Ed.* XIX, 21; *Nat. Ed.* XVII, 14.

───────. The experience of repeated financial crises in the last forty years has proved that the present method of issuing, through private agencies, notes secured by government bonds is both harmful and unscientific. . . . The issue of currency is fundamentally a governmental function. The system to be adopted should have as its basic principles soundness and elasticity. . . . Only by such means can the country be freed from the danger of recurring panics. The control should be lodged with the government, and should be safeguarded against manipulation by Wall Street or the large interests. It should be made impossible to use the machinery or perquisites of the currency system for any speculative purposes. The country must be safeguarded against the overexpansion or unjust contraction of either credit or circulating medium. (Before Progressive National Convention, Chicago, August 6, 1912.) *Mem. Ed.* XIX, 404; *Nat. Ed.* XVII, 292.

CURRENCY. *See also* BANKING; COINAGE; ELECTION OF 1896; GOLD STANDARD; PANIC OF 1907; SILVER.

CURRENT EVENTS. It is hard indeed for the average man to appreciate rightly the relative importance of the different movements going on about him. American historians very often fail signally in this respect. Questions of the tariff or of the currency, and the rise and fall of parties connected therewith absorb their attention. In reality all matters of this sort are of merely minor importance in our history. (*Independent,* November 24, 1892.) *Mem. Ed.* XIV, 287; *Nat. Ed.* XII, 247.

CURRENT EVENTS. *See also* HISTORY.

CURTIS, GEORGE WILLIAM. Mr. Curtis was not a mere critic. He was able to criticise so well, so justly, because he had been a doer of duties, and not a man that merely talked about them. I wonder how many of you realize that Mr. Curtis, who was so pre-eminently fitted for refined, cultivated society, never shirked the raw, rough work; that he did not shrink from taking part in the contest; that he was not frightened by the blood and sweat that came with contest. How many of you know that he was for many years the chairman of his party committee for his county; that he did all the detail work of practical politics himself; that he was a delegate to conventions —to State and national conventions—in one or two of which I had the great honor of sitting beside him; that he actually did all that work himself; that he did not merely talk about how it ought to be done if the conditions were entirely different from the conditions that actually existed, but that he went in himself to do the best he could with the means at hand. (At memorial meeting for G. W. Curtis, New York City, November 14, 1892.) *Mem. Ed.* XII, 483-484; *Nat. Ed.* XI, 227-228.

CURTIS, GEORGE WILLIAM. *See also* MUGWUMP.

CUSTOM. Where a bad custom has been in existence for any length of time, most people grow to regard it as part of the order of nature. (*Atlantic Monthly,* July 1892.) *Mem. Ed.* XVI, 199; *Nat. Ed.* XIV, 134.

CUSTOM. *See also* LAW.

CUSTOMS. *See* SOCIAL CONVENTIONS.

CYNICISM. There are, of course, men of such low moral type, or of such ingrained cynicism, that they do not believe in the possibility of making anything better, or do not care to see things better. There are also men who are slightly disordered mentally, or who are cursed with a moral twist which makes them champion reforms less from a desire to do good to others than as a kind of tribute to their own righteousness, for the sake of emphasizing their own superiority. From neither of these classes can we get any real help in the unending struggle for righteousness. (*Century,* June 1900.) *Mem. Ed.* XV, 378; *Nat. Ed.* XIII, 341.

D

DANTE. When Dante deals with the crimes which he most abhorred, simony and barratry, he flails offenders of his age who were of the same type as those who in our days flourish by political or commercial corruption; and he names his offenders, both those just dead and those still living, and puts them, popes and politicians alike, in hell. There have been trust magnates and politicians and editors and magazine-writers in our own country whose lives and deeds were no more edifying than those of the men who lie in the third and the fifth chasm of the eighth circle of the Inferno; yet for a poet to name those men would be condemned as an instance of shocking taste. . . .

An imitation of the letters of the times past, when the spirit has wholly altered, would be worse than useless; and the very qualities that help to make Dante's poem immortal would, if copied nowadays, make the copyist ridiculous. Nevertheless, it would be a good thing if we could, in some measure, achieve the mighty Florentine's high simplicity of soul, at least to the extent of recognizing in those around us the eternal qualities which we admire or condemn in the men who wrought good or evil at any stage in the world's previous history. Dante's masterpiece is one of the supreme works of art that the ages have witnessed; but he would have been the last to wish that it should be treated only as a work of art, or worshipped only for art's sake, without reference to the dread lessons it teaches mankind. (*Outlook*, August 26, 1911.) Mem. Ed. XIV, 446-447; Nat. Ed. XII, 104-105.

DARWIN, CHARLES. *See* SCIENCE.

DAVIS, RICHARD HARDING. As for Richard Harding Davis, although in his life he did much good work, he never did better work than in his last two years, when he served France and thereby served America with all the intensity of his virile Americanism. During the past three years, every man who has been a pacifist, or pro-German, and every man who has failed from the outset to strive with all his strength for preparedness, has been false to America, and false to humanity, and has deserved ill of this country, and ill of mankind. Long before this war began, Richard Harding Davis was striving for preparedness, and from the beginning of the war he realized that Germany had made herself the champion of all that was basest and most evil, and should be opposed by every lover of liberty, and believer in right, and that France, to a peculiar degree, symbolized in this contest the great cause, or group of causes to which, in the past, all of the Americans to whom our country owes most had dedicated their lives. (Introduction dated May 1917.) *For France,* edited by Charles Hanson Towne. (Doubleday, Page & Co., Garden City, 1917), p. x.

DEATH. Death is always and under all circumstances a tragedy, for if it is not, then it means that life itself has become one. But it is well to live bravely and joyously, and to face the inevitable end without flinching when we go to join the men and the tribes of immemorial eld. Death is the one thing certain for the nation as for the man, though from the loins of the one as from the loins of the other descendants may spring to carry on through the ages the work done by the dead. (To Spring Rice, March 12, 1900.) *The Letters and Friendships of Sir Cecil Spring Rice.* (Houghton Mifflin Co., Boston, 1929), I, 317.

——————. Only those are fit to live who do not fear to die; and none are fit to die who have shrunk from the joy of life and the duty of life. Both life and death are part of the same Great Adventure. Never yet was worthy adventure worthily carried through by the man who put his personal safety first. (*Metropolitan,* October 1918.) Mem. Ed. XXI, 263; Nat. Ed. XIX, 243.

——————. Well, friend, you and I are in the range of the rifle-pits; from now on until we ourselves fall—and that date cannot be so many years distant—we shall see others whom we love fall. It is idle to complain or to rail at the inevitable; serene and high of heart we must face our fate and go down into the darkness. (Letter written shortly before his death.) Mem. Ed. XXIV, 557; Bishop II, 476.

DEATH PENALTY. *See* CAPITAL PUNISHMENT.

DEBATE IN CONGRESS. Congress is the legislative body. To legislate means to make laws, not merely to talk about them. The laws should be made after debate, but the debate should be wholly subsidiary to the actual voting, and should be conducted in good faith with this object in view. Under the Reed rules there was ample opportunity for debate. In fact the pages of *The Congressional Record* show that there was more debate in the Fifty-first than in any preceding Congress.

When the debates of a legislative body occupy a series of volumes so large and so numerous as those of the "Encyclopædia Britannica," it is not worth while to answer the assertion that debate was strangled in that Congress. (*Forum*, December 1895.) *Mem. Ed.* XVI, 251; *Nat. Ed.* XIV, 177.

DEBATE. See also Congress; Filibustering; Reed, Thomas B.; Representative Government.

DEBATING CONTESTS. I have not the slightest sympathy with debating contests in which each side is arbitrarily assigned a given proposition and told to maintain it without the least reference to whether those maintaining it believe in it or not. I know that under our system this is necessary for lawyers, but I emphatically disbelieve in it as regards general discussion of political, social, and industrial matters. What we need is to turn out of our colleges young men with ardent convictions on the side of the right; not young men who can make a good argument for either right or wrong as their interest bids them. The present method of carrying on debates on such subjects as "Our Colonial Policy," or "The Need of a Navy," or "The Proper Position of the Courts in Constitutional Questions," encourages precisely the wrong attitude among those who take part in them. There is no effort to instill sincerity and intensity of conviction. On the contrary, the net result is to make the contestants feel that their convictions have nothing to do with their arguments. (1913.) *Mem. Ed.* XXII, 28; *Nat. Ed.* XX, 25.

DEBATING. See also Oratory.

DEBTOR IN AMERICA. The debtor, in America at least, is amply able to take care of his own interests. Our experience shows conclusively that the creditors only prosper when the debtors prosper, and the danger lies less in the accumulation of debts, than in their repudiation. Among us the communities which repudiate their debts, which inveigh loudest against their creditors, and which offer the poorest field for the operations of the honest banker (whom they likewise always call "money-lender") are precisely those which are least prosperous and least self-respecting. There are, of course, individuals here and there who are unable to cope with the money-lender, and even sections of the country where this is true; but this only means that a weak or thriftless man can be robbed by a sharp money-lender just as he can be robbed by the sharp producer from whom he buys or to whom he sells. (*Forum*, January 1897.) *Mem. Ed.* XIV, 145; *Nat. Ed.* XIII, 256.

DEBTOR. See also Currency; National Honor.

DECADENCE. Most emphatically there is such a thing as "decadence" of a nation, a race, a type; and it is no less true that we cannot give any adequate explanation of the phenomenon. Of course there are many partial explanations, and in some cases, as with the decay of the Mongol or Turkish monarchies, the sum of these partial explanations may represent the whole. But there are other cases, notably, of course, that of Rome in the ancient world, and, as I believe, that of Spain in the modern world, on a much smaller scale, where the sum of all the explanations is that they do not wholly explain. Something seems to have gone out of the people or peoples affected, and what it is no one can say. (To A. J. Balfour, March 8, 1905.) *Mem. Ed.* XXIV, 122; Bishop II, 105.

DECADENCE. See also Death; National Decay; Racial Decay; Roman Empire; Spain.

DECENCY AND EFFICIENCY. If I wished to accomplish anything for the country, my business was to combine decency and efficiency; to be a thoroughly practical man of high ideals who did his best to reduce those ideals to actual practice. This was my ideal, and to the best of my ability I strove to live up to it. (1913.) *Mem. Ed.* XXII, 107; *Nat. Ed.* XX, 91.

DECENCY AND STRENGTH. I desire to see in this country the decent men strong and the strong men decent, and until we get that combination in pretty good shape we are not going to be by any means as successful as we should be. (Before Holy Name Society, Oyster Bay, N. Y., August 16, 1903.) *Mem. Ed.* XV, 524; *Nat. Ed.* XIII, 590.

DECENCY AS A STANDARD. Measure iniquity by the heart, whether a man's purse be full or empty, partly full or partly empty. If the man is a decent man, whether well off or not well off, stand by him; if he is not a decent man stand against him, whether he be rich or poor. Stand against him in no spirit of vengeance, but only with the resolute purpose to make him act as decent citizens must act if this Republic is to be, and to be kept, what it shall become. (Speech at Oyster Bay, N. Y., July 4, 1906.) *Mem. Ed.* XVIII, 10; *Nat. Ed.* XVI, 9.

DECENCY. *See also* WEAKNESS.

DECLARATION OF INDEPENDENCE. The Declaration of Independence derived its peculiar importance, not on account of what America was, but because of what she was to become; she shared with other nations the present, and she yielded to them the past, but it was felt in return that to her, and to her especially, belonged the future. (At Dickinson, Dakota Territory, July 4, 1886.) Hermann Hagedorn, *Roosevelt in the Bad Lands*. (Houghton Mifflin Co., Boston, 1921), p 408.

—————————. I am afraid I have not got as much reverence for the Declaration of Independence as I should have because it has made certain untruths immortal. (Recorded by Butt in letter of July 24, 1908.) *The Letters of Archie Butt, Personal Aide to President Roosevelt.* (Doubleday, Page & Co., Garden City, N. Y., 1924), p. 68.

—————————. We Progressives hold that the words of the Declaration of Independence, as given effect to by Washington and as construed and applied by Abraham Lincoln, are to be accepted as real, and not as empty phrases. We believe that in very truth this is a government by the people themselves, that the Constitution is theirs, that the courts are theirs, that all the governmental agents and agencies are theirs. (At Madison Square Garden, N. Y. C., October 30, 1912.) *Mem. Ed.* XIX, 460; *Nat. Ed.* XVII, 337.

DECORATION DAY. *See* MEMORIAL DAY.

DEEDS—CREDIT FOR. In this world, in the long run, the job must necessarily fall to the man who both can and will do it when it must be done, even though he does it roughly or imperfectly. It is well enough to deplore and to strive against the conditions which make it necessary to do the job; but when once face to face with it, the man who fails either in power or will, the man who is half-hearted, reluctant, or incompetent, must give way to the actual doer, and he must not complain because the doer gets the credit and reward. (1900.) *Mem. Ed.* XIII, 405; *Nat. Ed.* X, 288.

DEEDS VERSUS WORDS. One of our besetting sins as a nation has been to encourage in our public servants, in our speech-making leaders of all kinds, the preaching of impossible ideals; and then to treat this as offsetting the fact that in practice these representatives did not live up to any ideals whatever. The vital need is that we as a nation shall say what we mean and shall make our public servants say what they mean; say it to other nations and say it to us, ourselves. Let us demand that we and they preach realizable ideals and that we and they live up to the ideals thus preached. Let there be no impassable gulf between exuberance of impossible promise and pitiful insufficiency in quality of possible performance. (1916.) *Mem. Ed.* XX, 530; *Nat. Ed.* XVIII, 455.

DEEDS. *See also* ACTION; BOASTING; CRITICISM; PRACTICALITY.

DEER, MULE. The mule-deer is a striking and beautiful animal. As is the case with our other species, it varies greatly in size, but is on the average heavier than either the whitetail or the true blacktail. The horns also average longer and heavier, and in exceptional heads are really noteworthy trophies. Ordinarily a full-grown buck has a head of ten distinct and well-developed points, eight of which consist of the bifurcations of the two main prongs into which each antler divides, while in addition there are two shorter basal or frontal points. But the latter are very irregular, being sometimes missing; while sometimes there are two or three of them on each antler. When missing it usually means that the antlers are of young animals that have not attained their full growth. (1905.) *Mem. Ed.* III, 207; *Nat. Ed.* III, 36.

—————————. The mule-deer differs widely from the whitetail in its habits, and especially in its gait and in the kind of country which it frequents. Although in many parts of its range it is found side by side with its whitetail cousin, the two do not actually associate together, and their propinquity is due simply to the fact that, the river-bottoms being a favorite haunt of the whitetail, long tongues of the distribution area of this species are thrust into the domain of its bolder, less stealthy, and less crafty kinsman. Throughout the plains country the whitetail is the deer of the river-bottoms, where the rank growth gives it secure hiding-places, as well as ample food. The mule-deer, on the contrary, never comes down into the dense growths of the river-bottoms. (1905.) *Mem. Ed.* III, 211; *Nat. Ed.* III, 39.

DEER, MULE—HUNTING THE. Ordinarily the mule-deer must be killed by long tramping among the hills, skilful stalking, and good shooting. The successful hunter should possess good eyes, good wind, and good muscles. He should know how to take cover and how to use his rifle. The work is sufficiently rough to test any man's endurance, and yet there is no such severe and intense toil as in following true mountain game, like the bighorn or white goat. As the hunter's one aim is to see the deer before it sees him, he can only use the horse to take him to the hunting-ground. Then he must go through the most likely ground and from every point of vantage scan with minute care the landscape round about, while himself unseen. If the country is wild and the deer have not been much molested, he will be apt to come across a band that is feeding. Under such circumstances it is easy to see them at once. But if lying down, it is astonishing how the gray of their winter coats fits in with the color of their surroundings. (1905.) *Mem. Ed.* III, 228; *Nat. Ed.* III, 53.

DEER, WHITETAIL. The whitetail deer is now, as it always has been, the most plentiful and most widely distributed of the American big game. It holds its own in the land better than any other species, because it is by choice a dweller in the thick forests and swamps, the places around which the tide of civilization flows, leaving them as islets of refuge for the wild creatures which formerly haunted all the country. The range of the whitetail is from the Atlantic to the Pacific, and from the Canadian to the Mexican borders, and somewhat to the north and far to the south of these limits. The animal shows a wide variability, both individually and locally, within these confines. (1905.) *Mem. Ed.* III, 178; *Nat. Ed.* III, 12.

DEER, WHITETAIL—HUNTING THE. Whitetail are comparatively easily killed with hounds, and there are very many places where this is almost the only way they can be killed at all. Formerly in the Adirondacks this method of hunting was carried on under circumstances which rendered those who took part in it objects of deserved contempt. The sportsman stood in a boat while his guides put out one or two hounds in the chosen forest side. After a longer or shorter run the deer took to the water; for whitetail are excellent swimmers, and when pursued by hounds try to shake them off by wading up or down stream or by swimming across a pond, and, if tired, come to bay in some pool or rapid. Once the unfortunate deer was in the water, the guide rowed the boat after it. If it was yet early in the season, and the deer was still in the red summer coat, it would sink when shot, and therefore the guide would usually take hold of its tail before the would-be Nimrod butchered it. If the deer was in the blue, the carcass would float, so it was not necessary to do anything quite so palpably absurd. But such sport, so far as the man who did the shooting was concerned, had not one redeeming feature. The use of hounds has now been prohibited by law. (1905.) *Mem. Ed.* III, 196; *Nat. Ed.* III, 27.

DEER HUNTING. A man who is hardy, resolute, and a good shot, has come nearer to realizing the ideal of a bold and free hunter than is the case with one who is merely stealthy and patient; and so, though to kill a white-tail is rather more difficult than to kill a black-tail, yet the chase of the latter is certainly the nobler form of sport, for it calls into play and either develops or implies the presence of much more manly qualities than does the other. Most hunters would find it nearly as difficult to watch in silence by a salt-lick throughout the night, and then to butcher with a shot-gun a whitetail, as it would be to walk on foot through rough ground from morning till evening, and to fairly approach and kill a black-tail; yet there is no comparison between the degree of credit to be attached to one feat and that to be attached to the other. Indeed, if difficulty in killing is to be taken as a criterion, a mink or even a weasel would have to stand as high up in the scale as a deer, were the animals equally plenty. (1885.) *Mem. Ed.* I, 129; *Nat. Ed.* I, 106.

DEFENSE. The only defensive that is worth anything is the offensive. (Campaign speech, New York City, October 5, 1898.) *Mem. Ed.* XVI, 445; *Nat. Ed.* XIV, 293.

———. Mere defensive by itself cannot permanently avail. The only permanently efficient defensive arm is one which can act offensively. (*Everybody's*, January 1915.) *Mem. Ed.* XX, 161; *Nat. Ed.* XVIII, 138.

DEFENSE, PASSIVE. Passive defense, giving the assailant complete choice of the time and place for attack, is always a most dangerous expedient. (*Atlantic Monthly*, October 1890.) *Mem. Ed.* XIV, 315; *Nat. Ed.* XII, 272.

DEFENSE MEASURES — INSISTENCE UPON. It is a fine alliance, that between the anglo-maniac mugwumps, the socialist working men, and corrupt politicians like Gorman, to prevent the increase of our Navy and coast defenses. The moneyed and semi-cultivated classes, especially of the Northeast, are doing their best to bring this country down to the Chinese level. If we ever come to nothing as a nation it will be because the teaching of Carl Schurz, President Eliot, the *Evening Post* and the futile sentimentalists of the international arbitration type, bears its legitimate fruit in producing a flabby, timid type of character, which eats away the great fighting features of our race. Hand in hand with the Chinese timidity and inefficiency of such a character would go the Chinese corruption. (To H. C. Lodge, April 29, 1896.) Lodge *Letters* I, 218.

DEFENSE OF A DEMOCRACY. We in America claim that a democracy can be as efficient for defense as an autocracy, as a despotism. It is idle to make this claim, it is idle to utter windy eloquence in Fourth of July speeches, and to prate in public documents about our greatness and our adherence to democratic principles and the mission we have to do good on the earth by spineless peacefulness, if we are not able, if we are not willing, to make our words count by means of our deeds. (*Metropolitan,* November 1915.) *Mem. Ed.* XX, 386; *Nat. Ed.* XVIII, 330.

DEFENSE. *See also* ARMY; MILITARY FORCES; MILITARY TRAINING; NATIONAL DEFENSE; NAVY; PACIFISM; PREPAREDNESS.

DEMAGOGUE. The demagogue, in all his forms, is as characteristic an evil of a free society as the courtier is of a despotism. (*Forum,* February 1895.) *Mem. Ed.* XV, 8; *Nat. Ed.* XIII, 7.

————. To play the demagogue for purposes of self-interest is a cardinal sin against the people in a democracy, exactly as to play the courtier for such purposes is a cardinal sin against the people under other forms of government. (1913.) *Mem. Ed.* XXII, 111; *Nat. Ed.* XX, 95.

————. When there is a great unrest, partly reasoning and partly utterly unreasoning and unreasonable, it becomes extremely difficult to beat a loud-mouthed demagogue, especially if he is a demagogue of great wealth. (To H. C. Lodge, November 9, 1911.) Lodge *Letters* II, 415.

DEMAGOGUES AND CORRUPTIONISTS. In the end the honest man, whether rich or poor, who earns his own living and tries to deal justly by his fellows, has as much to fear from the insincere and unworthy demagogue, promising much and performing nothing or else performing nothing but evil, who would set on the mob to plunder the rich, as from the crafty corruptionist, who, for his own ends, would permit the common people to be exploited by the very wealthy. If we ever let this government fall into the hands of men of either these two classes, we shall show ourselves false to America's past. Moreover, the demagogue and the corruptionist often work hand in hand. (Sixth Annual Message, Washington, Deember 3, 1906.) *Mem. Ed.* XVII, 420; *Nat. Ed.* XV, 358.

DEMOCRACY. The most genuine republican, if he has any common sense, does not believe in a democratic government for every race and in every age. (1888.) *Mem. Ed.* VIII, 418; *Nat. Ed.* VII, 360.

————. The principle of the sovereignty of the people is vital to all democracy. If the people fail to exercise that sovereignty with justice, self-control and practical good sense, then they show they are not fit for democracy. But if they are fit for democracy, then the sovereignty is and must be theirs, and theirs in fact and not merely in name. A free democracy fit for self-government must insist on governing itself and not being governed by others. Such a democracy can no more recognize the divine right of judges than the divine right of kings. It must itself declare what the laws and the constitution shall be. *Outlook,* November 15, 1913, p. 596.

DEMOCRACY—BELIEF IN. I had always been instinctively and by nature a democrat, but if I had needed conversion to the democratic ideal here in America the stimulus would have been supplied by what I saw of the attitude, not merely of the bulk of the men of greatest wealth, but of the bulk of the men who most prided themselves upon their education and culture, when we began in good faith to grapple with the wrong and injustice of our social and industrial system, and to hit at the men responsible for the wrong, no matter how high they stood in business or in politics, at the bar or on the bench. (1913.) *Mem. Ed.* XXII, 324; *Nat. Ed.* XX, 277.

————. The more I see of the Czar, the Kaiser, and the Mikado, the better I am content with democracy, even if we have to include the American newspaper as one of its assets—liability would be a better term. (To H. C. Lodge, June 16, 1905.) *Mem. Ed.* XXIII, 453; Bishop I, 394.

DEMOCRACY—DESPOTISM IN A. England, in the present century, has shown how complete may be the freedom of the individual under a nominal monarchy; and the Dreyfus incident in France would be proof enough, were any needed, that despotism of a peculiarly revolting type may grow rankly, even in a republic, if there is not in its citizens a firm and lofty purpose to do justice to all men and guard the rights of the weak as well as of the strong. (1900.) *Mem. Ed.* XIII, 302; *Nat. Ed.* X, 199.

DEMOCRACY—FOES OF. Every professional pacifist in America, every representative of commercialized greed, every apostle of timidity, every sinister creature who betrays his country by pandering to the anti-American feeling which masquerades under some species of hyphenated Americanism—all these men and women and their representatives in public life are at this moment working against democracy. If the democratic ideal fails, if democracy goes down, they will be primarily to blame. For democracy will assuredly go down if it once be shown that it is incompatible with national security. (*Metropolitan*, November 1915.) *Mem. Ed.* XX, 387; *Nat. Ed.* XVIII, 331.

DEMOCRACY—OBJECT OF. The true object of democracy should be to guarantee each man his rights, with the purpose that each shall thereby be enabled better to do his duty. . . . Democracy means failure if it merely substitutes a big privileged for a small privileged class, and if this big privileged class in its turn desires nothing more than selfish material enjoyment. The man who receives what he has not earned and does not earn, the man who does not render service in full for all that he has, is out of place in a democratic community. (*Outlook*, March 25, 1911.) *Mem. Ed.* XIX, 141; *Nat. Ed.* XVII, 100.

DEMOCRACY—PARTICIPATION IN A. The humblest among us, no matter what his creed, his birthplace, or the color of his skin, so long as he behaves in straight and decent fashion, must have guaranteed to him under the law his right to life and liberty, to protection from injustice, to the enjoyment of the fruits of his own labor, and to do his share in the work of self-government on the same terms with others of like fitness. (*Outlook*, August 24, 1912.) *Mem. Ed.* XIX, 414; *Nat. Ed.* XVII, 302.

DEMOCRACY—PROGRESS IN A. In popular government results worth having can only be achieved by men who combine worthy ideals with practical good sense; who are resolute to accomplish good purposes, but who can accommodate themselves to the give and take necessary where work has to be done, as almost all important work has to be done, by combination. (At the Harvard Union, Cambridge, February 23, 1907.) *Mem. Ed.* XV, 489; *Nat. Ed.* XIII, 565.

DEMOCRACY—SERVICE IN A. Unless democracy is based on the principle of service by everybody who claims the enjoyment of any right, it is not true democracy at all. The man who refuses to render, or is ashamed to render, the necessary service is not fit to live in a democracy. And the man who demands from another a service which he himself would esteem it dishonorable or unbecoming to render is to that extent not a true Democrat. No man has a right to demand a service which he does not regard as honorable to render; nor has he a right to demand it unless he pays for it in some way, *the payment to include respect for the man who renders it*. Democracy must mean mutuality of service rendered, and of respect for the service rendered. (*Metropolitan*, March 1918.) *Mem. Ed.* XXI, 372; *Nat. Ed.* XIX, 338.

DEMOCRACY—SUCCESS IN A. From the days when civilized man first began to strive for self-government and democracy success in this effort has depended primarily upon the ability to steer clear of extremes. (1918.) *Mem. Ed.* XXI, 377; *Nat. Ed.* XIX, 342.

DEMOCRACY, AMERICAN. We must make this nation a real democracy; an economic as well as political democracy free from every taint of either sectional or sectarian hatred; a democracy of true brotherhood which knows neither North nor South, East nor West, which recognizes the right of each man to worship his Creator as he chooses; a democracy which recognizes service and not pleasure as the ideal for every man and woman, which stands for each individual's performance of his own duty toward others even more than for his insistence upon his rights as against others. (At New York City, February 12, 1913.) *Mem. Ed.* XIX, 507; *Nat. Ed.* XVII, 377.

DEMOCRACY, AMERICAN—FEATURES OF. The distinctive features of the American system are its guarantees of personal independence and individual freedom; that is, as far as possible, it guarantees to each man his right to live as he chooses and to regulate his own private affairs as he wishes, without being interfered with or tyrannized over by an individual, or by an oligarchic minority, or by a Democratic majority; while, when the interests of the whole community are at stake, it is found best in the long run to let them be managed in accordance with the wishes of the majority of those presumably concerned. (1887.) *Mem. Ed.* VIII, 180; *Nat. Ed.* VII, 157.

DEMOCRACY, AMERICAN—OPPORTUNITY FOR. Here in America we the people have a continent on which to work out our destiny, and our faith is great that our men and women are fit to face the mighty days. Nowhere else in all the world is there such a chance for the triumph on a gigantic scale of the great cause of Democratic and popular government. If we fail, the failure will be lamentable, and our heads will be bowed with shame; for not only shall we fail for ourselves, but our failure will wreck the fond desires of all throughout the world who look toward us with the fond hope that here in this great Republic it shall be proved from ocean to ocean that the people can rule themselves, and thus ruling can gain liberty for and do justice both to themselves and to others. We who stand for the cause of the uplift of humanity and the betterment of mankind are pledged to eternal war against wrong whether by the few or by the many, by a plutocracy or by a mob. We believe that this country will not be a permanently good place for any of us to live in unless we make it a reasonably good place for all of us to live in. The sons of all of us will pay in the future if we of the present do not do justice to all in the present. Our cause is the cause of justice for all in the interest of all. (At Chicago, June 17, 1912.) *Mem. Ed.* XIX, 316; *Nat. Ed.* XVII, 230.

DEMOCRACY, AMERICAN — PRINCIPLES OF. We stand against all tyranny, by the few or by the many. We stand for the rule of the many in the interest of all of us, for the rule of the many in a spirit of courage, of common sense, of high purpose, above all in a spirit of kindly justice toward every man and every woman. We not merely admit, but insist, that there must be self-control on the part of the people, that they must keenly perceive their own duties as well as the rights of others; but we also insist that the people can do nothing unless they not merely have, but exercise to the full, their own rights. The worth of our great experiment depends upon its being in good faith an experiment—the first that has ever been tried—in true democracy on the scale of a continent, on a scale as vast as that of the mightiest empires of the Old World. Surely this is a noble ideal, an ideal for which it is worth while to strive, an ideal for which at need it is worth while to sacrifice much, for our ideal is the rule of all the people in a spirit of friendliest brotherhood toward each and every one of the people. (At Carnegie Hall, N. Y. C., March 20, 1912.) *Mem. Ed.* XIX, 223; *Nat. Ed.* XVII, 171.

——————. Our nation was founded to perpetuate democratic principles. These principles are that each man is to be treated on his worth as a man without regard to the land from which his forefathers came and without regard to the creed which he professes. If the United States proves false to these principles of civil and religious liberty, it will have inflicted the greatest blow on the system of free popular government that has ever been inflicted. (Before Knights of Columbus, New York City, October 12, 1915.) *Mem. Ed.* XX, 453; *Nat. Ed.* XVIII, 389.

DEMOCRACY, AMERICAN—RESPONSIBILITY OF. Our country—this great Republic—means nothing unless it means the triumph of a real democracy, the triumph of popular government, and, in the long run, of an economic system under which each man shall be guaranteed the opportunity to show the best that there is in him. That is why the history of America is now the central feature of the history of the world; for the world has set its face hopefully toward our democracy; and, O my fellow citizens, each one of you carries on your shoulders not only the burden of doing well for the sake of your own country, but the burden of doing well and of seeing that this nation does well for the sake of mankind. (At Osawatomie, Kan., August 31, 1910.) *Mem. Ed.* XIX, 10; *Nat. Ed.* XVII, 5.

——————. Our country offers the most wonderful example of democratic government on a giant scale that the world has ever seen; and the peoples of the world are watching to see whether we succeed or fail. We believe with all our hearts in democracy; in the capacity of the people to govern themselves; and we are bound to succeed, for our success means not only our own triumph, but the triumph of the cause of the rights of the people throughout the world, and the uplifting of the banner of hope for all the nations of mankind. (Before New York Republican State Convention, Saratoga, September 27, 1910.) *Mem. Ed.* XIX, 37; *Nat. Ed.* XVII, 28.

——————. The existence of this nation has no real significance, from the standpoint of humanity at large, unless it means the rule of the people, and the achievement of a greater measure of widely diffused popular well-being than has ever before obtained on a like scale.

Unless this is in very truth a government of, by, and for the people, then both historically and in world interest our national existence loses most of its point. Nominal republics with a high aggregate of industrial prosperity, and governed normally by rich traders and manufacturers in their own real or fancied interest, but occasionally by violent and foolish mobs, have existed in many previous ages. There is little to be gained by repeating on a bigger scale in the western hemisphere the careers of Tyre and Carthage on the shores of the Mediterranean. (*Outlook,* January 21, 1911.) *Mem. Ed.* XIX, 86; *Nat. Ed.* XVII, 53.

——————————. I hold that we of this nation are false to our professions, false to the traditions handed down to us by the founders and the preservers of the Republic, if we do not make it in very truth a real republic, a democracy in fact as well as in name, a democracy where each man stands on his worth as a man and is judged as such; a democracy in which the people really rule themselves, where their representatives do not rule them but honestly and efficiently manage the government for them. (At St. Louis, Mo., March 28, 1912.) *Mem. Ed.* XIX, 239; *Nat. Ed.* XVII, 176.

DEMOCRACY, AMERICAN—TEST OF. Our democracy is now put to a vital test; for the conflict is between human rights on the one side and on the other special privilege asserted as a property right. The parting of the ways has come. The Republican party must definitely stand on one side or the other. It must stand, by deeds, and not merely by empty phrases, for the rights of humanity, or else it must stand for special privilege. Our opponents are fond of calling themselves regular Republicans. In reality they have no title to membership in any party that is true to the principles of Abraham Lincoln. They are fighting for the cause of special privilege and their chief strength is drawn from the beneficiaries of intrenched economic and social injustice. (At Chicago, June 17, 1912.) *Mem. Ed.* XIX, 306; *Nat. Ed.* XVII, 221.

DEMOCRACY, ECONOMIC. Our whole experiment is meaningless unless we are to make this a democracy in the fullest sense of the word, in the broadest as well as the highest and deepest significance of the word. It must be made a democracy economically as well as politically. *Outlook,* September 3, 1910, p. 21.

——————————. There can be no real political democracy unless there is something approaching an economic democracy. A democracy must consist of men who are intellectually, morally, and materially fit to be their own masters. There can be neither political nor industrial democracy unless people are reasonably well-to-do, and also reasonably able to achieve the difficult task of self-mastery. (*Outlook,* November 18, 1914.) *Mem. Ed.* XIV, 220; *Nat. Ed.* XII, 237.

DEMOCRACY AND PRIVILEGE. I advocate genuine popular rule in nation, in State, in city, in county, as offering the best possible means for eliminating special privilege alike in politics and in business, and for getting a genuine equality of opportunity for every man to show the stuff there is in him. I do not demand equality of reward. There is wide inequality of service, and where this is the case it is but just that there should be inequality of reward, for it would be the rankest kind of injustice to reward the man who renders worthless service as well as we strive, however inadequately, to reward him who renders service that is literally priceless.

But I do ask that we endeavor so to shape our governmental policy as to bring about a measurable equality of opportunity for all men and all women so as to do justice to man and to woman, to big and to little, to rich and to poor. (At St. Louis, Mo., March 28, 1912.) *Mem. Ed.* XIX, 238; *Nat. Ed.* XVII, 175.

DEMOCRACY AND THE WORLD WAR. It is at least possible that the conflict will result in a growth of democracy in Europe, in at least a partial substitution of the rule of the people for the rule of those who esteem it their God-given right to govern the people. This, in its turn, would render it probably a little more unlikely that there would be a repetition of such disastrous warfare. I do not think that at present it would prevent the possibility of warfare. . . . The growth of the power of the people, while it would not prevent war, would at least render it more possible than at present to make appeals which might result in some cases in coming to an accommodation based upon justice; for justice is what popular rule must be permanently based upon and must permanently seek to obtain or it will not itself be permanent. (*Outlook,* September 23, 1914.) *Mem. Ed.* XX, 32; *Nat. Ed.* XVIII, 27.

——————————. When we went to war there was neither talk nor thought of "making the world safe for democracy"—if war for that purpose was necessary then it had been necessary for the preceding two years and a half. We went to war because for two years the

Germans had been murdering our unarmed men, women, and children, and had definitely announced their intention to continue the practice. After we had been at war a few weeks the President announced that our purpose was to make the world safe for democracy. This phrase, uttered by the President when we were already at war, solemnly pledged us to exert our whole strength, and suffer any losses, in a terrible crusade, not for our own benefit, but for the benefit of mankind as a whole. To make such a pledge lightly, or to abandon it when once made, would be infamous. Therefore we must keep it. (1917.) *Mem. Ed.* XXI, 10; *Nat. Ed.* XIX, 9.

DEMOCRACY. *See also* CITIZENSHIP; CIVIC DUTY; EDUCATION; EQUALITY; FRONTIER DEMOCRACY; GOVERNMENT; INDUSTRIAL DEMOCRACY; INITIATIVE; LEADERSHIP; LIBERTY; POWER; PRIVILEGE; REPUBLICAN GOVERNMENT; SELF-GOVERNMENT; SUFFRAGE; VOTING.

DEMOCRATIC IDEAL, THE. Let us be true to our democratic ideal, not by the utterance of cheap platitudes, not by windy oratory, but by living our lives in such manner as to show that democracy can be efficient in promoting the public welfare during periods of peace and efficient in securing national freedom in time of war. . . . The democratic ideal must be that of subordinating chaos to order, of subordinating the individual to the community, of subordinating individual selfishness to collective self-sacrifice for a lofty ideal, of training every man to realize that no one is entitled to citizenship in a great free commonwealth unless he does his full duty to his neighbor, his full duty in his family life, and his full duty to the nation; and unless he is prepared to do this duty not only in time of peace but also in time of war. It is by no means necessary that a great nation should always stand at the heroic level. But no nation has the root of greatness in it unless in time of need it can rise to the heroic mood. (1916.) *Mem. Ed.* XX, 532-533; *Nat. Ed.* XVIII, 456-457.

——————. Mutuality of respect and consideration, service and a reward corresponding as nearly as may be to the service—these make up the ideal of democracy. Such an ideal is as far from the stupid bourbonism of reaction as it is from the vicious lunacy of the Bolsheviki or I. W. W. type. (*Metropolitan,* March 1918.) *Mem. Ed.* XXI, 375; *Nat. Ed.* XIX, 340.

DEMOCRATIC PARTY. The Democratic party is now what it was twenty years ago; as long as the history of our State has been, as long as the history of our nation has lasted, the Democrats have been one and the same; from Jefferson, miscalled the Great, to Buchanan, the Little, it has been one and the same thing all the way through. (At Republican mass-meeting, 21st Assembly Dist., New York City, October 28, 1882.) *Mem. Ed.* XVI, 15; *Nat. Ed.* XIV, 13.

——————. There are a few of the members of the Democracy who do at times, at any rate, pay attention to reason and justice, but with the rank and file of that party as it is constituted I do not think much can ever be hoped for. (In New York Assembly, March 9, 1883.) *Mem. Ed.* XVI, 26; *Nat. Ed.* XIV, 19.

DEMOCRATIC PARTY AND PROGRESSIVE PARTY. From the Democratic party as at present constituted we are radically divided both because of the utter incoherence within that party itself, and because the doctrines to which it is at present committed are either fundamentally false or else set forth with a rhetorical vagueness which makes it utterly futile to attempt to reduce them to practice. The Democratic party can accomplish nothing of good unless it deliberately repudiates its campaign pledges—unless it deliberately breaks the promises it solemnly made in order to acquire power. Such repudiation necessarily means an intellectual dishonesty so great that no skill in rhetorical dialectics can cover or atone for it. To win power by definite promises, and then seek to retain it by the repudiation of those promises, would show a moral unfitness such as not to warrant further trust of any kind. Therefore we must proceed upon the assumption that the leaders of the democracy meant what they said when they were seeking to obtain office. Their only performance so far, at the time that this article is written, is in connection with the tariff and with a discreditable impotence in foreign affairs. As a means of helping to solve great industrial and social problems, the tariff is merely a red herring dragged across the trail to divert our people from the real issues. (*Century,* October 1913.) *Mem. Ed.* XIX, 539; *Nat. Ed.* XVII, 397.

DEMOCRATIC PARTY. *See also* COPPERHEADS; JEFFERSON, THOMAS; MADISON, JAMES; NEW FREEDOM; POLITICAL PARTIES; TAMMANY HALL; TARIFF; WILSON, WOODROW.

DENMARK—SOCIAL LEGISLATION IN. I was interested in the Old Age homes, and in the co-operative farming, although I could only get a glimpse of both; but I was rather puzzled to find that the very great growth of what I should call the wise and democratic use of the powers of the State toward helping raise the individual standard of social and economic well-being had not made the people more contented. It seems to me that the way Denmark has handled the problem of agricultural well-being, and the problem of dealing with the wage-workers who do manual labor, and of securing them against want in their old age, represents a higher and more intelligent social and governmental action than we have begun to have in America; yet I encountered much bitterness toward the national government among the large and growing Socialistic party. (To Sir George Otto Trevelyan, October 1, 1911.) *Mem. Ed.* XXIV, 277; Bishop II, 237.

DENOMINATIONAL SCHOOLS. See Public Schools; Schools.

DEPRESSION. See Hard Times; Panic.

DESERTION. There can be no graver crime than the crime of desertion from the army and navy, especially during war; it is then high treason to the Nation, and justly punishable by death. No man should be relieved from such a crime. (Message to Senate, March 11, 1902.) *Mem. Ed.* XXIII, 217; Bishop I, 189.

DESPOTISM. See Anarchists; Democracy; Revolution; Self-Government; Washington, George.

DEWEY, ADMIRAL GEORGE. Admiral Dewey has done more than add a glorious page to our history; more even than do a deed the memory of which will always be an inspiration to his countrymen, and especially his countrymen of his own profession. He has also taught us a lesson which should have profound practical effects, if only we are willing to learn it aright.

In the first place, he partly grasped and partly made his opportunity. Of course, in a certain sense, no man can absolutely make an opportunity.... Nevertheless when the chance does come, only the great man can see it instantly and use it aright. In the second place, it must always be remembered that the power of using the chance aright comes only to the man who has faithfully and for long years made ready himself and his weapons for the possible need. (*McClure's Magazine,* October 1899.) *Mem. Ed.* XII, 506; *Nat. Ed.* XIII, 420.

————————. Admiral Dewey performed one of the great feats of all time. At the very outset of the Spanish war he struck one of the two decisive blows which brought the war to a conclusion, and as his was the first fight, his success exercised an incalculable effect upon the whole conflict. He set the note of the war. He had carefully prepared for action during the months he was on the Asiatic coast. He had his plans thoroughly matured, and he struck the instant that war was declared. There was no delay, no hesitation. As soon as news came that he was to move, his war-steamers turned their bows toward Manila Bay. There was nothing to show whether or not Spanish mines and forts would be efficient; but Dewey, cautious as he was at the right time, had not a particle of fear of taking risks when the need arose. . . .

The work, however, was by no means done, and Dewey's diplomacy and firmness were given full scope for the year he remained in Manila waters, not only in dealing with Spaniards and insurgents, but in making it evident that we would tolerate no interference from any hostile European power. (*McClure's Magazine,* October 1899.) *Mem. Ed.* XII, 515; *Nat. Ed.* XIII, 428, 429.

DICKENS, CHARLES. Dickens was an ill-natured, selfish cad and boor, who had no understanding of what the word gentleman meant, and no appreciation of hospitality or good treatment. He was utterly incapable of seeing the high purpose and the real greatness which (in spite of the presence also of much that was bad or vile) could have been visible all around him here in America to any man whose vision was both keen and lofty. He could not see the qualities of the young men growing up here, though it was these qualities that enabled these men to conquer the West and to fight to a finish the great Civil War, and though they were to produce leadership like that of Lincoln, Lee, and Grant. Naturally he would think there was no gentleman in New York, because by no possibility could he have recognized a gentleman if he had met one. Naturally he would condemn all America because he had not the soul to see what America was really doing. (To Kermit Roosevelt, February 29, 1908.) *Mem. Ed.* XXI, 601; *Nat. Ed.* XIX, 540.

DICKENS' CHARACTERS. Dickens' characters are really to a great extent personified attributes rather than individuals. In consequence, while there are not nearly as many who are actually like people one meets, as for instance in Thackeray, there are a great many more who possess *characteristics* which we encounter continually, though rarely as strongly developed as in the fictional originals. So Dickens' characters last almost as Bunyan's do. For instance, Jefferson Brick and Elijah Pogram and Hannibal Chollop are all real personifications of certain bad tendencies in American life, and I am continually thinking of or alluding to some newspaper editor or Senator or homicidal rowdy by one of these three names. I never met any one exactly like Uriah Heep, but now and then we see individuals show traits which make it easy to describe them, with reference to those traits, as Uriah Heep. It is just the same with Micawber. Mrs. Nickleby is not quite a real person, but she typifies, in accentuated form, traits which a great many real persons possess, and I am continually thinking of her when I meet them. There are half a dozen books of Dickens which have, I think, furnished more characters which are the constant companions of the ordinary educated man around us, than is true of any other half-dozen volumes published within the same period. (To Theodore Roosevelt, Jr., May 20, 1906.) *Mem. Ed.* XXI, 565; *Nat. Ed.* XIX, 507.

―――――――. I quite agree with you about Tom Pinch. He is a despicable kind of character; just the kind of character Dickens liked, because he had himself a thick streak of maudlin sentimentality of the kind that, as somebody phrased it, "made him wallow naked in the pathetic." It always interests me about Dickens to think how much first-class work he did and how almost all of it was mixed up with every kind of cheap, second-rate matter. I am very fond of him. There are innumerable characters that he has created which symbolize vices, virtues, follies, and the like almost as well as the characters in Bunyan; and therefore I think the wise thing to do is simply to skip the bosh and twaddle and vulgarity and untruth, and get the benefit out of the rest. Of course one fundamental difference between Thackeray and Dickens is that Thackeray was a gentleman and Dickens was not. But a man might do some mighty good work and not be a gentleman in any sense. (To Kermit Roosevelt, February 23, 1908.) *Mem. Ed.* XXI, 600; *Nat. Ed.* XIX, 539.

DICTATORSHIP. See LIBERTY.

DIPLOMACY. Diplomacy is utterly useless where there is no force behind it; the diplomat is the servant, not the master, of the soldier. The prosperity of peace, commercial and material prosperity, gives no weight whatever when the clash of arms comes. (Address as Assistant Secretary of the Navy, Naval War College, June 1897.) *Mem. Ed.* XV, 255; *Nat. Ed.* XIII, 195.

DIPLOMACY. See also ALLIANCES; ARBITRATION; FOREIGN POLICY; JUSSERAND, J. J.

DIPLOMATIC SERVICE. As a matter of fact, I am anxious to have it understood that it is not necessary to be a multimillionaire in order to reach the highest positions in the American diplomatic service. (To Sir Cecil Arthur Spring-Rice, April 11, 1908.) *Mem. Ed.* XXIV, 128; Bishop II, 110.

―――――――. The American public rarely appreciate the high quality of the work done by some of our diplomats—work, usually entirely unnoticed and unrewarded, which redounds to the interest and the honor of all of us. (1913.) *Mem. Ed.* XXII, 404; *Nat. Ed.* XX, 347.

DIPLOMATIC SERVICE. See also AMBASSADORS; CONSULAR SERVICE; FOREIGN RELATIONS; WHITE, HENRY.

DIRECT ACTION. See ANARCHISTS; BOLSHEVISTS; INDUSTRIAL WORKERS OF THE WORLD.

DIRECT PRIMARY. See PRIMARIES.

DISARMAMENT. Harm and not good would result if the most advanced nations, those in which most freedom for the individual is combined with most efficiency in securing orderly justice as between individuals, should by agreement disarm and place themselves at the mercy of other peoples less advanced, of other peoples still in the stage of military barbarism or military despotism. Anything in the nature of general disarmament would do harm and not good if it left the civilized and peace-loving peoples, those with the highest standards of municipal and international obligation and duty, unable to check the other peoples who have no such standards, who acknowledge no such obligations. (To Andrew Carnegie, April 5, 1907.) *Presidential Addresses and State Papers* VI, 1191-1192.

―――――――. Disarmament of the free and liberty-loving nations would merely mean insuring the triumph of some barbarism or despotism, and if logically applied would mean the extinction of liberty and of all that makes civilization worth having throughout the world. (*Outlook*, September 23, 1914.) *Mem. Ed.* XX, 35; *Nat. Ed.* XVIII, 29.

———————. There is utter inconsistency between the ideal of making this nation the foremost commercial power in the world and of disarmament in the face of an armed world. There is utter inconsistency between the ideal of making this nation a power for international righteousness and at the same time refusing to make us a power efficient in anything save empty treaties and emptier promises. (New York *Times,* November 15, 1914.) *Mem. Ed.* XX, 107; *Nat. Ed.* XVIII, 92.

DISARMAMENT—DANGERS OF. Nothing would more promote iniquity, nothing would further defer the reign upon earth of peace and righteousness, than for the free and enlightened peoples which, though with much stumbling and many shortcomings, nevertheless strive toward justice, deliberately to render themselves powerless while leaving every despotism and barbarism armed and able to work their wicked will. The chance for the settlement of disputes peacefully, by arbitration, now depends mainly upon the possession by the nations that mean to do right of sufficient armed strength to make their purpose effective. (Sixth Annual Message, Washington, December 3, 1906.) *Mem. Ed.* XVII, 473; *Nat. Ed.* XV, 403.

———————. Unjust war is dreadful; a just war may be the highest duty. To have the best nations, the free and civilized nations, disarm and leave the despotisms and barbarisms with great military force, would be a calamity compared to which the calamities caused by all the wars of the nineteenth century would be trivial. Yet it is not easy to see how we can by international agreement state exactly which power ceases to be free and civilized and which comes near the line of barbarism or despotism. (1913.) *Mem. Ed.* XXII, 621; *Nat. Ed.* XX, 534.

DISARMAMENT — DESIRABILITY OF. If armaments were reduced while causes of trouble were in no way removed, wars would probably become somewhat more frequent just because they would be less expensive and less decisive. It is greatly to be desired that the growth of armaments should be arrested, but they cannot be arrested while present conditions continue. Mere treaties, mere bits of papers, with names signed to them and with no force back of them, have proved utterly worthless for the protection of nations, and where they are the only alternatives it is not only right but necessary that each nation should arm itself so as to be able to cope with any possible foe.

(New York *Times,* October 18, 1914.) *Mem. Ed.* XX, 64; *Nat. Ed.* XVIII, 54.

DISARMAMENT. *See also* ARBITRATION; ARMAMENTS; DEFENSE; NATIONAL DEFENSE; NAVAL ARMAMENTS; PACIFISM; PEACE; PREPAREDNESS; UNPREPAREDNESS.

DISCRIMINATION. *See* KNOW NOTHING MOVEMENT; RELIGIOUS DISCRIMINATION.

DISHONESTY IN PUBLIC SERVICE. We can as little afford to tolerate a dishonest man in the public service as a coward in the army. The murderer takes a single life; the corruptionist in public life, whether he be bribe-giver or bribe-taker, strikes at the heart of the commonwealth. (At unveiling of statue of General W. T. Sherman, Washington, October 15, 1903.) *Mem. Ed.* XXIII, 296; Bishop I, 257.

DISHONESTY. *See also* BRIBERY; CORRUPTION; HONESTY.

DISLOYALTY AND PREJUDICE. The disloyal man, whether his disloyalty is open or disguised, is our worst foe; but close behind him comes the man who, whether from wickedness or foolishness, assails his loyal fellow citizens because of the blood that flows in their veins. (1918.) *Mem. Ed.* XXI, 341; *Nat. Ed.* XIX, 312.

DISLOYALTY. *See also* LOYALTY; PREJUDICE.

DISTRIBUTION. *See* EFFICIENCY, NATIONAL.

DIVIDED ALLEGIANCE. *See* ALLEGIANCE.

DIVIDENDS. The public must not be expected to sacrifice its own interests and the interests of wage-workers in order to pay dividends on watered stock, or to secure promoters and managers against the consequences of their own folly. *Outlook,* July 5, 1913, p. 501.

———————. Dividends and wages should go up together; and the relation of rates to them should never be forgotten. This of course does not apply to dividends based on water; nor does it mean that if foolish people have built a road that renders no service, the public must nevertheless in some way guarantee a return on the investment; but it does mean that the interests of the honest investor are entitled to the same protection as the interests of the honest manager, the honest shipper, and the honest wage-earner. All these conflicting considerations should be carefully considered by legislatures before passing laws. One of the great objects in creating commissions should be the provision of disinterested, fair-minded experts who will really and wisely consider all these matters, and will shape their actions accordingly. (1913.) *Mem. Ed.* XXII, 570; *Nat. Ed.* XX, 490.

DIVIDENDS. See also CORPORATIONS; PROFITS; PROPERTY.

DIVINE RIGHT. See JUDGES; KINGS.

DIVISION OF POWERS. It is often said that ours is a government of checks and balances. But this should only mean that these checks and balances obtain as among the several different kinds of representatives of the people—judicial, executive, and legislative—to whom the people have delegated certain portions of their power. It does not mean that the people have parted with their power or cannot resume it. The "division of powers" is merely the division among the representatives of the powers delegated to them; the term must not be held to mean that the people have divided their power with their delegates. The power is the people's, and only the people's. It is right and proper that provision should be made rendering it necessary for the people to take ample time to make up their minds on any point; but there should also be complete provision to have their decision put into immediate and living effect when it has thus been deliberately and definitely reached. (Before Ohio Constitutional Convention, Columbus, February 21, 1912.) *Mem. Ed.* XIX, 166; *Nat. Ed.* XVII, 122.

———. In most positions the "division of powers" theory works unmitigated mischief. The only way to get good service is to give somebody power to render it, facing the fact that power which will enable a man to do a job well will also necessarily enable him to do it ill if he is the wrong kind of man. What is normally needed is the concentration in the hands of one man, or of a very small body of men, of ample power to enable him or them to do the work that is necessary; and then the devising of means to hold these men fully responsible for the exercise of that power by the people. This of course means that, if the people are willing to see power misused, it will be misused. But it also means that if, as we hold, the people are fit for self-government—if, in other words, our talk and our institutions are not shams—we will get good government. I do not contend that my theory will automatically bring good government. I do contend that it will enable us to get as good government as we deserve, and that the other way will not. (1913.) *Mem. Ed.* XXII, 205; *Nat. Ed.* XX, 176.

DIVISION OF POWERS. See also EXECUTIVE; GOVERNMENT; PRESIDENT; SPECIAL INTERESTS; SUPREME COURT.

DIVORCE. Multiplication of divorces means that there is something rotten in the community, that there is some principle of evil at work which must be counteracted and overcome or wide-spread disaster will follow. (At Pacific Theological Seminary, Spring 1911.) *Mem. Ed.* XV, 594; *Nat. Ed.* XIII, 631.

———. I do unqualifiedly condemn easy divorce. I know that the effect on the "Four Hundred" of easy divorce has been very bad. It has been shocking to me to hear young girls about to get married calmly speculating on how long it will be before they get divorces. (To Robert Grant, March 14, 1905.) Henry F. Pringle, *Theodore Roosevelt.* (Harcourt, Brace & Co., N. Y., 1931), p. 472.

———. In my judgment the whole question of marriage and divorce should be relegated to the authority of the National Congress. At present the wide differences in the laws of the different States on this subject result in scandals and abuses; and surely there is nothing so vitally essential to the welfare of the nation, nothing around which the nation should so bend itself to throw every safeguard, as the home life of the average citizen. The change would be good from every standpoint. (Sixth Annual Message, Washington, December 3, 1906.) *Mem. Ed.* XVII, 442; *Nat. Ed.* XV, 377.

DIVORCE COLONY. It is one colony of which you want to rid yourselves; I don't care what you do with those of your own State who seek divorces, but keep citizens of other States who want divorces out of Nevada. Don't allow yourselves to be deceived by the argument that such a colony brings money to your city. You can't afford to have that kind of money brought here. (At Reno, Nev., April 3, 1911.) *Mem. Ed.* XXIV, 364; Bishop II, 310.

DIVORCE. *See also* MARRIAGE.

DOCTORS. I think that all of us laymen, men and women, have a peculiar appreciation of what a doctor means; for I do not suppose there is one of us who does not feel that the family doctor stands in a position of close intimacy with each of us, in a position of obligation to him under which one is happy to rest to an extent hardly possible with any one else; and those of us, I think most of us, who are fortunate enough to have a family doctor who is a beloved and intimate friend, realize that there can be few closer ties of intimacy and affection in the world. And while, of course, even the greatest and best doctors can not assume that very intimate relation with more than a certain number of people (though it is to be said that more than any other man, the doctor does commonly assume such a relation to many people) . . . still with every patient with whom the doctor is thrown at all intimately he has this peculiar relation to a greater or less extent. The effect that the doctor has upon the body of the patient is in very many cases no greater than the effect that he has upon the patient's mind. (At United States Naval Medical School, Washington, D. C., March 25, 1905.) *Presidential Addresses and State Papers* III, 309.

——————. Of course it is almost needless to say that there is not and can not be any other lay profession the members of which occupy such a dual position, each side of which is of such importance—for the doctor has on the one hand to be the most thoroughly educated man in applied science that there is in the country, and on the other hand, as every layman knows, and as doubtless many a layman in the circle of acquaintance of each of you would gladly testify, the doctor gradually becomes the closest friend to more people than would be possible in any other profession. . . . The doctor must, therefore, to the greatest degree develop his nature along the two sides of his duties, although in the case of any other man you would call him a mighty good citizen if he developed only on one side. The scientific man who is really a first-class scientific man has a claim upon the gratitude of all the country; and the man who is a first-class neighbor, and is always called in in time of trouble by his neighbors, has an equal claim upon society at large. But the doctor has both claims. (Before Long Island Medical Society, Oyster Bay, N. Y., July 12, 1905.) *Presidential Addresses and State Papers* IV, 429-430.

DOLLAR WORSHIP. See Fortunes; Materialist; Millionaires; Money; Wealth.

DOMESTIC ECONOMY. See Home.

DOMESTIC SERVICE. It is as entirely right to employ housemaids, cooks, and gardeners as to employ lawyers, bankers, and business men or cashiers, factory-hands, and stenographers. But only on condition that we show the same respect to the individuals in one case as in the other cases!

Ultimately I hope that this respect will show itself in the forms of address, in the courtesy titles used, as well as the consideration shown, and the personal liberty expected and accorded. I am not demanding an instant change—I believe in evolution rather than revolution. But I am sure the change is possible and desirable; and even although it would be foolish and undesirable to set up the entirely new standard immediately, I hope we can work toward it. (*Metropolitan*, March 1918.) *Mem. Ed.* XXI, 374; *Nat. Ed.* XIX, 340.

DOOLEY, MR. Let me repeat that Dooley, especially when he writes about Teddy Rosenfelt, has no more interested and amused reader than said Rosenfelt himself. I have known that a few people have recently thought quite otherwise, as they have also told you that they thought; but this is not a feeling that I have shared in the least. On the contrary, I feel that what you have written about me, with exception too trivial to mention, has been written in just the nicest possible style—that what Dooley says shows "the good-natured affection that the boys in the army felt for old Grant and the people in Illinois for Lincoln." I hate to compare myself with two great men, even when I am only quoting you, and I do it of course merely to show how thoroughly I understand and appreciate our friend Mr. Dooley's attitude. (To Finley Peter Dunne, January 9, 1907.) *Mem. Ed.* XXIV, 40; Bishop II, 34.

DOUGHFACE. See Copperheads.

DRAFT. The draft has been admirably administered by General Crowder and is excellent in so far as it recognizes the principle of obligatory service; it is inadequate and unjust in so far as it is treated only as a temporary device, and in so far as it makes such service "selective," that is, in so far as it requires the haphazard selection of one man to make sacrifices while other men, not entitled to exemption, are relieved of duty at his expense. It is not too late to remedy this. A law should at once be passed making military training universal for our young men, and providing for its immediate application to all the young men between nineteen and twenty-one. (*Metropolitan*, September 1917.) *Mem. Ed.* XXI, 27; *Nat. Ed.* XIX, 23.

DRAFT   DUTY

————————. We ought to change the draft rules, so far as giving any special privileges to the young fellows between eighteen and twenty in the matter of college training, to fit them to be officers. To say that the nation will pay for all of them to go to college is a deception, and to believe it is a delusion. I do not believe in a selective draft for a favored class. I wish to see fair play for the workman's son who has not had the chance to learn so that he can go to college, but who has the natural ability to command and lead men. Only boys whose parents in the past have had the money to give them a special education can enter college at the present time, and it is unfair to the other boys to give these a special advantage. Let all go into the ranks together and after six months or a year of service let the best men be chosen out to enter the schools which will fit them to be officers. Of course, with the older men and at the beginning, we had to take those already available. But when we come to need the young fellows under twenty-one, let every man enter the ranks and stand on a fair footing with every one else, and be given promotion on his merits. Hitherto the men who came in under twenty-one, came in as volunteers, and they were entitled to try for any position they could get; but now we have at last done what we ought to have done in the beginning. Now let them all stand alike. (*Metropolitan,* November 1918.) *Mem. Ed.* XXI, 278; *Nat. Ed.* XIX, 257.

DRAFT. *See also* CONSCIENTIOUS OBJECTORS; MILITARY SERVICE; MILITARY TRAINING; PACIFISM; VOLUNTEER SYSTEM.

DRAMA. I know nothing of the drama except that I am ashamed to say I don't care to go to the theatre; and nevertheless I do very greatly care to read certain plays in my library. (To Joel E. Spingarn, August 28, 1917.) *Mem. Ed.* XXIV, 422; Bishop II, 359.

DRAMA. *See also* ABBEY THEATRE; LITERATURE; READING.

DREYFUS, ALFRED. Something recently happened which I want to speak about. I think it a rare thing for the whole nation to watch the trial of a single citizen of another nation. We have watched with indignation and regret the trial of Captain Dreyfus. It was less Dreyfus on trial than those who tried him. We should draw lessons from the trial. It was due in part to bitter religious prejudices of the French people. Those who have ever wavered from the doctrine of the separation of Church and State should ponder upon what has happened. Try to encourage every form of religious effort. Beware and do not ever oppose any man for any reason except worth or want of it. You cannot benefit one class by pulling another class down. (From speech at Walton, N. Y., September 13, 1899.) William Harding, *Dreyfus: The Prisoner of Devil's Island.* (Associated Publishing Company, 1899), p. 380.

DREYFUS, ALFRED. *See also* DEMOCRACY—DESPOTISM IN A.

DRINK. *See* LIQUOR; PROHIBITION; ROOSEVELT; TEMPERANCE.

DRUGS. *See* PURE FOOD LAW.

DUE PROCESS OF LAW. The object I have in view could probably be accomplished by an amendment of the State constitutions taking away from the courts the power to review the legislature's determination of a policy of social justice, by defining due process of law in accordance with the views expressed by Justice Holmes of the Supreme Court. But my proposal seems to me more democratic and, I may add, less radical. For under the method I suggest the people may sustain the court as against the legislature, whereas, if due process were defined in the Constitution, the decision of the legislature would be final. (At Carnegie Hall, N. Y. C., March 20, 1912.) *Mem. Ed.* XIX, 208; *Nat. Ed.* XVII, 157.

DUE PROCESS OF LAW. *See also* COURTS; JUDICIARY; LAW.

DUNNE, F. P. *See* DOOLEY, MR.

DUTY. Failure to perform duty to others is merely aggravated by failure to perform duty to ourselves. (*Metropolitan,* November 1915.) *Mem. Ed.* XX, 376; *Nat. Ed.* XVIII, 322.

————————. One of the prime needs is to remember that almost every duty is composed of two seemingly conflicting elements, and that over-insistence on one, to the exclusion of the other, may defeat its own end. (1913.) *Mem. Ed.* XXII, 194; *Nat. Ed.* XX, 166.

————————. Every good citizen, whatever his condition, owes his first service to those who are nearest to him, who are dependent upon him, to his wife and his children; next he owes his duty to his fellow citizens, and this duty he must perform both to his individual neighbor and to the State, which is simply a form of expression for all his neighbors combined. He must keep his self-respect and exact the respect of others. It is eminently wise and proper to strive for such leisure in our lives as will give a chance for self-improvement; but woe to the man who seeks, or trains up his children to seek, idleness instead of the chance to do good work. (At Labor Day Picnic, Chicago, September 3, 1900.) *Mem. Ed.* XVI, 517; *Nat. Ed.* XIII, 487.

DUTY—PERFORMANCE OF. What we as a people need more than aught else is the steady performance of the every-day duties of life, not with hope of reward, but because they are duties. (At Valley Forge, Pa., June 19, 1904.) *Mem. Ed.* XII, 618; *Nat. Ed.* XI, 333.

——————. We can make and keep this country worthy of the men who gave their lives to save it, only on condition that the average man among us on the whole does his duty bravely, loyally, and with common sense, in whatever position life allots to him. (At Gettysburg, Pa., May 30, 1904.) *Mem. Ed.* XII, 611; *Nat. Ed.* XI, 328.

——————. The prime requisite is to arouse among our people, individually and collectively, an understanding that the full performance of duty is not only right in itself but also the source of the profoundest satisfaction that can come in life. (*Outlook,* April 8, 1911.) *Mem. Ed.* XIV, 161; *Nat. Ed.* XII, 192.

DUTY AND RESPONSIBILITY. You can make up your minds to lead your lives well and nobly, doing first of all your duty to yourself and to those immediately dependent upon you, the duty of father to son, of husband to wife, of wife to husband, of parents to children—to do those duties first, and then to do the duties that lie beyond them, the duty of joining with your fellows in common work toward a common end, in the effort to achieve in common something worth achieving for the sake of all. You can lead that kind of life—and it is the only kind of life worth leading, and the only kind of life worth living—you can lead it only on condition of making up your mind that you will not expect always to have an easy time, to escape care, to escape responsibility, to escape the burdens that inevitably must be carried by every man and every woman whose shoulders are broad enough to enable him or her to play a part in the world. (At Occidental College, Los Angeles, March 22, 1911.) *Mem. Ed.* XV, 514; *Nat. Ed.* XIII, 581.

DUTY OF THE NATION. Keeping our own household straight is our first duty; but we have other duties. Just exactly as each man who is worth his salt must first of all be a good husband, a good father, a good bread-winner, a good man of business, and yet must in addition to that be a good citizen for the State at large —so a nation must first take care to do well its duties within its own borders, but must not make of that fact an excuse for failing to do those of its duties the performance of which lies without its own borders. (At Hartford, Conn., August 22, 1902.) *Mem. Ed.* XVIII, 355; *Nat. Ed.* XVI, 270.

——————. Our country should not shirk its duty to mankind. It can perform this duty only if it is true to itself. It can be true to itself only by definitely resolving to take the position of the just man armed; for a proud and self-respecting nation of freemen must scorn to do wrong to others, and must also scorn tamely to submit to wrong done by others. (1915.) *Mem. Ed.* XX, xxv; *Nat. Ed.* XVIII, xxiv.

DUTY. See also CITIZENSHIP; CIVIC DUTY; INTERNATIONAL DUTY; JOY OF LIVING; PLEASURE; RIGHTS; SERVICE; WOMEN.

E

EASE. See LEISURE; PLEASURE; STRENUOUS LIFE; WORK.

ECONOMIC DEMOCRACY. See DEMOCRACY.

ECONOMIC EVOLUTION. The prime need to-day is to face the fact that we are now in the midst of a great economic evolution. There is urgent necessity of applying both common sense and the highest ethical standard to this movement for better economic conditions among the mass of our people if we are to make it one of healthy evolution and not one of revolution. It is, from the standpoint of our country, wicked as well as foolish longer to refuse to face the real issues of the day. Only by so facing them can we go forward. (Before Progressive National Convention, Chicago, August 6, 1912.) *Mem. Ed.* XIX, 359; *Nat. Ed.* XVII, 255.

ECONOMIC EVOLUTION. See also BUSINESS; INDUSTRIAL REVOLUTION.

ECONOMIC POLICY. Stability of economic policy must always be the prime economic need of this country. This stability should not be fossilization. (Second Annual Message, Washington, December 2, 1902.) *Mem. Ed.* XVII, 167; *Nat. Ed.* XV, 144.

ECONOMIC REFORM. Economic reform must have a twofold object; first to increase general prosperity, because unless there is such general prosperity no one will be well off; and, second, to secure a fair distribution of this prosperity, so that the man of the people shall share in it. Introduction to *The Wisconsin Idea* by Charles McCarthy. (Macmillan Co., N. Y., 1912), p. x.

ECONOMICS. See MORALITY.

EDITORS. The editor, who stands as a judge in a community, should be one of the men to whom you would expect to look up, because his function as an editor makes him a more important man than the average merchant, the average business man, the average professional man can be. He wields great influence; and he cannot escape the responsibility of wielding it. If he wields it well, honor is his beyond the honor that comes to the average man who does well; if he wields it ill, shame should be his beyond the shame that comes to the average man who does ill. (At Milwaukee, Wis., September 7, 1910.) *Mem. Ed.* XV, 459; *Nat. Ed.* XIII, 546.

EDITORS. See also JOURNALIST; PRESS.

EDUCATED MEN—OBLIGATION OF. It is an evil thing for any man of education to forget that education should intensify patriotism, and that patriotism must not only be shown by striving to do good to the country from within, but by readiness to uphold its interests and honor, at any cost, when menaced from without. Educated men owe to the community the serious performance of this duty. (*The Bachelor of Arts*, March 1896.) *Mem. Ed.* XV, 236; *Nat. Ed.* XIII, 178.

——————. The educated man is entitled to no special privilege, save the inestimable privilege of trying to show that his education enables him to take the lead in striving to guide his fellows aright in the difficult task which is set to us of the twentieth century. (At University of Pennsylvania, Philadelphia, February 22, 1905.) *Mem. Ed.* XV, 348; *Nat. Ed.* XIII, 505.

EDUCATED MEN IN POLITICS. An educated man must not go into politics as such; he must go in simply as an American; and when he is once in, he will speedily realize that he must work very hard indeed, or he will be upset by some other American, with no education at all, but with much natural capacity. His education ought to make him feel particularly ashamed of himself if he acts meanly or dishonorably, or in any way falls short of the ideal of good citizenship, and it ought to make him feel that he must show that he has profited by it; but it should certainly give him no feeling of superiority until by actual work he has shown that superiority. In other words, the educated man must realize that he is living in a democracy and under democratic conditions, and that he is entitled to no more respect and consideration than he can win by actual performance. (*Atlantic Monthly*, August 1894.) *Mem. Ed.* XV, 52; *Nat. Ed.* XIII, 37.

EDUCATED MEN. See also CITIZENSHIP; CIVIC DUTY; DEMOCRACY.

EDUCATION. Education must be twofold. Of course if we do not have education in the school, the academy, the college, the university, and have it developed in the highest and wisest manner, we shall make but a poor fist of American citizenship. . . . But such education can never be all. It can never be more than half, and sometimes not that. Nothing can take the place of the education of the home; and that education must be largely the unconscious influence of character upon character. (Before Minnesota Legislature, St. Paul, April 4, 1903.) *Presidential Addresses and State Papers* I, 289.

——————. A literary education is simply one of many different kinds of education, and it is not wise that more than a small percentage of the people of any country should have an exclusively literary education. The average man must either supplement it by another education or else as soon as he has left an institution of learning, even though he has benefited by it, he must at once begin to train himself to do work along totally different lines. (At National University, Cairo, Egypt, March 28, 1910.) *Mem. Ed.* XVIII, 622; *Nat. Ed.* XVI, 451.

——————. A utilitarian education should undoubtedly be the foundation of all education. But it is far from advisable, it is far from wise, to have it the end of all education. Technical training will more and more be accepted as the prime factor in our educational system, a factor as essential for the farmer, the blacksmith, the seamstress, and the cook, as for the lawyer, the doctor, the engineer, and the stenographer. . . . Side by side with the need for the perfection of the individual in the technic of his special calling goes the need of broad human sympathy, and the need of lofty and generous emotion in that individual. Only thus can the citizenship of the modern state rise level to the complex modern social needs.

No technical training, no narrowly utilitarian study of any kind will meet this second class of needs. In part they can best be met by a training that will fit men and women to appreciate, and therefore to profit by, great poetry and those great expressions of the historian and the statesman which rivet our interest and stir our souls. (Presidential Address, American Historical Association, Boston, December 27, 1912.) *Mem. Ed.* XIV, 14; *Nat. Ed.* XII, 12-13.

——————. I doubt if there is any lesson more essential to teach in an industrial democracy like ours than the lesson that any failure to train the average citizen to a belief in the things of the spirit no less than the things of the body, must in the long run entail misfortune, shortcoming, possible disaster upon the Nation itself. . . . It is necessary that we should see that the children should be trained not merely in reading and writing, not merely in the elementary branches of learning strictly so defined; but trained industrially, trained adequately to meet the ever-increasing demands of the complex growth of our industrialism, trained agriculturally, trained in handicrafts, trained to be more efficient workers in every field of human activity. But they must be trained in more than that or the Nation will ultimately go down. They must be trained in the elementary branches of righteousness; they must be trained so that it shall come naturally to them to abhor that which is evil, or we never can see our democracy take the place which it must and shall take among the nations of the earth. (Before Religious Educational Association, White House, February 12, 1908.) *Presidential Addresses and State Papers* VII, 1652-1653.

EDUCATION—FUNCTION OF. Education should not confine itself to books. It must train executive power, and try to create that right public opinion which is the most potent factor in the proper solution of all political and social questions. Book learning is very important, but it is by no means everything; and we shall never get the right idea of education until we definitely understand that a man may be well trained in book-learning and yet, in the proper sense of the word, and for all practical purposes, be utterly uneducated; while a man of comparatively little book-learning may, nevertheless, in essentials, have a good education. (At semicentennial celebration, founding of Agricultural Colleges, Lansing, Mich., May 31, 1907.) *Mem. Ed.* XVIII, 185; *Nat. Ed.* XVI, 141.

EDUCATION—IMPROPER USE OF. Education is of good chiefly according to the use you put it to. If it teaches you to be so puffed with pride as to make you misestimate the relative values of things, it becomes a harm and not a benefit. There are few things less desirable than the arid cultivation, the learning and refinement which lead merely to that intellectual conceit which makes a man in a democratic community like ours hold himself aloof from his fellows and pride himself upon the weakness which he mistakes for supercilious strength. (At the Harvard Union, Cambridge, February 23, 1907.) *Mem. Ed.* XV, 488; *Nat. Ed.* XIII, 564.

EDUCATION—PROGRESS IN. Our progress in educational efficiency must come from two sources: from the great natural leader who happens to be an educator, and from the ordinary citizen who to common sense adds some power of vision, and who realizes the relation of the school to society. In pedagogy as in every other walk of life great natural leaders are scarce. Therefore the ordinary citizen of vision and common sense must concern himself with the changing problem of the school, and must insist that pedantic tradition does not keep our schools from performing their full public service. Foreword to *Democracy's High School* by William D. Lewis. (Houghton Mifflin Co., Boston, 1914), p. vi.

EDUCATION, INDUSTRIAL. Industrial training, training which will fit a girl to do work in the home, which will fit a boy to work in the shop if in a city, to work on a farm if in the country, is the most important of all training, aside from that which develops character; and it is a grave reproach to us as a nation that we have permitted our training to lead the children away from the farm and shop instead of toward them. We should try to provide the many with training in their professions, just as the few, the doctors, the ministers, the lawyers, are trained for their professions. In other words, the school system should be aimed primarily to fit the scholar for actual

EDUCATION

life rather than for a university. The exceptional individual, of the highest culture and most efficient training possible, is an important asset for the state. He should be encouraged and his development promoted; but this should not be done at the expense of all the other individuals who can do their work best on the farms and in the workshops; it is for the benefit of these individuals that our school system should be primarily shaped. (Letter to Herbert Myrick read at Springfield, Mass., November 12, 1908.) *Good Housekeeping,* December 1908, p. 626.

―――――――. Our industrial development depends largely upon technical education, including in this term all industrial education, from that which fits a man to be a good mechanic, a good carpenter, or blacksmith, to that which fits a man to do the greatest engineering feat. The skilled mechanic, the skilled workman, can best become such by technical industrial education. The far-reaching usefulness of institutes of technology and schools of mines or of engineering is now universally acknowledged, and no less far-reaching is the effect of a good building or mechanical trades-school, a textile, or watchmaking, or engraving school. All such training must develop not only manual dexterity but industrial intelligence. In international rivalry this country does not have to fear the competition of pauper labor as much as it has to fear the educated labor of specially trained competitors; and we should have the education of the hand, eye, and brain which will fit us to meet such competition. (Sixth Annual Message, Washington, December 3, 1906.) *Mem. Ed.* XVII, 437-438; *Nat. Ed.* XV, 373.

―――――――. To train boys and girls in merely literary accomplishments to the total exclusion of industrial, manual, and technical training, tends to unfit them for industrial work; and in real life most work is industrial.

The problem of furnishing well-trained craftsmen, or rather journeymen fitted in the end to become such, is not simple . . . and much care and forethought and practical common sense will be needed, in order to work it out in a fairly satisfactory manner. It should appeal to all our citizens.

I am glad that societies have already been formed to promote industrial education, and that their membership includes manufacturers and leaders of labor unions, educators and publicists, men of all conditions who are interested in education and in industry. It is such cooperation that offers most hope for a satisfactory solution of the question as to what is the best form of industrial school, as to the means by which it may be articulated with the public school system, and as to the way to secure for the boys trained therein the opportunity to acquire in the industries the practical skill which alone can make them finished journeymen. (At semicentennial celebration, founding of Agricultural Colleges, Lansing, Mich., May 31, 1907.) *Mem. Ed.* XVIII, 175; *Nat. Ed.* XVI, 132.

EDUCATION, LIBERAL. A cultural education must include the classics. It must not be based only on the classics. The Greek literature is one of the two noblest literatures in the world, the other being the English. Latin literature as such does not stand in the same rank with Greek; but it possesses an immense importance because the Latin civilization is the direct ancestor of modern Occidental civilization, and because the Latin tongue was for fifteen centuries the cultural tongue of Europe. With one or the other, and if possible with both, of these two classic languages and literatures every liberally educated man should be familiar. He should also be familiar with at least one of the great modern culture languages, such as French, Italian, German, Spanish or Portuguese, each of which has a noble literature. Every liberal course should also include a wide sweep of general history and pre-history, for a liberal scholar should certainly have vividly in mind the tremendous drama of man's progress through the ages. A competent knowledge of science must also be part of any really liberal education. But this does not mean the science taught in order to turn out a commercial chemist, an engineer or an electrician. It means that the man of liberal education should be a man who in addition to a broad classical training also possesses so broad a scientific training that the primary facts of the universe in which we live are vivid in his mind and form an integral portion of his stock of knowledge. The man with such broad liberal training is perhaps not apt to be a technical expert in any special vocation; for his training stands outside the most direct line to pecuniary reward. Yet he has a great place to fill, for he has been fitted to become a leader in public thought, and a true interpreter to the people of the development and meaning of our civilization in its most important aspects. (Statement sent to Conference on Classical Studies, Princeton University, June 2, 1917.) *Value of the Classics.* (Princeton University Press, 1917), pp. 137-138.

EDUCATION, SUBSIDIZED—ABUSE OF. By gifts to colleges and universities they

[149]

[wealthy men] are occasionally able to subsidize in their own interest some head of an educational body, who, save only a judge, should of all men be most careful to keep his skirts clear from the taint of such corruption. There are ample material rewards for those who serve with fidelity the Mammon of unrighteousness, but they are dearly paid for by that institution of learning whose head, by example and precept, teaches the scholars who sit under him that there is one law for the rich and another for the poor. (To Charles J. Bonaparte, January 2, 1908.) *Mem. Ed.* XXII, 515; *Nat. Ed.* XX, 443.

EDUCATION AND DEMOCRACY. A real democracy must see that the chance for an elementary education is open to every man and woman. This is the first essential. But it is also essential that there should be the amplest opportunity for every kind of higher education. The education of the mass, while the most important problem in democratic education, is in no way or shape by and of itself sufficient. Democracy comes short of what it should be just to the extent that it fails to provide for the exceptional individual the highest kind of exceptional training; for democracy as a permanent world force must mean not only the raising of the general level but also the raising of the standards of excellence to which only exceptional individuals can attain. The table land must be raised, but the high peaks must not be leveled down; on the contrary they too must be raised. Highly important though it is that the masons and bricklayers should be excellent, it is nevertheless a grave mistake to suppose that any excellence in the bricklayers will enable us to dispense with architects. *Outlook*, February 18, 1911, p. 344.

EDUCATION AND THE NATIONAL GOVERNMENT. The share that the National Government should take in the broad work of education has not received the attention and the care it rightly deserves. The immediate responsibility for the support and improvement of our educational systems and institutions rests and should always rest with the people of the several States acting through their State and local governments, but the nation has an opportunity in educational work which must not be lost and a duty which should no longer be neglected. (Eighth Annual Message, Washington, December 8, 1908.) *Mem. Ed.* XVII, 623; *Nat. Ed.* XV, 530.

EDUCATION FOR CITIZENSHIP. Education may not make a man a good citizen, but most certainly ignorance tends to prevent his being a good citizen. . . . No nation can permanently retain free government unless it can retain a high average of citizenship; and there can be no such high average of citizenship without a high average of education, using the word in its broadest and truest sense to include the things of the soul as well as the things of the mind. (At University of Pennsylvania, Philadelphia, February 22, 1905.) *Mem. Ed.* XV, 346; *Nat. Ed.* XIII, 504.

EDUCATION FOR LIFE. We of the United States must develop a system under which each individual citizen shall be trained so as to be effective individually as an economic unit, and fit to be organized with his fellows so that he and they can work in efficient fashion together. This question is vital to our future progress, and public attention should be focussed upon it. Surely it is eminently in accord with the principles of our democratic life that we should furnish the highest average industrial training for the ordinary skilled workman. But it is a curious thing that in industrial training we have tended to devote our energies to producing high-grade men at the top rather than in the ranks. Our engineering schools, for instance, compare favorably with the best in Europe, whereas we have done almost nothing to equip the private soldiers of the industrial army—the mechanic, the metal-worker, the carpenter. Indeed, too often our schools train away from the shop and the forge. (At semi-centennial celebration, founding of Agricultural Colleges, Lansing, Mich., May 31, 1907.) *Mem. Ed.* XVIII, 172; *Nat. Ed.* XVI, 130.

EDUCATION. *See aslo* CHINA; COLLEGE; LABOR—TRAINING OF; NORTHWEST ORDINANCE; PUBLIC SCHOOLS; SCHOOLS; TEACHERS; TEACHING; UNIVERSITY.

EDUCATION OF THE NEGRO. *See* NEGRO; TUSKEGEE INSTITUTE.

EFFICIENCY. We have no higher duty than to promote the efficiency of the individual. There is no surer road to the efficiency of the nation. (Before Ohio Constitutional Convention, Columbus, February 21, 1912.) *Mem. Ed.* XIX, 165; *Nat. Ed.* XVII, 121.

EFFICIENCY—REWARDS OF. Normally the man of great productive capacity who becomes rich by guiding the labor of many other men does so by enabling them to produce more than they could produce without his guidance; and both he and they share in the benefit, which comes also to the public at large. The superficial fact that the sharing may be unequal must never blind us to the underlying fact that there is this sharing, and that the benefit comes in some degree to each man concerned. Normally the wage-worker, the man of small means, and the average consumer, as well as the average producer, are all alike helped by making conditions such that the man of exceptional business ability receives an exceptional reward for his ability. Something can be done by legislation to help the general prosperity; but no such help of a permanently beneficial character can be given to the less able and less fortunate, save as the results of a policy which shall inure to the advantage of all industrious and efficient people who act decently; and this is only another way of saying that any benefit which comes to the less able and less fortunate must of necessity come even more to the more able and more fortunate. If, therefore, the less fortunate man is moved by envy of his more fortunate brother to strike at the conditions under which they have both, though unequally, prospered, the result will assuredly be that while danger may come to the one struck at, it will visit with an even heavier load the one who strikes the blow. Taken as a whole we must all go up or down together. (Fifth Annual Message, Washington, December 5, 1905.) *Mem. Ed.* XVII, 316; *Nat. Ed.* XV, 270.

EFFICIENCY, NATIONAL. National efficiency has many factors. It is a necessary result of the principle of conservation widely applied. In the end it will determine our failure or success as a nation. National efficiency has to do, not only with natural resources and with men, but it is equally concerned with institutions. The State must be made efficient for the work which concerns only the people of the State; and the nation for that which concerns all the people. There must remain no neutral ground to serve as a refuge for lawbreakers, and especially for lawbreakers of great wealth, who can hire the vulpine legal cunning which will teach them how to avoid both jurisdictions. (At Osawatomie, Kan., August 31, 1910.) *Mem. Ed.* XIX, 26; *Nat. Ed.* XVII, 18.

——————. In every respect this nation has to learn the lessons of efficiency in production and distribution, and of avoidance of waste and destruction; we must develop and improve instead of exhausting our resources. (Before Progressive National Convention, Chicago, August 6, 1912.) *Mem. Ed.* XIX, 378; *Nat. Ed.* XVII, 271.

EFFICIENCY AND MORALITY. Life is as if you were travelling a ridge crest. You have the gulf of inefficiency on one side and the gulf of wickedness on the other, and it helps not to have avoided one gulf if you fall into the other. It shall profit us nothing if our people are decent and ineffective. It shall profit us nothing if they are efficient and wicked. In every walk of life, in business, politics; if the need comes, in war; in literature, science, art, in everything, what we need is a sufficient number of men who can work well and who will work with a high ideal. (At Groton School, Groton, Mass., May 24, 1904.) *Mem. Ed.* XV, 480; *Nat. Ed.* XIII, 558.

EFFICIENCY. *See also* DECENCY; HONESTY; LABOR; POLITICS.

EFFORT. Nothing worth gaining is ever gained without effort. You can no more have freedom without striving and suffering for it than you can win success as a banker or a lawyer without labor and effort, without self-denial in youth and the display of a ready and alert intelligence in middle age. (Before the Liberal Club, Buffalo, N. Y., January 26, 1893.) *Mem. Ed.* XV, 64; *Nat. Ed.* XIII, 282.

EFFORT—LIFE OF. The life that is worth living, and the only life that is worth living, is the life of effort, the life of effort to attain what is worth striving for. (At Groton School, Groton, Mass., May 24, 1904.) *Mem. Ed.* XV, 479; *Nat. Ed.* XIII, 556.

EFFORT. *See also* IDEALS; LIFE; PLEASURE; STRENUOUS LIFE; STRIFE; WORK.

EIGHT-HOUR DAY. The idle man is a curse to the community, and cannot be a good citizen. But neither can the man who is exhausted by incessant and excessive toil be a good citizen. Men who work thirteen hours a day, including Sunday, week in and week out, simply have not the opportunity to develop themselves or to produce the kind of citizenship which it is absolutely essential for a democracy to possess if it intends to remain a real democracy. The eight-hour day is an ideal toward which we should strive to attain. We should apply it wherever the government has power, and should consistently endeavor to help in its achievement in private life. (*Outlook,* February 4, 1911.) *Mem. Ed.* XIX, 106; *Nat. Ed.* XVII, 70.

——————. I believe in the eight-hour day. It is the ideal toward which we should tend. But I believe that there must be common sense as well as common honesty in achieving the ideal. Mr. Wilson has laid down the principle that there is something sacred about the eight-hour day which makes it improper even to discuss it. If this is so, if it is applied universally, then Mr. Wilson is not to be excused for not applying it immediately where he has complete power and that is in his own household. If the principle of the eight-hour day is sacred and not to be changed under any circumstances, then the housemaid, who in Mr. Wilson's house arises at seven must be let off at three in the afternoon; and if Mr. Wilson's butler is kept up after a State dinner until ten, he must not come on until two of the following afternoon, and no hired man on a farm must get up to milk the cows in the morning unless he quits work before milking time arrives that same evening. Of course, the simple truth is that under one set of conditions an eight-hour day may be too long or at least may represent the very maximum of proper work; whereas there may be other conditions under which a man working more than eight hours one day gets one or two days of complete leisure following, or where the work is intermittent throughout the day, or is of so easy or varied a type that no exhaustion accompanies it, or where a rush of work for a few days will be compensated by complete leisure on certain other days. It is ridiculous to say that an engineer of a high-speed train under especially difficult conditions, an engineer of a low-speed train under very much easier conditions, a farm laborer in harvest time, a man engaged as a watchman through the quiet work of the night, or a man engaged in the exhausting work of a steel puddler in a continuous seven-days-a-week, night-and-day industry, should be governed by precisely the same rule, or by the same rigid application in detail of a second, general principle. (At Wilkes-Barre, Pa., October 14, 1916.) Theodore Roosevelt, *Americanism and Preparedness*. (New York, 1917), p. 68.

EIGHT-HOUR DAY IN GOVERNMENT SERVICE. The principle of the eight-hour day should as rapidly and as far as practicable be extended to the entire work carried on by the government; and the present law should be amended to embrace contracts on those public works which the present wording of the act has been construed to exclude. The general introduction of the eight-hour day should be the goal toward which we should steadily tend and the government should set the example in this respect. (Seventh Annual Message, Washington, December 3, 1907.) *Mem. Ed.* XVII, 511; *Nat. Ed.* XV, 435.

———. The more I had studied the subject the more strongly I had become convinced that an eight-hour day under the conditions of labor in the United States was all that could, with wisdom and propriety, be required either by the government or by private employers; that more than this meant, on the average, a decrease in the qualities that tell for good citizenship. I finally solved the problem, as far as government employees were concerned, by calling in Charles P. Neill, the head of the Labor Bureau; and, acting on his advice, I speedily made the eight-hour law really effective. (1913.) *Mem. Ed.* XXII, 527; *Nat. Ed.* XX, 452.

EIGHT-HOUR DAY. See also LABOR.

ELECTION OF 1884. Every now and then I meet an Independent who, taking it for granted that you and I were actuated by selfish motives, points out how much better for ourselves we would have done to have bolted. I always surprise him by saying that we have always been very well aware of that fact, and knew perfectly well that we had been pretty effectually killed as soon as Blaine was nominated. If our consciences would have permitted it I have not the slightest doubt that by bolting we could have done an immense amount for ourselves, and would have won a commanding position—at the cost, perfectly trivial in true Mugwump eyes, of black treachery to all our warmest and truest supporters and also at the cost of stultifying ourselves as regards all of our previous declarations in respect to the Democracy. (To H. C. Lodge, March 8, 1885.) Lodge *Letters* I, 28.

ELECTION OF 1884. See also BLAINE, JAMES G.; CLEVELAND, GROVER; MUGWUMPS; PARTY ALLEGIANCE.

ELECTION OF 1888. See CLEVELAND, GROVER.

ELECTION OF 1896.—Not since the Civil War has there been a Presidential election fraught with so much consequence to the country. The silver craze surpasses belief. The populists, populist-democrats, and silver- or populist-Republicans who are behind Bryan are impelled by a wave of genuine fanaticism; not only do they wish to repudiate their debts, but they really believe that somehow they are executing righteous justice on the moneyed oppressor; they feel the eternal and inevitable injustice of life, they do not realize and will not realize how that injustice is aggravated by their own extraordinary folly, and they wish, if they cannot lift themselves, at least to strike down those who are more fortunate or more prosperous. At present they are on the crest and were the election held now, they would carry the country; but I hope that before November the sober common sense of the great central western states, the pivotal states, will assert itself. McKinley's position is very hard; the main fight must be for sound finance; but he must stand by protection also, under penalty if he does, of making his new Democratic allies lukewarm, and if he does not, of making a much larger number of his old followers hostile. Matters are very doubtful; Bryan's election would be a great calamity, though we should in the end recover from it. (To Anna Roosevelt Cowles, July 26, 1896.) Cowles *Letters*, 188.

——————. This is no mere fight over financial standards. It is a semi-socialistic, agrarian movement, with free silver as a mere incident, supported mainly because it is hoped thereby to damage the well to do and thrifty. "Organized labor" is the chief support of Bryan in the big cities; and his utterances are as criminal as they are wildly silly. All the ugly forces that seethe beneath the social crust are behind him. The appeal for him is frankly on class and sectional hatred. It is as vicious a campaign as I have ever seen. And the worst of it is that the very people whom one would wish to help are those who are going most wrong, and are putting themselves in such a position that they must be resolutely opposed! (To Anna Roosevelt Cowles, September 27, 1896.) Cowles *Letters*, 194.

——————. We believe that the campaign should be waged on the moral, even more than the material, issue. Mr. Bryan and Mr. Altgeld are the embodiments of the two principles which our adversaries desire to see triumph; and in their ultimate analysis those principles are merely the negations of the two commandments, "Thou shalt not steal" and "Thou shalt do no murder." Mr. Bryan champions that system of dishonesty which would steal from the creditors of the nation half of what they have in good faith loaned and from the working men of the nation half of what by their honest toil they have earned. Mr. Altgeld condones and encourages the most infamous of murders and denounces the Federal Government and the Supreme Court for interfering to put a stop to the bloody lawlessness which would result in worse than murder. Both of them would substitute for the government of Washington and Lincoln, for the system of orderly liberty which we inherit from our forefathers and which we desire to bequeath to our sons, a red welter of lawlessnes and dishonesty as fantastic and as vicious as the Paris commune itself. (Before American Republican College League, Chicago, October 15, 1896.) *Mem. Ed.* XVI, 412; *Nat. Ed.* XIV, 273.

——————. In 1896, the issue was fairly joined, chiefly upon a question which as a party question was entirely new, so that the old lines of political cleavage were, in large part, abandoned. All other issues sank in importance when compared with the vital need of keeping our financial system on the high and honorable plane imperatively demanded by our position as a great civilized power. As the champion of such a principle President McKinley received the support not only of his own party, but of hundreds of thousands of those to whom he had been politically opposed. He triumphed, and he made good with scrupulous fidelity the promises upon which the campaign was won. (At banquet in honor of birthday of William McKinley, Canton, O., January 27, 1903.) *Mem. Ed.* XII, 496-497; *Nat. Ed.* XI, 239.

ELECTION OF 1896. *See also* BRYAN, WILLIAM J.; GOLD STANDARD; NATIONAL HONOR; POPULISM; SILVER.

ELECTION OF 1898. I haven't bothered myself a particle about the nomination, and have no idea whether it will be made or not. In the first place, I would rather have led this regiment than be Governor of New York three times over. In the next place, while on the whole I should like the Office of Governor and would not shirk it, the position will be one of such extreme difficulty, and I shall have to offend so many good friends of mine, that I should breathe a sigh of relief were it not offered to me.

It is a party position. I should be one of the big party leaders if I should take it. This means that I should have to treat with and work with the organization, and I should see and consult the leaders—not once, but continuously—and earnestly try to come to an agreement on all important questions with them; and of course the mere fact of my doing so would alienate many of my friends whose friendship I value. On the other hand, when we come to a matter like the Canal, or Life Insurance, or anything touching the Eighth Commandment and general decency, I could not allow any consideration of party to come in. And this would alienate those who, if not friends, were supporters. (Letter to F. E. Leupp, September 3, 1898.) Francis E. Leupp, *The Man Roosevelt*. (Appleton & Co., New York, 1904), p. 30.

———. First and foremost, this campaign is a campaign for good government, for good government both in the nation and the State. If I am elected governor I shall try to make good the promises, both expressed and implied, made on behalf of my candidacy, for I shall try to so administer the affairs of the State as to make each citizen a little prouder of the State, and I shall do my best to serve my party by helping it serve the people. So far as in me lies, I shall see that every branch of the government under me is administered with integrity and capacity, and when I deal with any public servant, I shall not be very patient with him if he lacks capacity, and short indeed will be his shrift if he lacks integrity. I shall feel most deeply my responsibilities to the people, and I shall do my best to show by my acts that I feel it even more deeply than my words express. (Campaign speech, New York City, October 5, 1898.) *Mem. Ed.* XVI, 441; *Nat. Ed.* XIV, 290.

ELECTION OF 1898. See also REPUBLICAN PARTY.

ELECTION OF 1900. I don't like some aspects of the political campaign at all. I believe we shall pull through, and of course there is always a large element of which we know nothing, so that it is always possible that there is a hidden force that will make a clean sweep either one way or the other; but the combination of all the lunatics, all the idiots, all the knaves, all the cowards and all the honest people who are hopelessly slow-witted is a formidable one to overcome when backed by the solid South. This is the combination that we now have to face. There is disaffection among the Irish and Germans, the disaffection being utterly unjustifiable. There is disaffection among the independents of the lunatic class under the lead of Carl Schurz, the Evening Post, etc., who, I am bound to say, in my judgment have done as much harm to the country as the worst Tammany men. Moreover, the best interests are curiously apathetic. They do not care to subscribe money. They take no interest in the campaign. In this State, Platt is going on the rule or ruin principle, acting with a folly almost as great as that of Carl Schurz or Godkin. So there is plenty of room for alarm. I think we shall win, of course events may take a turn that will make us win with a sweep; but at the present there are exceedingly ugly features in the situation. (To Anna Roosevelt Cowles, August 18, 1900.) Cowles *Letters*, 246.

———. There are several great issues at stake in this campaign, but of course the greatest issue of all is the issue of keeping the country on the plane of material well-being and honor to which it has been brought during the last four years. I do not claim that President McKinley's admirable administration and the wise legislation passed by Congress which he has sanctioned are solely responsible for our present well-being, but I do claim that it is this administration and this legislation which have rendered it possible for the American people to achieve such well-being. I insist furthermore that the one and only way to insure wide-spread industrial and social ruin would be now to reverse the policy under which we have so prospered, and to try that policy of financial disgrace and economic disaster which we rejected in '96. (At Grand Rapids, Mich., September 7, 1900.) *Mem. Ed.* XVI, 530; *Nat. Ed.* XIV, 346.

———. I feel that this contest is by no means one merely between Republicans and Democrats. We have a right to appeal to all good citizens who are far-sighted enough to see what the honor and the interest of the nation demand. To put into practice the principles embodied in the Kansas City platform would mean disaster to the nation; for that platform stands for reaction and disorder; for an upsetting of our financial system which would mean not only great suffering but the abandonment of the nation's good faith; and for a policy abroad which would imply the dishonor of the flag and an unworthy surrender of our national rights. Its success would mean unspeakable humiliation to men proud of their country, jealous of their country's good name, and desirous of securing the welfare of their fellow citizens. Therefore we have a right to appeal to all good men, North and South, East and West, whatever their politics may have been in the past, to stand with us, because we stand for the prosperity of the country and for the renown of the American flag. (Letter accepting nomination for Vice-Presidency, September 15, 1900.) *Mem. Ed.* XVI, 546-547; *Nat. Ed.* XIV, 360-361.

ELECTION OF 1900. See also GOLD STANDARD; REPUBLICAN PARTY; VICE-PRESIDENCY.

ELECTION OF 1904. To use the vernacular of our adopted West, you can bet your bed-

ELECTION OF 1904

rock dollar that if I go down it will be with colors flying and drums beating, and that I would neither truckle nor trade with any of the opposition if to do so guaranteed me the nomination and election. In the first place, I believe I shall win. In the next place—and what is infinitely more important—I am going to fight it out on the line I have chosen without deviating a hair's breadth from it, win or lose; for I am sure that the policies for which I stand are those in accordance with which this country must be governed, and up to which we must all of us live in public or private life, under penalty of grave disaster to the Nation. (Letter of January 27, 1904.) *Mem. Ed.* XXIII, 361; Bishop I, 313.

——————. To-morrow the National Convention meets, and barring a cataclysm I shall be nominated. There is a great deal of sullen grumbling, but it has taken more the form of resentment against what they think is my dictation as to details than against me personally. They don't dare to oppose me for the nomination and I suppose it is hardly likely the attempt will be made to stampede the Convention for any one. How the election will turn out no man can tell. Of course I hope to be elected, but I realize to the full how very lucky I have been, not only to be President but to have been able to accomplish so much while President, and whatever may be the outcome, I am not only content but very sincerely thankful for all the good fortune I have had. From Panama down I have been able to accomplish certain things which will be of lasting importance in our history. (To Kermit Roosevelt, June 21, 1904.) *Mem. Ed.* XXI, 527; *Nat. Ed.* XIX, 473.

——————. If elected I shall be very glad. If beaten I shall be sorry; but in any event I have had a first-class run for my money, and I have accomplished certain definite things. I would consider myself a hundred times over repaid if I had nothing more to my credit than Panama and the coaling-stations in Cuba. (To Rudyard Kipling, November 1, 1904.) *Mem. Ed.* XXIII, 384; Bishop I, 333.

——————. If elected I shall go into the Presidency unhampered by any pledge, promise or understanding of any kind, sort or description, save my promise, made openly to the American people, that so far as in my power lies I shall see to it that every man has a square deal, no less and no more. (Statement to the press, November 5, 1904.) *Mem. Ed.* XXIII, 385; Bishop I, 334.

——————. One of the things I am most pleased with in the recent election is that while I got, I think, a greater proportion of the Americans of Irish birth or parentage and of the Catholic religion than any previous Republican candidate, I got this proportion purely because they knew I felt in sympathy with them and in touch with them, and that they and I had the same ideals and principles, and not by any demagogic appeals about creed or race, or by any demagogic attack upon England. (To Finley Peter Dunne, November 1904.) *Mem. Ed.* XXIII, 400-401; Bishop I, 348.

——————. I am stunned by the overwhelming victory we have won. I had no conception that such a thing was possible. I thought it probable we should win, but was quite prepared to be defeated, and of course had not the slightest idea that there was such a tidal wave. . . . The only States that went against me were those in which no free discussion is allowed and in which fraud and violence have rendered the voting a farce. I have the greatest popular majority and the greatest electoral majority ever given to a candidate for President. (To Kermit Roosevelt, November 10, 1904.) *Mem. Ed.* XXIII, 386; Bishop I, 335.

ELECTION OF 1904. *See also* CAMPAIGN CONTRIBUTIONS.

ELECTION OF 1908. I have been informed that certain office-holders in your Department are proposing to go to the National Convention as delegates in favor of renominating me for the Presidency, or are proposing to procure my indorsement for such renomination by State conventions. This must not be. I wish you to inform such officers as you may find it advisable or necessary to inform in order to carry out the spirit of this instruction, that such advocacy of my renomination, or acceptance of an election as delegate for that purpose, will be regarded as a serious violation of official propriety and will be dealt with accordingly. (To Secretary of the Treasury, Postmaster-General, and Secretary of the Interior, November 19, 1907.) *Mem. Ed.* XXIV, 92; Bishop II, 79.

——————. As to the matter of my renomination, it seems to me that the proper ground to take is that any one who supposes that I have been scheming for it is not merely a fool, but shows himself to be a man of low morality. He reflects upon himself, not upon me. There has never been a moment when I could not have had the Republican nomination

[155]

with practical unanimity by simply raising one finger. . . .

The facts about the third-term agitation are that it does not come from any men high in public life, but from plain people who take no very great part in politics, and who seem to have been puzzled at my attitude in declining to run. The politicians, like the big business men, all cordially agree with me that I ought not to run again. . . .

Under such circumstances I would be exasperated, if I were not amused, at so much as anybody talking about the supposition that I was engaged in an effort to have the renomination forced upon me. As a matter of fact I doubt if Taft himself could be more anxious than I am that Taft be nominated, and that any stampede to me be prevented. I wish it on every account, personal and public, and I am bending every energy now to prevent the possibility of such a stampede; because if the convention were stampeded and I were nominated an exceedingly ugly situation would be created, a situation very difficult to meet at all and impossible to meet satisfactorily; whereas if, as I have every reason to believe, Taft is nominated almost by acclamation, certainly on the first ballot, everything is as it should be. (To Lyman Abbott, May 29, 1908.) *Mem. Ed.* XXIV, 100-102; Bishop II, 85-87.

――――――. I have naturally a peculiar interest in the success of Mr. Taft, and in seeing him backed by a majority in both houses of Congress which will heartily support his policies. For the last ten years, while I have been Governor of New York and President, I have been thrown into the closest intimacy with him, and he and I have on every essential point stood in heartiest agreement, shoulder to shoulder. We have the same views as to what is demanded by the National interest and honor, both within our own borders, and as regards the relations of this Nation with other nations. There is no fight for decency and fair dealing which I have waged in which I have not had his heartiest and most effective sympathy and support, and the policies for which I stand are his policies as much as mine. (To Conrad Kohrs, September 9, 1908.) *Presidential Addresses and State Papers* VII, 1784.

――――――. It is urgently necessary, from the standpoint of the public interest, to elect Mr. Taft, and a Republican Congress which will support him; and they seek election on a platform which specifically pledges the party, alike in its executive and legislative branches, to continue and develop the policies which have been not merely professed but acted upon during these seven years. These policies can be successfully carried through only by the hearty cooperation of the President and the Congress in both its branches, and it is therefore peculiarly important that there should obtain such harmony between them. To fail to elect Mr. Taft would be a calamity to the country; and it would be folly, while electing him, yet at the same time to elect a Congress hostile to him, a Congress which under the influence of partisan leadership would be certain to thwart and baffle him on every possible occasion. To elect Mr. Taft, and at the same time to elect a Congress pledged to support him, is the only way in which to perpetuate the policy of the Government as now carried on. I feel that all the aid that can be given to this policy by every good citizen should be given; for this is far more than a merely partisan matter. (To William B. McKinley, Republican Congressional Committee, September 9, 1908.) *Presidential Addresses and State Papers* VII, 1796.

――――――. If the result of my "renunciation" had been either the nomination of a reactionary in the place of Taft, or the turning over of the government to Bryan, I should have felt a very uncomfortable apprehension as to whether I did not deserve a place beside Dante's pope who was guilty of *il gran rifiuto*. Renunciation is so often the act of a weak nature, or the term by which a weak nature seeks to cover up its lack of strength, that I suppose that every man who feels that he ought to renounce something also tends to feel a little uncomfortable as to whether he is really acting in accordance with the dictates of a sound morality or from weakness. Yet feeling as I do about this people and about the proper standard for its chosen leaders, I would not have acted otherwise than as I did; and naturally the relief is very great to have the event justify me. (To Sir George Otto Trevelyan, November 6, 1908.) *Mem. Ed.* XXIV, 145; Bishop II, 124.

ELECTION OF 1908. *See also* PRESIDENCY AND THE THIRD TERM ISSUE; TAFT, WILLIAM H.

ELECTION OF 1910. Though I am bitterly disappointed with Taft, and consider much of his course absolutely inexplicable, I have felt that, as in so many other cases, I had to make the best of conditions as they actually were and do the best I possibly could to carry Congress and to carry the State of New York, with the entire understanding on my part that victory in either means the immense strengthening of Taft. In New York State I deliberately went in to put the close supporters of Taft in control of the Republican machinery, and have done and am now doing my best to elect a man whom, I assume, is a Taft man; because I felt that the one clear duty of a decent citizen was to try to put the Republican Party on a straight basis, and now to try to put that party in power in the State instead of turning the State over to Murphy of Tammany Hall, acting as the agent, ally and master of crooked finance.

I have never had a more unpleasant summer. The sordid baseness of much or most of the so-called Regulars, who now regard themselves as especially the Taft men, and the wild irresponsible folly of the ultra-Insurgents, make a situation which is very unpleasant. From a variety of causes, the men who are both sane and progressive, the men who make up the strength of the party, have been left so at sea during these months that they have themselves tended to become either sordid on the one hand, or wild on the other. I do not see how I could as a decent citizen have avoided taking the stand I have taken this year, and striving to reunite the party and to help the Republicans retain control of Congress and of the State of New York, while at the same time endeavoring to see that this control within the party was in the hands of sensible and honorable men who were progressives and not of a bourbon reactionary type. (To Elihu Root, October 21, 1910.) *Mem. Ed.* XXIV, 358; Bishop II, 305.

ELECTION OF 1912. I have played my part, and I have the very strongest objection to having to play any further part; I very earnestly hope that Taft will retrieve himself yet, and if, from whatever causes, the present condition of the party is hopeless, I most emphatically desire that I shall not be put in the position of having to run for the Presidency, staggering under a load which I cannot carry, and which has been put on my shoulders through no fault of my own. Therefore my present feeling is that Taft should be the next nominee, because, if the people approve of what he has done, they will elect him, and if they don't approve of what he has done, it is unfair to me to have me suffer for the distrust which others have earned, and for which I am in no way responsible. This represents not a settled conviction on my part, but my guess as to the situation from this distance. (To H. C. Lodge, April 11, 1910.) Lodge *Letters* II, 373.

—————————. I have refrained from saying that I would not be a candidate in 1912, not in the least from self-interest, for I should regard it as the greatest personal calamity to be forced into accepting the nomination, and if it is possible to avoid it, I do not intend to be so forced into accepting it; but because I do not wish to put myself in the position where if it becomes my plain duty to accept I shall be obliged to shirk such duty because of having committed myself. As things are now, I feel convinced that it will not become my duty to accept. They have no business to expect me to take command of a ship simply because the ship is sinking.

Were I nominated under present conditions, it would mean that I should be broken down by a burden for which I was not in any way responsible, but which would have to be carried by the nominee who succeeded Taft; and, on the other hand, I would face the sullen resentment of the many respectable people with no special information or imagination, who would think that in some way or other I had been treacherous to Taft. Often when one does not like conditions it is nevertheless necessary to play the game through under the conditions, because they cannot be changed until the game is over without making things even worse. As I feel now, I would refuse the nomination if it were offered me. (To Joseph B. Bishop, November 21, 1910.) *Mem. Ed.* XXIV, 361; Bishop II, 307.

—————————. You have struck the real reason of my nervousness on the subject. Of course the Wall Street crowd, and my enemies generally, think I have been scheming to be President. As a matter of fact there is nothing that I want less. Indeed this is not putting it strong enough. I feel that I did good work as President because the circumstances were such as to make me in sympathy with the men whom I really cared to represent. Now if I were again made President, it might be that the circumstances would be such that I could not do what was expected of me; and in any event I do not see how I could go out of the Presidency again with the credit I had when I left it this time. Moreover I have led such an active and vigorous life that I begin to feel rather old and to appreciate rest, now that I feel the right to it and so can enjoy it with a clear conscience, . . .

Now under these circumstances, if I consulted merely my own feelings, I would promptly announce that never under any circumstances would I consent to be President again. But I don't think that this would be right. I think the chances are a hundred to one that I never shall be President again—perhaps a thousand to one. But however improbable, it is possible that circumstances might arise when it would be unpatriotic of me, when it would represent going back on my principles and my friends, to refuse to be President. Moreover, what is much more likely, the threat of my possible Presidency may influence for good some worthy people who need just to be influenced! (To William Allen White, December 12, 1910.) *Mem. Ed.* XXIV, 362-363; Bishop II, 308-309.

───────────. As for the nomination, I should regard it from my personal standpoint as little short of a calamity. I not merely do not want it, but if I honorably can, I desire to avoid it. On the other hand, I certainly will not put myself in a position which would make it necessary for me to shirk a plain duty if it came unmistakably *as* a plain duty. As yet I am not convinced that it will so come, and, on the contrary, believe there is practically little or no chance of it. I will not be a candidate in any ordinary sense of the word, and my judgment is that the Federal office-holders together with the timid conservative people will give Taft the nomination. At any rate, as far as I am concerned, my anxieties are in this order: first, not to be nominated if it can honorably be avoided; and, second, if nominated, to have it made perfectly clear that it is in response to a genuine popular demand and because the public wishes me to serve them for their purpose, and not to gratify any ambition of mine. (To Joseph B. Bishop, December 13, 1911.) *Mem. Ed.* XXIV, 367; Bishop II, 312.

───────────. [Some individuals] have been to see me to urge me to make an announcement that I would refuse the nomination if offered to me! Of course I refused point blank. I told them that I emphatically did not want the nomination, and should regard it as a misfortune if it came, and that I did not believe there was any chance of its coming, but that I should certainly not definitely state that if it did come in the form of a duty I would refuse to perform the duty; in other words, that as Abraham Lincoln used to say, no man can justly ask me to cross such a bridge until I come to it. (To H. C. Lodge, December 13, 1911.) Lodge *Letters* II, 417.

───────────. There is, of course, always the danger that there may be a movement for me, the danger coming partly because the men who may be candidates are very anxious that the ticket shall be strengthened and care nothing for the fate of the man who strengthens it, and partly because there is a good deal of honest feeling for me among plain simple people who wish leadership, but who will not accept leadership unless they believe it to be sincere, fearless, and intelligent. I most emphatically do not wish the nomination. Personally I should regard it as a calamity to be nominated. In the first place, I might very possibly be beaten, and in the next place, even if elected I should be confronted with almost impossible conditions out of which to make good results. In the tariff, for instance, I would have to face the fact that men would keep comparing what I did, not with what the Democrats would or could have done but with an ideal, or rather with a multitude of entirely separate and really incompatible ideals. I am not a candidate, I will never be a candidate; but I have to tell the La Follette men and the Taft men that while I am absolutely sincere in saying that I am not a candidate and do not wish the nomination, yet that I do not feel it would be right or proper for me to say that under no circumstances would I accept it if it came; because, while wildly improbable, it is yet possible that there might be a public demand which would present the matter to me in the light of a duty which I could not shirk. (Letter of December 23, 1911.) Harold Howland, *Theodore Roosevelt and His Times.* (New Haven, 1921), p. 207.

───────────. I am sure that, from the personal standpoint, it would be rough on me to have me nominated, and I am as yet not sure that it would not be damaging from the public standpoint. I think a great many men would have a vague feeling that I was nominated to gratify my own ambition, and would pay no heed whatever to the circumstances of the nomination. The New York newspapers, for instance, would probably without a single exception assert that I had corruptly intrigued for the nomination, and keep up the assertion until they had deceived a good number of people. Very possibly I should be beaten if I ran, and if I was not beaten it might well be that I would be elected under circumstances which would render it impossible to put through any constructive programme—and if ever I hold the Presidency again I shall regard it as a capital misfortune unless I am able to hold it not merely for the sake of holding the office but for the sake of doing a job. (To Joseph B. Bishop, December 29, 1911.) *Mem. Ed.* XXIV, 367-368; Bishop II, 313.

───────────. I am always credited with far more political sagacity than I really possess. I act purely on public grounds and then this proves often to be good policy too. I assure you with all possible sincerity that I have not thought and am not thinking of the nomination, and that under no circumstances would I in the remotest degree plan to bring about my nomination. I do not want to be President again. I am not a candidate, I have not the slightest idea of becoming a candidate, and I do not for one moment believe that any such condition of affairs will arise that would make it necessary to consider me accepting the nomination. But as for the effect upon my own personal fortunes, I would not know how to consider it, because I would not have the vaguest idea what the effect would be, except that according to my own view it could not but be bad and unpleasant for me personally. From the personal standpoint I should view the nomination to the Presidency as a real and serious misfortune. Nothing would persuade me to take it, unless it appeared that the people really wished me to do a given job, which I could not honorably shirk. (To Lane, Dec. 1911 or Jan. 1912.) *The Letters of Franklin K. Lane.* (Houghton Mifflin Co., Boston, 1922), pp. 86-87.

——————. I am not and shall not be a candidate. I shall not seek the nomination, nor would I accept it if it came to me as the result of an intrigue. But I will not tie my hands by a statement which would make it difficult or impossible for me to serve the public by undertaking a great task if the people as a whole seemed definitely to come to the conclusion that I ought to do that task. In other words, as far as in me lies I am endeavoring to look at this matter purely from the standpoint of the public interest, of the interest of the people as a whole, and not in the least from my own standpoint.

If I should consult only my own pleasure and interest, I should most emphatically and immediately announce that I would under no circumstances run. I have had all the honor that any man can have from holding the office of President. From every personal standpoint there is nothing for me to gain either in running for the office or in holding the office once more, and there is very much to lose. . . .

If my position were only a pose, I should certainly act differently from the way I am acting, for I am well aware that the way I am acting is not the way in which to act if I desire to be made President. But my attitude is not a pose, I am acting as I do because, according to my lights, I am endeavoring, in a not too easy position, to do what I believe the interests of the people demand. From this standpoint I am convinced that although it is entirely proper for other men to seek the Presidency, it is neither wise nor proper for me to do so, the conditions being what they actually are. I have been President; I was President for nearly eight years; I am well known to the American people; I am to be judged not by words but by my acts; and whether the people like me or dislike me, they have these acts all before them for their decision. (To Frank A. Munsey, January 16, 1912.) *Mem. Ed.* XXIV, 368, 370; Bishop II, 314-315.

——————. It may be necessary for me to speak, and very possible I will have to speak before the first open primaries. I hope not, however. The trouble is that if I speak it looks as if I were making myself a candidate, and if I do not speak it looks as if I were acting furtively.

I write you, confidentially, that my own reading of the situation is that while there are a great many people in this country who are devoted to me, they do not form more than a substantial minority of the ten or fifteen millions of voters. I have had a great time; I have done my work. Unless I am greatly mistaken, the people have made up their mind that they wish some new instrument, that do not wish me; and if I know myself, I am sincere when I tell you that this does not cause one least little particle of regret to me. If it becomes necessary for me in the popular interest to attempt any job, of course I would attempt it; but nothing would persuade me to attempt it in my own interest and welfare, and as far as in me lies I shall endeavor to make it clear that such is the case. (To Joseph B. Bishop, January 29, 1912.) *Mem. Ed.* XXIV, 370; Bishop II, 315.

——————. In this fight I am standing for certain great principles, which I regard as vital to the present and future welfare of this Nation. My success is of value only as an incident to securing the triumph of these principles. Foremost among these principles is the right of the people to rule, and the duty of their representatives really to represent them, in nominating conventions no less than in executive or legislative offices. If the majority of the rank and file of the Republican party do not wish me nominated, then most certainly I do not wish to be nominated. *Outlook,* May 11, 1912, p. 62.

——————. When in February last I made up my mind that it was my duty to enter

[159]

this fight, it was after long and careful deliberation. I had become convinced that Mr. Taft had definitely and completely abandoned the cause of the people and had surrendered himself wholly to the biddings of the professional political bosses and of the great privileged interests standing behind them. I had also become convinced that unless I did make the fight it could not be made at all, and that Mr. Taft's nomination would come to him without serious opposition. The event has justified both my beliefs. (At Chicago, June 17, 1912.) *Mem. Ed.* XIX, 286; *Nat. Ed.* XVII, 205.

———. The American people are entitled to know that the charge of stealing the Chicago Convention of 1912 is more than campaign recrimination, and that the frauds complained of are much more serious than the mere repetition of loose practices which might have found unfortunate precedents in some previous conventions of both parties. Seriously and literally, President Taft's renomination was stolen for him from the American people and the ratification or rejection of that nomination raises the critical issue whether votes or fraud shall determine the selection of American Presidents. (*Outlook,* July 13, 1912.) *Mem. Ed.* XIX, 318; *Nat. Ed.* XVII, 232.

———. It is, of course, perfectly true that in voting for me or against me consideration must be paid to what I have done in the past and to what I propose to do. But it seems to me far more important that consideration should be paid to what the Progressive party proposes to do. (New York *Times,* October 18, 1912.) *Mem. Ed.* XIX, 454; *Nat. Ed.* XVII, 332.

———. We have fought a great fight. We have accomplished more in ninety days than ever any other party in our history accomplished in such a length of time. We have forced all parties and candidates to give at least lip-service to Progressive principles. In this brief campaign we have overthrown the powerful and corrupt machine that betrayed and strangled the Republican party. (At Chicago, December 10, 1912.) *Mem. Ed.* XIX, 473; *Nat. Ed.* XVII, 349.

ELECTION OF 1912. *See also* NEW FREEDOM; NEW NATIONALISM; PRESIDENCY AND THE THIRD TERM ISSUE; PROGRESSIVE PARTY; REPUBLICAN PARTY; TAFT, WILLIAM H.; WILSON, WOODROW.

ELECTION OF 1916. I am told that the proposal now among the Republican extremists is to renominate Taft next time. There are a great many Progressives, including myself, who under no circumstances would support Taft. Personally, it does not seem to me that I could support Wilson even against Taft; but there are plenty who would not stop even at that; and it does not seem to me to be wise to put him up, with the certainty that the Progressives as a whole will either come out for Wilson or run a third ticket. (To H. C. Lodge, February 6, 1915.) Lodge *Letters* II, 454.

———. I have been like an engine bucking a snow-drift. My progress was slower and slower; and finally I accumulated so much snow that I came to a halt and could not get through. I believe that there are some men who would support me against Wilson, for instance, or against a reactionary Republican, who would not support any one else. But I believe that there are a far larger number of men who would at once sink every other purpose, no matter what their convictions might be, for the purpose of smashing me once for all. According to the information at present before me, I believe that the bulk of our people would accept my candidacy as a proof of greedy personal ambition on my part, and would be bitterly hostile to me in consequence, and bitterly hostile therefore to the cause for which I stood. . . . Of course, if it was a duty impossible to avoid, I would fight in future as I have fought in the past. But I feel I have done my share; and, what is infinitely more important, I do not feel that I can be of use in a leading position any more. I think the people have made up their minds that they have had all they want of me, and that my championship of a cause or an individual, save in exceptional cases, is a damage rather than a benefit. (Letter of June 3, 1915.) *Mem. Ed.* XXIV, 449, 451; Bishop II, 382, 383.

———. It is my deliberate judgment that if the Republicans ever come to entertain the thought of nominating me next year, it will be because they know they will be defeated under me and intend that I shall receive the heaviest defeat they can give me, and they will nominate me with this purpose in view, thereby not only crushing the Progressives but definitely getting rid of me and enthroning the stand-patters in the Republican party.

It is perfectly evident to me that this people have made up their minds not only against the policies in which I believe but finally against me personally. The bulk of them are convinced that I am actuated by motives of personal ambition and that I am selfishly desirous of hurting Taft and Wilson and have not the good of the country at heart. Anything that you or any of my other close friends do that can be construed into putting me forward for the Presidency will absolutely confirm this opinion and will do me real and grave damage. (To George W. Perkins, September 3, 1915.) *Mem. Ed.* XXIV, 467; Bishop II, 397.

——————. Of course, it is possible that the Republicans will win without any assistance from the Progressives at all. It is also possible that they cannot win even with Progressive support. But on the assumption that there is need of trying to unite all the anti-Wilson forces into a coherent whole, I hope that the Republicans will take action such as will render it possible for the Progressives to go in with them. Unless there is a really vital national crisis I do not intend to separate myself from my Progressive supporters; but I shall do everything in my power to get them to act wisely. Incidentally I am as well aware of their shortcomings as of the shortcomings of other people. (To H. C. Lodge, November 27, 1915.) Lodge *Letters* II, 465.

——————. As you know, I feel that the course I have followed about hyphenated-Americanism, and especially the German-American vote, is such as absolutely to preclude the possibility of nominating me as a candidate, even though there had been such a possibility before, which in my judgment was not the case. I have followed the course I have followed in the last year, because I thought some man ought to say the kind of things I have said, and that without regard to his own future, and I was the man peculiarly blocked out for this task. (To H. C. Lodge, December 7, 1915.) Lodge *Letters* II, 466.

——————. Now, as for what you say about myself. I do not know whether anyone will believe it; but whether they do or not I am absolutely sincere in saying that the course I am following and have followed has been taken absolutely without regard to my own interests or the interests of any other individual. No politician desiring political preference would enter on a campaign to alienate the German-American vote and the pacificist vote and to wake up our people to unpleasant facts by telling them unpleasant truths. My judgment is now and has been from the beginning that this course would render me impossible as a candidate. Of two things at any rate I am sure. In the first place I not only do not desire but I will not take the nomination if it comes as the result of manipulation or of any manœuvers which would seem to make it appear that I am striving, for my own personal aggrandizement, to secure it. Unless there is a popular feeling in the Republican party in the country at large such as to make the Republican leaders feel that, not for my sake but for the sake of the party and the country, it is imperative to nominate me, why I won't even consider accepting the nomination. In the next place it is utterly idle to nominate me if the country is in a mood either of timidity or of that base and complacent materialism which finds expression in the phrase "Safety first." If the country is not determined to put honor and duty ahead of safety, then the people most emphatically do not wish me for President, and the party cannot afford to run me for President; for I will not take back by one finger's breadth anything I have said during the last eighteen months about national and international duty or apologize for anything I did while I was President. (Unless the country is somewhere near a mood of at least half-heroism it would be utterly useless to nominate me.) (To H. C. Lodge, February 4, 1916.) Lodge *Letters* II, 479.

——————. I will not enter into any fight for the nomination and I will not permit any factional fight to be made in my behalf. Indeed, I will go further and say that it would be a mistake to nominate me unless the country has in its mood something of the heroic—unless it feels not only devotion to ideals but the purpose measurably to realize those ideals in action.

This is one of those rare times which come only at long intervals in a nation's history, where the action taken determines the basis of the life of the generations that follow. Such times were those from 1776 to 1789, in the days of Washington, and from 1858 to 1865, in the days of Lincoln.

It is for us of to-day to grapple with the tremendous national and international problems of our own hour in the spirit and with the ability shown by those who upheld the hands of Washington and Lincoln. (Statement to press, Trinidad, B.W.I., March 9, 1916.) *Mem. Ed.* XIX, 560; *Nat. Ed.* XVII, 410.

——————. Disgust with the unmanly failure of the present [Wilson] administration, I believe, does not, and I know ought not to, mean that the American people will vote in a spirit of mere protest. They ought not to, and I believe they will not, be content merely to change the present administration for one equally timid, equally vacillating, equally lacking in vision, in moral integrity, and in high resolve. They should desire, and I believe they do desire, public servants and public policies signifying more than adroit cleverness in escaping action behind clouds of fine words, in refusal to face real internal needs, and in complete absorption of every faculty in devising constantly shifting hand-to-mouth and day-to-day measures for escape from our international duty by the abandonment of our national honor —measures due to sheer dread of various foreign powers, tempered by a sometimes harmonizing and sometimes conflicting dread of various classes of voters, especially hyphenated voters, at home. (Statement to press, Trinidad, B.W.I., March 9, 1916.) *Mem. Ed.* XIX, 561; *Nat. Ed.* XVII, 411.

―――――――――. Not only do I desire that no kind of faction fight be made to secure my nomination but I feel that it would be worse than worthless to have the nomination unless it comes of their own accord from the Republicans, because they feel they need me, and because they feel that the country is ripe for the kind of campaign which is the only campaign I would consent to make. After Lincoln became President the question of retaining the Union was of such absorbing consequence that for the next eighteen months he declined to consider even such a tremendous question as Slavery. He subordinated everything else to the question of the Union. There are certain tremendous national questions affecting our attitude as regards the primary duties of a nation, affecting perhaps the questions whether we are to continue as a nation, which transcend infinitely in importance any question of whether or not the Crane machine or any other machine is to be hurt, is to be opposed, or is to be made an issue in any way. I must not be used in any local fight for any local objects. (To Matthew Hale, April 3, 1916.) *Mem. Ed.* XXIV, 477; Bishop II, 406.

―――――――――. I wish to Heaven there was a better chance of developing some strong candidate against Wilson. There is a real movement to nominate me, simply because I am the only man who has stood openly against him in a way to show that I meant it. (To Frederick Scott Oliver, April 7, 1916.) *Mem. Ed.* XXIV, 479; Bishop II, 407.

―――――――――. The members of the Republican National Convention were unquestionably induced to nominate Mr. Hughes primarily because of the belief that his integrity and force of character and his long record of admirable public service would make him peculiarly acceptable not only to the rank and file of the Republican party but to the people generally. I do not believe that Mr. Hughes would have been nominated if it had not been for the fight on behalf of public decency and efficiency which the Progressive party has waged during the past four years.

In any event, and without any regard to what the personal feelings of any of us may be as regards the action of the Republican convention, I wish very solemnly to ask the representatives of the Progressive party to consider at this time only the welfare of the people of the United States. We shall prove false to our ideals and our professions if, in this grave crisis of the nation's life, we permit ourselves to be swerved from the one prime duty of serving with cool judgment and single-minded devotion the nation's needs.

Our own political fortunes, individually and collectively, are of no consequence whatever when compared with the honor and welfare of the people of the United States. Such things do not count when weighed in the balance against our duty to serve well the country in which, after we are dead, our children and our children's children are to live. (To Progressive National Committee, June 22, 1916.) *Mem. Ed.* XIX, 574; *Nat. Ed.* XVII, 422.

ELECTION OF 1916. *See also* HUGHES, CHARLES E.; PROGRESSIVE PARTY; WILSON, WOODROW.

ELECTION PLEDGES. The worth of a promise consists purely in the way in which the performance squares with it. That has two sides. In the first place, if a man is an honest man he will try just as hard to keep a promise made on the stump as one made off the stump. In the second place, if the people keep their heads they won't wish promises to be made which are impossible of performance. (At Symphony Hall, Boston, Mass., August 25, 1902.) *Presidential Addresses and State Papers,* I, 108.

―――――――――. A broken promise is bad enough in private life. It is worse in the field of politics. No man is worth his salt in public life who makes on the stump a pledge which he does not keep after election; and, if he makes such a pledge and does not keep it, hunt him out of public life. (At Osawatomie, Kan., August 31, 1910.) *Mem. Ed.* XIX, 11; *Nat. Ed.* XVII, 6.

ELECTION PLEDGES. *See also* COMPROMISE; PARTY PLATFORMS; PLATFORM PROMISES; POLITICAL PROMISES.

ELECTION REFORMS. It seems to me that one of the most important problems which this nation has to solve is that of honest elections, and I am for radical measures. . . .

I hope to see some day a national ballot-reform law for congressional and presidential elections, a law which shall not interfere in the least with State or local elections, and which shall not be in any wise sectional, bearing upon all States and districts alike, and which shall secure, in so far as legislation can secure, honest and pure elections; a law which shall threaten the evils that exist in one State or section as much as those that exist in another, which shall tell as heavily against "blocks of five" as against tissue ballots; which shall tell equally against the policy of bribery and the policy of the shotgun, against the purchase of elections by money no less than against the carrying of elections by violence and fraud. (Before Federal Club, New York City, March 6, 1891.) *Mem. Ed.* XVI, 190, 191; *Nat. Ed.* XIV, 126, 127.

————————. We should provide by national law for presidential primaries. We should provide for the election of United States senators by popular vote. We should provide for a short ballot; nothing makes it harder for the people to control their public servants than to force them to vote for so many officials that they cannot really keep track of any one of them, so that each becomes indistinguishable in the crowd around him. There must be stringent and efficient corrupt-practices acts, applying to the primaries as well as the elections; and there should be publicity of campaign contributions during the campaign. (Before Progressive National Convention, Chicago, August 6, 1912.) *Mem. Ed.* XIX, 363; *Nat. Ed.* XVII, 258.

ELECTION REFORMS. *See also* BALLOT; CAMPAIGN FUNDS; INITIATIVE; PRIMARIES; RECALL; REFERENDUM.

ELECTIONS. *See* BOSS; BRIBERY; CAMPAIGN CONTRIBUTIONS; CANDIDATES; CORRUPTION; MACHINE; MUNICIPAL ELECTIONS; PARTY SYSTEM; POLITICS; SENATORS; SUFFRAGE; VOTING.

ELECTRIC POWER. This century is bound to see an astounding development of the use of electrical power generated by running water. The development I believe will be extraordinary. We cannot foresee what the social conditions will be half a century hence. We cannot foresee how our people will feel, and what their needs will be fifty years hence, any more than the Supreme Court eighty years ago could see our needs of to-day. My aim is to hand over to our children and to our grandchildren the public property so unimpaired that they may then do whatever their needs then dictate. I realize absolutely that we must have that power developed in the present. For that reason I would allow the corporation leasing the power to lease it for any length of time necessary to insure them an ample return upon their money. Personally I would be delighted to see it made fifty years instead of twenty-five. Personally I should be glad to see the terms made as easy as possible, because the thing that concerns me is what I regard as the vital principle, the principle of not parting with the property, the principle of keeping it in the public hands, so that at the end of the next forty or fifty years of National development the people shall have it in their possession, and shall not find that they have developed a small number of wealthy men who own something that the public can no longer get except by revolution. (Before the Commonwealth Club, San Francisco, Cal., March 27, 1911.) *Transactions of the Commonwealth Club of California,* June 1912, p. 108.

ELEPHANTS. No other animal, not the lion himself, is so constant a theme of talk, and a subject of such unflagging interest round the camp-fires of African hunters and in the native villages of the African wilderness, as the elephant. Indeed the elephant has always profoundly impressed the imagination of mankind. It is, not only to hunters, but to naturalists, and to all people who possess any curiosity about wild creatures and the wild life of nature, the most interesting of all animals. Its huge bulk, its singular form, the value of its ivory, its great intelligence—in which it is only matched, if at all, by the highest apes, and possibly by one or two of the highest carnivora —and its varied habits, all combine to give it an interest such as attaches to no other living creature below the rank of man. In line of descent and in physical formation it stands by itself, wholly apart from all the other great land beasts, and differing from them even more widely than they differ from one another. (1910.) *Mem. Ed.* V, 231; *Nat. Ed.* IV, 199.

ELEVATED RAILROAD LEGISLATION. I have to say with shame that when I voted for this bill I did not act as I think I ought to have acted, and as I generally have acted on the floor of this House. For the only time that I ever voted here otherwise than in the way

I thought I honestly ought to, I did on that occasion. I have to confess that I weakly yielded, partly in a vindictive spirit toward the infernal thieves and conscienceless swindlers who have had the elevated railroad in charge, and partly to the popular voice of New York.

For the managers of the elevated railroad I have as little feeling as any man here. . . . I realize that they have done the most incalculable wrong to this community with their hired newspapers, with their corruption of the judiciary, with their corruption of past legislatures. . . .

Nevertheless, it is not a question of doing justice to them, it is a question of doing justice to ourselves. It is a question of standing by what we honestly think to be right, even if in so doing we antagonize the feelings of our constituents. (Speech on Governor Cleveland's veto, New York Assembly, March 2, 1883.) *Mem. Ed.* XVI, 19, 20.

ELIOT, CHARLES W. See Books—Lists of.

ELK—EXTERMINATION OF. The gradual extermination of this, the most stately and beautiful animal of the chase to be found in America, can be looked upon only with unmixed regret by every sportsman and lover of nature. Excepting the moose, it is the largest and, without exception, it is the noblest of the deer tribe. No other species of true deer, in either the Old or the New World, comes up to it in size and in the shape, length, and weight of its mighty antlers; while the grand, proud carriage and lordly bearing of an old bull make it perhaps the most majestic-looking of all the animal creation. The open plains have already lost one of their great attractions, now that we no more see the long lines of elk trotting across them; and it will be a sad day when the lordly, antlered beasts are no longer found in the wild, rocky glens and among the lonely woods of towering pines that cover the great Western mountain chains.

The elk has other foes besides man. The grizzly will always make a meal of one if he gets a chance; and against his ponderous weight and savage prowess hoofs and antlers avail but little. Still he is too clumsy and easily avoided ever to do very much damage in the herds. Cougars, where they exist, work more havoc. . . . But these great deer can hold their own and make head against all their brute foes; it is only when pitted against Man the Destroyer that they succumb in the struggle for life. (1885.) *Mem. Ed.* I, 252-253; *Nat. Ed.* I, 210-211.

ELK. See also Wapiti.

ELKHORN RANCH. My ranch . . . derived its name, "The Elkhorn," from the fact that on the ground where we built it were found the skulls and interlocked antlers of two wapiti bulls who had perished from getting their antlers fastened in battle. (1905.) *Mem. Ed.* III, 254; *Nat. Ed.* III, 75.

———————. The ranch-house stood on the brink of a low bluff overlooking the broad, shallow bed of the Little Missouri, through which at most seasons there ran only a trickle of water, while in times of freshet it was filled brimful with the boiling, foaming, muddy torrent. There was no neighbor for ten or fifteen miles on either side of me. The river twisted down in long curves between narrow bottoms bordered by sheer cliff walls, for the Bad Lands, a chaos of peaks, plateaus, and ridges, rose abruptly from the edges of the level, tree-clad, or grassy, alluvial meadows. In front of the ranch-house veranda was a row of cottonwood-trees with gray-green leaves which quivered all day long if there was a breath of air. From these trees came the far-away, melancholy cooing of mourning-doves, and little owls perched in them and called tremulously at night. In the long summer afternoons we would sometimes sit on the piazza, when there was no work to be done, for an hour or two at a time, watching the cattle on the sand-bars, and the sharply channelled and strangely carved amphitheatre of cliffs across the bottom opposite; while the vultures wheeled overhead, their black shadows gliding across the glaring white of the dry river-bed. (1913.) *Mem. Ed.* XXII, 116; *Nat. Ed.* XX, 99.

ELKHORN RANCH. See also Bad Lands; Chimney Butte Ranch; Ranch Life.

EMPLOYER-EMPLOYEE RELATIONS. Very much of our effort in reference to labor matters should be by every device and expedient to try to secure a constantly better understanding between employer and employee. Everything possible should be done to increase the sympathy and fellow-feeling between them, and every chance taken to allow each to look at all questions, especially at questions in dispute, somewhat through the other's eyes. If met with a sincere desire to act fairly by one another, and if there is, furthermore, power by each to appreciate the other's standpoint, the chance for trouble is minimized. (At Sioux Falls, S. D., April 6, 1903.) *Presidential Addresses and State Papers* I, 307.

———. All relations between employer and employee should be based on mutuality of respect and consideration; arrogance met by insolence, or an alternation of arrogance and insolence, offers but a poor substitute. (*Metropolitan,* March 1918.) *Mem. Ed.* XXI, 375; *Nat. Ed.* XIX, 340.

EMPLOYER-EMPLOYEE RELATIONS. *See also* CAPITAL AND LABOR; COLLECTIVE BARGAINING; INDUSTRIAL ARBITRATION; LABOR UNIONS; WORKERS.

EMPLOYERS. There are employers to-day who, like the great coal operators, speak as though they were lords of these countless armies of Americans, who toil in factory, in shop, in mill, and in the dark places under the earth. They fail to see that all these men have the right and the duty to combine to protect themselves and their families from want and degradation. They fail to see that the nation and the government, within the range of fair play and a just administration of the law, must inevitably sympathize with the men who have nothing but their wages, with the men who are struggling for a decent life, as opposed to men, however honorable, who are merely fighting for larger profits and an autocratic control of big business. (1913.) *Mem. Ed.* XXII, 547; *Nat. Ed.* XX, 470.

EMPLOYERS. *See also* BUSINESS; CAPITALISTS.

EMPLOYERS' LIABILITY. *See* WORKMEN'S COMPENSATION.

EMPLOYMENT, REGULAR. It is exceedingly difficult to make a good citizen out of a man who cannot count upon some steadiness and continuity in the work which means to him his livelihood. (*Outlook,* August 27, 1910.) *Mem. Ed.* XVIII, 197; *Nat. Ed.* XVI, 151.

EMPLOYMENT BUREAUS. The present method by which a man or a woman finds a job is about as primitive as an ox-team, and is expensive in waste, in time, and in the very life of the workers. The available work and the available workers in the community should be registered at some point where both can meet. Public employment bureaus should handle not merely common labor and the near-unemployable, but also the highest kinds of labor; and the men who run them should be treated as public officers, needing as high qualifications as the highest type of educator, alike as regards character, ability, devotion to the work, and trained intelligence; and ultimately these employment bureaus may very well co-operate with the public schools in directing into the proper channels the work of the scholars who are going into industry.

Public employment bureaus ought not to represent a kind of charity or merely a temporary aid in winter or in times of industrial depression; they should be a great permanent feature of the governmental work of the nation and of the municipality. Only through them can the labor market be so organized as to minimize the difficulties caused by seasonal and short-time work. (At New York City, January 26, 1915.) *Mem. Ed.* XVIII, 632-633; *Nat. Ed.* XVI, 461.

EMPLOYMENT. *See also* EIGHT-HOUR DAY; LABOR; SOCIAL INSURANCE; UNEMPLOYMENT; WAGES; WORKMEN'S COMPENSATION.

ENFORCEMENT OF LAW. *See* LAW.

ENGLAND—AMERICAN FEELING TOWARD. We have no feeling against England. On the contrary, we regard her as being well in advance of the great powers of Continental Europe, and we have more sympathy with her. In general, her success tells for the success of civilization, and we wish her well. But where her interests enlist her against the progress of civilization and in favor of the oppression of other nationalities who are struggling upward, our sympathies are immediately forfeited. (*The Bachelor of Arts,* March 1896.) *Mem. Ed.* XV, 234; *Nat. Ed.* XIII, 176.

ENGLAND—COMMONWEALTH OF. The whole history of the movement which resulted in the establishment of the Commonwealth of England will be misread and misunderstood if we fail to appreciate that it was the first modern, and not the last mediæval, movement; if we fail to understand that the men who figured in it and the principles for which they contended, are strictly akin to the men and the principles that have appeared in all similar great movements since: in the English Revolution of 1688; in the American Revolution of 1776; and the American Civil War of 1861. (1900.) *Mem. Ed.* XIII, 290; *Nat. Ed.* X, 190.

ENGLAND—ROOSEVELT'S ATTITUDE TOWARD. On the whole I am friendly to England. I do not at all believe in being over-effusive or in forgetting that fundamentally we are two different nations; but yet the fact remains, in the first place, that we are closer in feeling to her than to any other nation; and in the second place, that probably her interest and ours will run on rather parallel lines in the future. (To H. C. Lodge, June 19, 1901.) Lodge *Letters* I, 493.

——————. As regards England, I end the war more convinced than ever that there should be the closest alliance between the British Empire and the United States, but also I am more convinced than ever that neither one can afford for one moment to rely upon the other in a sufficiently tight place. (To Viscount Lee of Fareham, November 19, 1918.) *Mem. Ed.* XIII, 277; *Nat. Ed.* X, 179.

ENGLAND AND AMERICA. The day is past when an American was regarded as a poor relation; and if we remain self reliant and powerful it will never return. (To H. C. Lodge, September 10, 1909.) Lodge *Letters* II, 349.

ENGLAND IN THE WORLD WAR. Her women are working with all the steadfast courage and self-sacrifice that the women of France have shown. Her men from every class have thronged into the army. Her fisherfolk, and her seafarers generally, have come forward in such numbers that her fleet is nearly double as strong as it was at the outset of the war. Her mines and war factories have steadily enlarged their output, and it is now enormous, although many of the factories had literally to build from the ground up, and the very plant itself had to be created. Coal, food, guns, munitions, are being supplied with sustained energy. (1916.) *Mem. Ed.* XX, 259; *Nat. Ed.* XVIII, 223.

ENGLAND'S ENTRANCE INTO WAR. England's attitude in going to war in defense of Belgium's rights, according to its guaranty, was not only strictly proper but represents the only kind of action that ever will make a neutrality treaty or peace treaty or arbitration treaty worth the paper on which it is written. The published despatches of the British Government show that Sir Edward Grey clearly, emphatically, and scrupulously declined to commit his government to war until it became imperative to do so if Great Britain was to fulfil, as her honor and interest alike demanded, her engagements on behalf of the neutrality of Belgium. (New York *Times*, October 11, 1914.) *Mem. Ed.* XX, 52; *Nat. Ed.* XVIII, 45.

ENGLAND. *See also* ANGLOMANIA; ARBITRATION; BELGIUM; BOER WAR; COLONIAL SYSTEM; CROMWELL, OLIVER; GEORGE V; IMPERIALISM; INDIA; MONROE DOCTRINE; PANAMA CANAL; PARLIAMENTARY GOVERNMENT; REVOLUTIONARY WAR; WAR OF 1812; WORLD WAR.

ENGLISH LANGUAGE. *See* LANGUAGE.

ENGLISH NAVY. The English navy was mobilized with a rapidity and efficiency as great as that of the German army. It has driven every war-ship, except an occasional submarine, and every merchant ship of Germany off the seas, and has kept the ocean as a highway of life not only for England, but for France, and largely also for Russia. In all history there has been no such gigantic and successful naval feat accomplished as that which the seamen and shipwrights of England have to their credit during the last eighteen months. (1916.) *Mem. Ed.* XX, 258; *Nat. Ed.* XVIII, 222.

ENGLISH NAVY. *See also* NAVAL ARMAMENTS.

ENGLISH PEOPLE—DEVOTION OF. The colonial habit of thought dies hard. It is to be wished that those who are cursed with it would, in endeavoring to emulate the ways of the Old World, endeavor to emulate one characteristic which has been shared by every Old World nation, and which is possessed to a marked degree by England. Every decent Englishman is devoted to his country, first, last, and all the time. An Englishman may or may not dislike America, but he is invariably for England and against America when any question arises between them; and I heartily respect him for so being. (*The Bachelor of Arts*, March 1896.) *Mem. Ed.* XV, 238; *Nat. Ed.* XIII, 179.

ENGLISH-SPEAKING PEOPLES — FRIENDSHIP BETWEEN. I absolutely agree with you as to the importance, not only to ourselves but to all the free peoples of the civilized world, of a constantly growing friendship and understanding between the English-speaking peoples. One of the gratifying things in what has occurred during the last decade has been the growth in this feeling of good-will. All I can do to foster it will be done. I need hardly add that, in order to foster it, we need judgment and moderation no less than the good-will itself. The larger interests of the two nations are the same; and the fundamental, underlying traits of their characters are also the same. (To King Edward VII, March 9, 1905.) *Mem. Ed.* XXIV, 311; Bishop II, 262.

ENGLISH-SPEAKING PEOPLES — RELATIONS BETWEEN. A hundred years ago

ENTHUSIASM

the English-speaking peoples of Britain and America regarded one another as inveterate and predestined enemies, just as three centuries previously had been the case in Great Britain itself between those who dwelt in the northern half and those who dwelt in the southern half of the island. Now war is unthinkable between us. (New York *Times,* October 18, 1914.) *Mem. Ed.* XX, 68; *Nat. Ed.* XVIII, 58.

ENTHUSIASM. *See* FERVOR.

ENVY. The vice of envy is not only a dangerous but also a mean vice, for it is always a confession of inferiority. It may provoke conduct which will be fruitful of wrong-doing to others, and it must cause misery to the man who feels it. It will not be any the less fruitful of wrong and misery if, as is so often the case with evil motives, it adopts some high-sounding alias. (Before Young Men's Christian Association, New York City, December 30, 1900.) *Mem. Ed.* XV, 532; *Nat. Ed.* XIII, 496.

EPISCOPAL CHURCH. The Episcopal Church has a wonderful future ahead of it here. It is so closely akin to our civilization, and it appeals not so much to wealth (as is sometimes charged) as it does to conservatism. It just so happens that the conservative class is usually the wealthy class. While I should have liked one or two of my children to have become members of my church, I feel greatly comforted that they are in their mother's church. (Recorded by Butt in letter of January 20, 1909.) *The Letters of Archie Butt. Personal Aide to President Roosevelt.* (Doubleday, Page & Co., Garden City, N. Y., 1924), p. 298.

EQUALITY. Ours is a government of liberty by, through, and under the law. No man is above it and no man is below it. The crime of cunning, the crime of greed, the crime of violence, are all equally crimes, and against them all alike the law must set its face. This is not and never shall be a government either of a plutocracy or of a mob. It is, it has been, and it will be, a government of the people; including alike the people of great wealth and of moderate wealth, the people who employ others, the people who are employed, the wage-worker, the lawyer, the mechanic, the banker, the farmer; including them all, protecting each and every one if he acts decently and squarely, and discriminating against any one of them, no matter from what class he comes, if he does not act squarely and fairly, if he does not obey the law. (At Spokane, Wash., May 26, 1903.) *Mem. Ed.* XVIII, 20; *Nat. Ed.* XVI, 18.

EQUALITY

———————. This Government is based upon the fundamental idea that each man, no matter what his occupation, his race, or his religious belief, is entitled to be treated on his worth as a man, and neither favored nor discriminated against because of any accident in his position. (Letter accepting nomination for Presidency, September 12, 1904.) *Mem. Ed.* XVIII, 512; *Nat. Ed.* XVI, 384.

———————. The corner-stone of the Republic lies in our treating each man on his worth as a man, paying no heed to his creed, his birthplace, or his occupation, asking not whether he is rich or poor, whether he labors with head or hand; asking only whether he acts decently and honorably in the various relations of his life, whether he behaves well to his family, to his neighbors, to the State. We base our regard for each man on the essentials and not the accidents. We judge him not by his professions, but by his deeds; by his conduct, not by what he has acquired of this world's goods. Other republics have fallen, because the citizens gradually grew to consider the interests of a class before the interests of the whole; for when such was the case it mattered little whether it was the poor who plundered the rich or the rich who exploited the poor; in either event the end of the republic was at hand. (At Jamestown Exposition, April 26, 1907.) *Mem. Ed.* XII, 595; *Nat. Ed.* XI, 313.

———————. We should not take part in acting a lie any more than in telling a lie. We should not say that men are equal where they are not equal, nor proceed upon the assumption that there is an equality where it does not exist; but we should strive to bring about a measurable equality, at least to the extent of preventing the inequality which is due to force or fraud. (At the Sorbonne, Paris, April 23, 1910.) *Mem. Ed.* XV, 367; *Nat. Ed.* XIII, 521.

EQUALITY AND DEMOCRACY. We believe in a real, not a sham, democracy. We believe in democracy as regards political rights, as regards education, and, finally, as regards industrial conditions. By democracy we understand securing, as far as it is humanly possible to secure it, equality of opportunity, equality of the conditions under which each man is to show the stuff that is in him and to achieve the measure of success to which his own force of mind and character entitle him. Religiously this means that each man is to have the right, unhindered by the State, to worship his Creator as his conscience dictates, granting freely to

[167]

others the same freedom which he asks for himself. Politically we can be said substantially to have worked out our democratic ideals, and the same is true, thanks to the common schools, in educational matters. (At Cairo, Ill., October 3, 1907.) Mem. Ed. XVIII, 17; Nat. Ed. XVI, 15.

EQUALITY. See also CLASSES; DEMOCRACY; FREEDOM; LAW; LIBERTY; OPPORTUNITY; PRIVILEGE; REWARDS; SQUARE DEAL.

ETHICS. See CHARACTER; COURAGE; DUTY; HONESTY; IDEALS; JUSTICE; MORAL SENSE; MORALITY; RIGHT; RIGHTEOUSNESS; TEN COMMANDMENTS; TRUTH; VICE; VIRTUE.

ETIQUETTE. See SOCIAL CONVENTIONS.

EUGENICS. I wish very much that the wrong people could be prevented entirely from breeding; and when the evil nature of these people is sufficiently flagrant, this should be done. Criminals should be sterilized, and feeble-minded persons forbidden to leave offspring behind them. But as yet there is no way possible to devise which could prevent all undesirable people from breeding. The emphasis should be laid on getting desirable people to breed. This is no question of having enormous families for which the man and woman are unable to provide. I do not believe in or advocate such families. I am not encouraging shiftless people, unfit to marry, who have huge families. I am speaking of the ordinary, every-day Americans, the decent men and women who do make good fathers and mothers, and who ought to have good-sized families. (*Outlook,* January 3, 1914.) Mem. Ed. XIV, 172; Nat. Ed. XII, 201.

EUGENICS. See also BIRTH CONTROL; FAMILY; MARRIAGE; RACE SUICIDE.

EUROPE—ROOSEVELT'S VISIT TO. I should like then to spend a couple of months on a trip thru the hill towns of Italy, thru certain parts of Southern France, and finally a week or two in England. Whether or not I can make this tour depends upon what I shall have to do if I go to these countries. If it means that I have to make a kind of mock triumphal progress and spend my time at dismal and expensive entertainments which I shall loathe even more than the wretched creatures who feel obliged to give them, why I won't go, and shall simply come straight home. If I can travel purely as a private citizen of small means without seeing anybody but my old friends, why that I should prefer. I am inclined to think that if necessary I would compromise, and, to avoid seeming churlish, would be entirely willing to be presented privately at court, or call on the leading public men in the different countries, if this did not involve foolish and elaborate functions, and did give me time to see the sights I want to see and to call on the friends I want to call on. But all this can be settled later. (To H. C. Lodge, August 8, 1908.) Lodge *Letters* II, 311.

――――――――. I have rather a horror of ex-Presidents travelling around with no real business, and thereby putting unfortunate potentates who think they ought to show courtesy to the United States in a position where they feel obliged to entertain the said ex-Presidents, no matter how great a hero any one of them may be. If I could make the sovereigns and leading men of each country understand that I did not expect any attention and would be only too glad to be left to my own resources, and be permitted to call upon the people I already knew and a very few others whom I would like to know, why, that would be all right; but to make a kind of mock triumphal procession would offer about as unattractive an outing to me as could be imagined. (To Lord Curzon, August 18, 1908.) Mem. Ed. XXIV, 141; Bishop II, 121.

EUROPE—ROOSEVELT'S VISIT TO. See also DENMARK; FRANCE; GERMANY; GREY, SIR EDWARD; NORWAY; ROME; ROOSEVELT; WILLIAM II.

EUROPEAN COURTS — PRESENTATION OF AMERICANS AT. I have grown to have a constantly increasing horror of the Americans who go abroad desiring to be presented at court or to meet sovereigns. In very young people it is excusable folly; in older people it is mere snobbishness. . . . I cannot be too sincerely grateful that when Mrs. Roosevelt and I were abroad before I was President, we refused to be presented. I have a hearty respect for the right kind of a king and for the right kind of aristocracy, and for the right kind of Englishman who wishes to be presented or have his wife or daughter presented; but it is the business of an American to be a republican, a democrat, to behave in a simple and straightforward manner, and, without anything cheap or blatant about it, to be just what he is, a plain citizen of the American Republic; and he is thoroughly out of place, loses his dignity in the eyes of others, and loses his own self-respect, when he tries to play a rôle for which he is not suited, and which personally I think is less exalted than his own natural rôle. (To Whitelaw Reid, May 25, 1908.) *Mem. Ed.* XXIV, 130; Bishop II, 111.

EUROPEAN EXPANSION. *See* EXPANSION; IMPERIALISM.

EUROPEAN NATIONS AND THE UNITED STATES. I do not in the least misunderstand . . . the attitude of any European nation as regards us. We shall keep the respect of each of them just as long as we are thoroughly able to hold our own, and no longer. If we got into trouble, there is not one of them upon whose friendship we could count to get us out; what we shall need to count upon is the efficiency of our fighting men and particularly of our neighbor. (To Finley Peter Dunne, late 1904.) *Mem. Ed.* XXIII, 401; Bishop I, 348.

EUROPEAN UPPER CLASSES. The German upper classes, alone among the European upper classes—so far as I knew—really did not like the social type I represented. All the other people of the upper classes in Europe whom I met, even the extremely aristocratic Austrians, seemed eager to see me, just because I did represent something new to them. They regarded me as a characteristically American type, which however had nothing in common with the conventional American millionaire; to them it was interesting to meet a man who was certainly a democrat—a real, not a sham, democrat —both politically and socially, who yet was a gentleman, who had his own standards, and did not look down upon or feel defiant toward, or desire to offend, them, but who did not feel that his standards or position were in any way dependent upon their views and good-will. (To Sir George Otto Trevelyan, October 1, 1911.) *Mem. Ed.* XXIV, 288; Bishop II, 246.

EXAMPLES, WORTHY. Much of the usefulness of any career must lie in the impress that it makes upon, and the lessons that it teaches to, the generations that come after. (At unveiling of monument to General Phil Sheridan, Washington, November 25, 1908.) *Mem. Ed.* XII, 479; *Nat. Ed.* XI, 222.

EXAMPLES. *See also* FAME; HEROES.

EXECUTIVE, THE, AND LEGISLATION. In theory the Executive has nothing to do with legislation. In practice, as things now are, the Executive is or ought to be peculiarly representative of the people as a whole. As often as not the action of the Executive offers the only means by which the people can get the legislation they demand and ought to have. Therefore a good executive under the present conditions of American political life must take a very active interest in getting the right kind of legislation, in addition to performing his executive duties with an eye single to the public welfare. More than half of my work as governor was in the direction of getting needed and important legislation. I accomplished this only by arousing the people, and riveting their attention on what was done. (1913.) *Mem. Ed.* XXII, 322; *Nat. Ed.* XX, 276.

EXECUTIVE RESPONSIBILITY. I do not deal with public sentiment. I deal with the law. How I might act as a legislator or what kind of legislation I should advise has no bearing on my conduct as an executive officer charged with administering the law. (New York *Sun*, June 20, 1895.) *Mem. Ed.* XVI, 259; *Nat. Ed.* XIV, 181.

EXECUTIVE. *See also* ADMINISTRATION; CABINET; DIVISION OF POWERS; LAW; PRESIDENCY; PRESIDENT; SENATE; SUPREME COURT.

EXERCISE. A man whose business is sedentary should get some kind of exercise if he wishes to keep himself in as good physical trim as his brethren who do manual labor. (1913.) *Mem. Ed.* XXII, 48; *Nat. Ed.* XX, 42.

———————. It is hardly necessary at the present day to enter a plea for athletic exercise and manly outdoor sports. During the last twenty-five years there has been a wonderful growth of interest in and appreciation of healthy muscular amusements; and this growth can best be promoted by stimulating, within proper bounds, the spirit of rivalry on which all our games are based. The effect upon the physique of the sedentary classes, especially in the towns and cities, has already been very marked. We are much less liable than we were to reproaches on the score of our national ill health, of the bad constitutions of our men, and of the fragility and early decay of our women.

There are still plenty of people who look down on, as of little moment, the proper development of the body; but the men of good sense sympathize as little with these as they do with the even more noxious extremists who regard physical development as an end instead of a means. As a nation we have many tremendous problems to work out, and we need to bring every ounce of vital power possible to their solution. No people has ever yet done great and lasting work if its physical type was infirm and weak. (*North American Review*, August 1890.) *Mem. Ed.* XV, 516; *Nat. Ed.* XIII, 583.

EXERCISE. *See also* GYMNASTICS; OUTDOOR LIFE; SPORTS.

EXPANSION. Expansion is not only the handmaid of greatness, but, above all, it is the handmaid of peace. . . . Every expansion of a civilized power is a conquest for peace. . . . It means not only the extension of American influence and power, it means the extension of liberty and order, and the bringing nearer by gigantic strides of the day when peace shall come to the whole earth. . . .

When throughout the world barbarism has given place to civilization, then, and not till then, the reign of peace will be at hand; and expansion is at the moment the way in which this nation can best do its duty, can best help to bring about that hoped-for day. (Speech at Cincinnati, O., October 21, 1899.) *Mem. Ed.* XVI, 499-502; *Nat. Ed.* XIV, 336-339.

—————. As you know, I am an expansionist; and I am an expansionist because I believe that this people must play the part of a great people; because I believe it must do its share in the hard work of the world; because I don't think it is good for a nation, any more than for an individual, to spend all the time introspectively in the affairs of its own household merely. It will manage them all the better if it has outside interests. It must manage those interests from a double standpoint. It is bound to manage them from the standpoint of the honor of America and from the standpoint of the interests of the people governed. (At dinner to Chauncey M. Depew, March 11, 1899.) *Speeches at the Lotos Club.* (Lotos Club, New York, 1901), p. 329.

EXPANSION, AMERICAN. European nations war for the possession of thickly settled districts which, if conquered, will for centuries remain alien and hostile to the conquerors; we, wiser in our generation, have seized the waste solitudes that lay near us, the limitless forests and never-ending plains, and the valleys of the great, lonely rivers; and have thrust our own sons into them to take possession; and a score of years after each conquest we see the conquered land teeming with a people that is one with ourselves. (1887.) *Mem. Ed.* VIII, 197-198; *Nat. Ed.* VII, 171.

—————. Throughout a large part of our national career our history has been one of expansion, the expansion being of different kinds at different times. This expansion is not a matter of regret, but of pride. It is vain to tell a people as masterful as ours that the spirit of enterprise is not safe. The true American has never feared to run risks when the prize to be won was of sufficient value. No nation capable of self-government, and of developing by its own efforts a sane and orderly civilization, no matter how small it may be, has anything to fear from us. (At Minnesota State Fair, September 2, 1901.) *Mem. Ed.* XV, 337; *Nat. Ed.* XIII, 476.

—————. This work of expansion was by far the greatest work of our people during the years that intervened between the adoption of the Constitution and the outbreak of the Civil War. There were other questions of real moment and importance, and there were many which at the time seemed such to those engaged in answering them; but the greatest feat of our forefathers of those generations was the deed of the men who, with pack-train or wagon-train, on horseback, on foot, or by boat, pushed the frontier ever westward across the continent.

Never before had the world seen the kind of national expansion which gave our people all that part of the American continent lying west of the thirteen original States; the greatest landmark in which was the Louisiana Purchase. Our triumph in this process of expansion was indissolubly bound up with the success of our peculiar kind of Federal government; and this success has been so complete that because of its very completeness we now sometimes fail to appreciate not only the all-importance but the tremendous difficulty of the problem with which our nation was originally faced. (At Louisiana Purchase Exposition, St. Louis, April 30, 1903.) *Mem. Ed.* XII, 599; *Nat. Ed.* XI, 316-317.

EXPANSION, EUROPEAN. There is one feature in the expansion of the peoples of white, or European, blood during the past four centuries which should never be lost sight of, especially by those who denounce such expansion on moral grounds. On the whole, the movement has been fraught with lasting benefit to most of the peoples already dwelling in the lands over which the expansion took place. Of course any such general statement as this must be understood with the necessary reservations. Human nature being what it is, no movement lasting for four centuries and extending in one shape or another over the major part of the world could go on without cruel injustices being done at certain places and in certain times. Occasionally, although not very frequently, a mild and kindly race has been treated with wanton, brutal and ruthless inhumanity by the white intruders. Moreover, mere savages, whose type of life was so primitive as to be absolutely incompatible with the existence of civilization, inevitably died

[170]

out from the regions across which their sparse bands occasionally flitted, when these regions became filled with a dense population; they died out when they were kindly treated as quickly as when they were badly treated, for the simple reason that they were so little advanced that the conditions of life necessary to their existence were incompatible with any form of higher and better existence. It is also true that, even where great good has been done to the already existing inhabitants, where they have thriven under the new rule, it has sometimes brought with it discontent from the very fact that it has brought with it a certain amount of well-being and a certain amount of knowledge, so that people have learned enough to feel discontented and have prospered enough to be able to show their discontent. Such ingratitude is natural, and must be reckoned with as such; but it is also both unwarranted and foolish, and the fact of its existence in any given case does not justify any change of attitude on our part.

On the whole, and speaking generally, one extraordinary fact of this expansion of the European races is that with it has gone an increase in population and well-being among the natives of the countries where the expansion has taken place. (At celebration of Methodist Episcopal Church, Washington, January 18, 1909.) *Mem. Ed.* XVIII, 341-342; *Nat. Ed.* XVI, 258-259.

EXPANSION. *See also* AFRICA; BENTON, THOMAS HART; CANADIAN NORTHWEST; COLONIAL SYSTEM; CUBA; IMPERIALISM; INDIA; LOUISIANA PURCHASE; MANIFEST DESTINY; PHILIPPINES; SLAVERY; TEXAS; WESTWARD MOVEMENT.

EXPATRIATES. It is in those professions where our people have striven hardest to mould themselves in conventional European forms that they have succeeded least; and this holds true to the present day, the failure being of course most conspicuous where the man takes up his abode in Europe; where he becomes a second-rate European, because he is overcivilized, over-sensitive, overrefined, and has lost the hardihood and manly courage by which alone he can conquer in the keen struggle of our national life. Be it remembered, too, that this same being does not really become a European; he only ceases being an American, and becomes nothing. He throws away a great prize for the sake of a lesser one, and does not even get the lesser one. (*Forum*, April 1894.) *Mem. Ed.* XV, 22; *Nat. Ed.* XIII, 19.

EXPATRIATES. *See also* COSMOPOLITANS; FOREIGN WAYS.

EXPEDIENCY. *See* COMPROMISE; POLITICAL EXPEDIENCY.

EXPERIENCE. Americans learn only from catastrophes and not from experience. (1913.) *Mem. Ed.* XXII, 245; *Nat. Ed.* XX, 210.

EXPERIMENT—VALUE OF. It is far better to try experiments, even when we are not certain how these experiments will turn out, or when we are certain that the proposed plan contains elements of folly as well as elements of wisdom. Better "trial and error" than no trial at all. And the service test, the test of actual experiment, is the only conclusive test. It is only the attempt in actual practice to realize a realizable ideal that contains hope. Mere writing and oratory and enunciation of theory, with no attempt to secure the service test, amount to nothing. (1917.) *Mem. Ed.* XXI, 112; *Nat. Ed.* XIX, 115.

EXPERTS IN GOVERNMENT. We welcome leadership and advice, of course, and we are content to let experts do the expert business to which we assign them without fussy interference from us. But the expert must understand that he is carrying out our general purpose and not substituting his own for it. The leader must understand that he leads us, that he guides us, by convincing us so that we will follow him or follow his direction. He must not get it into his head that it is his business to drive us or to ride us. His business is to manage the government for us. (At St. Louis, Mo., March 28, 1912.) *Mem. Ed.* XIX, 237; *Nat. Ed.* XVII, 174.

EXPERTS. *See also* GOVERNMENT; LEADERS.

EXPLORATION—HAZARDS OF. In any expedition . . . there are bound to be unforeseen difficulties of every kind, and it is often absolutely impossible for the outside public to say whether a failure is due to some lack of forethought on the part of those engaged in the expedition, or to causes absolutely beyond human control. There is not and cannot be certainty in an affair of this kind—probably there cannot be certainty in any affair, but above all in what by its very nature is so hazardous. The slack or rash man is much more likely to fail than the man of forethought; but the hand of the Lord may be heavy upon the wise no less than upon the foolish.

There remains the question as to whether the great risks and hazards are warranted by the end sought to be achieved. I emphatically think they are warranted. This, however, is hardly a matter which can be settled by argument in such shape that it shall satisfy every one. People who greatly dread hazard or greatly disapprove of it, and who are not interested in knowledge as such, will naturally disapprove of taking even a small risk for widening at any point the domain of knowledge save where immediate and tangible remuneration is to follow. Naturally, such people, who are often very good people but who possess limited imaginative power, will never be appealed to by the men who prize life as a great adventure; the men who in one age first crossed the Atlantic, first sailed around the Cape of Good Hope, and first passed the Straits of Magellan and circumnavigated the globe; the men who, in another age, first penetrated to the North and South poles, who first crossed Africa, or who found their way for the first time to the forbidden city of the Dalai Lama. The difference is largely based upon difference of temperament, and argument can never reconcile wide temperamental distinctions. (*Outlook,* March 1, 1913.) *Mem. Ed.* XIV, 584-585; *Nat. Ed.* XII, 440-441.

EXPLORERS. The first geographical explorers of the untrodden wilderness, the first wanderers who penetrate the wastes where they are confronted with starvation, disease, and danger and death in every form, cannot take with them the elaborate equipment necessary in order to do the thorough scientific work demanded by modern scientific requirements. This is true even of exploration done along the course of unknown rivers; it is more true of the exploration . . . done across country, away from the rivers.

The scientific work proper of these early explorers must be of a somewhat preliminary nature; in other words the most difficult and therefore ordinarily the most important pieces of first-hand exploration are precisely those where the scientific work of the accompanying cartographer, geologist, botanist, and zoologist who works to most advantage in the wilderness must take his time, and therefore he must normally follow in the footsteps of, and not accompany, the first explorers. The man who wishes to do the best scientific work in the wilderness must not try to combine incompatible types of work nor to cover too much ground in too short a time. (1914.) *Mem. Ed.* VI, 332-333; *Nat. Ed.* V, 284.

——————. Many regions in the United States where life is now absolutely comfortable and easy-going offered most formidable problems to the first explorers a century or two ago. We must not fall into the foolish error of thinking that the first explorers need not suffer terrible hardships, merely because the ordinary travelers, and even the settlers who come after them do not have to endure such danger, privation, and wearing fatigue—although the first among the genuine settlers also have to undergo exceedingly trying experiences. The early explorers and adventurers make fairly well-beaten trails at heavy cost to themselves. Ordinary travellers, with little discomfort and no danger, can then traverse these trails; but it is incumbent on them neither to boast of their own experiences nor to misjudge the efforts of the pioneers because, thanks to these very efforts, their own lines fall in pleasant places. (1914.) *Mem. Ed.* VI, 165; *Nat. Ed.* V, 141.

EXPLORERS. *See also* BOONE, DANIEL; JESUITS; PEARY, ROBERT E.; PIONEERS; SOUTH AMERICA.

EXTRAVAGANCE. No laws which the wit of man can devise will avail to make the community prosperous if the average individual lives in such fashion that his expenditures always exceed his income. *Outlook,* October 5, 1912, p. 249.

EXTRAVAGANCE. *See also* LEISURE; THRIFT; WORK.

EXTREMES. *See* DEMOCRACY—SUCCESS IN A.

EXTREMISTS. It is always a difficult thing to state a position which has two sides with such clearness as to bring it home to the hearers. In the world of politics it is easy to appeal to the unreasoning reactionary, and no less easy to appeal to the unreasoning advocate of change, but difficult to get people to show for the cause of sanity and progress combined the zeal so easily aroused against sanity by one set of extremists and against progress by another set of extremists. So in the world of the intellect it is easy to take the position of the hard materialists who rail against religion, and easy also to take the position of those whose zeal for orthodoxy makes them distrust all action by men of independent mind in the search for scientific truth; but it is not so easy to make it understood that we both acknowledge our inestimable debt to the great masters of science, and yet are keenly alive to their errors and decline to surrender our judgment to theirs when they go wrong. (*Outlook,* December 2, 1911.) *Mem. Ed.* XIV, 430; *Nat. Ed.* XII, 123.

EXTREMISTS. *See also* LUNATIC FRINGE; RADICALS; REACTIONARIES.

F

FAILURE. A strong and wise people will study its own failures no less than its triumphs, for there is wisdom to be learned from the study of both, of the mistake as well as of the success. (Sixth Annual Message, Washington, December 3, 1906.) *Mem. Ed.* XVII, 474; *Nat. Ed.* XV, 404.

FAILURE. See also SUCCESS.

FALSEHOOD — EFFECT OF. Incessant falsehood inevitably produces in the public mind a certain disbelief in good men and a considerable disbelief in the charges against bad men; so that there results the belief that there are no men entirely good and no men entirely bad, and that they are all about alike and colored gray. (At Milwaukee, Wis., September 7, 1910.) *Mem. Ed.* XV, 460; *Nat. Ed.* XIII, 548.

FALSEHOOD. See also LIARS; TRUTH.

FAME. It makes small odds to any of us after we are dead whether the next generation forgets us, or whether a number of generations pass before our memory, steadily growing more and more dim, at last fades into nothing. On this point it seems to me that the only important thing is to be able to feel, when our time comes to go out into the blackness, that those survivors who care for us and to whom it will be a pleasure to think well of us when we are gone shall have that pleasure. Save in a few wholly exceptional cases, cases of men such as are not alive at this particular time, it is only possible in any event that a comparatively few people can have this feeling for any length of time. But it is a good thing if as many as possible feel it even for a short time, and it is surely a good thing that those whom we love should feel it as long as they too live. (To Oliver Wendell Holmes, December 5, 1904.) *Mem. Ed.* XXIII, 407; Bishop I, 353.

———. When America's history is written, when the history of the last century in America is written a hundred years hence, the name of no multimillionaire, who is nothing but a multimillionaire, will appear in that history, unless it appears in some foot-note to illustrate some queer vagary or extravagance. The men who will loom large in our history are the men of real achievement of the kind that counts. You can go over them—statesmen, soldiers, wise philanthropists . . . the writer, the man of science, of letters, of art, these are the men who will leave their mark on history. (At Pacific Theological Seminary, Spring 1911.) *Mem. Ed.* XV, 582; *Nat. Ed.* XIII, 621.

FAMILY. The life of the State rests and must ever rest upon the life of the family and the neighborhood. *Outlook,* April 10, 1909, p. 807.

FAMILY—IMPORTANCE OF THE. The man and woman who in peace-time fear or ignore the primary and vital duties and the high happiness of family life, who dare not beget and bear and rear the life that is to last when they are in their graves, have broken the chain of creation, and have shown that they are unfit for companionship with the souls ready for the Great Adventure. (*Metropolitan,* October 1918.) *Mem. Ed.* XXI, 263; *Nat. Ed.* XIX, 243.

FAMILY LIFE. Nothing else takes the place or can take the place of family life, and family life cannot be really happy unless it is based on duty, based on recognition of the great underlying laws of religion and morality, of the great underlying laws of civilization, the laws which if broken mean the dissolution of civilization. (At Pacific Theological Seminary, Spring 1911.) *Mem. Ed.* XV, 599; *Nat. Ed.* XIII, 636.

FAMILY LIFE—HAPPINESS IN. I am sure that when men and women come to their senses and are able to separate the things that are essential from the things that are non-essential in life, they will go back to the understanding that there is no form of happiness on the earth, no form of success of any kind, that in any way approaches the happiness of the husband and the wife who are married lovers and the father and mother of plenty of healthy children. No other form of success—political, literary, artistic, commercial—in any way approaches the kind of success open to most men and most women, the success of the man in making a home and of the woman in keeping it, the success of both in dwelling therein with mutual love, respect, and forbearance, and in bringing up as they should be brought up the children who bless and make holy the home. (*Outlook,* April 8, 1911.) *Mem. Ed.* XIV, 161; *Nat. Ed.* XII, 192.

———. The fundamental instincts are not only the basic but also the loftiest instincts in human nature. The qualities that make men and women eager lovers, faithful, duty-performing, hard-working husbands and wives, and wise and devoted fathers and mothers stand at the foundations of all possible social welfare, and also represent the loftiest heights of human happiness and usefulness. No other form of personal success and happiness or of individual service to the State compares with that which is represented by the love of the one man for the one woman, of their joint work as home-maker and home-keeper, and of their ability to bring up the children that are theirs. (*Metropolitan,* October 1917.) *Mem. Ed.* XXI, 167; *Nat. Ed.* XIX, 160.

FAMILY RELATIONSHIPS. There are men so selfish, so short-sighted, or so brutal, that they speak and act as if the fact of the man's earning money for his wife and children, while the woman bears the children, rears them, and takes care of the house for them and for the man, somehow entitles the man to be known as the head of the family, instead of a partner on equal terms with his wife, and entitles him to the exclusive right to dispose of the money and, as a matter of fact, to dispose of it primarily in his own interest. . . . Just as the prime work for the average man must be earning his livelihood and the livelihood of those dependent upon him, so the prime work for the average woman must be keeping the home and bearing and rearing her children. . . . The one way to honor this indispensable woman, the wife and mother, is to insist that she be treated as the full equal of her husband. (*Metropolitan,* May 1916.) *Mem. Ed.* XXI, 142, 146; *Nat. Ed.* XIX, 140, 143.

FAMILY. *See also* BIRTH CONTROL; CHILDREN; DIVORCE; EUGENICS; HOME; HUSBANDS; MARRIAGE; MOTHER.

FANATICISM. *See* ANTI-SEMITISM; BIGOTRY; RELIGIOUS DISCRIMINATION; TOLERANCE.

FAR EAST. *See* CHINA; JAPAN; OPEN DOOR; ORIENT; PHILIPPINES.

FARM AGENCIES—NEW TASKS FOR. Hitherto agricultural research, instruction, and agitation have been directed almost exclusively toward the production of wealth from the soil. It is time to adopt in addition a new point of view. Hereafter another great task before the National Department of Agriculture and the similar agencies of the various States must be to foster agriculture for its social results, or, in other words, to assist in bringing about the best kind of life on the farm for the sake of producing the best kind of men. The Government must recognize the far-reaching importance of the study and treatment of the problems of farm life alike from the social and the economic standpoints; and the Federal and State Departments of Agriculture should cooperate, at every point. (At semicentennial celebration, founding of Agricultural Colleges, Lansing, Mich., May 31, 1907.) *Mem. Ed.* XVIII, 180; *Nat. Ed.* XVI, 137.

FARM AGENCIES. *See also* AGRICULTURE—DEPARTMENT OF.

FARM LAND—TAXATION OF. To break up the big estates it might be best to try the graduated land tax, or else to equalize taxes as between used and unused agricultural land, which would prevent farm land being held for speculative purposes. There can without question be criticism of either proposal. If any better proposal can be made and *tried* we can cheerfully support it and be guided in our theories by the way it turns out. But we ought to insist on something being done—not merely talked about. Every one is agreed that we ought to get more people "back to the land"; but talk on the subject is utterly useless unless we put it in concrete shape and secure a "service test," even although it costs some money to furnish the means for doing what we say must be done. (1917.) *Mem. Ed.* XXI, 116; *Nat. Ed.* XIX, 118.

FARM LIFE—IMPROVEMENT OF. We have to grapple with one fact which has made both the strength and the weakness of the American farmer, and that is, his isolation. This isolation implies a lack both of the pleasure and of the inspiration which come from closer contact between people, and from a well-developed organization for social pleasures, for religious life, for education. On the other hand, it is to this isolation more than to anything else that we owe the strength of character so typical of the American farmer, who lives under a peculiarly individualistic system in the management alike of the farm and of the farm home.

The successfully managed family farm gives to the father, the mother, and the children better opportunities for useful work and for a happy life than any other occupation. Our object must be, so far as practicable, to do away with the disadvantages which are due to the isolation of the family farm, while conserving its many and great advantages. We wish to keep at its highest point the peculiarly American quality of individual efficiency, while at the same time bringing about that co-operation which indicates capacity in the mass. Both qualities can be used to increase the industrial and ethical proficiency of our people, for there is much the individual only can do for himself, and there is much also which must be done by all combined because the individual cannot do it. Our aim must be to supplement individualism on the farm and in the home with an associated effort in those country matters that require organized working together. (Letter to Herbert Myrick read at Springfield, Mass., November 12, 1908.) *Good Housekeeping,* December 1908, pp. 625-626.

───────────. It would be a calamity to have our farms occupied by a lower type of people than the hard-working, self-respecting, independent, and essentially manly and womanly men and women who have hitherto constituted the most typically American, and on the whole the most valuable, element in our entire nation. Ambitious native-born young men and women who now tend away from the farm must be brought back to it, and therefore they must have social as well as economic opportunities. Everything should be done to encourage the growth in the open farming country of such institutional and social movements as will meet the demand of the best type of farmers. There should be libraries, assembly-halls, social organizations of all kinds. The school-building and the teacher in the school-building should, throughout the country districts, be of the very highest type, able to fit the boys and girls not merely to live in, but thoroughly to enjoy and to make the most, of the country. The country church must be revived. All kinds of agencies, from rural free delivery to the bicycle and the telephone, should be ultilized to the utmost; good roads should be favored; everything should be done to make it easier for the farmer to lead the most active and effective intellectual, political, and economic life....

The farm grows the raw material for the food and clothing of all our citizens; it supports directly almost half of them; and nearly half the children of the United States are born and brought up on the farms. How can the life of the farm family be made less solitary, fuller of opportunity, freer from drudgery, more comfortable, happier, and more attractive? Such a result is most earnestly to be desired. How can life on the farm be kept on the highest level, and where it is not already on that level, be so improved, dignified, and brightened as to awaken and keep alive the pride and loyalty of the farmer's boys and girls, of the farmer's wife, and of the farmer himself? How can a compelling desire to live on the farm be aroused in the children that are born on the farm? All these questions are of vital importance not only to the farmer, but to the whole nation. (At semicentennial celebration, founding of Agricultural Colleges, Lansing, Mich., May 31, 1907.) *Mem. Ed.* XVIII, 177, 181; *Nat. Ed.* XVI, 134, 137.

───────────. One of the chief difficulties is the failure of country life, as it exists at present, to satisfy the higher social and intellectual aspirations of country people. Whether the constant draining away of so much of the best elements in the rural population into the towns is due chiefly to this cause or to the superior business opportunities of city life may be open to question. But no one at all familiar with farm life throughout the United States can fail to recognize the necessity for building up the life of the farm upon its social as well as upon its productive side.

It is true that country life has improved greatly in attractiveness, health, and comfort, and that the farmer's earnings are higher than they were. But city life is advancing even more rapidly, because of the greater attention which is being given by the citizens of the towns to their own betterment. For just this reason the introduction of effective agricultural cooperation throughout the United States is of the first importance. Where farmers are organized cooperatively they not only avail themselves much more readily of business opportunities and improved methods, but it is found that the organizations which bring them together in the work of their lives are used also for social and intellectual advancement. *Special Message from the President of the United States transmitting the report of the Country Life Commission, February 9, 1909.* (Washington, 1909), p. 5.

───────────. Rural free delivery, taken in connection with the telephone, the bicycle, and the trolley, accomplishes much toward lessening the isolation of farm life and making it brighter and more attractive. In the immediate past the lack of just such facilities as these has driven many of the more active and restless young men and women from the farms to the cities; for they rebelled at loneliness and lack of mental companionship. It is unhealthy and undesirable for the cities to grow at the expense of the country; and rural free delivery is not only a good thing in itself, but is good because it is one of the causes which check this unwholesome tendency toward the urban concentration of our population at the expense of the country districts. It is for the same reason that we sympathize with and approve of the policy of building good roads. The movement for good roads is one fraught with the greatest benefit to the country districts. (Third Annual Message, Washington, December 7, 1903.) *Mem. Ed.* XVII, 220; *Nat. Ed.* XV, 189.

FARM LIFE—PROBLEMS OF. There is no problem whose successful solution is fraught with greater returns, in the line of citizenship, as well as in material results, than the problems of rural life. These include better farm methods, better rural schools, better roads, better farm financing, more economical methods of marketing, and better farm life conditions for the men, women, and children on whose welfare and success the progress and prosperity of the nation depends. In these problems and those of social and industrial justice is also embodied no small part of the problem of the cost of living, although this will also be in part helped by our treatment of the trusts. (At Chicago, December 10, 1912.) *Mem. Ed.* XIX, 477; *Nat. Ed.* XVII, 353.

FARM LIFE. See also CITY; COUNTRY LIFE COMMISSION; ROADS.

FARM POPULATION. If there is one lesson taught by history it is that the permanent greatness of any State must ultimately depend more upon the character of its country population than upon anything else. No growth of cities, no growth of wealth can make up for a loss in either the number or the character of the farming population. In the United States more than in almost any other country we should realize this and should prize our country population. When this nation began its independent existence it was as a nation of farmers. The towns were small and were for the most part mere seacoast trading and fishing ports. The chief industry of the country was agriculture, and the ordinary citizen was in some way connected with it. In every great crisis of the past a peculiar dependence has had to be placed upon the farming population; and this dependence has hitherto been justified. But it cannot be justified in the future if agriculture is permitted to sink in the scale as compared with other employments. We cannot afford to lose that pre-eminently typical American, the farmer who owns his own farm. (At semicentennial celebration, founding of Agricultural Colleges, Lansing, Mich., May 31, 1907.) *Mem. Ed.* XVIII, 176; *Nat. Ed.* XVI, 133.

FARM PROBLEM—SOLUTION OF THE. Our object must be (1) to make the tenant-farmer a landowner; (2) to eliminate as far as possible the conditions which produce the shifting, seasonal, tramp type of labor, and to give the farm laborer a permanent status, a career as a farmer, for which his school education shall fit him, and which shall open to him the chance of in the end earning the ownership in fee of his own farm; (3) to secure co-operation among the small landowners, so that their energies shall produce the best possible results; (4) by progressive taxation or in other fashion to break up and prevent the formation of great landed estates, especially in so far as they consist of unused agricultural land; (5) to make capital available for the farmers, and thereby put them more on an equality with other men engaged in business; (6) to care for the woman on the farm as much as for the man, and to eliminate the conditions which now so often tend to make her life one of gray and sterile drudgery; (7) to do this primarily through the farmer himself, but also, when necessary, by the use of the entire collective power of the people of the country; for the welfare of the farmer is the concern of all of us. (1917.) *Mem. Ed.* XXI, 114; *Nat. Ed.* XIX, 116.

FARMER AND CONSUMER. The farmer, the producer of the necessities of life, can himself live only if he raises these necessities for a profit. On the other hand, the consumer who must have that farmer's product in order to live, must be allowed to purchase it at the lowest cost that can give the farmer his profit, and everything possible must be done to eliminate any middleman whose function does not tend to increase the cheapness of distribution of the product; and, moreover, everything must be done to stop all speculating, all gambling with the bread-basket which has even the slightest deleterious effect upon the producer and consumer. There must be legislation which will bring about a closer business relationship between the farmer and the consumer. (Before Progressive National Convention, Chicago, August 6, 1912.) *Mem. Ed.* XIX, 398; *Nat. Ed.* XVII, 288.

FARMER AND LABORER. The true welfare of the nation is indissolubly bound up with the welfare of the farmer and the wage-worker —of the man who tills the soil, and of the mechanic, the handicraftsman, the laborer. If we can insure the prosperity of these two classes we need not trouble ourselves about the prosperity of the rest. for that will follow as a matter of course. (At Pan-American Exposition, Buffalo, May 20, 1901.) *Mem. Ed.* XV, 314; *Nat. Ed.* XIII, 448.

———. It should be one of our prime objects to put both the farmer and the mechanic on a higher plane of efficiency and reward, so as to increase their effectiveness in the economic world, and therefore the dignity, the remuneration, and the power of their positions in the social world. (Seventh Annual Message, Washington, December 3, 1907.) *Mem. Ed.* XVII, 517; *Nat. Ed.* XV, 440.

FARMER COOPERATION. [The farmer] should be helped to cooperate in business fashion with his fellows, so that the money paid by the consumer for the product of the soil shall, to as large a degree as possible, go into the pockets of the man who raised that product from the soil. So long as the farmer leaves co-operative activities with their profit-sharing to the city man of business, so long will the foundations of wealth be undermined and the comforts of enlightenment be impossible in the country communities. (Before Progressive National Convention, Chicago, August 6, 1912.) *Mem. Ed.* XIX, 378; *Nat. Ed.* XVII, 271.

————————. The welfare of the farmer stands as the bedrock welfare of the entire Commonwealth. Hitherto he has not received the full share of industrial reward and benefit to which he is entitled. He can receive it only as the result of organization and co-operation. Along certain lines the government must itself co-operate with him; but normally most can be accomplished by co-operation among the farmers themselves, in marketing their products, in buying certain things which they particularly need, and in joint action along many lines. The States can wisely supplement such work of co-operation, but most of such work it cannot with wisdom itself undertake. (Before Republican State Convention, Saratoga Springs, N. Y., July 18, 1918.) *Mem. Ed.* XXI, 402; *Nat. Ed.* XIX, 364.

FARMER COOPERATIVES. Whenever farmers themselves have the intelligence and energy to work through co-operative societies this is far better than having the state undertake the work. Community self-help is normally preferable to using the machinery of government for tasks to which it is unaccustomed. This applies to the ownership of granaries, slaughter-houses, and the like. There are in Europe co-operative farmers' associations which own and run at a profit many such institutions; and when this is shown to be the case, the other owners of such agencies face the accomplished fact; and it often becomes possible for the farmers then to deal with them on a satisfactory basis.

In Europe these great farmer co-operative associations sometimes control the whole machinery by which their products are marketed. Each little district has its own co-operative group. The groups of all the districts in the state are united again in a large co-operative unit. In this way they do collectively what is beyond the power of any one farmer individually to accomplish. By sending their shipments to market they move them in great bulk-quantities at the lowest possible cost. They contract for long periods ahead and sell in the most advantageous market. Middlemen are eliminated. The labor of moving farm products is reduced to a minimum. . . .

A single farmer to-day is no match for the corporations, railroads, and business enterprises with which he must deal. Organized into co-operative associations, however, the farmers' power would be enormously increased. The principle upon which such co-operative groups are formed is very simple. The profits are divided partly in the shape of a rebate that is paid in proportion to the volume of business done for each member. The control, however, of the association does not depend upon the number of shares that a member may own but rests upon the democratic basis of one man, one vote. (1917.) *Mem. Ed.* XXI, 118-119; *Nat. Ed.* XIX, 119-120.

FARMERS—AID TO. I know what the work and what the loneliness of a farmer's life too often are. I do not want to help the farmer or to help his wife in ways that will soften either, but I do want to join with both, and try to help them and help myself and help all of us, not by doing away with the need of work, but by trying to create a situation in which work will be more fruitful, and in which the work shall produce and go hand in hand with opportunities for self-development. (*Outlook,* October 12, 1912.) *Mem. Ed.* XIX, 438; *Nat. Ed.* XVII, 318.

FARMERS—GOVERNMENT AID TO. We do not believe in confining governmental activity to the city. We believe that the problem of life in the open country is well-nigh the gravest problem before this nation. The eyes and thoughts of those working for social and industrial reform have been turned almost exclusively toward the great cities, and toward the solution of the questions presented by their teeming myriads of people and by the immense complexity of their life. Yet nothing is more certain than that there can be no permanent prosperity unless the men and women who live in the open country prosper. The problems of the farm, of the village, of the country church, and the country school, the problems of getting most value out of and keeping most value in the soil, and of securing healthy and happy and well-rounded lives for those who live upon it, are fundamental to our national welfare. (*Century Magazine,* October 1913.) *Mem. Ed.* XIX, 545; *Nat. Ed.* XVII, 402.

———————. We should . . . see that the help is given only to the man who is a real farmer and can really make use of it, but that it is extended in such a way as to be of genuine and material benefit.

This is the immediate need, and let us treat meeting this need as the opening wedge of a policy designed to prevent the growth of tenant farms at the expense of the farm owner who tills his own soil, and designed also to put a premium upon the permanent prosperity of the small farmer as compared with the big landowner. (February 15, 1918.) *Roosevelt in the Kansas City Star,* 105.

FARMERS—GOVERNMENT LOANS TO. As regards furnishing capital to the farmer, the first need is that we shall understand that this is essential, and is recognized to be essential in most civilized lands outside of Russia and the United States, but especially in Denmark, France, and Germany. Our farmers must have working capital. The present laws for providing farm loans do not meet the most important case of all, that of the tenant-farmer, and do not adequately provide for the landowning farmer. An immense amount of new capital—an amount to be reckoned in billions of dollars—is needed for the proper development of the farms of the United States, in order that our farmers may pass from the position of underproduction per acre, may improve and fertilize their lands, and so stock them as both to secure satisfactory returns upon the money invested and also enormously to increase the amount of food produced, while permanently enhancing the value of the land. Lack of capital on the part of the farmer inevitably means soil exhaustion and therefore diminished production. The farmer who is to prosper must have capital; only the prosperous can really meet the needs of the consumer; and in this, as in every other kind of honest business, the only proper basis of success is benefit to both buyer and seller, producer and consumer. (1917.) *Mem. Ed.* XXI, 116; *Nat. Ed.* XIX, 118.

FARMERS, TENANT. The number of tenants is rapidly growing. This is not good. Provision should be made to aid and increase the number of farm home-owners, for these make for a better agriculture and a stronger nation. (At Chicago, December 10, 1912.) *Mem. Ed.* XIX, 479; *Nat. Ed.* XVII, 354.

———————. In 1880, one farmer in four was a tenant; and at that time the tenant was still generally a young man to whom the position of tenant was merely an intermediate step between that of farm laborer and that of a farm owner. In 1910, over one farmer in three had become a tenant; and nowadays it becomes steadily more difficult to pass from the tenant to the owner stage. If the process continues unchecked, half a century hence we shall have deliberately permitted ourselves to plunge into the situation which brought chaos in Ireland, and which in England resulted in the complete elimination of the old yeomanry, so that nearly nine-tenth of English farmers to-day are tenants and the consequent class division is most ominous for the future. France and Germany are to-day distinctly better off than we are in this respect; and in New Zealand, where there is an excellent system of land distribution, only one-seventh of the farmers are tenants. . . .

The most important thing to do is to make the tenant-farmer a farm-owner. He must be financed so that he can acquire title to the land. In New Zealand the government buys land and sells it to small holders at the price paid with a low rate of interest. Perhaps our government could try this plan, or else could outright advance the money, charging three and a half per cent interest. Default in payments—which should of course be on easy terms—would mean that the land reverted to the government. (1917.) *Mem. Ed.* XXI, 112, 115; *Nat. Ed.* XIX, 114-115, 117.

FARMING. See AGRICULTURE.

FEAR. See COWARDICE; INTERNATIONAL FEAR.

"FEAR GOD AND TAKE YOUR OWN PART." Readers of Borrow will recognize in the . . . title of the book, a phrase used by the heroine of Lavengro.

Fear God; and take your own part! Fear God, in the true sense of the word, means love God, respect God, honor God; and all of this can only be done by loving our neighbor, treating him justly and mercifully, and in all ways endeavoring to protect him from injustice and cruelty; thus obeying, as far as our human frailty will permit, the great and immutable law of righteousness.

We fear God when we do justice to and demand justice for the men within our own borders. We are false to the teachings of righteousness if we do not do such justice and demand such justice. We must do it to the weak, and we must do it to the strong. We do not fear God if we show mean envy and hatred of those who are better off than we are; and still less do we fear God if we show a base arrogance toward and selfish lack of consideration for those who are less well off. We must apply the same standard of conduct alike to man and to woman, to rich man and to poor man, to employer and employee. (1916.) *Mem. Ed.* XX, 231; *Nat. Ed.* XVIII, 199.

——————. Let us quit trying to fool ourselves by indulging in cheap self-assertion or even cheaper sentimentality. We must have a period of self-searching. We must endeavor to recover our lost self-respect. Let us show in practical fashion that we fear God and therefore deal justly with all men; and let us also show that we can take our own part; for if we cannot take our own part we may be absolutely certain that no one else will try to take it for us. (*Metropolitan,* February 1916.) *Mem. Ed.* XX, 301; *Nat. Ed.* XVIII, 258.

——————. Fear God and take your own part! This is another way of saying that a nation must have power and will for self-sacrifice and also power and will for self-protection. There must be both unselfishness and self-expression, each to supplement the other, neither wholly good without the other. The nation must be willing to stand disinterestedly for a lofty ideal and yet it must also be able to insist that its own rights be heeded by others. Evil will come if it does not possess the will and the power for unselfish action on behalf of non-utilitarian ideals and also the will and the power for self-mastery, self-control, self-discipline. It must possess those high and stern qualities of soul which will enable it to conquer softness and weakness and timidity and train itself to subordinate momentary pleasure, momentary profit, momentary safety to the larger future. (1916.) *Mem. Ed.* XX, 528; *Nat. Ed.* XVIII, 453.

FEARLESSNESS. See COURAGE.

FEDERALIST, THE. Every young politician should of course read the *Federalist.* It is the greatest book of the kind that has ever been written. Hamilton, Madison, and Jay would have been poorly equipped for writing it if they had not possessed an extensive acquaintance with literature, and in particular if they had not been careful students of political literature; but the great cause of the value of their writings lay in the fact that they knew by actual work and association what practical politics meant. They had helped to shape the political thought of the country, and to do its legislative and executive work, and so they were in a condition to speak understandingly about it. (*Atlantic Monthly,* August 1894.) *Mem. Ed.* XV, 57; *Nat. Ed.* XIII, 42.

——————. The sneer of the professional politician at the theorist; at the man who gets his knowledge from books, is so silly that one does not have to pay much heed to it, especially before an audience of this kind. Read "The Federalist." It is one of the greatest—I hardly know whether I would not be right to say that it is on the whole the greatest book—dealing with applied politics that there ever has been—the creation of Hamilton helped by Madison and Jay; and you will see a book there consisting of a series of pamphlets which had an incalculable effect in procuring us our present National Government, which could not have had that effect if, on the one hand, the three writers had not been men trained in theory of politics and if, on the other hand, they had not been themselves veteran practical politicians. (Before the Liberal Club, Buffalo, N. Y., September 10, 1895.) *Mem. Ed.* XVI, 279-280; *Nat. Ed.* XIV, 199.

FEDERALIST PARTY — DECLINE OF. Distrust of the people . . . was the fatally weak streak in Federalism. In a government such as ours it was a foregone conclusion that a party which did not believe in the people would sooner or later be thrown from power unless there was an armed break-up of the system. The distrust was felt, and of course excited corresponding and intense hostility. Had the Federalists been united, and had they freely trusted in the people, the latter would have shown that the trust was well founded; but there was no hope for leaders who suspected each other and feared their followers. (1888.) *Mem. Ed.* VIII, 512-513; *Nat. Ed.* VII, 443.

FEDERALIST PARTY. *See also* MORRIS, GOUVERNEUR; WESTWARD MOVEMENT.

FEDERALISTS. *See* CONSTITUTION.

FELLOW-FEELING. Fellow-feeling, sympathy in the broadest sense, is the most important factor in producing a healthy political and social life. Neither our national nor our local civic life can be what it should be unless it is marked by the fellow-feeling, the mutual kindness, the mutual respect, the sense of common duties and common interests, which arise when men take the trouble to understand one another, and to associate together for a common object. (*Century,* January 1900.) *Mem. Ed.* XV, 404; *Nat. Ed.* XIII, 355.

———————. It is hard to benefit men from whom we are sundered by aloofness of spirit. The best work must be done by men whose sympathies are so broad and keen as literally to give fellow-feeling, and the understanding that can come only from fellow-feeling. Such fellow-feeling means a realization of the fundamental equality of all of us in need, in shortcoming, in aspiration—in short, in the fundamental things of our common brotherhood. *Outlook,* January 27, 1912, p. 163.

FELLOW-FEELING. *See also* BROTHERHOOD; CHARITY; COOPERATION; PHILANTHROPY.

FELLOWSHIP. It is an excellent thing to win a triumph for good government at a given election; but it is a far better thing gradually to build up that spirit of fellow-feeling among American citizens, which, in the long run, is absolutely necessary if we are to see the principles of virile honesty and robust common sense triumph in our civic life. (*Century,* January 1900.) *Mem. Ed.* XV, 420; *Nat. Ed.* XIII, 368.

———————. I need hardly say how earnestly I believe that men should have a keen and lively sense of their obligations in politics, of their duty to help forward great causes, and to struggle for the betterment of conditions that are unjust to their fellows, the men and women who are less fortunate in life. But in addition to this feeling there must be a feeling of real fellowship with the other men and women engaged in the same task, fellowship of work, with fun to vary the work; for unless there is this feeling of fellowship, of common effort on an equal plane for a common end, it will be difficult to keep the relations wholesome and natural. (1913.) *Mem. Ed.* XXII, 75; *Nat. Ed.* XX, 64.

FELLOWSHIP. *See also* CITIZENSHIP; CIVIC DUTY; POLITICS.

FERVOR. Religious fervor, or mere fervor for excellence in the abstract, is a great mainspring for good work in politics as in war, but it is no substitute for training, in either civil or military life; and if not accompanied by sound common sense and a spirit of broad tolerance, it may do as much damage as any other mighty force which is unregulated. (1900.) *Mem. Ed.* XIII, 425; *Nat. Ed.* X, 305.

FERVOR. *See also* TOLERANCE.

FIAT MONEY. *See* SILVER.

FIFTEENTH AMENDMENT. *See* NEGRO SUFFRAGE.

FIGHTING—PREPARATION FOR. Men cannot and will not fight well unless they are physically prepared; and they cannot and will not fight if, through the generations, they elaborately unfit themselves by weakening their own moral fibre. (*Metropolitan,* August 1915.) *Mem. Ed.* XX, 366; *Nat. Ed.* XVIII, 314.

FIGHTING EDGE, THE. Woe to the nation that does not make ready to hold its own in time of need against all who would harm it! And woe thrice over to the nation in which the average man loses the fighting edge, loses the power to serve as a soldier if the day of need should arise! (At University of Berlin, May 12, 1910.) *Mem. Ed.* XIV, 284; *Nat. Ed.* XII, 83.

FIGHTING MAN, THE. We despise and abhor the bully, the brawler, the oppressor, whether in private or public life; but we despise no less the coward and the voluptuary. No man is worth calling a man who will not fight rather than submit to infamy or see those that are dear to him suffer wrong. *Outlook,* May 7, 1910, p. 19.

FIGHTING QUALITIES. A peaceful and commercial civilization is always in danger of suffering the loss of the virile fighting qualities without which no nation, however cultured, however refined, however thrifty and prosperous can ever amount to anything. (*Forum,* July 1894.) *Mem. Ed.* XV, 46; *Nat. Ed.* XIII, 32.

FIGHTING VIRTUES. One of the prime dangers of civilization has always been its tendency to cause the loss of virile fighting virtues, of the fighting edge. When men get too comfortable and lead too luxurious lives, there is always danger lest the softness eat like an acid into their manliness of fibre. (At University of Berlin, May 12, 1910.) *Mem. Ed.* XIV, 275; *Nat. Ed.* XII, 76.

FIGHTING VIRTUES—LOSS OF. The curse of every ancient civilization was that its men in the end became unable to fight. Materialism, luxury, safety, even sometimes an almost modern sentimentality, weakened the fibre of each civilized race in turn; each became in the end a nation of pacifists, and then each was trodden under foot by some ruder people that had kept that virile fighting power the lack of which makes all other virtues useless and sometimes even harmful. (*Outlook*, February 14, 1917.) Mem. Ed. XIV, 48; Nat. Ed. XII, 169.

FIGHTING VIRTUES. See also BULLYING; COURAGE; COWARDICE; MANLINESS; MANLY VIRTUES; MILITARY TRAINING; PACIFIST; ROMAN EMPIRE; SOLDIERS.

FILIBUSTERING. Filibustering is like lynch-law; it is something which in extreme and exceptional instances may be defensible, but which when followed systematically produces nothing but anarchy and outrage and the paralysis of all the governmental functions of the body in which it takes place. When followed out systematically it should receive the severest censure. (Before Federal Club, New York City, March 6, 1891.) Mem. Ed. XVI, 195; Nat. Ed. XIV, 130.

——————. Filibustering has now become a recognized term by which to describe tactics of delay and obstruction in a legislative body. Of course such tactics are wholly indefensible except on revolutionary grounds. They are essentially improper. It should always be understood that it is discreditable to indulge in them save under circumstances which would justify any revolutionary proceeding; and such circumstances cannot occur once in a generation. . . . People cannot have free institutions if they lack the wisdom, self-command, and common sense to make use of them; and the people who condone and approve filibustering show that they lack all these qualities, and to that extent have forfeited their claim to be considered capable of governing themselves. (*Forum*, December 1895.) Mem. Ed. XVI, 250; Nat. Ed. XIV, 175.

FILIBUSTERING. See also DEBATE; REPRESENTATIVE GOVERNMENT.

FINANCE. See BANKING; CURRENCY; GOLD STANDARD; SILVER; TAXATION.

FINANCIERS. Allow me to say that you have with extraordinary keenness struck the exact situation about the central bank when you say that our big financiers are for the most part speculators, which is not true of the European big financiers. This is the keynote to our troubles; that is, we have to contend with the men who are in speculative, and not in legitimate business; or the men who, while in legitimate business, make illegitimate or speculative proceedings one main branch of their business. (To White, January 13, 1908.) Allan Nevins, *Henry White. Thirty Years of American Diplomacy*. (Harper & Bros., N. Y., 1930), pp. 294-295.

FINANCIERS. See also CAPITALISTS; WALL STREET.

FISHERIES. The Federal statute regulating interstate traffic in game should be extended to include fish. New Federal fish-hatcheries should be established. The administration of the Alaskan fur-seal service should be vested in the Bureau of Fisheries. (Eighth Annual Message, Washington, Dec. 8, 1908.) Mem. Ed. XVII, 628; Nat. Ed. XV, 534.

FIVE CENT FARE. See ELEVATED RAILROAD LEGISLATION.

FIVE FOOT BOOK SHELF. See BOOKS—LISTS OF.

FLAG—LOYALTY TO THE. We have room in this country for but one flag, the Stars and Stripes, and we should tolerate no allegiance to any other flag, whether a foreign flag or the red flag or black flag. We have room for but one loyalty, loyalty to the United States. (1918.) Mem. Ed. XXI, 329; Nat. Ed. XIX, 301.

FLAG-WAVING. Flag-waving, and uttering and applauding speeches, and singing patriotic songs, are excellent in so far as they are turned into cool foresight in preparation and grim resolution to spend and be spent when once the day of trial has come; but they are merely mischievous if they are treated as substitutes for preparedness in advance and for hard, efficient work and readiness for self-sacrifice during the crisis itself. (1917.) Mem. Ed. XXI, 7; Nat. Ed. XIX, 6.

FLAG. See also ALLEGIANCE; AMERICANISM; PATRIOTISM.

FLATTERY. A flatterer is not a good companion for any man; and the public man who rises only by flattering his constituents is just as unsafe a companion for them. (*Outlook*, March 25, 1911.) Mem. Ed. XIX, 146; Nat. Ed. XVII, 104.

FLATTERY. See also TRUTH.

FLOOD PREVENTION. Forests are the most effective preventers of floods, especially when they grow on the higher mountain slopes. The national forest policy, inaugurated primarily to avert or mitigate the timber famine which is now beginning to be felt, has been effective also in securing partial control of floods by retarding the run-off and checking the erosion of the higher slopes within the national forests. Still the loss from soil wash is enormous. It is computed that one-fifth of a cubic mile in volume, or one billion tons in weight of the richest soil matter of the United States, is annually gathered in storm rivulets, washed into the rivers, and borne into the sea. The loss to the farmer is in effect a tax greater than all other land taxes combined, and one yielding absolutely no return. (Before Deep Waterway Convention, Memphis, Tenn., October 4, 1907.) *Mem. Ed.* XVIII, 153; *Nat. Ed.* XVI, 116.

FLOOD PREVENTION. *See also* CONSERVATION; FOREST PROBLEM; INLAND WATERWAYS; MISSISSIPPI RIVER.

FLOWERS — ADMIRATION FOR. This morning Mother and I walked around the White House grounds as usual. I think I get more fond of flowers every year. The grounds are now at that high stage of beauty in which they will stay for the next two months. The buckeyes are in bloom, the pink dogwood, and the fragrant lilacs, which are almost the loveliest of the bushes; and then the flowers, including the lily-of-the-valley. (To Kermit Roosevelt, April 30, 1906.) *Mem. Ed.* XXI, 564; *Nat. Ed.* XIX, 506.

"FOES OF OUR OWN HOUSEHOLD." The foes of our own household are our worst enemies; and we can oppose them, not only by exposing and denouncing them, but by constructive work in planning and building for reforms which shall take into account both the economic and the moral factors in human advance. We of America can win to our great destiny only by service; not by rhetoric, and above all not by insincere rhetoric, and that dreadful mental double-dealing and verbal juggling which makes promises and repudiates them, and says one thing at one time, and the directly opposite thing at another time. Our service must be the service of deeds, the deeds of war and the deeds of peace. (1917.) *Mem. Ed.* XXI, 8; *Nat. Ed.* XIX, 7.

———. We must . . . remember that the demagogue is as dangerous a public enemy as the corruptionist himself, that the insincere radical is not a whit better than the insincere Tory, and that the enthusiastic fool will probably work even more mischief than the selfish reactionary. *All* of these men are among the foes of our own household! (*Metropolitan*, May 1917.) *Mem. Ed.* XXI, 98; *Nat. Ed.* XIX, 85.

FOOD ADULTERATION. *See* PURE FOOD LAW.

FOOTBALL. What I have to say with reference to all sports refers especially to football. The brutality must be done away with and the danger minimized. If necessary the college faculties must take a hand, and those of the different colleges must co-operate. The rules for football ought probably to be altered so as to do away with the present mass play, and, I think, also the present system of interference, while the umpires must be made to prevent slugging or any kind of foul play by the severest penalties. Moreover, professionalism must be stopped outright. It should be distinctly understood among the academies and colleges that no team will have anything to do with another upon which professionals are employed. *Harper's Weekly,* December 23, 1893, p. 1236.

———. It is to my mind simple nonsense, a mere confession of weakness, to desire to abolish a game because tendencies show themselves, or practices grow up, which prove that the game ought to be reformed. Take football, for instance. The preparatory schools are able to keep football clean and to develop the right spirit in the players without the slightest necessity ever arising to so much as consider the question of abolishing it. There is no excuse whatever for colleges failing to show the same capacity, and there is no real need for considering the question of the abolition of the game. If necessary, let the college authorities interfere to stop any excess or perversion, making their interference as little officious as possible, and yet as rigorous as is necessary to achieve the end. But there is no justification for stopping a thoroughly manly sport because it is sometimes abused, when the experience of every good preparatory school shows that the abuse is in no shape necessarily attendant upon the game. (At the Harvard Union, Cambridge, February 23, 1907.) *Mem. Ed.* XV, 483; *Nat. Ed.* XIII, 560.

———. One of the things I wish we could learn from you is how to make the game of football a rather less homicidal pastime. I do not wish to speak as a mere sentimentalist; but I do not think that killing should be a normal accompaniment of the game, and while we develop our football from Rugby, I wish we could go back and undevelop it, and get it nearer your game. I am not qualified to speak as an expert on the subject, but I wish we could make it more open and eliminate some features that certainly tend to add to the danger of the game as it is played in America now. On the Pacific slope we have been going back to your type of Rugby football. I would not have football abolished for anything, but I want to have it changed, just because I want to draw the teeth of the men who always clamor for the abolition of any manly game. I wish to deprive those whom I put in the mollycoddle class, of any argument against good sport. (At the Cambridge Union, Cambridge, Eng., May 26, 1910.) *Mem. Ed.* XV, 505; *Nat. Ed.* XIII, 573.

FOOTBALL. *See also* SPORTS.

FORAKER, JOSEPH B. I have seen the correspondence between Archbold and Foraker, published in the morning papers. Now, it is difficult for any man to advise another as to a given act in a campaign. Personally, if I were running for President, I should in view of these disclosures decline to appear upon the platform with Foraker, and I would have it understood in detail what is the exact fact, namely, that Mr. Foraker's separation from you and from me has been due not in the least to a difference of opinion on the negro question, which was merely a pretense, but to the fact that he was the attorney of the corporations, their hired representative in public life, and that therefore he naturally and inevitably opposed us in every way; that he opposed us when it came to appointments on the bench just as he opposed legislation that we asked for in Congress. I think it essential, if the bad effect upon the canvass of those disclosures is to be obviated, that we should show unmistakably how completely loose from us Mr. Foraker is. If this is not shown affirmatively, there is danger that the people will not see it and will simply think that all Republicans are tarred with the same brush. (To William H. Taft, September 19, 1908.) *Mem. Ed.* XXIV, 112; Bishop II, 96.

———. There are certain [issues] as to which you and I will continue to differ, but if I ever get the chance to speak publicly, I shall elaborate what I said in speaking of you in the libel suit.

Not only do I admire your entire courage and straightforwardness (in the railway-rate legislation I respected you a thousand times more than I did many of the men who voted for the bill), but I also grew steadily more and more to realize your absolute Americanism, and your capacity for generosity and disinterestedness. Besides, you knew the need that the freeman shall be able to fight, under penalty of ceasing to be a freeman.

Too many of our representatives in the Senate and the Lower House could not be persuaded to take any interest in any matter in which they or their districts were not personally concerned. But, as far as you were concerned when the question came up of dealing with the Philippines or Porto Rico or Panama, or the navy, or anything involving America's international good name, or the doing of our duty to help people who had no champion; I knew that if I could convince you that my view was right I could count upon your ardent championship of the cause. (To Foraker, June 28, 1916.) Julia B. Foraker, *I Would Live It Again.* (New York, Harper and Brothers, 1932), pp. 316-317.

FORCE. Force unbacked by righteousness is abhorrent. The effort to substitute for it vague declamation for righteousness unbacked by force is silly. The policeman must be put back of the judge in international law just as he is back of the judge in municipal law. The effective power of civilization must be put back of civilization's collective purpose to secure reasonable justice between nation and nation. (New York *Times,* September 27, 1914.) *Mem. Ed.* XX, 7; *Nat. Ed.* XVIII, 6.

———. The only way in which successfully to oppose wrong which is backed by might is to put over against it right which is backed by might. (1916.) *Mem. Ed.* XX, 261; *Nat. Ed.* XVIII, 224.

FORCE AND JUSTICE. Merely to trust to public opinion without organized force back of it is silly. Force must be put back of justice, and nations must not shrink from the duty of proceeding by any means that are necessary against wrong-doers. It is the failure to recognize these vital truths that has rendered the actions of our government during the last few years impotent to preserve world peace and fruitful only in earning for us the half-veiled derision of other nations. (New York *Times,* November 8, 1914.) *Mem. Ed.* XX, 85; *Nat. Ed.* XVIII, 74.

FORCE IN INTERNATIONAL RELATIONS. If it is impossible in the immediate future to devise some working scheme by which force shall be put behind righteousness in disinterested and effective fashion, where international wrongs are concerned, then the only alternative will be for each free people to keep itself in shape with its own strength to defend its own rights and interests, and meanwhile to do all that can be done to help forward the slow growth of sentiment which is assuredly, although very gradually, telling against international wrong-doing and violence. (New York *Times,* October 18, 1914.) *Mem. Ed.* XX, 66; *Nat. Ed.* XVIII, 57.

FORCE. *See also* LEAGUE FOR PEACE; RIGHT; TREATIES; WAR.

FORD, HENRY. For Mr. Ford personally, I feel not merely friendliness, but in many respects a very genuine admiration. There is much in the methods and very much in the purposes, with which he has conducted his business, notably in his relations to his working people, that commands my hearty sympathy and respect. Moreover, there is always something attractive to an American in the career of a man who has raised himself from the industrial ranks, until he is one of the captains of industry. But all that I have thus said, can with truth be said of many, perhaps of most of the Tories of the Revolutionary War and of many or most of the pacifists of the Civil War, the extremists among whom were popularly known as Copperheads. Many of these Tories and Civil War pacifists were men of fine character and upright purpose, who sincerely believed in the cause they advocated. They included all the men who were the pacifists of their day. These pacifists who formed so large a proportion of the old-time Tories and Copperheads abhorred and denounced the militarism of Washington in 1776 and of Lincoln in 1861. They were against all war and all preparedness for war. (At Detroit, Mich., May 19, 1916.) Theodore Roosevelt, *Righteous Peace through National Preparedness,* pp. 4-5.

————. If I get to Detroit it will be a great pleasure to accept your invitation to look at the work you are doing. As I have so frequently stated, I believe you are one of the men, the successful business men, who can do far more than any outsiders like myself in bringing about the right relations between the men who work with their hands, and those who supply the capital or the management in the business. But, my dear Mr. Ford, I trust you have not extended this invitation in ignorance of the position I have publicly taken about your attitude on behalf of pacifism. If you did not know my attitude when you wrote, I shall of course understand absolutely if you withdraw the invitation, for, as I supposed you knew, I am emphatically out of sympathy with you (just as I am radically out of sympathy with my friend, Miss Addams) as regards this pacifist agitation. If you do know my attitude and have sent the invitation knowing it, I wish you would give me the chance when I see you to make a very earnest appeal to you to use your good influence, not on behalf of a peace that will not bring righteousness, but on behalf of righteousness; for if that is obtained the peace worth having comes with it. (To Henry Ford, January 29, 1916.) *Mem. Ed.* XXIV, 469; Bishop II, 399.

FOREIGN LANGUAGE PRESS. I trust that Congress will pass a law refusing to allow a newspaper to be published in German or in the language of any other of our opponents while this war lasts, so that we shall know just what they are saying and doing. (Statement of August 10, 1917.) *Mem. Ed.* XXIV, 509; Bishop II, 435.

FOREIGN LANGUAGE PRESS. *See also* AMERICANIZATION; LANGUAGE.

FOREIGN POLICY Nine-tenths of wisdom is to be wise in time, and at the right time; and my whole foreign policy was based on the exercise of intelligent forethought and of decisive action sufficiently far in advance of any likely crisis to make it improbable that we would run into serious trouble. (1913.) *Mem. Ed.* XXII, 577; *Nat. Ed.* XX, 496.

FOREIGN POLICY—CHARACTER OF. The United States of America has not the option as to whether it will or will not play a great part in the world. It *must* play a great part. All that it can decide is whether it will play that part well or badly. And it can play it badly if it adopts the rôle either of the coward or of the bully. Nor will it help it in the end to avoid either part if it play the other. It must avoid both. Democratic America can be true to itself, true to the great cause of freedom and justice, only if it shows itself ready and willing to resent wrong from the strong, and scrupulously desirous of doing generous justice to both strong and weak. (*Outlook,* April 1, 1911.) *Mem. Ed.* XIX, 151; *Nat. Ed.* XVII, 108.

——————. We have become a great nation, forced by the fact of its greatness into relations with the other nations of the earth, and we must behave as beseems a people with such responsibilities. Toward all other nations, large and small, our attitude must be one of cordial and sincere friendship. We must show not only in our words, but in our deeds, that we are earnestly desirous of securing their good-will by acting toward them in a spirit of just and generous recognition of all their rights. But justice and generosity in a nation, as in an individual, count most when shown not by the weak but by the strong. While ever careful to refrain from wronging others, we must be no less insistent that we are not wronged ourselves. We wish peace, but we wish the peace of justice, the peace of righteousness. We wish it because we think it is right and not because we are afraid. No weak nation that acts manfully and justly should ever have cause to fear us, and no strong power should ever be able to single us out as a subject for insolent aggression. (Inaugural Address as President, Washington, March 4, 1905.) *Mem. Ed.* XVII, 312; *Nat. Ed.* XV, 267.

FOREIGN POLICY—CRITICISM OF WILSON'S. A policy of blood and iron is sometimes very wicked; but it rarely does as much harm, and never excites as much derision, as a policy of milk and water—and it comes dangerously near flattery to call the foreign policy of the United States under President Wilson and Mr. Bryan merely one of milk and water. Strength at least commands respect; whereas the prattling feebleness that dares not rebuke any concrete wrong, and whose proposals for right are marked by sheer fatuity, is fit only to excite weeping among angels and among men the bitter laughter of scorn. (New York *Times*, November 1, 1914.) *Mem. Ed.* XX, 78; *Nat. Ed.* XVIII, 66.

——————. The policy of milk-and-water is an even worse policy than the policy of blood-and-iron. To sink a hundred American men, women, and children on the *Lusitania*, in other words, to murder them, was an evil thing; but it was not quite as evil and it was nothing like as contemptible as it was for this nation to rest satisfied with governmental notes of protests couched in elegant English, and with vaguely implied threats which were not carried out. When a man has warned another man not to slap has wife's face, and the other man does it, the gentleman who has given the warning does not meet the situation by treating elocution as a substitute for action. (*Metropolitan,* August 1915.) *Mem. Ed.* XX, 359; *Nat. Ed.* XVIII, 308.

——————. For some years we have as a people shown an appalling unfitness for world leadership on behalf of the democratic ideal; for, especially during the last three years, we have played a mean and sordid part among the nations, and have been faithless to our obligations and to all the old-time ideals of American patriotism. (*Metropolitan,* May 1916.) *Mem. Ed.* XXI, 149; *Nat. Ed.* XIX, 146.

FOREIGN POLICY—DETERMINATION OF. As the nation, and not the several States, have to deal with foreign powers, the nation should have complete control over all questions likely to cause trouble with foreign powers, and therefore should have the complete and fully recognized ability to protect all aliens in their treaty rights. Yet in actual practice occasions have not infrequently arisen which have shown rather pitiable national shortcomings in this respect. (*Outlook,* April 1, 1911.) *Mem. Ed.* XIX, 152; *Nat. Ed.* XVII, 109.

FOREIGN POLICY, AMERICAN. America should have a coherent policy of action toward foreign powers, and this should primarily be based on the determination never to give offense when it can be avoided, always to treat other nations justly and courteously, and, as long as present conditions exist, to be prepared to defend our own rights ourselves. No other nation will defend them for us. No paper guaranty or treaty will be worth the paper on which it is written if it becomes to the interest of some other power to violate it, unless we have strength, and courage and ability to use that strength, back of the treaty. Every public man, every writer who speaks with wanton offensiveness of a foreign power or of a foreign people, whether he attacks England or France or Germany, whether he assails the Russians or the Japanese, is doing an injury to the whole American body politic. We have plenty of shortcomings at home to correct before we start out to criticise the shortcomings of others. Now and then it becomes imperatively necessary in the interests of humanity, or in our own vital interest, to act in a manner which will cause offense to some other power. This is a lamentable necessity; but when the necessity arises we must meet it and act as we are honorably bound to act, no matter what offense is given. We must always weigh well our duties in such a case, and consider the rights of others as well as our own rights, in the interest of the world at large. If after such consideration it is evident that we are bound to act along a certain line of policy, then it is mere weakness to refrain from doing so because offense is thereby given. But we must never act wantonly or brutally, or without regard to the essentials of genuine morality—a morality considering our interests as well as the interests of others, and considering the interests of future generations as well as of the present generation. We must so conduct ourselves that every big nation and every little nation that behaves itself shall never have to think of us with fear, and shall have confidence not only in our justice but in our courtesy. (*Outlook,* September 23, 1914.) *Mem. Ed.* XX, 28; *Nat. Ed.* XVIII, 24.

——————. Washington, Andrew Jackson, Lincoln and Grant have occupied exactly the right position as regards our duty in international affairs; and Jefferson, Buchanan and Wilson exactly the wrong position. The way to help us in the concrete to do what is right is to point out in the concrete the men at the head of affairs who do what is wrong. The War of 1812 was for us at best a draw and was fulfilled with humiliation and disgrace because of Jefferson's attitude and above all because Jefferson's attitude represented the American attitude. If men like Washington had been in charge of this government for the first sixteen years of the nineteenth century the War of 1812 would have been an overwhelming victory and probably would have been closed in 1812. Wilson and Bryan at the present day are contending for the proud pre-eminence of doing everything in their power in the last two years and a half to bring this nation to both impotence and infamy in its international relations—and Taft by his universal arbitration treaties and his Mexican policy ably paved the way for them. (To Julian Street, June 23, 1915.) *Mem. Ed.* XXIV, 452; Bishop II, 384.

FOREIGN RELATIONS. We cannot sit huddled within our own borders and avow ourselves merely an assemblage of well-to-do hucksters who care nothing for what happens beyond. Such a policy would defeat even its own end; for as the nations grow to have wider and wider interests and are brought into closer and closer contact, if we are to hold our own in the struggle for naval and commercial supremacy, we must build up our power within our own borders. (Before the Hamilton Club, Chicago, April 10, 1899.) *Mem. Ed.* XV, 272; *Nat. Ed.* XIII, 323.

——————. It is continually growing less and less possible for any great civilized nation to live purely for and by itself. Exactly as steam and electricity and the extraordinary agencies of modern industrialism have rendered more complex and more intimate the relations of all the individuals within each nation, so the same causes have rendered more complex and more intimate the relations of the various civilized nations with one another. (At New York City, October 3, 1913.) *Mem. Ed.* XVIII, 391; *Nat. Ed.* XVI, 292.

——————. The United States cannot again completely withdraw into its shell. We need not mix in all European quarrels nor assume all spheres of interest everywhere to be ours, but we ought to join with the other civilized nations of the world in some scheme that in a time of great stress would offer a likelihood of obtaining just settlements that will avert war. (Kansas City *Star,* November 17, 1918.) *Mem. Ed.* XXI, 445; *Nat. Ed.* XIX, 401.

FOREIGN RELATIONS—CONDUCT OF. Tame submission to foreign aggression of any kind is a mean and unworthy thing; but it is even meaner and more unworthy to bluster first, and then either submit or else refuse to make those preparations which can alone obviate the necessity for submission. (Address as Assistant Secretary of the Navy, Naval War College, June 1897.) *Mem. Ed.* XV, 253; *Nat. Ed.* XIII, 193.

——————. To be rich, unarmed, and yet insolent and aggressive, is to court well-nigh certain disaster. The only safe and honorable rule of foreign policy for the United States is to show itself courteous toward other nations, scrupulous not to infringe upon their rights, and yet able and ready to defend its own. This nation is now on terms of the most cordial good-will with all other nations. Let us make it a prime object of our policy to preserve these conditions. To do so it is necessary on the one hand to mete out a generous justice to all other peoples and show them courtesy and respect; and on the other hand, as we are yet a good way off from the millennium, to keep ourselves in such shape as to make it evident to all men that we desire peace because we think it is just and right and not from motives of weakness or timidity. (At Cairo, Ill., October 3, 1907.) *Mem. Ed.* XVIII, 16; *Nat. Ed.* XVI, 14.

——————. Whenever on any point we come in contact with a foreign power, I hope that we shall always strive to speak courteously and respectfully of that foreign power. Let us make it evident that we intend to do justice. Then let us make it equally evident that we will not tolerate injustice being done to us in return. Let us further make it evident that we use no words which we are not prepared to back up with deeds, and that while our speech is always moderate, we are ready and willing to make it good. Such an attitude will be the surest possible guarantee of that self-respecting peace, the attainment of which is and must ever be the prime aim of a self-governing people. (At Minnesota State Fair, September 2, 1901.) *Mem. Ed.* XV, 335; *Nat. Ed.* XIII, 475.

FOREIGN RELATIONS—PROMISES IN. The importance of a promise lies not in making it, but in keeping it; and the poorest of all positions for a nation to occupy in such a matter is readiness to make impossible promises at the same time that there is failure to keep promises which have been made, which can be kept, and which it is discreditable to break. (1913.) *Mem. Ed.* XXII, 613; *Nat. Ed.* XX, 527.

FOREIGN RELATIONS—RESPONSIBILITY IN. No nation can claim rights without acknowledging the duties that go with the rights. It is a contemptible thing for a great nation to render itself impotent in international action, whether because of cowardice or sloth, or sheer inability or unwillingness to look into the future. It is a very wicked thing for a nation to do wrong to others. But the most contemptible and most wicked course of conduct is for a nation to use offensive language or be guilty of offensive actions toward other people and yet fail to hold its own if the other nation retaliates; and it is almost as bad to undertake responsibilities and then not fulfil them. (1913.) *Mem. Ed.* XXII, 571; *Nat. Ed.* XX, 491.

FOREIGN RELATIONS AND PARTY POLITICS. The dealings of the United States with foreign powers should be considered from no partisan standpoint. Our party divisions affect ourselves purely; and when we are brought face to face with a foreign nation we should act as Americans merely. (*The Independent*, August 11, 1892.) *Mem. Ed.* XVI, 208; *Nat. Ed.* XIV, 140.

FOREIGN RELATIONS. *See also* ALLIANCES; AMBASSADORS; ARBITRATION; BIG STICK; DIPLOMACY; HAGUE COURT; "HANDS ACROSS THE SEA"; INTERNATIONAL DISPUTES; INTERNATIONAL DUTIES; INTERNATIONAL JUSTICE; INTERNATIONAL RELATIONS; LEAGUE OF NATIONS; PEACE; STATES' RIGHTS; WILSON, WOODROW; WORLD WAR.

FOREIGN SERVICE. *See* CONSULAR SERVICE; DIPLOMATIC SERVICE.

FOREIGN WAYS—IMITATION OF. I think there is only one thing more foolish than blind imitation of something that has done well abroad, and that is the narrow spirit that refuses to adopt anything just because it comes from abroad. (Before Iowa State Teachers' Association, Des Moines, Nov. 4, 1910.) *Mem. Ed.* XVIII, 451; *Nat. Ed.* XVI, 337.

FOREIGN WAYS. *See also* COSMOPOLITANS; EXPATRIATES.

FOREIGNERS — ATTITUDE TOWARD. The attitude of foreigners toward us is a matter of slight consequence. What really does concern us is the queer strained humility toward foreigners, and especially toward Englishmen, shown by certain small groups of Americans. We respect Englishmen; but we are a different people. It is right that others should worship at their own shrines; we ourselves worship at ours; but why should a few of our number run after strange gods, ignoring their own? (*Cosmopolitan*, December 1892.) *Mem. Ed.* XIV, 366; *Nat. Ed.* XII, 301.

FOREIGNERS. *See also* ALIENS; AMERICAN PEOPLE; IMMIGRATION.

FOREST AND GAME RESERVES. I have doubled or quadrupled the forest reserves of the country; have put through the reorganization of the forest service, placing it under the Agricultural Department; and I may add as a small incident, have created a number of reservations for preserving the wild things of nature, the beasts and birds as well as the trees. (To Sidney Brooks, December 28, 1908.) *Mem. Ed.* XXIV, 151; Bishop II, 129.

―――――――――. The practical common sense of the American people has been in no way made more evident during the last few years than by the creation and use of a series of large land reserves—situated for the most part on the great plains and among the mountains of the West—intended to keep the forests from destruction, and therefore to conserve the water-supply. These reserves are, and should be, created primarily for economic purposes. The semiarid regions can only support a reasonable population under conditions of the strictest economy and wisdom in the use of the water-supply, and in addition to their other economic uses the forests are indispensably necessary for the preservation of the water-supply and for rendering possible its useful distribution throughout the proper seasons. In addition, however, to this economc use of the wilderness, selected portions of it have been kept here and there in a state of nature, not merely for the sake of preserving the forests and the water, but for the sake of preserving all its beauties and wonders unspoiled by greedy and short-sighted vandalism. What has been actually accomplished in the Yellowstone Park affords the best possible object-lesson as to the desirability and practicability of establishing such wilderness reserves. This reserve is a natural breeding-ground and nursery for those stately and beautiful haunters of the wilds which have now vanished from so many of the great forests, the vast lonely plains, and the high mountain ranges, where they once abounded. (1905.) *Mem. Ed.* III, 271-272; *Nat. Ed.* III, 89-90.

FOREST CONSERVATION. Wise forest protection does not mean the withdrawal of forest resources, whether of wood, water, or grass, from contributing their full share to the welfare of the people, but, on the contrary, gives the assurance of larger and more certain supplies. The fundamental idea of forestry is the perpetuation of forests by use. Forest protection is not an end of itself; it is a means to increase and sustain the resources of our country and the industries which depend upon them. The preservation of our forests is an imperative business necessity. (First Annual Message, Washington, December 3, 1901.) *Mem. Ed.* XVII, 118; *Nat. Ed.* XV, 102.

FOREST CONSERVATION—NEED FOR. If the present rate of forest destruction is allowed to continue, with nothing to offset it, a timber famine in the future is inevitable. Fire, wasteful and destructive forms of lumbering, and the legitimate use, taken together, are destroying our forest resources far more rapidly than they are being replaced. It is difficult to imagine what such a timber famine would mean to our resources. And the period of recovery from the injuries which a timber famine would entail would be measured by the slow growth of the trees themselves. Remember that you can prevent such a timber famine occurring by wise action taken in time, but once the famine occurs there is no possible way of hurrying the growth of the trees necessary to relieve it. You have got to act in time or else the nation would have to submit to prolonged suffering after it had become too late for forethought to avail. (Before Forest Congress, Washington, D. C., January 5, 1905.) *Mem. Ed.* XVIII, 141; *Nat. Ed.* XVI, 105.

——————. We are consuming our forests three times faster than they are being reproduced. Some of the richest timber-lands of this continent have already been destroyed, and not replaced, and other vast areas are on the verge of destruction. Yet forests, unlike mines, can be so handled as to yield the best results of use, without exhaustion, just like grain-fields. (Before Deep Waterway Convention, Memphis, Tenn., October 4, 1907.) *Mem. Ed.* XVIII, 155; *Nat. Ed.* XVI, 117.

FOREST CONSERVATION — OBJECT OF. First and foremost, you can never afford to forget for one moment what is the object of the forest policy. Primarily that object is not to preserve forests because they are beautiful—though that is good in itself—not to preserve them because they are refuges for the wild creatures of the wilderness—though that too is good in itself—but the primary object of the forest policy as of the land policy of the United States, is the making of prosperous homes, is part of the traditional policy of home-making of our country. Every other consideration comes as secondary. The whole effort of the government in dealing with the forests must be directed to this end, keeping in view the fact that it is not only necessary to start the homes as prosperous, but to keep them so. That is the way the forests have need to be kept. You can start a prosperous home by destroying the forest, but you do not keep it. (Before Society of American Foresters, Washington, March 26, 1903.) *Mem. Ed.* XVIII, 127.

FOREST POLICY—HOSTILITY TO. Continual efforts are made by demagogues and by unscrupulous agitators to excite hostility to the forest policy of the government; and needy men who are short-sighted and unscrupulous join in the cry, and play into the hands of the corrupt politicians who do the bidding of the big and selfish exploiters of the public domain. One device of these politicians is through their representatives in Congress to cut down the appropriation for the forest service; and in consequence the administrative heads of the service, in the effort to be economical, are sometimes driven to the expedient of trying to replace the permanently employed experts by short-term men, picked up at haphazard, and hired only for the summer season. This is all wrong: first, because the men thus hired give very inferior service; and, second, because the government should be a model employer, and should not set a vicious example in hiring men under conditions that tend to create a shifting class of laborers who suffer from all the evils of unsteady employment, varied by long seasons of idleness. (1916.) *Mem. Ed.* IV, 9; *Nat. Ed.* III, 192.

FOREST PROBLEM, THE. The forest problem is in many ways the most vital internal problem of the United States. The more closely this statement is examined the more evident its truth becomes. In the arid regions of the West agricultural prosperity depends first of all upon the available water supply. Forest protection alone can maintain the stream flow necessary for irrigation in the West and prevent floods destructive to agriculture and manufactures in the East. The relation between forests and the whole mining industry is an extremely intimate one, for mines cannot be developed without timber, and usually not without timber close at hand.... The very existence of lumbering, the fourth great industry of the United States, depends upon the success of your work and our work as a nation in putting practical forestry into effective operation.

As it is with mining and lumbering, so it is in only less degree with transportation, manufacture, and commerce in general. The relation of all these industries to the forests is of the most intimate and dependent kind.... The forest resources of our country are already seriously depleted. They can be renewed and maintained only by the co-operation of the forester and the lumberman. (Before Society of American Foresters, Washington, March 26, 1903.) *Mem. Ed.* XVIII, 129.

FOREST RESERVES. It is not only necessary to establish a great system of storage reservoirs to prevent the flood waste of the waters; it is also necessary to preserve the forests on the mountains and among the foothills. This means that, in the first place, there must be a wide extension of the existing system of forest reserves, and, in the second place, that these forest reserves must be managed aright. They cannot be so managed while there is the present division among federal departments of the duties, and therefore, of the responsibilities, of their management.

We are just getting to understand what is involved in the preservation of our forests. Not only is an industry at stake which employs more than half a million of men, the lumber industry, but the whole prosperity and development of the West, and indeed ultimately of the entire country, is bound up with the preservation of the forests. Right use of the forests means the perpetuation of our supply both of wood and of water. Therefore we cannot afford to be satisfied with anything short of expert and responsible management of the national forest reserves and other national forest interests. The forest reserves must be cared for by the best trained foresters to be had, just as the storage reservoirs must be built and maintained by the best engineers. There is the same need of trained skill in handling the forests in your best interests as there is in building the great dams which will some day bring population and abounding prosperity to vast stretches of so-called desert in the West. (Letter of November 16, 1900; read before National Irrigation Congress, Chicago.) *The Forester,* December 1900, p. 289.

FOREST RESERVES — PURPOSE OF. Forest reserves are created for two principal purposes. The first is to preserve the water-supply. This is their most important use. The principal users of the water thus preserved are irrigation ranchers and settlers, cities and towns to whom their municipal water-supplies are of the very first importance, users and furnishers of water-power, and the users of water for domestic, manufacturing, mining, and other purposes. All these are directly dependent upon the forest reserves.

The second reason for which forest reserves are created is to preserve the timber-supply for various classes of wood users. Among the more important of these are settlers under the reclamation act and other acts, for whom a cheap and accessible supply of timber for domestic uses is absolutely necessary; miners and prospectors, who are in serious danger of losing their timber-supply by fire or through export by lumber companies when timber-lands adjacent to their mines pass into private ownership; lumbermen, transportation companies, builders, and commercial interests in general. (Fourth Annual Message, Washington, December 6, 1904.) *Mem. Ed.* XVII, 274; *Nat. Ed.* XV, 235-236.

FOREST. *See also* ARBOR DAY; CONSERVATION; NATURAL RESOURCES; PINCHOT, GIFFORD; TREES.

FORTUNES — ACQUISITION OF. It is probably true that the large majority of the fortunes that now exist in this country have been amassed not by injuring our people, but as an incident to the conferring of great bene-

[189]

fits upon the community; and this, no matter what may have been the conscious purpose of those amassing them. There is but the scantiest justification for most of the outcry against the men of wealth *as such;* and it ought to be unnecessary to state that any appeal which directly or indirectly leads to suspicion and hatred among ourselves, which tends to limit opportunity, and therefore to shut the door of success against poor men of talent, and, finally, which entails the possibility of lawlessness and violence, is an attack upon the fundamental properties of American citizenship. (At Minnesota State Fair, September 2, 1901.) *Mem. Ed.* XV, 332; *Nat. Ed.* XIII, 472.

──────────. We should discriminate in the sharpest way between fortunes well-won and fortunes ill-won; between those gained as an incident to performing great services to the community as a whole, and those gained in evil fashion by keeping just within the limits of mere law-honesty. Of course no amount of charity in spending such fortunes in any way compensates for misconduct in making them. (At Washington, April 14, 1906.) *Mem. Ed.* XVIII, 578; *Nat. Ed.* XVI, 421.

──────────. Great fortunes are usually made under very complex conditions both of effort and of surrounding, and the mere fact of the complexity makes it difficult to deal with the new conditions thus created. The contrast offered in a highly specialized industrial community between the very rich and the very poor is exceedingly distressing, and while under normal conditions the acquirement of wealth by an individual is necessarily of great incidental benefit to the community as a whole, yet this is by no means always the case. In our great cities there is plainly in evidence much wealth contrasted with much poverty, and some of the wealth has been acquired, or is used, in a manner for which there is no moral justification. . . .

Probably the large majority of the fortunes that now exist in this country have been amassed, not by injuring mankind, but as an incident to the conferring of great benefits on the community—whatever the conscious purpose of those amassing them may have been. The occasional wrongs committed or injuries endured are on the whole far outweighed by the mass of good which has resulted. The true questions to be asked are: Has any given individual been injured by the acquisition of wealth by any man? Were the rights of that individual, if they have been violated, insufficiently protected by law? If so, these rights, and all similar rights, ought to be guaranteed by additional legislation. (Annual Message as Governor, Albany, January 3, 1900.) *Mem. Ed.* XVII, 46-47; *Nat. Ed.* XV, 40-41.

FORTUNES—CONTROL OF. It is our clear duty to see, in the interest of the people, that there is adequate supervision and control over the business use of the swollen fortunes of today, and also wisely to determine the conditions upon which these fortunes are to be transmitted and the percentage that they shall pay to the government whose protecting arm alone enables them to exist. Only the nation can do this work. To relegate it to the States is a farce, and is simply another way of saying that it shall not be done at all. (At Harrisburg, Pa., October 4, 1906.) *Mem. Ed.* XVIII, 85; *Nat. Ed.* XVI, 71.

FORTUNES—LIMITATION ON SIZE OF. I wish it were in my power to devise some scheme to make it increasingly difficult to heap them [large fortunes] up beyond a certain amount. As the difficulties in the way of such a scheme are very great, let us at least prevent their being bequeathed after death or given during life to any one man in excessive amount. (Letter of April 26, 1906.) *Mem. Ed.* XXII, 563; *Nat. Ed.* XX, 484.

──────────. We believe that great fortunes, even when accumulated by the man himself, are of limited benefit to the country, and that they are detrimental rather than beneficial when secured through inheritance. We therefore believe in a heavily progressive inheritance tax—a tax which shall bear very lightly on small or ordinary inheritances, but which shall bear very heavily upon all inheritances of colossal size. We believe in a heavily graded income tax, along the same lines, but discriminating sharply in favor of earned, as compared with unearned, incomes. (*Century Magazine,* October 1913.) *Mem. Ed.* XIX, 549; *Nat. Ed.* XVII, 405.

FORTUNES. See also INHERITANCE TAX; MILLIONAIRES; MONEY; WEALTH.

FOURTEEN POINTS. The American people should insist that these fourteen points and any other points are stated in clear-cut language, and that there be a full understanding of just what is meant by them and a full knowledge of how far the American people approve of them before any foreign power is permitted to think that they represent America's position at the peace council. (Kansas City *Star,* October 17, 1918.) *Mem. Ed.* XXI, 417; *Nat. Ed.* XIX, 378.

———————. Our people ought emphatically to repudiate the "fourteen points" offered by President Wilson as a satisfactory basis for peace. We ought likewise to repudiate all of his *similar* proposals (some of his utterances have been satisfactory, but all of these have been contradicted by his other utterances, and no one can be sure which set of utterances will receive his ultimate adherence). Some of these fourteen points are mischievous under any interpretation. Most of them are worded in language so vague and so purely rhetorical that they may be construed with equal justice as having diametrically opposite meanings. Germany and Austria have eagerly approved these fourteen points; our own pro-Germans, pacifists, socialists, anarchists, and professional internationalists also approve them; but good citizens, who are also sound American nationalists, will insist upon all of them being put into straightforward and definite language—and then will reject most of them. (1918.) *Mem. Ed.* XXI, 256; *Nat. Ed.* XIX, 238.

FOURTEEN POINTS — CRITICISM OF THE. The first point forbids "all private international understandings of any kind," and says there must be "open covenants of peace, openly arrived at," and announces that "diplomacy shall always proceed frankly in the public view." . . .

This first one of the fourteen points offers such an illuminating opportunity to test promise as to the future by performance in the present that I have considered it at some length. . . .

The second in the fourteen points deals with freedom of the seas. It makes no distinction between freeing the seas from murder like that continually practiced by Germany and freeing them from blockade of contraband merchandise, which is the practice of a right universally enjoyed by belligerents, and at this moment practised by the United States. Either this proposal is meaningless or it is a mischievous concession to Germany.

The third point promises free trade among all the nations, unless the words are designedly used to conceal President Wilson's true meaning. This would deny to our country the right to make a tariff to protect its citizens, and especially its working men, against Germany or China or any other country. Apparently this is desired on the ground that the incidental domestic disaster to this country will prevent other countries from feeling hostile to us. The supposition is foolish. England practised free trade and yet Germany hated England particularly, and Turkey practised free trade without deserving or obtaining friendship from any one except those who desired to exploit her.

The fourth point provides that this nation, like every other, is to reduce its armaments to the lowest limit consistent with domestic safety. Either this is language deliberately used to deceive or else it means that we are to scrap our army and navy and prevent riot by means of a national constabulary, like the State constabulary of New York or Pennsylvania.

Point five proposes that colonial claims shall all be treated on the same basis. Unless the language is deliberately used to deceive, this means that we are to restore to our brutal enemy the colonies taken by our Allies while they were defending us from this enemy. The proposition is probably meaningless. If it is not, it is monstrous.

Point six deals with Russia. It probably means nothing, but if it means anything, it provides that America shall share on equal terms with other nations, including Germany, Austria, and Turkey, in giving Russia assistance. The whole proposition would not be particularly out of place in a college sophomore's exercise in rhetoric.

Point seven deals with Belgium and is entirely proper and commonplace.

Point eight deals with Alsace-Lorraine and is couched in language which betrays Mr. Wilson's besetting sin—his inability to speak in a straightforward manner. He may mean that Alsace and Lorraine must be restored to France, in which case he is right. He may mean that a plebiscite must be held, in which case he is playing Germany's evil game.

Point nine deals with Italy, and is right.

Point ten deals with the Austro-Hungarian Empire, and is so foolish that even President Wilson has since abandoned it.

Point eleven proposes that we, together with other nations, including apparently Germany, Austria, and Hungary, shall guarantee justice in the Balkan Peninsula. As this would also guarantee our being from time to time engaged in war over matters in which we had no interest whatever, it is worth while inquiring whether President Wilson proposes that we wage these wars with the national constabulary to which he desired to reduce our armed forces.

Point twelve proposes to perpetuate the infamy of Turkish rule in Europe, and as a sop to the conscience of humanity proposes to give the subject races autonomy, a slippery word which in a case like this is useful only for rhetorical purposes.

Point thirteen proposes an independent Poland, which is right; and then proposes that we guarantee its integrity in the event of future war, which is preposterous unless we intend to become a military nation more fit for overseas warfare than Germany is at present.

Point fourteen proposes a general association of nations to guarantee to great and small States alike political independence and territorial integrity. It is dishonorable to make this proposition so long as President Wilson continues to act as he is now acting in Haiti and San Domingo. In its essence Mr. Wilson's proposition for a league of nations seems to be akin to the holy alliance of the nations of Europe a century ago, which worked such mischief that the Monroe Doctrine was called into being especially to combat it. If it is designed to do away with nationalism, it will work nothing but mischief. If it is devised in sane fashion as an addition to nationalism and as an addition to preparing our own strength for our own defense, it may do a small amount of good; but it will certainly accomplish nothing if more than a moderate amount is attempted and probably the best first step would be to make the existing league of the Allies a going concern. (Kansas City *Star*, October 30, 1918.) *Mem. Ed.* XXI, 420-423; *Nat. Ed.*, XIX, 380-383.

FOURTEEN POINTS. *See also* LEAGUE OF NATIONS; OPEN COVENANTS; WORLD WAR—PEACE SETTLEMENT OF.

FOURTEENTH AMENDMENT. Actual experience with the Fourteenth Amendment to the National Constitution, . . . has shown us that an amendment passed by the people with one purpose may be given by the courts a construction which makes it apply to wholly different purposes and in a wholly different manner. The Fourteenth Amendment has been construed by the courts to apply to a multitude of cases to which it is positive the people who passed the amendment had not the remotest idea of applying it. (At Philadelphia, April 10, 1912.) *Mem. Ed.* XIX, 262; *Nat. Ed.* XVII, 196.

FOURTH OF JULY. It is announced that on the Fourth of July the celebration is to be by race groups—that is, by Scandinavians, Slavs, Germans, Italians, and so forth. In sport organizations it may be necessary to have such a kind of divided celebration in some places, but I most emphatically protest against such a type of celebration being general, and I doubt whether it is advisable to have it anywhere. On the contrary, I believe that we should make the Fourth of July a genuine Americanization day, and should use it to teach the prime lesson of Americanism, which is that there is no room in the country for the perpetuation of separate race groups or racial divisions; that we must all be Americans and nothing but Americans, and that therefore on the Fourth of July we should all get together simply as Americans and celebrate the day as such without regard to our several racial origins. (June 23, 1918.) *Roosevelt in the Kansas City Star,* 166.

FOX-HUNTING. Fox-hunting is a great sport, but it is as foolish to make a fetich of it as it is to decry it. The fox is hunted merely because there is no larger game to follow. As long as wolves, deer, or antelope remain in the land, and in a country where hounds and horsemen can work, no one would think of following the fox. It is pursued because the bigger beasts of the chase have been killed out. In England it has reached its present prominence only within two centuries; nobody followed the fox while the stag and the boar were common. At the present day, on Exmoor, where the wild stag is still found, its chase ranks ahead of that of the fox. It is not really the hunting proper which is the point in fox-hunting. It is the horsemanship, the galloping and jumping, and the being out in the open air. (1893.) *Mem. Ed.* II, 347; *Nat. Ed.* II, 298.

——————. As is always the case when an attempt is made to introduce anything new or out of the common, the effort to make riding to hounds a recognized amusement in the Northern States has given rise to a great deal of criticism, mostly of a singularly senseless sort, characterized by the sheerest and densest ignorance of the whole subject. Much of this criticism comes from men themselves too weak or too timid to do anything needing daring or involving the slightest personal risk, and who are actuated simply by jealousy of those who possess the attributes that they themselves lack. A favorite cry is that hunting is with us artificial and un-American. Of course it is artificial; so is every other form of sport in civilized countries, from tobogganing or ice-yachting to a game of base-ball. Anything more artificial than shooting quail on the wing over a trained setter could not be imagined. Hunting large game in the West with the rifle undoubtedly calls for the presence of a greater number of manly and hardy qualities in those who take part in it than is the case with riding to drag-hounds; but, unless the quarry is the grizzly bear, it does not need nearly as much personal daring. To object to hunting because they hunt in England is about as sensible as to object to lacrosse because the Indians play it. We do not have to concern ourselves in the least as to whether a pastime originated with Indians, or Englishmen, or Hottentots, for that matter, so long as it is attractive and health-giving. It goes without saying that the man who takes to hunting, not because it is a manly sport, but because it is done abroad, is a foolish snob; but, after all, he stands about on the same intellectual level with the man who refuses to take it up because it happens to be liked on the other side of the water.

To say the sport is un-American seems particularly absurd to such of us as happen to be in part of Southern blood, and whose forefathers, in Virginia, Georgia, or the Carolinas, have for six generations followed the fox with horse and hound. *Century,* July 1886, pp. 341-342.

――――――――. Fox-hunting is a first-class sport; but one of the most absurd things in real life is to note the bated breath with which certain excellent fox-hunters, otherwise of quite healthy minds, speak of this admirable but not over-important pastime. They tend to make it almost as much of a fetish as, in the last century, the French and German nobles made the chase of the stag, when they carried hunting and game-preserving to a point which was ruinous to the national life. Fox-hunting is very good as a pastime, but it is about as poor a business as can be followed by any man of intelligence. . . . Of course, in reality the chief serious use of fox-hunting is to encourage manliness and vigor, and to keep men hardy, so that at need they can show themselves fit to take part in work or strife for their native land. When a man so far confuses ends and means as to think that fox-hunting, . . . or whatever else the sport may be, is to be itself taken as the end, instead of as the mere means of preparation to do work that counts when the time arises, when the occasion calls—why, that man had better abandon sport altogether. (*St. Nicholas,* May 1900.) *Mem. Ed.* XV, 470-471; *Nat. Ed.* XIII, 403.

FRANCE—DEBT TO. In this great war France has suffered more and has achieved more than any other power. To her, more than to any other power, the final victory will be due. Civilization has in the past for immemorial centuries owed an incalculable debt to France; but for no single feat or achievement of the past does civilization owe as much to France as to what her sons and daughters have done in the world war now being waged by the free peoples against the powers of the Pit. (To Henry Bordeaux, June 27, 1918.) *Mem. Ed.* XXIV, 525; Bishop II, 449.

FRANCE—STATESMEN OF. It shows my own complacent Anglo-Saxon ignorance that I had hitherto rather looked down upon French public men, and have thought of them as people of marked levity. When I met them I found that they had just as solid characters as English and American public men, although with the attractiveness which to my mind makes the able and cultivated Frenchman really unique. (To Sir George Otto Trevelyan, October 1, 1911.) *Mem. Ed.* XXIV, 271; Bishop II, 232.

FRANCE AND THE WORLD WAR. The French feel with passionate conviction that this is the last stand of France, and that if she does not now succeed and is again trampled under foot, her people will lose for all time their place in the forefront of that great modern civilization of which the debt to France is literally incalculable. It would be impossible too highly to admire the way in which the men and women of France have borne themselves in this nerve-shattering time of awful struggle and awful suspense. They have risen level to the hour's needs, whereas in 1870 they failed so to rise. The high valor of the French soldiers has been matched by the poise, the self-restraint, the dignity, and the resolution with which the French people and the French Government have behaved. (New York *Times,* October 11, 1914.) *Mem. Ed.* XX, 55; *Nat. Ed.* XVIII, 47.

――――――――. France has shown a heroism and a loftiness of soul worthy of Joan of Arc herself. She was better prepared than either of her allies, perhaps because the danger to her was more imminent and more terrible, and therefore more readily understood; and since the first month of the war she has done everything that it was in human power to do. The unity, the quiet resolution, the spirit of self-sacrifice among her people—soldiers and civilians, men and women—are of a noble type. The soul of France, at this moment, seems purified of all dross; it burns like the clear flame of fire on a sacred tripod. Frenchmen are not only a gallant but a generous race. (1916.) *Mem. Ed.* XX, 257; *Nat. Ed.* XVIII, 221.

FRANCE. *See also* ALGECIRAS CONFERENCE; DREYFUS, ALFRED; FRENCH REVOLUTION; JUSSERAND, J. J.; WORLD WAR.

FRANCHISE. *See* NEGRO SUFFRAGE; SUFFRAGE; VOTING; WOMAN SUFFRAGE.

FRANCHISE TAX. After I was elected governor I had my attention directed to the franchise tax matter, looked into the subject, and came to the conclusion that it was a matter of plain decency and honesty that these companies should pay a tax on their franchises, inasmuch as they did nothing that could be considered as service rendered the public in lieu of a tax. This seemed to me so evidently the common sense and decent thing to do that I was hardly prepared for the storm of protest and anger which my proposal aroused. (1913.) *Mem. Ed.* XXII, 342; *Nat. Ed.* XX, 292.

———. On the one hand we have the perfectly simple savage who believes that you should tax franchises to the extent of confiscating them, and that it is the duty of all railroad corporations to carry everybody free and give him a chromo.

On the other, we have the scarcely less primitive mortal who believes that there is something sacred in a franchise and that there is no reason why it should pay its share of the public burdens at all.

Now, gentlemen, remember that the man who occupies the last position inevitably tends to produce the man who occupies the first position, and that the worst enemy of property is the man who, whether from unscrupulousness or from mere heedlessness and thoughtlessness, takes the ground that there is something sacrosanct about all property, that the owners of it are to occupy a different position in the community from all others and are to have their burdens not increased, but diminished, because of their wealth. (Before Independent Club, Buffalo, N. Y., May 15, 1899.) *Mem. Ed.* XVI, 487; *Nat. Ed.* XIV, 326.

FRANCHISE TAX—CONSTITUTIONALITY OF. I have just received a telegram to the effect that the Franchise Tax Law in New York has been declared constitutional by the Supreme Court. This was something very near my heart for I felt that the Franchise Tax Law was the most definite and important contribution to decent and intelligent government made by me while I was Governor. I am, therefore, very much pleased with the news. . . . The courts can be educated just as the public can be educated, and the suits you have carried on and the decisions you have secured in the United States Courts have had, I am convinced, a very profound effect elsewhere. Unless I am greatly mistaken one of the places where this effect is visible is this Franchise Tax decision. (To Philander C. Knox, April 28, 1903.) *Mem. Ed.* XXIII, 214; Bishop I, 187.

———. The great measure of my administration as Governor was the franchise tax. It was far more bitterly fought than the public-utilities bill; and mind you, it broke ground for the first time in New York in dealing with these big corporations, and it has been declared constitutional by the highest court in the land. (To Lawrence F. Abbott, November 27, 1907.) *Mem. Ed.* XXIV, 62; Bishop II, 53.

FREDERICK THE GREAT. As a soldier Frederick the Great ranks in that very, very small group which includes Alexander, Caesar, and Hannibal in antiquity, and Napoleon, and possibly Gustavus Adolphus, in modern times. He belonged to the ancient and illustrious house of Hohenzollern, which, after playing a strong and virile part in the Middle Ages, and after producing some men, like the great Elector, who were among the most famous princes of their time, founded the royal house of Prussia two centuries ago, and at last in our own day established the mighty German Empire as among the foremost of world powers. . . .

Not only must the military scholar always turn to the career of Frederick the Great for lessons in strategy and tactics; not only must the military administrator always turn to his career for lessons in organizing success; not only will the lover of heroism read the tales of his mighty feats as long as mankind cares for heroic deeds; but even those who are not attracted by the valor of the soldier must yet, for the sake of the greatness of the man, ponder and admire the lessons taught by his undaunted resolution, his inflexible tenacity of purpose, his farsighted grasp of lofty possibilities, and his unflinching, unyielding determination in following the path he had marked out. (At unveiling of statue of Frederick the Great, Washington, D. C., November 19, 1904.) *Presidential Addresses and State Papers* III, 101-103.

FREE COINAGE. *See* SILVER.

FREE INSTITUTIONS. *See* DEMOCRACY; GOVERNMENT; POPULAR RULE; SELF-GOVERNMENT.

FREE SPEECH. Free speech, exercised both individually and through a free press, is a necessity in any country where the people are themselves free. (May 7, 1918.) *Roosevelt in the Kansas City Star,* 148.

———. One of our cardinal doctrines is freedom of speech, which means freedom of speech about foreigners as well as about ourselves; and, inasmuch as we exercise this right with complete absence of restraint, we cannot expect other nations to hold us harmless unless in the last resort we are able to make our own words good by our deeds. One class of our citizens indulges in gushing promises to do everything for foreigners, another class offensively and improperly reviles them; and it is hard to say which class more thoroughly misrepresents the sober, self-respecting judgment of the American people as a whole. (1913.) *Mem. Ed.* XXII, 609; *Nat. Ed.* XX, 523.

FREE SPEECH—ATTEMPT TO LIMIT. The Senate Judiciary Committee has just recommended the passage of a law in which, among many excellent propositions to put down disloyalty, there has been adroitly inserted a provision that any one who uses "contemptuous or slurring language about the President" shall be punished by imprisonment for a long term of years and by a fine of many thousand dollars. This proposed law is sheer treason to the United States. Under its terms Abraham Lincoln would have been sent to prison for what he repeatedly said of Presidents Polk, Pierce, and Buchanan. . . . It is a proposal to make Americans subjects instead of citizens. It is a proposal to put the President in the position of the Hohenzollerns and Romanoffs. Government by the people means that the people have the right to do their own thinking and to do their own speaking about their public servants. They must speak truthfully and they must not be disloyal to the country, and it is their highest duty by truthful criticism to make and keep the public servants loyal to the country. . . .

Whenever the need arises I shall in the future speak truthfully of the President in praise or in blame, exactly as I have done in the past. . . . I am an American and a free man. My loyalty is due to the United States, and therefore it is due to the President, the Senators, the Congressmen, and all other public servants only and to the degree in which they loyally and efficiently serve the United States. (1918.) *Mem. Ed.* XXI, 325-327; *Nat. Ed.* XIX, 297-298.

FREE SPEECH. *See also* CRITICISM; LESE-MAJESTY; LIBERTY.

FREE TRADE. There is certainly a reaction in public sentiment against our doctrines, but this should not encourage cowardice in the ranks. It should rather make the advocates of free trade more persistent in their efforts to bring about the desired reform. The first and most prominent evil to be attacked is the prohibitory tariff on ships, and after that may be mentioned the tariff on art, which makes us the laughing stock of the world. (Before New York Free Trade Club, May 28, 1883.) *New York Times,* May 29, 1883.

——————. Thank God I am not a free-trader. In this country pernicious indulgence in the doctrine of free trade seems inevitably to produce fatty degeneration of the moral fibre. (To H. C. Lodge, December 27, 1895.) *Lodge Letters* I, 204.

——————. Free trade is one of the laissez-faire theories that has been abandoned by every serious student of economics; free trade is one of the laissez-faire theories the reliance on which has reduced England to her present position of scrap-heap industrialism. The English employer and the English workmen offer as fine natural material as is to be found anywhere, yet during the last forty years they have tended to fall behind their brethren in Germany, just because Germany abandoned laissez-faire doctrines and has taken decisive action in favor of wise organization, wise governmental supervision and intelligent cooperation as between the government and the individual. *Saturday Evening Post,* October 26, 1912, p. 4.

FREE TRADE. *See also* RECIPROCITY; TARIFF.

FREEDOM. Freedom is not a gift which can be enjoyed save by those who show themselves worthy of it. In this world no privilege can be permanently appropriated by men who have not the power and the will successfully to assume the responsibility of using it aright. . . . Freedom thus conceived is a constructive force, which enables an intelligent and good man to do better things than he could do without it; which is in its essence the substitution of self-restraint for external restraint—the substitution of a form of restraint which promotes progress for the form which retards it. This is the right view to take of freedom; but it can only be taken if there is a full recognition of the close connection between liberty and responsibility in every domain of human thought and action. (At Gettysburg, Pa., May 30, 1904.) *Mem. Ed.* XII, 609; *Nat. Ed.* XI, 326.

FREEDOM—FOES OF. Exactly as the reactionary is in the end the worst foe of order; exactly as the conscienceless and greedy man of wealth is in the end the worst foe of property and of honest and duty-performing holders of property, so the Anarchist and the wild Socialist, whose doctrines when applied necessarily lead to Anarchy and the I.W.W., and the crack-brained professional pacifists inevitably themselves are the worst enemies of freedom, of true democracy, and of righteousness. (November 26, 1917.) *Roosevelt in the Kansas City Star,* 57.

FREEDOM—NEGATION OF. No person should by contract be permitted to impose substantial restraints upon his liberty. Freedom to impose these restraints, if given to weak and needy people, simply amounts to defeating the very end of freedom. Academic freedom is the absolute negation of real freedom. Academic individualism defeats itself, whereas freedom in the fact makes for a rational individualism. (*Outlook,* March 11, 1911.) *Mem. Ed.* XIX, 133; *Nat. Ed.* XVII, 94.

FREEDOM—PRESERVATION OF. If freedom is worth having, if the right of self-government is a valuable right, then the one and the other must be retained exactly as our forefathers acquired them, by labor, and especially by labor in organiation; that is, in combination with our fellows who have the same interests and the same principles. (Before the Liberal Club, Buffalo, N. Y., January 26, 1893.) *Mem. Ed.* XV, 65; *Nat. Ed.* XIII, 282.

FREEDOM, INDIVIDUAL. The distinguishing feature of our American governmental system is the freedom of the individual; it is quite as important to prevent his being oppressed by many men as it is to save him from the tyranny of one. (1887.) *Mem. Ed.* VIII, 92; *Nat. Ed.* VII, 80.

———————. The one great reason for our having succeeded as no other people ever has, is to be found in that common sense which has enabled us to preserve the largest possible individual freedom on the one hand, while showing an equally remarkable capacity for combination on the other. We have committed plenty of faults, but we have seen and remedied them. Our very doctrinaires have usually acted much more practically than they have talked. (1888.) *Mem. Ed.* VIII, 373; *Nat. Ed.* VII, 323.

FREEDOM AND EQUALITY. Fundamentally, our chief problem may be summed up as the effort to make men, as nearly as they can be made, both free and equal; the freedom and equality necessarily resting on a basis of justice and brotherhood. It is not possible, with the imperfections of mankind, ever wholly to achieve such an ideal, if only for the reason that the shortcomings of men are such that complete and unrestricted individual liberty would mean the negation of even approximate equality, while a rigid and absolute equality would imply the destruction of every shred of liberty. Our business is to secure a practical working combination between the two. *Outlook,* September 3, 1910, p. 21.

FREEDOM. *See also* CONTRACT; DEMOCRACY; EQUALITY; FREE SPEECH; INDIVIDUALISM; LIBERTY; RELIGIOUS FREEDOM; SELF-GOVERNMENT; SLAVERY; TOLERANCE.

FREIGHT RATES. *See* RAILROAD RATES.

FRENCH IN AMERICA. *See* PARKMAN, FRANCIS.

FRENCH REVOLUTION. The French Revolution was in its essence a struggle for the abolition of privilege, and for equality in civil rights. . . . To the downtrodden masses of Continental Europe, the gift of civil rights and the removal of the tyranny of the privileged classes, even though accompanied by the rule of a directory, a consul, or an emperor, represented an immense political advance; but to the free people of England, and to the freer people of America, the change would have been wholly for the worse. (1888.) *Mem. Ed.* VIII, 403; *Nat. Ed.* VII, 347-348.

———————.There was never another great struggle, in the end productive of good to mankind, where the tools and methods by which that end was won were so wholly vile as in the French Revolution. Alone among movements of the kind, it brought forth no leaders entitled to our respect; none who were both great and good; none even who were very great, save, at its beginning, strange, strong, crooked Mirabeau, and at its close the towering world-genius who sprang to power by its means, wielded it for his own selfish purposes, and dazzled all nations over the wide earth by the glory of his strength and splendor. (1888.) *Mem. Ed.* VIII, 404-405; *Nat. Ed.* VII, 349.

———————. The excesses of the French Revolution were not only hideous in themselves, but were fraught with a menace to civilization which has lasted until our time and which has found its most vicious expression in the Paris Commune of 1871 and its would-be imitators here and in other lands. Nevertheless, there was hope for mankind in the French Revolution, and there was none in the system against which it was a protest, a system which had reached its highest development in Spain. Better the terrible flame of the French Revolution than the worse than Stygian hopelessness of the tyranny—physical, intellectual, spiritual—which brooded over the Spain of that day. (*Outlook,* December 2, 1911.) *Mem. Ed.* XIV, 422; *Nat. Ed.* XII, 116.

FRENCH REVOLUTION. *See also* MORRIS, GOUVERNEUR.

FRIENDS. See LOYALTY.

FRONTIER DEMOCRACY. The individualism of the backwoodsmen ... was tempered by a sound common sense, and capacity for combination. The first hunters might come alone or in couples, but the actual colonization was done not by individuals, but by groups of individuals. The settlers brought their families and belongings, either on pack-horses along the forest trails, or in scows down the streams; they settled in palisaded villages, and immediately took steps to provide both a civil and military organization. They were men of facts, not theories; and they showed their usual hard common sense in making a government. They did not try to invent a new system; they simply took that under which they had grown up, and applied it to their altered conditions....

They were also familiar with the representative system; and accordingly they introduced it into the new communities, the little forted villages serving as natural units of representation. They were already thoroughly democratic, in instinct and principle, and, as a matter of course, they made the offices elective and gave full play to the majority. (1889.) *Mem. Ed.* XI, 225-226; *Nat. Ed.* IX, 13.

FRONTIER LIFE. Out on the frontier, and generally among those who spend their lives in, or on the borders of the wilderness, life is reduced to its elemental conditions. The passions and emotions of these grim hunters of the mountains, and wild rough-riders of the plains, are simpler and stronger than those of people dwelling in more complicated states of society. As soon as the communities become settled and begin to grow with any rapidity, the American instinct for law asserts itself; but in the earlier stages each individual is obliged to be a law to himself and to guard his rights with a strong hand. Of course the transition periods are full of incongruities. Men have not yet adjusted their relations to morality and law with any niceness. They hold strongly by certain rude virtues, and on the other hand they quite fail to recognize even as shortcomings not a few traits that obtain scant mercy in older communities.... If the transition from the wild lawlessness of life in the wilderness or on the border to a higher civilization was stretched out over a term of centuries, he and his descendants would doubtless accommodate themselves by degrees to the changing circumstances. But unfortunately in the far West the transition takes place with marvellous abruptness, and at an altogether unheard-of speed, and many a man's nature is unable to change with sufficient rapidity to allow him to harmonize with his environment. In consequence, unless he leaves for still wilder lands, he ends by getting hanged instead of founding a family which would revere his name as that of a very capable although not in all respects a conventionally moral, ancestor. (1893.) *Mem. Ed.* II, 379-380; *Nat. Ed.* II, 325-326.

FRONTIER WARFARE. The history of the border wars, both in the ways they were begun and in the ways they were waged, makes a long tale of injuries inflicted, suffered, and mercilessly revenged. It could not be otherwise when brutal, reckless, lawless borderers, despising all men not of their own color, were thrown in contact with savages who esteemed cruelty and treachery as the highest of virtues, and rapine and murder as the worthiest of pursuits. Moreover, it was sadly inevitable that the law-abiding borderer as well as the white ruffian, the peaceful Indian as well as the painted marauder, should be plunged into the struggle to suffer the punishment that should only have fallen on their evil-minded fellows.

Looking back, it is easy to say that much of the wrongdoing could have been prevented; but if we examine the facts to find out the truth, not to establish a theory, we are bound to admit that the struggle was really one that could not possibly have been avoided. The sentimental historians speak as if the blame had been all ours, and the wrong all done to our foes, and as if it would have been possible by any exercise of wisdom to reconcile claims that were in their very essence conflicting; but their utterances are as shallow as they are untruthful. Unless we were willing that the whole continent west of the Alleghanies should remain an unpeopled waste, the hunting-ground of savages, war was inevitable; and even had we been willing, and had we refrained from encroaching on the Indians' lands, the war would have come nevertheless, for then the Indians themselves would have encroached on ours. (1889.) *Mem. Ed.* X, 78-79; *Nat. Ed.* VIII, 69-70.

FRONTIER. See also BOONE, DANIEL; CATTLEMAN; CLARK, GEORGE ROGERS; COWBOYS; EXPANSION; EXPLORERS; HOMESTEAD LAW; INDIANS; INDIVIDUALISM; JESUITS; LOUISIANA PURCHASE; MANIFEST DESTINY; MILITIA; NORTHWEST; PIONEER; SCOTCH-IRISH; SEVIER, J.; TEXAS; VIGILANTES; WAR OF 1812; WATAUGA SETTLEMENT; WEST; WESTWARD MOVEMENT.

FRONTIERSMEN. There was not only much that was attractive in their wild, free, reckless lives, but there was also very much good about the men themselves. They were—and such of them as are left still are—frank, bold, and self-reliant to a degree. They fear neither man, brute, nor element. They are generous and hospitable; they stand loyally by their friends, and pursue their enemies with bitter and vindictive hatred. For the rest, they differ among themselves in their good and bad points even more markedly than do men in civilized life, for out on the border virtue and wickedness alike take on very pronounced colors. A man who in civilization would be merely a backbiter becomes a murderer on the frontier; and, on the other hand, he who in the city would do nothing more than bid you a cheery good morning, shares his last bit of sun-jerked venison with you when threatened by starvation in the wilderness. (1888.) *Mem. Ed.* IV, 457; *Nat. Ed.* I, 351.

──────────. A single generation, passed under the hard conditions of life in the wilderness, was enough to weld together into one people the representatives of . . . numerous and widely different races; and the children of the next generation became indistinguishable from one another. Long before the first Continental Congress assembled, the backwoodsmen, whatever their blood, had become Americans, one in speech, thought, and character, clutching firmly the land in which their fathers and grandfathers had lived before them. They had lost all remembrance of Europe and all sympathy with things European; they had become as emphatically products native to the soil as were the tough and supple hickories out of which they fashioned the handles of their long, light axes. Their grim, harsh, narrow lives were yet strangely fascinating, and full of adventurous toil and danger; none but natures as strong, as freedom-loving, and as full of bold defiance as theirs could have endured existence on the terms which these men found pleasurable. Their iron surroundings made a mould which turned out all alike in the same shape. They resembled one another, and they differed from the rest of the world—even the world of America, and infinitely more, the world of Europe—in dress, in customs, and in the mode of life. (1889.) *Mem. Ed.* X, 101-102; *Nat. Ed.* VIII, 89.

──────────. The old race of Rocky Mountain hunters and trappers, of reckless, dauntless Indian fighters, is now fast dying out. Yet here and there these restless wanderers of the untrodden wilderness still linger, in wooded fastnesses so inaccessible that the miners have not yet explored them, in mountain valleys so far off that no ranchman has yet driven his herds thither. To this day many of them wear the fringed tunic or hunting-shirt, made of buckskin or homespun, and belted in at the waist—the most picturesque and distinctively national dress ever worn in America. . . .

These old-time hunters have been forerunners of the white advance throughout all our Western land. Soon after the beginning of the present century they boldly struck out beyond the Mississippi, steered their way across the flat and endless seas of grass, or pushed up the valleys of the great lonely rivers, crossed the passes that wound among the towering peaks of the Rockies, toiled over the melancholy wastes of sage-brush and alkali, and at last, breaking through the gloomy woodland that belts the coast, they looked out on the heaving waves of the greatest of all the oceans. They lived for months, often for years, among the Indians, now as friends, now as foes, warring, hunting, and marrying with them; they acted as guides for exploring parties, as scouts for the soldiers who from time to time were sent against the different hostile tribes. At long intervals they came into some frontier settlement or some fur company's fort, posted in the heart of the wilderness, to dispose of their bales of furs, or to replenish their stock of ammunition and purchase a scanty supply of coarse food and clothing.

From that day to this they have not changed their way of life. But there are not many of them left now. The basin of the upper Missouri was their last stronghold, being the last great hunting-ground of the Indians with whom the white trappers were always fighting and bickering, but who nevertheless by their presence protected the game that gave the trappers their livelihood. (1888.) *Mem. Ed.* IV, 455-456; *Nat. Ed.* I, 349-350.

FRONTIERSWOMEN. There are some striking exceptions; but, as a rule, the grinding toil and hardship of a life passed in the wilderness, or on its outskirts, drive the beauty and bloom from a woman's face long before her youth has left her. By the time she is a mother she is sinewy and angular, with thin, compressed lips and furrowed, sallow brow. But she has a hundred qualities that atone for the grace she lacks. She is a good mother and a hard-working housewife, always putting things to rights, washing and cooking for her stalwart spouse and offspring. She is faithful to her husband, and like the true American that she is, exacts faithfulness in return. Peril cannot daunt her, nor hardship and poverty appall her. Whether on the mountains in a log hut chinked with moss, in a sod or adobe hovel on the desolate prairie, or in a mere temporary camp, where the white-topped wagons have been drawn up in a protection-giving circle near some spring, she is equally at home. Clad in a dingy gown and a hideous sunbonnet she goes bravely about her work, resolute, silent, uncomplaining. The children grow up pretty much as fate dictates. Even when very small they seem well able to protect themselves. (1888.) *Mem. Ed.* IV, 476-477; *Nat. Ed.* I, 367-368.

G

GAME—EXTERMINATION OF. The rates of extermination of the different kinds of big game have been very unequal in different localities. Each kind of big game has had its own peculiar habitat in which it throve best, and each has also been found more or less plentifully in other regions where the circumstances were less favorable; and in these comparatively unfavorable regions it early tends to disappear before the advance of man. In consequence, where the ranges of the different game animals overlap and are intertwined, one will disappear first in one locality, and another will disappear first where the conditions are different. (1905.) *Mem. Ed.* III, 124; *Nat. Ed.* II, 497.

GAME HUNTING—ABUSE OF. The custom of shooting great bags of deer, grouse, partridges, and pheasants, the keen rivalry in making such bags, and their publication in sporting journals, are symptoms of a spirit which is most unhealthy from every standpoint. It is to be earnestly hoped that every American hunting or fishing club will strive to inculcate among its own members, and in the minds of the general public, that anything like an excessive bag, any destruction for the sake of making a record, is to be severely reprobated. . . . The professional market hunter who kills game for the hide, or for the feathers, or for the meat, or to sell antlers and other trophies; the market men who put game in cold storage; and the rich people, who are content to buy what they have not the skill to get by their own exertions—these are the men who are the real enemies of game. Where there is no law which checks the market hunters, the inevitable result of their butchery is that the game is completely destroyed and with it their own means of livelihood. (1905.) *Mem. Ed.* III, 269-270; *Nat. Ed.* III, 88.

GAME LAWS—NEED FOR. We need, in the interest of the community at large, a rigid system of game-laws rigidly enforced, and it is not only admissible, but one may almost say necessary, to establish, under the control of the State, great national forest reserves which shall also be breeding-grounds and nurseries for wild game; but I should much regret to see grow up in this country a system of large private game-preserves kept for the enjoyment of the very rich. One of the chief attractions of the life of the wilderness is its rugged and stalwart democracy; there every man stands for what he actually is and can show himself to be. (1893.) *Mem. Ed.* II, 412-413; *Nat. Ed.* II, 353-354.

————————. If we are really alive to our opportunities under our democratic social and political system, we can keep for ourselves—and by "ourselves" I mean the enormous bulk of men whose means range from moderate to very small—ample opportunity for the enjoyment of hunting and shooting, of vigorous and blood-stirring out-of-doors sport. If we fail to take advantage of our possibilities, if we fail to pass, in the interest of all, wise game laws, and to see that these game laws are properly enforced, we shall then have to thank ourselves if in the future the game is only found in the game preserves of the wealthy; and under such circumstances only these same wealthy people will have the chance to hunt it. (1905.) *Mem. Ed.* III, 211; *Nat. Ed.* III, 39.

GAME PRESERVES. The true way to preserve the mule-deer . . . as well as our other game, is to establish on the nation's property great nurseries and wintering grounds, such as the Yellowstone Park, and then to secure fair play for the deer outside these grounds by a wisely planned and faithfully executed series of game-laws. This is the really democratic method of solving the problem. Occasionally even yet some one will assert that the game "belongs to the people, and should be given over to them"—meaning thereby that there should be no game-laws, and that every man should be at liberty indiscriminately to kill every kind of wild animal, harmless, useless, or noxious, until the day when our woods become wholly bereft of all the forms of higher animal life. Such an argument can only be made from the standpoint of those big-game dealers in the cities who care nothing for the future, and desire to make money at the present day by a slaughter which in the last analysis only benefits the wealthy people who are able to pay for the game; for once the game has been destroyed, the livelihood of the professional gunner will be taken away. Most emphatically wild game not on private property does belong to the people, and the only way in which the people can secure their ownership is by protecting it in the interest of all against the vandal few. (1905.) *Mem. Ed.* III, 233-234; *Nat. Ed.* III, 58.

————————. Game reserves should not be established where they are detrimental to the interests of large bodies of settlers, nor yet should they be nominally established in regions so remote that the only men really interfered with are those who respect the law, while a premium is thereby put on the activity of the unscrupulous persons who are eager to break it. Similarly, game-laws should be drawn primarily in the interest of the whole people, keeping steadily in mind certain facts that ought to be self-evident to every one above the intellectual level of those well-meaning persons who apparently think that all shooting is wrong and that man could continue to exist if all wild animals were allowed to increase unchecked. (1910.) *Mem. Ed.* V, 13; *Nat. Ed.* IV, 11.

GAME PRESERVES—BENEFITS OF. The preservation of game and of wild life generally—aside from the noxious species—on these reserves is of incalculable benefit to the people as a whole. As the game increases in these national refuges and nurseries it overflows into the surrounding country. Very wealthy men can have private game-preserves of their own. But the average man of small or moderate means can enjoy the vigorous pastime of the chase, and indeed can enjoy wild nature, only if there are good general laws, properly enforced, for the preservation of the game and wild life, and if, furthermore, there are big parks or reserves provided for the use of all our people, like those of the Yellowstone, the Yosemite, and the Colorado. (1916.) *Mem. Ed.* IV, 10; *Nat. Ed.* III, 192.

GAME PRESERVES—TYPES OF. Game-preserving may be of two kinds. In one the individual landed proprietor, or a group of such individuals, erect and maintain a private game-preserve, the game being their property just as much as domestic animals. Such preserves often fill a useful purpose, and if managed intelligently and with a sense of public spirit and due regard for the interests and feelings of others, may do much good, even in the most democratic community. But wherever the population is sufficiently advanced in intelligence and character, a far preferable and more democratic way of preserving the game is by a system of public preserves, of protected nurseries and breeding-grounds, while the laws define the conditions under which all alike may shoot the game and the restrictions under which all alike must enjoy the privilege. It is in this way that the wild creatures of the forest and the mountain can best and most permanently be preserved. Even in the United States the enactment and observance of such laws has brought about a marked increase in the game of certain localities, as, for instance, New England, during the past thirty years. (Foreword to *The Master of Game* by Edward, second Duke of York; February 15, 1904.) *Mem. Ed.* XIV, 480-481; *Nat. Ed.* XII, 352.

GAME PROTECTION. It will be a real misfortune if our wild animals disappear from mountain, plain, and forest, to be found only, if at all, in great game preserves. It is to the interest of all of us to see that there is ample and real protection for our game as for our woodlands. A true democracy, really alive to its opportunities, will insist upon such game preservation, for it is to the interest of our people as a whole. (Introduction to A. G. Wallihan's *Camera Shots at Big Game*, dated May 31, 1901.) *Mem. Ed.* XIV, 580; *Nat. Ed.* XII, 437.

————————. In order to preserve the wild life of the wilderness at all, some middle ground must be found between brutal and senseless slaughter and the unhealthy sentimentalism which would just as surely defeat its own end by bringing about the eventual total extinction of the game. It is impossible to preserve the larger wild animals in regions thoroughly fit for agriculture; and it is perhaps too much to hope that the larger carnivores can be preserved for merely æsthetic reasons. But throughout our country there are large regions entirely unsuited for agriculture, where, if the people only have foresight, they can, through the power of the State, keep the game in perpetuity. There is no hope of preserving the bison permanently, save in large private parks; but all other game, including not merely deer, but the pronghorn, the splendid bighorn, and the stately and beautiful wapiti, can be kept on the public lands, if only the proper laws are passed, and if only these laws are properly enforced. (1905.) *Mem. Ed.* III, 252; *Nat. Ed.* III, 73.

————————. When genuinely protected, birds and mammals increase so rapidly that it becomes imperative to kill them. If, under such circumstances, their numbers are not kept down by legitimate hunting—and some foolish creatures protest even against legitimate hunting—it would be necessary to have them completely exterminated by paid butchers. But the foolish sentimentalists who do not see this are not as yet the really efficient foes of wild life and of sensible movements for its preservation. The game-hog, the man who commercializes the destruction of game, and the wealthy epicure—all of these, backed by the selfish ignorance which declines to learn, are the real foes with whom we must contend. True lovers of the chase, true sportsmen, true believers in hunting as a manly and vigorous pastime, recognize these men as their worst foes; and the great array of men and women who do not hunt, but who love wild creatures, who love all nature, must discriminate sharply between the two classes. (*Outlook,* January 20, 1915.) *Mem. Ed.* XIV, 570; *Nat. Ed.* XII, 428.

GAME. See also CONSERVATION; FOREST; HUNTING; WILD LIFE.

GAMES. See ATHLETICS; BOXING; FOOTBALL; GYMNASTICS; SPORTS.

GARFIELD, JAMES R. The appointment on March 4, 1907, of James R. Garfield as secretary of the interior led to a new era in the interpretation and enforcement of the laws governing the public lands. His administration of the Interior Department was beyond comparison the best we have ever had. It was based primarily on the conception that it is as much the duty of public-land officials to help the honest settler get title to his claim as it is to prevent the looting of the public lands. (1913.) *Mem. Ed.* XXII, 469; *Nat. Ed.* XX, 403.

GARFIELD, JAMES R. See also CABINET; CONSERVATION.

GARLAND, HAMLIN. Hamlin Garland is a man of letters and a man of action, a lover of nature and a lover of the life of men. For thirty years he has done good work; and never better work than he is doing now. The forests and the high peaks, the green prairies and the dry plains, he knows them as the city man knows his streets and he brings them vivid before the eyes of the reader. Moreover, he knows the men and women of the farms, the cattle-ranchers, and the little raw towns; he knew the old-time wilderness wanderers in their day; and their successors, the forest-rangers, the stockmen who own high-grade cattle, the officers of the law, are his friends today. His heart is tender with sympathy for those beaten down in the hard struggle for life, and aflame with indignation against every form of evil and opression. Whether the crime be one of cunnng or of brutal violence; whether it be by the rich man against the poor or by the mob against the doer of justice; whether it be by the white against the Indian or by the foul man-beast against the woman—it matters not, against all alike he bears burning testimony. And above all, his people are real men and real women; and those for whom he cares, we, who read of them, grow likewise to love; and we are more just and gentle toward our fellowmen, and toward the women who are our sisters, because of what he has written about them. (Appreciation by Theodore Roosevelt used as Foreword.) Hamlin Garland, *They of the High Trails.* (Harper & Bros., N. Y., 1916), p. viii.

GEORGE V. I like him thoroughly. He is a strong man. He is going to make himself felt, not only in England, but in the world, and he will keep well within the constitutional limitations. I don't think he has the tact of Edward, from what I hear; but that may come. But he struck me as one who has a thorough hold on himself and thorough knowledge of the people he is to rule. (Recorded by Butt in letter of June 30, 1910.) *Taft and Roosevelt. The Intimate Letters of Archie Butt.* (Doubleday, Doran & Co., Garden City, N. Y., 1930), I, 428.

GERMAN-AMERICANS. The American citizen of German birth or descent who is a good American and nothing but a good American, and whose whole loyalty is undividedly given to this country and its flag, stands on an exact level wth every other American, and is entitled to precisely the same consideration and treatment as if his ancestors had come over on the *Mayflower* or had settled on the banks of the James three centuries ago. I am partly of German blood, and I am exactly as proud of this blood as of the blood of other strains that flows in my veins. But—I am an American, and nothing else! (*Metropolitan,* October 1915.) *Mem. Ed.* XX, 325; *Nat. Ed.* XVIII, 278.

————. No man can retain his self-respect if he ostensibly remains as an American citizen while he is really doing everything he can do to subordinate the interests and duty of the United States to the interests of a foreign land. You made it evident that your whole heart is with the country of your preference, for Germany, and not with the country of your adoption, the United States. Under such circumstances you are not a good citizen here. But neither are you a good citizen of Germany. You should go home to Germany at once; abandon your American citizenship, if, as I understand, you possess it; and serve in the army, if you are able, or, if not, in any other position in which you can be useful. As far as I am concerned, I admit no divided allegiance in United States citizenship; and my views of hyphenated-Americans are those which were once expressed by the Emperor himself, when he said to Frederick Whitridge that he understood what Germans were; and he understood what Americans were; but he had neither understanding of nor patience with those who called themselves German-Americans. (To Viereck, March 15, 1915.) George Sylvester Viereck, *Roosevelt. A Study in Ambivalence.* (New York, 1919), p. 125.

GERMAN-AMERICANS — CONTRIBUTIONS OF. The German element has contributed much to our national life, and can yet do much more in music, in literature, in art, in sound constructive citizenship. In the greatest of our national crises, the Civil War, a larger percentage of our citizens of recent German origin, than of our citizens of old revolutionary stock, proved loyal to the great ideals of union and liberty. . . . I believe that this country has more to learn from Germany than from any other nation—and this as regards fealty to non-utilitarian ideals, no less than as regards the essentials of social and industrial efficiency, of that species of socialized governmental action which is absolutely necessary for individual protection and general well-being under the conditions of modern industrialism. (1916.) Mem. Ed. XX, 250; Nat. Ed. XVIII, 215.

GERMAN-AMERICANS — DISCRIMINATION AGAINST. It is an outrage to discriminate against a good American in civil life because he is of German blood. It is an even worse outrage for the Government to permit such discrimination against him in the army or in any of the organizations working under government supervision. Let us insist on the immediate stopping of such discriminations, which cruelly wound good Americans and tend to drive them back into the ranks of the half-loyal. (April 16, 1918.) *Roosevelt in the Kansas City Star,* 137.

GERMAN-AMERICANS—DUTY OF. As regards my friends, the Americans of German birth or descent, I can only say that they are in honor bound to regard all international matters solely from the standpoint of the interest of the United States, and of the demands of a lofty international morality. (*Independent,* January 4, 1915.) Mem. Ed. XX, 181; Nat. Ed. XVIII, 155.

GERMAN-AMERICANS, PROFESSIONAL. These men [professional German-Americans] have nothing in common with the great body of Americans who are in whole or in part of German blood, and who are precisely as good Americans as those of any other ancestry. There are not, and never have been, in all our land better citizens than the great mass of the men and women of German birth or descent who have been or are being completely merged in our common American nationality—a nationality distinct from any in Europe, for Americans who are good Americans are no more German-Americans than they are English-Americans or Irish-Americans or Scandinavian-Americans. They are Americans and nothing else. . . .

The professional German-Americans of this type are acting purely in the sinister interest of Germany. They have shown their eager readiness to sacrifice the interest of the United States whenever its interest conflicted with that of Germany. They represent that adherence to the politico-racial hyphen which is the badge and sign of moral treason to the Republic. (To Progressive National Committee, June 22, 1916.) Mem. Ed. XIX, 571; Nat. Ed. XVII, 420.

——————. The time has come to insist that they now drop their dual allegiance, and in good faith become outright Germans or outright Americans. They cannot be both; and those who pretend that they are both, are merely Germans who hypocritically pretend to be Americans in order to serve Germany and damage America. At the moment, the vital thing to remember about these half-hidden traitors is that to attack America's allies, while we are at death grips with a peculiarly ruthless and brutal foe, or to champion that foe as against our allies, or to apologize for that foe's infamous wrongdoing, or to clamor for an early and inconclusive peace, is to be false to the cause of liberty and to the United States.

In this war, either a man is a good American, and therefore is against Germany, and in favor of the allies of America, or he is not an American at all, and should be sent back to Germany where he belongs. (New York *Times,* September 10, 1917.) Mem. Ed. XXI, 36; Nat. Ed. XIX, 31.

GERMAN-AMERICANS IN WAR-TIME.
There is no permanent use in half-measures. It is silly to be lackadaisical over men of German origin having to fight the Germans of Prussianized Germany. Washington and most of his associates were of English origin; nevertheless they fought the British king. If they had not done so we would not now be a nation. If the Americans of German blood do not now fight against Germany and feel against Germany as strongly as the rest of us they are not fit to be Americans at all. (1918.) *Mem. Ed.* XXI, 330; *Nat. Ed.* XIX, 302.

GERMAN-AMERICANS. *See also* AMERICANS, HYPHENATED.

GERMAN DESIGNS ON LATIN AMERICA. I find that the Germans regard our failure to go forward in building up the navy this year as a sign that our spasm of preparation, as they think it, has come to an end; that we shall sink back, so that in a few years they will be in a position to take some step in the West Indies or South America which will make us either put up or shut up on the Monroe doctrine; they counting upon their ability to trounce us if we try the former horn of the dilemma. (To H. C. Lodge, March 27, 1901.) *Lodge Letters* I, 484.

GERMAN DISLIKE OF AMERICA. It was evident that, next to England, America was very unpopular in Germany. The upper classes, stiff, domineering, formal, with the organized army, the organized bureaucracy, the organized industry of their great, highly civilized and admirably administered country behind them, regarded America with a dislike which was all the greater because they could not make it merely contempt. They felt that we were entirely unorganized, that we had no business to be formidable rivals at all in view of our loose democratic governmental methods, and that it was exasperating to feel that our great territory, great natural resources, and strength of individual initiative enabled us in spite of our manifold shortcomings to be formidable industrial rivals of Germany; and, more incredible still, that thanks to our navy and our ocean-protected position, we were in a military sense wholly independent and slightly defiant. (To Sir George Otto Trevelyan, October 1, 1911.) *Mem. Ed.* XXIV, 287; Bishop II, 246.

GERMAN IMMIGRATION. It is almost exactly two hundred and twenty years ago that the first marked immigration from Germany to what were then the colonies in this western hemisphere began. As is inevitable with any pioneers those pioneers of the German race on this side of the ocean had to encounter bitter privation, had to struggle against want in many forms; had to meet and overcome hardship; for the people that go forth to seek their well-being in strange lands must inevitably be ready to pay as the price of success the expenditure of all that there is in them to overcome the obstacles in their way. . . .

Throughout our career of development the German immigration to this country went steadily onward, and they who came here, and their sons and grandsons, played an ever-increasing part in the history of our people—a part that culminated in the Civil War; for every lover of the Union must ever bear in mind what was done in this Commonwealth as in the Commonwealth of Missouri, by the folk of German birth or origin who served so loyally the flag that was theirs by inheritance or adoption. (At the Saengerfest, Baltimore, Md., June 15, 1903.) *Mem. Ed.* XVIII, 42-43; *Nat. Ed.* XVI, 36-37.

GERMAN INVASION OF BELGIUM. This crime of Germany was a crime against international good faith, a crime against the soul of international law and fair dealing. It is to this act of unforgivable treachery that every succeeding infamy is to be traced; from terrorism and indiscriminate slaughter on land to terrorism and indiscriminate massacre of non-combatants at sea. And this crime of Germany has been condoned by the recreant silence of neutral nations, and above all by the recreant silence of the United States and its failure to live bravely up to its solemn promises. (*Metropolitan,* October 1915.) *Mem. Ed.* XX, 333; *Nat. Ed.* XVIII, 286.

GERMAN INVASION OF BELGIUM. *See also* BELGIUM; HAGUE CONVENTIONS; WORLD WAR.

GERMAN LEADERS — POLICIES OF. Those responsible for Germany's policies at the present day are most ardent disciples of, and believers in, Frederick the Great and Bismarck, and not unnaturally have an intense contempt for the mock altruism of so many worthy people who will not face facts—a contempt which Bismarck showed for Motley when Motley very foolishly thrust upon him advice about how to deal with conquered France. Having been trained to believe only in loyalty to the national welfare, and in the kind of international morality characteristic of one pirate among his fellow pirates, they are unable to understand or appreciate the standards of international morality which men like Washington and Lincoln genuinely believed in, which have been practiced on a very large scale for two or three generations by your people in India, and latterly in Egypt and which are now being applied by our own people on a smaller scale in the Philippines and the West Indies. (To Sir George Otto Trevelyan, October 1, 1911.) *Mem. Ed.* XXIV, 266; Bishop II, 228.

GERMAN ORGANIZATION. The efficiency of the German organization, the results of the German preparation in advance, were strikingly shown in the powerful forward movement of the first six weeks of the war and in the steady endurance and resolute resourcefulness displayed in the following months.

Not only is the German organization, the German preparedness, highly creditable to Germany, but even more creditable is the spirit lying behind the organization. The men and women of Germany, from the highest to the lowest, have shown a splendid patriotism and abnegation of self. In reading of their attitude, it is impossible not to feel a thrill of admiration for the stern courage and lofty disinterestedness which this great crisis laid bare in the souls of the people. I most earnestly hope that we Americans, if ever the need may arise, will show similar qualities. (New York *Times*, October 11, 1914.) *Mem Ed.* XX, 54; *Nat. Ed.* XVIII, 46.

GERMAN PATRIOTISM. Our people need to pay homage to the great efficiency and the intense patriotism of Germany. But they need no less fully to realize that this patriotism has at times been accompanied by callous indifference to the rights of weaker nations, and that this efficiency has at times been exercised in a way that represents a genuine set-back to humanity and civilization. (*Everybody's*, January 1915.) *Mem. Ed.* XX, 155; *Nat. Ed.* XVIII, 133.

GERMAN PEOPLE — ADMIRATION FOR. I feel not merely respect but admiration for the German people. I regard their efficiency and their devoted patriotism and steady endurance as fraught with significant lessons to us. I believe that they have permitted themselves to be utterly misled, and have permitted their government to lead them in the present war into a course of conduct which, if persevered in, would make them the permanent enemy of all the free and liberty-loving nations of mankind and of civilization itself. But I believe that sooner or later they will recover their senses and make their government go right. I shall continue to cherish the friendliest feelings toward the Germans individually, and for Germany collectively as soon as Germany collectively comes to her senses. (1916.) *Mem. Ed.* XX, 252; *Nat. Ed.* XVIII, 217.

GERMAN PEOPLE AND GOVERNMENT. There are plenty of Americans like myself who immensely admire the efficiency of the Germans in industry and in war, the efficiency with which in this war they have subordinated the whole social and industrial activity of the state to the successful prosecution of the war, and who greatly admire the German people, and regard the Germain strain as one of the best and strongest strains in our composite American blood; but who feel that the German Government, the German governing class has in this war shown such ruthless and domineering disregard for the rights of others as to demand emphatic and resolute action (not merely words unbacked by action) on our part. Unfortunately, this ruthless and brutal efficiency has, as regards many men of the pacifist type, achieved precisely the purpose it was intended to achieve. (*Metropolitan*, August 1915.) *Mem. Ed.* XX, 356; *Nat. Ed.* XVIII, 305.

GERMAN SYMPATHIZERS. The men who oppose the war; who fail to support the government in every measure which really tends to the efficient prosecution of the war; and above all who in any shape or way champion the cause and the actions of Germany, show themselves to be the Huns within our own gates and the allies of the men whom our sons and brothers are crossing the ocean to fight. (October 1, 1917.) *Roosevelt in the Kansas City Star*, 8.

GERMAN UNREST—CAUSE OF. He [William II] kept saying that he thought it was the business of those who believe in monarchical government to draw the teeth of the Socialists by remedying all real abuses. I went over the problems at length with him from this standpoint. Of course it was not necessary or advisable that I should speak to him about one thing that had struck me much in Germany, namely, that the discontent was primarily political rather than economic; in other words, that the very real unrest among the lower classes sprung not from a sense that they were treated badly economically, but from the knowledge that it rested not with themselves, but with others as to how they should be treated, whether well or ill, and that this was galling to them. (To Sir George Otto

Trevelyan, October 1, 1911.) *Mem. Ed.* XXIV, 301; Bishop II, 257.

GERMAN WAR PLANS. The German war plans contemplate, as I happen to know personally, as possible courses of action, flank marches through both Belgium and Switzerland. They are under solemn treaty to respect the territories of both countries, and they have not the slightest thought of paying the least attention to these treaties unless they are threatened with war as the result of their violation. (To H. C. Lodge, September 12, 1911.) Lodge *Letters* II, 409.

GERMAN WOMEN. I hope it is not ungallant of me to say that the North German women of the upper classes were less attractive than the corresponding women of any country I visited. They have fine domestic qualities, and if only they keep these qualities, then the question of their attractiveness is, from the standpoint of the race, of altogether minor importance. But these domestic virtues seem to have been acquired at the cost of other attributes, which many other women, who are at least as good wives and mothers as the German women, do not find it necessary to sacrifice. Perhaps they are cowed in their home life. Their husbands, who also have fine qualities, not only wish to domineer over the rest of mankind—which is not always possible—but wish to, and do, domineer over their own wives. Whether because of this, or for some other reason, these same wives certainly did not seem attractive in the sense not only that their more southern neighbors were, but their more northern neighbors, like the Swedes. (To Sir George Otto Trevelyan, October 1, 1911.) *Mem. Ed.* XXIV, 293; Bishop II, 251.

GERMANY—CONDEMNATION OF. Germany has trampled under foot every device of international law for securing the protection of the weak and unoffending. She has shown an utter disregard of all considerations of pity, mercy, humanity, and international morality. She has counted upon the terror inspired by her ruthless brutality to protect her from retaliation or interference.

The outrages committed on our own people have been such as the United States has never before been forced to endure, and have included the repeated killing of our men, women and children. The sinking of the *Marina* and the *Cheming* the other day, with the attendant murder of six Americans, was but the most recent in an unbroken chain of injuries and insults, which by comparison make mere wrong to our property interests sink into absolute insignificance.

As long as neutrals keep silent, or speak apologetically, or take refuge in the futilities of the professional pacifists, there will be no cessation in these brutalities. (To F. W. Whitridge, December 15, 1916.) *Mem. Ed.* XXIV, 538; Bishop II, 460.

——————. In international relations, the Prussianized Germany of to-day stands for ruthless self-aggrandizement, and contempt for the rights of other nations. She stands for the rule of might over right; of power over justice. If Germany now conquered France and England, we would be the next victim; and if the conquest took place at this moment we would be a helpless victim. (1917.) *Mem. Ed.* XXI, 5; *Nat. Ed.* XIX, 5.

GERMANY—DEBT TO. From Germany this country has learned much. Germany has contributed a great element to the blood of our people, and it has given the most marked trend ever given to our scholastic and university system, to the whole system of training students and scholars. In taking what we should from Germany, from this great kindred nation, I wish that we could take especially the idealism which renders it natural to them to celebrate such an event as Schiller's life and writings; and also the keen, practical common-sense which enables them to turn their idealistic spirit into an instrument for producing the most perfect military and industrial organizations that this world has ever seen. (At Clark University, Worcester, Mass., June 21, 1905.) *Presidential Addresses and State Papers* IV, 393-394.

GERMANY—PEACE TERMS WITH. We should accept from Germany what our Allies have wrung from Austria and Turkey—unconditional surrender. This ought to be our war aim; and until this war aim is achieved the peace terms should be discussed only with our Allies and not with our enemies. In broad outline, it is possible now to state what these peace terms should include: Restitution by Germany of what she has taken and atonement for the wrong she has done; her complete military withdrawal from every foot of territory outside her own limits; and the giving not of "autonomy"—a slippery word used by slippery people to mean anything or nothing—but of complete independence to the races subject to the dominion of Germany, Austria, and Turkey. (1918.) *Mem. Ed.* XXI, 255; *Nat. Ed.* XIX, 237.

GERMANY — ROOSEVELT'S RECEPTION IN. It was curious and interesting to notice the contrast between my reception in Germany and my reception in the other countries of Europe which I had already visited or visited afterward. Everywhere else I was received, as I have said, with practically as much enthusiasm as in my own country when I was President. In Germany I was treated with proper civility, all the civility which I had a right to demand and expect; and no more. In Paris the streets were decorated with French and American flags in my honor. . . . In Berlin the authorities showed me every courtesy, and the people all proper civility. But excepting the university folk, they really did not want to see me. When I left Sweden I left a country where tens of thousands of people gathered on every occasion to see me; every station was jammed with them. When I came into Germany a few hundred might be at each station, or might not be. They were courteous, decorously enthusiastic, and that was all. It was just the same on our trip from Berlin to London. We were given the royal carriage, and every attention shown us by the officials; at each station there were a few score or a few hundred people, polite and mildly curious. . . .

The Germans did not like me, and did not like my country; and under the circumstances they behaved entirely correctly, showing me every civility and making no pretense of an enthusiasm which was not present. (To Sir George Otto Trevelyan, October 1, 1911.) *Mem. Ed.* XXIV, 286; Bishop II, 245, 246.

GERMANY—TREATMENT OF. As for crushing Germany or crippling her and reducing her to political impotence, such an action would be a disaster to mankind. The Germans are not merely brothers; they are largely ourselves. The debt we owe to German blood is great; the debt we owe to German thought and to German example, not only in governmental administration, but in all the practical work of life, is even greater. Every generous heart and every far-seeing mind throughout the world should rejoice in the existence of a stable, united, and powerful Germany, too strong to fear aggression and too just to be a source of fear to its neighbors. (New York *Times*, October 11, 1914.) *Mem. Ed.* XX, 58; *Nat. Ed.* XVIII, 49.

——————. Those of us who believe in unconditional surrender regard Germany's behavior during the last five years as having made her the outlaw among nations. In private life sensible men and women do not negotiate with an outlaw or grow sentimental about him, or ask for a peace with him on terms of equality if he will give up his booty. Still less do they propose to make a league with him for the future, and on the strength of this league to abolish the sheriff and take the constable. On the contrary, they expect the law officers to take him by force and to have him tried and punished. They do not punish him out of revenge, but because all intelligent persons know punishment to be necessary in order to stop certain kinds of criminals from wrong-doing and to save the community from such wrong-doing.

We ought to treat Germany in precisely this manner. It is a sad and dreadful thing to have to face some months or a year or so of additional bloodshed, but it is a much worse thing to quit now and have the children now growing up obliged to do the job all over again, with ten times as much bloodshed and suffering, when their turn comes. The surest way to secure a peace as lasting as that which followed the downfall of Napoleon is to overthrow the Prussianized Germany of the Hohenzollerns as Napoleon was overthrown. If we enter into a league of peace with Germany and her vassal allies, we must expect them to treat the arrangement as a scrap of paper whenever it becomes to their interest to do so. (Kansas City *Star*, October 26, 1918.) *Mem. Ed.* XXI, 418; *Nat. Ed.* XIX, 379.

GERMANY AND AMERICA. As an American I should advocate—as a matter of fact do advocate—keeping our navy at a pitch that will enable us to interfere promptly if Germany ventures to touch a foot of American soil. I would not go into the abstract rights or wrongs of it; I would simply say that we did not intend to have Germans on the continent, excepting as immigrants, whose children would become Americans of one sort or another, and if Germany intended to extend her empire here she would have to whip us first. (To Cecil Arthur Spring-Rice, August 11, 1897.) *Mem. Ed.* XXIII, 92; Bishop I, 78.

——————. Of all the nations of Europe it seems to me Germany is by far the most hostile to us. With Germany under the Kaiser we may at any time have trouble if she seeks to acquire territory in South America. (To F. C. Moore, February 5, 1898.) *Mem. Ed.* XXIII, 92; Bishop I, 79.

GERMANY AND DEMOCRACY. Germany stands as the antithesis of democracy. She exults in her belief that in England democracy has broken down. She exults in the fact that in America democracy has shown itself so utterly futile that it has not even dared to speak about wrong-doing committed against others, and has not dared to do more than speak, without acting, when the wrong was done against itself. (*Metropolitan,* November 1915.) *Mem. Ed.* XX, 386; *Nat. Ed.* XVIII, 330.

GERMANY AND ENGLAND. I do not believe that Germany consciously and of set purpose proposes to herself the idea of a conquest of England, but Germany has the arrogance of a very strong power, as yet almost untouched by that feeble aspiration toward international equity which one or two other strong powers, notably England and America, do at least begin to feel. Germany would like to have a strong navy so that whenever England does something she does not like she could at once assume toward England the tone she has assumed toward France. The Morocco incident shows how far Germany is willing to go in doing what she believes her interest and her destiny demand, in disregard of her own engagements and of the equities of other peoples. If she had a navy as strong as that of England, I do not believe that she would *intend* to use it for the destruction of England; but I do believe that incidents would be very likely to occur which might make her so use it. (To Sir George Otto Trevelyan, October 1, 1911.) *Mem. Ed.* XXIV, 296; Bishop II, 253.

GERMANY. See also ALGECIRAS CONFERENCE; ARBITRATION; BELGIUM; FREDERICK THE GREAT; HAGUE CONVENTIONS; *Lusitania*; MONROE DOCTRINE; PATRIOTISM; SUBMARINE WARFARE; WILLIAM II; WORLD WAR.

GETTYSBURG. As long as this Republic endures or its history is known, so long shall the memory of the Battle of Gettysburg likewise endure and be known; and as long as the English tongue is understood, so long shall Abraham Lincoln's Gettysburg speech thrill the hearts of mankind. . . .

He is but a poor American who, looking at this field, does not feel within himself a deeper reverence for the nation's past and a higher purpose to make the nation's future rise level to her past. Here fought the chosen sons of the North and the South, the East and the West. (At Gettysburg, Pa., May 30, 1904.) *Mem. Ed.* XII, 607, 608; *Nat. Ed.* XI, 324, 325.

GIRAFFE. See ANIMALS—PROTECTIVE COLORATION OF.

GLADSTONE, WILLIAM. Mr. Gladstone's wide range of scholarship, and extensive—possibly more extensive than profound—acquaintance with many different branches of learning, none would deny; yet it is perhaps not unfair to say that his speculations attract attention less for their own merits than because of the fame their author has won as an orator and politician. (*Cosmopolitan,* December 1892.) *Mem. Ed.* XIV, 370; *Nat. Ed.* XII, 304.

GOAT, WHITE. Of all American game the white goat is the least wary and most stupid. In places where it is much hunted it of course gradually grows wilder and becomes difficult to approach and kill; and much of its silly tameness is doubtless due to the inaccessible nature of its haunts, which renders it ordinarily free from molestation; but aside from this it certainly seems as if it was naturally less wary than either deer or mountain-sheep. The great point is to get above it. All its foes live in the valleys, and while it is in the mountains, if they strive to approach it at all, they must do so from below. It is in consequence always on the watch for danger from beneath; but it is easily approached from above, and then, as it generally tries to escape by running uphill, the hunter is very apt to get a shot.

Its chase is thus laborious rather than exciting; and to my mind it is less attractive than is the pursuit of most of our other game. Yet it has an attraction of its own, after all; while the grandeur of the scenery amid which it must be carried on, the freedom and hardihood of the life, and the pleasure of watching the queer habits of the game, all combine to add to the hunter's enjoyment. (1893.) *Mem. Ed.* II, 115-116; *Nat. Ed.* II, 101-102.

——————. The white goat is the only game beast of America which has not decreased in numbers since the arrival of the white man. Although in certain localities it is now decreasing, yet, taken as a whole, it is probably quite as plentiful now as it was fifty years back; for in the early part of the present century there were Indian tribes who hunted it perseveringly to make the skins into robes, whereas now they get blankets from the traders and no longer persecute the goats. The early trappers and mountain-men knew but little of the animal. Whether they were after beaver or were hunting big game or were merely exploring, they kept to the valleys; there was no inducement for them to climb to the tops of the mountains; so it resulted that there was no animal with which the old hunters were so unfamiliar as with the white goat. The professional hunters of to-day likewise bother it but little; they do not care to undergo severe toil for an animal with worthless flesh and a hide of little value —for it is only in the late fall and winter that the long hair and fine wool give the robe any beauty.

So the quaint, sturdy, musky beasts, with their queer and awkward ways, their boldness and their stupidity, with their white coats and big black hoofs, black muzzles, and sharp, gently curved, span-long black horns, have held their own well among the high mountains that they love. (1893.) *Mem. Ed.* II, 118-119; *Nat. Ed.* II, 104.

GOETHALS, GEORGE W. The work [of digging the Panama Canal] as a whole has been done under the direction of an army officer, Colonel Goethals, whose name is not very familiar to the people here in the United States; and yet, I think, this country at this time owes as much to him as any country in the world owes to any public men now performing a public duty. I am not speaking hyperbolically. I have had some historical training myself, and I am using exactly the words that I think describe the case, when I say what I have said. I believe that, excepting a certain number of men who have taken part in the wars which founded and perpetuated this Republic, there is no body of our citizens of similar size which has more emphatically deserved well of the Republic than the men engaged in doing that work down at Panama, men like Doctor Gorgas, Mr. Bishop, all the engineer officers, and above all Colonel Goethals. It is he to whom we owe most—to whom we owe more than to any other one man for what has been done down there. . . .

And remember, Colonel Goethals does not profit pecuniarily by doing that wonderful work in our interest. He will finish it as part of his duty as an army officer and then take any other detail to which he is assigned; and so far from being properly rewarded by this government, he will be uncommonly lucky if he is not ferociously attacked should any effort be made to recognize his great services by giving him some special promotion. (At Harvard University, Cambridge, December 14, 1910.) *Mem. Ed.* XV, 556-557; *Nat. Ed.* XIII, 602-603.

GOLD STANDARD. We . . . believe in the gold standard as fixed by the usage and verdict of the business world, and in a sound monetary system, as matters of principle; as matters not of momentary political expediency, but of permanent organic policy. In 1896 and again in 1900 far-sighted men, without regard to their party fealty in the past, joined to work against what they regarded as a debased monetary system. The policies which they championed have been steadfastly adhered to by the Administration; and by the act of March 14, 1900, Congress established the single gold standard as the measure of our monetary value. (Letter accepting nomination for Presidency, September 12, 1904.) *Mem. Ed.* XVIII, 508-509; *Nat. Ed.* XVI, 380-381.

GOLD STANDARD. See also CURRENCY; SILVER.

GOLDEN RULE. See TEN COMMANDMENTS.

GOOD GOVERNMENT. See GOVERNMENT.

GORKY, MAXIM. The Gorky class of realistic writer of poems and short stories is a class of beings for whom I have no very great regard *per se;* but I would not have the slightest objection to receiving him, and indeed would be rather glad to receive him, if he was merely a member of it. But in addition he represents the very type of fool academic revolutionist which tends to bring to confusion and failure the great needed measures of social, political, and industrial reform. (Letter of April 23, 1906.) *Mem. Ed.* XXIV, 15; Bishop II, 12.

GOVERNING CLASS, THE. The weakling and the coward are out of place in a strong and free community. In a republic like ours the governing class is composed of the strong men who take the trouble to do the work of government; and if you are too timid or too fastidious or too careless to do your part in this work, then you forfeit your right to be considered one of the governing and you become one of the governed instead—one of the driven cattle of the political arena. (At the Harvard Union, Cambridge, February 23, 1907.) *Mem. Ed.* XV, 487; *Nat. Ed.* XIII, 563.

———————. Mr. Taft's position is perfectly clear. It is that we have in this country a special class of persons wiser than the people, who are above the people, who cannot be reached by the people, but who govern them and ought to govern them; and who protect various classes of the people from the whole people. That is the old, old doctrine which has been acted upon for thousands of years abroad; and which here in America has been acted upon sometimes openly, sometimes secretly, for forty years by many men in public and in private life, and I am sorry to say by many judges; a doctrine which has in fact tended to create a bulwark for privilege, a bulwark unjustly protecting special interests against the rights of the people as a whole. This doctrine is to me a dreadful doctrine; for its effect is, and can only be, to make the courts the shield of privilege against popular rights. Naturally, every upholder and beneficiary of crooked privilege loudly applauds the doctrine. It is behind the shield of that doctrine that crooked clauses creep into laws, that men of wealth and power control legislation. The men of wealth who praise this doctrine, this theory, would do well to remember that to its adoption by the courts is due the distrust so many of our wage-workers now feel for the courts. I deny that that theory has worked so well that we should continue it. I most earnestly urge that the evils and abuses it has produced cry aloud for remedy; and the only remedy is in fact to restore the power to govern directly to the people, and to make the public servants directly responsible to the whole people—and to no part of them, to no "class" of them. (At Carnegie Hall, New York City, March 20, 1912.) *Mem. Ed.* XIX, 213; *Nat. Ed.* XVII, 162.

GOVERNMENT—THE PEOPLE AND THE. The attempt has recently been made to improve on Abraham Lincoln's statement that "this is a government of the people, for the people, by the people." As a substitute therefor it is proposed that this government shall hereafter be a government of the people, for the people, by a representative part of the people.

It is always a dangerous matter to try to improve on Lincoln when we deal with the rights and duties of the people, and this particular attempt at improvement is not a happy one. In substance it of course means nothing except that this is to be a government of the whole people by a part of the people. We have had such a government in various parts of this Union from time to time, and stripped of verbiage it simply means a government of the people by the bosses; a government of the whole people against instead of for the interest of the whole people by a part of the people which does the bidding of the holders of political and financial privilege. (At St. Louis, Mo., March 28, 1912.) *Mem. Ed.* XIX, 234; *Nat. Ed.* XVII, 172.

————————. We propose that the people shall control both the legislatures and the courts, not to pervert the Constitution, but to overthrow those who themselves pervert the Constitution into an instrument for perpetuating injustice, instead of making it what it must and shall be made, the most effective of all possible means for securing to the people of the whole country the right everywhere to create conditions which will tend for the uplift of the ordinary, the average men, women, and children of the United States. (Before National Conference of Progressive Service, Portsmouth, R. I., July 2, 1913.) *Mem. Ed.* XIX, 527; *Nat. Ed.* XVII, 387.

————————. We hold that all the agencies of government belong to the people, that the Constitution is theirs, and that the courts are theirs. The people should exercise their power, not to overthrow either the Constitution or the courts, but to overthrow those who would pervert them into agents against the popular welfare. We believe that where a public servant misrepresents the people, the people should have the right to remove him from office, and that where the legislature enacts a law which it should not enact or fails to enact a law which it should enact, the people should have the right on their own initiative to supply the omission. We do not believe that either power should be loosely or wantonly used, and we would provide for its exercise in a way which would make its exercise safe; but the power is necessary, and it should be provided. (*Century Magazine*, October 1913.) *Mem. Ed.* XIX, 550; *Nat. Ed.* XVII, 405.

GOVERNMENT, AMERICAN. This great Republic of ours shall never become the government of a plutocracy, and it shall never become the government of a mob. God willing, it shall remain what our fathers who founded it meant it to be—a government in which each man stands on his worth as a man, where each is given the largest personal liberty consistent with securing the well-being of the whole, and where, so far as in us lies, we strive continually to secure for each man such equality of opportunity that in the strife of life he may have a fair chance to show the stuff that is in him. (At Jamestown Exposition, Va., April 26, 1907.) *Mem. Ed.* XII, 595; *Nat. Ed.* XI, 314.

GOVERNMENT, FREE. Free government is only for nations that deserve it; and they lose all right to it by licentiousness, no less than by servility. If a nation cannot govern itself, it makes comparatively little difference whether its inability springs from a slavish and craven distrust of its own powers, or from sheer incapacity on the part of its citizens to exercise self-control and to act together. Self-governing freemen must have the power to accept necessary compromises, to make necessary concessions, each sacrificing somewhat of prejudice, even of principle, and every group must show the necessary subordination of its particular interests to the interests of the community as a whole. When the people will not or cannot work together; when they permit groups of extremists to decline to accept anything that does not coincide with their own extreme views, or when they let power slip from their hands through sheer supine indifference; then they have themselves chiefly to blame if the power is grasped by stronger hands. (1900.) *Mem. Ed.* XIII, 424; *Nat. Ed.* X, 304.

————————. It is no light task for a nation to achieve the temperamental qualities without which the institutions of free government are but an empty mockery. Our people are now successfully governing themselves, because for more than a thousand years they have been slowly fitting themselves, sometimes consciously, sometimes unconsciously, toward this end. (First Annual Message, Washington, December 3, 1901.) *Mem. Ed.* XVII, 128; *Nat. Ed.* XV, 110-111.

————————. All of us, you and I, all of us together, want to rule ourselves, and we don't wish to have any body of outsiders rule us. That is what free government means. If people cannot rule themselves, then they are not fit for free government, and all talk about democracy is a sham.

And this is aside from the fact that in actual life here in the United States experience has shown that the effort to substitute for the genuine rule of the people something else always means the rule of privilege in some form or other, sometimes political privilege, sometimes financial privilege, often a mixture of both. (At St. Louis, Mo., March 28, 1912.) *Mem. Ed.* XIX, 236; *Nat. Ed.* XVII, 173.

GOVERNMENT, GOOD. The end is good government, obtained through genuine popular rule. Any device that under given conditions achieves this end is good for those conditions, and the value of each device must be tested purely by the answer to the question, Does it or does it not secure the end in view? One of the worst faults that can be committed by practical men engaged in the difficult work of self-government is to make a fetich of a name, or to confound the means with the end. The end is to secure justice, equality of opportunity in industrial as well as in political matters, to safeguard the interests of all the people, and work for a system which shall promote the general diffusion of well-being and yet give ample rewards to those who in any walk of life and in any kind of work render exceptional service to the community as a whole. (*Outlook*, January 21, 1911.) *Mem. Ed.* XIX, 97; *Nat. Ed.* XVII, 62.

GOVERNMENT, GOOD—ENDS OF. The ends of good government in our democracy are to secure by genuine popular rule a high average of moral and material well-being among our citizens. (Before Ohio Constitutional Convention, Columbus, February 21, 1912.) *Mem. Ed.* XIX, 169; *Nat. Ed.* XVII, 124.

GOVERNMENT, GOOD — ESSENTIALS FOR. There isn't any great genius needed to carry on our government well. We need ability, but it is the kind of ability that is common enough among average citizens, only it is the ability carried to a greater degree of perfection than the average man possesses. You want to have a man of ability just as you want to have a man of ability as the engineer of a first-class flying express-train. In the next place you want a man of honesty, and when I say "honesty" I do not mean merely that the man won't steal himself. I don't mean merely that kind of timid honesty which travels in blinders and if told that there is corruption on the right and left hand, says with nervous haste, "But I don't see it," because he can't see it. I mean truculent, aggressive honesty. (At Elmira, N. Y., October 14, 1910.) *Mem. Ed.* XIX, 45; *Nat. Ed.* XVII, 35.

GOVERNMENT, GOOD—FOUNDATION OF. There never can be, there never will be a good government in which the average citizen is not a decent man in private life. It is a contradiction in terms to speak of a good government if the good government does not rest upon cleanliness and decency in the home, respect of husband and wife for one another, tenderness of the man for those dependent upon him, performance of duty by woman and by man, and the proper education of the children who are to make the next generation. The vital things in life are the things that foolish people look upon as commonplace. The vital deeds of life are those things which it lies within the reach of each of us to do, and the failure to perform which means the destruction of the State. (At Montgomery, Ala., October 24, 1905.) *Presidential Addresses and State Papers* IV, 529.

————————. It cannot be too often repeated that there is no patent device for securing good government; that after all is said and done, after we have given full credit to every

[210]

scheme for increasing our material prosperity, to every effort of the lawmaker to provide a system under which each man shall be best secured in his own rights, it yet remains true that the great factor in working out the success of this giant republic of the Western continent must be the possession of those qualities of essential virtue and essential manliness which have built up every great and mighty people of the past, and the lack of which always has brought, and always will bring, the proudest of nations crashing down to ruin. (At Pan-American Exposition, Buffalo, May 20, 1901.) *Mem. Ed.* XV, 312; *Nat. Ed.* XIII, 446.

―――――――. In achieving good government the fundamental factor must be the character of the average citizen; that average citizen's power of hatred for what is mean and base and unlovely; his fearless scorn of cowardice and his determination to war unyieldingly against the dark and sordid forces of evil. (At Antietam, Md., September 17, 1903.) *Mem. Ed.* XII, 624; *Nat. Ed.* XI, 337.

GOVERNMENT, INVISIBLE. The selfish opposition of the great corporation lawyers and of their clients is entirely intelligent; for these men alone are the beneficiaries of the present reign of hidden, of invisible, government, and they rely primarily on well-meaning but reactionary courts to thwart the forward movement. (*Century Magazine,* October 1913.) *Mem. Ed.* XIX, 551; *Nat. Ed.* XVII, 407.

GOVERNMENT, POPULAR. In every great crisis of the kind we face to-day, we find arrayed on one side the men who with fervor and broad sympathy and lofty idealism stand for the forward movement, the men who stand for the uplift and betterment of mankind, and who have faith in the people; and over against them the men of restricted vision and contracted sympathy, whose souls are not stirred by the wrongs of others. Side by side with the latter, appear the other men who lack all intensity of conviction, who care only for the pleasure of the day; and also those other men who distrust the people, who if dishonest wish to keep the people helpless so as to exploit them, and who if honest so disbelieve in the power of the people to bring about wholesome reform that every appeal to popular conscience and popular intelligence fills them with an angry terror. According to their own lights, these men are often very respectable, very worthy, but they live on a plane of low ideals. In the atmosphere they create impostors flourish, and leadership comes to be thought of only as success in making money, and the vision of heaven becomes a sordid vision, and all that is highest and purest in human nature is laughed at, and honesty is bought and sold in the market-place. (At Chicago, June 17, 1912.) *Mem. Ed.* XIX, 312; *Nat. Ed.* XVII, 227.

―――――――. For years I accepted the theory, as most of the rest of us then accepted it, that we already had popular government; that this was a government by the people. I believed the power of the boss was due only to the indifference and short-sightedness of the average decent citizen. Gradually it came over me that while this was half the truth, it was only half the truth, and that while the boss owed part of his power to the fact that the average man did not do his duty, yet that there was the further fact to be considered, that for the average man it had already been made very difficult instead of very easy for him to do his duty. I grew to feel a keen interest in the machinery for getting adequate and genuine popular rule, chiefly because I found that we could not get social and industrial justice without popular rule, and that it was immensely easier to get such popular rule by the means of machinery of the type of direct nominations at primaries, the short ballot, the initiative, referendum, and the like. (*Outlook,* October 12, 1912.) *Mem. Ed.* XIX, 436; *Nat. Ed.* XVII, 316.

GOVERNMENT, POPULAR — FITNESS FOR. Many eminent lawyers who more or less frankly disbelieve in our entire American system of government for, by, and of the people, . . . believe, and sometimes assert, that the American people are not fitted for popular government, and that it is necessary to keep the judiciary "independent of the majority or all of the people"; that there must be no appeal to the people from the decision of a court in any case; and that therefore the judges are to be established as sovereign rulers over the people.

I take absolute issue with all those who hold such a position. I regard it as a complete negation of our whole system of government; and if it became the dominant position in this country, it would mean the absolute upsetting of both the rights and the rule of the people.

If the American people are not fit for popular government, and if they should of right be the servants and not the masters of the men whom they themselves put in office, then Lincoln's work was wasted and the whole system of government upon which this great democratic Republic rests is a failure.

I believe, on the contrary, with all my heart

that the American people are fit for complete self-government, and that, in spite of all our failings and shortcomings, we of this Republic have more nearly realized than any other people on earth the ideal of justice attained through genuine popular rule. (Before Ohio Constitutional Convention, Columbus, February 21, 1912.) *Mem. Ed.* XIX, 188; *Nat. Ed.* XVII, 140.

GOVERNMENT, STRONG. A strong people need never fear a strong man or a strong government; for a strong government is the most efficient instrument, and a strong man the most efficient servant, of a strong people. It is an admission of popular weakness to be afraid of strong public servants and of an efficient governmental system. But it is an even more culpable weakness for the people not to shape their governmental system so that they retain in their own hands absolute control over both their servants and their agencies of government. *Outlook,* November 15, 1913, p. 590.

——————. In the past free peoples have generally split and sunk on that great rock of difficulty caused by the fact that a government which recognizes the liberties of the people is not usually strong enough to preserve the liberties of the people against outside aggression. Washington and Lincoln believed that ours was a strong people and therefore fit for a strong government. They believed that it was only weak peoples that had to fear strong governments, and that to us it was given to combine freedom and efficiency. (*Outlook,* September 23, 1914.) *Mem. Ed.* XX, 30; *Nat. Ed.* XVIII, 26.

GOVERNMENT AND THE INDIVIDUAL. While we are not to be excused if we fail to do whatever is possible through the agency of government, we must keep ever in mind that no action of the government, no action by combination among ourselves, can take the place of the individual qualities to which in the long run every man must owe the success he can make of life. There never has been devised, and there never will be devised, any law which will enable a man to succeed save by the exercise of those qualities which have always been the prerequisites of success—the qualities of hard work, of keen intelligence, of unflinching will. Such action can supplement those qualities but it cannot take their place. No action by the State can do more than supplement the initiative of the individual; and ordinarily the action of the State can do no more than to secure to each individual the chance to show under as favorable conditions as possible the stuff that there is in him. (At Providence, R. I., August 23, 1902.) *Mem. Ed.* XVIII, 80-81; *Nat. Ed.* XVI, 67-68.

GOVERNMENT. *See also* ADMINISTRATION; BUREAUCRACY; DIVISION OF POWERS; EXPERTS; INITIATIVE; LEGISLATION; MUNICIPAL GOVERNMENT; PARLIAMENTARY GOVERNMENT; POPULAR RULE; PRIMARIES; RECALL; REFERENDUM; REPUBLICAN GOVERNMENT; SELF-GOVERNMENT.

GOVERNMENT CONTROL OF BUSINESS. I do not believe in the government interfering with private business more than is necessary. I do not believe in the government undertaking any work which can with propriety be left in private hands. But neither do I believe in the government flinching from overseeing any work when it becomes evident that abuses are sure to obtain therein unless there is governmental supervision. (Fifth Annual Message, Washington, December 5, 1905.) *Mem. Ed.* XVII, 321; *Nat. Ed.* XV, 275.

——————. [The] extension of the national power to oversee and secure correct behavior in the management of all great corporations engaged in interstate business will . . . render far more stable the present system by doing away with those grave abuses which are not only evil in themselves but are also evil because they furnish an excuse for agitators to inflame well-meaning people against all forms of property, and to commit the country to schemes of wild, would-be remedy which would work infinitely more harm than the disease itself. The government ought not to conduct the business of the country; but it ought to regulate it so that it shall be conducted in the interest of the public. (At Harrisburg, Pa., October 4, 1906.) *Mem. Ed.* XVIII, 87; *Nat. Ed.* XVI, 73.

GOVERNMENT CONTROL. *See also* BUSINESS; COMBINATIONS; CORPORATIONS; INDUSTRIAL COMMISSION; INSURANCE COMPANIES; INTERSTATE COMMERCE COMMISSION; MONOPOLIES; RAILROADS; SHERMAN ANTI-TRUST ACT; TRUSTS.

GOVERNMENT EMPLOYEES — CARE OF. The National Government should be a model employer. It should demand the highest quality of service from its employees and should care for them properly in return. Congress should adopt legislation providing limited but definite compensation for accidents to all workmen within the scope of the Federal power, including employees in navy-yards and arsenals. (At Jamestown Exposition, Va., June 10, 1907.) *Mem. Ed.* XVIII, 242; *Nat. Ed.* XVI, 179.

GOVERNMENT EMPLOYEES. *See also* CIVIL SERVICE; EIGHT-HOUR DAY; LABOR UNIONS; MERIT SYSTEM; OPEN SHOP.

GOVERNMENT OF LAW AND MEN. Ours is a government of laws, but every one should keep always before him the fact that no law is worth anything unless there is the right kind of man behind it. In tropical America there are many republics whose constitutions and laws are practically identical with ours, yet some of these republics have, throughout their governmental career, alternated between despotism and anarchy, and have failed in striking fashion at every point where in equally striking fashion we have succeeded. The difference was not in the laws or the institutions, for they were the same. The difference was in the men who made up the community, in the men who administered the laws, and in the men who put in power the administrators. (*Outlook*, January 21, 1911.) *Mem. Ed.* XIX, 98; *Nat. Ed.* XVII, 63.

————. This is a government of law, but it is also, as every government always has been and always must be, a government of men; for the worth of a law depends as much upon the men who interpret and administer it as upon the men who have enacted it. (*Outlook*, March 4, 1911.) *Mem. Ed.* XIX, 126; *Nat. Ed.* XVII, 88.

GOVERNMENT OF LAW AND MEN. *See also* CONSTITUTION; COURTS; JUDICIARY; JUSTICE; LAW; LEGALISM.

GOVERNMENT OWNERSHIP. Government ownership should be avoided wherever possible; our purpose should be to steer between the anarchy of unregulated individualism and the deadening formalism and inefficiency of wide-spread State ownership. From time to time it has been found, and will be found, necessary for the government to own and run certain businesses, the uninterrupted prosecution of which is necessary to the public welfare and which cannot be adequately controlled in any other way, but normally this is as inadvisable as to permit such business concerns to be free from all government supervision and direction. Normally, and save where the necessity is clearly shown, our aim should be to encourage and stimulate private action and co-operation, subject to government control. (Before Republican State Convention, Saratoga Springs, N. Y., July 18, 1918.) *Mem. Ed.* XXI, 400; *Nat. Ed.* XIX, 363.

GOVERNMENT OWNERSHIP. *See also* INDIVIDUALISM; MUNICIPAL OWNERSHIP; RAILROADS; SOCIALISM.

GOVERNMENT REGULATION. It is not possible to lay down a hard-and-fast rule, logically perfect, as to when the State shall interfere, and when the individual must be left unhampered and unhelped.

We have exactly the same right to regulate the conditions of life and work in factories and tenement-houses that we have to regulate fire-escapes and the like in other houses. In certain communities the existence of a thoroughly efficient department of factory inspection is just as essential as the establishment of a fire department. How far we shall go in regulating the hours of labor, or the liabilities of employers, is a matter of expediency, and each case must be determined on its own merits, exactly as it is a matter of expediency to determine what so-called "public utilities" the community shall itself own and what ones it shall leave to private or corporate ownership, securing to itself merely the right to regulate. (At Labor Day Picnic, Chicago, September 3, 1900.) *Mem. Ed.* XVI, 513; *Nat. Ed.* XIII, 484.

GOVERNMENT REGULATION. *See also* INDIVIDUALISM; LAISSEZ-FAIRE; LIBERTY.

GOVERNMENTAL ACTION. We decline to be bound by the empty, little cut-and-dried formulas of bygone philosophies, useful once, perhaps, but useless now. Our purpose is to shackle greedy cunning as we shackle brutal force, and we are not to be diverted from this purpose by the appeal to the dead dogmas of a vanished past. We propose to lift the burdens from the lowly and the weary, from the poor and the oppressed. We propose to stand for the sacred rights of childhood and womanhood. Nay, more, we propose to see that manhood is not crushed out of the men who toil, by excessive hours of labor, by underpayment, by injustice and oppression. When this purpose can only be secured by the collective action of our people through their governmental agencies, we propose so to secure it.

We brush aside the arguments of those who seek to bar action by the repetition of some formula about "States' rights" or about "the history of liberty" being "the history of the limitation of governmental power," or about the duty of the courts finally to determine the meaning of the Constitution. We are for human rights and we intend to work for them in efficient fashion. Where they can be best obtained by the application of the doctrines of States' rights, then we are for States' rights. Where, in order to obtain them, it is necessary to invoke the power of the nation, then we shall invoke to its uttermost limits that mighty power. (At Madison Square Garden, New York City, October 30, 1912.) *Mem. Ed.* XIX, 458; *Nat. Ed.* XVII, 336.

GOVERNMENTAL POLICY. Our whole governmental policy should be shaped to secure a more even justice as between man and man, and better conditions such as will permit each man to do the best there is in him. In other words, our governmental ideal is to secure as far as possible the even distribution of justice. (At Pacific Theological Seminary, Spring 1911.) *Mem. Ed.* XV, 627; *Nat. Ed.* XIII, 661.

——————. To sum up, then, our position is, after all, simple. We believe that the government should concern itself chiefly with the matters that are of most importance to the average man and average woman, and that it should be its special province to aid in making the conditions of life easier for these ordinary men and ordinary women, who compose the great bulk of our people. To this end we believe that the people should have direct control over their own governmental agencies; and that when this control has been secured, it should be used with resolution, but with sanity and self-restraint, in the effort to make conditions of life and labor a little easier, a little fairer and better for the men and women of the nation. (*Century,* October 1913.) *Mem. Ed.* XIX, 553; *Nat. Ed.* XVII, 409.

GOVERNMENTAL POWER—CONCENTRATION OF. Governmental power should be concentrated in the hands of a very few men, who would be so conspicuous that no citizen could help knowing all about them; and the elections should not come too frequently. Not one decent voter in ten will take the trouble annually to inform himself as to the character of the host of petty candidates to be balloted for, but he will be sure to know all about the mayor, comptroller, etc. It is not to his credit that we can only rely, and that without much certainty, upon his taking a spasmodic interest in the government that affects his own well-being; but such is the case, and accordingly we ought, as far as possible, to have a system requiring on his part intermittent and not sustained action. (*Century,* November 1886.) *Mem. Ed.* XV, 139; *Nat. Ed.* XIII, 98.

GOVERNMENTAL POWER — EXTENSION OF. So long as governmental power existed exclusively for the king and not at all for the people, then the history of liberty was a history of the limitation of governmental power. But now the governmental power rests in the people, and the kings who enjoy privilege are the kings of the financial and industrial world; and what they clamor for is the limitation of governmental power, and what the people sorely need is the extension of governmental power. . . . The only way in which our people can increase their power over the big corporation that does wrong, the only way in which they can protect the working man in his conditions of work and life, the only way in which the people can prevent children working in industry or secure women an eight-hour day in industry, or secure compensation for men killed or crippled in industry, is by extending, instead of limiting, the powers of government.

There is no analogy whatever from the standpoint of real liberty, and of real popular need, between the limitations imposed by the people on the power of an irresponsible monarch or a dominant aristocracy, and the limitations sought to be imposed by big financiers, by big corporation lawyers, and by well-meaning students of a dead-and-gone system of political economy on the power of the people to right social wrongs and limit social abuses, and to secure for the humble what, unless there is an extension of the powers of government, the arrogant and the powerful will certainly take from the humble. (At San Francisco, September 14, 1912.) *Mem. Ed.* XIX, 420, 423; *Nat. Ed.* XVII, 307, 309.

GOVERNMENTAL POWER — LIMITATION OF. There once was a time in history when the limitation of governmental power meant increasing liberty for the people. In the present day the limitation of governmental power, of governmental action, means the enslavement of the people by the great corporations who can only be held in check through the extension of governmental power. (At San Francisco, September 14, 1912.) *Mem. Ed.* XIX, 427; *Nat. Ed.* XVII, 313.

GOVERNMENTAL POWER. *See also* CONGRESS; CONSTITUTION; COURTS; DIVISION OF POWERS; EXECUTIVE; JUDICIARY; PRESIDENT.

GOVERNMENTAL THEORY. I do not fear to depart from our theory of government, when experience shows that the theory in some particular case works badly. (In New York Assembly, March 12, 1884.) *Mem. Ed.* XVI, 59; *Nat. Ed.* XIV, 36.

GOVERNOR OF NEW YORK. Compared with the great game of which Washington is the centre, my own work here is parochial. But it is interesting too; and so far I seem to have been fairly successful in overcoming the centrifugal forces always so strong in the Republican party. I am getting on well with Senator Platt, and I am apparently satisfying the wishes of the best element in our own party; of course I have only begun, but so far I think the state is the better, and the party the stronger, for my administration. (To Hay, February 7, 1899.) William R. Thayer, *The Life and Letters of John Hay*. (Houghton Mifflin Co., Boston, 1915), II, 338.

——————. So far I am getting along well but it means an infinity of hard work and a great deal of resolution with no small amount of tact and good nature. The satisfaction which I have is that I don't look for anything more in politics. People are continually writing me that my career has only begun, and they make me almost angry, for my usefulness in my present office is largely conditional in the fact that I don't expect to hold another, and so nobody has got a twist on me in any way. I could not get along at all if I had to try and shape my course with a view to favors to come, either from the people or from the politicians. I hope to keep the party united and to make a good Governor, and if I can go out having done that, I shall be more than contented. (To Andrew D. White, February 10, 1899.) *Mem. Ed.* XXIII, 139; Bishop I, 119.

——————. Oh Lord! I wish there were more of you. I think I have made a pretty good Governor, but I am quite honest in saying that I think you would have made a better one; for in just such matters as trusts and the like you have the ideas to work out whereas I have to try to work out what I get from you and men like you. (To Root, December 15, 1899.) Philip C. Jessup, *Elihu Root*. (Dodd, Mead & Co., N. Y., 1938), I, 210.

——————. I have thoroughly enjoyed being Governor. I have kept every promise, expressed or implied, I made on the stump and I feel that the Republican party is stronger before the State because of my incumbency. Certainly everything is being managed now on a perfectly straight basis and every office is as clean as a whistle. Now, I should like to be Governor for another term, especially if we are able to take hold of the canal in serious shape. (To Senator T. C. Platt, February 1, 1900.) *Mem. Ed.* XXIII, 157; Bishop I, 135.

——————. I have been pretty successful as Governor. . . . I have got the departmental work of the State on a really high plane of execution. I have committed myself to a great policy in reference to the canals. There is ample work left for me to do in another term—work that will need all my energy and capacity—in short, work well worth any man's doing. I understand perfectly that in New York with the Republican party shading on the one hand into corrupt politicians, and on the other hand, into a group of impracticables of the Godkin-Parkhurst type who are essentially quite as dishonest, the task of getting results is one of incredible difficulty, and the danger of being wrecked very great, and this without regard to one's own capacities. For instance, if the machine were very strong and could get the complete upper hand, they would undoubtedly like to throw me over, while the *Evening Post* style of independent always tends to be so angered at my securing good results along lines which he does not understand, that he will join Tammany to try to destroy me, as he did when I ran before. But this is simply the inevitable risk in such a state as this. It is not possible to count on a political career in New York as it is in Massachusetts, and the only thing to do is to face the fact, do good work while the chance lasts, and show good humor when, as inevitably must happen, the luck turns, and for no fault of one's own, one is thrown out. (To H. C. Lodge, February 2, 1900.) Lodge *Letters* I, 447.

——————. It is not the business of a Governor to "carry out the wishes of the organization" unless these wishes coincide with the good of the Party and of the State. If they do, then he ought to have them put into effect; if they do not, then as a matter of course he ought to disregard them. To pursue any other course would be to show servility; and a servile man is always an undesirable—not to say a contemptible—public servant. A Governor should, of course, try in good faith to work with the organization; but under no circumstances should he be servile to it, or "carry out its wishes" unless his own best judgment is that they ought to be carried out. I am a good organization man myself, as I understand the word "organization," but it is in the highest degree foolish to make a fetish of the word "organization" and to treat any man or any small group of men as embodying the organization. The organization should strive to give effective, intelligent, and honest leadership to and representation of the Republican Party, just as the Republican Party strives to give wise and upright government to the State. When what I have said ceases to be true of either organization or party, it means that the organization or party is not performing its duty, and is losing the reason for its existence. (To T. C. Platt, August 20, 1900.) William R. Thayer, *Theodore Roosevelt*. (Houghton Mifflin Co., Boston, 1919), p. 146.

——————. My desire was to achieve results, and not merely to issue manifestoes of virtue. It is very easy to be efficient if the efficiency is based on unscrupulousness, and it is still easier to be virtuous if one is content with the purely negative virtue which consists in not doing anything wrong, but being wholly unable to accomplish anything positive for good. My favorite quotation from Josh Billings again applies: It is so much easier to be a harmless dove than a wise serpent. My duty was to combine both idealism and efficiency. At that time the public conscience was still dormant as regards many species of political and business misconduct, as to which during the next decade it became sensitive. I had to work with the tools at hand and to take into account the feeling of the people, which I have already described. (1913.) *Mem. Ed.* XXII, 328; *Nat. Ed.* XX, 281.

GOVERNOR OF NEW YORK. See also ELECTION OF 1898; FRANCHISE TAX.

GRAND ARMY OF THE REPUBLIC. You men of the Grand Army by your victory not only rendered all Americans your debtors for evermore, but you rendered all humanity your debtors. If the Union had been dissolved, if the great edifice built with the blood and sweat and tears by mighty Washington and his compeers had gone down in wreck and ruin, the result would have been an incalculable calamity, not only for our people—and most of all for those who in such event would have seemingly triumphed—but for all mankind. The great American Republic would have become a memory of derision; and the failure of the experiment of self-government by a great people on a great scale would have delighted the heart of every foe of republican institutions. . . . It was because you, the men who wear the button of the Grand Army, triumphed in those dark years, that every American now holds his head high. (At Antietam, Md., September 17, 1903.) *Mem. Ed.* XII, 620; *Nat. Ed.* XI, 335.

——————.You men of the Grand Army, you men who fought through the Civil War, not only did you justify your generation, not only did you render life worth living for our generation, but you justified the wisdom of Washington and Washington's colleagues. If this Republic had been founded by them only to be split asunder into fragments when the strain came, then the judgment of the world would have been that Washington's work was not worth doing. It was you who crowned Washington's work, as you carried to achievement the high purpose of Abraham Lincoln. (At Osawatomie, Kan., August 31, 1910.) *Mem. Ed.* XIX, 10; *Nat. Ed.* XVII, 5.

——————. The veterans of the Grand Army of the Republic . . . deserve honor and recognition such as is paid to no other citizens of the Republic; for to them the republic owes its all; for to them it owes its very existence. It is because of what you and your comrades did in the dark years that we of to-day walk, each of us, head erect, and proud that we belong, not to one of a dozen little squabbling contemptible commonwealths, but to the mightiest nation upon which the sun shines. (At Osawatomie, Kan., August 31, 1910.) *Mem. Ed.* XIX, 12; *Nat. Ed.* XVII, 7.

GRAND ARMY OF THE REPUBLIC. See also CIVIL WAR; VETERANS.

GRAND CANYON. In the Grand Canyon, Arizona has a natural wonder which, so far as I know, is in kind absolutely unparalleled throughout the rest of the world. I want to ask you to do one thing in connection with it in your own interest and in the interest of the country—to keep this great wonder of nature as it now is. I was delighted to learn of the wisdom of the Santa Fe railroad people in deciding not to build their hotel on the brink of the canyon. I hope you will not have a building of any kind, not a summer cottage, a hotel, or anything else, to mar the wonderful grandeur, the sublimity, the great loneliness and beauty of the canyon. Leave it as it is. You can not improve on it. The ages have been at work on it, and man can only mar it. What you can do is to keep it for your children, your children's children, and for all who come after you, as one of the great sights which every American if he can travel at all should see. We have gotten past the stage, my fellow-citizens, when we are to be pardoned if we treat any part of our country as something to be skinned for two or three years for the use of the present generation, whether it is the forest, the water, the scenery. Whatever it is, handle it so that your children's children will get the benefit of it. (At Grand Canyon, Arizona, May 6, 1903.) *Presidential Addresses and State Papers* I, 370.

GRANT, ULYSSES S. In the Union armies there were generals as brilliant as Grant, but none with his iron determination. This quality he showed as President no less than as general. He was no more to be influenced by a hostile majority in Congress into abandoning his attitude in favor of a sound and stable currency than he was to be influenced by check or repulse into releasing his grip on beleaguered Richmond. It is this element of unshakable strength to which we are apt specially to refer when we praise a man in the simplest and most effective way, by praising him as a man. It is the one quality which we can least afford to lose. It is the only quality the lack of which is as unpardonable in the nation as in the man. It is the antithesis of levity, fickleness, volatility, of undue exaltation, of undue depression, of hysteria and neuroticism in all their myriad forms. (At Galena, Ill., April 27, 1900.) *Mem. Ed.* XII, 462; *Nat. Ed.* XIII, 433.

―――――――. Grant was no brawler, no lover of fighting for fighting's sake. He was a plain, quiet man, not seeking for glory; but a man who, when aroused, was always in deadly earnest, and who never shrank from duty. He was slow to strike, but he never struck softly. He was not in the least of the type which gets up mass-meetings, makes inflammatory speeches or passes inflammatory resolutions, and then permits overforcible talk to be followed by overfeeble action. His promise squared with his performance. His deeds made good his words. . . .

Part of Grant's great strength lay in the fact that he faced facts as they were, and not as he wished they might be. He was not originally an abolitionist, and he probably could not originally have defined his views as to State sovereignty; but when the Civil War was on, he saw that the only thing to do was to fight it to a finish and establish by force of arms the constitutional right to put down rebellion. (At Galena, Ill., April 27, 1900.) *Mem. Ed.* XII, 465, 470; *Nat. Ed.* XIII, 436, 440.

GREAT ADVENTURE, THE. See DEATH; LIFE.

GREAT BRITAIN. See BOER WAR; ENGLAND; INDIA; MONROE DOCTRINE; NAVAL ARMAMENTS; PANAMA CANAL; PARLIAMENTARY GOVERNMENT; REVOLUTIONARY WAR; WAR OF 1812; WORLD WAR.

GREAT MEN. See MORAL INFLUENCE.

GREATNESS — SOURCE OF. Greatness comes only through labor and courage, through the iron willingness to face sorrow and death, the tears of women and the blood of men, if only thereby it is possible to serve a lofty ideal. (1916.) *Mem. Ed.* XX, 259; *Nat. Ed.* XVIII, 223.

GREATNESS. See also NATIONAL GREATNESS; SUCCESS.

GREECE, ANCIENT. I am not quite sure that I agree even with your carefully guarded statement as to your liking to have lived in Greece in the classic age. The proviso you put in includes a great deal! We should have to get rid not only of our present conventions of morality, but of what has come to be our ordinary instincts of humanity, in order to tolerate even the best and simplest of the society of that day; and we should have to lose entirely the beautiful love of husband and wife, with all that it has so incalculably meant for the home. What a strange thing it is that those wonderful Greeks, so brilliant that I suppose Galton is right in placing the average Athenian in point of intellect as far above the average civilized man of our countries as the latter is above the upper-class barbarian, yet lacked the self-restraint and political common sense necessary to enable them to hold their own against any strong aggressive power. (To Sir George Otto Trevelyan, October 7, 1905.) *Mem. Ed.* XXIV, 180; Bishop II, 154.

GREEK—STUDY OF. See EDUCATION, LIBERAL.

GREEK LITERATURE. See LATIN LITERATURE.

GREENBACKS. See CURRENCY.

GREGORY, LADY. See ABBEY THEATRE.

GREY, SIR EDWARD. I thoroughly enjoyed my stay in England. The men I met were delightful, and I felt at home with them. As a whole, they had my ideals and ways of looking at life. But the twenty-four hours I really most enjoyed not only in England but in all Europe were those I spent with Edward Grey the last twenty-four hours I was in England. He is very fond of birds, and I had been anxious to hear and see the English birds which I knew so well in the books. He took me down to the valley of the Itchen, which we tramped along, and then motored to an inn near the New Forest where we took tea—having already eaten our lunch on a bank—and then tramped through the New Forest, reaching the inn on the other side of it about nine in the evening, tired and happy and ready for a warm bath, a hot supper, and bed. Grey is not a brilliant man like Balfour, or a born leader like Lloyd George, but he is the kind of high-minded public servant, as straight in all private as in all public relations, whom it is essential for a country to have, and I do not remember ever meeting anyone else except Leonard Wood to whom I took so strong a fancy on such short acquaintance. (To David Gray, October 5, 1911.) *Saturday Evening Post*, December 26, 1931, p. 65.

GREY, SIR EDWARD. *See also* BELGIUM.

GRIZZLY. *See* BEARS.

GUNNERY. *See* MARKSMANSHIP; NAVY—EFFICIENCY OF.

GYMNASTICS. There is little point in the mere development of strength. The point lies in developing a man who can do something with his strength; who not only has the skill to turn his muscles to advantage, but the heart and the head to direct that skill, and to direct it well and fearlessly. Gymnastics and calisthenics are very well in their way as substitutes when nothing better can be obtained, but the true sports for a manly race are sports like running, rowing, playing football and baseball, boxing and wrestling, shooting, riding, and mountain-climbing. *Harper's Weekly*, December 23, 1893, p. 1236.

GYMNASTICS. *See also* SPORTS.

H

HAGUE CONFERENCES. In such matter as the Hague Conference business the violent extremists who favor the matter are to be dreaded almost or quite as much as the Bourbon reactionaries who are against us. . . . I hope to see real progress made at the next Hague Conference. If it is possible in some way to bring about a stop, complete or partial, to the race in adding to armaments, I shall be glad; but I do not yet see my way clear as regards the details of such a plan. We must always remember that it would be a fatal thing for the great free peoples to reduce themselves to impotence and leave the despotisms and barbarians armed. It would be safe to do so if there were some system of international police; but there is now no such system. (To Andrew Carnegie, August 5, 1906.) *Mem. Ed.* XXIV, 25; Bishop II, 21.

——————. It was well worth going into these Hague conferences, but only on condition of clearly understanding how strictly limited was the good that they accomplished. The hysterical people who treated them as furnishing a patent peace panacea did nothing but harm, and partially offset the real but limited good the conferences actually accomplished. Indeed, the conferences undoubtedly did a certain amount of damage because of the preposterous expectations they excited among well-meaning but ill-informed and unthinking persons. These persons really believed that it was possible to achieve the millennium by means that would not have been very effective in preserving peace among the active boys of a large Sunday-school —let alone grown-up men in the world as it actually is. A pathetic commentary on their attitude is furnished by the fact that the fifteen years that have elapsed since the first Hague conference have seen an immense increase of war, culminating in the present war, waged by armies, and with bloodshed, on a scale far vaster than ever before in the history of mankind. (*Everybody's*, January 1915.) *Mem. Ed.* XX, 149; *Nat. Ed.* XVIII, 128.

HAGUE CONVENTIONS. The Hague conventions were treaties entered into by us with, among other nations, Belgium and Germany. Under our Constitution such a treaty becomes part of "the supreme law of the land," binding upon ourselves and upon the other nations that make it. For this reason we should never lightly enter into a treaty, and should both observe it, and demand its observance by others when made. The Hague conventions were part of the Supreme Law of our Land, under the Constitution. Therefore Germany violated the *supreme law of our land* when she brutally wronged Belgium; and we permitted it without a word of protest. (*Metropolitan*, February 1916.) *Mem. Ed.* XX, 281; *Nat. Ed.* XVIII, 241.

HAGUE CONVENTIONS — APPLICATION OF. They forbid the violation of neutral territory, and, of course, the subjugation of unoffending neutral nations, as Belgium has been subjugated. They forbid such destruction as that inflicted on Louvain, Dinant, and other towns in Belgium, the burning of their priceless public libraries and wonderful halls and churches, and the destruction of cathedrals such as that at Rheims. They forbid the infliction of heavy pecuniary penalties and the taking of severe punitive measures at the expense of civilian populations. They forbid the bombardment—of course including the dropping of bombs from aeroplanes—of unfortified cities and of cities whose defenses were not at the moment attacked. They forbid such actions as have been committed against various cities, Belgian, French, and English, not for military reason but for the purpose of terrorizing the civilian population by killing and wounding men, women, and children who were non-combatants. All of these offenses have been committed by Germany. (*Independent*, January 4, 1915.) *Mem. Ed.* XX, 177; *Nat. Ed.* XVIII, 152.

HAGUE CONVENTIONS — OBSERVANCE OF. The United States and the great powers now at war were parties to the international code created in the regulations annexed to The Hague conventions of 1899 and 1907. As President, acting on behalf of this government, and in accordance with the unanimous wish of our people, I ordered the signature of the United States to these conventions. Most emphatically I would not have permitted such a farce to have gone through if it had entered my head that this government would not consider itself bound to do all it could to see that the regulations to which it made itself a party were actually observed when the necessity for their observance arose. I cannot imagine any sensible nation thinking it worth while to sign future Hague conventions if even such a powerful neutral as the United States does not care enough about them to protest against their open breach. Of the present neutral powers the United States of America is the most disinterested and the strongest, and should therefore bear the main burden of responsibility in this matter.

It is quite possible to make an argument to the effect that we never should have entered into The Hague conventions, because our sole duty is to ourselves and not to others, and our sole concern should be to keep ourselves at peace, at any cost, and not to help other powers that are oppressed, and not to protest against wrong-doing. I do not myself accept this view; but in practice it is the view taken by the present administration, apparently with at the moment the approval of the mass of our people. Such a policy, while certainly not exalted, and in my judgment neither far-sighted nor worthy of a high-spirited and lofty-souled nation, is yet in a sense understandable, and in a sense defensible. (New York *Times*, November 8, 1914.) *Mem. Ed.* XX. 87; *Nat. Ed.* XVIII, 75.

HAGUE CONVENTIONS—SIGNING OF. I took the action I did in directing these conventions to be signed on the theory and with the belief that the United States intended to live up to its obligations, and that our people understood that living up to solemn obligations, like any other serious performance of duty, means willingness to make effort and to incur risk. If I had for one moment supposed that signing these Hague conventions meant literally nothing whatever beyond the expression of a pious wish which any power was at liberty to disregard with impunity, in accordance with the dictation of self-interest, I would certainly not have permitted the United States to be a party to such a mischievous farce. (*Independent*, January 4, 1915.) *Mem. Ed.* XX, 178; *Nat. Ed.* XVIII, 153.

HAGUE COURT—DEPENDENCE UPON. We must refuse to be misled into abandoning the policy of efficient self-defense, by any unfounded trust that The Hague court, as now constituted, and peace or arbitration treaties of the existing type, can in the smallest degree accomplish what they never have accomplished and never can accomplish. Neither the existing Hague court nor any peace treaties of the existing type will exert even the slightest influence in saving from disaster any nation that does not preserve the virile virtues and the long-sightedness that will enable it by its own might to guard its own honor, interest, and national life. (New York *Times*, October 4, 1914.) *Mem. Ed.* XX, 47; *Nat. Ed.* XVIII, 41.

————————. Important though it is that we should get the Hague Tribunal to act . . . where it can properly act, it is very much more important that we have a first-class navy and an efficient, though small, army. No Hague Court will save us if we come short in these respects. (To L. F. Abbott, January 1903.) Lawrence F. Abbott, *Impressions of Theodore Roosevelt*. (Doubleday, Page & Co., Garden City, N. Y., 1919), p. 107.

HAGUE COURT—PLACE OF. Questions between nations continually arise which are not of first-class importance; which, for instance, refer to some illegal act by or against a fishing-schooner, to some difficulty concerning contracts, to some question of the interpretation of a minor clause in a treaty, or to the sporadic action of some hot-headed or panic-struck official. In these cases, where neither nation wishes to go to war, The Hague court has furnished an easy method for the settlement of the dispute without war. This does not mark a very great advance; but it is an advance, and was worth making.

The fact that it is the only advance that The Hague court has accomplished make the hysterical outbursts formerly indulged in by the ultrapacifists concerning it seem in retrospect exceedingly foolish. While I had never shared the hopes of these ultrapacifists, I had hoped for more substantial good than has actually come from The Hague conventions. This was because I accept promises as meaning something. (*Independent,* January 4, 1915.) *Mem. Ed.* XX, 176; *Nat. Ed.* XVIII, 151.

HAGUE COURT—SERVICE OF. The Hague court has served a very limited, but a useful, purpose. Some, although only a small number, of the existing peace and arbitration treaties have served a useful purpose. But the purpose and the service have been strictly limited. Issues often arise between nations which are not of first-class importance, which do not affect their vital honor and interest, but which, if left unsettled, may eventually cause irritation that will have the worst possible results. The Hague court and the different treaties in question provide instrumentalities for settling such disputes, where the nations involved really wish to settle them but might be unable to do so if means were not supplied. This is a real service and one well worth rendering. These treaties and The Hague court have rendered such service again and again in time past. It has been a misfortune that some worthy people have anticipated too much and claimed too much in reference to them, for the failure of the excessive claims has blinded men to what they really have accomplished. To expect from them what they cannot give is merely shortsighted. To assert that they will give what they cannot give is mischievous. (New York *Times,* October 4, 1914.) *Mem. Ed.* XX, 46; *Nat. Ed.* XVIII, 40.

HAGUE COURT—WEAKNESS OF. The supreme difficulty in connection with developing the peace work of The Hague arises from the lack of any executive power, of any police power, to enforce the decrees of the court. (Before Nobel Prize Committee, Christiania, Norway, May 5, 1910.) *Mem. Ed.* XVIII, 414; *Nat. Ed.* XVI, 309.

HAGUE TREATIES. In practice The Hague treaties have proved and will always prove useless while there is no sanction of force behind them. For the United States to proffer "good offices" to the various powers entering such a great conflict as the present one accomplishes not one particle of good; to refer them, when they mutually complain of wrongs, to a Hague court which is merely a phantom does less than no good. The Hague treaties can accomplish nothing, and ought not have been entered into, unless in such a case as this of Belgium there is willingness to take efficient action under them. There could be no better illustration of how extremely complicated and difficult a thing it is in practice instead of in theory to make even a small advance in the cause of peace. (New York *Times,* October 4, 1914.) *Mem. Ed.* XX, 44; *Nat. Ed.* XVIII, 37.

————. I have been frantically denounced by the pacifists because I would not enter into these treaties. But the reason was simply that I would not enter into any treaty I did not intend to keep and think we could keep. I regard with horror the fact that this Government has not protested under the Hague Conventions as to the outrageous wrongs inflicted upon Belgium. (I would have made the protest effective!) I agree absolutely with you that no treaty of the kind should hereafter ever be made unless the Powers signing it bind themselves to uphold its terms by force if necessary. (To Sir Edward Grey, February 1, 1915.) *Twenty-five Years* by Viscount Grey of Fallodon. (Hodder & Stoughton, London, 1925), II, 149.

HAGUE TREATIES. *See also* ARBITRATION; BELGIUM; NEUTRALITY; PROMISES; STRAUS, OSCAR S.; TREATIES; WILSON, WOODROW; WORLD WAR.

HAITI. At this moment Hayti is more backward than any other West Indian island, her average negro citizen is less well off than the corresponding negro in any of the other islands, and the general social condition is worse and contains less promise than in any other island; and all because the other islands have been through a process of evolution instead of revolution. There was ample moral warrant for the Haytian revolution at the end of the eighteenth century; nevertheless, its success was a curse, for its success, with the dreadful accompanying atrocities, put off the day when emancipation came to the other islands; and, moreover, in a short time emancipation would have inevitably come to Hayti anyhow, with comparatively little shock and dislocation; and then there would have been left in the island, as in the other islands, an element naturally fit for uplifting leadership. (*Outlook,* June 4, 1910.) *Mem. Ed.* XIV, 190; *Nat. Ed.* XII, 218.

HAITI. *See also* OPEN COVENANTS; SLAVERY; SUFFRAGE.

HALE, NATHAN. *See* ANDRÉ, JOHN.

HAMILTON, ALEXANDER. *See Federalist, The;* JEFFERSON, THOMAS; MORRIS, GOUVERNEUR; ROOT, ELIHU.

"HANDS ACROSS THE SEA." I have never used in peace or in war any such expression as "hands across the sea," and I emphatically disapprove of what it signifies save in so far as it means cordial friendship between us and every other nation that acts in accordance with the standards that we deem just and right. On this ground all Americans, no matter what their race origins, ought to stand together. It is not just that they should be asked to stand with any foreign power on the ground of community of origin between some of them and the citizens of that foreign power. (*Metropolitan,* October 1915.) *Mem. Ed.* XX, 329; *Nat. Ed.* XVIII, 282.

"HANDS ACROSS THE SEA." *See also* FOREIGN RELATIONS; INTERNATIONAL RELATIONS.

HANNA, MARK. No man had larger traits than Hanna. He was a big man in every way and as forceful a personality as we have seen in public life in our generation. I think that not merely for myself, but the whole party and the whole country have reason to be very grateful to him for the way in which, after I came into office, under circumstances which were very hard for him, he resolutely declined to be drawn into the position which a smaller man of meaner cast would inevitably have taken; that is, the position of antagonizing public policies if I was identified with them. He could have caused the widest disaster to the country and the public if he had attacked and opposed the policies referring to Panama, the Philippines, Cuban reciprocity, Army reform, the Navy, and the legislation for regulating corporations. But he stood by them just as loyally as if I had been McKinley. (To Elihu Root, February 16, 1904.) *Mem. Ed.* XXIII, 363-364; Bishop I, 315.

HAPPINESS. Happiness cannot come to any man capable of enjoying true happiness unless it comes as the sequel to duty well and honestly done. (At Groton School, Groton, Mass., May 24, 1904.) *Mem. Ed.* XV, 479; *Nat. Ed.* XIII, 557.

HAPPINESS—SOURCE OF. If you are to play any part in the world, if you are to have great happiness, you must make up your mind that you are not going to shrink from risks, that you are going to face the fact that effort, and painful effort, will often be necessary; and you must count for your happiness, not on avoiding everything that is unpleasant, but of possessing in you the power to overcome and trample it under foot. If you have small, shallow souls, shallow souls and shallow hearts, I will not say you will be unhappy; you can obtain the bridge-club standards of happiness, and you can go through life without cares and without sorrows, and without conscious effort, in so far as your brains will enable you to do so; but you have richly deserved the contempt of everybody whose respect is worth having. (At Occidental College, Los Angeles, Cal., March 22, 1911.) *Mem. Ed.* XV, 514; *Nat. Ed* XIII, 580.

HAPPINESS, PERSONAL. I cannot expect most people to believe that I have not for years been happier than since election. I have worked very hard and practically without intermission for a long time. Now what I most desire is to be free from engagements and stay out here with Mother and without too much to do, and since election I have been quite busy but it is not exhausting labor and will diminish rather than increase. We have had ten lovely days here. I have ridden once or twice. Two or three times I have taken Mother for a row and we have walked together and sat by the wood-fire in the late afternoon and evening. I was going to say that I have been as happy as a king, but as a matter of fact I have been infinitely happier than any of the kings I know, poor devils! (To Kermit Roosevelt, November 11, 1914.) *Mem. Ed.* XXIV, 418; Bishop II, 356.

HAPPINESS. *See also* CHILDREN; FAMILY LIFE; IDEALS; JOY OF LIVING; LOVE; PLEASURE; SUCCESS.

HARD TIMES. The slightest acquaintance with our industrial history should teach even the most short-sighted that the times of most suffering for our people as a whole, the times when business is stagnant, and capital suffers from shrinkage and gets no return from its investments, are exactly the times of hardship, and want, and grim disaster among the poor. If all the existing instrumentalities of wealth could be abolished, the first and severest suffering would come among those of us who are least well off at present. The wage-worker is well off only when the rest of the country is well off; and he can best contribute to this general well-being by showing sanity and a firm purpose to do justice to others. (At State Fair, Syracuse, N. Y., September 7, 1903.) *Mem. Ed.* XVIII, 65; *Nat. Ed.* XVI, 55.

――――――. When hard times come it is inevitable that the President under whom they come should be blamed. There are foolish people who supported me because we had heavy crops; and there are now foolish people who oppose me because extravagant speculations, complicated here and there with dishonesty, have produced the inevitable reaction. (To Hamlin Garland, November 23, 1907.) *Mem. Ed.* XXIV, 58; Bishop II, 49.

HARD TIMES. *See also* CURRENCY; PANIC; PROSPERITY.

HARRIS, JOEL CHANDLER. Georgia has done a great many things for the Union; but she has never done more than when she gave Mr. Joel Chandler Harris to American literature. I suppose he is one of those literary people who insist that art should have nothing to do with morals, and will condemn me as a Philistine for not agreeing with them; but I want to say that one of the great reasons why I like what he has written is because after reading it I rise up with the purpose of being a better man, a man who is bound to strive to do what is in him for the cause of decency and for the cause of righteousness. Gentlemen, I feel too strongly to indulge in any language of mere compliment, of mere flattery. Where Mr. Harris seems to me to have done one of his greatest services is that he has written what exalts the South in the mind of every man who reads it, and yet what has not even a flavor of bitterness toward any other part of the Union. There is not an American anywhere who can read Mr. Harris's stories—I am not speaking at the moment of his wonderful folk tales, but of his stories—who does not rise up a better citizen for having read them, who does not rise up with a more earnest desire to do his part in solving American problems aright. (Before Piedmont Club, Atlanta, Ga., October 20, 1905.) *Presidential Addresses and State Papers* IV, 501.

――――――. Fond though I am of the brer rabbit stories I think I am even fonder of your other writings. I doubt if there is a more genuinely pathetic tale in all our literature than "Free Joe." Moreover I have felt that all that you write serves to bring our people closer together. I know, of course, the ordinary talk is that an artist should be judged purely by his art; but I am rather a Philistine and like to feel that the art serves a good purpose. Your art is not only an art addition to our sum of national achievement, but it has also always been an addition to the forces that tell for decency, and above all for the blotting out of sectional antagonism. (To Joel Chandler Harris, October 12, 1903.) *Mem. Ed.* XXI, 505; *Nat. Ed.* XIX, 448.

HARRISON, BENJAMIN. I saw the President yesterday and had a long talk with him. . . . The conclusion of the talk was rather colorless, as usual. Heavens, how I like positive men! (To H. C. Lodge, May 9, 1890.) *Lodge Letters* I, 99.

HARRISON, BENJAMIN. *See also* CIVIL SERVICE COMMISSIONER.

HARTFORD CONVENTION. It is idle to try to justify the proceedings of the Hartford Convention, or of the Massachusetts and Connecticut legislatures. The decision to keep the New England troops as an independent command was of itself sufficient ground for condemnation; moreover, it was not warranted by any show of superior prowess on the part of the New Englanders, for a portion of Maine continued in possession of the British till the close of the war. The Hartford resolutions were so framed as to justify seceding or not seceding as events turned out. (1888.) *Mem. Ed.* VIII, 538; *Nat. Ed.* VII, 465.

HATRED. The poorest of all emotions for any American citizen to feel is the emotion of hatred toward his fellows. Let him feel a just and righteous indignation where that just and righteous indignation is called for; let him not hesitate to inflict punishment where the punishment is needed in the interest of the public; but let him beware of demanding mere vengeance; and above all of inciting the masses of the people to such demand. (Speech at Oyster Bay, N. Y., July 4, 1906.) *Mem. Ed.* XVIII, 8; *Nat. Ed.* XVI, 7.

HATRED. *See also* CLASS HATRED.

HAWAII—ANNEXATION OF. We should annex Hawaii immediately. It was a crime against the United States, it was a crime against white civilization, not to annex it two years and a half ago. The delay did damage that is perhaps irreparable; for it means that at the critical period of the island's growth the influx of population consisted, not of white Americans, but of low-caste laborers drawn from the yellow races. (*Century,* November 1895.) *Mem. Ed.* XVI, 347; *Nat. Ed.* XIV, 247-248.

——————————. If the United States desires to become what it undoubtedly should become, the great power of the Pacific, then our people must heartily back up President McKinley's course in preparing the annexation treaty. We must take Hawaii just as we must continue to build a navy equal to the needs of America's greatness. If we do not take Hawaii ourselves we will have lost the right to dictate what shall be her fate. We cannot play hot and cold at the same moment. Hawaii cannot permanently stand alone, and we have no right to expect other powers to be blind to their own interests because we are blind to ours. If Hawaii does not become American then we may as well make up our minds to see it become European or Asiatic. *Gunton's Magazine,* January 1898, p. 4.

HAWAII—FORTIFICATION OF. In my judgment immediate steps should be taken for the fortification of Hawaii. This is the most important point in the Pacific to fortify in order to conserve the interests of this country. It would be hard to overstate the importance of this need. (Fifth Annual Message, Washington, December 5, 1905.) *Mem. Ed.* XVII, 391; *Nat. Ed.* XV, 333.

HAWAIIAN POLICY. In Hawaii our aim must be to develop the Territory on the traditional American lines. We do not wish a region of large estates tilled by cheap labor; we wish a healthy American community of men who themselves till the farms they own. All our legislation for the islands should be shaped with this end in view; the well-being of the average home-maker must afford the true test of the healthy development of the islands. (First Annual Message, Washington, December 3, 1901.) *Mem. Ed.* XVII, 126; *Nat. Ed.* XV, 109.

HAY, JOHN. John Hay's death was very sudden and removes from American life a man whose position was literally unique. The country was the better because he lived, for it was a fine thing to have set before our young men the example of success contained in the career of a man who had held so many and such important public positions, while there was not in his nature the slightest touch of the demagogue, and who in addition to his great career in political life had also left a deep mark in literature. (To Henry Cabot Lodge, July 11, 1905.) *Mem. Ed.* XXIII, 425; Bishop I, 369.

——————————. John Hay was one of a very limited number of American public men who have possessed marked literary ability and that high and fine quality of intellectual eminence which Matthew Arnold would have characterized as "distinction." In consequence of a rather curious tradition of American public life, ambassadors and ministers have frequently been appointed because they were distinguished men of letters. There would have been nothing unusual in Hay's having come purely in this class. But John Hay, in addition to serving abroad in various diplomatic positions, including that of ambassador at the Court of St. James, began his public career by being the private secretary of Abraham Lincoln during the tremendous crisis of the Civil War and ended it by being secretary of state during the years which saw the United States, for good or evil, forced to take her part among the great powers of the world and begin to deal with world questions. (*Harvard Graduates' Magazine,* December 1915.) *Mem. Ed.* XII, 503; *Nat. Ed.* XI, 244.

——————————. As secretary of state, Hay occupied a unique position. To a high standard of personal integrity, which made him expect and believe that the nation should observe the same standard of national integrity, he added a fastidiousness of temper, of taste, of refinement, which was a very real benefit to American public life when exhibited in high public place by a man of signal and conceded capacity as a public servant. The sensitive refinement of nature, like the sheer massiveness of Lincoln's character, made it impossible for Hay to tolerate what was meretricious or sentimental or offensive to morals. . . .

Hay's services as secretary of state were great; but it may be doubted whether his services as Lincoln's biographer were not even greater. At any rate, the monumental work, in which he was partner with Nicolay, taken together with the two volumes of Lincoln's letters which they subsequently edited, will always remain a storehouse, wherein not merely the American historians of the period of the Civil War, but American politicians anxious to deal in proper fashion with national problems, will find a wealth of material that they can find nowhere else. (*Harvard Graduates' Magazine*, December 1915.) *Mem. Ed.* XII, 504, 505; *Nat. Ed.* XI, 246, 247.

HAY-HERRAN TREATY. The Hay-Herran treaty, if it erred at all, erred in the direction of an over-generosity toward the Colombian Government. In our anxiety to be fair we had gone to the very verge in yielding to a weak nation's demands what that nation was helplessly unable to enforce from us against our will. The only criticisms made upon the Administration for the terms of the Hay-Herran treaty were for having granted too much to Colombia, not for failure to grant enough. Neither in the Congress nor in the public press, at the time that this treaty was formulated, was there complaint that it did not in the fullest and amplest manner guarantee to Colombia everything that she could by any color of title demand. (Message to Congress, January 4, 1904.) *Presidential Addresses and State Papers* II, 713.

HAY-PAUNCEFOTE TREATY. Under the Hay-Pauncefote treaty it was explicitly provided that the United States should control, police, and protect the canal which was to be built, keeping it open for the vessels of all nations on equal terms. The United States thus assumed the position of guarantor of the canal and of its peaceful use by all the world. The guarantee included as a matter of course the building of the canal. The enterprise was recognized as responding to an international need. (Message to Congress, January 4. 1904.) *Presidential Addresses and State Papers* II, 712.

HAY, JOHN. See also PANAMA CANAL.

HAYS, WILL H. Hays is a trump. He is all right. He may make mistakes, but he won't make many. The party seems to be united on him and that's something well worth while. Now we've got to back him up. With Hays at work and on the job, I think we'll get results. For one thing, there's only one party now. Most of the Progressives have come back. Most of the others will follow. Those that won't return would sooner or later have quit even the Progressive Party—they're just natural-born Mavericks who won't stay long in any herd, and won't stay branded.

Hays will, I'm sure, weld the party firmly together. The day of factions has gone. But we have all got to help him. (February or March 1918; recorded by Leary.) *Talks with T. R.* From the diaries of John J. Leary, Jr. (Houghton Mifflin Co., Boston, 1920), p. 9.

HAZING—PUNISHMENT FOR. I heartily disapprove of the practice of hazing, and, in common with all those interested in the welfare of the Academy, wish to see this practice thoroughly eradicated there. But the punishment of dismissal is altogether disproportionate to the culpability involved in some forms of hazing. In many cases, these amount to nothing more than exhibitions of boyish mischief attended with no consequence of any moment to those hazed, and indicating on the part of the hazers only some exuberance of animal spirits. Unquestionably they ought to be punished, for under any circumstances hazing constitutes a breach of the rules, and the future officers of our Navy must be taught, first of all and as a foundation for all other merits, strict and unquestioning obedience. But to punish those faults of youth by depriving the young man concerned of his career in life is to commit a glaring injustice. (To chairmen of Naval Committees of Senate and House, February 1, 1906.) *Mem. Ed.* XXIV, 5; Bishop II, 3.

HEALTH, PUBLIC. No people are more vitally interested than working men and working women in questions affecting the public health. The pure-food law must be strengthened and efficiently enforced. In the National Government one department should be intrusted with all the agencies relating to the public health, from the enforcement of the pure-food law to the administration of quarantine. This department, through its special health service, would co-operate intelligently with the various State and municipal bodies established for the same end. There would be no discrimination against us for any one set of therapeutic methods, against or for any one school of medicine or system of healing; the aim would be merely to secure under one administrative body efficient sanitary regulation in the interest of the people as a whole. (Before Progressive National Convention, Chicago, August 6, 1912.) *Mem. Ed.* XIX, 377; *Nat. Ed.* XVII, 270.

HEARST, WILLIAM RANDOLPH. Hearst's nomination is a very, very bad thing. I do not think he will be elected, and yet I cannot blind myself to his extraordinary popularity among the "have-nots," and the chance there is for him because of the great agitation and unrest which we have witnessed during the last eighteen months—an agitation and unrest in large part due simply to the evil preaching of men like himself, but also due to the veritable atrocities committed by some wealthy men and by the attitude of the Bourbon reactionaries who endeavor to prevent any remedy of the evils due to the lack of supervision of wealth. (To H. C. Lodge, October 1, 1906.) *Lodge Letters* II, 239.

HEARST PAPERS. The Hearst papers play the German game when they oppose the war, assail our allies, and clamor for an inconclusive peace, and they play the German game when they assail the men who truthfully point out the shortcomings which, unless corrected, will redound to Germany's advantage and our terrible disadvantage. But the administration has taken no action against the Hearst papers. (1918.) *Mem. Ed.* XXI, 323; *Nat. Ed.* XIX, 295.

HEBREWS. See ANTI-SEMITISM; JEWS.

HERO WORSHIP. It is of little use for us to pay lip-loyalty to the mighty men of the past unless we sincerely endeavor to apply to the problems of the present precisely the qualities which in other crises enabled the men of that day to meet those crises. (At Osawatomie, Kan., August 31, 1910.) *Mem. Ed.* XIX, 13; *Nat. Ed.* XVII, 7.

HEROES. It is a good thing for all Americans, and it is an especially good thing for young Americans, to remember the men who have given their lives in war and peace to the service of their fellow countrymen, and to keep in mind the feats of daring and personal prowess done in time past by some of the many champions of the nation in the various crises of her history. (Preface to *Hero Tales,* with H. C. Lodge, 1895.) *Mem. Ed.* IX, xxi; *Nat. Ed.* X, xxiii.

HEROES, NATIONAL. In the long run every great nation instinctively recognizes the men who peculiarly and preëminently represent its own type of greatness. Here in our country we have had many public men of high rank—soldiers, orators, constructive statesmen, and popular leaders. We have even had great philosophers who were also leaders of popular thought. Each of these men has had his own group of devoted followers, and some of them have at times swayed the nation with a power such as the foremost of all hardly wielded. (At Galena, Ill., April 27, 1900.) *Mem. Ed.* XII, 458; *Nat. Ed.* XIII, 430.

———. The worst ill that can befall us is to have our own souls corrupted, and it is a debasing thing for a nation to choose as its heroes the men of mere wealth. (At Pacific Theological Seminary, Spring 1911.) *Mem. Ed.* XV, 581; *Nat. Ed.* XIII, 620.

HEROES, WAR-TIME. The men who have died of pneumonia or fever in the hospitals, the men who have been killed in accidents on the airplane training-fields are as much heroes as those who were killed at the front, and their shining souls shall hereafter light up all to a clearer and greater view of the duties of life. (*Kansas City Star,* November 13, 1918.) *Mem. Ed.* XXI, 370; *Nat. Ed.* XIX, 337.

HEROIC TYPE. We should . . . keep in mind that the hero cannot win save for the forethought, energy, courage, and capacity of countless other men. Yet we must keep in mind also that all this forethought, energy, courage, and capacity will be wasted unless at the supreme moment some man of the heroic type arises capable of using to the best advantage the powers lying ready to hand. (*McClure's Magazine,* October 1899.) *Mem. Ed.* XII, 515; *Nat. Ed.* XIII, 427.

HEROIC VIRTUES. Thrift, industry, obedience to law, and intellectual cultivation are essential qualities in the make-up of any successful people; but no people can be really great unless they possess also the heroic virtues which are as needful in time of peace as in time of war, and as important in civil as in military life. (Preface to *Hero Tales,* with H. C. Lodge, 1895.) *Mem. Ed.* IX, xxi; *Nat. Ed.* X, xxiii.

HEROIC VIRTUES. *See also* VIRTUES.

HEROISM. *See* COURAGE.

HEWITT, ABRAM S. Now, if an opportunity comes, I shall be more than glad to do as you suggest about Mr. Hewitt. I say "if an opportunity comes," because, as you with your great experience of public life know, it is not possible to foretell just how the chance will shape itself. It may be that when an opportunity to give Mr. Hewitt what he deserves arises there will be some imperative necessity to recognize the claim of someone else. I say this only because I do not want even impliedly to promise more than I am able to perform. But I want to add that I would particularly like, for my own sake, to satisfy my own feeling as to the recognition of the highest quality of citizenship, to pay the compliment, to give the acknowledgment, to Mr. Hewitt.

Now can you indicate at all specifically the kind of thing you would suggest? I do not believe I ought to offer him a position in the

[225]

Cabinet, even though an opportunity arose. Short of that there is nothing I would not gladly offer him; and as far as I am personally concerned, I should be only too delighted to have him in the Cabinet. But from the political standpoint, both as regards him and myself, I should doubt the wisdom of so doing. (To D. M. Dickinson, March 26, 1902.) Allan Nevins, *Abram S. Hewitt. With some account of Peter Cooper.* (Harper & Bros., N. Y., 1935), p. 599.

HISTORIANS. There are two kinds of historians: one, the delver, the bricklayer, the man who laboriously gathers together bare facts; and the other, the builder, the architect, who out of these facts makes the great edifice of history. Both are indispensable; but it is only the latter who can be called an historian in the highest sense. Without a thorough and full knowledge of the details, generalization is mere folly, and the man who tries to generalize on insufficient or misunderstood data is many degrees worse than the man who does not try to generalize at all, but merely gathers data. Nevertheless it is the generalizer really able to handle the subject who does the permanent work. (*Bookman,* June 1897.) *Mem. Ed.* XIV, 326-327; *Nat. Ed.* XII, 280-281.

——————. The great historian is necessarily a man of imagination, and, however accurate he may be, he cannot be, in the broadest sense, truthful, unless, like Gibbon, Macaulay, and others, he has the power to visualize to himself what he has found in the past,—unless he has the power not merely to visualize it himself, but to put it down in words so that his readers can visualize it also. (Lecture, March 21, 1911.) *Bulletin of Throop Polytechnic Institute,* July 1911, pp. 6-7.

HISTORIANS — MATERIALS FOR. The great historian of the future will have easy access to innumerable facts patiently gathered by tens of thousands of investigators, whereas the great historian of the past had very few facts, and often had to gather most of these himself. The great historian of the future cannot be excused if he fails to draw on the vast storehouses of knowledge that have been accumulated, if he fails to profit by the wisdom and work of other men, which are now the common property of all intelligent men. He must use the instruments which the historians of the past did not have ready to hand. Yet even with these instruments he cannot do as good work as the best of the elder historians unless he has vision and imagination, the power to grasp what is essential and to reject the infinitely more numerous non-essentials, the power to embody ghosts, to put flesh and blood on dry bones, to make dead men living before our eyes. In short, he must have the power to take the science of history and turn it into literature. (Presidential Address, American Historical Association, Boston, December 27, 1912.) *Mem. Ed.* XIV, 12; *Nat. Ed.* XII, 11.

HISTORIANS—POSITION OF. The great historian of the future must essentially represent the ideal striven after by the great historians of the past. The industrious collector of facts occupies an honorable, but not an exalted, position, and the scientific historian who produces books which are not literature must rest content with the honor, substantial, but not of the highest type, that belongs to him who gathers material which some time some great master shall arise to use. (At Oxford University, England, June 7, 1910.) *Mem. Ed.* XIV, 69; *Nat. Ed.* XII, 28.

HISTORIANS—TASK OF. The great historian must be able to paint for us the life of the plain people, the ordinary men and women, of the time of which he writes. He can do this only if he possesses the highest kind of imagination. Collections of figures no more give us a picture of the past than the reading of a tariff report on hides or woollens gives us an idea of the actual lives of the men and women who live on ranches or work in factories. The great historian will in as full measure as possible present to us the every-day life of the men and women of the age which he describes. Nothing that tells of this life will come amiss to him. The instruments of their labor and the weapons of their warfare, the wills that they wrote, the bargains that they made, and the songs that they sang when they feasted and made love: he must use them all. He must tell us of the toil of the ordinary man in ordinary times, and of the play by which that ordinary toil was broken. He must never forget that no event stands out entirely isolated. He must trace from its obscure and humble beginnings each of the movements that in its hour of triumph has shaken the world. (Presidential Address, American Historical Association, Boston, December 27, 1912.) *Mem. Ed.* XIV, 21; *Nat. Ed.* XII, 19.

HISTORIANS, AMERICAN—CRITICISM OF. Unfortunately with us it is these small men who do most of the historic teaching in the colleges. They have done much real harm in preventing the development of students who might

[226]

have a large grasp of what history should really be. They represent what is in itself the excellent revolt against superficiality and lack of research, but they have grown into the opposite and equally noxious belief that research is all in all, that accumulation of facts is everything, and that the ideal history of the future will consist not even of the work of one huge pedant but of a multitude of articles by a multitude of small pedants. They are honestly unconscious that all they are doing is to gather bricks and stones, and that whether their work will or will not amount to anything really worthy depends entirely upon whether or not some great masterbuilder hereafter arrives who will be able to go over their material, to reject the immense majority of it, and out of what is left to fashion some edifice of majesty and beauty instinct with the truth that both charms and teaches. A thousand of them would not in the aggregate begin to add to the wisdom of mankind what another Macaulay, should one arise, would add. The great historian must of course have the scientific spirit which gives the power of research, which enables one to marshal and weigh the facts; but unless his finished work is literature of a very high type small will be his claim to greatness. (To Sir George Otto Trevelyan, January 23, 1904.) *Mem. Ed.*, XXIV, 164; Bishop II, 140.

HISTORIANS. *See also* BRYCE, LORD; CARLYLE, THOMAS; MACAULAY, LORD; MAHAN, A. T.; PARKMAN, FRANCIS; TREVELYAN, SIR GEORGE OTTO.

HISTORICAL KNOWLEDGE — EXTENSION OF. The last two generations have seen such immense additions to our archaeological and historical knowledge as completely to revolutionize our sense of values and proportions in this matter. We now know that the pre-history of man, during the period after he had become clearly human but before he had reached the lower levels of civilization or had learned to leave written records, covered a period of certainly two hundred thousand years, and probably twice as long. We have pushed the domain of actual history so far back into the past that Sennacherib and Nebuchadnezzar, together with the later Judean kings and the great prophets, stand about in the middle of the age covered by written records; the first rulers of whom we have clear knowledge beside the Nile and the Euphrates were separated by almost as long a period of time from the last Assyrian, Babylonian and Egyptian sovereigns as is the period that divides these latter from us. (*Outlook*, February 14, 1917.) *Mem. Ed.* XIV, 38-39; *Nat. Ed.* XII, 160-161.

HISTORY. If the proper study of mankind is man, then the proper study of a Nation is its own history, and all true patriots should encourage in every way the associations which record the great deeds, and the successes and failures alike, of the forefathers of their people. (Address before the State Historical Society of Wisconsin, January 24, 1893.) Theodore Roosevelt, *The Northwest in the Nation*. (Wisconsin State Historical Society, 1893), p. 93.

——————. I do not believe that any man can adequately appreciate the world of to-day unless he has some knowledge of—a little more than a slight knowledge—some feeling for and of—the history of the world of the past. (Charter Day Address, Berkeley, Cal., March 23, 1911.) University of California *Chronicle*, April 1911, p. 134.

——————. [A feature] of the growth in the position of science in the eyes of everyone, and of the greatly increased respect naturally resulting for scientific methods, has been a certain tendency for scientific students to encroach on other fields. This is particularly true of the field of historical study. Not only have scientific men insisted upon the necessity of considering the history of man, especially in its early stages, in connection with what biology shows to be the history of life, but furthermore there has arisen a demand that history shall itself be treated as a science. Both positions are in their essence right; but as regards each position, the more arrogant among the invaders of the new realm of knowledge take an attitude to which it is not necessary to assent. As regards the latter of the two positions, that which would treat history henceforth merely as one branch of scientific study, we must of course cordially agree that accuracy in recording facts and appreciation of their relative worth and inter-relationship are just as necessary in historical study as in any other kind of study. The fact that a book, though interesting, is untrue, of course removes it at once from the category of history, however much it may still deserve to retain a place in the always desirable group of volumes which deal with entertaining fiction. But the converse also holds, at least to the extent of permitting us to insist upon what would seem to be the elementary fact that a book which is written to be read should be readable. This rather obvious truth seems to have been forgotten by some of the more zealous scientific historians, who apparently hold that the worth of a historical book is directly in proportion to the impossibility of reading it, save as a painful duty. Now I am willing that history shall be treated as a branch of science, but only on condition that it also remains a branch of literature. (At Oxford University, England, June 7, 1910.) *Mem. Ed.* XIV, 67; *Nat. Ed.* XII, 27.

―――――――. The immediate past I suppose can hardly be written of sufficiently dispassionately, because to write it truthfully you would have to give great offense to so many good people, who simply happened unfortunately to be in positions where any one would have done badly under the existing conditions, and who therefore did badly; and it would be hard upon them to hold them up to scorn or obloquy for what really wasn't their fault. In consequence it would be a very difficult thing to teach the lessons of history from what has occurred while the men who did the deeds are still living. (At Conference on Military History, American Historical Association, Boston, December 28, 1912.) *Mem. Ed.* XVIII, 313; *Nat. Ed.* XVI, 235.

―――――――. The history of man himself is by far the most absorbing of all histories, and it cannot be understood without some knowledge of his prehistory. Moreover, the history of the rest of the animal world also yields a drama of intense and vivid interest to all scholars gifted with imagination. The two histories—the prehistory of humanity and the history of the culminating phase of non-human mammalian life—were interwoven during the dim ages when man was slowly groping upward from the bestial to the half-divine. (1916.) *Mem. Ed.* IV, 139; *Nat. Ed.* III, 303.

HISTORY—LESSONS OF. It is a very poor thing, whether for nations or individuals, to advance the history of great deeds done in the past as an excuse for doing poorly in the present; but it is an excellent thing to study the history of the great deeds of the past, and of the great men who did them, with an earnest desire to profit thereby so as to render better service in the present. In their essentials, the men of the present day are much like the men of the past, and the live issues of the present can be faced to better advantage by men who have in good faith studied how the leaders of the nation faced the dead issues of the past. (Introduction to A. B. Lapsley's *Writings of Abraham Lincoln;* September 1905.) *Mem. Ed.* XII, 446; *Nat. Ed.* XI, 205.

HISTORY—PRESENTATION OF. History can never be truthfully presented if the presentation is purely emotional. It can never be truthfully or usefully presented unless profound research, patient, laborious, painstaking, has preceded the presentation. No amount of self-communion and of pondering on the soul of mankind, no gorgeousness of literary imagery, can take the place of cool, serious, widely extended study. The vision of the great historian must be both wide and lofty. But it must be sane, clear, and based on full knowledge of the facts and of their interrelations. . . . Many hard-working students, alive to the deficiencies of this kind of romance-writing, have grown to distrust not only all historical writing that is romantic, but all historical writing that is vivid. They feel that complete truthfulness must never be sacrificed to color. In this they are right. They also feel that complete truthfulness is incompatible with color. In this they are wrong. The immense importance of full knowledge of a mass of dry facts and gray details has so impressed them as to make them feel that the dryness and the grayness are in themselves meritorious. (Presidential Address, American Historical Association, Boston, December 27, 1912.) *Mem. Ed.* XIV, 5; *Nat. Ed.* XII, 5.

HISTORY—TEACHING OF. A number of women teachers in Chicago are credited with having proposed, in view of war, hereafter to prohibit in the teaching of history any reference to war and battles. Intellectually, of course, such persons show themselves unfit to be retained as teachers a single day, and indeed unfit to be pupils in any school more advanced than a kindergarten. But it is not their intellectual, it is also their moral shortcomings which are striking. The suppression of the truth is, of course, as grave an offense against morals as is the suggestion of the false or even the lie direct; and these teachers actually propose to teach untruths to their pupils.

True teachers of history must tell the facts of history; and if they do not tell the facts both about the wars that were righteous and the wars that were unrighteous, and about the causes that led to these wars and to success or defeat in them, they show themselves morally unfit to train the minds of boys and girls. If in addition to telling the facts they draw the lessons that should be drawn from the facts, they will give their pupils a horror of all wars that are entered into wantonly or with levity or in a spirit of mere brutal aggression or save under dire necessity. But they will also teach that among the noblest deeds of mankind are those that have been done in great wars for liberty, in wars of self-defense, in wars for the relief of oppressed peoples, in wars for putting an end to wrong-doing in the dark places of the globe. (New

HISTORY, AMERICAN. It is hard indeed for the average man to appreciate rightly the relative importance of the different movements going on about him. American historians very often fail signally in this respect. Questions of the tariff or of the currency, and the rise and fall of parties connected therewith absorb their attention. In reality all matters of this sort are of merely minor importance in our history. The conquest of this continent by the white race; which branch of the white race should win for itself the right to make this conquest; the struggle between the different European nationalities, and between all of them and the original red lords of the land; the establishment of national independence; the building of the National Government; the long contest over slavery; the war for the preservation of the Union —these are the really great matters with which American history deals. (*Independent,* November 24, 1892.) *Mem. Ed.* XIV, 287; *Nat. Ed.* XII, 247.

HISTORY, MILITARY. I do not believe it is possible to treat military history as something entirely apart from the general national history. I will go a little further than that: I think it is utterly idle to try to understand the German victories in 1866 and 1870 unless you study the German history from the time when Stein and Scharnhorst began the reforms until those reforms reached their culmination under Roon and Moltke. I don't think that any study of the last sixty days' military operations in the Balkans would help you to understand what was done if you didn't study carefully the history of the Balkan people for at least a generation previous to this war that we have seen going on before our eyes. I am perfectly clear that the military history must be written primarily— not entirely, but primarily—by military men, and for that reason, I have felt that it should be written under the observation of the general staff, but I feel that there should be the collaboration of civilians with the military writers, and if those civilian writers are of the proper type some of the most important lessons will be taught by them, and they will be among the most important lessons because they will be lessons that the military man can't with propriety teach. They will be criticisms of the American Government and the American people. I don't wish to see the military history written by the general staff alone, because the general staff can't with propriety tell the whole truth about the government and about the people, to the government and to the people. (At Conference on Military History, American Historical Association, Boston, December 28, 1912.) *Mem. Ed.* XVIII, 310-311; *Nat. Ed.* XVI, 233-234.

HISTORY, NATIONAL. A nation's greatness lies in its possibility of achievement in the present, and nothing helps it more than the consciousness of achievement in the past. (*Forum,* February 1895.) *Mem. Ed.* XV, 14; *Nat. Ed.* XIII, 12.

HISTORY AND CITIZENSHIP. History, taught for a directly and immediately useful purpose to pupils and the teachers of pupils, is one of the necessary features of a sound education in democratic citizenship. (Presidential Address, American Historical Association, Boston, December 27, 1912.) *Mem. Ed.* XIV, 7; *Nat. Ed.* XII, 7.

HISTORY. *See also* ARCHAEOLOGY; CURRENT EVENTS; INSCRIPTIONS; MONGOL INVASIONS; PRIMITIVE SOCIETY.

HOHENZOLLERNS. *See* FREDERICK THE GREAT; WILLIAM II.

HOLIDAYS. *See* CHRISTMAS; FOURTH OF JULY; MEMORIAL DAY; THANKSGIVING DAY.

HOLLAND. I thoroughly enjoyed my stay in Holland, both at The Hague and Amsterdam. The people were charming, and the crowd behaved exactly as if I was still President and home in America. . . . There was one thing I found really consoling about Holland. After the beginning of the eighteenth century it had gone steadily down-hill, and was very low indeed at the close of the Napoleonic wars. Since then it has steadily risen, and though the nation itself is small I was struck by the power and alertness and live spirit of the people as individuals and collectively. They had completely recovered themselves. When I feel melancholy about some of the tendencies in England and the United States, I like to think that they probably only represent temporary maladies, and that ultimately our people will recover themselves and achieve more than they have ever achieved; and Holland shows that national recovery can really take place. (To Sir George Otto Trevelyan, October 1, 1911.) *Mem. Ed.* XXIV, 275; Bishop II, 235.

HOME—IMPORTANCE OF THE. Tariffs, the currency, all kinds of other things that convulse the country and attract every one's attention, are not of any real consequence compared with having the right kind of men and women in the homes of the country. (Before Iowa State Teachers' Association, Des Moines, November 4, 1910.) *Mem. Ed.* XVIII, 454; *Nat. Ed.* XVI, 340.

HOME—SUBSTITUTES FOR THE. Nothing outside of home can take the place of home. The school is an invaluable adjunct to the home, but it is a wretched substitute for it. The family relation is the most fundamental, the most important of all relations. (At semicentennial celebration, founding of Agricultural Colleges, Lansing, Mich., May 31, 1907.) *Mem. Ed.* XVIII, 189; *Nat. Ed.* XVI, 144.

──────── . No institution will take the place of a home, and all proposals for rearing and educating children outside the home and supplying the place of parents by "trained educators" indicate a morbid pathological condition in the woman making the proposal. (*Outlook,* January 3, 1914.) *Mem. Ed.* XIV, 174; *Nat. Ed.* XII, 203.

HOME—WOMAN'S PLACE IN THE. I emphatically believe that for the great majority of women the really indispensable industry in which they should engage is the industry of the home. There are exceptions, of course, but exactly as the first duty of the normal man is the duty of being the home maker, so the first duty of the normal woman is to be the home keeper; and exactly as no other learning is as important for the average man as the learning which will teach him how to make his livelihood, so no other learning is as important for the average woman as the learning which will make her a good housewife and mother. (At semicentennial celebration, founding of Agricultural Colleges, Lansing, Mich., May 31, 1907.) *Mem. Ed.* XVIII, 187; *Nat. Ed.* XVI, 142.

HOME LIFE. No piled-up wealth, no splendor of material growth, no brilliance of artistic development, will permanently avail any people unless its home life is healthy, unless the average man possesses honesty, courage, common sense, and decency, unless he works hard and is willing at need to fight hard; and unless the average woman is a good wife, a good mother, able and willing to perform the first and greatest duty of womanhood, able and willing to bear, and to bring up as they should be brought up, healthy children, sound in body, mind, and character, and numerous enough so that the race shall increase and not decrease. (Before National Congress of Mothers, Washington, March 13, 1905.) *Mem. Ed.* XVIII, 226; *Nat. Ed.* XVI, 165.

HOME LIFE, ROOSEVELT'S. I tell you, Kermit, it was a great comfort to feel, all during the last days when affairs looked doubtful, that no matter how things came out the really important thing was the lovely life I have with Mother and with you children, and that compared to this home life everything else was of very small importance from the standpoint of happiness. (To Kermit Roosevelt, November 10, 1904.) *Mem. Ed.* XXIII, 387; Bishop I, 336.

HOME LIFE AND CITIZENSHIP. The basis of good citizenship is the home. A man must be a good son, husband, and father, a woman a good daughter, wife, and mother, first and foremost. There must be no shirking of duties in big things or in little things. The man who will not work hard for his wife and his little ones, the woman who shrinks from bearing and rearing many healthy children, these have no place among the men and women who are striving upward and onward. (Before Young Men's Christian Association, New York City, December 30, 1900.) *Mem. Ed.* XV, 533; *Nat. Ed.* XIII, 497.

HOME-MAKER AND HOME-KEEPER. Exactly as it is true that no nation will prosper unless the average man is a home-maker; that is, unless at some business or trade or profession, he earns enough to make a home for himself and his wife and children, and is a good husband and father; so no nation can exist at all unless the average woman is the home-keeper, the good wife, and unless she is the mother of a sufficient number of healthy children to insure the race going forward and not backward. (*Metropolitan,* May 1916.) *Mem. Ed.* XXI, 145; *Nat. Ed.* XIX, 142.

HOME. See also CHILDREN; FAMILY; HAPPINESS; LABOR CONDITIONS; MARRIAGE; SAGAMORE HILL; TEACHERS; WOMEN.

HOMES COMMISSION. See HOUSING.

HOMESTEAD LAW. Much of our prosperity as a nation has been due to the operation of the homestead law. On the other hand, we should recognize the fact that in the grazing region the man who corresponds to the homesteader may be unable to settle permanently if only allowed to use the same amount of pastureland that his brother, the homesteader, is allowed to use of arable land. One hundred and sixty acres of fairly rich and well-watered soil, or a much smaller amount of irrigated land, may keep a family in plenty, whereas no one could get a living from 160 acres of dry pastureland capable of supporting at the outside only one head of cattle to every ten acres. In the past great tracts of the public domain have been fenced in by persons having no title thereto, in direct defiance of the law forbidding the maintenance or construction of any such unlawful inclosure of public land. For various reasons there has been little interference with such inclosures in the past, but ample notice has now been given the trespassers, and all the resources at the command of the government will hereafter be used to put a stop to such trespassing. (Second Annual Message, Washington, December 2, 1902.) *Mem. Ed.* XVII, 188; *Nat. Ed.* XV, 162.

HONESTY. You cannot have unilateral honesty. The minute that a man is dishonest along certain lines, even though he pretends to be honest along other lines, you can be sure that it is only a pretense, it is only expediency; and you cannot trust to the mere sense of expediency to hold a man straight under heavy pressure. I very early made up my mind that it was a detriment to the public to have in public life any man whose attitude was merely that he would be as honest as the law made it necessary for him to be. The kind of honesty which essentially consists merely in too great acuteness to get into jail is a mighty poor type of honesty upon which to rely; because, up near the borderline between what can and what cannot be punished by law, there come many occasions when the man can defile the public service, can defy the public conscience, can in spirit be false to his oath, and yet technically keep his skirts clear. (At Pacific Theological Seminary, Spring 1911.) *Mem. Ed.* XV, 620; *Nat. Ed.* XIII, 654.

──────────. We firmly believe that the American people feel hostility to no man who has honestly won success. We firmly believe that the American people ask only justice, justice each for himself and justice each for all others. They are against wickedness in rich man and poor man alike. They are against lawless and murderous violence exactly as they are against the sordid materialism which seeks wealth by trickery and cheating, whether on a large or a small scale. They wish to deal honestly and in good faith with all men. They recognize that the prime national need is for honesty, honesty in public life and in private life, honesty in business and in politics, honesty in the broadest and deepest significance of the word. (At Madison Square Garden, New York City, October 30, 1912.) *Mem. Ed.* XIX, 462; *Nat. Ed.* XVII, 339.

HONESTY—NEED FOR. If you have not honesty in the average private citizen, in the average public servant, then all else goes for nothing. The abler a man is, the more dexterous, the shrewder, the bolder, why the more dangerous he is if he has not the root of right living and right thinking in him—and that in private life, and even more in public life. Exactly as in time of war, although you need in each fighting man far more than courage, yet all else counts for nothing if there is not that courage upon which to base it, so in our civil life, although we need that the average man in private life, that the average public servant, shall have far more than honesty, yet all other qualities go for nothing or for worse than nothing unless honesty underlies them—honesty in public life and honesty in private life; not only the honesty that keeps its skirts technically clear, but the honesty that is such according to the spirit as well as the letter of the law; the honesty that is aggressive, the honesty that not merely deplores corruption—it is easy enough to deplore corruption—but that wars against it and tramples it under foot. I ask for that type of honesty, I ask for militant honesty, for the honesty of the kind that makes those who have it discontented with themselves as long as they have failed to do everything that in them lies to stamp out dishonesty wherever it can be found, in high place or in low. (At Washington, October 25, 1903.) *Mem. Ed.* XV, 465; *Nat. Ed.* XIII, 552.

HONESTY AND COURAGE. It is, of course, not enough that a public official should be honest. No amount of honesty will avail if he is not also brave and wise. The weakling and the coward cannot be saved by honesty alone; but without honesty the brave and able man is merely a civic wild beast who should be hunted down by every lover of righteousness. (*Outlook,* May 12, 1900.) *Mem. Ed.* XV, 444; *Nat. Ed.* XIII, 389.

HONESTY AND EFFICIENCY. It is not difficult to be virtuous in a cloistered and negative way. Neither is it difficult to succeed, after a fashion, in active life, if one is content to disregard the considerations which bind honorable and upright men. But it is by no means easy to combine honesty and efficiency; and yet it is absolutely necessary, in order to do any work really worth doing. (1897.) *Mem. Ed.* XV, xix; *Nat. Ed.* XIII, xvii.

HONESTY IN GOVERNMENT. The man who debauches our public life ... is a greater foe to our well-being as a nation than is even the defaulting cashier of a bank, or the betrayer of a private trust. No amount of intelligence and no amount of energy will save a nation which is not honest, and no government can ever be a permanent success if administered in accordance with base ideals. (*Forum,* July 1894.) *Mem. Ed.* XV, 40; *Nat. Ed.* XIII, 27.

———. Without honesty popular government is a repulsive farce. *Outlook,* November 11, 1911, p. 610.

HONESTY IN POLITICS. I would rather go out of politics feeling that I had done what was right than stay in with the approval of all men, knowing in my heart that I had acted as I ought not to. (In the New York Assembly, March 2, 1883.) *Mem. Ed.* XVI, 21.

———. Before discussing questions dealing with the right of the people to rule and to secure social and industrial justice it is necessary to settle once for all that when the decision has been made by the people it shall not be reversed by force and fraud. We have a right to ask every honest man among our opponents, whatever may be his views as to the principles we advocate, heartily to support us in this fight for the elementary, the fundamental honesties of politics. The first and greatest issue before us is the issue of theft. Every honest citizen should join with us in the fight for honesty against theft and corruption. (At Chicago, June 17, 1912.) *Mem. Ed.* XIX, 305; *Nat. Ed.* XVII, 221.

HONESTY IN PUBLIC LIFE. You cannot have honesty in public life unless the average citizen demands honesty in public life. (Before the Hamilton Club, Chicago, September 8, 1910.) *Mem. Ed.* XV, 453; *Nat. Ed.* XIII, 541.

———. Honesty is not so much a credit as an absolute prerequisite to efficient service to the public. ... The number of public servants who actually take bribes is not very numerous outside of certain well-known centres of festering corruption. But the temptation to be dishonest often comes in insidious ways. There are not a few public men who, though they would repel with indignation an offer of a bribe, will give certain corporations special legislative and executive privileges because they have contributed heavily to campaign funds; will permit loose and extravagant work because a contractor has political influence; or, at any rate, will permit a public servant to take public money without rendering an adequate return, by conniving at inefficient service on the part of men who are protected by prominent party leaders. (*Outlook,* May 12, 1900.) *Mem. Ed.* XV, 443; *Nat. Ed.* XIII, 388.

———. If you habitually suffer your public representatives to be dishonest you will gradually lose all power of insisting upon honesty. If you let them continually do little acts that are not quite straight you will gradually induce in their minds the mental attitude which will make it hopeless to get from them anything that is not crooked. (At Pacific Theological Seminary, Spring 1911.) *Mem. Ed.* XV, 625; *Nat. Ed.* XIII, 659.

HONESTY OF THINKING. It is always best to look facts squarely in the face, without blinking them, and to remember that, as has been well said, in the long run even the most uncomfortable truth is a safer companion than the pleasantest falsehood. (*The Sewanee Review,* August 1894.) *Mem. Ed.* XIV, 235; *Nat. Ed.* XIII, 204.

HONESTY VERSUS BRILLIANCY. Honesty we must have; no brilliancy, no "smartness," can take its place. Indeed, in our home affairs, both in the State and in the municipality, it has always seemed to me that what we need is, not so much genius as the homely, every-day virtues of common sense and common honesty. (Campaign Speech, New York City, October 5, 1898.) *Mem. Ed.* XVI, 448; *Nat. Ed.* XIV, 295.

HONESTY. See also BRIBERY; BUSINESS; CHARACTER; CORRUPTION; ELECTION REFORMS; FALSEHOOD; MENTAL ACUTENESS; TEN COMMANDMENTS; TRUTH; VIRTUES.

HONOR. See NATIONAL HONOR.

HOOVER, HERBERT. Mr. Hoover has been appointed as the man to lead us of this Nation in the vitally important matter of producing and saving as much food as we possibly can in order that we can send abroad the largest possible amount for the use of our suffering allies and for the use of our own gallant soldiers. Mr. Hoover's preëminent services in Belgium pointed him out as of all the men in this country the man most fit for the very position to which he has been appointed. Let us give him our most hearty and loyal support. (October 30, 1917.) *Roosevelt in the Kansas City Star,* p. 38.

HORSEBACK RIDING. A good rider is a good rider all the world over; but an Eastern or English horsebreaker and Western broncobuster have so little in common with each other as regards style or surroundings and are so totally out of place in doing each other's work, that it is almost impossible to get either to admit that the other has any merits at all as a horseman, for neither could sit in the saddle of the other or could without great difficulty perform his task. (1888.) *Mem. Ed.* IV, 399; *Nat. Ed.* I, 302.

——————. Cross-country riding in the rough is not a difficult thing to learn; always provided the would-be learner is gifted with or has acquired a fairly stout heart, for a constitutionally timid person is peculiarly out of place in the hunting field. A really finished cross-country rider, a man who combines hand and seat, heart and head, is of course rare. . . . It is comparatively easy to acquire a light hand and a capacity to sit fairly well down in the saddle; and when a man has once got these, he will find no especial difficulty in following the hounds on a trained hunter; and after he has once taken to the sport, he will hardly give it up again of his own free will, for there is no other that is so manly and health-giving, while at the same time yielding so much fun and excitement. While he is learning horsemanship, by the way, the tyro had best also learn to show a wise tolerance for styles of riding other than that he adopts. At some of the meets, although unfortunately not by any means at all of them, he will see a few outsiders, who are not regular members of the hunt; and because one of these, perhaps, rides an army saddle, wears a slouch hat, and has a long-tailed horse, the man whose rig is of the swellest very probably looks down on him, while the slouch-hatted horseman, in return, and quite as illogically, affects to despise, as a mark of effeminacy, the faultless get-up of the regular hunt member. The feeling is quite as absurd on one side as on the other, and is in violation of the cardinal American doctrine of "live and let live." It is perfectly right and proper that the man who wishes to and can afford it should have both himself and his horse turned out in the very latest style; only he should then make up his mind to live well in the front, for it is hardly the thing for a man with a very elaborate get-up to be always pottering about in the rear or riding along roads. On the other hand, there are plenty of men who cannot or will not come except in the dress which happens to suit their own ideas; and certainly their appearance does not concern anybody else but themselves. It is the true policy to welcome warmly any man who cares for the sport, provided he is plucky, good-tempered, and rides his own line; and whether he wears a stiff silk hat, or a broad-brimmed felt one, has nothing whatever to do with the question. *Century,* July 1886, p. 339.

——————. The cowboy's scorn of every method of riding save his own is as profound and as ignorant as is that of the school rider, jockey, or foxhunter. The truth is that each of these is best in his own sphere and is at a disadvantage when made to do the work of any of the others. For all-around riding and horsemanship, I think the West Point graduate is somewhat ahead of any of them. Taken as a class, however, and compared with other classes as numerous, and not with a few exceptional individuals, the cowboy, like the Rocky Mountain stage-driver, has no superiors anywhere for his own work; and they are fine fellows, these iron-nerved reinsmen and rough-riders. (1893.) *Mem. Ed.* II, 350; *Nat. Ed.* II, 300.

HORSEBACK RIDING. See also COWBOYS.

HORSEMANSHIP, ROOSEVELT'S. You are all off about my horsemanship; as you would say if you saw me now. Almost all of our horses on the ranch being young, I had to include in my string three that were but partially broken; and I have had some fine circuses with them. One of them had never been saddled but once before, and he proved vicious, and besides bucking, kept falling over backwards with me; finally he caught me, giving me an awful slam, from which my left arm has by no means recovered. Another bucked me off going down hill; but I think I have cured him, for I put him through a desperate course of sprouts when I got on again. The third I nearly lost in swimming him across a swollen creek, where the flood had carried down a good deal of drift timber. However, I got him through all right in the end, after a regular ducking. Twice one of my old horses turned a somersault while galloping after cattle; once in a prairie dog town, and once while trying to prevent the herd from stampeding in a storm at night. I tell you, I like gentle and well broken horses if I am out for pleasure, and I do not get on any other, unless, as in this case, from sheer necessity. (To H. C. Lodge, June 5, 1885.) *Lodge Letters* I, 30.

HOURS OF LABOR. See EIGHT-HOUR DAY.

HOUSING. We of this country are just beginning to appreciate the social problems which have developed while our cities have been growing so marvelously and while our people have been over-absorbed in their industrial and commercial tasks. We are now becoming conscious of some of the unevenness which has naturally resulted from the rapidity of material growth, the over-absorption in material things; we are beginning to think of the neighbors and the neighborhoods which have been neglected. In a democracy like ours, it is an ill thing for all of us, if any of us suffer from unwholesome surroundings or from lack of opportunity for good home life, good citizenship and useful industry.

It seems to me that your suggestions for the improvement of housing conditions in American cities are wise. Washington is not worse than other cities, but simply like them, in the fact that the living conditions of its less resourceful citizens need to be studied and improved. In appointing the Homes Commission I sought to begin for the National Capital such work as was accomplished for New York City by the several tenement house committees organized there at various times. Doubtless the work which has been inaugurated in Washington by the Homes Commission will need to be continued and extended, as you suggest, by a special philanthropic organization or by subsequent commissions officially appointed. (To C. F. Weller, Secretary, The President's Homes Commission, September 8, 1908.) Charles F. Weller, *Neglected Neighbors*. (J. C. Winston Co., Phila., 1909), p. 1.

HOWE, JULIA WARD. I pin my faith to woman suffragists of the type of the late Julia Ward Howe. Julia Ward Howe was one of the foremost citizens of this Republic; she rendered service to the people such as few men in any generation render; and yet she did, first of all, her full duty in the intimate home relations that must ever take precedence of all other relations. There was never a better wife or mother; her children rose up to call her blessed, and the Commonwealth should call her blessed for the children she bore and reared, for the character she transmitted to them, and the training she gave them in her household. We are fortunate in being able to point to such a woman as exemplifying all that we mean when we insist that the good woman's primary duties must be those of the home and the family, those of wife and mother; but that the full performance of these duties may be helped and not hindered if she also possesses a sense of duty to the public, and the power and desire to perform this duty. (*Outlook*, February 3, 1912.) *Mem. Ed.* XVIII, 280; *Nat. Ed.* XVI, 211-212.

——————. She was in the highest sense a good wife and a good mother; and therefore she fulfilled the primary law of our being. She brought up with devoted care and wisdom her sons and her daughters. At the same time she fulfilled her full duty to the Commonwealth from the public standpoint.

She preached righteousness and she practised righteousness. She sought the peace that comes as the handmaiden of well-doing. She preached that stern and lofty courage of soul which shrinks neither from war nor from any other form of suffering and hardship and danger if it is only thereby that justice can be served. She embodied that trait more essential than any other in the make-up of the men and women of this Republic—the valor of righteousness. (1916.) *Mem. Ed.* XX, 221; *Nat. Ed.* XVIII, 189.

HUERTA, VICTORIANO. See MEXICO.

HUGHES, CHARLES E. As between Mr. Hughes and Mr. Wilson, who can doubt which is the man who will, with austere courage, stand for the national duty?

Mr. Wilson's words have contradicted one another; and all his words have been contradicted by his acts.

Mr. Wilson's promise has not borne the slightest reference to his performance.

We have against him in Mr. Hughes a man whose public life is a guarantee that whatever he says he will make good, and that all his words will be borne out by his deeds.

Against Mr. Wilson's combination of grace in elocution, with futility in action; against his record of words unbacked by deeds or betrayed by deeds, we set Mr. Hughes' rugged and uncompromising straight-forwardness of character and action in every office he has held.

We put the man who thinks and speaks directly, and whose words have always been made good, against the man whose adroit and facile elocution is used to conceal his plans or his want of plans. *Collier's*, October 14, 1916, p. 43.

HUGHES, CHARLES E.—NOMINATION OF. You have, of course, seen the result of the Presidential nominations here. I am having my own troubles with my fellow Progressives. They are wild to have me run on a third ticket. They feel that the Republican Convention was a peculiarly sordid body, a feeling with which I heartily sympathize. They feel that Mr. Hughes was nominated largely in consequence of the German-Americans who were against me, and largely also for the very reason that nobody

[234]

knew anything of his views on living subjects of the day,—and a nomination made for such a cause is in my own judgment evidence of profound political immorality on the part of those making it. But Hughes is an able, upright man whose instincts are right, and I believe in international matters he will learn with comparative quickness, especially as I hope he will put Root into office as Secretary of State. Under these circumstances there is in my mind no alternative but to support him. At his worst he will be better than Wilson, and there is always the chance that he will do very well indeed. (To James Bryce, June 19, 1916.) *Mem. Ed.* XXIV, 485; Bishop II, 413.

―――――――――. In my judgment the nomination of Mr. Hughes meets the conditions set forth in the statement of the Progressive National Committee, issued last January, and in my own statements. Under existing conditions the nomination of a third ticket would, in my judgment, be merely a move in the interest of the election of Mr. Wilson.

I regard Mr. Hughes as a man whose public record is a guaranty that "he will not merely stand for a programme of clean-cut, straight-out Americanism before election, but will resolutely and in good faith put it through if elected." He is beyond all comparison better fitted to be President than Mr. Wilson. (To Progressive National Committee, June 22, 1916.) *Mem. Ed.* XIX, 570; *Nat. Ed.* XVII, 419.

HUGHES CAMPAIGN. I cannot make his fight for him or tell him how to fight. He must do his own battling, make his own plans. His danger is that he will not carry the fight to Wilson. If he does that he is safe. But if he allows Wilson to get the jump on him he is beaten. Wilson will do it with him if he does not watch out. As matters stand, and if the election were held to-morrow, Hughes is beaten.

Here is the cruelty of this nomination of Hughes: For years he has been out of touch with real things; he knows nothing of the great things the Progressive Party movement stood for and did; he is out of touch with the man in the street; out of touch with national and world politics. He is nominated at a time when we needed an advocate—not a judge.

I cannot but support Hughes. You see that as clearly as I do. It is the only thing for me to do because it is the right thing to do. . . .

A term on the bench takes the punch out of many men; it slows them up. It may be that way with Hughes; I don't know. But I do know that he must fight to win. (In conversation with Leary, 1916.) *Talks with T. R.* From the diaries of John J. Leary, Jr. (Houghton Mifflin Co., Boston, 1922), pp. 56-57.

HUGHES, CHARLES E. *See also* ELECTION OF 1916.

HUMAN RIGHTS. *See* PROPERTY RIGHTS.

HUMANITY—TRAITS OF. We have lost the faculty simply and naturally to recognize that the essential traits of humanity are shown alike by big men and by little men, in the lives that are now being lived and in those that are long ended. (*Outlook,* August 26, 1911.) *Mem. Ed.* XIV, 442; *Nat. Ed.* XII, 100.

HUMANITY. *See also* BROTHERHOOD; CHARITY; FELLOW-FEELING.

HUNTER—QUALIFICATIONS OF THE. The qualities that make a good soldier are, in large part, the qualities that make a good hunter. Most important of all is the ability to shift for oneself, the mixture of hardihood and resourcefulness which enables a man to tramp all day in the right direction, and, when night comes, to make the best of whatever opportunities for shelter and warmth may be at hand. Skill in the use of the rifle is another trait; quickness in seeing game, another; ability to take advantage of cover, yet another; while patience, endurance, keenness of observation, resolution, good nerves, and instant readiness in an emergency, are all indispensable to a really good hunter. (1905.) *Mem. Ed.* III, 189; *Nat. Ed.* III, 21.

―――――――――. In addition to being a true sportsman and not a game-butcher, in addition to being a humane man as well as keen-eyed, strong-limbed, and stout-hearted, the big-game hunter should be a field naturalist. If possible, he should be an adept with the camera; and hunting with the camera will tax his skill far more than hunting with rifle, while the results in the long run give much greater satisfaction. Wherever possible he should keep a note-book, and should carefully study and record the habits of the wild creatures, especially when in some remote regions to which trained scientific observers but rarely have access. (1905.) *Mem. Ed.* III, 173-174; *Nat. Ed.* III, 8-9.

―――――――――. The mere fair-weather hunter, who trusts entirely to the exertions of others, and does nothing more than ride or walk about under favorable circumstances, and shoot at what somebody else shows him, is a hunter in name only. Whoever would really deserve the title must be able at a pinch to shift for himself, to grapple with the difficulties and hardships of wilderness life unaided, and not only to hunt, but at times to travel for days, whether on foot or on horseback, alone. However, after one has passed one's novitiate, it is pleasant to be comfortable when the comfort does not interfere with the sport; and although a man sometimes likes to hunt alone, yet often it is well to be with some old mountain hunter, a master of woodcraft, who is a first-rate hand at finding game, creeping upon it, and tracking it when wounded. With such a companion one gets much more game, and learns many things by observation instead of by painful experience. (1893.) *Mem. Ed.* II, 163; *Nat. Ed.* II, 142.

——————. Not only should the hunter be able to describe vividly the chase and the life habits of the quarry, but he should also draw the wilderness itself and the life of those who dwell or sojourn therein. We wish to see before us the cautious stalk and the headlong gallop; the great beasts as they feed or rest or run or make love or fight; the wild hunting camps; the endless plains shimmering in the sunlight; the vast, solemn forests; the desert and the marsh and the mountain chain; and all that lies hidden in the lonely lands through which the wilderness wanderer roams and hunts game. (1905.) *Mem. Ed.* III, 298; *Nat. Ed.* III, 112.

HUNTERS OF THE PLAINS. Most of the so-called hunters are not worth much. There are plenty of men hanging round the frontier settlements who claim to be hunters, and who bedizen themselves in all the traditional finery of the craft, in the hope of getting a job at guiding some "tenderfoot"; and there are plenty of skin-hunters, or meat-hunters, who, after the Indians have been driven away and when means of communication have been established, mercilessly slaughter the game in season and out, without more skill than they possess; but these are all mere temporary excrescences, and the true old Rocky Mountain hunter and trapper, the plainsman, or mountain man, who, with all his faults, was a man of iron nerve and will, is now almost a thing of the past. . . .

The old hunters were a class by themselves. They penetrated, alone or in small parties, to the farthest and wildest haunts of the animals they followed, leading a solitary, lonely life, often never seeing a white face for months and even years together. They were skilful shots, and were cool, daring, and resolute to the verge of recklessness. On anything like even terms, they very greatly overmatched the Indians by whom they were surrounded, and with whom they waged constant and ferocious war. In the government expeditions against the plains tribes they were of absolutely invaluable assistance as scouts. They rarely had regular wives or white children, and there are none to take their places, now that the greater part of them have gone. For the men who carry on hunting as a business where it is perfectly safe have all the vices of their prototypes, but, not having to face the dangers that beset the latter, so neither need nor possess the stern, rough virtues that were required in order to meet and overcome them. The ranks of the skin-hunters and meat-hunters contain some good men; but, as a rule, they are a most unlovely race of beings, not excelling even in the pursuit which they follow because they are too shiftless to do anything else; and the sooner they vanish the better. (1885.) *Mem. Ed.* I, 30-32; *Nat. Ed.* I, 25-26.

HUNTERS. See also Adventurer; Selous, F. C.; Washington, George; Wilderness.

HUNTING. It is still a moot question whether it is better to hunt on horseback or on foot; but the course of events is rapidly deciding it in favor of the latter method. Undoubtedly, it is easier and pleasanter to hunt on horseback; and it has the advantage of covering a great deal of ground. But it is impossible to advance with such caution, and it is difficult to shoot as quickly, as when on foot; and where the deer are shy and not very plenty, the most enthusiastic must, slowly and reluctantly but surely, come to the conclusion that a large bag can only be made by the still-hunter who goes on foot. Of course, in the plains country it is not as in the mountainous or thickly wooded regions, and the horse should almost always be taken as a means of conveyance to the hunting-grounds and from one point to another; but the places where game is expected should, as a rule, be hunted over on foot. This rule is by no means a general one, however. There are still many localities where the advantage of covering a great deal of ground more than counterbalances the disadvantage of being on horseback. (1885.) *Mem. Ed.* I, 120-121; *Nat. Ed.* I, 99.

——————. The older I grow the less I care to shoot anything except "varmints." I do not think it at all advisable that the gun should be given up, nor does it seem to me that shooting wild game under proper restrictions can be legitimately opposed by any who are willing that domestic animals shall be kept for food; but there is altogether too much shooting, and if we can only get the camera in place of the gun and have the sportsman sunk somewhat in the naturalist and lover of wild things, the next generation will see an immense change for the better in the life of our woods and waters. (Letter to Mr. Job used as Introduction.) Herbert K. Job, *Wild Wings*. (Houghton Mifflin Co., Boston, 1905), p. xiii.

HUNTING—HARDSHIPS IN. Of course in hunting one must expect much hardship and repeated disappointment; and in many a camp, bad weather, lack of shelter, hunger, thirst, or ill success with game, renders the days and nights irksome and trying. Yet the hunter worthy of the name always willingly takes the bitter if by so doing he can get the sweet, and gladly balances failure and success, spurning the poorer souls who know neither. (1893.) *Mem. Ed.* II, 105; *Nat. Ed.* II, 92-93.

HUNTING—PLEASURES OF. In hunting, the finding and killing of the game is after all but a part of the whole. The free, self-reliant, adventurous life, with its rugged and stalwart democracy; the wild surroundings, the grand beauty of the scenery, the chance to study the ways and habits of the woodland creatures—all these unite to give to the career of the wilderness hunter its peculiar charm. The chase is among the best of all national pastimes; it cultivates that vigorous manliness for the lack of which in a nation, as in an individual, the possession of no other qualities can possibly atone. (1893.) *Mem. Ed.* II, xxxi; *Nat. Ed.* II, xxix.

——————. Personally I feel that the chase of any animal has in it two chief elements of attraction. The first is the chance given to be in the wilderness; to see the sights and hear the sounds of wild nature. The second is the demand made by the particular kind of chase upon the qualities of manliness and hardihood. As regards the first, some kinds of game, of course, lead the hunter into particularly remote and wild localities; and the farther one gets into the wilderness, the greater is the attraction of its lonely freedom. Yet to camp out at all implies some measure of this delight. The keen, fresh air, the breath of the pine forests, the glassy stillness of the lake at sunset, the glory of sunrise among the mountains, the shimmer of the endless prairies, the ceaseless rustle of the cottonwood-leaves where the wagon is drawn up on the low bluff of the shrunken river—all these appeal intensely to any man, no matter what may be the game he happens to be following. But there is a wide variation, and indeed contrast, in the qualities called for in the chase itself, according as one quarry or another is sought. (1905.) *Mem. Ed.* III, 188-189; *Nat. Ed.* III, 21.

HUNTING—PREFERENCE IN. I have always liked "horse and rifle," and being, like yourself, "ein echter Amerikaner," prefer that description of sport which needs a buckskin shirt to that whose votaries adopt the red coat. A buffalo is nobler game than an anise seed bag, the Anglomaniacs to the contrary notwithstanding. (To H. C. Lodge, August 12, 1884.) Lodge *Letters* I, 7.

HUNTING—SKILL IN. I always make it a rule to pace off the distance after a successful shot, whenever practicable—that is, when the animal has not run too far before dropping—and I was at first both amused and somewhat chagrined to see how rapidly what I had supposed to be remarkably long shots shrank under actual pacing. It is a good rule always to try to get as near the game as possible, and in most cases it is best to risk startling it in the effort to get closer rather than to risk missing it by a shot at long range. At the same time, I am a great believer in powder-burning, and, if I cannot get near, will generally try a shot anyhow, if there is a chance of the rifle's carrying to it. In this way a man will now and then, in the midst of many misses, make a very good long shot, but he should not try to deceive himself into the belief that these occasional long shots are to be taken as samples of his ordinary skill. Yet it is curious to see how a really truthful man will forget his misses, and his hits at close quarters, and, by dint of constant repetition, will finally persuade himself that he is in the habit of killing his game at three or four hundred yards. (1885.) *Mem. Ed.* I, 38; *Nat. Ed.* I, 32.

——————. In killing dangerous game, steadiness is more needed than good shooting. No game is dangerous unless a man is close up, for nowadays hardly any wild beast will charge from a distance of a hundred yards, but will rather try to run off; and if a man is close it is easy enough for him to shoot straight if he does not lose his head. A bear's brain is about the size of a pint bottle; and any one can hit a pint bottle offhand at thirty or forty feet. I have had two shots at bears at close quarters, and each time I fired into the brain, the bullet in one case striking fairly between the eyes, . . . and in the other going in between the eye and ear. A novice at this kind of sport will find it best and safest to keep in mind the old Norse viking's advice in reference to a long sword: "If you go in close enough your sword will be long enough." If a poor shot goes in close enough he will find that he shoots straight enough. (1885.) *Mem. Ed.* I, 290; *Nat. Ed.* I, 241.

HUNTING BOOKS. A really first-class hunting book ... ought to be written by a man of prowess and adventure, who is a fair out-of-doors naturalist; who loves nature, who loves books, and who possesses the gift of seeing what is worth seeing and of portraying it with vivid force and yet with refinement. Such men are rare; and it is not always easy for them to command an audience. (N. Y. *Times Review of Books,* October 13, 1918.) *Mem. Ed.* XIV, 550-551; *Nat. Ed.* XII, 410.

——————. The average big-game hunter writes a book about as interesting as a Baedeker, and nothing like as useful. I doubt if there is a less attractive type of literary output than an annotated game-bag, or record of slaughter, from which we are able to gather nothing of value as to the lives of the animals themselves, and very little even from the dreary account of the author's murderous prowess. Some of the books by the best men err in exasperating fashion owing to a morbid kind of modesty which makes the writer too self-conscious to tell frankly and fully what he himself has done. This is sometimes spoken of as a good trait, but it is not a good trait. It is not as repellent as conceit or vulgarity, separate or combined, or as that painful trait, the desire to be "funny"; but it is a very bad trait, nevertheless. If a hunter thinks he ought not to tell what he himself has done, then he had much better not write a book at all. ... If the hunter does write, and is a keen observer, he should remember that, if he is worth listening to at all, his listeners will be particularly interested in hearing of any noteworthy experience that has happened to him personally. (*Outlook,* September 16, 1911.) *Mem. Ed.* XIV, 503-504; *Nat. Ed.* XII, 371-372.

HUNTING IN LATER YEARS. My trip with the boys in Arizona was a great success, although it is rather absurd for me now to be going on such trips, for a stout, rheumatic, elderly gentleman is not particularly in place sleeping curled up in a blanket on the ground, and eating the flesh of a cougar because there is nothing else available. (To Arthur Lee, September 2, 1913.) *Mem. Ed.* XXIV, 414; Bishop II, 352.

HUNTING IN SOUTH AFRICA. South Africa was the true hunters' paradise. If the happy hunting-grounds were to be found anywhere in this world, they lay between the Orange and the Zambesi, and extended northward here and there to the Nile countries and Somaliland. Nowhere else were there such multitudes of game, representing so many and such widely different kinds of animals, of such size, such beauty, such infinite variety. We should have to go back to the fauna of the Pleistocene to find its equal. Never before did men enjoy such hunting as fell to the lot of those roving adventurers who first penetrated its hidden fastnesses, camped by its shrunken rivers, and galloped over its sun-scorched wastes; and, alas that it should be written, no man will ever see the like again. Fortunately, its memory will forever be kept alive in some of the books that the great hunters have written about it. (1905.) *Mem. Ed.* III, 301; *Nat. Ed.* III, 114.

HUNTING IN THE WILDERNESS. Hunting in the wilderness is of all pastimes the most attractive, and it is doubly so when not carried on merely as a pastime. Shooting over a private game-preserve is of course in no way to be compared to it. The wilderness hunter must not only show skill in the use of the rifle and address in finding and approaching game, but he must also show the qualities of hardihood, self-reliance, and resolution needed for effectively grappling with his wild surroundings. The fact that the hunter needs the game, both for its meat and for its hide, undoubtedly adds a zest to the pursuit. (1893.) *Mem. Ed.* II, 19; *Nat. Ed.* II, 17.

HUNTING TROPHIES. If it is morally right to kill an animal to eat its body, then it is morally right to kill it to preserve its head. A good sportsman will not hesitate as to the relative value he puts upon the two, and to get the one he will go a long time without eating the other. (1905.) *Mem. Ed.* III, 311; *Nat. Ed.* III, 122.

HUNTING WITH HOUNDS. Of all sports possible in civilized countries, riding to hounds is perhaps the best if followed as it should be, for the sake of the strong excitement, with as much simplicity as possible, and not merely as a fashionable amusement. It tends to develop moral no less than physical qualities; the rider needs nerve and head; he must possess daring and resolution, as well as a good deal of bodily skill and a certain amount of wiry toughness and endurance. (1893.) *Mem. Ed.* II, 354; *Nat. Ed.* II, 304.

HUNTING WITH THE CAMERA. More and more, as it becomes necessary to preserve the game, let us hope that the camera will largely supplant the rifle. It is an excellent thing to have a nation proficient in marksmanship, and it is highly undesirable that the rifle should be wholly laid by. But the shot is, after all, only a small part of the free life of the wilderness. The chief attractions lie in the physical hardihood for which the life calls, the sense of limitless freedom which it brings, and the remoteness and wild charm and beauty of primitive nature. All of this we get exactly as much in hunting with the camera as in hunting with the rifle; and of the two, the former is the kind of sport which calls for the higher degree of skill, patience, resolution, and knowledge of the life history of the animal sought. (Introduction to A. G. Wallihan's *Camera Shots at Big Game,* dated May 31, 1901.) Mem. Ed. XIV, 581; *Nat. Ed.* XII, 437.

HUNTING. *See also* Antelope; Bear; Buffalo; Deer; Elk; Fox; Game; Moose; Rifle; Sheep; Wapiti; Wild Life.

HUSBANDS. A man must think well before he marries. He must be a tender and considerate husband and realize that there is no other human being to whom he owes so much of love and regard and consideration as he does to the woman who with pain bears and with labor rears the children that are his. No words can paint the scorn and contempt which must be felt by all right-thinking men, not only for the brutal husband, but for the husband who fails to show full loyalty and consideration to his wife. Moreover, he must work, he must do his part in the world. (1913.) Mem. Ed. XXII, 194; *Nat. Ed.* XX, 166.

——————. Whenever a man thinks that he has outgrown the woman who is his mate, he will do well carefully to consider whether his growth has not been downward instead of upward, whether the facts are not merely that he has fallen away from his wife's standard of refinement and of duty. (1913.) Mem. Ed. XXII, 201; *Nat. Ed.* XX, 172.

HUSBANDS. *See also* Family; Home; Marriage; Women.

HYPHENATED AMERICANS. *See* Allegiance; American People; Americans, Hyphenated; Citizenship; German-Americans; Irish-Americans.

HYPOCRISY. Hypocrisy is as revolting in a nation as in a man; and in the long run, I do not believe it pays either man or nation. *Outlook,* December 30, 1911, p. 1047.

——————. Reform is always held back by hypocrisy. *Outlook,* November 11, 1911, p. 611.

HYPOCRISY—CONDEMNATION OF. I do not like the thief, big or little; I do not like him in business and I do not like him in politics; but I dislike him most when, to shield himself from the effects of his wrong-doing, he claims that, after all, he is a "religious man." He is not a religious man, save in the sense that the Pharisee was a religious man in the time of the Saviour. The man who advances the fact that he goes to church and reads the Bible as an offset to the fact that he has acted like a scoundrel in his public and private relations, only writes his own condemnation in larger letters than before. (At Pacific Theological Seminary, Spring 1911.) Mem. Ed. XV, 614; *Nat. Ed.* XIII, 649.

HYPOCRISY IN POLITICS. It does make me flame with indignation when men who pretend to be especially the custodians of morals, and who sit in judgment from an Olympian height of virtue on the deeds of other men, themselves offend in a way that puts them on a level with the most corrupt scoundrel in a city government. (To William R. Nelson, late 1910.) *Roosevelt in the Kansas City Star,* p. xx.

HYSTERIA. Hysteria does not tend toward edification; and in this country hysteria is unfortunately too often the earmark of the ultrapacifist. (*Outlook,* September 23, 1914.) Mem. Ed. XX, 25; *Nat. Ed.* XVIII, 21.

HYSTERICS. It is not merely schoolgirls that have hysterics; very vicious mob-leaders have them at times and so do well-meaning demagogues when their heads are turned by the applause of men of little intelligence and their minds inflated with the possibility of acquiring solid leadership in the country. The dominant note in Mr. Bryan's utterances and in the campaign waged in his behalf is the note of hysteria. (Before American Republican College League, Chicago, October 15, 1896.) Mem. Ed. XVI, 394; *Nat. Ed.* XIV, 258.

I

IDEAL—THE PRACTICAL AND THE. All my life in politics, I have striven to make the necessary working compromise between the ideal and the practical. If a man does not have an ideal and try to live up to it, then he becomes a mean, base and sordid creature, no matter how successful. If, on the other hand, he does not work practically, with the knowledge that he is in the world of actual men and must get results, he becomes a worthless head-in-the-air creature, a nuisance to himself and to everybody else. (To Kermit Roosevelt, January 27, 1915.) *Mem. Ed.* XXIV, 419; Bishop II, 356.

IDEAL. *See also* COMPROMISE; PRACTICALITY.

IDEALISM—NEED OF. Surely all of us . . . ought to realize the need in this country of a loftier idealism than we have had in the past; and the further and even greater need that we should in actual practice live up to the ideals we profess. The things of the body have a rightful place and a great place. But the things of the soul should have an even greater place. There has been in the past in this country far too much of that gross materialism which, in the end, eats like an acid into all the finer qualities of our souls. (*Metropolitan,* November 1918.) *Mem. Ed.* XXI, 272; *Nat. Ed.* XIX, 252.

IDEALISM—PLEA FOR. When I speak of lofty idealism, I mean ideals to be realized. I abhor that mock idealism which finds expression only in phrase and vanishes when the phrase has been uttered. I am speaking of the idealism which will permit no man in public or private to say anything lofty as a cloak for base action. I am asking for the idealism which will demand that every promise expressed or implied be kept, that every profession of decency, of devotion that is lofty in words, should be made good by deeds. I am asking for an idealism which shall find expression beside the hearthstone and in the family and in the councils of the state and the nation, and I ask you men in this great crisis, and I ask you women who have now come into the political arena, to stand shoulder to shoulder with your husbands and brothers and sons. I ask you to see that when those who have gone abroad to endure every species of hardship, to risk their lives, to give their lives, when those of them who live come home, that they shall come home to a nation which they can be proud to have fought for or could be proud to have died for. (At Saratoga, N. Y., July 17, 1918.) *Mem. Ed.* XXIV, 529; Bishop II, 452.

IDEALISM, APPLIED. The only idealism worth considering in the workaday business of this world is applied idealism. This is merely another way of saying that permanent good to humanity is most apt to come from actually trying to reduce ideals to practice, and this means that the ideals must be substantially or at least measurably realizable. (1918.) *Mem. Ed.* XXI, 346; *Nat. Ed.* XIX, 316.

IDEALISTS — RESPONSIBILITY OF. There can be nothing worse for the community than to have the men who profess lofty ideals show themselves so foolish, so narrow, so impracticable, as to cut themselves off from communion with the men who are actually able to do the work of governing, the work of business, the work of the professions. It is a sad and evil thing if the men with a moral sense group themselves as impractical zealots, while the men of action gradually grow to discard and laugh at all moral sense as an evidence of impractical weakness. (At Harvard University, Cambridge, June 28, 1905.) *Mem. Ed.* XVIII, 441; *Nat. Ed.* XVI, 328.

IDEALS. Be practical as well as generous in your ideals. Keep your eyes on the stars, but remember to keep your feet on the ground. Be truthful; a lie implies fear, vanity, or malevolence; be frank; furtiveness and insincerity are faults incompatible with true manliness. Be honest, and remember that honesty counts for nothing unless back of it lie courage and efficiency. If in this country we ever have to face a state of things in which on one side stand the men of high ideals who are honest, good, well-meaning, pleasant people, utterly unable to put those ideals into shape in the rough field of practical life, while on the other side are grouped the strong, powerful, efficient men with no ideals: then the end of the Republic will be near. (At Groton School, Groton, Mass., May 24, 1904.) *Mem. Ed.* XV, 480; *Nat. Ed.* XIII, 557.

————. Our ideals should be high, and yet they should be capable of achievement in practical fashion; and we are as little to be excused if we permit our ideals to be tainted with what is sordid and mean and base, as if we allow our power of achievement to atrophy and become either incapable of effort or capable only of such fantastic effort as to accomplish nothing of permanent good. The true doctrine to preach to this nation, as to the individuals composing this nation, is not the life of ease, but the life of effort. If it were in my power to promise the people of this land anything, I would not promise them pleasure. I would promise them that stern happiness which comes from the sense of having done in practical fashion a difficult work which was worth doing. (At Pilgrim Memorial Monument, Provincetown, Mass., August 20, 1907.) *Mem. Ed.* XVIII, 92-93; *Nat. Ed.* XVI, 78.

―――――――. If this nation has not the right kind of ideal in every walk of life, if we have not in our souls the capacity for idealism, the power to strive after ideals, then we are gone. No nation ever amounted to anything if it did not have within its soul the power of fealty to a lofty ideal. (At Pacific Theological Seminary, Spring, 1911.) *Mem. Ed.* XV, 589; *Nat. Ed.* XIII, 627.

IDEALS—ADHERENCE TO. When questions involve deep and far-reaching principles, then I believe that the real expediency is to be found in straightforward and unflinching adherence to principle, and this without regard to what may be the temporary effect. (To Baron d'Estournelles de Constant, September 1, 1903.) *Mem. Ed.* XXIII, 290; Bishop I, 252.

IDEALS — ATTAINMENT OF. We must realize, on the one hand, that we can do little if we do not set ourselves a high ideal, and, on the other, that we will fail in accomplishing even this little if we do not work through practical methods and with a readiness to face life as it is, and not as we think it ought to be. (Inaugural Address as Governor, Albany, January 2, 1899.) *Mem. Ed.* XVII, 4; *Nat. Ed.* XV, 4.

IDEALS—DEVOTION TO. We must not prove false to the memories of the nation's past. We must not prove false to the fathers from whose loins we sprang, and to their fathers, the stern men who dared greatly and risked all things that freedom should hold aloft an undimmed torch in this wide land. They held their worldly well-being as dust in the balance when weighed against their sense of high duty, their fealty to lofty ideals. Let us show ourselves worthy to be their sons. Let us care, as is right, for the things of the body; but let us show that we care even more for the things of the soul. Stout of heart, and pledged to the valor of righteousness, let us stand four-square to the winds of destiny, from whatever corner of the world they blow. (1916.) *Mem. Ed.* XX, 262; *Nat. Ed.* XVIII, 225.

IDEALS, REALIZABLE. If there is one thing with which I have no sympathy, it is with the type of oration very frequently delivered to graduating classes, sometimes, I regret to say, delivered from pulpits, which preaches an ideal so fantastic that those listening listen with a merely intellectual pleasure, and without the slightest intention of trying in real life to realize it. To preach an ideal like that does not do good; it does harm; for it is an evil thing to teach people that precept and practice have no close relation. The moment that any person grows to believe that the abstract conception of conduct is not in any real way to be approached in actual life, that person has received serious harm.... I want you to have ideals that you can achieve, and yet ideals that shall mean on your part a steady spiritual life within you if you try to reach them. I want you to have your eyes on the stars, but remember that your feet are on the ground; and never to let yourselves get into the frame of mind which accepts the abstract deification of certain attributes in theory as an excuse for falling far short in actual life of what you can actually accomplish. (At Commencement of National Cathedral School, Washington, D. C., June 6, 1906.) *Presidential Addresses and State Papers* V, 776-777.

―――――――. If we consciously or carelessly preach ideals which cannot be realized and which we do not intend to have realized, then so far from accomplishing a worthy purpose we actually tend to weaken the morality we ostensibly preach....

Harm is always done by preaching an ideal which the preacher and the hearer know cannot be followed, which they know it is not intended to have followed; for then the hearer confounds all ideals with the false ideal to which he is listening; and because he finds that he is not expected to live up to the doctrine to which he has listened he concludes that it is needless to live up to any doctrine at all.

Now I do not mean for a moment that the ideal preached should be a low one; I do not mean for a moment that it is ever possible entirely to realize even for the very best man or woman the loftiest ideal; but I do mean that the ideal should not be preached except with sincerity, and that it should be preached in such a fashion as to make it possible measurably to approach it. (At Pacific Theological Seminary, Spring 1911.) *Mem. Ed.* XV, 575, 577; *Nat. Ed.* XIII, 615, 616.

―――――――. The vital thing for the nation no less than the individual to remember is that, while dreaming and talking both have their uses, these uses must chiefly exist in seeing the dream realized and the talk turned into action. It is well that there should be some ideals so high as never to be wholly possible of realization; but unless there is a sincere effort measurably to realize them, glittering talk about them represents merely a kind of self-indulgence which ultimately means atrophy of will power. Ideals that are so lofty as always to be unrealizable, have a place, sometimes an exceedingly important place, in the history of mankind, if the attempt partially to realize them is made; but in the long run what most helps forward the common run of humanity in this workaday world is the possession of realizable ideals and the sincere attempt to realize them.

For similar reasons mere closet theorizing about the work of governing or bettering men is only rarely of any use, and is never of as much use as a working hypothesis that is being translated into practice. It is not mere documentation, mere historical or philosophical research, but experimentation, the service test, the test by trial and error, which counts most in the ceaseless struggle for the slow, partial, never very satisfactory, but never-to-be-abandoned uplift of our brother man and sister woman. (Stafford Little Lecture at Princeton University, November 1917.) Theodore Roosevelt, *National Strength and International Duty.* (Princeton, N. J., 1917), pp. 33-34.

IDEALS AS GUIDE IN POLITICS. I certainly have not yet found any new principle, of importance, in public life, and so far as I have been able to get, I have become more and more a convinced believer in the doctrine flouted a few years ago by a then eminent statesman, that, after all, the Decalogue and the Golden Rule are the two guides to conduct upon which we should base our actions in political affairs. I do not mean to speak in a spirit of cant. I am about the last person who would advocate holding up to any body of men an impractical theory of life; for I steadily feel more and more that if you make your theory impractical you will make your practice imperfect, and that if you set up a theory to which no man can live, you will in practice condone a course of life on the part of your public men which falls far short of what it is your right and duty to insist upon. (Before Independent Club, Buffalo, N. Y., May 15, 1899.) *Mem. Ed.* XVI, 482; *Nat. Ed.* XIV, 322.

IDEALS. *See also* CHARACTER; DEMOCRATIC IDEAL; HONESTY; JUSTICE; MORAL SENSE; MORALITY; TEN COMMANDMENTS.

IDLERS. The idler, rich or poor, is at best a useless and is generally a noxious member of the community. (At Labor Day Picnic, Chicago, September 3, 1900.) *Mem. Ed.* XVI, 516; *Nat. Ed.* XIII, 487.

——————. There is no room in our healthy American life for the mere idler, for the man or the woman whose object it is throughout life to shirk the duties which life ought to bring. Life can mean nothing worth meaning, unless its prime aim is the doing of duty, the achievement of results worth achieving. (At State Fair, Syracuse, N. Y., September 7, 1903.) *Mem. Ed.* XVIII, 67; *Nat. Ed.* XVI, 57.

IDLERS. *See also* LEISURE; PLEASURE; WORK.

IGNORANCE. Viewed from any angle, ignorance is the costliest crop that can be raised in any part of this Union. (At Tuskegee Institute, Tuskegee, Ala., October 24, 1905.) *Mem. Ed.* XVIII, 472; *Nat. Ed.* XVI, 352.

IGNORANCE. *See also* EDUCATION.

IMMIGRANTS—AID TO. If we leave the immigrant to be helped by representatives of foreign governments, by foreign societies, by a press and institutions conducted in a foreign language and in the interest of foreign governments, and if we permit the immigrants to exist as alien groups, each group sundered from the rest of the citizens of the country, we shall store up for ourselves bitter trouble in the future. (Before Knights of Columbus, New York City, October 12, 1915.) *Mem. Ed.* XX, 465; *Nat. Ed.* XVIII, 399.

IMMIGRANTS — ASSIMILATION OF. Where immigrants, or the sons of immigrants, do not heartily and in good faith throw in their lot with us, but cling to the speech, the customs, the ways of life, and the habits of thought of the Old World which they have left, they thereby harm both themselves and us. If they remain alien elements, unassimilated, and with interests separate from ours, they are mere obstructions to the current of our national life, and, moreover, can get no good from it themselves. In fact, though we ourselves also suffer from their perversity, it is they who really suffer most. It is an immense benefit to the European immigrant to change him into an American citizen. To bear the name of American is to bear the most honorable of titles; and whoever does not so believe has no business to bear the name at all, and, if he comes from Europe, the sooner he goes back there the better. Besides, the man who does not become Americanized nevertheless fails to remain a European, and becomes nothing at all. The immigrant cannot possibly remain what he was, or continue to be a member of the Old World society. If he tries to retain his old language, in a few generations it becomes a barbarous jargon; if he tries to retain his old customs and ways of life, in a few generations he becomes an uncouth boor. He has cut himself off from the Old World, and cannot retain his connection with it; and if he wishes ever to amount to anything he must throw himself heart and soul, and without reservation, into the new life to which he has come. (*Forum*, April 1894.) *Mem. Ed.* XV, 26; *Nat. Ed.* XIII, 22.

——————. We should insist that if the immigrant who comes here does in good faith become an American and assimilates himself to us he shall be treated on an exact equality with every one else, for it is an outrage to discriminate against any such man because of creed or birthplace or origin.

But this is predicated upon the man's becoming in very fact an American and nothing but an American. If he tries to keep segregated with men of his own origin and separated from the rest of America, then he isn't doing his part as an American. There can be no divided allegiance here. . . . We have room for but one language here, and that is the English language, for we intend to see that the crucible turns our people out as Americans, of American nationality, and not as dwellers in a polyglot boarding-house; and we have room for but one soul loyalty, and that is loyalty to the American people. (To President of the American Defense Society, January 3, 1919; last message, read at meeting in New York, January 5, 1919.) *Mem. Ed.* XXIV, 554; Bishop II, 474.

IMMIGRANTS — DISCRIMINATION AGAINST. Any discrimination against aliens is a wrong, for it tends to put the immigrant at a disadvantage and to cause him to feel bitterness and resentment during the very years when he should be preparing himself for American citizenship. If an immigrant is not fit to become a citizen, he should not be allowed to come here. If he is fit, he should be given all the rights to earn his own livelihood, and to better himself, that any man can have. (Before Knights of Columbus, New York City, October 12, 1915.) *Mem. Ed.* XX, 464; *Nat. Ed.* XVIII, 398.

IMMIGRANTS—OBLIGATION OF. We should provide for every immigrant, by day-schools for the young and night-schools for the adult, the chance to learn English; and if after, say, five years he has not learned English, he should be sent back to the land from whence he came. . . . We should demand full performance of duty from them. Every man of them should be required to serve a year with the colors, like our native-born youth, before being allowed to vote. Nothing would do more to make him feel an American among his fellow Americans, on an equality of rights, of duties, and of loyalty to the flag. (New York *Times*, September 10, 1917.) *Mem. Ed.* XXI, 54; *Nat. Ed.* XIX, 46.

IMMIGRANTS—RIGHTS OF. The Americans of other blood must remember that the man who in good faith and without reservations gives up another country for this must in return receive exactly the same rights, not merely legal, but social and spiritual, that other Americans proudly possess. We of the United States belong to a new and separate nationality. We are all Americans and nothing else, and each, without regard to his birthplace, creed, or national origin, is entitled to exactly the same rights as all other Americans. (July 15, 1918.) *Roosevelt in the Kansas City Star*, 180.

IMMIGRANTS—TREATMENT OF. Never under any condition should this Nation look at an immigrant as primarily a labor unit. He should always be looked at primarily as a future citizen and the father of other citizens who are to live in this land as fellows with our children and our children's children. Our immigration laws, permanent or temporary, should always be constructed with this fact in view. (December 1, 1917.) *Roosevelt in the Kansas City Star*, 58.

——————. The immigrant must not be allowed to drift or to be put at the mercy of the exploiter. Our object is not to imitate one of the older racial types, but to maintain a new American type and then to secure loyalty to this type. We cannot secure such loyalty unless we make this a country where men shall feel that they have justice and also where they shall feel that they are required to perform the duties imposed upon them. . . .

We cannot afford to continue to use hundreds of thousands of immigrants merely as industrial assets while they remain social outcasts and menaces any more than fifty years ago we could afford to keep the black man merely as an industrial asset and not as a human being. We cannot afford to build a big industrial plant and herd men and women about it without care for their welfare. We cannot afford to permit squalid overcrowding or the kind of living system which makes impossible the decencies and necessities of life. We cannot afford the low wage rates and the merely seasonal industries which mean the sacrifice of both individual and family life and morals to the industrial machinery. (Before Knights of Columbus, New York City, October 12, 1915.) *Mem. Ed.* XX, 468; *Nat. Ed.* XVIII, 402.

IMMIGRANTS. *See also* ALIENS; ALLEGIANCE; AMERICANS, HYPHENATED; CITIZENSHIP; LANGUAGE; LUTHERAN CHURCH; PUBLIC SCHOOLS.

IMMIGRATION. We cannot have too much immigration of the right sort and we should have none whatever of the wrong sort. Of course, it is desirable that even the right kind of immigration should be properly distributed in this country. We need more of such immigration for the South; and special effort should be made to secure it. Perhaps it would be possible to limit the number of immigrants allowed to come in any one year to New York and other Northern cities, while leaving unlimited the number allowed to come to the South; always provided, however, that a stricter effort is made to see that only immigrants of the right kind come to our country anywhere. (Fifth Annual Message, Washington, December 5, 1905.) *Mem. Ed.* XVII, 372-373; *Nat. Ed.* XV, 318.

IMMIGRATION—REGULATION OF. It is urgently necessary to check and regulate our immigration, by much more drastic laws than now exist; and this should be done both to keep out laborers who tend to depress the labor market, and to keep out races which do not assimilate readily with our own, and unworthy individuals of all races. (*Forum*, April 1894.) *Mem. Ed.* XV, 27; *Nat. Ed.* XIII, 23.

IMMIGRATION — RESTRICTION OF. I wish Congress would revise our laws about immigration. Paupers and assisted immigrants of all kinds should be kept out; so should every variety of Anarchists. And if Anarchists do come, they should be taught, as speedily as possible, that the first effort to put their principles into practice will result in their being shot down.... We must soon try to prevent too many laborers coming here and underselling our own workmen in the labor market; a good round head tax on each immigrant, together with a rigid examination into his character, would work well. (Before Federal Club, New York City, December 13, 1888.) *Mem. Ed.* XVI, 137-138; *Nat. Ed.* XIV, 85.

————. Many working men look with distrust upon laws which really would help them; laws for the intelligent restriction of immigration, for instance. I have no sympathy with mere dislike of immigrants; there are classes and even nationalities of them which stand at least on an equality with the citizens of native birth, as the last election showed. But in the interest of our working men we must in the end keep out laborers who are ignorant, vicious, and with low standards of life and comfort, just as we have shut out the Chinese. (*Review of Reviews*, January 1897.) *Mem. Ed.* XVI, 380; *Nat. Ed.* XIII, 164.

————. The prime need is to keep out all immigrants who will not make good American citizens. The laws now existing for the exclusion of undesirable immigrants should be strengthened. Adequate means should be adopted, enforced by sufficient penalties, to compel steamship companies engaged in the passenger business to observe in good faith the law which forbids them to encourage or solicit immigration to the United States. Moreover, there should be a sharp limitation imposed upon all vessels coming to our ports as to the number of immigrants in ratio to the tonnage which each vessel can carry. This ratio should be high enough to insure the coming hither of as good a class of aliens as possible. (Fifth Annual Message, Washington, December 5, 1905.) *Mem. Ed.* XVII, 373; *Nat. Ed.* XV, 319.

IMMIGRATION — RESTRICTION OF ORIENTAL. There has always been a strong feeling in California against the immigration of Asiatic laborers, whether these are wage-workers or men who occupy and till the soil. I believe this to be fundamentally a sound and proper attitude, an attitude which must be insisted upon, and yet which can be insisted upon in such a manner and with such courtesy and such sense of mutual fairness and reciprocal obligation and respect as not to give any just cause of offense to Asiatic peoples. (1913.) *Mem. Ed.* XXII, 429; *Nat. Ed.* XX, 368.

IMMIGRATION POLICY. Our present immigration laws are unsatisfactory. We need every honest and efficient immigrant fitted to become an American citizen, every immigrant who comes here to stay, who brings here a strong body, a stout heart, a good head, and a resolute purpose to do his duty well in every way and to bring up his children as law-abiding and God-fearing members of the community. But there should be a comprehensive law enacted with the object of working a threefold improvement over our present system. First, we should aim to exclude absolutely not only all persons who are known to be believers in anarchistic principles or members of anarchistic societies, but also all persons who are of a low moral tendency or of unsavory reputation....

The second object of a proper immigration law ought to be to secure by a careful and not merely perfunctory educational test some intelligent capacity to appreciate American institutions and act sanely as American citizens. This would not keep out all anarchists, for many of them belong to the intelligent criminal class. But it would do what is also in point, that is, tend to decrease the sum of ignorance, so potent in producing the envy, suspicion, malignant passion, and hatred of order, out of which anarchistic sentiment inevitably springs. Finally, all persons should be excluded who are below a certain standard of economic fitness to enter our industrial field as competitors with American labor. There should be proper proof of personal capacity to earn an American living and enough money to insure a decent start under American conditions. This would stop the influx of cheap labor, and the resulting competition which gives rise to so much of bitterness in American industrial life. (First Annual Message, Washington, December 3, 1901.) *Mem. Ed.* XVII, 110-111; *Nat. Ed.* XV, 95-96.

IMMIGRATION. See also AMERICAN PEOPLE; CHINESE IMMIGRATION; GERMAN IMMIGRATION; JAPANESE EXCLUSION.

IMPARTIALITY. See NEUTRALITY.

IMPERIALISM. Nations that expand and nations that do not expand may both ultimately go down, but the one leaves heirs and a glorious memory, and the other leaves neither. The Roman expanded, and he has left a memory which has profoundly influenced the history of mankind, and he has further left as the heirs of his body, and, above all, of his tongue and culture, the so-called Latin peoples of Europe and America. Similarly to-day it is the great expanding peoples which bequeath to future ages the great memories and material results of their achievements, and the nations which shall have sprung from their loins, England standing as the archetype and best exemplar of all such mighty nations. But the peoples that do not expand leave, and can leave, nothing behind them. (1900.) *Mem. Ed.* XV, 290-291; *Nat. Ed.* XIII, 339.

——————. It is as idle to apply to savages the rules of international morality which obtain between stable and cultured communities, as it would be to judge the fifth-century English conquest of Britain by the standards of to-day. Most fortunately, the hard, energetic, practical men who do the rough pioneer work of civilization in barbarous lands, are not prone to false sentimentality. The people who are, are the people who stay at home. Often these stay-at-homes are too selfish and indolent, too lacking in imagination, to understand the race-importance of the work which is done by their pioneer brethren in wild and distant lands; and they judge them by standards which would only be applicable to quarrels in their own townships and parishes. Moreover, as each new land grows old, it misjudges the yet newer lands, as once it was itself misjudged. The home-staying Englishman of Britain grudges to the Africander his conquest of Matabeleland; and so the home-staying American of the Atlantic States dislikes to see the Western miners and cattlemen win for the use of their people the Sioux hunting-grounds. Nevertheless, it is the men actually on the borders of the longed-for ground, the men actually in contact with the savages, who in the end shape their own destinies. (1894.) *Mem. Ed.* XI, 274-275; *Nat. Ed.* IX, 57.

——————. Russia has expanded in Asia, England in Asia, Africa and Australia, and France and Germany in Africa, all with the strides of giants during the years that have just passed. In every instance the expansion has taken place because the race was a great race. It was a sign and proof of greatness in the expanding nation, and moreover bear in mind that in each instance it was of incalculable benefit to mankind. In Australia a great sister commonwealth to our own has sprung up. In India a peace like the Roman peace has been established, and the country made immeasurably better. So it is in Egypt, in Algiers and at the Cape, while Siberia, before our very eyes, is being changed from the seat of wandering tribes of ferocious nomads into a great civilized country. When great nations fear to expand, shrink from expansion, it is because their greatness is coming to an end. Are we still in the prime of our lusty youth, still at the beginning of our glorious manhood, to sit down among the outworn people, to take our place with the weak and craven? A thousand times no! A thousand times rather face any difficulty—rather meet and overcome any danger—than turn the generous and vigorous blood of our national life into the narrow channels of ignominy and fear. (At Akron, O., September 23, 1899.) Thomas W. Handford, *Theodore Roosevelt, The Pride of the Rough Riders.* (Chicago, 1899), pp. 190-191.

IMPERIALISM—JUSTIFICATION OF. It is infinitely better for the whole world that Russia should have taken Turkestan, that France should have taken Algiers, and that England should have taken India. The success of an Algerian or of a Sepoy revolt would be a hideous calamity to all mankind, and those who abetted it, directly or indirectly, would be traitors to civilization. And so exactly the same reasoning applies to our own dealings with the Philippines. (At Lincoln Club Dinner, New York City, February 13, 1899.) *Mem. Ed.* XVI, 476; *Nat. Ed.* XIV, 317.

IMPERIALISM—OPPONENTS OF. There are some anti-expansionists whose opposition to expansion takes the form of opposition to American interests; and with these gentry there is no use dealing at all. Whether from credulity, from timidity, or from sheer lack of patriotism, their attitude during the war was as profoundly un-American as was that of the "Copperheads" in 1861. Starting from the position of desiring to avoid war even when it had become inevitable if our national honor was to be preserved, they readily passed into a frame of mind which made them really chagrined at every American triumph, while they showed very poorly concealed satisfaction over every American shortcoming; and now they permit their hostility to the principle of expansion to lead them into persistent effort to misrepresent what is being done in the islands and parts of islands which we have actually conquered. (*Outlook*, January 7, 1899.) *Mem. Ed.* XII, 518-519; *Nat. Ed.* XI, 248-249.

IMPERIALISM, AMERICAN. The simple truth is that there is nothing even remotely resembling "imperialism" or "militarism" involved in the present development of that policy of expansion which has been part of the history of America from the day when she became a nation. The words mean absolutely nothing as applied to our present policy in the Philippines; for this policy is only imperialistic in the sense that Jefferson's policy in Louisiana was imperialistic; only military in the sense that Jackson's policy toward the Seminoles or Custer's toward the Sioux embodied militarism....

There is no more militarism or imperialism in garrisoning Luzon until order is restored than there was imperialism in sending soldiers to South Dakota in 1890 during the Ogillallah outbreak. The reasoning which justifies our having made war against Sitting Bull also justifies our having checked the outbreaks of Aguinaldo and his followers, directed, as they were against Filipino and American alike. (Letter accepting nomination for Vice-Presidency, September 15, 1900.) *Mem. Ed.* XVI, 556-557; *Nat. Ed.* XIV, 368-369.

IMPERIALISM AND PEACE. With a barbarous nation peace is the exceptional condition. On the border between civilization and barbarism war is generally normal because it must be under the conditions of barbarism. Whether the barbarian be the Red Indian on the frontier of the United States, the Afghan on the border of British India, or the Turkoman who confronts the Siberian Cossack, the result is the same. In the long run civilized man finds he can keep the peace only by subduing his barbarian neighbor; for the barbarian will yield only to force, save in instances so exceptional that they may be disregarded....

Every expansion of civilization makes for peace. In other words, every expansion of a great civilized power means a victory for law, order, and righteousness. This has been the case in every instance of expansion during the present century, whether the expanding power were France or England, Russia or America. In every instance the expansion has been of benefit, not so much to the power nominally benefited, as to the whole world. In every instance the result proved that the expanding power was doing a duty to civilization far greater and more important than could have been done by any stationary power. (1900.) *Mem. Ed.* XV, 286-287; *Nat. Ed.* XIII, 336.

IMPERIALISM. *See also* AFRICA; COLONIAL SYSTEM; EXPANSION; INDIA.

IMPERIALIST WAR. The very causes which render this struggle between savagery and the rough front rank of civilization so vast and elemental in its consequence to the future of the world, also tend to render it in certain ways peculiarly revolting and barbarous. It is primeval warfare, and it is waged as war was waged in the ages of bronze and of iron. All the merciful humanity that even war has gained during the last two thousand years is lost. It is a warfare where no pity is shown to noncombatants, where the weak are harried without ruth, and the vanquished maltreated with merciless ferocity. A sad and evil feature of such warfare is that the whites, the representatives of civilization, speedily sink almost to the level of their barbarous foes, in point of hideous brutality. (1894.) *Mem. Ed.* XI, 276; *Nat. Ed.* IX, 58.

IMPERIALIST WAR. *See also* WARS OF CONQUEST.

IMPRESSIONISTS. *See* PAINTING.

"IN GOD WE TRUST." When the question of the new coinage came up we looked into the law and found there was no warrant therein for putting "IN GOD WE TRUST" on the coins. As the custom, although without legal warrant, had grown up, however, I might have felt at liberty to keep the inscription had I approved of its being on the coinage. But as I did not approve of it, I did not direct that it should again be put on. Of course the matter of the law is absolutely in the hands of Congress, and any direction of Congress in the matter will be immediately obeyed. At present, as I have said, there is no warrant in law for the inscription.

My own feeling in the matter is due to my very firm conviction that to put such a motto on coins, or to use it in any kindred manner, not only does no good but does positive harm, and is in effect irreverence which comes dangerously close to sacrilege. A beautiful and solemn sentence such as the one in question should be treated and uttered only with that fine reverence which necessarily implies a certain exaltation of spirit. Any use which tends to cheapen it, and above all, any use which tends to secure its being treated in a spirit of levity, is from every standpoint profoundly to be regretted. . . .

As regards its use on the coinage we have actual experience by which to go. In all my life I have never heard any human being speak reverently of this motto on the coins or show any sign of its having appealed to any high emotion in him. But I have literally hundreds of times heard it used as an occasion of, and incitement to, the sneering ridicule which it is above all things undesirable that so beautiful and exalted a phrase should excite. For example, throughout the long contest, extending over several decades, on the free-coinage question, the existence of this motto on the coins was a constant source of jest and ridicule; and this was unavoidable. Every one must remember the innumerable cartoons and articles based on phrases like "In God we trust for the other eight cents"; "In God we trust for the short weight"; "In God we trust for the thirty-seven cents we do not pay"; and so forth, and so forth. (Letter of November 11, 1907.) *Mem. Ed.* XXIV, 83; Bishop II, 71.

INCOME TAX. There is every reason why, when next our system of taxation is revised, the National Government should impose a graduated inheritance tax, and, if possible, a graduated income tax. The man of great wealth owes a peculiar obligation to the State, because he derives special advantages from the mere existence of government. Not only should he recognize this obligation in the way he leads his daily life and in the way he earns and spends his money, but it should also be recognized by the way in which he pays for the protection the State gives him. On the one hand, it is desirable that he should assume his full and proper share of the burden of taxation; on the other hand, it is quite as necessary that in this kind of taxation, where the men who vote the tax pay but little of it, there should be clear recognition of the danger of inaugurating any such system save in a spirit of entire justice and moderation. Whenever we, as a people, undertake to remodel our taxation system along the lines suggested, we must make it clear beyond peradventure that our aim is to distribute the burden of supporting the government more equitably than at present; that we intend to treat rich man and poor man on a basis of absolute equality, and that we regard it as equally fatal to true democracy to do or permit injustice to the one as to do or permit injustice to the other. (Sixth Annual Message, Washington, December 3, 1906.) *Mem. Ed.* XVII, 432-433; *Nat. Ed.* XV, 368-369.

―――――――――. I speak diffidently about the income tax because one scheme for an income tax was declared unconstitutional by the Supreme Court by a five to four vote; and in addition it is a difficult tax to administer in its practical workings, and great care would have to be exercised to see that it was not evaded by the very man whom it is most desirable to have taxed, for if so evaded it would of course be worse than no tax at all, as the least desirable of all taxes is the tax which bears heavily upon the honest as compared with the dishonest man. Nevertheless, a graduated income tax of the proper type would be a desirable permanent feature of Federal taxation, and I still hope that one may be devised which the Supreme Court will declare constitutional. (Before National Editorial Association, Jamestown, Va., June 10, 1907.) *Presidential Addresses and State Papers* VI, 1319-1320.

―――――――――. The Constitutional Amendment about the income tax is all right; but an income tax must always have in it elements of gross inequality and must always be to a certain extent a tax on honesty. A heavily progressive inheritance tax—national (and heavy) only on really great fortunes going to single individuals—would be far preferable to a national income tax. But whether we can persuade the people to adopt this view I don't know. (To H. C. Lodge, September 10, 1909.) Lodge *Letters* II, 346.

INCOME TAX. *See also* WEALTH.

INDEPENDENCE DAY. *See* FOURTH OF JULY.

INDEPENDENCE SPIRIT — PERVERSION OF. The separatist feeling is ingrained in the fibre of our race, and though in itself a most dangerous failing and weakness, is yet merely a perversion and distortion of the defiant and self-reliant independence of spirit which is one of the chief of the race virtues. (1887.) *Mem. Ed.* VIII, 39; *Nat. Ed.* VII, 33.

INDEPENDENCE SPIRIT. *See also* SLAVERY.

INDEPENDENT, THE, IN POLITICS. I now wish to speak for a moment to those Republicans who call themselves the Independents and work outside of the party. They always claim that they wish to purify the Republican party. They say that to do that they must defeat our candidates. There is a better way to teach those on the inside—that is, when they put up good candidates elect them. (At Republican mass-meeting, 21st Assembly Dist., N. Y., October 28, 1882.) *Mem. Ed.* XVI, 16; *Nat. Ed.* XIV, 14.

――――――. The independent, if he cannot take part in the regular organizations, is bound to do just as much active constructive work (not merely the work of criticism) outside; he is bound to try to get up an organization of his own and to try to make that organization felt in some effective manner. Whatever course the man who wishes to do his duty by his country takes in reference to parties or to independence of parties, he is bound to try to put himself in touch with men who think as he does, and to help make their joint influence felt in behalf of the powers that go for decency and good government. He must try to accomplish things; he must not vote in the air unless it is really necessary. (*Forum,* July 1894.) *Mem. Ed.* XV, 44; *Nat. Ed.* XIII, 31.

――――――. I took the best mugwump stand: my own conscience, my own judgment, were to decide in all things. I would listen to no argument, no advice. I took the isolated peak on every issue, and my people left me. When I looked around, before the session was well under way, I found myself alone. I was absolutely deserted. The people didn't understand. The men from Erie, from Suffolk, from anywhere, would not work with me. "He won't listen to anybody," they said, and I would not. My isolated peak had become a valley; every bit of influence I had was gone. The things I wanted to do I was powerless to accomplish. What did I do? I looked the ground over and made up my mind that there were several other excellent people there, with honest opinions of the right, even though they differed from me. I turned in to help them, and they turned to and gave me a hand. And so we were able to get things done. We did not agree in all things, but we did in some, and those we pulled at together. That was my first lesson in real politics. It is just this: if you are cast on a desert island with only a screw-driver, a hatchet, and a chisel to make a boat with, why, go make the best one you can. It would be better if you had a saw, but you haven't. So with men. Here is my friend in Congress who is a good man, a strong man, but cannot be made to believe in some things which I trust. It is too bad that he doesn't look at it as I do, but he does not, and we have to work together as we can. There is a point, of course, where a man must take the isolated peak and break with it all for clear principle, but until it comes he must work, if he would be of use, with men as they are. As long as the good in them overbalances the evil, let him work with that for the best that can be got. (In conversation with Mr. Riis.) Jacob H. Riis, *Theodore Roosevelt: The Citizen.* (The Outlook Co., N. Y., 1904), pp. 58-60.

INDEPENDENT, THE. *See also* Boss; Compromise; Machine; Mugwumps; Organization; Party Allegiance; Party System; Politics.

INDIA. In India we encounter the most colossal example history affords of the successful administration by men of European blood of a thickly populated region in another continent. It is the greatest feat of the kind that has been performed since the break-up of the Roman Empire. Indeed, it is a greater feat than was performed under the Roman Empire. Unquestionably mistakes have been made; it would indicate qualities literally superhuman if so gigantic a task had been accomplished without mistakes. It is easy enough to point out shortcomings; but the fact remains that the successful administration of the Indian Empire by the English has been one of the most notable and most admirable achievements of the white race during the past two centuries. On the whole it has been for the immeasurable benefit of the natives of India themselves. Suffering has been caused in particular cases and at particular times to these natives; much more often, I believe, by well-intentioned ignorance or bad judgment than by any moral obliquity. But on the whole there has been a far more resolute effort to do justice, a far more resolute effort to secure fair treatment for the humble and the oppressed during the days of English rule in India than during any other period of recorded Indian history. England does not draw a penny from India for English purposes; she spends for India the revenues raised in India; and they are spent for the benefit of the Indians themselves. Undoubtedly India is a less pleasant place than formerly for the heads of tyrannical states. There is now little or no room in it for successful freebooter chieftains, for the despots who lived in gorgeous splendor while under their cruel rule the immense mass of their countrymen festered in sodden misery. But the

[248]

mass of the people have been and are far better off than ever before, and far better off than would now be if English control were overthrown or withdrawn. Indeed, if English control were now withdrawn from India, the whole peninsula would become a chaos of bloodshed and violence; all the weaker peoples, and the most industrious and law-abiding, would be plundered and forced to submit to indescribable wrong and oppression; and the only beneficiaries among the natives would be the lawless, violent, and bloodthirsty. I have no question that there are reforms to be advanced—this is merely another way of saying that the government has been human; I have also no question that there is being made and will be made a successful effort to accomplish these reforms. But the great salient fact is that the presence of the English in India . . . has been for the advantage of mankind. (At celebration of Methodist Episcopal Church, Washington, January 18, 1909.) *Mem. Ed.* XVIII, 345-347; *Nat. Ed.* XVI, 261-263.

INDIAN DIFFICULTIES—CAUSE OF. When I went West, the last great Indian wars had just come to an end, but there were still sporadic outbreaks here and there, and occasionally bands of marauding young braves were a menace to outlying and lonely settlements. Many of the white men were themselves lawless and brutal, and prone to commit outrages on the Indians. Unfortunately, each race tended to hold all the members of the other race responsible for the misdeeds of a few, so that the crime of the miscreant, red or white, who committed the original outrage too often invited retaliation upon entirely innocent people, and this action would in its turn arouse bitter feeling which found vent in still more indiscriminate retaliation. (1913.) *Mem. Ed.* XXII, 132; *Nat. Ed.* XX, 113.

INDIAN LANDS. During the past century a good deal of sentimental nonsense has been talked about our taking the Indians' land. Now, I do not mean to say for a moment that gross wrong has not been done the Indians both by government and individuals, again and again. The government makes promises impossible to perform, and then fails to do even what it might toward their fulfillment; and where brutal and reckless frontiersmen are brought into contact with a set of treacherous, revengeful and fiendishly cruel savages a long series of outrages by both sides is sure to follow. But as regards taking the land, at least from the Western Indians, the simple truth is that the latter never had any real ownership in it at all. Where the game was plenty, there they hunted; they followed it when it moved away to new hunting-grounds, unless they were prevented by stronger rivals, and to most of the land on which we found them they had no stronger claim than that of having a few years previously butchered the original occupants. When my cattle came to the Little Missouri, the region was only inhabited by a score or so of white hunters; their title to it was quite as good as that of most Indian tribes to the lands they claim; yet nobody dreamed of saying that these hunters owned the country. Each could eventually have kept his own claim of 160 acres, and no more. The Indians should be treated in just the same way that we treat the white settlers. Give each his little claim; if, as would generally happen, he declined this, why, then let him share the fate of the thousands of white hunters and trappers who have lived on the game that the settlement of the country has exterminated, and let him, like these whites, who will not work, perish from the face of the earth which he cumbers.

The doctrine seems merciless, and so it is; but it is just and rational for all that. It does not do to be merciful to a few at the cost of justice to the many. (1885.) *Mem. Ed.* I, 18-20; *Nat. Ed.* I, 16.

——————. Much maudlin nonsense has been written about the governmental treatment of the Indians, especially as regards taking their land. For the simple truth is that they had no possible title to most of the lands we took, not even that of occupancy, and at the most were in possession merely by virtue of having butchered the previous inhabitants. For many of its actions toward them the government does indeed deserve the severest criticism; but it has erred quite as often on the side of too much leniency as on the side of too much severity. From the very nature of things, it was wholly impossible that there should not be much mutual wrong-doing and injury in the intercourse between the Indians and ourselves. It was equally out of the question to let them remain as they were, and to bring the bulk of their number up to our standard of civilization with sufficient speed to enable them to accommodate themselves to the changed conditions of their surroundings. (1887.) *Mem. Ed.* VIII, 44; *Nat. Ed.* VII, 38.

——————. The question which lay at the root of our difficulties was that of the occupation of the land itself, and to this there could be no solution save war. The Indians had no ownership of the land in the way in which we understand the term. The tribes lived far apart; each had for its hunting-ground all the territory from which it was not barred by rivals. Each looked with jealousy upon all interlopers, but each was prompt to act as an interloper when occasion offered. Every good hunting-ground was claimed by many nations. It was rare, indeed, that any tribe had an uncontested title to a large tract of land; where such title existed, it rested not on actual occupancy and cultivation, but on the recent butchery of weaker rivals. For instance, there were a dozen tribes, all of whom hunted in Kentucky, and fought each other there, all of whom had equally good titles to the soil, and not one of whom acknowledged the right of any other; as a matter of fact, they had therein no right, save the right of the strongest. The land no more belonged to them than it belonged to Boone and the white hunters who first visited it. (1889.) *Mem. Ed.* X, 80; *Nat. Ed.* VIII, 70.

INDIAN POLICY. It was wholly impossible for our policy to be always consistent. Nowadays we undoubtedly ought to break up the great Indian reservations, disregard the tribal governments, allot the land in severalty (with, however, only a limited power of alienation), and treat the Indians as we do other citizens, with certain exceptions, for their sakes as well as ours. But this policy, which it would be wise to follow now, would have been wholly impracticable a century since. Our central government was then too weak either effectively to control its own members or adequately to punish aggressions made upon them; and even if it had been strong, it would probably have proved impossible to keep entire order over such a vast, sparsely peopled frontier, with such turbulent elements on both sides. The Indians could not be treated as individuals at that time. There was no possible alternative, therefore, to treating their tribes as nations, exactly as the French and English had done before us. Our difficulties were partly inherited from these, our predecessors, were partly caused by our own misdeeds, but were mainly the inevitable result of the conditions under which the problem had to be solved; no human wisdom or virtue could have worked out a peaceable solution. As a nation, our Indian policy is to be blamed, because of the weakness it displayed, because of its short-sightedness, and its occasional leaning to the policy of the sentimental humanitarians; and we have often promised what was impossible to perform; but there has been little wilful wrong-doing. Our government almost always tried to act fairly by the tribes. (1889.) *Mem. Ed.* X, 91-92; *Nat. Ed.* VIII, 80.

——————. In my judgment the time has arrived when we should definitely make up our minds to recognize the Indian as an individual and not as a member of a tribe. The General Allotment Act is a mighty pulverizing engine to break up the tribal mass. It acts directly upon the family and the individual. Under its provisions some 60,000 Indians have already become citizens of the United States. We should now break up the tribal funds, doing for them what allotment does for the tribal lands; that is, they should be divided into individual holdings. There will be a transition period during which the funds will in many cases have to be held in trust. This is the case also with the lands. A stop should be put upon the indiscriminate permission to Indians to lease their allotments. The effort should be steadily to make the Indian work like any other man on his own ground. The marriage laws of the Indians should be made the same as those of the whites.

In the schools the education should be elementary and largely industrial. The need of higher education among the Indians is very, very limited. On the reservations care should be taken to try to suit the teaching to the needs of the particular Indian. (First Annual Message, Washington, December 3, 1901.) *Mem. Ed.* XVII, 150-151; *Nat. Ed.* XV, 129-130.

——————. Wherever the effort is to jump the ordinary Indian too far ahead and yet send him back to the reservation, the result is usually failure. To be useful the steps for the ordinary boy or girl, in any save the most advanced tribes, must normally be gradual. Enough English should be taught to enable such a boy or girl to read, write, and cipher so as not to be cheated in ordinary commercial transactions. Outside of this the training should be industrial, and, among the Navajos, it should be the kind of industrial training which shall avail in the home cabins and in tending flocks and herds and irrigated fields. The Indian should be encouraged to build a better house; but the house must not be too different from his present dwelling, or he will as a rule, neither build it nor live in it. The boy should be taught what will be of actual use to him among his fellows, and not what might be of use to a skilled mechanic in a big city, who can work only with first-class appliances; and the agency farmer should strive steadily to teach the young men out in the field how to better their stock and practically to increase the yield of their rough agriculture. The girl should be taught domestic science, not as it would be practised in a first-class hotel or a wealthy private home, but as she must practise it in a hut with no conveniences, and with intervals of sheep-herding. If the boy and girl are not so taught, their after-lives will normally be worthless both to themselves and to others. If they are so taught, they will normally themselves rise and will be the most effective of home missionaries for their tribe. (1916.) *Mem. Ed.* IV, 40-41; *Nat. Ed.* III, 218-219.

INDIAN WARS. The difficulty and duration of a war with an Indian tribe depend less upon the numbers of the tribe itself than upon the nature of the ground it inhabits. The two Indian tribes that have caused the most irritating and prolonged struggle are the Apaches, who live in the vast, waterless, mountainous deserts of Arizona and New Mexico, and whom we are at this present moment engaged in subduing, and the Seminoles, who, from among the impenetrable swamps of Florida, bade the whole United States army defiance for seven long years; and this although neither Seminoles nor Apaches ever brought much force into the field, nor inflicted such defeats upon us as have other Indian tribes, like the Creeks and Sioux. (1887.) *Mem. Ed.* VIII, 155; *Nat. Ed.* VII, 135.

——————. It is idle folly to speak of . . . [the Indian wars] as being the fault of the United States Government; and it is even more idle to say that they could have been averted by treaty. Here and there, under exceptional circumstances or when a given tribe was feeble and unwarlike, the whites might gain the ground by a treaty entered into of their own free will by the Indians, without the least duress; but this was not possible with warlike and powerful tribes when once they realized that they were threatened with serious encroachment on their hunting-grounds. Moreover, looked at from the standpoint of the ultimate result, there was little real difference to the Indian whether the land was taken by treaty or by war. In the end the Delaware fared no better at the hands of the Quaker than the Wampanoag at the hands of the Puritan; the methods were far more humane in the one case than in the other, but the outcome was the same in both. No treaty could be satisfactory to the whites, no treaty served the needs of humanity and civilization, unless it gave the land to the Americans as unreservedly as any successful war. (1894.) *Mem. Ed.* XI, 272-273; *Nat. Ed.* IX, 55.

INDIAN WELFARE—RESPONSIBILITY FOR. The Indians must be treated with intelligent and sympathetic understanding, no less than with justice and firmness; and until they become citizens, absorbed into the general body politic, they must be the wards of the nation, and not of any private association, lay or clerical, no matter how well-meaning. (1914.) *Mem. Ed.* VI, 148; *Nat. Ed.* V, 126.

INDIANS. I suppose I should be ashamed to say that I take the Western view of the Indian. I don't go so far as to think that the only good Indians are the dead Indians, but I believe nine out of every ten are, and I shouldn't like to inquire too closely into the case of the tenth. The most vicious cowboy has more moral principle than the average Indian. Turn three hundred low families of New York into New Jersey, support them for fifty years in vicious idleness, and you will have some idea of what the Indians are. Reckless, revengeful, fiendishly cruel, they rob and murder, not the cowboys, who can take care of themselves, but the defenseless, lone settlers on the plains. (At New York, January 1886.) Hermann Hagedorn, *Roosevelt in the Bad Lands*. (Houghton Mifflin Co., Boston, 1921), p. 355.

——————. They were trained to the use of arms from their youth up and war and hunting were their two chief occupations, the business as well as the pleasure of their lives. They were not as skillful as the white hunters with the rifle—though more so than the average regular soldier—nor could they equal the frontiersman in feats of physical prowess, such as boxing and wrestling; but their superior endurance and the ease with which they stood fatigue and exposure made amends for this. A white might outrun them for eight or ten miles; but on a long journey they could tire out any man, and any beast except a wolf. Like most barbarians, they were fickle and inconstant, not to be relied on for pushing through a long campaign and after a great victory apt to go off to their homes, because each man desired to secure his own plunder and tell his own tale of glory. They are often spoken of as undisciplined; but in reality their discipline in the battle itself was very high. They attacked, retreated, rallied, or repelled a charge at the signal of command; and they were able to fight in open order in thick covers without losing touch of each other—a feat that no European regiment was then able to perform. (1889.) *Mem. Ed.* X, 74-75; *Nat. Ed.* VIII, 65-66.

INDIANS—ABILITY AMONG. Always when I have seen Indians in their homes, in mass, I was struck by the wide cultural and intellectual difference among the different tribes, as well as among the different individuals of each tribe, and both by the great possibilities for their improvement and by the need of showing common sense even more than good intentions if this improvement is to be achieved. Some Indians can hardly be moved forward at all. Some can be moved forward both fast and far. To let them entirely alone usually means their ruin. To interfere with them foolishly, with whatever good intentions, and to try to move all of them forward in a mass, with a jump, means their ruin. A few individuals in every tribe, and most of the individuals in some tribes, can move very far forward at once; the non-reservation schools do excellently for these. Most of them need to be advanced by degrees; there must be a half-way house at which they can halt, or they may never reach their final destination and stand on a level with the white man. (1916.) *Mem. Ed.* IV, 39; *Nat. Ed.* III, 217.

―――――――. Of course all Indians should not be forced into the same mould. Some can be made farmers; others mechanics; yet others have the soul of the artist. Let us try to give each his chance to develop what is best in him. . . .

A few Indians may be able to turn themselves into ordinary citizens in a dozen years. Give these exceptional Indians every chance; but remember that the majority must change gradually, and that it will take generations to make the change complete. Help them to make it in such fashion that when the change is accomplished we shall find that the original and valuable elements in the Indian culture have been retained, so that the new citizens come with full hands into the great field of American life, and contribute to that life something of marked value to all of us, something which it would be a misfortune to all of us to have destroyed. (1916.) *Mem. Ed.* IV, 56; *Nat. Ed.* III, 231-232.

INDIANS—MISSIONARIES TO THE. Exceptional qualities of courage, hard-headed common sense, sympathy, and understanding are needed by the missionary who is to do really first-class work; even more exceptional than are the qualities needed by the head of a white congregation under present conditions. The most marked successes have been won by men, themselves of lofty and broad-minded spirituality, who have respected the advances already made by the Indian toward a higher spiritual life, and instead of condemning these advances have made use of them in bringing his soul to a loftier level. One very important service rendered by the missionaries is their warfare on what is evil among the white men on the reservations; they are most potent allies in warring against drink and sexual immorality, two of the greatest curses with which the Indian has to contend. . . . Many of the missionaries, including all who do most good, are active in protecting the rights of each Indian to his land. Like the rest of us, the missionary needs to keep in mind the fact that the Indian criminal is on the whole more dangerous to the well-meaning Indian than any outsider can at present be. (1916.) *Mem. Ed.* IV, 52; *Nat. Ed.* III, 228.

INDIANS. *See also* BUFFALO; JESUITS; PRIMITIVE SOCIETY; WAR OF 1812; WESTWARD MOVEMENT.

INDIVIDUALISM. No amount of legislation or of combination can supply the lack of individual initiative—the lack of individual energy, honesty, thrift, and industry. (Annual Message, Albany, January 2, 1899.) *Mem. Ed.* XVII, 9; *Nat. Ed.* XV, 9.

―――――――. Individual initiative, the reign of individualism, may be crushed out just as effectively by the unchecked growth of private monopoly if the state does not interfere at all, as it would be crushed out under communism, or as it would disappear, together with everything else that makes life worth living, if we adopted the tenets of the extreme Socialists. *Outlook,* June 19, 1909, p. 392.

―――――――. Under modern industrial conditions absence of governmental regulation and control means such swollen development of a few personalities that all other personalities are dwarfed, are stunted and fettered, and their power of initiative, their power of self-help, largely atrophied. Absolute liberty for each individual to do what he wishes in the modern industrial world means for the mass of men much what, a thousand years ago, similar liberty for the strong in a military age meant for the multitude in that day. It is as necessary to possess the power of control over the industrial baronage of the twentieth century as it was to impose such control on the mediaeval baronage of the sword; and the movement is one for real as against nominal liberty now just as truly as in the Middle Ages. It is as necessary to shackle cunning in the present as ever it was to shackle physical force in the past. *Outlook,* January 28, 1911, p. 145.

INDIVIDUALISM

INDIVIDUALISM—ABUSE OF. On the border each man was a law unto himself, and good and bad alike were left in perfect freedom to follow out to the uttermost limits their own desires; for the spirit of individualism so charactersitic of American life reached its extreme of development in the backwoods. The whites who wishes peace, the magistrates and leaders, had little more power over their evil and unruly fellows than the Indian sachems had over the turbulent young braves. Each man did what seemed best in his own eyes, almost without let or hindrance; unless, indeed, he trespassed upon the rights of his neighbors, who were ready enough to band together in their own defense, though slow to interfere in the affairs of others. (1889.) *Mem. Ed.* X, 83; *Nat. Ed.* VIII, 73.

INDIVIDUALISM—RESTRICTION OF. I am a strong individualist by personal habit, inheritance and conviction; but it is a mere matter of common sense to recognize that the State, the community, the citizens acting together, can do a number of things better than if they were left to individual action. The individualism which finds its expression in the abuse of physical force is checked very early in the growth of civilization, and we of to-day should, in our turn, strive to shackle or destroy that individualism which triumphs by greed and cunning, which exploits the weak by craft instead of ruling them by brutality. We ought to go with any man in the effort to bring about justice and the equality of opportunity; to turn the tool user more and more into the tool owner; to shift burdens so that they can be more equitably borne. (At the Sorbonne, Paris, April 23, 1910.) *Mem. Ed.* XV, 366; *Nat. Ed.* XIII, 520.

——————. It is curious to see how difficult it is to make some men understand that insistence upon one factor does not and must not mean failure fully to recognize other factors. The selfish individual needs to be taught that we must now shackle cunning by law exactly as a few centuries back we shackled force by law. Unrestricted individualism spells ruin to the individual himself. But so does the elimination of individualism, whether by law or custom. (1913.) *Mem. Ed.* XXII, 191; *Nat. Ed.* XX, 164.

INDIVIDUALISM AND COLLECTIVE ACTION. A fundamental requisite of social efficiency is a high standard of individual energy and excellence; but this is in no wise inconsistent with power to act in combination for aims which can not so well be achieved by the individual acting alone. (Second Annual Message, Washington, December 2, 1902.) *Mem. Ed.* XVII, 163; *Nat. Ed.* XV, 141.

INDIVIDUALISM. *See also* COLLECTIVE ACTION; COLLECTIVISM; COMPETITION; CONTRACT; COOPERATION; EQUALITY; FREEDOM; FRONTIER DEMOCRACY; GOVERNMENT; LAISSEZ-FAIRE; POLITICAL ISSUES; SOCIALISM.

INDUSTRIAL ARBITRATION

INDUSTRIAL ARBITRATION. I suppose every thinking man rejoices when by mediation or arbitration it proves possible to settle troubles in time to avert the suffering and bitterness caused by strikes. Moreover a conciliation committee can do best work when the trouble is in its beginning, or at least has not come to a head. When the break has actually occurred, damage has been done, and each side feels sore and angry; and it is difficult to get them together—difficult to make either forget its own wrongs and remember the rights of the other. If possible the effort at conciliation or mediation or arbitration should be made in the earlier stages, and should be marked by the wish on the part of both sides to try to come to a common agreement which each shall think in the interests of the other as well as of itself. (At Sioux Falls, S. D., April 6, 1903.) *Presidential Addresses and State Papers* I, 308.

——————. The exercise of a judicial spirit by a disinterested body representing the Federal Government, such as would be provided by a commission on conciliation and arbitration, would tend to create an atmosphere of friendliness and conciliation between contending parties; and the giving each side an equal opportunity to present fully its case in the presence of the other would prevent many disputes from developing into serious strikes or lockouts, and, in other cases, would enable the commission to persuade the opposing parties to come to terms.

In this age of great corporate and labor combinations, neither employers nor employees should be left completely at the mercy of the stronger party to a dispute, regardless of the righteousness of their respective claims. (Sixth Annual Message, Washington, December 3, 1906.) *Mem. Ed.* XVII, 424-425; *Nat. Ed.* XV, 362.

——————. Congress [should] favorably consider the matter of creating the machinery for compulsory investigation of such industrial controversies as are of sufficient magnitude and of sufficient concern to the people of the country as a whole to warrant the Federal Government in taking action. . . .

Each successive step creating machinery for the adjustment of labor difficulties must be taken with caution, but we should endeavor to make progress in this direction. (Seventh Annual Message, Washington, December 3, 1907.) *Mem. Ed.* XVII, 511-512; *Nat. Ed.* XV, 436.

——————. When any labor trouble becomes of such size as to involve the public, the public has a right to interfere, to insist that there shall be no intereference with the welfare and safety of the public, and therefore to insist on arbitration, that is, for just decision by the Government, after an investigation conducted through a commission which will get all the facts and lay them before the Executive and Legislative representatives of the public for what action they deem necessary. These were the principles which by actual deed, when I was President, I upheld in the teeth of violent opposition from the most powerful corporations in the land, representing the employers' interest. The opposition of these great employing corporations was asserted in every possible way against me throughout the period when I held public office or was a candidate for public office. I absolutely disregarded it, because I thought that only by disregarding it could I do my duty to the country. (At Battle Creek, Mich., September 30, 1916.) Theodore Roosevelt, *Americanism and Preparedness.* (New York, 1917), p. 50.

INDUSTRIAL ARBITRATION. *See also* Coal Strike; Collective Bargaining; Labor; Strikes.

INDUSTRIAL COMMISSION — PLAN FOR. We propose, we Progressives, to establish an interstate commission having the same power over industrial concerns that the Interstate Commerce Commission has over railroads, so that whenever there is in the future a decision rendered in such important matters as the recent suits against the Standard Oil, . . . we will have a commission which will see that the decree of the court is really made effective; that it is not made a merely nominal decree. (At Milwaukee, Wis., October 14, 1912.) *Mem. Ed.* XIX, 448; *Nat. Ed.* XVII, 326.

——————. What is needed is the application to all industrial concerns and all cooperating interests engaged in interstate commerce in which there is either monopoly or control of the market of the principles on which we have gone in regulating transportation concerns engaged in such commerce. The antitrust law should be kept on the statute-books and strengthened so as to make it genuinely and thoroughly effective against every big concern tending to monopoly or guilty of antisocial practices. At the same time, a national industrial commission should be created which should have complete power to regulate and control all the great industrial concerns engaged in interstate business—which practically means all of them in this country. This commission should exercise over these industrial concerns like powers to those exercised over the railways by the Interstate Commerce Commission, and over the national banks by the comptroller of the currency, and additional powers if found necessary.

The establishment of such a commission would enable us to punish the individual rather than merely the corporation, just as we now do with banks, where the aim of the government is, not to close the bank, but to bring to justice personally any bank official who has gone wrong.

Any corporation voluntarily coming under the commission should not be prosecuted under the antitrust law as long as it obeys in good faith the orders of the commission. The commission would be able to interpret in advance, to any honest man asking the interpretation, what he may do and what he may not do in carrying on a legitimate business. Any corporation not coming under the commission should be exposed to prosecution under the antitrust law, and any corporation violating the orders of the commission should also at once become exposed to such prosecution; and when such a prosecution is successful, it should be the duty of the commission to see that the decree of the court is put into effect completely and in good faith, so that the combination is absolutely broken up, and is not allowed to come together again, nor the constituent parts thereof permitted to do business save under the conditions laid down by the commission. This last provision would prevent the repetition of such gross scandals as those attendant upon the present Administration's prosecution of the Standard Oil and the Tobacco Trusts. (Before Progressive National Committee, Chicago, August 6, 1912.) *Mem. Ed.* XIX, 387-389; *Nat. Ed.* XVII, 279-280.

——————. Our proposal . . . is to create a commission like the Interstate Commerce Commission, and through this commission to supervise the big industrial concerns doing an interstate business, just as the government now supervises railroads and banks. We will thereby prevent the eggs from being scrambled, and, if necessary, unscramble them effectively.

The antitrust law will remain on the books, and it will be strengthened by prohibiting agreements to divide territory or limit output, by prohibiting a refusal to sell to customers who buy from business rivals, by prohibiting the custom of selling below cost in certain areas while maintaining higher prices in other areas, by prohibiting the use of the power of transportation to aid or injure special business concerns—in short, by prohibiting these and all other unfair trade practices. The Interstate Industrial Commission will give us an efficient instrument for seeing that the law is carried out in letter and in spirit, and for effectively punishing not only every corporation, but every individual who violates the provisions of the law. (At Oyster Bay, N. Y., November 2, 1912.) *Mem. Ed.* XIX, 469; *Nat. Ed.* XVII, 346.

INDUSTRIAL COMMISSION — WORK OF. An industrial commission should do as the Interstate Commerce Commission should do, that is, remember always its dual duty, the duty to the corporation and individual controlled no less than to the public. It is an absolute necessity that the investors, the owners, of an honest, useful, and decently managed concern, should have reasonable profit. It is impossible to run business unless this is done. Unless the business man prospers, there will be no prosperity for the rest of the community to share. He must have certainty of law and opportunity for honest and reasonable profit under the law. (*Century Magazine*, October 1913.) *Mem. Ed.* XIX, 548; *Nat. Ed.* XVII, 404.

INDUSTRIAL COMMISSION. See also BUSINESS; COMBINATIONS; CORPORATIONS; MONOPOLIES; SHERMAN ANTI-TRUST ACT; TRUSTS.

INDUSTRIAL COOPERATION. There must to-day be some species of collective control of industry; which means that the tool-users shall become the tool-owners; but which also means that they will assuredly break down themselves and their business unless they are willing to pay for skilled management a price, in some measure, corresponding to the high value of the service rendered, and unless they are willing to give a just reward to whatever necessary capital they cannot themselves supply. This means an effort toward a combination of the proper functions of the corporation with the wise activities of the labor-union (and I emphasize proper in one case and wise in the other). (1917.) *Mem. Ed.* XXI, 70; *Nat. Ed.* XIX, 60.

INDUSTRIAL COOPERATION. See also COLLECTIVISM; COOPERATION.

INDUSTRIAL DEMOCRACY — MEANING OF. Let me again repeat that industrial democracy does not mean handing over the control of matters requiring expert knowledge to masses of men who lack that knowledge; and therefore it does mean that it cannot come until the men in the ranks have sufficient self-knowledge and self-control to accept and demand expert leadership as part of the necessary division of labor. If democracy, whether in industry or politics, refuses to employ experts, it will simply show that it is unfit to survive. At the outset, at least, the share of the workers in control would not be on the business side proper of the management, but over the conditions of daily work—the essentially human side of the industrial process. . . .

It is only by experiments in the actual work of business that we shall find the exact methods by which, and the exact degree to which, we can measurably realize the ideal. For full success, the trial should be made in a business in which the workers are of a high type in skill, intelligence, and character, and are fairly accustomed to act together. The government could well afford to experiment along these lines in some of its work. (1917.) *Mem. Ed.* XXI, 94; *Nat. Ed.* XIX, 81.

INDUSTRIAL DEMOCRACY. See also DEMOCRACY, ECONOMIC.

INDUSTRIAL EDUCATION. See EDUCATION.

INDUSTRIAL FATALITIES. Of course industry inevitably takes toll of life. Far more lives have been lost in this country by men engaged in bridge-building, tunnel-digging, mining, steel-manufacturing, the erection of sky-scrapers, the operations of the fishing-fleet, and the like, than in all our battles in all our foreign wars put together. Such loss of life no more justifies us in opposing righteous wars than in opposing necessary industry. There was certainly far greater loss of life, and probably greater needless and preventable and uncompensated loss of life, in the industries out of which Mr. Carnegie made his gigantic fortune than has occurred among our troops in war during the time covered by Mr. Carnegie's activities on behalf of peace. (*Everybody's*, January 1915.) Mem. Ed. XX, 143; Nat. Ed. XVIII, 123.

INDUSTRIAL FATALITIES. *See also* Workmen's Compensation.

INDUSTRIAL JUSTICE. The fundamental need in dealing with our people, whether laboring men or others, is not charity but justice; we must all work in common for the common end of helping each and all, in a spirit of the sanest, broadest, and deepest brotherhood.

It was not always easy to avoid feeling very deep anger with the selfishness and shortsightedness shown both by the representatives of certain employers' organizations and by certain great labor federations or unions. (1913.) Mem. Ed. XXII, 561; Nat. Ed. XX, 482.

―――――. Here in America we have in many ways been more backward than in most countries of middle and western Europe, because our situation was such that we could shut our eyes to unpleasant truths and yet temporarily prosper. But our system, or rather no-system, of attempting to combine political democracy with industrial autocracy, and tempering the evil of the boss and the machine politician by the evil of the doctrinaire and the demagogue, has now begun to creak and strain so as to threaten a breakdown.

Surely the time has come when we should with good nature and practical common sense set ourselves to the practical work of solving the problem. This means that we must disregard equally the apostles of ultracollectivism and the doctrinaires of ultraindividualism. It also means that we must rebuke with equal emphasis the men who can see nothing wrong in what is done by capitalists and corporations, and the other men who can see nothing wrong in what is done by labor leaders and tradesunions. (1917.) Mem. Ed. XXI, 86; Nat. Ed. XIX, 74.

INDUSTRIAL JUSTICE. *See also* Brotherhood; Fellowship; Justice; Social and Industrial Justice.

INDUSTRIAL LEGISLATION. *See* Labor Legislation; Social Insurance; Social Legislation.

INDUSTRIAL PEACE. *See* Nobel Peace Prize.

INDUSTRIAL PROBLEMS — NEW TYPES OF. We are now forced to face problems not only new in degree, but new in kind. We must face these problems in the spirit of Washington and Lincoln; but our methods in industrial life must differ as completely from those that obtained in the times of those two great men of the past as the weapons of warfare now differ from the flint-locks of Washington's soldiers, or the muzzle-loading smoothbores of Lincoln's day. We must quit the effort to meet modern conditions by flint-lock legislation. (At Cooper Union, N. Y. C., November 3, 1916.) Mem. Ed. XX, 517; Nat. Ed. XVIII, 444.

INDUSTRIAL REVOLUTION. Over a century ago the "industrial revolution" began to turn the industrial world into one of big business, in which the dominant features were massed capital on a hitherto unheard-of scale, and laborers employed, also in enormous masses, by the capitalist, without personal touch or sense of responsibility on his part. The new system was inaugurated in England. France and Germany speedily followed suit. In the United States, the change from the old system of unlimited cutthroat competition among the multitude of small, weak concerns, to the new system of concentration (without either co-operation or control), got under full headway about the time of the Civil War; in economically backward countries like Russia and Spain it was yet later.

There was much that was beneficial in the change. It produced an immense increase of population and aggregate wealth; it was everywhere accompanied or followed by a great spread of education and community effort; and it probably, on the whole, raised the standard of attainable luxury and comfort for the workers in the industrial countries, compared to what it remained in the backward countries such as Spain and Russia.

But it was accompanied by evils so numerous and so grave that to this day one of our heaviest tasks is the struggle to do away with them. The movement substituted for the old social contrast between privileged patrician and unprivileged plebeian an even more offensive and violent industrial contrast between the man of one type of specialized capacity who possessed capital and the men of all other types of capacity who did not possess capital. (1917.) Mem. Ed. XXI, 84-85; Nat. Ed. XIX, 73-74.

INDUSTRIAL WORKERS OF THE WORLD. The I. W. W. and the "direct-action" anarchists and apologists for anarchy are never concerned for justice. They are concerned solely in seeing one kind of criminal

INDUSTRIAL WORKERS escape justice, precisely as certain big business men and certain corporation lawyers have in the past been concerned in seeing another kind of criminal escape justice. . . . Murder is murder, and it is rather more evil, when committed in the name of a professed social movement. The reactionaries have in the past been a great menace to this republic; but at this moment it is the I. W. W., the Germanized Socialists, the Anarchists, the foolish creatures who always protest again the suppression of crime, the pacifists and the like, who are the really grave danger. These are the Bolsheviki of America. (Letter of December 19, 1917.) *Mem. Ed.* XXIV, 541; Bishop II, 463.

———————. The leaders of the I. W. W. are no more victims of social wrong, are no more protesters against social evil, than are so many professional gunmen. There are plenty of honest, misled men among the rank and file of all these organizations; and plenty of wrongs from which these men suffer; but these men can be helped, and these wrongs remedied, only if we set our faces like flint against the evil leaders who would hurl our social organism into just such an abyss as that which has engulfed Russia. (1918.) *Mem. Ed.* XXI, 385; *Nat. Ed.* XIX, 349.

INDUSTRIAL WRONGS — REMEDY FOR. The convictions to which I have come have not been arrived at as the result of study in the closet or the library, but from the knowledge I have gained through hard experience during the many years in which, under many and varied conditions, I have striven and toiled with men. I believe in a larger use of the governmental power to help remedy industrial wrongs, because it has been borne in on me by actual experience that without exercise of such power many of the wrongs will go unremedied. (Before Progressive National Convention, Chicago, August 6, 1912.) *Mem. Ed.* XIX, 409; *Nat. Ed.* XVII, 297.

INEFFICIENCY. See EFFICIENCY.

INFANT MORTALITY. A high percentage of infant mortality does not mean the weeding out of the unfit; it means the existence of conditions which greatly impair the vitality of even those who survive. Moreover, the moral effect is at least as great as the physical. (*Metropolitan*, February 1916.) *Mem. Ed.* XX, 297; *Nat. Ed.* XVIII, 255.

INFLATION. See CURRENCY.

INHERITANCE. See NATIONAL INHERITANCE.

INHERITANCE TAX. In the near future our national legislators should enact a law providing for a graduated inheritance tax by which a steadily increasing rate of duty should be put upon all moneys or other valuables coming by gift, bequest, or devise to any individual or corporation. It may be well to make the tax heavy in proportion as the individual benefited is remote of kin. In any event, in my judgment the pro rata of the tax should increase very heavily with the increase of the amount left to any one individual after a certain point has been reached. It is most desirable to encourage thrift and ambition, and a potent source of thrift and ambition is the desire on the part of the bread-winner to leave his children well off. This object can be attained by making the tax very small on moderate amounts of property left; because the prime object should be to put a constantly increasing burden on the inheritance of those swollen fortunes which it is certainly of no benefit to this country to perpetuate. (Sixth Annual Message, Washington, December 3, 1906.) *Mem. Ed.* XVII, 433-434; *Nat. Ed.* XV, 369-370.

———————. It is eminently right that the nation should fix the terms upon which the great fortunes are inherited. They rarely do good and they often do harm to those who inherit them in their entirety. (Eighth Annual Message, Washington, December 8, 1908.) *Mem. Ed.* XVII, 588; *Nat. Ed.* XV, 500.

———————. I believe we should have a Federal Inheritance Tax, aimed only at the very large fortunes, which cannot be adequately reached by State Inheritance taxes, if they are sufficiently high and the graduation sufficiently marked. (To H. C. Lodge, July 26, 1909.) Lodge *Letters* II, 341.

INHERITANCE TAX—PURPOSE OF. I feel that we shall ultimately have to consider the adoption of some such scheme as that of a progressive tax on all fortunes, beyond a certain amount either given in life or devised or bequeathed upon death to any individual—a tax so framed as to put it out of the power of the owner of one of these enormous fortunes to hand on more than a certain amount to any one individual; the tax, of course, to be imposed by the National and not the State Government. Such taxation should, of course, be aimed merely at the inheritance or transmission in their entirety of those fortunes swollen beyond all healthy limits. (At Washington, April 14, 1906.) *Mem. Ed.* XVIII, 578; *Nat. Ed.* XVI, 421.

———————. I do not believe that any advantage comes either to the country as a whole or to the individuals inheriting the money by permitting the transmission in their entirety of such enormous fortunes as have been accumulated in America. The tax could be made to bear more heavily upon persons residing out of the country than upon those residing within it. Such a heavy progressive tax is of course in no shape or way a tax on thrift or industry, for thrift and industry have ceased to possess any measurable importance in the acquisition of the swollen fortunes of which I speak long before the tax would in any way seriously affect them. Such a tax would be one of the methods by which we should try to preserve a measurable equality of opportunity for the people of the generation growing to manhood. (Before National Editorial Association, Jamestown, Va., June 10, 1907.) *Presidential Addresses and State Papers* VI, 1322-1323.

INHERITANCE TAX. *See also* FORTUNES; INCOME TAX; WEALTH.

INITIATIVE AND REFERENDUM. The opponents of the referendum and initiative, . . . would do well to remember that the movement in favor of the two is largely due to the failure of the representative bodies really to represent the people. There has been a growing feeling that there should be more direct popular action as an alternative, not to the action of an ideal legislative body, but to the actions of legislative bodies as they are now too often found in very fact to act. . . .

On the other hand, the advocates of the initiative and referendum should, in their turn, remember that those measures are in themselves merely means and not ends; that their success or failure is to be determined not on *a priori* reasoning but by actually testing how they work under varying conditions; and, above all, that it is foolish to treat these or any other devices for obtaining good government and popular rule as justifying sweeping condemnation of all men and communities where other governmental methods are preferred (*Outlook,* January 21, 1911.) *Mem. Ed.* XIX, 94, 96; *Nat. Ed.* XVII, 60, 61.

———————. I believe in the initiative and the referendum, which should be used not to destroy representative government, but to correct it whenever it becomes misrepresentative. Here again I am concerned not with theories but with actual facts. If in any State the people are themselves satisfied with their present representative system, then it is of course their right to keep that system unchanged; and it is nobody's business but theirs. But in actual practice it has been found in very many States that legislative bodies have not been responsive to the popular will. Therefore I believe that the State should provide for the possibility of direct popular action in order to make good such legislative failure. The power to invoke such direct action, both by initiative and by referendum, should be provided in such fashion as to prevent its being wantonly or too frequently used. I do not believe that it should be made the easy or ordinary way of taking action. In the great majority of cases it is far better that action on legislative matters should be taken by those specially delegated to perform the task; in other words, that the work should be done by the experts chosen to perform it. But where the men thus delegated fail to perform their duty, then it should be in the power of the people themselves to perform the duty. (Before Ohio Constitutional Convention, Columbus, February 21, 1912.) *Mem. Ed.* XIX, 180; *Nat. Ed.* XVII, 134.

INITIATIVE AND REFERENDUM—APPLICATION OF. The initiative and referendum may if applied in a given manner in a given community work real benefit, or they may be so applied as to work harm. I am sorry that they are advocated as though they were a panacea for everything, and sorry where they are opposed in such a way as to convey the entirely wrong impression that the big man, the fine public servant who opposes them has allied himself with the forces of reaction. (To H. C. Lodge, December 13, 1911.) Lodge *Letters* II, 417.

INITIATIVE AND REFERENDUM—EXPERIENCE WITH. Oregon has already tried the principle of the initiative and the referendum, and it seems to have produced good results—certainly in the case of the referendum, and probably in the case of the initiative. This, of course, does not necessarily mean that the principle would work well in all other communities, and under our system it is difficult to see at present how it could normally have more than a State-wide application. In Switzerland it has been applied both in the cantons, or states, and in the federal or national government, and it seems on the whole to have worked fairly well. (*Outlook,* January 21, 1911.) *Mem. Ed.* XIX, 91; *Nat. Ed.* XVII, 58.

INITIATIVE AND REFERENDUM — FUNCTION OF. The "initiative and referendum," . . . are so framed that if the legislatures obey the command of some special interest, and obstinately refuse the will of the majority, the majority may step in and legislate directly. No man would say that it was best to conduct all legislation by direct vote of the people — it would mean the loss of deliberation, of patient consideration — but, on the other hand, no one whose mental arteries have not long since hardened can doubt that the proposed changes are needed when the legislatures refuse to carry out the will of the people. The proposal is a method to reach an undeniable evil. (At Carnegie Hall, New York City, March 20, 1912.) *Mem. Ed.* XIX, 202; *Nat. Ed.* XVII, 153.

INITIATIVE AND REFERENDUM — ROLE OF. There are plenty of cases in which, on a given issue of sufficient importance, it is better that the people should decide for themselves rather than trust the decision to a body of representatives — and our present-day acceptance of this fact is shown by our insistence upon a direct vote of the State when the State adopts a new constitution. But ordinary citizens in private life — such as the present writer, and most of his readers — neither can nor ought to spend their time in following all the minutiæ of legislation. This work they ought to delegate to the legislators, who are to make it their special business; and if scores of bills are habitually presented for popular approval or disapproval at every election, it is not probable that good will come, and it is certain that the percentage of wise decisions by the people will be less than if only a few propositions of really great importance are presented. It is necessary to guard not only against the cranks and well-meaning busybodies with fads, but also against the extreme laxity with which men are accustomed to sign petitions. . . . A much larger proportion of men should be required to petition for an initiative than for a referendum, but in each case the regulations both as to the number of names required and as to additional guarantees where necessary should be such as to forbid the invocation of this method of securing popular action unless the measure is one of real importance, as to which there is a deep-rooted popular interest. (*Outlook,* January 21, 1911.) *Mem. Ed.* XIX, 90; *Nat. Ed.* XVII, 57.

————. Action by the initiative or referendum ought *not* to be the normal way of legislation; I think the Legislature should be given an entirely free hand. But I believe the people should have the power to reverse or supplement the work of the Legislature, *whenever it becomes necessary. Outlook,* March 30, 1912, p. 721.

INITIATIVE. *See also* MINORITY DEMANDS; RECALL; REFERENDUM; REPRESENTATIVE GOVERNMENT.

INJUNCTION—RIGHT OF. As for the right of injunction, it is absolutely necessary to have this power lodged in the courts; though of course any abuse of the power is strongly to be reprobated. During the four and a half years that I have been President I do not remember an instance where the Government has invoked the right of injunction against a combination of laborers. We have invoked it certainly a score of times against combinations of capital; I think possibly oftener. But understand me, gentlemen, if ever I thought it necessary, if I thought a combination of laborers were doing wrong, I would apply an injunction against them just as quick as against so many capitalists. (At interview granted members of Executive Council, American Federation of Labor, March 21, 1906.) *Mem. Ed.* XXIV, 20; Bishop II, 16.

INJUNCTIONS. There has been demand for depriving courts of the power to issue injunctions in labor disputes. Such special limitation of the equity powers of our courts would be most unwise. It is true that some judges have misused this power; but this does not justify a denial of the power any more than an improper exercise of the power to call a strike by a labor leader would justify the denial of the right to strike. The remedy is to regulate the procedure by requiring the judge to give due notice to the adverse parties before granting the writ, the hearing to be ex parte if the adverse party does not appear at the time and place ordered. What is due notice must depend upon the facts of the case; it should not be used as a pretext to permit violation of law or the jeopardizing of life or property. Of course, this would not authorize the issuing of a restraining order or injunction in any case in which it is not already authorized by existing law. (Fifth Annual Message, Washington, December 5, 1905.) *Mem. Ed.* XVII, 332; *Nat. Ed.* XV, 284-285.

————. I believe it would be wrong altogether to prohibit the use of injunctions. It is criminal to permit sympathy for criminals to weaken our hands in upholding the law; and if men seek to destroy life or property by mob violence there should be no impairment of the

INJUNCTIONS

power of the courts to deal with them in the most summary and effective way possible. . . .

In this matter of injunctions there is lodged in the hands of the judiciary a necessary power which is nevertheless subject to the possibility of grave abuse. It is a power that should be exercised with extreme care and should be subject to the jealous scrutiny of all men, and condemnation should be meted out as much to the judge who fails to use it boldly when necessary as to the judge who uses it wantonly or oppressively. Of course, a judge strong enough to be fit for his office will enjoin any resort to violence or intimidation, especially by conspiracy, no matter what his opinion may be of the rights of the original quarrel. There must be no hesitation in dealing with disorder. But there must likewise be no such abuse of the injunctive power as is implied in forbidding laboring men to strive for their own betterment in peaceful and lawful ways; nor must the injunction be used merely to aid some big corporation in carrying out schemes for its own aggrandizement. (Sixth Annual Message, Washington, December 3, 1906.) *Mem. Ed.* XVII, 406-407; *Nat. Ed.* XV, 347.

——————————. The process of injunction is an essential adjunct of the court's doing its work well; and as preventive measures are always better than remedial, the wise use of this process is from every standpoint commendable. But where it is recklessly or unnecessarily used, the abuse should be censured, above all by the very men who are properly anxious to prevent any effort to shear the courts of this necessary power. The court's decision must be final; the protest is only against the conduct of individual judges in needlessly anticipating such final decision, or in the tyrannical use of what is nominally a temporary injunction to accomplish what is in fact a permanent decision. (Seventh Annual Message, Washington, December 3, 1907.) *Mem. Ed.* XVII, 507-508; *Nat. Ed.* XV, 432.

INJUNCTIONS—ABUSE OF. The worst injunctions, so far as my remembrance goes, in the whole history of the United States have been granted in West Virginia. Ten years ago some of the injunctions then granted by Judge Jackson read as the veriest travesty upon justice. Under the pressure of an unenlightened capitalistic opinion, the West Virginian courts have rendered decisions . . . which themselves serve as the most striking object-lessons of the need of the wide-spread application of Progressive principles. (Before National Conference of Progressive Service, Portsmouth, R. I., July 2,

INLAND WATERWAYS

1913.) *Mem. Ed.* XIX, 521; *Nat. Ed.* XVII, 381.

INJUNCTIONS. *See also* LABOR.

INLAND WATERWAYS—IMPORTANCE OF. While . . . the improvement of inland navigation is a vital problem, there are other questions of no less consequence connected with our waterways. One of these relates to the purity of waters used for the supply of towns and cities, to the prevention of pollution by manufacturing and other industries, and to the protection of drainage areas from soil wash through forest covering or judicious cultivation. With our constantly increasing population this question becomes more and more pressing, because the health and safety of great bodies of citizens are directly involved.

Another important group of questions concerns the irrigation of arid lands, the prevention of floods, and the reclamation of swamps. Already many thousands of homes have been established on the arid regions, and the population and wealth of seventeen States and Territories have been largely increased through irrigation. Yet this means of national development is still in its infancy, and it will doubtless long continue to multiply homes and increase the productiveness and power of the nation. The reclamation of overflow lands and marshes, both in the interior and along the coasts, has already been carried on with admirable results, but in this field, too, scarcely more than a good beginning has yet been made. Still another fundamentally important question is that of water-power. (Before Deep Waterway Convention, Memphis, Tenn., October 4, 1907.) *Mem. Ed.* XVIII, 152; *Nat. Ed.* XVI, 115.

INLAND WATERWAYS — IMPROVEMENT OF. Until the work of river improvement is undertaken in a modern way it cannot have results that will meet the needs of this modern nation. These needs should be met without further dilly-dallying or delay. The plan which promises the best and quickest results is that of a permanent commission authorized to co-ordinate the work of all the government departments relating to waterways, and to frame and supervise the execution of a comprehensive plan. Under such a commission the actual work of construction might be intrusted to the reclamation service; or to the military engineers acting with a sufficient number of civilians to continue the work in time of war; or it might be divided between the reclamation service and the corps of engineers. Funds should be provided from current revenues if it

[260]

is deemed wise—otherwise from the sale of bonds. The essential thing is that the work should go forward under the best possible plan, and with the least possible delay. We should have a new type of work and a new organization for planning and directing it. The time for playing with our waterways is past. The country demands results. (Eighth Annual Message, Washington, December 8, 1908.) *Mem. Ed.* XVII, 617-618; *Nat. Ed.* XV, 525.

——————. Facility of cheap transportation is an essential in our modern civilization, and we cannot afford any longer to neglect the great highways which nature has provided for us. These natural highways, the waterways, can never be monopolized by any corporation. They belong to all the people, and it is in the power of no one to take them away. . . . Year by year transportation problems become more acute, and the time has come when the rivers really fit to serve as arteries of trade should be provided with channels deep enough and wide enough to make the investment of the necessary money profitable to the public. The National Government should undertake this work. Where the immediately abutting land is markedly benefited, and this benefit can be definitely localized, I trust that there will be careful investigation to see whether some way can be devised by which the immediate benficiaries may pay a portion of the expenses—as is now the custom as regards certain classes of improvements in our municipalities; and measures should be taken to secure from the localities specially benefited proper terminal facilities. The expense to the nation of entering upon such a scheme of river improvement as that which I believe it should undertake, will necessarily be great. Many cautious and conservative people will look askance upon the project, and from every standpoint it is necessary, if we wish to make it successful, that we should enter upon it only under conditions which will guarantee the nation against waste of its money, and which will insure us against entering upon any project until after the most elaborate expert examination, and reliable calculation of the proportion between cost and benefit. (Before Deep Waterway Convention, Memphis, Tenn., October 4, 1907.) *Mem. Ed.* XVIII, 148-149; *Nat. Ed.* XVI, 111-112.

INLAND WATERWAYS COMMISSION. The preliminary report of the Inland Waterways Commission was excellent in every way. It outlines a general plan of waterway improvement which when adopted will give assurance that the improvements will yield practical results in the way of increased navigation and water transportation. In every essential feature the plan recommended by the commission is new. In the principle of co-ordinating all uses of the waters and treating each waterway system as a unit; in the principle of correlating water traffic with rail and other land traffic; in the principle of expert initiation of projects in accordance with commercial foresight and the needs of a growing country; and in the principle of cooperation between the States and the Federal Government in the administration and use of waterways, etc.; the general plan proposed by the commission is new, and at the same time sane and simple. The plan deserves unqualified support. I regret that it has not yet been adopted by Congress, but I am confident that ultimately it will be adopted. (1908.) *Mem. Ed.* XXII, 464; *Nat. Ed.* XX, 399.

INLAND WATERWAYS. *See also* CONSERVATION; FLOOD PREVENTION; MISSISSIPPI RIVER; WATER POWER.

INSANITY PLEA—CRITICISM OF. I have scant sympathy with the plea of insanity advanced to save a man from the consequences of crime, when unless that crime had been committed it would have been impossible to persuade any responsible authority to commit him to an asylum as insane. (Letter of August 8, 1904.) *Mem. Ed.* XXII, 425; *Nat. Ed.* XX, 365.

INSCRIPTIONS—VALUE OF. It is only of recent years that the importance of inscriptions has been realized. To the present-day scholar they are invaluable. Even to the layman, some of them turn the past into the present with startling clearness. The least imaginative is moved by the simple inscription on the Etruscan sarcophagus, "I, the great lady"; a lady so haughty that no other human being was allowed to rest near her; and yet now nothing remains but this proof of the pride of the nameless one. (Presidential Address, American Historical Association, Boston, December 27, 1912.) *Mem. Ed.* XIV, 10; *Nat. Ed.* XII, 9.

INSULAR POSSESSIONS — ADMINISTRATION OF. In making appointments to the insular service, the appointing power must feel all the time that he is acting for the country as a whole, in the interest of the good name of our people as a whole, and any question of mere party expediency must be wholly swept aside, and the matter looked at solely from the standpoint of the honor of our own nation and the welfare of the islands. (At Hartford,

Conn., August 22, 1902.) *Mem. Ed.* XVIII, 357; *Nat. Ed.* XVI, 272.

———————. Politics should have as little to do with the choice of our colonial administrators as it should have to do with the choice of an admiral or a general. We cannot afford to trifle with our own honor or with the interests of the great alien communities over which we have assumed supervision.... We cannot afford to let politicians do with our public service in our dependencies what they have done for the consular service; still less can we afford to let doctrinaires, or honest, ignorant people, decide the difficult and delicate questions bound to arise in administering the new provinces. (*Outlook*, January 7, 1899.) *Mem. Ed.* XII, 526; *Nat. Ed.* XI, 255.

INSULAR POSSESSIONS. *See also* HAWAII; PHILIPPINES; PORTO RICO; WOOD, LEONARD.

INSURANCE COMPANIES — REGULATION OF. Recent events have emphasized the importance of an early and exhaustive consideration of this question, to see whether it is not possible to furnish better safeguards than the several States have been able to furnish against corruption of the flagrant kind which has been exposed. It has been only too clearly shown that certain of the men at the head of these large corporations take but small note of the ethical distinction between honesty and dishonesty; they draw the line only this side of what may be called law-honesty, the kind of honesty necessary in order to avoid falling into the clutches of the law. Of course the only complete remedy for this condition must be found in an aroused public conscience, a higher sense of ethical conduct in the community at large, and especially among business men and in the great profession of the law, and in the growth of a spirit which condemns all dishonesty, whether in rich man or in poor man, whether it takes the shape of bribery or of blackmail. But much can be done by legislation which is not only drastic but practical. There is need of a far stricter and more uniform regulation of the vast insurance interests of this country. The United States should in this respect follow the policy of other nations by providing adequate national supervision of commercial interests which are clearly national in character. (Fifth Annual Message, Washington, December 5, 1905.) *Mem. Ed.* XVII, 337-338; *Nat. Ed.* XV, 289.

INSURGENTS. *See* INDEPENDENT; MACHINE; MUGWUMPS; PARTY ALLEGIANCE; POLITICS; PROGRESSIVE MOVEMENT.

INTELLECT. Intellect is a great thing. A sound mind is a great thing, just as a sound body is a great thing. But more than body and more than mind is what we call character. That is what counts ultimately with the individual and with the nation. I am sure all of us here have known a great many men of large intellect, of whom we distinctly preferred to see as little as possible. Some of the men who have left the most unenviable reputations in our history were men of marked intellect; because, of course, a man who possesses intellect greatly developed without having his moral sense equally developed is a more dangerous wild beast. Sound morality and good principles count for more than intellect. (Address, October 11, 1897.) *Two Hundredth Anniversary of the Old Dutch Church of Sleepy Hollow.* (First Reformed Church, Tarrytown, N. Y., 1898), p. 106.

INTELLECTUAL ACUTENESS AND MORALITY. I intend to try ... to warn you—oh, how I wish I could warn all my countrymen!—against that most degrading of processes, the deification of any man for what we are pleased to term smartness, the deification of mere intellectual acuteness, wholly unaccompanied by moral responsibility, wholly without reference to whether it is exercised in accordance or not in accordance with the elementary rules of morality. (Before Independent Club, Buffalo, N. Y., May 15, 1899.) *Mem. Ed.* XVI, 484; *Nat. Ed.* XIV, 324.

INTELLECTUAL ACUTENESS. *See also* CHARACTER; MORAL SENSE; VIRTUES.

INTELLECTUAL LEADERSHIP—NEED OF. We can well do without the hard intolerance and arid intellectual barrenness of what was worst in the theological systems of the past, but there has never been greater need of a high and fine religious spirit than at the present time. So, while we can laugh good-humoredly at some of the pretensions of modern philosophy in its various branches, it would be worse than folly on our part to ignore our need of intellectual leadership. (At University of Berlin, May 12, 1910.) *Mem. Ed.* XIV, 283; *Nat. Ed.* XII, 82.

INTELLECTUAL LEADERSHIP. *See also* EDUCATED MEN; LEADERSHIP.

INTELLIGENCE. No man can reach the front rank if he is not intelligent and if he is not trained with intelligence; but mere intelligence, by itself, is worse than useless, unless it is guided by an upright heart, unless there are also strength and courage behind it. Morality, decency, clean living, courage, manliness, self-respect—these qualities are more important in the make-up of a people than any mental subtlety. (At National University, Cairo, Egypt, March 28, 1910.) Mem. Ed. XVIII, 621; Nat. Ed. XVI, 451.

INTELLIGENCE. *See also* CHARACTER; COURAGE; MENTAL ACUTENESS; MORALITY; REASON.

INTEMPERANCE. *See* LIQUOR; PROHIBITION; TEMPERANCE.

INTERESTS. *See* NATIONAL INTERESTS; NEW NATIONALISM; SPECIAL INTERESTS.

INTERNATIONAL AGREEMENTS. The prime fact to consider in securing any peace agreement worth entering into, or that will have any except a mischievous effect, is that the nations entering into the agreement shall make no promises that ought not to be made, that they shall in good faith live up to the promises that are made, and that they shall put their whole strength unitedly back of these promises against any nation which refuses to carry out the agreement, or which, if it has not made the agreement, nevertheless violates the principles which the agreement enforces. In other words, international agreements intended to produce peace must proceed much along the lines of The Hague conventions; but a power signing them, as the United States signed The Hague conventions, must do so with the intention in good faith to see that they are carried out, and to use force to accomplish this, if necessary. (*Independent,* January 4, 1915.) Mem. Ed. XX, 180; Nat. Ed. XVIII, 155.

INTERNATIONAL AGREEMENTS. *See also* PROMISES; TREATIES.

INTERNATIONAL ARBITRATION. *See* ARBITRATION.

INTERNATIONAL COURT—PROPOSAL FOR. It is necessary to devise means for putting the collective and efficient strength of all the great powers of civilization back of any well-behaved power which is wronged by another power. In other words, we must devise means for executing treaties in good faith, by the establishment of some great international tribunal, and by securing the enforcement of the decrees of this tribunal through the action of a posse comitatus of powerful and civilized nations, all of them being bound by solemn agreement to coerce any power that offends against the decrees of the tribunal. That there will be grave difficulties in successfully working out this plan I would be the first to concede, and I would be the first to insist that to work it out successfully would be impossible unless the nations acted in good faith. But the plan is feasible, and it is the only one which at the moment offers any chance of success. (New York *Times,* November 8, 1914.) Mem. Ed. XX, 85; Nat. Ed. XVIII, 73.

———. All the civilized powers which are able and willing to furnish and to use force, when force is required to back up righteousness—and only the civilized powers who possess virile manliness of character and the willingness to accept risk and labor when necessary to the performance of duty are entitled to be considered in this matter—should join to create an international tribunal and to provide rules in accordance with which that tribunal should act. These rules would have to accept the *status quo* at some given period; for the endeavor to redress all historical wrongs would throw us back into chaos. They would lay down the rule that the territorial integrity of each nation was inviolate; that it was to be guaranteed absolutely its sovereign rights in certain particulars, including, for instance, the right to decide the terms on which immigrants should be admitted to its borders for purposes of residence, citizenship, or business; in short, all its rights in matters affecting its honor and vital interest. Each nation should be guaranteed against having any of these specified rights infringed upon. They would not be made arbitrable, any more than an individual's right to life and limb is made arbitrable; they would be mutually guaranteed. All other matters that could arise between these nations should be settled by the international court. The judges should act not as national representatives, but purely as judges, and in any given case it would probably be well to choose them by lot, excluding, of course, the representatives of the powers whose interests were concerned. Then, and most important, the nations should severally guarantee to use their entire military force, if necessary, against any nation which defied the decrees of the tribunal or which violated any of the rights which in the rules it was expressly stipulated should be reserved to the several nations, the rights to their territorial integrity and the like. . . .

In addition to the contracting powers, a certain number of outside nations should be named as entitled to the benefits of the court. These nations should be chosen from those which are as civilized and well-behaved as the great contracting nations, but which, for some reason or other, are unwilling or unable to guarantee to help execute the decrees of the court by force. They would have no right to take part in the nomination of judges, for no people are entitled to do anything toward establishing a court unless they are able and willing to face the risk, labor, and self-sacrifice necessary in order to put police power behind the court. But they would be treated with exact justice; and in the event of any one of the great contracting powers having trouble with one of them, they would be entitled to go into court, have a decision rendered, and see the decision supported, precisely as in the case of a dispute between any two of the great contracting powers themselves. . . . [In addition] there are various . . . states which have never been entitled to the consideration as civilized, orderly, self-respecting powers which would entitle them to be treated on terms of equality in the fashion indicated. As regards these disorderly and weak outsiders, it might well be that after a while some method would be devised to deal with them by common agreement of the civilized powers; but until this was devised and put into execution they would have to be left as at present.

Of course, grave difficulties would be encountered in devising such a plan and in administering it afterward, and no human being can guarantee that it would absolutely succeed. But I believe that it could be made to work and that it would mark a very great improvement over what obtains now. (*Independent,* January 4, 1915.) *Mem. Ed.* XX, 184-187; *Nat. Ed.* XVIII, 158-161.

INTERNATIONAL COURT. See also ARBITRATION TREATIES; FORCE; HAGUE COURT; LEAGUE FOR PEACE; LEAGUE OF NATIONS; PEACE.

INTERNATIONAL COURTESY. Courtesy among individuals is a good thing, but international courtesy is quite as good a thing. If there is any one quality to be deprecated in a public man and in a public writer alike, it is the using of language which without any corresponding gain to ourselves tends to produce irritation among nations with whom we ought to be on friendly terms. Nations are now brought much nearer together than they formerly were. Steam, electricity, the immense spread of the newspaper press in all countries, the way in which so much of what is written in any country is translated into the language of another country, all of these facts have tended to bring peoples closer together now. That ought to and I think in the future will tell predominantly for good; but it does not help us in the least to be brought closer together with other peoples if they merely find our unamiable traits more strongly marked than they thought. We can rest assured that no man ever thinks better of us because we point out his salient defects; and no nation is ever won to a kindlier feeling toward us if we adopt toward it a tone which we would resent if adopted toward us. (Before Periodical Publishers' Association, Washington, D. C., April 7, 1904.) *Presidential Addresses and State Papers* III, 7-8.

INTERNATIONAL CRITICISM. International criticism may be of value in three ways. First, it may help the country criticised (and that it may do, even though in large part inaccurate); second, it may help outsiders, by holding up to their view an example, either to follow or avoid; third, it may throw a flood of light on the mental condition of the critic himself. *Eclectic Magazine,* November 1888, p. 578.

INTERNATIONAL DISPUTES — SETTLEMENT OF. It is our duty, *so far as is now possible,* so far as human nature in the present-day world will permit, to try to provide peaceful substitutes for war as a method for the settlement of international disputes. But progress in this direction is merely hindered by the folly that believes in putting peace above righteousness; while it is of course even worse to pretend so to believe. The greatest service this nation can render to righteousness is to behave with scrupulous justice to other nations, and yet to keep ready to hold its own if necessary. (*Outlook,* September 9, 1911.) *Mem. Ed.* XVIII, 426; *Nat. Ed.* XVI, 318.

————. I have always championed every practical measure to bring nearer the day when we shall be able to substitute other methods than those of war for the settlement of international disputes. I have always sought in every way to further the cause of the peace and righteousness throughout the world. But as yet, friends, it would be an act of criminal folly for the great free nations not to remember that we must make might the servant of right instead of divorcing might from right. As yet no movement for peace amounts to anything unless the peoples behind it possess in addition to the love of justice, the power and the determination in time of need to use the potential force that is theirs. (At Buenos Aires, Argentina, November 12, 1913.) *American Ideals. Speeches . . . of Dr. Emilio Frers and of Col. Theodore Roosevelt.* (Buenos Aires, 1914), p. 22.

INTERNATIONAL DISPUTES. *See also* ARBITRATION; FORCE; WAR.

INTERNATIONAL DUTIES. An American who is loyal to this great American nation has two duties, and only two, in international matters. In the first place, he is bound to serve the honor and the interest of the United States. In the second place, he is bound to treat all other nations in accordance with their conduct at any given time, and in accordance with the ultimate needs of mankind at large; and not in accordance with the interests of the European nation from which some or all of his ancestors have come. If he does not act along these lines, he is derelict in his duty to his fellow citizens and he is guilty of betraying the interests of his country. (*Metropolitan,* October 1915.) *Mem. Ed.* XX, 330; *Nat. Ed.* XVIII, 283.

INTERNATIONAL DUTIES — AVOIDANCE OF. We must clearly grasp the fact that mere selfish avoidance of duty to others, even although covered by such fine words as "peace" and "neutrality," is a wretched thing and an obstacle to securing the peace of righteousness throughout the world. (New York *Times,* November 8, 1914.) *Mem. Ed.* XX, 84; *Nat. Ed.* XVIII, 73.

INTERNATIONAL DUTIES—PERFORMANCE OF. It is impossible for us much longer to blind ourselves to the fact that we have international relations, and that we have no choice save to perform our international duties. We may perform them well or badly, but perform them we must; we may meet the problems that we have to face either wisely or foolishly, but meet them we have to. All that we can decide is whether we shall do our work well or ill. (*Outlook,* May 31, 1913.) *Mem. Ed.* XIV, 225; *Nat. Ed.* XII, 242.

INTERNATIONAL DUTIES AND RIGHTS. Whether we desire it or not, we must henceforth recognize that we have international duties no less than international rights. (First Annual Message, Washington, December 3, 1901.) *Mem. Ed.* XVII, 135; *Nat. Ed.* XV, 117.

INTERNATIONAL DUTY. The other type of duty is the international duty, the duty owed by one nation to another. I hold that the laws of morality which should govern individuals in their dealings one with the other, are just as binding concerning nations in their dealings one with the other. (At Oxford University, England, June 7, 1910.) *Mem. Ed.* XIV, 105; *Nat. Ed.* XII, 58.

——————. There can be no higher international duty than to safeguard the existence and independence of industrious, orderly states, with a high personal and national standard of conduct, but without the military force of the great powers; states, for instance, such as Belgium, Holland, Switzerland, the Scandinavian countries, Uruguay, and others. (*Outlook,* September 23, 1914.) *Mem. Ed.* XX, 14; *Nat. Ed.* XVIII, 12.

——————. I believe in International Duty. I hold that we cannot assert that we are entirely guiltless of responsibility for the outrages committed on well-behaved nations, particularly on Belgium, and on non-combatants, particularly on women and children, in the present war. Prior to the war we had become parties to the various conventions and treaties designed to mitigate the horrors of war, and to limit the offenses that can, with impunity, be committed by belligerents either on neutrals or non-combatants. When we declined to take any action under these conventions and treaties we ourselves treated them as "scraps of paper." Such being the case while our guilt is not as great as that of the strong and ruthless nations who committed the misdeeds, we nevertheless occupy, in some respects, an even meaner position. For we possess strength, and yet we refuse to make ready this strength and we refuse to use it for righteousness. We possess strength, and yet we decline to put it behind our plighted word when the interests and honor of others are involved.

Performance of international duty to others means that in international affairs, in the commonwealth of nations, we shall not only refrain from wronging the weak, but shall, according to our capacity, and as opportunity offers, stand up for the weak when the weak are wronged by the strong. Most emphatically it does not mean that we shall submit to wrongdoing by other nations. To do so is a proof not of virtue, but of weakness, and of a mean and abject national spirit. To submit to wrongdoing is to encourage wrongdoing; and it is, therefore, itself, a form of iniquity—and a peculiarly objectionable form of iniquity, for it is based on cowardice. (At Kansas City, Mo., May 30, 1916.) *The Progressive Party; Its Record from January to July 1916.* (Progressive National Committee, 1916), p. 58.

INTERNATIONAL DUTY. *See also* Belgium; Foreign Policy; Hague Conventions; Neutrality; World War.

INTERNATIONAL FEAR. It is idle merely to make speeches and write essays against this fear, because at present the fear has a real basis. At present each nation has cause for the fear it feels. Each nation has cause to believe that its national life is in peril unless it is able to take the national life of one or more of its foes or at least hopelessly to cripple that foe. The causes of the fear must be removed or, no matter what peace may be patched up to-day or what new treaties may be negotiated to-morrow, these causes will at some future day bring about the same results, bring about a repetition of this same awful tragedy. (New York *Times,* October 11, 1914.) *Mem. Ed.* XX, 59; *Nat. Ed.* XVIII, 50.

INTERNATIONAL GUARANTEES. Fear of national destruction will prompt men to do almost anything, and the proper remedy for outsiders to work for is the removal of the fear. If Germany were absolutely freed from danger of aggression on her eastern and western frontiers, I believe that German public sentiment would refuse to sanction such acts as those against Belgium. The only effective way to free it from this fear is to have outside nations like the United States in good faith undertake the obligation to defend Germany's honor and territorial integrity, if attacked, exactly as they would defend the honor and territorial integrity of Belgium, or of France, Russia, Japan, or England, or any other well-behaved, civilized power, if attacked. (*Independent,* January 4, 1915.) *Mem. Ed.* XX, 182; *Nat. Ed.* XVIII, 156.

————. I very earnestly hope that this nation will ultimately adopt a dignified and self-respecting policy in international affairs. I earnestly hope that ultimately we shall live up to every international obligation we have undertaken—exactly as we did live up to them during the seven and a half years while I was president. I earnestly hope that we shall ourselves become one of the joint guarantors of world peace . . . and that we shall hold ourselves ready and willing to act as a member of the international posse comitatus to enforce the peace of righteousness as against any offender big or small. This would mean a great practical stride toward relief from the burden of excessive military preparation. It would mean that a long step had been taken toward at least minimizing and restricting the area and extent of possible warfare. It would mean that all liberty-loving and enlightened peoples, great and small, would be freed from the haunting nightmare of terror which now besets them when they think of the possible conquest of their land. (New York *Times,* November 8, 1914.) *Mem. Ed.* XX, 96; *Nat. Ed.* XVIII, 83.

INTERNATIONAL GUARANTEES. *See also* Belgium; Hague Treaties; League for Peace; League of Nations.

INTERNATIONAL JUSTICE. The prime lesson of this war is that no nation can preserve its own self-respect, or the good-will of other nations, unless it keeps itself ready to exact justice from others, precisely as it should keep itself eager and willing to do justice to others. (New York *Times,* October 11, 1914.) *Mem. Ed.* XX, 50; *Nat. Ed.* XVIII, 43.

————. I have certainly never hesitated, and at this moment am not hesitating, to condemn my own country and my own countrymen when it and they are wrong. I would just as unhesitatingly condemn England, France, or Russia if any one of them should in the future behave as Germany is now behaving. I shall stand by Germany in the future on any occasion when its conduct permits me so to do. We must not be vindictive, or prone to remember injuries; we need forgiveness, and we must be ready to grant forgiveness. When an injury is past and is atoned for, it would be wicked to hold it in mind. We must do justice as the facts at the moment demand. (1916.) *Mem. Ed.* XX, 254; *Nat. Ed.* XVIII, 218.

INTERNATIONAL JUSTICE—CHARACTER OF. Justice and fair dealing among nations rest upon principles identical with those which control justice and fair dealing among the individuals of which nations are composed, with the vital exception that each nation must do its own part in international police work. If you get into trouble here you can call for the police; but if Uncle Sam gets into trouble, he has got to be his own policeman, and I want to see him strong enough to encourage the peaceful aspirations of other peoples in connection with us. I believe in national friendships and heartiest good-will to all nations; but national friendships, like those between men, must be founded on respect as well as on liking, on forbearance as well as upon trust. (At Osawatomie, Kan., August 31, 1910.) *Mem. Ed.* XIX, 21; *Nat. Ed.* XVII, 14.

INTERNATIONAL JUSTICE. *See also* Big Stick; "Hands Across the Sea."

INTERNATIONAL LAW

INTERNATIONAL LAW—NATURE OF.
There is no such thing as international law in the sense that there is municipal law or law within a nation. Within the nation there is always a judge, and a policeman who stands back of the judge. The whole system of law depends first upon the fact that there is a judge competent to pass judgment, and second upon the fact that there is some competent officer whose duty it is to carry out this judgment, by force if necessary. In international law there is no judge, unless the parties in interest agree that one shall be constituted; and there is no policeman to carry out the judge's orders. In consequence, as yet each nation must depend upon itself for its own protection. (1913.) *Mem. Ed.* XXII, 436; *Nat. Ed.* XX, 374.

INTERNATIONAL LAW AND WORLD PEACE. World peace must rest on the willingness of nations with courage, cool foresight, and readiness for self-sacrifice to defend the fabric of international law. No nation can help in securing an organized, peaceful, and justice-doing world community until it is willing to run risks and make efforts in order to secure and maintain such a community. (1916.) *Mem. Ed.* XX, 235; *Nat. Ed.* XVIII, 203.

INTERNATIONAL LAW. See also CONTRABAND; HAGUE CONVENTIONS; MONROE DOCTRINE; MUNITIONS; NEUTRALITY.

INTERNATIONAL MORALITY—INEFFECTIVENESS OF. It would be untrue to say that nations have not at times proved themselves capable of acting with great disinterestedness and generosity toward other peoples; but such conduct is not very common at the best, and although it often may be desirable, it certainly is not always so. If the matter in dispute is of great importance, and if there is a doubt as to which side is right, then the strongest party to the controversy is pretty sure to give itself the benefit of that doubt; and international morality will have to take tremendous strides in advance before this ceases to be the case. (1887.) *Mem. Ed.* VIII, 194; *Nat. Ed.* VII, 168.

INTERNATIONAL MORALITY. See also IMPERIALISM.

INTERNATIONAL OPINION — FORCE OF. I believe that international opinion can do something to arrest wrong; but only if it is aroused and finds some method of clear and forceful expression. (New York *Times,* October 4, 1914.) *Mem. Ed.* XX, 44; *Nat. Ed.* XVIII, 38.

INTERNATIONAL RELATIONS

INTERNATIONAL POLICE POWER. The supreme difficulty in connection with developing the peace work of The Hague arises from the lack of any executive power, of any police power to enforce the decrees of the court. In any community of any size the authority of the courts rests upon actual or potential force; on the existence of a police, or on the knowledge that the able-bodied men of the country are both ready and willing to see that the decrees of judicial and legislative bodies are put into effect. In new and wild communities where there is violence, an honest man must protect himself; and until other means of securing his safety are devised, it is both foolish and wicked to persuade him to surrender his arms while the men who are dangerous to the community retain theirs. He should not renounce the right to protect himself by his own efforts until the community is so organized that it can effectively relieve the individual of the duty of putting down violence. So it is with the nations. Each nation must keep well prepared to defend itself until the establishment of some form of international police power, competent and willing to prevent violence as between nations. *Outlook,* May 7, 1910, p. 20.

——————. The futility of international agreements in great crises has come from the fact that force was not back of them.

What is needed in international matters is to create a judge and then to put police power back of the judge.

So far the time has not been ripe to attempt this. Surely now, in view of the awful cataclysm of the present war, such a plan could at least be considered; and it may be that the combatants at the end will be willing to try it in order to secure at least a chance for the only kind of peace that is worth having, the peace that is compatible with self-respect. (New York *Times,* October 18, 1914.) *Mem. Ed.* XX, 62-63; *Nat. Ed.* XVIII, 53.

INTERNATIONAL POLICE POWER. See also DEFENSE; DISARMAMENT; HAGUE COURT; LEAGUE FOR PEACE; LEAGUE OF NATIONS; PREPAREDNESS.

INTERNATIONAL RELATIONS—BASIS OF. It is a mistake, and it betrays a spirit of foolish cynicism, to maintain that all international governmental action is, and must ever be, based upon mere selfishness, and that to advance ethical reasons for such action is always a sign of hypocrisy. This is no more necessarily true of the action of governments than of the action of individuals. It is a sure sign of a base nature always to ascribe base motives for the actions of others. Unquestionably no nation can afford to disregard proper considerations of self-interest, any more than a private individual can do so.... A really great nation must often act, and as a matter of fact, often does act, toward other nations in a spirit not in the least of mere self-interest, but paying heed chiefly to ethical reasons; and as the centuries go by this disinterestedness in international action, this tendency of the individuals comprising a nation to require that nation to act with justice toward its neighbors, steadily grows and strengthens. (Sixth Annual Message, Washington, December 3, 1906.) *Mem. Ed.* XVII, 450; *Nat. Ed.* XV, 383.

INTERNATIONAL RELATIONS—CONDUCT OF. In international affairs this country should behave toward other nations exactly as an honorable private citizen behaves toward other private citizens. We should do no wrong to any nation, weak or strong, and we should submit to no wrong. (Before Progressive National Convention, Chicago, August 6, 1912.) *Mem. Ed.* XIX, 407; *Nat. Ed.* XVII, 295.

――――――. The questions arising in connection with our international relations must to-day, as always, be settled exactly along the lines of general policy laid down by Washington, under penalty of risking grave national discredit and disgrace. (*Century Magazine,* October 1913.) *Mem. Ed.* XIX, 532; *Nat. Ed.* XVII, 391.

INTERNATIONAL RELATIONS—PROGRESS IN. The world has moved so far that it is no longer necessary to believe that one nation can rise only by thrusting another down. All far-sighted statesmen, all true patriots, now earnestly wish that the leading nations of mankind, as in their several ways they struggle constantly toward a higher civilization, a higher humanity, may advance hand in hand, united only in a generous rivalry to see which can best do its allotted work in the world. I believe that there is a rising tide in human thought which tends for righteous international peace; a tide which it behooves us to guide through rational channels to sane conclusions. (At Jamestown Exposition, Va., April 26, 1907.) *Mem. Ed.* XII, 586; *Nat. Ed.* XI, 306.

――――――. Two centuries ago there was the greatest suspicion and malevolence exhibited by all the people, high and low, of each European country, for all the people, high and low, of every other European country, with but few exceptions. The cultivated people of the different countries, however, had already begun to treat with one another on good terms. But when, for instance, the Huguenots were exiled from France, and great numbers of Huguenot workmen went to England, their presence excited the most violent hostility, manifesting itself even in mob violence, among the English workmen. The men were closely allied by race and religion, they had practically the same type of ancestral culture, and yet they were unable to get on together. Two centuries have passed, the world has moved forward, and now there could be no repetition of such hostilities. In the same way a marvellous progress has been made in the relations of Japan with the Occidental nations. (To Baron Kentaro Kaneko, May 23, 1907.) Julian Street, *Mysterious Japan.* (Doubleday, Page & Co., Garden City, N. Y., 1921), p. 224.

INTERNATIONAL RELATIONS. *See also* ALLIANCE; ARBITRATION; BIG STICK; DIPLOMACY; FORCE; FOREIGN POLICY; FOREIGN RELATIONS; "HANDS ACROSS THE SEA"; PEACE; WAR.

INTERNATIONALISM. The man who loves other nations as much as he does his own, stands on a par with the man who loves other women as much as he does his own wife. (1916.) *Mem. Ed.* XX, 233; *Nat. Ed.* XVIII, 201.

INTERNATIONALISM AND NATIONALISM. The cult of absolute internationalism *as a substitute for nationalism* is the cult of a doctrine of fatal sterility. It had much vogue up to the beginning of this war among the professional "intellectuals," especially among bright, clever young college men of superficial cultivation. It was of real damage to these, and therefore it, to a certain extent, damaged the country; for it inevitably emasculates its sincere votaries, and therefore deprives their country of whatever aid they could otherwise give in the effort to build a vigorous civilization, based, as every civilization worth calling such must be, on a spirit of intense nationalism.

The damage done, because of the way such sham internationalism destroys the creative fibre of the intellectuals, is chiefly of negative character. It deprives the nation of a growth-force which ought to be a valuable asset. But it works in positively mischievous fashion among the powerful sinister men who are not sincere devotees of the cult, but who use it as a cloak behind which they war on all civilization, or else deliberately adopt a pretense of belief in it in order to weaken other nations and make them an easier prey. (1918.) *Mem. Ed.* XXI, 352; *Nat. Ed.* XIX, 321.

───────────. To substitute internationalism for nationalism means to do away with patriotism, and is as vicious and as profoundly demoralizing as to put promiscuous devotion to all other persons in the place of steadfast devotion to a man's own family. Either effort means the atrophy of robust morality. . . . The professional internationalist is a man who, under a pretense of diffuse attachment for everybody hides the fact that in reality he is incapable of doing his duty by anybody. (Lafayette Day exercises, New York City, September 6, 1918.) *Mem. Ed.* XXI, 410; *Nat. Ed.* XIX, 372.

INTERNATIONALISM. *See also* ALLEGIANCE; AMERICANISM; COSMOPOLITANS; EXPATRIATES; NATIONALISM; PATRIOTISM.

INTERSTATE COMMERCE — NATIONAL REGULATION OF. No more important subject can come before the Congress than this of the regulation of interstate business. This country cannot afford to sit supine on the plea that under our peculiar system of government we are helpless in the presence of the new conditions, and unable to grapple with them or to cut out whatever of evil has arisen in connection with them. The power of the Congress to regulate interstate commerce is an absolute and unqualified grant, and without limitations other than those prescribed by the Constitution. The Congress has constitutional authority to make all laws necessary and proper for executing this power, and I am satisfied that this power has not been exhausted by any legislation now on the statute-books. It is evident, therefore, that evils restrictive of commercial freedom and entailing restraint upon national commerce fall within the regulative power of the Congress and that a wise and reasonable law would be a necessary and proper exercise of congressional authority to the end that such evils should be eradicated. (Second Annual Message, Washington, December 2, 1902.) *Mem. Ed.* XVII, 165; *Nat. Ed.* XV, 142-143.

───────────. Under a wise and far-seeing interpretation of the interstate commerce clause of the Constitution, I maintain that the National Government should have complete power to deal with all of this wealth which in any way goes into the commerce between the States— and practically all of it that is employed in the great corporations does thus go in. The national legislators should most scrupulously avoid any demagogic legislation about the business use of this wealth, and should realize that it would be better to have no legislation at all than legislation couched either in a vindictive spirit of hatred toward men of wealth or else drawn with the recklessness of impracticable visionaries. But, on the other hand, it shall and must ultimately be understood that the United States Government, on behalf of the people of the United States, has and is to exercise the power of supervision and control over the business use of this wealth—in the first place, over all the work of the common carriers of the nation, and in the next place over the work of all the great corporations which directly or indirectly do any interstate business whatever—and this includes almost all of the great corporations. (At Harrisburg, Pa., October 4, 1906.) *Mem. Ed.* XVIII, 85-86; *Nat. Ed.* XVI, 72.

───────────. I most strongly hold the view that the States should not, and cannot permanently, be allowed to exercise any power, directly or indirectly, over interstate commerce. Wherever commerce is interstate the national power is not only supreme but sole. . . . All questions of the regulation of traffic through any State, if that traffic is interstate, belong, under the Constitution, to the National Government. The encouragement to the States to act on their own initiative in this matter has come chiefly from the failure of the National Government to act; the failure of Congress to provide laws sufficiently far-reaching; and the nullification of these laws, when enacted, by decisions like that in the Knight Sugar Case. When, by what ordinary men regard as a mere legal subtlety, the power of the National Congress over great corporations engaged in interstate commerce is reduced to a nullity, it is inevitable that the State governments should themselves try to step in and take the place which the highest Federal court, in the decision which has become the supreme law of the land, has declared to be vacant so far as the National Government is concerned. A decision like that in the Knight Case invites each State to act for itself, and therefore invites industrial chaos. (*Outlook,* March 11, 1911.) *Mem. Ed.* XIX, 138; *Nat. Ed.* XVII, 98.

───────────. The National Government exercises control over inter-State commerce railways, and it can in similar fashion, through an appropriate governmental body, exercise control over all industrial organizations engaged in inter-State commerce. This control should be exercised, not by the courts, but by an administrative bureau or board such as the Bureau of

Corporations or the Inter-State Commerce Commission; for the courts cannot with advantage permanently perform executive and administrative functions. *Outlook,* November 18, 1911, p. 656.

───────────. The Constitution was framed more for the purpose of giving to the government complete power over interstate commerce than for any other object. Every trust magnate in the country can rest in safety if he can have the law relegated to the States instead of to the nation. All danger to him will vanish forthwith. (*Outlook,* July 27, 1912.) *Mem. Ed.* XIX, 356; *Nat. Ed.* XVII, 253.

INTERSTATE COMMERCE. *See also* BUSINESS; CORPORATIONS; INDUSTRIAL COMMISSION; KNIGHT CASE; NORTHERN SECURITIES CASE; RAILROADS; TRUSTS.

INTERSTATE COMMERCE LAW—ACCOMPLISHMENTS UNDER THE. It was framed on the theory that certain monopolies—for every railway is, because of its very nature, to a certain extent a monopoly, or has a certain monopolistic tendency—because of their tremendous power as business entities and of the impossibility of the individual man grappling with them on even terms, should be rigidly supervised and controlled by the agent of the people as a whole, that is, by the National Government. We are as yet very far from having achieved the best possible results under the Inter-State Commerce Law, but we have steadily improved both the law and its administration and are accomplishing far more for the control of those monopolies called railways under the Inter-State Commerce Law than is now being accomplished, or can by any possibility be accomplished, in the way of control of other business monopolies by the Anti-Trust Law or any alteration thereof. *Outlook,* June 3, 1911, p. 240.

INTERSTATE COMMERCE LAW—STRENGTHENING OF THE. The interstate commerce law has rather amusingly falsified the predictions, both of those who asserted that it would ruin the railroads and of those who asserted that it did not go far enough and would accomplish nothing. During the last five months the railroads have shown increased earnings and some of them unusual dividends; while during the same period the mere taking effect of the law has produced an unprecedented, a hitherto unheard-of number of voluntary reductions in freights and fares by the railroads. Since the founding of the Commission there has never been a time of equal length in which anything like so many reduced tariffs have been put into effect. (Sixth Annual Message, Washington, December 3, 1906.) *Mem. Ed.* XVII, 427; *Nat. Ed.* XV, 364.

───────────. We passed a law giving vitality to the Interstate Commerce Commission, and for the first time providing some kind of efficient control by the National Government over the great railroads. (To Sydney Brooks, December 28, 1908.) *Mem. Ed.* XXIV, 152. Bishop II, 131.

INTERSTATE INDUSTRIAL COMMISSION. *See* INDUSTRIAL COMMISSION.

INTERVENTION. I never said that I would refuse to run the risk of shedding a drop of blood to protect American property; that doctrine if carried out logically would mean that no policeman ought ever to arrest a burglar or a pickpocket, for burglary and highway robbing are only offences against property, whereas interference with them undoubtedly means incurring the risk of bloodshed. Nor did I say that all American citizens should leave the country, abandoning their property to the good-will of the contending factions. My position was the direct reverse. My position was that if Americans had a right to be in a country, they could stay there, and every resource of the government would be exhausted to protect them. Nor did I refuse to act at all until foreign powers acted, nor either ask or accept their co-operation in action; still less did I follow a course which was certain to produce anarchy and make existing conditions worse, so as to force intervention. I protected the rights of our own people, while nevertheless examining their claims so carefully as to insure us against protecting any of them in wrong-doing. (At New York City, October 3, 1913.) *Mem. Ed.* XVIII, 403-404; *Nat. Ed.* XVI, 302-303.

INTERVENTION. *See also* CUBA; SANTO DOMINGO; VENEZUELA.

INTOLERANCE. *See* ANTI-SEMITISM; CLASS JEALOUSY; DISLOYALTY; RELIGIOUS DISCRIMINATION; TOLERANCE.

INTOXICATING LIQUORS. *See* LIQUOR; PROHIBITION; TEMPERANCE.

INVESTORS. *See* CORPORATIONS; DIVIDENDS; SPECULATOR; STOCK-WATERING.

INVISIBLE GOVERNMENT. *See* GOVERNMENT.

IRELAND—RACIAL ANTAGONISM IN. There is no language in which to paint the hideous atrocities committed in the Irish wars of Elizabeth; and the worst must be credited to the highest English officials. In Ireland the antagonism was fundamentally racial; whether the sovereign of England were Catholic or Protestant made little difference in the burden of wrong which the Celt was forced to bear. (1900.) *Mem. Ed.* XIII, 297; *Nat. Ed.* X, 196.

IRISH-AMERICANS. We welcome the German or the Irishman who becomes an American. We have no use for the German or Irishman who remains such. We do not wish German-Americans and Irish-Americans who figure as such in our social and political life; we want only Americans, and, provided they are such, we do not care whether they are of native or of Irish or of German ancestry. We have no room in any healthy American community for a German-American vote or an Irish-American vote, and it is contemptible demagogy to put planks into any party platform with the purpose of catching such a vote. We have no room for any people who do not act and vote simply as Americans, and as nothing else. (*Forum,* April 1894.) *Mem. Ed.* XV, 24; *Nat. Ed.* XIII, 21.

IRISH-AMERICANS — CONTRIBUTION OF. The people who have come to this country from Ireland have contributed to the stock of our common citizenship qualities which are essential to the welfare of every great nation. They are a masterful race of rugged character, a race the qualities of whose womanhood have become proverbial, while its men have the elemental, the indispensable virtues of working hard in time of peace and fighting hard in time of war. (Before Society of Friendly Sons of St. Patrick, New York City, March 17, 1905.) *Mem. Ed.* XVIII, 49; *Nat. Ed.* XVI, 42.

IRISH-AMERICANS. *See also* ALLEGIANCE; AMERICANS, HYPHENATED; CITIZENSHIP; TAMMANY HALL.

IRISH DRAMA. *See* ABBEY THEATRE.

IRISH LITERATURE. *See* CELTIC LITERATURE.

IRRIGATION. I believe to the last point in the vital necessity of storing the floods and preserving the forests, especially throughout the plains and Rocky Mountain regions. The problem of the development of the greater West is in large part a problem of irrigation. I earnestly believe in the national government giving generous aid to the movement, for it is not possible, and if it were possible, it would not be wise to have this storage work done merely through private ownership; and owing to the peculiar necessities of the case, much of the work must be done by the National and not by any State government. (Letter of November 16, 1900; read before National Irrigation Congress, Chicago). *The Forester,* December 1900, p. 289.

———. Irrigation works should be built by the National Government. The lands reclaimed by them should be reserved by the government for actual settlers, and the cost of construction should so far as possible be repaid by the land reclaimed. The distribution of the water, the division of the streams among irrigators, should be left to the settlers themselves in conformity with State laws and without interference with those laws or with vested rights. The policy of the National Government should be to aid irrigation in the several States and Territories in such manner as will enable the people in the local communities to help themselves, and as will stimulate needed reforms in the State laws and regulations governing irrigation. (First Annual Message, Washington, December 3, 1901.) *Mem. Ed.* XVII, 122-123; *Nat. Ed.* XV, 106.

IRRIGATION—PROGRESS IN. Not of recent years has any more important law been put upon the statute books of the Federal Government than the law a year ago providing for the first time that the National Government should interest itself in aiding and building up a system of irrigated agriculture in the Rocky Mountains and plains States. Here the government had to a large degree to sit at the feet of Gamaliel in the person of Utah; for what you had done and learned was of literally incalculable benefit to those engaged in framing and getting through the national irrigation law. Irrigation was first practiced on a large scale in this State. The necessity of the pioneers here led to the development of irrigation to a degree absolutely unknown before on this continent. . . . We all know that when you once get irrigation applied rain is a very poor substitute for it. The Federal Government must co-operate with Utah and Utah people for a further extension of the irrigated area. Many of the simpler problems of obtaining and applying water have already been solved and so well solved that, as I have said, some of the most important provisions of the Federal act, such as the control of the irrigating works by the communities they serve, such as making the water appurtenant to the land not a source of speculation apart from the land, were based upon the experience of Utah. Of course the control of the larger streams which flow through more than one State must come under the Federal Government. (At Salt Lake City, Utah, May 29, 1903.) *Presidential Addresses and State Papers* II, 442.

——————. In legislation I succeeded in getting through the national irrigation act in the development of the semiarid States of the great plains and Rockies; I think this achievement in importance comes second only to the creation of the homestead act; and indeed in those particular States it is more important than the homestead act. (To Sydney Brooks, December 28, 1908.) *Mem. Ed.* XXIV, 151; Bishop II, 130.

IRRIGATION. *See also* CONSERVATION; FOREST PROBLEM; INLAND WATERWAYS; RECLAMATION.

ISTHMUS OF PANAMA. *See* PANAMA CANAL.

ITALY. *See* ROME; SOCIALISM; VICTOR EMMANUEL; WORLD WAR.

J

JACKSON, ANDREW. Jackson had precisely the qualities fitted to render him a man of mark in this turbulent backwoods community [Tennessee]. The Indian fighters, game-hunters, and frontier farmers who made up the population had many faults and short-comings; but they were, after all, essentially a manly race, and they respected the young lawyer both for his indomitable courage and physical prowess, and for the resolute determination with which he stood by his friends and upheld the cause of order—as order was understood in that place and at that time. (*Chautauquan,* January 1891.) *Mem. Ed.* XII, 438; *Nat. Ed.* XI, 197.

——————. The two great reasons for Jackson's success throughout his political career were to be found in the strength of the feeling in his favor among the poorer and least educated classes of voters, and in the ardent support given him by the low politicians, who, by playing on his prejudices and passions, moulded him to their wishes, and who organized and perfected in their own and his interests a great political machine, founded on the "spoils system." (1887.) *Mem. Ed.* VIII, 87-88; *Nat. Ed.* VII, 76.

——————. As President, Jackson did much good and much evil. He was wholly incapable of distinguishing between a public and a private foe. To him an enemy of his own was of necessity an enemy of the nation, and he followed both with inveterate hostility. . . .

Jackson had many faults, but he was devotedly attached to the Union, and he had no thought of fear when it came to defending his country. By his resolute and defiant bearing and his fervent championship of the Federal Government he overawed the Disunionist party and staved off for thirty years the attempt at secession. . . .

With the exception of Washington and Lincoln, no man has left a deeper mark on American history; and though there is much in his career to condemn, yet all true lovers of America can unite in paying hearty respect to the memory of a man who was emphatically a true American, who served his country valiantly on the field of battle against a foreign foe, and who upheld with the most stanch devotion the cause of the great Federal Union. (*Chautauquan,* January 1891.) *Mem. Ed.* XII, 443; *Nat. Ed.* XI, 202.

JACKSON AT NEW ORLEANS. The only really noteworthy feat of arms of the war [of 1812] took place at New Orleans, and the only military genius that the struggle developed was Andrew Jackson. His deeds are worthy of all praise, and the battle he won was in many ways so peculiar as to make it well worth a much closer study than it has yet received. It was by far the most prominent event of the war; it was a victory which reflected high honor on the general and soldiers who won it, and it was in its way as remarkable as any of the great battles that took place about the same time in Europe. (1883.) *Mem. Ed.* VII, xxxiii; *Nat. Ed.* VI, xxix.

——————. He had hereditary wrongs to avenge on the British, and he hated them with an implacable fury that was absolutely devoid of fear. Born and brought up among the lawless characters of the frontier, and knowing well how to deal with them, he was able to establish and preserve the strictest martial law in the city without in the least quelling the spirit of the citizens. To a restless and untiring energy he united sleepless vigilance and genuine military genius. Prompt to attack whenever the chance offered itself, seizing with ready grasp the slightest vantage-ground, and never giving up a foot of earth that he could keep, he yet had the patience to play a defensive game when it so suited him, and with consummate skill he always followed out the scheme of warfare that was best adapted to his wild soldiery. In after-years he did to his country some good and more evil; but no true American can think of his deeds at New Orleans without profound and unmixed thankfulness. (1882.) *Mem. Ed.* VII, 429; *Nat. Ed.* VI, 377-378.

JAPAN—COOPERATION WITH. She and the United States have great interests on and in the Pacific. These interests in no way conflict. They can be served to best purpose for each nation by the heartiest and most friendly co-operation between them on a footing of absolute equality. There is but one real chance of friction. This should be eliminated, not by pretending to ignore facts, but by facing them with good-natured and courteous wisdom—for, as Emerson somewhere says, "in the long run the most unpleasant truth is a safer travelling companion than the most agreeable falsehood." Each country should receive exactly the rights which it grants. Travellers, scholars, men engaged in international business, all sojourners for health, pleasure, and study, should be heartily welcomed in both countries. From neither country should there be any emigration of workers of any kind to, or any settlement in mass in, the other country. (*Metropolitan*, March 1915.) *Mem. Ed.* XX, 481; *Nat. Ed.* XVIII, 412.

————————. To speak only of the nation concerning which there has been most recent talk of war, I not only have a great respect and admiration for the Japanese, but I very strongly feel that we have much to learn from them. I regard a good understanding between Japan and the United States as of capital consequence to this country, and as of the first importance from the standpoint of preserving peace in the Pacific. . . . But there should be the closest and friendliest relations between the two countries, conducted on a basis of absolute equality and of mutual regard and respect. (*Outlook*, April 1, 1911.) *Mem. Ed.* XIX, 158; *Nat. Ed.* XVII, 114.

JAPAN—FUTURE OF. I have, from the beginning, favoured Japan and have done all that I could do, consistent with international law, to advance her interests. I thoroughly admire and believe in the Japanese. They have always told me the truth, and the Russians have not. Moreover, they have the kind of fighting stock that I like; but there is one thing that I hope will be impressed upon them, and that is the necessity for a broad, intelligent self-restrained attitude at the close of this war. I am confident that Japan will prove to the end, as she has proven so far, victorious; but then she will have before her a very great problem, and it is the solution of this problem that I fear.

If Japan is careful, and is guided by the best minds in her empire, she can become one of the leaders of the family of great nations; but if she is narrow and insular, if she tries to gain from her victory more than she ought to have, she will array against her all of the great Powers, and you know very well that however determined she may be, she cannot successfully face an allied world. (To George Kennan, early 1905.) Tyler Dennett, *Roosevelt and the Russo-Japanese War.* (Doubleday, Page & Co., Garden City, N. Y., 1925), pp. 160-161.

JAPAN—PROGRESS OF. If the Japanese win out, not only the Slav, but all of us will have to reckon with a great new force in eastern Asia. The victory will make Japan by itself a formidable power in the Orient, because all the other powers having interests there will have divided interests, divided cares, double burdens, whereas Japan will have but one care, one interest, one burden. If, moreover, Japan seriously starts in to reorganize China and makes any headway, there will result a real shifting of the centre of equilibrium as far as the white races are concerned. Personally I believe that Japan will develop herself, and seek to develop China, along paths which will make the first, and possibly the second, great civilized powers; but the civilisation must, of course, be of a different type from our civilisations. I do not mean that the mere race taken by itself would cause such a tremendous difference. I have met Japanese, and even Chinese, educated in our ways, who in all their emotions and ways of thought were well-nigh identical with us. But the weight of their own ancestral civilization will press upon them, and will prevent their ever coming into exactly our mould. (To Spring Rice, March 19, 1904.) *The Letters and Friendships of Sir Cecil Spring Rice.* (Houghton Mifflin Co., Boston, 1929), I, 398.

————————. As for Japan, she has risen with simply marvelous rapidity, and she is as formidable from the industrial as from the military standpoint. She is a great civilized nation; though her civilization is in some important respects not like ours. There are some things she can teach us, and some things she can learn

[273]

from us. She will be as formidable an industrial competitor as, for instance, Germany, and in a dozen years I think she will be the leading industrial nation of the Pacific. The way she has extended her trade and prepared for the establishment of new steamship lines to all kinds of points in the Pacific has been astonishing, for its has gone right on even through the time of this war. Whether her tremendous growth in industrialism will in course of time modify and perhaps soften the wonderful military spirit she has inherited from the days of the Samurai supremacy it is hard to say. Personally, I think it will; but the effect will hardly be felt for a generation to come. Still, her growing industrial wealth will be to a certain extent a hostage for her keeping the peace. We should treat her courteously, generously and justly, but we should keep our navy up and make it evident that we are not influenced by fear. I do not believe she will look toward the Philippines until affairs are settled on the mainland of Asia in connection with China, even if she ever looks toward them, and on the mainland in China her policy is the policy to which we are already committed. (To H. C. Lodge, June 16, 1905.) Lodge *Letters* II, 153.

——————. Japan's sudden rise into a foremost position among the occidental civilized powers has been an extraordinary phenomenon. There has been nothing in the past in any way approaching it. No other nation in history has ever so quickly entered the circle of civilized powers. It took the yellow-haired barbarians of the North who overthrew Rome six or eight centuries before the civilization they built up even began to approach the civilization they had torn down; whereas Japan tore down nothing and yet reached the level of her western neighbors in half a century. Moreover, she entered the circle of the higher civilization bearing gifts in both hands. Her appreciation of art and nature, her refinement of life, and many of her social conventions, together with her extraordinary and ennobling patriotism, convey lessons to us of America and Europe which we shall do well to learn. Every thoughtful American who dwells on the relations between Japan and the United States must realize that each has something to learn from the other. (Written July 1918.) Theodore Roosevelt, *Japan's Part*. (Japan Society, N. Y., 1919), p. 5.

JAPAN AND THE UNITED STATES. Exactly as the educated classes in Europe, among the several nations, grew to be able to associate together generations before it was possible for such association to take place among the men who had no such advantages of education, so it is evident we must not press too fast in bringing the labouring classes of Japan and America together. Already in these fifty years we have completely attained the goal as between the educated and the intellectual classes of the two countries. We must be content to wait another generation before we shall have made progress enough to permit the same close intimacy between the classes who have had less opportunity for cultivation, and whose lives are less easy, so that each has to feel, in earning its daily bread, the pressure of the competition of the other. I have become convinced that to try to move too far toward all at once is to incur jeopardy of trouble. This is just as true of one nation as of the other. If scores of thousands of American miners went to Saghalin, or of American mechanics to Japan or Formosa, trouble would almost certainly ensue. Just in the same way scores of thousands of Japanese labourers, whether agricultural or industrial, are certain chiefly because of the pressure caused thereby, to be a source of trouble if they should come here or to Australia. (To Baron Kentaro Kaneko, May 23, 1907.) Julian Street, *Mysterious Japan*. (Doubleday, Page & Co., Garden City, N. Y., 1921), p. 225.

——————. The Japanese certainly object to Americans acquiring land in Japan at least as much as the Americans of the far Western States object to the Japanese acquiring land on our soil. The Americans who go to Japan and the Japanese who come to America should be of the same general class—that is, they should be travellers, students, teachers, scientific investigators, men engaged in international business, men sojourning in the land for pleasure or study. As long as the emigration from each side is limited to classes such as these, there will be no settlement in mass, and therefore no difficulty. Wherever there is settlement in mass—that is, wherever there is a large immigration of urban or agricultural laborers, or of people engaged in small local business of any kind—there is sure to be friction. It is against the interests of both nations that such unrestricted immigration or settlement in mass should be allowed as regards either nation. This is the cardinal fact in the situation; it should be freely recognized by both countries, and can be accepted by each not only without the slightest loss of self-respect, but with the certainty that its acceptance will tend to preserve mutual respect and friendliness. (*Outlook*, May 8, 1909.) *Mem. Ed.* XVIII, 383; *Nat. Ed.* XVI, 289.

——————. I cannot too strongly express my indignation with, and abhorrence of, reckless public writers and speakers who, with coarse and vulgar insolence, insult the Japanese people and thereby do the greatest wrong not only to Japan but to their own country. . . . It is eminently undesirable that Japanese and Americans should attempt to live together in masses; any such attempt would be sure to result disastrously, and the far-seeing statesmen of both countries should join to prevent it.

But this is not because either nation is inferior to the other; it is because they are different. The two peoples represent two civilizations which, although in many respects equally high, are so totally distinct in their past history that it is idle to expect in one or two generations to overcome this difference. One civilization is as old as the other; and in neither case is the line of cultural descent coincident with that of ethnic descent. Unquestionably the ancestors of the great majority both of the modern Americans and the modern Japanese were barbarians in that remote past which saw the origins of the cultured peoples to which the Americans and the Japanese of to-day severally trace their civilizations. But the lines of development of these two civilizations, of the Orient and the Occident, have been separate and divergent since thousands of years before the Christian era. (1913.) *Mem. Ed.* XXII, 432; *Nat. Ed.* XX, 371.

——————. The astounding thing, the thing unprecedented in all history, is that two civilized peoples whose civilizations had developed for thousands of years on almost wholly independent lines, should within half a century grow so close together. Fifty years ago there was no intellectual or social community at all between the two nations. Nowadays, the man of broad cultivation, whether in statesmanship, science, art, or philosophy, who dwells in one country, is as much at home in the other as is a Russian in England, or a Spaniard in the United States, or an Italian in Sweden; the men of this type, whether Japanese or Europeans, or North or South Americans, are knit together in a kind of freemasonry of social and intellectual taste. (*Metropolitan,* March 1915.) *Mem. Ed.* XX, 478; *Nat. Ed.* XVIII, 411.

——————. There is always time to point out the elemental fact that this country should feel for Japan a peculiar admiration and respect, and that one of the cardinal principles of our foreign policy should be to secure and retain her friendship, respect, and good-will. There is not the slightest real or necessary conflict of interest between the United States and Japan in the Pacific; her interest is in Asia, ours in America; neither has any desire nor excuse for acquiring territory in the other continent. Japan is playing a great part in the civilized world; a good understanding between her and the United States is essential to international progress, and it is a grave offense against the United States for any man by word or deed to jeopardize this good understanding. (Written July 1918.) Theodore Roosevelt, *Japan's Part,* (Japan Society, N. Y., 1919), p. 13.

JAPAN IN THE WORLD WAR. In this war Japan has played a great and useful part. That she had her special and peculiar grievances against Germany goes without saying. So had we. She took these grievances into account precisely as we took our grievances into account. But she ranged herself on the side of humanity and freedom and justice exactly as we did. Her duty has been, first of all, to drive Germany from the Pacific and to police and protect the Orient. If she had not done this it is probable that at the present moment a British and American force would be besieging Kiao-Chau and that our commerce would be suffering from German raids in the Pacific. Great Britain and the United States are able to keep their fleets out of the Pacific at this moment because the Japanese fleet is there. But she has done much more than this. Gradually, as the war has grown she has extended her assistance all over the globe. Her volunteers have appeared in that most hazardous of all military branches, the air service, at the extreme fighting front. She has sent her destroyers to protect English and American troop ships and cargo ships in the Atlantic Ocean, the North Sea and the Mediterranean. (Written July 1918.) Theodore Roosevelt, *Japan's Part,* (Japan Society, N. Y., 1919), pp. 5-6.

JAPAN. *See also* ORIENT; PATRIOTISM; PHILIPPINES; RUSSO-JAPANESE WAR; "YELLOW PERIL."

JAPANESE—REGARD FOR. The Japanese I am inclined to welcome as a valuable factor in the civilization of the future. But it is not to be expected that they should be free from prejudice against and distrust of the white race. (To Sir George Otto Trevelyan, May 13, 1905.) *Mem. Ed.* XXIII, 438; Bishop I, 381.

JAPANESE

──────────. What wonderful people the Japanese are! They are quite as remarkable industrially as in warfare. In a dozen years the English, Americans and Germans, who now dread one another as rivals in the trade of the Pacific, will have each to dread the Japanese more than they do any other nation. In the middle of this war they have actually steadily increased their exports to China, and are proceeding in the establishment of new lines of steamers in new points of Japanese trade expansion throughout the Pacific. Their lines of steamers are not allowed to compete with one another, but each competes with some foreign line, and usually the competition is to the advantage of the Japanese. The industrial growth of the nation is as marvellous as its military growth. It is now a great power and will be a greater power. As I have always said, I cannot pretend to prophesy what the results, as they affect the United States, Australia, and the European Powers with interests in the Pacific, will ultimately be. I believe that Japan will take its place as a great civilised power of a formidable type, and with motives and ways of thought which are not quite those of the powers of our race. My own policy is perfectly simple, though I have not the slightest idea whether I can get my country to follow it. I wish to see the United States treat the Japanese in a spirit of all possible courtesy, and with generosity and justice. At the same time I wish to see our navy constantly built up, and each ship kept at the highest possible point of efficiency as a fighting unit. If we follow this course we shall have no trouble with the Japanese or any one else. But if we bluster; if we behave rather badly to other nations; if we show that we regard the Japanese as an inferior and alien race, and try to treat them as we have treated the Chinese; and if at the same time we fail to keep our navy at the highest point of efficiency and size—then we shall invite disaster. (To Spring Rice, June 16, 1905.) *The Letters and Friendships of Sir Cecil Spring Rice.* (Houghton Mifflin Co., Boston, 1920.) I, 472-473.

JAPANESE EXCLUSION. In California the question became acute in connection with the admission of the Japanese. I then had and now have a hearty admiration for the Japanese people. I believe in them; I respect their great qualities; I wish that our American people had many of these qualities. Japanese and American students, travellers, scientific and literary men, merchants engaged in international trade, and the like can meet on terms of entire equality and should be given the freest access each to the country of the other. But the Japanese themselves would not tolerate the intrusion into their country of a mass of Americans who would displace Japanese in the business of the land. I think they are entirely right in this position. I would be the first to admit that Japan has the absolute right to declare on what terms foreigners shall be admitted to work in her country, or to own land in her country, or to become citizens of her country. America has and must insist upon the same right. The people of California were right in insisting that the Japanese should not come thither in mass, that there should be no influx of laborers, of agricultural workers, or small tradesmen—in short, no mass settlement or immigration. (1913.) *Mem. Ed.* XXII, 429; *Nat. Ed.* XX, 368.

──────────. As yet the differences between the Japanese who work with their hands and the Americans who work with their hands are such that it is absolutely impossible for them, when brought into contact with one another in great numbers, to get on. Japan would not permit any immigration in mass of our people into her territory, and it is wholly inadvisable that there should be such immigration of her people into our territory. This is not because either side is inferior to the other but because they are different. As a matter of fact, these differences are sometimes in favor of the Japanese and sometimes in favor of the Americans. But they are so marked that at this time, whatever may be the case in the future, friction and trouble are certain to come if there is any immigration in mass of Japanese into this country, exactly as friction and trouble have actually come in British Columbia from this cause, and have been prevented from coming in Australia only by the most rigid exclusion laws. Under these conditions the way to avoid trouble is not by making believe that things which are not so are so but by courteously and firmly facing the situation. (New York *Times,* November 15, 1914.) *Mem. Ed.* XX, 119; *Nat. Ed.* XVIII, 102.

JAPANESE EXCLUSION—DEFENSE OF. He [Admiral Yamamoto] kept insisting that the Japanese must not be kept out save as we keep out Europeans. I kept explaining to him that what we had to do was to face facts; that if American laboring men came in and cut down the wages of Japanese laboring men they would be shut out of Japan in one moment; and that Japanese laborers must be excluded from the United States on economic grounds. I told him emphatically that it was not pos-

JAPANESE EXCLUSION

sible to admit Japanese laborers into the United States. I pointed out to him those rules which Secretary Wilson quoted in his memorandum, which show that the Japanese Government has already in force restrictions against American laborers coming into Japan, save in the old treaty ports. I pointed out that under our present treaty we had explicitly reserved the right to exclude Japanese laborers. (To Elihu Root, July 13, 1907.) *Mem. Ed.* XXIV, 75; Bishop II, 65.

JAPANESE EXCLUSION — NECESSITY OF. One practical problem of statesmanship, . . . must be to keep on good terms with these same Japanese and their kinsmen on the mainland of Asia, and yet to keep the white man in America and Australia out of home contact with them. It is equally to the interest of the British Empire and of the United States that there should be no immigration in mass from Asia to Australia or to North America. It can be prevented, and an entirely friendly feeling between Japan and the English speaking peoples preserved, if we act with sufficient courtesy and at the same time with sufficient resolution. (To A. J. Balfour, March 5, 1908.) *Mem. Ed.* XXIV, 128; Bishop II, 110.

JAPANESE EXCLUSION — REASON FOR. An effort to mix together, out of hand, the peoples representing the culminating points of two such lines of divergent cultural development would be fraught with peril; and this, I repeat, because the two are different, not because either is inferior to the other. Wise statesmen, looking to the future, will for the present endeavor to keep the two nations from mass contact and intermingling, precisely because they wish to keep each in relations of permanent good-will and friendship with the other. (1913.) *Mem. Ed.* XXII, 433; *Nat. Ed.* XX, 372.

———. It has taken many centuries for Europeans to achieve a common standard such as to permit of the free immigration of the workers of one nation into another nation, and there is small cause for wonder in the fact that a few decades have been insufficient to bring it about between Japan and the American and Australian commonwealths. Japan would not, and could not, at this time afford to admit into competition with her own people masses of immigrants, industrial or agricultural workers, or miners or small tradesmen, from the United States. It would be equally unwise for the United States to admit similar groups from Japan. This does not mean that either side is inferior; it means that they are different. (*Metropolitan,* March 1915.) *Mem. Ed.* XX, 479; *Nat. Ed.* XVIII, 411.

JEFFERSON

JAPANESE EXCLUSION—RIGHT OF. I admit in the fullest way every nation's right to keep out any classes of immigrants who come in to work or to live. As you know, I never liked our having abandoned this right in the present treaty with the Japanese. (To H. C. Lodge, October 20, 1911.) Lodge *Letters* II, 412.

JAPANESE IMMIGRATION — NATIONAL CONTROL OVER. I insisted upon the two points: (1) that the nation and not the individual States must deal with matters of such international significance and must treat foreign nations with entire courtesy and respect; and (2) that the nation would at once, and in efficient and satisfactory manner, take action that would meet the needs of California. I both asserted the power of the nation and offered a full remedy for the needs of the State. This is the right, and the only right, course. The worst possible course in such a case is to fail to insist on the right of the nation, to offer no action of the nation to remedy what is wrong, and yet to try to coax the State not to do what it is mistakenly encouraged to believe it has the power to do, when no other alternative is offered. (1913.) *Mem. Ed.* XXII, 431; *Nat. Ed.* XX, 370.

JAPANESE IMMIGRATION. See also IMMIGRATION.

JAPANESE IN CALIFORNIA. I am utterly disgusted at the manifestations which have begun to appear on the Pacific slope in favor of excluding the Japanese exactly as the Chinese are excluded. The California State Legislature and various other bodies have acted in the worst possible taste and in the most offensive manner to Japan. Yet the Senators and Congressmen from these very States were lukewarm about the Navy last year. It gives me a feeling of disgust to see them challenge Japanese hostility and justify by their actions any feeling the Japanese might have against us, while at the same time refusing to take steps to defend themselves against the formidable foe whom they are ready with such careless insolence to antagonize. (To H. C. Lodge, May 15, 1905.) Lodge *Letters* II, 122.

JAY, JOHN. See *Federalist, The.*

JEFFERSON, THOMAS. Thank Heaven, I have never hesitated to criticise Jefferson; he was infinitely below Hamilton. I think the worship of Jefferson a discredit to my country; and I have as small use for the ordinary Jeffersonian as for the ordinary defender of the house of Stuart—and I am delighted to notice that you share this last prejudice with me. I think Jefferson *on the whole* did harm in public life. . . . He did thoroughly believe in the people, just as Abraham Lincoln did, just as Chatham and Pitt believed in England. . . . Jefferson led the people wrong, and followed them when they went wrong; and though he had plenty of imagination and of sentimental inspiration, he had neither courage nor farsighted common sense, where the interests of the nation were at stake. (To Frederick Scott Oliver, August 9, 1906.) *Mem. Ed.* XXIV, 27-28; Bishop II, 23-24.

———————. The more I study Jefferson the more profoundly I distrust him and his influence, taken as a whole. (To H. C. Lodge, September 21, 1907.) Lodge *Letters* II, 282.

———————. Heaven knows how cordially I despise Jefferson, but he did have one great virtue which his Federalist opponents lacked—he stood for the plain people, whom Abraham Lincoln afterward represented.

By the way, speaking of Jefferson, isn't it humiliating to realize that Jefferson—who I think was, not even excepting Buchanan, the most incompetent chief executive we ever had, and whose well-nigh solitary service as President to his country, the acquisition of Louisiana, was rendered by adopting the Federalist principles which he had most fiercely denounced—isn't it humiliating to think that he should have been, as President, rather more popular than Washington himself at the very close of his administration, and that almost all the State legislatures, excluding Massachusetts but including Rhode Island and Vermont, should have petitioned him to serve for another term and should have sent him formal messages of grateful thanks for his services after his term was over? (To Justice W. H. Moody, September 21, 1907.) *Mem. Ed.* XXIV, 82; Bishop II, 71.

———————. Jefferson was fond of science, and in appreciation of the desirability of non-remunerative scientific observation and investigation he stood honorably distinguished among the public men of the day. To him justly belongs the credit of originating . . . [the] first exploring expedition ever undertaken by the United States Government. (1896.) *Mem. Ed.* XII, 359; *Nat. Ed.* IX, 504.

JEFFERSON ADMINISTRATION. Jefferson, though a man whose views and thories had a profound influence upon our national life, was perhaps the most incapable executive that ever filled the presidential chair; being almost purely a visionary, he was utterly unable to grapple with the slightest actual danger, and, not even excepting his successor, Madison, it would be difficult to imagine a man less fit to guide the State with honor and safety through the stormy times that marked the opening of the present century. Without the prudence to avoid war or the forethought to prepare for it, the Administration drifted helplessly into a conflict in which only the navy prepared by the Federalists twelve years before, and weakened rather than strengthened during the intervening time, saved us from complete and shameful defeat. (1882.) *Mem. Ed.* VII, 424; *Nat. Ed.* VI, 373.

JEFFERSON, THOMAS. *See also* DEMOCRATIC PARTY; MADISON, JAMES; POPULARITY; WESTWARD MOVEMENT.

JESUITS IN AMERICA. Inspired by a fervent devotion to their church and religion, which was akin both to that of the early Christian martyrs and to that of the most warlike crusaders, these early Jesuits were among the pioneers in the exploration of the New World, and baptized and converted to at least nominal Christianity scores of tribes from the Bay of Fundy to Lake Superior and the mouth of the Mississippi. They suffered every conceivable kind of danger, discomfort, and hardship; they braved toil and peril like knights errant of the Middle Ages, and they met the most terrible deaths with cheerful, resolute composure. At one time is looked as though they might build up a great empire in the interior of this continent, with converted tribes of Indian warriors as its buttresses; and yet the fabric which they so laboriously reared proved unsubstantial and crumbled without in any way fulfilling its promise. Most of the Indians whom they had converted lapsed into heathenism, and most of the remainder remained Christians in little save the name. The lasting services they rendered were less as pioneers of Christianity than as explorers and map-makers. (*Independent*, November 24, 1892.) *Mem. Ed.* XIV, 289-290; *Nat. Ed.* XII, 249.

JEWS—PERSECUTION OF. The lamentable and terrible suffering to which so many of the Jewish people in other lands have been subjected, makes me feel it my duty, as the head of the American people, not only to express my deep sympathy for them, as I now do, but at the same time to point out what fine qualities of citizenship have been displayed by the men of Jewish faith and race, who having come to this country, enjoy the benefits of free institutions and equal treatment before the law. I feel very strongly that if any people are oppressed anywhere, the wrong inevitably reacts in the end on those who oppress them; for it is an immutable law in the spiritual world that no one can wrong others and yet in the end himself escape unhurt. (To Jacob H. Schiff, November 16, 1905; read at Carnegie Hall, New York City, November 30, 1905.) *The Two Hundred and Fiftieth Anniversary of the Settlement of the Jews in the United States.* (N. Y. Cooperative Society, 1906), p. 18.

JEWS IN AMERICA. I am glad to be able to say, in addressing you on this occasion, that while the Jews of the United States, who now number more than a million, have remained loyal to their faith and their race traditions, they have become indissolubly incorporated in the great army of American citizenship, prepared to make all sacrifice for the country, either in war or peace, and striving for the perpetuation of good government and for the maintenance of the principles embodied in our Constitution. They are honorably distinguished by their industry, their obedience to law, and their devotion to the national welfare. They are engaged in generous rivalry with their fellow-citizens of other denominations in advancing the interests of our common country. This is true not only of the descendants of the early settlers and those of American birth, but of a great and constantly increasing proportion of those who have come to our shores within the last twenty-five years as refugees reduced to the direst straits of penury and misery. All Americans may well be proud of the extraordinary illustration of the wisdom and strength of our governmental system thus afforded. In a few years, men and women hitherto utterly unaccustomed to any of the privileges of citizenship have moved mightily upward toward the standard of loyal, self-respecting American citizenship; of that citizenship which not merely insists upon its rights, but also eagerly recognizes its duty to do its full share in the material, social, and moral advancement of the nation. (To Jacob H. Schiff, November 16, 1905; read at Carnegie Hall, New York City, November 30, 1905.) *The Two Hundred and Fiftieth Anniversary of the Settlement of the Jews in the United States.* (N. Y. Cooperative Society, 1906), pp. 19-20.

JEWS. *See also* ANTI-SEMITISM; DREYFUS, ALFRED; KISHINEFF MASSACRE.

JINGOES. *See* AMERICAN, THE BLATANT.

JINGOISM. *See* NATIONALISM; PATRIOTISM.

JIU JITSU. Yesterday afternoon we had Professor Yamashita up here to wrestle with Grant. It was very interesting, but of course jiu jitsu and our wrestling are so far apart that it is difficult to make any comparison between them. Wrestling is simply a sport with rules almost as conventional as those of tennis, while jiu jitsu is really meant for practice in killing or disabling our adversary. In consequence, Grant did not know what to do except to put Yamashita on his back, and Yamashita was perfectly content to be on his back. Inside of a minute Yamashita had choked Grant, and inside of two minutes more he got an elbow hold on him that would have enabled him to break his arm; so that there is no question but that he could have put Grant out. So far this made it evident that the jiu jitsu man could handle the ordinary wrestler. But Grant, in the actual wrestling and throwing was about as good as the Japanese, and he was so much stronger that he evidently hurt and wore out the Japanese. With a little practice in the art I am sure that one of our big wrestlers or boxers, simply because of his greatly superior strength, would be able to kill any of those Japanese, who though very good men for their inches and pounds are altogether too small to hold their own against big, powerful, quick men who are as well trained. (To Kermit Roosevelt, February 24, 1905.) *Mem. Ed.* XXI, 535; *Nat. Ed.* XIX, 480.

JONES, JOHN PAUL. I feel that the place of all others in which the memory of the dead hero will most surely be a living force is here in Annapolis, where year by year we turn out the midshipmen who are to officer in the future the Navy, among whose founders the dead man stands first. Moreover, the future naval officers, who live within these walls, will find in the career of the man whose life we this day celebrate, not merely a subject for admiration and respect, but an object lesson to be taken into their innermost hearts. Every officer in our Navy should know by heart the deeds of John Paul Jones. Every officer in our Navy should feel in each fiber of his being the eager desire to emulate the energy, the professional capacity, the indomitable determination, and dauntless scorn of death which marked John Paul Jones above all his fellows. *Address of President Roosevelt on the Occasion of the Reinterment* *of the Remains of John Paul Jones at Annapolis, Md., April 24, 1906.* (Government Printing Office, 1906), pp. 4-5.

JOURNALISM, YELLOW. Yellow journalism . . . deifies the cult of the mendacious, the sensational, and the inane, and, . . . throughout its wide but vapid field, does as much to vulgarize and degrade the popular taste, to weaken the popular character, and to dull the edge of the popular conscience, as any influence under which the country can suffer. These men sneer at the very idea of paying heed to the dictates of a sound morality; as one of their number has cynically put it, they are concerned merely with selling the public whatever the public will buy—a theory of conduct which would justify the existence of every keeper of an opium den, of every foul creature who ministers to the vices of mankind. *Outlook,* March 6, 1909, p. 510.

——————. Of all the forces that tend for evil in a great city like New York, probably none are so potent as the sensational papers. (*Atlantic Monthly,* September 1897.) *Mem. Ed.* XV, 160; *Nat. Ed.* XIII, 125.

JOURNALISM. *See also* PRESS.

JOURNALIST. In our country I am inclined to think that almost, if not quite, the most important profession is that of the newspaper man, including the man of the magazines, especially the cheap magazines, and the weeklies; and I speak as a member of the brotherhood myself.

The newspaper men—publishers, editors, reporters—are just as much public servants as are the men in the government service themselves, whether these men be elected or appointed officers. Now, we have always held in higher honor the public man who did his duty, and we have always felt that the public man who did not do his duty was deserving of a peculiar degree of reprobation. And just the same way about the newspaper man. The editor, the publisher, the reporter, who honestly and truthfully puts the exact facts before the public, who does not omit for improper reasons things that ought to be stated, who does not say what is not true, who does not color his facts so as to give false impressions, who does not manufacture his facts, who really is ready, in the first place, to find out what the truth is, and, in the next place, to state it accurately—that man occupies one of the most honorable positions in the community. (At Milwaukee, Wis., September 7, 1910.) *Mem. Ed.* XV, 456; *Nat. Ed.* XIII, 544.

JOURNALIST—POWER OF THE. The power of the journalist is great, but he is entitled neither to respect nor admiration because of that power unless it is used aright. He can do, and he often does, great good. He can do, and he often does, infinite mischief. All journalists, all writers, for the very reason that they appreciate the vast possibilities of their profession, should bear testimony against those who deeply discredit it. Offenses against taste and morals, which are bad enough in a private citizen, are infinitely worse if made into instruments for debauching the community through a newspaper. Mendacity, slander, sensationalism, inanity, vapid triviality, all are potent factors for the debauchery of the public mind and conscience. The excuse advanced for vicious writing, that the public demands it and that the demand must be supplied, can no more be admitted than if it were advanced by the purveyors of food who sell poisonous adulterations. (At the Sorbonne, Paris, April 23, 1910.) *Mem. Ed.* XV, 362; *Nat. Ed.* XIII, 517.

JOURNALIST—SERVICE OF THE. Exactly as I put as the first requisite of the man in public life that he should be honest, so I put as the first requisite of the man writing for the newspaper that he should tell the truth. Now, it is important that he should tell the whole truth, for there can be no greater service rendered than the exposure of corruption in either public life or in business, or in that intricate web of public life and business which exists too often in America to-day. . . .

If an article is published in a magazine, exposing corruption, and the article tells the truth, I do not care what it is, the writer has rendered the greatest possible service by writing it; but I want to be certain that he is telling the truth. (At Milwaukee, Wis., September 7, 1910.) *Mem. Ed.* XV, 459; *Nat. Ed.* XIII, 547.

JOURNALIST. *See also* EDITORS; MUCKRAKERS.

JOY OF LIVING. With all my heart I believe in the joy of living; but those who achieve it do not seek it as an end in itself, but as a seized and prized incident of hard work well done and of risk and danger never wantonly courted, but never shirked when duty commands that they be faced. (*Metropolitan,* October 1918.) *Mem. Ed.* XXI, 264; *Nat. Ed.* XIX, 244.

JOY OF LIVING. *See also* DUTY; LIFE; STRENUOUS LIFE; WORK.

JUDGES—CHARACTER OF. The judge who by word or deed makes it plain that the corrupt corporation, the law-defying corporation, the law-defying rich man, has in him a sure and trustworthy ally, the judge who by misuse of the process of injunction makes it plain that in him the wage-worker has a determined and unscrupulous enemy, the judge who when he decides in an employers' liability or a tenement-house factory case shows that he has neither sympathy for nor understanding of those fellow citizens of his who most need his sympathy and understanding; these judges work as much evil as if they pandered to the mob, as if they shrank from sternly repressing violence and disorder. The judge who does his full duty well stands higher, and renders a better service to the people, than any other public servant; he is entitled to greater respect; and if he is a true servant of the people, if he is upright, wise and fearless, he will unhesitatingly disregard even the wishes of the people if they conflict with the eternal principles of right as against wrong. He must serve the people; but he must serve his conscience first. All honor to such a judge; and all honor cannot be rendered him if it is rendered equally to his brethren who fall immeasurably below the high ideals for which he stands. (To Charles J. Bonaparte, January 2, 1908.) *Mem. Ed.* XXII, 522; *Nat. Ed.* XX, 449.

JUDGES—CONTROL OVER. We are unfit to be called a free people if we permanently surrender the right to shape our destinies, and place this right in the hands of any man not responsible to us. I do not believe that it is wise or safe to pretend that we have self-government and yet by indirect methods to permit outsiders to rob us of self-government. I believe that the only ultimate safety to our people is in self-control, not in control from the outside. I do not believe in snap judgments; I do not believe in permitting the determination of a moment to be transmuted into a permanent policy; but I do believe that the serious, sober, well-thought-out judgment of the people must be given effect; I do believe that this people must ultimately control its own destinies, and cannot surrender the right of ultimate control to a judge any more than to a legislator or an executive. As a matter of expediency it may be, and in my opinion it is, desirable that the control by the people over the judge shall be exercised more cautiously and in different fashion than the control by the people over the legislator and the executive; but the control must be there, the power must exist in the people to see to it that the judge, like the legislator and the executive, becomes in the long run representative of and answerable to the well-thought-out judgment of the people as a whole. (At New York City, October 20, 1911.) *Mem. Ed.* XVIII, 274; *Nat. Ed.* XVI, 207.

JUDGES—CRITICISM OF. Exactly as he is no true patriot who fails to uphold the judge who is a far-seeing and fearless public servant, so he is no true patriot who hesitates to point out the facts when the judge does not serve the people. Ours is a government of the people, and no man has a right to be in public life who is not in a high and true sense the servant of the people; and the doctrine that there shall not be honest, fearless, and temperate criticism of any judge is not only unworthy of being held by any free man who respects himself, but is a betrayal of the cause of good government; for only thus can there be proper discrimination in the public mind between the wise judge who serves the people and his equally honest brother who, because he lacks the statesmanlike qualities or clings to outworn (that is, to fossilized) political theories, does damage to the people. (*Outlook,* November 5, 1910.) *Mem. Ed.* XII, 532; *Nat. Ed.* XI, 260.

———————. It is absolutely necessary that there should be discrimination between, and therefore intelligent criticism of, the judges who by their power of interpretation are the final arbiters in deciding what shall be the law of the land. Men ought not to be classed together for praise or blame because they occupy one kind of public office. The bonds that knit them in popular esteem or popular disfavor should be based, not upon the offices they hold, but upon the way in which they fill these offices. Chief Justice Taney was, I doubt not, in private life as honorable a man as Chief Justice Marshall; but during his long term of service as chief justice his position on certain vital questions represented a resolute effort to undo the work of his mighty predecessor. If, on these positions, one of these two great justices was right, then the other was wrong; if one is entitled to praise, then the other must be blamed. (*Outlook,* March 4, 1911.) *Mem. Ed.* XIX, 125; *Nat. Ed.* XVII, 87.

JUDGES—DIVINE RIGHT OF. The doctrine of the divine right of judges to rule the people is every whit as ignoble as the doctrine of the divine right of kings; and this doctrine is now chiefly and powerfully upheld by the legal and financial representatives of privilege. We believe that the American people has about made up its mind that it is to be master within its own house, and that its representatives are in good faith to represent it and not to attempt to impose their wills upon it against its will. (At Chicago, December 10, 1912.) *Mem. Ed.* XIX, 479; *Nat. Ed.* XVII, 354.

JUDGES—POLITICS OF. Nothing has been so strongly borne in on me concerning lawyers on the bench as that the *nominal* politics of the man has nothing to do with his actions on the bench. His *real* politics are all important. (To H. C. Lodge, September 4, 1906.) Lodge *Letters* II, 228.

JUDGES—POWER OF. Under our American system of government the judge occupies a position such as he occupies nowhere else in the world, a position that makes him, so far as the negative side of legislation is concerned, the most important legislative official in the country.... I emphatically believe that we have been wise in giving great power to our judges, including this power of judicial interpretation of statutes to see whether they conform to the fundamental law of the land. But I also firmly believe that like any other power, this power can be abused, and that it is a power which the people have temporarily parted with and not one which they have permanently alienated. (At New York City, October 20, 1911.) *Mem. Ed.* XVIII, 266; *Nat. Ed.* XVI, 200.

JUDGES—RECALL OF. The question of applying the recall in any shape is one of expediency merely. Each community has a right to try the experiment for itself in whatever shape it pleases....

I do not believe in adopting the recall save as a last resort, when it has become clearly evident that no other course will achieve the desired result.

But either the recall will have to be adopted or else it will have to be made much easier than it now is to get rid, not merely of a bad judge, but of a judge who, however virtuous, has grown so out of touch with social needs and facts that he is unfit longer to render good service on the bench. It is nonsense to say that impeachment meets the difficulty. In actual practice we have found that impeachment does not work, that unfit judges stay on the bench in spite of it, and indeed because of the fact that impeachment is the only remedy that can be used against them. Where such is the actual fact it is idle to discuss the theory of the case. Impeachment as a remedy for the ills of which the people justly complain is a complete failure. A quicker, a more summary, remedy is needed. (Before Ohio Constitutional Convention, Columbus, February 21, 1912.) *Mem. Ed.* XIX, 185; *Nat. Ed.* XVII, 137.

———————. In a great many States there has been for many years a real recall of judges as regards appointments, promotions, reappointments, and re-elections; and this recall was through the turn of a thumbscrew at the end of a long-distance rod in the hands of great interests. I believe that a just judge would feel far safer in the hands of the people than in the hands of those interests. (At Carnegie Hall, New York City, March 20, 1912.) *Mem. Ed.* XIX, 215; *Nat. Ed.* XVII, 164.

JUDGES—RESPONSIBILITY OF. [Our opponents] speak as if the judges were somehow imposed on us by Heaven, and were responsible only to Heaven. As a matter of fact judges are human just like other people, and in this country they will either be chosen by the people and responsible to the people, or they will be chosen by, and responsible to, the bosses and the special interests and the political and financial beneficiaries of privilege. (At Philadelphia, April 10, 1912.) *Mem. Ed.* XIX, 270; *Nat. Ed.* XVII, 203.

JUDGES—SALARIES OF. I most earnestly urge upon the Congress the duty of increasing the totally inadequate salaries now given to our judges. On the whole there is no body of public servants who do as valuable work, nor whose moneyed reward is so inadequate compared to their work. Beginning with the Supreme Court, the judges should have their salaries doubled. It is not befitting the dignity of the nation that its most honored public servants should be paid sums so small compared to what they would earn in private life that the performance of public service by them implies an exceedingly heavy pecuniary sacrifice. (Eighth Annual Message, Washington, December 8, 1908.) *Mem. Ed.* XVII, 593; *Nat. Ed.* XV, 504.

JUDGES AS LEGISLATORS. We stand for an upright judiciary. But where the judges claim the right to make our laws by finally interpreting them, by finally deciding whether or not we have the power to make them, we claim the right ourselves to exercise that power. We forbid any men, no matter what their official position may be, to usurp the right which is ours, the right which is the people's. We recognize in neither court nor Congress nor President, any divine right to override the will of the people expressed with due deliberation in orderly fashion and through the forms of law. (At Madison Square Garden, New York City,

October 30, 1912.) *Mem. Ed.* XIX, 460; *Nat. Ed.* XVII, 337.

JUDGES AS PUBLIC SERVANTS. Taken as a whole, the judges of the country are, and have been, more useful public servants than any other public men. A wise and upright judge can render, and does render, in the long run, rather better service than can be rendered even by the right type of executive or legislative officer; and I believe that we find a larger proportion of men who reach the proper official standard among judges than among the members of any other class of public servants.

Yet, while not merely granting that this is the fact, but insisting upon it, it remains true that the judges are public servants just as other officials are, that they are, or should be, responsible to the public just as other officials are (for it is idle to call a man a servant of the public unless he is responsible to the public) and that therefore there should be criticism of them just as of other officials. In the case of judges it is even more essential than in the case of other public officials that the criticism should be wise and temperate, and, above all, that it should be absolutely truthful. (*Outlook,* March 4, 1911.) *Mem. Ed.* XIX, 117; *Nat. Ed.* XVII, 80.

JUDGES. *See also* CONSTITUTION; LEGALISM; MARSHALL, JOHN; RECALL.

JUDICIAL DECISION—SUBJECTS FOR. We hold emphatically that . . . [social and industrial legislation] are not properly matters for final judicial decision. The judges have no special opportunity and no especial ability to determine the justice or injustice, the desirability or undesirability, of legislation of such a character. Indeed, in most cases, although not in all, the judges in the higher courts are so out of touch with the conditions of life affected by social and industrial legislation on behalf of the humble that they are peculiarly unfit to say whether the legislation is wise or the reverse. Moreover, whether they are fit or unfit, it is not their province to decide what the people ought or ought not to desire in matters of this kind. They are not lawmakers; they were not elected or appointed for such purpose. They are not censors of the public in this matter. (*Century Magazine,* October 1913.) *Mem. Ed.* XIX, 552; *Nat. Ed.* XVII, 407.

——————. It was this case [Tenement Cigar Case] which first waked me to a dim and partial understanding of the fact that the courts were not necessarily the best judges of what should be done to better social and industrial conditions. The judges who rendered this decision were well-meaning men. They knew nothing whatever of tenement-house conditions; they knew nothing whatever of the needs, or of the life and labor, of three-fourths of their fellow citizens in great cities. They knew legalism but not life. . . . This decision completely blocked tenement-house reform legislation in New York for a score of years. It was one of the most serious setbacks which the cause of industrial and social progress and reform ever received. (1913.) *Mem. Ed.* XXII, 98; *Nat. Ed.* XX, 84.

JUDICIAL DECISION. *See also* LAW; RECALL.

JUDICIAL REVIEW. *See* COURTS; LAW.

JUDICIARY—CRITICISM OF. There is one consideration which should be taken into account by the good people who carry a sound proposition to an excess in objecting to any criticism of a judge's decision. The instinct of the American people as a whole is sound in this matter. They will not subscribe to the doctrine that any public servant is to be above all criticism. If the best citizens, those most competent to express their judgment in such matters, and above all those belonging to the great and honorable profession of the bar, so profoundly influential in American life, take the position that there shall be no criticism of a judge under any circumstances, their view will not be accepted by the American people as a whole. . . . Just and temperate criticism, when necessary, is a safeguard against the acceptance by the people as a whole of that intemperate antagonism toward the judiciary which must be combated by every right-thinking man, and which, if it became wide-spread among the people at large, would constitute a dire menace to the Republic. (Sixth Annual Message, Washington, December 3, 1906.) *Mem. Ed* XVII, 410; *Nat. Ed.* XV, 350.

——————. Unless the Federal judiciary is willing to submit to temperate criticism where it goes completely wrong, and to amend its shortcomings by its own action, then sooner or later there is certain to be dangerous agitation against it. (To H. C. Lodge, September 12, 1910.) *Lodge Letters* II, 391.

JUDICIARY—DEMANDS UPON. We have a right to demand that our judiciary should be kept beyond reproach, and we have a right to demand that, if we find men against whom there is not only suspicion, but almost a certainty that they have had collusion with men whose interest was in conflict with those of the public, they shall at least be required to bring positive facts with which to prove there has not been such collusion, and they ought themselves to have been the first to demand such an investigation. (In Assembly Chamber, Albany, April 6, 1882.) *Mem. Ed.* XVI, 12; *Nat. Ed.* XIV, 11.

JUDICIARY—INDEPENDENCE OF. On the one hand, the very men who by their actions seek to degrade the judiciary into the position of a servile register of the popular whim of the moment will cheerfully render lip-loyalty to the theory that a judge should be upright and independent. On the other hand, the very men who strive hardest to prevent the judge from being a real popular servant, and who wish, on the contrary, to make him an instrument for defeating the popular will in the interests of a special class, are always loudest in their assertion that they are really championing the cause of popular rights. The men whose patriotism is really rational and sincere, the men who really believe in the just rule of the people, and neither in the selfish rule of a plutocracy nor the selfish rule of a mob, stand as equally opposed to the extremists of both classes. (*Outlook,* February 25, 1911.) *Mem. Ed.* XIX, 115; *Nat. Ed.* XVII, 78.

_____. An independent and upright judiciary which fearlessly stands for the right, even against popular clamor, but which also understands and sympathizes with popular needs, is a great asset of popular government. (Before Ohio Constitutional Convention, Columbus, February 21, 1912.) *Mem. Ed.* XIX, 184; *Nat. Ed.* XVII, 136.

JUDICIARY. *See also* CONSTITUTION; COURTS; DIVISION OF POWERS; GOVERNMENT; JUSTICE; LAW; LEGALISM; POPULAR RULE; SUPREME COURT.

JUSSERAND, J. J. It is the simple and literal truth to say that in my judgment we owe it to you more than to any other one man that the year which has closed has not seen a war between France and Germany, which, had it begun, would probably have extended to take in a considerable portion of the world. In last May and June the relations between the two countries were so strained that such a war was imminent. Probably the only way it could have been avoided was by an international conference, and such a conference could only have been held on terms compatible with France's honour and dignity. You were the man most instrumental in having just this kind of conference arranged for. I came into the matter most unwillingly, and I could not have come into it at all if I had not possessed entire confidence alike in your unfailing soundness of judgment and in your high integrity of personal conduct. Thanks to the fact that these are the two dominant notes in your personality, my relationship with you has been such as I think has very, very rarely obtained between any Ambassador at any time and the head of the Government to which that Ambassador was accredited; and certainly no Ambassador and head of a Government could ever stand to one another on a footing at once more pleasant and more advantageous to their respective countries than has been the case with you and me. If, in these delicate Morocco negotiations, I had not been able to treat you with the absolute frankness and confidence that I did, no good result could possibly have been obtained, and this frankness and confidence were rendered possible only because of the certainty that you would do and advise what was wisest to be done and advised, and that you would treat all that was said and done between us two as a gentleman of the highest honour treats what is said and done in the intimate personal relations of life. If you had been capable of adopting one line of conduct as a private individual and another as a public man I should have been wholly unable to assume any such relations with you; nor, on the other hand, however high your standard of honour, could I have assumed them had I not felt complete confidence in the soundness and quickness of your judgment. The service you rendered was primarily one to France, but it was also a service to the world at large; and in rendering it you bore yourself as the ideal public servant should bear himself; for such a public servant should with trained intelligence know how to render the most effective service to his own country while yet never deviating by so much as a hand's breadth from the code of mutual good faith and scrupulous regard for the rights of others which should obtain between nations no less than between gentlemen. I do not suppose that you will ever gain any personal advantage, and perhaps not even any personal recognition, because of what you have done in the past year, but I desire that you should at least know my appreciation of it. (To Jusserand, April 25, 1906.) J. J. Jusserand, *What Me Befell.* (Houghton Mifflin Co., Boston, 1933), pp. 325-326.

———————. The Ambassador has been here for fifteen years, and he has fulfilled as very, very few Ambassadors have ever done, the two prime functions of an Ambassador—showing genuine devotion to his own country, and showing genuine purpose to do all that can be done for the country to which he is accredited. The Ambassador has proved himself as able a servant of France as France has ever had in her long line of able servants. And he has also proved himself as loyal a friend of America as even France has produced since 1778.

We greet the Ambassador and through him we pay homage to France. Thank heaven, at last we stand shoulder to shoulder with France, as one hundred and forty years ago, in our hour of dark trial, the forefathers of the French of today stood shoulder to shoulder with our forefathers here. (At New York City, December 8, 1917.) *Year Book of the Pennsylvania Society 1918.* (Penna. Society, N. Y., 1918), p. 45.

JUSTICE. The first requisite for the welfare of any community is justice; not merely legal justice, but ethical justice, moral justice, the kind of justice meant by the ordinary man when he says that he wishes fair play or a square deal. In order to get this justice it is absolutely necessary that there should be order; and there can be no order unless there is law, and unless the law is rigidly and honestly enforced. Crimes of greed and violence and crimes of greed and cunning must alike be repressed, for it makes no difference what form wrong-doing takes so long as it is wrong-doing; and important though it is to have good legislative and executive officers, it is even more important to have an upright, fearless, and independent judiciary, bent with whole-hearted and intelligent zeal upon serving the interests of all the people.

Justice is based upon law and order, and without law and order there can be no justice. The triumph of disorder and lawlessness is certain in the end to mean not only the undoing of the reputable rich but the undoing of the reputable poor; and indeed the undoing of everybody, reputable or disreputable, for not even scoundrels can permanently flourish in a society in which the conditions have passed a certain degree of anarchy. But it must never be forgotten that law and order are not in themselves ends, but means toward obtaining justice. . . . Without law and order there can be no permanent justice; but law and order are good only when used to bring about such justice. (*Outlook,* February 25, 1911.) *Mem. Ed.* XIX, 110; *Nat. Ed.* XVII, 74.

———————. We cannot afford to rest satisfied until all that the government can do has been done to secure fair dealing and equal justice as between man and man. In the great part which hereafter, whether we will or not, we must play in the world at large, let us see to it that we neither do wrong nor shrink from doing right because the right is difficult; that on the one hand we inflict no injury, and that on the other we have a due regard for the honor and the interest of our mighty nation; and that we keep unsullied the renown of the flag which beyond all others of the present time or of the ages of the past stands for confident faith in the future welfare and greatness of mankind. (At Colorado Springs, Col., August 2, 1901.) *Mem. Ed.* XV, 327; *Nat. Ed.* XIII, 458.

———————. We need to check the forces of greed, to insure just treatment alike of capital and of labor, and of the general public, to prevent any man, rich or poor, from doing or receiving wrong, whether this wrong be one of cunning or of violence. Much can be done by wise legislation and by resolute enforcement of the law. But still more must be done by steady training of the individual citizen, in conscience and character, until he grows to abhor corruption and greed and tyranny and brutality and to prize justice and fair dealing. (At Harrisburg, Pa., October 4, 1906.) *Mem. Ed.* XVIII, 89; *Nat. Ed.* XVI, 75.

JUSTICE—ATTAINMENT OF. The ideal of elemental justice meted out to every man is the ideal we should keep ever before us. It will be many a long day before we attain to it, and unless we show not only devotion to it, but also wisdom and self-restraint in the exhibition of that devotion, we shall defer the time for its realization still further. (Before Republican Club of New York City, February 13, 1905.) *Mem. Ed.* XVIII, 465; *Nat. Ed.* XVI, 346.

———————. This is a democracy, a government by the people, and the people have supreme power if they choose to exercise it. The people can get justice peaceably, if they really desire it; and if they do not desire it enough to show the wisdom, patience, and cool-headed determination necessary in order to get it peaceably, through the orderly process of law, then they haven't the slightest excuse for trying to get it by riot and murder. (To Victor A. Olander, Secretary-Treasurer, Illinois

State Federation of Labor, July 17, 1917.) *Mem. Ed.* XXI, 176; *Nat. Ed.* XIX, 169.

JUSTICE—DEPARTMENT OF. The Department of Justice is now in very fact the Department of Justice, and justice is meted out with an even hand to great and small, rich and poor, weak and strong. Those who have denounced you and the action of the Department of Justice are either misled or else are the very wrong-doers, and the agents of the very wrong-doers, who have for so many years gone scot-free and flouted the laws with impunity. Above all, you are to be congratulated upon the bitterness felt and exprest towards you by the representatives and agents of the great law-defying corporations of immense wealth who, until within the last half dozen years, have treated themselves and have expected others to treat them as being beyond and above all possible check from law. (To Bonaparte, December 23, 1907.) Joseph B. Bishop, *Charles J. Bonaparte.* (Charles Scribner's Sons, N. Y., 1922), p. 150.

JUSTICE—MEANING OF. Justice consists not in being neutral between right and wrong, but in finding out the right and upholding it, wherever found, against the wrong. (1916.) *Mem. Ed.* XX, 239; *Nat. Ed.* XVIII, 206.

JUSTICE — PROGRESS TOWARD. We know that there are in life injustices which we are powerless to remedy. But we know also that there is much injustice which can be remedied, and this injustice we intend to remedy. We know that the long path leading upward toward the light cannot be traversed at once, or in a day, or in a year. But there are certain steps that can be taken at once. These we intend to take. Then, having taken these first steps, we shall see more clearly how to walk still further with a bolder stride. We do not intend to attempt the impossible. But there is much, very much, that is possible in the way of righting wrong and remedying injustice, and all that is possible we intend to do. We intend to strike down privilege, to equalize opportunity, to wrest justice from the hands that do injustice, to hearten and strengthen men and women for the hard battle of life. (At Madison Square Garden, New York City, October 30, 1912.) *Mem. Ed.* XIX, 461; *Nat. Ed.* XVII, 338.

JUSTICE AND LEGALISM. Our prime concern is to get justice. When the spirit of mere legalism, the spirit of hair-splitting technicality, interferes with justice, then it is our highest duty to war against this spirit, whether it shows itself in the courts or anywhere else. The judge has no more right than any other official to be set up over the people as an irremovable and irresponsible despot. He has no more right than any other official to decide for the people what the people ought to think about questions of vital public policy, such as the proper handling of corporations and the proper methods of securing the welfare of farmers, wage workers, small business men, and small professional men. (Introduction dated July 1, 1912.) William L. Ransom, *Majority Rule and the Judiciary.* (Scribner's, N. Y., 1912), pp. 4-5.

————————. Here again I ask you not to think of the mere legal formalism, but to think of the great immutable principles of justice, the great immutable principles of right and wrong, and to ponder what it means to men dependent for their livelihood, and to the women and children dependent upon these men, when the courts of the land deny them the justice to which they are entitled. (Before Ohio Constitutional Convention, Columbus, February 21, 1912.) *Mem. Ed.* XIX, 196; *Nat. Ed.* XVII, 147.

JUSTICE AND MERCY. It is even more necessary to temper mercy with justice than justice with mercy. (*Review of Reviews,* January 1897.) *Mem. Ed.* XVI, 382; *Nat. Ed.* XIII, 165.

JUSTICE. See also COURTS; FORCE; INDUSTRIAL JUSTICE; INTERNATIONAL JUSTICE; LAW; LOYALTY; LYNCHING; MARSHALL, JOHN; SOCIAL AND INDUSTRIAL JUSTICE; SQUARE DEAL; SUPREME COURT.

JUVENILE COURTS. The work of the juvenile court is really a work of character-building. It is now generally recognized that young boys and young girls who go wrong should not be treated as criminals, not even necessarily as needing reformation, but rather as needing to have their characters formed, and for this end to have them tested and developed by a system of probation. (Fourth Annual Message, Washington, December 6, 1904.) *Mem. Ed.* XVII, 266; *Nat. Ed.* XV, 229.

K

KAISER WILHELM. *See* William II.

KINGS. You are quite right about my preferring a beetle to a throne; that is, if you use the word "beetle" as including a field-mouse or a weasel. I would not say this aloud, because

I have been awfully well treated by kings; but in modern days a king's business is not a man's job. He is kept as a kind of national pet, treated with consideration and distinction, but not allowed to have any say in the running of the affairs of the national household. (To Charles G. Washburn, March 5, 1913.) *Mem. Ed.* XXIV, 308; Bishop II, 260.

——————. I do not mean that he fails to serve a useful purpose, just as the flag serves a useful purpose. Only a very foolish creature will talk of the flag as nothing but a bit of dyed or painted bunting, because it is a symbol of enormous consequence in the life and thought of the people. Similarly, the king may serve a purpose of enormous usefulness as a symbol, and I have no question that for many peoples, it would be a misfortune not to have such a symbol, such a figurehead. I am not speaking of the king from the standpoint of his usefulness to the community, which I fully admit; I am merely saying that from his own standpoint, if he is a man of great energy, force and power, it must be well-nigh intolerable to have to content himself with being simply king in the figurehead or symbol fashion. (To Sir George Otto Trevelyan, October 1, 1911.) *Mem. Ed.* XXIV, 250-251; Bishop II, 214.

——————. Kings and such are fundamentally just as funny as American politicians. (To H. C. Lodge, September 14, 1905.) *Lodge Letters* II, 200.

KINGS—DIVINE RIGHT OF. The doctrine of the divine right of kings, which represented the extreme form of loyalty to the sovereign, was vicious, unworthy of the [English] race, and to be ranked among degrading superstitions. It is now so dead that it is easy to laugh at it; but it was . . . a real power for evil. (1900.) *Mem. Ed.* XIII, 301; *Nat. Ed.* X, 199.

KINGS—POWER OF. It would be very attractive to be a king with the power of a dictator, and the ability to wield that power, to be a Frederick the Great, for instance, or even a man like the old Kaiser William, who if not exactly a great man yet had the qualities which enabled him to use and be used by Bismarck, Moltke, and von Roon. But the ordinary king—and I speak with cordial liking of all the kings I met—has to play a part in which the dress parade is ludicrously out of proportion to the serious effort; there is a quite intolerable quantity of sack to the amount of bread. If he is a decent, straight, honorable fellow, he can set a good example—and yet if he is not, most of his subjects, including almost all the clergymen, feel obliged to be blind and to say that he is; and he can exercise a certain small influence for good on public affairs in an indirect fashion. But he can play no part such as is played by the real leaders in the public life of to-day, if he is a constitutional monarch. (To Sir George Otto Trevelyan, October 1, 1911.) *Mem. Ed.* XXIV, 250; Bishop II, 214.

KINGS. See also PRESIDENCY; ROYALTY.

KISHINEFF MASSACRE. I need not dwell upon the fact so patent as the widespread indignation with which the American people heard of the dreadful outrages upon the Jews in Kishineff. I have never in my experience in this country known of a more immediate or a deeper expression of sympathy for the victims and of horror over the appalling calamity that has occurred.

It is natural that while the whole civilized world should express such a feeling, it should yet be most intense and most widespread in the United States; for all the great Powers I think I may say that the United States is that country in which from the beginning of its natural career most has been done in the way of acknowledging the debt due to the Jewish race and of endeavoring to do justice to those American citizens who are of Jewish ancestry and faith. (At White House, June 15, 1903.) Simon Wolf, *The Presidents I Have Known.* (Washington, 1918), p. 193.

KITCHENER, LORD. He is a strong man, but exceedingly bumptious, and everlastingly posing as a strong man. . . . Kitchener is a very powerful fellow, just about as powerful as Leonard Wood but nothing like as attractive personally, and nothing like as modest. He suddenly attacked me on the subject of the Panama Canal, saying that it was a great mistake not to have made it a sea-level canal. I at first answered in a noncommittal way, but he kept on the subject and in a very loud voice repeated that it was a great mistake, that it was very foolish on our part, not to have had it a sea-level canal, and he could not understand why we did not build one. I said that our engineers on the ground reported that there were altogether too many difficulties and too few advantages in a sea-level canal, to which he responded: "I never regard difficulties, or pay heed to protests like that; all I would do in such a case would be to say, 'I order that a sea-level canal be dug, and I wish to hear nothing more about it.'" I answered, "If you say so, I have no doubt you would have given such an order; but I wonder if you remember the conversation between Glendower and Hotspur, when Glendower says, 'I can call spirits from the vasty deep,' and Hotspur answers, 'So can I, and so can any man; but will they come?' " I think he did not entirely understand the quotation, and he reiterated that he would have ordered it to be a sea-level canal and would have listened to no protests from engineers. (To David Gray, October 5, 1911.) *Saturday Evening Post,* December 26, 1931, p. 5.

KNIGHT CASE. The effect of this decision was not merely the absolute nullification of the antitrust law, so far as industrial corporations were concerned, but was also in effect a declaration that, under the Constitution, the National Government could pass no law really effective for the destruction or control of such combinations.

This decision left the National Government, that is, the people of the nation, practically helpless to deal with the large combinations of modern business. The courts in other cases asserted the power of the Federal Government to enforce the antitrust law so far as transportation rates by railways engaged in interstate commerce were concerned. But so long as the trusts were free to control the production of commodities without interference from the general government, they were well content to let the transportation of commodities take care of itself—especially as the law against rebates was at that time a dead letter; and the court by its decision in the Knight case had interdicted any interference by the President or by Congress with the production of commodities. It was on the authority of this case that practically all the big trusts in the United States . . . were formed. (1913.) *Mem. Ed.* XXII, 486-487; *Nat. Ed.* XX, 418-419.

KNIGHT CASE. *See also* INTERSTATE COMMERCE; NORTHERN SECURITIES CASE.

KNOW - NOTHING MOVEMENT. The Know-nothing Movement in every form is entirely repugnant to true Americanism and this is, perhaps, especially the case when it is directed not merely against American citizens of foreign origin, but also against even native-born Americans of a different creed. We Americans give to men of all races equal and exact justice. That has been our boast as a nation ever since the day when the Puritan of Massachusetts and the Catholic of Maryland sat in the same hall and signed the same Declaration of Independence. On the roll of honor where we have engraved the names of the nation's statesmen and soldiers, patriots and commonwealth-builders, no distinction is known of creed or of race origin, nor even of birthplace. (At Boston, Mass., November 1893.) *Mem. Ed.* XV, 34-35; *Nat. Ed.* XIII, 276.

KNOWLEDGE—THIRST FOR. On this trip—here while visiting this castle [Count Wiltczek's, near Vienna], just as at Cairo—I was helped for the first time in my life by the fact that I had always gratified my thirst for useless information. I have never demanded of knowledge anything except that it shall be useless. Now this means that while I know nothing that the average scholar does not know, yet that I know a good deal as to which the average politician or man of affairs is abysmally ignorant; and as naturally my life has been chiefly led among politicians and men of affairs, when it was not led among frontiersmen, there are a great many things I have studied about which I have rarely or never had a chance to speak. . . . Until I went abroad this time I doubt if I had ever derived the slightest benefit, however small, from such things as a knowledge of Moslem travels in the thirteenth century, or Magyar history, or the Mongol conquests, or the growth of the races of Middle Europe and the deeds of their great men. On this occasion, however, my knowledge of these things really added to my pleasure, and brought me into touch with people. For instance, Wiltczek hugely enjoyed finding that, besides a general interest in sport and in mediæval ways and customs, I had taken it for granted that his family, if not Czeck, was of Polish origin, and descended from the Piasts and from Boleslav the Glorious; that when he showed me a portrait of Batory, I was familiar with that Hungarian king of Poland and his wars against Ivan the Terrible; that I knew the details of Rudolph's fight with Ottocar of Bohemia; and so on and so on. (To Sir George Otto Trevelyan, October 1, 1911.) *Mem. Ed.* XXIV, 256; Bishop II, 219.

KNOWLEDGE. *See also* EDUCATION; EXPLORATION; SCHOLARSHIP; UNIVERSITY.

KNOX, PHILANDER C. *See* NORTHERN SECURITIES CASE.

L

LA FOLLETTE, ROBERT M. Thanks to the movement for genuinely democratic popular government which Senator La Follette led to overwhelming victory in Wisconsin, that state has become literally a laboratory for wise experimental legislation aiming to secure the social and political betterment of the people as a whole. Nothing is easier than to demand, on the stump, or in essays and editorials, the abolition of injustice and the securing to each man of his rights. But actually to accomplish practical and effective work along the line of such utterances is so hard that the average public man, and average public writer, have not even attempted it; and unfortunately too many of the men in public life who have seemed to attempt it have contented themselves with enacting legislation which, just because it made believe to do so much, in reality accomplished very little.

But in Wisconsin there has been a successful effort to redeem the promises by performances, and to reduce theories into practice. . . .

The Wisconsin reformers have accomplished the extraordinary results for which the whole nation owes them so much, primarily because they have not confined themselves to dreaming dreams and then to talking about them. They have had power to see the vision, of course; if they did not have in them the possibility of seeing visions, they could accomplish nothing; but they have tried to make their ideals realizable, and then they have tried, with an extraordinary measure of success, actually to realize them. As soon as they decided that a certain object was desirable they at once set to work practically to study how to develop the constructive machinery through which it could be achieved. Introduction to *The Wisconsin Idea* by Charles McCarthy. (Macmillan Co., N. Y., 1912), pp. vii-viii.

LABOR. It has never been any effort on my part to respect the first-class railway man or blacksmith or carpenter or cow-hand as much as I respect a competent banker or lawyer; indeed, I have always felt a certain impatience with any one who does not admire physical address and daring; and there are many men who work with their hands among those whose judgment I desire on any question relating to the essential needs, social, political, and industrial, of our civilization. I do not mean that a man should limit himself simply to doing physical work, or adopt the principles of the well-meaning but unbalanced enthusiasts who would require every man always to do manual work in addition to his other labor. Such conduct is not idealism but folly. I do mean, however, that, in my judgment, it is best, where possible, to combine physical and mental efficiency, and that the highest type of citizen is most apt to be a man who can thus combine them; and I mean, furthermore, that the high type of man who in driving an engine or erecting a building or handling deep-sea fishing-craft shows the necessary moral, intellectual, and physical qualities demanded by his task ought to be instantly accepted as standing upon as high a plane of citizenship as any human being in the community. But he can never stand on such a plane unless he regards his work with such devotion that he is not content to do less than his very best. He ought to join with his fellows in a union, or in some similar association, for mutual help and betterment, and in that association he should strive to raise higher his less competent brothers; but he should positively decline to allow himself to be dragged down to their level, and if he does thus permit himself to be dragged down, the penalty is the loss of individual, of class, and finally of national efficiency. (*Outlook,* February 4, 1911.) *Mem. Ed.* XIX, 102; *Nat. Ed.* XVII, 67.

LABOR. *See also* CHILD LABOR; CONVICT LABOR; DOMESTIC SERVICE; EMPLOYMENT; IMMIGRATION; LEISURE; UNEMPLOYMENT; WORK.

LABOR—DUTY TOWARD. The first charge on the industrial statesmanship of the day is to prevent human waste. The dead weight of orphanage and depleted craftsmanship, of crippled workers and workers suffering from trade diseases, of casual labor, of insecure old age, and of household depletion due to industrial conditions are, like our depleted soils, our gashed mountainsides and flooded river-bottoms, so many strains upon the national structure, draining the reserve strength of all industries and showing beyond all peradventure the public element and public concern in industrial health.

Ultimately we desire to use the government to aid, as far as can safely be done, in helping the industrial tool-users to become in part tool-owners, just as our farmers now are. Ultimately the government may have to join more efficiently than at present in strengthening the hands of the working men who already stand at a high level, industrially and socially, and who are able by joint action to serve themselves. But the most pressing and immediate need is to deal with the cases of those who are on the level, and who are not only in need themselves, but because of their need tend to jeopardize the welfare of those who are better off. (Before Progressive National Convention, Chicago, August 6, 1912.) *Mem. Ed.* XIX, 372, *Nat. Ed.* XVII, 266.

LABOR—DUTY TOWARD. *See also* SQUARE DEAL; WORKERS.

LABOR—EFFICIENCY OF. The wage-worker should not only receive fair treatment; he should give fair treatment. In order that prosperity may be passed around it is necessary that the prosperity exist. In order that labor shall receive its fair share in the division of reward it is necessary that there be a reward to divide. Any proposal to reduce efficiency by insisting that the most efficient shall be limited in their output to what the least efficient can do is a proposal to limit by so much production, and therefore to impoverish by so much the public, and specifically to reduce the amount that can be divided among the producers. This is all wrong. Our protest must be against unfair division of the reward for production. . . . But increased productiveness is not secured by excessive labor amid unhealthy surroundings. The contrary is true. Shorter hours, and healthful conditions, and opportunity for the wage-worker to make more money, and the chance for enjoyment as well as work, all add to efficiency. My contention is that there should be no penalization of efficient productiveness, brought about under healthy conditions; but that every increase of production brought about by an increase in efficiency should benefit all the parties to it, including wage-workers as well as employers or capitalists, men who work with their hands as well as men who work with their heads. (1913.) *Mem. Ed.* XXII, 556; *Nat. Ed.* XX, 477.

LABOR—ORGANIZATION OF. I believe emphatically in organized labor. I believe in organizations of wage-workers. Organization is one of the laws of our social and economic development at this time. But I feel that we must always keep before our minds the fact that there is nothing sacred in the name itself. To call an organization an organization does not make it a good one. The worth of an organization depends upon its being handled with the courage, the skill, the wisdom, the spirit of fair dealing as between man and man, and the wise self-restraint which, I am glad to be able to say, your Brotherhood has shown. (Before Brotherhood of Locomotive Firemen, Chattanooga, Tenn., September 8, 1902.) *Mem. Ed.* XVIII, 201-202; *Nat. Ed.* XVI, 152.

——————. Wage-workers have an entire right to organize and by all peaceful and honorable means to endeavor to persuade their fellows to join with them in organizations. They have a legal right, which, according to circumstances, may or may not be a moral right, to refuse to work in company with men who decline to join their organizations. They have under no circumstances the right to commit violence upon those, whether capitalists or wage-workers, who refuse to support their organizations, or who side with those with whom they are at odds. (Fourth Annual Message, Washington, December 6, 1904.) *Mem. Ed.* XVII, 253; *Nat. Ed.* XV, 217.

——————. It is essential that there should be organizations of labor. This is an era of organization. Capital organizes and therefore labor must organize. My appeal for organized labor is twofold; to the outsider and the capitalist I make my appeal to treat the laborer fairly, to recognize the fact that he must organize, that there must be such organization, that the laboring man must organize for his own protection, and that it is the duty of the rest of us to help him and not hinder him in organizing. That is one-half of the appeal that I make.

Now, the other half is to the labor man himself. My appeal to him is to remember that as he wants justice, so he must do justice. I want every labor man, every labor leader, every organized union man, to take the lead in denouncing crime or violence. I want them to take the lead in denouncing disorder and in denouncing the inciting of riot; that in this country we shall proceed under the protection of our laws and with all respect to the laws, and I want the labor men to feel in their turn that exactly as justice must be done them so they must do justice. That they must bear their duty as citizens, their duty to this great country of ours, and that they must not rest content unless they do that duty to the fullest degree. (At Milwaukee, Wis., October 14, 1912.) *Mem. Ed.* XIX, 447; *Nat. Ed.* XVII, 325.

——————. While we must repress all illegalities and discourage all immoralities, whether of labor organizations or of corporations, we must recognize the fact that to-day the organization of labor into trade-unions and federations is necessary, is beneficent, and is one of the greatest possible agencies in the attainment of a true industrial, as well as a true political, democracy in the United States. (1913.) *Mem. Ed.* XXII, 547; *Nat. Ed.* XX, 470.

——————. Labor has as much right as capital to organize. It is tyranny to forbid the exercise of this right, just as it is tyranny to misuse the power acquired by organization. The people of the United States do not believe in tyranny and do believe in cooperation. (June 27, 1918.) *Roosevelt in the Kansas City Star*, 171.

LABOR—ORGANIZATION OF. *See also* CAPITAL AND LABOR; COLLECTIVE BARGAINING; COMBINATIONS; LABOR UNIONS.

LABOR—PROGRESSIVE PLANK ON. In the Progressive National platform we inserted the following plank:

"The supreme duty of the nation is the conservation of human resources through an enlightened measure of social and industrial justice. We pledge ourselves to work unceasingly in State and nation for:

"Effective legislation looking to the prevention of industrial accidents, occupational diseases, overwork, involuntary unemployment, and other injurious effects incident to modern industry;

"The fixing of minimum safety and health standards for the various occupations, and the exercise of the public authority of State and nation, including the Federal control over interstate commerce and the taxing power, to maintain such standards;

"The prohibition of child labor;

"Minimum-wage standards for working women, to provide a living scale in all industrial occupations;

"The prohibition of night-work for women and the establishment of an eight-hour day for women and young persons;

"One day's rest in seven for all wage-workers;

"The eight-hour day in continuous twenty-four-hour industries;

"The abolition of the convict contract-labor system; substituting a system of prison production for governmental consumption only; and the application of prisoners' earnings to the support of their dependent families;

"Publicity as to wages, hours, and conditions of labor; full reports upon industrial accidents and diseases, and the opening to public inspection of all tallies, weights, measures, and check systems on labor products;

"Standards of compensation for death by industrial accident and injury and trade diseases which will transfer the burden of lost earnings from the families of working people to the industry, and thus to the community;

"The protection of home life against the hazards of sickness, irregular employment, and old age through the adoption of a system of social insurance adapted to American use;

"The development of the creative labor power of America by lifting the last load of illiteracy from American youth and establishing continuation schools for industrial education under public control, and encouraging agricultural education and demonstration in rural schools;

"The establishment of industrial research laboratories to put the methods and discoveries of science at the service of American producers.

"We favor the organization of the workers, men and women, as a means of protecting their interests and of promoting their progress."

These propositions are definite and concrete. They represent for the first time in our political history the specific and reasoned purpose of a great party to use the resources of the government in sane fashion for industrial betterment. (*Century Magazine,* October 1913.) *Mem. Ed.* XIX, 544; *Nat. Ed.* XVII, 400.

LABOR—PROTECTION OF. The minute that the democracy becomes convinced that the workman and the peasant are suffering from competition with cheap labor, whether this cheap labor take the form of alien immigration, or of the importation of goods manufactured abroad by low-class working men, or of commodities produced by convicts, it at once puts a stop to the competition. We keep out the Chinese, very wisely; we have put an end to the rivalry of convict contract labor with free labor; we are able to protect ourselves, whenever necessary, by heavy import duties, against the effect of too cheap labor in any foreign country; and, finally, in the Civil War, we utterly destroyed the system of slavery, which really was threatening the life of the free working man in a way in which it cannot possibly be threatened by any conceivable development of the "capitalistic" spirit. (*Forum,* January 1897.) *Mem. Ed.* XIV, 138; *Nat. Ed.* XIII, 250.

——————. No body of officials, no matter how well-meaning and personally honest, no matter whether they be legislators, judges, or executives, have any right to say that we, the people, shall not make laws to protect women and children, and also men in hazardous industry, to protect men, women and children from working under unhealthy conditions or for manifestly excessive hours, or to prevent the conditions of life in tenement-houses from becoming intolerable. *Outlook,* January 6, 1912, p. 44.

——————. By the time I became President I had grown to feel with deep intensity of conviction that governmental agencies must find their justification largely in the way in which they are used for the practical betterment of living and working conditions among the mass of the people. I felt that the fight was really for the abolition of privilege; and one of the first stages in the battle was necessarily

[291]

to fight for the rights of the working man. For this reason I felt most strongly that all that the government could do in the interest of labor should be done. (1913.) *Mem. Ed.* XXII, 526; *Nat. Ed.* XX, 452.

LABOR—PROTECTION OF. *See also* CONTRACT; SOCIAL INSURANCE; SQUARE DEAL; WORKERS; WORKMEN'S COMPENSATION.

LABOR—RIGHTS OF. There can be no doubt but that labor must have a new voice in the management of industrial affairs. The right of labor to collective bargaining, and in that right, the further right to know exactly how the books stand in every industrial concern is going to be a vital political question and the Republican party should take a constructive stand. It cannot afford to talk about constitutional rights of capital and try to dam the moving current of the times. I am satisfied that many Republicans who did not believe these things three and six years ago, are going to believe them now. And I feel that if you will give the Republican organization a free opportunity for development it will develop into a constructive liberty party. (To Will H. Hays, May 15, 1918.) *Mem. Ed.* XXIV, 523; Bishop II, 446.

LABOR—TRAINING OF. Progress cannot permanently consist in the abandonment of physical labor, but in the development of physical labor so that it shall represent more and more the work of the trained mind in the trained body. To provide such training, to encourage in every way the production of the men whom it alone can produce, is to show that as a nation we have a true conception of the dignity and importance of labor. The calling of the skilled tiller of the soil, the calling of the skilled mechanic, should alike be recognized as professions, just as emphatically as the callings of lawyer, of doctor, of banker, merchant, or clerk. The printer, the electrical worker, the house-painter, the foundryman, should be trained just as carefully as the stenographer or the drug clerk. They should be trained alike in head and in hand. They should get over the idea that to earn twelve dollars a week and call it "salary" is better than to earn twenty-five dollars a week and call it "wages." The young man who has the courage and the ability to refuse to enter the crowded field of the so-called professions and to take to constructive industry is almost sure of an ample reward in earnings, in health, in opportunity to marry early, and to establish a home with reasonable freedom from worry. (At semicentennial celebration, founding of Agricultural Colleges, Lansing, Mich., May 31, 1907.) *Mem. Ed.* XVIII, 174; *Nat. Ed.* XVI, 131.

LABOR—TRAINING OF. *See also* EDUCATION, INDUSTRIAL.

LABOR—TREATMENT OF. While I am President I wish the labor man to feel that he has the same right of access to me that the capitalist has; that the doors swing open as easily to the wage-worker as to the head of a big corporation—*and no easier*. Anything else seems to be not only un-American, but as symptomatic of an attitude which will cost grave trouble if persevered in. (Letter of November 26, 1903.) *Mem. Ed.* XXII, 566; *Nat. Ed.* XX, 486.

————. Hereafter in a very real sense labor should be treated, both as regards conditions of work and conditions of reward, as a partner in the enterprises in which he is associated; housing and living conditions must be favorable; effort must be made to see that the work is interesting, there must be insurance against old age, sickness and involuntary unemployment; and a share in the money reward for increased business success, whether it comes from efficiency shown in speeding up or from labor-saving machinery or from any other cause. And on the other side there must be no restriction of output, no levelling down, no failure by the man to exert his full powers, and to receive the full reward to which his individual excellence entitles him, and no failure to recognize that unless there is a proper reward for the capital invested and for the management provided, absolute industrial disaster will result to every human being in this country. (Before Republican State Convention, Saratoga Springs, N. Y., July 18, 1918.) *Mem. Ed.* XXI, 401; *Nat. Ed.* XIX, 364.

LABOR—TREATMENT OF. *See also* CAPITAL AND LABOR; CONTRACT; SQUARE DEAL; WORKERS.

LABOR—WAGES AND HOURS OF. We stand for a living wage. Wages are subnormal if they fail to provide a living for those who devote their time and energy to industrial occupations. The monetary equivalent of a living wage varies according to local conditions, but must include enough to secure the elements of a normal standard of living—a standard high enough to make morality possible, to provide for education and recreation, to care for immature members of the family, to maintain the family during periods of sickness, and to permit of reasonable saving for old age.

Hours are excessive if they fail to afford the worker sufficient time to recuperate and return to his work thoroughly refreshed. We hold that the night labor of women and children is abnormal and should be prohibited; we hold that the employment of women over forty-eight hours per week is abnormal and should be prohibited. We hold that the seven-day working week is abnormal, and we hold that one day of rest in seven should be provided by law. We hold that the continuous industries, operating twenty-four hours out of twenty-four, are abnormal, and where, because of public necessity or of technical reasons (such as molten metal), the twenty-four hours must be divided into two shifts of twelve hours or three shifts of eight, they should by law be divided into three of eight. (Before Progressive National Convention, Chicago, August 6, 1912.) *Mem. Ed.* XIX, 374; *Nat. Ed.* XVII, 268.

LABOR—WAGES AND HOURS OF. *See also* EIGHT-HOUR DAY; WAGES.

LABOR AGITATORS—DANGER OF. Of course the worst foes of America are the foes to that orderly liberty without which our Republic must speedily perish. The reckless labor agitator who arouses the mob to riot and bloodshed is in the last analysis the most dangerous of the working man's enemies. This man is a real peril; and so is his sympathizer, the legislator, who to catch votes denounces the judiciary and the military because they put down mobs. (*Forum,* February 1895.) *Mem. Ed.* XV, 7; *Nat. Ed.* XIII, 7.

LABOR AGITATORS. *See also* CLASS LINES; INDUSTRIAL WORKERS OF THE WORLD.

LABOR CONDITIONS—IMPROVEMENT OF. We wish to reshape social and industrial conditions so that it shall no longer be possible for masses of men—still less, masses of women and children—to be worked for excessive hours, or under conditions disastrous to their health, or at their own personal risk to life and limb, or for a wage too small to permit the living of a self-respecting life. (*Outlook,* February 4, 1911.) *Mem. Ed.* XIX, 101; *Nat. Ed.* XVII, 66.

——————. New York State should put a stop to manufacturing in tenement houses. I know perfectly well that trouble would be caused, dislocation of industry, hardship, when that was done, but I am convinced by thirty years' experience of work in New York that we can not work the reform that must be worked without putting a stop to manufacturing in tenement houses. This State leads in the amount of manufacturing carried on in tenement houses. The Labor Law contains no provisions to prevent the employment of children nor to restrict the working hours of minors or women in tenements. It provides merely that work of certain specified articles (41 in number), may not be carried on in a tenement living-room without a license. No one knows the actual extent of home work in New York City, as the inadequate force of inspectors of the State Labor Department can not cover all the tenements where work may be carried on. Any of you who have had actual experience, as I have had, in acting with legislatures . . . know that after passing a law which they are reluctant to pass, one of their favorite methods of nullifying that law is to refuse a sufficient appropriation to have it carried really into effect. The incomplete figures from the labor records show over 12,000 tenements licensed for home work. Actual experience has shown that under present conditions home work is a serious menace both for the workers and for the public. A home workshop is neither a home nor a factory. The institution of the home from earliest times has surrounded itself with peculiar rights and traditions. To make it a "factory annex" is an invasion of the home which should not be tolerated. The home workshop is a factory without a closing hour. I mean that literally. Home work and congestion, bad ventilation and dark rooms go hand in hand. (Before Civic Forum and the Child Welfare League, Carnegie Hall, N. Y. C., October 20, 1911.) Theodore Roosevelt, *The Conservation of Womanhood and Childhood.* (Funk & Wagnalls Co., N. Y., 1912), pp. 21-24.

——————. When I plead the cause of the crippled brakeman on a railroad, of the overworked girl in a factory, of the stunted child toiling at inhuman labor, of all who work excessively or in unhealthy surroundings, of the family dwelling in the squalor of a noisome tenement, of the worn-out farmer in regions where the farms are worn out also; when I protest against the unfair profits of unscrupulous and conscienceless men or against the greedy exploitation of the helpless by the beneficiaries of privilege; in all these cases I am not only fighting for the weak, I am also fighting for the strong.

The sons of all of us will pay in the future if we of the present do not do justice in the present.

If the fathers cause others to eat bitter bread, the teeth of their own sons shall be set on edge. (At Louisville, Ky., April 3, 1912.) *Mem. Ed.* XIX, 254; *Nat. Ed.* XVII, 189.

LABOR CONDITIONS — REGULATION OF. The right to regulate the use of wealth in the public interest is universally admitted. Let us admit also the right to regulate the terms and conditions of labor, which is the chief element of wealth, directly in the interest of the common good. The fundamental thing to do for every man is to give him a chance to reach a place in which he will make the greatest possible contribution to the public welfare. . . . No man can be a good citizen unless he has a wage more than sufficient to cover the bare cost of living, and hours of labor short enough so that after his day's work is done he will have time and energy to bear his share in the management of the community, to help in carrying the general load. We keep countless men from being good citizens by the conditions of life with which we surround them. We need comprehensive workmen's compensation acts, both State and national laws to regulate child labor and work for women, and, especially, we need in our common schools not merely education in book-learning, but also practical training for daily life and work. We need to enforce better sanitary conditions for our workers and to extend the use of safety appliances for our workers in industry and commerce, both within and between the States. (At Osawatomie, Kan., August 31, 1910.) *Mem. Ed.* XIX, 24; *Nat. Ed.* XVII, 17.

——————. We also maintain that the nation and the several States have the right to regulate the terms and conditions of labor, which is the chief element of wealth, directly in the interest of the common good. It is our prime duty to shape the industrial and social forces so that they may tell for the material and moral upbuilding of the farmer and the wage-worker, just as they should do in the case of the business man. (Before Ohio Constitutional Convention, Columbus, February 21, 1912.) *Mem. Ed.* XIX, 177; *Nat. Ed.* XVII, 131.

LABOR CONDITIONS. *See also* CHILD LABOR; CONVICT LABOR; DOMESTIC SERVICE; EIGHT-HOUR DAY; WAGES; WORKMEN'S COMPENSATION.

LABOR DISPUTES—PUBLIC INTEREST IN. In all great labor struggles, not only are the capitalists and the employees parties in interest, but there is another party, and that third party is the people as a whole. You here are the party in interest, and peculiarly so in a controversy . . . where a public-service corporation is involved which has a peculiar and special connection with the government and with the people. (At Columbus, O., September 10, 1910.) *Mem. Ed.* XVIII, 217.

——————. In any labor disturbance of a size or character to jeopardize the public welfare, there are three parties in interest—the property-owners, the wage-earners, and the general public. I refuse to assent to the view that either the owners of the property or the workers have interests paramount to the general interest of the public at large. This position was formerly taken by the owners, who insisted that the property was theirs, and that the government had nothing whatever to do with their management of it, except to furnish them protection if they were threatened by lawless violence on the part of the workers. I then declined to accept this view. In exactly the same way I now decline to accept any claim put forth in their turn by the workers that they must not be interfered with by the government, and that the public has no rights which it can assert—as against the will of the workers—to do whatever they choose in the premises. One view is precisely as untenable as the other. The public servant who is worth his salt will do what is right, no matter which side is hurt, and will pay no heed to the threats of either side when the question is one affecting the public interests. (1917.) *Mem. Ed.* XXI, 78; *Nat. Ed.* XIX, 67.

LABOR DISPUTES—USE OF POLICE IN. While this feeling against the police is entirely improper, it is perfectly natural; because in labor disturbances the action of the police, when it has been called out, in nineteen-twentieths of the cases is against the interest of the wrong-doing wage-worker, and not against the interest of the wrong-doing capitalist. The wage-worker is right in resenting this fact. But he is wholly wrong in failing to see where the trouble comes in. He makes his attack on the wrong point. The trouble is not that the government represses the wrong-doing of one side. The trouble is that it does not also repress the wrong-doing of the other side. The protest should be not against the efficient use of the police power but against the failure to use it with equal efficiency against both sides. The trouble is not in the use of the police force to restore order. No government has any warrant for existing, if it cannot keep order, and suppress disorder and violence. This is the first step to take, and until it has been taken all further progress is impossible. The trouble is that the government is apt to *confine* itself to keeping order, whereas it ought by rights to treat keeping order, not as in itself an end, but as a means for securing justice. (1917.) *Mem. Ed.* XXI, 73; *Nat. Ed.* XIX, 63.

LABOR DISPUTES. *See also* ALTGELD, JOHN PETER; COAL STRIKE; COLLECTIVE BARGAINING; EMPLOYER-EMPLOYEE RELATIONS; INDUSTRIAL ARBITRATION; INJUNCTIONS; STRIKES.

LABOR EXCHANGES. We have only begun to realize that, as regards the father, the man, we must help him to help himself; help him to learn the vitally important and difficult business of co-operation; help him to learn industrial citizenship by beginning to exercise industrial power; and also help him along many different lines by outright governmental action—insurance against sickness, accident, and undeserved unemployment, provision for old age, provision against overwork and unsanitary conditions. To this end we shall ultimately need a system of nationally federated labor exchanges, co-ordinated with the schools, so that both the capacity of the pupil and the demands of industry may be considered. (*Metropolitan,* May 1917.) *Mem. Ed.* XXI, 97; *Nat. Ed.* XIX, 84.

LABOR EXCHANGES. *See also* EMPLOYMENT BUREAUS.

LABOR LEADERS. *See* CAPITALIST AND LABOR LEADER.

LABOR LEGISLATION. In nothing do we need to exercise cooler judgment than in labor legislation. Such legislation is absolutely necessary, alike from the humanitarian and the industrial standpoints, and it is as much our duty to protect the weaker wage-workers from oppression as to protect helpless investors from fraud. But we must beware above all things of that injudicious and ill-considered benevolence which usually in the long run defeats its own ends. To discourage industry and thrift ultimately amounts to putting a premium on poverty and shiftlessness. It is neither of benefit to the individual nor to society needlessly to handicap superior ability and energy, and to reduce their possessor to the level of work and gain suited for his less able and energetic rivals. (Annual Message as Governor, Albany, January 3, 1900.) *Mem. Ed.* XVII, 55; *Nat. Ed.* XV, 48.

LABOR LEGISLATION—PURPOSE OF. It is not only highly desirable but necessary that there should be legislation which shall carefully shield the interests of wage-workers, and which shall discriminate in favor of the honest and humane employer by removing the disadvantage under which he stands when compared with unscrupulous competitors who have no conscience and will do right only under fear of punishment. (At Minnesota State Fair, September 2, 1901.) *Mem. Ed.* XV, 331; *Nat. Ed.* XIII, 472.

LABOR LEGISLATION. *See also* CHILD LABOR; HOUSING; SOCIAL INSURANCE; WORKMEN'S COMPENSATION.

LABOR PARTY. The difficulty with the Labor-Party idea is that it is based upon a false premise. It is based on the theory that the interests of so-called labor are different from the interests of the community as a whole. That is a foolish doctrine, just as foolish as it would be to try and maintain that the interests of the manufacturer or other employer are different from those of the rest of the community. It is entirely a selfish and wicked doctrine, and, if successful, would work hardships on labor more than on any other group in the community. (Fall 1917; reported by Leary.) *Talks with T. R.* From the diaries of John J. Leary, Jr. (Houghton Mifflin Co., Boston, 1920), p. 151.

LABOR PROBLEM—NATURE OF THE. The labor problem is a human and a moral as well as an economic problem; . . . a fall in wages, an increase in hours, a deterioration of labor conditions mean wholesale moral as well as economic degeneration, and the needless sacrifice of human lives and human happiness; while a rise of wages, a lessening of hours, a bettering of conditions, mean an intellectual, moral, and social uplift of millions of American men and women. (1913.) *Mem. Ed.* XXII, 547; *Nat. Ed.* XX, 470.

LABOR RELATIONS—VIOLENCE IN. In every way I shall support the law-abiding and upright representatives of labor; and in no way can I better support them than by drawing the sharpest possible line between them on the one hand, and, on the other hand, those preachers of violence who are themselves the worst foes of the honest laboring man. (Letter of April 22, 1907.) *Mem. Ed.* XXIV, 73; Bishop II, 62.

————. Violence must be vigorously repressed; but the law must be enforced by lawful methods. This means that the government must supply the police, and must not only eliminate the mob on one side, but must eliminate on the other the private mine-guard and imported thug. Moreover, the police power should always be exercised in conjunction with a thoroughgoing and impartial governmental inquiry into the causes of the strike; and until this government commission has had time to investigate the facts and make its findings, it would be wise to forbid the importing of strike-breakers—for the imported strike-breaker stands on an entirely different footing from the non-unionist (or unionist) who refuses to go on strike. (1917.) *Mem. Ed.* XXI, 77; *Nat. Ed.* XIX, 66.

——————. I hold, with the utmost intensity of conviction, that it is absolutely impossible for us to succeed along the lines of an orderly democracy, a democracy which shall be industrial as well as political, unless we treat the repression of crime, including crimes of violence, and the insistence on justice obtained through the enforcement of law, as prime necessities. I, of course, refuse, under any conditions, to accept the fact that certain persons decline "to unionize and strike" as warranting their murder, or as warranting any kind of violence against them. But I go much further than this. I will aid in every way in my power to secure, by governmental as well as private action, the remedying of all the wrongs of labor, and in so acting I shall pay no heed to any capitalistic opposition. But I refuse to treat any industrial condition as warranting riot and murder; and I condemn all persons, whether representatives of organized labor or not, who attempt to palliate or excuse such crimes, or who fail to condemn them in clear-cut and unequivocal fashion. I heartily believe in organized labor, just as, and even more than, I believe in organized capital; I am very proud of being an honorary member of one labor organization; but I will no more condone crime or violence by a labor organization or by working men than I will condone crime or wrongdoing by a corporation or by capitalists. (To Victor A. Olander, Secretary-Treasurer, Illinois State Federation of Labor, July 17, 1917.) *Mem. Ed.* XXI, 175; *Nat. Ed.* XIX, 168.

LABOR RELATIONS. *See also* EMPLOYER-EMPLOYEE RELATIONS; INDUSTRIAL ARBITRATION; NOBEL PEACE PRIZE; STRIKES.

LABOR-SAVING MACHINERY. When the tool-user has some ownership in and some control over the tool, the matter of opposition to labor-saving machinery will largely solve itself; for then a substantial part of the benefit will come to the working man, instead of having it all come as profit to the capitalist, while the working man may see his job vanish. (1917.) *Mem. Ed.* XXI, 94; *Nat. Ed.* XIX, 81.

LABOR UNIONS. I am a believer in unions. I am an honorary member of one union. But the union must obey the law just as the corporation must obey the law. Just as every man, rich or poor, must obey the law. As yet, no action has been called for by me and most certainly if action is called for I shall try to do justice under the law to every man, so far as I have power. But the first essential is the preservation of law and order, the suppression of violence by mobs or individuals. (To Chicago Strikers, May 1905.) *Mem. Ed.* XXIII, 505; Bishop I, 440.

——————. Labor organizations are like other organizations, like organizations of capitalists; sometimes they act very well, and sometimes they act very badly. We should consistently favor them when they act well, and as fearlessly oppose them when they act badly. I wish to see labor organizations powerful; and the minute that any organization becomes powerful it becomes powerful for evil as well as for good; and when organized labor becomes sufficiently powerful the State will have to regulate the collective use of labor just as it must regulate the collective use of capital. Therefore the very success of the effort we are making to increase the power of labor means that among labor leaders and among other citizens there must be increased vigilance and courage in unhesitatingly rebuking anything that labor does that is wrong. (*Outlook*, February 4, 1911.) *Mem. Ed.* XIX, 108; *Nat. Ed.* XVII, 72.

——————. No straightforward man can believe, and no fearless man will assert, that a trade-union is always right. That man is an unworthy public servant who by speech or silence, by direct statement or cowardly evasion, invariably throws the weight of his influence on the side of the trade-union, whether it is right or wrong. It has occasionally been my duty to give utterance to the feelings of all right-thinking men by expressing the most emphatic disapproval of unwise or even immoral actions by representatives of labor. (1913.) *Mem. Ed.* XXII, 546; *Nat. Ed.* XX, 469.

LABOR UNIONS—FAULTS OF. The worst faults of trades-unionism to-day are largely, and probably mainly, due to past and present misconduct and shortcoming by the capitalists, the corporations. Trades-unionism grew up as an effort to organize the resistance of labor to capitalistic exaction; and it has acquired or inherited many of the vices against which it warred. Corporations and labor-unions are alike bound to serve the commonwealth. Each must recognize in the future its public duty; and this can only come as the result of the state becoming the partner of both, a partner sincerely anxious to help both, but determined that each shall do its duty. (1917.) *Mem. Ed.* XXI, 91; *Nat. Ed.* XIX, 79.

LABOR UNIONS—NEED FOR. In our cities, or where men congregate in masses, it is often necessary to work in combination, that is, through associations; and here it is that we can see the great good conferred by labor organizations, by trade-unions. Of course, if managed unwisely, the very power of such a union or organization makes it capable of doing much harm; but, on the whole, it would be hard to overestimate the good these organizations have done in the past, and still harder to estimate the good they can do in the future if handled with resolution, forethought, honesty, and sanity. (At Labor Day Picnic, Chicago, September 3, 1900.) *Mem. Ed.* XVI, 512; *Nat. Ed.* XIII, 484.

LABOR UNIONS—PRAISE OF. There are certain labor-unions, certain bodies of organized labor—notably those admirable organizations which include the railway conductors, the locomotive engineers and the firemen—which to my mind embody almost the best hope that there is for healthy national growth in the future. (*Review of Reviews,* January 1897.) *Mem. Ed.* XVI, 379; *Nat. Ed.* XIII, 163.

LABOR UNIONS—PROGRESS OF. [I] think—and this is a belief which has been borne upon me through many years of practical experience—that the trade-union is growing constantly in wisdom as well as in power, and is becoming one of the most efficient agencies toward the solution of our industrial problems, the elimination of poverty and of industrial disease and accidents, the lessening of unemployment, the achievement of industrial democracy, and the attainment of a larger measure of social and industrial justice.

If I were a factory employee, a workman on the railroads or a wage-earner of any sort, I would undoubtedly join the union of my trade. If I disapproved of its policy, I would join in order to fight that policy; if the union leaders were dishonest, I would join in order to put them out. I believe in the union and I believe that all men who are benefited by the union are morally bound to help to the extent of their power in the common interests advanced by the union. (1913.) *Mem. Ed.* XXII, 549; *Nat. Ed.* XX, 472.

LABOR UNIONS—RECOGNITION OF. If I were a wage-worker, I should certainly join a union; but when I was in I would remember that I was first of all an American citizen. . . . In our modern industrial system the union is just as necessary as the corporation, and in the modern field of industrialism it is often an absolute necessity that there should be collective bargaining by the employees with the employers; and such collective bargaining is but one of the many benefits conferred by wisely and honestly organized unions that act properly. . . . The union has the same right to exist that the corporation has, and it is unfair to refuse to deal with it as it is to refuse to deal with the corporation. Show your willingness to give the union its full rights, and you will be stronger when you set your faces like flint, as I have set mine, against the union when it is wrong. (At Columbus, O., September 10, 1910.) *Mem. Ed.* XVIII, 218.

LABOR UNIONS AND THE GOVERNMENT. In the employment and dismissal of men in the government service I can no more recognize the fact that a man does or does not belong to a union as being for or against him than I can recognize the fact that he is a Protestant or a Catholic, a Jew or a Gentile, as being for or against him. (Statement to Executive Council, Amer. Fed. of Labor, September 29, 1903.) *Mem. Ed.* XXIII, 289; Bishop I, 251.

————. There is no objection to employees of the government forming or belonging to unions; but the government can neither discriminate for nor discriminate against non-union men who are in its employment, or who seek to be employed under it. Moreover, it is a very grave impropriety for government employees to band themselves together for the purpose of extorting improperly high salaries from the government. (Fourth Annual Message, Washington, December 6, 1904.) *Mem. Ed.* XVII, 255-256; *Nat. Ed.* XV, 219-220.

————. I believe in trade-unions. I always prefer to see a union shop. But my private preferences cannot control my public actions. The government can recognize neither union men nor non-union men as such, and is

[297]

bound to treat both exactly alike. (1913.) *Mem. Ed.* XXII, 550; *Nat. Ed.* XX, 472.

LABOR UNIONS. *See also* COLLECTIVE BARGAINING; COMBINATIONS; EMPLOYER-EMPLOYEE RELATIONS; INDUSTRIAL ARBITRATION; INJUNCTIONS; OPEN SHOP; STRIKES.

LAFAYETTE, MARQUIS DE. To Lafayette ... America owes as much as to any of her own children, for his devotion to us was as disinterested and sincere as it was effective; and it is a pleasant thing to remember that we, in our turn, not only repaid him materially, but, what he valued far more, that our whole people yielded him all his life long the most loving homage a man could receive. No man ever kept pleasanter relations with a people he had helped than Lafayette did with us. (1888.) *Mem. Ed.* VIII, 340; *Nat. Ed.* VII, 294.

LAFAYETTE, MARQUIS DE. *See also* POPULARITY.

LAISSEZ-FAIRE. It is perfectly true that the laissez-faire doctrine of the old school of political economists is receiving less and less favor; but after all, if we look at events historically, we see that every race, as it has grown to civilized greatness, has used the power of the State more and more. A great State cannot rely on mere unrestricted individualism, any more than it can afford to crush out all individualism. Within limits, the mercilessness of private commercial warfare must be curbed as we have curbed the individual's right of private war proper. (*Sewanee Review,* August 1894.) *Mem. Ed.* XIV, 247-248; *Nat. Ed.* XIII, 215.

———. The *laissez-faire* doctrine of the English political economists three-quarters of a century ago ... can be applied with profit, if anywhere at all, only in a primitive community under primitive conditions, in a community such as the United States at the end of the eighteenth century, a community before the days of Fulton, Morse and Edison. To apply it now in the United States at the beginning of the twentieth century, with its highly organized industries, with its railways, telegraphs, and telephones, means literally and absolutely to refuse to make a single effort to better any one of our social or industrial conditions. (At San Francisco, September 14, 1912.) *Mem. Ed.* XIX, 420; *Nat. Ed.* XVII, 307.

LAISSEZ-FAIRE. *See also* COMPETITION; CONTRACT; FREE TRADE; GOVERNMENT CONTROL; INDIVIDUALISM; LIBERTY; POLITICAL ISSUES.

LAND—SETTLEMENT OF. *See* HOMESTEAD LAW; INDIAN LANDS; MANIFEST DESTINY; WESTWARD MOVEMENT.

LAND RESERVES. *See* FOREST RESERVES.

LANDS, PUBLIC. *See* PUBLIC LANDS.

LANGUAGE, ENGLISH. We have room for but one language, the language of Washington and Lincoln, the language of the Declaration of Independence and the Gettysburg speech; the English language. English should be the only language used or taught in the primary schools, public or private; in higher schools of learning other modern languages should be taught, on an equality with one another; but the language of use and instruction should be English. We should require by law that within a reasonable length of time, a time long enough to prevent needless hardship, every newspaper should be published in English. The language of the church and the Sunday-school should be English. The government should provide night schools free for every immigrant who comes here, require him to attend them, and return him to his own country unless at the end of five years he has learned to speak and read English. (1918.) *Mem. Ed.* XXI, 329; *Nat. Ed.* XIX, 301.

LANGUAGE, ENGLISH, IN SCHOOLS. We stand unalterably in favor of the public-school system in its entirety. We believe that English, and no other language, is that in which all the school exercises should be conducted. (*Forum,* April 1894.) *Mem. Ed.* XV, 25; *Nat. Ed.* XIII, 21.

LANGUAGE DIFFERENCES. It would be not merely a misfortune but a crime to perpetuate differences of language in this country, for it would mean failure on our part to become in reality a nation. Many of the newspapers published in foreign tongues are of high character and have done and are doing capital work, by helping the immigrants who speak these tongues during the transition period before they become citizens. These papers deserve hearty recognition for their work. But it must be recognized as transition work, and therefore its usefulness must be recognized as conditioned upon its finally coming to an end. This is as true of the use of a foreign language in schools and churches as in newspapers. (New York *Times,* September 10, 1917.) *Mem. Ed.* XXI, 46; *Nat. Ed.* XIX, 39.

LANGUAGE. *See also* AMERICANIZATION; CITIZENSHIP; FOREIGN LANGUAGE PRESS; IMMIGRANTS; SPELLING REFORM.

LARK—SONG OF THE. I spoke above of the sweet singing of the Western meadow-lark and plains skylark; neither of them kin to the true skylark, by the way, one being a cousin of the grackles and hang-birds, and the other a kind of pipit. To me both of these birds are among the most attractive singers to which I have ever listened; but with all bird music much must be allowed for the surroundings and much for the mood and the keenness of sense of the listener. The lilt of the little plains skylark is neither very powerful nor very melodious; but it is sweet, pure, long-sustained, with a ring of courage befitting a song uttered in highest air. . . .

I doubt if any man can judge dispassionately the bird songs of his own country; he can not disassociate them from the sights and sounds of the land that is so dear to him.

This is not a feeling to regret, but it must be taken into account in accepting any estimate of bird music—even in considering the reputation of the European skylark and nightingale. To both of these birds I have often listened in their own homes; always with pleasure and admiration, but always with a growing belief that relatively to some other birds they were ranked too high. They are pre-eminently birds with literary associations; most people take their opinions of them at second-hand, from the poets. (1893.) *Mem. Ed.* II, 59; *Nat. Ed.* II, 52.

LARK AND NIGHTINGALE. No one can help liking the lark; it is such a brave, honest, cheery bird, and, moreover, its song is uttered in the air, and is very long-sustained. But it is by no means a musician of the first rank. The nightingale is a performer of a very different and far higher order; yet, though it is indeed a notable and admirable singer, it is an exaggeration to call it unequalled. In melody, and above all in that finer, higher melody where the chords vibrate with the touch of eternal sorrow, it cannot rank with such singers as the wood-thrush and hermit-thrush. (1893.) *Mem. Ed.* II, 60-61; *Nat. Ed.* II, 53.

LARK. *See also* MEADOW-LARK.

LATIN—STUDY OF. *See* EDUCATION, LIBERAL.

LATIN AMERICA—FUTURE OF. In the century that has passed the development of North America has, on the whole, proceeded faster than the development of South America; but in the century that has now opened I believe that no other part of the world will see such extraordinary development in wealth, in population, in all that makes for progress, as will be seen from the northern boundary of Mexico, through all Central and South America, and I can assure you that the people of this nation look with the most profound satisfaction upon the great growth that has already taken place in the countries which you represent—a growth alike in political stability and in the material well-being which can only come when there is political stability. (At Bureau of American Republics, Washington, May 11, 1908.) *Mem. Ed.* XVIII, 374; *Nat. Ed.* XVI, 280.

——————. I believe that the century that is opening will see South America, will see Latin America, so grow in power and prosperity as to make this growth the central feature in the growth of the world in the twentieth century, precisely as the growth of North America was the central feature in the growth of the civilized world during the nineteenth century. As the several countries of Latin America thus grow in orderly strength and well-being, they will themselves naturally and inevitably assume for themselves the guardianship of the [Monroe] doctrine; and if, and so long as, this orderly growth continues, our responsibility for the doctrine and the need for exercising the responsibility will gradually, step by step, cease until we either share it with many others or the need for its assertion altogether vanishes. (At New York City, October 3, 1913.) *Mem. Ed.* XVIII, 399-400; *Nat. Ed.* XVI, 299.

LATIN AMERICA. *See also* BRAZIL; COLOMBIA; CUBA; GERMANY; HAITI; INTERVENTION; MEXICO; MONROE DOCTRINE; PANAMA; PORTO RICO; SANTO DOMINGO; SOUTH AMERICA; VENEZUELA.

LATIN LITERATURE — CHARACTER OF. Latin literature was not really an expression of the soul of the Latin race at all, and this will seem strange only to the men who have not succeeded in freeing their thought from the narrow type of scholastic education prevalent in our universities and schools up to the present day. Latin literature was merely an elegant accomplishment developed by small groups of Latin-speaking men who self-consciously set themselves to the production of a literature and an art modelled on Greek lines. The result of the efforts of these men has had a profound effect upon the civilization of the last two thousand years throughout the world; but this effect has come merely because the race to which this artificial literature belonged was a race of conquerors, of administrators, of empire-builders. Greek literature and art, Greek philosophy, Greek thought, have profoundly shaped the after-destinies of the world, although the Greek was trampled under foot by the Roman. But Roman literature, Latin literature, would not be heard of at this day if it were not for the fact that the Latin stamped his character on all occidental and central Europe. (Before Amer. Acad. and Nat. Inst. of Arts and Letters, New York City, November 16, 1916.) *Mem. Ed.* XIV, 452; *Nat. Ed.* XII, 328.

LAW—INTERPRETATION OF. There is no need of discussing the question whether or not judges have a right to make law. The simple fact is that by their interpretation they inevitably *do* make the law in a great number of cases. Therefore it is vital that they should make it aright. (*Outlook,* March 4, 1911.) *Mem. Ed.* XIX, 122; *Nat. Ed.* XVII, 84.

———————. I believe in the cumulative value of the law and in its value as an impersonal, disinterested basis of control. I believe in the necessity for the courts' interpretation of the law as law without the power to change the law or to substitute some other thing than law for it. But I agree with every great jurist, from Marshall downward, when I say that every judge is bound to consider two separate elements in his decision of a case, one the terms of the law, and the other the conditions of actual life to which the law is to be applied. Only by taking both of these elements into account is it possible to apply the law as its spirit and intent demand that it be applied. Both law and life are to be considered in order that the law and the Constitution shall become, in John Marshall's words, "a living instrument and not a dead letter." Justice between man and man, between the State and its citizens, is a living thing, whereas legalistic justice is a dead thing. (Before Ohio Constitutional Convention, Columbus, February 21, 1912.) *Mem. Ed.* XIX, 184; *Nat. Ed.* XVII, 137.

———————. The power to interpret is the power to establish; and if the people are not to be allowed finally to interpret the fundamental law, ours is not a popular government. (Before Ohio Constitutional Convention, Columbus, February 21, 1912.) *Mem. Ed.* XIX, 190; *Nat. Ed.* XVII, 141.

LAW—OBEDIENCE TO. All individuals, rich or poor, private or corporate, must be subject to the law of the land; and the Government will hold them to a rigid obedience thereto. The biggest corporation, like the humblest private citizen, must be held to strict compliance with the will of the people as expressed in the fundamental law. The rich man who does not see that this is in his interests is indeed short-sighted. When we make him obey the law, we insure for him the absolute protection of the law. *Outlook,* September 27, 1902, p. 206.

———————. No man is above the law and no man is below it; nor do we ask any man's permission when we require him to obey it. Obedience to the law is demanded as a right; not asked as a favor. (Third Annual Message, Washington, December 7, 1903.) *Mem. Ed.* XVII, 200; *Nat. Ed.* XV, 172.

———————. Individual capitalist and individual wage-worker, corporation and union, are alike entitled to the protection of the law, and must alike obey the law. (Fifth Annual Message, Washington, December 5, 1905.) *Mem. Ed.* XVII, 335; *Nat. Ed.* XV, 287.

———————. We ask no man's permission when we require him to obey the law; neither the permission of the poor man nor yet of the rich man. (At State Fair, Syracuse, N. Y., September 7, 1903.) *Mem. Ed.* XVIII, 64; *Nat. Ed.* XVI, 55.

———————. Having made a real democracy, we must remember that however good we make the law, more important still is it that the people themselves shall show loyalty in support of the law. I wish to see this made a real democracy, because I believe that our people have the capacity for self-control, for self-mastery. Ever in government there must be control somewhere, mastery somewhere. Ever in government there must be loyalty and obedience to law if law is to prevail. Our purpose should be twofold. We should take from the boss, from the big financier, from the judge himself where the judge even though well-meaning acts against the cause of justice, the power to misrepresent us. We should give that power into the hands of the people. Then we should make it understood by the people that power is a curse to the holder if it is abused, that we the people must show obedience to the law, loyalty to our ideals, self-control, self-mastery, self-restraint. We must act with justice and broad generosity and charity toward one another and toward all men if we are to make this Republic what it must and shall be made, the nation in all the earth where each man can in best and freest fashion live his own life unwronged by others and proudly careful to wrong no other man. (Before National Conference of Progressive Service, Portsmouth, R. I., July 2, 1913.) *Mem. Ed.* XIX, 507; *Nat. Ed.* XVII, 378.

LAW—RESISTANCE TO. Resistance to the law is justified only on grounds that justify a revolution. (At Buffalo, N. Y., September 11, 1895.) *Mem. Ed.* XVI, 297.

LAW—RESPECT FOR. No nation ever yet retained its freedom for any length of time after losing its respect for the law, after losing the law-abiding spirit, the spirit that really makes orderly liberty. (At Galena, Ill., April 27, 1900.) *Mem. Ed.* XII, 466; *Nat. Ed.* XIII, 437.

LAW, CRIMINAL. Centuries ago it was especially needful to throw every safeguard round the accused. The danger then was lest he should be wronged by the State. The danger is now exactly the reverse. Our laws and customs tell immensely in favor of the criminal and against the interests of the public he has wronged. Some antiquated and outworn rules which once safeguarded the threatened rights of private citizens, now merely work harm to the general body politic. The criminal law of the United States stands in urgent need of revision. The criminal process of any court of the United States should run throughout the entire territorial extent of our country. The delays of the criminal law, no less than of the civil, now amount to a very great evil. (Fifth Annual Message, Washington, December 5, 1905.) *Mem. Ed.* XVII, 365-366; *Nat Ed.* XV, 312-313.

——————. The two great evils in the execution of our criminal laws to-day are sentimentality and technicality. For the latter the remedy must come from the hands of the legislatures, the courts, and the lawyers. The other must depend for its cure upon the gradual growth of a sound public opinion which shall insist that regard for the law and the demands of reason shall control all other influences and emotions in the jury-box. Both of these evils must be removed or public discontent with the criminal law will continue. (Seventh Annual Message, Washington, December 3, 1907.) *Mem. Ed.* XVII, 506; *Nat. Ed.* XV, 431.

LAW, MUNICIPAL AND INTERNATIONAL. The whole fabric of municipal law, of law within each nation, rests ultimately upon the judge and the policeman; and the complete absence of the policeman, and the almost complete absence of the judge, in international affairs, prevents there being as yet any real homology between municipal and international law. (1913.) *Mem. Ed.* XXII, 605; *Nat. Ed.* XX, 520.

LAW AND CIVILIZATION. The first essential of civilization is law. Anarchy is simply the handmaiden and forerunner of tyranny and despotism. Law and order enforced with justice and by strength lie at the foundations of civilization. Law must be based upon justice, else it cannot stand, and it must be enforced with resolute firmness, because weakness in enforcing it means in the end that there is no justice and no law, nothing but the rule of disorderly and unscrupulous strength. Without the habit of orderly obedience to the law, without the stern enforcement of the laws at the expense of those who defiantly resist them, there can be no possible progress, moral or material, in civilization. (At Minnesota State Fair, September 2, 1901.) *Mem. Ed.* XV, 338; *Nat. Ed.* XIII, 477.

LAW AND CUSTOM. Law is largely crystallized custom, largely a mass of remedies which have been slowly evolved to meet the wrongs with which humanity has become thoroughly familiar. (Annual Message as Governor, Albany, January 3, 1900.) *Mem. Ed.* XVII, 50; *Nat. Ed.* XV, 44.

LAW AND LIBERTY. Ours is a government of liberty, by, through, and under the law. Lawlessness and connivance at lawbreaking—whether the lawbreaking take the form of a crime of greed and cunning or of a crime of violence—are destructive not only of order, but of the true liberties which can only come through order. If alive to their true interests rich and poor alike will set their faces like flint against the sprit which seeks personal advantage by overriding the laws, without regard to whether this spirit shows itself in the form of bodily violence by one set of men or in the form of vulpine cunning by another set of men. (At State Fair, Syracuse, N. Y., September 7, 1903.) *Mem. Ed.* XVIII, 63; *Nat. Ed.* XVI, 54.

LAW. *See also* CHARACTER; CONSTITUTION; COURTS; CROMWELL, OLIVER; DUE PROCESS; EQUALITY; INTERNATIONAL LAW; JUDGES;

JUDICIARY; JUSTICE; LAWYERS; LEGALISM; MARSHALL, JOHN; ORDER; PUBLIC OPINION; RECALL; SUPREME COURT.

LAW ENFORCEMENT. We would refuse to gain a victory at the price of joining those who believe that legislators should recklessly pass a law that is not intended to be enforced, and that executive officers should carry out this law only so far as they think expedient. We stand for the honest enforcement of law, and in the long run I have faith that the American people will approve of that stand, because the honest enforcement of law is vital to the ultimate well-being of our great Republic. (At Buffalo, N. Y., September 11, 1895.) *Mem. Ed.* XVI, 298.

──────────. The administration of the government, the enforcement of the laws, must be fair and honest. The laws are not to be administered either in the interest of the poor man or the interest of the rich man. They are simply to be administered justly; in the interest of justice to each man be he rich or be he poor—giving immunity to no violator, whatever form the violation may assume. Such is the obligation which every public servant takes, and to it he must be true under penalty of forfeiting the respect both of himself and of his fellows. (At Charleston Exposition, S. C., April 9, 1902.) *Mem. Ed.* XVIII, 36; *Nat. Ed.* XVI, 30.

──────────. No city or State, still less the nation, can be injured by the enforcement of law. As long as public plunderers when detected can find a haven of refuge in any foreign land and avoid punishment, just so long encouragement is given them to continue their practices. If we fail to do all that in us lies to stamp out corruption we cannot escape our share of responsibility for the guilt. The first requisite of successful self-government is unflinching enforcement of the law and the cutting out of corruption. (Third Annual Message, Washington, December 7, 1903.) *Mem. Ed.* XVII, 209; *Nat. Ed.* XV, 180.

──────────. I will go to the limit in enforcing the law against the wealthiest man or the wealthiest corporation if I think he or it has done wrong. (Letter of March 20, 1906.) *Mem. Ed.* XXIV, 13; Bishop II, 10.

──────────. I shall enforce the laws; I shall enforce them against men of vast wealth just exactly as I enforce them against ordinary criminals; and I shall not flinch from this course, come weal come woe. (To David Scull, August 16, 1907.) *Mem. Ed.* XXIV, 52; Bishop II, 45.

LAW ENFORCEMENT. *See also* CAPITAL PUNISHMENT; COURTS; CRIME; JUSTICE; JUVENILE COURTS; LYNCHING; SUPREME COURT.

LAWS—ADMINISTRATION OF. Bad laws are evil things, good laws are necessary; and a clean, fearless, common-sense administration of the laws is even more necessary. (At Pan-American Exposition, Buffalo, N. Y., May 20, 1901.) *Mem. Ed.* XV, 315; *Nat. Ed.* XIII, 449.

LAWS—IMPORTANCE OF. It is a capital error to fail to recognize the vital need of good laws. It is also a capital error to believe that good laws will accomplish anything unless the average man has the right stuff in him. . . .

Even after we have all the good laws necessary, the chief factor in any given man's success or failure must be that man's own character, it must not be inferred that I am in the least minimizing the importance of these laws, the real and vital need for them. The struggle for individual advancement and development can be brought to naught, or indefinitely retarded, by the absence of law or by bad law. It can be immeasurably aided by organized effort on the part of the State. Collective action and individual action, public law and private character, are both necessary. It is only by a slow and patient inward transformation such as these laws aid in bringing about that men are really helped upward in their struggle for a higher and a fuller life. (1913.) *Mem. Ed.* XXII, 192; *Nat. Ed.* XX, 164, 165.

──────────. I hope that not only you and I but all our people may ever remember that while good laws are necessary, while it is necessary to have the right kind of governmental machinery, yet that the all-important matter is to have the right kind of man behind the law.

A State cannot rise without proper laws, but the best laws that the wit of man can devise will amount to nothing if the State does not contain the right kind of man, the right kind of woman.

A good constitution, and good laws under the constitution, and fearless and upright officials to administer the law—all these are necessary; but the prime requisite in our national life is, and must always be, the possession by the average citizen of the right kind of character. (Before Ohio Constitutional Convention, Columbus, February 21, 1912.) *Mem. Ed.* XIX, 196; *Nat. Ed.* XVII, 147.

LAWS—VALUE OF. We need good laws just as a carpenter needs good instruments. If he has not tools, the best carpenter alive cannot do good work. But the best tools will not make a good carpenter, any more than to give a coward a rifle will make him a good soldier. (*Outlook*, March 25, 1911.) *Mem. Ed.* XIX, 148; *Nat. Ed.* XVII, 106.

LAWS—VIOLATION OF. Every time a law is broken, every individual in the community has the moral tone of his life lowered. (At Tuskegee Institute, Tuskegee, Ala., October 24, 1905.) *Mem. Ed.* XVIII, 473; *Nat. Ed.* XVI, 352.

LAWS. See also ADMINISTRATION; LEGISLATION; PROSPERITY.

LAWYERS—CONTRIBUTION OF. A lawyer is not like a doctor. No real good for the community comes from the development of legalism, from the development of that kind of ability shown by the great corporation lawyers who lead our bar; whereas good does come from medical development. The high-priced lawyer means, when reduced to his simplest expression, that justice tends to go to the man with the longest purse. (Letter to W. R. Nelson, July 1912.) *Roosevelt in the Kansas City Star,* p. xxiii.

LAWYERS AS STATESMEN. There is not a greater delusion than the belief that a lawyer is, *per se,* also a statesman. On the contrary, the mere lawyer is rather more unfit than, say, the mere dentist, or mere bricklayer, or mere banker, to be a public man. The ablest lawyer often has had public experience of one type or another which makes him more apt than the ordinary business man to be able to excel in public life; but it is not because he is a lawyer at all; it is because he has great ability and a certain knowledge of public affairs. I could go still further and say that to be a great lawyer is, while a good thing in a judge, very far from being the most important thing. (To H. C. Lodge, April 11, 1910.) Lodge *Letters* II, 374.

LAWYERS. See also JUSTICE; LAW; LEGALISM.

LEADERS—DEMANDS UPON. We, the men who compose the great bulk of the community, wish to govern ourselves. We welcome leadership, but we wish our leaders to understand that they derive their strength from us, and that, although we look to them for guidance, we expect this guidance to be in accordance with our interests and our ideals. *Outlook,* July 9, 1910, p. 508.

LEADERS—DUTY OF. A council of war never fights, and in a crisis the duty of a leader is to lead and not to take refuge behind the generally timid wisdom of a multitude of councillors. (1913.) *Mem. Ed.* XXII, 623; *Nat. Ed.* XX, 535.

LEADERS—NEED FOR. In order to succeed we need leaders of inspired idealism, leaders to whom are granted great visions, who dream greatly and strive to make their dreams come true; who can kindle the people with the fire from their own burning souls. The leader for the time being, whoever he may be, is but an instrument, to be used until broken and then to be cast aside; and if he is worth his salt he will care no more when he is broken than a soldier cares when he is sent where his life is forfeit in order that the victory may be won. In the long fight for righteousness the watchword for all of us is spend and be spent. It is of little matter whether any one man fails or succeeds; but the cause shall not fail, for it is the cause of mankind. (At Carnegie Hall, New York City, March 20, 1912.) *Mem. Ed.* XIX, 222; *Nat. Ed.* XVII, 170.

LEADERS—RESPONSIBILITY OF. Doing our duty is, of course, incumbent on every one of us alike; yet the heaviest blame for dereliction should fall on the man who sins against the light, the man to whom much has been given, and from whom, therefore, we have a right to expect much in return. We should hold to a peculiarly rigid accountability those men who in public life, or as editors of great papers, or as owners of vast fortunes, or as leaders and moulders of opinion in the pulpit, or on the platform, or at the bar, are guilty of wrongdoing, no matter what form that wrong-doing may take. (At Pan-American Exposition, Buffalo, N. Y., May 20, 1901.) *Mem. Ed.* XV, 313; *Nat. Ed.* XIII, 447.

LEADERS—RISE OF. If during the lifetime of a generation no crisis occurs sufficient to call out in marked manner the energies of the strongest leader, then of course the world does not and cannot know of the existence of such a leader; and in consequence there are long periods in the history of every nation during which no man appears who leaves an indelible mark in history. If, on the other hand, the crisis is one so many-sided as to call for the development and exercise of many distinct attributes, it may be that more than one man will appear in order that the requirements shall be fully met. (At banquet in honor of birthday of William McKinley, Canton, O., January 27, 1903.) *Mem. Ed.* XII, 493; *Nat. Ed.* XI, 236.

LEADERS. See also BOSSES; CONGRESSIONAL LEADERS; EXPERTS; MORAL INFLUENCE; ROOSEVELT.

LEADERSHIP—FAILURE OF. There can be no greater misfortune for a free nation than to find itself under incapable leadership when confronted by a great crisis. This is peculiarly the case when the crisis is not merely one in its own history, but is due to some terrible world cataclysm—such a cataclysm as at this moment has overwhelmed civilization. (At Cooper Union, New York City, November 3, 1916.) *Mem. Ed.* XX, 515; *Nat. Ed.* XVIII, 442.

LEADERSHIP, POLITICAL. When I left the Presidency I was prepared, and of course am now prepared, not to be a leader at all; I don't see how an outsider can be a leader; that is the business of the President and the party leaders who hold office; but it is folly to try to be a leader when all that those who appeal to you really desire is that your leadership shall count in getting them elected, but shall be instantly thrown aside when it comes to dealing with party policy after once they have been elected, and no longer need your assistance. (To H. C. Lodge, April 11, 1910.) Lodge *Letters* II, 370.

LEADERSHIP IN A DEMOCRACY. There can be no greater mistake from the democratic point of view, nothing more ruinous can be imagined from the point of view of a true democracy, than to believe that democracy means absence of leadership. Of course it is hard to tell exactly how much can be done in any given case by the leadership that is differentiated from the mass work. (Before Amer. Acad. and Nat. Inst. of Arts and Letters, New York City, November 16, 1916.) *Mem. Ed.* XIV, 451; *Nat. Ed.* XII, 328.

LEADERSHIP IN THE PROGRESSIVE PARTY. In the matter of leadership, both local and national, we may trust the events of the next year or two to develop our ablest and most resourceful man; and for every position the leader must be chosen, not in the least with reference to his own desires, but solely with regard to the needs of the people, for the Progressive party is the servant of the people. No man should come into this party with the idea that he can establish a claim on it; he must be content with the opportunity it offers for service and for sacrifice. (At Chicago, December 10, 1912.) *Mem. Ed.* XIX, 481; *Nat. Ed.* XVII, 356.

LEADERSHIP. See also INTELLECTUAL LEADERSHIP; POLITICIANS.

LEAGUE FOR PEACE. An efficient world league for peace is as yet in the future; and it may be, although I sincerely hope not, in the far future. (*Everybody's,* January 1915.) *Mem. Ed.* XX, 158; *Nat. Ed.* XVIII, 136.

————. It is our duty to try to work for a great world league for righteous peace enforced by power; but no such league is yet in sight. At present the prime duty of the American people is to abandon the inane and mischievous principle of watchful waiting— that is, of slothful and timid refusal either to face facts or to perform duty. Let us act justly toward others; and let us also be prepared with stout heart and strong hand to defend our rights against injustice from others. (*Everybody's,* January 1915.) *Mem. Ed.* XX, 167; *Nat. Ed.* XVIII, 143.

————. Before we make such a league for the future, let us in the present live up to our engagements under The Hague conventions and without delay protest on behalf of Belgium. If we are not willing to undergo the modest risk implied in thus keeping the promise we have already made, then for heaven's sake let us avoid the hypocrisy of proposing a new world league, under which we would guarantee to send armies over to coerce great military powers which decline to abide by the decisions of an arbitral court. Above all, let us avoid the infinite folly, the discreditable folly, of agitating for such an agreement until we have a naval and military force sufficient to entitle us to speak with the voice of authority when fronted with great military nations in international matters. Let us not live in a realm of childish make-believe. Let us not make new and large promises in a spirit of grandiloquent and elocutionary disregard of facts unless and until we are willing by deeds to make good the promises we have already made but have refrained from executing. (*Metropolitan,* August 1915.) *Mem. Ed.* XX, 355; *Nat. Ed.* XVIII, 304.

LEAGUE FOR PEACE — POSSIBILITY OF. The only alternative to war, that is to hell, is the adoption of some plan substantially like that which I herein advocate and which has itself been called utopian. It is possible that it is utopian for the time being; that is, that nations are not ready as yet to accept it. But it is also possible that after this war has come to an end the European contestants will be sufficiently sobered to be willing to consider some such proposal, and that the United States will abandon the folly of the pacifists and be willing to co-operate in some practical effort for the only kind of peace worth having, the peace of justice and righteousness. The proposal is not in the least utopian, if by utopian we understand something that is theoretically desirable but impossible. What I propose is a working and realizable utopia. My proposal is that the efficient civilized nations—those that are efficient in war as well as in peace—shall join in a world league for the peace of righteousness. This means that they shall by solemn covenant agree as to their respective rights which shall not be questioned; that they shall agree that all other questions arising between them shall be submitted to a court of arbitration; and that they shall also agree—and here comes the vital and essential point of the whole system—to act with the combined military strength of all of them against any recalcitrant nation, against any nation which transgresses at the expense of any other nation the rights which it is agreed shall not be questioned, or which on arbitrable matters refuses to submit to the decree of the arbitral court. (*Independent,* January 4, 1915.) Mem. Ed. XX, 172; Nat. Ed. XVIII, 148.

LEAGUE FOR PEACE—SUPPORTERS OF. There is one point about those gentlemen who support a League for International World Peace that is worth while considering. Six months ago or more I outlined that programme which they announced they had just discovered the other day. But I then very emphatically stated that it was a programme for the future and that our first business was to make good the promises we had already made and to put ourselves in position to defend our own rights. These gentlemen declined to say a word in favor of our fitting ourselves to go into *defensive* war in our own interest; and yet they actually wish to make us at this time promise to undertake *offensive* war in the interests of other people! It is a striking illustration of the recklessness with which the average American is willing to make any kind of a promise without any thought of how it can be carried out. (To E. A. Van Valkenberg, June 29, 1915.) Mem. Ed. XXIV, 454; Bishop II, 386.

LEAGUE FOR PEACE AS ALTERNATIVE TO FORCE. The great civilized nations of the world which do possess force, actual or immediately potential, should combine by solemn agreement in a great World League for the Peace of Righteousness. . . . Such a world agreement offers the only alternative to each nation's relying purely on its own armed strength; for a treaty unbacked by force is in no proper sense of the word an alternative. Of course, if there were not reasonable good faith among the nations making such an agreement, it would fail. But it would not fail merely because one nation did not observe good faith. It would be impossible to say that such an agreement would at once and permanently bring universal peace. But it would certainly mark an immense advance. It would certainly mean that the chances of war were minimized and the prospects of limiting and confining and regulating war immensely increased. At present force, as represented by the armed strength of the nations, is wholly divorced from such instrumentalities for securing peace as international agreements and treaties. In consequence, the latter are practically impotent in great crises. There is no connection between force, on the one hand, and any scheme for securing international peace or justice on the other. (New York *Times,* October 18, 1914.) Mem. Ed. XX, 64; Nat. Ed. XVIII, 55.

LEAGUES FOR PEACE VERSUS ALLIANCES. It is because I believe our attitude should be one of sincere good-will toward all nations that I so strongly feel that we should endeavor to work for a league of peace among all nations rather than trust to alliances with any particular group. Moreover, alliances are very shifty and uncertain. Within twenty years England has regarded France as her immediately dangerous opponent; within ten years she has felt that Russia was the one power against which she must at all costs guard herself; and during the same period there have been times when Belgium has hated England with a peculiar fervor. Alliances must be based on self-interest and must continually shift. But in such a world league as that of which we speak and dream, the test would be conduct and not merely selfish interest, and so there would be no shifting of policy. (New York *Times,* November 29, 1914.) Mem. Ed. XX, 198; Nat. Ed. XVIII, 170.

LEAGUE FOR PEACE. *See also* MILITARY TRAINING; NATIONAL DEFENSE; PEACE; PREPAREDNESS.

LEAGUE OF NATIONS. I am not at all sure about the future. . . . I don't put much faith in the League of Nations, or any corresponding cure-all. (To Rider Haggard, December 6, 1918.) *Mem. Ed.* XXIV, 547; Bishop II, 468.

──────────. For the moment the point as to which we are foggy is the League of Nations. We all of us earnestly desire such a League, only we wish to be sure that it will help and not hinder the cause of world peace and justice. There is not a young man in this country who has fought, or an old man who has seen those dear to him fight, who does not wish to minimize the chance of future war. But there is not a man of sense who does not know that in any such movement if too much is attempted the result is either failure or worse than failure. (Dictated January 3, 1919; printed January 13, 1919.) *Roosevelt in the Kansas City Star,* 292.

LEAGUE OF NATIONS — ADMISSION TO. President Wilson's announcement was a notice to the malefactors that they would not be punished for the murders. Let us treat the League of Nations only as an addition to, and not as a substitute for, thorough preparedness and intense nationalism on our part. Let none of the present international criminals be admitted until a sufficient number of years has passed to make us sure it has repented. Make conduct the test of admission to the league. In every crisis judge each nation by its conduct. Therefore, at the present time let us stand by our friends and against our enemies. (October 30, 1918.) *Roosevelt in the Kansas City Star,* 248.

LEAGUE OF NATIONS—MEMBERSHIP IN. Test the proposed future League of Nations so far as concerns proposals to disarm, and to trust to anything except our own strength for our own defense, by what the nations are actually doing at the present time. Any such league would have to depend for its success upon the adhesion of the nine nations which are actually or potentially the most powerful military nations, and these nine nations include Germany, Austria, Turkey, and Russia. The first three have recently and repeatedly violated, and are now actively and continuously violating, not only every treaty, but every rule of civilized warfare and of international good faith. During the last year Russia, under the dominion of the Bolshevists, has betrayed her allies, has become the tool of the German autocracy.... What earthly use is it to pretend that the safety of the world would be secured by a league in which these four nations would be among the nine leading partners? Long years must pass before we can again trust any promises these four nations make. Any treaty of any kind or sort which we make with them should be made with the full understanding that they will cynically repudiate it whenever they think it to their interest to do so. Therefore, unless our folly is such that it will not depart from us until we are brayed in a mortar, let us remember that any such treaty will be worthless unless our own prepared strength renders it unsafe to break it. (Lafayette Day exercises, New York City, September 6, 1918.) *Mem. Ed.* XXI, 411; *Nat. Ed.* XIX, 372.

──────────. Probably the first essential would be to limit the league at the outset to the Allies, to the peoples with whom we have been operating and with whom we are certain we can co-operate in the future. Neither Turkey nor Austria need now be considered as regards such a league, and we should clearly understand that Bolshevist Russia is, and that Bolshevist Germany would be, as undesirable in such a league as the Germany and Russia of the Hohenzollerns and Romanoffs....

The league, therefore, would have to be based on the combination among the Allies of the present war—together with any peoples like the Czecho-Slovaks, who have shown that they are fully entitled to enter into such a league if they desire to do so. (November 17, 1918.) *Roosevelt in the Kansas City Star,* 263.

LEAGUE OF NATIONS—ROOSEVELT'S PROPOSAL FOR. Would it not be well to begin with the League which we actually have in existence, the League of the Allies who have fought through this great war? Let us at the peace table see that real justice is done as among these Allies and that while the sternest reparation is demanded from our foes for such horrors as those committed in Belgium, Northern France, Armenia and the sinking of the *Lusitania,* nothing should be done in the spirit of mere vengeance. Then let us agree to extend the privileges of the League, as rapidly as their conduct warrants it, to other nations, doubtless discriminating between those who would have a guiding part in the League and the weak nations who would be entitled to the privileges of membership, but who would not be entitled to a guiding voice in the councils. (Dictated January 3, 1919; printed January 13, 1919.) *Roosevelt in the Kansas City Star,* 293.

LEAGUE OF NATIONS AND NATIONAL DEFENSE. Above all, let us treat any such agreement or covenant as a mere addition or supplement to and never as a substitute for the preparation in advance of our own armed power. Next time that we behave with the ignoble folly we have shown during the last four years we may not find allies to do what France and England and Italy have done for us. They have protected us with their navies and armies, their blood and their treasure, while we first refused to do anything and then slowly and reluctantly began to harden and make ready our giant but soft and lazy strength. (1918.) *Mem. Ed.* XXI, 351; *Nat. Ed.* XIX, 320.

LEAGUE OF NATIONS AND NATIONAL DUTIES. The vital military need of this country as regards its future international relations is the immediate adoption of the policy of permanent preparedness based on universal training. This is its prime duty from the standpoint of American nationalism and patriotism. Then, as an addition or supplement to, but under no conditions as substitute for, the policy of permanent preparedness, we can afford cautiously to enter into and try out the policy of a league of nations. There is no difficulty whatever in prattling cheerfully about such a league or in winning applause by rhetoric concerning it prior to the effort to make it work in practice; but there will be much difficulty in making it work at all when any serious strain comes, and it will prove entirely unworkable if the effort is made to unload upon it, in the name of internationalism, duties which in the present state of the world will be efficiently performed by the free nations only if they perform them as national duties. (October 15, 1918.) *Roosevelt in the Kansas City Star,* 229.

LEAGUE OF NATIONS AND NATIONAL RIGHTS. [There are] certain matters of such vital national interest that they cannot be put before any international tribunal. This country must settle its own tariff and industrial policies, and the question of admitting immigrants to work or to citizenship, and all similar matters, the exercise of which was claimed as a right when in 1776 we became an independent Nation. We will not surrender our independence to a league of nations any more than to a single nation. Moreover, no international court must be intrusted with the decision of what is and what is not justiciable.

In the articles of agreement the non-justiciable matters should be as sharply defined as possible, and until some better plan can be devised, the nation itself must reserve to itself the right, as each case arises, to say what these matters are. (December 2, 1918.) *Roosevelt in the Kansas City Star,* 279.

LEAGUE OF NATIONS. See also FOURTEEN POINTS; NEUTRALITY; WORLD WAR.

LEAGUE TO ENFORCE PEACE. It is mere hypocrisy to promise to put a stop to wrongdoing in the future unless we are willing to undergo the labor and peril necessary to stop wrongdoing in the present. In our own country nothing but harm was done by the worthy persons who, a couple of years ago, formed a league to enforce peace in the future, while at the same time they nervously declared that they would have nothing to do with enforcing peace by stopping international wrong in the present. (December 2, 1917.) *Roosevelt in the Kansas City Star,* 61.

LEARNING. See KNOWLEDGE; SCHOLARSHIP; UNIVERSITY.

LEE, ROBERT E. General Lee has left us the memory, not merely of his extraordinary skill as a general, his dauntless courage and high leadership in campaign and battle, but also of that serene greatness of soul characteristic of those who most readily recognize the obligations of civic duty. Once the war was over he instantly undertook the task of healing and binding up the wounds of his countrymen, in the true spirit of those who feel malice toward none and charity toward all; in that spirit which from the throes of the Civil War brought forth the real and indissoluble Union of to-day. It was eminently fitting that this great man, this war-worn veteran of a mighty struggle, who, at its close, simply and quietly undertook his duty as a plain, every-day citizen, bent only upon helping his people in the paths of peace and tranquillity, should turn his attention toward educational work; toward bringing up in fit fashion the younger generation, the sons of those who had proved their faith by their endeavor in the heroic days. (To Committee of Arrangement for celebration of 100th anniversary of birth of Robert E. Lee; January 16, 1907.) *Mem. Ed.* XII, 472-473; *Nat. Ed.* XI, 217-218.

LEGALISM. The stick-in-the-bark legalism, the legalism that subordinates equity to technicalities, should be recognized as a potent enemy of justice. *Outlook,* August 17, 1912, p. 855.

———————. The stickler for technicalities, the man who treats precedents, however outrageous, as always binding, instead of as signposts put up for his consideration, will often do as much harm as the other man who permits himself to be swayed either by special sympathy for or special antipathy toward a certain class of his fellow men, whether those who possess much property or those who do not—

and antipathy toward one is just as bad as antipathy toward the other.

Plenty of poor men who are criminals of the worst type escape punishment because of technicalities, just as plenty of rich men do. (*Outlook*, March 11, 1911.) Mem. Ed. XIX, 130; Nat. Ed. XVII, 91.

LEGALISM. *See also* CONSTITUTION; COURTS; JUDGES; JUDICIARY; JUSTICE; LAW; LAWYERS; POPULAR RULE.

LEGISLATION — POPULAR DEMAND FOR. We have heard a great deal about the people demanding the passage of this bill. Now, anything that the people demand that is right, it is most clearly and most emphatically the duty of this legislature to do; but we should never yield to what they demand if it is wrong. (In New York Assembly, Albany, March 2, 1883.) Mem. Ed. XVI, 20.

LEGISLATION—SPHERE OF. No hard-and-fast rule can be laid down as to where our legislation shall stop in interfering between man and man, between interest and interest. All that can be said is that it is highly undesirable, on the one hand, to weaken individual initiative, and, on the other hand, that in a constantly increasing number of cases we shall find it necessary in the future to shackle cunning as in the past we have shackled force. (At Minnesota State Fair, September 2, 1901.) Mem. Ed. XV, 331; Nat. Ed. XIII, 471.

LEGISLATION, CLASS. Legislation to be permanently good for any class must also be good for the nation as a whole, and legislation which does injustice to any class is certain to work harm to the nation. (At State Fair, Syracuse, N. Y., September 7, 1903.) Mem. Ed. XVIII, 66; Nat. Ed. XVI, 56.

LEGISLATION, SPECIAL. In a federal Union it is most unwise to pass laws which shall benefit one part of the community to the hurt of another part, when the latter receives no compensation. (1887.) Mem. Ed. VIII, 68; Nat. Ed. VII, 59.

—————. No special law should be passed where passing a general law will serve the purpose. (Annual Message as Governor, Albany, January 2, 1899.) Mem. Ed. XVII, 24; Nat. Ed. XV, 21.

LEGISLATION AND THE INDIVIDUAL. Primarily the man must rely on himself. Yet the fact remains that along certain lines a great deal can be gained by legislation. Legislation cannot make a man prosperous, for it cannot make him honest or thrifty or industrious, but it can sometimes secure the fruits of honesty, thrift, and industry to the rightful owners. (Campaign Speech, New York City, October 5, 1898.) Mem. Ed. XVI, 449; Nat. Ed. XIV, 296.

—————. Legislation to be thoroughly effective for good must proceed upon the principle of aiming to get for each man a fair chance to allow him to show the stuff there is in him. No legislation can make some men prosperous; no legislation can give wisdom to the foolish, courage to the timid, strength to the shiftless. All that legislation can do, and all that honest and fearless administration of the laws can do is to give each man as good a chance as possible to develop the qualities he has in him, and to protect him so far as is humanly possible against wrong of any kind at the hands of his fellows. (At Jamestown, N. D., April 7, 1903.) *Presidential Addresses and State Papers* I, 323.

LEGISLATION. *See also* ADMINISTRATION; CONGRESS; INDIVIDUALISM; INDUSTRIAL PROBLEMS; LABOR LEGISLATION; LAISSEZ-FAIRE; LAWS; PROSPERITY; SOCIAL LEGISLATION; SPECIAL INTERESTS; SUPREME COURT.

LEGISLATIVE MINORITY — POWER OF. Legislative government is, as its name implies, government by the enactment of laws after debate. The debate is to be used for the purpose of assisting legislation, for procuring wise legislation. The minute it is perverted from these legitimate and lawful ends, and used to stop all legislation, or any legislation of which the minority disapproves, it becomes improper and should be suppressed with a strong hand. We have been tending to develop legislative bodies wherein the majority should only be able to do such things as the minority chose to permit. The establishment of such a principle, of course, upsets our whole theory of government. If the minority is as powerful as the majority there is no use of having political contests at all, for there is no use in having a majority. (Before Federal Club, New York City, March 6, 1891.) Mem. Ed. XVI, 193; Nat. Ed. XIV, 129.

LEGISLATIVE MINORITY. *See also* DEBATE; FILIBUSTERING.

LEGISLATORS—CHARACTER OF. The character of a legislator, if bad, soon becomes a matter of common notoriety, and no dishonest legislator can long keep his reputation good with honest men. If the constituents wish to know the character of their member, they can easily find it out, and no member will be dishonest if he thinks his constituents are looking at him; he presumes upon their ignorance or indifference. (*Century*, January 1885.) Mem. Ed. XV, 86; Nat. Ed. XIII, 52.

LEGISLATORS—SERVICE OF. The history of free government is in large part the history of those representative bodies in which, from the earliest times, free government has found its loftiest expression. They must ever hold a peculiar and exalted position in the record which tells how the great nations of the world have endeavored to achieve and preserve orderly freedom. No man can render to his fellows greater service than is rendered by him who, with fearlessness and honesty, with sanity and disinterestedness, does his life-work as a member of such a body. Especially is this the case when the legislature in which the service is rendered is a vital part in the governmental machinery of one of those world powers to whose hands, in the course of the ages, is intrusted a leading part in shaping the destinies of mankind. (Inaugural Address as Vice-President, Washington, March 4, 1901.) Mem. Ed. XVII, 89; Nat. Ed. XV, 77.

LEGISLATORS AND THEIR CONSTITUENTS. As a rule, and where no matter of vital principle is involved, a member is bound to represent the views of those who have elected him; but there are times when the voice of the people is anything but the voice of God, and then a conscientious man is equally bound to disregard it. In the long run, and on the average, the public will usually do justice to its representatives; but it is a very rough, uneven, and long-delayed justice. That is, judging from what I have myself seen of the way in which members were treated by their constituents, I should say that the chances of an honest man being retained in public life were about ten per cent better than if he were dishonest, other things being equal. This is not a showing very creditable to us as a people; and the explanation is to be found in the shortcomings peculiar to the different classes of our honest and respectable voters. (*Century*, January 1885.) Mem. Ed. XV, 96; Nat. Ed. XIII, 61.

LEGISLATORS. See also CONGRESSMEN; REPRESENTATIVES; SENATORS.

LEGISLATURE—WORK OF A. Remember what a legislative body is. It is a body whose first duty is to act, not to talk. The talking comes in merely as an adjunct to the acting. (Before Federal Club, New York City, March 6, 1891.) Mem. Ed. XVI, 193; Nat. Ed. XIV, 129.

LEGISLATURE. See also CONGRESS; DEBATE; DIVISION OF POWERS; FILIBUSTERING; REPRESENTATIVE GOVERNMENT; SENATE.

LEISURE—USE OF. We believe in every kind of honest and lawful pleasure, so long as the getting it is not made man's chief business; and we believe heartily in the good that can be done by men of leisure who work hard in their leisure, whether at politics or philanthropy, literature or art. But a leisure class whose leisure simply means idleness is a curse to the community, and in so far as its members distinguish themselves chiefly by aping the worst— not the best—traits of similar people across the water, they become both comic and noxious elements of the body politic. (*Forum*, April 1894.) Mem. Ed. XV, 24; Nat. Ed. XIII, 20.

——————. A man can be freed from the necessity of work only by the fact that he or his fathers before him have worked to good purpose. If the freedom thus purchased is used aright, and the man still does actual work, though of a different kind, whether as a writer or a general, whether in the field of politics or in the field of exploration and adventure, he shows he deserves his good fortune. But if he treats this period of freedom from the need of actual labor as a period, not of preparation, but of mere enjoyment, even though perhaps not of vicious enjoyment, he shows that he is simply a cumberer of the earth's surface, and he surely unfits himself to hold his own with his fellows if the need to do so should again arise. A mere life of ease is not in the end a very satisfactory life, and, above all, it is a life which ultimately unfits those who follow it for serious work in the world. (Before the Hamilton Club, Chicago, April 10, 1899.) Mem. Ed. XV, 268; Nat. Ed. XIII, 320.

——————. There is so much that is enthrallingly interesting in life, there is so much that is individually well worth doing, that I think all men of sound mind and character have a feeling of utter contempt for the idler—for the small soul who stands aside from the stress and strain of that life where the great issues are faced, where the great defeats are suffered and the great successes won; for the man who is content to whirl in an eddy on one side, because it is quiet in the eddy, while there

[309]

are waves on the main stream. To all college-bred men I would preach the doctrine of work. If you are fortunate enough to have means which will enable you to lead a life of leisure, remember that the life of leisure, if it is to be worth living, is not to be a life of idleness. We need men who are able to lead lives of leisure, because we need to have done an immense amount of work that is not remunerative; and much of that work—probably the most of it—must be done by men of leisure. We need men of leisure and men of means, then, to work out and fully develop the national life; and these men should understand that they are bound to work as hard as anybody else in the land, the only difference being that their work is of a different kind. (At Commencement, Columbia University, N. Y. C., 1899.) *Columbia University Quarterly*, September 1899, pp. 380-381.

LEISURE. *See also* IDLERS; STRENUOUS LIFE; WORK.

LESE-MAJESTY. I contemptuously refuse to recognize any American adaptation of the German doctrine of lese-majesty. I am concerned only with the welfare of my beloved country and with the effort to beat down the German horror in the interest of the orderly freedom of all the nations of mankind. If the administration does the work of war with all possible speed and efficiency, and stands for preparedness as a permanent policy, and heartily supports our allies to the end, and insists upon complete victory as a basis for peace, I shall heartily support it. If the administration moves in the direction of an improper peace, of the peace of defeat and of cowardice, or if it wages war feebly and timidly, I shall oppose it and shall endeavor to wake the American people to their danger. (1918.) *Mem. Ed.* XXI, 328; *Nat. Ed.* XIX, 299.

LESE-MAJESTY. *See also* CRITICISM; PRESIDENT; SERVILITY.

LEWIS AND CLARK EXPEDITION. *See* JEFFERSON, THOMAS.

LIARS. The liar is no whit better than the thief, and if his mendacity takes the form of slander, he may be worse than most thieves. It puts a premium upon knavery untruthfully to attack an honest man, or even with hysterical exaggeration to assail a bad man with untruth. An epidemic of indiscriminate assault upon character does not good, but very great harm. The soul of every scoundrel is gladdened whenever an honest man is assailed, or even when a scoundrel is untruthfully assailed. (At Washington, April 14, 1906.) *Mem. Ed.* XVIII, 572; *Nat. Ed.* XVI, 416.

LIARS. *See also* FALSEHOOD; TRUTH.

LIBEL SUIT, BARNES. I have felt that this libel suit which has just ended was really as much a fight for those who have fought with me during the last three years as for myself. It has justified in court by legal evidence all we said about boss rule and crooked business three years ago. I do not grudge the money it has cost me, but I think the service was really worth rendering; but I do very strongly feel that in a way it excuses me from doing too much more. (Letter of June 3, 1915.) *Mem. Ed.* XXIV, 450; Bishop II, 383.

LIBEL SUIT, BARNES—VERDICT IN. I have been more moved and touched than I can express by what you have done, and I want to say to you that I appreciate to the full the obligation that you men, representing every sphere of political belief, have put me under. There is only one return that I can make, and that, I assure you, I will try to make to the best of my ability. I will try all my life to act in public and private affairs so that no one of you will have cause to regret the verdict you have given this morning. I thank you from my heart. You have put on me a solemn duty to behave as a decent American citizen should, and I shall try to my utmost to fulfil that duty. (To jury, May 22, 1915.) *Mem. Ed.* XXIV, 434; Bishop II, 369.

LIBERAL EDUCATION. *See* EDUCATION.

LIBERALS. *See* EXTREMISTS; LUNATIC FRINGE; PROGRESSIVE; RADICALS; REFORMERS.

LIBERTY. True liberty shows itself to best advantage in protecting the rights of others, and especially of minorities. (At Oxford University, England, June 7, 1910.) *Mem. Ed.* XIV, 102; *Nat. Ed.* XII, 56.

———————. Throughout past history Liberty has always walked between the twin terrors of Tyranny and Anarchy. They have stalked like wolves beside her, with murder in their red eyes, ever-ready to tear each other's throats, but even more ready to rend in sunder Liberty herself. (1918.) *Mem. Ed.* XXI, 377; *Nat. Ed.* XIX, 342.

LIBERTY—ABUSE OF. The extreme doctrinaires, who are fiercest in declaiming in favor of freedom, are in reality its worst foes, far more dangerous than any absolute monarchy ever can be. When liberty becomes license, some form of one-man power is not far distant.

The one great reason for our having succeeded as no other people ever has, is to be found in that common sense which has enabled us to preserve the largest possible individual freedom on the one hand, while showing an equally remarkable capacity for combination on the other. (1887.) *Mem. Ed.* VIII, 373; *Nat. Ed.* VII, 322-323.

———————. No small part of the trouble that we have comes from carrying to an extreme the national virtue of self-reliance, of independence in initiative and action. It is wise to conserve this virtue and to provide for its fullest exercise, compatible with seeing that liberty does not become a liberty to wrong others. Unfortunately, this is the kind of liberty that the lack of all effective regulation inevitably breeds. (Seventh Annual Message, Washington, December 3, 1907.) *Mem. Ed.* XVII, 486; *Nat. Ed.* XV, 414.

LIBERTY—PRESERVATION OF. As yet no nation can hold its place in the world, or can do any work really worth doing, unless it stands ready to guard its rights with an armed hand. That orderly liberty which is both the foundation and the capstone of our civilization can be gained and kept only by men who are willing to fight for an ideal; who hold high the love of honor, love of faith, love of flag, and love of country. (Address as Assistant Secretary of the Navy, Naval War College, June 1897.) *Mem. Ed.* XV, 244; *Nat. Ed.* XIII, 185.

LIBERTY AND GOVERNMENT REGULATION. Our opponents are fond of saying that the governmental regulation which we advocate interferes with "liberty." This is the argument of which certain judges and certain lawyers are most fond. It is the "liberty" which every reactionary court wishes to guarantee to the employer who makes money from the lifeblood of those he employs; the "liberty" of the starving girl to starve slowly in a sweat-shop, or to accept employment where she hazards life and limb, at her own risk, in the service of others. Well, it was Lincoln who said that the reactionaries of his day "sighed for that perfect liberty—the liberty of making slaves of other people." (At New York City, February 12, 1913.) *Mem. Ed.* XIX, 493; *Nat. Ed.* XVII, 366.

LIBERTY. *See also* ANARCHY; CONTRACT; CROMWELL, OLIVER; DEMOCRACY; EQUALITY; FREEDOM; INDIVIDUALISM; LAISSEZ-FAIRE; LAW; ORDER; RELIGIOUS FREEDOM; TOLERANCE; SELF-GOVERNMENT; SLAVERY.

LIBERTY LOANS. It is the duty of every man, of every woman in this country, who can possibly afford to do so, to buy Liberty Bonds in order that guns, ammunition, food and clothes may be promptly and freely furnished to our soldiers who go to the front. . . .

The highest human service is that of the man who offers his life to his country. Next to that come the services in factory and farm and office which help to keep the great national war machinery efficiently working. And the outstanding and fundamental need, without which nothing can be accomplished, is the need for money; money from rich and poor; money in large sums and small. The motto you have adopted is excellent: "If you can't enlist—invest.—Buy Liberty Bonds."

I myself have invested in these bonds. There is every reason for buying them. The patriotic reason is enough. But here in addition there is offered the best security in the world, an investment backed by all the credit of the Government and people of the United States. We ourselves, we the people, are behind every promise our Government makes, because in the last analysis it is we who are the Government. If the security of the Government should fail it would be because we, the people, were in such plight as no longer to be interested in any security. (To Guy Emerson, May 22, 1917.) Printed broadside.

———————. Today we are gathered to back up the Government in its call to our people to subscribe to the Fourth Liberty Loan. It is our duty not only to subscribe to it, but to oversubscribe to it, and thereby to make our own men on the other side and our enemies on the other side understand how heartily and loyally the people of the United States are back of this war. Moreover, in asking our people to subscribe to this loan I am asking them to display wisdom, but not self-sacrifice. There are plenty of war activities where there must be some sacrifice. Of course, the men at the front and their mothers and wives at home are making the supreme sacrifice and are rendering the supreme service. All that the rest of us can do is simply to back up these men at the front. Of course, when we give money for war charities or cheerfully pay our taxes or do any of the hundred things we ought to do to aid in the war, we are making to some extent a sacrifice—

although it is too trivial a sacrifice to be even alluded to in connection with the sacrifice made by the men at the front. But in subscribing to the Liberty bonds we are benefiting ourselves. The interest is good and the security is the very best in the world. Whoever subscribes is certain to get his money back, unless Uncle Sam bursts up, and in that event it won't matter, because every one of us will burst up, too. In other words, the security is the best in the world, and we are helping ourselves and encouraging habits of thrift and foresight and prudence at the same time that we are helping Uncle Sam. The bonds are so arranged that everyone can take them and every human being in the country ought to take either a Liberty bond or Thrift stamps. We should make the bondholders and the people interchangeable terms. It is not the obligation of the Government officials to raise and furnish the money. That, my fellow-citizens, is your obligation and duty. We must in the heartiest and most generous spirit raise the money. Then, when it has been raised, it is the duty of the officials to see that it is well and wisely spent. (At Baltimore, Md., September 28, 1918.) *An Address by Colonel Theodore Roosevelt at Baltimore in opening the campaign for the Fourth Liberty Loan,* pp. 3-4.

LIBERTY OF SPEECH. See FREE SPEECH.

LIFE. Life is a long campaign where every victory merely leaves the ground free for another battle, and sooner or later defeat comes to every man, unless death forestalls it. But the final defeat does not and should not cancel the triumphs, if the latter have been substantial and for a cause worth championing. (To Sir George Otto Trevelyan, March 9, 1905.) *Mem. Ed.* XXIII, 419; Bishop I, 364.

——————. Life is a great adventure, and I want to say to you, accept it in such a spirit. I want to see you face it ready to do the best that lies in you to win out; and resolute, if you do not win out, to go down without complaining, doing the best that is in you, and abiding by the result. What is true of the boy is also true of the girl; what is true of the young man is true of the young woman, the fundamental facts are the same.

Nothing worth having normally comes unless there is willingness to pay for it; and perhaps the highest good that comes from training of the kind which you get here is not merely training of the body, not merely the training of the mind, but the training of what counts for more than body, more than mind—the training of character, especially in the two ways of giving you the proper perspective (so that you may see what are the important and what the unimportant things) and of giving you the type of soul which will make you willing to strive, and to pay the necessary penalty, for achieving the things that are really worth while. (At Occidental College, Los Angeles, Cal., March 22, 1911.) *Mem. Ed.* XV, 511; *Nat. Ed.* XIII, 578.

——————. The life even of the most useful man, of the best citizen, is not to be hoarded if there be need to spend it. I felt, and feel, this about others; and of course also about myself. (1913.) *Mem. Ed.* XXII, 297; *Nat. Ed.* XX, 254.

——————. It is impossible to win the great prizes of life without running risks, and the greatest of all prizes are those connected with the home. No father and mother can hope to escape sorrow and anxiety, and there are dreadful moments when death comes very near those we love, even if for the time being it passes by. But life is a great adventure, and the worst of all fears is the fear of living. (1913.) *Mem. Ed.* XXII, 394; *Nat. Ed.* XX, 338.

——————. Only those are fit to live who do not fear to die; and none are fit to die who have shrunk from the joy of life and the duty of life. Both life and death are parts of the same Great Adventure. Never yet was worthy adventure worthily carried through by the man who put his personal safety first. Never yet was a country worth living in unless its sons and daughters were of that stern stuff which bade them die for it at need; and never yet was a country worth dying for unless its sons and daughters thought of life not as something concerned only with the selfish evanescence of the individual, but as a link in the great chain of creation and causation, so that each person is seen in his true relations as an essential part of the whole, whose life must be made to serve the larger and continuing life of the whole. Therefore it is that the man who is not willing to die, and the woman who is not willing to send her man to die, in a war for a great cause, are not worthy to live. (*Metropolitan,* October 1918.) *Mem. Ed.* XXI, 263; *Nat. Ed.* XIX, 243.

LIFE. See also DEATH; EDUCATION; EFFICIENCY AND MORALITY; EFFORT; JOY OF LIVING; STRENUOUS LIFE.

LIFE IMPRISONMENT. See CAPITAL PUNISHMENT.

LIMITATION OF ARMAMENTS. See Armaments; Disarmament; Naval Armaments.

LINCOLN, ABRAHAM. For some reason or other he is to me infinitely the most real of the dead Presidents. So far as one who is not a great man can model himself upon one who was, I try to follow out the general lines of policy which Lincoln laid down. I do not like to say this in public, for I suppose it would seem as if I were presuming, but I know you will understand the spirit in which I am saying it. I wish to Heaven I had his invariable equanimity. I try my best not to give expression to irritation, but sometimes I do get deeply irritated. (To Henry S. Pritchett, December 14, 1904.) *Mem. Ed.* XXIII, 405; Bishop I, 352.

——————. He grew to know greatness, but never ease. Success came to him, but never happiness, save that which springs from doing well a painful and a vital task. Power was his, but not pleasure. The furrows deepened on his brow, but his eyes were undimmed by either hate or fear. His gaunt shoulders were bowed, but his steel thews never faltered as he bore for a burden the destinies of his people. His great and tender heart shrank from giving pain; and the task allotted him was to pour out like water the life-blood of the young men, and to feel in his every fiber the sorrow of the women. Disaster saddened but never dismayed him. As the red years of war went by they found him ever doing his duty in the present, ever facing the future with fearless front, high of heart, and dauntless of soul. Unbroken by hatred, unshaken by scorn, he worked and suffered for the people. Triumph was his at the last; and barely had he tasted it before murder found him, and the kindly, patient, fearless eyes were closed forever. (Address at Hodgenville, Ky., February 12, 1903.) *Mem. Ed.* XII, 451; *Nat. Ed.* XI, 210.

——————. Greatly though we now regard Abraham Lincoln, my countrymen, the future will put him on an even higher pinnacle than we have put him. In all history I do not believe that there is to be found an orator whose speeches will last as enduringly as certain of the speeches of Lincoln; and in all history, with the sole exception of the man who founded this Republic, I do not think there will be found another statesman at once so great and so single-hearted in his devotion to the weal of his people. We cannot too highly honor him; and the highest way in which we can honor him is to see that our homage is not only homage of words; that to lip loyalty we join the loyalty of the heart. (At Freeport, Ill., June 3, 1903.) *Mem. Ed.* XII, 449-450; *Nat. Ed.* XI, 208-209.

——————. It is a great comfort to me to read the life and letters of Abraham Lincoln. I am more and more impressed every day, not only with the man's wonderful power and sagacity, but with his literally endless patience, and at the same time his unflinching resolution. (To Kermit Roosevelt, October 2, 1903.) *Mem. Ed.* XXI, 501; *Nat. Ed.* XIX, 444.

——————. I am very busy now, facing the usual endless worry and discouragement, and trying to keep steadily in mind that I must not only be as resolute as Abraham Lincoln in seeking to achieve decent ends, but as patient, as uncomplaining, and as even-tempered in dealing, not only with knaves, but with the well-meaning foolish people, educated and uneducated, who by their unwisdom give the knaves their chance. (To Theodore Roosevelt, Jr., October 4, 1903.) *Mem. Ed.* XXI, 504; *Nat. Ed.* XIX, 447.

——————. In reading his works and addresses, one is struck by the fact that as he went higher and higher all personal bitterness seemed to die out of him. In the Lincoln-Douglas debates one can still catch now and then a note of personal antagonism; the man was in the arena, and as the blows were given and taken you can see that now and then he had a feeling against his antagonist. When he became President and faced the crisis that he had to face, from that time on I do not think that you can find an expression, a speech, a word of Lincoln's, written or spoken, in which bitterness is shown to any man. His devotion to the cause was so great that he neither could nor would have feeling against any individual. (At N. Y. Avenue Presbyterian Church, Washington, D. C., November 16, 1903.) *Mem. Ed.* XII, 457; *Nat. Ed.* XI, 216.

——————. Throughout his entire life, and especially after he rose to leadership in his party, Lincoln was stirred to his depths by the sense of fealty to a lofty ideal; but throughout his entire life, he also accepted human nature as it is, and worked with keen, practical good sense to achieve results with the instruments at hand. It is impossible to conceive of a man farther removed from baseness, farther removed from corruption, from mere self-seeking; but it is also impossible to conceive of a man of more sane and healthy mind—a man less under the influence of that fantastic and diseased morality (so fantastic and diseased as to be in reality profoundly immoral) which makes a man in this workaday world refuse to do what is possible because he cannot accomplish the impossible. (Introduction to A. B. Lapsley's *Writings of Abraham Lincoln;* September 1905.) Mem. Ed. XII, 447; Nat. Ed. XI, 206.

──────────. Lincoln was a great radical. He was of course a wise and cautious radical —otherwise he could have done nothing for the forward movement. But he was the efficient leader of this forward movement. (1917.) Mem. Ed. XXI, 60; Nat. Ed. XIX, 51.

──────────. Lincoln was a radical compared to Buchanan and Fillmore; he was a conservative compared to John Brown and Wendell Phillips; and he was right in both positions. The men and forces whom and which he had to overcome were those behind Buchanan and Fillmore; to overcome them was vital to the nation; and they would never have been overcome under the leadership of men like Brown and Phillips. Lincoln was to the full as conscientious as the extremists who regarded him as an opportunist and a compromiser; and he was far wiser and saner, and therefore infinitely better able to accomplish practical results on a national scale. (*Outlook,* January 14, 1911.) Mem. Ed. XIX, 81; Nat. Ed. XVII, 49.

LINCOLN AND HAMILTON. Lincoln, who . . . conscientiously carried out the Hamiltonian tradition, was superior to Hamilton just because he was a politician and was a genuine democrat, and therefore suited to lead a genuine democracy. He was infinitely superior to Jefferson. (To Frederick Scott Oliver, August 9, 1906.) Mem. Ed. XXIV, 28; Bishop II, 23.

LINCOLN SCHOOL OF POLITICAL THOUGHT. Men who understand and practice the deep underlying philosophy of the Lincoln school of American political thought are necessarily Hamiltonian in their belief in a strong and efficient National Government and Jeffersonian in their belief in the people as the ultimate authority, and in the welfare of the people as the end of government. (1913.) Mem. Ed. XXII, 481; Nat. Ed. XX, 414.

LINCOLN'S PATRONAGE PROBLEMS. I have had a most vivid realization of what it must have meant to Abraham Lincoln, in the midst of the heart-breaking anxieties of the Civil War, to have to take up his time trying to satisfy the candidates for postmaster at Chicago, or worse still in meeting the demands of the Germans or the Irish, or one ·section or another of Republicans or War Democrats, that such and such an officer should be given promotion or some special position. It is of course easy for the mugwump or goo-goo who has no knowledge whatever of public affairs to say that the proper thing is to refuse to deal with such men or to pay any heed to such considerations. But in practical life one has to work with the instruments at hand, and it is impossible wholly to disregard what have by long usage come to be established customs. Lincoln had to face the fact that great bodies of his supporters would have been wholly unable to understand him if he had refused to treat them with consideration when they wished to discuss such questions of patronage. (To Sir George Otto Trevelyan, May 13, 1905.) Mem. Ed. XXIV, 175; Bishop II, 149.

LINCOLN, ABRAHAM. *See also* GRAND ARMY OF THE REPUBLIC; JEFFERSON, THOMAS; REPUBLICAN PARTY; WASHINGTON, GEORGE; WILSON, WOODROW.

LIQUOR. *See* PROHIBITION; PROHIBITIONISTS; ROOSEVELT; SALOON; TEMPERANCE.

LIQUOR LAW—ENFORCEMENT OF. It is perfectly true that we have honestly enforced the Sunday liquor laws, like other laws, and we intend to enforce them as long as we are in office. If the lawgivers of the State believe that a working man should only labor six days a week, and that on the seventh he should be given an opportunity to rest and innocently enjoy himself, the only way to carry out their intent is to arrest and punish his trade rivals who defy the law, violate it with impunity, and therefore force other working men also to labor on the seventh day or to be left behind by their competitors. If it is the intention of the people of this State to legalize all work on the seventh day, so that toil may be uninterrupted from week's end to week's end and unbroken by so much as a single day's rest, why, let them enact laws to that effect; but while the present Sunday laws are on the statute-book this board of police commissioners will honestly endeavor to execute them. (Before N. Y. Preachers' Meeting, January 20, 1896.) Mem. Ed. XVI, 317-318; Nat. Ed. XIV, 223-224.

LIQUOR LAW. *See also* POLICE COMMISSIONER.

LIQUOR PROBLEM—COMPLEXITY OF.
Any man who studies the social condition of the poor knows that liquor works more ruin than any other one cause. He knows also, however, that it is simply impracticable to extirpate the habit entirely, and that to attempt too much often merely results in accomplishing too little; and he knows, moreover, that for a man alone to drink whiskey in a barroom is one thing, and for men with their families to drink light wines or beer in respectable restaurants is quite a different thing. (*Atlantic Monthly,* September 1897.) *Mem. Ed.* XV, 163; *Nat. Ed.* XIII, 128.

LIQUOR TAX—DEFENSE OF. The people who drink and sell liquor are, of all others, those who should be made to contribute in every possible way to pay the running expenses of the state, for there can be no hardship involved in paying heavily for the use of what is at best a luxury, and frequently a pernicious luxury. (Before Union League Club, New York City, January 11, 1888.) *Mem. Ed.* XVI, 129; *Nat. Ed.* XIV, 77.

LIQUOR TRAFFIC BILL. I think that no more terrible curse could be inflicted upon this community than the passage of a prohibitory law. In a community governed on the principle of popular sovereignty it is idle to hope for the enforcement of a law where nineteen-twentieths of the people do not believe in the justice of its provisions. In the country districts you doubtless can, and I believe you practically do, enforce a total prohibition of the liquor traffic. But in the city of New York I am understating the case when I say that nineteen out of every twenty citizens would be against any such provision; that they would recognize the utter folly and futility of trying to stop the liquor traffic absolutely and entirely. With us prohibition would be a great wrong, pure and simple. If you wish to put a premium upon intemperance, pass the prohibitory amendment so that it can affect that city. When I say nineteen out of twenty people, I do not mean those who are disreputable; I mean a great majority of decent law-abiding citizens. (In New York Assembly, January 24, 1884.) *Mem. Ed.* XVI, 35; *Nat. Ed.* XIV, 27.

——————. As a mere matter of party policy, I do not believe in passing this law. It would be absolutely null; its provisions would be absolutely nugatory in the great cities; it would be of the greatest possible harm to morality. Remember what I have said before. I believe a majority of the decent and intelligent citizens of New York will agree with me in saying that they would consider it quite as bad in New York to be at the mercy of the Prohibitionists as to be at the mercy of the liquor-sellers; for they think that to have the Prohibitionists establish their rule would mean simply that the liquor-sellers would be given free play, and the Prohibitionists would have bound our hands and bound the hands of decent people, so that we could not defend ourselves. You would have forged a weapon wherewith those whom you profess to be attacking would strike us; you would have hindered us from defending ourselves; that is all you would have done, granting that you are able to carry this Prohibition amendment. And mind you, I do not believe that the people of this State would ever reach such a height of folly as to be willing to pass it. (In New York Assembly, January 24, 1884.) *Mem. Ed.* XVI, 38; *Nat. Ed.* XIV, 29-30.

LITERATURE. Literature may be defined as that which has permanent interest because both of its substance and its form, aside from the mere technical value that inheres in a special treatise for specialists. (Presidential Address, American Historical Association, Boston, December 27, 1912.) *Mem. Ed.* XIV, 7; *Nat. Ed.* XII, 6.

——————. There is enough of horror and grimness and sordid squalor in real life with which an active man has to grapple; and when I turn to the world of literature—of books considered as books, and not as instruments of my profession—I do not care to study suffering unless for some sufficient purpose. (1916.) *Mem. Ed.* IV, 190; *Nat. Ed.* III, 346.

——————. Normally I only care for a novel if the ending is good and I quite agree with you that if the hero has to die he ought to die worthily and nobly, so that our sorrow at the tragedy shall be tempered with the joy and pride one always feels when a man does his duty well and bravely. There is quite enough sorrow and shame and suffering and baseness in real life, and there is no need for meeting it unnecessarily in fiction. (To Kermit Roosevelt, November 19, 1905.) *Mem. Ed.* XXI, 553; *Nat. Ed.* XIX, 496.

——————. We are apt to speak of the judgment of "posterity" as final; but "posterity" is no single entity, and the "posterity" of one age has no necessary sympathy with the judgments of the "posterity" that preceded it by a few centuries. Montaigne, in a very amusing and, on the whole, sound essay on training children, mentions with pride that when young he read Ovid instead of wasting his time on " 'King Arthur,' 'Lancelot du Lake,' . . . and such idle time-consuming and wit-besotting trash of books, wherein youth doth commonly amuse itself." Of course the trashy books which he had specially in mind were the romances which Cervantes not long afterward destroyed at a stroke. But Malory's book and others were then extant; and yet Montaigne, in full accord with the educated taste of his day, saw in them nothing that was not ridiculous. His choice of Ovid as representing a culture and wisdom immeasurably greater and more serious shows how much the judgment of the "posterity" of the sixteenth century differed from that of the nineteenth, in which the highest literary thought was deeply influenced by the legends of Arthur's knights and hardly at all by anything Ovid wrote. (*Outlook,* April 30, 1910.) *Mem. Ed.* XIV, 473; *Nat. Ed.* XII, 345.

LITERATURE — ROOSEVELT'S PREFERENCE IN. I happen to be devoted to Macbeth, whereas I very seldom read Hamlet (though I like parts of it). Now I am humbly and sincerely conscious that this is a demerit in me and not in Hamlet; and yet it would not do me any good to pretend that I like Hamlet as much as Macbeth when, as a matter of fact, I don't. I am very fond of simple epics and of ballad poetry, from the Nibelungenlied and the Roland song through "Chevy Chase" and "Patrick Spens" and "Twa Corbies" to Scott's poems and Longfellow's "Saga of King Olaf" and "Othere." On the other hand, I don't care to read dramas as a rule; I cannot read them with enjoyment unless they appeal to me very strongly. They must almost be Æschylus or Euripides, Goethe or Molière, in order that I may not feel after finishing them a sense of virtuous pride in having achieved a task. Now I would be the first to deny that even the most delightful old English ballad should be put on a par with any one of scores of dramatic works by authors whom I have not mentioned; I know that each of these dramatists has written what is of more worth than the ballad; only, I enjoy the ballad, and I don't enjoy the drama; and therefore the ballad is better for me, and this fact is not altered by the other fact that my own shortcomings are to blame in the matter. I still read a number of Scott's novels over and over again, whereas if I finish anything by Miss Austen I have a feeling that duty performed is a rainbow to the soul. But other booklovers who are very close kin to me, and whose taste I know to be better than mine, read Miss Austen all the time—and, moreover, they are very kind, and never pity me in too offensive a manner for not reading her myself. (1913.) *Mem. Ed.* XXII, 379; *Nat. Ed.* XX, 325.

LITERATURE, AMERICAN. American literature must naturally develop on its own lines. Politically, Americans, unlike Canadians and Australians, are free from the colonial spirit which accepts, as a matter of course, the inferiority of the colonist as compared to the man who stays at home in the mother country. We are not entirely free as yet, however, from this colonial idea in matters social and literary. Sometimes it shows itself in an uneasy self-consciousness, whether of self-assertion or self-depreciation; but it always tacitly admits the assumption that American literature should in some way be tried by the standard of contemporary British literature. (*Bookman,* February 1896.) *Mem. Ed.* XIV, 357-358; *Nat. Ed.* XII, 294.

LITERATURE, NATIONAL. Next to developing original writers in its own time, the most fortunate thing, from the literary standpoint, which can befall any people is to have revealed to it some new treasure-house of literature. This treasure-house may be stored with the writings of another people in the present, or else with the writings of a buried past. But a few generations ago, in that innocent age when Blackstone could speak of the "Goths, Huns, Franks, and Vandals"—incongruous gathering —as "Celtic" tribes, the long-vanished literatures of the ancestors of the present European nations, the epics, the sagas, the stories in verse or prose, were hardly known to, or regarded by, their educated and cultivated descendants. Gradually, and chiefly in the nineteenth century, these forgotten literatures, or fragments of them, were one by one recovered. They are various in merit and interest, in antiquity and extent. . . . In some there is but one great poem; in some all the poems or stories are of one type; in others, as in the case of the Norse sagas, a wide range of history, myth, and personal biography is covered. (*Century,* January 1907.) *Mem. Ed.* XIV, 384; *Nat. Ed.* XII, 131.

LITERATURE. *See also* BOOKS; BROWNING, ROBERT; CELTIC LITERATURE; COPYRIGHT LAW; DRAMA; HISTORY; LATIN LITERATURE; MAHAN, A. T.; NATURALISTS; POETRY; READING; SCIENCE.

LIVING WAGE. *See* WAGES.

LLOYD GEORGE, DAVID. I was anxious to meet both Lloyd George and John Burns, and I took a real fancy to both. John Burns struck me as having a saner judgment, Lloyd George being very emotional; but of course Lloyd George was the most powerful statesman I met in England—in fact, the man of power. (To David Gray, October 5, 1911.) *Saturday Evening Post,* December 26, 1931, p. 5.

LLOYD GEORGE, DAVID. *See also* GREY, SIR EDWARD.

LOANS. *See* LIBERTY LOANS.

LOBBY. *See* LEGISLATION; PRIVILEGE; SPECIAL INTERESTS.

LODGE, GEORGE CABOT. Of all the men with whom I have been intimately thrown he was the man to whom I would apply the rare name of genius. He was an extraordinary student and scholar; he walked forever through the arch of the past experience of all the great minds of the ages. Any language which he cared to study was his, and he studied every language which held anything he wished. I have never met another man with so thorough and intimate a knowledge of so many great literatures, nor another man who so revelled in enjoyment of the best that he read. He never read for any reason except to find out something he wished to know, or, far more frequently, to gratify his wonderful love, his passion, for high thought finely expressed. A great poem, a great passage in prose, kindled his soul like a flame. Yet he was unaffectedly modest about the well-nigh infinitely wide knowledge, as deep as it was wide, in which his being was steeped. It seemed as if he did not realize how very much he knew. He never made any show of it; unless it came out incidentally and naturally no one ever knew of it; indeed he was really humble-minded in the eager simplicity with which he sought to learn from others who had not even a small fraction of his hoarded wealth of fact and thought. (Introduction to *Poems and Dramas of G. C. Lodge;* 1911.) Mem. Ed. XII, 576-577; Nat. Ed. XI, 297-298.

LODGE, HENRY CABOT. Lodge has violent enemies. But he is a boss or the head of a machine only in the sense that Henry Clay and Webster were bosses and heads of political machines; that is, it is a very great injustice to couple his name with the names of those commonly called bosses. I know Massachusetts politics well. I know Lodge's share in them, and I know what he has done in the Senate. He and I differ radically on certain propositions, as for instance, on the pending rate bill and on the arbitration treaties of a couple of years ago; but I say deliberately that during the twenty years he has been in Washington he has been on the whole the best and most useful servant of the public to be found in either house of Congress.

I say also that he has during that period led politics in Massachusetts in the very way which, if it could only be adopted in all our States, would mean the elimination of graft, of bossism, and of every other of the evils which are most serious in our politics. Lodge is a man of very strong convictions, and this means that when his convictions differ from mine I am apt to substitute the words "narrow" and "obstinate" for "strong"; and he has a certain aloofness and coldness of manner that irritate people who don't live in New England. But he is an eminently fit successor of Webster and Sumner in the Senatorship of Massachusetts. He is a bigger man than Sumner, but of course he has not dealt with any such crisis as Sumner dealt with. He is not as big a man intellectually as Webster, but he is a far better man morally; and the type of citizenship which he represents is from the standpoint of the United States better than either of theirs. (Letter of February 23, 1906.) Mem. Ed. XXIV, 9; Bishop II, 6.

LODGE'S WAR ADDRESSES. Your volume of war addresses is of permanent interest and value; and I am very glad indeed that it is dedicated to Corinne. It is the kind of volume which must be used by the future historian who is honest if he wishes to get Wilson into proper perspective. (To H. C. Lodge, May 26, 1917.) Lodge Letters II, 526.

LONG, JOHN D. I don't suppose I shall ever again have a chief under whom I shall enjoy serving as I have enjoyed serving under you, nor one toward whom I shall feel the same affectionate regard. It is a good thing for a man to have, as I have had in you, a chief whose whole conduct in office, as seen by those most intimately connected with him, has been guided solely by resolute disinterestedness and single-minded devotion to the public interest. I hate to leave you more than I can say. I deeply appreciate, and am deeply touched by, the confidence you have put in me, and the more than generous and kindly spirit you have always shown toward me. I have grown not merely to respect you as my superior officer, but to value your friendship very highly; and I trust I have profited by association with one of the most high-minded and upright public servants it has ever been my good fortune to meet. (To Secretary Long, May 6, 1898.) *Papers of John Davis Long.* (Mass. Hist. Soc., 1939), p. 115.

LOUISIANA PURCHASE. This immense region was admittedly the territory of a foreign power, of a European kingdom. None of our people had ever laid claim to a foot of it. Its acquisition could in no sense be treated as rounding out any existing claims. When we acquired it we made evident once for all that consciously and of set purpose we had embarked on a career of expansion, that we had taken our place among those daring and hardy nations who risk much with the hope and desire of winning high position among the great powers of the earth. As is so often the case in nature, the law of development of a living organism showed itself in its actual workings to be wiser than the wisdom of the wisest. (At Louisiana Purchase Exposition, St. Louis, April 30, 1903.) *Mem. Ed.* XII, 598-599; *Nat. Ed.* XI, 316.

LOVE. There is no other such happiness on earth as there is for a true lover, and a sweet, fair girl beloved. (To H. C. Lodge, October 10, 1891.) Lodge *Letters* I, 117.

———. I think that the love of the really happy husband and wife—*not* purged of passion, but with passion heatened to a white heat of intensity and purity and tenderness and consideration, and with many another feeling added thereto—is the loftiest and most ennobling influence that comes into the life of any man or woman, even loftier and more ennobling than wise and tender love for children. The cheapest, most degrading, and most repulsive cynicism is that which laughs at, or describes as degraded, this relation. (To L. F. Abbott, October 21, 1909.) Lawrence F. Abbott, *Impressions of Theodore Roosevelt.* (Doubleday, Page & Co., Garden City, N. Y., 1919), p. 189.

LOVE OF COUNTRY. The man shows little wisdom and a low sense of duty who fails to see that love of country is one of the elemental virtues, even though scoundrels play upon it for their own selfish ends. (*Forum,* April 1894.) *Mem. Ed.* XV, 15; *Nat. Ed.* XIII, 13.

———. Love of country is an elemental virtue, like love of home, or like honesty or courage. No country will accomplish very much for the world at large unless it elevates itself. The useful member of a community is the man who first and foremost attends to his own rights and his own duties, and who therefore becomes better fitted to do his share in the common duties of all. The useful member of the brotherhood of nations is that nation which is most thoroughly saturated with the national idea, and which realizes most fully its rights as a nation and its duties to its own citizens. This is in no way incompatible with a scrupulous regard for the rights of other nations, or a desire to remedy the wrongs of suffering peoples. (*The Bachelor of Arts,* March 1896.) *Mem. Ed.* XV, 229; *Nat. Ed.* XIII, 172.

LOVE OF COUNTRY. *See also* ALLEGIANCE; AMERICANISM; LOYALTY; NATIONALISM; PATRIOTISM; TREASON.

LOWELL, JAMES RUSSELL. I have all of Lowell with me [in Africa]; I care more and more for his Biglow Papers, especially the second series; I like his literary essays; but what a real mugwump he gradually became, as he let his fastidiousness, his love of ease and luxury, and his shrinking from the necessary roughness of contact with the world grow upon him! I think his sudden painting of Dante as a mugwump is deliciously funny. I suppose that his character was not really strong, and that he was permanently injured by association with the Charles Eliot Norton type, and above all by following that impossible creature, Godkin. (To H. C. Lodge, September 10, 1909.) Lodge *Letters* II, 347.

LOYALTY. Our loyalty is due entirely to the United States. It is due to the President only and exactly to the degree in which he efficiently serves the United States. It is our duty to support him when he serves the United States well. It is our duty to oppose him when he serves it badly. (April 6, 1918.) *Roosevelt in the Kansas City Star,* 130.

———. We hold that our loyalty is due solely to the American Republic, and to all our public servants exactly in proportion as they efficiently and faithfully serve the Republic. Our opponents, in flat contradiction of Lincoln's position, hold that our loyalty is due to the President, not the country; to one man, the servant of the people, instead of to the people themselves. In practice they adopt the fetishism of all believers in absolutism, for every man who parrots the cry of "stand by the President" without adding the proviso "so far as he serves the Republic" takes an attitude

LOYALTY

as essentially unmanly as that of any Stuart royalist who championed the doctrine that the king could do no wrong. No self-respecting and intelligent freeman can take such an attitude. (1918.) *Mem. Ed.* XXI, 321; *Nat. Ed.* XIX, 293.

LOYALTY, DIVIDED. Any man who tries to combine loyalty to this country with loyalty to some other country inevitably, when the strain arises, becomes disloyal to this country. (New York *Times,* September 10, 1917.) *Mem. Ed.* XXI, 40; *Nat. Ed.* XIX, 34.

——————. The larger Americanism demands that we insist that every immigrant who comes here shall become an American citizen and nothing else; if he shows that he still remains at heart more loyal to another land, let him be promptly returned to that land; and if, on the other hand, he shows that he is in good faith and whole-heartedly an American, let him be treated as on a full equality with the native-born. This means that foreign-born and native-born alike should be trained to absolute loyalty to the flag, and trained so as to be able effectively to defend the flag. The larger Americanism demands that we refuse to be sundered from one another along lines of class or creed or section or national origin; that we judge each American on his merits as a man; that we work for the well-being of our bodily selves, but also for the well-being of our spiritual selves; that we consider safety, but that we put honor and duty ahead of safety. (*Metropolitan,* February 1916.) *Mem. Ed.* XX, 301; *Nat. Ed.* XVIII, 258.

LOYALTY TO CLASS OR NATION. I have no patience with the man, whether a multimillionaire or a wage-worker, whether the member of a big corporation or the member of a labor-union, who does not recognize the fact that as an American citizen his first loyalty is due to the nation, and to his fellow citizens no matter what position they occupy as long as those fellow citizens are decent men. His first loyalty must be to the nation and to decency in citizenship. He cannot be a good citizen if he puts loyalty to any other organization above loyalty to the nation, if he puts loyalty to any class above loyalty to good citizenship as such. (At Pacific Theological Seminary, Spring 1911.) *Mem. Ed.* XV, 634; *Nat. Ed.* XIII, 667.

LOYALTY TO FRIENDS OR JUSTICE. I entirely appreciate loyalty to one's friends, but loyalty to the cause of justice and honor stands above it. (To a Senator from Oregon, May 15, 1905.) *Mem. Ed.* XXIII, 508; Bishop I, 443.

LUSITANIA

LOYALTY. See also ALLEGIANCE; AMERICANISM; AMERICANS, HYPHENATED; CITIZENSHIP; DISLOYALTY; IMMIGRANTS; NATIONALISM; PATRIOTISM; TREASON.

LUNATIC FRINGE. It is vitally necessary to move forward and to shake off the dead hand, often the fossilized dead hand, of the reactionaries; and yet we have to face the fact that there is apt to be a lunatic fringe among the votaries of any forward movement. (*Outlook,* March 29, 1913.) *Mem. Ed.* XIV, 406; *Nat. Ed.* XII, 148.

——————. Among the wise and high-minded people who in self-respecting and genuine fashion strive earnestly for peace, there are the foolish fanatics always to be found in such a movement and always discrediting it—the men who form the lunatic fringe in all reform movements. (1913.) *Mem. Ed.* XXII, 247; *Nat. Ed.* XX, 212.

——————. The various admirable movements in which I have been engaged, have always developed among their members a large lunatic fringe; and I have had plenty of opportunity of seeing individuals who in their revolt against sordid baseness go into utterly wild folly. (To H. C. Lodge, February 27, 1913.) Lodge *Letters* II, 434.

LUNATIC FRINGE. See also PAINTING; POLITICAL QUACKS; REFORM; REFORMERS.

LUSITANIA—**SINKING OF THE.** This represents not merely piracy, but piracy on a vaster scale of murder than old-time pirates ever practised. This is the warfare which destroyed Louvain and Dinant and hundreds of men, women, and children in Belgium. It is warfare against innocent men, women, and children, travelling on the ocean, and our own fellow countrymen and countrywomen, who are among the sufferers. It seems inconceivable that we can refrain from taking action in this matter, for we owe it not only to humanity but to our own self-respect. (Statement to press, May 8, 1915.) *Mem. Ed.* XXIV, 443; Bishop II, 376.

LUSITANIA **CRISIS — AMERICAN WEAKNESS IN.** To sink a hundred American men, women, and children on the *Lusitania,* in other words, to murder them, was an evil thing; but it was not quite as evil and it

[319]

was nothing like as contemptible as it was for this nation to rest satisfied with governmental notes of protest couched in elegant English, and with vaguely implied threats which were not carried out. (*Metropolitan*, August 1915.) *Mem. Ed.* XX, 359; *Nat. Ed.* XVIII, 308.

LUSITANIA CRISIS—PROPER COURSE IN. Without twenty-four hours' delay this country should and could take effective action. It should take possession of all the interned German ships, including the German war-ships, and hold them as a guaranty that ample satisfaction shall be given us. Furthermore it should declare that in view of Germany's murderous offenses against the right of neutrals all commerce with Germany shall be forthwith forbidden and all commerce of every kind permitted and encouraged with France, England, Russia, and the rest of the civilized world. (Statement to press, May 1915.) *Mem. Ed.* XX, 444; *Nat. Ed.* XVIII, 380.

LUSITANIA CRISIS — ROOSEVELT'S STAND ON. I have felt as regards the *Lusitania* business that as an honorable man I could not keep silent, although I thoroughly realized that what I said would offend the pacifists, would offend the good, short-sighted men who do not fully understand international relations, and would make envenomed enemies of the great bulk of these Americans of German descent or birth from whom in the past I have had rather more than my normal proportion of support. This was to me a matter of principle, a matter of national duty, of duty which I owed my country; and I did not think that I was warranted in considering my own personal fortune in the matter. (Letter of June 3, 1915.) *Mem. Ed.* XXIV, 449; Bishop II, 382.

LUSITANIA CRISIS—WILSON'S FAILURE IN. As for the *Lusitania*, . . . President Wilson has failed, and has caused the American people to fail, in performing national and international duty in a world crisis. There was not the slightest occasion for diplomacy or meditation. The facts were uncontroverted. Germany did what she said she intended to do and what President Wilson has informed her he would hold her to a "strict accountability" for doing. What was needed was not thought or words but action. The time for thought or for words had passed. The thought should have come in before we sent the "strict accountability" letter. If the President had acted at that time, . . . Germany would have stood before the civilized world, not as a warrior, but as a murderer. I do not think it is an opportune time to talk. I have expressed myself as clearly as I know how. (To Charles F. Amidon, May 29, 1915.) *Mem. Ed.* XXIV, 447; Bishop II, 380.

——————. I have a perfect horror of words that are not backed up by deeds. I have a perfect horror of denunciation that ends in froth. All denunciations of Germany, all ardent expressions of sympathy for the Allies amount to precisely and exactly nothing if we are right in preserving a complete political neutrality between right and wrong. If Wilson is not wrong in his action, or rather inaction, about the *Lusitania* and Belgium, then the wise and proper thing for our people is to keep their mouths shut about both deeds. The loose tongue and the unready hand make a poor combination. We are justified in denouncing the action of Germany only if we make it clearly evident that Wilson has shamelessly and scandalously misinterpreted us. I don't think that the American people believe that he has misrepresented us; I think they are behind him. I think they are behind him largely because their leaders have felt that in this crisis the easy thing to do was to minister to our angered souls by words of frothy denunciation and minister to our soft bodies by taking precious good care that there was no chance of our having to turn these words into deeds. (To Owen Wister, July 7, 1915.) *Mem. Ed.* XXIV, 459; Bishop II, 391.

——————. When that ship was sunk scores of women and children, including American women and children, paid with their lives the penalty of a brutal and murderous attack by a war-ship which was acting in pursuance of the settled policy of the German Government. President Wilson sat supine and complacent, making on the following night his celebrated statement about a nation "being too proud to fight," a statement that under the circumstances could only be taken as meaning that the murder of American women and children would be accepted by American men as justifying nothing more than empty declamation. These men, women, and children of the *Lusitania* were massacred because the German Government believed that the Wilson administration did not intend to back up its words with deeds. The result showed that they were right in their belief. Eight months have gone by since then. American ships were sunk and torpedoed before and afterward; other American lives were lost; and the President wrote other notes upon the subject; but he never pressed the *Lusitania* case; and the only explanation must be found in his fear lest the Germans might refuse to disavow their action. (*Metropolitan,* January 1916.) *Mem. Ed.* XX, 313; *Nat. Ed.* XVIII, 268.

LUTHERAN CHURCH. The Lutheran Church came to the territory which is now the United States very shortly after the first permanent settlements were made within our limits; for when the earliest settlers came to dwell around the mouth of the Delaware they brought the Lutheran worship with them, and so with the earliest German settlers who came to Pennsylvania and afterward to New York and the mountainous region in the western part of Virginia and the States south of it. From that day to this the history of the growth in population of this Nation has consisted largely, in some respects mainly of the arrival of successive waves of newcomers to our shores; and the prime duty of those already in the land is to see that their own progress and development are shared by these newcomers. It is a serious and dangerous thing for any man to tear loose from the soil, from the religion in which he and his forbears have taken root, and to be transplanted into a new land. He should receive all possible aid in the new land; and the aid can be tendered him most effectively by those who can appeal to him on the ground of spiritual kinship. Therefore the Lutheran Church can do most in helping upward and onward so many of the newcomers to our shores; and it seems to me that it should be, I am tempted to say, well nigh the prime duty of this Church to see that the immigrant, especially the immigrant of Lutheran faith from the Old World, whether he comes from Scandinavia or Germany, or whether he belonged to one of the Lutheran countries of Finland, or Hungary, or Austria, may be not suffered to drift off with no friendly hand extended to him out of all the church communion, away from all the influences that tend toward safeguarding and uplifting him, and that he find ready at hand in this country those eager to bring him into fellowship with the existing bodies. (At Lutheran Place Memorial Church, Washington, D. C., January 29, 1905.) *Presidential Addresses and State Papers* III, 205-206.

LYNCHING. The men who head a lynching-party, and the officers who fail to protect criminals threatened with lynching, always advance as their excuse that public sentiment sanctions their action. The chief offenders often insist that they have taken such summary action because they fear lest the law be not enforced against the offender. In other words, they put public sentiment ahead of law in the first place; and in the second they offer, as a partial excuse for so doing, the fact that too often laws are not enforced by the men elected or appointed to enforce them. The only possible outcome of such an attitude is lawlessness, which gradually grows until it becomes mere anarchy. The one all-important element in good citizenship in our country is obedience to law. (*Forum,* September 1895.) *Mem. Ed.* XVI, 268-269; *Nat. Ed.* XIV, 189-190.

─────────────. One of the greatest blots on American civilization is lynch law. If you study the statistics of lynching you will see that lynching cases tend—it is not a regular rule, it is a tendency, however—they tend to be most numerous in the States where it is most difficult legally to punish with death a murderer. Where the law persistently miscarries you are certain to have these dreadful efforts to remedy the miscarriage of the law or to anticipate its miscarriage by remedies far worse even than the disease. We must put down lynch law; and as a first step we should provide for the swift and sure and heavy punishment of the worst offenders; above all, those crimes which are the crimes of fiends. If we could only remember that exactly as justice must be tempered with mercy, so we must not let justice be overthrown by a false spirit of mercy! It is not true mercy of course; for the feeling that prompts men to let a criminal escape from paying the penalty of his misdeeds is mere sentimentality, mere shortsightedness. It is not mercy as mercy should rightly be understood. (At Albany, N. Y., November 20, 1900.) *Proceedings of the New York State Conference of Charities and Correction at the First Annual Session.* (Albany, N. Y., 1901), pp. 7-8.

─────────────. All thoughtful men must feel the gravest alarm over the growth of lynching in this country, and especially over the peculiarly hideous forms so often taken by mob violence when colored men are the victims— on which occasions the mob seems to lay most weight, not on the crime, but on the color of the criminal. In a certain proportion of these cases the man lynched has been guilty of a crime horrible beyond description; a crime so horrible that as far as he himself is concerned he has forfeited the right to any kind of sympathy whatsoever. The feeling of all good citizens that such a hideous crime shall not be hideously punished by mob violence is due not in the least to sympathy for the criminal, but to a very lively sense of the train of dreadful consequences which follows the course taken by the mob in exacting inhuman vengeance for an inhuman wrong. . . .

Every effort should be made under the law to expedite the proceedings of justice in the case of such an awful crime. But it can not be necessary in order to accomplish this to deprive any citizen of those fundamental rights to be heard in his own defense which are so dear to us all and which lie at the root of our liberty. It certainly ought to be possible by the proper administration of the laws to secure swift vengeance upon the criminal; and the best and immediate efforts of all legislators, judges, and citizens should be addressed to securing such reforms in our legal procedure as to leave no vestige of excuse for those misguided men who undertake to reap vengeance through violent methods. (To W. T. Durbin, Governor of Indiana, August 6, 1903.) *Presidential Addresses and State Papers* II, 524-525.

———————. Lawlessness in the United States is not confined to any one section; lynching is not confined to any one section; and there is perhaps no body of American citizens who have deserved so well of the entire American people as the public men, the publicists, the clergymen, the countless thousands of high-minded private citizens, who have done such heroic work in the South in arousing public opinion against lawlessness in all its forms, and especially against lynching. I very earnestly hope that their example will count in the North as well as in the South, for there are just as great evils to be warred against in one region of our country as in another, though they are not in all places the same evils. (At Tuskegee Institute, Tuskegee, Ala., October 24, 1905.) *Mem. Ed.* XVIII, 473; *Nat. Ed.* XVI, 352-353.

———————. Governor [of Arkansas], you spoke of a hideous crime that is often hideously avenged. The worst enemy of the negro race is the negro criminal, and, above all, the negro criminal of that type; for he has committed not only an unspeakably dreadful and infamous crime against the victim, but he has committed a hideous crime against the people of his own color; and every reputable colored man, every colored man who wishes to see the uplifting of his race, owes it as his first duty to himself and to that race to hunt down that criminal with all his soul and strength. Now for the side of the white man. To avenge one hideous crime by another hideous crime is to reduce the man doing it to the bestial level of the wretch who committed the bestial crime. The horrible effects of the lynchings are not for that crime at all, but for other crimes. And above all other men, Governor, you and I and all who are exponents and representatives of the law, owe it to our people, owe it to the cause of civilization and humanity, to do everything in our power, officially and unofficially, directly and indirectly, to free the United States from the menace and reproach of lynch-law. (At Little Rock, Ark., October 25, 1905.) *Mem. Ed.* XXIII, 507; Bishop I, 442.

———————. In that part of my message about lynching . . . I speak of the grave and evil fact that the negroes too often band together to shelter their own criminals, which action had an undoubted effect in helping to precipitate the hideous Atlanta race-riots. I condemn such attitude strongly, for I feel that it is fraught with the gravest danger to both races. Here, where I have power to deal with it, I find this identical attitude displayed among the negro troops. I should be recreant to my duty if I failed by deeds as well as words to emphasize with the utmost severity my disapproval of it. (To Silas McBee, November 27, 1906.) *Mem. Ed.* XXIV, 34; Bishop II, 28.

———————. Lawlessness grows by what it feeds upon; and when mobs begin to lynch for rape they speedily extend the sphere of their operations and lynch for many other kinds of crimes, so that two-thirds of the lynchings are not for rape at all; while a considerable proportion of the individuals lynched are innocent of all crime. . . .

The members of the white race . . . should understand that every lynching represents by just so much a loosening of the bands of civilization; that the spirit of lynching inevitably throws into prominence in the community all the foul and evil creatures who dwell therein. No man can take part in the torture of a human being without having his own moral nature permanently lowered. Every lynching means just so much moral deterioration in all the children who have any knowledge of it, and therefore just so much additional trouble for the next generation of Americans. (Sixth Annual Message, Washington, December 3, 1906.) *Mem. Ed.* XVII, 412, 414; *Nat. Ed.* XV, 351, 353.

LYNCHING. *See also* VIGILANTES.

M

MACAULAY, LORD. I am rather a fanatic about Macaulay. Of course in a man with such an active life, and a man who wrote so much, there will be occasional expressions or convictions with which I do not agree; but in most cases I think these were matters as to which it was impossible that he and I should have the same understanding. In all the essentials he seems to me more and more as I grow older a *very* great political philosopher and statesman, no less than one of the two or three very greatest historians. Of course I am undoubtedly partly influenced by the fact that he typifies common sense mixed with high idealism, but also the same and tempered radicalism which seem to me to make for true progress. (To Sir George Otto Trevelyan, March 19, 1913.) *Mem. Ed.* XXIV, 207; Bishop II, 177.

——————. I always take in my saddle-pocket some volume (I am too old now to be satisfied merely with a hunter's life), and among the most worn are the volumes of Macaulay. Upon my word, the more often I read him, whether the History or the Essays, the greater my admiration becomes. I read him primarily for pleasure, as I do all books; but I get any amount of profit from him, incidentally. Of all the authors I know I believe I should first choose him as the man whose writings will most help a man of action who desires to be both efficient and decent, to keep straight and yet be of some account in the world. (To Sir George Otto Trevelyan, September 10, 1909.) *Mem. Ed.* XXIV, 202; Bishop II, 173.

MACAULAY'S "HISTORY." I . . . reread Macaulay's "History." When I had finished it I felt a higher regard for him as a great writer, and as in the truest sense of the word a great philosophical historian, than I have ever felt before. It is a pretty good test of such a history to have a President who is also a candidate for the presidency read it in the midst of a campaign. (To Sir George Otto Trevelyan, November 24, 1904.) *Mem. Ed.* XXIV, 169; Bishop II, 144.

MACHINE, POLITICAL. The terms machine and machine politician are now undoubtedly used ordinarily in a reproachful sense; but it does not at all follow that this sense is always the right one. On the contrary, the machine is often a very powerful instrument for good; and a machine politician really desirous of doing honest work on behalf of the community is fifty times as useful an ally as is the average philanthropic outsider. Indeed, it is of course true, that any political organization (and absolutely no good work can be done in politics without an organization) is a machine; and any man who perfects and uses this organization is himself, to a certain extent, a machine politician. In the rough, however, the feeling against machine politics and politicians is tolerably well justified by the facts, although this statement really reflects most severely upon the educated and honest people who largely hold themselves aloof from public life, and show a curious incapacity for fulfilling their public duties. . . .

The reason why the word machine has come to be used, to a certain extent, as a term of opprobrium is to be found in the fact that these organizations are now run by the leaders very largely as business concerns to benefit themselves and their followers, with little regard to the community at large. This is natural enough. The men having control and doing all the work have gradually come to have the same feeling about politics that other men have about the business of a merchant or manufacturer; it was too much to expect that if left entirely to themselves they would continue disinterestedly to work for the benefit of others. Many a machine politician who is to-day a most unwholesome influence in our politics is in private life quite as respectable as any one else; only he has forgotten that his business affects the State at large, and, regarding it as merely his own private concern, he has carried into it the same selfish spirit that actuates in business matters the majority of the average mercantile community. (*Century,* November 1886.) *Mem. Ed.* XV, 114; *Nat. Ed.* XIII, 76.

——————. Such words as "boss" and "machine" now imply evil, but both the implication the words carry and the definition of the words themselves are somewhat vague. A leader is necessary; but his opponents always call him a boss. An organization is necessary; but the men in opposition always call it a machine. Nevertheless, there is a real and deep distinction between the leader and the boss, between organizations and machines. A political leader who fights openly for principles, and who keeps his position of leadership by stirring the consciences and convincing the intellects of his followers, so that they have confidence in him and will follow him because they can achieve greater results under him than under any one else, is doing work which is indispensable in a democracy. . . . The machine is simply another name for the kind of organization which is certain to grow up in a party or sec-

[323]

tion of a party controlled by . . . [bosses] and by their henchmen, whereas, of course, an effective organization of decent men is essential in order to secure decent politics. (1913.) *Mem. Ed.* XXII, 178; *Nat. Ed.* XX, 152.

MACHINE, POLITICAL, IN NEW YORK CITY. In New York City, as in most of our other great municipalities, the direction of political affairs has been for many years mainly in the hands of a class of men who make politics their regular business and means of livelihood. These men are able to keep their grip only by means of the singularly perfect way in which they have succeeded in organizing their respective parties and factions; and it is in consequence of the clockwork regularity and efficiency with which these several organizations play their parts, alike for good and for evil, that they have been nicknamed by outsiders "machines," while the men who take part in and control, or, as they would themselves say, "run" them, now form a well-recognized and fairly well-defined class in the community, and are familiarly known as machine politicians. (*Century*, November 1886.) *Mem. Ed.* XV, 114; *Nat. Ed.* XIII, 76.

MACHINES, POLITICAL — ALLIANCE BETWEEN. Our fight is a fundamental fight against both of the old corrupt party machines, for both are under the dominion of the plunder league of the professional politicians who are controlled and sustained by the great beneficiaries of privilege and reaction. How close is the alliance between the two machines is shown by the attitude of that portion of those northeastern newspapers, including the majority of the great dailies in all the northeastern cities—Boston, Buffalo, Springfield, Hartford, Philadelphia, and, above all, New York—which are controlled by or representative of the interests which, in popular phrase, are conveniently grouped together as the Wall Street interests. The large majority of these papers supported Judge Parker for the presidency in 1904; almost unanimously they supported Mr. Taft for the Republican nomination this year; the large majority are now supporting Professor Wilson for the election. Some of them still prefer Mr. Taft to Mr. Wilson, but all make either Mr. Taft or Mr. Wilson their first choice; and one of the ludicrous features of the campaign is that those papers supporting Professor Wilson show the most jealous partisanship for Mr. Taft whenever they think his interests are jeopardized by the Progressive movement—that, for instance, any electors will obey the will of the majority of the Republican voters at the primaries, and vote for me instead of obeying the will of the Messrs. Barnes-Penrose-Guggenheim combination by voting for Mr. Taft. (Before Progressive National Convention, Chicago, August 6, 1912.) *Mem. Ed.* XIX, 359; *Nat. Ed.* XVII, 255.

MACHINES, POLITICAL — ROOSEVELT'S RELATIONS WITH. When, after the Spanish War, I got to a position of such importance that a good deal of consideration had to be paid me, I was very successful; and, as President, I was able to do a great deal that I wished to do. This was done merely because I utilized the reformers without letting them grow perfectly wild-eyed; and I yet kept in some kind of relations with the machine men, so as to be on a living basis with them, although I had to thwart them at every turn. But, when I got back from Africa, I found that everything had split. Taft had thrown in his lot with the sordid machine crowd, as had most of my former efficient political supporters. (To Kermit Roosevelt, January 27, 1915.) *Mem. Ed.* XXIV, 420; Bishop II, 357.

MACHINES, POLITICAL. *See also* BOSS; BRIBERY; CORRUPTION; ELECTION REFORMS; GOVERNOR OF NEW YORK; INDEPENDENT; ORGANIZATION; PARTY ALLEGIANCE; PARTY SYSTEM; PLATT, T. C.; POLITICAL PARTIES; POLITICIANS; POLITICS; PRIMARIES; ROOSEVELT'S POLITICAL CAREER; SALOON; TAMMANY HALL.

McKINLEY, WILLIAM. McKinley is a man hardly even of moderate means. He is about as well off say as a division superintendent of the New York Central railroad. He lives in a little house at Canton just as such a division superintendent who had retired would live in a little house in Auburn or some other small New York city or big country town. He comes from the typical hard-working farmer stock of our country. In every instinct and feeling he is closely in touch with, and the absolute representative of, the men who make up the immense bulk of our Nation—the small merchants, clerks, farmers and mechanics who formed the backbone of the patriotic party under Washington in the Revolution; of the Republican Party under Lincoln at the time of the Civil War. His one great anxiety while President has been to keep in touch with this body of people and to give expression to their desires and sentiments. He has been so successful that within a year he has been re-elected by an overwhelming majority, a majority including the bulk of the wage-workers and the very great bulk of the farmers. He has been to a high degree accessible to everyone. At his home anyone could see him just as easily as anyone else could be seen. All that was necessary was, if he was engaged, to wait until his engagement was over. More than almost any public man I have ever met, he has avoided exciting personal enmities. I have never heard him denounce or assail any man or any body of men. There is in the country at this time the most widespread confidence in and satisfaction with his policies. (To H. C. Lodge, September 9, 1901.) Lodge *Letters* I, 499.

——————. It is not too much to say that at the time of President McKinley's death he was the most widely loved man in all the United States; while we have never had any public man of his position who has been so wholly free from the bitter animosities incident to public life. His political opponents were the first to bear the heartiest and most generous tribute to the broad kindliness of nature, the sweetness and gentleness of character which so endeared him to his close associates. To a standard of lofty integrity in public life he united the tender affections and home virtues which are all-important in the make-up of national character. A gallant soldier in the great war for the Union, he also shone as an example to all our people because of his conduct in the most sacred and intimate of home relations. There could be no personal hatred of him, for he never acted with aught but consideration for the welfare of others. No one could fail to respect him who knew him in public or private life. (First Annual Message, Washington, December 3, 1901.) *Mem. Ed.* XVII, 93-94; *Nat. Ed.* XV, 81-82.

——————. It was given to President McKinley to take the foremost place in our political life at a time when our country was brought face to face with problems more momentous than any whose solution we have ever attempted, save only in the Revolution and in the Civil War; and it was under his leadership that the nation solved these mighty problems aright. Therefore he shall stand in the eyes of history not merely as the first man of his generation, but as among the greatest figures in our national life, coming second only to the men of the two great crises in which the Union was founded and preserved.

No man could carry through successfully such a task as President McKinley undertook, unless trained by long years of effort for its performance. Knowledge of his fellow citizens, ability to understand them, keen sympathy with even their innermost feelings, and yet power to lead them, together with far-sighted sagacity and resolute belief both in the people and in their future—all these were needed in the man who headed the march of our people during the eventful years from 1896 to 1901. These were the qualities possessed by McKinley and developed by him throughout his whole history previous to assuming the presidency. (At banquet in honor of birthday of William McKinley, Canton, O., January 27, 1903.) *Mem. Ed.* XII, 494; *Nat. Ed.* XI, 237.

——————. No other President in our history has seen high and honorable effort crowned with more conspicuous personal success. No other President entered upon his second term feeling such right to a profound and peaceful satisfaction. Then by a stroke of horror, so strange in its fantastic iniquity as to stand unique in the black annals of crime, he was struck down....

He won greatness by meeting and solving the issues as they arose—not by shirking them—meeting them with wisdom, with the exercise of the most skilful and cautious judgment, but with fearless resolution when the time of crisis came. He met each crisis on its own merits; he never sought excuse for shirking a task in the fact that it was different from the one he had expected to face. The long public career, which opened when as a boy he carried a musket in the ranks and closed when as a man in the prime of his intellectual strength he stood among the world's chief statesmen, came to what it was because he treated each triumph as opening the road to fresh effort, not as an excuse for ceasing from effort. (At banquet in honor of birthday of William McKinley, Canton, O., January 27, 1903.) *Mem. Ed.* XII, 500-501; *Nat. Ed.* XI, 242-243.

McKINLEY, WILLIAM. See also ELECTION OF 1896; ELECTION OF 1900; *Maine*.

MADISON, JAMES. In the Constitutional Convention Madison, a moderate federalist, was the man who, of all who were there, saw things most clearly as they were, and whose theories most closely corresponded with the principles finally adopted; and although even he was at first dissatisfied with the result, and both by word and by action interpreted the Constitution in widely different ways at different times, still this was Madison's time of glory; he was one of the statesmen who do extremely useful work, but only at some single given crisis. While the Constitution was being formed and adopted, he stood in the very front; but in his later career he sunk his own individuality, and became a mere pale shadow of Jefferson. (1888.) *Mem. Ed.* VIII, 379; *Nat. Ed.* VII, 327-328.

———————. Excepting Jefferson, we have never produced an Executive more helpless than Madison, when it came to grappling with real dangers and difficulties. Like his predecessor, he was only fit to be President in a time of profound peace; he was utterly out of place the instant matters grew turbulent, or difficult problems arose to be solved, and he was a ridiculously incompetent leader for a war with Great Britain. He was entirely too timid to have embarked on such a venture of his own accord, and was simply forced into it by the threat of losing his second term. (1888.) *Mem. Ed.* VIII, 531-532; *Nat. Ed.* VII, 459-460.

MADISON, JAMES. See also *Federalist, The*.

MAHAN, A. T. Admiral Mahan belonged in that limited class of men whose honorable ambition it is to render all the service in their power to the cause which they espouse, and who care to achieve distinction and reward for themselves only by the success with which they render this service to the cause. He emphatically belonged among those invaluable workers, the only ones whose work really adds to the sum of mankind's achievement, of whom Ruskin spoke when he said that the only work worth doing was that done by the men who labored primarily for the sake of the labor itself and not for the fee. (*Outlook*, January 13, 1915.) *Mem. Ed.* XII, 554; *Nat. Ed.* XI, 278.

———————. Mahan's really great success came in Europe, and especially in England, before it came here. The American public took him at his true worth only with reluctance, and after educated and far-seeing Englishmen had hailed him with relief and enthusiasm as the man of genius who was able to bring home to the minds of the people as a whole truths to which they would not listen when told by less gifted men. In dealing with our naval officers, in working for the navy from within the navy, Mahan was merely one among a number of first-class men; and many of these other first-class men were better than he was in the practical handling of the huge and complicated instruments of modern war. But in the vitally important task of convincing the masters of all of us—the people as a whole—of the importance of a true understanding of naval needs, Mahan stood alone. There was no one else in his class or anywhere near it. (*Outlook*, January 13, 1915.) *Mem. Ed.* XII, 556; *Nat. Ed.* XI, 279.

MAHAN'S *INFLUENCE OF SEA POWER UPON HISTORY*. Captain Mahan has written distinctively the best and most important, and also by far the most interesting, book on naval history which has been produced on either side of the water for many a long year. Himself an officer who has seen active service and borne himself with honor under fire, he starts with an advantage that no civilian can possess. On the other hand, he does not show the shortcomings which make the average military man an exasperatingly incompetent military historian. His work is in every respect scholarly, and has not a trace of the pedantry which invariably mars mere self-conscious striving after scholarship. He is thoroughly conversant with his subject, and has prepared himself for it by exhaustive study and research, and he approaches it in, to use an old-fashioned phrase, an entirely philosophical spirit. He subordinates detail to mass-effects, trying always to grasp and make evident the essential features of a situation; and he neither loses sight of nor exaggerates the bearing which the history of past struggles has upon our present problems. (*Atlantic Monthly,* October 1890.) *Mem. Ed.* XIV, 306; *Nat. Ed.* XII, 264.

MAHAN'S *LIFE OF NELSON*. Captain Mahan has met the requirements necessary for an historian of the first class. He knows all the minute details of the subject so well that he can with an unsparing hand exercise the all-important right of rejection. Out of the immense mass of trivialities he selects the essential and the essential only. Nelson lived and died in a light as fierce and brilliant as any that ever beat upon a throne, and there is not a single fact of importance in reference to his career now left to be gathered by the most industrious gleaner in the stubble of historical literature. All the facts of importance are practically uncontested. In consequence Captain Mahan has been able almost entirely to discard footnotes, the necessary bane of the ordinary historian even of the first rank. The facts with which he deals are uncontested; but the power and vividness with which he sets them forth, and the unerring sagacity of his deductions from them, are new, and are all his own. He writes with careful self-restraint, and with careful suppression of all that is in any way redundant, or aside from his main theme. His style is concise and clear; it is simple, and yet it rises level to the needs of the feats of wonderful heroism which he describes. In short, the book has the vigor and the simplicity that mark the classic in any tongue. Biography, like portrait-painting, is perhaps the most difficult branch of the art of which it is a part; and Captain Mahan has written the best of all naval biographies, about the greatest of all sea-captains, the man who was himself the embodiment of sea power in action. (*Bookman,* June 1897.) *Mem. Ed.* XIV, 327-328; *Nat. Ed.* XII, 281.

MAINE—SINKING OF THE. Being a Jingo, as I am writing confidentially, I will say, to relieve my feelings, that I would give anything if President McKinley would order the fleet to Havana to-morrow. This Cuban business ought to stop. The *Maine* was sunk by an act of dirty treachery on the part of the Spaniards, I believe; though we shall never find out definitely, and officially it will go down as an accident. (Letter of February 16, 1898.) *Mem. Ed.* XXIII, 99; Bishop I, 85.

———. Let me again earnestly urge that you advise the President against our conducting any examination in conjunction with the Spaniards as to the *Maine's* disaster. I myself doubt whether it will be possible to tell definitely how the disaster occurred by an investigation, and it may be that we could do it as well in conjunction with the Spaniards as alone. But I am sure we could never convince the people at large of this fact. . . . I was informed that both Speaker Reed and Senator Hale had stated that we should cease building any more battleships, in view of the disaster to the *Maine.* I cannot believe that the statement is true, for of course *such an attitude, if supported by the people, would mean that we had reached the last pitch of national cowardice and baseness.* I earnestly wish that you could see your way clear now, without waiting a day, to send in a special message, stating that in view of the disaster to the *Maine* (and perhaps in view of the possible needs of this country) instead of recommending one battleship you ask for two, or better still, that four battleships be authorized immediately by Congress. (To Secretary John D. Long, February 19, 1898.) *Mem. Ed.* XXIII, 99; Bishop I, 85.

———. Of course I have nothing to say as to the policy of the Government, but I hope this incident [*Maine*] will not be treated by itself, but as part of the whole Cuban business. There is absolutely but one possible solution of a permanent nature to that affair, and that is Cuban independence. The sooner we make up our minds to this the better. If we can attain our object peacefully, of course we should try to do so; but we should attain it one way or the other anyhow. (To Henry White, March 9, 1898.) *Mem. Ed.* XXIII, 101; Bishop I, 86.

MAINE. See also CUBA; SPANISH-AMERICAN WAR.

MAJORITY—TYRANNY OF THE. The majority in a democracy has no more right to tyrannize over a minority than, under a different system, the latter would have to oppress the former; and . . . if there is a moral principle at stake, the saying that the voice of the people is the voice of God may be quite as untrue, and do quite as much mischief, as the old theory of the divine right of kings. (1887.) *Mem. Ed.* VIII, 91; *Nat. Ed.* VII, 80.

MAJORITY. See also MINORITY; POPULAR RULE; PRIVILEGE.

"MALEFACTORS OF GREAT WEALTH." Too much cannot be said against the men of wealth who sacrifice everything to getting wealth. There is not in the world a more ignoble character than the mere money-getting American, insensible to every duty, regardless of every principle, bent only on amassing a fortune, and putting his fortune only to the basest uses—whether these uses be to speculate in stocks and wreck railroads himself, or to allow his son to lead a life of foolish and expensive idleness and gross debauchery, or to purchase some scoundrel of high social position, foreign or native, for his daughter. Such a man is only the more dangerous if he occasionally does some deed like founding a college or endowing a church, which makes those good people who are also foolish forget his real iniquity. These men are equally careless of the working men, whom they oppress, and of the State, whose existence they imperil. There are not very many of them, but there is a very great number of men who approach more or less closely to the type, and, just in so far as they do so approach, they are curses to the country. (*Forum,* February 1895.) *Mem. Ed.* XV, 10; Nat. Ed. XIII, 9.

"MALEFACTORS OF GREAT WEALTH" AND THE PANIC OF 1907. It may well be that the determination of the government (in which, gentlemen, it will not waver) to punish certain malefactors of great wealth, has been responsible for something of the trouble; at least to the extent of having caused these men to combine to bring about as much financial stress as possible, in order to discredit the policy of the government and thereby secure a reversal of that policy, so that they may enjoy unmolested the fruits of their own evil-doing. . . . I regard this contest as one to determine who shall rule this free country—the people through their governmental agents, or a few ruthless and domineering men whose wealth makes them peculiarly formidable because they hide behind the breastworks of corporate organization. (At Pilgrim Memorial Monument, Provincetown, Mass., August 20, 1907.) *Mem. Ed.* XVIII, 99; *Nat. Ed.* XVI, 84.

"MALEFACTORS OF GREAT WEALTH." *See also* CORPORATIONS; FORTUNES; MONOPOLIES; TRUSTS; WALL STREET; WEALTH.

MANHOOD—QUALITIES OF. We need . . . the iron qualities that must go with true manhood. We need the positive virtues of resolution, of courage, of indomitable will, of power to do without shrinking the rough work that must always be done, and to persevere through the long days of slow progress or of seeming failure which always come before the final triumph, no matter how brilliant. But we need more than these qualities. This country cannot afford to have its sons less than men; but neither can it afford to have them other than good men. (At Colorado Springs, Col., August 2, 1901.) *Mem. Ed.* XV, 326; *Nat. Ed.* XIII, 457.

MANIFEST DESTINY. The general feeling in the West . . . crystallized into what became known as the "Manifest Destiny" idea, which reduced to its simplest terms, was: that it was our manifest destiny to swallow up the land of all adjoining nations who were too weak to withstand us; a theory that forthwith obtained immense popularity among all statesmen of easy international morality. . . . The hearty Western support given to the movement was due to entirely different causes, the chief among them being the fact that the Westerners honestly believed themselves to be indeed created the heirs of the earth, or at least of so much of it as was known by the name of North America, and were prepared to struggle stoutly for the immediate possession of their heritage. (1887.) *Mem. Ed.* VIII, 31-32; *Nat. Ed.* VII, 27-28.

MANIFEST DESTINY. *See also* EXPANSION; WESTWARD MOVEMENT.

MANLINESS. The ideal citizen of a free state must have in him the stuff which in time of need will enable him to show himself a first-class fighting man who scorns either to endure or to inflict wrong. American society is sound at core and this means that at the bottom we, as a people, accept as the basis of sound morality not slothful ease and soft selfishness and the loud timidity that fears every species of risk and hardship, but the virile strength of manliness which clings to the ideal of stern, unflinching performance of duty, and which follows whithersoever that ideal may lead. (*New York Times,* November 8, 1914.) *Mem. Ed.* XX, 99; *Nat. Ed.* XVIII, 86.

MANLINESS. *See also* CHARACTER; FIGHTING VIRTUES; SERVILITY.

MANLY VIRTUES, THE. Every citizen should be taught, both in public and in private life, that while he must avoid brawling and quarrelling, it is his duty to stand up for his rights. He must realize that the only man who is more contemptible than the blusterer and bully is the coward. No man is worth much to the commonwealth if he is not capable of feeling righteous wrath and just indignation, if he is not stirred to hot anger by misdoing, and is not impelled to see justice meted out to the wrong-doers. No man is worth much anywhere if he does not possess both moral and physical courage. (*Forum,* July 1894.) *Mem. Ed.* XV, 46; *Nat. Ed.* XIII, 32.

MANLY VIRTUES. *See also* COURAGE; COWARDICE; FIGHTING QUALITIES; ROMAN EMPIRE; WEAKNESS.

MANUAL TRAINING. *See* EDUCATION, INDUSTRIAL.

MARINA—SINKING OF THE. *See* GERMANY.

MARKSMANSHIP. The officers and enlisted men on board the ships must in their turn, by the exercise of unflagging and intelligent zeal, keep themselves fit to get the best use out of the weapons of war intrusted to their care. The instrument is always important, but the man who uses it is more important still. We must constantly endeavor to perfect our navy in all its duties in time of peace, and above all in manoeuvring in a seaway and in marksmanship with the great guns. In battle the only shots that count are those that hit, and marksmanship is a matter of long practice and of intelligent reasoning. (At Haverhill, Mass., August 26, 1902.) *Presidential Addresses and State Papers* I, 121.

MARKSMANSHIP. *See also* NAVY—EFFICIENCY OF.

MARRIAGE. [I] believe that the greatest privilege and greatest duty for any man is to be happily married, and that no other form of success or service, for either man or woman, can be wisely accepted as a substitute or alternative. (1913.) *Mem. Ed.* XXII, 67; *Nat. Ed.* XX, 58.

———————. I think the highest life, the ideal life, is the married life. But there are both unmarried men and unmarried women who perform service of the utmost consequence to the whole people; and it is equally foolish and wicked for a man to slur the unmarried woman when he would not dream of slurring the unmarried man. Bishop Brent, in the Philippines, is unmarried. He has done admirable work there, just as Jane Addams has done at Hull House. When the *Times* says that it dislikes to see Miss Addams "Held up in the limelight as an example for all other women to follow" it speaks offensively, and its words are true only in the sense that they would be true if it had used them about Bishop Brent or the late Phillips Brooks. Again and again I have heard Bishop Brent held up as an example, and I have held him up as an example myself; and so of the late Phillips Brooks. And in just the same way, I am heartily glad to say, I have heard Jane Addams held up as an example and have thus held her up myself. The cases of the three stand on the same plane; all three by their lives have added to, and are adding to, our heritage of good in this country; and it is an absurdity to say that in recognizing this fact as regards one of them we are in any shape or way explicitly or implicitly failing to take the position that we ought, as a matter of course, to take about marriage and the happy married life. *Mr. Roosevelt's Speech on Suffrage, delivered at St. Johnsbury, Vt., August 30, 1912,* p. 2.

———————. When the ordinary decent man does not understand that to marry the woman he loves, as early as he can, is the most desirable of all goals, the most successful of all forms of life entitled to be called really successful; when the ordinary woman does not understand that all other forms of life are but makeshift and starveling substitutes for the life of the happy wife, the mother of a fair-sized family of healthy children; then the state is rotten at heart. (1916.) *Mem. Ed.* IV, 77; *Nat. Ed.* III, 250.

MARRIAGE—FEDERAL CONTROL OF. As to there being a cessation of the movement for Federal control of marriage, including divorce and polygamy, so far as I know there never was such cessation; personally I have always favored such control. There was a strong agitation to give the national Government complete control over marriage and divorce. This was strongly opposed by a majority of the Representatives in the two Houses of Congress from the different States, and in but two or three instances is it possible that those opposing it, whether Democrats or Republicans, could have been influenced by any thought whatever concerning the Mormons. Personally I then favored the proposal, and have always favored it since, because I believed and still believe that this is one of several directions in which the power of the general government could with advantage be increased. (To Isaac Russell, February 17, 1911.) *Collier's,* April 15, 1911, p. 28.

MARRIAGE—JOYS OF. The only full life for man or woman is led by those men and women who together, with hearts both gentle and valiant, face lives of love and duty, who see their children rise up to call them blessed and who leave behind them their seed to inherit the earth. Dealing with averages, it is the bare truth to say that no celibate life approaches such a life in point of usefulness, no matter what the motive for the celibacy—religious, philanthropic, political, or professional. The mother comes ahead of the nun—and also of the settlement or hospital worker; and if either man or woman must treat a profession as a substitute for, instead of as an addition to or basis for, marriage, then by all means the profession or other "career" should be abandoned. (1916.) *Mem. Ed.* IV, 78; *Nat. Ed.* III, 250.

MARRIAGE AND CHILDREN. In a small group there may be good and sufficient explanations why the individual men and women have remained unmarried; and the fact that those that marry have no children, or only one or two children, may be cause only for sincere and respectful sympathy. But if, in a community of a thousand men and a thousand women, a large proportion of them remain unmarried, and if of the marriages so many are sterile, or with only one or two children, that the population is decreasing, then there is something radically wrong with the people of that community as a whole. The trouble may be partly physical, partly due to the strange troubles which accompany an overstrained intensity of life. But even in this case the root trouble is probably moral; and in all probability the whole trouble is moral, and is due to a complex tissue of causation in which coldness, love of ease, striving after social position, fear of pain, dislike of hard work, and sheer inability to get life values in their proper perspective all play a part. (*Metropolitan,* October 1917.) *Mem. Ed.* XXI, 166; *Nat. Ed.* XIX, 160.

MARRIAGE AS A PARTNERSHIP. The one way to honor this indispensable woman, the wife and mother, is to insist that she be treated as the full equal of her husband. The birth-pangs make all men the debtors of all women; and the man is a wretched creature who does not live up to this obligation. Marriage should be a real partnership, a partnership of the soul, the spirit, and the mind, no less than of the body. An immediately practical feature of this partnership should be the full acknowledgment that the woman who keeps the home has exactly the same right to a say in the disposal of the money as the man who earns the money. Earning the money is not one whit more indispensable than keeping the home. Indeed, I am inclined to put it in the second place. The husband who does not give his wife, as a matter of right, her share in the disposal of the common funds is false to his duty. It is not a question of favor at all. Aside from the money to be spent on common account, for the household and the children, the wife has just the same right as the husband to her pin-money, her spending-money. It is not his money that he gives to her as a gift. It is hers as a matter of right. He may earn it; but he earns it because she keeps the house; and she has just as much right to it as he has. This is not a hostile right; it is a right which it is every woman's duty to ask and which it should be every man's pride and pleasure to give without asking. He is a poor creature if he grudges it; and she in her turn is a poor creature is she does not insist upon her rights, just exactly as she is worse than a poor creature if she does not do her duty. (*Metropolitan,* May 1916.) *Mem. Ed.* XXI, 147; *Nat. Ed.* XIX, 144.

MARRIAGE. *See also* BIRTH CONTROL; CHILDREN; DIVORCE; FAMILY; HAPPINESS; HOME; HUSBANDS; LOVE; MORMONS; MOTHER; SEX INSTINCT; WOMEN.

MARSHALL, JOHN. The three men to whom throughout our national history we as a people owe most are two Presidents, Washington and Lincoln, and one chief justice, Marshall. Marshall is the one man whose services to the nation entitle him to be grouped with the two great Presidents, and he owes this to the fortunate fact that not only did he as a man deserve to rank with them as men, but that his office as an office deserved to rank, and did rank, with the great offices which they held. (*Outlook,* March 4, 1911.) *Mem. Ed.* XIX, 116; *Nat. Ed.* XVII, 80.

———————. John Marshall is one of the six or eight foremost figures of American statesmanship. He stands among the men who actually did the constructive work of building a coherent national fabric out of the loose jumble of exhausted and squabbling little commonwealths left on the Atlantic coast by the ebb of the Revolutionary War. This was an incredibly difficult work, because it had to be forced on a suspicious, short-sighted, and reluctant people by a small number of really great leaders. (*Outlook,* July 18, 1917.) *Mem. Ed.* XII, 427; *Nat. Ed.* XI, 189.

———————. Marshall himself was in the best sense of the term a self-made man. As a very young man he served in the Continental army under Washington, honorably but without special distinction. He earned his living as a hard-working Virginia lawyer. . . .

Marshall was an entirely democratic man in every sense of the word which makes it a word of praise. He had not a particle of arrogance in dealing with others; was simple, straightforward, and unaffected, being at ease in the courtroom or in any public gathering, with any neighbor of no matter what social standing. There was about him none of that starched self-consciousness which men who are more anxious to seem great than to be great are so apt to mistake for dignity. (*Outlook,* July 18, 1917.) *Mem. Ed.* XII, 428-429; *Nat. Ed.* XI, 190-191.

MARSHALL'S CONTRIBUTION. It was the appointment of Marshall and the exercise by that great man of his extraordinary personal influence which gave the Supreme Court its great power in our government, and which thereby also gave an enormous impetus to the growth among us of that spirit which made and kept us a nation, a great, free, united people, instead of permitting us to dissolve into a snarl of jangling and contemptible little independent commonwealths, with governments oscillating between the rule of a dictator, the rule of an oligarchy, and the rule of a mob. Those who on abstract grounds insist that the courts never have anything to do with the embodiment of public policy into law ought to pay heed to the simple fact that, under Marshall, the Supreme Court of the United States worked a tremendous revolution, not merely in ordinary law, but in the fundamental constitutional law of the land. . . . Marshall, in his first constitutional opinion, in an argument which, as Chancellor Kent said, approached to the precision and certainty of a mathematical demonstration, held that the Supreme Court possessed in itself the ultimate power to declare whether or not an Act of Congress was void. Nowadays the authority of the court to decide that an Act of the Legislative Department, whether of the nation or of any of the States, is repugnant to the Constitution seems self-evident. But no such power was expressly prescribed in the Constitution, and not only Jefferson but Jackson, with an emphasis amounting to violence, denounced Marshall's position and asserted that no such power existed. The reason why Marshall was so great a chief justice, the reason why he was a public servant whose services were of such incalculable value to our people, is to be found in the very fact that he thus read into the Constitution what was necessary in order to make the Constitution march. (*Outlook*, March 4, 1911.) *Mem. Ed.* XIX, 124; *Nat. Ed.* XVII, 85.

MARSHALL, JOHN. *See also* SUPREME COURT.

MARTINIQUE—DESCRIPTION OF. We of the North dwell in a rather drab world, and on a holiday it is well to see such sights as those of Martinique: the gay dresses and good looks of the working women, the only less picturesque quality of their mates, the quaint, many-hued houses, the beauty of the landscape outside the city, and within the city the great park or savanna with its rows of noble trees, the taverns with their tables outside under the colonnades, the little shops, and all the queer mixture of what is French with what is utterly exotic. The market was a really bewildering place, because of the color—always the color—and the strangeness, not only of the buyers and the sellers, but of many of the wares bought and sold. (1917.) *Mem. Ed.* IV, 291; *Nat. Ed.* III, 431.

MATERIALISM, SCIENTIFIC. No grotesque repulsiveness of mediæval superstition, even as it survived into nineteenth-century Spain and Naples, could be much more intolerant, much more destructive of all that is fine in morality, in the spiritual sense, and indeed in civilization itself, than that hard dogmatic materialism of to-day which often not merely calls itself scientific but arrogates to itself the sole right to use the term. If these pretensions affected only scientific men themselves, it would be a matter of small moment, but unfortunately they tend gradually to affect the whole people, and to establish a very dangerous standard of private and public conduct in the public mind. (*Outlook*, December 2, 1911.) *Mem. Ed.* XIV, 418; *Nat. Ed.* XII, 113.

————————. At present we are in greater danger of suffering in things spiritual from a wrong-headed scientific materialism than from religious bigotry and intolerance; just as at present we are threatened rather by what is vicious among the ideas that triumphed in the Revolution than we are from what is vicious in the ideas that it overthrew. But this is merely because victorious evil necessarily contains more menace than defeated evil; and it will not do to forget the other side, nor to let our protest against the evil of the present drive us into championship of the evil of the past. (*Outlook*, December 2, 1911.) *Mem. Ed.* XIV, 421; *Nat. Ed.* XII, 116.

MATERIALIST. [There are men] who measure everything by the shop-till, the people who are unable to appreciate any quality that is not a mercantile commodity, who do not understand that a poet may do far more for a country than the owner of a nail factory, who do not realize that no amount of commercial prosperity can supply the lack of the heroic virtues, or can in itself solve the terrible social problems which all the civilized world is now facing. The mere materialist is above all things, short-sighted. . . . To men of a certain kind, trade and property are far more sacred than life or honor, of far more consequence than the great thoughts and lofty emotions, which alone make a nation mighty. They believe, with a faith almost touching in its utter feebleness, that "the Angel of Peace, draped in a garment of untaxed calico," has given her final message to men when she has implored them to devote all their energies to producing oleomargarine at a quarter of a cent less a firkin, or to importing woollens for a fraction less than they can be made at home. These solemn prattlers strive after an ideal in which they shall happily unite the imagination of a green-grocer with the heart of a Bengalee baboo. They are utterly incapable of feeling one thrill of generous emotion, or the slightest throb of that pulse which gives to the world statesmen, patriots, warriors, and poets, and which makes a nation other than a cumberer of the world's surface. (*Forum*, February 1895.) *Mem. Ed.* XV, 11, 12; *Nat. Ed.* XIII, 10.

MATERIALIST—STANDARDS OF THE. There are not a few men of means who have made the till their fatherland, and who are always ready to balance a temporary interruption of money-making, or a temporary financial and commercial disaster, against the self-sacrifice necessary in upholding the honor of the nation and the glory of the flag. (Address as Assistant Secretary of the Navy, Naval War College, June 1897.) *Mem. Ed.* XV, 247; *Nat. Ed.* XIII, 188.

——————. [I do not wish] to be judged by . . . the standards of that particular kind of money-maker whose soul has grown hard while his body has grown soft; that is, who is morally ruthless to others and physically timid about himself. (To Sir Edward Grey, November 15, 1912.) *Mem. Ed.* XXIV, 402; Bishop II, 342.

MATERIALIST. See also FORTUNES; MILLIONAIRES; MONEY; PROFITS; PROSPERITY; WEALTH.

MAYOR — ROOSEVELT'S CANDIDACY FOR. See ROOSEVELT.

MEADOW-LARK. The meadow-lark is a singer of a higher order, deserving to rank with the best. Its song has length, variety, power and rich melody; and there is in it sometimes a cadence of wild sadness, inexpressibly touching. Yet I cannot say that either song would appeal to others as it appeals to me; for to me it comes forever laden with a hundred memories and associations; with the sight of dim hills reddening in the dawn, with the breath of cool morning winds blowing across lonely plains, with the scent of flowers on the sunlit prairie, with the motion of fiery horses, with all the strong thrill of eager and buoyant life. (1893.) *Mem. Ed.* II, 60; *Nat. Ed.* II, 52-53.

MEDIATION. See COLLECTIVE BARGAINING; INDUSTRIAL ARBITRATION; STRIKES.

MEDICINE. See DOCTORS; TUBERCULOSIS.

MELTING POT. See AMERICAN PEOPLE; IMMIGRATION.

MEMORIAL DAY. On this day, the 30th of May, we call to mind the deaths of those who died that the nation might live, who wagered all that life holds dear for the great prize of death in battle, who poured out their blood like water in order that the mighty national structure raised by the far-seeing genius of Washington, Franklin, Marshall, Hamilton, and the other great leaders of the Revolution, great framers of the Constitution, should not crumble into meaningless ruins. (At Arlington, Va., May 30, 1902.) *Presidential Addresses and State Papers* I, 57.

——————. This is Memorial Day. You have to-day decorated the graves of gallant men who paid by their death for the lack of wisdom and foresight shown by their forefathers. This is the day of homage to heroism. But it is also a day of mourning. For forty years prior to the Civil War our people refused to face facts and soberly bend their energies to make war impossible. Heroes shed their blood, and women walked all their lives in the shadow, because there had been such lack of foresight, such slothful, lazy optimism. (At Kansas City, Mo., May 30, 1916.) *The Progressive Party; Its Record from January to July.* (Progressive National Committee, 1916), p. 69.

MEMORIALS. See MONUMENTS; WHITE HOUSE.

MENTAL ACUTENESS. The kind of mental acuteness that is shown merely by a thorough study of the best methods of escaping successful criminal procedure is not the kind of mental acuteness that you value in your friend, in the man with whom you have business relations; and it should be the last type of mental ability, the last type of moral attitude, which you tolerate in a public man. (At Pacific Theological Seminary, Spring 1911.) *Mem. Ed.* XV, 621; *Nat. Ed.* XIII, 655.

MENTAL ACUTENESS. See also CHARACTER; HONESTY; INTELLIGENCE; MORAL SENSE.

MERCANTILISM. See COLONIAL SYSTEM.

MERCHANT MARINE. It is discreditable to us as a nation that our merchant marine should be utterly insignificant in comparison to that of other nations which we overtop in other forms of business. We should not longer submit to conditions under which only a trifling portion of our great commerce is carried in our own ships. To remedy this state of things would not merely serve to build up our shipping interests, but it would also result in benefit to all who are interested in the permanent establishment of a wider market for American products, and would provide an auxiliary force for the navy. Ships work for their own countries just as railroads work for their terminal points. Shipping lines, if established to the principal countries with which we have dealings, would be of political as well as commercial benefit. From every standpoint it is unwise for the United States to continue to rely upon the ships of competing nations for the distribution of our goods. It should be made advantageous to carry American goods in American-built ships. (First Annual Message, Washington, December 3, 1901.) *Mem. Ed.* XVII, 114; *Nat. Ed.* XV, 98-99.

———. To the spread of our trade in peace and the defense of our flag in war a great and prosperous merchant marine is indispensable. We should have ships of our own and seamen of our own to convey our goods to neutral markets, and in case of need to reinforce our battle-line. It cannot but be a source of regret and uneasiness to us that the lines of communication with our sister republics of South America should be chiefly under foreign control. It is not a good thing that American merchants and manufacturers should have to send their goods and letters to South America via Europe if they wish security and despatch. Even on the Pacific, where our ships have held their own better than on the Atlantic, our merchant flag is now threatened through the liberal aid bestowed by other governments on their own steamlines. (Fifth Annual Message, Washington, December 5, 1905.) *Mem. Ed.* XVII, 370; *Nat. Ed.* XV, 316.

MERCY. *See* JUSTICE; LYNCHING.

MERIT SYSTEM. I think it is mere idle chatter to talk of the merit system as being undemocratic and un-American. The spoils system is emphatically undemocratic, for the spoils system means the establishing and perpetuation of a grasping and ignorant oligarchy. The merit system is essentially democratic and essentially American, and in line with the utterances and deeds of our forefathers of the days of Washington and Madison. (Before Civil Service Reform Association, Baltimore, February 23, 1889.) *Mem. Ed.* XVI, 146; *Nat. Ed.* XIV, 89.

———. The merit system is the system of fair play, of common sense, and of common honesty; and therefore it is essentially American and essentially democratic. (*Century,* February 1890.) *Mem. Ed.* XVI, 174; *Nat. Ed.* XIV, 112.

———. The upholders of the merit system . . . maintain that offices should be held for the benefit of the whole public, and not for the benefit of that particular section of the public which enters into politics as a lucrative, though rather dirty, game; they believe that the multitude of small government positions, of which the duties are wholly unconnected with political questions, should be filled by candidates selected, not for political reasons, but solely with reference to their special fitness for the duty they seek to perform; and, furthermore, they believe that the truly American and democratic way of filling these offices is by an open and manly rivalry, into which every American citizen has a right to enter, without any more regard being paid to his political than to his religious creed, and without being required to render degrading service to any party boss, or do aught save show by common-sense practical tests that he is the man best fitted to perform the particular service needed. (*Century,* February 1890.) *Mem. Ed.* XVI, 158-159; *Nat. Ed.* XIV, 99-100.

———. The merit system of making appointments is in its essence as democratic and American as the common-school system itself. It simply means that in clerical and other positions where the duties are entirely non-political, all applicants should have a fair field and no favor, each standing on his merits as he is able to show them by practical test. . . .

Whenever the conditions have permitted the application of the merit system in its fullest and widest sense, the gain to the government has been immense. The navy-yards and postal service illustrate, probably better than any other branches of the government, the great gain in economy, efficiency, and honesty due to the enforcement of this principle. (First Annual Message, Washington, December 3, 1901.) *Mem. Ed.* XVII, 148; *Nat. Ed.* XV, 127-128.

MERIT SYSTEM. *See also* APPOINTMENTS; CIVIL SERVICE; PATRONAGE; SPOILS SYSTEM.

METHODIST CHURCH. Since the days of the Revolution not only has the Methodist Church increased greatly in the old communities of the thirteen original States, but it has played a peculiar and prominent part in the pioneer growth of our country, and has in consequence assumed a position of immense importance throughout the vast region west of the Alleghanies which has been added to our Nation since the days when the Continental Congress first met. . . .

In the hard and cruel life of the border, with its grim struggle against the forbidding forces of wild nature and wilder men, there was much to pull the frontiersman down. If left to himself, without moral teaching and moral guidance, without any of the influences that tend toward the uplifting of man and the subduing of the brute within him, sad would have been his, and therefore our, fate. From this fate we have been largely rescued by the fact that together with the rest of the pioneers went the

[333]

pioneer preachers; and all honor be given to the Methodists for the great proportion of these pioneer preachers whom they furnished. (At bi-centennial celebration of birth of John Wesley, New York City, February 26, 1903.) *Presidential Addresses and State Papers* I, 243-244.

METHODIST MISSION IN ROME. [Their] work was not only good in itself, but it was good from the standpoint of those who wish well to the Catholic Church, as I do, for it tended to introduce a spirit of rivalry in service, for rivalry in good conduct, which in the long run is as advantageous to the church as to the people, but which of course is peculiarly abhorrent to the narrow and intolerant priestly reactionaries, who, whenever and wherever they have the upper hand in the church, make it the baleful enemy of mankind. There was, however, one Methodist in town, taking charge of a congregation, who was of an utterly different type. I have no doubt that he had a certain amount of sincerity, and a great deal of energy, and there were places where I suppose he could have done good. But he was a crude, vulgar, tactless creature, cursed with the thirst of self-advertisement, and utterly unable to distinguish between notoriety and fame. He found that he could attract attention best by frantic denunciations of the Pope, and so he preached sermons in which he pleasantly alluded to the Pope as "the whore of Babylon," and even indulged in attacks on the other Protestant bodies in Rome, denouncing the Episcopalian and Presbyterian churches, and assailing the Young Men's Christian Association because it was under the Waldensian leadership. (To Sir George Otto Trevelyan, October 1, 1911.) *Mem. Ed.* XXIV, 227; Bishop II, 195.

MEXICAN FACTIONS — SUPPORT TO. There was no reason whatever for any American to uphold Huerta; but to antagonize him on moral grounds, and then to endeavor to replace him by a polygamous bandit, was not compatible with any intelligent system of international ethics. Nor did any betterment follow from dropping this bandit, and putting the power of the United States Government behind another bandit. It may be entirely proper to take the view that we have no concern with the morality of any chief who is for the time being the ruler of Mexico. But to do as President Wilson has done and actively take sides against Huerta and for Villa, condemning the former for misdeeds, and ignoring the far worse misdeeds of the latter, and then to abandon Villa and support against him Carranza, who was responsible for exactly the same kind of hideous outrages against Americans, and insults to the American flag, is an affront to all who believe in straightforward sincerity in American public life. (*Metropolitan,* March 1915.) *Mem. Ed.* XX, 422; *Nat. Ed.* XVIII, 362.

MEXICAN HOSTILITY TOWARD UNITED STATES. There is no government in the world for which the Mexican people now feel the profound contempt that they feel for the United States Government; and we owe this contempt to the way in which our governmental authorities have behaved during the last five years, but especially during the last three years. Well-meaning people praise President Wilson for having preserved "peace" with Mexico, and avoided the "hostility" of Mexico. As a matter of fact his action has steadily increased Mexican hostility, has not prevented the futile and infamous little "war" in which we first took and then abandoned Vera Cruz, and has been responsible for death, outrage, and suffering which have befallen hundreds of Americans and hundreds of thousands of Mexicans during the carnival of crime and bloodshed with which this "peace" has prevented interference. (*Metropolitan,* March 1915.) *Mem. Ed.* XX, 421; *Nat. Ed.* XVIII, 361.

MEXICAN RELATIONS—ROOSEVELT'S STAND ON. To avoid the chance of anything but wilful misrepresentation, let me emphasize my position. I hold that it was not our affair to interfere one way or the other in the purely internal affairs of Mexico, so far as they affected only Mexican citizens; because if the time came when such interference was absolutely required it could only be justified if it were thoroughgoing and effective. Moreover, I hold that it was our clear duty to have interfered promptly and effectively on behalf of American citizens who were wronged, instead of behaving as President Wilson and Secretary Bryan actually did behave. To our disgrace as a nation, they forced American citizens to claim and accept from British and German officials and officers the protection which our own government failed to give. When we did interfere in Mexican internal affairs to aid one faction, we thereby made ourselves responsible for the deeds of that faction, and we have no right to try to shirk that responsibility. Messrs. Wilson and Bryan declined to interfere to protect the rights of Americans or of other foreigners in Mexico. But they interfered as between the Mexicans themselves in the interest of one faction and with the result of placing that faction in power. They therefore bound themselves to accept responsibility for the deeds and misdeeds of that faction, and of the further factions into which it then split, in so far as Mr. Wilson sided with one of these as against the other. (New York *Times,* December 6, 1914.) *Mem. Ed.* XX, 397; *Nat. Ed.* XVIII, 341.

MEXICAN WAR. *See* TEXAS; WARS.

MEXICO—AMERICAN DUTY IN. A prime duty, of course, is to secure livable conditions in Mexico. To permit such conditions as have obtained in Mexico for the past five years is to put a premium upon European interference; for where we shirk our duty to ourselves, to honest and law-abiding Mexicans, and to all European foreigners within Mexico, we cannot expect permanently to escape the consequences. (*Metropolitan,* February 1916.) *Mem. Ed.* XX, 280; *Nat. Ed.* XVIII, 241.

MEXICO—WILSON'S POLICY IN. We are told we have kept the peace in Mexico. As a matter of fact we have twice been at war in Mexico within the last two years. Our failure to prepare, our failure to take action of a proper sort on the Mexican border has not averted bloodshed; it has invited bloodshed. It has cost the loss of more lives than were lost in the Spanish War. Our Mexican failure is merely the natural fruit of the policies of pacificism and anti-preparedness. (1916.) *Mem. Ed.* XX, 225; *Nat. Ed.* XVIII, 193.

——————————. His conduct rendered the United States an object of international derision because of the way in which its affairs were managed. President Wilson made no declaration of war. He did not in any way satisfy the requirements of common international law before acting. He invaded a neighboring state, with which he himself insisted we were entirely at peace, and occupied the most considerable seaport of the country after military operations which resulted in the loss of the lives of perhaps twenty of our men and five or ten times that number of Mexicans; and then he sat supine, and refused to allow either the United States or Mexico to reap any benefit from what had been done. It is idle to say that such an amazing action was not war. It was an utterly futile war and achieved nothing; but it was war. We had ample justification for interfering in Mexico and even for going to war with Mexico, if after careful consideration this course was deemed necessary. But the President did not even take notice of any of the atrocious wrongs Americans had suffered, or deal with any of the grave provocations we had received. His statement of justification was merely that "we are in Mexico to serve mankind, if we can find a way." Evidently he did not have in his mind any particular idea of how he was to "serve mankind," for, after staying eight months in Mexico, he decided that he could not "find a way" and brought his army home. He had not accomplished one single thing. In all our history there has been no more extraordinary example of queer infirmity of purpose in an important crisis than was shown by President Wilson in this matter. His business was either not to interfere at all or to interfere hard and effectively. This was the sole policy which should have been allowed by regard for the dignity and honor of the government of the United States and the welfare of our people. In the actual event President Wilson interfered, not enough to quell civil war, not enough to put a stop to or punish the outrages on American citizens, but enough to incur fearful responsibilities. Then, having without authority of any kind, either under the Constitution or in international law or in any other way, thus interfered, and having interfered to worse than no purpose, and having made himself and the nation partly responsible for the atrocious wrongs committed on Americans and on foreigners generally in Mexico by the bandit chiefs whom he was more or less furtively supporting, President Wilson abandoned his whole policy and drew out of Mexico to resume his "watchful waiting." (*Everybody's,* January 1915.) *Mem. Ed.* XX, 144-146; *Nat. Ed.* XVIII, 124-125.

MEXICO. *See also* VILLA, PANCHO; WATCHFUL WAITING; WILSON, WOODROW.

MEYER, GEORGE VON L. I trust it is not necessary for me to say what a keen satisfaction and comfort I have taken out of your being Postmaster General. You are one of the Cabinet Ministers upon whom I lean. You always spare me trouble, you never make a mistake, and you are a constant source of strength to the administration. (To Meyer, summer 1907.) M. A. De Wolfe Howe, *George von Lengerke Meyer.* (Dodd, Mead & Co., N. Y., 1919), p. 363.

MEYER, GEORGE VON L. *See also* AMBASSADORS.

MIDDLE CLASS, THE. In most countries the Bourgeoisie—the moral, respectable, commercial, middle class—are looked upon with a certain contempt which is justified by their timidity and unwarlikeness. But the minute a middle class produces men like Hawkins and Frobisher on the seas, or men such as the average Union soldier in the Civil War, it acquires the hearty respect of others which it merits. (To Edward S. Martin, November 26, 1900.) *Mem. Ed.* XXIII, 6; Bishop I, 4.

MIDDLE CLASS IN POLITICS. This class is composed of the great bulk of the men who range from well-to-do up to very rich; and of these the former generally and the latter almost universally neglect their political duties, for the most part rather pluming themselves upon their good conduct if they so much as vote on election day. This largely comes from the tremendous wear and tension of life in our great cities. Moreover, the men of small means with us are usually men of domestic habits; and this very devotion to home, which is one of their chief virtues, leads them to neglect their public duties. They work hard, as clerks, mechanics, small tradesmen, etc., all day long, and when they get home in the evening they dislike to go out. If they do go to a ward meeting, they find themselves isolated, and strangers both to the men whom they meet and to the matter on which they have to act; for in the city a man is quite as sure to know next to nothing about his neighbors as in the country he is to be intimately acquainted with them. In the country the people of a neighborhood, when they assemble in one of their local conventions, are already well acquainted, and therefore able to act together with effect; whereas in the city, even if the ordinary citizens do come out, they are totally unacquainted with one another, and are as helplessly unable to oppose the disciplined ranks of the professional politicians as is the case with a mob of freshmen in one of our colleges when in danger of being hazed by the sophomores. (*Century,* November 1886.) *Mem. Ed.* XV, 119; *Nat. Ed.* XIII, 80.

MIDDLE CLASS. See also BOURGEOISIE; FORTUNES; MATERIALIST; MONEY; WEALTH.

MIGHT. See FORCE; RIGHT.

MILITARISM. Militarism is a real factor for good or for evil in most European countries. In America it has not the smallest effect one way or the other; it is a negligible quantity. There are undoubtedly states of society where militarism is a grave evil, and there are plenty of circumstances in which the prime duty of man may be to strive against it. But it is not righteous war, not even war itself, which is the absolute evil, the evil which is evil always and under all circumstances. Militarism which takes the form of a police force, municipal or national, may be the prime factor for upholding peace and righteousness. Militarism is to be condemned or not purely according to the conditions. (*Outlook,* May 15, 1909.) *Mem. Ed.* XIV, 414; *Nat. Ed.* XII, 321.

———. There are nations who only need to have peaceful ideals inculcated, and to whom militarism is a curse and a misfortune. There are other nations, like our own, so happily situated that the thought of war is never present to their minds. They are wholly free from any tendency improperly to exalt or to practice militarism. These nations should never forget that there must be military ideals no less than peaceful ideals. (1913.) *Mem. Ed.* XXII, 269; *Nat. Ed.* XX, 230.

MILITARISM, EUROPEAN. It is of course worth while for sociologists to discuss the effect of this European militarism on "social values," but only if they first clearly realize and formulate the fact that if the European militarism had not been able to defend itself against and to overcome the militarism of Asia and Africa, there would have been no "social values" of any kind in our world to-day, and no sociologists to discuss them. (American Sociological Society, *Papers,* 1915.) *Mem. Ed.* XX, 273; *Nat. Ed.* XVIII, 235.

MILITARISM AND PREPAREDNESS. As yet, as events have most painfully shown, there is nothing to be expected by any nation in a great crisis from anything except its own strength. Under these circumstances it is criminal in the United States not to prepare. Critics have stated that in advocating universal military service on the Swiss plan in this country, I am advocating militarism. I am not concerned with mere questions of terminology. The plan I advocate would be a corrective of every evil which we associate with the name of militarism. It would tend for order and self-respect among our people. Not the smallest evil among the many evils that exist in America is due to militarism. Save in the crisis of the Civil War there has been no militarism in the United States and the only militarist President we have ever had was Abraham Lincoln. (New York *Times,* November 29, 1914.) *Mem. Ed.* XX, 203; *Nat. Ed.* XVIII, 174.

MILITARISM AND THE WORLD WAR. We nations who are outside ought to recognize both the reality of this fear felt by each nation for others, together with the real justification for its existence. Yet we cannot sympathize with that fear-born anger which would vent itself in the annihilation of the conquered. The right attitude is to limit militarism, to destroy the menace of militarism, but to preserve the national integrity of each nation. (New York *Times,* October 11, 1914.) *Mem. Ed.* XX, 57; *Nat. Ed.* XVIII, 48.

MILITARISM. See also ARMAMENTS; DISARMAMENT; MILITARY SERVICE; PACIFISM; PREPAREDNESS; WAR.

MILITARY ACADEMY. See WEST POINT.

MILITARY ADVICE—VARIETY OF. It is unnecessary for me to say that military men differ among themselves in wisdom and farsightedness, precisely as civilians do. The civilian heads of a government, when faced by a great military crisis, have to show their own wisdom primarily in sifting out the very wise military advice from the very unwise military advice which they will receive. This is especially true in a service where promotion is chiefly by seniority and where a large number of the men who rise high owe more to the possession of a sound stomach than to the possession of the highest qualities of head and heart. The military advice which you have received in this matter is strikingly unwise. I do not know whether those giving it openly advocated the principle of universal obligatory military training two and a half years ago—not within the last few months when people everywhere have been waking up to the matter—but two and a half years ago. If they did not, then they themselves are partly responsible for the condition of unpreparedness which renders it expedient from every standpoint that we should utilize every military asset in the country. (To Secretary Newton D. Baker, April 22, 1917.) *Mem. Ed.* XXI, 213; *Nat. Ed.* XIX, 201.

MILITARY EXPENDITURES. It is treachery to the Republic for statesmen—and for professional officers—to propose and to acquiesce in unsound half-measures which necessitate large continuing expenditures, but which do not provide for adequate national defense. (*Metropolitan,* February 1916.) *Mem. Ed.* XX, 296; *Nat. Ed.* XVIII, 254.

MILITARY EXPENDITURES — WASTE OF. At present the United States does not begin to get adequate return in the way of efficient preparation for defense from the amount of money appropriated every year. Both the Executive and Congress are responsible for this—and of course this means that the permanent and ultimate responsibility rests on the people. It is really less a question of spending more money than of knowing how to get the best results for the money that we do spend. Most emphatically there should be a comprehensive plan both for defense and for expenditure. The best military and naval authorities—not merely the senior officers but the best officers—should be required to produce comprehensive plans for battleships, for submarines, for air-ships, for proper artillery, for a more efficient Regular Army, and for a great popular reserve behind the army. Every useless military post should be forthwith abandoned; and this cannot be done save by getting Congress to accept or reject plans for defense and expenditure in their entirety. If each congressman or senator can put in his special plea for the erection or retention of a military post for non-military reasons, and for the promotion or favoring of some given officer or group of officers also for non-military reasons, we can rest assured that good results can never be obtained. Here, again, what is needed is not plans by outsiders but the insistence by outsiders upon the army and navy officers being required to produce the right plans, being backed up when they do produce the right plans, and being held to a strict accountability for any failure, active or passive, in their duty. (New York *Times,* November 29, 1914.) *Mem. Ed.* XX, 205; *Nat. Ed.* XVIII, 176.

MILITARY FORCES—ADVANCEMENT IN. In the Army and the Navy the chance for a man to show great ability and rise above his fellows does not occur on the average more than once in a generation. When I was down at Santiago it was melancholy for me to see how fossilized and lacking in ambition, and generally useless, were most of the men of my age and over, who had served their lives in the Army. The Navy for the last few years has been better, but for twenty years after the Civil War there was less chance in the Navy than in the Army to practise, and do, work of real consequence. (To Theodore Roosevelt, Jr., Jan. 21, 1904.) *Mem. Ed.* XXI, 516; *Nat. Ed.* XIX, 458.

MILITARY FORCES—EFFICIENCY OF. By the establishment of army and navy manœuvres I have, I think, much increased the efficiency of the army and doubled the efficiency of the navy. (To Sydney Brooks, December 28, 1908.) *Mem. Ed.* XXIV, 153; Bishop II, 131.

MILITARY FORCES—PRAISE OF. No American can overpay the debt of gratitude we all of us owe to the officers and enlisted men of the army and of the navy. (1913.) *Mem. Ed.* XXII, 299; *Nat. Ed.* XX, 255.

MILITARY FORCES — SUPPORT OF.
There is no class of our citizens, big or small, who so emphatically deserve well of the country as the officers and the enlisted men of the army and navy. . . . But they must be heartily backed up, heartily supported, and sedulously trained. They must be treated well, and, above all, they must be treated so as to encourage the best among them by sharply discriminating against the worst. The utmost possible efficiency should be demanded of them. They are emphatically and in every sense of the word men. (New York *Times,* November 22, 1914.) *Mem. Ed.* XX, 130; *Nat. Ed.* XVIII, 112.

MILITARY FORCES. See also ARMY; DESERTION; NAVY.

MILITARY HISTORY. See HISTORY.

MILITARY LEADERS. See DEWEY, ADMIRAL; FREDERICK THE GREAT; GRANT, U. S.; JONES, JOHN PAUL; LEE, R. E.; NAPOLEON; PERSHING, J.; SHERIDAN, P. H.; WAYNE, ANTHONY.

MILITARY POLICY, NATIONAL. We should consider our national military policy as a whole. We must prepare a well-thought-out strategic scheme, planned from the standpoint of our lasting national interests, and steadily pursued by preparation and the study of experts, through a course of years. (*Metropolitan,* February 1916.) *Mem. Ed.* XX, 283; *Nat. Ed.* XVIII, 243.

MILITARY POLICY. See also DEFENSE; DISARMAMENT; NATIONAL DEFENSE; PREPAREDNESS.

MILITARY SERVICE. A man has no more right to escape military service in time of need than he has to escape paying his taxes. We do not beseech a man to "volunteer" to pay his taxes, or scream that it would be "an infringement of his liberty" and "contrary to our traditions" to make him pay them. We simply notify him how much he is to pay, and when, and where. We ought to deal just as summarily with him as regards the even more important matter of personal service to the commonwealth in time of war. He is not fit to live in the State unless when the State's life is at stake he is willing and able to serve it in any way that it can best use his abilities, and, as an incident, to fight for it if the State believes it can best use him in such fashion. Unless he takes this position he is not fit to be a citizen and should be deprived of the vote. Universal service is the practical, democratic method of dealing with this problem. (*Metropolitan,* February 1916.) *Mem. Ed.* XX, 299; *Nat. Ed.* XVIII, 256.

——————. In any small group of men it may happen that, for good and sufficient reasons, it is impossible for any of the members to go to war: two or three may be physically unfit, two or three may be too old or too young, and the remaining two or three may be performing civil duties of such vital consequence to the commonwealth that it would be wrong to send them to the front. In such case no blame attaches to any individual, and high praise may attach to all. But if in a group of a thousand men more than a small minority are unwilling and unfit to go to war in the hour of the nation's need, then there is something radically wrong with them, spiritually or physically, and they stand in need of drastic treatment. (*Metropolitan,* October 1917.) *Mem. Ed.* XXI, 166; *Nat. Ed.* XIX, 160.

MILITARY SERVICE—BENEFITS OF.
Universal military service, wherever tried, has on the whole been a benefit and not a harm to the people of the nation, so long as the demand upon the average man's life has not been for too long a time. . . . The short military training given has been found to increase in marked fashion the social and industrial efficiency, the ability to do good industrial work, of the man thus trained. It would be well for the United States from every standpoint immediately to provide such strictly limited universal military training. (*Everybody's,* January 1915.) *Mem. Ed.* XX, 150; *Nat. Ed.* XVIII, 129.

——————. The efficiency of the average man in civil life would be thereby greatly increased. He would be trained to realize that he is a partner in this giant democracy, and has duties to the other partners. He would first learn how to obey and then how to command. He would acquire habits of order, of cleanliness, of self-control, of self-restraint, of respect for himself and for others. The whole system would be planned with especial regard to the conditions and needs of the farmer and the working man. The average citizen would become more efficient in his work and a better man in his relations to his neighbors. We would secure far greater social solidarity and mutual understanding and genuine efficiency among our citizens in time of peace. . . .

Universal service would be in every way beneficial to the State and would be quite as beneficial from the standpoint of those who consider the interest of the State in time of peace as from the standpoint of those who are interested in the welfare of the State in time of war. The normal tests of military efficiency are the very tests which would test a man's efficiency for industry and for the ordinary tasks of civil life. If a large percentage of men are unfit for military service it shows that they are also poorly fit for industrial work. (*Metropolitan,* February 1916.) *Mem. Ed.* XX, 294, 297; *Nat. Ed.* XVIII, 253, 255.

MILITARY SERVICE, OBLIGATORY AND VOLUNTARY. I most heartily favor universal obligatory military training and service, not only as regards this war, but as a permanent policy of the government. Selective obligatory military service, as a "temporary" expedient, is better than having resort *only* to volunteering; but it is a mischievous error to use it in order to prevent *all* volunteering. Universal obligatory service, as a permanent policy, is absolutely just, fair, democratic and efficient. But it needs a period of perhaps two years in order to produce first class results; and so does the "selective" substitute for it. It is folly not to provide by volunteering for the action that ought to be taken during these two years. (Volunteering to serve in the ranks of the regular army or national guard of course in no way meets the need.)

The vice of the volunteer system lies chiefly not in the men who do volunteer, but in the men who don't. A chief, altho not the only, merit in the obligatory system lies in its securing preparedness in advance. By our folly in not adopting the obligatory system as soon as this war broke out, we have forfeited this prime benefit of preparedness. You now propose to use its belated adoption as an excuse for depriving us of the benefits of the volunteer system. This is a very grave blunder. The only right course under existing conditions is to combine the two systems. My proposal is to use the volunteer system so that we can at once avail ourselves of the services of men who would otherwise be exempt, and to use the obligatory as the permanent system so as to make all serve who ought to serve. You propose to use the belated adoption of the obligatory system as a reason for refusing the services of half the men of the nation who are most fit to serve, who are most eager to serve, and whose services can be utilized at once. (To Secretary Newton D. Baker, April 22, 1917.) *Mem. Ed.* XXI, 208; *Nat. Ed.* XIX, 197.

MILITARY SERVICE AND UNIVERSAL SUFFRAGE. Universal suffrage can be justified only if it rests on universal service. We stand against all privilege not based on the full performance of duty; and there is no more contemptible form of privilege than the privilege of existing in smug, self-righteous, peaceful safety because other, braver, more self-sacrificing men give up safety and go to war to preserve the nation. If a man is too conscientious to fight, then the rest of us ought to be too conscientious to let him vote in a democratic land which can permanently exist only if the average man is willing in the last resort to fight for it, and die for it. (At Minneapolis, Minn., September 28, 1917.) *Mem. Ed.* XXI, 185; *Nat. Ed.* XIX, 176.

MILITARY SERVICE IN A DEMOCRACY. A democracy should not be willing to hire somebody else to do its fighting. The man who claims the right to vote should be a man able and willing to fight at need for the country which gives him the vote. I believe in democracy in time of peace; and I believe in it in time of war. I believe in universal service. Universal service represents the true democratic ideal. No man, rich or poor, should be allowed to shirk it. In time of war every citizen of the Republic should be held absolutely to serve the Republic whenever the Republic needs him or her. The pacifist and the hyphenated American should be sternly required to fight and made to serve in the army and to share the work and danger of their braver and more patriotic countrymen; and any dereliction of duty on their part should be punished with the sharpest rigor. (*Metropolitan,* November 1915.) *Mem. Ed.* XX, 390; *Nat. Ed.* XVIII, 334.

MILITARY SERVICE. See also CONSCIENTIOUS OBJECTORS; DRAFT; PACIFISTS; PREPAREDNESS; UNPREPAREDNESS.

MILITARY SUPREMACY. Another thing that makes one feel irritated is the way that people insist on speaking as if what has occurred during the last three or four hundred years represented part of the immutable law of nature. The military supremacy of the whites is an instance in point. From the rise of the Empire of Genghis Khan to the days of Selim, the Mongol and Turkish tribes were unquestionably the military superiors of the peoples of the Occident, and when they came into conflict it was the former who almost always appeared as invaders and usually as victors. Yet people speak of the Japanese victories over the Russians as if they had been without precedent throughout the ages. (To A. J. Balfour, March 5, 1908.) *Mem. Ed.* XXIV, 127; Bishop II, 109.

[339]

MILITARY SUPREMACY. *See also* MONGOL INVASIONS.

MILITARY TRAINING. Universal training in time of peace may avert war, and if war comes will certainly avert incalculable waste and extravagance and bloodshed and possible ultimate failure. (1916.) *Mem. Ed.* XX, 260; *Nat. Ed.* XVIII, 224.

———. Now, Americans do make splendid soldiers. They shoot well naturally. But they have got to be helped by training, or their natural capacity will count for nothing. Go out and try the experiment yourself—some of you use the rifle—try to reach the target by the light of original reason, without practice, and see how far you will get in the experiment. Although the regular army men are very good men, they are only men after all. You have got to give them the right tools, and you have got to give them a chance to practise with those tools. We must have our navy exercised in fleets, our army exercised in great evolutions as an army.

We need an army, we need a navy, because we have got to work out a great destiny; and we have a right to demand that this country, when it meets its great destiny, shall be so fitted, so armed, so equipped that it can make a record which shall be a source of pride to each and every American within its borders. If we do not prepare thoroughly in advance we can never make such a record, and then shame will cover us, and we ourselves, who fail to prepare, will be responsible for the shame. (At dinner to Chauncey M. Depew, March 11, 1899.) *Speeches at the Lotos Club.* (Lotos Club, New York, 1901), p. 332.

———. I am . . . heart and soul for the proposal of the Administration for universal obligatory military training and service. I would favor it for three million men. You can call it conscription if you wish, and I would say yes. (Statement to press, April 9, 1917.) *Mem. Ed.* XXIV, 497; Bishop II, 424.

———. Now and then the ultra-pacifists point out the fact that war is bad because the best men go to the front and the worst stay at home. There is a certain truth in this. I do not believe that we ought to permit pacifists to stay at home and escape all risk, while their braver and more patriotic fellow countrymen fight for the national well-being. It is for this reason that I wish that we would provide for universal military training for our young men, and in the event of serious war make all men do their part instead of letting the whole burden fall upon the gallant souls who volunteer. But as there is small likelihood of any such course being followed in the immediate future, I at least hope that we will so prepare ourselves in time of peace as to make our navy and army thoroughly efficient; and also to enable us in time of war to handle our volunteers in such shape that the loss among them shall be due to the enemy's bullets instead of, as is now the case, predominantly to preventable sickness which we do not prevent. (*Everybody's*, January 1915.) *Mem. Ed.* XX, 142; *Nat. Ed.* XVIII, 122.

MILITARY TRAINING—DEPENDENCE ON. Devotion to country or to religion adds immensely to the efficiency of a soldier, but is a broken reed by itself. Officers whose only qualifications are religious or patriotic zeal are better than officers who seek service to gratify their vanity, or who are appointed through political favor; but until they have really learned their business, and unless they are eager and able to learn it, this is all that can be said of them. (1900.) *Mem. Ed.* XIII, 407; *Nat. Ed.* X, 290.

MILITARY TRAINING—INDUSTRIAL AND. The adoption at once of the policy of obligatory universal military training will be the performance of a great public duty.

For three years the foremost advocates of this policy have pointed out that it can advantageously be combined with a certain amount of industrial training. It is earnestly to be hoped that this element of industrial training will be incorporated in the law. Of course, in such case the length of service with the colors in the field, aside from preliminary training in the higher school grades, ought to be a year, so as to avoid superficiality. Credit should be given the graduates of certain scholastic institutions or to individuals who speedily attain a high degree of proficiency, and for them the time of service could be shortened. All officers or other candidates for officers' training schools would be chosen from among the best of the men who had gone through the training, without regard to anything except their fitness. This would represent the embodiment in our army of the democratic principle which insists upon an equal chance for all, equal justice for all, and the need for leadership, and therefore for special rewards for leadership. (July 3, 1918.) *Roosevelt in the Kansas City Star*, 173.

MILITARY TRAINING — NEED FOR. The average citizen of a civilized community

MILITARY TRAINING

requires months of training before he can be turned into a good soldier, and . . . raw levies —no matter how patriotic—are, under normal conditions, helpless before smaller armies of trained and veteran troops, and cannot strike a finishing-blow even when pitted against troops of their own stamp. (1900.) *Mem. Ed.* XIII, 332; *Nat. Ed.* X, 226.

―――――――. Good ships and good guns are simply good weapons, and the best weapons are useless save in the hands of men who know how to fight with them. (First Annual Message, Washington, December 3, 1901.) *Mem. Ed.* XVII, 140; *Nat. Ed.* XV, 121.

―――――――. Steadily remember that ample material is useless unless we prepare in advance the highly trained personnel to handle it. This applies all the way through from battle-cruisers and submarines to coast guns and field-artillery and aeroplanes. (*Metropolitan,* February 1916.) *Mem. Ed.* XX, 292; *Nat. Ed.* XVIII, 251.

MILITARY TRAINING — VALUE OF. Training of our young men in field manœuvres and in marksmanship, as is done in Switzerland, and to a slightly less extent in Australia, would be of immense advantage to the physique and morale of our whole population. It would not represent any withdrawal of our population from civil pursuits, such as occurs among the great military states of the European Continent. In Switzerland, for instance, the ground training is given in the schools, and the young man after graduating serves only some four months with the branch of the army to which he is attached, and after that only about eight days a year, not counting his rifle practice. All serve alike, rich and poor, without any exceptions; and all whom I have ever met, the poor even more than the rich, are enthusiastic over the beneficial effects of the service and the increase in self-reliance, self-respect, and efficiency which it has brought. (New York *Times,* November 8, 1914.) *Mem. Ed.* XX, 98; *Nat. Ed.* XVIII, 85.

―――――――. Universal training would give our young men the discipline, the sense of orderly liberty and of loyalty to the interests of the whole people which would tell in striking manner for national cohesion and efficiency. It would tend to enable us in time of need to mobilize not only troops but workers and financial resources and industry itself and to co-ordinate all the factors in national life. There can be no such mobilization and co-ordination until we appreciate the necessity and value of national organization; and universal service would be a most powerful factor in bringing about such general appreciation.

As a result of it, every man, whether he carried a rifle or labored on public works or managed a business or worked on a railway, would have a clearer conception of his obligations to the State. (*Metropolitan,* February 1916.) *Mem. Ed.* XX, 298; *Nat. Ed.* XVIII, 256.

MILITARY TRAINING, AMERICAN. If ever we have a great war, the bulk of our soldiers will not be men who have had any opportunity to train soul and mind and body so as to meet the iron needs of an actual campaign. Long continued and faithful drill will alone put these men in shape to begin to do their duty, and failure to recognize this on the part of the average man will mean laziness and folly and not the possession of efficiency. Moreover, if men have been trained to believe, for instance, that they can "arbitrate questions of vital interest and national honor," if they have been brought up with flabbiness of moral fibre as well as flabbiness of physique, then there will be need of long and laborious and faithful work to give the needed tone to mind and body. But if the men have in them the right stuff, it is not so very difficult. (1913.) *Mem. Ed.* XXII, 278; *Nat. Ed.* XX, 238.

MILITARY TRAINING, SWISS. It is absolutely our duty to prepare for our own defense.

This country needs something like the Swiss system of war training for its young men. Switzerland is one of the most democratic governments in the world, and it has given its young men such an efficient training as to insure entire preparedness for war, without suffering from the least touch of militarism. Switzerland is at peace now primarily because all the great military nations that surround it know that its people have no intention of making aggression on anybody and yet that they are thoroughly prepared to hold their own and are resolute to fight to the last against any invader who attempts either to subjugate their territory or by violating its neutrality to make it a battle-ground. (New York *Times,* November 15, 1914.) *Mem. Ed.* XX, 104; *Nat. Ed.* XVIII, 90.

―――――――. I am certain that the only permanently safe attitude for this country as regards national preparedness for self-defense is along the lines of obligatory universal service on the Swiss model. Switzerland is the most democratic of nations. Its army is the most

MILITARY TRAINING

democratic army in the world. There isn't a touch of militarism or aggressiveness about Switzerland. It has been found as a matter of actual practical experience in Switzerland that the universal military training has made a very marked increase in social efficiency and in the ability of the man thus trained to do well for himself in industry. The man who has received the training is a better citizen, is more self-respecting, more orderly, better able to hold his own, and more willing to respect the rights of others, and at the same time he is a more valuable and better-paid man in his business. (Before Knights of Columbus, New York City, October 12, 1915.) *Mem. Ed.* XX, 466; *Nat. Ed.* XVIII, 400.

MILITARY TRAINING AND NATIONAL DEFENSE. Until an efficient world league for peace is in more than mere process of formation the United States must depend upon itself for protection where its vital interests are concerned. All the youth of the nation should be trained in warlike exercises and in the use of arms—as well as in the indispensable virtues of courage, self-restraint, and endurance—so as to be fit for national defense. (*New York Times,* November 22, 1914.) *Mem. Ed.* XX, 124; *Nat. Ed.* XVIII, 107.

―――――――. Think what Grmany did to her foes in the first ninety days, in the first thirty days of this war, and you will have an idea of the appalling disaster that will some day befall us unless we turn seriously to the solution of the problem of self-defense.

There is but one such solution. It is the adoption of the principle of universal military training of our young men in advance, in time of peace, with as a corollary the acceptance of the obligation of universal service in time of war. This is the only democratic system. This is the only efficient system. (*Metropolitan,* September 1917.) *Mem. Ed.* XXI, 26; *Nat. Ed.* XIX, 22.

MILITARY TRAINING AND PREPAREDNESS. It is . . . evident that this preparedness for the tasks of peace forms the only sound basis for that indispensable military preparedness which rests on universal military training and which finds expression in universal obligatory service in time of war. Such universal obligatory training and service are the necessary complements of universal suffrage and represent the realization of the true American, the democratic, ideal in both peace and war. (To Progressive National Committee, dated June 22, 1916.) *Mem. Ed.* XIX, 565; *Nat. Ed.* XVII, 415.

MILITIA

―――――――. You seem to think, if I understand your letter aright, that "preparedness" is in some way designed to make your boys food for cannon. Now, as a matter of fact, the surest way to prevent your boys from being food for cannon is to have them, and all the other young men of the country—my boys, for instance, and the boys of all other fathers and mothers throughout the country,—so trained, so prepared, that it will not be safe for any foreign foe to attack us. Preparedness no more invites war than fire insurance invites a fire. (Letter of February 9, 1916.) *Mem. Ed.* XXI, 152; *Nat. Ed.* XIX, 149.

MILITARY TRAINING. See also DEFENSE; DRAFT; FIGHTING EDGE; MARKSMANSHIP; NATIONAL DEFENSE; NAVAL PERSONNEL; PACIFISM; PEACE; PREPAREDNESS; SOLDIERS; TRAINING CAMPS; VOLUNTEER SYSTEM.

MILITIA. This proposal [for universal military training] does not represent anything more than carrying out the purpose of the second amendment to the Federal Constitution, which declares that a well-regulated militia is necessary to the security of a free nation. The Swiss army is a well-regulated militia; and, therefore, it is utterly different from any militia we have ever had. (*Everybody's,* January 1915.) *Mem. Ed.* XX, 164; *Nat. Ed.* XVIII, 140.

MILITIA—INEFFECTIVENESS OF. [We must remember] the old lesson that, whether by sea or land, a small, well-officered, and well-trained force, cannot, except very rarely, be resisted by a greater number of mere militia; and that in the end it is true economy to have the regular force prepared beforehand, without waiting until we have been forced to prepare it by the disasters happening to the irregulars. (1882.) *Mem. Ed.* VII, 145; *Nat. Ed.* VI, 128.

MILITIA, FRONTIER. The frontier virtue of independence and of impatience of outside direction found a particularly vicious expression in the frontier abhorrence of regular troops, and advocacy of a hopelessly feeble militia system. The people were foolishly convinced of the efficacy of their militia system, which they loudly proclaimed to be the only proper mode of national defense. While in the actual presence of the Indians the stern necessities of border warfare forced the frontiersmen into a certain semblance of discipline. As soon as the immediate pressure was relieved, however, the whole militia system sank into a mere farce. At certain stated occasions there were musters for company or regimental drill. These training days were treated as occasions for frolic and merrymaking. (1896.) *Mem. Ed.* XII, 302-303; *Nat. Ed.* IX, 455.

MILITIA AND REGULAR ARMY.—Under modern conditions, in a great civilized state, the regular army is composed of officers who have as a rule been carefully trained to their work; who possess remarkably fine physique, and who are accustomed to the command of men and to taking the lead in emergencies; and the enlisted men have likewise been picked out with great care as to their bodily development; have been drilled until they handle themselves, their horses, and their weapons admirably, can cook for themselves, and are trained to the endurance of hardship and exposure under the conditions of march and battle. An ordinary volunteer or militia regiment from an ordinary civilized community, on the other hand, no matter how enthusiastic or patriotic, or how intelligent, is officered by lawyers, merchants, business men, or their sons, and contains in its ranks clerks, mechanics, or farmers' lads of varying physique, who have to be laboriously taught how to shoot and how to ride, and above all, how to cook and to take care of themselves and make themselves comfortable in the open, especially when tired out by long marches, and when the weather is bad. At the outset such a regiment is, of course, utterly inferior to a veteran regular regiment, but after it has been in active service in the field for a year or two, so that its weak men have been weeded out, and its strong men have learned their duties—which can be learned far more rapidly in time of war than in time of peace—it becomes equal to any regiment. (1900.) *Mem. Ed.* XIII, 333-334; *Nat. Ed.* X, 227.

MILITIA. *See also* NATIONAL GUARD; ROUGH RIDERS; SOLDIERS; WAR OF 1812.

MILLIONAIRES. I do not think the average American multimillionaire a very high type, and I do not much admire him. But in his place he is well enough. (To Sir George Otto Trevelyan, March 9, 1905.) *Mem. Ed.* XXIV, 171; Bishop II, 147.

──────────. I wish it distinctly to be understood that I have not the smallest prejudice against multimillionaires. I like them. But I always feel this way when I meet one of them: You have made millions—good; that shows you must have something in you; I wish you would show it.

I do regard it as a realizable ideal for our people as a whole to demand, not of the millionaire—not at all—but of their own children and of themselves, that they shall get the millionaire in his proper perspective, and, when they once do that, ninety-five per cent of what is undesirable in the power of the millionaire will disappear. (At Pacific Theological Seminary, Spring 1911.) *Mem. Ed.* XV, 584; *Nat. Ed.* XIII, 622.

──────────. I decline to recognize the mere multimillionaire, the man of mere wealth, as an asset of value to any country; and especially as not an asset to my own country. If he has earned or uses his wealth in a way that makes him of real benefit, of real use—and such is often the case—why, then he does become an asset of worth. But it is the way in which it has been earned or used, and not the mere fact of wealth, that entitles him to the credit. (At the Sorbonne, Paris, April 23, 1910.) *Mem. Ed.* XV, 359; *Nat. Ed.* XIII, 514.

──────────. The very luxurious, grossly material life of the average multimillionaire whom I know does not appeal to me in the least, and nothing could hire me to lead it. It is an exceedingly nice thing to have money enough to be able to take a hunting trip in Africa after big game (if you are not able to make it pay for itself in some other way). It is an exceedingly nice thing, if you are young, to have one or two good jumping horses and to be able to occasionally hunt—although Heaven forfend that any one for whom I care should treat riding to hounds as the serious business of life! It is an exceedingly nice thing to have a good house and to be able to purchase good books and good pictures, and especially to have that house isolated from others. But I wholly fail to see where any real enjoyment comes from a dozen automobiles, a couple of hundred horses, and a good many different houses luxuriously upholstered. From the standpoint of real pleasure I should selfishly prefer my old-time ranch on the Little Missouri to anything in Newport. (To Sir Cecil Arthur Spring-Rice, April 11, 1908.) *Mem. Ed.* XXIV, 129; Bishop II, 111.

──────────. Now, a word to my fellow reformers. If they permit themselves to adopt an attitude of hate and envy toward the millionaire they are just about as badly off as if they adopt an attitude of mean subservience to him. It is just as much a confession of inferiority to feel mean hatred and defiance of a man as it is to feel a mean desire to please

[343]

him overmuch. In each case it means that the man having the emotion is not confident in himself, that he lacks self-confidence, self-reliance, that he does not stand on his own feet; and, therefore, in each case it is an admission that the man is not as good as the man whom he hates and envies, or before whom he truckles.

So that I shall preach as an ideal neither to truckle to nor to hate the man of mere wealth, because if you do either you admit your inferiority in reference to him; and if you admit that you are inferior as compared to him you are no good American, you have no place in this Republic. (At Pacific Theological Seminary, Spring 1911.) *Mem. Ed.* XV, 584; *Nat. Ed.* XIII, 623.

MILLIONAIRES. *See also* CAPITALIST; FAME; FORTUNES; "MALEFACTORS OF GREAT WEALTH"; MATERIALIST; WEALTH.

MILTON, JOHN. I have had a good deal of time for reading, naturally, and among other things have gone over Milton's prose works. What a radical republican, and what a stanch partisan, and what an intense Protestant the fine old fellow was; subject to the inevitable limitations of his time and place, he was curiously modern too. He advocated liberty of conscience to a degree that few were then able to advocate, or at least few of those who were not only philosophers like Milton, but also like Milton in active public life, and his plea for liberty of the press is good reading now. His essay on divorce is curious rather than convincing, and while it is extremely modern in some ways it is not modern at all in the contemptuous arrogance of its attitude toward women. (To Sir George Otto Trevelyan, November 23, 1906.) *Mem. Ed.* XXIV, 187; Bishop II, 160.

MINERAL FUELS — CONSERVATION OF. The mineral fuels of the eastern United States have already passed into the hands of large private owners, and those of the West are rapidly following. This should not be, for such mineral resources belong in a peculiar degree to the whole people. Under private control there is much waste from shortsighted methods of working, and the complete utilization is often sacrificed for a greater immediate profit. The mineral fuels under our present conditions are as essential to our prosperity as the forests will always be. The difference is that the supply is definitely limited, for coal does not grow and trees do. It is obvious that the mineral fuels should be conserved, not wasted, and that enough of them should remain in the hands of the Government to protect the people against unjust or extortionate prices so far as that can still be done. What has been accomplished in the regulation of the great oil fields of the Indian Territory offers a striking example of the good results of such a policy. Last summer, accordingly, I withdrew most of the coal-bearing public lands temporarily from disposal, and asked for the legislation necessary to protect the public interest by the conservation of the mineral fuels; that is, for the power to keep the fee in the Government and to lease the coal, oil, and gas rights under proper regulation. No such legislation was passed, but I still hope that we shall ultimately get it. (Before National Editorial Association, Jamestown, Va., June 10, 1907.) *Presidential Addresses and State Papers* VI, 1314-1315.

MINERAL FUELS. *See also* OIL.

MINERS. *See* COAL STRIKE.

MINES. *See* CONSERVATION; FOREST PROBLEM.

MINING CONDITIONS IN WEST VIRGINIA. The government should not content itself merely with restoring law and order; although this is the essential first step, it is only the first step; and when law and order have been obtained a system of fair play must be established or the evil will return with increasing violence. What is needed is the thorough rooting out of the conditions which brought about the dreadful state of affairs in the West Virginia bituminous fields. . . .

They say that the laborer has the freedom, or as they phrase it the "right" to sell his labor as he thinks best, and that any law controlling this right is unconstitutional. Literally and exactly this decision stands on a par with one which in the name of freedom should guarantee the laborer the right to sell himself into slavery. It represents nothing whatever but the effort, the successful effort, to suppress the workers' end of an economic controversy by denying him just law; and in actual practice this has been supplemented in West Virginia by the issuance of oppressive injunctions against the laborer. (Before National Conference of Progressive Service, Portsmouth, R. I., July 2, 1913.) *Mem. Ed.* XIX, 520, 524; *Nat. Ed.* XVII, 381, 384.

MINORITIES. *See* LIBERTY.

MINORITY—TYRANNY OF A. I have scant patience with this talk of the tyranny of the majority. Wherever there is tyranny of the

[344]

majority, I shall protest against it with all my heart and soul. But we are to-day suffering from the tyranny of minorities. It is a small minority that is grabbing our coal-deposits, our water-powers, and our harbor fronts. A small minority is battening on the sale of adulterated foods and drugs. It is a small minority that lies behind monopolies and trusts. It is a small minority that stands behind the present law of master and servant, the sweat-shops, and the whole calendar of social and industrial injustice. It is a small minority that is to-day using our convention system to defeat the will of a majority of the people in the choice of delegates to the Chicago Convention.

The only tyrannies from which men, women, and children are suffering in real life are the tyrannies of minorities.

If the majority of the American people were in fact tyrannous over the minority, if democracy had no greater self-control than empire, then indeed no written words which our forefathers put into the Constitution could stay that tyranny. (At Carnegie Hall, New York City, March 20, 1912.) *Mem. Ed.* XIX, 200; *Nat. Ed.* XVII, 151.

——————. For twenty-five years here in New York State, in our efforts to get social and industrial justice, we have suffered from the tyranny of a small minority. We have been denied, now by one court, now by another, as in the Bakeshop Case, where the courts set aside the law limiting the hours of labor in bakeries —the "due process" clause again—as in the Workmen's Compensation Act, as in the Tenement-House Cigar-Factory Case—in all these and many other cases we have been denied by small minorities, by a few worthy men of wrong political philosophy on the bench, the right to protect our people in their lives, their liberty, and their pursuit of happiness. As for "consistency"—why, the record of the courts, in such a case as the income tax, for instance, is so full of inconsistencies as to make the fear expressed of "inconsistency" on the part of the people seem childish. (At Carnegie Hall, New York City, March 20, 1912.) *Mem. Ed.* XIX, 214; *Nat. Ed.* XVII, 162.

——————. I shall protest against the tyranny of the majority whenever it arises, just as I shall protest against every other form of tyranny. But at present we are not suffering in any way from the tyranny of the majority. We suffer from the tyranny of the bosses and of the special interests, that is, from the tyranny of minorities. Mr. Choate, Mr. Milburn, and their allies are acting as the servants and spokesmen of the special interests and are standing cheek by jowl with the worst representatives of politics when they seek to keep the courts in the grasp of privilege and of the politicians; for this is all they accomplish when they prevent them from being responsible in proper fashion to the people. (At Philadelphia, April 10, 1912.) *Mem. Ed.* XIX, 270; *Nat. Ed.* XVII, 202.

MINORITY. *See also* COURTS; FILIBUSTERING; GOVERNMENT; LEGISLATIVE MINORITY; POPULAR RULE; PRIVILEGE; REFERENDUM; REPRESENTATIVE GOVERNMENT; SPECIAL INTERESTS.

MISSIONARIES. America has for over a century done its share of missionary work. We who stay at home should as a matter of duty give cordial support to those who in a spirit of devotion to all that is highest in human nature, spend the best part of their lives in trying to carry civilization and Christianity into lands which have hitherto known little or nothing of either. The work is vast, and it is done under many and widely varied conditions. . . .

I hope there will be the most hearty support of these men, who in far-off regions are fighting for progress in things of the spirit no less than in things of the body. Let us help them to make the missions centres of industrial no less than of ethical teaching; for unless we raise the savage in industrial efficiency we cannot permanently keep him on a high plane of moral efficiency, nor yet can we render him able to hold his own in the world. (At celebration of Methodist Episcopal Church, Washington, January 18, 1909.) *Mem. Ed.* XVIII, 349-350; *Nat. Ed.* XVI, 264-266.

——————. Mission work among savages offers many difficulties, and often the wisest and most earnest effort meets with dishearteningly little reward; while lack of common sense, and of course, above all, lack of a firm and resolute disinterestedness, insures the worst kind of failure. There are missionaries who do not do well, just as there are men in every conceivable walk of life who do not do well; and excellent men who are not missionaries, including both government officials and settlers, are only too apt to jump at the chance of criticising a missionary for every alleged sin of either omission or commission. Finally, zealous missionaries, fervent in the faith, do not always find it easy to remember that savages can only be raised by slow steps, that an empty adherence to forms and ceremonies amounts to nothing, that industrial training is an essential in any permanent upward movement, and that the gradual elevation of mind and character is a prerequisite to the achievement of any kind of Christianity which is worth calling such. Nevertheless, after all this has been said, it remains true that the good done by missionary effort in Africa has been incalculable. . . . Over most of Africa the problem for the white man is to govern, with wisdom and firmness, and when necessary with severity, but always with an eye single to their own interests and development, the black and brown races. To do this needs sympathy and devotion no less than strength and wisdom, and in the task the part to be played by the missionary and the part to be played by the official are alike great, and the two should work hand in hand. (1910.) *Mem. Ed.* V, 102-103; *Nat. Ed.* IV, 88.

MISSIONARIES. See also AFRICA; JESUITS.

MISSISSIPPI RIVER—DEVELOPMENT OF. We should undertake the complete development and control of the Mississippi as a national work, just as we have undertaken the work of building the Panama Canal. We can use the plant, and we can use the human experience, left free by the completion of the Panama Canal in so developing the Mississippi as to make it a mighty highroad of commerce, and a source of fructification and not of death to the rich and fertile lands lying along its lower length. (Before Progressive National Convention, Chicago, August 6, 1912.) *Mem. Ed.* XIX, 405; *Nat. Ed.* XVII, 294.

MITCHELL, JOHN. See COAL STRIKE.

MOB RULE. See POPULAR RULE.

MOB VIOLENCE. See VIOLENCE.

MOCKING-BIRD. The mocking-bird is a singer that has suffered much in reputation from its powers of mimicry. On ordinary occasions, and especially in the daytime, it insists on playing the harlequin. But when free in its own favorite haunts at night in the love season it has a song, or rather songs, which are not only purely original but are also more beautiful than any other bird music whatsoever. Once I listened to a mocking-bird singing the live-long spring night, under the full moon, in the magnolia tree; and I do not think I shall ever forget its song. (1893.) *Mem. Ed.* II, 61; *Nat. Ed.* II, 54.

———. The mocking-bird is as conspicuous as it is attractive, and when at its best it is the sweetest singer of all birds; though its talent for mimicry and a certain odd perversity in its nature often combine to mar its performances. The way it flutters and dances in the air when settling in a tree-top, its alert intelligence, its good looks, and the comparative ease with which it can be made friendly and familiar, all add to its charm. (1905.) *Mem. Ed.* III, 318; *Nat. Ed.* III, 128.

"MOLLYCODDLE." In the long run the "sissy" and the "mollycoddle" are as undesirable members of society as the crook and the bully. I don't like the crook and the bully. Don't misunderstand me; I will abate both of them when I get the chance at them. But, after all, there is the possibility that you can reform the crook or the bully, but you cannot reform the "sissy" or the "mollycoddle," because there is not anything there to reform. With a nation, as with an individual, weakness, cowardice, and flabby failure to insist upon what is right, even if a certain risk comes in insisting, may be as detrimental, not only from the standpoint of the individual or the nation, but from the standpoint of humanity at large, as wickedness itself. (Before Panama-Pacific Historical Congress, Palo Alto, Cal., July 23, 1915.) *The Pacific Ocean in History. Papers and Addresses.* (Macmillan Co., N. Y., 1917), p. 149.

MONARCHS. See KINGS; ROYALTY.

MONETARY STANDARD. See CURRENCY; GOLD STANDARD; SILVER.

MONEY. Money is a good thing. It is a foolish affectation to deny it. But it is not the only good thing, and after a certain amount has been amassed it ceases to be the chief even of material good things. It is far better, for instance, to do well a bit of work which is well worth doing, than to have a large fortune. (Before Young Men's Christian Association, New York City, December 30, 1900.) *Mem. Ed.* XV, 532; *Nat. Ed.* XIII, 496.

———. It is a false statement, and therefore it is a disservice to the cause of morality, to tell any man that money does not count. If he has not got it he will find that it does count tremendously. If he is worth his salt and is desirous of caring for mother and sisters, wife and children, he will not only find that it counts but he will realize that he has acted with infamy and with baseness if he has not appreciated the fact that it does count. Of course, when I speak of money I mean what money stands for. It counts tremendously. No man has any right to the respect of his fellows if through any fault of his own he has failed to keep those dependent upon him in reasonable comfort. It is his duty not to despise money. It is his duty to regard money, up to the point where his wife and children and any other people dependent upon him have food, clothing, shelter, decent surroundings, the chance for the children to get a decent education, the chance for the children to train themselves to do their life-work aright, a chance for wife and children to get reasonable relaxation. (At Pacific Theological Seminary, Spring 1911.) *Mem. Ed.* XV, 578; *Nat. Ed.* XIII, 617.

——————. The very fact that I grant in the fullest degree the need of having enough money, which means the need of sufficient material achievement to enable you and those dependent upon you to lead your lives healthily and under decent conditions . . . entitles me to have you accept what I say at its face value when I add that this represents only the beginning, and that after you have reached this point your worth as a unit in the commonwealth, your worth to others and your worth to yourself, depends infinitely less upon having additional money than it depends upon your possessing certain other things, things of the soul and the spirit. . . . After the man and the woman have reached the point where they have a home in which the elemental needs are met and where in addition they have accumulated the comparatively small amount of money necessary to meet the primal needs of the spirit and of the intellect—after this point is reached it is my deliberate judgment that money, instead of being the prime factor, is one of the minor factors, both in usefulness and in happiness. (At Pacific Theological Seminary, Spring 1911.) *Mem. Ed.* XV, 580; *Nat. Ed.* XIII, 619-620.

——————. I feel very strongly that one great lesson to be taught here in America is that while the first duty of every man is to earn enough for his wife and children, that when once this has been accomplished no man should treat money as the primary consideration. He is very foolish unless he makes it the first consideration, up to the point of supporting his family; but normally, thereafter it should come secondary. (To John St. Loe Strachey, November 28, 1908.) *Mem. Ed.* XXIV, 147; Bishop II, 126.

MONEY. See also FORTUNES; MATERIALIST; SUCCESS; WEALTH.

MONEYED MEN. The moneyed classes, especially those of large fortune, whose ideal tends to the mere money, are not fitted for any predominant guidance in a really great nation. I do not dislike but I certainly have no especial respect or admiration for and no trust in, the typical big moneyed man of my country. I do not regard them as furnishing sound opinion as regards either foreign or domestic policies. (To Frederick Scott Oliver, August 9, 1906.) *Mem. Ed.* XXIV, 28; Bishop II, 24.

MONEYED MEN — ROOSEVELT'S INDEPENDENCE OF. Unfortunately, the strength of my public position before the country is also its weakness. I am genuinely independent of the big monied men in all matters where I think the interests of the public are concerned, and probably I am the first President of recent times of whom this could be truthfully said. I think it right and desirable that this should be true of the President. But where I do not grant any favors to these big monied men which I do not think the country requires that they should have, it is out of the question for me to expect them to grant favors to me in return. I treat them precisely as I treat other citizens; that is, I consider their interests so far as my duty requires and so far as I think the needs of the country warrant. In return, they will support me, in so far as they are actuated purely by public spirit, simply accordingly as they think I am or am not doing well; and so far as they are actuated solely by their private interests they will support me only on points where they think it is to their interest to do so. (To H. C. Lodge, September 27, 1902.) Lodge *Letters* I, 534.

MONEYED MEN. See also BUSINESS, BIG; CAPITALISTS; CORPORATIONS; MILLIONAIRES; WALL STREET.

MONGOL INVASIONS. It is extraordinary to see how ignorant even the best scholars of America and England are of the tremendous importance in world history of the nation-shattering Mongol invasions. A noted Englishman of letters not many years ago wrote a charming essay on the thirteenth century—an essay showing his wide learning, his grasp of historical events, and the length of time that he had devoted to the study of the century. Yet the essayist not only never mentioned but was evidently ignorant of the most stupendous fact of the century—the rise of Genghis Khan and the spread of the Mongol power from the Yellow Sea to the Adriatic and the Persian

Gulf. Ignorance like this is partly due to the natural tendency among men whose culture is that of western Europe to think of history as only European history and of European history as only the history of Latin and Teutonic Europe. . . . It is this ignorance, of course accentuated among those who are not scholars, which accounts for the possibility of such comically absurd remarks as the one not infrequently made at the time of the Japanese-Russian War, that for the first time since Salamis Asia had conquered Europe. As a matter of fact the recent military supremacy of the white or European races is a matter of only some three centuries. For the four preceding centuries, that is, from the beginning of the thirteenth to the seventeenth, the Mongol and Turkish armies generally had the upper hand in any contest with European foes, appearing in Europe always as invaders and often as conquerors; while no ruler of Europe of their days had to his credit such mighty feats of arms, such wide conquests, as Genghis Khan, as Timour the Limper, as Bajazet, Selim, and Amurath, as Baber and Akbar. (Foreword to J. Curtin's *The Mongol;* dated September 1907.) *Mem. Ed.* XIV, 58; *Nat. Ed.* XII, 178.

MONGOL INVASIONS. See also MILITARY SUPREMACY.

MONOPOLIES — OBJECTION TO. The very reason why we object to State ownership, that it puts a stop to individual initiative and to the healthy development of personal responsibility, is the reason why we object to an unsupervised, unchecked monopolistic control in private hands. *Outlook,* June 19, 1909, p. 394.

MONOPOLIES — PROSECUTION OF. Monopolies can, although in rather cumbrous fashion, be broken up by lawsuits. Great business combinations, however, cannot possibly be made useful instead of noxious industrial agencies merely by lawsuits, and especially by lawsuits supposed to be carried on for their destruction and not for their control and regulation. (1913.) *Mem. Ed.* XXII, 490; *Nat. Ed.* XX, 422.

MONOPOLIES IN NEW YORK. There is an issue in this State of great importance, and they who defend it have to some extent brought it into disrepute, that is anti-monopoly. But nevertheless there is no question that there is a vital spirit underlying it; that we as a people are suffering from new dangers; that as our fathers fought with slavery and crushed it, in order that it would not seize and crush them, so we are called on to fight new forces, and we cannot do it unless our hands are held up, and those who act outside of legislative halls give us the support through which alone we can act. (At Republican mass-meeting, 21st Assembly Dist., New York, October 28, 1882.) *Mem. Ed.* XVI, 16; *Nat. Ed.* XIV, 14.

MONOPOLY. All business into which the element of monopoly in any way or degree enters, and where it proves in practice impossible totally to eliminate this element of monopoly, should be carefully supervised, regulated, and controlled by governmental authority; and such control should be exercised by administrative, rather than by judicial, officers. . . . Where regulation by competition (which is, of course, preferable) proves insufficient, we should not shrink from bringing governmental regulation to the point of control of monopoly prices if it should ever become necessary to do so, just as in exceptional cases railway rates are now regulated.

In emphasizing the part of the administrative department in regulating combinations and checking absolute monopoly, I do not, of course, overlook the obvious fact that the legislature and the judiciary must do their part. The legislature should make it clear exactly what methods are illegal, and then the judiciary will be in a better position to punish adequately and relentlessly those who insist on defying the clear legislative decrees.

I do not believe any absolute private monopoly is justified, but if our great combinations are properly supervised, so that immoral practices are prevented, absolute monopoly will not come to pass, as the laws of competition and efficiency are against it. (Before Ohio Constitutional Convention, Columbus, February 21, 1912.) *Mem. Ed.* XIX, 174; *Nat. Ed.* XVII, 129.

———. The true way of dealing with monopoly is to prevent it by administrative action before it grows so powerful that even when courts condemn it they shrink from destroying it. (1913.) *Mem. Ed.* XXII, 492; *Nat. Ed.* XX, 423.

MONOPOLY—LEGALIZATION OF. Our opponents have said that we intend to legalize monopoly. Nonsense. They have legalized monopoly. At this moment the Standard Oil and Tobacco Trust monopolies are legalized; they are being carried on under the decree of the Supreme Court. Our proposal is really to break up monopoly. Our proposal is to lay down certain requirements, and then require the commerce commission—the industrial commission

—to see that the trusts live up to those requirements. Our opponents have spoken as if we were going to let the commission declare what the requirements should be. Not at all. We are going to put the requirements in the law and then see that the commission requires them to obey that law. (At Milwaukee, Wis., October 14, 1912.) *Mem. Ed.* XIX, 449; *Nat. Ed.* XVII, 326.

MONOPOLY. *See also* BUSINESS; COMBINATIONS; COMPETITION; CORPORATIONS; GOVERNMENT CONTROL; GOVERNMENT REGULATION; INDUSTRIAL COMMISSION; NORTHERN SECURITIES CASE; TRUSTS.

MONROE DOCTRINE. The Monroe Doctrine may be briefly defined as forbidding European encroachment on American soil. It is not desirable to define it so rigidly as to prevent our taking into account the varying degrees of national interest in varying cases. The United States has not the slightest wish to establish a universal protectorate over other American States, or to become responsible for their misdeeds. If one of them becomes involved in an ordinary quarrel with a European power, such quarrel must be settled between them in any one of the usual methods. But no European State is to be allowed to aggrandize itself on American soil at the expense of any American State. Furthermore, no transfer of an American colony from one European State to another is to be permitted, if, in the judgment of the United States, such transfer would be hostile to its own interests. (*The Bachelor of Arts,* March 1896.) *Mem. Ed.* XV, 226; *Nat. Ed.* XIII, 169.

————. The Monroe Doctrine should be the cardinal feature of the foreign policy of all the nations of the two Americas, as it is of the United States. . . . The Monroe Doctrine is a declaration that there must be no territorial aggrandizement by any non-American power at the expense of any American power on American soil. It is in nowise intended as hostile to any nation in the Old World. Still less is it intended to give cover to any aggression by one New World power at the expense of any other. It is simply a step, and a long step, toward assuring the universal peace of the world by securing the possibility of permanent peace on this hemisphere. (First Annual Message, Washington, December 3, 1901.) *Mem. Ed.* XVII, 134; *Nat. Ed.* XV, 116.

————. There are certain essential points which must never be forgotten as regards the Monroe Doctrine. In the first place we must as a nation make it evident that we do not intend to treat it in any shape or way as an excuse for aggrandizement on our part at the expense of the republics to the south. We must recognize the fact that in some South American countries there has been much suspicion lest we should interpret the Monroe Doctrine as in some way inimical to their interests, and we must try to convince all the other nations of this continent once and for all that no just and orderly government has anything to fear from us. There are certain republics to the south of us which have already reached such a point of stability, order, and prosperity that they themselves, though as yet hardly consciously, are among the guarantors of this doctrine. These republics we now meet not only on a basis of entire equality, but in a spirit of frank and respectful friendship, which we hope is mutual. If all of the republics to the south of us will only grow as those to which I allude have already grown, all need for us to be especial champion of the doctrine will disappear, for no stable and growing American republic wishes to see some great non-American military power acquire territory in its neigborhood. All that this country desires is that the other republics on this continent shall be happy and prosperous; and they cannot be happy and prosperous unless they maintain order within their boundaries and behave with a just regard for their obligations toward outsiders. (Fifth Annual Message, Washington, December 5, 1905.) *Mem. Ed.* XVII, 352-353; *Nat. Ed.* XV, 301-302.

————. It is in no sense a doctrine of one-sided advantage; it is to be invoked only in the interest of all our commonwealths in the Western Hemisphere. It should be invoked by our nations in a spirit of mutual respect, and on a footing of complete equality of both right and obligation. Therefore, as soon as any country of the New World stands on a sufficiently high footing of orderly liberty and achieved success, of self-respecting strength, it becomes a guarantor of the doctrine on a footing of complete equality. I congratulate the countries of South America that I have visited and am about to visit that their progress is such, in justice, political stability and material prosperity, as to make them also the sponsors of the Monroe Doctrine, so that, as regards them, all that the United States has to do is to stand ready, as one of the great brotherhood of American nations, to join with them in upholding the doctrine should they at any time desire, in the interest of the Western

Hemisphere, that we should do so. (At Montevideo, November 1913.) J. H. Zahm, *Through South America's Southland*. (D. Appleton & Co., N. Y., 1916), pp. 143-144.

———————. Ninety years ago, when the doctrine was first proclaimed, the only American nation that had sufficient strength to gain a scanty and discourteous hearing from the Old World was the United States of America. At that time the only hearing even the United States received was both scanty and discourteous; nevertheless, it could at times make itself heard and heeded; and therefore the guardianship of the doctrine had to rest with the United States. But times have changed. Certain of the Latin American nations have grown with astonishing speed to a position of assured and orderly political development, material prosperity, readiness to do justice to others and potential strength to enforce justice from the others. These nations are able to enforce order at home and respect abroad. These nations have so developed their institutions that they themselves do not wrong others, and that they are able to repel wrong from others. Every such nation, when once it has achieved such a position, should become itself a sponsor and guarantor of the doctrine; and its relations with the other sponsors and guarantors should be those of equality. (At Buenos Aires, Argentina, November 12, 1913.) *American Ideals. Speeches . . . of Dr. Emilio Frers and of Col. Theodore Roosevelt*. (Buenos Aires, 1914), p. 23.

———————. This doctrine was perfectly simple. It declared that the soil of the Western Hemisphere was no longer to be treated as a subject for territorial conquest or acquisitions by old-world powers. I wish you to remember just what the Monroe Doctrine is. If any man tells you that it is dead, ask him if he really means that Old-World powers are to be permitted to acquire territory by conquest or colonization in the Western Hemisphere. Unless he so believes, he cannot assert that the doctrine is dead. So far from its being dead, I think it is a great deal more alive than ever before. I believe that there is a less chance than ever before of the American nations permitting any species of conquest or colonization on this Continent by Old-World powers. Moreover, I believe that the time has now come when the doctrine in reality has the guarantee not only of the United States, my own country, but of your country, Chile, and of every other American nation which has risen to a sufficient point of economic well-being, of stable and orderly government, of power to do justice to others and to exact justice from others; and therefore of potential armed strength to enable it thus to act as a guarantor of the doctrine.

In other words, keep these two facts distinctly in your minds: 1) the doctrine itself; 2) the question as to who the guarantor or guarantors of that doctrine shall be. I am wholly unable to understand how any farsighted patriot of the two Americas could fail to recognize the vital importance of the doctrine to the liberty and well-being of the nations of the Western Hemisphere. The only differences that can arise are as to the methods of its enforcement, and as to who shall be its guarantors. On these points there must of necessity be change as conditions change. (At Santiago, November 24, 1913.) *Souvenir of the visit of Colonel Mr. Theodore Roosevelt, ex-President of the United States of America, to Chile*. (Santiago de Chile, 1914), pp. 44-45.

MONROE DOCTRINE — APPLICATION OF. The great nations of southernmost South America, Brazil, the Argentine, and Chile, are now so far advanced in stability and power that there is no longer any need of applying the Monroe Doctrine as far as they are concerned; and this also relieves us as regards Uruguay and Paraguay, the former of which is well advanced and neither of which has any interests with which we need particularly concern ourselves. As regards all these powers, therefore, we now have no duty save that doubtless if they got into difficulties and desired our aid we would gladly extend it, just as, for instance, we would to Australia and Canada. But we can now proceed on the assumption that they are able to help themselves and that any help we should be required to give would be given by us as an auxiliary rather than as a principal. (New York *Times*, November 22, 1914.) *Mem. Ed.* XX, 127; *Nat. Ed.* XVIII, 109.

———————. We need bother with the Monroe Doctrine only so far as the approaches to the Panama Canal are concerned, that is, so far as concerns the territories between our Southern border and, roughly speaking, the Equator. (*Metropolitan*, November 1915.) *Mem. Ed.* XX, 389; *Nat. Ed.* XVIII, 333.

MONROE DOCTRINE—IMPLICATIONS OF. We have not the slightest desire to secure any territory at the expense of any of our neighbors. We wish to work with them hand in hand, so that all of us may be uplifted together, and we rejoice over the good fortune of any of them, we gladly hail their material prosperity and political stability, and are concerned and alarmed if any of them fall into industrial or political chaos. We do not wish to see any Old World military power grow up on this continent, or to be compelled to become a military power ourselves. The peoples of the Americas can prosper best if left to work out their own salvation in their own way. (First Annual Message, Washington, December 3, 1901.) *Mem. Ed.* XVII, 135; *Nat. Ed.* XV, 117.

──────────. We can not permanently adhere to the Monroe Doctrine unless we succeed in making it evident in the first place that we do not intend to treat it in any shape or way as an excuse for aggrandizement on our part at the expense of the republics to the south of us; second, that we do not intend to permit it to be used by any of these republics as a shield to protect that republic from the consequences of its own misdeeds against foreign nations; third, that inasmuch as by this doctrine we prevent other nations from interfering on this side of the water, we shall ourselves in good faith try to help those of our sister republics, which need such help, upward toward peace and order. (At Chautauqua, N. Y., August 11, 1905.) *Presidential Addresses and State Papers* IV, 440.

──────────. Foolish people say that the Monroe Doctrine is outworn, without taking the trouble to understand what the Monroe Doctrine is. As a matter of fact, to abandon the Monroe Doctrine would be to invite overwhelming disaster. In its essence the Monroe Doctrine amounts to saying that we shall not permit the American lands around us to be made footholds for foreign military powers who would in all probability create out of them points of armed aggression against us. We must therefore make up our mind that we will police and defend the Panama Canal and its approaches, preserve order and safeguard civilization in the territories adjacent to the Caribbean Sea, and see that none of these territories great or small, are seized by any military empire of the Old World which can use them to our disadvantage. (*Metropolitan,* February 1916.) *Mem. Ed.* XX, 280; *Nat. Ed.* XVIII, 240.

MONROE DOCTRINE—JUSTIFICATION OF. The Monroe Doctrine should not be considered from any purely academic standpoint, but as a broad, general principle of living policy. It is to be justified not by precedent merely, but by the needs of the nation and the true interests of Western civilization. (*The Bachelor of Arts,* March 1896.) *Mem. Ed.* XV, 224; *Nat. Ed.* XIII, 168.

MONROE DOCTRINE — OPPOSITION TO. There are many upright and honorable men who take the wrong side, that is, the anti-American side, of the Monroe Doctrine because they are too short-sighted or too unimaginative to realize the hurt to the nation that would be caused by the adoption of their views. There are other men who take the wrong view simply because they have not thought much of the matter, or are in unfortunate surroundings, by which they have been influenced to their own moral hurt. There are yet other men in whom the mainspring of the opposition to that branch of American policy known as the Monroe Doctrine is sheer timidity. This is sometimes the ordinary timidity of wealth. Sometimes, however, it is peculiarly developed among educated men whose education has tended to make them overcultivated and oversensitive to foreign opinion. They are generally men who undervalue the great fighting qualities, without which no nation can ever rise to the first rank. . . . Those wealthy men who wish the abandonment of the Monroe Doctrine because its assertion may damage their business, bring discredit to themselves, and, so far as they are able, discredit to the nation of which they are a part. (*The Bachelor of Arts,* March 1896.) *Mem. Ed.* XV, 235; *Nat. Ed.* XIII, 177.

MONROE DOCTRINE — ROOSEVELT'S VIEW OF. I regard the Monroe Doctrine as being equivalent to open door in South America. That is, I do not want the United States or any European power to get territorial possessions in South America but to let South America gradually develop on its own lines, with an open door to all outside nations, save as the individual countries enter into individual treaties with one another. (To Baron H. S. von Sternberg, October 11, 1901.) *Mem. Ed.* XXIII, 184; Bishop I, 158.

──────────. I am having my hands full . . . in endeavoring to make our people act on a rational interpretation of the Monroe Doctrine. No such policy as that of the Monroe Doctrine can remain fossilized while the nation grows. Either it must be abandoned or it must be modified to meet the changing needs of national life. I believe with all my heart in the Monroe Doctrine and have, for instance, formally notified Germany to that effect. But I also believe that we must make it evident on the one hand that we do not intend to use the Monroe Doctrine as a pretence for self-aggrandizement at the expense of the Latin-American republics, and on the other hand that we do not intend it to be used as a warrant for letting any of these republics remain as small bandit-nests of a wicked and inefficient type. (To Spring Rice, July 24, 1905.) *The Letters and Friendships of Sir Cecil Spring Rice.* (Houghton Mifflin Co., Boston, (1929), I, 480.

MONROE DOCTRINE AND ENGLAND.
As far as England is concerned I do not care a rap whether she subscribes to the Monroe Doctrine or not, because she is the one power with which any quarrel on that doctrine would be absolutely certain to result to our immediate advantage. She could take the Philippines and Porto Rico, but they would be a very poor offset for the loss of Canada. I should regard a war with England as a calamity because of its future results to both powers and especially to England; but its immediate effect would be beneficial to the United States. (To H. C. Lodge, June 19, 1901.) Lodge *Letters* I, 494.

MONROE DOCTRINE AND INTERNATIONAL LAW. The Monroe Doctrine is not international law; but there is no necessity that it should be. All that is needful is that it should continue to be a cardinal feature of American policy on this continent; and the Spanish-American states should, in their own interests, champion it as strongly as we do. We do not by this doctrine intend to sanction any policy of aggression by one American commonwealth at the expense of any other, nor any policy of commercial discrimination against any foreign power whatsoever. Commercially, as far as this doctrine is concerned, all we wish is a fair field and no favor; but if we are wise we shall strenuously insist that under no pretext whatsoever shall there be any territorial aggrandizement on American soil by any European power, and this, no matter what form the territorial aggrandizement may take. (At Minnesota State Fair, September 2, 1901.) *Mem. Ed.* XV, 335; *Nat. Ed.* XIII, 475.

──────────. The Monroe Doctrine is not international law, and though I think one day it may become such, this is not necessary as long as it remains a cardinal feature of our foreign policy and as long as we possess both the will and the strength to make it effective. This last point, my fellow-citizens, is all important, and is one which as a people we can never afford to forget. I believe in the Monroe Doctrine with all my heart and soul; I am convinced that the immense majority of our fellow-countrymen so believe in it; but I would infinitely prefer to see us abandon it than to see us put it forward and bluster about it, and yet fail to build up the efficient fighting strength which in the last resort can alone make it respected by any strong foreign power whose interest it may ever happen to be to violate it. (At Chicago, Ill., April 2, 1903.) *Presidential Addresses and State Papers* I, 265.

──────────. The Monroe Doctrine lays down the rule that the western hemisphere is not hereafter to be treated as subject to settlement and occupation by Old World powers. It is not international law; but it is a cardinal principle of our foreign policy. (1913.) *Mem. Ed.* XXII, 575; *Nat. Ed.* XX, 495.

MONROE DOCTRINE AND THE CANAL.
As to the Monroe Doctrine. If we invite foreign powers to a joint ownership, a joint guaranty [of a canal], of what so vitally concerns us but a little way from our borders, how can we possibly object to similar joint action say in Southern Brazil or Argentina, where our interests are so much less evident? If Germany has the same right that we have in the canal across Central America, why not in the partition of any part of Southern America? To my mind, we should consistently refuse to all European powers the right to control, in any shape, any territory in the the Western Hemisphere which they do not already hold. (To Secretary John Hay, February 18, 1900.) *Mem. Ed.* XXIII, 168; Bishop I, 145.

MONROE DOCTRINE AND THE NAVY.
The Monroe Doctrine is as strong as the United States navy, and no stronger. (1916.) *Mem. Ed.* XX, 261; *Nat. Ed.* XVIII, 225.

──────────. The Monroe Doctrine won't be observed by foreign nations with sufficient strength to disregard it when once it becomes their interest to disregard it, unless we have a navy sufficient to make our assertion of the Doctrine good.

The Monroe Doctrine, unbacked by a navy, is an empty boast; and there exist but few more contemptible characters, individual or national, than the man or the nation who boasts and when the boast is challenged, fails to make good. (At Naval War College, Newport, R. I., July 22, 1908.) *Mem. Ed.* XVIII, 333; *Nat. Ed.* XVI, 252.

MONROE DOCTRINE. See also BIG STICK; LATIN AMERICA; NAVY; SANTO DOMINGO; VENEZUELA.

MONUMENTS. We have not too many monuments of the past; let us keep every bit of association with that which is highest and best of the past as a reminder to us, equally of what we owe to those who have gone before and of how we should show our appreciation. (At N. Y. Avenue Presbyterian Church, Washington, D. C., November 16, 1903.) *Mem. Ed.* XII, 456; *Nat. Ed.* XI, 215.

MONUMENTS. *See also* OBELISKS; WHITE HOUSE.

MOODY, WILLIAM H. It is the universal testimony of all who knew him that as justice he grew and developed with extraordinary rapidity. As district attorney of Massachusetts, as congressman, as secretary of the navy, and as attorney-general he had rendered signal service to his country; indeed, his record as attorney-general can be compared without fear with the record of any other man who ever held that office. Much was rightly expected of him when he was made justice of the Supreme Court; but what he did and the attitude he took during his lamentably short term of office showed that these expectations would be far more than realized. He was not a man who was misled by a formula. His clear eye always saw into the heart of things. No devotion to the theory of national power prevented his deciding in favor of the rights of any State wherever it was obvious that through the exercise of its rights by the State lay the only chance of securing the rights of the people. On the other hand, no theory as to the rights of the States caused him to refrain from giving effect to a just expression of the popular will when that popular will could find effective expression only by the exercise of the powers of the Federal Government. It is not a difficult thing to find an upright man who as judge will do justice between individuals; but it is a very difficult thing to find the far-seeing statesman who on the bench will with wisdom and firmness shape the course of governmental action so that the national and State governments shall completely cover the whole field of governmental action in order that there shall be left no neutral ground wherein astute men, protected by contradictory judicial decisions, may work wickedness uncontrolled by either State or nation. Mr. Justice Moody was one of these men. He rendered noteworthy service to the country even during his short term on the bench, and had he been able to continue on the bench he would have rendered such service as hardly any other man now in public life can hope to render. (*Outlook*, November 5, 1910.) *Mem. Ed.* XII, 535-536; *Nat. Ed.* XI, 262-263.

MOOSE. The true way to kill the noble beast, however, is by fair still-hunting. There is no grander sport than still-hunting the moose, whether in the vast pine and birch forests of the Northeast, or among the stupendous mountain masses of the Rockies. The moose has wonderfully keen nose and ears, though its eyesight is not remarkable. Most hunters assert that it is the wariest of all game, and the most difficult to kill. I have never been quite satisfied that this was so; it seems to me that the nature of the ground wherein it dwells helps it even more than do its own sharp senses. (1893.) *Mem. Ed.* II, 200; *Nat. Ed.* II, 173.

MORAL INFLUENCE OF GREAT MEN. Every great nation owes to the men whose lives have formed part of its greatness not merely the material effect of what they did, not merely the laws they placed upon the statute-books or the victories they won over armed foes, but also the immense but indefinable moral influence produced by their deeds and words themselves upon the national character. (*Forum*, February 1895.) *Mem. Ed.* XV, 3; *Nat. Ed.* XIII, 3.

MORAL INFLUENCE. *See also* HEROES; LEADERS; LEADERSHIP.

MORAL SENSE. If courage and strength and intellect are unaccompanied by the moral purpose, the moral sense, they become merely forms of expression for unscrupulous force and unscrupulous cunning. If the strong man has not in him the lift toward lofty things his strength makes him only a curse to himself and to his neighbor. All this is true in private life, and it is no less true in public life. (At Colorado Springs, Col., August 2, 1901.) *Mem. Ed.* XV, 326; *Nat. Ed.* XIII, 457.

———————. If a man's efficiency is not guided by a moral sense, then the more efficient he is the worse he is, the more dangerous to the body politic. Courage, intellect, all the masterful qualities, serve but to make a man more evil if they are used merely for that man's own advancement, with brutal indifference to the rights of others. It speaks ill for the community if the community worships these qualities and treats their possessors as heroes regardless of whether the qualities are used rightly or wrongly. It makes no difference as to the precise way in which this sinister efficiency is shown. It makes no difference whether such a man's force and ability betray themselves in the career of money-maker or politician, soldier or orator, journalist or popular leader. If the man works for evil, then the more successful he is the more he should be despised and condemned by all upright and far-seeing men. (At the Sorbonne, Paris, April 23, 1910.) *Mem. Ed.* XV, 363; *Nat. Ed.* XIII, 518.

MORAL SENSE. See also CHARACTER; CONSCIENCE; COURAGE; INTELLIGENCE; MENTAL ACUTENESS.

MORALITY. Morality, to count, must include the two elements of uprightness and efficiency. You need the zeal, and the knowledge without which zeal amounts to so little; and I need not say, gentlemen, that to be efficient without also being upright is merely to be additionally dangerous to the community. The abler a man is, the worse he is from the public standpoint if his ability is not guided by conscience. (At Harvard University, Cambridge, December 14, 1910.) *Mem. Ed.* XV, 555; *Nat. Ed.* XIII, 601.

MORALITY, NATIONAL. No prosperity and no glory can save a nation that is rotten at heart. We must ever keep the core of our national being sound, and see to it that not only our citizens in private life, but, above all, our statesmen in public life, practice the old commonplace virtues which from time immemorial have lain at the root of all true national well-being. (At Minnesota State Fair, September 2, 1901.) *Mem. Ed.* XV, 334; *Nat. Ed.* XIII, 474.

————. The most perfect machinery of government will not keep us as a nation from destruction if there is not within us a soul. No abounding material prosperity shall avail us if our spiritual senses atrophy. The foes of our own household shall surely prevail against us unless there be in our people an inner life which finds its outward expression in a morality not very widely different from that preached by the seers and prophets of Judea when the grandeur that was Greece and the glory that was Rome still lay in the future. (1917.) *Mem. Ed.* XXI, 132; *Nat. Ed.* XIX, 132.

MORALITY, POLITICAL AND PRIVATE. I do not for one moment admit that political morality is different from private morality, that a promise made on the stump differs from a promise made in private life. I do not for one moment admit that a man should act deceitfully as a public servant in his dealings with other nations, any more than that he should act deceitfully in his dealings as a private citizen with other private citizens. I do not for one moment admit that a nation should treat other nations in a different spirit from that in which an honorable man would treat other men. (At the Sorbonne, Paris, April 23, 1910.) *Mem. Ed.* XV, 374; *Nat. Ed.* XIII, 527.

MORALITY AND ECONOMICS. It is a mistake of the gravest kind to believe that any moral question can be completely solved along purely economic lines; but it is an equally grave mistake not to recognize that no movement of moral reform can permanently avail unless it has the proper economic foundation. *Outlook*, July 15, 1911, p. 570.

MORALITY. See also CORRUPTION; EFFICIENCY; IDEALISM; IDEALS; INTELLECTUAL ACUTENESS; INTERNATIONAL MORALITY; RELIGION; SPIRITUAL DEVELOPMENT; SUCCESS; VIRTUES; WEAKNESS.

MORMONS. Any effort, openly or covertly, to reintroduce polygamy in the Mormon Church would merely mean that that Church had set its face toward destruction. The people of the United States will not tolerate polygamy; and if it were found that, with the sanction and approval or connivance of the Mormon Church people, polygamous marriages are now being entered into among Mormons, or if entered into are treated on any other footing than bigamous marriages are treated everywhere in the country, then the United States Government would unquestionably itself in the end take control of the whole question of polygamy, and there could be but one outcome to the struggle. In such event, the Mormon Church would be doomed, and if there be any Mormons who advocate in any shape or way disobedience to, or canceling of, or the evading of, the manifesto forbidding all further plural marriages, that Mormon is doing his best to secure the destruction of the Church. . . . The Mormon has the same right to his form of religious belief that the Jew and the Christian have to theirs; but, like the Jew and the Christian, he must not practise conduct which is in contravention of the law of the land. I have known monogamous Mormons whose standard of domestic life and morality and whose attitude toward the relations of men and women was as high as that of the best citizens of any other creed; indeed, among these

Mormons the standard of sexual morality was unusually high. Their children were numerous, healthy and well brought up; their young men were less apt than their neighbors to indulge in that course of vicious sexual dissipation so degrading to manhood and so brutal in the degradation it inflicts on women; and they were free from that vice, more destructive to civilization than any other can possibly be, the artificial restriction of families, the practice of sterile marriage; and which ultimately means destruction of the nation. (To Isaac Russell, February 17, 1911.) *Collier's*, April 15, 1911, p. 28.

MOROCCO. *See* ALGECIRAS CONFERENCE; JUSSERAND, J. J.

MORRIS, GOUVERNEUR. Morris was a true republican, and an American to the core. He was alike free from truckling subserviency to European opinion,—a degrading remnant of colonialism that unfortunately still lingers in certain limited social and literary circles,—and from the uneasy self-assertion that springs partly from sensitive vanity, and partly from a smothered doubt as to one's real position. Like most men of strong character, he had no taste for the "cosmopolitanism" that so generally indicates a weak moral and mental make-up. He enjoyed his stay in Europe to the utmost, and was intimate with the most influential men and charming women of the time; but he was heartily glad to get back to America, refused to leave it again, and always insisted that it was the most pleasant of all places in which to live. While abroad he was simply a gentleman among gentlemen. He never intruded his political views or national prejudices upon his European friends; but he was not inclined to suffer any imputation on his country. (1888.) *Mem. Ed.* VIII, 418; *Nat. Ed.* VII, 360.

——————. There has never been an American statesman of keener intellect or more brilliant genius. Had he possessed but a little more steadiness and self-control he would have stood among the two or three very foremost. He was gallant and fearless. He was absolutely upright and truthful; the least suggestion of falsehood was abhorrent to him. His extreme, aggressive frankness, joined to a certain imperiousness of disposition, made it difficult for him to get along well with many of the men with whom he was thrown in contact. In politics he was too much of a free lance ever to stand very high as a leader. He was very generous and hospitable; he was witty and humorous, a charming companion, and extremely fond of good living. He had a proud, almost hasty temper, and was quick to resent an insult. He was strictly just; and he made open war on all traits that displeased him, especially meanness and hypocrisy. He was essentially a strong man, and he was an American through and through. (1888.) *Mem. Ed.* VIII, 543; *Nat. Ed.* VII, 469.

MORRIS, GOUVERNEUR, AND THE CONVENTION. Morris played a very prominent part in the convention. He was a ready speaker, and among all the able men present there was probably no such really brilliant thinker. In the debates he spoke more often than any one else, although Madison was not far behind him; and his speeches betrayed, but with marked and exaggerated emphasis, both the virtues and the shortcomings of the Federalist school of thought. They show us, too, why he never rose to the first rank of statesmen. His keen, masterful mind, his far-sightedness, and the force and subtlety of his reasoning were all marred by his incurable cynicism and deep-rooted distrust of mankind. He throughout appears as *advocatus diaboli;* he puts the lowest interpretation upon every act, and frankly avows his disbelief in all generous and unselfish motives. His continual allusions to the overpowering influence of the baser passions, and to their mastery of the human race at all times, drew from Madison, although the two men generally acted together, a protest against his "forever inculcating the utter political depravity of men, and the necessity for opposing one vice and interest as the only possible check to another vice and interest." (1888.) *Mem. Ed.* VIII, 379; *Nat. Ed.* VII, 328.

MORRIS, GOUVERNEUR, AND THE FEDERALIST PARTY. Gouverneur Morris, like his far greater friend and political associate, Alexander Hamilton, had about him that "touch of the purple" which is always so strongly attractive. He was too unstable and erratic to leave a profound mark upon our political developments, but he performed two or three conspicuous feats, he rendered several marked services to the country, and he embodied to a peculiar degree both the qualities which made the Federalist party so brilliant and so useful, and those other qualities which finally brought about its downfall. Hamilton and even Jay represented better what was highest in the Federalist party. Gouverneur Morris stood for its weakness as well as for its strength. Able, fearless, and cultivated, deeply devoted to his people, and of much too tough fibre ever to be misled into losing his affection for things American because of American faults and shortcomings, as was and is the case with weaker natures, he was able to render distinguished service to his country. (Preface, April 1898.) *Mem. Ed.* VIII, 273; *Nat. Ed.* VII, 237.

MORRIS, GOUVERNEUR, AND THE FRENCH REVOLUTION. In his whole attitude towards the revolution, Morris represents better than any other man the clear-headed, practical statesman, who is genuinely devoted to the cause of constitutional freedom. He was utterly opposed to the old system of privilege on the one hand, and to the wild excesses of the fanatics on the other. The few liberals of the revolution were the only men in it who deserve our true respect. The republicans who champion the deeds of the Jacobins are traitors to their own principles; for the spirit of Jacobinism, instead of being identical with, is diametrically opposed to the spirit of true liberty. Jacobinism, socialism, communism, nihilism, and anarchism,—these are the real foes of a democratic republic, for each one, if it obtains control, obtains it only as the sure forerunner of a despotic tyranny and of some form of the one-man power.

Morris, an American, took a clearer and truer view of the French Revolution than did any of the contemporary European observers. Yet while with them it was the all-absorbing event of the age, with him, as is evident by his writings, it was merely an important episode; for to him it was dwarfed by the American Revolution of a decade or two back. (1888.) *Mem. Ed.* VIII, 495; *Nat. Ed.* VII, 427.

MORRIS, GOUVERNEUR, AND THE WAR OF 1812. In fact, throughout the War of 1812 he appeared as the open champion of treason to the nation, of dishonesty to the nation's creditors, and of cringing subserviency to a foreign power. It is as impossible to reconcile his course with his previous career and teachings as it is to try to make it square with the rules of statesmanship and morality. His own conduct affords a conclusive condemnation of his theories as to the great inferiority of a government conducted by the multitude, to a government conducted by the few who should have riches and education. Undoubtedly he was one of these few; he was an exceptionally able man, and a wealthy one; but he went farther wrong at this period than the majority of our people—the "mob" as he would have contemptuously called them—have ever gone at any time; for though every State in turn, and almost every statesman, has been wrong upon some issue or another, yet in the long run the bulk of the people have always hitherto shown themselves true to the cause of right. Morris strenuously insisted upon the need of property being defended from the masses; yet he advocated repudiation of the national debt, which he should have known to be quite as dishonest as the repudiation of his individual liabilities, and he was certainly aware that the step is a short one between refusing to pay a man what *ought* to be his and taking away from him what actually *is* his. (1888.) *Mem. Ed.* VIII, 536; *Nat. Ed.* VII, 464.

MORRIS, WILLIAM—POEMS OF. Last night I was reading the poems of William Morris. Of course they are rather absurd and one gets tired of them very soon; but there are some of them which have a kind of pre-Raphaelite attraction of their own. (To Sir George Otto Trevelyan, September 1905.) *Mem. Ed.* XXIV, 178; Bishop II, 152.

MOTHER, THE. The welfare of the woman is even more important than the welfare of the man; for the mother is the real Atlas, who bears aloft in her strong and tender arms the destiny of the world. She deserves honor and consideration such as no man should receive. She forfeits all claim to this honor and consideration if she shirks her duties. But the average American woman does not shirk them; and it is a matter of the highest obligation for us to see that they are performed under conditions which make for her welfare and happiness and for the welfare and happiness of the children she brings into the world. *Outlook,* August 27, 1910, p. 922.

——————. No man, not even the soldier who does his duty, stands quite on the level with the wife and mother who has done her duty. (*Outlook,* April 8, 1911.) *Mem. Ed.* XIV, 162; *Nat. Ed.* XII, 193.

MOTHER, THE. *See also* BIRTH CONTROL; CHILDREN; FAMILY; HOME; MARRIAGE; WOMEN.

MOUNTAIN CLIMBING. Mountaineering is among the manliest sports; and it is to be hoped that some of our young men with a taste for hard work and adventure among the high hills will attempt the conquest of these great untrodden mountains of their own continent. As with all pioneer work, there would be far more discomfort and danger, far more need to display resolution, hardihood, and wisdom in such an attempt than in any expedition on well-known and historic ground like the Swiss Alps; but the victory would be a hundred-fold better worth winning. (1893.) *Mem. Ed.* II, 415; *Nat. Ed.* II, 356.

MUCK-RAKERS. In Bunyan's "Pilgrim's Progress" you may recall the description of the Man with the Muck-rake, the man who could look no way but downward, with the muck-rake in his hand; who was offered a celestial crown for his muck-rake, but who would neither look up nor regard the crown he was offered, but continued to rake to himself the filth of the floor.

In "Pilgrim's Progress" the Man with the Muck-rake is set forth as the example of him whose vision is fixed on carnal instead of on spiritual things. Yet he also typifies the man who in this life consistently refuses to see aught that is lofty, and fixes his eyes with solemn intentness only on that which is vile and debasing. Now, it is very necessary that we should not flinch from seeing what is vile and debasing. There is filth on the floor, and it must be scraped up with the muck-rake; and there are times and places where this service is the most needed of all the services than can be performed. But the man who never does anything else, who never thinks or speaks or writes, save of his feats with the muck-rake, speedily becomes, not a help to society, not an incitement to good, but one of the most potent forces for evil. (At Washington, April 14, 1906.) *Mem. Ed.* XVIII, 571; *Nat. Ed.* XVI, 415.

——————. Muck-rakers who rake up much that ought to be raked up deserve well of the community, and the magazines and newspapers who publish their writings do a public service. But they must write the truth and the service they do must be real. The type of magazine which I condemn is what may be called the Ananias muck-raker type. No paper bought and owned by the special interests can be viler, or can play a more contemptible part in American politics, than the Ananias muck-raker type of magazine, the type of magazine of which the proprietor, editor, and writer seek to earn their livelihood by telling that what they know to be scandalous falsehoods about honest men. No boodling alderman, no convicted private or public thief serving his term in stripes in the penitentiary, is a baser and more degraded being than the writers of whom I speak. And they render this ill service, this worst of bad services to the public; they confuse the mind of the public as between honest and dishonest men. (At Pacific Theological Seminary, Spring 1911.) *Mem. Ed.* XV, 637; *Nat. Ed.* XIII, 668-669.

MUCK-RAKING. I want to let in light and air, but I do not want to let in sewer-gas. If a room is fetid and the windows are bolted I am perfectly contented to knock out the windows, but I would not knock a hole into the drain-pipe. In other words, I feel that the man who in a yellow newspaper or in a yellow magazine makes a ferocious attack on good men or even attacks bad men with exaggeration or for things they have not done, is a potent enemy of those of us who are really striving in good faith to expose bad men and drive them from power. I disapprove of the whitewash-brush quite as much as of mud-slinging, and it seems to me that the disapproval of one in no shape or way implies approval of the other. (To Ray Stannard Baker, April 9, 1906.) *Mem. Ed.* XXIV, 14; Bishop II, 11.

——————. Some persons are sincerely incapable of understanding that to denounce mud-slinging does not mean the indorsement of whitewashing; and both the interested individuals who need whitewashing, and those others who practise mud-slinging, like to encourage such confusion of ideas. One of the chief counts against those who make indiscriminate assault upon men in business or men in public life, is that they invite a reaction which is sure to tell powerfully in favor of the unscrupulous scoundrel who really ought to be attacked, who ought to be exposed, who ought, if possible, to be put in the penitentiary. (At Washington, April 14, 1906.) *Mem. Ed.* XVIII, 573; *Nat. Ed.* XVI, 416.

MUCK-RAKING. *See also* JOURNALISM, YELLOW.

MUGWUMPS. There is nothing that I have more regretted in the present campaign than the fact that many of those with whom we were proud to act in time past, have now felt obliged to go over to the camp of those who are, as we firmly believe, the most bitter foes of the very principles which Independent Republicanism has so stoutly upheld. Beyond question, many of our brother Independents have done what they conscientiously believe to be right; most certainly. We cannot question the honesty of purpose and the sincerity of motive that actuate men like Carl Schurz, George William Curtis, and Horace White; but I think these gentlemen have been drawn into a course of action

[357]

which, in the end, they must most bitterly regret, and into contact and companionship with men whom they must heartily despise, and I think they themselves would be among the first to see the evil results to the whole community that would inevitably follow in the fortunately exceedingly improbable event of their being able to accomplish the defeat of the Republican nominee. (Before Young Republican Club of Brooklyn, N. Y., October 18, 1884.) *Mem. Ed.* XVI, 73-74; *Nat. Ed.* XIV, 41.

——————. I regard this dishonest jealousy of decent men on the part of people who claim to be good, and this wholesale abuse, as two of the most potent forces for evil now existent in our nation. The foul and coarse abuse of an avowed partisan, willing to hurt the nation for the sake of personal or party gain, is bad enough; but it receives the final touch when steeped in the mendacious hypocrisy of the mugwump, the mis-called Independent. (To H. C. Lodge, July 11, 1889.) Lodge *Letters* I, 83.

MUGWUMPS. See also ELECTION OF 1884; INDEPENDENT.

MUIR, JOHN. Our greatest nature-lover and nature-writer, the man who has done most in securing for the American people the incalculable benefit of appreciation of wild nature in his own land, is John Burroughs. Second only to John Burroughs, and in some respects ahead even of John Burroughs, was John Muir. Ordinarily, the man who loves the woods and the mountains, the trees, the flowers, and the wild things, has in him some indefinable quality of charm which appeals even to those sons of civilization who care for little outside of paved streets and brick walls. John Muir was a fine illustration of this rule. . . . His was a dauntless soul, and also one brimming over with friendliness and kindliness. (*Outlook*, January 6, 1915.) *Mem. Ed.* XII, 566; *Nat. Ed.* XI, 288.

MULE-DEER. See DEER.

MUNICIPAL ADMINISTRATION. In spite of the fact that the urban growth is as yet small in the South, the time seems not very far distant when the average American, instead of living in the country, will live in a city or town, and when a very large number of Americans will live in cities of such size as show all the effects, for good and for evil, which accompany the crowding together of masses of people in limited areas.

Under such circumstances, it behooves every American interested in public life and public affairs to study as carefully as he can the phenomena of the life in these cities, and the administration of them. In this study of our own cities, nothing will help us more than an intelligent comparison with foreign cities. We desire to know whether certain phenomena appearing with us are constant and inevitable accompaniments of urban growth, or whether they are merely special to our peculiar conditions. An unintelligent comparison is of little use, and there is still less use in reasoning upon conclusions drawn from conditions wholly different from those which exist with us, and recklessly applied to our own circumstances; but if the conclusions are drawn carefully, and with ample allowance for different conditions, and if the comparison is really accurate the American civic student is put in possession of invaluable data. (*Atlantic Monthly*, April 1895.) *Mem. Ed.* XIV, 206; *Nat. Ed.* XII, 224-225.

MUNICIPAL ELECTIONS. A non-partisan ticket usually (although not always) [is] the right kind of ticket in municipal affairs, provided it represents not a bargain among factions but genuine non-partisanship with the genuine purpose to get the right men in control of the city government on a platform which deals with the needs of the average men and women, the men and women who work hard and who too often live hard. (1913.) *Mem. Ed.* XXII, 202; *Nat. Ed.* XX, 173.

MUNICIPAL GOVERNMENT — PARTICIPATION IN. Above all, every young man should realize that it is a disgrace to him not to take active part in some way in the work of governing the city. Whoever fails to do this, fails notably in his duty to the Commonwealth. (1891.) *Mem. Ed.* IX, 420; *Nat. Ed.* X, 534.

MUNICIPAL GOVERNMENT. See also CIVIC DUTY; LAW; POLICE COMMISSIONER; TAMMANY HALL.

MUNICIPAL OFFICERS — QUALIFICATIONS OF. What you want in your municipal authorities is, first and foremost, absolute honesty. Their views upon any conceivable question of public policy come second to that. You must have in an executive officer willingness to be faithful to his oath of office; willingness, again, to show the common virtues; willingness to behave with that measure of probity which you exact from every successful business man, from every reputable lawyer. (Before Liberal Club of Buffalo, N. Y., September 10, 1895.) *Mem. Ed.* XVI, 274; *Nat. Ed.* XIV, 195.

MUNICIPAL OWNERSHIP. I would point out to the advocates of municipal ownership that it is doubly incumbent upon them to take the most efficient means of rebuking municipal corruption and of insisting upon a high standard of continuous fidelity to duty among municipal employees. Only if the government ... of a municipality is honest will it be possible ever to justify fully the workings of municipal ownership. (Message to Legislature, April 21, 1899.) Murat Halstead, *The Life of Theodore Roosevelt.* (Akron, O., 1902), p. 131.

MUNICIPAL PROGRAM. This was nineteen years ago, but it makes a pretty good platform in municipal politics even to-day—smash corruption, take the municipal service out of the domain of politics, insist upon having a mayor who shall be a working man's mayor even more than a business man's mayor, and devote all attention possible to the welfare of the children. (1913.) *Mem. Ed.* XXII, 204; *Nat. Ed.* XX, 175.

MUNICIPAL SELF-GOVERNMENT. We believe that municipalities should have complete self-government as regards all the affairs that are exclusively their own, including the important matter of taxation, and that the burden of municipal taxation should be so shifted as to put the weight of land taxation upon the unearned rise in value of the land itself rather than upon the improvements, the buildings; the effort being to prevent the undue rise of rent. We regard it as peculiarly the province of the government to supervise tenement-houses, to secure proper living conditions, and to erect parks and playgrounds in the congested districts, and to use the schools as social centres. (*Century*, October 1913.) *Mem. Ed.* XIX, 549; *Nat. Ed.* XVII, 405.

MUNICIPAL WASTE. Waste is the largest single element in municipal finance. It persists largely because taxpayers cannot properly analyze public outlays. It could be greatly lessened by a system of public accounts and reports which would separate the wasteful from the useful outlays and subject them frequently and in a concise form to the scrutiny of taxpayers. (At Merchants' Association dinner, New York City, May 25, 1900.) *Mem. Ed.* XVI, 505.

MUNITION PLANTS. We should at once begin governmental encouragement and control of our munition plants. To make war on them is to make war on the United States; and those doing so should be treated accordingly and all who encourage them should be treated accordingly. The existing plants should be encouraged in every legitimate way, and provision made to encourage their continuance after the war. But it is most unfortunate that they are situated so near the seacoast. The establishment of munition plants farther inland should be provided for, without delay. Pittsburgh is as far east as any plant should by rights be placed. This whole matter of providing and regulating the output of munitions is one in which Germany should especially stand as our model. Let us study carefully what she has done, and then develop and adapt to our own needs the schemes which she has found successful, supplementing them with whatever additional measures our own experience may indicate as advisable. (*Metropolitan*, February 1916.) *Mem. Ed.* XX, 291; *Nat. Ed.* XVIII, 250.

MUNITIONS—SALE OF. It has been the settled policy of Germany to drive all other countries out of the business of manufacturing arms and supplies because, of course, if this were once substantially accomplished, the rest of the world would be completely helpless before Germany. . . .

It was Germany which for decades supplied Turkey with the means of keeping the Christians of her European and Asiatic provinces in a state of dreadful subjection. . . . Essen has been the centre of military supplies to belligerents and has exported on an enormous scale to belligerents in all the modern wars, making vast profits from this traffic even in the late Balkan wars. Germany has consistently followed this course, even when one of the belligerents alone had access to her markets and the other, with which she was nominally in sympathy, had no such access. . . . In short, Germany has thriven enormously on the sale of arms to belligerents when she was a neutral; she insisted that such sale be sanctioned by The Hague conventions; she, so far as possible, desires to prevent other nations from manufacturing arms; and if she is successful in this effort she will have taken another stride to world dominion. The professional pacifists, hyphenated Americans, and beef and cotton Americans; in short, all the representatives of American mollycoddleism, American greed, and downright treachery to America, in seeking to prevent shipments of munitions to the Allies, are playing the game of a brutal militarism against Belgium and against their own country. (*Metropolitan*, October 1915.) *Mem. Ed.* XX, 338-339; *Nat. Ed.* XVIII, 290-291.

MUNITIONS—SHIPMENT OF. The manufacture and shipment of arms and ammunition to any belligerent is moral or immoral, according to the use to which the arms and munitions are to be put. If they are to be used to prevent the redress of hideous wrongs inflicted on Belgium then it is immoral to ship them. If they are to be used for the redress of those wrongs and the restoration of Belgium to her deeply wronged and unoffending people, then it is eminently moral to send them. (Statement to press, May 1915.) *Mem. Ed.* XX, 444; *Nat. Ed.* XVIII, 380.

——————. The professional pacifists, the cotton Americans, the beef barons, and the German-Americans—in other words, the hyphenated Americans, the greedy materialists, and all the mollycoddles of both sexes—advocate the prohibition of the shipment of munitions to the Allies who are engaged in fighting Belgium's battles. They thereby take a stand which, not merely in the concrete case of the moment but in all future cases, would immensely benefit powerful and aggressive nations which cynically disregard the rules of international morality at the expense of the peaceful and industrial nations which have no thought of aggression and which act toward their neighbors with honorable good faith.

From the standpoint of international law, . . . we have the absolute right to make such shipments. Washington and Lincoln, in fact all our Presidents and secretaries have peremptorily refused to allow this right to be questioned. The right has been insisted upon by Germany in her own interest, more strongly than by any other nation, up to the beginning of the present war. (*Metropolitan*, October 1915.) *Mem. Ed.* XX, 342; *Nat. Ed.* XVIII, 293.

MUNITIONS. *See also* CONTRABAND; NEUTRAL RIGHTS; NEUTRALITY; WORLD WAR.

MURRAY, JOSEPH. He was by nature as straight a man, as fearless and as stanchly loyal, as any one whom I have ever met, a man to be trusted in any position demanding courage, integrity, and good faith. He did his duty in the public service, and became devotedly attached to the organization which he felt had given him his chance in life. . . . It was to him that I owe my entry into politics. I had at that time neither the reputation nor the ability to have won the nomination for myself, and indeed never would have thought of trying for it. (1913.) *Mem. Ed.* XXII, 72, 73; *Nat. Ed.* XX, 62, 63.

MUSIC. *See* PLEASURE.

N

NAPOLEON. I do not think there is a more impressive sepulchre on earth than . . . [Napoleon's] tomb; it is grandly simple. I am not very easily awestruck, but it certainly gave me a solemn feeling to look at the plain, red stone bier which contained what had once been the mightiest conqueror the world ever saw. He was a great fighter, at least, though otherwise I suppose an almost unmixed evil. Hannibal alone is his equal in military genius; and Cæsar in cruel power and ambition. What a child such a mere butcher as Tamerlane, Genghis Khan or Attila would have been in his hands! (To Anna Roosevelt, September 5, 1881.) *Cowles Letters*, 49.

NAPOLEON. *See also* FRENCH REVOLUTION; REVOLUTIONS; SELF-GOVERNMENT.

NATIONAL ART. *See* ART.

NATIONAL CHARACTER. It is character that counts in a nation as in a man. It is a good thing to have a keen, fine intellectual development in a nation, to produce orators, artists, successful business men; but it is an infinitely greater thing to have those solid qualities which we group together under the name of character —sobriety, steadfastness, the sense of obligation toward one's neighbor and one's God, hard common sense, and, combined with it, the lift of generous enthusiasm toward whatever is right. These are the qualities which go to make up true national greatness. (At Galena, Ill., April 27, 1900.) *Mem. Ed.* XII, 466; *Nat. Ed.* XIII, 437.

——————. Good laws in the State, like a good organization in an army, are the expressions of national character. Leaders will be developed in military and in civil life alike; and weapons and tactics change from generation to generation, as methods of achieving good government change in civic affairs; but the fundamental qualities which make for good citizenship do not change any more than the fundamental qualities which make good soldiers. (At Antietam, Md., September 17, 1903.) *Mem. Ed.* XII, 622; *Nat. Ed.* XI, 337.

——————. Just as in private life many of the men of strongest character are the very men of loftiest and most exalted morality, so I believe that in national life, as the ages go by, we shall find that the permanent national types will more and more tend to become those in

[360]

which, though intellect stands high, character stands higher; in which rugged strength and courage, rugged capacity to resist wrongful aggression by others, will go hand in hand with a lofty scorn of doing wrong to others. (At Oxford University, England, June 7, 1910.) *Mem. Ed.* XIV, 101; *Nat. Ed.* XII, 55.

——————. The prime work for this nation at this moment is to rebuild its own character. Let us find our own souls; let us frankly face the world situation to-day as it affects ourselves and as it affects all other countries. (*Metropolitan*, February 1916.) *Mem. Ed.* XX, 300; *Nat. Ed.* XVIII, 258.

——————. If a nation is not proudly willing and able to fight for a just cause—for the lives of its citizens, for the honor of its flag, even for the rescue of some oppressed foreign nationality—then such a nation will always be an ignoble nation, and this whether it achieves the sordid prosperity of those who are merely successful hucksters, or whether it kills its virility by an exclusive appreciation of grace, ease, and beauty. Strength, courage, and justice must come first. (Before Amer. Acad. and Nat. Inst. of Arts and Letters, New York City, November 16, 1916.) *Mem. Ed.* XIV, 453; *Nat. Ed.* XII, 329.

NATIONAL CHARACTER — GROWTH OF. The men who have profoundly influenced the growth of our national character have been in most cases precisely those men whose influence was for the best and was strongly felt as antagonistic to the worst tendency of the age. The great writers, who have written in prose or verse, have done much for us. The great orators whose burning words on behalf of liberty, of union, of honest government, have rung through our legislative halls, have done even more. Most of all has been done by the men who have spoken to us through deeds and not words, or whose words have gathered their especial charm and significance because they came from men who did speak in deeds. (*Forum*, February 1895.) *Mem. Ed.* XV, 14; *Nat. Ed.* XIII, 12.

NATIONAL CHARACTER. *See also* CHARACTER; HEROES.

NATIONAL DECAY. If our population decreases; if we lose the virile, manly qualities, and sink into a nation of mere hucksters, putting gain above national honor, and subordinating everything to mere ease of life; then we shall indeed reach a condition worse than that of the ancient civilizations in the years of their decay. But at present no comparison could be less apt than that of Byzantium, or Rome in its later years, with a great modern state where the thronging millions who make up the bulk of the population are wage-earners, who themselves decide their own destinies; a state which is able in time of need to put into the field armies, composed exclusively of its own citizens, more numerous than any which the world has ever before seen, and with a record of fighting in the immediate past with which there is nothing in the annals of antiquity to compare. (*Forum*, January 1897.) *Mem. Ed.* XIV, 150; *Nat. Ed.* XIII, 259-260.

——————. It needs but little of the vision of a seer to foretell what must happen in any community if the average woman ceases to become the mother of a family of healthy children, if the average man loses the will and the power to work up to old age and to fight whenever the need arises. If the homely commonplace virtues die out, if strength of character vanishes in graceful self-indulgence, if the virile qualities atrophy, then the nation has lost what no material prosperity can offset. (At Oxford University, England, June 7, 1910.) *Mem. Ed.* XIV, 86; *Nat. Ed.* XII, 42.

NATIONAL DECAY. *See also* DEATH; DECADENCE; ROMAN EMPIRE.

NATIONAL DEFENSE. We can afford as a people to differ on the ordinary party questions; but if we are both farsighted and patriotic we cannot afford to differ on the all-important question of keeping the national defenses as they should be kept; of not alone keeping up, but of going on with building up of, the United States Navy, and of keeping our small Army at least at its present size and making it the most efficient for its size that there is on the globe. Remember, you here who are listening to me, that to applaud patriotic sentiments and to turn out to do honor to the dead heroes who by land or by sea won honor for our flag is only worthwhile if we are prepared to show that our energies do not exhaust themselves in words; if we are prepared to show that we intend to take to heart the lessons of the past and make things ready so that if ever, which heaven forbid, the need should arise, our fighting men on sea and ashore shall be able to rise to the standard established by their predecessors in our services of the past. *Address of President Roosevelt on the Occasion of the Reinterment of the Remains of John Paul Jones at Annapolis, Md., April 24, 1906.* (Government Printing Office, 1906), pp. 18-20.

———————. A nation that cannot take its own part is at times almost as fertile a source of mischief in the world at large as is a nation which does wrong to others, for its very existence puts a premium on such wrong-doing. Therefore, a nation must fit itself to defend its honor and interest against outside aggression; and this necessarily means that in a free democracy every man fit for citizenship must be trained so that he can do his full duty to the nation in war no less than in peace. (1916.) *Mem. Ed.* XX, 232; *Nat. Ed.* XVIII, 200.

———————. The only kind of peace worth having is the peace of righteousness and justice; the only nation that can serve other nations is the strong and valiant nation; and the only great international policies worth considering are those whose upholders believe in them strongly enough to fight for them. . . . A nation is utterly contemptible if it will not fight in its own defense. A nation is not wholly admirable unless in time of stress it will go to war for a great ideal wholly unconnected with its immediate material interest. (1916.) *Mem. Ed.* XX, 261; *Nat. Ed.* XVIII, 225.

———————. Nations are made, defended, and preserved, not by the illusionists, but by the men and women who practise the homely virtues in time of peace, and who in time of righteous war are ready to die, or to send those they love best to die, for a shining ideal. (1918.) *Mem. Ed.* XXI, 357; *Nat. Ed.* XIX, 325.

NATIONAL DEFENSE—PLANS FOR. It is not desirable that civilians, acting independently of and without the help of military and naval advisers, shall prepare minute or detailed plans as to what ought to be done for our national defense. But civilians are competent to advocate plans in outline exactly as I have here advocated them. Moreover, and most important, they are competent to try to make public opinion effective in these matters. A democracy must have proper leaders. But these leaders must be able to appeal to a proper sentiment in the democracy. It is the prime duty of every right-thinking citizen at this time to aid his fellow counrymen to understand the need of working wisely for peace, the folly of acting unwisely for peace, and, above all, the need of real and thorough national preparedness against war. (New York *Times,* November 29, 1914.) *Mem. Ed.* XX, 208; *Nat. Ed.* XVIII, 178.

NATIONAL DEFENSE. See also ARMY; DEFENSE; HAWAII; LEAGUE OF NATIONS; MILITARY TRAINING; NAVY; PACIFISM; PANAMA CANAL; PREPAREDNESS; SELF-PRESERVATION.

NATIONAL DUTY. Let this nation fear God and take its own part. Let it scorn to do wrong to great or small. Let it exercise patience and charity toward all other peoples, and yet at whatever cost unflinchingly stand for the right when the right is menaced by the might which backs wrong. (1916.) *Mem. Ed.* XX, 260; *Nat. Ed.* XVIII, 224.

NATIONAL DUTY. See also DUTY; "FEAR GOD AND TAKE YOUR OWN PART"; LEAGUE OF NATIONS.

NATIONAL EFFICIENCY. In this stage of the world's history to be fearless, to be just, and to be efficient are the three great requirements of National life. National efficiency is the result of natural resources well handled, of freedom of opportunity for every man, and of the inherent capacity, trained ability, knowledge and will, collectively and individually, to use that opportunity. (Message to Congress, January 22, 1909.) *Presidential Addresses and State Papers* VIII, 2095.

NATIONAL EXISTENCE. While the nation that has dared to be great, that has had the will and the power to change the destiny of the ages, in the end must die, yet no less surely the nation that has played the part of the weakling must also die; and whereas the nation that has done nothing leaves nothing behind it, the nation that has done a great work really continues, though in changed form, to live forevermore. (At Minnesota State Fair, September 2, 1901.) *Mem. Ed.* XV, 333; *Nat. Ed.* XIII, 473.

———————. I really believe that people sometimes think of "new" nations as being suddenly created out of nothing; they certainly speak as if they were not aware that the newest and the oldest nations and races must of course have identically the same length of racial pedigree. They talk, moreover, of the "destruction" of the inhabitants of Mexico, and of the "destruction" of the inhabitants of Tasmania, as if the processes were alike. In Tasmania the people were absolutely destroyed; none of their blood is left. But the bulk of the blood of Mexico, and a part of the blood of the governing classes of Mexico (including Diaz), is that of the Mexicans whom Cortez and his successors conquered. In the same way Australia and Canada and the United States are "new" commonwealths only in the sense that Syracuse and Cyrene were new compared with Athens and

Corinth. (To A. J. Balfour, March 5, 1908.) *Mem. Ed.* XXIV, 127; Bishop II, 109.

———————. No nation deserves to exist if it permits itself to lose the stern and virile virtues; and this without regard to whether the loss is due to the growth of a heartless and all-absorbing commercialism, to prolonged indulgence in luxury and soft effortless ease, or to the deification of a warped and twisted sentimentality. *Outlook,* May 7, 1910, p. 19.

NATIONAL GREATNESS. It is not what we have that will make us a great nation; it is the way in which we use it.

I do not undervalue for a moment our material prosperity; like all Americans, I like big things; big prairies, big forests and mountains, big wheat-fields, railroads,—and herds of cattle, too,—big factories, steamboats, and everything else. But we must keep steadily in mind that no people were ever yet benefited by riches if their prosperity corrupted their virtue. It is of more importance that we should show ourselves honest, brave, truthful, and intelligent, than that we should own all the railways and grain elevators in the world. We have fallen heirs to the most glorious heritage a people ever received, and each one must do his part if we wish to show that the nation is worthy of its good fortune. Here we are not ruled over by others, as in the case of Europe; we rule ourselves. All American citizens, whether born here or elsewhere, whether of one creed or another, stand on the same footing; we welcome every honest immigrant no matter from what country he comes, provided only that he leaves off his former nationality, and remains neither Celt nor Saxon, neither Frenchman nor German, but becomes an American, desirous of fulfilling in good faith the duties of American citizenship. (At Dickinson, Dakota Territory, July 4, 1886.) Hermann Hagedorn, *Roosevelt in the Bad Lands.* (Houghton Mifflin Co., Boston, 1921), pp. 409-410.

———————. If we are to be a really great people, we must strive in good faith to play a great part in the world. We cannot avoid meeting great issues. All that we can determine for ourselves is whether we shall meet them well or ill. (Before the Hamilton Club, Chicago, April 10, 1899.) *Mem. Ed.* XV, 271; *Nat. Ed.* XIII, 322.

———————. Normally, the nation that achieves greatness, like the individual who achieves greatness, can do so only at the cost of anxiety and bewilderment and heart-wearing effort. Timid people, people scant of faith and hope, and good people who are not accustomed to the roughness of the life of effort—are almost sure to be disheartened and dismayed by the work and the worry, and overmuch cast down by the shortcomings, actual or seeming, which in real life always accompany the first stages even of what eventually turn out to be the most brilliant victories. (At Hartford, Conn., August 22, 1902.) *Mem. Ed.* XVIII, 359-360; Nat. Ed. XVI, 274.

———————. I would not pretend for a moment . . . that merely military proficiency on land or sea would by itself make this or any other nation great. First and foremost come the duties within the gates of our own household; first and foremost our duty is to strive to bring about a better administration of justice, cleaner, juster, more equitable methods in our political, business, and social life, the reign of law, the reign of that orderly liberty which was the first consideration in the minds of the founders of this Republic. Our duties at home are of the first importance. But our duties abroad are of vital consequence also. This nation may fail, no matter how well it keeps itself prepared against the possibility of disaster from abroad; but it will certainly fail if we do not thus keep ourselves prepared. (At Naval War College, Newport, R. I., July 22, 1908.) *Mem. Ed.* XVIII, 338; *Nat. Ed.* XVI, 256.

———————. In any nation those citizens who possess the pride in their nationality, without which they cannot claim to be good citizens, must feel a particular satisfaction in the deeds of every man who adds to the sum of worthy national achievement. The great nations of antiquity, of the middle ages, and of modern times were and are great in each several case, not only because of the collective achievements of each people as a whole, but because of the sum of the achievemnts of the men of special eminence; and this whether they excelled in warcraft or statecraft, as road-makers or cathedral builders, as men of letters, men of art, or men of science. The field of effort is almost limitless; and preeminent success in any part of it is not only a good thing for humanity as a whole, but should be especially prized by the nation to which the man achieving the success belongs. (At Saint-Gaudens Exhibition, Corcoran Art Gallery, Washington, D. C., December 15, 1908.) *Mem. Ed.* XII, 559; *Nat. Ed.* XI, 282.

———————. The precise form of government, democratic or otherwise, is the instrument, the tool, with which we work. It is important to have a good tool. But, even if it is the best possible, it is only a tool. No implement can ever take the place of the guiding intelligence that wields it. A very bad tool will ruin the work of the best craftsman; but a good tool in bad hands is no better. In the last analysis the all-important factor in national greatness is national character. (At Oxford University, England, June 7, 1910.) *Mem. Ed.* XIV, 97; *Nat. Ed.* XII, 52.

NATIONAL GREATNESS—SOURCE OF. No nation can achieve real greatness if its people are not both essentially moral and essentially manly; both sets of qualities are necessary. It is an admirable thing to possess refinement and cultivation, but the price is too dear if they must be paid for at the cost of the rugged fighting qualities which make a man able to do a man's work in the world, and which make his heart beat with that kind of love of country which is shown not only in readiness to try to make her civic life better, but also to stand up manfully for her when her honor and influence are at stake in a dispute with a foreign power. (*The Bachelor of Arts,* March 1896.) *Mem. Ed.* XV, 235; *Nat. Ed.* XIII, 177.

——————. Ultimately no nation can be great unless its greatness is laid on foundations of righteousness and decency. We cannot do great deeds as a nation unless we are willing to do the small things that make up the sum of greatness, unless we believe in energy and thrift, unless we believe that we have more to do than simply accomplish material prosperity, unless, in short, we do our full duty as private citizens interested alike in the honor of the State. (At Grant's Tomb, New York City, May 30, 1899.) *Mem. Ed.* XVI, 494; *Nat. Ed.* XIV, 333.

——————. The greatness of our nation in the past has rested upon the fact that the people had power, and that they used it aright for great and worthy ends. Washington and Lincoln, each in the degree that his generation rendered possible, trusted to and believed in the people, steadfastly refused to represent anything save what was highest and best in the people, and by appealing to this highest and best brought it out and made it prominent. Each called upon his countrymen to lay down their lives for an ideal, and then called upon the survivors to perform the even harder task of leading their lives in such shape as to realize the ideal for which the dead men had died. (*Outlook,* March 25, 1911.) *Mem. Ed.* XIX, 146; *Nat. Ed.* XVII, 105.

——————. No nation can be great unless its sons and daughters have in them the quality to rise level to the needs of heroic days. Yet this heroic quality is but the apex of a pyramid of which the broad foundations must solidly rest on the performance of duties so ordinary that to impatient minds they seem commonplace. (*Metropolitan,* October 1918.) *Mem. Ed.* XXI, 264; *Nat. Ed.* XIX, 244.

NATIONAL GUARD. Now that the organized militia, the National Guard, has been incorporated with the army as a part of the national forces, it behooves the government to do every reasonable thing in its power to perfect its efficiency. It should be assisted in its instruction and otherwise aided more liberally than heretofore. The continuous services of many well-trained regular officers will be essential in this connection. Such officers must be specially trained at service schools best to qualify them as instructors of the National Guard. (Eighth Annual Message, Washington, December 8, 1908.) *Mem. Ed.* XVII, 637; *Nat. Ed.* XV, 542.

NATIONAL GUARD. *See also* MILITIA.

NATIONAL HEROES. *See* HEROES.

NATIONAL HONOR. A really great people, proud and high-spirited, would face all the disasters of war rather than purchase that base prosperity which is bought at the price of national honor. (Address as Assistant Secretary of the Navy, Naval War College, June 1897.) *Mem. Ed.* XV, 242; *Nat. Ed.* XIII, 184.

——————. Until we put honor and duty first, and are willing to risk something in order to achieve righteousness both for ourselves and for others, we shall accomplish nothing; and we shall earn and deserve the contempt of the strong nations of mankind. (To Samuel T. Dutton, chairman of Committee on Armenian Outrages, November 24, 1915.) *Mem. Ed.* XX, 446; *Nat. Ed.* XVIII, 383.

NATIONAL HONOR—DANGER TO. In this presidential election we confront a danger graver than any that has menaced the country from its birth, save at the time of the election of 1860 alone. On the result next month depends whether we shall hang our heads with shame because our country has become the dupe and willing prey of dishonest demagogues, because we have announced that we do not wish to pay our just debts, because we have announced that we do not wish to enforce our

NATIONAL HONOR

laws and are willing to account the national honor as nothing in the balance against successful trickery; or else we shall stand prouder than ever of our citizenship in that great republic whose boast it has been that at last this nation, alone of all nations through the ages, has solved the problem of preserving orderly liberty, of standing stoutly for the rights of the individual, while yet being careful to allow no man to be wronged, and of guarding with jealous care that national honor which can be seriously hurt only by our own folly or our own weakness. (Before American Republican College League, Chicago, October 15, 1896.) *Mem. Ed.* XVI, 396; *Nat. Ed.* XIV, 260.

NATIONAL HONOR—DEFENSE OF. No nation should ever wage war wantonly, but no nation should ever avoid it at the cost of the loss of national honor. A nation should never fight unless forced to; but it should always be ready to fight. The mere fact that it is ready will generally spare it the necessity of fighting. (Address as Assistant Secretary of the Navy, Naval War College, June 1897.) *Mem. Ed.* XV, 256; *Nat. Ed.* XIII, 195.

NATIONAL HONOR — MAINTENANCE OF. When a question of national honor or of national right or wrong is at stake, no question of financial interest should be considered for a moment. (*The Bachelor of Arts*, March 1896.) *Mem. Ed.* XV, 236; *Nat. Ed.* XIII, 178.

————. In every nation there is, as there has been from time immemorial, a good deal of difficulty in combining the policies of upholding the national honor abroad, and of preserving a not too heavily taxed liberty at home. (1900.) *Mem. Ed.* XIII, 300; *Nat. Ed.* X, 198.

NATIONAL HONOR. *See also* PEACE; RIGHTEOUSNESS; WORLD WAR.

NATIONAL INHERITANCE. In this country of ours no man can permanently leave to his descendants the right to live softly; and if he could leave such a right it would in the end prove to be a right not worth having. The inheritance really worth while which we can transmit to our children and to our children's children is the ability to do work that counts, not the means of avoiding work—the ability for efficient effort, not the opportunity for the slothful avoidance of all effort. (At Chicago, June 17, 1912.) *Mem. Ed.* XIX, 310; *Nat. Ed.* XVII, 225.

NATIONAL OBLIGATIONS

————. We inherit as freemen this fair and mighty land only because our fathers and forefathers had iron in their blood. We can leave our heritage undiminished to those who come after us only if we in our turn show a resolute and rugged manliness in the dark days of trial that have come upon us. (*Metropolitan*, January 1918.) *Mem. Ed.* XXI, 283; *Nat. Ed.* XIX, 261.

NATIONAL INHERITANCE. *See also* AMERICAN PEOPLE; LEISURE; WORK.

NATIONAL INTERESTS. It is right that the United States should regard primarily its own interests. But I believe that I speak for a considerable number of my countrymen when I say that we ought not solely to consider our own interests. Above all, we should not do as the present administration does; for it refuses to take any concrete action in favor of any nation which is wronged; and yet it also refuses to act so that we may ourselves be sufficient for our own protection. (New York *Times*, November 8, 1914.) *Mem. Ed.* XX, 92; *Nat. Ed.* XVIII, 79.

NATIONAL LITERATURE. *See* LITERATURE.

NATIONAL MORALITY. *See* INTERNATIONAL MORALITY; MORALITY.

NATIONAL OBLIGATIONS—FULFILLMENT OF. President Wilson and Secretary Bryan . . . take the view that when the United States assumes obligations in order to secure small and unoffending neutral nations or noncombatants generally against hideous wrong, its action is not predicated on any intention to make the guaranty effective. They take the view that when we are asked to redeem in the concrete promises we made in the abstract, our duty is to disregard our obligations and to preserve ignoble peace for ourselves by regarding with cold-blooded and timid indifference the most frightful ravages of war committed at the expense of a peaceful and unoffending country. This is the cult of cowardice. That Messrs. Wilson and Bryan profess it and put it in action would be of small consequence if only they themselves were concerned. The importance of their action is that it commits the United States. (*Independent*, January 4, 1915.) *Mem. Ed.* XX, 178; *Nat. Ed.* XVIII, 153.

NATIONAL OBLIGATIONS. *See also* INTERNATIONAL AGREEMENTS; PROMISES; TREATIES.

[365]

NATIONAL PARKS. See Forest Reserves; Grand Canyon; Yellowstone Park.

NATIONAL PROBLEMS — SOLUTION OF. The conditions which have told for our marvellous material well-being, which have developed to a very high degree our energy, self-reliance and individual initiative, have also brought the care and anxiety inseparable from the accumulation of great wealth in industrial centres. Upon the success of our experiment much depends, not only as regards our own welfare, but as regards the welfare of mankind. If we fail, the cause of free self-government throughout the world will rock to its foundations, and therefore our responsibility is heavy, to ourselves, to the world as it is to-day, and to the generations yet unborn. There is no good reason why we should fear the future, but there is every reason why we should face it seriously, neither hiding from ourselves the gravity of the problems before us nor fearing to approach those problems with the unbending, unflinching purpose to solve them aright.

Yet, after all, though the problems are new, though the tasks set before us differ from the tasks set before our fathers who founded and preserved this Republic, the spirit in which these tasks must be undertaken and these problems faced, if our duty is to be well done, remains essentially unchanged. (Inaugural Address as President, Washington, March 4, 1905.) *Mem. Ed.* XVII, 313; *Nat. Ed.* XV, 268.

NATIONAL REPUTATION. Other peoples have been as devoted to liberty, and yet, because of lack of hard-headed common sense and of ability to show restraint and subordinate individual passions for the general good, have failed so signally in the struggle of life as to become a byword among the nations. Yet other peoples, again, have possessed all possible thrift and business capacity, but have been trampled underfoot, or have played a sordid and ignoble part in the world, because their business capacity was unaccompanied by any of the lift toward nobler things which marks a great and generous nation. The stern but just rule of judgment for humanity is that each nation shall be known by its fruits; and if there are no fruits, if the nation has failed, it matters but little whether it has failed through meanness of soul or through lack of robustness of character. We must judge a nation by the net result of its life and activity. (At Union League, Philadelphia, November 22, 1902.) *Mem. Ed.* XVIII, 480; *Nat. Ed.* XVI, 357.

NATIONAL RESPONSIBILITY. We are a great nation and we are compelled, whether we will or not, to face the responsibilities that must be faced by all great nations. It is not in our power to avoid meeting them. All that we can decide is whether we shall meet them well or ill. (At Lincoln Club dinner, New York City, February 13, 1899.) *Mem. Ed.* XVI, 474; *Nat. Ed.* XIV, 315.

———————. American citizens must understand that they cannot advocate or acquiesce in an evil course of action and then escape responsibility for the results. (*Everybody's,* January 1915.) *Mem. Ed.* XX, 159; *Nat. Ed.* XVIII, 136.

NATIONAL RESPONSIBILITY. See also International Duty.

NATIONAL RIGHTS. See League of Nations; States' Rights.

NATIONAL SELF-DETERMINATION. See Fourteen Points.

NATIONAL SELF-RELIANCE. No friendliness with other nations, no good-will for them or by them, can take the place of national self-reliance. No alliance, no inoffensive conduct on our part, would supply, in time of need, the failure in ability to hold our own with the strong hand. We must work out our own destiny by our own strength. (At Galena, Ill., April 27, 1900.) *Mem. Ed.* XII, 469; *Nat. Ed.* XIII, 439-440.

NATIONAL SELF-RELIANCE. See also Alliances; Defense; Preparedness.

NATIONAL SELF-RESPECT. No amount of material prosperity can atone for lack of national self-respect; and in no way can national self-respect be easier lost than through a peace obtained or preserved unworthily, whether through cowardice or through sluggish indifference. (*Century Magazine,* November 1895.) *Mem. Ed.* XVI, 348; *Nat. Ed.* XIV, 248.

NATIONAL SOLIDARITY. See Sectionalism.

NATIONAL UNITY. I ask you to help strike the note that shall unite our people. As a people we must be united. If we are not united we shall slip into the gulf of measureless disaster. We must be strong in purpose for our own defense and bent on securing justice within our borders. If as a nation we are split into warring camps, if we teach our citizens not to look upon one another as brothers but as enemies divided by the hatred of creed for creed or of those of one race against those of another race, surely we shall fail and our great democratic experiment on this continent will go down in crushing overthrow. (Before Knights of Columbus, New York City, October 12, 1915.) *Mem. Ed.* XX, 471; *Nat. Ed.* XVIII, 404.

──────────. This war has shown us in vivid and startling fashion the danger of allowing our people to separate along lines of racial origin and linguistic cleavage. We shall be guilty of criminal folly if we fail to insist on the complete and thoroughgoing unification of our people. (1918.) *Mem. Ed.* XXI, 330; *Nat. Ed.* XIX, 301.

NATIONAL UNITY. *See also* AMERICAN PEOPLE; RACIAL UNITY.

NATIONAL UNSELFISHNESS. National unselfishness and self-sacrifice, national self-mastery, and the development of national power, can never be achieved by words alone. National unselfishness—which is another way of saying service rendered to internationalism—can become effective only if the nation is willing to sacrifice something, is willing to face risk and effort and endure hardship in order to render service. (1916.) *Mem. Ed.* XX, 529; *Nat. Ed.* XVIII, 454.

NATIONAL UNSELFISHNESS. *See also* INTERNATIONAL DUTY.

NATIONALISM. We can help humanity at large very much to the extent that we are national—in the proper sense, not in the chauvinistic sense—that we are devoted to our own country first. I prize the friendship of the man who cares for his family more than he cares for me; if he does not care for his family any more than he cares for me, I know that he cares for me very little. What is true in individual relations is no less true in the world at large. (Before Amer. Acad. and Nat. Inst. of Arts and Letters, New York City, November 16, 1916.) *Mem. Ed.* XIV, 451; *Nat. Ed.* XII, 327.

──────────. I do not ask for overcentralization; but I do ask that we work in a spirit of broad and far-reaching nationalism when we work for what concerns the people as a whole. We are all Americans. (*Outlook*, January 14, 1911.) *Mem. Ed.* XIX, 83; *Nat. Ed.* XVII, 51.

──────────. We must resolutely refuse to permit our great nation, our great America, to be split into a score of little replicas of European nationalities, and to become a Balkan Peninsula on a larger scale. We are a nation, and not a hodge-podge of foreign nationalities. We are a people, and not a polyglot boarding-house. We must insist on a unified nationality, with one flag, one language, one set of national ideals. We must shun as we would shun the plague all efforts to make us separate in groups of separate nationalities. We must all of us be Americans, and nothing but Americans; and all good Americans must stand on an equality of consideration and respect, without regard to their creed or to the land from which their forebears came. (1918.) *Mem. Ed.* XXI, 335; *Nat. Ed.* XIX, 306.

──────────. There is no limit to the greatness of the future before America, before our beloved land. But we can realize it only if we are Americans, if we are nationalists, with all the fervor of our hearts and all the wisdom of our brains. We can serve the world at all only if we serve America first and best. We must work along our own national lines in every field of achievement. We must feel in the very marrow of our being that our loyalty is due only to America, and that it is not diluted by loyalty for any other nation or all other nations. (1918.) *Mem. Ed.* XXI, 358; *Nat. Ed.* XIX, 326.

NATIONALISM, AMERICAN. The first essential here in the United States is that we shall be one nation and that the American nation. We are a new nation, by blood akin to but different from every one of the nations of Europe. We have our own glorious past, we are a nation with a future such as no other nation in the world has before it, if only we, the men and women of to-day, do our full duty and bring up our sons and daughters to do their full duty, as Americans, and as nothing else. (At Springfield, O., May 25, 1918.) *Mem. Ed.* XXIV, 523; Bishop II, 447.

──────────. Let us trust for our salvation to a sound and intense American nationalism.

The horse-sense of the matter is that all agreements to further the cause of sound internationalism must be based on recognition of the fact that, as the world is actually constituted, our present prime need is this sound and intense American nationalism. The first essential of this sound nationalism is that the nation shall trust to its own fully prepared strength for its own defense. So far as possible, its strength must also be used to secure justice for others and must never be used to wrong others. But unless we possess and prepare the strength, we can neither help ourselves nor others. (1918.) *Mem. Ed.* XXI, 350; *Nat. Ed.* XIX, 319.

NATIONALISM AND INTERNATIONALISM. Patriotism stands in national matters as love of family does in private life. Nationalism corresponds to the love a man bears for his wife and children. Internationalism corresponds to the feeling he has for his neighbors generally. The sound nationalist is the only type of really helpful internationalist, precisely as in private relations it is the man who is most devoted to his own wife and children who is apt in the long run to be the most satisfactory neighbor. To substitute internationalism for nationalism means to do away with patriotism, and is as vicious and as profoundly demoralizing as to put promiscuous devotion to all other persons in the place of steadfast devotion to a man's own family. (Lafayette Day exercises, New York City, September 6, 1918.) *Mem. Ed.* XXI, 410; *Nat. Ed.* XIX, 372.

————. I heartily favor true internationalism as an addition to, but never as substitute for, a fervid and intensely patriotic nationalism. I will gladly back any wise and honest effort to create a league of nations, but only on condition that it is treated as an addition to, and not as a substitute for, the full preparedness of our own strength for our own defense. (October 15, 1918.) *Roosevelt in the Kansas City Star*, 231.

NATIONALISM VERSUS PARTICULARISM. The minute that the spirit which finds its healthy development in local self-government, and is the antidote to the dangers of an extreme centralization, develops into mere particularism, into inability to combine effectively for achievement of a common end, then it is hopeless to expect great results. Poland and certain republics of the Western Hemisphere are the standard examples of failure of this kind; and the United States would have ranked with them, and her name would have become a byword of derision, if the forces of union had not triumphed in the Civil War. (At Oxford University, England, June 7, 1910.) *Mem. Ed.* XIV, 86; *Nat. Ed.* XII, 42.

NATIONALISM. *See also* ALLEGIANCE; AMERICAN PEOPLE; AMERICANISM; BIG STICK; CITIZENSHIP; INDEPENDENCE SPIRIT; INTERNATIONALISM; LOYALTY; NEW NATIONALISM; PATRIOTISM; STATES' RIGHTS.

NATIONALITY, DUAL. Surely it ought not to be necessary to say that the rights of every citizen in this land are as great and as sacred as those of any other citizen. The United States cannot with self-respect permit its organic and fundamental law to be overridden by the laws of a foreign country. It cannot acknowledge any such theory as this of "a dual nationality"—which, incidentally, is a self-evident absurdity. (*Metropolitan*, June 1915.) *Mem. Ed.* XX, 438; *Nat. Ed.* XVIII, 375.

NATIONALITY. *See also* ALLEGIANCE; CITIZENSHIP.

NATIONALS—PROTECTION OF. *See* INTERVENTION.

NATURAL GAS. *See* MINERAL FUELS.

NATURAL HISTORY. The time has passed when we can afford to accept as satisfactory a science of animal life whose professors are either mere roaming field collectors or mere closet catalogue writers who examine and record minute differences in "specimens" precisely as philatelists examine and record minute differences in postage-stamps—and with about the same breadth of view and power of insight into the essential. Little is to be gained by that kind of "intensive" collecting and cataloguing which bears fruit only in innumerable little pamphlets describing with meticulous care unimportant new sub-species, or new "species" hardly to be distinguished from those already long known. (Introduction to *Tropical Wild Life in British Guiana* by William Beebe and others; dated December 10, 1916.) *Mem. Ed.* XIV, 521; *Nat. Ed.* XII, 386.

NATURAL HISTORY — ROOSEVELT'S INTEREST IN. I can no more explain why I like "natural history" than why I like California canned peaches; nor why I do not care for that enormous brand of natural history which deals with invertebrates any more than why I do not care for brandied peaches. All I can say is that almost as soon as I began to read at all I began to like to read about the natural history of beasts and birds and the more formidable or interesting reptiles and fishes. (*American Museum Journal*, May 1918.) *Mem. Ed.* VI, 443; *Nat. Ed.* V, 384.

NATURAL HISTORY—TEACHING OF. I don't believe for a minute that some of these men who are writing nature stories and putting the word "truth" prominently in their prefaces know the heart of the wild things. Neither do

I believe that certain men who, while they may say nothing specifically about truth, do claim attention as realists because of their animal stories, have succeeded in learning the real secrets of the life of the wilderness. They don't know, or if they do know, they indulge in the wildest exaggeration under the mistaken notion that they are strengthening their stories.

As for the matter of giving these books to the children for the purpose of teaching them the facts of natural history—why, it's an outrage. If these stories were written as fables, published as fables, and put into the children's hands as fables, all well and good. As it is, they are read and believed because the writer not only says they are true, but lays stress upon his pledge. There is no more reason why the children of the country should be taught a false natural history than why they should be taught a false physical geography. (*Everybody's Magazine,* June 1907.) *Mem. Ed.* VI, 424; *Nat. Ed.* V, 367.

NATURAL HISTORY. *See also,* NATURALISTS; NATURE STUDY; SCIENCE.

NATURAL RESOURCES. If in a given community unchecked popular rule means unlimited waste and destruction of the natural resources—soil, fertility, water-power, forests, game, wild life generally—which by right belong as much to subsequent generations as to the present generation, then it is sure proof that the present generation is not yet really fit for self-control; that it is not yet really fit to exercise the high and responsible privilege of a rule which shall be both by the people and for the people. The term "for the people" must always include the people unborn as well as the people now alive, or the democratic ideal is not realized. (1916.) *Mem. Ed.* IV, 228; *Nat. Ed.* III, 378.

——————. The steadily increasing drain on . . . natural resources has promoted to an extraordinary degree the complexity of our industrial and social life. Moreover, this unexampled development has had a determining effect upon the character and opinions of our people. The demand for efficiency in the great task has given us vigor, effectiveness, decision, and power, and a capacity for achievement which in its own lines has never yet been matched. So great and so rapid has been our material growth that there has been a tendency to lag behind in spiritual and moral growth; but that is not the subject upon which I speak to you to-day. Disregarding for the moment the question of moral purpose, it is safe to say that the prosperity of our people depends directly on the energy and intelligence with which our natural resources are used. It is equally clear that these resources are the final basis of national power and perpetuity. Finally, it is ominously evident that these resources are in the course of rapid exhaustion. (At Conference on the Conservation of Natural Resources, Washington, May 13, 1908.) *Mem. Ed.* XVIII, 162; *Nat. Ed.* XVI, 123.

NATURAL RESOURCES. *See also* CONSERVATION; FOREST; GAME; INLAND WATERWAYS; IRRIGATION; PUBLIC LANDS; RECLAMATION; SOIL CONSERVATION; WATER POWER; WILD LIFE.

NATURAL SELECTION. *See* PROGRESS.

NATURALISTS. Nowadays the field naturalist—who is usually at all points superior to the mere closet naturalist—follows a profession as full of hazard and interest as that of the explorer or of the big-game hunter in the remote wilderness. He penetrates to all the out-of-the-way nooks and corners of the earth; he is schooled to the performance of very hard work, to the endurance of fatigue and hardship, to encountering all kinds of risks, and to grappling with every conceivable emergency. In consequence he is exceedingly competent, resourceful and self-reliant, and the man of all others to trust in a tight place. (1910.) *Mem. Ed.* V, 402; *Nat. Ed.* IV, 346.

——————. The outdoor naturalist, the faunal naturalist, who devotes himself primarily to a study of the habits and of the life histories of birds, beasts, fish, and reptiles, and who can portray truthfully and vividly what he has seen, could do work of more usefulness than any mere collector, in this upper Paraguay country. The work of the collector is indispensable; but it is only a small part of the work that ought to be done; and after collecting has reached a certain point the work of the field observer with the gift for recording what he has seen becomes of far more importance. (1914.) *Mem. Ed.* VI, 71; *Nat. Ed.* V, 60.

——————. Specialization, like every other good thing, can be carried to excess; and no forms of specialization are less desirable than those which make of the outdoor naturalist a mere collector of "specimens," and of the indoor naturalist a mere laborious cataloguer and describer of these specimens when collected. The outdoor naturalist ought to be able to do all the indoor work too; and he ought to have the power to see and to portray the life histories of the shy creatures of the far-off wilderness.

But it is well if he can go even beyond this.

No man leads a hardier or more adventurous life than the collecting naturalist whose quest takes him to the uttermost parts of the earth. He works in the wildest lands, and on the shifting borders where the raw outskirts of civilization merge into savagery. He works with the wild men of the forest and the desert, and with the men only one degree less wild who do the most primitive work of civilization on the borders of the forest and the desert. If he has eyes to see he will have many a tale to tell; and if he can tell it aright the tale becomes an addition to that shelf of true stories of adventure in strange lands which is so fascinating a part of the great library of worth-while literature. (*American Museum Journal,* December 1918.) *Mem. Ed.* XIV, 525; *Nat. Ed.* XII, 389.

NATURALISTS. *See also* BEEBE, WILLIAM; BURROUGHS, JOHN; MUIR, JOHN; NATURE FAKERS; SCIENCE; SELOUS, F. C.; SOUTH AMERICA.

NATURE. It is an incalculable added pleasure to any one's sum of happiness if he or she grows to know, even slightly and imperfectly, how to read and enjoy the wonder-book of nature. (1905.) *Mem. Ed.* III, 313; *Nat. Ed.* III, 124.

NATURE — HARSHNESS OF. The very pathetic myth of "beneficent nature" could not deceive even the least wise being if he once saw for himself the iron cruelty of life in the tropics. Of course "nature"—in common parlance a wholly inaccurate term, by the way, especially when used as if to express a single entity—is entirely ruthless, no less so as regards types than as regards individuals, and entirely indifferent to good or evil, and works out her ends or no ends with utter disregard of pain and woe. (1914.) *Mem. Ed.* VI, 142; *Nat. Ed.* V, 121.

———. Death by violence, death by cold, death by starvation—these are the normal endings of the stately and beautiful creatures of the wilderness. The sentimentalists who prattle about the peaceful life of nature do not realize its utter mercilessness; although all they would have to do would be to look at the birds in the winter woods, or even at the insects on a cold morning or cold evening. Life is hard and cruel for all the lower creatures, and for man also in what the sentimentalists call a "state of nature." The savage of today shows us what the fancied age of gold of our ancestors was really like; it was an age when hunger, cold violence, and iron cruelty were the ordinary accompaniments of life. (1910.) *Mem. Ed.* V, 196; *Nat. Ed.* IV, 169.

NATURE—JOY IN. The lack of power to take joy in outdoor nature is as real a misfortune as the lack of power to take joy in books. *Outlook,* September 23, 1911, p. 162.

NATURE. *See also* ADVENTURE; BOOK-LOVERS; OUTDOOR LIFE; WILD LIFE; WILDERNESS.

NATURE FAKERS. The modern "nature-faker" is of course an object of derision to every scientist worthy of the name, to every real lover of the wilderness, to every faunal naturalist, to every true hunter or nature-lover. But it is evident that he completely deceives many good people who are wholly ignorant of wild life. Sometimes he draws on his own imagination for his fictions; sometimes he gets them second-hand from irresponsible guides or trappers or Indians. (*Everybody's Magazine,* September 1907.) *Mem. Ed.* VI, 435; *Nat. Ed.* V, 377.

———. I wish to express my hearty appreciation of your warfare against the sham nature-writers—those whom you have called "the yellow journalists of the woods." From the days of Aesop to the days of Reinecke Fuchs, and from the days of Reinecke Fuchs to the present time, there has been a distinct and attractive place in literature for those who write avowed fiction in which the heroes are animals with human or semihuman attributes. This fiction serves a useful purpose in many ways, even in the way of encouraging people to take the right view of outdoor creatures; but it is unpardonable for any observer of nature to write fiction and then publish it as truth, and he who exposes and wars against such action is entitled to respect and support. (To John Burroughs, October 2, 1905. Preface to *Outdoor Pastimes of an American Hunter.*) *Mem. Ed.* III, xxix; *Nat. Ed.* II, 390.

———. Once more let me say that if the fairy-tale mark were put on the stories of these writers, criticism would pass. Apparently, however, they wish to be known as teachers, or possibly they have a feeling of pride that springs from the belief that their readers will think of them as of those who have tramped the wilds and met nature in its gentleness and in its fierceness face to face. (*Everybody's Magazine,* June 1907.) *Mem. Ed.* VI, 430; *Nat. Ed.* V, 372.

NATURE STORIES. The preservation of the useful and beautiful animal and bird life of the country depends largely upon creating in the young an interest in the life of the woods and fields. If the child mind is fed with stories that are false to nature, the children will go to the haunts of the animal only to meet with disappointment. The result will be disbelief, and the death of interest. The men who misinterpret nature and replace facts with fiction, undo the work of those who in the love of nature interpret it aright. (*Everybody's Magazine,* June 1907.) *Mem. Ed.* VI, 432; *Nat. Ed.* V, 374.

NATURE STUDY. The great book of nature contains many pages which are hard to read, and at times conscientious students may well draw different interpretations of the obscure and least-known texts. It may not be that either observer is at fault, but what is true of an animal in one locality may not be true of the same animal in another, and even in the same locality two individuals of the same species may differ widely in their traits and habits. (1905.) *Mem. Ed.* III, 122; *Nat. Ed.* II, 495.

——————. The ordinary naturalist, if he goes into the haunts of the big game, is apt to find numerous small animals of interest, and he naturally devotes an altogether disproportionate share of his time to these. Yet such time is almost wasted; for the little animals, and especially the insects and small birds, remain in the land long after the big game has vanished, and can then be studied at leisure by hosts of observers. The observation of the great beasts of the marsh and the mountain, the desert and the forest, must be made by those hardy adventurers, who, unless explorers by profession, are almost certainly men to whom the chase itself is a dominant attraction. (Foreword to F. C. Selous' *African Nature Notes and Reminiscences;* dated May 23, 1907.) *Mem. Ed.* XIV, 485; *Nat. Ed.* XII, 356.

——————. Undoubtedly wild creatures sometimes show very unexpected traits, and individuals among them sometimes perform fairly startling feats or exhibit totally unlooked-for sides of their characters in their relations with one another and with man. We much need a full study and observation of all these animals, undertaken by observers capable of seeing, understanding, and recording what goes on in the wilderness; and such study and observation cannot be made by men of dull mind and limited power of appreciation. The highest type of student of nature should be able to see keenly and write interestingly and should have an imagination that will enable him to interpret the facts. But he is not a student of nature at all who sees not keenly but falsely, who writes interestingly and untruthfully, and whose imagination is used not to interpret facts but to invent them. (*Everybody's Magazine,* September 1907.) *Mem. Ed.* VI, 434-435; *Nat. Ed.* V, 376.

NATURE STUDY AND PHOTOGRAPHY. The photographer plays an exceedingly valuable part in nature study, but our appreciation of the great value of this part must never lead us into forgetting that as a rule even the best photograph renders its highest service when treated as material for the best picture, instead of as a substitute for the best picture; and that the picture itself, important though it is, comes entirely secondary to the text in any book worthy of serious consideration either from the standpoint of science or the standpoint of literature. Of course this does not mean any failure to appreciate the absolute importance of photographs; . . . what I desire is merely that we keep in mind, when books are treated seriously, the relative values of the photograph, the picture, and the text. (1910; Appendix of *African Game Trails.*) *Mem. Ed.* VI, 375-376; *Nat. Ed.* V, 323-324.

NATURE STUDY. See also NATURAL HISTORY; SCIENCE.

NAVAL ACADEMY. See ANNAPOLIS; WEST POINT.

NAVAL ARMAMENTS. I don't want this country to lead the race for big ships, but it seems to me well nigh criminal for us to fall behind. I think the ship provided for last year and the ship to be provided for this year, two in all, should be at least eighteen thousand tons apiece. Japan's new battleship, the Satsuma, is of this size, which is the Dreadnaught size. I do not think we can afford to take any chances with our navy. (To Congressman Foss, December 19, 1906.) Thomas A. Bailey, *Theodore Roosevelt and the Japanese-American Crisis.* (Stanford University Press, 1934), p. 120.

——————. I should like to see the British Navy kept at its present size but only on condition that the Continental and Japanese Navies are not built up. I do not wish to see it relatively weaker to them than is now the case. As regards our own Navy, I believe in number of units it is now as large as it need be, and I should advocate merely the substitution of efficient for inefficient units. This would mean allowing for about one new battleship a year, and of course now and then for a cruiser, collier, or a few torpedo-boat destroyers. (To Reid, August 7, 1906.) Royal Cortissoz, *The Life of Whitelaw Reid.* (Charles Scribner's Sons, N. Y., 1921), II, 343.

NAVAL ARMAMENTS — LIMITATION OF.

I have been thinking more and more that we might at least be able to limit the size of battleships, and I should put the limit below the size of the Dreadnaught. Let the English have the two or three of the Dreadnaught stamp that they have already built, but let all nations agree that hereafter no ship to exceed say fifteen thousand tons shall be built. I am inclined to think that, although not a very large, this would be a very real advance, and it is possible that the powers would agree to it, for surely they must be a little appalled by going into an era of competition in size of ships. Germany, which, as you know, has been extremely lukewarm in all Hague matters, might be inclined to agree with us in limiting the size of battleships, because her coasts are shallow and it is a disadvantage to her to have to build large ships. (To Carnegie, September 6, 1906.) Burton J. Hendrick, *The Life of Andrew Carnegie*. (Doubleday, Doran & Co., Garden City, N. Y., 1932), II, 307-308.

——————. I entirely agree with his [Victor Emmanuel] position about disarmament. It would be an admirable thing if we could get the nations not to improve their arms. Ask the King if it would not be possible to get them to agree hereafter not to build any ships of more than a certain size. Of course the United States has not any army and can do nothing to decrease the size of armaments on land; but I will be glad to follow any practical suggestion as to putting a stop to the increase of armaments at sea. I think that the reduction in the size of ships as above outlined would be a practicable, though a small, step. (To White, September 13, 1906.) Allan Nevins, *Henry White, Thirty Years of American Diplomacy*. (Harper & Bros., N. Y., 1930), p. 254.

——————. While President I had sounded, unofficially and informally, Germany and England as well as others powers to see if we could not limit the size of armaments, at least by limiting the size of ships; but had found that while all the other powers were willing, Germany and England would not consent; Germany taking the ground that the *status quo* put her at an improper disadvantage, and England saying—as I believe quite properly—that naval superiority was vital to her existence and that if Germany intended to alter the *status quo* she could not agree under any consideration to refrain from a policy of ship-building which would prevent such alteration from coming into effect. I added that while I had no proposition to make myself I did wish that the German authorities would seriously consider whether it was worth while for them to keep on with a building program which was the real cause why other nations were forced into the very great expense attendant upon modern naval preparation. (To Sir George Otto Trevelyan, October 1, 1911.) *Mem. Ed.* XXIV, 267; Bishop II, 229.

NAVAL EXPENDITURES. Our ships should be the best of their kind—this is the first desideratum; but, in addition, there should be plenty of them. We need a large navy, composed not merely of cruisers, but containing also a full proportion of powerful battleships, able to meet those of any other nation. It is not economy—it is niggardly and foolish shortsightedness—to cramp our naval expenditures, while squandering money right and left on everything else, from pensions to public buildings. (*Atlantic Monthly*, October 1890.) *Mem. Ed.* XIV, 315; *Nat. Ed.* XII, 272.

NAVAL OFFICERS. The business of a naval officer is one which, above all others, needs daring and decision, and if he must err on either side the nation can best afford to have him err on the side of too much daring rather than too much caution. (Report as Assistant Secretary of the Navy, May 1897.) *Mem. Ed.* XXIII, 86; Bishop I, 73.

NAVAL PERSONNEL. Taken as a whole there are no better citizens of this country than the officers and enlisted men of our navy. *Outlook*, January 7, 1911, p. 15.

——————. No navy in the world has such fine stuff out of which to make man-of-war's men. But they must be heartily backed up, heartily supported, and sedulously trained. They must be treated well, and, above all, they must be treated so as to encourage the best among them by sharply discriminating against the worst. The utmost possible efficiency should be demanded of them. They are emphatically and in every sense of the word men; and real men resent with impatient contempt a policy under which less than their best is demanded. The finest material is utterly worthless without the best personnel. In such a highly specialized service as the navy constant training of a purely military type is an absolute necessity. (New York *Times*, November 22, 1914.) *Mem. Ed.* XX, 130; *Nat. Ed.* XVIII, 112.

——————. History, modern and ancient, has invariably shown that an efficient personnel is the greatest factor toward an effective navy. No matter how well equipped in other respects a navy may be, though its fleet may be composed of powerful, high-speed battleships, manoeuvred by complicated tactics based upon the latest development of naval science, yet it is grievously handicapped if directed by admirals and captains who lack experience in their duties and who are hampered by long deprivation of independent action and responsibility. To oppose such a fleet to one equally good, led by officers more active and more experienced in their duties, is to invite disaster. (Message to Congress, December 17, 1906.) *Presidential Addresses and State Papers* V, 1011.

NAVAL PERSONNEL — EFFICIENCY OF. I have no question that the officers and men of our Navy now are in point of fighting capacity better than in the times of Drake and Nelson; and morally and in physical surroundings the advantage is infinitely in our favor. (To Theodore Roosevelt, Jr., November 14, 1906.) *Mem. Ed.* XXI, 574; *Nat. Ed.* XIX, 515.

NAVAL PERSONNEL—TRAINING OF. Exactly as it is of no use to give an army the best arms and equipment if it is not also given the chance to practise with its arms and equipment, so the finest ships and the best natural sailors and fighters are useless to a navy if the most ample opportunity for training is not allowed. Only incessant practice will make a good gunner; though, inasmuch as there are natural marksmen as well as men who never can become good marksmen, there should always be the widest intelligence displayed in the choice of gunners. Not only is it impossible for a man to learn how to handle a ship or do his duty aboard her save by long cruises at sea, but it is also impossible for a good single-ship captain to be an efficient unit in a fleet unless he is accustomed to manœuvre as part of a fleet. . . . A thoroughly good navy takes a long time to build up, and the best officer embodies always the traditions of a first-class service. Ships take years to build, crews take years before they become thoroughly expert, while the officers not only have to pass their early youth in a course of special training, but cannot possibly rise to supreme excellence in their profession unless they make it their life-work. (*McClure's Magazine,* October 1899.) *Mem. Ed.* XII, 513-515; *Nat. Ed.* XIII, 426, 427.

————. Though the sea-mechanic has replaced the sailorman, yet it is almost as necessary as ever that a man should have the sea habit in order to be of use aboard ship; and it is infinitely more necessary than in former times that a man-of-war's-man should have especial training with his guns before he can use them aright. In the old days cannon were very simple; sighting was done roughly; and the ordinary merchant seaman speedily grew fit to do his share of work on a frigate. Nowadays men must be carefully trained for a considerable space of time before they can be of any assistance whatever in handling and getting good results from the formidable engines of destruction on battle-ship, cruiser, and torpedo-boat. Crews cannot be improvised. To get the very best work out of them, they should all be composed of trained and seasoned men; and in any event they should not be sent against a formidable adversary unless each crew has for a nucleus a large body of such men filling all the important positions. From time immemorial it has proved impossible to improvise so much as a makeshift navy for use against a formidable naval opponent. Any such effort must meet with disaster. (*Century,* November 1899.) *Mem. Ed.* XV, 297-298; *Nat. Ed.* XIII, 411-412.

————. The ships will be absolutely useless if the men aboard them are not so trained that they can get the best possible service out of the formidable but delicate and complicated mechanisms intrusted to their care. The markmanship of our men has improved so during the last five years that I deem it within bounds to say that the navy is more than twice as efficient, ship for ship, as half a decade ago. The navy can only attain proper efficiency if enough officers and men are provided, and if these officers and men are given the chance (and required to take advantage of it) to stay continually at sea and to exercise the fleets singly and above all in squadron, the exercise to be of every kind and to include unceasing practice at the guns, conducted under conditions that will test marksmanship in time of war. (Sixth Annual Message, Washington, December 3, 1906.) *Mem. Ed.* XVII, 475; *Nat. Ed.* XV, 405.

NAVAL PREPAREDNESS. The first and most essential form of preparedness should be making the navy efficient. (*Everybody's,* January 1915). *Mem. Ed.* XX, 160; *Nat. Ed.* XVIII, 137.

————. In public as in private life a bold front tends to insure peace and not strife. If we possess a formidable navy, small is the chance indeed that we shall ever be dragged into a war to uphold the Monroe Doctrine. If we do not possess such a navy, war may be forced on us at any time.

It is certain, then, that we need a first-class navy. It is equally certain that this should not be merely a navy for defense. Our chief harbors should, of course, be fortified and put in condition to resist the attack of an enemy's fleet; and one of our prime needs is an ample force of torpedo boats to use primarily for coast defense. But in war the mere defensive never pays, and can never result in anything but disaster. It is not enough to parry a blow. The surest way to prevent its repetition is to return it. No master of the prize ring ever fought his way to supremacy by mere dexterity in avoiding punishment. He had to win by inflicting punishment. If the enemy is given the choice of time and place to attack, sooner or later he will do irreparable damage, and if he is at any point beaten back, why, after all, it is merely a repulse, and there are no means of following it up and making it a rout. (Address as Assistant Secretary of the Navy, Naval War College, June 1897.) *Mem. Ed.* XV, 253; *Nat. Ed.* XIII, 193.

―――――――. Those well-meaning but fatuous advocates of peace who would try to prevent the unbuilding of our navy utterly misread the temper of their countrymen. We Americans are ourselves both proud and high-spirited, and we are not always by any means far-sighted. If our honor or our interest were menaced by a foreign power, this nation would fight, wholly without regard to whether or not its navy was efficient. In the event of a crisis arising, the peace advocates who object to our building up the navy would be absolutely powerless to prevent this country going to war. All they could do would be to prevent its being successful in the war. (*Outlook,* May 8, 1909.) *Mem. Ed.* XVIII, 385; *Nat. Ed.* XVI, 291.

NAVAL PREPAREDNESS — DEMAND FOR. It is difficult for me to restrain my indignation at the cowardice of so many of the men to whom we ought to look for aid in any movement on behalf of Americanism. . . . More important than any other question is, it seems to me, the matter of providing an adequate coast defense and an adequate Navy. (To H. C. Lodge, March 13, 1896.) Lodge *Letters* I, 215.

―――――――. Let us at once take action to make us the second naval power in the world. Let us take the action this year, not the year after next. Do it now. The navy is our first line of defense. It is from the national standpoint literally criminal to neglect it. (*Metropolitan,* February 1916.) *Mem. Ed.* XX, 290; *Nat. Ed.* XVIII, 249.

NAVAL PREPAREDNESS — RESULTS OF. No small part of the respect and good will inspired by the United States in the world at large during recent years has been due to the known preparedness for war of the United States navy. *Outlook,* January 7, 1911, p. 15.

NAVAL VESSELS. *See* BATTLESHIPS; SUBMARINES; TORPEDO BOATS.

NAVY—DEPENDENCE ON. We all of us earnestly hope that the occasion for war may not arise, but if it has to come then this nation must win; and . . . in winning the prime factor must of necessity be the United States Navy. If the navy fails us then we are doomed to defeat. It should therefore be an object of prime importance for every patriotic American to see that the navy is built up; and that it is kept to the highest point of efficiency both in personnel and material. Above all, it can not be too often repeated to those representatives of the nation in whose hands the practical application of the principle lies, that in modern naval war the chief factor in achieving triumph is what has been done in the way of thorough preparation and training before the beginning of the war. It is what has been done before the outbreak of war that counts most. (At Annapolis, Md., May 2, 1902.) *Presidential Addresses and State Papers* I, 33-34.

―――――――. Unless the United States is prepared to take a place beside China, it will keep its navy and its little army at the highest point of efficiency; if we cannot protect our own interests with our own navy, then all the arbitration and other treaties that all the international philanthropists of the world can devise will not, in even the smallest degree, protect us. If we believe otherwise, we shall have a bitter awakening; and if ever that bitter awakening comes, I trust that our people will remember the foolish philanthropists and the recreant congressmen and other public servants at whose doors the responsibility will lie. (*Outlook,* May 31, 1913.) *Mem. Ed.* XIV, 228; *Nat. Ed.* XII, 244.

―――――――. If, as an aftermath of this war, some great Old World power or combination of powers made war on us because we objected to their taking and fortifying Magdalena Bay or St. Thomas, our chance of securing justice would rest exclusively on the efficiency of our fleet and army, especially the fleet. No arbitration treaties, or peace treaties, of the kind recently negotiated at Washington by the bushelful, and no tepid goodwill of neutral powers, would help us in even the smallest degree. If our fleet were conquered, New York and San Francisco would be seized and probably each would be destroyed as Louvain was destroyed unless it were put to ransom as Brussels has been put to ransom. Under such circumstances outside powers would undoubtedly remain neutral exactly as we have remained neutral as regards Belgium. (New York *Times,* September 27, 1914.) *Mem. Ed.* XX, 11; *Nat. Ed.* XVIII, 9.

NAVY—EFFICIENCY OF. I have for some time been much interested in the development of our gun practice. It looks very much as if we were behind the age in this all-important branch of naval work—the very branch in which we possessed the decisive superiority that mainly contributed to our victories in 1812. . . . I am certain that a board of experts who know something of what foreign navies can achieve in gun practice, as well as from practical experience what our people can do, could from personal inspection of our training ships and our cruisers, not merely give valuable hints in the way of improving the gun practice, but also get information that would be of great assistance to us. (To Secretary Long, January 4, 1898.) *Papers of John Davis Long.* (Mass. Hist. Soc., 1939), p. 40.

——————. It is not possible to improvise a navy after war breaks out. The ships must be built and the men trained long in advance. Some auxiliary vessels can be turned into makeshifts which will do in default of any better for the minor work, and a proportion of raw men can be mixed with the highly trained, their shortcomings being made good by the skill of their fellows; but the efficient fighting force of the navy will be found almost exclusively in the warships that have been regularly built and in the officers and men who through years of faithful performance of sea duty have been trained to handle their formidable but complex and delicate weapons with the highest efficiency. (First Annual Message, Washington, December 3, 1901.) *Mem. Ed.* XVII, 137; *Nat. Ed.* XV, 118.

——————. Not only should our navy be as large as our position and interest demand, but it should be kept continually at the highest point of efficiency and should never be used save for its own appropriate military purposes. (New York *Times,* November 22, 1914.) *Mem. Ed.* XX, 131; *Nat. Ed.* XVIII, 113.

NAVY—FUNCTION OF THE. There are always a certain number of well-meaning, amiable individuals—coupled with others not quite so well-meaning—who like to talk of having a navy merely for defense, who advocate a coast-defense navy. Such advocacy illustrates a habit of mind as old as human nature itself—the desire at the same time to do something, and not to do it, than which there is no surer way of combining the disadvantages of leaving it undone and of trying to do it. A purely defensive navy, a mere coast-defense navy, would be almost worthless. (At Naval War College, Newport, R. I., July 22, 1908.) *Mem. Ed.* XVIII, 330; *Nat. Ed.* XVI, 250.

——————. The navy must primarily be used for offensive purposes. Forts, not the navy, are to be used for defense. The only permanently efficient type of defensive is the offensive. A portion, and a very important portion, of our naval strength must be used with our own coast ordinarily as a base, its striking radius being only a few score miles, or a couple of hundred at the outside. . . . But the prime lesson of the war, as regards the navy, is that the nation with a powerful seagoing navy, although it may suffer much annoyance and loss, yet is able on the whole to take the offensive and do great damage to a nation with a less powerful navy. (New York *Times,* November 22, 1914.) *Mem. Ed.* XX, 128; *Nat. Ed.* XVIII, 110.

——————. The navy is our first line of defense, but it must be remembered that it can be used wisely for defense only as an offensive arm. Parrying is never successful from the standpoint of defense. The attack is the proper method of efficient defense. For some years we have been using the navy internationally as a bluff defensive force, or rather asserting that it would be so used and could be so used. Its real value is as an offensive force in the interest of any war undertaken for our own defense. Freedom of action by the fleet is the secret of real naval power. This cannot be attained until we have at our disposal an effective military establishment which would enable us when threatened to repel any force disembarking on our coast. This is fundamental. It is only by creating a sufficient army that we can employ our fleet on its legitimate functions. The schemes of the navy must always be correlated with the plans of the army, and both of them with the plans of the State Department, which should never under any circumstances undertake any scheme of foreign policy without considering what our military situation is and may be made. (*Metropolitan,* February 1916.) *Mem. Ed.* XX, 283; *Nat. Ed.* XVIII, 243.

NAVY

NAVY—NEED FOR. A great Navy does not make for war but for peace. It is the cheapest kind of insurance. No coast fortifications can really protect our coasts; they can only be protected by a formidable fighting Navy. (To Secretary John D. Long, September 30, 1897.) *Mem. Ed.* XXIII, 97; Bishop I, 83.

———————. If we intend to claim to be a great nation then we must fit ourselves so that we may be ready at need to make good that claim. That can only be done by building up and maintaining at the highest point of efficiency the United States navy. (At Naval War College, Newport, R. I., July 22, 1908.) *Mem. Ed.* XVIII, 333; *Nat. Ed.* XVI, 253.

———————. Our own navy should be ample to protect our own coasts and to maintain the Monroe Doctrine. There are in Europe and Asia several great military commonwealths, each one of which will in all probabilitiy always possess a far more formidable army than ours, even though, as I earnestly hope, we adopt some development of universal military training on the lines of the Swiss system. Therefore, it is of the highest consequence that our navy should be second to that of Great Britain. (December 17, 1918.) *Roosevelt in the Kansas City Star,* 286.

NAVY — ROOSEVELT'S LABORS FOR THE. During my term as President I have more than doubled the navy of the United States, and at this moment our battle fleet is doing what no other similar fleet of a like size has ever done— that is, circumnavigating the globe—and is also at this moment in far more efficient battle trim, from the standpoint of battle tactics, and even from the standpoint of gunnery, than when it started out a year ago, while the individual ships are each just a trifle more efficient. (To Sydney Brooks, December 28, 1908.) *Mem. Ed.* XXIV, 150; Bishop II, 129.

NAVY, AMERICAN. The navy of the United States is the right arm of the United States and is emphatically the peacemaker. Woe to our country if we permit that right arm to become palsied or even to become flabby, and inefficient. (New York *Times,* November 22, 1914.) *Mem. Ed.* XX, 135; *Nat. Ed.* XVIII, 116.

NAVY, AMERICAN—DIVISION OF. One closing legacy. Under no circumstances divide the battleship fleet between the Atlantic and Pacific oceans prior to the finishing of the Panama Canal. Malevolent enemies of the navy will try to lead public opinion in a matter like this without regard to the dreadful harm they may do the country; and good, entirely ignorant, men may be thus misled. I should obey no direction of Congress and pay heed to no popular sentiment, no matter how strong, if it went wrong in such a vital matter as this. When I sent the fleet around the world there was a wild clamor that some of it should be sent to the Pacific, and equally wild clamor that some of it should be left in the Atlantic. I disregarded both. At first it seemed as if popular feeling was nearly a unit against me. It is now nearly a unit in favor of what I did. (To William H. Taft, March 3, 1909.) *Mem. Ed.* XXIV, 139; Bishop II, 119.

NAVY, AMERICAN—PROGRAM FOR. In building . . . [our] navy, we must remember two things: First, that our ships and guns should be the very best of their kind; and second, that no matter how good they are, they will be useless unless the man in the conning-tower and the man behind the guns are also the best of their kind. It is mere folly to send men to perish because they have arms with which they cannot win. With poor ships, were an Admiral Nelson and Farragut rolled in one, he might be beaten by any first-class fleet; and he surely would be beaten if his opponents were in any degree his equals in skill and courage; but without this skill and courage no perfection of material can avail, and with them very grave shortcomings in equipment may be overcome. The men who command our ships must have as perfect weapons ready to their hands as can be found in the civilized world, and they must be trained to the highest point in using them. They must have skill in handling the ships, skill in tactics, skill in strategy, for ignorant courage cannot avail; but without courage neither will skill avail. They must have in them the dogged ability to bear punishment, the power and desire to inflict it, the daring, the resolution, the willingness to take risks and incur responsibility which have been possessed by the great captains of all ages, and without which no man can ever hope to stand in the front rank of fighting men. (Address as Assistant Secretary of the Navy, Naval War College, June 1897.) *Mem. Ed.* XV, 252; *Nat. Ed.* XIII, 192.

NAVY, AMERICAN—SERVICE OF. Never since the beginning of our country's history has the navy been used in an unjust war. Never has it failed to render great and sometimes vital service to the Republic. It has not been too strong for our good, though often not strong enough to do all the good it should have done. Our possession of the Philippines, our interest in the trade of the Orient, our building the Isthmian Canal, our insistence upon the Monroe Doctrine, all demand that our navy shall be of adequate size and for its size of unsurpassed efficiency. (At University of Pennsylvania, Philadelphia, February 22, 1905.) *Mem. Ed.* XV, 344; *Nat. Ed.* XIII, 502.

NAVY, AMERICAN AND BRITISH. I am speaking purely as an American. No man in this country who is both intelligent or informed has the slightest fear that Great Britain will ever invade us or try to go to war with us. The British navy is not in the slightest degree a menace to us. I can go a little further than this. There is in Great Britain a large pacifist and defeatist party which behaves exactly like our own pacifists, pro-Germans, Germanized Socialists, defeatists, and Bolsheviki. If this party had its way and Great Britain abandoned its fleet, I should feel, so far from the United States being freed from the necessity of building up a fleet, that it behooved us to build a much stronger one than is at present necessary. (December 24, 1918.) *Roosevelt in the Kansas City Star,* 288.

NAVY, ASSISTANT SECRETARY OF THE—APPOINTMENT AS. As soon as I received the news of my appointment I thought of you, and knew you would be pleased. Of course, it was Lodge who engineered it, at the end as at the beginning; working with his usual untiring loyalty and energy. Platt did his best to defeat me; and Gorman, with the help of the Populists, came near causing serious trouble in the Senate. However, I went through; and without making a promise, or even request of any kind, save to ask Olcott and Doty to vouch for my efficiency, etc., as you know. I am very glad to get out of this place; for I have done all that could be done, and now the situation has become literally intolerable. I do not object to any amount of work and worry, where I have a fair chance to win or lose on my merits; but here, at the last, I was playing against stacked cards. (To White, April 16, 1897.) Allan Nevins, *Henry White, Thirty Years of American Diplomacy.* (Harper & Bros., N. Y., 1930), p. 121.

NAVY AS GUARANTOR OF PEACE. So far from being in any way a provocation to war, an adequate and highly trained navy is the best guarantee against war, the cheapest and most effective peace insurance. The cost of building and maintaining such a navy represents the very lightest premium for insuring peace which this nation can possibly pay. (First Annual Message, Washington, December 3, 1901.) *Mem. Ed.* XVII, 136; *Nat. Ed.* XV, 117.

————. Our navy is the surest guarantee of peace and the cheapest insurance against war, and those who, in whatever capacity, have helped to build it up during the past twenty years have been in good faith observing and living up to one of the most important of the principles which Washington laid down for the guidance of his countrymen. (At University of Pennsylvania, Philadelphia, February 22, 1905.) *Mem. Ed.* XV, 344; *Nat. Ed.* XIII, 502.

————. I wish to reiterate, and to say with just as much earnestness as I have spoken to-day on other subjects, that I want a first-class fighting navy because it is the most effective guarantee of peace that this country can have. Uncle Sam can well afford to pay for his peace and safety so cheap an insurance policy as is implied in the maintenance of the United States navy. There is not a more paying investment that he makes. (At Naval War College, Newport, R. I., July 22, 1908.) *Mem. Ed.* XVIII, 337; *Nat. Ed.* XVI, 256.

————. A strong navy is the surest guaranty of peace that America can have, and the cheapest insurance against war that Uncle Sam can possibly pay. (*Outlook,* May 8, 1909.) *Mem. Ed.* XVIII, 386; *Nat. Ed.* XVI, 291.

NAVY. *See also* BATTLE FLEET; CHAPLAINS; DESERTION; ENGLISH NAVY; LONG, JOHN D.; MAHAN, A. T.; *Maine;* MARKSMANSHIP; MERCHANT MARINE; MILITARY FORCES; MILITARY HISTORY; MONROE DOCTRINE; PACIFISM; PEACE; PREPAREDNESS; WAR OF 1812.

NEGRO. You colored men and women must set your faces like flint against those who would preach to you the gospel of envy, hatred, and bitterness. May you realize that the way in which you can help your fellow citizens as well as the members of your race, is not by empty declarations, least of all by preaching vindictiveness and hatred, but by leading your lives as every-day citizens in such fashion that they shall add to the sum total of good citizenship. When you succeed in getting the ordinary white man of the community to realize that the ordinary colored man is a good citizen you have a friend in him, and that white man is benefited so greatly that there is only one person who receives a greater benefit, and that is the colored man himself. (Before National Negro Business League, New York City, August 19, 1910.) *Report of the Eleventh Annual*

Convention of the National Negro Business League. (Nashville, 1911), p. 193.

NEGRO—DUTY OF THE EDUCATED. Remember . . . that no help can permanently avail you save as you yourselves develop capacity for self-help. You young colored men and women educated at Tuskegee must by precept and example lead your fellows toward sober, industrious, law-abiding lives. You are in honor bound to join hands in favor of law and order and to war against all crime, and especially against all crime by men of your own race; for the heaviest wrong done by the criminal is the wrong to his own race. You must teach the people of your race that they must scrupulously observe any contract into which they in good faith enter, no matter whether it is hard to keep or not. If you save money, secure homes, become taxpayers, and lead clean, decent, modest lives, you will win the respect of your neighbors of both races. Let each man strive to excel his fellows only by rendering substantial service to the community in which he lives. The colored people have many difficulties to pass through, but these difficulties will be surmounted if only the policy of reason and common sense is pursued. You have made real and great progress. (At Tuskegee Institute, Tuskegee, Ala., October 24, 1905.) *Mem. Ed.* XVIII, 474; *Nat. Ed.* XVI, 353.

NEGRO—EDUCATION OF THE. The white man, if he is wise, will decline to allow the negroes in a mass to grow to manhood and womanhood without education. Unquestionably education such as is obtained in our public schools does not do everything toward making a man a good citizen; but it does much. . . . Of course the best type of education for the colored man, taken as a whole, is such education as is conferred in schools like Hampton and Tuskegee; where the boys and girls, the young men and young women, are trained industrially as well as in the ordinary public-school branches. The graduates of these schools turn out well in the great majority of cases, and hardly any of them become criminals, while what little criminality there is never takes the form of that brutal violence which invites lynch-law. Every graduate of these schools—and for the matter of that every other colored man or woman—who leads a life so useful and honorable as to win the good-will and respect of those whites whose neighbor he or she is, thereby helps the whole colored race as it can be helped in no other way; for next to the negro himself, the man who can do most to help the negro is his white neighbor who lives near him; and our steady effort should be to better the relations between the two. (Sixth Annual Message, Washington, December 3, 1906.) *Mem. Ed.* XVII, 415-416; *Nat. Ed.* XV, 354-355.

NEGRO—FUTURE OF THE. It is true of the colored man, as it is true of the white man, that in the long run his fate must depend far more upon his own effort than upon the efforts of any outside friend. Every vicious, venal, or ignorant colored man is an even greater foe to his own race than to the community as a whole. The colored man's self-respect entitles him to do that share in the political work of the country which is warranted by his individual ability and integrity and the position he has won for himself. But the prime requisite of the race is moral and industrial uplifting.

Laziness and shiftlessness, these, and above all, vice and criminality of every kind, are evils more potent for harm to the black race than all acts of oppression of white men put together. The colored man who fails to condemn crime in another colored man, who fails to co-operate in all lawful ways in bringing colored criminals to justice, is the worst enemy of his own people, as well as an enemy to all the people. Law-abiding black men should, for the sake of their race, be foremost in relentless and unceasing warfare against lawbreaking black men. If the standards of private morality and industrial efficiency can be raised high enough among the black race, then its future on this continent is secure. The stability and purity of the home is vital to the welfare of the black race, as it is to the welfare of every race. (At Lincoln dinner, Republican Club of New York City, February 13, 1905.) *Mem. Ed.* XVIII, 465; *Nat. Ed.* XVI, 346.

——————. He has a hard road to travel anyhow. He is certain to be treated with much injustice, and although he will encounter among white men a number who wish to help him upward and onward, he will encounter only too many who, if they do him no bodily harm, yet show a brutal lack of consideration for him. Nevertheless, his one safety lies in steadily keeping in view that the law of service is the great law of life, above all in this Republic, and that no man of color can benefit either himself or the rest of his race, unless he proves by his life his adherence to this law. Such a life is not easy for the white man, and it is very much less easy for the black man; but it is even more important for the black man, and for the black man's people, that he should lead it. (Preface to E. J. Scott and L. B. Stowe's

Booker T. Washington; dated August 28, 1916.) *Mem. Ed.* XII, 549; *Nat. Ed.* XI, 274.

NEGRO—OPPORTUNITIES FOR THE. It is . . . to the interest of the colored people that they clearly realize that they have opportunities for economic development here in the South not now offered elsewhere. Within the last twenty years the industrial operations of the South have increased so tremendously that there is a scarcity of labor almost everywhere; so that it is the part of wisdom for all who wish the prosperity of the South to help the negro to become in the highest degree useful to himself, and therefore to the community in which he lives. The South has always depended, and now depends, chiefly upon her native population for her work. (At Tuskegee Institute, Tuskegee, Ala., October 24, 1905.) *Mem. Ed.* XVIII, 471; *Nat. Ed.* XVI, 351.

NEGRO—SQUARE DEAL FOR THE. It is a good thing that the guard around the tomb of Lincoln should be composed of colored soldiers. It was my own good fortune at Santiago to serve beside colored troops. A man who is good enough to shed his blood for the country is good enough to be given a square deal afterward. More than that no man is entitled to, and less than that no man shall have. (At Lincoln Monument, Springfield, Ill., June 4, 1903.) *Mem. Ed.* XVIII, 459.

NEGRO, THE, AND THE OLD PARTIES. For many years the attitude of the Democratic party toward the colored man has been one of brutality, and the attitude of the Republican party toward him one of hypocrisy. One party has brutally denied him, not only his rights, but all hope of ever being treated aright; the other has hypocritically pretended to be zealous for his rights, but has acted only in ways that did him harm and not good. . . . For nearly half a century the Republican party has proceeded on the theory that the colored man in the South, in order to secure him his political rights, should be encouraged to antagonize the white man in the South; for nearly half a century the Democratic party has encouraged the white man of the South to trample on the colored man. The Republican policy has utterly and miserably failed in its object; it has not only done no good to the colored man, but has harmed him, has also harmed the white man of the South, and through the votes of the colored man of the South in the national convention has finally destroyed the Republican party itself. The Democratic party has succeeded in its policy, but at the cost of the utmost damage not only to the colored man, but also to those in whose interest the policy was supposed to be carried on—the white men of the South themselves. One of the greatest services that can be performed for the white men of the South is to emancipate them from their slavery to the Democratic party, As regards the colored man, I need hardly point out that the Democratic party is, as it always has been, his consistent foe; and no man who supports the Democratic party and its candidates in this contest can honestly say that he is the friend of the colored man, or entitled to be listened to when he pretends to be such. (*Outlook,* August 24, 1912.) *Mem. Ed.* XIX, 412, 415; *Nat. Ed.* XVII, 300, 302.

NEGRO, THE, AND THE PROGRESSIVE PARTY. Unlike the Democratic party, the Progressive party stands for justice and fair dealing toward the colored man; and, unlike the Republican party, it proposes to secure him justice and fair dealing in the only practicable way, by encouraging in every part of the country good feeling between the white men and the colored men who are neighbors, and by appealing in every part of the country to the white men who are the colored man's neighbors, and who alone can help him, to give him such help, not because they are forced by outsiders to do so, but as a matter of honorable obligation freely recognized on their own part. The plans already tried by the Republican and Democratic parties have failed utterly and hopelessly. No other plan than the one we propose offers the remotest chance of benefiting either the white man or the colored man of the South. Therefore it is merely the part of wisdom to try our plan, which is to try for the gradual re-enfranchisement of the worthy colored man of the South by frankly giving the leadership of our movement to the wisest and justest white men of the South. . . .

In the South we propose to proceed just as we are proceeding in the North, by appealing to what is best in the best men in the country, the most upright and honest and far-sighted citizens. The average American objects to being driven, but he is susceptible to any appeal made frankly to his sense of honor and justice. We no more propose to try, or pretend to try, to dragoon the people of Georgia or Louisiana than the people of New York or Illinois. We feel that when the movement is allowed to come from within, the men of the right type from the South Atlantic and Gulf States will act as their brethren elsewhere act; and then the colored man who is a good citizen will have the same chance in one place as in another.

(*Outlook,* August 24, 1912.) *Mem. Ed.* XIX, 415, 417; *Nat. Ed.* XVII, 303, 304.

NEGRO, THE, IN THE NORTH. The attitude of the North toward the negro is far from what it should be and there is need that the North also should act in good faith upon the principle of giving to each man what is justly due him, of treating him on his worth as a man, granting him no special favors, but denying him no proper opportunity for labor and the reward of labor. (At Lincoln dinner, Republican Club of New York City, February 13, 1905.) *Mem. Ed.* XVIII, 463; *Nat. Ed.* XVI, 344.

NEGRO APPOINTMENTS. So far as I legitimately can I shall always endeavor to pay regard to the likes and dislikes of the people of each locality, but I cannot consent by my action to take the position that the door of hope—the door of opportunity—is to be shut upon all men, no matter how worthy, purely upon the grounds of color. Such an attitude would according to my conviction be fundamentally wrong. . . . The question simply is whether it is to be declared that under no circumstances shall any man of color, no matter how good a citizen, no matter how upright and honest, no matter how fair in his dealings with all his fellows, be permitted to hold any office under our government. I certainly cannot assume such an attitude, and you must permit me to say that in my view it is an attitude no one should assume, whether he looks at it from the standpoint of the true interest of the white men of the South or of the colored men of the South —not to speak of any other section in the Union. It seems to me that it is a good thing from every standpoint to let the colored man know that if he shows in marked degree the qualities of good citizenship—the qualities which in a white man we feel are entitled to reward—then he himself will not be cut off from all hope of similar reward. (To R. G. Rhett, November 10, 1902.) *Mem. Ed.* XXIII, 195; Bishop I, 168.

————. Concerning Federal appointments in the South. Frankly, it seems to me that my appointments speak for themselves and that my policy is self-explanatory. So far from feeling that they need the slightest apology or justification, my position is that on the strength of what I have done I have the right to claim the support of all good citizens who wish not only a high standard of Federal service but fair and equitable dealing to the South as well as to the North, and a policy of consistent justice and good-will toward all men. In making appointments I have sought to consider the feelings of the people of each locality so far as I could consistently do so without sacrificing principle. The prime tests I have applied have been those of character, fitness and ability, and when I have been dissatisfied with what has been offered within my own party lines I have without hesitation gone to the opposite party. . . . I certainly cannot treat mere color as a permanent bar to holding office, any more than I could so treat creed or birthplace—always provided that in other respects the applicant or incumbent is a worthy and well-behaved American citizen. (To Clark Howell, February 23, 1903.) *Mem. Ed.* XXIII, 196; Bishop I, 169.

NEGRO PROBLEM—NATURE OF THE. It is in the South that we find in its most acute phase one of the gravest problems before our people: the problem of so dealing with the man of one color as to secure him the rights that no one would grudge him if he were of another color. To solve this problem it is, of course, necessary to educate him to perform the duties a failure to perform which will render him a curse to himself and to all around him. . . .

The problem is so to adjust the relations between two races of different ethnic type that the rights of neither be abridged nor jeoparded; that the backward race be trained so that it may enter into the possession of true freedom, while the forward race is enabled to preserve unharmed the high civilization wrought out by its forefathers. The working out of this problem must necessarily be slow; it is not possible in offhand fashion to obtain or to confer the priceless boons of freedom, industrial efficiency, political capacity, and domestic morality. Nor is it only necessary to train the colored man; it is quite as necessary to train the white man, for on his shoulders rests a well-nigh unparalleled sociological responsibility. It is a problem demanding the best thought, the utmost patience, the most earnest effort, the broadest charity, of the statesman, the student, the philanthropist; of the leaders of thought in every department of our national life. (At Lincoln dinner, Republican Club of New York City, February 13, 1905). *Mem. Ed.* XVIII, 462, 464; *Nat. Ed.* XVI, 344, 345.

NEGRO PROBLEM—ROOSEVELT AND THE. The most damaging thing to me any one can do is to give the impression that in what I have been trying to do for the negro I have been actuated by political motives. That is why

I have been so insistent that neither you nor any one else shall take any step to secure a negro or any other delegation from the South. I do not want the nomination unless it comes freely from the people of the Republican States, because they believe in me, and because they believe I can carry their States. And in the South I want to make it as clear as a bell that I have acted in the way I have on the negro question simply because I hold myself the heir of the policies of Abraham Lincoln and would be incapable of abandoning them to serve political or personal ends. (To a member of the Republican National Committee, March 13, 1903.) *Mem. Ed.* XXIII, 285; Bishop I, 247.

NEGRO PROBLEM — SOLUTION OF THE. The negroes were formerly held in slavery. This was a wrong which legislation could remedy, and which could not be remedied except by legislation. Accordingly they were set free by law. This having been done, many of their friends believed that in some way, by additional legislation, we could at once put them on an intellectual, social, and business equality with the whites. The effort has failed completely. In large sections of the country the negroes are not treated as they should be treated, and politically in particular the frauds upon them have been so gross and shameful as to awaken not merely indignation but bitter wrath; yet the best friends of the negro admit that his hope lies, not in legislation, but in the constant working of those often unseen forces of the national life which are greater than all legislation. (*Reviews of Reviews,* January 1897.) *Mem. Ed.* XVI, 377.

———. I have not been able to think out any solution of the terrible problem offered by the presence of the negro on this continent, but of one thing I am sure, and that is that inasmuch as he is here and can neither be killed nor driven away, the only wise and honorable and Christian thing to do is to treat each black man and each white man strictly on his merits as a man, giving him no more and no less than he shows himself worthy to have. I say I am "sure" that this is the right solution. Of course I know that we see through a glass dimly, and, after all, it may be that I am wrong; but if I am, then all my thoughts and beliefs are wrong, and my whole way of looking at life is wrong. At any rate, while I am in public life, however short a time that may be, I am in honor bound to act up to my beliefs and convictions. I do not intend to offend the prejudices of any one else, but neither do I intend to allow their prejudices to make me false to my principles. (To Albion W. Tourgee, November 8, 1901.) *Mem. Ed.* XXIII, 192; Bishop I, 166.

———. Neither I nor any other man can say that any given way of approaching that problem will present in our time even an approximately perfect solution, but we can safely say that there can never be such solution at all unless we approach it with the effort to do fair and equal justice among all men; and to demand from them in return just and fair treatment for others. Our effort should be to secure to each man, whatever his color, equality of opportunity, equality of treatment before the law. As a people striving to shape our actions in accordance with the great law of righteousness we cannot afford to take part in or be indifferent to the oppression or maltreatment of any man who, against crushing disadvantages, has by his own industry, energy, self-respect, and perseverance struggled upward to a position which would entitle him to the respect of his fellows, if only his skin were of a different hue. (At Lincoln dinner, Republican Club of New York City, February 13, 1905.) *Mem. Ed.* XVIII, 463; *Nat. Ed.* XVI, 345.

NEGRO SUFFRAGE. I have always felt that the passage of the Fifteenth Amendment at the time it was passed was a mistake; but to admit this is very different from admitting that it is wise, even if it were practicable, now to repeal that amendment. . . .

There is no white man from a Southern district in which blacks are numerous who does not tell you, either defiantly or as a joke, that any white man is allowed to vote, no matter how ignorant and degraded, and that the negro vote is practically suppressed because it *is* the negro vote. To acquiesce in this state of things because it is not possible at the time to attempt to change it without doing damage is one thing. It's quite another thing to do anything which will seem formally to approve it. (To Henry S. Pritchett, December 14, 1904.) *Mem. Ed.* XXIII, 403, 404; Bishop I, 350, 351.

NEGRO. *See also* ABOLITIONISTS; BROWNSVILLE RIOT; HAITI; LYNCHING; SLAVERY; TUSKEGEE INSTITUTE; WASHINGTON, BOOKER T.

NEUTRAL NATIONS—DUTY OF. I entirely agree with his [M. Renault's] thesis that neutrals who sign conventions have a duty to stand up for them. I shall never accept the view that neutrality between right and wrong is proper. I shall never accept the view that all wars are to be condemned alike, or that all kinds of peace are to be glorified. I put righteousness as the end. Usually peace is the means to righteousness; but occasionally war offers the only means by which righteousness can be achieved. (To J. J. Jusserand, April 2, 1915.) *Mem. Ed.* XXIV, 440; Bishop II, 374.

——————————. In my view the really unprecedented folly was in exercising our loose tongues in a way thoroughly to irritate Germany and yet to do nothing whatever to back up these aforesaid tongues by governmental action. If it was our duty to remain neutral politically, it was emphatically our duty to remain morally neutral. Any political neutrality not based on moral reasons is no more and no less admirable than the neutrality of Pontius Pilate or of the backwoodsman who saw his wife fighting the bear. Either The Hague Conventions meant something or they did not mean something. Either they can be construed according to their spirit or by legalistic device the letter can be twisted so as to give a faint shadow of justification for violating the spirit. If they meant nothing, then it was idiocy for us to have gone into them. If they meant anything, Wilson and Bryan are not to be excused for failure to try to make them good by whatever action was necessary; and political neutrality when they were violated was a crime against the world and a thoroughly base and dishonorable thing on our part. (To Owen Wister, July 7, 1915.) *Mem. Ed.* XXIV, 458; Bishop II, 389.

NEUTRAL NATIONS. *See also* BELGIUM; HAGUE CONVENTIONS; TREATIES.

NEUTRAL RIGHTS. The United States senator or governor of a State, or other public representative, who takes the position that our citizens should not, in accordance with their lawful rights, travel on such ships, and that we need not take action about their deaths, occupies a position precisely and exactly as base and as cowardly (and I use these words with scientific precision) as if his wife's face were slapped on the public streets and the only action he took was to tell her to stay in the house. (1916.) *Mem. Ed.* XX, 246; *Nat. Ed.* XVIII, 212.

NEUTRAL RIGHTS—PROTECTION OF. The administration should represent American interests; it should see that while we perform our duties as neutrals we should be protected in our rights as neutrals; and one of these rights is the trade in contraband. To prohibit this is to take part in the war for the benefit of one belligerent at the expense of another and to our own cost.

Of course it would be an ignoble action on our part after having conspicuously failed to protest against the violation of Belgian neutrality to show ourselves over-eager to protest against comparatively insignificant violations of our own neutral rights. But we should never have put ourselves in such a position as to make insistence on our own rights seem disregard for the rights of others. The proper course for us to pursue was on the one hand, scrupulously to see that we did not so act as to injure any contending nation, unless required to do so in the name of morality and of our solemn treaty obligations, and also fearlessly to act on behalf of other nations which were wronged, as required by these treaty obligations; and, on the other hand, with courteous firmness to warn any nation which, for instance, seized or searched our ships against the accepted rules of international conduct that this we could not permit and that such a course should not be persevered in by any nation which desired our good-will. (New York *Times,* November 22, 1914.) *Mem. Ed.* XX, 123; *Nat. Ed.* XVIII, 106.

——————————. I blame the Administration, but I blame even more the American people, who stand supine and encourage their representatives to permit unchecked the murder of women and children and other non-combatants rather than to take a policy which might, forsooth, jeopardize the life of some strong fighting man. (*Metropolitan,* January 1916.) *Mem. Ed.* XX, 317; *Nat. Ed.* XVIII, 272.

NEUTRAL RIGHTS—VIOLATION OF. [The violation of Belgian neutrality] was not the only one. The Japanese and English forces not long after violated Chinese neutrality in attacking Kiao-Chau. It has been alleged and not denied that the British ship *Highflier* sunk the *Kaiser Wilhelm der Grosse* in neutral Spanish waters, this being also a violation of The Hague conventions; and on October 10th the German Government issued an official protest about alleged violations of the Geneva convention by the French. Furthermore, the methods employed in strewing portions of the seas with floating mines have been such as to warrant the most careful investigation by any neutral nations which treat neutrality pacts and Hague conventions as other than merely dead letters. Not a few offenses have been committed against our own people. If, instead of observing a timid and spiritless neutrality, we had lived up to our obligations by taking action in all of these cases without regard to which power it was that was alleged to have done wrong, we would have followed the only course that would both have told for world righteousness and have served our own self-respect. (New York *Times,* November 29, 1914.) *Mem. Ed.* XX, 194; *Nat. Ed.* XVIII, 166.

NEUTRAL TRADE. It is thoroughly immoral in any way to help Germany win a triumph which would result in making the subjugation of Belgium perpetual. It is highly moral, it is from every standpoint commendable, to sell arms which shall be used in endeavoring to secure the freedom of Belgium and to create a condition of things which will make it impossible that such a crime against humanity as its subjugation by Germany shall ever be repeated, whether by Germany or by any other power. (*Metropolitan,* October 1915.) *Mem. Ed.* XX, 343; *Nat. Ed.* XVIII, 294.

NEUTRAL TRADE. *See also* CONTRABAND; MUNITIONS.

NEUTRALITY. As for neutrality, it is well to remember that it is never moral, and may be a particularly mean and hideous form of immorality. It is in itself merely unmoral; that is, neither moral nor immoral; and at times it may be wise and expedient. But it is never anything of which to be proud; and it may be something of which to be heartily ashamed. It is a wicked thing to be neutral between right and wrong. Impartiality does not mean neutrality. (1916.) *Mem. Ed.* XX, 239; *Nat. Ed.* XVIII, 206.

———. There is no meaner moral attitude than that of a timid and selfish neutrality between right and wrong. (*Metropolitan,* August 1915.) *Mem. Ed.* XX, 351; *Nat. Ed.* XVIII, 301.

———. The milk-and-water statesmanship of the American Government during the past year has been a direct aid to the statesmanship of blood-and-iron across the water; it may not be as wicked, but it is far more contemptible. The United States has signally and culpably failed to keep its promises made in The Hague conventions, and to stand for the right. Instead, it has taken refuge in the world-old neutrality between right and wrong which is always so debasing for the man practising it. As has been well said, such a neutral is the ignoblest work of God. (*Metropolitan,* November 1915.) *Mem. Ed.* XX, 382; *Nat. Ed.* XVIII, 327.

NEUTRALITY—GUARANTY OF. It is eminently desirable to guarantee the neutrality of small civilized nations which have a high social and cultural status and which are so advanced that they do not fall into disorder or commit wrong-doing on others. But it is eminently undesirable to guarantee the neutrality or sovereignty of an inherently weak nation which is impotent to preserve order at home, to repel assaults from abroad, or to refrain from doing wrong to outsiders. It is even more undesirable to give such a guaranty with no intention of making it really effective. . . . To enter into a joint guaranty of neutrality which in emergencies can only be rendered effective by force of arms is to incur a serious responsibility which ought to be undertaken in a serious spirit. To enter into it with no intention of using force, or of preparing force, in order at need to make it effective, represents the kind of silliness which is worse than wickedness. (New York *Times,* November 22, 1914.) *Mem. Ed.* XX, 125; *Nat. Ed.* XVIII, 108.

NEUTRALITY, BELGIAN. Our course toward foreign nations has combined unworthy submission to wrongs against ourselves, with selfish refusal to keep our word and do right by others. Under the sixth article of the Constitution treaties are "the supreme law of the land." The Hague conventions were treaties of this kind. They included a guaranty from Germany that she would not violate the territory of neutral nations (including the territory of Belgium) and a guaranty by Belgium that if an attempt was made to violate her territory she would fight to prevent the violation. Germany broke her solemn promise to us, and offended against the Supreme law of our land. Belgium kept her solemn promise made by her to us, to Germany, to France, Russia, and England. We shirked our duty by failing to take any action, even by protest, against the wrong-doer and on behalf of the wronged, by permitting this violation of our law, of the law which we guaranteed, of "the supreme law of the land," and by announcing through our President that we would be "neutral in thought as well as in deed" between the oppressor and the oppressed. (1916.) *Mem. Ed.* XX, 246; *Nat. Ed.* XVIII, 212.

NEUTRALITY, BELGIAN—VIOLATION OF. I feel in the strongest way that we should have interfered, at least to the extent of the most emphatic diplomatic protest and at the very outset—and then by whatever further action was necessary—in regard to the violation of the neutrality of Belgium; for this act was the earliest and the most important and, in its consequences the most ruinous of all the violations and offenses against treaties committed by any combatant during the war. . . . Inasmuch as, in the first and greatest and the most ruinous case of violation of neutral rights and of international morality, this nation, under the guidance of Messrs. Wilson and Bryan, kept timid silence and dared not protest, it would be—and is—an act of deliberate bad faith to protest only as regards subsequent and less important violations. Of course, if, as a people, we frankly take the ground that our actions are based upon nothing whatever but our own selfish and shortsighted interest, it is possible to protest only against violations of neutrality that at the moment unfavorably affect our own interests. (New York *Times,* November 29, 1914.) *Mem. Ed.* XX, 193, 194; *Nat. Ed.* XVIII, 166, 167.

NEUTRALITY AND PEACE. The kind of "neutrality" which seeks to preserve "peace" by timidly refusing to live up to our plighted word and to denounce and take action against such wrong as that committed in the case of Belgium, is unworthy of an honorable and powerful people. Dante reserved a special place of infamy in the inferno for those base angels who dared side neither with evil nor with good. Peace is ardently to be desired, but only as the handmaid of righteousness. The only peace of permanent value is the peace of righteousness. There can be no such peace until well-behaved, highly civilized small nations are protected from oppression and subjugation. (1915.) *Mem. Ed.* XX, xxii; *Nat. Ed.* XVIII, xxi.

————. President Wilson has been much applauded by all the professional pacifists because he has announced that our desire for peace must make us secure it for ourselves by a neutrality so strict as to forbid our even whispering a protest against wrong-doing, lest such whispers might cause disturbance to our ease and well-being. We pay the penalty of this action . . . on behalf of peace for ourselves, by forfeiting our right to do anything on behalf of peace for the Belgians in the present. We can maintain our neutrality only by refusal to do anything to aid unoffending weak Powers which are dragged into the gulf of bloodshed and misery through no fault of their own. (*Outlook,* September 23, 1914.) *Mem. Ed.* XX, 23; *Nat. Ed.* XVIII, 19.

NEUTRALITY AND THE LEAGUE. By all means go into any wise league or covenant among nations to abolish neutrality (for of course a league to enforce peace is merely another name for a league to abolish neutrality in every possible war). But let us first understand what we are promising, and count the cost and determine to keep our promises. (1918.) *Mem. Ed.* XXI, 351; *Nat. Ed.* XIX, 320.

NEUTRALITY IN THE WORLD WAR. When I had the great pleasure and honor of being associated with you and other men whom I highly regarded in the effort to bring about peace between Russia and Japan, I could in good faith act as a neutral. But neutrality in the present war is a crime against humanity and against the future of the race. . . . If I had had the power I would have made this nation actively interfere, if possible at the head of all neutral nations, on the ground of the violation of The Hague Conventions as regards Belgium. (To Baron Rosen, August 7, 1915.) *Mem. Ed.* XXIV, 461; Bishop II, 392.

NEUTRALITY. See also ARBITRATION; BELGIUM; CONTRABAND; JUSTICE; LEAGUE FOR PEACE; *Lusitania;* PACIFISM; PEACE; PREPAREDNESS; WORLD WAR.

NEW ENGLAND. On the whole, the New Englanders have exerted a more profound and wholesome influence upon the development of our common country than has ever been exerted by any other equally numerous body of our people. They have led the nation in the path of civil liberty and sound governmental administration. But too often they have viewed the nation's growth and greatness from a narrow and provincial standpoint, and have grudgingly acquiesced in, rather than led the march toward, continental supremacy. In shaping the nation's policy for the future, their sense of historic perspective seemed imperfect. They could not see the all-importance of the valley of the Ohio, or of the valley of the Columbia, to the republic of the years to come. The value of a county in Maine offset, in their eyes, the value of these vast, empty regions. (1894.) *Mem. Ed.* XI, 321-322; *Nat. Ed.* IX, 97-98.

NEW FREEDOM, THE. The worth of any such phrase as this of our scholarly and well-intentioned President lies in its interpretation. A careful study of the articles that have appeared by President Wilson dealing with this subject since he was President has left us somewhat puzzled as to what he really does mean; but of course I assume that there must be meaning, and if this assumption is warranted, then the "New Freedom" means nothing whatever but the old license translated into terms of pleasant rhetoric. The "New Freedom" is nothing whatever but the right of the strong to prey on the weak, of the big men to crush down the little men, and to shield their iniquity beneath the cry that they are exercising freedom. The "New Freedom" when practically applied turns out to be that old kind of dreadful freedom which leaves the unscrupulous and powerful free to make slaves of the feeble. There is but one way to interfere with this freedom to inflict slavery on others, and that is by invoking the supervisory, the regulatory, the controlling, and directing power of the government. (Before National Conference of Progressive Service, Portsmouth, R. I., July 2, 1913.) *Mem. Ed.* XIX, 519; *Nat. Ed.* XVII, 380.

───────────. A patient and sincere effort to find out what Mr. Wilson means by the "New Freedom" leaves me in some doubt whether it has any meaning at all. But if there is any meaning, the phrase means and can mean only freedom for the big man to prey unchecked on the little man, freedom for unscrupulous exploiters of the public and of labor to continue unchecked in a career of cut-throat commercialism, wringing their profits out of the laborers whom they oppress and the business rivals and the public whom they outwit. This is the only possible meaning that the phrase can have if reduced to action. It is, however, not probable that it has any meaning at all. It certainly can have no meaning of practical value if its coiner will not translate it out of the realm of magniloquent rhetoric into specific propositions affecting the intimate concerns of our social and industrial life to-day. To discriminate against a very few big men because of their efficiency, without regard to whether their efficiency is used in a social or antisocial manner, may perhaps be included in Mr. Wilson's meaning; but this would be absolutely useless from every aspect, and harmful from many aspects, while all the other big unscrupulous men were left free to work their wicked will. The line should be drawn on conduct, not on size. The man who behaves badly should be brought to book, whether he is big or little; but there should be no discrimination against efficiency, if the results of the efficiency are beneficial to the wage-earners and the public.

We have waited for a year to see such propositions made, and until they are made and put into actual practice, and until we see how they work, the phrase "New Freedom" must stand as any empty flourish of rhetoric, having no greater and no smaller value than all the similar flourishes invented by clever phrase-makers whose concern is with diction and not action. (*Century*, October 1913.) *Mem. Ed.* XIX, 541-542; *Nat. Ed.* XVII, 398-399.

NEW NATIONALISM, THE. [I] ask that we work in a spirit of broad and far-reaching nationalism when we work for what concerns our people as a whole. We are all Americans. Our common interests are as broad as the continent. I speak to you here in Kansas exactly as I would speak in New York or Georgia, for the most vital problems are those which affect us all alike. The National Government belongs to the whole American people, and where the whole American people are interested, that interest can be guarded effectively only by the National Government. The betterment which we seek must be accomplished, I believe, mainly through the National Government.

The American people are right in demanding that New Nationalism, without which we cannot hope to deal with new problems. The New Nationalism puts the national need before sectional or personal advantage. It is impatient of the utter confusion that results from local legislatures attempting to treat national issues as local issues. It is still more impatient of the impotence which springs from overdivision of governmental powers, the impotence which makes it possible for local selfishness or for legal cunning, hired by wealthy special interests, to bring national activities to a deadlock. This New Nationalism regards the executive power as the steward of the public welfare. It demands of the judiciary that it shall be interested primarily in human welfare rather than in property, just as it demands that the representative body shall represent all the people rather than any one class or section of the people. (At Osawatomie, Kan., August 31, 1910.) *Mem. Ed.* XIX, 26; *Nat. Ed.* XVII, 19.

───────────. The New Nationalism represents the struggle of freemen to gain and to hold the right of self-government as against the special interests, who twist the methods of free government into machinery for defeating the popular will. At every stage, and under all circumstances, the essence of the struggle is to equalize opportunity, to destroy privilege, and to give to the life and the citizenship of every individual in the commonwealth the highest possible value, both to himself and to the nation. (At Cleveland, O., November 5, 1910.) *Mem. Ed.* XIX, 69.

NEW NATIONALISM, THE. *See also* PROGRESSIVE PARTY.

NEW ORLEANS—BATTLE OF. See JACKSON, ANDREW.

NEW YORK ASSEMBLY—ROOSEVELT'S SERVICE IN. All I can say . . . is this: as I served you last year, so will I serve you this. If you are satisfied with what I did last year, you may return me; if not, I will take my dismissal. The duties of an assemblyman are not of a very high nature. I think all one needs to have there is honesty and courage. I certainly shall do the best I can to serve you with these qualities. And I use honesty not in the sense of merely refraining from taking that which is not your own, though I wish some of my fellow assemblymen had adopted that principle. I use it also in the higher sense, that of carrying private morality into public life. It is not always necessary to vote strictly within party lines, and I am happy to say that though I generally vote in the Republican party, still I wish to feel when I return that every citizen in the district can feel that I have served him to the best of my ability. I shall certainly try to please you and make every man feel as far as possible that I have served the cause of good government in the city and State of New York. (At Republican mass-meeting 21st Assembly Dist., New York City, October 28, 1882.) *Mem. Ed.* XVI, 14; *Nat. Ed.* XIV, 12.

——————. In the legislature the problems with which I dealt were mainly problems of honesty and decency and of legislative and administrative efficiency. They represented the effort, the wise, the vitally necessary effort, to get efficient and honest government. But as yet I understood little of the effort which was already beginning, for the most part under very bad leadership, to secure a more genuine social and industrial justice. Nor was I especially to blame for this. The good citizens I then knew best, even when themselves men of limited means—men like my colleague Billy O'Neill, and my backwoods friends Sewall and Dow—were no more awake than I was to the changing needs the changing times were bringing. Their outlook was as narrow as my own, and, within its limits, as fundamentally sound. (1913.) *Mem. Ed.* XXII, 94-95; *Nat. Ed.* XX, 81.

NEW YORK ASSEMBLY. See also LIQUOR TRAFFIC BILL; MURRAY, JOSEPH; O'NEILL, BILLY; ROOSEVELT.

NEW YORK CITY. For all its motley population, there is a most wholesome underlying spirit of patriotism in the city, if it can only be roused. Few will question this who saw the great processions on land and water, and the other ceremonies attendant upon the celebration of the one hundredth anniversary of the adoption of the federal Constitution. (1891.) *Mem. Ed.* IX, 422; *Nat. Ed.* X, 536.

——————. Uncharitableness and lack of generosity have never been New York failings; the citizens are keenly sensible to any real, tangible distress or need. A blizzard in Dakota, an earthquake in South Carolina, a flood in Pennsylvania—after any such catastrophe hundreds of thousands of dollars are raised in New York at a day's notice, for the relief of the sufferers; while, on the other hand, it is a difficult matter to raise money for a monument or a work of art. (1891.) *Mem. Ed.* IX, 422; *Nat. Ed.* X, 535.

——————. [I] feel that in a peculiar degree New York is not representative of the country, and what is more that almost each considerable section of New York is peculiarly unrepresentative of the state as a whole. The commercial and business world, the world of Wall Street, of the banks, of the big mercantile houses, and of the clubs, has absolutely no touch with the world of the East Side; just exactly as the little knots of idealistic reformers, who mean well but do not know, have no kind of touch with the great and rather sordid political machines of the city, which emphatically do know, and often do not mean well at all. (To Anna Roosevelt Cowles, October 16, 1902.) Cowles *Letters*, 252.

NEW YORK CITY—GOVERNMENT OF. During three years' service in the State Legislature fully half my time was occupied in dealing with the intricate municipal misgovernment of this city, and it became evident to me that there could be no great or effective change for the better in our City Government except through the unsparing use of the knife wielded by some man who could act unhampered by the political interests which sustain the present abuses, and without fear of either personal or political consequences. It is not enough that the Mayor refrain from making bad appointments or that he play a passively good part; to work a real reform he must devote his whole energy to actively grappling with and rooting out the countless evils and abuses already existing.

The chief reason for the continuance of these evils and abuses lies in the fact that hitherto no man having power has dared to deal with them without reference to the effect upon National and State politics. Many excellent gentle-

NEW YORK CITY

men have deplored their existence and would have been glad to remedy them; but every effort against the spoilsmen who are eating up the substance of the city has been checked by the consideration that to assail them would affect unfavorably the control of some convention or the success of some election. (Letter accepting nomination for Mayor, New York *Times,* October 17, 1886.) *Mem. Ed.* XVI, 111-112; *Nat. Ed.* XIV, 68-69.

NEW YORK CITY. *See also* MACHINE; POLICE; SALOON; TAMMANY HALL.

NEW YORK LEGISLATURE. Few persons realize the magnitude of the interests affected by State legislation in New York. It is no mere figure of speech to call New York the Empire State; and many of the laws most directly and immediately affecting the interests of its citizens are passed at Albany, and not at Washington. In fact, there is at Albany a little home rule parliament which presides over the destinies of a commonwealth more populous than any one of two-thirds of the kingdoms of Europe, and one which, in point of wealth, material prosperity, variety of interests, extent of territory, and capacity for expansion, can fairly be said to rank next to the powers of the first class. (*Century,* January 1885.) *Mem. Ed.* XV, 81; *Nat. Ed.* XIII, 47.

NEWELL, F. H. *See* CONSERVATION.

NEWSPAPERS. *See* JOURNALISM; PRESS.

NIGHTINGALE. *See* LARK.

NOBEL PEACE PRIZE. The medal and diploma will be prized by me throughout my life, and by my children after my death. I have turned over the money to a committee, including the Chief Justice of the Supreme Court of the United States and the Secretaries of Agriculture and Commerce and Labor, in trust, to be used as a foundation for promoting the cause of industrial peace in this country. In our modern civilization it is as essential to secure a righteous peace based upon sympathy and fair dealing between the different classes of society as it is to secure such a peace among the nations of the earth; and therefore I have felt that the use I have made of the amount of the Nobel Prize was one peculiarly in accordance with the spirit of the gift. (To Nobel Prize Committee, January 8, 1907.) *Mem. Ed.* XXIII, 485; Bishop I, 422.

——————. I think it eminently just and proper that in most cases the recipient of the prize should keep for his own use the prize in its entirety. But in this case, while I did not act officially as President of the United States, it was nevertheless only because I was President that I was enabled to act at all; and I felt that the money must be considered as having been given me in trust for the United States. I therefore used it as a nucleus for a foundation to forward the cause of industrial peace, as being well within the general purpose of your committee; for in our complex industrial civilization of to-day the peace of righteousness and justice, the only kind of peace worth having, is at least as necessary in the industrial world as it is among nations. There is at least as much need to curb the cruel greed and arrogance of part of the world of capital, to curb the cruel greed and violence of part of the world of labor, as to check a cruel and unhealthy militarism in international relationships. (Before Nobel Prize Committee, Christiania, Norway, May 5, 1910.) *Mem. Ed.* XVIII, 410; *Nat. Ed.* XVI, 305.

NORTH AND SOUTH. I believe that the North has hearty sympathy with the trials of the South and is generously glad to assist the South whenever the South does not render it impossible by "superfluity of naughtiness." (To Henry S. Pritchett, December 14, 1904.) *Mem. Ed.* XXIII, 404; Bishop I, 351.

NORTH. *See also* CIVIL WAR; COPPERHEADS; NEGRO.

NORTHERN SECURITIES CASE. I know the stress you are under, but as regards this Northern Securities business no stress must make us go one hand's breadth out of our path. I should hate to be beaten in this contest; but I should not merely hate, I should not be able to bear being beaten under circumstances which implied ignominy. To give any color for misrepresentation to the effect that we were now weakening in the Northern Securities matter would be ruinous. The Northern Securities suit is one of the great achievements of my administration. I look back upon it with great pride, for through it we emphasize in signal fashion, as in no other way could be emphasized, the fact that the most powerful men in this country were held to accountability before the law. Now we must not spoil the effect of this lesson. (To George B. Cortelyou, August 11, 1904.) *Mem. Ed.* XXIII, 374-375; Bishop I, 324-325.

——————. During the last few years the National Government has taken very long strides in the direction of exercising and securing this adequate control over the great corporations, and it was under the leadership of one of the most honored public men in our country, one of Pennsylvania's most eminent sons—the present Senator, and then Attorney-General, Knox—that the new departure was begun. Events have moved fast during the last five years, and it is curious to look back at the extreme bitterness which not merely the spokesmen and representatives of organized wealth, but many most excellent conservative people then felt as to the action of Mr. Knox and of the Administration.

Many of the greatest financiers of this country were certain that Mr. Knox's Northern Securities suit, if won, would plunge us into the worst panic we had ever seen. They denounced as incitement to anarchy, as an apology for socialism, the advocacy of policies that either have now become law or are in fair way of becoming law; and yet these same policies, so far from representing either anarchy or socialism, were in reality the antidotes to anarchy, the antidotes to socialism. (At Harrisburg, Pa., October 4, 1906.) *Mem. Ed.* XVIII, 86; *Nat. Ed.* XVI, 72-73.

————————. By a vote of five to four the Supreme Court reversed its decision in the Knight case, and in the Northern Securities case sustained the government. The power to deal with industrial monopoly and suppress it and to control and regulate combinations, of which the Knight case had deprived the Federal Government, was thus restored to it by the Northern Securities case. After this later decision was rendered, suits were brought by my direction against the American Tobacco Company and the Standard Oil Company. Both were adjudged criminal conspiracies, and their dissolution ordered. The Knight case was finally overthrown. The vicious doctrine it embodied no longer remains as an obstacle to obstruct the pathway of justice when it assails monopoly. Messrs. Knox, Moody, and Bonaparte, who successively occupied the position of attorney-general under me, were profound lawyers and fearless and able men; and they completely established the newer and more wholesome doctrine under which the Federal Government may now deal with monopolistic combinations and conspiracies. . . .

From the standpoint of giving complete control to the National Government over big corporations engaged in interstate business, it would be impossible to overestimate the importance of the Northern Securities decision and of the decisions afterward rendered in line with it in connection with the other trusts whose dissolution was ordered. The success of the Northern Securities case definitely established the power of the government to deal with all great corporations. Without this success the National Government must have remained in the impotence to which it had been reduced by the Knight decision as regards the most important of its internal functions. (1913.) *Mem. Ed.* XXII, 489-490; *Nat. Ed.* XX, 420-422.

————————. I talked over the matter in full with Knox. He believed that the Knight case would not have been decided over again as it actually was decided, and that if we could differentiate the Northern Securities case from it, we could secure what would be in fact (although not in name) a reversal of it. This I felt it imperative to secure. The Knight case practically denied the Federal Government power over corporations, because it whittled to nothing the meaning of "commerce between the States." It had to be upset or we could not get any efficient control by the National Government. (In conversation with Mr. Washburn.) Charles G. Washburn, *Theodore Roosevelt, The Logic of His Career*. (Houghton Mifflin Co., Boston, 1916), p. 67.

NORTHWEST, THE OLD. The old Northwest, the middle or northern west of to-day, was the true child of the federal government, and the states now composing it, the states lying around the Great Lakes and in the valley of the upper Mississippi, sprang into being owing to the direct action of the union founded by Washington. It was a striking instance of historic justice that in the second great crisis of this nation's history, the Northwest, the child of the union, should have saved the union, and should have developed in Abraham Lincoln the one American who has the right to stand alongside of Washington; while it was from the Northwest that those great soldiers sprang, under whose victorious leadership the Northern armies fought to a finish, once and for all, the terrible civil war. It was the Northwest which preserved the union in the times that tried men's souls, and it is the Northwest which to-day typifies alike in inner life and in bodily prosperity those conditions which give us ground for the belief that our union will be perpetual, and that this great nation has before it a career such as in all the ages of the past has never been vouchsafed to any other. (Address before the State Historical Society of Wisconsin, January 24, 1893.) Theodore Roosevelt, *The Northwest in the Nation*. (Wisconsin State Historical Society, 1893), p. 99.

NORTHWEST ORDINANCE OF 1785. Congress regarded the territory as forming a treasury chest, and was anxious to sell the land in lots, whether to individuals or to companies. In 1785, it passed an ordinance of singular wisdom, which has been the basis of all our subsequent legislation on the subject.

This ordinance was another proof of the way in which the nation applied its collective power to the subdual and government of the Northwest, instead of leaving the whole matter to the working of unrestricted individualism, as in the Southwest. The pernicious system of acquiring title to public lands in vogue among the Virginians and North Carolinians was abandoned. Instead of making each man survey his own land and allowing him to survey it when, how, and where he pleased, with the certainty of producing endless litigation and trouble, Congress provided for a corps of government surveyors, who were to go about this work systematically. (1894.) *Mem. Ed.* XII, 20-21; *Nat. Ed.* IX, 213.

NORTHWEST ORDINANCE OF 1787. The Ordinance of 1787 was so wide-reaching in its effects, was drawn in accordance with so lofty a morality and such far-seeing statesmanship, and was fraught with such weal for the nation, that it will ever rank among the foremost of American State papers, coming in that little group which includes the Declaration of Independence, the Constitution, Washington's Farewell Address, and Lincoln's Emancipation Proclamation and Second Inaugural. It marked out a definite line of orderly freedom along which the new States were to advance. It laid deep the foundation for that system of widespread public education so characteristic of the Republic and so essential to its healthy growth. It provided that complete religious freedom and equality which we now accept as part of the order of nature, but which were then unknown in any important European nation. It guaranteed the civil liberty of all citizens. It provided for an indissoluble Union, a Union which should grow until it could relentlessly crush nullification and secession; for the States founded under it were the creatures of the nation, and were by the compact declared forever inseparable from it. (1894.) *Mem. Ed.* XII, 27-28; *Nat. Ed.* IX, 218-219.

NORTHWEST. *See also* CANADIAN NORTHWEST; CLARK, GEORGE ROGERS.

NORWAY. Norway is as funny a kingdom as was ever imagined outside of opéra bouffe—although it isn't opéra bouffe at all, for the Norwegians are a fine, serious, powerful lot of men and women. But they have the most genuinely democratic society to be found in Europe, not excepting Switzerland; there are only two or three states in the American Union which are as real democracies. They have no nobles, hardly even gentry; they are peasants and small townspeople—farmers, sailors, fisherfolk, mechanics, small traders. On this community a royal family is suddenly plumped down. It is much as if Vermont should offhand try the experiment of having a king. Yet it certainly seemed as if the experiment were entirely successful.

I was interested to find that the Norwegians in America had on the whole advised a constitutional kingdom rather than a republic, on the ground that the king would not in any way interfere with the people having complete self-government and yet would give an element of stability to the government, preventing changes from being too violent and making a rallying-point; one philosophic leader pointing out that this was not necessary in America, where people had grown to accept the republic as a historic ideal, in itself a symbol and pledge of continuity, but that in Norway the republic would not stand for any such ideal of historic continuity, and moreover would be looked down on by its monarchic neighbors—the last being a touch of apprehension on the score of possible international social inequality which was both amusing and interesting.

For such a kingdom, constituted of such materials and with such theories, the entire royal family, king, queen, and prince, were just exactly what was needed. They were as simple and unpretentious as they were good and charming. . . .

I had to speak to the Nobel Committee, at the University, at a huge "Banquet" of the canonical—and unspeakably awful type—and thoroughly enjoyed seeing the vigorous, self-reliant people; they lined the streets in dense masses, and had a peculiar barking cheer, unlike any I ever heard elsewhere. But we enjoyed most the family life—it was real family life—of our host and hostess; it was not only very pleasant, but restful, in the palace; we felt as if we were visiting friends, who were interesting and interested, and who wished us to be comfortable in any way we chose. (To Sir George Otto Trevelyan, October 1, 1911.) *Mem. Ed.* XXIV, 278, 281; Bishop II, 238, 240.

NOVELS. *See* BOOKS; LITERATURE; READING.

NULLIFICATION. At this time it is not necessary to discuss nullification as a constitutional dogma; it is an absurdity too great to demand serious refutation. The United States has the same right to protect itself from death by nullification, secession, or rebellion that a man has to protect himself from death by assassination. Calhoun's hair-splitting and metaphysical disquisitions on the constitutionality of nullification have now little more practical interest than have the extraordinary arguments and discussions of the schoolmen of the Middle Ages. (1887.) *Mem. Ed.* VIII, 72; *Nat. Ed.* VII, 62-63.

NULLIFICATION. See also STATES' RIGHTS.

O

OBELISKS. An obelisk should be left in Egypt; it is absurd, it is shockingly inappropriate, to plump down such an obelisk in Paris, New York, or London, where it is utterly out of place and has no reason for its presence. (*Outlook,* September 30, 1911.) *Mem. Ed.* XIV, 56; *Nat. Ed.* XII, 176.

OFFICE. No people is wholly civilized where a distinction is drawn between stealing an office and stealing a purse. *Outlook,* June 12, 1912, p. 480.

OFFICE—CONDUCT IN. I have named you as District Attorney. Now there is one thing, and one thing only, that I demand. That is, that you keep clear of factional politics, and indeed do just as little political work as possible, and confine your attention to making the best record as district attorney that has been made by any district attorney of Delaware. There must not be a single legitimate or well-founded complaint against you. You will of course show neither fear nor favor in anything you do. Any offender of any kind whose case may be brought to your attention, or whom you can reach, is to be prosecuted with absolute indifference as to whether he is Republican or Democrat, Addicks man or anti-Addicks man. I have liked you and I think well of you, but under the circumstances of your appointment and the way in which it was fought, I have a right to demand that you walk even more guardedly than the ordinary public official walks, and that you show yourself a model officer in point of fearlessness and integrity, industry and ability.

The question of your confirmation will come up when the Senate reconvenes. You can help yourself in it more than any other man can possibly help you; and you can help yourself only by making a record which will be a just source of pride to you and to me. (To William M. Byrne, March 23, 1903.) *Mem. Ed.* XXIII, 278; Bishop I, 241.

OFFICE—MALFEASANCE IN. Any man holding an executive or legislative position who is false to his oath of office, who is guilty of misfeasance or malfeasance, we hold to be a traitor to the whole people; and we have not permitted and will not permit any such man to remain in office where it is in our power to remove him. (Before New York Republican State Convention, Saratoga, September 27, 1910.) *Mem. Ed.* XIX, 33; *Nat. Ed.* XVII, 25.

OFFICE — RECOMMENDATIONS FOR. In each recommendation I made I simply write about the men who have been under me, just as their commanding officers might write of them, or as I write about the men in my own regiment. Of course, I cannot say that they are better than their competitors, but I give the reasons why I regard them as good. Most emphatically I should regret being the cause of injustice to any one and would never want any recommendation of mine heeded if it means injustice to somebody else. (To Anna Roosevelt Cowles, December 29, 1899.) Cowles *Letters,* 229.

OFFICE—TENURE OF. It goes without saying that in a well-ordered government the great bulk of the employees in the civil service, the men whose functions are merely to execute faithfully routine departmental work, should hold office during good behavior, and should be appointed without reference to their politics; but if the higher public servants, such as the heads of departments and foreign ministers, are not in complete accord with their chief, the only result can be to introduce halting indecision and vacillation into the counsels of the nation, without abating by one iota the virulence of party passion. (1888.) *Mem. Ed.* VIII, 497-498; *Nat. Ed.* VII, 429-430.

————. I want it thoroughly understood that no presidential appointee has a prescriptive right to hold office. I intend to consult only the public welfare in making appointments. As long as a man proves himself fit and efficient his position is safe. When he shows himself unfit and inefficient he will be removed. (In conversation with a Representative from Illinois, late 1901.) *Mem. Ed.* XXIII, 180; Bishop I, 155.

OFFICE. See also APPOINTMENTS; CAMPAIGN EXPENSES; CAMPAIGN FUNDS; CANDIDATES; CIVIL SERVICE; NEGRO APPOINTMENTS; PATRONAGE; SPOILS SYSTEM.

OFFICERS. See ARMY OFFICERS; NAVAL OFFICERS.

OIL AND COAL CONSERVATION. In the Eastern United States the mineral fuels have already passed into the hands of large private owners, and those of the West are rapidly following. It is obvious that these fuels should be conserved and not wasted, and it would be well to protect the people against unjust and extortionate prices, so far as that can still be done. What has been accomplished in the great oil-fields of the Indian Territory by the action of the Administration offers a striking example of the good results of such a policy. In my judgment the government should have the right to keep the fee of the coal, oil, and gas fields in its own possession and to lease the rights to develop them under proper regulations; or else, if the Congress will not adopt this method, the coal deposits should be sold under limitations, to conserve them as public utilities, the right to mine coal being separated from the title to the soil. (Seventh Annual Message, Washington, December 3, 1907.) *Mem. Ed.* XVII, 530; *Nat. Ed.* XV, 451-452.

OIL. *See also* MINERAL FUELS.

OLD AGE INSURANCE. *See* SOCIAL INSURANCE.

O'NEILL, BILLY. My closest friend for the three years I was there [in the New York Assembly] was Billy O'Neill, from the Adirondacks. He kept a small crossroads store. He was a young man, although a few years older than I was, and, like myself, had won his position without regard to the machine. He had thought he would like to be assembly-man, so he had taken his buggy and had driven around Franklin County visiting everybody, had upset the local ring, and came to the legislature as his own master. There is surely something in American traditions that does tend toward real democracy in spite of our faults and shortcomings. In most other countries two men of as different antecedents, ancestry, and surroundings as Billy O'Neill and I would have had far more difficulty in coming together. I came from the biggest city in America and from the wealthiest ward of that city, and he from a backwoods county where he kept a store at a crossroads. In all the unimportant things we seemed far apart. But in all the important things we were close together. (1913.) *Mem. Ed.* XXII, 78; *Nat. Ed.* XX, 67.

O'NEILL, BUCKY. There was Bucky O'Neill, of Arizona, captain of Troop A, the mayor of Prescott, a famous sheriff throughout the West for his feats of victorious warfare against the Apache, no less than against the white road-agents and man-killers. . . . He was a wild, reckless fellow, soft spoken, and of dauntless courage and boundless ambition; he was stanchly loyal to his friends, and cared for his men in every way. . . .

It was Doctor Church who first gave me an idea of Bucky O'Neill's versatility, for I happened to overhear them discussing Aryan word-roots together, and then sliding off into a review of the novels of Balzac, and a discussion as to how far Balzac could be said to be the founder of the modern realistic school of fiction. (1899.) *Mem. Ed.* XIII, 14, 31; *Nat. Ed.* XI, 12, 27.

——————. The most serious loss that I and the regiment could have suffered befell just before we charged. Bucky O'Neill was strolling up and down in front of his men, smoking his cigarette, for he was inveterately addicted to the habit. He had a theory that an officer ought never to take cover—a theory which was, of course, wrong, though in a volunteer organization the officers should certainly expose themselves very fully, simply for the effect on the men; our regimental toast on the transport running: "The officers; may the war last until each is killed, wounded, or promoted." As O'Neill moved to and fro, his men begged him to lie down, and one of the sergeants said: "Captain, a bullet is sure to hit you." O'Neill took his cigarette out of his mouth, and blowing out a cloud of smoke laughed and said: "Sergeant, the Spanish bullet isn't made that will kill me." A little later he discussed for a moment with one of the regular officers the direction from which the Spanish fire was coming. As he turned on his feet a bullet struck him in the mouth and came out at the back of his head; so that even before he fell his wild and gallant soul had gone out into the darkness. (1899.) *Mem. Ed.* XIII, 93; *Nat. Ed.* XI, 79.

OPEN COVENANTS. The first point [of the Fourteen Points] forbids "all private international understandings of any kind," and says there must be "open covenants of peace, openly arrived at," and announced that "diplomacy shall always proceed frankly in the public view." The President has recently waged war on Haiti and San Domingo and rendered democracy within these two small former republics not merely unsafe, but non-existent. He has kept all that he has done in the matter absolutely secret. If he means what he says, he will at once announce what open covenant of peace he has openly arrived at with these two little republics, which he has deprived of their right of self-determination. He will also announce what public international understanding, if any, he now has with these two republics, whose soil he is at present occupying with the armed forces of the United

States and hundreds of whose citizens have been killed by these armed forces. If he has no such public understanding, he will tell us why, and whether he has any private international understanding, or whether he invaded and conquered them and deprived them of the right of self-determination without any attempt to reach any understanding, either private or public. (Kansas City *Star,* October 30, 1918.) *Mem. Ed.* XXI, 420; *Nat. Ed.* XIX, 380.

OPEN COVENANTS. *See also* FOURTEEN POINTS; PEACE TREATIES.

OPEN DOOR. We advocate the "open door" with all that it implies; not merely the procurement of enlarged commercial opportunities on the coasts, but access to the interior by the waterways with which China has been so extraordinarily favored. Only by bringing the people of China into peaceful and friendly community of trade with all the peoples of the earth can the work now auspiciously begun be carried to fruition. In the attainment of this purpose we necessarily claim parity of treatment, under the conventions, throughout the empire for our trade and citizens with those of all other powers. (First Annual Message, Washington, December 3, 1901.) *Mem. Ed.* XVII, 159; *Nat. Ed.* XV, 137.

———. The Open Door policy in China was an excellent thing, and I hope it will be a good thing for the future, so far as it can be maintained by general diplomatic agreement; but . . . the Open Door policy, as a matter of fact, completely disappears as soon as a powerful nation determines to disregard it, and is willing to run the risk of war rather than forego its intention. (To W. H. Taft, December 22, 1910.) Foster Rhea Dulles, *Forty Years of American-Japanese Relations.* (D. Appleton-Century Co., N. Y., 1937), p. 87.

OPEN DOOR. *See also* CHINA.

OPEN SHOP IN GOVERNMENT SERVICE. I am President of all the people of the United States, without regard to creed, color, birthplace, occupation, or social condition. My aim is to do equal and exact justice as among them all. In the employment and dismissal of men in the Government service I can no more recognize the fact that a man does or does not belong to a union as being for or against him than I can recognize the fact that he is a Protestant or a Catholic, a Jew or a Gentile, as being for or against him. (Interview with members of executive council, American Federation of Labor, September 29, 1903.) *Mem. Ed.* XXII, 551; *Nat. Ed.* XX, 473.

OPEN SHOP. *See also* COLLECTIVE BARGAINING; GOVERNMENT EMPLOYEES; LABOR.

OPINION. *See* INTERNATIONAL OPINION; PUBLIC OPINION.

OPPORTUNISM. *See* COMPROMISE.

OPPORTUNITY. In a certain sense, no man can absolutely make an opportunity. . . . Nevertheless, when the chance does come, only the great man can see it instantly and use it aright. In the second place, it must always be remembered that the power of using the chance aright comes only to the man who has faithfully and for long years made ready himself and his weapons for the possible need. Finally, and most important of all, it should ever be kept in mind that the man who does a great work must almost invariably owe the possibility of doing it to the faithful work of other men, either at the time or long before. Without his brilliancy their labor might be wasted, but without their labor his brilliancy would be of no avail. (*McClure's Magazine,* October 1899.) *Mem. Ed.* XII, 506; *Nat. Ed.* XIII, 420.

OPPORTUNITY—EQUALITY OF. Practical equality of opportunity for all citizens, when we achieve it, will have two great results. First, every man will have a fair chance to make of himself all that in him lies, to reach the highest point to which his capacities, unassisted by special privilege of his own and unhampered by the special privilege of others, can carry him, and to get for himself and his family substantially what he has earned. Second, equality of opportunity means that the commonwealth will get from every citizen the highest service of which he is capable. No man who carries the burden of the special privileges of another can give to the commonwealth that service to which it is fairly entitled. (At Osawatomie, Kan., August 31, 1910.) *Mem. Ed.* XIX, 15; *Nat. Ed.* XVII, 9.

———. Our fundamental purpose must be to secure genuine equality of opportunity. No man should receive a dollar unless that dollar has been fairly earned. Every dollar received should represent a dollar's worth of service rendered. (Before Ohio Constitutional Convention, Columbus, February 21, 1912.) *Mem. Ed.* XIX, 176; *Nat. Ed.* XVII, 130.

OPPORTUNITY AND REWARD. More and more we must shape conditions so that each man shall have a fair chance in life; that so far as we can bring it about . . . each man shall start in life on a measurable equality of opportunity with other men, unhelped by privilege himself, unhindered by privilege in others....

I do not mean for a moment that we should try to bring about the impossible and undesirable condition, of giving to all men equality of reward. As long as human nature is what it is there will be inequality of service, and where there is inequality of service there ought to be inequality of reward. That is justice. Equal reward for unequal service is injustice. All I am trying to help bring about is such a condition of affairs that there shall be measurable approximation to a higher reward than at present for the right kind of service, and a lesser reward than at present for some forms of activity that do not represent real service at all. (At Pacific Theological Seminary, Spring 1911.) *Mem. Ed.* XV, 627; *Nat. Ed.* XIII, 660.

OPPORTUNITY. *See also* NEW NATIONALISM; PRIVILEGE; SQUARE DEAL.

OPTIMISM. Optimism is a good characteristic, but if carried to an excess it becomes foolishness. (Seventh Annual Message, Washington, December 3, 1907.) *Mem. Ed.* XVII, 526; *Nat. Ed.* XV, 448.

─────────. I am an optimist, but I hope I am a reasonably intelligent one. I recognize that all the time there are numerous evil forces at work, and that in places and at times they outweigh the forces that tend for good. Hitherto, on the whole, the good have come out ahead, and I think that they will in the future; but I am not so sure that I can afford to look at the coming years with levity. (To Wister, February 27, 1895.) Owen Wister, *Roosevelt, The Story of a Friendship.* (Macmillan Co., N. Y., 1930), p. 39.

OPTIMISM. *See also* PESSIMISM.

OPTIMIST AND PESSIMIST. A foolish optimist is only less noxious than an utter pessimist; and the pre-requisite for any effort, whether hopeful or hopeless, to better our conditions is an accurate knowledge of what these conditions are. (*Forum,* January 1897.) *Mem. Ed.* XIV, 134; *Nat. Ed.* XIII, 246.

ORATORY. I think very little of mere oratory. I feel an impatient contempt for the man of words if he is merely a man of words. The great speech must always be the speech of a man with a great soul, who has a thought worth putting into words, and whose acts bear out the words he utters; and the occasion must demand the speech. (To H. C. Lodge, July 19, 1908.) *Lodge Letters* II, 302.

ORATORY. *See also* ACTION; DEBATING.

ORDER. The one all-important foundation of our system of orderly liberty is obedience to law. (*Outlook,* December 21, 1895.) *Mem. Ed.* XV, 150; *Nat. Ed.* XIII, 305.

ORDER AND LIBERTY. No people can permanently remain free unless it possesses the stern self-control and resolution necessary to put down anarchy. Order without liberty and liberty without order are equally destructive; special privilege for the few and special privilege for the many are alike profoundly anti-social; the fact that unlimited individualism is ruinous, in no way alters the fact that absolute state ownership and regimentation spells ruin of a different kind. All of this ought to be trite to reasonably intelligent people—even if they are professional intellectuals—but in practice an endless insistence on these simple fundamental truths is endlessly necessary. (1918.) *Mem. Ed.* XXI, 377; *Nat. Ed.* XIX, 342.

─────────. We must realize that the reactionaries among us are the worst foes of order, and the revolutionaries the worst foes of liberty; and unless we can preserve both order and liberty the republic is doomed. (1918.) *Mem. Ed.* XXI, 383; *Nat. Ed.* XIX, 347.

ORDER AND STABILITY. I believe with all my heart in order and stability, but I hold that in a people fit for self-government both can best be produced by giving the people full power. If they exercise this power badly, then they show that they are not fit for self-government. *Outlook,* November 15, 1913, p. 590.

ORDER. *See also* ANARCHY; LAW; LIBERTY.

ORGANIZATION, PARTY. When once a band of one hundred and fifty or two hundred honest, intelligent men, who mean business and know their business, is found in any district, whether in one of the regular organizations or outside, you can guarantee that the local politicians of that district will begin to treat it with a combination of fear, hatred, and respect, and that its influence will be felt. (Before the Liberal Club, Buffalo, N. Y., January 26, 1893.) *Mem. Ed.* XV, 70. *Nat. Ed.* XIII, 287.

─────────. I am not against the organization and never have been against it because it was a party organization, but I have been against it because it was an organization for private plunder. That is what I am against....

I have no quarrel with any man who has been in the organization for what he has done in the past if he's straight now. There are a good many things everybody sees are improper now that only a few thought were improper a short time back. It's like the lottery—Harvard College and many of your old churches about here were financed by lotteries in the old days. Times have changed.

If the organization is straight, runs straight, if its leaders and the men in it run straight, I have no objection to it. I will work with it just so long as it is straight and I won't worry over the possibility that some of its members have not always held as high views as they do now. (Fall 1916; reported by Leary.) *Talks with T. R.* From the diaries of John J. Leary, Jr. (Houghton Mifflin Co., Boston, 1920), pp. 6-7.

ORGANIZATION, PARTY. *See also* Boss; Democratic Party; Governor of New York; Independent; Machine; Party Allegiance; Party System; Political Parties; Politicians; Politics; Primaries; Republican Party; Roosevelt's Political Career; Tammany Hall.

ORIENT—AMERICAN INTERESTS IN. Our interests are as great in the Pacific as in the Atlantic. The welfare of California, Oregon, and Washington is as vital to the nation as the welfare of New England, New York, and the South Atlantic States. The awakening of the Orient means very much to all the nations of Christendom, commercially no less than politically; and it would be short-sighted statesmanship on our part to refuse to take the necessary steps for securing a proper share to our people of this commercial future. The possession of the Philippines has helped us, as the securing of the open door in China has helped us. Already the government has taken the necessary steps to provide for the laying of a Pacific cable under conditions which safeguard absolutely the interests of the American public. Our commerce with the East is growing rapidly. Events have abundantly justified, alike from the moral and material standpoint, all that we have done in the Far East as a sequel to our war with Spain. (At Hartford, Conn., August 22, 1902.) *Mem. Ed.* XVIII, 364-365; *Nat. Ed.* XVI, 278.

ORIENT. *See also* China; Japan; Open Door; Philippines.

ORIENTAL IMMIGRATION. *See* Chinese Immigration; Immigration; Japanese Exclusion.

OUSEL, THE. The ousels are to my mind well-nigh the most attractive of all our birds, because of their song, their extraordinary habits, their whole personality. They stay through the winter in the Yellowstone because the waters are in many places open. We heard them singing cheerfully, their ringing melody having a certain suggestion of the winter wren's. Usually they sang while perched on some rock on the edge or in the middle of the stream; but sometimes on the wing; and often just before dipping under the torrent, or just after slipping out from it to some ledge of rock or ice....

I cannot understand why the Old World ousel should have received such comparatively scant attention in the books, whether from nature writers or poets; whereas our ousel has greatly impressed all who know him. John Muir's description comes nearest doing him justice. To me he seems a more striking bird than, for instance, the skylark; though of course, I not only admire but am very fond of the skylark. (1905.) *Mem. Ed.* III, 286; *Nat. Ed.* III, 101-102.

OUTDOOR LIFE. Only a few men, comparatively speaking, lead their lives in the wilderness; only a few others, again speaking comparatively, are able to take their holidays in the shape of hunting trips in the wilderness. But all who live in the country, or who even spend a month now and then in the country, can enjoy outdoor life themselves and can see that their children enjoy it in the hardy fashion which will do them good. Camping out, and therefore the cultivation of the capacity to live in the open, and the education of the faculties which teach observation, resourcefulness, self-reliance, are within the reach of all who really care for the life of the woods, the fields, and the waters. Marksmanship with the rifle can be cultivated with small cost or trouble; and if any one passes much time in the country he can, if only he chooses, learn much about horsemanship. (1905.) *Mem. Ed.* III, 313; *Nat. Ed.* III, 124.

————. I am not disposed to undervalue manly outdoor sports, or to fail to appreciate the advantage to a nation, as well as to an individual, of such pastimes; but they must be pastimes and not business, and they must not be carried to excess. There is much to be said for the life of a professional hunter in lonely lands; but the man able to be something more, should be that something more—an explorer, a naturalist, or else a man who makes his hunting trips merely delightful interludes in his life-work. (1905.) *Mem. Ed.* III, 310; *Nat. Ed.* III, 122.

OUTDOOR LIFE. *See also* Adventure; Horseback Riding; Hunting; Mountain Climbing; Nature; Ranch Life; Sports; Strenuous Life; Vigor; Wilderness.

P

PACIFIC INTERESTS. *See* CHINA; HAWAII; JAPAN; OPEN DOOR; ORIENT; PHILIPPINES.

PACIFISM. The precepts and teachings upon which the pacifists rely apply not to war, but to questions arising from or concerning individual and mob violence and the exercise of the internal police power. In so far as sincere and logical pacifists are concerned, they recognize this fact. There are schools of pacifists who decline to profit by the exercise of the police power, who decline to protect not merely themselves, but those dearest to them, from any form of outrage and violence. The individuals of this type are at least logical in their horror even of just war. If a man deliberately takes the view that he will not resent having his wife's face slapped, that he will not by force endeavor to save his daughter from outrage, and that he disapproves of the policeman who interferes by force to save a child kidnapped by a black-hander, or a girl run off by a white-slaver, then he is logical in objecting to war. Of course, to my mind, he occupies an unspeakably base and loathsome position, and is not fit to cumber the world—in which, as a matter of fact, he exists at all only because he is protected by the maintenance by others of the very principle which he himself repudiates and declines to share.

Such a position I hold to be as profoundly immoral as it is profoundly unpatriotic. But, at least, the men holding it are trying logically to apply the principles which they profess to follow. (1916.) *Mem. Ed.* XX, 240; *Nat. Ed.* XVIII, 207.

——————. If the man who objects to war also objects to the use of force in civil life . . . his position is logical, although both absurd and wicked. If the college presidents, politicians, automobile manufacturers, and the like, who during the past year or two have preached pacifism in its most ignoble and degrading form are willing to think out the subject and are both sincere and fairly intelligent, they must necessarily condemn a police force or a posse comitatus just as much as they condemn armies; and they must regard the activities of the sheriff and the constable as being essentially militaristic and therefore to be abolished. (American Sociological Society, *Papers,* 1915.) *Mem. Ed.* XX, 270; *Nat. Ed.* XVIII, 232.

PACIFISM—BASIS OF. The professional pacifists, the leaders in the pacifist movement in the United States, do particular harm by giving well-meaning but uninformed people who do not think deeply what seems to them a convincing excuse for failure to show courage and resolution. Those who preach sloth and cowardice under the high-sounding name of "peace" give people a word with which to cloak, even to themselves, their failure to perform unpleasant duty. For a man to stand up for his own rights, or especially for the rights of somebody else, means that he must have virile qualities: courage, foresight, willingness to face risk and undergo effort. It is much easier to be timid and lazy. The average man does not like to face death and endure hardship and labor. (1916.) *Mem. Ed.* XX, 238; *Nat. Ed.* XVIII, 205.

——————. There are plenty of politicians . . . who find it to their profit to pander to the desire common to most men to live softly and easily and avoid risk and effort. Timid and lazy men, men absorbed in money-getting, men absorbed in ease and luxury, and all soft and slothful people naturally hail with delight anybody who will give them high-sounding names behind which to cloak their unwillingness to run risks or to toil and endure. Emotional philanthropists to whom thinking is a distasteful form of mental exercise enthusiastically champion this attitude. . . . These men and women are delighted to pass resolutions in favor of anything with a lofty name, provided always that no demand is ever made upon them to pay with their bodies to even the smallest degree in order to give effect to these lofty sentiments. (American Sociological Society, *Papers,* 1915.) *Mem. Ed.* XX, 267; *Nat. Ed.* XVIII, 229.

PACIFISM—EVILS OF. The professional pacifists of the United States are seeking to make the United States follow in the footsteps of China. They represent what has been on the whole the most evil influence at work in the United States for the last fifty years; and for five years they have in international affairs shaped our governmental policy. These men, whether politicians, publicists, college presidents, capitalists, labor leaders, or self-styled philanthropists, have done everything they could to relax the fibre of the American character and weaken the strength of the American will. They teach our people to seek that debasing security which is to be found in love of ease, in fear of risk, in the craven effort to avoid any duty that is hard or hazardous—a security which purchases peace in the present not only at the cost of humiliation in the present but at the cost of disaster in the future. . . . They not only make us work for our own undoing, and for the ultimate ruin of the great democratic experiment for which our great American Republic stands; but they also render us utterly powerless to work for others. We have refused to do our duty by Belgium; we refuse to do our duty by Armenia; because we have deified peace at any price, because we have preached and practised that evil pacifism which is the complement to and the encouragement of alien militarism. Such pacifism puts peace above righteousness, and safety in the present above both duty in the present and safety in the future. (To Samuel T. Dutton, chairman of Committee on Armenian Outrages, November 24, 1915.) *Mem. Ed.* XX, 450; *Nat. Ed.* XVIII, 386.

PACIFISM—RESULTS OF. I call the attention of the ultrapacifists to the fact that in the last half-century all the losses among our men caused by "militarism," as they call it, that is, by the arms of an enemy in consequence of our going to war, have been far less than the loss caused among these same soldiers by applied pacifism, that is, by our government having yielded to the wishes of the pacifists and declined in advance to make any preparations for war. The professional peace people have benefited the foes and ill-wishers of their country; but it is probably the literal fact to say that in the actual deed, by the obstacles they have thrown in the way of making adequate preparation in advance, they have caused more loss of life among American soldiers, fighting for the honor of the American flag, during the fifty years since the close of the Civil War than has been caused by the foes whom we have fought during that period. (*Everybody's,* January 1915.) *Mem. Ed.* XX, 143; *Nat. Ed.* XVIII, 123.

———. Not the smallest particle of good has come from the peace propaganda of the last ten years as carried on in America. Literally, this agitation of the professional pacifists during these ten years has not represented the smallest advance toward securing the peace of righteousness. It has, on the other hand, represented a very considerable and real deterioration in the American character. I do not think it is a permanent deterioration. I think that we shall recover and become heartily ashamed of our lapse from virile manliness. But there has been a distinct degeneracy in the moral fibre of our people owing to this peace propaganda, a distinct increase in moral flabbiness, a distinct increase in hysteria and sentimental untruthfulness. . . . The persons who seek to persuade our people that by doing nothing, by passing resolutions that cost nothing, and by writing eloquent messages and articles that mean nothing, and by complacently applauding elocution that means less than nothing, some service is thereby rendered to humanity, are not only rendering no such service, but are weakening the spring of national character. This applies to the publicists and politicians who write messages and articles and make speeches of this kind; it applies to the newspaper editors and magazine writers who applaud such utterances; and most of all it applies to those of our people who insist upon the passage of treaties that cannot and will not be enforced, while they also inveigh against preparedness, and shudder at action on behalf of our own rights. (*Metropolitan,* August 1915.) *Mem. Ed.* XX, 351; *Nat. Ed.* XVIII, 301.

PACIFISM AND MORALITY. The professional pacifists in and out of office who at peace congresses pass silly resolutions which cannot be, and ought not to be, lived up to, and enter into silly treaties which ought not to be, and cannot be kept, are not serving God, but Baal. They are not doing anything for anybody. If in addition these people, when the concrete case arises, as in Belgium or Armenia, fear concretely to denounce and antagonize the wrong-doer, they become not merely passive, but active, agents of the devil. The professional pacifists who applauded universal arbitration treaties and disarmament proposals prior to the war, since the war have held meetings and parades in this country on behalf of peace, and have gone on silly missions to Europe on behalf of peace—and the peace they sought to impose on heroes who were battling against infamy was a peace conceived in the interests of the authors of the infamy. They did not dare to say that they stood only for a peace that should right the wrongs of Belgium. They did not dare to denounce the war of aggression by Germany against Belgium. Their souls were too small, their timidity too great. They were even afraid to applaud the war waged by Belgium in its own defense. These pacifists have served morality, have shown that they feared God, exactly as the Pharisees did, when they made broad their philacteries and uttered long prayers in public, but did not lift a finger to lighten the load of the oppressed. (1916.) *Mem. Ed.* XX, 236; *Nat. Ed.* XVIII, 203.

PACIFISM AND PEACE. The ultrapacifists are capable of taking any position, yet I suppose that few among them now hold that there was value in the "peace" which was obtained by the concert of European powers when they prevented interference with Turkey while the Turks butchered some hundreds of thousands of Armenian men, women, and children. In the same way I do not suppose that even the ultrapacifists really feel that "peace" is triumphant in Belgium at the present moment. . . . We can maintain our neutrality only by refusal to do anything to aid unoffending weak powers which are dragged into the gulf of bloodshed and misery through no fault of their own. It is a grim comment on the professional pacifist theories as hitherto developed that, according to their view, our duty to preserve peace for ourselves necessarily means the abandonment of all effective effort to secure peace for other unoffending nations which through no fault of their own are trampled down by war. (*Outlook,* September 23, 1914.) *Mem. Ed.* XX, 22; *Nat. Ed.* XVIII, 19, 20.

———————. The great danger to peace so far as this country is concerned arises from such pacifists as those who have made and applauded our recent all-inclusive arbitration treaties, who advocate the abandonment of our policy of building battleships and the refusal to fortify the Panama Canal. It is always possible that these persons may succeed in impressing foreign nations with the belief that they represent our people. If they ever do succeed in creating this conviction in the minds of other nations, the fate of the United States will speedily be that of China and Luxembourg, or else it will be saved therefrom only by long-drawn war, accompanied by incredible bloodshed and disaster. . . . In such a war the prime fact to be remembered is that the men really responsible for it would not be those who would pay the penalty. The ultrapacifists are rarely men who go to battle. Their fault or their folly would be expiated by the blood of countless thousands of plain and decent American citizens of the stamp of those, North and South alike, who in the Civil War laid down all they had, including life itself, in battling for the right as it was given to them to see the right. (New York *Times,* September 27, 1914.) *Mem. Ed.* XX, 12, 13; *Nat. Ed.* XVIII, 10, 11.

———————. The truth is that the advocates of world-wide peace, like all reformers, should bear in mind Josh Billings's astute remark that "it is much easier to be a harmless dove than a wise serpent." The worthy pacifists have completely forgotten that the Biblical injunction is twosided and that we are bidden not only to be harmless as doves but also to be wise as serpents. The ultrapacifists have undoubtedly been an exceedingly harmless body so far as obtaining peace is concerned. They have exerted practically no influence in restraining wrong, although they have sometimes had a real and lamentable influence in crippling the forces of right and preventing them from dealing with wrong. An appreciable amount of good work has been done for peace by genuine lovers of peace, but it has not been done by the feeble folk of the peace movement, loquacious but impotent, who are usually unfortunately prominent in the movement and who excite the utter derision of the great powers of evil. (New York *Times,* October 4, 1914.) *Mem. Ed.* XX, 42; *Nat. Ed.* XVIII, 36.

PACIFISM AND PREPAREDNESS. There are some *doctrinaires* whose eyes are so firmly fixed on the golden vision of universal peace that they cannot see the grim facts of real life until they stumble over them, to their own hurt, and, what is much worse, to the possible undoing of their fellows. . . . But after all these people, though often noisy, form but a small minority of the whole. They would be swept like chaff before the gust of popular fury which would surely come if ever the nation really saw and felt a danger or an insult. The real trouble is that in such a case this gust of popular fury would come too late. Unreadiness for war is merely rendered more disastrous by readiness to bluster; to talk defiance and advocate a vigorous policy in words, while refusing to back up these words by deeds, is cause for humiliation. It has always been true, and in this age it is more than ever true, that it is too late to prepare for war when the time for peace has passed. (Address as Assistant Secretary of the Navy, Naval War College, June 1897.) *Mem. Ed.* XV, 247; *Nat. Ed.* XIII, 188.

———————. It has actually been proposed by some of these shivering apostles of the gospel of national abjectness that, in view of the destruction that has fallen on certain peaceful powers of Europe, we should abandon all efforts at self-defense, should stop building battleships, and cease to take any measures to defend ourselves if attacked. It is difficult seriously to consider such a proposition. It is precisely and exactly as if the inhabitants of a village in whose neighborhood highway robberies had occurred should propose to meet the crisis by depriving the local policeman of his revolver and club. (New York *Times,* November 1, 1914.) *Mem. Ed.* XX, 74; *Nat. Ed.* XVIII, 63.

———. A few of the professional pacifists now support the government's plan for a half-preparation, for pretending to meet needs without meeting them. But the extreme pacifists can always be trusted to insist on the nadir of folly. They do not wish to see this nation even pretend to act with self-respect. It is natural that they should wage a sham battle with a sham, for all their utterances are those of men who dwell in a world of windy make-believe. Their argument is that we should have no preparedness whatever, that we should not prepare for defense, nor bear arms, nor be able to use force, and that this nation must "influence others by example rather than by exciting fear," and must secure its safety "not by carrying arms, but by an upright, honorable course.". . . To argue with these gentlemen is to waste time, for there can be no greater waste of time than to debate about non-debatable things. (*Metropolitan,* February 1916.) *Mem. Ed.* XX, 289; *Nat. Ed.* XVIII, 248.

PACIFISM IN WAR-TIME. Whatever may have been our judgment in normal times we are convinced that to-day . . . professional pacifists should be regarded as traitors to the great cause of justice and humanity. The only peace is the peace of overwhelming victory. (Statement to press, September 20, 1917.) *Mem. Ed.* XXIV, 511; Bishop II, 436.

PACIFIST AGITATION—EFFECTS OF. We of the United States have had a twofold duty imposed on us during the last year. We have owed a duty to ourselves. We have owed a duty to others. We have failed in both. Primarily both failures are due to the mischievous effects of the professional pacifist agitation which became governmental nearly five years ago when the then Administration at Washington sought to negotiate various all-inclusive arbitration treaties under which we abandoned the right to stand up for our own vital interest and national honor. Very reluctantly we who believe in peace, but in the peace of righteousness, have been forced to the conclusion that the most prominent leaders of the peace agitation of the past ten years in this country, so far as they have accomplished anything that was not purely fatuous, have accomplished nothing but mischief. This result of the activities of these professional pacifist agitators has been due mainly to the fact that they have consistently placed peace ahead of righteousness, and have resolutely refused to look facts in the face if they thought the facts were unpleasant. (*Metropolitan,* November 1915.) *Mem. Ed.* XX, 375; *Nat. Ed.* XVIII, 321.

PACIFIST INACTION. The fact that these male and female professional peace enthusiasts who have screamed so busily for peace during the past year have been afraid to make any concrete protest against wrong is doubtless due primarily to sheer fear on their part. They were afraid of the trouble and effort implied in acting about Mexico. Above all, they are afraid of Germany. Those of them who are politicians are afraid of the German-American vote; for these professional pacifists have no sense of national honor and are great encouragers of hyphenated Americanism. But in addition they are terrorized, they are cowed, by the ruthless spirit of German militarism. (*Metropolitan,* August 1915.) *Mem. Ed.* XX, 355; *Nat. Ed.* XVIII, 305.

———. Those very apostles of pacifism who, when they can do so with safety, scream loudest for peace, have made themselves objects of contemptuous derision by keeping silence in this crisis. . . . They are supported by the men who insist that all that we are concerned with is escaping even the smallest risk that might follow upon the performance of duty to any one except ourselves. This last is not a very exalted plea. It is, however, defensible. But if, as a nation, we intend to act in accordance with it, we must never promise to do anything for any one else. (*Independent,* January 4, 1915.) *Mem. Ed.* XX, 179; *Nat. Ed.* XVIII, 154.

———. Professional pacifists attack evil only when it can be done with entire safety to themselves. In the present great crisis, the professional pacifists have confined themselves to trying to prevent the United States from protecting its honor and interest and the lives of its citizens abroad; and in their loud denunciations of war they have been careful to use language which would apply equally to terribly wronged peoples defending all that was dear to them against cynical and ruthless oppression, and to the men who were responsible for this cynical and ruthless oppression. They dare not speak for righteousness in the concrete. They dare not speak against the most infamous wrong in the concrete. They work hand in glove with these exponents of hyphenated Americanism who are seeking to turn this country into an ally and tool of alien militarism. (*Metropolitan,* January 1916.) *Mem. Ed.* XX, 305; *Nat. Ed.* XVIII, 262.

PACIFIST MOVEMENT. The pacifist movement in this country has not only been one of extreme folly and immorality, but has been bolstered by consistent and unwearied falsification of the facts, laudation of shallow and unprincipled demagogues, and condemnation of the upright public servants who fearlessly tell the truth. (1916.) *Mem. Ed.* XX, 236; *Nat. Ed.* XVIII, 203.

PACIFIST MOVEMENT—FAILURE OF. There are . . . men who put peace ahead of righteousness, and who care so little for facts that they treat fantastic declarations for immediate universal arbitration as being valuable, instead of detrimental, to the cause they profess to champion, and who seek to make the United States impotent for international good under the pretense of making us impotent for international evil. All the men of this kind, and all of the organizations they have controlled, since we began our career as a nation, all put together, have not accomplished one hundredth part as much for both peace and righteousness, have not done one-hundredth part as much either for ourselves or for other peoples, as was accomplished by the people of the United States when they fought the war with Spain and with resolute good faith and common sense worked out the solution of the problems which sprang from the war. (1913.) *Mem. Ed.* XXII, 305; *Nat. Ed.* XX, 260.

───────. All the actions of the ultra-pacifists for a generation past, all their peace congresses and peace conventions, have amounted to precisely and exactly nothing in advancing the cause of peace. The peace societies of the ordinary pacifist type have in the aggregate failed to accomplish even the smallest amount of good, have done nothing whatever for peace, and the very small effect they have had on their own nations has been, on the whole, slightly detrimental. Although usually they have been too futile to be even detrimental, their unfortunate tendency has so far been to make good men weak and to make virtue a matter of derision to strong men. (1915.) *Mem. Ed.* XX, xxii; *Nat. Ed.* XVIII, xxii.

PACIFIST MOVEMENT—LEADERS OF. There are persons who are against preparedness for war and who believe in the avoidance of national duty, who nevertheless are honest in their belief and who may not be cowardly or weak, but only foolish and misguided; and there are hundreds of thousands of good and reasonably brave men and women who simply have not thought of the matter at all and who are misguided by their leaders. But of most of these leaders it is not possible to take so charitable a view. The fundamental characteristic of the peace-at-any-price men is sheer, downright physical or moral timidity. Very many of the leaders among the men who protest against preparedness and who are hostile to manly action on our part—hostile to the insistence in good faith upon the observance of The Hague conventions and upon respect for the lives and property of our citizens in Mexico and on the high seas—are easily cowed by any exhibition of ruthless and brutal force, and never venture to condemn wrong-doers who make themselves feared. This fact might just as well be faced. To it is due the further fact that the professional pacifist usually turns up as the ally of the most cynical type of international wrongdoer. (*Metropolitan*, August 1915.) *Mem. Ed.* XX, 349; *Nat. Ed.* XVIII, 300.

PACIFIST PROGRAM. Amiable but fatuous persons . . . pass resolutions demanding universal arbitration for everything, and the disarmament of the free civilized powers and their abandonment of their armed forces; or else they write well-meaning, solemn little books, or pamphlets or editorials, and articles in magazines or newspapers, to show that it is "an illusion" to believe that war ever pays, because it is expensive. This is precisely like arguing that we should disband the police and devote our sole attention to persuading criminals that it is "an illusion" to suppose that burglary, highway robbery and white slavery are profitable. It is almost useless to attempt to argue with these well-intentioned persons, because they are suffering under an obsession and are not open to reason. They go wrong at the outset, for they lay all the emphasis on peace and none at all on righteousness. They are not all of them physically timid men; but they are usually men of soft life; and they rarely possess a high sense of honor or a keen patriotism. They rarely try to prevent their fellow countrymen from insulting or wronging the people of other nations; but they always ardently advocate that we, in our turn, shall tamely submit to wrong and insult from other nations. As Americans their folly is peculiarly scandalous, because if the principles they now uphold are right, it means that it would have been better that Americans should never have achieved their independence, and better that, in 1861, they should have peacefully submitted to seeing their country split into half a dozen jangling confederates and slavery made perpetual. (1913.) *Mem. Ed.* XXII, 606; *Nat. Ed.* XX, 521.

PACIFIST PROPAGANDA. This country will never be able to find its own soul or to play a part of high nobility in the world until it realizes the full extent of the damage done to it, materially and morally, by the ignoble peace propaganda for which these men and the others like them, whether capitalists, labor leaders, college professors, politicians or publicists, are responsible. (*Metropolitan,* January 1916.) *Mem. Ed.* XX, 321; *Nat. Ed.* XVIII, 275.

―――――――. It would be impossible to overstate the damage done to the moral fibre of our country by the professional pacifist propaganda, the peace-at-any-price propaganda, which had been growing in strength for the previous decade and which for the first two and a half years of the war was potent in influencing us as a people to play a part which was wholly unworthy of the teachings of the great men of our past. The professional pacifist movement was heavily financed by certain big capitalists. This was not merely admitted but blazoned abroad by some among them; whereas the accusations that the munition-makers, or any other interested persons, played any important part in the movement for preparedness were malicious falsehoods, well known to be such by those who uttered them. The professional pacifists during these two and a half years have occupied precisely the position of the copperheads during the time of Abraham Lincoln. (At Lincoln, Neb., June 14, 1917.) *Mem. Ed.* XXI, 189; *Nat. Ed.* XIX, 180.

PACIFISTS. A class of professional non-combatants is as hurtful to the real, healthy growth of a nation as is a class of fire-eaters; for a weakness or folly is nationally as bad as a vice, or worse. . . . No man who is not willing to bear arms and to fight for his rights can give a good reason why he should be entitled to the privilege of living in a free community. (1887.) *Mem. Ed.* VIII, 29; *Nat. Ed.* VII, 26.

―――――――. The man who will not fight to avert or undo wrong is but a poor creature; but, after all, he is less dangerous than the man who fights on the side of wrong. Again and again in a nation's history the time may, and indeed sometimes must, come when the nation's highest duty is war. (At Galena, Ill., April 27, 1900.) *Mem. Ed.* XII, 459; *Nat. Ed.* XIII, 431.

―――――――. These persons would do no harm if they affected only themselves. Many of them are, in the ordinary relations of life, good citizens. . . . But . . . they are able to do harm because they affect our relations with foreign powers, so that other men pay the debt which they themselves have really incurred. It is the foolish, peace-at-any-price persons who try to persuade our people to make unwise and improper treaties, or to stop building up the navy. But if trouble comes and the treaties are repudiated, or there is a demand for armed intervention, it is not these people who will pay anything; they will stay at home in safety, and leave brave men to pay in blood, and honest men to pay in shame, for their folly. (1913.) *Mem. Ed.* XXII, 608; *Nat. Ed.* XX, 523.

―――――――. The professional pacifist, who exalts peace above righteousness, is not only a traitor to the memory of the two greatest Americans [Washington and Lincoln], but has no claim to have any part in governing or in voting in the nation which one founded and the other preserved. (1917.) *Mem. Ed.* XXI, 56; *Nat. Ed.* XIX, 48.

PACIFISTS—ACTIVITIES OF. During the past year the activities of our professional pacifists have been exercised almost exclusively on behalf of hideous international iniquity. They have struck hands with those evil enemies of America, the hyphenated Americans, and with the greediest representatives of those Americans whose only god is money. They have sought to make this country take her stand against right that was downtrodden, and in favor of wrong that seemed likely to be successful. Every man or woman who has clamored for peace without daring to say that peace would be a crime unless Belgium was restored to her own people and the repetition of such wrong-doing as that from which she has suffered provided against, has served the devil and not the Lord. Every man or woman who in the name of peace now advocates the refusal on the part of the United States to furnish arms and munitions of war to those nations who have had the manliness to fight for the redressing of Belgium's wrongs, is serving the devil and not the Lord. (*Metropolitan,* October 1915.) *Mem. Ed.* XX, 324; *Nat. Ed.* XVIII, 278.

PACIFISTS — ERROR OF. Well-meaning persons who treat peace pageants, peace parades, peace conferences, and minor movements of similar nature as of consequence, are guilty of an error which makes their conduct foolish. Those of them who champion the exaltation of peace above righteousness and the abandonment of national power of self-defense—without which there never has been and never will be either national heroism or national manliness—will do well to study China. . . .

If our people really believed what the pacifists and the German-fearing politicians advocate, if they really feared war above anything else and really had sunk to the Chinese level —from which the best and bravest and most honorable Chinamen are now striving to lift their people—then it would be utterly hopeless to help the United States. In such case, the best thing that could befall it would be to have the Germans, or the Japanese, or some other people that still retains virility, come over here to rule and oppress a nation of feeble pacifists, unfit to be anything but hewers of wood and drawers of water for their masters. (*Metropolitan*, August 1915.) *Mem. Ed.* XX, 368, 369; *Nat. Ed.* XVIII, 315, 316.

PACIFISTS—FOLLY OF. The ultrapacifists have been fond of prophesying the immediate approach of a universally peaceful condition throughout the world, which will render it unnecessary to prepare against war because there will be no more war. This represents in some cases well-meaning and pathetic folly. In other cases it represents mischievous and inexcusable folly. But it always represents folly. At best, it represents the inability of some well-meaning men of weak mind, and of some men of strong but twisted mind, either to face or to understand facts. (*Everybody's*, January 1915.) *Mem. Ed.* XX, 146; *Nat. Ed.* XVIII, 126.

PACIFISTS—INFLUENCE OF. There is . . . an element of a certain numerical importance among our people, including the members of the ultrapacifist group, who by their teachings do some real, although limited, mischief. They are a feeble folk, these ultrapacifists, morally and physically; but in a country where voice and vote are alike free, they may, if their teachings are not disregarded, create a condition of things where the crop they have sowed in folly and weakness will be reaped with blood and bitter tears by the brave men and highhearted women of the nation. (New York *Times,* November 1, 1914.) *Mem. Ed.* XX, 71; *Nat. Ed.* XVIII, 61.

————. In our country the men who in time of peace speak loudest about war are usually the ultrapacifists whose activities have been shown to be absolutely futile for peace, but who do a little mischief by persuading a number of well-meaning persons that preparedness for war is unnecessary. (New York *Times,* November 29, 1914.) *Mem. Ed.* XX, 207; *Nat. Ed.* XVIII, 178.

————. The American professional pacifists, the American men and women of the peace-at-any-price type, who join in meetings to "denounce war" or with empty words "protest" on behalf of the Armenians or other tortured and ruined peoples carry precisely the weight that an equal number of Chinese pacifists would carry if at a similar meeting they went through similar antics in Peking. They do not wear pigtails; but it is to be regretted that they do not carry some similar outward and visible sign of their inward and spiritual disgrace. They accomplish nothing for peace; and they do accomplish something against justice. They do harm instead of good; and they deeply discredit the nation to which they belong. (To Samuel T. Dutton, chairman of Committee on Armenian Outrages, November 24, 1915.) *Mem. Ed.* XX, 446; *Nat. Ed.* XVIII, 383.

PACIFISTS — OBJECTION TO. "Blessed are the peacemakers," not merely the peacelovers; for action is what makes thought operative and valuable. Above all, the peace-prattlers are in no way blessed. On the contrary, only mischief has sprung from the activities of the professional peace-prattlers, the ultrapacifists, who, with the shrill clamor of eunuchs, preach the gospel of the milk and water of virtue and scream that belief in the efficacy of diluted moral mush is essential to salvation. It seems necessary every time I state my position to guard against the counterwords of wilful folly by reiterating that my disagreement with the peace-at-any-price men, the ultrapacifists, is not in the least because they favor peace. I object to them, first, because they have proved themselves futile and impotent in working for peace, and, second, because they commit what is not merely the capital error but the crime against morality of failing to uphold righteousness as the all-important end toward which we should strive. In actual practice they advocate the peace of unrighteousness just as fervently as they advocate the peace of righteousness. I have as little sympathy as they have for the men who deify mere brutal force, who insist that power justifies wrong-doing, and who declare that there is no such thing as international morality. But the ultrapacifists really play into the hands of these men. To condemn equally might which backs right and might which overthrows right is to render positive service to wrongdoers. It is as if in private life we condemned alike both the policeman and the dynamiter or black-hand kidnapper or white-slaver whom he has arrested. To denounce the nation that wages war in self-defense, or from a generous desire to relieve the oppressed, in the

[401]

same terms in which we denounce war waged in a spirit of greed or wanton folly stands on an exact par with denouncing equally a murderer and the policeman who, at peril of his life and by force of arms, arrests the murderer. In each case the denunciation denotes not loftiness of soul but weakness both of mind and of morals. (New York *Times,* November 29, 1914.) *Mem. Ed.* XX, 191; *Nat. Ed.* XVIII, 164.

——————. My prime objection to the pacifist is not that he won't fight in the long run. Even the pacifist, if you kick him long enough, will fight. The trouble is that prolonged and pernicious indulgence in pacifism renders a man unfit to accomplish anything when he does fight. The pacifist does not keep the country out of war—he merely keeps the country unfit to do its duty in war by making it prepare after the war has come. (At Trinity College, Hartford, June 16, 1918.) *Commencement at Trinity College.* (Hartford, Conn., 1918), p. 11.

PACIFISTS—POSITION OF EXTREME. A Yale professor—he might just as well have been a Harvard professor—is credited in the press with saying the other day that he wishes the United States would take the position that if attacked it would not defend itself, and would submit unresistingly to any spoliation. The professor said that this would afford such a beautiful example to mankind that war would undoubtedly be abolished. Magazine writers, and writers of syndicate articles published in reputable papers, have recently advocated similar plans. Men who talk this way are thoroughly bad citizens. Few members of the criminal class are greater enemies of the Republic. (*Everybody's,* January 1915.) *Mem. Ed.* XX, 158; *Nat. Ed.* XVIII, 136.

PACIFISTS — RESPONSIBILITY OF. [The] deeds . . . done by the nominally Christian powers in Europe, . . . things done wholesale, things done retail, have been such as we had hoped would never again occur in civilized warfare. They are far worse than anything that has occurred in such warfare since the close of the Napoleonic contests a century ago. . . . For all of this, the pacifists who dare not speak for righteousness, and who possess such an unpleasant and evil prominence in the United States, must share the responsibility with the most brutal type of militarists. The weak and timid milk-and-water policy of the professional pacifists is just as responsible as the blood-and-iron policy of the ruthless and unscrupulous militarist for the terrible recrudescence of evil on a gigantic scale in the civilized world. (To Samuel T. Dutton, chairman of Committee on Armenian Outrages, November 24, 1915.) *Mem. Ed.* XX, 448; *Nat. Ed.* XVIII, 385.

PACIFISTS—TYPES OF. [Some of] the leading apostles of applied pacifism are not timid men; on the contrary they are brutal, violent men, who are perfectly willing to fight, but only for themselves and not for the nation. These rough-neck pacifists have always been the potent allies of the parlor or milk-and-water pacifists; although they stand at the opposite end of the developmental scale. The parlor pacifist, the white-handed or sissy type of pacifist, represents decadence, represents the rotting out of the virile virtues among people who typify the unlovely senile side of civilization. The rough-neck pacifist, on the contrary, is a mere belated savage, who has not been educated to the virtues of national patriotism and of willingness to fight for the national flag and the national ideal. . . .

There remains the pacifist, the conscientious objector, who really does conscientiously object to war and who is sincere about it. As regards these men we must discriminate sharply between the men deeply opposed to war so long as it is possible honorably to avoid it, who are ardent lovers of peace, but who put righteousness above peace; and the other men who, however sincerely, put peace above righteousness, and thereby serve the devil against the Lord. (At Minneapolis, Minn., September 28, 1917.) *Mem. Ed.* XXI, 181; *Nat. Ed.* XIX, 173.

PACIFISTS. *See also* CONSCIENTIOUS OBJECTORS; DISARMAMENT; DRAFT; FIGHTING EDGE; FORD, HENRY; HYSTERIA; MANLY VIRTUES; MILITARY SERVICE; MILITARY TRAINING; NATIONAL DEFENSE; NAVY; PEACE; PREPAREDNESS; RIGHTEOUSNESS; UNPREPAREDNESS; WAR.

PAINTING, MODERN. Probably we err in treating most of these pictures seriously. It is likely that many of them represent in the painters the astute appreciation of the power to make folly lucrative which the late P. T. Barnum showed with his faked mermaid. There are thousands of people who will pay small sums to look at a faked mermaid; and now and then one of this kind with enough money will buy a Cubist picture, or a picture of a misshapen nude woman, repellent from every standpoint. . . .

In this recent art exhibition the lunatic fringe was fully in evidence, especially in the rooms devoted to the Cubists and the Futurists, or Near-Impressionists. I am not entirely certain which of the two latter terms should be used in connection with some of the various pictures and representations of plastic art—and, frankly, it is not of the least consequence. The Cubists are entitled to the serious attention of all who find enjoyment in the colored puzzle-pictures of the Sunday newspapers. Of course there is no reason for choosing the cube as a symbol, except that it is probably less fitted than any other mathematical expression for any but the most formal decorative art. There is no reason why people should not call themselves Cubists, or Octagonists, or Parallelpipedonists, or Knights of the Isosceles Triangle, or Brothers of the Cosine, if they so desire; as expressing anything serious and permanent, one term is as fatuous as another. . . .

As for many of the human figures in the pictures of the Futurists, they show that the school would be better entitled to the name of the "Past-ists." I was interested to find that a man of scientific attainments who had likewise looked at the pictures had been struck, as I was, by their resemblance to the later work of the palaeolithic artists of the French and Spanish caves. There are interesting samples of the strivings for the representation of the human form among artists of many different countries and times, all in the same stage of palaeolithic culture, to be found in a recent number of the "Revue d'Ethnographie." The palaeolithic artist was able to portray the bison, the mammoth, the reindeer, and the horse with spirit and success, while he still stumbled painfully in the effort to portray man. This stumbling effort in his case represented progress, and he was entitled to great credit for it. Forty thousand years later, when entered into artificially and deliberately, it represents only a smirking pose of retrogression, and is not praiseworthy. So with much of the sculpture. A family group of precisely the merit that inheres in a structure made of the wooden blocks in a nursery is not entitled to be reproduced in marble. (*Outlook*, March 29, 1913.) *Mem. Ed.* XIV, 405-408; *Nat. Ed.* XII, 147-150.

PAINTING. See also ART.

PANAMA. Panama was a great sight. In the first place it was strange and beautiful with its mass of luxuriant tropic jungle, with the treacherous tropic rivers trailing here and there through it; and it was lovely to see the orchids and brilliant butterflies and the strange birds and snakes and lizards, and finally the strange old Spanish towns and the queer thatch and bamboo huts of the ordinary natives. In the next place it is a tremendous sight to see the work on the canal going on. From the chief engineer and the chief sanitary officer down to the last arrived machinist or time-keeper, the five thousand Americans at work on the Isthmus seemed to me an exceptionally able, energetic lot, some of them grumbling, of course, but on the whole a mighty good lot of men. The West Indian negroes offer a greater problem, but they are doing pretty well also. I was astonished at the progress made. (To Theodore Roosevelt, Jr., November 20, 1906.) *Mem. Ed.* XXI, 578; *Nat. Ed.* XIX, 519.

——————. It certainly adds to one's pleasure to have read history and to appreciate the picturesque. When on Wednesday we approached the coast, and the jungle-covered mountains looked clearer and clearer until we could see the surf beating on the shores, while there was hardly a sign of human habitation, I kept thinking of the four centuries of wild and bloody romance, mixed with abject squalor and suffering, which had made up the history of the Isthmus until three years ago. I could see Balboa crossing at Darien, and the wars between the Spaniards and the Indians, and the settlement and the building up of the quaint walled Spanish towns; and the trade, across the seas by galleon, and over land by pack-train and river canoe, in gold and silver, in precious stones; and then the advent of the buccaneers, and of the English seamen, of Drake and Frobisher and Morgan, and many, many others, and the wild destruction they wrought. Then I thought of the rebellion against the Spanish dominion, and the uninterrupted and bloody wars that followed, the last occurring when I became President; wars, the victorious heroes of which have their pictures frescoed on the quaint rooms of the palace at Panama City, and in similar palaces in all capitals of these strange, turbulent little half-caste civilizations. Meanwhile the Panama railroad had been built by Americans over a half century ago, with appalling loss of life, so that it is said, of course with exaggeration, that every sleeper laid represented the death of a man. Then the French canal company started work, and for two or three years did a good deal, until it became evident that the task far exceeded its powers; and then to miscalculation and inefficiency was added the hideous greed of adventurers, trying each to save something from the general wreck, and the company closed with infamy and scandal. (To Kermit Roosevelt, November 20, 1906.) *Mem. Ed.* XXI, 575; *Nat. Ed.* XIX, 516.

[403]

PANAMA

PANAMA — RECOGNITION OF. I confidently maintain that the recognition of the Republic of Panama was an act justified by the interests of collective civilization. If ever a government could be said to have received a mandate from civilization to effect an object the accomplishment of which was demanded in the interest of mankind, the United States holds that position with regard to the interoceanic canal. Since our purpose to build the canal was definitely announced, there have come from all quarters assurances of approval and encouragement, in which even Colombia herself at one time participated; and to general assurances were added specific acts and declarations. In order that no obstacle might stand in our way, Great Britain renounced important right under the Clayton-Bulwer treaty and agreed to its abrogation, receiving in return nothing but our honorable pledge to build the canal and protect it as an open highway. . . .

That our position as the mandatory of civilization has been by no means misconceived is shown by the promptitude with which the powers have, one after another, followed our lead in recognizing Panama as an independent State. (Message to Congress, January 4, 1904.) *Presidential Addresses and State Papers* II, 750-752.

PANAMA AND THE UNITED STATES. The people of the United States and the people of the Isthmus and the rest of mankind will all be the better because we dig the Panama Canal and keep order in its neighborhood. And the politicians and revolutionists at Bogota are entitled to precisely the amount of sympathy we extend to other inefficient bandits. (To Cecil Arthur Spring-Rice, January 18, 1904.) *Mem. Ed.* XXIII, 343; Bishop I, 297.

—————————. The sole desire of the United States as regards the Republic of Panama is to see it increase in wealth, in numbers, in importance, until it becomes, as I so earnestly hope it will become, one of the republics whose history reflects honor upon the entire Western world. Such progress and prosperity . . . can come only through the preservation of both order and liberty; through the observance of those in power of all their rights, obligations, and duties to their fellow citizens, and through the realization of those out of power that the insurrectionary habit, the habit of civil war, ultimately means destruction to the republic. (Speech at Panama, November 1906.) *Mem. Ed.* XXIII, 520; Bishop I, 452.

PANAMA CANAL. The canal will be of great benefit to America, and of importance to all the world. It will be of advantage to us industrially and also as improving our military position. It will be of advantage to the countries of tropical America. It is earnestly to be hoped that all of these countries will do as some of them have already done with signal success, and will invite to their shores commerce and improve their material conditions by recognizing that stability and order are the prerequisites of successful development. No independent nation in America need have the slightest fear of aggression from the United States. It behooves each one to maintain order within its own borders and to discharge its just obligations to foreigners. When this is done, they can rest assured that, be they strong or weak, they have nothing to dread from outside interference. (Second Annual Message, Washington, December 2, 1902.) *Mem. Ed.* XVII, 176-177; *Nat. Ed.* XV, 152.

—————————. To my mind this building of the canal through Panama will rank in kind, though not of course in degree, with the Louisiana Purchase and the acquisition of Texas. I can say with entire conscientiousness that if in order to get the treaty through and start building the canal it were necessary for me forthwith to retire definitely from politics, I should be only too glad to make the arrangement accordingly; for it is the amount done in office, and not length of time in office, that makes office worth having. (To Samuel W. Small, December 29, 1903.) *Mem. Ed.* XXIII, 340; Bishop I, 295.

—————————. The one thing evident is to do nothing at present. If under the treaty of 1846 we have a color of right to start in and build a canal, my offhand judgment would favor such proceeding. It seems that the great bulk of the best engineers are agreed that that route is the best; and I do not think that the Bogota lot of obstructionists should be allowed permanently to bar one of the future highways of civilization. Of course, under the terms of the Act we could now go ahead with Nicaragua, and perhaps would technically be required to do so. But what we do now will be of consequence, not merely decades, but centuries hence, and we must be sure that we are taking the right step before we act. (To John Hay, August 19, 1903.) *Mem. Ed.* XXIII, 319; Bishop I, 276.

—————————. Every action we took was not only open and straightforward, but was rendered absolutely necessary by the misconduct of Colombia. Every action we took was in accordance with the highest principles of national, international, and private morality. The honor of the United States, and the interest not only of the United States but of the world, demanded the building of the Canal. The Canal could not have been built, it would not now have been begun, had our government not acted precisely as it did act in 1903. No action ever taken by the government, in dealing with any foreign power since the days of the Revolution, was more vitally necessary to the well-being of our people, and no action we ever took was taken with a higher regard for the standards of honor, of courage, and of efficiency which should distinguish the attitude of the United States in all its dealings with the rest of the world. (*Metropolitan*, February 1915.) *Mem. Ed.* XX, 513; *Nat. Ed.* XVIII, 441.

PANAMA CANAL — BUILDING OF. I have good reason to believe that they [the Germans] will back England very strongly in energetic protests if we abrogate the Clayton-Bulwer treaty, or attempt to build the canal on our own hook. Now my own view, if I had the power, would be that we should tell Great Britain that we wanted to be friendly and would like a treaty that would keep their self respect as well as ours, but yet which would permit us to handle the canal as outlined by the amended treaty of last year. If this is impossible I would then abrogate the Clayton-Bulwer treaty anyhow. But I would not take the last step unless I had counted the cost and unless I was prepared to back up words by deeds, to keep on building the navy and to make our army such that we could send out a formidable expeditionary force of small size. The Germans at present I know count with absolute confidence upon our inability to assemble an army of thirty thousand men which would be in any way a match for a German army of the same size.

I think Lord Lansdowne's position is both mischievous and ridiculous, but I also think we should be exceedingly cautious about embroiling ourselves with England, from whom we have not the least little particle of danger to fear in any way or shape; while the only power which may be a menace to us in anything like the immediate future is Germany. Before we abrogate the Clayton-Bulwer treaty we want to be sure of the position we intend taking should Germany and England combine against us. (To H. C. Lodge, March 27, 1901.) Lodge *Letters* I, 485.

———————. The government of the United States would have been guilty of folly and weakness, amounting in their sum to a crime against the nation, had it acted otherwise than it did when the revolution of November 3 last took place in Panama. This great enterprise of building the interoceanic canal cannot be held up to gratify the whims, or out of respect to the governmental impotence, or to the even more sinister and evil political peculiarities, of people who, though they dwell afar off, yet, against the wish of the actual dwellers on the Isthmus, assert an unreal supremacy over the territory. The possession of a territory fraught with such peculiar capacities as the Isthmus in question carries with it obligations to mankind. The course of events has shown that this canal cannot be built by private enterprise, or by any other nation than our own; therefore it must be built by the United States. (Third Annual Message, Washington, December 7, 1903.) *Mem. Ed.* XVII, 247; *Nat. Ed.* XV, 212.

———————. Now we have taken hold of the job. We have difficulties with our own people, of course. I haven't a doubt that it will take a little longer and cost a little more than men now appreciate, but I believe that the work is being done with a very high degree both of efficiency and honesty; and I am immensely struck by the character of American employees who are engaged, not merely in superintending the work, but in doing all the jobs that need skill and intelligence. The steam shovels, the dirt trains, the machine shops, and the like, are all filled with American engineers, conductors, machinists, boiler-makers, carpenters. From the top to the bottom these men are so hardy, so efficient, so energetic, that it is a real pleasure to look at them. (To Kermit Roosevelt, November 20, 1906.) *Mem. Ed.* XXI, 576; *Nat. Ed.* XIX, 517.

———————. Where the slanderers are of foreign origin, I have no concern with them. Where they are Americans, I feel for them the heartiest contempt and indignation; because, in a spirit of wanton dishonesty and malice, they are trying to interfere with, and hamper the execution of, the greatest work of the kind ever attempted, and are seeking to bring to naught the efforts of their countrymen to put to the credit of America one of the giant feats of the ages. The outrageous accusations of these slanderers constitute a gross libel upon a body of public servants who, for trained intelligence, expert ability, high character, and devotion to duty, have never been excelled anywhere. There is not a man among them directing the work on the Isthmus who has obtained his position on any other basis than merit alone, and not one who has used his position in any way for his own personal or pecuniary advantage. (Special Message to Congress, December 17, 1906.) *Mem. Ed.* XXIII, 523; Bishop I, 455.

──────────. The digging of the Panama Canal, the success with which it has been dug, has curiously enough, made, I think, a deeper impression abroad than at home. Unfortunately —and with a certain amount of justification— there has grown up a feeling that there is danger of corruption in work undertaken among us by the government for the public, and the total failure of all previous efforts by other nations, to accomplish anything on the Panama Canal had given rise in Europe to much cynical disbelief in our power to do the work. But it has been done; the success is literally astounding. It has been done with as near absolute cleanness, as near absolute honesty, as it is humanly possible to do any work, public or private. We have put down there men at small salaries—improperly small salaries—who have handled hundreds of millions of dollars, without the slightest suspicion of financial corruption on the part of any government servant holding a position of any importance in connection with the work. Moreover, the work has been done with the utmost efficiency. (At Harvard University, Cambridge, December 14, 1910.) *Mem. Ed.* XV, 554-555; *Nat. Ed.* XIII, 600-601.

PANAMA CANAL — FORTIFICATION OF. As you know, I am heartily friendly to England, but I cannot help feeling that the State Department has made a great error in the canal treaty [Hay-Pauncefote Treaty]. We really make not only England but all the great continental powers our partners in the transaction, and I do not see why we should dig the canal if we are not to fortify it so as to insure its being used for ourselves and against our foes in time of war. (To A. T. Mahan, February 14, 1900.) *Mem. Ed.* XXIII, 167; Bishop I, 143.

──────────. When the treaty [Hay-Pauncefote Treaty] is adopted, as I suppose it will be, I shall put the best face possible on it, and shall back the Administration as heartily as ever; but oh, how I wish you and the President would drop the treaty and push through a bill to build *and fortify* our own canal. . . . If that canal is open to the warships of an enemy, it is a menace to us in time of war; it is an added burden, an additional strategic point to be guarded by our fleet. If fortified by us, it becomes one of the most potent sources of our possible sea strength. Unless so fortified it strengthens against us every nation whose fleet is larger than ours. One prime reason for fortifying our great seaports is to unfetter our fleet, to release it for offensive purposes; and the proposed canal would fetter it again, for our fleet would have to watch it, and therefore do the work which a fort should do; and what it could do much better. (To Secretary John Hay, February 18, 1900.) *Mem. Ed.* XXIII, 168; Bishop I, 144.

──────────. My view of the canal business is just this: If we fortified it, then in the event of a war with a stronger naval power, she cannot use it and we probably can. If we do not fortify it, then if our opponent is weaker than we are we still have another vital point to watch. But if she is stronger she can seize the canal and use it to our detriment. If the proposed canal had existed in the Spanish war, the Oregon it is true could have gotten through it, but we should then have spent six weeks of wild anxiety, during which we should either have had to watch the canal with a formidable detachment, or else to have run the risk of seeing Cervera go through it and then vanish into the Pacific, leaving us uncertain whether he meant to lay waste Puget Sound or sail over to attack Dewey. (To William S. Cowles, February 26, 1900.) *Cowles Letters,* 236.

──────────. If the Panama Canal were not fortified, in time of war we should either have to abandon it to any enterprising enemy, or else paralyze our fleet by employing it to defend the Canal. If it is adequately fortified, our fleet can absolutely disregard it save in so far as it fulfils the vital requisite of a first-class naval base. War-vessels are inefficient substitutes for forts; and the poorest way to use a navy is to string the vessels in small groups in the ports along a coast, for then the enemy's navy can get them in detail. An unfortified Panama Canal would be a great source of weakness to this country; a fortified Panama Canal would enormously increase our strength. If our people are wise, they will hold those senators and congressmen who vote against the fortification of the Canal as unfaithful public servants who betray our country's interest at a vital point. With the possible exception of Hawaii, there is no other spot so necessary to fortify as the Panama Canal. We should have very few naval bases. These few should be thoroughly fortified and strongly held, and among them the two most important are those above mentioned. (*Outlook,* April 1, 1911.) *Mem. Ed.* XIX, 156; *Nat. Ed.* XVII, 112.

PANAMA CANAL—INTERNATIONALIZATION OF. The Panama Canal must not be internationalized. It is our canal; we built it; we fortified it, and we will protect it, and we will not permit our enemies to use it in war. In time of peace all nations shall use it alike, but in time of war our interest at once becomes dominant. (Kansas City *Star,* December 2, 1918.) Mem. Ed. XXI, 449; Nat. Ed. XIX, 404.

PANAMA CANAL — ROOSEVELT AND THE. At present I feel that there are two alternatives. (1) To take up Nicaragua; (2) in some shape or way to interfere when it becomes necessary so as to secure the Panama route without further dealing with the foolish and homicidal corruptionists in Bogotá. I am not inclined to have any further dealings whatever with those Bogotá people. (To John Hay, September 15, 1903.) Dwight C. Miner, *The Fight for the Panama Route.* (Columbia University Press, N. Y. 1940), p. 351.

──────────. Just at the moment I am more concerned about Panama than anything else. Of course, to me, the situation is simple. In its essence it is exactly as if a road-agent had tried to hold up a man, and the man was quick enough to take his gun away. Under such circumstances I would regard it as the wildest sentimental folly for outsiders to claim that the road-agent did not intend to shoot, and that it was his gun and ought to be given back to him. By every consideration of equity, and of legitimate national and international interest, what we have done was right. And it will be a lamentable thing if a twisted party feeling should join with mere hysteria to prevent at this time the fulfilling of what has been accomplished. (To Chase S. Osborn, December 9, 1903.) Mem. Ed. XXIII, 338; Bishop I, 293.

──────────. The Panama Canal I naturally take special interest in, because I started it. If I had acted strictly according to precedent, I should have turned the whole matter over to Congress; in which case, Congress would be ably debating it at this moment, and the canal would be fifty years in the future. Fortunately the crisis came at a period when I could act unhampered. Accordingly I took the Isthmus, started the canal, and then left Congress—not to debate the canal, but to debate me. And in portions of the public press the debate still goes on as to whether or not I acted properly in taking the canal. But while the debate goes on the canal does too; and they are welcome to debate me as long as they wish, provided that we can go on with the canal. (Charter Day Address, Berkeley, Cal., March 23, 1911.) University of California *Chronicle,* April 1911, p. 139.

──────────. My own part in it may perhaps be explained by the fact that I deemed it better not to have half a century of debate prior to starting in on the canal; I thought that instead of debating for half a century before building the canal it would be better to build the canal first and debate me for a half-century afterward. (At memorial exercises for Joseph H. Choate, New York City, January 19, 1918.) Mem. Ed. XII, 545; Nat. Ed. XI, 271.

PANAMA CANAL — ROOSEVELT'S VISIT TO. I went over everything that I could possibly go over in the time at my disposal. I examined the quarters of married and single men, white men and negroes. I went over the ground of the Gatun and La Boca dams; went through Panama and Colon, and spent a day in the Culebra cut, where the great work is being done. There the huge steam-shovels are hard at it; scooping huge masses of rock and gravel and dirt previously loosened by the drillers and dynamite blasters, loading it on trains which take it away to some dump, either in the jungle or where the dams are to be built. They are eating steadily into the mountain, cutting it down and down. Little tracks are laid on the side-hills, rocks blasted out, and the great ninety-five ton steam-shovels work up like mountain howitzers until they come to where they can with advantage begin their work of eating into and destroying the mountainside. With intense energy men and machines do their task, the white men supervising matters and handling the machines, while the tens of thousands of black men do the rough manual labor where it is not worth while to have machines do it. It is an epic feat, and one of immense significance. (To Kermit Roosevelt, November 20, 1906.) Mem. Ed. XXI, 576; Nat. Ed. XIX, 517.

PANAMA CANAL—START OF. The opening stage of the securing and digging of the Panama Canal . . . [was] the abrogation of the Clayton-Bulwer Treaty; unless that treaty had been abrogated the canal must either have remained unbuilt or have been built at the cost of a substantial measure of estrangement between Great Britain and ourselves. It was a real triumph to have secured the abrogation of the treaty—accomplished partly through Mr. Hay, partly through Ambassador Choate, partly through Lord Pauncefote, and partly through Mr. Balfour himself. (At memorial exercises for Joseph H. Choate, New York City, January 19, 1918.) *Mem. Ed.* XII, 544; *Nat. Ed.* XI, 270.

PANAMA CANAL TOLLS. We have a perfect right to permit our coastwise traffic (with which there can be no competition by the merchant marine of any foreign nation—so that there is no discrimination against any foreign marine) to pass through that Canal on any terms we choose, and I personally think that no toll should be charged on such traffic. Moreover, in time of war, where all treaties between warring nations, save those connected with the management of the war, at once lapse, the Canal would, of course, be open to the use of our war-ships and closed to the war-ships of the nation with which we were engaged in hostilities. But at all times the Canal should be opened on equal terms to the ships of all nations, including our own, engaged in international commerce. That was the understanding of the treaty when it was adopted, and the United States must always, as a matter of honorable obligation, and with scrupulous nicety, live up to every understanding which she has entered into with any foreign power. (Before Progressive National Convention, Chicago, August 6, 1912.) *Mem. Ed.* XIX, 407; *Nat. Ed.* XVII, 295.

PANAMA CANAL ZONE. We have not the slightest intention of establishing an independent colony in the middle of the state of Panama, or of exercising any greater governmental functions than are necessary to enable us conveniently and safely to construct, maintain and operate the canal under the rights given us by the treaty. Least of all do we desire to interfere with the business and prosperity of the people of Panama. (To W. H. Taft, October 19, 1904.) Hugh G. Miller, *The Isthmian Highway*. (Macmillan Co., N. Y., 1929), p. 29.

PANAMA CANAL ZONE — PAYMENT FOR. Ten million dollars was the price stipulated by Colombia herself as payment to those in possession of the Isthmus, and it was the price we actually did pay to those who actually were in possession of the Isthmus. The only difference was that, thanks to the most just and proper revolution which freed Panama from the intolerable oppression and wrong-doing of Colombia, we were able to give this ten million dollars to the men who themselves dwelt on the Isthmus, instead of to alien taskmasters and oppressors of theirs.

The proposal now is that after having paid ten million dollars to the rightful owners of the Isthmus we shall in addition pay twenty-five million dollars to their former taskmasters and oppressors; a sum two and a half times what these tricky oppressors originally asked, a sum which is to be paid to them merely because they failed in carrying to successful completion what must truthfully be characterized as a bit of international villainy as wicked as it was preposterous. In point of good sense and sound morality, the proposal is exactly on a par with paying a discomfited burglar a heavy sum for the damage done his feelings by detecting him and expelling him from the house. . . .

The people of the United States should remember that the United States paid fifty million dollars to Panama and the French company for every real right of every sort or description which existed on the Isthmus. There would have been no value even to these rights unless for the action that the United States then intended to take, and has since actually taken. The property of the French company would not have been worth any more than any other scrap-heap save for our subsequent action, and the right to cross the Isthmus of Panama would have been valueless to Colombia or to any other nation or body of men if we had failed to build a canal across it and had built one somewhere else. The whole value then and now of any right upon that Isthmus depended upon the fact that we then intended to spend and now have spent in building the Canal some three hundred and seventy-five million dollars. (*Metropolitan*, February 1915.) *Mem. Ed.* XX, 485, 486; *Nat. Ed.* XVIII, 416, 417.

PANAMA REVOLUTION. I cast aside the proposition made at this time to foment the secession of Panama. Whatever other governments can do, the United States cannot go into the securing by such underhand means, the cession. Privately, I freely say to you that I should be delighted if Panama were an independent State, or if it made itself so at this moment; but for me to say so publicly would amount to an instigation of a revolt, and therefore I cannot say it. (To Albert Shaw, October 10, 1903.) *Mem. Ed.* XXIII, 322; Bishop I, 279.

————————. I did not foment the revolution on the Isthmus. . . . It is idle folly to speak of there having been a conspiracy with us. The people of the Isthmus are a unit for the canal, and in favor of separation from the Colombians. The latter signed their death-warrant when they acted in such infamous manner about the signing of the treaty. Unless Congress overrides me, which I do not think probable, Colombia's grip on Panama is gone forever. (To Albert Shaw, November 6, 1903.) *Mem. Ed.* XXIII, 333; Bishop I, 288.

———————. Everything goes on there as we would wish; I am about to receive Mr. Bunau-Varilla. It is reported that we have made the revolution; it is not so, but for months such an occurrence was probable and I was ready for it. It is all for the best; such a revolution is quicker and not more bloody than our arbitration. If the Colombians try to send troops by sea against Panama, the American squadron has for its instructions to divert those ships to some place where they can do no mischief. Our own ships will avoid with the utmost care any action which might look like actual war against Colombia. (In conversation, November 11, 1903.) J. J. Jusserand, *What Me Befell.* (Houghton Mifflin Co., Boston, 1933), pp. 253-254.

———————. The revolution in Panama, or secession of Panama, is just like the secession of Greece from Turkey at the beginning of the last century, and of the other Christian States from Turkey later on in the century. Panama has suffered oppression for years. Not only was its secession justifiable but if it had had the power it would not have been warranted in standing such oppression for twenty-four hours. No body of men of courage and power, trained as you and I and our fellow citizens have been trained in self-government, in liberty, and in law-abiding habits, would submit for one day to the oppression habitual under Colombian rule in Panama.

Finally, when Colombia, which had plundered Panama, and misgoverned and misruled her, declined to ratify the treaty for the canal —which meant giving up Panama's last hope— the people of Panama rose literally as one man. When once this rising had occurred our Government was bound by every consideration of honor and humanity, and of national and international interest, to take exactly the steps that it took. (To David D. Thompson, December 22, 1903.) *Mem. Ed.* XXIII, 340; Bishop I, 294.

———————. I hesitate to refer to the injurious insinuations which have been made of complicity by this government in the revolutionary movement in Panama. They are as destitute of foundation as of propriety. The only excuse for my mentioning them is the fear lest unthinking persons might mistake for acquiescence the silence of mere self-respect. I think proper to say, therefore, that no one connected with this Government had any part in preparing, inciting, or encouraging the late revolution on the Isthmus of Panama, and that save from the reports of our military and naval officers, . . . no one connected with this Government had any previous knowledge of the revolution except such as was accessible to any person of ordinary intelligence who read the newspapers and kept up a current acquaintance with public affairs.

By the unanimous action of its people, without the firing of a shot—with a unanimity hardly before recorded in any similar case—the people of Panama declared themselves an independent republic. Their recognition by this Government was based upon a state of facts in no way dependent for its justification upon our action in ordinary cases. (Message to Congress, January 4, 1904.) *Presidential Addresses and State Papers* II, 743.

———————. Some people say that I fomented insurrection in Panama. There had been innumerable revolutions in Panama prior to the time that I became President. While I was President I kept my foot down on these revolutions so that when the revolution referred to did occur, I did not have to foment it; I simply lifted my foot. (In conversation with William H. Childs, aboard steamer from Europe, June 1914.) Frederick S. Wood, *Roosevelt As We Knew Him.* (J. C. Winston Co., Phila., 1927), p. 153.

———————. Even had I desired to foment a revolution—which I did not—it would have been unnecessary for me to do so. The Isthmus was seething with revolution. Any interference from me would have had to take the shape of preventing a revolution, not of creating one. All the people residing on the Isthmus ardently desired the revolution. The citizens of Panama desired it. . . . When the revolution had occurred, and was successful, and Panama was an independent republic, I certainly did prevent Colombia from carrying on a bloody war on the Isthmus in the effort to overthrow the revolutionists. I certainly did refuse to do what Colombia requested, that is, to use the army and navy of the United States against our friends in the interests of the foes who had just been trying to blackmail us. We were solemnly pledged to keep transit across the Isthmus open. Again and again we landed forces in time of revolutionary disturbance to secure this object. If Colombia had attempted the reconquest of the Isthmus, there would have been a far more bloody contest than ever before on the Isthmus, and the only way by which that contest could have been carried on would have been by using the railroad line and interrupting transit across the Isthmus.

It is therefore perfectly true that I prevented any attempt by Colombia to land troops on the Isthmus and plunge the Isthmus into a long-drawn-out and bloody war. (*Metropolitan*, February 1915.) Mem. Ed. XX, 502; Nat. Ed. XVIII, 431.

——————. On the "consent of the governed" theory, Panama was entitled to govern itself. The people of the Isthmus, the people of the Republic of Panama, were being oppressed by an alien people, who misgoverned them, for the interest of outsiders, and who were now jeopardizing their entire future for corrupt purposes. It has been said that I raised my hand and caused revolution. The simile is inexact. There were a dozen fuses always burning and leading up to revolutionary explosions in Panama. I came to the conclusion that I was absolved from all further duty to stamp out those fuses.... The government of the United States never took the smallest part, directly or indirectly, in fomenting or encouraging any revolutionary movement in Panama. Any statement to the contrary is a wicked and slanderous falsehood, to support which there is not merely no proof, but not a particle of just suspicion can be adduced in support of any such thing. (Before Panama-Pacific Historical Congress, Palo Alto, Cal., July 23, 1915.) *The Pacific Ocean in History. Papers and Addresses.* (Macmillan Co., N. Y., 1917), p. 145.

PANAMA. *See also* COLOMBIA; GOETHALS, GEORGE W.; HAY-HERRAN TREATY; HAY-PAUNCEFOTE TREATY; KITCHENER, LORD; MONROE DOCTRINE; NATIONAL DEFENSE; NAVY.

PANIC OF 1903. *See* CURRENCY.

PANIC OF 1907. In the fall of 1907 there were severe business disturbances and financial stringency, culminating in a panic which arose in New York and spread over the country. The damage actually done was great, and the damage threatened was incalculable. Thanks largely to the action of the government, the panic was stopped before, instead of being merely a serious business check, it became a frightful and nation-wide calamity, a disaster fraught with untold misery and woe to all our people. (1913.) Mem. Ed. XXII, 498; Nat. Ed. XX, 429.

——————. Of course I am gravely harassed and concerned over the situation. Every kind of suggestion is made to me, almost always impractically. I am doing everything I have power to do; but the fundamental fact is that the public is suffering from a spasm of lack of confidence. Most of this lack of confidence is absolutely unreasonable, and therefore we can do nothing with it. There is a part for which there is substantial basis, however. There has been so much trickery and dishonesty in high places; the exposures about Harriman, Rockefeller, Heinze, Barney, Morse, Ryan, the insurance man, and others, have caused such a genuine shock to people that they have begun to be afraid that every bank really has something rotten in it. In other words, they have passed thru the period of unreasoning trust and optimism into unreasoning distrust and pessimism.

I shall do everything I can up to the very verge of my power to restore confidence, to give the banks a chance to get currency into circulation. Whether I can accomplish what I seek to do I cannot say. Of course if I do not I shall be held responsible for the conditions. . . . There is nothing that I have done that I would not do over again, and I am absolutely positive that the principles which I have sought to enforce are those that must obtain if this Government is to endure. But, as you say, the very people whom I have been seeking to protect by exposing what is rotten in trusts and railroads, when the dinner-pail becomes empty will feel they would rather have full dinner-pails, and watered stocks and other things against which they used to declaim, rather than to go thru the period of discomfort when readjustment takes place. (To Douglas Robinson, November 16, 1907.) Mem. Ed. XXIV, 56; Bishop II, 48.

——————. You say that the fear of investors in railway securities must be dispelled; and you say that the people now have the impression that the greatest business interests (those of railroads) are imperilled. I am inclined to think that this is the case. If so, the responsibility lies primarily and overwhelmingly upon the railway and corporation people —that is, the manipulators of railroad and other corporation stocks—who have been guilty of such scandalous irregularities during the last few years. Secondarily it lies, of course, with the agitators and visionaries to whom the misdeeds of the conscienceless speculators I have named gave the chance to impress the people as a whole. Not one word of mine; not one act, administrative or legislative, of the National Government, is responsible, directly or indirectly, in any degree whatsoever for the present situation. I trust I have stated this with sufficient emphasis, for it would be quite impossible to overemphasize it. (To Henry L. Higginson, March 28, 1907.) *Mem. Ed.* XXIV, 46; Bishop II, 39.

──────────. I would have been derelict in my duty, I would have shown myself a timid and unworthy public servant, if in that extraordinary crisis I had not acted precisely as I did act [in regard to the Tennessee Coal and Iron Company]. In every such crisis the temptation to indecision, to non-action, is great, for excuses can always be found for non-action, and action means risk and the certainty of blame to the man who acts. But if the man is worth his salt he will do his duty, he will give the people the benefit of the doubt, and act in any way which their interests demand and which is not affirmatively prohibited by law, unheeding the likelihood that he himself, when the crisis is over and the danger past, will be assailed for what he has done. (1913.) *Mem. Ed.* XXII, 504; *Nat. Ed.* XX, 433.

PANIC OF 1907 — RESPONSIBILITY FOR. Whether I am or am not in any degree responsible for the panic, I shall certainly be held responsible. At present most of those who hold me responsible are people who are bitterly against me anyhow; but of course the feeling will spread to those who have been my friends, because when the average man loses his money he is simply like a wounded snake and strikes right and left at anything, innocent or the reverse, that presents itself as conspicuous in his mind.

Whether I can do anything to allay the panic I do not know. All the reactionaries wish to take advantage of the moment by having me announce that I will abandon my policies, at least in effect. Inasmuch as I believe that these policies are absolutely necessary, I shall not abandon them no matter what may be the stress for the time being. (To Dr. Alexander Lambert, December 1, 1907.) *Mem. Ed.* XXIV, 53; Bishop II, 45.

PANIC OF 1907 AND THE ROOSEVELT POLICIES. I am perfectly certain that in the end the Nation will have to come to my policies, or substantially to my policies, simply because the Republic cannot endure unless the governmental actions are founded on these policies, for they represent nothing whatever but aggressive honesty and fair treatment for all—not make-believe fair treatment, but genuine fair treatment. I do not think that my policies had anything to do with producing the conditions which brought on the panic; but I do think that very possibly the assaults and exposures which I made, and which were more or less successfully imitated in the several States, have brought on the panic a year or two sooner than would otherwise have been the case. The panic would have been infinitely worse, however, had it been deferred. (To Hamlin Garland, November 23, 1907.) *Mem. Ed.* XXIV, 58; Bishop II, 50.

PANIC OF 1907. *See also* CURRENCY; HARD TIMES; "MALEFACTORS OF GREAT WEALTH"; TENNESSEE COAL AND IRON COMPANY.

PAPER MONEY. *See* CURRENCY; SILVER.

PARAGUAY. *See* MONROE DOCTRINE.

PARDON. *See* CAPITAL PUNISHMENT; CRIMINALS.

PARENTS. *See* CHILDREN; FAMILY; HOME; HUSBANDS; MARRIAGE; MOTHER; WOMEN.

PARKMAN, FRANCIS. It is a fortunate thing when some great historic event, or chain of events, is commemorated by a great historian; and it is a matter for no small congratulation that the greatest historian whom the United States has yet produced should have found ready to his hand the all-important and singularly dramatic struggle which decided whether the destiny of the North American continent should be shaped by the French or the English race.

Mr. Parkman has now finished the work to which he has devoted his life. He has portrayed from the beginning the history of the French power in North America, through all its phases, to the time when it went down in the final struggle with England. He has published different volumes under different titles; but now that they are completed they form a connected whole, under the general title of "France and England in North America." (*Independent,* November 24, 1892.) *Mem. Ed.* XIV, 286; *Nat. Ed.* XII, 246.

──────────. Mr. Parkman has done a great work which there is no need of any one trying to do again. He has shown all the qualities of the historian, capacity for wide and deep research, accuracy in details combined with power to subordinate these details to the general effect, a keen perception of the essential underlying causes and results, and the mastery of a singularly clear, pure, and strong style. He has had a great subject, he has considered it philosophically, and has treated it with knowledge, with impartiality, and with enthusiasm. He has now brought to an end the life task he set himself. He has produced a great book, and added to the sum of the successful efforts of his countrymen in a way that is given to but few of them to add. (*Independent*, November 24, 1892.) Mem. Ed. XIV, 294; Nat. Ed. XII, 253.

PARLIAMENTARY GOVERNMENT. The English, or so-called "responsible," theory of parliamentary government is one entirely incompatible with our own governmental institutions. It could not be put into operation here save by absolutely sweeping away the United States Constitution. Incidentally, I may say it would be to the last degree undesirable, if it were practicable. But this is not the point upon which I wish to dwell; the point is that it was wholly impracticable to put it into operation, and that an agitation favoring this kind of government was from its nature unintelligent. (*Atlantic Monthly*, August 1894.) Mem. Ed. XV, 58; Nat. Ed. XIII, 43.

———. The English parliamentary system [is] a system admirable for England, taking into account the English national character, the customs and ways of looking at things inherited generation after generation by both the English people and their public men, and especially the fact that there are in England two parties; but a system which has not worked well in a government by groups, where the people do not mind changing their leaders continually, and are so afraid of themselves that, unlike the English and Americans, they do not dare trust any one man with a temporary exercise of large power for fear they will be weak enough to let him assume it permanently. (To Sir George Otto Trevelyan, October 1, 1911.) Mem. Ed. XXIV, 271; Bishop II, 232.

PARLIAMENTARY PRACTICE. See Debate; Filibustering; Legislative Minority.

PAROCHIAL SCHOOLS. See Schools.

PARTISANSHIP. I do not think partisanship should ever obscure the truth. (To Mrs. Theodore Roosevelt, Sr., September 14, 1881.) Cowles *Letters*, 50.

———. There are certain considerations of good citizenship which rise above all questions of mere partisanship. *Outlook*, July 12, 1913, p. 555.

PARTY ALLEGIANCE. I am a loyal party man, but I believe very firmly that I can best render aid to my party by doing all that in me lies to make that party responsive to the needs of the State, responsive to the needs of the people. (At New York State Bar Association banquet, January 18, 1899.) Mem. Ed. XVI, 467; Nat. Ed. XIV, 308.

———. A man cannot act both without and within the party; he can do either, but he cannot possibly do both. Each course has its advantages and each has its disadvantages, and one cannot take the advantages or the disadvantages separately. I went in with my eyes open to do what I could within the party; I did my best and got beaten; and I propose to stand by the result. It is impossible to combine the functions of a guerilla chief with those of a colonel in the regular army; one has a greater independence of action, the other is able to make what action he does take vastly more effective. In certain contingencies, the one can do most good; in certain contingencies the other; but there is no use in accepting a commission and then trying to play the game out on a lone hand. (Interview, Boston *Herald*, July 20, 1884.) Mem. Ed. XVI, 71; Nat. Ed. XIV, 39.

———. I recognize that at times it is necessary to leave the party, that it is right at times to bolt. I have done that myself, but I insist this much, that there shall be adequate cause for leaving the party, that there shall be a proper time chosen, and that we shall be absolutely certain that the results reached will be proper. (Before Republican meeting, Malden, Mass., October 20, 1884.) Mem. Ed. XVI, 86; Nat. Ed. XIV, 50.

———. Often the mere fact of having a good deal of record is more against a man than for him, when the question is as to how people will vote; for my experience is that usually people are more apt to let their dislikes than their likings cause them to break away from their party ties in matters of voting. In other words, the people of the opposite party who like what I have done are less apt for that reason to leave their candidate than the people of my own party who dislike what I have done are apt to leave me. (To Henry White, April 4, 1904.) Mem. Ed. XXIII, 364; Bishop I, 316.

PARTY ALLEGIANCE—ABUSE OF. The party man who offers his allegiance to party as an excuse for blindly following his party, right or wrong, and who fails to try to make that party in any way better, commits a crime against the country; and a crime quite as serious is committed by the independent who makes his independence an excuse for easy self-indulgence, and who thinks that when he says he belongs to neither party he is excused from the duty of taking part in the practical work of party organizations. The party man is bound to do his full share in party management. He is bound to attend the caucuses and the primaries, to see that only good men are put up, and to exert his influence as strenuously against the foes of good government within his party, as, through his party machinery, he does against those who are without the party. (*Forum,* July 1894.) *Mem. Ed.* XV, 44; *Nat. Ed.* XIII, 30.

PARTY ALLEGIANCE AND INDEPENDENCE. [A man] has got to preserve his independence on the one hand; and on the other, unless he wishes to be a wholly ineffective crank, he has got to have some sense of party allegiance and party responsibility, and he has got to realize that in any given exigency it may be a matter of duty to sacrifice one quality, or it may be a matter of duty to sacrifice the other.

If it is difficult to lay down any fixed rules for party action in the abstract; it would, of course, be wholly impossible to lay them down for party action in the concrete, with reference to the organizations of the present day. I think we ought to be broad-minded enough to recognize the fact that a good citizen, striving with fearlessness, honesty, and common sense to do his best for the nation, can render service to it in many different ways, and by connection with many different organizations. (Before the Liberal Club, Buffalo, N. Y., January 26, 1893.) *Mem. Ed.* XV, 67; *Nat. Ed.* XIII, 284.

——————. A man of sound political instincts can no more subscribe to the doctrine of absolute independence of party on the one hand than to that of unquestioning party allegiance on the other. No man can accomplish much unless he works in an organization with others, and this organization, no matter how temporary, is a party for the time being. But that man is a dangerous citizen who so far mistakes means for ends as to become servile in his devotion to his party, and afraid to leave it when the party goes wrong. To deify either independence or party allegiance merely as such is a little absurd. It depends entirely upon the motive, the purpose, the result. . . . The truth is, simply, that there are times when it may be the duty of a man to break with his party, and there are other times when it may be his duty to stand by his party, even though, on some points, he thinks that party wrong; he must be prepared to leave it when necessary, and he must not sacrifice his influence by leaving it unless it is necessary. If we had no party allegiance, our politics would become mere windy anarchy, and, under present conditions, our government could hardly continue at all. If we had no independence, we should always be running the risk of the most degraded kind of despotism— the despotism of the party boss and the party machine. (*Atlantic Monthly,* August 1894.) *Mem. Ed.* XV, 60; *Nat. Ed.* XIII, 45.

PARTY ALLEGIANCE. *See also* CITIZENSHIP; CIVIC DUTY; INDEPENDENT; MACHINE; MUGWUMPS; POLITICS.

PARTY PLATFORMS. It is in large part a sequel to . . . crooked control that there has been so long a record of failure on the part of both the old parties to redeem their platform pledges. I very earnestly hope that the Progressive party will bear this fact in mind when it comes to building its platform. Not only should the platform be right, but it should be so clearly drawn as to make the intentions of those who draw it perfectly understood by the average man; it should deal wisely and boldly with the new issues confronting our people; and, finally, it should scrupulously refrain from promising anything that cannot be performed, and should clearly show that it intends as a matter of honorable obligation to carry out every promise made. To make a promise which cannot be carried out or which would hopelessly damage the country if carried out is equivalent to announcing in advance that, not only this promise, but all the other promises in the platform, are meant to be broken, and are for campaign uses only. No party, and no candidate, should receive the support of the people if the platform shows on its face the corrupt insincerity of those making it. (*Outlook,* July 27, 1912.) *Mem. Ed.* XIX, 348; *Nat. Ed.* XVII, 246.

PARTY PLATFORMS. *See also* COMPROMISE; ELECTION PLEDGES; PLATFORM PROMISES; POLITICAL PROMISES.

PARTY SYSTEM—CRITICISM OF. Present party conditions insure the absolute powerlessness of the people when faced by a bipartisan combine of the two boss-ridden party machines, whose hostility each to the other is only nominal compared to the hostility of both to the people at large.

The second fundamental fact of the situation

partly depends upon this first fact. Where neither party ventures to have any real convictions upon the vital issues of the day it is normally impossible to use either as an instrument for meeting these vital issues. (*Century Magazine,* October 1913.) Mem. Ed. XIX, 532; Nat. Ed. XVII, 390.

——————. Four years ago I declined to make a fetich of the Republican party, when to do so meant dishonor to the nation, and this year I declined to make a fetich of the Progressive party when to do so meant dishonor to honor. I agree with you that issues and men are the things that count. A party is good only as a means to an end. Nevertheless, we have to face the fact that has been made strikingly evident during the past four years that with ninety per cent of our country-men the party name of itself has a certain fetichistic power, and we would be very foolish if we did not take this into account in endeavoring to work for good results. Moreover, it is unfortunately true that the dead hand of a party sometimes paralyzes its living members. The ancestral principles of the Democratic party are so bad it seems to be entirely impossible for it to be useful to the country except in spasms. (To a Mrs. Nicholson, of Oregon, July 18, 1916.) Corinne Roosevelt Robinson, *My Brother Theodore Roosevelt,* 308.

PARTY SYSTEM—FUNCTION OF. It is only through the party system that free governments are now successfully carried on, and yet we must keep ever vividly before us that the usefulness of a party is strictly limited by its usefulness to the State, and that in the long run, he serves his party best who most helps to make it instantly responsive to every need of the people, and to the highest demands of that spirit which tends to drive us onward and upward. (Inaugural Address as Governor, Albany, January 2, 1899.) Mem. Ed. XVII, 4; Nat. Ed. XV, 4.

PARTY SYSTEM. See also Boss; Independent; Machine; Organization; Platt, T. C.; Political Parties; Politics; Primaries.

PATRIOTIC CELEBRATIONS. See Fourth of July; Memorial Day.

PATRIOTIC SOCIETIES. Societies that cultivate patriotism in the present by keeping alive the memory of what we owe to the patriotism of the past, fill an indispensable function in this Republic. (Before Society of the Sons of the American Revolution, Washington, D. C., May 2, 1902.) *Presidential Addresses and State Papers* I, 36.

PATRIOTIC SONGS. Probably no one capable of feeling a generous thought of love for country can really judge quite dispassionately the songs which recite the great deeds done by the men of his own land. We Americans hold very high the memory of the men who "proved their truth by their endeavor," in the days of Lincoln and Grant, of Lee and Jackson and Farragut. It may be true that we cannot estimate what is said or sung of these with the absolute indifference of pure criticism; and of necessity it must appeal to us as it cannot appeal to others. Nevertheless, making every allowance for this feeling, it may still be safely said that on the whole no other contest has produced such poetry as our own Civil War. (*Cosmopolitan,* December 1892.) Mem. Ed. XIV, 376; Nat. Ed. XII, 309.

PATRIOTISM. Patriotism should be an integral part of our every feeling at all times, for it is merely another name for those qualities of soul which make a man in peace or in war, by day or by night, think of his duty to his fellows, and of his duty to the nation through which their and his loftiest aspirations must find their fitting expression. (1916.) Mem. Ed. XX, 234; Nat. Ed. XVIII, 201.

——————. Never yet was there a country worth living in which did not develop among her sons something at least of that nobility of soul which makes men not only serve their country when they are starving, but when death has set its doom on their faces. (At Cooper Union, New York City, November 3, 1916.) Mem. Ed. XX, 522; Nat. Ed. XVIII, 448.

——————. I believe in that ardent patriotism which will make a nation true to itself by making it secure justice for all within its own borders, and then so far as may be, aid in every way in securing just and fair treatment for all the nations of mankind. (*Metropolitan,* May 1916.) Mem. Ed. XXI, 149; Nat. Ed. XIX, 146.

——————. Patriotism is an affair of deeds, and patriotic words are good only in so far as they result in deeds. . . . Patriotism means service to the nation; and only those who render such service are fit to enjoy the privilege of citizenship. (At Lincoln, Neb., June 14, 1917.) Mem. Ed. XXI, 191; Nat. Ed. XIX, 181, 182.

[414]

──────────. Patriotism stands in national matters as love of family does in private life. Nationalism corresponds to the love a man bears for his wife and children. (Lafayette Day exercises, New York City, September 6, 1918.) *Mem. Ed.* XXI, 410; *Nat. Ed.* XIX, 372.

PATRIOTISM—DEMANDS UPON. America will cease to be a great nation whenever her young men cease to possess energy, daring, and endurance, as well as the wish and the power to fight the nation's foes. No citizen of a free State should wrong any man; but it is not enough merely to refrain from infringing on the rights of others; he must also be able and willing to stand up for his own rights and those of his country against all comers, and he must be ready at any time to do his full share in resisting either malice domestic or foreign levy. (Preface to Hero Tales, with H. C. Lodge, 1895.) *Mem. Ed.* IX, xxii; *Nat. Ed.* X, xxiii.

──────────. Patriotism is as much a duty in time of war as in time of peace, and it is most of all a duty in any and every great crisis. To commit folly or do evil, to act inconsiderately and hastily or wantonly and viciously, in the name of patriotism, represents not patriotism at all, but a use of the name to cloak an attack upon the thing. Such baseness or folly is wrong, at every time and on every occasion. But patriotism itself is not only in place on every occasion and at every time, but is peculiarly the feeling which should be stirred to its deepest depths at every serious crisis. . . . Patriotism, for far from being incompatible with performance of duty to other nations, is an indispensable prerequisite to doing one's duty toward other nations. Fear God; and take your own part! If this nation had feared God it would have stood up for the Belgians and Armenians; if it had been able and willing to take its own part there would have been no murderous assault on the *Lusitania,* no outrages on our men and women in Mexico. True patriotism carries with it not hostility to other nations but a quickened sense of responsible good-will toward other nations, a good-will of acts and not merely of words. (1916.) *Mem. Ed.* XX, 234-235; *Nat. Ed.* XVIII, 202-203.

──────────. The policies of Americanism and preparedness taken together mean applied patriotism. Our first duty as citizens of the nation is owed to the United States, but if we are true to our principles, we must also think of serving the interests of mankind at large. In addition to serving our own country, we must shape the policy of our country so as to secure the cause of international right, righteousness, fair play and humanity. (At Lewiston, Me., August 1916.) Corinne Roosevelt Robinson, *My Brother Theodore Roosevelt,* 320.

──────────. In America to-day all our people are summoned to service and sacrifice. Pride is the portion only of those who know bitter sorrow or the foreboding of bitter sorrow. But all of us who give service, and stand ready for sacrifice, are the torch-bearers. We run with the torches until we fall, content if we can then pass them to the hands of other runners. The torches whose flame is brightest are borne by the gallant men at the front, and by the gallant women whose husbands and lovers, whose sons and brothers are at the front. These men are high of soul, as they face their fate on the shell-shattered earth, or in the skies above or in the waters beneath; and no less high of soul are the women with torn hearts and shining eyes; the girls whose boy lovers have been struck down in their golden morning, and the mothers and wives to whom word has been brought that henceforth they must walk in the shadow.

These are the torch-bearers; these are they who have dared the Great Adventure. (*Metropolitan,* October 1918.) *Mem. Ed.* XXI, 267; *Nat. Ed.* XIX, 246.

PATRIOTISM—FOUNDATION OF. There can be no genuine feeling of patriotism of the kind that makes all men willing and eager to die for the land, unless there has been some measure of success in making the land worth living in for all alike, whatever their station, so long as they do their duty; and on the other hand, no man has a right to enjoy any benefits whatever from living in the land in time of peace, unless he is trained physically and spiritually so that if duty calls he can and will do his part to keep the land against all alien aggression. (At Cooper Union, New York City, November 3, 1916.) *Mem. Ed.* XX, 518; *Nat. Ed.* XVIII, 445.

PATRIOTISM—FUTURE OF. There are philosophers who assure us that, in the future, patriotism will be regarded not as a virtue at all, but merely as a mental stage in the journey toward a state of feeling when our patriotism will include the whole human race and all the world. This may be so; but the age of which these philosophers speak is still several eons distant. In fact, philosophers of this type are so very advanced that they are of no practical service to the present generation. It may be, that in ages so remote that we cannot now understand any of the feelings of those who will dwell in them, patriotism will no longer be regarded as a virtue, exactly as it may be that in those remote ages people will look down upon and disregard monogamic marriage; but as things now are and have been for two or three thousand years past, and are likely to be for two or three thousand years to come, the words "home" and "country" mean a great deal. Nor do they show any tendency to lose their significance. (*Forum,* April 1894.) *Mem. Ed.* XV, 19; *Nat. Ed.* XIII, 16-17.

PATRIOTISM—MEANING OF. Patriotism means to stand by the country. It does not mean to stand by the President or any other public official save exactly to the degree in which he himself stands by the country. It is patriotic to support him in so far as he efficiently serves the country. It is unpatriotic not to oppose him to the exact extent that by inefficiency or otherwise he fails in his duty to stand by the country. In either event, it is unpatriotic not to tell the truth—whether about the President or about any one else—save in the rare cases where this would make known to the enemy information of military value which would otherwise be unknown to him. (1918.) *Mem. Ed.* XXI, 316; *Nat. Ed.* XIX, 289.

PATRIOTISM, GERMAN AND JAPANESE. We should in all humility imitate not a little of the spirit so much in evidence among the Germans and the Japanese, the two nations which in modern times have shown the most practical type of patriotism, the greatest devotion to the common weal, the greatest success in developing their economic resources and abilities from within, and the greatest far-sightedness in safeguarding the country against possible disaster from without. (New York *Times,* November 29, 1914.) *Mem. Ed.* XX, 205; *Nat. Ed.* XVIII, 176.

PATRIOTISM AND COSMOPOLITANISM. The man who has in him real fighting blood is sure to be more deeply stirred by the deeds of his own people than by those of any other folk, though to these likewise he may pay glad and sincere homage. Every man to his own! We Americans cannot but feel our blood run quickest at the recital of the prowess of our own forefathers. Of course, if this feeling does not exist by nature it cannot be cultivated—there can be no self-conscious simulation of Americanism; but the man in whom intense love of country is wanting is a very despicable creature, no matter how well equipped with all the minor virtues and graces, literary, artistic, and social. (*Cosmopolitan,* December 1892.) *Mem. Ed.* XIV, 380; *Nat. Ed.* XII, 313.

————————. I am no advocate of a foolish cosmopolitanism. I believe that a man must be a good patriot before he can be, and as the only possible way of being, a good citizen of the world. Experience teaches us that the average man who protests that his international feeling swamps his national feeling, that he does not care for his country because he cares so much for mankind, in actual practice proves himself the foe of mankind; that the man who says that he does not care to be a citizen of any one country, because he is a citizen of the world, is in very fact usually an exceedingly undesirable citizen of whatever corner of the world he happens at the moment to be in. . . . However broad and deep a man's sympathies, however intense his activities, he need have no fear that they will be cramped by love of his native land. . . . So far from patriotism being inconsistent with a proper regard for the rights of other nations, I hold that the true patriot, who is as jealous of the national honor as a gentleman is of his own honor, will be careful to see that the nation neither inflicts nor suffers wrong, just as a gentleman scorns equally to wrong others or to suffer others to wrong him. (At the Sorbonne, Paris, April 23, 1910.) *Mem. Ed.* XV, 373-374; *Nat. Ed.* XIII, 526-527.

————————. Each people can do justice to itself only if it does justice to others, but each people can do its part in the world movement for all only if it first does its duty within its own household. The good citizen must be a good citizen of his own country first before he can with advantage be a citizen of the world at large. *Outlook,* May 14, 1910, p. 74.

PATRIOTISM. *See also* ALLEGIANCE; AMERICANISM; AMERICANS, HYPHENATED; BIG STICK; COSMOPOLITANS; FLAG; GERMAN PATRIOTISM; INTERNATIONALISM; LOVE OF COUNTRY; LOYALTY; NATIONALISM.

PATRONAGE. I feel sure that the possession of the patronage damages rather than benefits a party; but it is certainly also true that for one party to refrain from all use of patronage, while not by law enacting that its opponent must likewise refrain, would work little lasting benefit to the public service, and would probably insure party defeat. . . .

PATRONAGE — PEACE

It is therefore perfectly plain that the remedy lies in changing the system. For honest politicians to refrain from meddling with patronage, while leaving dishonest politicians full liberty to do so, is in the long run to work harm rather than good. The offices must be taken out of reach of all politicians, good or bad, by some permanent system of law. (*Century,* February 1890.) *Mem. Ed.* XVI, 167, 168; *Nat. Ed.* XIV, 107.

——————. I have done all I could, and I think I may say more than any other President has ever done, in the direction of getting rid of the system of appointing and removing men for political considerations. But enough remains to cause me many hours of sordid and disagreeable work, which yet must be done under penalty of losing the good-will of men with whom it is necessary that I should work. (To Sir George Otto Trevelyan, May 13, 1905.) *Mem. Ed.* XXIV, 174; Bishop II, 149.

——————. The use of government offices as patronage is a handicap difficult to overestimate from the standpoint of those who strive to get good government. Any effort for reform of any sort, national, State, or municipal, results in the reformers immediately finding themselves face to face with an organized band of drilled mercenaries who are paid out of the public chest to train themselves with such skill that ordinary good citizens when they meet them at the polls are in much the position of militia matched against regular troops. Yet these citizens themselves support and pay their opponents in such a way that they are drilled to overthrow the very men who support them. . . . Patronage does not really help a party. It helps the bosses to get control of the machinery of the party—as in 1912 was true of the Republican party—but it does not help the party. On the average, the most sweeping party victories in our history have been won when the patronage was against the victors. All that the patronage does is to help the worst element in the party retain control of the party organization. (1913.) *Mem. Ed.* XXII, 158; *Nat. Ed.* XX, 135, 136.

PATRONAGE. *See also* APPOINTMENTS; CIVIL SERVICE REFORM; OFFICE; SPOILS SYSTEM.

PAUNCEFOTE, SIR JULIAN. *See* HAY-PAUNCEFOTE TREATY; PANAMA CANAL.

PEACE. Peace is generally good in itself, but it is never the highest good unless it comes as the handmaid of righteousness; and it becomes a very evil thing if it serves merely as a mask for cowardice and sloth, or as an instrument to further the ends of despotism or anarchy. *Outlook,* May 7, 1910, p. 19.

——————. Work for peace will never be worth much unless accompanied by courage, effort, and self-sacrifice. (*Independent,* January 4, 1915.) *Mem. Ed.* XX, 179; *Nat. Ed.* XVIII, 154.

——————. Scant attention is paid to the weakling or the coward who babbles of peace; but due heed is given to the strong man with sword girt on thigh who preaches peace, not from ignoble motives, not from fear or distrust of his own powers, but from a deep sense of moral obligation. (1900.) *Mem. Ed.* XV, 286; *Nat. Ed.* XIII, 335.

——————. Our business is to create the beginnings of international order out of the world of nations as these nations actually exist. We do not have to deal with a world of pacifists and therefore we must proceed on the assumption that treaties will never acquire sanctity until nations are ready to seal them with their blood. We are not striving for peace in heaven. That is not our affair. What we were bidden to strive for is "peace on earth and good-will toward men." To fulfil this injunction it is necessary to treat the earth as it is and men as they are, as an indispensable prerequisite to making the earth a better place in which to live and men better fit to live in it. It is inexcusable moral culpability on our part to pretend to carry out this injunction in such fashion as to nullify it; and this we do if we make believe that the earth is what it is not and if our professions of bringing good-will toward men are in actual practice shown to be empty shams. Peace congresses, peace parades, the appointment and celebration of days of prayer for peace, and the like, which result merely in giving the participants the feeling that they have accomplished something and are therefore to be excused from hard, practical work for righteousness, are empty shams. (New York *Times,* November 29, 1914.) *Mem. Ed.* XX, 199; *Nat. Ed.* XVIII, 171.

——————. Peace is not a question of names. It is a question of facts. If murders occur in a city, and if the police force is so incompetent that no record is made of them officially, that does not interfere with the fact that murders have been committed and that life is unsafe. In just the same way, if lives are taken by violence between nations, it is not of the slightest consequence whether those responsible for the government of the nation whose citizens have lost their lives do or do not assert that the nation is at peace. During the last three years we have been technically at peace. But during those three years more of our citizens have been killed by Mexicans, Germans, Austrians, and Haytians than were killed during the entire Spanish War. (1916.) *Mem. Ed.* XX, 244; *Nat. Ed.* XVIII, 210.

──────────────. Peace, like Freedom, is not a gift that tarries long in the hands of cowards, or of those too feeble or too short-sighted to deserve it, and we ask to be given the means to insure that honorable peace which alone is worth having. (To Guy Emerson, Spring 1916.) Corinne Roosevelt Robinson, *My Brother Theodore Roosevelt,* 293.

PEACE—ACQUISITION OF. Remember that peace itself, that peace after which all men crave, is merely the realization in the present of what has been bought by strenuous effort in the past. Peace represents stored-up effort of our fathers or of ourselves in the past. It is not a means—it is an end. You do not get peace by peace; you get peace as the result of effort. If you strive to get it by peace you will lose it, that is all. If we ever grow to regard peace as a permanent condition; if we ever grow to feel that we can afford to let the keen, fearless, virile qualities of heart and mind and body be lost, then we will prepare the way for inevitable and shameful disaster in the future. (At Lincoln Club dinner, New York City, February 13, 1899.) *Mem. Ed.* XVI, 475; *Nat. Ed.* XIV, 315.

──────────────. No paper scheme designed to secure peace without effort and safety without service and sacrifice will either make this country safe or enable it to do its international duty toward others. (August 4, 1918.) *Roosevelt in the Kansas City Star,* 195.

PEACE—AMERICAN INFLUENCE FOR. Last summer the United States had the honor to take what was on the whole the leading part in the Peace Conference at The Hague. We were able to play that part solely because during the preceding year we had fought to a victorious conclusion the most righteous foreign war in which any nation has been engaged for half a century.

Our power to further the cause of peace as among the civilized nations of the world has been immeasurably increased because we have shown ourselves able and willing to do our part in policing the world, in keeping order in the world's waste spaces. . . . When a coward or a weakling preaches peace but little good results; but, as was shown at The Hague last year, when a mighty people, not afraid to do its duty in the world, stands up for peace, the good result is immediately manifest. (At Cincinnati, O., October 21, 1899.) *Mem. Ed.* XVI, 501; *Nat. Ed.* XIV, 338.

──────────────. We are glad indeed that we are on good terms with all the other peoples of mankind, and no effort on our part shall be spared to secure a continuance of these relations. And remember, gentlemen, that we shall be a potent factor for peace largely in proportion to the way in which we make it evident that our attitude is due, not to weakness, not to inability to defend ourselves, but to a genuine repugnance to wrongdoing, a genuine desire for self-respecting friendship with our neighbors. The voice of the weakling or the craven counts for nothing when he clamors for peace; but the voice of the just man armed is potent. We need to keep in a condition of preparedness, especially as regards our navy, not because we want war, but because we desire to stand with those whose plea for peace is listened to with respectful attention. (At banquet of Chamber of Commerce, New York City, November 11, 1902.) *Mem. Ed.* XXIII, 265; Bishop I, 230.

──────────────. Our voice is now potent for peace, and is so potent because we are not afraid of war. But our protestations upon behalf of peace would neither receive nor deserve the slightest attention if we were impotent to make them good. (Fourth Annual Message, Washington, December 6, 1904.) *Mem. Ed.* XVII, 303; *Nat. Ed.* XV, 260.

PEACE—ATTAINMENT OF. The one permanent move for obtaining peace, which has yet been suggested, with any reasonable chance of attaining its object, is by an agreement among the great powers, in which each should pledge itself not only to abide by the decisions of a common tribunal but to back with force the decisions of that common tribunal. The great civilized nations of the world which do possess force, actual or immediately potential, should combine by solemn agreement in a great World League for the Peace of Righteousness. (New York *Times,* October 18, 1914.) *Mem. Ed.* XX, 64; *Nat. Ed.* XVIII, 54.

──────────────. I very sincerely believe in peace. I hold the man, who, in a spirit of levity or wantonness or brutality or mere fancied self-interest, goes to war, to be an abhorrent brute.

But, as the world now is, I am convinced that peace will only come on the same terms on which we get it in great cities—that is, by doing everything to cultivate justice and gentleness and fair dealing between man and man and between man and woman, and at the same time having a court backed by physical force, that is backed by the police power, to which one can appeal against the brutal, the disorderly, the homicidal. (To Alfred Noyes, November 28, 1914.) Lord Charnwood, *Theodore Roosevelt*. (Atlantic Monthly Press, Boston, 1923), p. 197.

——————. Every peace body, whether religious or humanitarian, philosophic or political; and all advocates of peace whether in public or private life, work nothing but mischief, and, save in so far as mere silliness prevents it, very serious mischief, unless they put righteousness first and peace next. Every league that calls itself a Peace League is championing immorality unless it clearly and explicitly recognizes the duty of putting righteousness before peace and of being prepared and ready to enforce righteousness by war if necessary; and it is idle to promise to wage offensive war on behalf of others until we have shown that we are able and willing to wage defensive war on behalf of ourselves. The man who fears death more than dishonor, more than failure to perform duty, is a poor citizen; and the nation that regards war as the worst of all evils and the avoidance of war as the highest good is a wretched and contemptible nation, and it is well that it should vanish from the face of the earth. (*Metropolitan*, August 1915.) Mem. Ed. XX, 368; Nat. Ed. XVIII, 316.

——————. Kindly people who know little of life and nothing whatever of the great forces of international rivalry have exposed the cause of peace to ridicule by believing that serious wars could be avoided through arbitration treaties, peace treaties, neutrality treaties, and the action of The Hague court, without putting force behind such treaties and such action. The simple fact is that none of these existing treaties and no function of The Hague court hitherto planned and exercised have exerted or could exert the very smallest influence in maintaining peace when great conflicting international passions are aroused and great conflicting national interests are at stake. (New York *Times*, October 4, 1914.) Mem. Ed. XX, 45; Nat. Ed. XVIII, 39.

PEACE—DESIRE FOR. As a civilized people we desire peace, but the only peace worth having is obtained by instant readiness to fight when wronged—not by unwillingness or inability to fight at all. (Preface to *Hero Tales*, with H. C. Lodge, 1895.) Mem. Ed. IX, xxi; Nat. Ed. X, xxiii.

PEACE—FALSE ADVOCATES OF. Peace is a great good; and doubly harmful, therefore, is the attitude of those who advocate it in terms that would make it synonymous with selfish and cowardly shrinking from warring against the existence of evil. The wisest and most far-seeing champions of peace will ever remember that, in the first place, to be good it must be righteous, for unrighteous and cowardly peace may be worse than any war; and, in the second place, that it can often be obtained only at the cost of war. (1900.) Mem. Ed. XV, 282; Nat. Ed. XIII, 332.

——————. In the history of our country the peace advocates who treat peace as more than righteousness will never be, and never have been, of service, either to it or to mankind. The true lovers of peace, the men who have really helped onward the movement for peace, have been those who followed, even though afar off, in the footsteps of Washington and Lincoln, and stood for righteousness as the supreme end of national life. (*Outlook*, September 9, 1911.) Mem. Ed. XVIII, 426; Nat. Ed. XVI, 319.

——————. Unfortunately, many of those often well-meaning persons who claim a leading position among the advocates of international peace have harmed their cause in the eyes of all really far-sighted and patriotic citizens by advocating for America a position which would be abjectly unworthy of her standing among the nations. This category includes those who opposed our war with Spain, those who opposed the subsequent enforcement of law and order in the Philippines, those who opposed the building up of the navy, and those who now oppose the fortification of the Panama Canal. Some of these men are misguided men of good character; others, however, are merely men who do not possess any keen sense of international honor, and who are perfectly willing to see this nation expose itself to the chance of discredit and disaster, because their own small souls would be unaffected by a national defeat which would make most Americans bow their heads with bitterness and shame. As regards these men, I should not have the slightest objection to their inviting the disaster that would come upon them if their wishes were fulfilled, were it not for the fact that the rest of us would unfortunately have to share in the disaster. It is somewhat exasperating to reflect that we have to protect these particular peace advocates of the crazy type from themselves, and, in spite of their shrieking protests, guard them and their children against suffering their share of the national humiliation they do their best to bring about. (*Outlook*, April 1, 1911.) Mem. Ed. XIX, 153; Nat. Ed. XVII, 110.

PEACE—FRIENDS OF. It is those among us who would go to the front . . . —as I and my four sons would go—who are the really farsighted and earnest friends of peace. We desire measures taken in the real interest of peace because we, who at need would fight, but who earnestly hope never to be forced to fight, have most at stake in keeping peace. We object to the actions of those who do most talking about the necessity of peace because we think they are really a menace to the just and honorable peace which alone this country will in the long run support. We object to their actions because we believe they represent a course of conduct which may at any time produce a war in which we and not they would labor and suffer. (*New York Times,* September 27, 1914.) Mem. Ed. XX, 12; Nat. Ed. XVIII, 11.

————————. The effective workers for the peace of righteousness were men like Stein, Cavour, and Lincoln; that is, men who dreamed great dreams, but who were also pre-eminently men of action, who stood for the right, and who knew that the right would fail unless might was put behind it. The prophets of pacifism have had nothing whatever in common with these great men; and whenever they have preached mere pacifism, whenever they have failed to put righteousness first and to advocate peace as the handmaiden of righteousness, they have done evil and not good. (*Everybody's,* January 1915.) Mem. Ed. XX, 148; Nat. Ed. XVIII, 127.

PEACE—GUARANTEES OF. What we need is not to promise action in the nebulous future but to act now in the living present. Any promise of ours about entering into international peace leagues or guaranteeing the peace of the world or protecting small nationalities hereafter is worse than worthless, is mischievous and hypocritical, unless we make our words good by action in the case that is uppermost in the present. Until we can and do guarantee peace in Mexico let us not talk loudly and make empty gestures about guaranteeing the peace of the world. Unless we are willing to run some risk and make some effort to right the wrongs of Belgium in the present let us refrain from indulging in insincere declamation about protecting small nations in similar cases in the future. And let us make no absurd promises about "enforcing" peace at some remote period in the future until by foresight and labor and service and self-sacrifice we have shown that we have spiritually prepared ourselves to make our words good and until materially we have made ready our vast but soft and lazy strength. (To Charles W. Farnham, January 19, 1917.) Mem. Ed. XXIV, 539; Bishop II, 461.

PEACE—INTERNATIONAL COOPERATION FOR. We should endeavor to devise some method of action, in common with other nations, whereby there shall be at least a reasonable chance of securing world peace and, in any event, of narrowing the sphere of possible war and its horrors. To do this it is equally necessary unflinchingly to antagonize the position of the men who believe in nothing but brute force exercised without regard to the rights of other nations, and unhesitatingly to condemn the well-meaning but unwise persons who seek to mislead our people into the belief that treaties, mere bits of paper, when unbacked by force and when there is no one responsible for their enforcement, can be of the slightest use in a serious crisis. (*New York Times,* September 27, 1914.) Mem. Ed. XX, 6; Nat. Ed. XVIII, 6.

PEACE—NEED FOR. Peace must be the normal condition, or the nation will come to a bloody doom. Twice in great crises, in 1776 and 1861, and twice in lesser crises, in 1812 and 1898, the nation was called to arms in the name of all that makes the words "honor," "freedom," and "justice" other than empty sounds. On each occasion the net result of the war was greatly for the benefit of mankind. But on each occasion this net result was of benefit only because after the war came peace, came justice and order and liberty. If the Revolution had been followed by bloody anarchy, if the Declaration of Independence had not been supplemented by the adoption of the Constitution, if the freedom won by the sword of Washington had not been supplemented by the stable and orderly government which Washington was instrumental in founding, then we should have but added to the chaos of the world, and our victories would have told against and not for the betterment of mankind. So it was with the Civil War. If the four iron years had not been followed by peace, they would not have been justified. (At Galena, Ill., April 27, 1900.) Mem. Ed. XII, 460; Nat. Ed. XIII, 431.

[420]

PEACE—PRESERVATION OF. We are a great peaceful nation; a nation of merchants and manufacturers, of farmers and mechanics; a nation of workingmen, who labor incessantly with head or hand. It is idle to talk of such a nation ever being led into a course of wanton aggression. If we forget that in the last resort we can only secure peace by being ready and willing to fight for it, we may some day have bitter cause to realize that a rich nation which is slothful, timid, or unwieldy is an easy prey for any people which still retains those most valuable of all qualities, the soldierly virtues. . . .

Peace is a goddess only when she comes with sword girt on thigh. The ship of state can be steered safely only when it is always possible to bring her against any foe with "her leashed thunders gathering for the leap." (Address as Assistant Secretary of the Navy, Naval War College, June 1897.) *Mem. Ed.* XV, 241; *Nat. Ed.* XIII, 183

——————. The true end of every great and free people should be self-respecting peace; and this nation most earnestly desires sincere and cordial friendship with all others. Over the entire world, of recent years, wars between the great civilized powers have become less and less frequent. Wars with barbarous or semi-barbarous peoples come in an entirely different category, being merely a most regrettable but necessary international police duty which must be performed for the sake of the welfare of mankind. Peace can only be kept with certainty where both sides wish to keep it; but more and more the civilized peoples are realizing the wicked folly of war and are attaining that condition of just and intelligent regard for the rights of others which will in the end, we hope and believe, make the world-wide peace possible. (First Annual Message, Washington, December 3, 1901.) *Mem. Ed.* XVII, 133; *Nat. Ed.* XV, 115.

PEACE—ROOSEVELT'S WORK FOR. My past words, and the acts wherein I have striven to make those words good, afford proof of my sincerity in the cause of peace. I will do all I can to bring about such a league of, or understanding among, the great powers as will forbid one of them, or any small power, to engage in unrighteous, foolish or needless war; to secure an effective arbitral tribunal, with power to enforce at least certain of its decrees; to secure an agreement to check the waste of money on growing and excessive armaments. If, as is probable, so much cannot be secured at once, I will do all I can to help in the movement, rapid or slow, towards the desired end. But I will not be, and you would not wish me to be, put in the attitude of advocating the impossible, or, above all, of seeming to be insincere. (To Carnegie, February 18, 1910.) Burton J. Hendrick, *The Life of Andrew Carnegie.* (Doubleday, Doran & Co., Garden City, N. Y., 1932), II, 327.

——————. In my own judgment the most important service that I rendered to peace was the voyage of the battle fleet round the world. (1913.) *Mem. Ed.* XXII, 622; *Nat. Ed.* XX, 535.

——————. No man can possibly be more anxious for peace than I am. I ask those individuals who think of me as a firebrand to remember that during the seven and a half years I was President not a shot was fired at any soldier of a hostile nation by any American soldier or sailor, and there was not so much as a threat of war. . . . When I left the presidency, there was not a cloud on the horizon—and one of the reasons why there was not a cloud on the horizon was that the American battle fleet had just returned from its sixteen months' trip around the world, a trip such as no other battle fleet of any power had ever taken, which it had not been supposed could be taken, and which exercised a greater influence for peace than all the peace congresses of the last fifty years. With Lowell I most emphatically believe that peace is not a gift that tarries long in the hands of cowards; and the fool and the weakling are no improvement on the coward. (New York *Times*, November 15, 1914.) *Mem. Ed.* XX, 105-106; *Nat. Ed.* XVIII, 91.

PEACE—VALUE OF. Peace is of true value only if we use it in part to make ready to face with untroubled heart, with fearless front, whatever the future may have in store for us. The peace which breeds timidity and sloth is a curse and not a blessing. (At Lincoln Club dinner, New York City, February 13, 1899.) *Mem. Ed.* XVI, 475; *Nat. Ed.* XIV, 316.

PEACE AND RIGHTEOUSNESS. Until people get it firmly fixed in their minds that peace is valuable chiefly as a means to righteousness, and that it can only be considered as an end when it also coincides with righteousness, we can do only a limited amount to advance its coming on this earth. (To Carl Schurz, September 8, 1905.) *Mem. Ed.* XXII, 620; *Nat. Ed.* XX, 533.

——————. Peace is normally a great good, and normally it coincides with righteous-

PEACE

ness; but it is righteousness and not peace which should bind the conscience of a nation as it should bind the conscience of an individual; and neither a nation nor an individual can surrender conscience to another's keeping. (Sixth Annual Message, Washington, December 3, 1906.) *Mem. Ed.* XVII, 472; *Nat. Ed.* XV, 402.

——————. It is one of our prime duties as a nation to seek peace. It is an even higher duty to seek righteousness. It is also our duty not to indulge in shams, not to make believe we are getting peace by some patent contrivance which sensible men ought to know cannot work in practice, and which if we sought to make it work might cause irretrievable harm. (*Outlook,* September 9, 1911.) *Mem. Ed.* XVIII, 416; *Nat. Ed.* XVI, 310.

——————. There is one thing in connection with this war [Spanish-American] which it is well that our people should remember, our people who genuinely love the peace of righteousness, the peace of justice—and I would be ashamed to be other than a lover of the peace of righteousness and of justice. The true preachers of peace, who strive earnestly to bring nearer the day when peace shall obtain among all peoples, and who really do help forward the cause, are men who never hesitate to choose righteous war when it is the only alternative to unrighteous peace. (1913.) *Mem. Ed.* XXII, 304; *Nat. Ed.* XX, 260.

——————. There can be no nobler cause for which to work than the peace of righteousness; and high honor is due those serene and lofty souls who with wisdom and courage, with high idealism tempered by sane facing of the actual facts of life, have striven to bring nearer the day when armed strife between nation and nation, between class and class, between man and man shall end throughout the world. Because all this is true, it is also true that there are no men more ignoble or more foolish, no men whose actions are fraught with greater possibility of mischief to their country and to mankind, than those who exalt unrighteous peace as better than righteous war. (1913.) *Mem. Ed.* XXII, 604; *Nat. Ed.* XX, 519.

——————. Peace is worthless unless it serves the cause of righteousness. Peace which consecrates militarism is of small service. Peace obtained by crushing the liberty and life of just and unoffending peoples is as cruel as the most cruel war. (*Outlook,* September 23, 1914.) *Mem. Ed.* XX, 14; *Nat. Ed.* XVIII, 12.

PEACE-AT-ANY-PRICE

——————. I abhor war. In common with all other thinking men I am inexpressibly saddened by the dreadful contest now waging in Europe. I put peace very high as an agent for bringing about righteousness. But if I must choose between righteousness and peace I choose righteousness. Therefore, I hold myself in honor bound to do anything in my power to advance the cause of the peace of righteousness throughout the world. (New York *Times,* October 4, 1914.) *Mem. Ed.* XX, 41; *Nat. Ed.* XVIII, 35.

——————. Let us as a nation understand that peace is worth having only when it is the handmaiden of international righteousness and of national self-respect. (Statement to press, May 1915.) *Mem. Ed.* XX, 444; *Nat. Ed.* XVIII, 381.

——————. Washington loved peace. Perhaps Lincoln loved peace even more. But when the choice was between peace and righteousness, both alike trod undaunted the dark path that led through terror and suffering and the imminent menace of death to the shining goal beyond. We treasure the lofty words these men spoke. We treasure them because they were not merely words, but the high expression of deeds still higher; the expression of a serene valor that was never betrayed by a cold heart or a subtle and selfish brain. (At Cooper Union, New York City, November 3, 1916.) *Mem. Ed.* XX, 519; *Nat. Ed.* XVIII, 445.

PEACE-AT-ANY-PRICE. There is . . . no more utterly useless and often utterly mischievous citizen, than the peace-at-any-price, universal-arbitration type of being, who is always complaining either about war or else about the cost of the armaments which act as the insurance against war. (1913.) *Mem. Ed.* XXII, 245; *Nat. Ed.* XX, 210.

——————. It is we ourselves, it is the American people, who are responsible for the public sentiment which permits unworthy action on the part of our governmental representatives. The peace propaganda of the past ten years in this country has steadily grown more noisy. It received an enormous impetus when five years ago, by the negotiation of peace-at-any-price or all-inclusive arbitration treaties, and in the last year by the ratification of the thirty-odd peace-at-any-price arbitration-commission treaties, it was made part of our national governmental policy. It is the literal truth to say that this peace-at-any-price propaganda has probably, on the whole, worked more mischief to the United States than all the crookedness in business and politics combined during the same

[422]

period. It has represented more positive deterioration in the American character. Millions of plain Americans, who do not have the opportunity to know the facts or to think them out for themselves, have been misled in this matter. They are not to blame; but the leaders and organizers of that movement, its upholders and apologists on the stump and in the pulpit and in the press, are very greatly to blame. Really good and high-minded clergymen, capable of foresight and brave enough to risk being misrepresented, have stood steadfastly against the odious creed which puts peace ahead of righteousness. But every cheap man in the pulpit, like every cheap demagogue on the stump, has joined in the "peace-at-any-price" cry.... The man who preaches peace at any price, non-resistance to all wrong, disarmament and the submission of everything to arbitration, no matter how sincere and honest he may be, is rendering a worse service to his fellow countrymen than any exponent of crooked business or crooked politics. The deification of peace without regard to whether it is either wise or righteous does not represent virtue. It represents a peculiarly base and ignoble form of evil. (*Metropolitan*, August 1915.) *Mem. Ed.* XX, 345-347; *Nat. Ed.* XVIII, 296-297.

PEACE CONGRESSES—ACCOMPLISHMENTS OF. We must explicitly recognize that all the peace congresses and the like that have been held of recent years have done no good whatever to the cause of world peace. All their addresses and resolutions about arbitration and disarmament and such matters have been on the whole slightly worse than useless. Disregarding The Hague conventions, it is the literal fact that none of the peace congresses that have been held for the last fifteen or twenty years—to speak only of those of which I myself know the workings—have accomplished the smallest particle of good. In so far as they have influenced free, liberty-loving, and self-respecting nations not to take measures for their own defense they have been positively mischievous. In no respect have they achieved anything worth achieving; and the present World War proves this beyond the possibility of serious question. (*Independent*, January 4, 1915.) *Mem. Ed.* XX, 175; *Nat. Ed.* XVIII, 151.

PEACE OF JUSTICE. The steady aim of this nation, as of all enlightened nations, should be to strive to bring ever nearer the day when there shall prevail throughout the world the peace of justice. There are kinds of peace which are highly undesirable, which are in the long run as destructive as any war.... Many times peoples who were slothful or timid or short-sighted, who had been enervated by ease or by luxury, or misled by false teachings, have shrunk in unmanly fashion from doing duty that was stern and that needed self-sacrifice, and have sought to hide from their own minds their shortcomings, their ignoble motives, by calling them love of peace. The peace of tyrannous terror, the peace of craven weakness, the peace of injustice, all these should be shunned as we shun unrighteous war. The goal to set before us as a nation, the goal which should be set before all mankind, is the attainment of the peace of justice, of the peace which comes when each nation is not merely safeguarded in its own rights, but scrupulously recognizes and performs its duty toward others. (Fourth Annual Message, Washington, December 6, 1904.) *Mem. Ed.* XVII, 296; *Nat. Ed.* XV, 254.

————————. We wish peace, but we wish the peace of justice, the peace of righteousness. We wish it because we think it is right and not because we are afraid. No weak nation that acts manfully and justly should ever have cause to fear us, and no strong power should ever be able to single us out as a subject for insolent aggression. (Inaugural Address as President, Washington, March 4, 1905.) *Mem. Ed.* XVII, 312; *Nat. Ed.* XV, 268.

————————. We must endeavor earnestly but with sanity to try to bring around better world conditions. We must try to shape our policy in conjunction with other nations so as to bring nearer the day when the peace of righteousness, the peace of justice and fair dealing, will be established among the nations of the earth. With this object in view, it is our duty carefully to weigh the influences which are at work or may be put to work in order to bring about this result and in every effective way to do our best to further the growth of these influences. When this has been done no American administration will be able to assert that it is reduced to humiliating impotence even to protest against such wrong as that committed on Belgium, because, forsooth, our "neutrality" can only be preserved by failure to help right what is wrong—and we shall then as a people have too much self-respect to enter into absurd, all-inclusive arbitration treaties, unbacked by force, at the very moment when we fail to do what is clearly demanded by our duty under The Hague treaties. (New York *Times*, October 18, 1914.) *Mem. Ed.* XX, 61; *Nat. Ed.* XVIII, 52.

PEACE SOCIETIES. None of our peace bodies ... have ventured to denounce Germany for

[423]

her destruction of Belgium, which is, on the whole, the most hideous crime against peace and civilization that has been perpetrated since the close of the Napoleonic wars. They hold little futile peace-parades, and send round peace postage-stamps with a dove on them, and get up petitions for peace in the public schools; but they do not venture for one moment to condemn any man who has done wrong, or to do more than raise a feeble clamor to the effect that peace must be obtained by tame acquiescence in wrong. (To Alfred Noyes, November 28, 1914.) Lord Charnwood, *Theodore Roosevelt.* (Atlantic Monthly Press, Boston, 1923), pp. 197-198.

PEACE TREATIES—DEPENDENCE ON. At this moment there is a very grave crisis in Europe, and before the war clouds now gathering, all the peace and arbitration treaties, and all the peace and arbitration societies, and all the male and female shrieking sisterhood of Carnegies and the like, are utterly powerless. If war is averted, it will be only because Germany thinks that France has a first-class army and will fight hard, and that England is ready and able to render her some prompt assistance. (To H. C. Lodge, September 12, 1911.) Lodge *Letters* II, 409.

――――――. What befell Antwerp and Brussels will surely some day befall New York or San Francisco, and may happen to many an inland city also, if we do not shake off our supine folly, if we trust for safety to peace treaties unbacked by force. . . . We must stand absolutely for righteousness. But to do so is utterly without avail unless we possess the strength and the loftiness of spirit which will back righteousness with deeds and not mere words. We must clear the rubbish from off our souls and admit that everything that has been done in passing peace treaties, arbitration treaties, neutrality treaties, Hague treaties, and the like, with no sanction of force behind them, amounts to literally and absolutely zero, to literally and absolutely nothing, in any time of serious crisis. We must recognize that to enter into foolish treaties which cannot be kept is as wicked as to break treaties which can and ought to be kept. (New York *Times,* November 1, 1914.) *Mem. Ed.* XX, 79, 81; *Nat. Ed.* XVIII, 68, 69.

PEACE WITHOUT VICTORY. President Wilson has announced himself in favor of peace without victory, and now he has declared himself against universal service—that is, against all efficient preparedness by the United States.

Peace without victory is the natural ideal of the man who is too proud to fight.

When fear of the German submarine next moves Mr. Wilson to declare for "peace without victory" between the tortured Belgians and their cruel oppressors and taskmasters; when such fear next moves him to utter the shameful untruth that each side is fighting for the same things, and to declare for neutrality between wrong and right; let him think of the prophetess Deborah, who, when Sisera mightily oppressed the children of Israel with his chariots of iron, and when the people of Meroz stood neutral between the oppressed and the oppressor, sang of them:

"Curse ye Meroz, said the angel of the Lord, curse ye bitterly the inhabitants thereof; because they came not to the help of the Lord against the wrongdoings of the mighty."

President Wilson has earned for the nation the curse of Meroz for he has not dared to stand on the side of the Lord against the wrongdoings of the mighty. (Statement, January 29, 1917.) *Mem. Ed.* XXIV, 490; Bishop II, 418.

――――――. Every decent citizen should make the pacifist and the home Hun realize that agitation for a premature peace, for a peace without victory, is seditious. Shame on every man, and above all on every public servant and every leader of public opinion, who endeavors to weaken the determination of America to see the war through and at all costs secure an overwhelming triumph for the principles for which we contend. If Germany is left unbeaten, the Western Hemisphere will stand in cowering dread of an assault by Germany's ruthless and barbarous autocracy. The liberties of the free peoples of the world are at stake. (October 23, 1917.) *Roosevelt in the Kansas City Star,* 31.

PEACE. *See also* ALLIANCES; ARBITRATION; ARMAMENTS; BATTLE FLEET; DEFENSE; DISARMAMENT; EXPANSION; FOURTEEN POINTS; HAGUE CONVENTIONS; IMPERIALISM; INTERNATIONAL COURT; LEAGUE FOR PEACE; LEAGUE OF NATIONS; LUNATIC FRINGE; NATIONAL DEFENSE; NEUTRAL RIGHTS; NEUTRALITY; NOBEL PEACE PRIZE; PACIFISM; PACIFIST; PREPAREDNESS; RIGHTEOUSNESS; TREATIES; UNPREPAREDNESS; WAR; WORLD WAR.

PEARY, ROBERT E. Probably few outsiders realize the well-nigh incredible toil and hardship entailed in such an achievement as Peary's; and fewer still understand how many years of careful training and preparation there must be before the feat can be even attempted with any chance of success. A "dash for the pole" can be successful only if there have been many preliminary years of painstaking, patient toil. Great physical hardihood and endurance, an iron will and unflinching courage, the power of command, the thirst for adventure, and a keen and farsighted intelligence—all these must go to the make-up of the successful arctic explorer; and these, and more than these, have gone to the make-up of the chief of successful arctic explorers, of the man who succeeded where hitherto even the best and the bravest had failed.

Commander Peary has made all dwellers in the civilized world his debtors; but, above all, we, his fellow Americans, are his debtors. He has performed one of the great feats of our time; he has won high honor for himself and for his country. (Introduction to R. E. Peary's *The North Pole,* March 12, 1910.) *Mem. Ed.* XIV, 582; *Nat. Ed.* XII, 438.

PEDAGOGY. *See* EDUCATION.

PENDLETON ACT. *See* CIVIL SERVICE REFORM.

PENOLOGY. *See* CRIME; CRIMINALS.

PEOPLE, THE. *See* AMERICAN PEOPLE; CONSTITUTION; COURTS; DEMOCRACY; GOVERNMENT; NATIONAL GREATNESS; POPULAR RULE; PUBLIC OFFICIALS; REPRESENTATIVES; SELF-GOVERNMENT.

PERSEVERANCE. The lesson of unyielding, unflinching, unfaltering perseverance in the course upon which the nation has entered is one very necessary for a generation whose preachers sometimes dwell overmuch on the policies of the moment. (At Galena, Ill., April 27, 1900.) *Mem. Ed.* XII, 462; *Nat. Ed.* XIII, 434.

―――――. Sometimes in life, both at school and afterwards, fortune will go against any one, but if he just keeps pegging away and doesn't lose his courage things always take a turn for the better in the end. (To Kermit Roosevelt, December 3, 1904.) *Mem. Ed.* XXI, 531; *Nat. Ed.* XIX, 477.

PERSHING, JOHN J. My dear General, you are the American most to be envied of all the Americans since the close of the Civil War. You have done the great deed in the great crisis, and you have made all of us debtors always. Of course, all the wars in which our nation has taken part, even in the Civil War itself, had nothing to show in any way resembling this war, or the fighting that you have yourself conducted. (To General Pershing, September 27, 1918.) *Mem. Ed.* XXIV, 535-536; Bishop II, 457.

PESSIMISM. It is foolish to look at the future with blind and careless optimism; quite as foolish as to gaze at it only through the dun-colored mists that surround the preachers of pessimism. (*The Sewanee Review,* August 1894.) *Mem. Ed.* XIV, 235; *Nat. Ed.* XIII, 204.

PESSIMIST, THE. There is no place among us for the mere pessimist; no man who looks at life with a vision that sees all things black or gray can do aught healthful in moulding the destiny of a mighty and vigorous people. But there is just as little use for the foolish optimist who refuses to face the many and real evils that exist, and who fails to see that the only way to insure the triumph of righteousness in the future is to war against all that is base, weak, and unlovely in the present. (At Pan-American Exposition, Buffalo, N. Y., May 20, 1901.) *Mem. Ed.* XV, 307; *Nat. Ed.* XIII, 442.

PESSIMIST. *See also* OPTIMIST.

PETROLEUM. *See* MINERAL FUELS; OIL.

PHILANTHROPY. The soup-kitchen style of philanthropy is worse than useless, for in philanthropy as everywhere else in life almost as much harm is done by soft-headedness as by hard-heartedness. The highest type of philanthropy is that which springs from the feeling of brotherhood, and which, therefore, rests on the self-respecting, healthy basis of mutual obligation and common effort. The best way to raise anyone is to join with him in an effort whereby both you and he are raised by each helping the other. (*McClure's,* March, 1901.) *Mem. Ed.* XV, 198; *Nat. Ed.* XIII, 261.

―――――. Undoubtedly the best type of philanthropic work is that which helps men and women who are willing and able to help themselves; for fundamentally this aid is simply what each of us should be all the time both giving and receiving. Every man and woman in the land ought to prize above almost every other quality the capacity for self-help; and yet every man and woman in the land will at some time or other be sorely in need of the help of others, and at some time or other will find that he or she can in turn give help even to the strongest. The quality of self-help is so splendid a quality that nothing can compensate for its loss; yet, like every virtue, it can be twisted into a fault, and it becomes a fault if carried to the point of cold-hearted arrogance, of inability to understand that now and then the strongest may be in need of aid, and that for this reason alone, if for no other, the strong should always be glad of the chance in turn to aid the weak. (*Century,* October 1900.) *Mem. Ed.* XV, 427-428; *Nat. Ed.* XIII, 374-375.

———————Philanthropy has undoubtedly been a good deal discredited both by the exceedingly noxious individuals who go into it with ostentation to make a reputation, and by the only less noxious persons who are foolish and indiscriminate givers. Anything that encourages pauperism, anything that relaxes the manly fiber and lowers self-respect, is an unmixed evil. The soup-kitchen style of philanthropy is as thoroughly demoralizing as most forms of vice or oppression, and it is of course particularly revolting when some corporation or private individual undertakes it, not even in a spirit of foolish charity, but for purposes of self-advertisement. In a time of sudden and wide-spread disaster, caused by a flood, a blizzard, an earthquake, or an epidemic, there may be ample reason for the extension of charity on the largest scale to every one who needs it. But these conditions are wholly exceptional, and the methods of relief employed to meet them must also be treated as wholly exceptional. (*Century,* October 1900.) *Mem. Ed.* XV, 433-434; *Nat. Ed.* XIII, 379-380.

PHILANTHROPY. *See also* BROTHERHOOD; CHARITY; FELLOW-FEELING; SELF-HELP.

PHILIPPINE INDEPENDENCE. The talk about the Filipinos having practically achieved their independence is, of course, the veriest nonsense. Aguinaldo, who has turned against us, owed his return to the islands to us. It was our troops and not the Filipinos who conquered the Spaniards, and as a consequence, it was to us the islands fell, and we shall show ourselves not merely weaklings unfit to take our place among the great nations of the world, but traitors to the cause of the advancement of mankind if we flinch from doing aright the task which destiny has intrusted to our hand.

We have no more right to leave the Filipinos to butcher one another and sink slowly back into savagery than we would have the right, in an excess of sentimentality, to declare the Sioux or Apaches free to expel all white settlers from the lands they once held. The Filipinos offer excellent material for the future; with our aid they may be brought up to the level of self-government, but at present they cannot stand alone for any length of time. A weak nation can be pardoned for giving up a work which it does badly, but a strong nation cannot be pardoned for flinching from a great work because, forsooth, there are attendant difficulties and hardships. (At Akron, O., September 23, 1899.) Thomas W. Handford, *Theodore Roosevelt, The Pride of the Rough Riders.* (Chicago, 1899), p. 187-188.

———————. There is no question as to our not having gone far enough and fast enough in granting self-government to the Filipinos; the only possible danger has been lest we should go faster and further than was in the interest of the Filipinos themselves. Each Filipino at the present day is guaranteed his life, his liberty and the chance to pursue happiness as he wishes, so long as he does not harm his fellows, in a way which the Islands have never known before during all their recorded history. (At Memphis, Tenn., November 19, 1902.) *Mem. Ed.* XXIII, 267; Bishop I, 232.

———————. In dealing with the Philippines, I have first the jack fools who seriously think that any group of pirates and head-hunters needs nothing but independence in order that it may be turned forthwith into a dark-hued New England town-meeting; and then the entirely practical creatures who join with these extremists because I do not intend that the Islands shall be exploited for corrupt purposes. (To Rudyard Kipling, November 1, 1904.) *Mem. Ed.* XXIII, 383; Bishop I, 332.

———————. Real progress toward self-government is being made in the Philippine Islands. The gathering of a Philippine legislative body and Philippine assembly marks a process absolutely new in Asia, not only as regards Asiatic colonies of European powers but as regards Asiatic possessions of other Asiatic powers; and, indeed, always excepting the striking and wonderful example afforded by the great empire of Japan, it opens an entirely new departure when compared with anything which has happened among Asiatic powers which are their own masters. . . . The Filipino people, through their officials, are therefore making real steps in the direction of self-government. I hope and believe that these steps mark the beginning of a course which will continue till the Filipinos become fit to decide for themselves whether they desire to be an independent nation. But it is well for them (and well also for those Americans who during the past decade have done so much damage to the Filipinos by agitation for an immediate independence for which they were totally unfit) to remember that self-government depends, and must depend, upon the Filipinos themselves. All we can do is to give them the opportunity to develop the capacity for self-government. (Eighth Annual Message, Washington, December 8, 1908.) *Mem. Ed.* XVII, 631-632; *Nat. Ed.* XV, 537-538.

──────────. As regards the Philippines my belief was that we should train them for self-government as rapidly as possible, and then leave them free to decide their own fate. I did not believe in setting the time-limit within which we would give them independence, because I did not believe it wise to try to forecast how soon they would be fit for self-government; and once having made the promise I would have felt that it was imperative to keep it. . . . The people of the islands have never developed so rapidly, from every standpoint, as during the years of the American occupation. The time will come when it will be wise to take their own judgment as to whether they wish to continue their association with America or not. There is, however, one consideration upon which we should insist. Either we should retain complete control of the islands, or absolve ourselves from all responsibility for them. Any half and half course would be both foolish and disastrous. We are governing and have been governing the islands in the interests of the Filipinos themselves. If after due time the Filipinos themselves decide that they do not wish to be thus governed, then I trust that we will leave; but when we do leave it must be distinctly understood that we retain no protectorate—and above all that we take part in no joint protectorate—over the islands, and give them no guaranty, of neutrality or otherwise; that is, in short, we are absolutely quit of responsibility for them, of every kind and description. (1913.) *Mem. Ed.* XXII, 571-573; *Nat. Ed.* XX, 491-493.

──────────. The present administration was elected on the outright pledge of giving the Filipinos independence. Apparently its course in the Philippines has proceeded upon the theory that the Filipinos are now fit to govern themselves. Whatever may be our personal and individual beliefs in this matter, we ought not as a nation to break faith or even to seem to break faith. I hope therefore that the Filipinos will be given their independence at an early date and without any guaranty from us which might in any way hamper our future action or commit us to staying on the Asiatic coast. I do not believe we should keep any foothold whatever in the Philippines. Any kind of position by us in the Philippines merely results in making them our heel of Achilles if we are attacked by a foreign power. They can be of no compensating benefit to us. If we were to retain complete control over them and to continue the course of action which in the past sixteen years has resulted in such immeasurable benefit for them, then I should feel that it was our duty to stay and work for them in spite of the expense incurred by us and the risk we thereby ran. But inasmuch as we have now promised to leave them and as we are now abandoning our power to work efficiently for and in them, I do not feel that we are warranted in staying in the islands in an equivocal position, thereby incurring great risk to ourselves without conferring any real compensating advantage, of a kind which we are bound to take into account, on the Filipinos themselves. If the Filipinos are entitled to independence, then we are entitled to be freed from all the responsibility and risk which our presence in the islands entails upon us. (New York *Times,* November 22, 1914.) *Mem. Ed.* XX, 126; *Nat. Ed.* XVIII, 108.

──────────. I administered the Islands absolutely without regard to politics. . . . I . . . peremptorily refused to promise independence, save in the very careful language I used on the one or two occasions when I spoke of the subject, because to promise independence without the sharpest qualification is inevitably taken as meaning Independence in the near future. (To Forbes, January 4, 1915.) W. Cameron Forbes, *The Philippine Islands.* (Houghton Mifflin Co., Boston, 1928), II, 344.

PHILIPPINE WAR. The war in the Philippines is absolutely and without qualification a national war. With characteristic pervision of the facts, our opponents have spoken as though this war was unnecessary, as if it were now waged by President McKinley on his own authority, and without the warrant of Congress. In the first place, what we have done was inevitable, so far as the administration and the American people at large were concerned. There was just one chance of avoiding war. If the anti-expansionists, the peace-at-any-price people, had not delayed the treaty in the Senate, if by their loose invective they had not misled the Tagals, we should probably never have had any war in the Philippines. Aguinaldo's proclamation proves beyond shadow of doubt that the insurgents have held out on the strength of the hoped-for aid from the Democratic party and from the anti-expansionists here in our own home. (At Cincinnati, O., October 21, 1899.) *Mem. Ed.* XVI, 502; *Nat. Ed.* XIV, 339.

PHILIPPINES — ADMINISTRATION OF THE. Most assuredly . . . all that I can do will be done to see that the Philippine Islands are administered in the interest, moral and spiritual no less than material and intellectual, of their inhabitants, and wherever possible, in accordance with the wishes of the Filipinos. . . . When we took over the islands there was practically no indication of system at all, so far as the bulk of the people were concerned. There was no foundation on which to build. We had to start absolutely new. (Letter of August 5, 1902.) *Mem. Ed.* XXIII, 223; Bishop I, 194.

——————. During these eight sessions of Congress I have succeeded in getting the administration of the civil government in the Philippine Islands put upon a satisfactory basis. (To Sydney Brooks, December 28, 1908.) *Mem. Ed.* XXIV, 151; Bishop II, 130.

PHILIPPINES—AMERICAN DUTY IN THE. We may not wish the Philippines, and may regret that circumstances have forced us to take them; but we have taken them, and stay there we must for the time being—whether this temporary stay paves the way for permanent occupation, or whether it is to last only until some more satisfactory arrangement, whether by native rule or otherwise, takes its place. Discussion of theories will not avail much; we have a bit of very practical work to be done, and done it must be, somehow. (*Outlook,* January 7, 1899.) *Mem. Ed.* XII, 519; *Nat. Ed.* XI, 249.

——————. If the men who have counseled national degradation, national dishonor, by urging us to leave the Philippines and put the Aguinaldan oligarchy in control of those islands, could have their way, we should merely turn them over to rapine and bloodshed until some stronger, manlier power stepped in to do the task we had shown ourselves fearful of performing. But, as it is, this country will keep the islands and will establish therein a stable and orderly government, so that one more fair spot of the world's surface shall have been snatched from the forces of darkness. Fundamentally the cause of expansion is the cause of peace. (1900.) *Mem. Ed.* XV, 289-290; *Nat. Ed.* XIII, 338.

——————. In the Philippines we have brought peace, and we are at this moment giving them such freedom and self-government as they could never under any conceivable conditions have obtained had we turned them loose to sink into a welter of blood and confusion, or to become the prey of some strong tyranny without or within. The bare recital of the facts is sufficient to show that we did our duty; and what prouder title to honor can a nation have than to have done its duty? We have done our duty to ourselves, and we have done the higher duty of promoting the civilization of mankind. . . . We are not trying to subjugate a people; we are trying to develop them and make them a law-abiding, industrious, and educated people, and we hope ultimately a self-governing people. (At Minnesota State Fair, September 2, 1901.) *Mem. Ed.* XV, 337, 340; *Nat. Ed.* XIII, 477, 479.

——————. I have never felt that the Philippines were of any special use to us. But I have felt that we had a great task to perform there and that a great nation is benefited by doing a great task. It was our bounden duty to work primarily for the interests of the Filipinos; but it was also our bounden duty, inasmuch as the entire responsibility lay upon us, to consult our own judgment and not theirs in finally deciding what was to be done. It was our duty to govern the islands or to get out of the islands. It was most certainly not our duty to take the responsibility of staying in the islands without governing them. Still less was it—or is it—our duty to enter into joint arrangements with other powers about the islands; arrangements of confused responsibility and divided power of the kind sure to cause mischief. I had hoped that we would continue to govern the islands until we were certain that they were able to govern themselves in such fashion as to do justice to other nations and to repel injustice committed on them by other nations. (New York *Times,* November 22, 1914.) *Mem. Ed.* XX, 125; *Nat. Ed.* XVIII, 107.

PHILIPPINES—ANNEXATION OF THE. The taking of the Philippines was inevitable. The outbreak was rendered inevitable by the conduct of those who opposed the taking of the Philippines, and who gave moral aid and comfort to Aguinaldo and his men. . . . We are doing but our simple duty in introducing the reign of law, order, and peace into the Philippines and we cannot shrink from it without shame and dishonor. The path of expansion is the path of national honor, the path toward universal peace. (At Cincinnati, October 21, 1899.) *Mem. Ed.* XVI, 504; *Nat. Ed.* XIV, 341.

PHILIPPINES—PROTECTION OF THE. It may be that the Japanese have designs on the Philippines. I hope not; I am inclined to believe not; for I like the Japanese, and wish them well, as they have much in their character to admire. But I believe we should put our naval and military preparations in such shape that we can hold the Philippines against

PHILIPPINES

any foe. If we do this, and act justly towards, and speak courteously of, our foreign neighbors, we shall have taken the only effective steps to make our position good. (To Congressman J. A. T. Hull, March 16, 1905.) Tyler Dennett, *Roosevelt and the Russo-Japanese War.* (Doubleday, Page & Co., Garden City, N. Y., 1925), p. 162.

―――――――. I would unquestionably advocate the retention of the Islands upon the condition that first, no promise of independence is authoritatively given, and second and even more important, that our policy of armament should be made to conform with the requirements of the situation. In other words, this means that the government of the people must in emphatic manner take the proper attitude toward our position as a world power, and therefore toward the establishment and maintenance of a great naval and military programme, which alone would be adequate to maintain such a position. (To Forbes, May 23, 1916.) W. Cameron Forbes, *The Philippine Islands.* (Houghton Mifflin Co., Boston, 1928), II, 345.

PHILIPPINES—TREATMENT OF THE. We must treat them [the Philippines] with absolute justice, but we must treat them also with firmness and courage. They must be made to realize that justice does not proceed from a sense of weakness on our part, that we are the masters. Weakness in any form or shape, as you gentlemen, who all your lives have upheld the honor of the flag ashore and afloat, know, is the unpardonable sin in dealing with such a problem as that with which we are confronted in the Philippines. The insurrection must be stamped out as mercifully as possible; but it must be stamped out.

We have put an end to a corrupt mediaeval tyranny, and by that very fact we have bound ourselves to see that no savage anarchy takes its place. What the Spaniard has been taught the Malay must learn—that the American flag is to float unchallenged where it floats now. But remember this, that when this has been accomplished our task has only just begun. Where we have won entrance by the prowess of our soldiers we must deserve to continue by the righteousness, the wisdom, and the even-handed justice of our rule. (At Lincoln Club dinner, New York City, February 13, 1899.) *Mem. Ed.* XVI, 476-477; *Nat. Ed.* XIV, 317.

―――――――. Their population includes half-caste and native Christians, warlike Moslems, and wild pagans. Many of their people are utterly unfit for self-government, and show no signs of becoming fit. Others may in time become fit but at present can only take part in self-government under a wise supervision, at once firm and beneficent. We have driven Spanish tyranny from the islands. If we now let it be replaced by savage anarchy, our work has been for harm and not for good. I have scant patience with those who fear to undertake the task of governing the Philippines, and who openly avow that they do fear to undertake it, or that they shrink from it because of the expense and trouble; but I have even scanter patience with those who make a pretense of humanitarianism to hide and cover their timidity, and who cant about "liberty" and the "consent of the governed," in order to excuse themselves for their unwillingness to play the part of men. (Before the Hamilton Club, Chicago, April 10, 1899.) *Mem. Ed.* XV, 279; *Nat. Ed.* XIII, 329.

PHILIPPINES. *See also* IMPERIALISM; ORIENT; SPANISH-AMERICAN WAR.

PHILOSOPHY. *See* BROWNING, ROBERT.

PHOTOGRAPHS. I do not want to begin to have new photographs taken. If I do it in one case, I must do it in others. In the first place, it is an intolerable nuisance; and in the next place it creates a false impression. People do not realize that I do not like to sit for photographs and that it is only a good-natured acquiescence on my part when I do. Now there is not the slightest need of a new photograph. Dozens of excellent ones have been taken. (To Richard Watson Gilder, November 18, 1904.) *Mem. Ed.* XXIII, 408; Bishop I, 354.

PHOTOGRAPHY. *See* HUNTING; NATURE STUDY.

PHYSICAL TRAINING. *See* EXERCISE; GYMNASTICS; MILITARY TRAINING; SPORTS.

PHYSICIANS. *See* DOCTORS.

PIGSKIN LIBRARY. There was one other bit of impedimenta, less usual for African travel, but perhaps almost as essential for real enjoyment even on a hunting trip, if it is to be of any length. This was the "Pigskin Library," so called because most of the books were bound in pigskin. They were carried in a light aluminum and oilcloth case, which, with its contents, weighed a little less than sixty pounds, making a load for one porter. . . .

It represents in part Kermit's taste, in part mine; and, I need hardly say, it also represents in no way all the books we most care for, but

[429]

merely those which, for one reason or another, we thought we should like to take on this particular trip. (1910.) *Mem. Ed.* V, 24-26; *Nat. Ed.* IV, 22.

PIGSKIN LIBRARY. *See also* BOOKS.

PINCHOT, GIFFORD. So much for what we are trying to do in utilizing our public lands for the public; in securing the use of the water, the forage, the coal, and the timber for the public. In all four movements my chief adviser, and the man first to suggest to me the courses which have actually proved so beneficial, was Mr. Gifford Pinchot, the chief of the National Forest Service. Mr. Pinchot, also suggested to me a movement supplementary to all of these movements; one which will itself lead the way in the general movement which he represents and with which he is actively identified, for the conservation of all our natural resources. This was the appointment of the Inland Waterways Commission. (Before National Editorial Association, Jamestown, Va., June 10, 1907.) *Presidential Addresses and State Papers* VI, 1317-1318.

———————. Especial credit is due to the initiative, the energy, the devotion to duty, and the far-sightedness of Gifford Pinchot, to whom we owe so much of the progress we have already made in handling this matter of the co-ordination and conservation of natural resources. If it had not been for him this convention neither would nor could have been called. (At Conference on the Conservation of Natural Resources, Washington, May 13, 1908.) *Mem. Ed.* XVIII, 165; *Nat. Ed.* XVI, 126.

———————. Gifford Pinchot is the man to whom the nation owes most for what has been accomplished as regards the preservation of the natural resources of our country. He led, and indeed during its most vital period embodied, the fight for the preservation through use of our forests. He played one of the leading parts in the effort to make the National Government the chief instrument in developing the irrigation of the arid West. He was the foremost leader in the great struggle to co-ordinate all our social and governmental forces in the effort to secure the adoption of a rational and far-seeing policy for securing the conservation of all our national resources. . . . Taking into account the varied nature of the work he did, its vital importance to the nation and the fact that as regards much of it he was practically breaking new ground, and taking into account also his tireless energy and activity, his fearlessness, his complete disinterestedness, his single-minded devotion to the interests of the plain people, and his extraordinary efficiency, I believe it is but just to say that among the many, many public officials who under my administration rendered literally invaluable service to the people of the United States, he, on the whole, stood first. (1913.) *Mem. Ed.* XXII, 447; *Nat. Ed.* XX, 385.

PINCHOT, GIFFORD. *See also* CONSERVATION.

PIONEER PREACHERS. The pioneer preachers warred against the forces of spiritual evil with the same fiery zeal and energy that they and their fellows showed in the conquest of the rugged continent. They had in them the heroic spirit, the spirit that scorns ease if it must be purchased by failure to do duty, the spirit that courts risk and a life of hard endeavor if the goal to be reached is really worth attaining. Great is our debt to these men and scant the patience we need show toward their critics. At times they seemed hard and narrow to those whose training and surroundings had saved them from similar temptations; and they have been criticised, as all men, whether missionaries, soldiers, explorers, or frontier settlers, are criticised when they go forth to do the rough work that must inevitably be done by those who act as the first harbingers, the first heralds, of civilization in the world's dark places. It is easy for those who stay at home in comfort, who never have to see humanity in the raw, or to strive against the dreadful naked forces which appear clothed, hidden, and subdued in civilized life—it is easy for such to criticise the men who, in rough fashion, and amid grim surroundings, make ready the way for the higher life that is to come afterward; but let us all remember that the untempted and the effortless should be cautious in passing too heavy judgment upon their brethren who may show hardness, who may be guilty of shortcomings, but who nevertheless do the great deeds by which mankind advances. (At Carnegie Hall, New York City, February 26, 1903.) *Presidential Addresses and State Papers* I, 245.

PIONEER VIRTUES. The pioneer days are over, save in a few places; and the more complex life of to-day calls for a greater variety of good qualities than were needed on the frontier. There is need at present to encourage the development of new abilities which can be brought to high perfection only by a kind of training useless in pioneer times; but these new qualities can only supplement, and never supplant, the old, homely virtues; the need for the special and distinctive pioneer virtues is as great as ever. In other words, as our civilization grows older and more complex, while it is true that we need new forms of trained ability, and need to develop men whose lives are devoted wholly to the pursuit of special objects, it is yet also true that we need a greater and not a less development of the fundamental frontier virtues. (*Outlook*, September 10, 1910.) *Mem. Ed.* XVIII, 23; *Nat. Ed.* XVI, 21.

PIONEERS. They were above all a people of strong, virile character, certain to make their weight felt either for good or for evil. They had many virtues which can fairly be called great, and their faults were equally strongly marked. They were not a thrifty people, nor one given to long-sustained, drudging work; there were not then, nor are there now, to be found in this land such comfortable, prosperous homes and farms as those which dot all the country where dwell the men of northeastern stock. They were not, as a rule, even ordinarily well educated; the public school formed no such important feature in their life as it did in the life of their fellow citizens farther north. They had narrow, bitter prejudices and dislikes; the hard and dangerous lives they had led had run their character into a stern and almost forbidding mould. They valued personal prowess very highly, and respected no man who did not possess the strongest capacity for self-help, and who could not shift for himself in any danger. They felt an intense, although perhaps ignorant, pride in and love for their country, and looked upon all the lands hemming in the United States as territory which they or their children should some day inherit; for they were a race of masterful spirit, and accustomed to regard with easy tolerance any but the most flagrant violations of law. They prized highly such qualities as courage, loyalty, truth and patriotism, but they were, as a whole, poor, and not overscrupulous of the rights of others, nor yet with the nicest sense of money obligations. . . . Their passions, once roused, were intense, and if they really wished anything they worked for it with indomitable persistency. There was little that was soft or outwardly attractive in their character: it was stern, rude and hard, like the lives they led: but it was the character of those who were every inch men, and who were Americans through to the very heart's core. (1887.) *Mem. Ed.* VIII, 16-17; *Nat. Ed.* VII, 14-15.

———. The pioneers, though warlike and fond of fighting, were primarily settlers; their soldiering came in as a purely secondary occupation. They were not a band of mere adventurers, living by the sword and bent on nothing but conquest. They were a group of hard-working, hard-fighting freemen who had come in with their wives and children to possess the land. They were obliged to use all their wit and courage to defend what they had already won without wasting their strength by grasping at that which lay beyond. The very conditions that enabled so small a number to make a permanent settlement forbade their trying unduly to extend its bounds. (1889.) *Mem. Ed.* X, 343; *Nat. Ed.* VIII, 299.

———. Boone and his fellow hunters were the heralds of the oncoming civilization, the pioneers in that conquest of the wilderness which has at last been practically achieved in our own day. Where they pitched their camps and built their log huts or stockaded hamlets towns grew up, and men who were tillers of the soil, not mere wilderness wanderers, thronged in to take and hold the land. Then, ill at ease among the settlements for which they had themselves made ready the way, and fretted even by the slight restraints of the rude and uncouth semicivilization of the border, the restless hunters moved onward into the yet unbroken wilds where the game dwelt and the red tribes marched forever to war and hunting. Their untamable souls ever found something congenial and beyond measure attractive in the lawless freedom of the lives of the very savages against whom they warred so bitterly.

Step by step, often leap by leap, the frontier of settlement was pushed westward; and ever from before its advance fled the warrior tribes of the red men and the scarcely less intractable array of white Indian fighters and game-hunters. (1893.) *Mem. Ed.* II, 7-8; *Nat. Ed.* II, 7.

———. The wood choppers, game hunters, and Indian fighters, who first came over the mountains, were only the forerunners of the more regular settlers who followed them; but these last had much the same attributes as their predecessors. For many years after the settlements were firmly rooted, the life of the settlers was still subject to all the perils of the wilderness. Above all, the constant warfare in which they were engaged for nearly thirty-five years, and which culminated in the battle of New Orleans, left a deep and lasting imprint on their character. Their incessant wars were waged almost wholly by the settlers them-

[431]

selves, with comparatively little help from the federal government, and with hardly any regular troops as allies. . . . The chief effect of this long-continued and harassing border warfare was to make more marked the sullen and almost defiant self-reliance of the pioneer, and to develop his peculiarly American spirit of individual self-sufficiency, his impatience of outside interference or control, to a degree not known elsewhere, even on this continent. It also gave a distinct military cast to his way of looking at territory which did not belong to him. He stood where he was because he was a conqueror; he had wrested his land by force from its rightful Indian lords; he fully intended to repeat the same feat as soon as he should reach the Spanish lands lying to the west and southwest; he would have done so in the case of French Louisiana if it had not been that the latter was purchased, and was thus saved from being taken by force of arms. This belligerent, or, more properly speaking, piratical way of looking at neighboring territory, was very characteristic of the West, and was at the root of the doctrine of "manifest destiny." (1887.) *Mem. Ed.* VIII, 13-14; *Nat. Ed.* VII, 11-13.

——————. No continent is ever really conquered, or thoroughly explored, by a few leaders, or exceptional men, although such men can render great service. The real conquest, the thorough exploration and settlement, is made by a nameless multitude of small men of whom the most important are, of course, the home-makers. Each treads most of the time in the footsteps of his predecessors, but for some few miles, at some time or other, he breaks new ground; and his house is built where no house has ever stood before. Such a man, the real pioneer, must have no strong desire for social life and no need, probably no knowledge, of any luxury, or of any comfort save of the most elementary kind. The pioneer who is always longing for the comfort and luxury of civilization, and especially of great cities, is no real pioneer at all. (1914.) *Mem. Ed.* VI, 311-312; *Nat. Ed.* V, 265.

PIONEERS—EXAMPLE OF. We need to keep in mind the lesson taught by the American pioneer. It is a lesson that is to be found in the fact that the pioneer is so good an American. He is an American, first and foremost. The man of the West throughout the successive stages of Western growth has always been one of the two or three most typical figures, indeed I am tempted to say the most typical figure, in American life; and no man can really understand our country, and appreciate what it really is and what it promises, unless he has the fullest and closest sympathy with the ideals and aspirations of the West. (*Outlook*, September 10, 1910.) *Mem. Ed.* XVIII, 28; *Nat. Ed.* XVI, 25.

PIONEERS—RESPONSIBILITIES OF. It always seems to me that those who dwell in a new territory, and whose actions, therefore, are peculiarly fruitful, for good and for bad alike, in shaping the future, have in consequence, peculiar responsibilities. You have already been told, very truthfully and effectively, of the great gifts and blessings you enjoy; and we all of us feel, most rightly and properly, that we belong to the greatest nation that has ever existed on this earth—a feeling I like to see, for I wish every American always to keep the most intense pride in his country, and people. But as you already know your rights and privileges so well, I am going to ask you to excuse me if I say a few words to you about your duties. Much has been given to us, and so, much will be expected of us; and we must take heed to use aright the gifts entrusted to our care. . . .

We, grangers and cowboys alike, have opened a new land; and we are the pioneers, and as we shape the course of the stream near its head, our efforts have infinitely more effect, in bending it in any given direction, than they would have if they were made farther along. In other words, the first comers in a land can, by their individual efforts, do far more to channel out the course in which its history is to run than can those who come after them; and their labors, whether exercised on the side of evil or on the side of good, are far more effective than if they had remained in old settled communities. (At Dickinson, Dakota Territory, July 4, 1886.) Hermann Hagedorn, *Roosevelt in the Bad Lands.* (Houghton Mifflin Co., Boston, 1921), p. 408.

PIONEERS. *See also* BOONE, DANIEL; CLARK, GEORGE ROGERS; EXPANSION; EXPLORERS; FRONTIER; FRONTIERSMEN; INDIANS; INDIVIDUALISM; MANIFEST DESTINY; METHODIST CHURCH; NORTHWEST; SCOTCH-IRISH; SEVIER, JOHN; TEXAS; WEST; WESTWARD MOVEMENT.

PLAINS, THE. *See* COWBOYS; HUNTERS; PRAIRIE.

PLATFORM PROMISES. It shows a thoroughly unhealthy state of mind when the public pardons with a laugh failure to keep a distinct pledge, on the ground that a politician cannot be expected to confine himself to the truth when on the stump or the platform. A man should no more be excused for lying on the stump than for lying off the stump. Of course matters may so change that it may be impossible for him, or highly inadvisable for the country, that he should try to do what he in good faith said he was going to do. But the necessity for the change should be made very evident, and it should be well understood that such a case is the exception and not the rule. As a rule, and speaking with due regard to the exceptions, it should be taken as axiomatic that when a man in public life pledges himself to a certain course of action he shall as a matter of course do what he said he would do, and shall not be held to have acted honorably if he does otherwise. (*Outlook,* July 28, 1900.) *Mem. Ed.* XV, 401-402; *Nat. Ed.* XIII, 399.

PLATFORM PROMISES. *See also* COMPROMISE; ELECTION PLEDGES; PARTY PLATFORMS; POLITICAL PROMISES.

PLATT, THOMAS C. Senator Platt had the same inborn capacity for the kind of politics which he liked that many big Wall Street men have shown for not wholly dissimilar types of finance. It was his chief interest, and he applied himself to it unremittingly. He handled his private business successfully; but it was politics in which he was absorbed, and he concerned himself therewith every day in the year. He had built up an excellent system of organization, and the necessary funds came from corporations and men of wealth. . . . The majority of the men with a natural capacity for organization leadership of the type which has generally been prevalent in New York politics turned to Senator Platt as their natural chief and helped build up the organization, until under his leadership it became more powerful and in a position of greater control than any other Republican machine in the country, excepting in Pennsylvania. . . . It would be an entire mistake to suppose that Mr. Platt's lieutenants were either all bad men or all influenced by unworthy motives. He was constantly doing favors for men. He had won the gratitude of many good men. In the country districts especially, there were many places where his machine included the majority of the best citizens, the leading and substantial citizens, among the inhabitants. Some of his strongest and most efficient lieutenants were disinterested men of high character. (1913.) *Mem. Ed.* XXII, 317-318; *Nat. Ed.* XX, 271-272.

———————. Though we shall have a good deal of friction from time to time, I do not believe it very likely that he will come to a definite break with me, because I like him personally, I always tell him the truth, and I genuinely endeavor to help him, if I can, with proper regard for the interest of the State and party. (To H. C. Lodge, December 11, 1899.) Lodge *Letters* I, 426-427.

PLATT AMENDMENT. When the acceptance of the Platt Amendment was required from Cuba by the action of the Congress of the United States, this Government thereby definitely committed itself to the policy of treating Cuba as occupying a unique position as regards this country. It was provided that when the island became a free and independent republic she should stand in such close relations with us as in certain respects to come within our system of international policy; and it necessarily followed that she must also to a certain degree become included within the lines of our economic policy. Situated as Cuba is, it would not be possible for this country to permit the strategic abuse of the island by any foreign military power. It is for this reason that certain limitations have been imposed upon her financial policy, and that naval stations have been conceded by her to the United States. (Message to Congress, November 10, 1903.) *Presidential Addresses and State Papers* II, 645-646.

PLAYGROUNDS. It is an excellent thing to have rapid transit, but it is a good deal more important, if you look at matters with a proper perspective, to have ample playgrounds in the poorer quarters of the city, and to take the children off the streets so as to prevent them growing up toughs. In the same way it is an admirable thing to have clean streets; indeed, it is an essential thing to have them; but it would be a better thing to have our schools large enough to give ample accommodation to all who should be pupils and to provide them with proper playgrounds. (To Jacob Riis, late 1894.) *Mem. Ed.* XXII, 204; *Nat. Ed.* XX, 174.

———————. It is a poor type of school nowadays that has not a good playground attached. It is not so long since, in my own city, at least, that this was held as a revolutionary doctrine, especially in the crowded quarters where playgrounds were most needed. People said they did not need playgrounds. It was a new-fangled idea. They expected to make good citizens of the boys and girls who, when they were not in school, were put upon the streets in the crowded quarters of New York to play at the kind of games alone that they could play at in the streets. We have passed that stage. I think we realize what a good, healthy playground means to children. I think we understand not only the effect for good upon their bodies, but for good minds. We need a healthy body. We need to have schools physically developed. (At Philadelphia, Pa., November 22, 1902.) *Proceedings of the Dedication of the New Buildings of the Central High School,* (Board of Public Education, 1910), pp. 63-64.

——————. City streets are unsatisfactory playgrounds for children because of the danger, because most good games are against the law, because they are too hot in summer, and because in crowded sections of the city they are apt to be schools of crime. Neither do small back yards nor ornamental grass plots meet the needs of any but the very small children. Older children who would play vigorous games must have places especially set aside for them; and, since play is a fundamental need, playgrounds should be provided for every child as much as schools. This means that they must be distributed over the cities in such a way as to be within walking distance of every boy and girl, as most children can not afford to pay carfare. (To Cuno H. Rudolph, Washington Playground Association, February 16, 1907.) *Presidential Addresses and State Papers* VI, 1163.

PLAYS. See ABBEY THEATRE; DRAMA.

PLEASURE. It is a good thing that life should gain in sweetness, but only provided that it does not lose in strength. Ease and rest and pleasure are good things, but only if they come as the reward of work well done, of a good fight well won, of strong effort resolutely made and crowned by high achievement. The life of mere pleasure, of mere effortless ease, is as ignoble for a nation as for an individual. The man is but a poor father who teaches his sons that ease and pleasure should be their chief objects in life; the woman who is a mere petted toy, incapable of serious purpose, shrinking from effort and duty, is more pitiable than the veriest overworked drudge. So he is but a poor leader of the people, but a poor national adviser, who seeks to make the nation in any way subordinate effort to ease, who would teach the people not to prize as the greatest blessing the chance to do any work, no matter how hard, if it becomes their duty to do it. (At Pilgrim Memorial Monument, Provincetown, Mass., August 20, 1907.) *Mem. Ed.* XVIII, 92; *Nat. Ed.* XVI, 77.

——————. I wish that everywhere in our country we could see clubs and associations including all our citizens, similar in character to that society which has furnished the reason for the assembling of this great audience to-night. No greater contribution to American social life could possibly be made than by instilling into it the capacity for Gemüthlichkeit. No greater good can come to our people than to encourage in them a capacity for enjoyment which shall discriminate sharply between what is vicious and what is pleasant. Nothing can add more to our capacity for healthy social enjoyment than, by force of example no less than by precept, to encourage the formation of societies which by their cultivation of music, vocal and instrumental, give great lift to the artistic side, the æsthetic side, of our nature; and especially is that true when we remember that no man is going to go very far wrong if he belongs to a society where he can take his wife with him to enjoy it. (At the Saengerfest, Baltimore, Md., June 15, 1903.) *Mem. Ed.* XVIII, 44; *Nat. Ed.* XVI, 38.

PLEASURE—SOURCE OF. You cannot get the highest pleasure in life without toil and effort and risk, and yours is a poor soul if you fail to pay the price for them. (At Occidental College, Los Angeles, March 22, 1911.) *Mem. Ed.* XV, 513; *Nat. Ed.* XIII, 579.

PLEASURE AND VICE. The influence of the Puritan has been most potent for strength and for virtue in our national life. But his sombre austerity left one evil: the tendency to confound pleasure and vice, a tendency which, in the end, is much more certain to encourage vice than to discourage pleasure—a tendency especially strong among the rigid formalists, including the ultrasabbatarian formalists, who remain true only to what is least desirable in Puritanism. . . . If the natural desire of young people for pleasure is not given a healthy outlet it is only too apt to find an unhealthy outlet. (1917.) *Mem. Ed.* XXI, 139, 140; *Nat. Ed.* XIX, 138.

PLEASURE. See also DUTY; EFFORT; HAPPINESS; IDEALS; JOY OF LIVING; LEISURE; PURITANISM; SERVICE; WORK.

PLUTOCRACY. See ARISTOCRACY; GOVERNMENT, AMERICAN; POPULAR RULE.

POE, EDGAR ALLAN. He is our one supereminent genius. In spite of the persistent effort to belittle him, and I must say it has come largely from New England, he still remains the most eminent literary character we have produced. I do not think that the New England school has tried to belittle him because he was not from New England, but their rules for literature are so adjusted that it will not permit of such an irregular genius as Poe. Even as sane a man as Holmes declared Poe to be one fifth genius and four fifths guff. If any man was ever about five fifths genius, that man was Poe. (Recorded by Butt in letter of October 10, 1908.) *The Letters of Archie Butt.* (Doubleday, Page & Co., Garden City, N. Y., 1924), p. 124.

POETRY. Poetry is of course one of those arts in which the smallest amount of work of the very highest class is worth an infinity of good work that is not of the highest class. The touch of the purple makes a poem out of verse, and if it is not there, there is no substitute. (*Outlook,* August 12, 1905.) *Mem. Ed.* XIV, 360; *Nat. Ed.* XII, 296.

——————. Personally, I don't care a rap whether we call the Flight of a Tartar Tribe, or certain passages in the Confessions of an Opium-Eater, prose or vers libres. I think that it might help the eye to have parts of them arranged as the Spoon River Anthology is arranged, in irregular lines. But in any event I enjoy what seems to me to be the rhythm, and the beauty and majesty of the diction. I enjoy Wordsworth's sonnets and I enjoy Shakespeare's sonnets; and I don't care in the least if some one proves to me that Shakespeare did not write sonnets but something else. On the other hand, I loathe Wordsworth's Excursion, and not Matthew Arnold himself would persuade me to read it. I delight in the saga of King Olaf and Othere and Belisarius, and Simon Danz, and the Mystery of the Sea; and I don't care for Evangeline or any of Longfellow's plays; and I cannot give any reasoned-out explanations in either case. (To Joel E. Spingarn, August 28, 1917.) *Mem. Ed.* XXIV, 422; Bishop II, 359.

POETRY. See also PATRIOTIC SONGS; READING.

POETS. See BROWNING, ROBERT; DANTE; LODGE, GEORGE CABOT; MILTON, JOHN; MORRIS, WILLIAM; ROBINSON, E. A.; WHITMAN, WALT.

POLAR EXPLORATION. See PEARY, ROBERT E.

POLICE—EFFICIENCY OF. There is every possible reason for seeing that the efficiency of the police is not impaired, for such impairment is always at the expense of law-abiding and upright men, whether rich or poor. There can be no possible justification for seeking to impair this efficiency. If the police power is used oppressively, or improperly, let us by all means put a stop to the practice and punish those responsible for it; but let us remember that a brute will be just as much of a brute whether he is inefficient or efficient. Either abolish the police, or keep them at the highest point of efficiency. To follow any other course is foolish. A bad man in a uniform may perhaps use his weapon to evil purpose; but it would be childish because of this fact to insist that all policemen, instead of having automatic revolvers, be armed with flintlock pistols. We must give the individual policeman the best arms possible, in order that he may not be at a disadvantage when pitted against a criminal; and then see to it that under no circumstances are these arms used unless the need is imperative, and the justification complete. Exactly the same rule applies as regards the efficiency of the police force as a whole. (1917.) *Mem. Ed.* XXI, 73; *Nat. Ed.* XIX, 63.

POLICE, NEW YORK. In spite of their wide diversity of race origin, and in spite of some very evident shortcomings, the New York police as a body are a first-class set of men, and Americans through and through. They are brave, well disciplined, and efficient, and they have a very strong esprit de corps. In time past they have been corrupt, but this was because of the system under which they worked, and we accomplished an enormous amount toward putting a complete stop to this corruption. The prime reason why we succeeded so well in our efforts to improve a body of men who had been terribly demoralized was because we treated them on their merits, wholly without regard to their creed or the birthplace of their parents, rewarding the good man and punishing the bad, without heeding anything save the virtues or faults of either. (*Munsey's,* June 1897.) *Mem. Ed.* XVI, 330; *Nat. Ed.* XIV, 234-235.

POLICE COMMISSIONER — ROOSEVELT AS. Personally, I think I can best serve the Republican party by taking the police force absolutely out of politics. Our duty is to preserve order, to protect life and property, to arrest criminals, and to secure honest elections. In striving to attain these ends we recognize no party; we pay no heed to any man's political predilections, whether he is within or without the police force. In the past, "politics," in the base sense of the term, has been the curse of the police force of New York; and the present board has done away with such politics. . . .

On entering office we found—what indeed had long been a matter of common notoriety—that various laws, and notably the excise law, were enforced rigidly against people who had no political pull, but were not enforced at all against the men who had a political pull, or who possessed sufficient means to buy off the high officials who controlled, or had influence in, the Police Department. All that we did was to enforce these laws, not against some wrong-doers, but honestly and impartially against all wrong-doers. We did not resurrect dead laws; we did not start a crusade to enforce blue laws. (*Forum*, September 1895.) *Mem. Ed.* XVI, 263-264; *Nat. Ed.* XIV, 184-186.

——————. When we took up the task of reforming the New York police we did it with our eyes open. We realized fully the heavy odds against which we had to fight, and the almost incredible difficulties which beset our path. It was not a reform which could be accomplished at a blow, for we had to change not only the force itself, but the whole system; and the wrong-doing of decades cannot be undone in six or eight months. It must be remembered that the corruption of the Police Department, though the worst part, was only a part of the corruption of the entire city government, and of all that portion of our many-sided social and civic life which came into contact with the city government. . . . There were hundreds of interests each of which had thrived and fattened through the dishonesty and favoritism of the administration of the Police Department. We did not single out any one interest; we made war on all alike; and in consequence we attracted, as we knew we would attract, the venomous enmity of the tens of thousands of men whose financial gains we interfered with as soon as we began to administer the department along the lines of honesty and of rigid observance of law. Against this active and interested hostility of men whose sense of injury was very concrete, there was nothing to put save the vague and impersonal support of a community which believed in right in the abstract, but was inclined to be rather tepid in its belief. Wherever we struck a concrete wrong we roused a foe whose hostility was sure to be active with the malignity of personal suffering, while in each case the general public could not itself be keenly conscious of any direct individual benefit to its members arising from the correction of the wrong. (Before N. Y. Preachers' Meeting, January 20, 1896.) *Mem. Ed.* XVI, 303-304; *Nat. Ed.* XIV, 211-212.

——————. When the Mayor asked me to take the place first, I refused, and when I finally accepted I told him that I felt I must have colleagues with whom I could work; that with you I was sure I could join in doing my best for the City's welfare, and that the other two men should be men of your character and stamp. I need not say how heartily I agree in your view that the members of the Board should be united, and that the affairs of the Department should be administered solely with a view to the interests of the public. (To Avery D. Andrews, April 25, 1895.) Frederick S. Wood, *Roosevelt As We Knew Him*. (John C. Winston Co., Phila., 1927), p. 29.

——————. I have had my hands full as usual with both my regular police work and with politics since I last wrote you. Gradually and in spite of great difficulties with two of my colleagues I am getting this force into good shape; but I am quite sincere when I say that I do not believe that any other man in the United States, not even the President, has had as heavy a task as I have had during the past ten months. In itself the work was herculean, even had I been assisted by an honest and active public sentiment and had I received help from the Press and the politicians. As a matter of fact, public sentiment is apathetic and likes to talk about virtue in the abstract, but it does not want to obtain the virtue if there is any trouble about it. (To Anna Roosevelt Cowles, February 25, 1896.) *Cowles Letters*, 174.

——————. In managing the Police Department I speedily found what every man must find that we could draw help from every source, from every church, and could expect to find foes in every nationality and in every church, and that we were bound no more to flinch from any set of foes, because they represented a given race or religion than we were bound to uphold any man who did his duty without regard to the religion which he professed or to the land from which his ancestors came. I would decline to show one least bit of favor more to the man of my creed or of my origin than I would to the last emigrant from Ireland or from Russia. All I demand of him is that he shall not act as either Protestant, or Jew, as Irishman, German or Russian, but that he shall be a plain American and nothing else. If he is that I will treat him precisely as if his

———————. This is the last office I shall ever hold. I have offended so many powerful interests and so many powerful politicians that no political preferment in future will be possible for me. All the liquor interests, including the great breweries, and all the party bosses will oppose me, and no political party will venture to defy an opposition so fatal as that is. I realized this when I began my fight for the enforcement of the Sunday law and against police bribery and corruption, but it was the only course I could honestly pursue and I am willing to abide by the consequences. (In conversation with Joseph B. Bishop, early 1897.) *Mem. Ed.* XXIII, 80; Bishop I, 68.

POLICE COMMISSIONER. *See also* LIQUOR LAW.

POLICE POWER. *See* INTERNATIONAL POLICE POWER.

POLITICAL ASSESSMENTS. Experience . . . has convinced me that the talk so often heard about the injustice of not allowing clerks to make "voluntary contributions"—which the law in no wise prevents—is all nonsense. Government employees do not as a rule contribute simply from a desire to help the political cause in which they believe. The so-called "voluntary contributions" are nine times out of ten made from some personal motives; that is, either in the hope of being retained in office or else with the object of gaining some advantage over the other clerks. In other words, the employees are coerced into making them for fear their position will be jeopardized if they fail to do so. It is probably safe to say that 90 per cent of the money collected for political purposes from minor governmental employees represents simply so much blackmail. This particular species of robbery is mean enough at best, and one of its meanest features is the fact that the men most apt to contribute money, the men most susceptible to pressure are those of opposite political faith to the dominant party. Those who agree in politics with the party in control feel some assurance of protection if they refuse to be coerced into parting with their money, but the unfortunates of opposite political faith feel they have no power behind the throne on which to rely, are nervously afraid of giving offense, and yield helplessly when threatened. The amount paid is not absolutely very great in any individual case, but to a poor clerk barely able to get along the loss of 3 per cent of his salary may mean just the difference between having and not having a winter overcoat for himself, a warm dress for his wife, or a Christmas tree for his children. Such a forced payment is a piece of cruel injustice and iniquity. *Report of Commissioner Roosevelt concerning political assessments . . . in the New York Customs District, January 1890.* (Washington, 1890), p. 7.

———————. We believe thoroughly that the American people are at heart sound, and that they have a contempt for that meanest of blackmailing which consists of robbing government clerks of a portion of their salaries in the interests of politicians, and that if the details of wrong-doing can be made public enough, this mere publicity will act as the greatest of possible checks. (Before Boston Civil Service Reform Association, February 20, 1893.) *Mem. Ed.* XVI, 228; *Nat. Ed.* XIV, 157.

———————. Government employees, as a whole, are hard-working, not overpaid men, with families to support, and there is no meaner species of swindling than to blackmail them for the sake of a political organization. . . .

Moreover, it is the poorest and most helpless class who are most apt to be coerced into paying. . . . Another thing to be kept in mind, in dealing with these cases of political blackmail, is that really but a comparatively small portion of the funds obtained goes to the benefit of the party organization. A certain proportion gets lost in the transit, and when the collecting officers and clubs are of low character this proportion becomes very large indeed. The money that is collected is used, in the great majority of cases, not to further the welfare of the party as a whole, but to further the designs of certain individuals in it, who are quite as willing to use the funds they have obtained against their factional foes in their own organization as against the common party foe without. (*Atlantic Monthly*, July 1892.) *Mem. Ed.* XVI, 204-205; *Nat. Ed.* XIV, 138-139.

———————. We now have a sweeping Federal law forbidding the collection of these assessments among national office-holders. Under this law the evil has been greatly diminished; yet it still exists to some extent, and it is most rife in presidential years. . . .

During the past three years the commission has recommended the indictment of some thirty different individuals for violations of the law against making political assessments. Indictments have been procured in ten or twelve cases. It is simply a question of time when we shall get some conspicuous offender convicted, and either heavily fined or imprisoned. Whenever we can make a strong case against any individual collecting political assessments, we intend to ask for his indictment, and we shall often get it, and this alone will serve to frighten other offenders. Of the men thus indicted, eventually we shall be able to convict a certain proportion. Moreover, we find that a very great deal can be done to stop the assessments by mere publicity. Throughout the approaching campaign we intend, whenever we find an individual or an organization trying to assess government office-holders, publicly, through the press, to call the attention of everybody to what is being done, and to invite any information which will enable us to prosecute the offenders; at the same time assuring the people solicited that they need not contribute one dollar unless they wish, and that they will be amply protected if they refuse to contribute at all. (*Atlantic Monthly,* July 1892.) *Mem. Ed.* XVI, 199, 201; *Nat. Ed.* XIV, 134, 136.

———————. I cannot say that we [the Civil Service Commissioners] succeeded in stopping political assessments outright. We did not. They went on to altogether too great an extent; but I firmly believe that we succeeded in greatly reducing the evil, and in checking it to a greater extent than it had ever before been checked. We made government clerks feel that they surely would be protected, that they would not have to pay assessments or contribute to any political party unless of their own free will; and we inspired would-be wrong-doers with sufficient fear to make them avoid those open methods by which alone they could hope to collect any very great funds. The minute they were obliged to work in the dark, by subterfuges and in an underhand way, they could only collect a comparatively small amount, for they could collect only from the clerks who were weakest and most timid. No man with an ounce of pluck in him had to pay. (Before Boston Civil Service Reform Association, February 20, 1893.) *Mem. Ed.* XVI, 229; *Nat. Ed.* XIV, 158.

POLITICAL ASSESSMENTS. *See also* CAMPAIGN EXPENSES; CAMPAIGN FUNDS.

POLITICAL ASSOCIATES. All that can rightly be asked of one's political associates is that they shall be honest men, good Americans, and substantially in accord as regards their political ideas. (*Forum,* July 1894.) *Mem. Ed.* XV, 46; *Nat. Ed.* XIII, 32.

POLITICAL ASSOCIATES. *See also* AMERICANS, HYPHENATED; AMERICANS IN POLITICS; CLASS LINES; COLLEGE EDUCATION; EDUCATED MEN; GERMAN-AMERICANS; GOVERNING CLASS; IRISH-AMERICANS.

POLITICAL DUTIES. The first duty of an American citizen, then, is that he shall work in politics; his second duty is that he shall do that work in a practical manner; and his third is that it shall be done in accord with the highest principles of honor and justice. Of course, it is not possible to define rigidly just the way in which the work shall be made practical. Each man's individual temper and convictions must be taken into account. To a certain extent his work must be done in accordance with his individual beliefs and theories of right and wrong. To a yet greater extent it must be done in combination with others, he yielding or modifying certain of his own theories and beliefs so as to enable him to stand on a common ground with his fellows, who have likewise yielded or modified certain of their theories and beliefs. (Before the Liberal Club, Buffalo, N. Y., January 26, 1893.) *Mem. Ed.* XV, 65; *Nat. Ed.* XIII, 283.

POLITICAL DUTIES—NEGLECT OF. However refined and virtuous a man may be, he is yet entirely out of place in the American body politic unless he is himself of sufficiently coarse fibre and virile character to be more angered than hurt by an insult or injury; the timid good form a most useless as well as a most despicable portion of the community. Again, when a man is heard objecting to taking part in politics because it is "low," he may be set down as either a fool or a coward: it would be quite as sensible for a militiaman to advance the same statement as an excuse for refusing to assist in quelling a riot. Many cultured men neglect their political duties simply because they are too delicate to have the element of "strike back" in their natures, and because they have an unmanly fear of being forced to stand up for their own rights when threatened with abuse or insult. (*Century,* November 1886.) *Mem. Ed.* XV, 121; *Nat. Ed.* XIII, 82.

———————. It ought to be axiomatic in this country that every man must devote a reasonable share of his time to doing his duty in the political life of the community. No man has a right to shirk his political duties under whatever plea of pleasure or business; and while such shirking may be pardoned in those of small means, it is entirely unpardonable in those among whom it is most common—in the people whose circumstances give them freedom in the struggle for life. In so far as the community grows to think rightly, it will likewise grow to regard the young man of means who shirks his duty to the State in time of peace as being only one degree worse than the man who thus shirks it in time of war (Before the Liberal Club, Buffalo, N. Y., January 26, 1893.) *Mem. Ed.* XV, 63; *Nat. Ed.* XIII, 281.

POLITICAL DUTIES. *See also* CITIZENSHIP; CIVIC DUTY; DEMOCRACY; POLITICS—PARTICIPATION IN.

POLITICAL EXPEDIENCY. Political expediency is right enough in its place; but not when it conflicts with vital national interest.— (1918.) *Mem. Ed.* XXI, 362; *Nat. Ed.* XIX, 329.

POLITICAL EXPEDIENCY. *See also* POLITICS—SUCCESS IN.

POLITICAL HONESTY. *See* BRIBERY; CORRUPTION; ELECTION REFORMS; HONESTY; SPOILS SYSTEM.

POLITICAL ISSUES. If a party raises an issue which it knows is a false issue, merely for the hope of carrying an election, then that party shows in the most striking way that it is the enemy of the country and unfit to be intrusted with its government. The squaring of one's deeds with one's words is the quality above all others which we should exact from public men and from the spokesmen of great parties, whether these spokesmen appear upon the stump or speak through the platforms of their parties. If the spokesmen of a party do not and cannot believe what they say, whether in the way of denunciation or promise, and especially if they promise what they know they cannot perform, and what is palpably intended not to result in performance, but in vote-getting at the moment, then they insult the conscience and the intelligence of every freeman fit to exercise a freeman's privilege. (At Akron, O., September 23, 1899.) Thomas W. Handford, *Theodore Roosevelt. The Pride of the Rough Riders.* (Chicago, 1899), pp. 179-180.

POLITICAL ISSUES, RECENT. Most of the issues which nine times out of ten most concern the average man and average woman of our Republic have reached their present form only within the lifetime of the men who are now of middle age. They are due to the profound social and economic changes of the last half-century, to the exhaustion of the soil and of our natural resources, to the rapid growth of manufacturing towns and great trading cities, and to the relative lowering of the level of life in many country districts, both from the standpoint of interest and the standpoint of profit. Whether we approach the problem having in view only the interests of the wage-worker or of the farmer or of the small business man, or having in view the interests of the public as a whole, we are obliged to face certain new facts. One is that in their actual workings the old doctrines of extreme individualism and of a purely competitive industrial system have completely broken down. Another is that if we are to grapple efficiently with the evils of to-day, it will be necessary to invoke the use of governmental power to a degree hitherto unknown in this country, and, in the interest of the democracy, to apply principles which the purely individualistic democracy of a century ago would not have recognized as Democratic. (*Century,* October 1913.) *Mem. Ed.* XIX, 532; *Nat. Ed.* XVII, 391.

POLITICAL JUDGMENT. The judgment on practical affairs, political and social, of the men who keep aloof from conditions of practical life, is apt to be valueless to those other men who do wage effective war against the forces of baseness and of evil. From the political standpoint an education that leads you into the ranks of the educated ineffectives is a harm, not a good. It is a harm to all of you here if it serves you as an excuse for refusing to mingle with your fellows, for standing aloof from the broad sweep of our national life in a curiously impotent spirit of fancied superiority. (At the Harvard Union, Cambridge, February 23, 1907.) *Mem. Ed.* XV, 489; *Nat. Ed.* XIII, 565.

POLITICAL LEADERS. *See* BOSSES; LEADERS; POLITICIANS; ROOSEVELT; STATESMEN.

POLITICAL PARTIES. A party is much more than its candidate or its platform. It is even more than the men who, in the aggregate, compose it at the moment; for it is a bundle of traditions, tendencies, and principles as well. (*Century,* November 1895.) *Mem. Ed.* XVI, 349; *Nat. Ed.* XIV, 249.

———. A party should not contain utterly incongruous elements, radically divided on the real issues, and acting together only on false and dead issues insincerely painted

[439]

as real and vital. It should not in the several States as well as in the nation be prostituted to the service of the baser type of political boss. It should be so composed that there should be a reasonable agreement in the actions by it both in the nation and in the several States.

Judged by these standards, both of the old parties break down. Neither can longer be trusted to do the work so urgently needed by the country. They have been shown to be utterly reactionary by the platforms of their conventions, by the actions of both sets of bosses in the various States, and also by the legislative work of the standpat Republican senators and of the Democratic Fitzgerald-Underwood alliance in control of the House of Representatives. Any real and lasting success for the people must be based on the liberalization of the party as well as of the party's candidates. (*Outlook*, July 27, 1912.) Mem. Ed. XIX, 347; Nat. Ed. XVII, 245.

POLITICAL PARTIES—STRENGTH OF. The strength of our political organizations arises from their development as social bodies; many of the hardest workers in their ranks are neither office-holders nor yet paid henchmen, but merely members who have gradually learned to identify their fortunes with the party whose hall they have come to regard as the headquarters in which to spend the most agreeable of their leisure moments. Under the American system it is impossible for a man to accomplish anything by himself; he must associate himself with others, and they must throw their weight together. This is just what the social functions of the political clubs enable their members to do. (*Century*, November 1886.) Mem. Ed. XV, 129; Nat. Ed. XIII, 89.

POLITICAL PARTIES—SUCCESS OF. If they [political organizations] are to be successful they must necessarily be democratic, in the sense that each man is treated strictly on his merits as a man. No one can succeed who attempts to go in on any other basis; above all, no one can succeed if he goes in feeling that, instead of merely doing his duty, he is conferring a favor upon the community, and is therefore warranted in adopting an attitude of condescension toward his fellows. (*Century*, January 1900.) Mem. Ed. XV, 416; Nat. Ed. XIII, 365.

POLITICAL PARTIES. *See also* BOSS; CAMPAIGN CONTRIBUTIONS; CAMPAIGN FUNDS; DEMOCRATIC PARTY; FEDERALIST PARTY; KNOW NOTHING MOVEMENT; LABOR PARTY; MACHINE; ORGANIZATION; PARTY ALLEGIANCE; PARTY SYSTEM; POPULISTS; PROGRESSIVE PARTY; REPUBLICAN PARTY; WHIG PARTY.

POLITICAL PROMISES. It is always easy for an individual or a party to make promises; the strain comes when the party or individual has to make them good. (Before Civil Service Reform Association, Baltimore, February 23, 1889.) Mem. Ed. XVI, 145; Nat. Ed. XIV, 88.

——————. I believe that the root-vice in our political life is the demand by part of the public that a candidate shall make impossible promises, and the grin of cynical amusement and contempt with which another portion of the public regards his breaking even the promises he could keep; and one attitude is as bad as the other. (To L. F. Abbott, October 21, 1909.) Lawrence F. Abbott, *Impressions of Theodore Roosevelt*. (Doubleday, Page & Co., Garden City, N. Y., 1919), p. 190.

POLITICAL PROMISES. *See also* COMPROMISE; ELECTION PLEDGES; PARTY PLATFORMS; PLATFORM PROMISES.

POLITICAL QUACKS. When there is a good deal of misery and of injustice, even though it is mainly due to the faults of the individuals themselves, or to the mere operation of nature's laws, the quack who announces he has a cure-all for it is a dangerous person. (To H. C. Lodge, August 10, 1899.) Lodge *Letters* I, 416.

POLITICAL QUACKS. *See also* LUNATIC FRINGE.

POLITICAL REVOLUTIONS. *See* REVOLUTIONS.

POLITICAL THEORY. *See* FEDERALIST, THE.

POLITICIANS. A politician who really serves his country well, and deserves his country's gratitude, must usually possess some of the hardy virtues which we admire in the soldier who serves his country well in the field. (*Forum*, July 1894.) Mem. Ed. XV, 47; Nat. Ed. XIII, 33.

——————. A politician may be and often is a very base creature, and if he cares only for party success, if he panders to what is evil in the people, and still more if he cares only for his own success, his special abilities merely render him a curse. But among free peoples, and especially among the free peoples who speak English, it is only in very exceptional circumstances that a statesman can be efficient, can be of use to the country, unless he is also (not as a substitute, but in addition) a politician. (To Frederick Scott Oliver, August 9, 1906.) *Mem. Ed.* XXIV, 27; Bishop II, 23.

──────────. Every man who has been in practical politics grows to realize that politicians, big and little, are no more all of them bad than they are all of them good. Many of these men are very bad men indeed, but there are others among them—and some among those held up to special obloquy, too—who, even although they may have done much that is evil, also show traits of sterling worth which many of their critics wholly lack. There are few men for whom I have ever felt a more cordial and contemptuous dislike than for some of the bosses and big professional politicians with whom I have been brought into contact. On the other hand, in the case of some political leaders who were most bitterly attacked as bosses, I grew to know certain sides of their characters which inspired in me a very genuine regard and respect. (1913.) *Mem. Ed.* XXII, 184; *Nat. Ed.* XX, 157.

POLITICIANS—LEADERSHIP OF. An honest, courageous, and far-sighted politician is a good thing in any country. But his usefulness depends chiefly upon his being able to express the wishes of a population wherein the politician forms but a fragment of the leadership, where the business man and landowner, the engineer and man of technical knowledge, the men of a hundred different pursuits, represent the average type of leadership. No people has ever permanently amounted to anything if its only public leaders were clerks, politicians, and lawyers. (At National University, Cairo, Egypt, March 28, 1910.) *Mem. Ed.* XVIII, 622; *Nat. Ed.* XVI, 452.

POLITICIANS—THE PEOPLE AND. If the citizens can be thoroughly waked up, and a plain, naked issue of right and wrong presented to them, they can always be trusted. The trouble is that in ordinary times the self-seeking political mercenaries are the only persons who both keep alert and understand the situation; and they commonly reap their reward. The mass of vicious and ignorant voters—especially among those of foreign origin—forms a trenchant weapon forged ready to their hand, and presents a standing menace to our prosperity; and the selfish and shortsighted indifference of decent men is only one degree less dangerous. (1891.) *Mem. Ed.* IX, 419; *Nat. Ed.* X, 533.

POLITICIANS. *See also* BOSSES; BUREAUCRACY; *Federalist, The;* LEADERS; MACHINE; ORGANIZATION; STATESMEN.

POLITICS—BETTERMENT OF. We have proceeded upon the assumption that the decalogue and the golden rule are peculiarly applicable to political life, and, also, that if a public official was worth his salt he was bound to try to show that the purification of politics was not an iridescent dream. (Before Liberal Club of Buffalo, N. Y., September 10, 1895.) *Mem. Ed.* XVI, 273-274; *Nat. Ed.* XIV, 194.

──────────. No man who is worth his salt has any right to abandon the effort to better our politics merely because he does not find it pleasant, merely because it entails associations which to him happen to be disagreeable. Let him keep right on, taking the buffets he gets good-humoredly, and repaying them with heartiness when the chance arises. Let him make up his mind that he will have to face the violent opposition of the spoils politician, and also, too often, the unfair and ungenerous criticism of those who ought to know better. Let him be careful not to show himself so thin-skinned as to mind either; let him fight his way forward, paying only so much regard to both as is necessary to enable him to win in spite of them. He may not, and indeed probably will not, accomplish nearly as much as he would like to, or as he thinks he ought to: but he will certainly accomplish something; and if he can feel that he has helped to elevate the type of representative sent to the municipal, the State, or the national legislature from his district, or to elevate the standard of duty among the public officials in his own ward, he has a right to be profoundly satisfied with what he has accomplished. (*Forum*, July 1894.) *Mem. Ed.* XV, 47; *Nat. Ed.* XIII, 33.

──────────. Clean politics is simply one form of applied good citizenship. No man can be a really good citizen unless he takes a lively interest in politics from a high standpoint. (*Outlook*, July 28, 1900.) *Mem. Ed.* XV, 432; *Nat. Ed.* XIII, 379.

──────────. The best lesson that any people can learn is that there is no patent cure-all which will make the body politic perfect. *Outlook*, April 10, 1909, p. 807.

POLITICS—COOPERATION IN. Under our form of government, no man can accomplish anything by himself; he must work in combination with others. (*Century,* January 1885.) *Mem. Ed.* XV, 97; *Nat. Ed.* XIII, 62.

POLITICS—EFFICIENCY IN. The one thing which corrupt machine politicians most desire is to have decent men frown on the activity, that is, on the efficiency, of the honest man who genuinely wishes to reform politics.

If efficiency is left solely to bad men, and if virtue is confined solely to inefficient men, the result cannot be happy. (1913.) *Mem. Ed.* XXII, 106; *Nat. Ed.* XX, 91.

POLITICS—IMPROVEMENT OF. For the last twenty years our politics have been better and purer, though with plenty of corruption and jobbery left still. There are shoals of base, ignorant, vicious "heelers" and "ward workers," who form a solid, well-disciplined army of evil, led on by abler men whose very ability renders them dangerous. Some of these leaders are personally corrupt; others are not, but do almost as much harm as if they were, because they divorce political from private morality. (1891.) *Mem. Ed.* IX, 419; *Nat. Ed.* X, 533.

———————. Personally I am inclined to think that in public life we are on the whole a little better and not a little worse than we were thirty years ago, when I was serving in the New York legislature. I think the conditions are a little better in national, in State, and in municipal politics. Doubtless there are points in which they are worse, and there is an enormous amount that needs reformation. But it does seem to me as if, on the whole, things had slightly improved. (1913.) *Mem. Ed.* XXII, 83; *Nat. Ed.* XX, 71.

POLITICS—INDEPENDENCE IN. It is well for a man if he is able conscientiously to feel that his views on the great questions of the day, on such questions as the tariff, finance, immigration, the regulation of the liquor traffic, and others like them, are such as to put him in accord with the bulk of those of his fellow citizens who compose one of the greatest parties; but it is perfectly supposable that he may feel so strongly for or against certain principles held by one party, or certain principles held by the other, that he is unable to give his full adherence to either. In such a case I feel that he has no right to plead this lack of agreement with either party as an excuse for refraining from active political work prior to election. (Before the Liberal Club, Buffalo, N. Y., January 26, 1893.) *Mem. Ed.* XV, 67; *Nat. Ed.* XIII, 285.

POLITICS—INTEREST IN. The trouble is always in rousing the people sufficiently to make them take an *effective* interest—that is, making them sufficiently in earnest to be willing to give a little of their time to the accomplishment of the object they have in view. (*Century*, January 1885.) *Mem. Ed.* XV, 86; *Nat. Ed.* XIII, 52.

———————. Of recent years there has been among men of character and good standing a steady growth of interest in, and of a feeling of responsibility for, our politics. This otherwise most healthy growth has been at times much hampered and warped by the political ignorance and bad judgment of the leaders in the movement. Too often the educated men who without having had any practical training as politicians yet turn their attention to politics, are and remain utterly ignorant of the real workings of our governmental system, and in their attitude toward our public men oscillate between excessive credulity concerning their idol of the moment and jealous, ignorant prejudice against those with whom they temporarily disagree. . . .

Neither the unintelligent and rancorous partisan, nor the unintelligent and rancorous independent, is a desirable member of the body politic; and it is unfortunately true of each of them that he seems to regard with special and sour hatred, not the bad man, but the good man with whom he politically differs. (1891.) *Mem. Ed.* IX, 419-420; *Nat. Ed.* X, 533-534.

———————. The man who is content to let politics go from bad to worse, jesting at the corruption of politicians, the man who is content to see the maladministration of justice without an immediate and resolute effort to reform it, is shirking his duty and is preparing the way for infinite woe in the future. Hard, brutal indifference to the right, and an equally brutal short-sightedness as to the inevitable results of corruption and injustice, are baleful beyond measure; and yet they are characteristic of a great many Americans who think themselves perfectly respectable, and who are considered thriving, prosperous men by their easy-going fellow-citizens. (*Forum*, February 1895.) *Mem. Ed.* XV, 10-11; *Nat. Ed.* XIII, 9-10.

POLITICS—PARTICIPATION IN. Every man who wishes well to his country is in honor bound to take an active part in political life. If he does his duty and takes that active part he will be sure occasionally to commit mistakes and to be guilty of shortcomings. For these mistakes and shortcomings he will receive the unmeasured denunciation of the critics who commit neither because they never do anything but criticise. Nevertheless he will have the satisfaction of knowing that the salvation of the country ultimately lies, not in the hands of his critics, but in the hands of those who, however imperfectly, actually do the work of the nation.... The man who wishes to do good in his community must go into active politcial life. If he is a Republican, let him join his local Republican association; if a Democrat, the Democratic association; if an Independent, then let him put himself in touch with those who think as he does. In any event let him make himself an active force and make his influence felt. Whether he works within or without party lines he can surely find plenty of men who are desirous of good government, and who, if they act together, become at once a power on the side of righteousness. (*Forum,* July 1894.) *Mem. Ed.* XV, 42-43; *Nat. Ed.* XIII, 29-30.

—————. It may be accepted as a fact, however unpleasant, that if steady work and much attention to detail are required, ordinary citizens, to whom participation in politics is merely a disagreeable duty, will always be beaten by the organized army of politicians to whom it is both duty, business, and pleasure, and who are knit together and to outsiders by their social relations. On the other hand, average citizens do take a spasmodic interest in public affairs; and we should therefore so shape our governmental system that the action required by the voters should be as simple and direct as possible, and should not need to be taken any more often than is necessary. (*Century,* November 1886.) *Mem. Ed.* XV, 139; *Nat. Ed.* XIII, 98.

—————. The people who say that they have not time to attend to politics are simply saying that they are unfit to live in a free community. Their place is under a despotism; or if they are content to do nothing but vote, you can take despotism tempered by an occasional plebiscite.... It makes one feel half angry and half amused, and wholly contemptuous, to find men of high business or social standing in the community saying that they really have not got time to go to ward meetings, to organize political clubs, and to take a personal share in all the important details of practical politics; men who further urge against their going the fact that they think the condition of political morality low, and are afraid that they may be required to do what is not right if they go into politics. (Before the Liberal Club, Buffalo, N. Y., January 26, 1893.) *Mem. Ed.* XV, 64, 65; *Nat. Ed.* XIII, 282, 283.

—————. Two of the evil elements in our government against which good citizens have to contend are: 1, the lack of continuous activity on the part of these good citizens themselves; and, 2, the ever-present activity of those who have only an evil self-interest in political life. It is difficult to interest the average citizen in any particular movement to the degree of getting him to take an efficient part in it. He wishes the movement well, but he will not, or often cannot, take the time and the trouble to serve it efficiently; and this whether he happens to be a mechanic or a banker, a telegraph operator or a storekeeper. He has his own interests, his own business, and it is difficult for him to spare the time to go around to the primaries, to see to the organization, to see to getting out the vote—in short, to attend to all the thousand details of political management. (1913.) *Mem. Ed.* XXII, 158; *Nat. Ed.* XX, 136.

POLITICS—SUCCESS IN. The men who wish to work for decent politics must work practically, and yet must not swerve from their devotion to a high ideal. They must actually do things, and not merely confine themselves to criticising those who do them. They must work disinterestedly, and appeal to the disinterested element in others, although they must also do work which will result in the material betterment of the community. They must act as Americans through and through, in spirit and hope and purpose, and, while being disinterested, unselfish, and generous in their dealings with others, they must also show that they possess the essential manly virtues of energy, of resolution, and of indomitable personal courage. (*Forum,* July 1894.) *Mem. Ed.* XV, 49; *Nat. Ed.* XIII, 35.

—————. I believe in being thoroughly practical in politics, and in paying all proper heed to political considerations. As things actually are in this world, I do not feel that a man can accomplish much for good in public life unless he does so. But I believe still more strongly that when we come to root questions affecting the welfare of the entire nation, it is out of the question for an honorable man, whether in public or private life, to consider political expediency at all. (To Dr. B. Lawton Wiggins, late 1906.) *Mem. Ed.* XXIV, 35; Bishop II, 29.

POLITICS, PRACTICAL. I am not an impractical theorist; I am a practical politician. But I do not believe that practical politics and foul politics are necessarily synonymous terms. I never expect to get absolute perfection; and I have small sympathy with those people who are always destroying good men and good causes because they are not the best of all possible men and all possible causes; but on a naked issue of right and wrong, such as the performance or non-performance of one's official duty, it is not possible to compromise. (*Forum,* September 1895.) *Mem. Ed.* XVI, 262; *Nat. Ed.* XIV, 184.

――――――. I personally think that practical politics are a most sordid business unless they rest on a basis of honest and disinterested sentiment (though of course I appreciate to the full that with this disinterested sentiment there must also go intelligent self-interest.) (To Sir George Otto Trevelyan, September 12, 1905.) *Mem. Ed.* XXIII, 481; Bishop I, 418-419.

――――――. Resolved into its ultimate elements, the view of the spoils politician is that politics is a dirty game, which ought to be played solely by those who desire, by hook or by crook, by fair play or by foul play, to win pecuniary reward, and who are quite indifferent as to whether this pecuniary reward takes the form of money or of office. Politics can not possibly be put upon a healthy basis until this idea is absolutely eradicated. At present the ordinary office-seeking ward workers and a very large percentage of office-holders have grown to believe that it is part of the natural order of things that those who hold or seek to hold the office should exercise the controlling influence in political contests. The civil-service law is doing much to disabuse them of this idea, and the further it can be extended and the more rigidly it can be executed the healthier the result will be. The ward worker, who is simply in politics for the offices, is a curse to the community, and the sooner this is recognized the better. His political activity is purely unhealthy and mischievous. Take it out of the power of any politician to give him any office and he will cease from his noxious labors in a very short space of time. *Report of Commissioner Roosevelt concerning political assessments . . . in the Federal offices at Baltimore, Md., May 1, 1891.* (Washington, 1891), p. 4.

――――――. Practical politics must not be construed to mean dirty politics. On the contrary, in the long run the politics of fraud and treachery and foulness are unpractical politics, and the most practical of all politicians is the politician who is clean and decent and upright. But a man who goes into the actual battles of the political world must prepare himself much as he would for the struggle in any other branch of our life. He must be prepared to meet men of far lower ideals than his own, and to face things, not as he would wish them, but as they are. He must not lose his own high ideal, and yet he must face the fact that the majority of the men with whom he must work have lower ideals. He must stand firmly for what he believes, and yet he must realize that political action, to be effective, must be the joint action of many men, and that he must sacrifice somewhat of his own opinions to those of his associates if he ever hopes to see his desires take practical shape. (*Forum,* July 1894.) *Mem. Ed.* XV, 41; *Nat. Ed.* XIII, 28.

――――――. It is a pleasant but a dangerous thing to associate merely with cultivated, refined men of high ideals and sincere purpose to do right, and to think that one has done all one's duty by discussing politics with such associates. It is a good thing to meet men of this stamp; indeed it is a necessary thing, for we thereby brighten our ideals, and keep in touch with the people who are unselfish in their purposes; but if we associate with such men exclusively we can accomplish nothing. The actual battle must be fought out on other and less pleasant fields. The actual advance must be made in the field of practical politics among the men who represent or guide or control the mass of the voters, the men who are sometimes rough and coarse, who sometimes have lower ideals than they should, but who are capable, masterful, and efficient. It is only by mingling on equal terms with such men, by showing them that one is able to give and to receive heavy punishment without flinching, and that one can master the details of political management as well as they can, that it is possible for a man to establish a standing that will be useful to him in fighting for a great reform. (*Forum,* July 1894.) *Mem. Ed.* XV, 42; *Nat. Ed.* XIII, 28-29.

――――――. I believe in political organizations, and I believe in practical politics. If a man is not practical, he is of no use anywhere. But when politicians treat practical politics as foul politics, and when they turn what ought to be a necessary and useful political organization into a machine run by professional spoilsmen of low morality in their own interest, then it is time to drive the politician from public life, and either to mend or destroy the machine, according as the necessity may determine. (1913.) *Mem. Ed.* XXII, 215; *Nat. Ed.* XX, 184.

POLITICS AS A CAREER. Never get the political bee in your bonnet. Never try to shape your course so that you shall secure a reelection or a continuance of a political career. (To A.

W. Merrifield, September 25, 1889.) *Collier's,* September 27, 1919.

——————. American politics are of a kaleidoscopic character. There is no use in looking ahead as regards one's personal interests, though there is every use in shaping one's career so as to conduct it along firmly settled great principles and policies. (To Anna Roosevelt Cowles, February 2, 1900.) Cowles *Letters,* 233.

——————. I did not then [in 1880] believe, and I do not now believe, that any man should ever attempt to make politics his only career. It is a dreadful misfortune for a man to grow to feel that his whole livelihood and whole happiness depend upon his staying in office. Such a feeling prevents him from being of real service to the people while in office, and always puts him under the heaviest strain of pressure to barter his convictions for the sake of holding office. A man should have some other occupation—I had several other occupations—to which he can resort if at any time he is thrown out of office, or if at any time he finds it necessary to choose a course which will probably result in his being thrown out, unless he is willing to stay in at cost to his conscience. (1913.) *Mem. Ed.* XXII, 67; *Nat. Ed.* XX, 58.

——————. Although I have been pretty steadily in politics since I left college, I have always steadfastly refused to regard politics as a career, for save under exceptional circumstances I do not believe that any American can afford to try to make this his definite career in life. With us politics are of a distinctly kaleidoscopic nature. Nobody can tell when he will be upset; and if a man is to be of real use he ought to be able at times philosophically to accept defeat and to go on about some other kind of useful work, either permanently or at least temporarily until the chances again permit him to return to political affairs. (To John St. Loe Strachey, February 12, 1906.) *Mem. Ed.* XXIV, 7; Bishop II, 4.

POLITICS. *See also* APPOINTMENTS; BOSS; BRIBERY; CIVIC DUTY; CIVIL SERVICE REFORM; COMPROMISE; CORRUPTION; EDUCATED MEN; HONESTY; INDEPENDENT; KNOW NOTHING MOVEMENT; LEADERS; MACHINE; MIDDLE CLASS; OFFICE; ORGANIZATION; PARTY ALLEGIANCE; PATRONAGE; ROOSEVELT'S POLITICAL CAREER; SPOILS SYSTEM; WALL STREET.

POLYGAMY. *See* MARRIAGE—FEDERAL CONTROL OF; MORMONS.

"POLYGLOT BOARDING HOUSE." *See* AMERICANISM; AMERICANIZATION; IMMIGRATION; LANGUAGE; NATIONALISM.

POPULAR GOVERNMENT. *See* DEMOCRACY; GOVERNMENT; SELF-GOVERNMENT.

POPULAR RULE. As for the principles for which I stand.... Fundamentally, these principles are, first, that the people have the right to rule themselves, and can do so better than any outsiders can rule them; and, second, that it is their duty so to rule in a spirit of justice toward every man and every woman within our borders, and to use the Government, so far as possible, as an instrument for obtaining not merely political but industrial justice. *Outlook,* June 29, 1912, p. 480.

——————. The first essential in the Progressive programme is the right of the people to rule. But a few months ago our opponents were assuring us with insincere clamor that it was absurd for us to talk about desiring that the people should rule, because, as a matter of fact, the people actually do rule. Since that time the actions of the Chicago Convention, and to an only less degree of the Baltimore Convention, have shown in striking fashion how little the people do rule under our present conditions. (Before Progressive National Convention, Chicago, August 6, 1912.) *Mem. Ed.* XIX, 363; *Nat. Ed.* XVII, 258.

——————. If there is any worse form of government than that of a plutocracy, it is one which oscillates between control by a plutocracy and control by a mob. It ought not to be necessary to point out that popular rule is the antithesis of mob rule; just as the fact that the nation was in arms during the Civil War meant that there was no room in the country for armed mobs. Popular rule means not that the richest man in the country is given less than his right to a share in the work of guiding the government; on the contrary, it means that he is guaranteed just as much right as any one else, *but no more*—in other words, that each man will have his full share as a citizen, and only just so much more as his abilities entitle him to by enabling him to render to his fellow citizens services more important than the average man can render. On the other hand, the surest way to bring about mob rule is to have a government based on privilege, the kind of government desired not only by the beneficiaries of privilege, but by many honest reactionaries of dim vision; for the exasperation caused by such a government is sure in the end to produce a violent reaction and accompanying excesses. (*Outlook,* January 21, 1911.) *Mem. Ed.* XIX, 86; *Nat. Ed.* XVII, 53.

——————. I believe in adopting every device for popular government which is in theory good and when the practice bears out the theory. It is of course true that each is only a device, and that its worth must be shown in actual practice; and it is also true that where, as with us, the people are masters, the most vital need is that they shall show self-mastery as well as the power to master their servants. But it is often impossible to establish genuine popular rule and get rid of privilege, without the use of new devices to meet new needs. I think that this is the situation which now confronts us in the United States, and that the adoption in principle of the programme on which the Progressives, especially in the West, are tending to unite offers us the best chance to achieve the desired result. (*Outlook,* January 21, 1911.) *Mem. Ed.* XIX, 99; *Nat. Ed.* XVII, 64.

——————. The great fundamental issue now before the Republican party and before our people can be stated briefly. It is, Are the American people fit to govern themselves, to rule themselves, to control themselves? I believe they are. My opponents do not. I believe in the right of the people to rule. I believe the majority of the plain people of the United States will, day in and day out, make fewer mistakes in governing themselves than any smaller class or body of men, no matter what their training, will make in trying to govern them. I believe, again, that the American people are, as a whole, capable of self-control and of learning by their mistakes. Our opponents pay lip-loyalty to this doctrine; but they show their real beliefs by the way in which they champion every device to make the nominal rule of the people a sham. (At Carnegie Hall, New York City, March 20, 1912.) *Mem. Ed.* XIX, 200; *Nat. Ed.* XVII, 151.

——————. I believe in a larger opportunity for the people themselves directly to participate in government and to control their governmental agents, because long experience has taught me that without such control many of their agents will represent them badly. By actual experience in office I have found that, as a rule, I could secure the triumph of the causes in which I most believed, not from the politicians and the men who claim an exceptional right to speak in business and government, but by going over their heads and appealing directly to the people themselves. (Before Progressive National Convention, Chicago, August 6, 1912.) *Mem. Ed.* XIX, 409; *Nat. Ed.* XVII, 297.

——————. If the people are not sovereign over their own officials, then we do not live in a real democracy; for a government based on the divine right of irresponsible judges, no matter how learned and well-meaning, is as flat a negation of popular rule and democracy as is a system based on the divine right of kings. (Before National Conference of Progressive Service, Portsmouth, R. I., July 2, 1913.) *Mem. Ed.* XIX, 523; *Nat. Ed.* XVII, 383.

——————. The first essential to settle is who shall speak with authority. In democracies our answer is, the people. This necessarily means the majority of the people. Majorities change, however. The shifting of a small percentage of votes may, and as a matter of fact continually does, reverse the position of majority and minority in almost all democracies. It is therefore essential to secure forms of government under which two purposes shall be served. First, the people shall have ample opportunity deliberately to make up their minds, so that the course of action decided upon will not be due merely to whim. . . . When once the people have thus deliberately made up their minds, their decision must be rendered really, and not nominally effective, and this without undue delay. The people should have ample time to think over a matter before coming to a definite decision. Once they have reached their decision, their action should be real and effective, and their power complete. The power should always be exercised with due regard for the rights of the minority. No democracy is worth calling such unless the majority possess the power; but no democracy will endure as a democracy unless that power is exercised with wisdom and self-restraint, and with consideration for the rights and interests of minorities. One of the great tests of democracy is this willingness of those who possess the power to exercise it with moderation and with a proper regard for the rights of others. *Outlook,* November 15, 1913, p. 590.

POPULAR RULE. *See also* Boss Rule; Class Lines; Constitution; Courts; Democracy; Federalist Party; Governing Class; Government; Judges; Privilege; Representative Government; Self-Government.

POPULARITY. Popularity is a good thing, but it is not something for which to sacrifice studies or athletics or good standing in any way; and sometimes to seek it overmuch is to lose it. (To Theodore Roosevelt, Jr., October 11, 1905.) *Mem. Ed.* XXI, 550; *Nat. Ed.* XIX, 493.

———————. I do not attach any real importance to the seeming popularity which I for the moment enjoy. I don't see how it can work out for permanent good, and, as you know, I care nothing whatever for popularity, excepting as a means to an end. Of course I like to have the good-will and respect of those for whom I care, but wide popular acclaim, it seems to me, counts for almost nothing unless it can be turned to good tangible account, in the way of getting substantial advance along the lines of clean and wise government. I have never cared in the least for the kind of popularity which Lafayette so thoroughly enjoyed, and which Jefferson enjoyed, popularity which the popular man basks in for and of itself, without reference to transmuting it into any positive achievement. I want to accomplish things. Now I don't for a moment believe that popularity of the kind that at the moment I seem to enjoy will avail when there is a tide of bitter popular feeling against a party or an organization. I may be mistaken, but this is my present view. (To H. C. Lodge, May 5, 1910.) Lodge *Letters* II, 380.

POPULARITY. See also ROOSEVELT'S POPULARITY.

POPULATION. See BIRTH CONTROL; RACE SUICIDE.

POPULISM. Thrift, industry, and business energy are qualities which are quite incompatible with true Populistic feeling. Payment of debts, like the suppression of riots, is abhorrent to the Populistic mind. . . . Populism never prospers save where men are unprosperous, and your true Populist is especially intolerant of business success. If a man is a successful business man he at once calls him a plutocrat.

He makes only one exception. A miner or speculator in mines may be many times a millionaire and yet remain in good standing in the Populist party. The Populist has ineradically fixed in his mind the belief that silver is a cheap metal, and that silver money is, while not fiat money, still a long step toward it. Silver is connected in his mind with scaling down debts, the partial repudiation of obligations, and other measures aimed at those odious moneyed tyrants who lend money to persons who insist upon borrowing, or who have put their ill-gotten gains in savings-banks and kindred wicked institutions for the encouragement of the vice of thrift. These pleasurable associations quite outweigh, with the Populist, the fact that the silver man himself is rich. (*Review of Reviews,* September 1896.) *Mem. Ed.* XVI, 361-362; *Nat. Ed.* XIII, 147-148.

POPULISTS. The Populists really represent very little except an angry but loose discontent with affairs as they actually are, and a readiness to grasp after any remedy proposed either by charlatanism or by an ignorance as honest as it is abysmal. The Populist party, therefore, waxes and wanes inversely as prosperity increases or declines; that is, the folly of certain voters seems to grow in inverse ratio to their need of displaying wisdom. At present, affairs over the country seem to be on the mend, and the Populist party is therefore losing power. (*Century,* November 1895.) *Mem. Ed.* XVI, 341-342; *Nat. Ed.* XIV, 243.

PORTO RICO. We had a most interesting two days at Porto Rico. We landed on the south side of the island and were received by the Governor and the rest of the administration, including nice Mr. Laurance Grahame; then were given a reception by the Alcalde and people of Ponce; and then went straight across the island in automobiles to San Juan on the north shore. It was an eighty mile trip and really delightful. The road wound up to the high mountains of the middle island, through them, and then down again to the flat plain on the north shore. The scenery was beautiful. It was as thoroughly tropical as Panama but much more livable. There were palms, tree-ferns, bananas, mangoes, bamboos, and many other trees and multitudes of brilliant flowers. There was one vine called the dream-vine with flowers as big as great white water-lilies, which close up tight in the day-time and bloom at night. There were vines with masses of brilliant purple and pink flowers, and others with masses of little white flowers, which at night-time smell deliciously. There were trees studded over with huge white flowers, and others, the flamboyants such as I saw in the campaign at Santiago, are a mass of large scarlet blossoms in June, but which now had shed them. I thought the tree-ferns especially beautiful. The towns were just such as you saw in Cuba, quaint, brilliantly colored, with the old church or cathedral fronting the plaza, and the plaza always full of flowers. Of course the towns are dirty, but they are not nearly as dirty and offensive as those of Italy; and there is something pathetic and childlike about the people. We are giving them a good government and the island is prospering. (To Kermit Roosevelt, November 23, 1906.) *Mem. Ed.* XXI, 579; *Nat. Ed.* XIX, 520.

———————. In Porto Rico the task was simple. The island could not be independent. It became in all essentials a part of the Union. It has been given all the benefits of our economic and financial system. Its inhabitants have been given the highest individual liberty, while yet their government has been kept under the supervision of officials so well chosen that the island can be appealed to as affording a model for all such experiments in the future; and this result was mainly owing to the admirable choice of instruments by President McKinley when he selected the governing officials. (At banquet in honor of birthday of William McKinley, Canton, O., January 27, 1903.) *Mem. Ed.* XII, 498; *Nat. Ed.* XI, 240.

———————. There is a matter to which I wish to call your special attention, and that is, the desirability of conferring full American citizenship upon the people of Porto Rico. I most earnestly hope that this will be done. I can not see how any harm can possibly result from it, and it seems to me a matter of right and justice to the people of Porto Rico. They are loyal, they are glad to be under our flag, they are making rapid progress along the path of orderly liberty. Surely we should show our appreciation of them, our pride in what they have done, and our pleasure in extending recognition for what has thus been done, by granting them full American citizenship. (Message to Congress, December 11, 1906.) *Presidential Addresses and State Papers* V, 998.

PORTO RICO—ADMINISTRATION OF. Porto Rico, it is a pleasure to say, may now serve as an example of the best methods of administering our insular possessions. Sometimes we have to learn by experience what to avoid. It is much pleasanter when one can turn to an experience for the purpose of learning what to follow; and the last is true of our experience in Porto Rico. So excellent has been the administration of the island, so excellent the effect of the legislation concerning it, that their very excellence has caused most of us to forget all about it. There is no opportunity for head-lines about Porto Rico. You don't need to use large letters in order to say that Porto Rico continues quiet and prosperous. There is hardly a ripple of failure upon the stream of our success there; and as we don't have to think of remedies, we follow our usual custom in these matters, and don't think of it at all. (At Hartford, Conn., August 22, 1902.) *Mem. Ed.* XVIII, 356; *Nat. Ed.* XVI, 271.

———————. Under the wise administration of the present governor and council, marked progress has been made in the difficult matter of granting to the people of the island the largest measure of self-government that can with safety be given at the present time. It would have been a very serious mistake to have gone any faster than we have already gone in this direction. The Porto Ricans have complete and absolute autonomy in all their municipal governments, the only power over them possessed by the insular government being that of removing corrupt or incompetent municipal officials. This power has never been exercised save on the clearest proof of corruption or of incompetence—such as to jeopardize the interests of the people of the island; and under such circumstances it has been fearlessly used to the immense benefit of the people. It is not a power with which it would be safe, for the sake of the island itself, to dispense at present. . . . The governor and council are co-operating with all of the most enlightened and most patriotic of the people of Porto Rico in educating the citizens of the island in the principles of orderly liberty. They are providing a government based upon each citizen's self-respect, and the mutual respect of all citizens; that is, based upon a rigid observance of the principles of justice and honesty. It has not been easy to instil into the minds of people unaccustomed to the exercise of freedom, the two basic principles of our American system; the principle that the majority must rule, and the principle that the minority has rights which must not be disregarded or trampled upon. Yet real progress has been made in having these principles accepted as elementary, as the foundations of successful self-government. (Message to Congress, December 11, 1906.) *Presidential Addresses and State Papers* V, 998-1000.

PORTSMOUTH—TREATY OF. *See* RUSSO-JAPANESE WAR.

POST OFFICE INVESTIGATION. I would far rather incur the hostility of a Congressman or a Senator than do something we ought not to do. The Post-Office Department is now under fire and there is much baseless distrust of it in the popular mind. Really, you and I are not responsible for the misconduct. It happened before either of us came into office; but as long as this feeling exists we can a hundredfold better afford to incur the hostility of any politician than to give the slightest ground for belief that we are managing the Department primarily as a political machine. If the real or fancied need of any politician comes in conflict with what you regard as the good of the service or as equity to any individuals, disregard that politician utterly and if he complains send him to me. I shall take up any such case myself. (To Postmaster-General Henry C. Payne, September 4, 1903.) *Mem. Ed.* XXIII, 291; Bishop I, 253.

POWER. Power invariably means both responsibility and danger. (Inaugural Address as President, Washington, March 4, 1905.) *Mem. Ed.* XVII, 312; *Nat. Ed.* XV, 268.

——————. Our chief usefulness to humanity rests on our combining power with high purpose. Power undirected by high purpose spells calamity; and high purpose by itself is utterly useless if the power to put it into effect is lacking. (*Outlook,* September 9, 1911.) *Mem. Ed.* XVIII, 426; *Nat. Ed.* XVI, 319.

POWER—CONCENTRATION OF. The danger to American democracy lies not in the least in the concentration of administrative power in responsible and accountable hands. It lies in having the power insufficiently concentrated, so that no one can be held responsible to the people for its use. Concentrated power is palpable, visible, responsible, easily reached, quickly held to account. Power scattered through many administrators, many legislators, many men who work behind and through legislators and administrators, is impalpable, is unseen, is irresponsible, cannot be reached, cannot be held to account. (Eighth Annual Message, Washington, December 8, 1908.) *Mem. Ed.* XVII, 586; *Nat. Ed.* XV, 498.

POWER AND RESPONSIBILITY. Power always brings with it responsibility. You cannot have power to work well without having so much power as to be able to work ill, if you turn yourselves that way. (At Milwaukee, Wis., September 7, 1910.) *Mem. Ed.* XV, 457; *Nat. Ed.* XIII, 545.

POWER. *See also* AUTHORITY; ROOSEVELT'S POWER; SOVEREIGNTY.

POWERS OF GOVERNMENT. *See* COURTS; DIVISION OF POWERS; GOVERNMENTAL POWER; PRESIDENT.

PRACTICAL POLITICS. *See* POLITICS.

PRACTICALITY. A man, to amount to anything, must be practical. He must actually do things, not talk about doing them, least of all cavil at how they are accomplished by those who actually go down into the arena, and actually face the dust and the blood and the sweat, who actually triumphed in the struggle. The man must have the force, the power, the will to accomplish results, but he must have also the lift toward lofty things which shall make him incapable of striving for aught unless that for which he strives is something honorable and high—something well worth striving for. (At Valley Forge, Pa., June 19, 1904.) *Mem. Ed.* XII, 619; *Nat. Ed.* XI, 334.

——————. It is to the men who work in practical fashion with their fellows, and not to those who, whether because they are impractical or incapable, cannot thus work, that we owe what success we have had in dealing with every problem which we have either solved or started on the path of solution during the last decade. (At the Harvard Union, Cambridge, February 23, 1907.) *Mem. Ed.* XV, 492; *Nat. Ed.* XIII, 567.

PRACTICALITY. *See also* ACTION; CRITICISM; DEEDS.

PRAIRIE, THE. Nowhere, not even at sea, does a man feel more lonely than when riding over the far-reaching, seemingly never-ending plains; and after a man has lived a little while on or near them, their very vastness and loneliness and their melancholy monotony have a strong fascination for him. The landscape seems always the same, and after the traveller has plodded on for miles and miles he gets to feel as if the distance was indeed boundless. As far as the eye can see there is no break; either the prairie stretches out into perfectly level flats, or else there are gentle, rolling slopes, whose crests mark the divides between the drainage systems of the different creeks; and when one of these is ascended, immediately another precisely like it takes its place in the distance, and so roll succeeds roll in a succession as interminable as that of the waves of the ocean. Nowhere else does one seem so far off from all mankind; the plains stretch out in death-like and measureless expanse, and as he journeys over them they will for many miles be lacking in all signs of life. Although he can see so far, yet all objects on the outermost verge of the horizon, even though within the ken of his vision, look unreal and strange; for there is no shade to take away from the bright glare, and at a little distance things seem to shimmer and dance in the hot rays of the sun. The ground is scorched to a dull brown, and against its monotonous expanse any objects stand out with a prominence that makes it difficult to judge of the distance at which they are. A mile off one can see, through the strange shimmering haze, the shadowy white outlines of something which looms vaguely up till it looks as large as the canvas top of a prairie wagon; but as the horseman comes nearer it shrinks and dwindles and takes clearer form, until at last it changes into the ghastly staring skull of some mighty buffalo, long dead and gone to join the rest of his vanished race. (1885.) *Mem. Ed.* I, 183; *Nat. Ed.* I, 151.

PRAIRIE. See also CATTLEMAN; COWBOYS; HUNTERS.

PREACHERS. See JESUITS; MISSIONARIES; PIONEER PREACHERS; RELIGIOUS TEACHERS.

PREHISTORIC MAN. See NATURE; PRIMITIVE SOCIETY.

PREJUDICE. See ANTI-SEMITISM; BIGOTRY; RELIGIOUS DISCRIMINATION; TOLERANCE.

PREPAREDNESS. Unjust war is to be abhorred; but woe to the nation that does not make ready to hold its own in time of need against all who would harm it; and woe thrice over to the nation in which the average man loses the fighting edge, loses the power to serve as a soldier if the day of need should arise. *Outlook,* May 14, 1910, p. 73.

————————. I advocate that our preparedness take such shape as to fit us to resist aggression, not to encourage us in aggression. I advocate preparedness that will enable us to defend our own shores and to defend the Panama Canal and Hawaii and Alaska, and prevent the seizure of territory at the expense of any commonwealth of the western hemisphere by any military power of the Old World. I advocate this being done in the most democratic manner possible. (New York *Times,* November 15, 1914.) *Mem. Ed.* XX, 121; *Nat. Ed.* XVIII, 104.

————————. In this country there is not the slightest danger of an overdevelopment of warlike spirit, and there never has been any such danger. In all our history there has never been a time when preparedness for war was any menace to peace. On the contrary, again and again we have owed peace to the fact that we were prepared for war; and in the only contest which we have had with a European power since the Revolution, the War of 1812, the struggle and all its attendant disasters were due solely to the fact that we were not prepared to face, and were not ready instantly to resent, an attack upon our honor and interest; while the glorious triumphs at sea which redeemed that war were due to the few preparations which we had actually made. (Address as Assistant Secretary of the Navy, Naval War College, June 1897.) *Mem. Ed.* XV, 240; *Nat. Ed.* XIII, 182.

————————. Our people as a whole are unquestionably very short sighted about making preparations. Under such circumstances it is always possible that we may find ourselves pitted against a big military power where we shall need to develop fighting material at the very outset. (To General Frederick Funston, March 30, 1901.) *Mem. Ed.* XXIII, 125; Bishop I, 108.

————————. The indispensable thing for every free people to do in the present day is with efficiency to prepare against war by making itself able physically to defend its rights and by cultivating that stern and manly spirit without which no material preparation will avail.

The last point is all-essential. It is not of much use to provide an armed force if that force is composed of poltroons and ultrapacifists. Such men should be sent to the front, of course, for they should not be allowed to shirk the danger which their braver fellow countrymen willingly face, and under proper discipline some use can be made of them; but the fewer there are of them in a nation the better the army of that nation will be. (*Everybody's,* January 1915.) *Mem. Ed.* XX, 158; *Nat. Ed.* XVIII, 136.

————————. I am, as you know, a most ardent believer in national preparedness against war as a means of securing that honorable and self-respecting peace which is the only peace desired by all high-spirited people. But it is an absolute impossibility to secure such preparedness in full and proper form if it is an isolated feature of our policy. The lamentable fate of Belgium has shown that no justice in legislation or success in business will be of the slightest avail if the nation has not prepared in advance the strength to protect its rights. But it is equally true that there cannot be this preparation in advance for military strength unless there is a solid basis of civil and social life behind it. There must be social, economic, and military preparedness all alike, all harmoniously developed; and above all there must be spiritual and mental preparedness.

There must be not merely preparedness in

things material; there must be preparedness in soul and mind. To prepare a great army and navy without preparing a proper national spirit would avail nothing. And if there is not only a proper national spirit but proper national intelligence, we shall realize that even from the standpoint of the army and navy some civil preparedness is indispensable. (Before Knights of Columbus, New York City, October 12, 1915.) *Mem. Ed.* XX, 460; *Nat. Ed.* XVIII, 395.

―――――――. There is no use in saying that we will fit ourselves to defend ourselves a little, but not much. Such a position is equivalent to announcing that, if necessary, we shall hit, but we shall only hit soft. The only right principle is to prepare thoroughly or not at all. The only right principle is to avoid hitting if it is possible to do so, but never under any circumstances to hit soft. To go to war a little, but not much, is the one absolutely certain way to ensure disaster. To prepare a little but not much, stands on a par with a city developing a fire department which, after a fire occurs, can put it out a little, but not much.

Yet at this moment the majority of our political leaders either keep silent on the vital issues before our people, or else engage in conflicts which are almost meaningless because the men ranged on one side advocate total unpreparedness and the men ranged on the other side nervously deny that they desire any real and thoroughgoing preparedness. Such a condition of affairs speaks badly for this nation. (At Detroit, Mich., May, 1916.) Theodore Roosevelt, *Righteous Peace through National Preparedness*, pp. 8-9.

―――――――. When this war is over it is possible that some one of the combatants, being fully armed, will assail us because we offer ourselves as a rich and helpless prize. On the other hand it is also possible that there will be temporary exhaustion among the combatants, and a willingness, even on the part of the most brutal and ruthless, to go through the form of saying that they are peaceful and harmless. In such event there will be real danger lest our people be influenced by the foolish apostles of unpreparedness to accept this condition as permanent, and once more to shirk our duty of getting ready.

I wish to say, with all the emphasis in my power, that if peace in Europe should come tomorrow, it ought not, in the smallest degree, to affect our policy of preparedness. As a matter of fact, we probably cannot now prepare in any way that will have a material effect upon the present war. Our folly has been such that it is now too late for us to do this. All we can now do is to prepare so that the war shall leave no aftermath of horror and disaster for our nation. If we fail so to prepare then assuredly some day we or our children will have bitter cause to rue our folly. (At Kansas City, Mo., May 30, 1916.) *The Progressive Party; Its Record from January to July 1916.* (Progressive National Committee, 1916), p. 55.

―――――――. When we have closed the giant war we must prepare for the giant tasks of peace. First and foremost we should act on Washington's advice, and in time of peace prepare against war so that never again shall we be caught in such humiliating inability to defend ourselves and assert our rights as has been the case during the last four years. (Before Republican State Convention, Saratoga Springs, N. Y., July 18, 1918.) *Mem. Ed.* XXI, 399; *Nat. Ed.* XIX, 362.

PREPAREDNESS — BENEFITS OF. We can, if we have sufficient good sense and foresight, not only successfully safeguard ourselves against attack from without, but can, and ought to, do it in such a manner as immeasurably to increase our moral and material efficiency in our every-day lives. Proper preparation for self-defense will be of immense incidental help in solving our spiritual and industrial problems. (*Metropolitan*, February 1916.) *Mem. Ed.* XX, 294; *Nat. Ed.* XVIII, 252.

―――――――. Military preparedness meets two needs. In the first place, it is a partial insurance against war. In the next place, it is a partial guaranty that if war comes the country will certainly escape dishonor and will probably escape material loss. . . .

The first thing to understand is the fact that preparedness for war does not always insure peace but that it very greatly increases the chances of securing peace. Foolish people point out nations which, in spite of preparedness for war, have seen war come upon them, and then exclaim that preparedness against war is of no use. Such an argument is precisely like saying that the existence of destructive fires in great cities shows that there is no use in having a fire department. A fire department, which means preparedness against fire, does not prevent occasional destructive fires, but it does greatly diminish and may completely minimize the chances for wholesale destruction by fire. Nations that are prepared for war occasionally suffer from it; but if they are unprepared for it they suffer far more often and far more

[451]

radically. (*Everybody's*, January 1915.) *Mem. Ed.* XX, 136; *Nat. Ed.* XVIII, 117.

PREPAREDNESS — DEPENDENCE ON.
If we are not all of us Americans and nothing else, scorning to divide along lines of section, of creed, or of national origin, then the Nation itself will crumble to dust. If we are not thoroughly prepared, if we have not developed a strength which respects the rights of others but which is also ready to enforce from others respect for its own rights, then sooner or later we shall have to submit to the will of an alien conqueror. (Telegram to Senator Jackson of Maryland, June 8, 1916.) Lodge *Letters* II, 488.

───────────. We cannot permanently hold a leading place in the world unless we prepare. But there is far more than world-position at stake. Our mere safety at home is at stake. We cannot prevent ourselves from sooner or later sinking into precisely the position China now occupies in the presence of Japan, unless we prepare. The probabilities are overwhelming that the next time we fight a formidable foe we shall not again find allies whose interest it will be to protect us, and to shield us from the consequences of our feebleness and shortsightedness, as France and England have for seven months—indeed for three years—been doing. This means that ruin will surely in the end befall us unless we ourselves so prepare our strength that against a formidable opponent we shall be able to do for ourselves what the English and French armies and navies are now doing for us. Let us make no mistake. Unless we beat Germany in Europe, we shall have to fight her deadly ambition on our own coasts and in our own continent. A great American army in Europe now is the best possible insurance against a great European or Asiatic army in our own country a couple of years, or a couple of decades, hence. (*Metropolitan,* September 1917.) *Mem. Ed.* XXI, 22; *Nat. Ed.* XIX, 18-19.

───────────. Though it is a bad thing for a nation to arouse fear it is an infinitely worse thing to excite contempt; and every editor or writer or public man who tells us that we ought not to have battleships and that we ought to trust entirely to well-intentioned foolish all-inclusive arbitration treaties and abandon fortifications and not keep prepared, is merely doing his best to bring contempt upon the United States and to insure disaster in the future. (New York *Times,* October 4, 1914.) *Mem. Ed.* XX, 38; *Nat. Ed.* XVIII, 32.

───────────. The American pacifist has been the potent ally of the German militarist and the silly tool of the Hun within our gates. In the future we shall gain the respect and friendship of well-disposed nations and the respect and fear of ill-disposed nations by prepared strength; and professions of pacifism and of general good intentions, if we fail to prepare our strength, will conciliate nobody, will make us despised by everybody, and will expose us to the hostility of the forces of evil throughout the world. (*Metropolitan,* September 1918.) *Mem. Ed.* XXI, 314; *Nat. Ed.* XIX, 287.

PREPAREDNESS—ESSENTIALS OF.
We owe it to ourselves as a nation effectively to safeguard ourselves against all likelihood of disaster at the hands of a foreign foe. We should bring our navy up to the highest point of preparedness, we should handle it purely from military considerations, and should see that the training was never intermitted. We should make our little regular army larger and more effective than at present. We should provide for it an adequate reserve. In addition, I most heartily believe that we should return to the ideal held by our people in the days of Washington although never lived up to by them. We should follow the example of such typical democracies as Switzerland and Australia and provide and require military training for all our young men. Switzerland's efficient army has unquestionably been the chief reason why in this war there has been no violation of her neutrality. (New York *Times,* November 8, 1914.) *Mem. Ed.* XX, 97; *Nat. Ed.* XVIII, 84.

───────────. We should devote ourselves as a preparative to preparedness, alike in peace and war, to secure the three elemental things: one, a common language, the English language; two, the increase in our social loyalty—citizenship absolutely undivided, a citizenship which acknowledges no flag except of the United States and which emphatically repudiates all duality of national loyalty; and third, an intelligent and resolute effort for the removal of industrial and social unrest, an effort which shall aim equally to secure every man his rights and to make every man understand that unless he in good faith performs his duties he is not entitled to any rights at all. (Before Knights of Columbus, New York City, October 12, 1915.) *Mem. Ed.* XX, 465; *Nat. Ed.* XVIII, 399.

───────────. It takes months to build guns and ships now, where it then [in 1812] took days, or at the most, weeks; and it takes far longer now to train men to the management of the vast and complicated engines with which war is waged. Therefore preparation is much more difficult, and requires a much longer time; and yet wars are so much quicker, they last so comparatively short a period, and can be begun so instantaneously that there is very much less time than formerly in which to make preparations. . . . Even if the enemy did not interfere with our efforts, which they undoubtedly would, it would, therefore, take from three to six months after the outbreak of a war, for which we were unprepared, before we could in the slightest degree remedy our unreadiness. During this six months it would be impossible to overestimate the damage that could be done by a resolute and powerful antagonist. Even at the end of that time we would only be beginning to prepare to parry his attack, for it would be two years before we could attempt to return it. Since the change in military conditions in modern times there has never been an instance in which a war between any two nations has lasted more than about two years. In most recent wars the operations of the first ninety days have decided the result of the conflict. All that followed has been a mere vain effort to strive against the stars in their courses by doing at the twelfth hour what it was useless to do after the eleventh.

We must therefore make up our minds once for all to the fact that it is too late to make ready for war when the fight has once begun. The preparation must come before that. (Address as Assistant Secretary of the Navy, Naval War College, June 1897.) *Mem. Ed.* XV, 249-250; *Nat. Ed.* XIII, 189-190.

——————. If we had been wise enough to begin thoroughgoing preparations two and a half years ago, after this great war broke out, and if, as the main feature thereof, we had introduced the principle of obligatory universal military training and service (and had also done such elementary things as running the Springfield factory at full speed, in which case we would now be a million rifles to the good), there would be scant need of a volunteer force now, for we would have been able to put a couple of million men, well armed and equipped, into the field, and would have finished this war at once. Nine-tenths of wisdom is being wise in time. But we were not wise in time. We did not prepare in advance the instruments which would alone be thoroughly satisfactory, and which cannot possibly be improvised to meet immediate needs. Therefore, let us use every instrument that is available to meet the immediate needs. Let us not advance our unwisdom in the past as a justification for fresh unwisdom in the present. If the people of a town do not prepare a fire company until a fire breaks out, they are selfish. But they are more foolish still if when the fire breaks out they then decline to try to put it out with any means at hand, on the ground that they prefer to wait and drill a fire company. Your military advisers are now giving you precisely such advice. Put out the fire with the means available, and at the same time start the drill of the fire company. (To Secretary Newton D. Baker, April 22, 1917.) *Mem. Ed.* XXI, 210; *Nat. Ed.* XIX, 199.

PREPAREDNESS — EXPENDITURES FOR. Our danger is always that we shall spend too little, and not too much, in keeping ourselves prepared for foreign war. (1887.) *Mem. Ed.* VIII, 108; *Nat. Ed.* VII, 94.

PREPAREDNESS — EXTENT OF. Our people need to remember that half-preparation is no preparation at all. A great many well-meaning people are of the same mind as a philanthropist who wrote me the other day to the effect that he believed in some preparedness, but not much. This is like building a bridge half-way across a stream, but not all the way. I regret to state that this seems to be the attitude which our government now takes as a substitute for its attitude of a year ago, when its view was that preparedness was "hysterical," immoral and unnecessary. The only proper attitude is that there shall be no preparedness at all that is not necessary, but that in so far as there is need for preparedness the need shall be fully met. (*Metropolitan*, February 1916.) *Mem. Ed.* XX, 285; *Nat. Ed.* XVIII, 244-245.

PREPAREDNESS—FOES OF. The fundamental fact is that the real foes of preparedness in this country are its make-believe friends who are for a half—or rather for a tenth—measure of preparedness, of sham preparedness. Bryan is not the real foe. He and his followers, including his Republican and Progressive followers, are too unspeakably silly permanently to delude the country. It is Wilson who is the real danger. Uncle Sam finds himself unarmed, among nations each of which is armed with a high-power rifle. Bryan says he should not have any weapon. Wilson says that this is all wrong; that Uncle Sam should be armed; that he is in great danger; that there is need; that he should be amply prepared for self-defense; and that therefore he should be given a muzzle-loading flintlock musket. Now, we ought to

[453]

make our people understand that it is really rather more dangerous to send a man armed only with a muzzle-loading flintlock musket against a man with a high-power rifle than it is to send him totally unarmed. (To H. C. Lodge, February 4, 1916.) Lodge *Letters* II, 477.

PREPAREDNESS — NEGLECT OF. The blindest can now see that had we, in August, 1914, when the Great War began, ourselves begun actively to prepare, we would now be in a position such that every one knew our words would be made good by our deeds. In such case no nation would dream of interfering with us or of refusing our demands; and each of the warring nations would vie with the others to keep us out of the war. Immediate preparedness at the outset of the war would have meant that there would never have been the necessity for sending the "strict accountability" note. It would have meant that there never would have been the murder of the thousands of men, women, and children on the high seas. It would have meant that we would now be sure of peace for ourselves. It would have meant that we would now be ready to act the part of peacemaker for others. (1916.) *Mem. Ed.* XX, 227; *Nat. Ed.* XVIII, 194.

———. When the World War broke out over a year ago, it was simply inexcusable for this people not at once to begin the work of preparation. If we had done so, we would now have been able to make our national voice felt effectively in helping to bring about peace with justice—and no other peace ought to be allowed. But not one thing has been done by those in power to make us ready. . . .

Men are not to be seriously blamed for failure to see or foresee what is hidden from all but eyes that are almost prophetic. The most far-seeing Americans, since the days of Washington, have always stood in advance of popular feeling in the United States so far as national preparedness against war is concerned. But on the other hand not a few of the leaders have been much less advanced than the people they led. And under right leadership the people have always been willing to grapple with facts that were fairly obvious. They have refused to do this when the official leadership was wrong. (*Metropolitan*, November 1915.) *Mem. Ed.* XX, 378, 379; *Nat. Ed.* XVIII, 323, 325.

———. As yet we, as a people, acting through our governmental authorities, have not taken one step to avert disaster in the future by introducing a permanent policy of preparedness. By actual test the system, or rather no-system, upon which during the last three years we have been told we could rely has proved entirely worthless. The measures under which we are now acting are temporary makeshifts, announced to be such. We have been caught utterly unprepared in a terrible emergency because we did nothing until the emergency actually arose; and now our government announces that what we are doing is purely temporary; that we shall stop doing it as soon as the emergency is over, and will then remain equally unprepared for the next emergency. (1917.) *Mem. Ed.* XXI, 6; *Nat. Ed.* XIX, 5.

———. We are utterly unprepared. The things we are now doing, even when well done, are things which we ought to have begun doing three years ago. We can now only partially offset our folly in failing to prepare during these last three years, in failing to heed the lesson writ large across the skies in letters of flame and blood. Nine-tenths of wisdom consists in being wise in time! Now we must fight without proper preparation. But we must prepare as well as we can at this late date. (At Lincoln, Neb., June 14, 1917.) *Mem. Ed.* XXI, 190; *Nat. Ed.* XIX, 181.

PREPAREDNESS—PEACE INSURANCE BY. Fit to hold our own against the strong nations of the earth, our voice for peace will carry to the ends of the earth. Unprepared, and therefore unfit, we must sit dumb and helpless to defend ourselves, protect others, or preserve peace. (Eighth Annual Message, Washington, December 8, 1908.) *Mem. Ed.* XVII, 638; *Nat. Ed.* XV, 543.

———. The fact that unpreparedness does not mean peace ought to be patent to every American who will think of what has occurred in this country during the last seventeen years. In 1898 we were entirely unprepared for war. No big nation, save and except our opponent, Spain, was more utterly unprepared than we were at that time, nor more utterly unfit for military operations. This did not, however, mean that peace was secured for a single additional hour. Our army and navy had been neglected for thirty-three years. This was due largely to the attitude of the spiritual forebears of those eminent clergymen, earnest social workers, and professionally humanitarian and peace-loving editors, publicists, writers for syndicates, speakers for peace congresses, pacifist college presidents, and the like who have recently come forward to protest against any inquiry into the military condition of this nation, on the ground that to supply our ships and forts with sufficient ammunition and to fill up the depleted ranks of the army and navy, and in other ways to prepare against war, will tend to interfere with peace. In 1898 the gentlemen of this sort had had their way for thirty-three years. Our army and navy had been grossly neglected. But the unpreparedness due to this neglect had not the slightest effect of any kind in preventing the war. The only effect it had was to cause the unnecessary and useless loss of thousands of lives in the war. Hundreds of young men perished in the Philippine trenches because, while the soldiers of Aguinaldo had modern rifles with smokeless powder, our troops had only the old black-powder Springfield. Hundreds more, nay thousands, died or had their health impaired for life in fever camps here in our own country and in the Philippines and Cuba, and suffered on transports, because we were entirely unprepared for war, and therefore no one knew how to take care of our men. The lives of these brave young volunteers were the price that this country paid for the past action of men like the clergymen, college presidents, editors, and humanitarians in question—none of whom, by the way, risked their own lives. (*Everybody's*, January 1915.) *Mem. Ed.* XX, 141-142; *Nat. Ed.* XVIII, 121-122.

───────────. The most certain way for a nation to invite disaster is to be opulent, self-assertive, and unarmed. A nation can no more prepare for self-defense when war actually threatens than a spoiled college "sissy" of the pacifist type can defend himself if a young tough chooses to insult him; and unlike the sissy, the nation cannot under such conditions appeal to the police. Now and then to insure a house means that some scoundrel burns the house down in order to get insurance. But we do not in consequence abandon insurance against fire. Now and then a nation prepares itself for a war of aggression. But this is no argument against preparedness in order to repel aggression. Preparedness against war is the only efficient form of national peace insurance. (*Metropolitan*, August 1915.) *Mem. Ed.* XX, 372; *Nat. Ed.* XVIII, 319.

PREPAREDNESS—SUBSTITUTES FOR. You will be worthless in war if you have not prepared yourselves for it in peace. You will be utterly unable to rise to the needs of the crisis if you have not by long years of steady and patient work fitted yourselves to get the last ounce of work out of every man, every gun, and every ship in the fleet; if you have not practised steadily on the high seas until each ship can do its best, can show at its best, alone or in conjunction with others in fleet formation. Remember that no courage can ever atone for lack of that preparedness which makes the courage valuable; and yet if the courage is there, if the dauntless heart is there, its presence will sometimes make up for other shortcomings; while if with it are combined the other military qualities the fortunate owner becomes literally invincible. (At Annapolis, Md., April 24, 1906.) *Mem. Ed.* XVIII, 328; *Nat. Ed.* XVI, 248-249.

PREPAREDNESS, BROOMSTICK. In the fall of 1917 the enormous majority of our men in the encampments were drilling with broomsticks or else with rudely whittled guns. As late as the beginning of December they had in the camps almost only wooden machine-guns and wooden field-cannon. In the camps I saw barrels mounted on sticks on which zealous captains were endeavoring to teach their men how to ride a horse. At that time we had one or two divisions of well-trained infantry in France—which would have been simply lapped up if placed against the army of any formidable military power. At that time, eight months after we had gone to war, the army we had gathered in the cantonments had neither the rifles, the machine-guns, the cannon, the tanks, nor the airplanes which would have enabled them to make any fight at all against any army of any military power that could have landed on our shores. It would have been as helpless against an invading army as so many savages armed with stone-headed axes. We were wholly unable to defend ourselves a year after we had gone to war. We owed our safety only to the English, French, and Italian fleets and armies.

The cause was our refusal to prepare in advance. . . . We paid the price later with broomstick rifles, logwood cannon, soldiers without shoes, and epidemics of pneumonia in the camps. We are paying the price now in shortage of coal and congestion of transportation, and in the double cost of necessary war-supplies. (1918.) *Mem. Ed.* XXI, 290-291; *Nat. Ed.* XIX, 267.

───────────. Let Uncle Sam prepare to defend himself. Let him realize from the experience of the immediate past that, unless he prepares long in advance, he will be utterly helpless if suddenly menaced with war by a great military nation. Broomstick preparedness is of value only from the political standpoint.

Fine words will never save us from a foreign

conqueror. Only deeds will save us; and then only if we prepare for these deeds in advance. (1918.) *Mem. Ed.* XXI, 298; *Nat. Ed.* XIX, 274.

PREPAREDNESS, NAVAL. There is a loose popular idea that we could defend ourselves by some kind of patent method, invented on the spur of the moment. This is sheer folly. There is no doubt that American ingenuity could do something, but not enough to prevent the enemy from ruining our coasting-trade and threatening with destruction half our coast towns. Proper forts, with heavy guns, could do much; but our greatest need is the need of a fighting-fleet. Forts alone could not prevent the occupation of any town or territory outside the range of their guns, or the general wasting of the seaboard; while a squadron of heavy battleships, able to sail out and attack the enemy's vessels as they approached, and possessing the great advantage of being near their own base of supplies, would effectually guard a thousand miles of coast. (*Atlantic Monthly,* October 1890.) *Mem. Ed.* XIV, 315; *Nat. Ed.* XII, 272.

——————. It can . . . be taken for granted that there must be adequate preparation for conflict, if conflict is not to mean disaster. Furthermore, this preparation must take the shape of an efficient fighting navy. We have no foe able to conquer or overrun our territory. Our small army should always be kept in first-class condition, and every attention should be paid to the National Guard; but neither on the North nor on the South have we neighbors capable of meanacing us with invasion or long resisting a serious effort on our part to invade them. The enemies we may have to face will come from over sea; they may come from Europe, or they may come from Asia. (Address as Assistant Secretary of the Navy, Naval War College, June 1897.) *Mem. Ed.* XV, 252; *Nat. Ed.* XIII, 192.

PREPAREDNESS, SOCIAL AND INDUSTRIAL. Let us prepare not merly in military matters, but in our social and industrial life. There can be no sound relationship toward other nations unless there is also sound relationship among our own citizens within our own ranks. Let us insist on the thorough Americanization of the newcomers to our shores, and let us also insist on the thorough Americanization of ourselves. Let us encourage the fullest industrial activity, and give the amplest industrial reward to those whose activities are most important for securing industrial success, and at the same time let us see that justice is done and wisdom shown in securing the welfare of every man, woman, and child within our borders. (1916.) *Mem. Ed.* XX, 261; *Nat. Ed.* XVIII, 225.

——————. It is our great duty to combine preparedness for peace, efficiency in securing both industrial success and industrial justice, with preparedness against war. We need not in servile fashion follow exactly the example set abroad, but if we are wise we will profit by what has been achieved, notably among great industrial nations, like Germany, in these matters. (*Metropolitan,* February 1916.) *Mem. Ed.* XX, 295; *Nat. Ed.* XVIII, 253.

——————. The question of more real consequence to this nation than any other at this moment is the question of preparedness. The first step must be preparedness against war. Of course there can be no efficient military preparedness against war without preparedness for social and industrial efficiency in peace. Germany, which is the great model for all other nations in matters of efficiency, has shown this, and if this democracy is to endure, it must emulate German efficiency—adding thereto the spirit of democratic justice and of international fair play. Moreover, and finally, there can be no preparedness in things material, whether of peace or war, without also preparedness in things mental and spiritual. There must be preparedness of the soul and the mind in order to make full preparedness of the body, although it is no less true that the mere fact of preparing the body also prepares the soul and the mind. There is the constant action and reaction of one kind of preparation upon another in nations as in individuals. (*Metropolitan,* February 1916.) *Mem. Ed.* XX, 278; *Nat. Ed.* XVIII, 239.

——————. Preparedness does not mean merely a man with a gun. It means that too; but it means a great deal more. It means that in this country we must secure conditions which will make the farmer and the working man understand that it is in a special sense their country; that the work of preparedness is entered into for the defense of the country which belongs to them, to all of us, and the government of which is administered in their interest, in the interest of all of us. . . . We in America who are striving for preparedness must make it evident that the preparedness is to serve the people as a whole. The war on the other side has shown that there can be no efficient army in the field unless the men behind are trained and efficient and unless they are whole-heartedly loyal in their patriotic devotion to their country. (To S. S. Menken, January 10, 1917; read before National Security League, Washington, January 26, 1917.) *Proceedings of the Congress of Constructive Patriotism.* (New York, 1917), pp. 173-174.

―――――――. With the individual military training there must go industrial preparedness, by encouragement and supervision, on the part of the Government, of every industry which could be useful in time of war. The industries should be kept ready to render service immediately upon the outbreak of war. The railroads of the country, and indeed the transportation generally, should be handled at all times with the idea that the Government would immediately control it in the event of war. All munition plants, automobile factories, and the like, should be continually exercised by sample orders. Expert workers should be card-catalogued, so that the Government would know exactly what to do with its men wherever the need arose; and in all workshops, and in such matters as aviation and transportation by train or automobile, women should be given the chance in time of war to replace the men who ought to go to the front, in the fighting line, into the position of danger. It should be understood clearly that in time of war the Government would regulate every business in the interest of the Nation as a whole, and would tolerate no practice inconsistent with the welfare of the Nation and the success of the war, permitting neither excessive profit-making on the part of employers nor abuses by employers, nor strikes on the part of employees, so long as the war lasted. *National Service,* March 1917, pp. 71-72.

PREPAREDNESS AGAINST WAR. Intelligent foresight in preparation and known capacity to stand well in battle are the surest safeguards against war. (Preface to *Hero Tales* with H. C. Lodge, 1895.) *Mem. Ed.* IX, xxi; *Nat. Ed.* X, xxiii.

―――――――. We ask for an armament fit for the nation's needs, not primarily to fight, but to avert fighting. Preparedness deters the foe, and maintains right by the show of ready might without the use of violence. (Address as Assistant Secretary of the Navy, Naval War College, June 1897.) *Mem. Ed.* XV, 259; *Nat. Ed.* XIII, 198.

―――――――. This nation is a great peaceable nation, both by the temper of its people and by its fortunate geographical situation, and is freed from the necessity of maintaining such armaments as those that cramp the limbs of the powers of Continental Europe. Nevertheless, events have shown that war is always a possibility even for us. Now, the surest way to avert war, if it can be averted, is to be prepared to do well if forced to go into war. If we don't prepare for war in advance, then other powers will have a just contempt for us. They will fail to understand that with us unreadiness does not mean timidity; and they may at any time do things which would force us to make war, and which they would carefully refrain from doing if they were sure we were ready to resent them. (Campaign Speech, New York City, October 5, 1898.) *Mem. Ed.* XVI, 443; *Nat. Ed.* XIV, 292.

―――――――. A world league for peace is not now in sight. Until it is created the prime necessity for each free and liberty-loving nation is to keep itself in such a state of efficient preparedness as to be able to defend by its own strength both its honor and its vital interest. The most important lesson for the United States to learn from the present war is the vital need that it shall at once take steps thus to prepare.

Preparedness against war does not always avert war or disaster in war any more than the existence of a fire department, that is, of preparedness against fire, always averts fire. But it is the only insurance against war and the only insurance against overwhelming disgrace and disaster in war. Preparedness usually averts war and usually prevents disaster in war; and always prevents disgrace in war. Preparedness, so far from encouraging nations to go to war, has a marked tendency to diminish the chance of war occurring. (1915.) *Mem. Ed.* XX, xxiv; *Nat. Ed.* XVIII, xxiii.

―――――――. Preparedness for War is in reality preparedness against War. There is nothing more important for our people to understand than that sooner or later disaster, shame and disgrace will come to us if we do not keep ourselves in shape to guard our own vital rights —and it is well to remember that the right to national self-respect is as vital as any material right. Preparedness against War renders it likely that if it should come it will not bring disaster and disgrace. Moreover, such preparedness is the only possible method by which the United States can be made an agent in producing the Peace of Righteousness. Impotence is never impressive; and though it is a bad thing to arouse the emotion of fear in others, it is an infinitely worse thing to arouse the emotion of contempt. (To Mr. Van Zile, January 8, 1915.) Edward

S. Van Zile, *The Game of Empires.* (Moffat, Yard & Co., N. Y., 1915), p. 7.

───────────. Preparedness will probably prevent these boys from having "to face the cannon"; but if other nations become convinced that the mothers of this country have raised their boys to be *afraid* to face the cannon, then you can be absolutely certain that, sooner or later, these other nations will come over and treat us just as the military powers of the Old World have treated the Chinese. (Letter of February 9, 1916.) *Mem. Ed.* XXI, 155; *Nat. Ed.* XIX, 151.

───────────. If America's strength is fully prepared in advance, she will in all probability never have to go to war and will be a potent factor in preserving the peace of justice throughout the world. (April 12, 1918.) *Roosevelt in the Kansas City Star,* 135.

PREPAREDNESS AND MILITARISM. Our people are not military. We need normally only a small standing army; but there should be behind it a reserve of instructed men big enough to fill it up to full war strength, which is over twice the peace strength. Moreover, the young men of the country should realize that it is the duty of every one of them to prepare himself so that in time of need he may speedily become an efficient soldier—a duty now generally forgotten, but which should be recognized as one of the vitally essential parts of every man's training. (1913.) *Mem. Ed.* XXII, 269; *Nat. Ed.* XX, 231.

───────────. As far as the United States is concerned, I believe we should keep our navy to the highest possible point of efficiency and have it second in size to that of Great Britain alone, and we should then have universal obligatory military training for all our young men for a period of, say, nine months during some one year between the ages of nineteen and twenty-three inclusive. This would not represent militarism, but an antidote against militarism. It would not represent a great expense. On the contrary, it would mean to give to every citizen of our country an education which would fit him to do his work as a citizen as no other type of education could. (Kansas City *Star,* November 17, 1918.) *Mem. Ed.* XXI, 447; *Nat. Ed.* XIX, 402.

───────────. I very strongly believe that never again should we be caught unprepared as we have been caught unprepared this time. I believe that all our young men should be trained to arms as the Swiss are trained. But I would regard it as an unspeakable calamity for this Nation to have to turn its whole energies into . . . exaggerated militarism. (May 12, 1918.) *Roosevelt in the Kansas City Star,* 153.

PREPAREDNESS AND SOCIAL VALUES. In December last I was asked to address the American Sociological Congress on "the effect of war and militarism on social values." In sending my answer I pointed out that infinitely the most important fact to remember in connection with the subject in question is that if an unscrupulous, warlike, and militaristic nation is not held in check by the warlike ability of a neighboring non-militaristic and well-behaved nation, then the latter will be spared the necessity of dealing with its own "moral and social values" because it won't be allowed to deal with anything. Until this fact is thoroughly recognized, and the duty of national preparedness by justice-loving nations explicitly acknowledged, there is very little use of solemnly debating such questions as the one which the sociological congress assigned me—which, in detail, was "How war and militarism affect such social values as the sense of the preciousness of human life; care for child welfare; the conservation of human resources; upper-class concern for the lot of the masses; interest in popular education; appreciation of truth-telling and truth-printing; respect for personality and regard for personal rights." It seems to me positively comic to fail to appreciate, with the example of Belgium before our eyes, that the real question which modern peace-loving nations have to face is not how the militaristic or warlike spirit within their own borders will affect these "values," but how failure on their part to be able to resist the militarism of an unscrupulous neighbor will affect them. (American Sociological Society, *Papers,* 1915.) *Mem. Ed.* XX, 264; *Nat. Ed.* XVIII, 227.

PREPAREDNESS FOR WAR. A service will do well or ill at the outbreak of war very much in proportion to the way it has been prepared to meet the outbreak during the preceding months. Now, it is often impossible to say whether the symptoms that seem to forebode war will or will not be followed by war. . . . Therefore, when war threatens, preparations must be made in any event; for the evil of what proves to be the needless expenditure of money in one instance is not to be weighed for a moment against the failure to prepare in the other. But only a limited number of men have the moral courage to make these preparations, because there is always risk to the individual making them. Laws and regulations must be stretched when an emergency arises, and yet there is always some danger to the person who stretches them; and, moreover, in time of sudden need, some indispensable article can very possibly only be obtained at an altogether exorbitant price. If war comes, and the article, whether it be a cargo of coal, or a collier, or an auxiliary naval vessel, proves its usefulness, no complaint is ever made. But if the war does not come, then some small demagogue, some cheap economist, or some undersized superior who is afraid of taking the responsibility himself, may blame the man who bought the article and say that he exceeded his authority; that he showed more zeal than discretion in not waiting for a few days, etc. These are the risks which must be taken, and the men who take them should be singled out for reward and for duty. (*McClure's Magazine,* October 1899.) *Mem. Ed.* XII, 507-508; *Nat. Ed.* XIII, 421-422.

——————. I had been preaching preparedness for years; but for the last year I have been earnestly advocating that we prepare in such fashion as to make ourselves able to count decisively if we do have to interfere. (To Baron Rosen, August 7, 1915.) *Mem. Ed.* XXIV, 461; Bishop II, 392.

——————. If we go to war, we are not to be excused if we do not prepare instantly and to the utmost of all our strength. . . . We must strike hard at Germany with the most formidable expeditionary force that can be raised. (At Hartford, Conn., March 1, 1917.) *Mem. Ed.* XXIV, 491; Bishop II, 419.

PREPAREDNESS IN A DEMOCRACY. Autocracy may use preparedness for the creation of an aggressive and provocative militarism that invites and produces war; but in a democracy preparedness means security against aggression and the best guaranty of peace. (*New York Times,* November 29, 1914.) *Mem. Ed.* XX, 211; *Nat. Ed.* XVIII, 181.

——————. I believe that our people will make democracy successful. They can only do so if they show by their actions that they understand the responsibilities that go with democracy. The first and the greatest of these responsibilities is the responsibility of national self-defense. We must be prepared to defend a country governed in accordance with the democratic ideal or else we are guilty of treason to that ideal. To defend the country it is necessary to organize the country in peace, or it cannot be organized in war.

A riot of unrestricted individualism in time of peace means impotence for sustained and universal national effort toward a common end in war-time. Neither business man nor wage-worker should be permitted to do anything detrimental to the people as a whole; and if they act honestly and efficiently they should in all ways be encouraged. There should be social cohesion. We must devise methods by which under our democratic government we shall secure the socialization of industry which autocratic Germany has secured, so that business may be encouraged and yet controlled in the general interest, and the wage-workers guaranteed full justice and their full share of the reward of industry, and yet required to show the corresponding efficiency and public spirit that justify their right to an increased reward. But the vital fact to remember is that ultimately it will prove worse than useless to have our people prosper unless they are able to defend this prosperity; to fight for it. (*Metropolitan,* November 1915.) *Mem. Ed.* XX, 387; *Nat. Ed.* XVIII, 331.

——————. The professional pacifists who have so actively worked for the dishonor of the American name and the detriment of the American nation (and who incidentally have shown themselves the basest allies and tools of triumphant wrong) would do well to bear in view the elementary fact that the only possible way by which to enable us to live at peace with other nations is to develop our strength in order that we may defend our own rights. Above all, let them realize that a democracy more than any other human government needs preparation in advance if peace is to be safeguarded against war. So far as self-defense is concerned, universal military training and, in the event of need, universal military service, represent the highest expression of the democratic ideal in government. (*Metropolitan,* February 1916.) *Mem. Ed.* XX, 277; *Nat. Ed.* XVIII, 238.

——————. It is always hard to make a democracy prepare in advance against dangers which only the far-sighted see to be imminent. Even in France there were well-meaning men, who but a few years ago did not realize the danger that hung over their land, and who then strove against adequate preparedness. In England, which was by no means in the same danger as France, there were far more of these men—just as there are far more of them in our own country than in England. Almost all these men, both in France and in England, are now, doing everything in their power to atone for the error they formerly committed, an error for which they and their fellow countrymen have paid a bitter price of blood and tears. In our land, however, the men of this stamp have not learned these lessons, and with evil folly are endeavoring to plunge the nation into an abyss of disaster by preventing it from so preparing as to remove the chance of disaster. France has learned her lesson in the hard school of invasion and necessity; England has been slower to learn, because the war was not in her home territory; and our own politicians, and to a lamentably large degree our own people, are fatuously unable to profit by what has happened, because they lack the power to visualize either the present woe of others or the future danger to themselves. (1916.) *Mem. Ed.* XX, 256; *Nat. Ed.* XVIII, 221.

——————. Let us be true to our democratic ideal, not by the utterance of cheap platitudes, not by windy oratory, but by living our lives in such manner as to show that democracy can be efficient in promoting the public welfare during periods of peace and efficient in securing national freedom in time of war. If a free government cannot organize and maintain armies and navies which can and will fight as well as those of an autocracy or a despotism, it will not survive. We must have a first-class navy and a first-class professional army. We must also secure universal and obligatory military training for all our young men. Our democracy must prove itself effective in making the people healthy, strong, and industrially productive, in securing justice, in inspiring intense patriotism, and in making every man and woman within our borders realize that if they are not willing at time of need to serve the nation against all comers in war, they are not fit to be citizens of the nation in time of peace. (1916.) *Mem. Ed.* XX, 532; *Nat. Ed.* XVIII, 456-457.

PREPAREDNESS. *See also* ARBITRATION; ARMAMENTS; ARMY; BIG STICK; DEFENSE; DISARMAMENT; FIGHTING EDGE; MILITARISM; MILITARY SERVICE; MILITARY TRAINING; NATIONAL DEFENSE; NATIONAL SELF-RELIANCE; NAVAL ARMAMENTS; NAVY; PACIFISM; PEACE; RIGHTEOUSNESS; SOLDIERLY QUALITIES; TRAINING CAMPS; UNPREPAREDNESS; WAR; WEAKNESS; WORLD WAR.

PRESIDENCY. Perhaps the two most striking things in the presidency are the immense power of the President, in the first place; and in the second place, the fact that as soon as he has ceased being President he goes right back into the body of the people and becomes just like any other American citizen. While he is in office he is one of the half-dozen persons throughout the whole world who have most power to affect the destinies of the world.

He can set fleets and armies in motion; he can do more than any save one or two absolute sovereigns to affect the domestic welfare and happiness of scores of millions of people. Then when he goes out of office he takes up his regular round of duties like any other citizen, or if he is of advanced age retires from active life to rest, like any other man who has worked hard to earn his rest. (Written early in 1900; published in *The Youth's Companion*, November 6, 1902.) *Mem. Ed.* XV, 222; *Nat. Ed.* XIII, 313-314.

——————. To me there is something fine in the American theory that a private citizen can be chosen by the people to occupy a position as great as that of the mightiest monarch, and to exercise a power which may for the time being surpass that of Czar, Kaiser, or Pope, and that then, after having filled this position, the man shall leave it as an unpensioned private citizen, who goes back into the ranks of his fellow citizens with entire self-respect, claiming nothing save what on his own individual merits he is entitled to receive. But it is not in the least fine, it is vulgar and foolish, for the President or ex-President to make believe, and, of all things in the world, to feel pleased if other people make believe, that he is a kind of second-rate or imitation king. . . . The effort to combine incompatibles merely makes a man look foolish. The positions of President and King are totally different in kind and degree; and it is silly, and worse than silly, to forget this. It is not of much consequence whether other people accept the American theory of the Presidency; but it is of very much consequence that the American people, including especially any American who has held the office, shall accept the theory and live up to it. (To Sir George Otto Trevelyan, October 1, 1911.) *Mem. Ed.* XXIV, 230-240; Bishop II, 205.

——————. A President has a great chance; his position is almost that of a king and a prime minister rolled into one; once he has left office he cannot do very much; and he is a fool if he fails to realize it all and to be profoundly thankful for having had the great chance. No President ever enjoyed himself in the Presidency as much as I did; and no President after leaving the office took as much joy in life as I am taking. (To Lady Delamere, March 7, 1911.) Lord Charnwood, *Theodore Roosevelt*. (Atlantic Monthly Press, Boston, 1923), p. 223.

[460]

PRESIDENCY—REELECTION TO THE.
Of course I should like to be reelected President, and I shall be disappointed, although not very greatly disappointed, if I am not; and so far as I legitimately can I pay heed to considerations of political expediency—in fact I should be unfit for my position, or for any position of political leadership, if I did not do so. But when questions involve deep and far-reaching principles, then I believe that the real expediency is to be found in straightforward and unflinching adherence to principle, and this without regard to what may be the temporary effect. . . . I should be sorry to lose the Presidency, but I should be a hundredfold more sorry to gain it by failing in every way in my power to try to put a stop to lynching and to brutality and wrong of any kind; or by failing on the one hand to make the very wealthiest and most powerful men in the country obey the law and handle their property (so far as it is in my power to make them) in the public interest; or, on the other hand, to fail to make the laboring men in their turn obey the law, and realize that envy is as evil a thing as arrogance, and that crimes of violence and riot shall be as sternly punished as crimes of greed and cunning. (To Baron d'Estournelles de Constant, September 1, 1903.) *Mem. Ed.* XXIII, 290; Bishop I, 252.

——————. The other day in a very kindly editorial you spoke of me as saying that I would do anything in the world not dishonorable or improper or in violation of my conscience to be reelected as President. I forget the exact word, but this was the sense. It seems to me that this is calculated to convey a somewhat wrong impression of what I said. I do not believe in playing the hypocrite. Any strong man fit to be President would desire a renomination and reelection after his first term. Lincoln was President in so great a crisis that perhaps he neither could nor did feel any personal interest in his own reelection. I trust and believe that if the crisis were a serious one I should be incapable of considering my own well-being for a moment in such a contingency. I should like to be elected President just precisely as John Quincy Adams, or McKinley, or Cleveland, or John Adams, or Washington himself, desired to be elected. It is pleasant to think that one's countrymen thought well of one. But I shall not do anything whatever to secure my nomination or election save to try to carry on the public business in such shape that decent citizens will believe I have shown wisdom, integrity and courage. If they believe this with sufficient emphasis to secure my nomination and election—and on no other terms can I or would I, be willing to secure either—why I shall be glad. If they do not I shall be sorry, but I shall not be very much cast down because I shall feel that I have done the best that was in me, and that there is nothing I have yet done of which I have cause to be ashamed, or which I have cause to regret; and that I can go out of office with the profound satisfaction of having accomplished a certain amount of work that was both beneficial and honorable for the country. (To L. Clarke Davis, fall 1903.) *Mem. Ed.* XXIII, 293; Bishop I, 255.

PRESIDENCY—RESPONSIBILITIES OF THE. Altogether, there are few harder tasks than that of filling well and ably the office of President of the United States. The labor is immense, the ceaseless worry and harassing anxiety are beyond description. But if the man at the close of his term is able to feel that he has done his duty well; that he has solved after the best fashion of which they were capable the great problems with which he was confronted, and has kept clean and in good running order the governmental machinery of the mighty Republic, he has the satisfaction of feeling that he has performed one of the great world-tasks, and that the mere performance is in itself the greatest of all possible rewards. (Written early in 1900; published in *The Youth's Companion*, November 6, 1902.) *Mem. Ed.* XV, 223; *Nat. Ed.* XIII, 314-315.

——————. I know I need not tell you that I appreciate to the full the burdens placed upon me. All that in me lies to do will be done to make my work a success. That I shall be able to solve with entire satisfaction to myself or any one else each of the many problems confronting me, I cannot of course hope for, but I shall do my best in each case, and in a reasonable number of cases I shall hope to meet with success. At any rate, I want you to know one thing. I can conscientiously say that my purpose is entirely single. I want to make a good President and to keep the administration upright and efficient; to follow policies external and internal which shall be for the real and ultimate benefit of our people as a whole, and all party considerations will be absolutely secondary. (To Richard Olney, September 23, 1901.) *Mem. Ed.* XXIII, 175-176; Bishop I, 151.

PRESIDENCY—SUCCESSION TO THE. It is a dreadful thing to come into the Presidency this way; but it would be a far worse thing to be morbid about it. Here is the task, and I have got to do it to the best of my ability; and that is all there is about it. (To H. C.

Lodge, September 23, 1901.) Lodge *Letters* I, 506.

———. On three previous occasions the Vice-President had succeeded to the Presidency on the death of the President. In each case there had been a reversal of party policy, and a nearly immediate and nearly complete change in the personnel of the higher offices, especially the Cabinet. I had never felt that this was wise from any standpoint. If a man is fit to be President, he will speedily so impress himself in the office that the policies pursued will be his anyhow, and he will not have to bother as to whether he is changing them or not; while as regards the offices under him, the important thing for him is that his subordinates shall make a success in handling their several departments. The subordinate is sure to desire to make a success of his department for his own sake, and if he is a fit man, whose views on public policy are sound, and whose abilities entitle him to his position, he will do excellently under almost any chief with the same purposes.

I at once announced that I would continue unchanged McKinley's policies for the honor and prosperity of the country, and I asked all the members of the Cabinet to stay. (1913.) *Mem. Ed.* XXII, 396; *Nat. Ed.* XX, 339.

PRESIDENCY AND THE THIRD TERM ISSUE. A wise custom which limits the President to two terms regards the substance and not the form, and under no circumstances will I be a candidate for or accept another nomination. (Statement, November 8, 1904.) *Mem. Ed.* XXIII, 386; Bishop I, 334.

———. I did not make my announcement that I would not accept another term, without thinking it carefully over and coming to a definite and final conclusion. If you will recall the words I used you will remember that I not merely stated that I would not be a candidate; I added that I would not under any circumstances accept the nomination. And I would not. (To Joseph Bucklin Bishop, March 23, 1905.) *Mem. Ed.* XXIII, 496; Bishop I, 432.

———. Most emphatically, I do not wish to run again for President. As I think I have made this remark in public, and in private letters which were not marked private, several hundred times, in addition to saying it quite as often in private conversation, it really does not seem advisable to say anything more at present. I find that it is absolutely useless to try to correct untruths or misrepresentations even of the most flagrant kind in the newspapers. If I should say anything whatever about not running again it would cause a furore for one week and then the next week they would say I was intriguing for a nomination and would expect a denial. (To W. Emlen Roosevelt, November 9, 1907.) *Mem. Ed.* XXIV, 91; Bishop II, 78.

———. There are still a great many people bound to try to force a third term. As I have tried to explain to them, and as I have succeeded in convincing most of them, my value as an asset to the American people consists chiefly in a belief in my disinterestedness and and trustworthiness, in the belief that I mean what I say, and that my concern is for the good of the country; and if they should now nominate me, even under the circumstances that would force me to take the nomination, I could only take it as the least of two evils, and with the bitter knowledge that many good people would have their faith in me shaken, and that therefore my influence for good would be measurably, and perhaps greatly, diminished. (To Reid, June 13, 1908.) Royal Cortissoz, *The Life of Whitelaw Reid.* (Charles Scribner's Sons, N. Y., 1921), II, 391.

———. There is very much to be said in favor of the theory that the public has a right to demand as long service from any man who is doing good service as it thinks will be useful; and during the last year or two I have been rendered extremely uncomfortable both by the exultation of my foes over my announced intention to retire, and by the real uneasiness and chagrin felt by many good men because, as they believed, they were losing quite needlessly the leader in whom they trusted, and who they believed could bring to a successful conclusion certain struggles which they regarded as of vital concern to the national welfare. Moreover, it was of course impossible to foresee, and I did not foresee, when I made my public announcement of my intention, that the leadership I then possessed would continue (so far as I am able to tell) unbroken, as has actually been the case; and that the people who believed in me and trusted me and followed me would three or four years later still feel that I was the man of all others whom they wished to see President. Yet such I think has been the case; and therefore, when I felt obliged to insist on retiring and abandoning the leadership, now and then I felt ugly qualms as to whether I was not refusing to do what I ought to do and abandoning great work on a mere fantastic point of honor.

There are strong reasons why my course

should be condemned; yet I think that the countervailing reasons are still stronger. Of course, when I spoke I had in view the precedent set by Washington and continued ever since, the precedent which recognizes the fact that as there inheres in the Presidency more power than in any other office in any great republic or constitutional monarchy of modern times, it can only be saved from abuse by having the people as a whole accept as axiomatic the position that no man has held it for more than a limited time. I don't think that any harm comes from the concentration of power in one man's hands, provided the holder does not keep it for more than a certain, definite time, and then returns to the people from whom he sprang. (To Sir George Otto Trevelyan, June 19, 1908.) *Mem. Ed.* XXIV, 107-109; Bishop II, 92-93.

———————. I have thoroughly enjoyed the job. I never felt more vigorous, so far as the work of the office is concerned, and if I had followed my own desires I should have been only too delighted to stay as President. I had said that I would not accept another term, and I believe the people think that my word is good, and I should be mighty sorry to have them think anything else. However, for the very reason that I believe in being a strong President and making the most of the office and using it without regard to the little, feeble, snarling men who yell about executive usurpation, I also believe that it is not a good thing that any one man should hold it too long. (To Sewall, June 25, 1908.) William W. Sewall, *Bill Sewall's Story of T. R.* (Harper & Bros., N. Y., 1919), p. 113.

———————. My theory has been that the presidency should be a powerful office, and the President a powerful man, who will take every advantage of it; but, as a corollary, a man who can be held accountable to the people, after a term of four years, and who will not in any event occupy it for more than a stretch of eight years. (To Corinne Roosevelt Robinson, June 26, 1908.) Robinson, *My Brother Theodore Roosevelt*, 244.

———————. It is so easy for a man to deceive himself into doing what others want him to do when it coincides with his own wishes. In my own case, I could so easily have persuaded myself that I was really needed to carry out my own policies. I sometimes felt that it was weakness which made me adhere to my resolution, taken nearly four years ago now. Nine-tenths of my reasoning bade me accept another term, and only one-tenth, but that one-tenth was the still small voice, kept me firm. (Recorded by Butt in letter of October 10, 1908.) *The Letters of Archie Butt, Personal Aide to President Roosevelt.* (Doubleday, Page & Co., Garden City, N. Y., 1924), p. 125.

———————. I am the only man in the United States who can speak of the presidency without the thrill that always comes to the man who has never been in the White House. To go to the White House simply for the sake of being President doesn't interest me in the least. There are so many things that I haven't yet done and that I want so much to do. I want to take some time now, in the next few years, to do some of those things. I have done something in geography and something in ornithology, and something in other lines. I want to put myself in position where I can be rightfully recognized as a scientist in one or two of these lines.

Most men in this country think of the presidency as the supreme thing, and that is natural and all right. But I've had that, and another term could not add anything to what I have had there. Of course, if there were a big job of work to be done, which the people of the country wanted me to handle, that would be a different thing. But then it would be going back in order to do a particular thing, and one that I had not done before. It would not be going back simply for the sake of being President again. There is a far greater probability that another term in the White House, unless under the exceptional conditions I spoke about, would detract from my record, than there is that it would add to the record. (August 24, 1910, reported by Davis.) Oscar King Davis, *Released for Publication.* (Houghton Mifflin Co., Boston, 1925), pp. 200-201.

———————. I've had eight years of the Presidency. I know all the honor and pleasure of it and all of its sorrows and dangers. I have nothing more to gain by being President again and I have a great deal to lose. I am *not* going to do it, unless I get a mandate from the American people. (In conversation with Herbert Knox Smith, 1911.) *Mem. Ed.* XIX, xiv; *Nat. Ed.* XVII, xiii.

———————. The Presidency is a great office, and the power of the President can be effectively used to secure a renomination, especially if the President has the support of certain great political and financial interests. It is for this reason, and this reason alone, that the wholesome principle of continuing in office, so

[463]

long as he is willing to serve, an incumbent who has proved capable, is not applicable to the Presidency. Therefore, the American people have wisely established a custom against allowing any man to hold that office for more than two consecutive terms. But every shred of power which a President exercises while in office vanishes absolutely when he has once left office. An ex-President stands precisely in the position of any other private citizen, and has not one particle more power to secure a nomination or election than if he had never held the office at all—indeed, he probably has less because of the very fact that he has held the office. Therefore the reasoning on which the anti-third term custom is based has no application whatever to an ex-President, and no application whatever to anything except consecutive terms. As a barrier of precaution against more than two consecutive terms the custom embodies a valuable principle. Applied in any other way it becomes a mere formula, and like all formulas a potential source of mischievous confusion. (1913.) *Mem. Ed.* XXII, 441; *Nat. Ed.* XX, 379.

——————. I believe that it is well to have a custom of this kind, to be generally observed, but that it would be very unwise to have it definitely hardened into a Constitutional prohibition. It is not desirable ordinarily that a man should stay in office twelve consecutive years as President; but most certainly the American people are fit to take care of themselves, and stand in no need of an irrevocable self-denying ordinance. They should not bind themselves never to take action which under some quite conceivable circumstances it might be to their great interest to take. It is obviously of the last importance to the safety of a democracy that in time of real peril it should be able to command the service of every one among its citizens in the precise position where the service rendered will be most valuable. It would be a benighted policy in such event to disqualify absolutely from the highest office a man who while holding it had actually shown the highest capacity to exercise its powers with the utmost effect for the public defense. If, for instance, a tremendous crisis occurred at the end of the second term of a man like Lincoln, as such a crisis occurred at the end of his first term, it would be a veritable calamity if the American people were forbidden to continue to use the services of the one man whom they knew, and did not merely guess, could carry them through the crisis. The third term tradition has no value whatever except as it applies to a third consecutive term. While it is well to keep it as a custom, it would be a mark both of weakness and unwisdom for the American people to embody it into a Constitutional provision which could not do them good and on some given occasion might work real harm. (1913.) *Mem. Ed.* XXII, 442-443; *Nat. Ed.* XX, 379-380.

PRESIDENT—CONGRESS AND THE. It is eminently desirable that the President and the majority leaders in Congress shall be in such touch that the President will back whatever legislation they put through and will not veto it, even though, as of course must be the case, he continually disapproves of things more or less substantial in the various bills. (To H. C. Lodge, July 18, 1905.) *Lodge Letters* II, 169.

——————. I have a very strong feeling that it is a President's duty to get on with Congress if he possibly can, and that it is a reflection upon him if he and Congress come to a complete break. For seven sessions I was able to prevent such a break. This session, however, they felt that it was safe utterly to disregard me because I was going out and my successor had been elected; and I made up my mind that it was just a case where the exception to the rule applied and that if I did not fight and fight hard, I should be put in a contemptible position; while inasmuch as I was going out on the fourth of March I did not have to pay heed to our ability to co-operate in the future. The result has, I think, justified my wisdom. I have come out ahead so far, and I have been full President right up to the end, which hardly any other President has ever been. (To Theodore Roosevelt, Jr., January 31, 1909.) *Mem. Ed.* XXIV, 156; Bishop II, 134.

PRESIDENT—CRITICISM OF THE. The President is merely the most important among a large number of public servants. He should be supported or opposed exactly to the degree which is warranted by his good conduct or bad conduct, his efficiency or inefficiency in rendering loyal, able, and disinterested service to the Nation as a whole. Therefore it is absolutely necessary that there should be full liberty to tell the truth about his acts, and this means that it is exactly necessary to blame him when he does wrong as to praise him when he does right. Any other attitude in an American citizen is both base and servile. To announce that there must be no criticism of the President, or that we are to stand by the President, right or wrong, is not only unpatriotic and servile, but is morally treasonable to the American public. Nothing but the truth should be spoken about him or any one else. But it is even more important to tell the truth, pleasant or unpleasant, about him than about any one else. (May 7, 1918.) *Roosevelt in the Kansas City Star,* 149.

PRESIDENT—DUTY OF THE. [I] am ready and eager to do my part, so far as I am able, in solving the problems which must be solved, if we of this, the greatest democratic Republic upon which the sun has ever shone, are to see its destinies rise to the high level of our hopes and its opportunities. This is the duty of every citizen; but it is peculiarly my duty, for any man who has ever been honored by being made President of the United States is thereby forever after rendered the debtor of the American people, and is in honor bound throughout his life to remember this as his prime obligation; and in private life, as much as in public life, so to carry himself that the American people may never have cause to feel regret that once they placed him at their head. (Remarks on return from Africa and Europe, June 18, 1910.) *Mem. Ed.* XIX, 5; *Nat. Ed.* XVII, 3.

—————————. It is one of the chief duties —and it is the highest privilege—of a President of the United States to be the active leader and exponent of policies which will help the people to obtain such legislative and administrative reforms as are required to meet any reasonable popular demand which makes for the common good. *Outlook,* April 20, 1912, p. 852.

—————————. The President's duty is to act so that he himself and his subordinates shall be able to do efficient work for the people, and this efficient work he and they cannot do if Congress is permitted to undertake the task of making up his mind for him as to how he shall perform what is clearly his sole duty. (1913.) *Mem. Ed.* XXII, 414; *Nat. Ed.* XX, 355.

PRESIDENT—LOYALTY TO THE. Our loyalty is due entirely to the United States. It is due to the President only and exactly to the degree in which he efficiently serves the United States. It is our duty to support him when he serves the United States well. It is our duty to oppose him when he serves it badly. This is true about Mr. Wilson now and it has been true about all our Presidents in the past. It is our duty at all times to tell the truth about the President and about every one else, save in the cases where to tell the truth at the moment would benefit the public enemy. (1918.) *Mem. Ed.* XXI, 325; *Nat. Ed.* XIX, 297.

PRESIDENT—POWERS OF THE. The theory which I have called the Jackson-Lincoln theory of the Presidency [implies] . . . that occasionally great national crises arise which call for immediate and vigorous executive action, and that in such cases it is the duty of the President to act upon the theory that he is the steward of the people, and that the proper attitude for him to take is that he is bound to assume that he has the legal right to do whatever the needs of the people demand, unless the Constitution or the laws explicitly forbid him to do it. (1913.) *Mem. Ed.* XXII, 530; *Nat. Ed.* XX, 455.

—————————. Although many men must share with the President the responsibility for different individual actions, and although Congress must of course also very largely condition his usefulness, yet the fact remains that in his hands is infinitely more power than in the hands of any other man in our country during the time that he holds the office; that there is upon him always a heavy burden of responsibility; and that in certain crises this burden may become so great as to bear down any but the strongest and bravest man.

It is easy enough to give a bad administration; but to give a good administration demands the most anxious thought, the most wearing endeavor, no less than very unusual powers of mind. The chances for error are limitless, and in minor matters, where from the nature of the case it is absolutely inevitable that the President should rely upon the judgment of others, it is certain that under the best Presidents some errors will be committed. (Written early in 1900; published in *The Youth's Companion,* November 6, 1902.) *Mem. Ed.* XV, 216; *Nat. Ed.* XIII, 308-309.

—————————. Now, my ambition is that, in however small a way, the work I do shall be along the Washington and Lincoln lines. While President I have *been* President, emphatically; I have used every ounce of power there was in the office and I have not cared a rap for the criticisms of those who spoke of my 'usurpation of power'; for I know that the talk was all nonsense and that there was no usurpation. I believe that the efficiency of this Government depends upon its possessing a strong central executive, and wherever I could establish a precedent for strength in the executive, as I did for instance as regards the external affairs in the case of sending the fleet around the world, taking Panama, settling affairs of Santo Domingo and Cuba; or as I did in internal affairs in settling the anthracite-coal strike, in keeping order in Nevada this year when the Federation of Miners threatened anarchy, or as I have done in bringing the big corporations to book—why, in all these cases I have felt not merely that my action was right in itself, but that in showing the strength of, or in giving strength to, the executive, I was establishing a precedent of value. I believe in a strong executive; I believe in power; but I believe that responsibility should go with power, and that it is not well that the strong executive should be a perpetual executive. Above all and beyond all I believe as I have said before that the salvation of this country depends upon Washington and Lincoln representing the type of leader to which we are true. I hope that in my acts I have been a good President, a President who has deserved well of the Republic; but most of all, I believe that whatever value my service may have, comes even more from what I am than from what I do. (To Sir George Otto Trevelyan, June 19, 1908.) *Mem. Ed.* XXIV, 110; Bishop II, 94.

——————. I have a definite philosophy about the Presidency. I think it should be a very powerful office, and I think the President should be a very strong man who uses without hesitation every power that the position yields; but because of this very fact I believe that he should be sharply watched by the people, held to a strict accountability by them, and that he should not keep the office too long. (To H. C. Lodge, July 19, 1908.) Lodge *Letters* II, 304.

——————. My view was that every executive officer, and above all every executive officer in high position, was a steward of the people bound actively and affirmatively to do all he could for the people, and not to content himself with the negative merit of keeping his talents undamaged in a napkin. I declined to adopt the view that what was imperatively necessary for the nation could not be done by the President unless he could find some specific authorization to do it. My belief was that it was not only his right but his duty to do anything that the needs of the nation demanded unless such action was forbidden by the Constitution or by the laws. Under this interpretation of executive power I did and caused to be done many things not previously done by the President and the heads of the departments. I did not usurp power, but I did greatly broaden the use of executive power. In other words, I acted for the public welfare, I acted for the common well-being of all our people, whenever and in whatever manner was necessary, unless prevented by direct constitutional or legislative prohibition. I did not care a rap for the mere form and show of power; I cared immensely for the use that could be made of the substance. (1913.) *Mem. Ed.* XXII, 404-405; *Nat. Ed.* XX, 347-348.

PRESIDENT — ROOSEVELT AS. One thing I want you to understand at the start— I feel myself just as much a constitutionally elected President of the United States as McKinley was. I was voted for as Vice-President, it is true, but the Constitution provides that in case of the death or inability of the President the Vice-President shall serve as President, and therefore, due to the act of a madman, I am President and shall act in every word and deed precisely as if I and not McKinley had been the candidate for whom the electors cast the vote for President. I have no superstitions and no misgivings on that score. That should be understood. (Statement to newspaper correspondents, September 1901.) David S. Barry, *Forty Years in Washington.* (Little, Brown & Co., Boston, 1924), p. 267.

——————. I don't know anything about seven years. But this I do know—I am going to be President for three years, and I am going to do my utmost to give the country a good President during that period. I am going to be full President, and I would rather be full President for three years than half a President for seven years. Now, mind you, I am no second Grover Cleveland. I admire certain of his qualities, but I have no intention of doing with the Republican party what he did with the Democratic party. I intend to work with my party and to make it strong by making it worthy of popular support. (In conversation with Joseph B. Bishop, September 20, 1901.) *Mem. Ed.* XXIII, 174; Bishop I, 150.

——————. I am going to be President of the United States and not of any section. (In conversation with Southern Congressmen, September 21, 1901.) *Mem. Ed.* XXIII, 179; Bishop I, 154.

——————. Most emphatically I shall endeavor to do absolute justice. But you must let me say that in doing justice I should be ashamed to take into consideration whether what I did was popular or not. I hope I shall not have to take any part at all in a matter that purely refers to President McKinley's administration, and with which I have nothing whatever to do; but if I do have to take it up I shall decide the case absolutely on its merits, and I shall no more consider whether a majority of the people are for or against a given man than I should consider it if I were a judge sitting upon the bench deciding the rights or wrongs of a particular case. (To a Western editor, December 10, 1901.) *Mem. Ed.* XXIII, 198-199; Bishop I, 172.

——————. I suppose few Presidents can form the slightest idea whether their policies have met with approval or not—certainly I cannot. But as far as I can see those policies have been right, and I hope that time will justify them. If it does not, why, I must abide the fall of the dice, and that is all there is about it. (To Corinne Roosevelt Robinson, September 23, 1903.) *Mem. Ed.* XXIII, 292; Bishop I, 254.

——————. I enjoy being President, and I like to do the work and have my hand on the lever. But it is very worrying and puzzling, and I have to make up my mind to accept every kind of attack and misrepresentation. (To Kermit Roosevelt, October 2, 1903.) *Mem. Ed.* XXI, 501; *Nat. Ed.* XIX, 444.

——————. I certainly would not be willing to hold the Presidency at the cost of failing to do the things which make the real reason why I care to hold it at all. I had much rather be a real President for three years and a half than a figurehead for seven years and a half. I think I can truthfully say that I now have to my credit a sum of substantial achievement—and the rest must take care of itself. (To Sir George Otto Trevelyan, May 28, 1904.) *Mem. Ed.* XXIV, 161; Bishop II, 138.

——————. I have done a good many things in the past three years, and the fact that I did them is doubtless due partly to accident and partly to temperament. Naturally, I think I was right in doing them, for otherwise I would not have done them. It is equally natural that some people should have been alienated by each thing I did, and the aggregate of all that have been alienated may be more than sufficient to overthrow me. (To Rudyard Kipling, November 1, 1904.) *Mem. Ed.* XXIII, 383; Bishop I, 332.

——————. Of course I greatly enjoyed inauguration day, and indeed I have thoroughly enjoyed being President. But I believe I can also say that I am thoroughly alive to the tremendous responsibilities of my position. Life is a long campaign where every victory merely leaves the ground free for another battle, and sooner or later defeat comes to every man, unless death forestalls it. But the final defeat does not and should not cancel the triumphs, if the latter have been substantial and for a cause worth championing. (To Sir George Otto Trevelyan, March 9, 1905.) *Mem. Ed.* XXIV, 171; Bishop II, 146.

——————. No man is fit to hold the position of President of the United States at all unless as President he feels that he represents no party but the people as a whole. So far as in me lies I have tried and shall try so to handle myself that every decent American citizen can feel that I have at least made the effort. Each man has got to carry out his own principles in his own way. If he tries to model himself on some one else he will make a poor show of it. My own view has been that if I must choose between taking risks by not doing a thing or by doing it, I will take the risks of doing it. (At banquet, Dallas, Tex., April 5, 1905.) *Presidential Addresses and State Papers* III, 320.

——————. I have finished my career in public life; I have enjoyed it to the full; I have achieved a large proportion of what I set out to achieve; and I am almost ashamed to say that I do not mind in the least retiring to private life. No President has ever enjoyed himself as much as I have enjoyed myself, and for the matter of that I do not know any man of my age who has had as good a time. Of course if I had felt that I could conscientiously keep on in the Presidency I should have dearly liked to have tried again; and I shall miss a very little having my hands on the levers of the great machine; but I am really almost uneasy to find that I do not mind the least bit in the world getting out. (To E. S. Martin, November 6, 1908.) *Mem. Ed.* XXIV, 144; Bishop II, 123.

——————. The most important factor in getting the right spirit in my Administration, next to the insistence upon courage, honesty, and a genuine democracy of desire to serve the plain people, was my insistence upon the theory that the executive power was limited only by specific restrictions and prohibitions appearing in the Constitution or imposed by the Congress under its Constitutional powers. (1913.) *Mem. Ed.* XXII, 404; *Nat. Ed.* XX, 347.

——————. In internal affairs I cannot say that I entered the Presidency with any deliberately planned and far-reaching scheme of social betterment. I had, however, certain strong convictions; and I was on the lookout for every opportunity of realizing those convictions. I was bent upon making the government the most efficient possible instrument in helping the people of the United States to better themselves in every way, politically, socially, and industrially. I believed with all my heart in real and thoroughgoing democracy, and I wished to make this democracy industrial as well as political, although I had only partially formulated the methods I believed we should follow. I believed in the people's rights, and therefore in national rights and States' rights just exactly to the degree in which they severally secured popular rights. I believed in invoking the national power with absolute freedom for every national need; and I believed that the Constitution should be treated as the greatest document ever devised by the wit of man to aid a people in exercising every power necessary for its own betterment, and not as a straitjacket cunningly fashioned to strangle growth. As for the particular methods of realizing these various beliefs, I was content to wait and see what method might be necessary in each given case as it arose; and I was certain that the cases would arise fast enough. (1913.) *Mem. Ed.* XXII, 438; *Nat. Ed.* XX, 376.

——————. Of course, we can never be absolutely certain, but my usefulness to this country depended so largely upon conditions of national and international politics that its real need of me has probably passed. My great usefulness as President came in connection with the Anthracite Coal Strike, the voyage of the battle fleet around the world, the taking of Panama, the handling of Germany in the Venezuela business, England in the Alaska boundary matter, the irrigation business in the West, and finally, I think, the toning up of the Government service generally. (To E. A. Van Valkenburg, September 5, 1916.) *Mem. Ed.* XXIV, 486; Bishop II, 413.

PRESIDENT—THE PEOPLE AND THE. Any man who has occupied the office of President realizes the incredible amount of administrative work with which the President has to deal even in time of peace. He is of necessity a very busy man, a much-driven man, from whose mind there can never be absent, for many minutes at a time, the consideration of some problem of importance, or of some matter of less importance which yet causes worry and strain. Under such circumstances, it is not easy for a President, even in times of peace, to turn from the affairs that are of moment to all the people and consider affairs that are of moment to but one person. (To the Editor of the *Review of Reviews,* January 1, 1909.) Ferdinand C. Iglehart, *Theodore Roosevelt, The Man As I Knew Him.* (The Christian Herald, N. Y., 1919), p. 30.

——————. The course I followed, of regarding the executive as subject only to the people, and, under the Constitution, bound to serve the people affirmatively in cases where the Constitution does not explicitly forbid him to render the service, was substantially the course followed by both Andrew Jackson and Abraham Lincoln. Other honorable and well-meaning Presidents, such as James Buchanan, took the opposite and, as it seems to me, narrowly legalistic view that the President is the servant of Congress rather than of the people, and can do nothing, no matter how necessary it be to act, unless the Constitution explicitly commands the action. Most able lawyers who are past middle-age take this view, and so do large numbers of well-meaning, respectable citizens. (1913.) *Mem. Ed.* XXII, 411; *Nat. Ed.* XX, 352.

PRESIDENT—TITLE OF THE. I would rather not be called Excellency, and this partly because the title does not belong to me and partly from vanity! The President of the United States ought to have no title; and if he did have a title it ought to be a bigger one. Whenever an important prince comes here he is apt to bring a shoal of "Excellencies" in his train. Just as I should object to having the simple dignity of the White House changed for such attractions as might lie in a second-rate palace, so I feel that the President of a great democratic republic should have no title but President. He could not have a title that would not be either too much or too little. Let him be called the President, and nothing more. (To Sir George Otto Trevelyan, May 13, 1905.) *Mem. Ed.* XXIV, 174; Bishop II, 148-149.

PRESIDENT AND HIS SUBORDINATES. The Jackson-Lincoln view is that a President who is fit to do good work should be able to form his own judgment as to his own subordinates, and, above all, of the subordinates standing highest and in closest and most intimate touch with him. My secretaries and their subordinates were responsible to me, and I accepted the responsibility for all their deeds. As long as they were satisfactory to me I stood by them against every critic or assailant, within or without Congress; and as for getting Congress to make up my mind for me about them, the thought would have been inconceivable to me. (1913.) *Mem. Ed.* XXII, 413; *Nat. Ed.* XX, 354.

PRESIDENT. See also CABINET; DIVISION OF POWERS; EXECUTIVE; GOVERNMENT; LESE MAJESTY; ROOSEVELT'S POLITICAL CAREER; SECRET SERVICE; WHITE HOUSE.

PRESIDENTIAL ELECTIONS. See ELECTION OF 1884; 1896; 1900; 1904; 1908; 1912; 1916.

PRESIDENTS — POSITION OF FORMER. When people have spoken to me as to what America should do with its ex-Presidents, I have always answered that there was one ex-President as to whom they need not concern themselves in the least, because I would do for myself. It would be to me personally an unpleasant thing to be pensioned and given some honorary position. I emphatically do not desire to clutch at the fringe of departing greatness. Indeed, to me there is something rather attractive, something in the way of living up to a proper democratic ideal, in having a President go out of office just as I shall go, and become absolutely and without reservation a private man, and do any honorable work which he finds to do. (To John St. Loe Strachey, November 28, 1908.) *Mem. Ed.* XXIV, 146; Bishop II, 125.

——————————. When I start on this African trip I shall have ceased to be President, and shall be simply a private citizen, like any other private citizen. Not only do I myself believe, but I am firmly convinced that the great mass of the American people believe, that when the President leaves public office he should become exactly like any other man in private life. He is entitled to no privileges, but, on the other hand, he is also entitled to be treated no worse than any one else. Now, it will be an indefensible wrong, a gross impropriety from every standpoint, for any newspaper to endeavor to have its representatives accompany me on this trip, or to fail to give me the complete privacy to which every citizen who acts decently and behaves himself is entitled. (To Melville E. Stone, December 2, 1908.) *Mem. Ed.* XXIV, 143; Bishop II, 123.

PRESIDENTS. See also CLEVELAND, GROVER; GRANT, U. S.; HARRISON, BENJAMIN; JACKSON, ANDREW; JEFFERSON, THOMAS; LINCOLN, ABRAHAM; MCKINLEY, WILLIAM; MADISON, JAMES; TAFT, W. H.; TYLER, JOHN; VAN BUREN, MARTIN; WASHINGTON, GEORGE; WILSON, WOODROW.

PRESS—CONTROL OF THE. The big newspaper, owned or controlled in Wall Street, which is everlastingly preaching about the iniquity of laboring men, which is quite willing to hound politicians for their misdeeds, but which with raving fury defends all the malefactors of great wealth, stands on an exact level with, and neither above nor below, that other newspaper whose whole attack is upon men of wealth, which declines to condemn, or else condemns in an apologetic, perfunctory, and wholly inefficient manner, outrages committed by labor. *Outlook,* June 19, 1909, p. 395.

——————————. That portion of the daily press which is controlled by the special interests, and particularly that portion of the New York City daily press which is responsive to Wall Street sentiment, has come to regard the judiciary as in a special sense the bulwark of property; and inasmuch as the special interests naturally put property rights above popular rights, their representatives in the press make it their particular concern to extol those judges who take the same view. They are therefore very severe in their denunciations of any man who has anything to say in criticism of a judicial decision which favors property rights and is against popular rights. But if the decision is the other way, the same papers and individuals immediately reverse their former attitude and themselves become the most violent and bitter critics of the judge. (*Outlook,* February 25, 1911.) *Mem. Ed.* XIX, 113; *Nat. Ed.* XVII, 76.

——————————. In New York City the press, directly or indirectly influenced by and responsive to those special interests which are as a matter of rough convenience designated as the Wall Street interests, is naturally very large, and any man engaged in the effort to bring about a genuine betterment of social, political, and industrial conditions, especially if he lives in New York or the neighborhood, must accept as a matter of course the virulent hostility of this portion of the press; and the hostility shown by certain papers which pride themselves upon representing the educated classes is marked by as much mendacity as is the case with the newspapers which are frankly "yellow." (*Outlook,* March 25, 1911.) *Mem. Ed.* XIX, 144; *Nat. Ed.* XVII, 103.

——————————. We who in this contest are fighting for the rights of the plain people, we who are fighting for the right of the people to rule themselves, need offer no better proof of the fact that we are fighting for all citizens, no matter what their politics, than that which is afforded by the action of that portion of the press which is controlled by privilege, by the great special interests in business. Newspapers of this type are found in every part of the country, in San Francisco, in Cincinnati, in Chicago and St. Louis, in Boston and Philadelphia. But they are strongest in New York. Some of these newspapers are nominally Democratic, some nominally Republican, some nominally independent. But in reality they are true only to the real or fancied interests of the great capitalist class by certain of whose members they are controlled. Sometimes the interests of this capitalist class are identical with those of the country as a whole, and in that case these papers serve the interests of the commonwealth. Sometimes the interests of the capitalist class are against the interests of the people as a whole, and in that case these papers are hostile to the interests of the commonwealth. But neither their acting favorably to nor their acting adversely to the interests of the commonwealth is anything more than an incident to their support of the interests to which they are bound. The great and far-reaching evil of their action is that they choke and foul the only channels of information open to so many honest and well-meaning citizens. (At Chicago, June 17, 1912.) *Mem. Ed.* XIX, 311, *Nat. Ed.* XVII, 226.

PRESS—INFLUENCE OF THE. Our newspapers, including those who professedly stand as representatives of the highest culture of the community, have been in the habit of making such constant and reckless assaults upon the characters of even very good public men, as to greatly detract from their influence when they attack one who is really bad. They paint every one with whom they disagree black. As a consequence the average man, who knows they are partly wrong, thinks they may also be partly right; he concludes that no man is absolutely white, and at the same time that no one is as black as he is painted; and takes refuge in the belief that all alike are gray. It then becomes impossible to rouse him to make an effort either for a good man or against a scoundrel. Nothing helps dishonest politicians as much as this feeling; and among the chief instruments in its production we must number certain of our newspapers who are loudest in asserting that they stand on the highest moral plane. As for the other newspapers, those of frankly "sensational" character, such as the two which at present claim to have the largest circulation in New York, there is small need to characterize them; they form a very great promotive to public corruption and private vice, and are on the whole the most potent of all the forces for evil which are at work in the city. (*Century*, January 1885.) *Mem. Ed.* XV, 91; *Nat. Ed.* XIII, 56.

PRESS—LIBERTY OF THE. I think that if there is one thing we ought to be careful about it is in regard to interfering with the liberty of the press. We have all of us at times suffered from the liberty of the press, but we have to take the good and the bad. I think we certainly ought to hesitate very seriously before passing any law that will interfere with the broadest public utterance. I think it is a great deal better to err a little bit on the side of having too much discussion and having too virulent language used by the press, rather than to err on the side of having them not say what they ought to say, especially with reference to public men and measures. (In New York Assembly, March 27, 1883.) *Mem. Ed.* XVI, 30; *Nat. Ed.* XIV, 22.

PRESS. *See also* DEMOCRACY; EDITORS; FOREIGN LANGUAGE PRESS; FREE SPEECH; JOURNALISM; JOURNALIST; MUCK-RAKING; SLANDER.

PRESSURE GROUPS. *See* PRIVILEGE; SPECIAL INTERESTS.

PRIMARIES—ADVOCACY OF. We should at once introduce in this State the system of direct nominations in the primaries, so that the people shall be able themselves to decide who the candidates shall be, instead of being limited merely to choosing between candidates with whose nomination they have had nothing to do. (Before New York Republican State Convention, Saratoga, September 27, 1910.) *Mem. Ed.* XIX, 36; *Nat. Ed.* XVII, 28.

——————. I believe in providing for direct nominations by the people, including therein direct preferential primaries for the election of delegates to the national nominating conventions. Not as a matter of theory, but as a matter of plain and proved experience, we find that the convention system, while it often records the popular will, is also often used by adroit politicians as a method of thwarting the popular will. In other words, the existing machinery for nominations is cumbrous, and is not designed to secure the real expression of the popular desire. Now, as good citizens we are all of us willing to acquiesce cheerfully in a nomination secured by the expression of a majority of the people, but we do not like to acquiesce in a nomination secured by adroit political management in defeating the wish of the majority of the people. (Before Ohio Constitutional Convention, Columbus, February 21, 1912.) *Mem. Ed.* XIX, 179; *Nat. Ed.* XVII, 133.

——————. The movement for direct primaries is spreading fast. Whether it shall apply to all elective officials or to certain categories of them is a matter which must be decided by the actual experience of each State when the working of the scheme is tested in practice. (*Outlook,* January 21, 1911.) *Mem. Ed.* XIX, 88; *Nat. Ed.* XVII, 55.

PRIMARIES—EXPERIENCE WITH. If the direct primary merely means additional expense without compensating advantage in wise and just action, the gain will be nil. At present there are cities where the direct primary obtains, in which, as far as I can see, the boss system is about as firmly rooted as in those cities where the direct primary has not been introduced. (*Outlook,* January 21, 1911.) *Mem. Ed.* XIX, 98; *Nat. Ed.* XVII, 64.

——————. It is instructive to compare the votes of States where there were open primaries and the votes of States where there were not. In Illinois, Pennsylvania, and Ohio we had direct primaries, and the Taft machine was beaten two to one. Between and bordering on these States were Michigan, Indiana, and Kentucky. In these States we could not get direct primaries, and the politicians elected two delegates to our one. In the first three States the contests were absolutely open, absolutely honest. The rank and file expressed their wishes, and there was no taint of fraud about what they did. In the other three States the contest was marked by every species of fraud and violence on the part of our opponents, and half the Taft delegates in the Chicago Convention from these States had tainted titles. The entire Wall Street press at this moment is vigorously engaged in denouncing the direct primary system and upholding the old convention system, or, as they call it, the "old representative system." They are so doing because they know that the bosses and the powers of special privilege have tenfold the chance under the convention system that they have when the rank and file of the people can express themselves at the primaries. The nomination of Mr. Taft at Chicago was a fraud upon the rank and file of the Republican party; it was obtained only by defrauding the rank and file of the party of their right to express their choice; and such fraudulent action does not bind a single honest member of the party. (Before Progressive National Convention, Chicago, August 6, 1912.) *Mem. Ed.* XIX, 366; *Nat. Ed.* XVII, 266.

PRIMARIES—OBJECT OF. In the State the primary should be of the simplest form (consistent with preventing fraud) that will enable each individual voter to act directly on the nomination of elective officers; in the Nation Presidential primaries should be so framed that the voters may choose their delegates to the National conventions, and at the same time express their *preference* for nominees for the Presidency. At the present moment our political machines are using their power to defraud the people out of their right to make nominations. *Outlook,* March 30, 1912, p. 720.

——————. Then there is the direct primary—the real one, not the New York one—and that, too, the Progressives offer as a check on the special interests. Most clearly of all does it seem to me that this change is wholly good—for every State. The system of party government is not written in our constitutions, but it is none the less a vital and essential part of our form of government. In that system the party leaders should serve and carry out the will of their own party. There is no need to show how far that theory is from the facts, or to rehearse the vulgar thieving partnerships of the corporations and the bosses, or to show how many times the real government lies in the hands of the boss, protected from the commands and the revenge of the voters by his puppets in office and the power of patronage. We need not be told how he is thus intrenched nor how hard he is to overthrow. The facts stand out in the history of nearly every State in the Union. They are blots on our political system. The direct primary will give the voters a method ever ready to use, by which the party leader shall be made to obey their command. The direct primary, if accompanied by a stringent corrupt-practices act, will help break up the corrupt partnership of corporations and politicians. (At Carnegie Hall, New York City, March 20, 1912.) *Mem. Ed.* XIX, 203; *Nat. Ed.* XVII, 153.

PRIMARIES AND PARTY CONTROL. The principle of direct primaries is essential to proper party control. . . . The prime and simple reason for direct primaries is that the average voter must have the right to choose his own leaders. We do not propose to do away with organization or with leadership, but we propose to make the organization and the leadership responsive to the demands of the average citizen. We propose that a leader shall really be a leader and not a driver; and the only way to make him a leader instead of a driver is to give the average man complete power within his party organization, which power can be secured for him through the direct primary and through the direct primary alone. This would make the leader far more wary than at present of disregarding popular feeling; ordinarily he would lead, just as at present; but the people would have what they do not now have, the power to assert their wishes over him whenever they became sufficiently stirred. *Outlook,* July 12, 1913, pp. 555-556.

PRIMITIVE MAN. *See* IMPERIALISM; INDIANS; NATURE.

PRIMITIVE SOCIETY—STUDY OF. The scientific study of the origins of primitive society and of the ruder cultures has in the past fifty years come to assume a high importance. Already the slowly gathered results of the work of the archaeologist, the ethnographer, and the physical anthropologist are in various ways, direct as well as indirect, profoundly influencing popular opinion. Sometimes consciously, more often unconsciously, our views on many vital questions are being modified by conclusions reached by specialists in these fields of research. Their discoveries and conclusions are such as cannot today be ignored by any of the men on whose activities intellectual and moral progress depends. This is especially true of the social workers, the economists, the historians, and those merchants, missionaries, and administrators who are confronted with the problems which invariably arise as soon as civilized nations are brought into contact with savage or barbarous races.

Yet many intelligent men, especially among those who delight to style themselves "practical," are entirely unconscious of the deep importance of this new knowledge. Such men, even though they may appreciate certain types of learning, regard the time spent in the investigation of prehistoric or ancient civilizations, or of the wearisome and often repellent details of modern savagery, as time wasted. The man of limited mental horizon and defective imagination is apt to ask himself what antiquity has to do with us of today, or what good is gained by costly and sometimes perilous expeditions sent to remote parts of the earth for the purpose of recording the habits of foul or dangerous barbarians. . . . Man needs to know the truth about himself—as much of it, that is, as he can grasp—if he is to make the most of himself. It is only by the painstaking collection of the details of old civilizations, by the patient working out of the rude racial and cultural beginnings which led up to the ancient civilizations, and by studying races yet in their childhood, that the modern investigator can comprehend the nature of the remote past from which we of today have sprung, and from which we are separated by a wide gulf of time and change. Only thus can we grow to understand the laws—or some of the laws—by which that progress has been governed. (Introduction, dated August 10, 1916.) *Harvard African Studies I, Varia Africana I.* (Peabody Museum, Cambridge, Mass., 1917.)

PRISONERS. See CONVICT LABOR; CRIMINALS.

PRIVILEGE. We must set our faces against privilege; just as much against the kind of privilege which would let the shiftless and lazy laborer take what his brother has earned as against the privilege which allows the huge capitalist to take toll to which he is not entitled. (*Outlook,* March 27, 1909.) *Mem. Ed.* XVIII, 569; *Nat. Ed.* XIX, 112.

―――――――――. Privilege should not be tolerated because it is to the advantage of a minority; nor yet because it is to the advantage of a majority. (At Oxford University, June 7, 1910.) *Mem. Ed.* XIV, 102; *Nat. Ed.* XII, 56.

―――――――――. We will not submit to privilege in the form of wealth. Just as little will we submit to the privilege of a mob. (1918.) *Mem. Ed.* XXI, 381; *Nat. Ed.* XIX, 346.

PRIVILEGE—DEFENDERS OF. In private most of the beneficiaries of special privilege, and not a few other persons, freely defend it; advancing the usual argument, that only a limited number of persons are fit to lead humanity, and that these persons should be permitted to accumulate wealth and power without let or hindrance, because this is really to the benefit of everybody—a position by the way, fundamentally identical with that of the *laissez faire* school of economists who until recently held unchecked sway in so many institutions of learning. In a nation founded on the principle of popular government such a position as this cannot be publicly upheld by public men. *Outlook,* January 28, 1911, p. 145.

―――――――――. In attacking special privilege, in attacking the great moneyed interests which have exercised so sinister a control over our political and social life, we have to count not only upon the open and avowed opposition of our enemies, but on their much more dangerous indirect opposition. (*Outlook,* March 25, 1911.) *Mem. Ed.* XIX, 144; *Nat. Ed.* XVII, 103.

PRIVILEGE—DESTRUCTION OF. In every wise struggle for human betterment one of the main objects, and often the only object, has been to achieve in large measure equality of opportunity. In the struggle for this great end, nations rise from barbarism to civilization, and through it people press forward from one stage of enlightenment to the next. One of the chief factors in progress is the destruction of special privilege. The essence of any struggle for healthy liberty has always been, and must always be, to take from some one man or class of men the right to enjoy power, or wealth, or position, or immunity, which has not been earned by service to his or their fellows. (At Osawatomie, Kan., August 31, 1910.) *Mem. Ed.* XIX, 14; *Nat. Ed.* XVII, 9.

——————, We who war against privilege pay heed to no outworn system of philosophy. We demand of our leaders to-day understanding of and sympathy with the living and the vital needs of those in the community whose needs are greatest. We are against privilege in every form. We believe in striking down every bulwark of privilege. Above all we are against the evil alliance of special privilege in business with special business in politics. We believe in giving the people a free hand to work in efficient fashion for true justice. To the big man and to the little man, in all the relations of life, we pledge justice and fair dealing. . . . We who stand for the cause of progress are fighting to make this country a better place to live in for those who have been harshly treated by fate; and if we succeed it will also really be a better place for those who are already well off. None of us can really prosper permanently if masses of our fellows are debased and degraded, if they are ground down and forced to live starved and sordid lives, so that their souls are crippled like their bodies and the fine edge of their every feeling blunted. We ask that those of our people to whom fate has been kind shall remember that each is his brother's keeper, and that all of us whose veins thrill with abounding vigor shall feel our obligation to the less fortunate who work wearily beside us in the strain and stress of our eager modern life. (At Chicago, June 17, 1912.) *Mem. Ed.* XIX, 314-315; *Nat. Ed.* XVII, 228-230.

PRIVILEGE—FORMS OF. Much of what we are fighting against in modern civilization is privilege. We fight against privilege when it takes the form of a franchise to a street-railway company to enjoy the use of the streets of a great city without paying an adequate return; when it takes the form of a great business combination which grows rich by rebates which are denied to other shippers; when it takes the form of a stock-gambling operation which results in the watering of railway securities so that certain inside men get an enormous profit out of a swindle on the public. All these represent various forms of illegal, or, if not illegal, then antisocial, privilege. (*Outlook,* March 20, 1909.) *Mem. Ed.* XVIII, 561; *Nat. Ed.* XIX, 104.

PRIVILEGE—TYRANNY OF. Whenever there is tyranny by the majority I shall certainly fight it. But the tyrannies from which we have been suffering in this country have, ninety-nine times out of a hundred, been tyrannies by a minority; that is, tyranny by privilege. Sometimes, as in the case of some public-utility franchise or other bit of grabbing by a few what belongs to the many, the tyranny is primarily commercial; at other times, it is primarily political. This, for instance, is true at the present day in those States where the people have been denied the right to vote at primaries in order to express their preferences for President. (At St. Louis, Mo., March 28, 1912.) *Mem. Ed.* XIX, 236; *Nat. Ed.* XVII, 174.

PRIVILEGE AND DEMOCRATIC GOVERNMENT. The democracy, if it is to come to its own in this country, must set its face like steel against privilege and all the beneficiaries of privilege. It must war to cut out special privilege from our frame of government, and in doing so it must count upon the envenomed hostility, not only of the great industrial corporations and individuals who are the beneficiaries of privilege, but of their servants and adherents in the press and in public life. (*Outlook,* March 25, 1911.) *Mem. Ed.* XIX, 145; *Nat. Ed.* XVII, 104.

PRIVILEGE AND POPULAR RULE. In our government we cannot permanently succeed unless the people really do rule. We have tried the other experiment. The present system means the rule of the powers of political and industrial privilege, and for that we propose to substitute the right of the people to rule themselves and their duty to rule so as to bring nearer the day when every man and every woman within the boundaries of this great land of ours shall have fair play, equal rights, shall receive and shall give justice, social and industrial, justice for every man, for every woman within our borders. (At St. Louis, Mo., March 28, 1912.) *Mem. Ed.* XIX, 239; *Nat. Ed.* XVII, 176.

——————. There never has been a clearer line-up than this between the plain people of the country on the one side, and on the other the powers that prey, the representatives of special privilege in the world of business and their tools and instruments in the world of politics. There can be no compromise in such a contest. It is natural that the representatives of special privilege, who know that special privilege cannot continue if the people really rule, should resort unblushingly to every kind of trickery and dishonesty in order to perpetuate their hold upon the party, and should be eager callously to destroy the party if necessary to prevent its being controlled by its rank and file. But for this very reason we feel we have a right solemnly to appeal to all honest men to stand with us on what has now become a naked issue of right and wrong. There can be no yielding, no flinching on our part. We have the people behind us overwhelmingly. We have justice and honesty on our side. We are warring against bossism, against privilege social and industrial; we are warring for the elemental virtues of honesty and decency, of fair dealing as between man and man; we are warring to save the Republican party; and the only reward for which we ask is to put our party in such shape that it shall be of the highest possible service to the people of the United States. (At Chicago, June 17, 1912.) *Mem. Ed.* XIX, 297; *Nat. Ed.* XVII, 214.

PRIVILEGE. *See also* CORRUPTION; DEMOCRACY; EQUALITY; FREEDOM; FRENCH REVOLUTION; LIBERTY; NEW NATIONALISM; OPPORTUNITY; SERVICE; SPECIAL INTERESTS; SUPREME COURT; TARIFF; WEALTH.

PRIZE-FIGHTING. A prize-fight is simply brutal and degrading. The people who attend it, and make a hero of the prize-fighter, are—excepting boys who go for fun and don't know any better—to a very great extent, men who hover on the borderline of criminality; and those who are not are speedily brutalized, and are never rendered more manly. They form as ignoble a body as do the kindred frequenters of rat-pit and cock-pit. The prize-fighter and his fellow professional athletes of the same ilk are, together with their patrons in every rank of life, the very worst foes with whom the cause of general athletic development has to contend. (*North American Review,* August 1890.) *Mem. Ed.* XV, 522; *Nat. Ed.* XIII, 588.

————. Boxing is a fine sport, but this affords no justification of prize-fighting, any more than the fact that a cross-country run or a ride on a wheel is healthy justifies such a demoralizing exhibition as a six-day race. When any sport is carried on primarily for money—that is, as a business—it is in danger of losing much that is valuable, and of acquiring some exceedingly undesirable characteristics. In the case of prize-fighting, not only do all the objections which apply to the abuse of other professional sports apply in aggravated form, but in addition the exhibition has a very demoralizing and brutalizing effect. (Annual Message as Governor, Albany, January 3, 1900.) *Mem. Ed.* XVII, 65-66; *Nat. Ed.* XV, 57.

————. Naturally, being fond of boxing, I grew to know a good many prize-fighters, and to most of those I knew I grew genuinely attached. I have never been able to sympathize with the outcry against prize-fighters. The only objection I have to the prize-ring is the crookedness that has attended its commercial development. Outside of this I regard boxing, whether professional or amateur, as a first-class sport, and I do not regard it as brutalizing. Of course matches can be conducted under conditions that make them brutalizing. But this is true of football games and of most other rough and vigorous sports. Most certainly prize-fighting is not half as brutalizing or demoralizing as many forms of big business and of the legal work carried on in connection with big business. Powerful, vigorous men of strong animal development must have some way in which their animal spirits can find vent. (1913.) *Mem. Ed.* XXII, 51; *Nat. Ed.* XX, 44.

PRIZE-FIGHTING. *See also* BOXING.

PRODUCTION. *See* EFFICIENCY; PROFITS.

PROFITS. There can be no delusion more fatal to the nation than the delusion that the standard of profits, of business prosperity, is sufficient in judging any business or political question—from rate legislation to municipal government. (Fifth Annual Message, Washington, December 5, 1905.) *Mem. Ed.* XVII, 327; *Nat. Ed.* XV, 280.

PROFITS—RESTRICTION OF. We need maximum production; and improper restriction of profits, and, therefore, improperly low prices, will put a stop to maximum production. It is criminal to halt the work of building the navy or fitting out our training camps because of refusal to allow a fair profit to the business men who alone can do the work speedily and effectively; and it is equally mischievous not to put a stop to the making of unearned and improper fortunes out of the war by heavy progressive taxation on the excess war profits—taxation as heavy as that which England now imposes; and as regards the proper profits that are permitted and encouraged, we should insist on a reasonably equitable division between the capitalists, the managers, and the wage-workers. (1917.) *Mem. Ed.* XXI, 9; *Nat. Ed.* XIX, 8.

PROFITS. *See also* MATERIALIST.

[474]

PROFITS AND PROFITEERING. Profiteering out of the war should be stopped; but it is more common sense to say that proper profit-making should be encouraged, for, unless there is a profit, the business cannot run, labor cannot be paid, and neither the public nor the government can be served. And the misery into which this country was plunged before our business was artificially stimulated by the outbreak of the World War shows the need of a protective tariff. (Before Republican State Convention, Saratoga Springs, N. Y., July 18, 1918.) *Mem. Ed.* XXI, 401; *Nat. Ed.* XIX, 363.

————————. Above all—and I want to say this especially to every business man or possible business man—during wartime the question of money making, especially for the big man, should be treated as wholly secondary to the question of service to the nation. For at this time serving the nation may literally mean saving the nation. There is one form of money making that is peculiarly abhorrent at a time like this, and that is the making of excess profits out of anything connected with the war. Indeed, to make excessive profits out of anything during wartime is poor citizenship; there is too much suffering, too much hardship, too much glad and gallant facing of danger and death for us to have sympathy with the man who sits at ease and makes too much money. The man who makes a big fortune during wartime ought to be required to show cause why he should not be regarded as leaving an unsavory heritage to his children. No man worth his salt ought to devote his time primarily to making money at a crisis like this. There should not be more than a legitimate profit for any man, and, above all, not for any big man, made out of anything connected with the war. Do not misunderstand me; most emphatically there must be a legitimate profit; if there is not a legitimate profit then the big industries, absolutely indispensable to the winning of the war, cannot be run. (Address before graduating class, Peirce School, 1918.) *Great Orations.* (Peirce School, Philadelphia, 1922), pp. 18-19.

PROFITEERS. I suppose that war always does bring out what is highest and lowest in human nature. The contractors who furnish poor materials to the army or the navy in time of war stand on a level of infamy only one degree above that of the participants in the white-slave traffic (1913.) *Mem. Ed.* XXII, 264; *Nat. Ed.* XX, 226.

————————. As for the persons who base their actions upon greed in such a crisis as this, little needs to be said. The beef baron or the representative of the cotton interests who wishes to ignore the butchery of our women and children, and the sinking of our ships by German submarines, and to take sides against the Allies so that he may make money by the sale of cotton and beef, is faithless to every consideration of honor and decency. (*Metropolitan,* October 1915.) *Mem. Ed.* XX, 330; *Nat. Ed.* XVIII, 283.

————————. At the moment the profiteers, and all men who make fortunes out of this war, represent the worst types of reactionary privilege. (1918.) *Mem. Ed.* XXI, 383; *Nat. Ed.* XIX, 347.

————————. The unpardonable profit is that of the man, especially the rich man, who, having preached pacifism and unpreparedness, now, when war comes, sees brave men face a death which pacifism and unpreparedness have made infinitely more probable while he himself and his sons profit by these other men's courage and sit at home in the ease and safety secured by the fact that these others face death. The worst profiteers in this country are the men and the sons of the men who decline to face the death which their own actions have made more probable for others. (August 9, 1918.) *Roosevelt in the Kansas City Star,* 199.

PROFITEERS AND SLACKERS. At this moment we can only lay the foundation in outline; but there are certain things that we should do at once in connection with the war. One of them is to stop all profiteering by capitalists; and another is to stop all slacking and loafing, whether by individual workmen or as a result of union action. Of these two perhaps the profiteer is worse; but the slacker is almost as bad. As for the profiteer, any man who makes a fortune out of this war ought to be held up to derision and scorn. No man should come out of this war materially ahead of what he was when we went into it. There must be the reward for capital necessary in order to make it profitable to do the necessary work, and to cover the necessity risk; this is indispensable, and the government should see that neither demagogy nor ignorance interferes with this necessary reward. But we heartily approve, as a war measure, of heavy progressive taxation of all profits, beyond the reasonable profits necessary for the continuance of industry, and our governmental authorities would do well to see whether it is not possible to put a tax on unused land. (*Metropolitan,* November

1918.) *Mem. Ed.* XXI, 274; *Nat. Ed.* XIX, 253.

PROGRESS. We, ourselves, are not certain that progress is assured; we only assert that it may be assured if we but live wise, brave, and upright lives. We do not know whether the future has in store for us calm or unrest. We cannot know beyond peradventure whether we can prevent the higher races from losing their nobler traits and from being overwhelmed by the lower races. On the whole, we think that the greatest victories are yet to be won, the greatest deeds yet to be done, and that there are yet in store for our peoples, and for the causes that we uphold, grander triumphs than have ever yet been scored. But be this as it may, we gladly agree that the one plain duty of every man is to face the future as he faces the present, regardless of what it may have in store for him, turning toward the light as he sees the light, to play his part manfully, as a man among men. (*Sewanee Review*, August 1894.) *Mem. Ed.* XIV, 256-257; *Nat. Ed.* XIII, 222.

———. It is but rarely that great advances in general social well-being can be made by the adoption of some far-reaching scheme, legislative or otherwise; normally they come only by gradual growth, and by incessant effort to do first one thing, then another, and then another. Quack remedies of the universal cure-all type are generally as noxious to the body politic as to the body corporal. (*Review of Reviews*, January 1897.) *Mem. Ed.* XVI, 378; *Nat. Ed.* XIII, 162.

———. When one is in the midst of the strife, with the dust, and the blood and the rough handling, and is receiving blows (and if he is worth anything, is returning them), it is difficult always to see perfectly straight in the direction the right lies. Perhaps we must always advance a little by zigzags; only we must always advance; and the zigzags should go toward the right goal. (At New York State Bar Association Banquet, January 18, 1899.) *Mem. Ed.* XVI, 468; *Nat. Ed.* XIV, 309.

———. Mankind has moved slowly upward through the ages, sometimes a little faster, sometimes a little slower, but rarely indeed by leaps and bounds. At times a great crisis comes in which a great people, perchance led by a great man, can at white heat strike some mighty blow for the right—make a long stride in advance along the path of justice and of orderly liberty. But normally we must be content if each of us can do something—not all that we wish, but something—for the advancement of those principles of righteousness which underlie all real national greatness, all true civilization and freedom. (At Providence, R. I., August 23, 1902.) *Mem. Ed.* XVIII, 80; *Nat. Ed.* XVI, 66-67.

———. It is a rather irritating delusion—the delusion that somehow or other we are all necessarily going to move forward in the long run no matter what the temporary checks may be. I have a very firm faith in this general forward movement, considering only men of our own race for the past score or two centuries, and I hope and believe that the movement will continue for an indefinite period to come; but no one can be sure; there is certainly nothing inevitable or necessary about the movement. (To A. J. Balfour, March 5, 1908.) *Mem. Ed.* XXIV, 125; Bishop II, 107.

———. The important thing is generally the "next step." We ought not to take it unless we are sure that it is advisable; but we should not hesitate to take it when once we are sure; and we can safely join with others who also wish to take it, without bothering our heads overmuch as to any somewhat fantastic theories they may have concerning, say, the two hundredth step, which is not yet in sight. (*Outlook*, March 27, 1909.) *Mem. Ed.* XVIII, 565; *Nat. Ed.* XIX, 109.

———. It often happens that the good conditions of the past can be regained, not by going back, but by going forward. We cannot re-create what is dead; we cannot stop the march of events; but we can direct this march, and out of the new conditions develop something better than the past knew. (*Outlook*, August 27, 1910.) *Mem. Ed.* XVIII, 194; *Nat. Ed.* XVI, 149.

———. The surest way to stop progress is to lull ourselves into supineness, whether by the cultivation of a flabby optimism, or of that refined shrinking from the sight or knowledge of evil and suffering which may itself be a very unpleasant form of vicious self-indulgence. *Outline*, July 15, 1911, p. 570.

———. Our hope lies in progress, for if we try to remain stationary we shall surely go backward; and yet as soon as we leave the ground on which we stand in order to advance there is always danger that we shall plunge into some abyss. (*Outlook*, December

2, 1911.) *Mem. Ed.* XIV, 432; *Nat. Ed.* XII, 125.

PROGRESS AND NATURAL SELECTION. In civilized societies the rivalry of natural selection works against progress. Progress is made in spite of it, for progress results not from the crowding out of the lower classes by the upper, but on the contrary from the steady rise of the lower classes to the level of the upper, as the latter tend to vanish, or at most barely hold their own. In progressive societies it is often the least fit who survive; but, on the other hand, they and their children often tend to grow more fit. . . .

It is plain that the societies and sections of societies where the individual's happiness is on the whole highest, and where progress is most real and valuable, are precisely these where the grinding competition and the struggle for mere existence is least severe. Undoubtedly in every progressive society there must be a certain sacrifice of individuals so that there must be a certain proportion of failures in every generation; but the actual facts of life prove beyond shadow of doubt that the extent of this sacrifice has nothing to do with the rapidity or worth of the progress. The nations that make most progress may do so at the expense of ten or fifteen individuals out of a hundred, whereas the nations that make least progress, or even go backwards, may sacrifice almost every man out of the hundred. (*North American Review*, July 1895.) *Mem. Ed.* XIV, 112-113; *Nat. Ed.* XIII, 227-228.

PROGRESS. See also DEMOCRACY; EXPANSION; LUNATIC FRINGE; PRIMITIVE SOCIETY; REFORM; REVOLUTION.

PROGRESSIVE, THE. Every man who fights fearlessly and effectively against special privilege in any form is to that extent a Progressive. Every man who, directly or indirectly, upholds privilege and favors the special interests, whether he acts from evil motives or merely because he is puzzle-headed or dull of mental vision, or lacking in social sympathy, or whether he simply lacks interest in the subject, is a reactionary.

Every man is to that extent a Progressive if he stands for any form of social justice, whether it be securing proper protection for factory girls against dangerous machinery, for securing a proper limitation of hours of labor for women and children in industry, for securing proper living conditions for those who dwell in the thickly crowded regions of our great cities, for helping, so far as legislation can help, all the conditions of work and life for wage-workers in great centres of industry, or for helping by the action both of the National and State Governments, so far as conditions will permit, the men and women who dwell in the open country to increase their efficiency both in production on their farms and in business arrangements for the marketing of their produce, and also to increase the opportunities to give the best possible expression to their social life. (At Louisville, Ky., April 3, 1912.) *Mem. Ed.* XIX, 243; *Nat. Ed.* XVII, 180.

PROGRESSIVE MOVEMENT. This new movement is a movement of truth, sincerity, and wisdom, a movement which proposes to put at the service of all our people the collective power of the people, through their governmental agencies, alike in the nation and in the several States. We propose boldly to face the real and great questions of the day, and not skilfully to evade them as do the old parties. (Before Progressive National Convention, Chicago, August 6, 1912.) *Mem. Ed.* XIX, 358; *Nat. Ed.* XVII, 254.

——————. I am in this cause with my whole heart and soul. I believe that the Progressive movement is for making life a little easier for all our people; a movement to try to take the burdens off the men and especially the women and children of this country. I am absorbed in the success of that movement.

Friends, I ask you now this evening to accept what I am saying as absolutely true, when I tell you I am not thinking of my own success. I am not thinking of my life or of anything connected with me personally. I am thinking of the movement. (At Milwaukee, Wis., October 14, 1912.) *Mem. Ed.* XIX, 442; *Nat. Ed.* XVII, 321.

——————. I suppose I had a natural tendency to become a Progressive, anyhow. That is, I was naturally a democrat, in believing in fair play for everybody. But I grew toward my present position, not so much as the result of study in the library or the reading of books—although I have been very much helped by such study and by such reading—as by actually living and working with men under many different conditions and seeing their needs from many different points of view. (*Outlook*, October 12, 1912.) *Mem. Ed.* XIX, 435; *Nat. Ed.* XVII, 315.

——————. It seems to me . . . that the time is ripe, and over-ripe, for a genuine Pro-

[477]

gressive movement, nation-wide and justice-loving, sprung from and responsible to the people themselves, and sundered by a great gulf from both of the old party organizations, while representing all that is best in the hopes, beliefs, and aspirations of the plain people who make up the immense majority of the rank and file of both the old parties. (Before Progressive National Convention, Chicago, August 6, 1912.) *Mem. Ed.* XIX, 362; *Nat. Ed.* XVII, 258.

PROGRESSIVE MOVEMENT—NATURE OF. Those of us who believe in Progressive Nationalism are sometimes dismissed with the statement that we are "radicals." So we are; we are radicals in such matters as eliminating special privilege and securing genuine popular rule, the genuine rule of the democracy. But we are not overmuch concerned with matters of mere terminology. We are not in the least afraid of the word "conservative," and, wherever there is any reason for caution, we are not only content but desirous to make progress slowly and in a cautious. conservative manner. . . .

The great movement of our day, the Progressive National movement against special privilege and in favor of an honest and efficient political and industrial democracy, is as emphatically a wise and moral movement as the movement of half a century ago in which Lincoln was the great and commanding figure. (*Outlook*, January 14, 1911.) *Mem. Ed.* XIX, 81; *Nat. Ed.* XVII, 49.

PROGRESSIVE MOVEMENT—OBJECTS OF. One of the prime objects which the Progressives have in view in seeking to secure the highest governmental efficiency of both the National and the State Governments is to safeguard and guarantee the vital interests of the wage-workers. We believe in property rights; normally and in the long run property rights and human rights coincide; but where they are at variance we are for human rights first and for property rights second. (*Outlook*, February 4, 1911.) *Mem. Ed.* XIX, 101; *Nat. Ed.* XVII, 66.

——————. Our aim, the aim of those of us who stand for true progress, for true Nationalism, for true democracy, is not only to give the people power, but, ourselves as part of the people, to try to see that the power is used aright, that it is used with wisdom, with courage, with self-restraint, and in a spirit of the broadest kindliness and charity toward all men. (*Outlook*, March 25, 1911.) *Mem. Ed.* XIX, 146; *Nat. Ed.* XVII. 105.

——————. The Progressive movement which culminated last August in the creation of the Progressive party is no mere sign of temporary political discontent, it is a manifestation of the eternal forces of human growth, a manifestation of the God-given impulse implanted in mankind to make a better race and a better earth. Its purpose is to establish in this world the rights of man, the right not only to religious and political but to economic freedom; and to make these rights real and living. (At New York City, February 12, 1913.) *Mem. Ed.* XIX, 485; *Nat. Ed.* XVII, 359.

——————. Personally, I should like to see the initiative and referendum, with proper safeguards, adopted generally in the States of the Union, and personally I am sorry that the New England town meeting has not spread throughout the Union. But I certainly do not intend to part company from other Progressives who fail to sympathize with me in either view, and I do intend to insist with all the strength I have that each device is a device and nothing more, is a means and not an end. The end is good government, obtained through genuine popular rule. Any device that under given conditions achieves this end is good for those conditions, and the value of each device must be tested purely by the answer to the question, Does it or does it not secure the end in view? One of the worst faults that can be committed by practical men engaged in the difficult work of self-government is to make a fetich of a name, or to confound the means with the end. The end is to secure justice, equality of opportunity in industrial as well as in political matters, to safeguard the interests of all the people, and work for a system which shall promote the general diffusion of well-being and yet give ample rewards to those who in any walk of life and in any kind of work render exceptional service to the community as a whole. (*Outlook*, January 21, 1911.) *Mem. Ed.* XIX, 97; *Nat. Ed.* XVII, 62.

PROGRESSIVE MOVEMENT—ORIGIN OF. Now there has sprung up a feeling deep in the hearts of the people—not of the bosses and professional politicians, not of the beneficiaries of special privilege—a pervading belief of thinking men that when the majority of the people do in fact, as well as theory, rule, then the servants of the people will come more quickly to answer and obey, not the commands of the special interests, but those of the whole people. To reach toward that end the Progressives of the Republican party in certain States have formulated certain proposals for change in the form of the State government—certain new "checks and balances" which may check and balance the special interests and their allies. (At Carnegie Hall, N. Y., March 20, 1912.) *Mem. Ed.* XIX, 202; *Nat. Ed.* XVII, 152.

PROGRESSIVE MOVEMENT AND STATES' RIGHTS. We Progressives stand for the rights of the people. When these rights can best be secured by insistence upon States' rights, then we are for States' rights; when they can best be secured by insistence upon national rights, then we are for national rights. Interstate commerce can be effectively controlled only by the nation. The States cannot control it under the Constitution, and to amend the Constitution by giving them control of it would amount to a dissolution of the government. (Before Progressive National Committee, Chicago, August 6, 1912.) *Mem. Ed.* XIX, 385; *Nat. Ed.* XVII, 277.

——————. There is thus one group composed of those who understand Progressive Nationalism and heartily approve it because they believe it tends toward the abolition of special privilege and of political corruption and toward the development of a genuine democracy; and another group composed of those who cordially fear and fight it because they wish to preserve special privilege and evade control. There is yet another group who are not in the movement because they *misunderstand* it. One of the most frequently advanced allegations about the movement, made for the purpose of discrediting it in the minds of good men who do not know the facts, is that it stands for "overcentralization" and for the destruction of States' rights. Nothing could be further from the truth. . . .

The advocates of a Progressive Nationalism emphatically plead for efficient State action as well as for efficient national action. All they demand is that both State and national action be in the interest of, and not against the interest of, the people. The most efficient possible development of State power is not only not incompatible with but is likely to accompany the most efficient possible development of national power. (*Outlook,* January 14, 1911.) *Mem. Ed.* XIX, 82-83; *Nat. Ed.* XVII, 50-51.

PROGRESSIVE PARTY. Fundamentally the reason for the existence of the Progressive party is found in two facts: first, the absence of real distinctions between the old parties which correspond to those parties; and, second, the determined refusal of the men in control of both parties to use the party organizations and their control of the government for the purpose of dealing with the problems really vital to our people. (*Century,* October 1913.) *Mem. Ed.* XIX, 529; *Nat. Ed.* XVII, 388.

——————. The Progressive Party in this country embodies the Progressive movement, the movement which concerns itself with the rights of all men and women, and especially with the welfare of all who toil. The Progressive Movement is greater than the Progressive Party; yet the Progressive Party is at present the only instrument through which that movement can be advanced. Our effort is to make this country economically as well as politically a genuine democracy. The leaders of both the old parties at times pay lip service to the principles and the purposes of our party; but it is only lip service. Our purposes are the purposes of Thomas Jefferson when he founded the Democratic Party; although the lapse of a century has shown that the extreme individualism and the minimized government control which in that day served to achieve his purposes are in our day no longer serviceable. Both our purposes and our principles are those of Abraham Lincoln and of the Republicans of his day. All we have done has been to apply these principles in actual fact to the living problems of today; instead of praising them as applied to the dead problems of half a century back, and repudiating them with abhorrence when they are invoked on behalf of the men, women and children who toil in the Twentieth Century. (Introduction dated September 12, 1913.) S. J. Duncan-Clark, *The Progressive Movement.* (Boston, 1913), p. xiii.

——————. The Progressive Party was founded primarily to meet the great awakening of conscience which we have seen in the American people during the last few years. Thoughtful men and women have grown to realize that it is impossible that either our present political or industrial conditions shall continue unchanged if the Republic itself is to live and prosper. Self-government is incompatible with dishonest government; and a political democracy and a business oligarchy cannot permanently exist in the same country side by side. We are accused by our enemies of being hostile to business. So far is this from being true that we are the only true and real friends of business. The men of great wealth who are careless of the welfare of the average citizens of our country are laying up an evil harvest for their own children. It is not merely the part of justice, but the part of wisdom to remember that in the long run we here will all go up or go down together, and that the growth of misery in any one great class will ultimately make its baleful effects felt through all classes. We wish the business man to prosper, and, alone among the great parties, we propose a rational common-sense plan which will secure him prosperity at the same time that it secures us against possible wrongdoing by him. We hold that the right type of business man is the man who makes money by serving others, and if the service is great, we wish the reward to be great. We draw the line on conduct, not on size. We do not intend to destroy big business; where it is useful to the people we intend to keep it, but we intend so to supervise and control it that we can be sure that it will be useful. The more successful a man is, the better pleased we are, provided his success is achieved, not by hurting others, but by benefiting others. (At Philadelphia, March 13, 1913.) *The Story of the Progressive Movement in Pennsylvania,* p. 45.

——————. We stand for every principle set forth in our platform. We stand for the purging of the roll of American public life by driving out of politics the big bosses who thwart the popular will, who rely on corruption as a political instrument, and who serve the cause of privilege. But the function of the new party is not limited to securing the enactment of the measures advocated in the party's platform, and the retirement of a few bosses. Our purpose is to keep up a continuous campaign for social and industrial justice and for genuine government by the people, and for the people. Such a campaign cannot be expected from any party which is partly reactionary; and at their best both of the old parties are partly, and they are usually dominantly, reactionary. Just as in the days of Jefferson, the Democratic was the Progressive party, so in the days of Lincoln, the Republican was the Progressive party; but in both of them now the machinery is in the hands of the representatives of reaction. Our function is to bring about the needed realignment of political parties along national and rational lines. Substantially the old parties are but wings of the same party of reaction and privilege. There is now no natural definite difference between them. They are two organizations maintained to secure special privileges and benefits, and not organizations to promote causes and principles. This has made possible the rule of the bipartisan bosses, and has deprived the people of effective means of correcting unsatisfactory conditions. Ultimately all the Progressives who still cling to the two old parties will have to come with us in order to effect the needed improvements in political conditions, in the efficiency of government, and in financial and industrial standards. (At Chicago, December 10, 1912.) *Mem. Ed.* XIX, 474; *Nat. Ed.* XVII, 350.

PROGRESSIVE PARTY — APPEAL OF. The Progressive party is making its appeal to all our fellow citizens without any regard to their creed or to their birthplace. We do not regard as essential the way in which a man worships his God or as being affected by where he was born. We regard it as a matter of spirit and purpose. (At Milwaukee, Wis., October 14, 1912.) *Mem. Ed.* XIX, 445; *Nat. Ed.* XVII, 323.

——————. We stand shoulder to shoulder in a spirit of real brotherhood. We recognize no differences of class, creed, or birthplace. We recognize no sectionalism. Our appeal is made to the Easterner no less than to the Westerner. Our appeal is made to the Southerner no less than to the Northerner. We appeal to the men who wore the gray just as we appeal to the men who wore the blue. We appeal to the sons of the men who followed Lee no less than to the sons of the men who followed Grant; for the memory of the great deeds of both is now part of the common heritage of honor which belongs to all our people, wherever they dwell. (At Madison Square Garden, New York, October 30, 1912.) *Mem. Ed.* XIX, 461; *Nat. Ed.* XVII, 338.

PROGRESSIVE PARTY—BIRTH OF. I think the time has come when not only men who believe in Progressive principles, but all men who believe in those elementary maxims of public and private morality which must underlie every form of successful free government, should join in our movement. I, therefore, ask you to go to your several homes to find out the sentiment of the people at home and then again come together, I suggest by mass convention, to nominate for the presidency a Progressive on a Progressive platform that will enable us to appeal to Northerner and Southerner, Easterner and Westerner, Republican and Democrat alike, in the name of our common American citizenship. If you wish me to make the fight, I will make it, even if only one State should support me.

I am in this fight for certain principles, and

the first and most important of these goes back to Sinai, and is embodied in the commandment, "Thou shalt not steal." Thou shalt not steal a nomination. Thou shalt neither steal in politics nor in business. Thou shalt not steal from the people the birthright of the people to rule themselves. (At Chicago, June 22, 1912.) *Mem. Ed.* XXIV, 392; Bishop II, 334.

PROGRESSIVE PARTY—DUTY OF. Our task is to profit by the lessons of the past, and to check in time the evils that grow around us, lest our failure to do so may cause dreadful disaster to the people. We must not sit supine and helpless. We must not permit the brutal selfishness of arrogance and the brutal selfishness of envy, each to run unchecked its evil course. If we do so, then some day smouldering hatred will suddenly kindle into a consuming flame, and either we or our children will be called on to face a crisis as grim as any which this Republic has ever seen.

It is our business to show that nine-tenths of wisdom consists in being wise in time. Woe to our nation if we let matters drift, if in our industrial and political life we let an unchecked and utterly selfish individualistic materialism riot to its appointed end! That end would be wide-spread disaster, for it would mean that our people would be sundered by those dreadful lines of division which are drawn when the selfish greed of the *haves* is set over against the selfish greed of the *have-nots*. There is but one way to prevent such a division, and that is to forestall it by the kind of a movement in which we are now engaged. (At Madison Square Garden, New York, October 30, 1912.) *Mem. Ed.* XIX, 456; *Nat. Ed.* XVII, 334.

PROGRESSIVE PARTY—FUTURE OF. My immediate and acute trouble is over. The Progressive party cannot in all human probability make another fight as a national party; and, if it does, there will be no expectation that I will have to lead. I am through my hard and disagreeable work. I do not mean that there won't come unpleasant and disagreeable things in connection with the party; but there won't be any such heart-breaking and grinding work as I had last summer. The trouble was that most of my lieutenants, who were good, fine fellows, as disinterested and upright as possible, could not realize that the rank and file had left them; and they felt that I was going back on them if I refused to head the old-style type of fight. I had to make it; and that was all there was to it. (To Kermit Roosevelt, January 27, 1915.) *Mem. Ed.* XXIV, 419; Bishop II, 356.

——————. The Progressive Party has come a cropper. Many causes have brought about the result. Over platform of 1912 was rather too advanced for the average man. Our typical leadership was also a little advanced along the lines of morality and loftiness of aim for the average man to follow. Moreover, we inevitably attracted great multitudes of cranks, who would like us to go into a kind of modified I. W. W. movement, to the emotionalists in this state who represented fundamentally the same type as the Englishmen who in multitudes supported the Tichborne claimant a generation ago. Finally, we have to deal with certain political habits that have become very deep-rooted in our people. The average man is a Democrat or a Republican and he is this as a matter of faith, not as a matter of morals. He no more requires a reason for so being than an adherent of the blue or green factions of the Byzantine Circus required a reason. He has grown to accept as correlative to this attitude entire willingness to punish his party by voting for the opposite party. Having done this, he returns to his own party. (To Charles J. Bonaparte, November 7, 1914.) *Mem. Ed.* XXIV, 416; Bishop II, 353-354.

——————. It would be utter silliness for the Progressive Party, as such, to go into the next campaign. In spite of every effort of the leaders it died in 1914 and it is mere folly to keep it alive. (To S. H. Clark, December 23, 1918.) *Mem. Ed.* XXIV, 547-548; Bishop II, 468.

PROGRESSIVE PARTY — OPPONENTS OF. The fundamental concern of the privileged interests is to beat the new party. Some of them would rather beat it with Mr. Wilson; others would rather beat it with Mr. Taft; but the difference between Mr. Wilson and Mr. Taft they consider as trivial, as a mere matter of personal preference. Their real fight is for either, as against the Progressives. They represent the allied reactionaries of the country, and they are against the new party because to their unerring vision it is evident that the real danger to privilege comes from the new party, and from the new party alone. The men who presided over the Baltimore and the Chicago Conventions, and the great bosses who controlled the two conventions, Mr. Root and Mr. Parker, Mr. Barnes and Mr. Murphy, Mr. Penrose and Mr. Taggart, Mr. Guggenheim and Mr. Sullivan, differ from one another of course on certain points. But these are the differences which one corporation lawyer has with another corporation lawyer when acting for different corporations. They come together at once as against a common enemy when the dominion of both is threatened by the supremacy of the people of the United States, now aroused to the need of a national alignment on the vital economic issues of this generation. (Before Progressive National Convention, Chicago, August 6, 1912.) *Mem. Ed.* XIX, 360; *Nat. Ed.* XVII, 256.

————————. The great majority of capitalists ... and of the big corporation lawyers so intimately connected with them, are naturally hostile to us. Their hostility did not surprise me. The men who are most benefited by privilege unless they are exceptionally disinterested and far-sighted, cannot be expected to feel friendly toward those who assail privilege. But associated with them are many men whose selfish interest in privilege is far less obvious. I genuinely regret that we have had with us so small a percentage of the men for whom life has been easy, who belong to or are intimately associated with the leisured and monied classes; so small a proportion of the class which furnishes the bulk of the membership in the larger social, business and professional clubs, and which supplies the majority of the heads of our great educational institutions and of the men generally, who take the lead in upholding the cause of virtue when only the minor moralities and the elegancies of life are at issue. My concern and regret are primarily for these men themselves. They could do us good by joining with us, for it is earnestly to be wished that this movement for social justice shall number among its leaders at least a goodly proportion of men whose leadership is obviously disinterested, who will themselves receive no material benefit from the changes which as a matter of justice they advocate. Yet the good to the people would be small compared to the good which these men would do to their own class by casting in their lot with us as we battle for the rights of humanity, as we battle for social and industrial justice, as we champion the cause of those who most need champions and for whom champions have been too few. (At Chicago, June 17, 1912.) *Mem. Ed.* XIX, 308-309; *Nat. Ed.* XVII, 223-224.

————————. I would like to say just a word to a portion of our friends, the enemy—the bulk of the very wealthy men. The bulk of the very wealthy business men have been short-sightedly opposed to us. I wish that they would remember that it is a great deal safer for them in the long run to trust to fair play from honest men rather than to receiving unfair advantages from crooked men. Sooner or later they will have it beaten in on them that any man who will steal for them will steal from them. It is a good deal safer to trust not to getting privileges to which they are not entitled, but to men who won't do any injustice for them, and because of that very fact can be trusted not to do any injustice to them. (At Philadelphia, March 13, 1913.) *The Story of the Progressive Movement in Pennsylvania*, pp. 41-42.

————————. We Progressives were fighting for elementary social and industrial justice, and we had with us the great majority of the practical idealists of the country. But we had against us both the old political organizations and ninety-nine per cent at the very least of the corporate wealth of the country, and therefore the great majority of the newspapers. Moreover we were not able to reach the hearts of the materialists, or to stir the imagination of the well-meaning somewhat sodden men who lack vision and prefer to travel in a groove. We were fought by the Socialists as bitterly as by the representatives of the two old parties, and this for the very reason that we stand equally against government by a plutocracy and government by a mob. (To Sir Edward Grey, November 15, 1913.) *Mem. Ed.* XXIV, 408; Bishop II, 347.

PROGRESSIVE PARTY — PLATFORM OF. At the outset I wish to explain that the Progressive platform is our covenant with the people, binding the party and its candidates in state and nation to the pledges made therein. We regard it as a contract which we wish to enter into with the American people, and if given the power it is our purpose to carry into effect every one of the proposals that constitute the obligations of this contract. Furthermore, this platform is a program in which is set forth the concrete measures that we advocate. In this it differs fundamentally from the Democratic platform, which, as the leader of that party, admits, "is not a program." We Progressives are more fortunate. Our platform states explicitly what we propose and definitely what we intend to do with regard to the vital issues of the day. It is entirely sincere and practical. We do not have to apologize for it or speak of it in language so carefully guarded as to convey the impression that we are endeavoring neither to repudiate it nor to support it. We stand squarely on our platform and ask that it be adopted by the American people. And I am glad that we Progressives have the right, in view of our platform, to make the same serious and sober appeal to the women that we make to the men. *Saturday Evening Post,* October 26, 1912, p. 3.

PROGRESSIVE PARTY—SERVICE OF.
The Progressive movement has been given an incalculable impetus by what the Progressive party has done. Our strongest party antagonists have accepted and enacted into law, or embodied in their party platforms, very many of our most important principles. Much has been accomplished in awakening the public to a better understanding of the problems of social and industrial welfare.

Yet it has become entirely evident that the people under existing conditions are not prepared to accept a new party.

It is impossible for us Progressives to abandon our convictions. But we are faced with the fact that as things actually are the Progressive national organization no longer offers the means whereby we can make these convictions effective in our national life. Under such circumstances our duty is to do the best we can, and not to sulk because our leadership is rejected. That we ourselves continue to believe that the course we advocated was in the highest interest of the American people is aside from the question.

It is unpatriotic to refuse to do the best possible merely because the people have not put us in position to do what we regard as the very best. It remains for us, good-humoredly and with common sense, to face the situation and endeavor to get out of it the best that it can be made to yield from the standpoint of the interests of the nation as a whole. (To Progressive National Committee, June 22, 1916.) *Mem. Ed.* XIX, 566; *Nat. Ed.* XVII, 416.

PROGRESSIVE PARTY CONVENTION OF 1916.
The delegates who go to Chicago will have it in their power to determine the character of the administration which is to do or leave undone the mighty tasks of the next four years. That administration can do an incalculable amount to make or mar our country's future. The men chosen to decide such a question ought not to be politicians of the average type and parochial outlook; still less should they be politicians controlled by sinister influence from within or without. They should be the very best men that can be found in our country, whose one great mission should be to declare in unequivocal terms for a programme of clean-cut, straight-out, national Americanism, in deeds not less than in words, and in internal and international matters alike, and to choose as their candidate a man who will not merely stand for such a programme before election, but will resolutely and in good faith put it through if elected.

These men should be men of rugged independence, who possess the broadest sympathy with and understanding of the needs and desires of their fellows; their loyalty should be neither to classes nor to sections, but to the whole of the United States and to all the people that dwell therein. They should be controlled by no man and no interest and their own minds should be open. (Statement to press, Trinidad, B. W. I., March 9, 1916.) *Mem. Ed.* XIX, 562; *Nat. Ed.* XVII, 412.

PROGRESSIVE PARTY. See also ARMAGEDDON; BEVERIDGE, ALBERT J.; DEMOCRATIC PARTY; ELECTION OF 1912; ELECTION OF 1916; HAYS, WILL H.; LA FOLLETTE, ROBERT M.; LABOR; LEADERSHIP; NEW NATIONALISM; REFORMERS; REPUBLICAN PARTY; TAFT, W. H.; TARIFF.

PROGRESSIVE PRINCIPLES.
We Progressives believe that the people have the right, the power, and the duty to protect themselves and their own welfare; that human rights are supreme over all other rights; that wealth should be the servant, not the master, of the people.

We believe that unless representative government does absolutely represent the people it is not representative government at all.

We test the worth of all men and all measures by asking how they contribute to the welfare of the men, women, and children of whom this nation is composed.

We are engaged in one of the great battles of the age-long contest waged against privilege on behalf of the common welfare.

We hold it a prime duty of the people to free our government from the control of money in politics.

For this purpose we advocate, not as ends in themselves, but as weapons in the hands of the people, all governmental devices which will make the representatives of the people more easily and certainly responsible to the people's will. (Before Ohio Constitutional Convention, Columbus, February 21, 1912.) *Mem. Ed.* XIX, 164; *Nat. Ed.* XVII, 120.

———. We believe in securing for the people the direct election of United States senators exactly as the people have already secured in actual practice the direct election of the President. We believe in securing for the people the right of nominating candidates for office, from the President down, by direct primaries, because the convention system, good in its day, has been twisted from its purpose, so that the delegates to the conventions when chosen under the present methods by pressure of money and patronage, often deliberately misrepresent instead of representing the popular will.

We believe in securing to the people the exercise of a real and not merely a nominal control over their representatives in office, this control to include the power to secure the enactment of laws which the people demand, and the rejection of laws to which the people are opposed if after due effort it is found impossible to get from the legislature and the courts a real representation of the deliberate popular judgment in these matters. (At Louisville, Ky., April 3, 1912.) *Mem. Ed.* XIX, 242; *Nat. Ed.* XVII, 178.

──────. Our movement is one of resolute insistence upon the rights and full acknowledgment of the duties of every man and every woman within this great land of ours. We war against the forces of evil, and the weapons we use are the weapons of right. We do not set greed against greed or hatred against hatred. Our creed is one that bids us to be just to all, to feel sympathy for all, and to strive for an understanding of the needs of all. Our purpose is to smite down wrong. But toward those who have done the wrong we feel only the kindliest charity that is compatible with causing the wrong to cease. We preach hatred to no man, and the spirit in which we work is as far removed from vindictiveness as from weakness. We are resolute to do away with the evil, and we intend to proceed with such wise and cautious sanity as will cause the very minimum of disturbance that is compatible with achieving our purpose. (At Madison Square Garden, New York, October 30, 1912.) *Mem. Ed.* XIX, 457; *Nat. Ed.* XVII, 335.

PROGRESSIVE PRINCIPLES—ATTAINMENT OF. The promotion of genuine popular government in America, the defense of human rights, and the establishment of social and industrial justice, so that every force in the community may be directed towards securing for the average man and average woman a higher and better and fuller life in the things of the body no less than those of the mind and soul, . . . [require] a new and radical application of the old principles of justice and common honesty, which are as eternal as life itself. New methods and new machinery are needed for carrying these principles into our National existence; and also a broader sympathy, so that our justice may be generous and human, and not merely legalistic. *Outlook,* March 30, 1912, p. 720.

PROGRESSIVE PRINCIPLES — SURVIVAL OF. What the future of the Progressive Party will be, nobody can say, but I am very confident that our principles in some shape or other will triumph. At present, however, I do not see how the party can triumph under me; but I have to continue to take a certain interest in it until a new man of sufficient power comes along. (To Sir Henry Lucy, December 18, 1912.) *Mem. Ed.* XXIV, 409; Bishop II, 348.

──────. Sooner or later the national principles championed by the Progressives of 1912, must in their general effect be embodied in the structure of our national existence. With all my heart I shall continue to work for these great ideals, shoulder to shoulder with the men and women who in 1912 championed them; and I am sure that these men and women will show a like loyalty to the other, the fundamental, ideals which the events of the last two years have proven to be vital to the permanency of our national existence. (To Progressive National Committee, June 22, 1916.) *Mem. Ed.* XIX, 566; *Nat. Ed.* XVII, 415.

PROGRESSIVE PRINCIPLES. *See also* BUSINESS; COMBINATIONS; CONSTITUTION; CORPORATIONS; COURTS; INITIATIVE; JUDICIARY; LABOR; MONOPOLIES; NEW NATIONALISM; PRIMARIES; RECALL; REFERENDUM; TARIFF; TRUSTS.

PROHIBITION. I think the average liquor-seller would infinitely rather see a prohibitory law passed, which he knows he can avoid, than see some practical measure passed which he knows would be enforced, and the enforcement of which he fears. You do not frighten the liquor-seller by telling him his traffic will be annulled in New York; he knows better; he knows you can't stop it entirely, and he is willing to have you try, because he knows you will fail. You do frighten him if you set to work coolly and with common sense to regulate his traffic, to see that as far as it *can* be made, just so far it *shall* be made decent; to see that the evils resulting from it shall be reduced to a minimum. (In New York Assembly, January 24, 1884.) *Mem. Ed.* XVI, 39; *Nat. Ed.* XIV, 30.

──────. If ever there was a wicked attitude it is that of these fanatic extremists who advocate a law so drastic that it cannot be enforced, knowing perfectly well that lawlessness and contempt of law follow. . . . To pass prohibitory laws to govern localities where the sentiment does not sustain them is simply equivalent to allowing free liquor, plus lawlessness, and is the very worst possible way of solving the problem. My experience with prohibitionists, however, is that the best way to deal with them is to ignore them. (To W. H. Taft, July 16, 1908.) Henry F. Pringle, *Theodore Roosevelt*. (Harcourt, Brace & Co., N. Y., 1931), p. 142.

———————. In answer to your question I wish to state that at the outbreak of the war I advocated prohibiting the use of all hard grains, of all grains that can be used in food products, for the making of alcoholic liquor. I am sure that this would have eliminated much of the evil of intemperance which now seriously handicaps our preparations for war. When we must feed our army and help the armies of our allies not a bushel of grain should be permitted to be made into intoxicating liquor. Neither the men in the army nor the men engaged in doing vital work for the army in connection with railroads, factories, mines and shipyards should be allowed to waste strength and health in drink at this time. The same reasons that render it necessary to prohibit the sale of liquor to soldiers in uniform, or within a given number of miles from a military camp, and to stop its use on battleships, apply to extending similar protection for all citizens engaged in the work of railroads, factories, mines and shipyards. (To Clarence True Wilson, December 12, 1917.) *Christian Advocate*, January 17, 1918, p. 70.

PROHIBITION — ENFORCEMENT OF. I have been in States where prohibition is nominally enforced. In those States, in certain districts where the people who believe in prohibition are greatly in excess of the people who do not believe in it, it is to a certain extent enforced. In all other sections the law is almost a dead letter. In all other sections drunkenness is if anything increased—the crimes resulting from drunkenness are if anything made more frequent by the very presence of the prohibitory clause in the Constitution. (In New York Assembly, January 24, 1884.) *Mem. Ed.* XVI, 36; *Nat. Ed.* XIV, 28.

PROHIBITION. *See also* LIQUOR LAW; LIQUOR TAX; TEMPERANCE.

PROHIBITIONISTS. The liquor men and temperance people invariably subordinate all greater issues to the one in which they are immediately interested. (To H. C. Lodge, September 12, 1906.) Lodge *Letters* II, 231.

———————. Many of the Prohibitionists are honestly and earnestly desirous of doing all they can to check this evil. But it seems to me that within that party there are many men who are so utterly impracticable that they are quite as responsible as any of the liquor-dealers for much of the evil that now results from the liquor traffic. I say that deliberately, and repeat it again, that many of the extreme Prohibitionists do quite as much harm to decency and morality as do the extremists of the other side; for they side with the liquor-sellers to prevent any law being enacted that will practically result in the minimizing of the evils of the traffic. (In New York Assembly, January 24, 1884.) *Mem. Ed.* XVI, 36; *Nat. Ed.* XIV, 28.

PROHIBITIONISTS AND THE LIQUOR TAX. It is a rudimentary axiom of political economy to raise revenue when practicable by a tax on mere luxuries and superfluities; and if there is a single article that it is right to tax, it is whiskey. The people who drink and sell liquor are, of all others, those who should be made to contribute in every possible way to pay the running expenses of the State, for there can be no hardship involved in paying heavily for the use of what is at best a luxury, and frequently a pernicious luxury. The very fact that the third party (the Prohibitionists) have declared in favor of removing the tax should make us set our faces against it; for experience has invariably shown that these same third party Prohibitionists are the most valuable allies the liquor-sellers possess, and are the consistent opponents of every rational scheme for dealing with the liquor question. (Before Union League Club, New York, January 11, 1888.) *Mem. Ed.* XVI, 129; *Nat. Ed.* XIV, 77.

PROMISES. A man is worthless unless he has in him a lofty devotion to an ideal, and he is worthless also unless he strives to realize this ideal by practical methods. He must promise, both to himself and to others, only what he can perform; but what really can be performed he must promise, and such promise he must at all hazards make good. (*Outlook*, July 28, 1900.) *Mem. Ed.* XV, 402-403; *Nat. Ed.* XIII, 400.

———————. Promises that are idly given and idly broken represent profound detriment to the morality of nations. Until no promise is idly entered into and until promises that have once been made are kept, at no matter what cost of risk and effort and positive loss, just so long will distrust and suspicion and wrongdoing rack the world. (New York *Times*, November 29, 1914.) *Mem. Ed.* XX, 200; *Nat. Ed.* XVIII, 171.

———. It is idle to make promises on behalf of a movement for world peace unless we intend to live up to them. If so, the first step is to live up to the promises we have already made, and not to try to sneak out of them on the ground that to fulfil them means to abandon our "policy of refusal to be entangled in foreign alliances." (*Metropolitan*, August 1915.) *Mem. Ed.* XX, 361; *Nat. Ed.* XVIII, 309.

PROMISES — VALUE OF. The one fact which all of us need to keep steadfastly before our eyes is the need that performance should square with promise if good work is to be done, whether in the industrial or in the political world. Nothing does more to promote mental dishonesty and moral insincerity than the habit either of promising the impossible, or of demanding the performance of the impossible, or, finally, of failing to keep a promise that has been made; and it makes not the slightest difference whether it is a promise made on the stump or off the stump. Remember that there are two sides to the wrong thus committed. There is, first, the wrong of failing to keep a promise made, and, in the next place, there is the wrong of demanding the impossible, and therefore forcing or permitting weak or unscrupulous men to make a promise which they either know, or should know, cannot be kept. . . . We can do a great deal when we undertake, soberly, to do the possible. When we undertake the impossible, we too often fail to do anything at all. (At Labor Day Picnic, Chicago, September 3, 1900.) *Mem. Ed.* XVI, 519; *Nat. Ed.* XIII, 489-490.

———. National promises, made in treaties, in Hague conventions, and the like are like the promises of individuals. The sole value of the promise comes in the performance. Recklessness in making promises is in practice almost or quite as mischievous and dishonest as indifference to keeping promises; and this as much in the case of nations as in the case of individuals. Upright men make few promises, and keep those they make. (1915.) *Mem. Ed.* XX, xxii; *Nat. Ed.* XVIII, xxii.

PROMISES. See also ARBITRATION; BIG STICK; COMPROMISE; ELECTION PLEDGES; FOREIGN RELATIONS; NATIONAL OBLIGATIONS; PARTY PLATFORMS; PLATFORM PROMISES; POLITICAL PROMISES; TREATIES.

PRONGBUCK. The prongbuck is the most characteristic and distinctive of American game animals. Zoologically speaking, its position is unique. It is the only hollow-horned ruminant which sheds its horns, or rather the horn sheaths. We speak of it as an antelope, and it does of course represent on our prairies the antelopes of the Old World; but it stands apart from all other horned animals. Its place in the natural world is almost as lonely as that of the giraffe. In all its ways and habits it differs as much from deer and elk as from goat and sheep. Now that the buffalo has gone, it is the only game really at home on the wide plains. It is a striking-looking little creature, with its prominent eyes, single-pronged horns, and the sharply contrasted white, brown, and reddish of its coat. The brittle hair is stiff, coarse, and springy; on the rump it is brilliantly white, and is erected when the animal is alarmed and excited, so as to be very conspicuous. In marked contrast to deer, antelope never seek to elude observation; all they care for is to be able themselves to see. As they have good noses and wonderful eyes, and as they live by preference where there is little or no cover, shots at them are usually obtained at far longer range than is the case with other game. (1905.) *Mem. Ed.* III, 123; *Nat. Ed.* II, 496.

PRONGBUCK — HUNTING THE. The prongbucks are almost the only game that can be hunted as well during the heat of the day as at any other time. They occasionally lie down for two or three hours about noon in some hollow where they cannot be seen, but usually there is no place where they are sure they can escape observation even when resting; and when this is the case they choose a somewhat conspicuous station and trust to their own powers of observation, exactly as they do when feeding. . . .

Prongbucks are very fast runners indeed, even faster than deer. They vary greatly in speed, however, precisely as is the case with deer; in fact, I think that the average hunter makes altogether too little account of this individual variation among different animals of the same kind. (1905.) *Mem. Ed.* III, 136, 139; *Nat. Ed.* II, 507, 509.

PROPERTY. The true friend of property, the true conservative, is he who insists that property shall be the servant and not the master of the commonwealth; who insists that the creature of man's making shall be the servant and not the master of the man who made it. The citizens of the United States must effectively control the mighty commercial forces which they have themselves called into being. (At Osawatomie, Kan., August 31, 1910.) *Mem. Ed.* XIX, 17; *Nat. Ed.* XVII, 11.

————————. I believe in shaping the ends of government to protect property as well as human welfare. Normally, and in the long run, the ends are the same; but whenever the alternative must be faced, I am for men and not for property, as you were in the Civil War. I am far from underestimating the importance of dividends; but I rank dividends below human character. Again, I do not have any sympathy with the reformer who says he does not care for dividends. Of course, economic welfare is necessary, for a man must pull his own weight and be able to support his family. I know well that the reformers must not bring upon the people economic ruin, or the reforms themselves will go down in the ruin. But we must be ready to face temporary disaster, whether or not brought on by those who will war against us to the knife. Those who oppose all reform will do well to remember that ruin in its worst form is inevitable if our national life brings us nothing better than swollen fortunes for the few and the triumph in both politics and business of a sordid and selfish materialism. (At Osawatomie, Kan., August 31, 1910.) *Mem. Ed.* XIX, 27; *Nat. Ed.* XVII, 20.

————————. You cannot protect property without finding that you are protecting the property of some people who are not very straight. You cannot war against the abuses of property without finding that there are some people warring beside you whose motives you would frankly repudiate. But in each case be sure that you keep your own motives and your own conduct straight. When it becomes necessary to curb a great corporation, curb it. I will do my best to help you do it. But I will do it in no spirit of anger or hatred to the men who own or control that corporation; and if any seek in their turn to do wrong to the men of means, to do wrong to the men who own corporations, I will turn around and fight for them in defense of their rights just as hard as I fight against them when I think that they are doing wrong. (At Oyster Bay, N. Y., July 4, 1906.) *Mem. Ed.* XVIII, 9; *Nat. Ed.* XVI, 8.

PROPERTY—ABUSES OF. Our purpose is to build up rather than to tear down. We show ourselves the truest friends of property when we make it evident that we will not tolerate the abuses of property. We are steadily bent on preserving the institution of private property; we combat every tendency toward reducing the people to economic servitude; and we care not whether the tendency is due to a sinister agitation directed against all property, or whether it is due to the actions of those members of the predatory classes whose antisocial power is immeasurably increased because of the very fact that they possess wealth. (At Jamestown Exposition, April 26, 1907.) *Mem. Ed.* XII, 595; *Nat. Ed.* XI, 313.

PROPERTY—USES OF. The use and abuse of property. The use of it is to use it as any honest man would use his property in reference to his brother. Its abuse is to use it as any honest man would not use his property in reference to his brother. All that the legislature, all that our public bodies, have to do is to see that our policy as a State, that the policy of the legislatures and the policy of the nation is shaped along those lines; that when a measure comes up in our State legislature, it shall be treated absolutely on its merits. (Before Independent Club, Buffalo, May 15, 1899.) *Mem. Ed.* XVI, 489; *Nat. Ed.* XIV, 328.

PROPERTY RIGHTS. Violent excess is sure to provoke violent reaction; and the worst possible policy for our country would be one of violent oscillation between reckless upsetting of property rights, and unscrupulous greed manifested under pretense of protecting those rights. *Outlook,* September 3, 1910, p. 24.

————————. One great problem that we have before us is to preserve the rights of property; and these can only be preserved if we remember that they are in less jeopardy from the Socialist and the Anarchist than from the predatory man of wealth. It has become evident that to refuse to invoke the power of the Nation to restrain the wrongs committed by the man of great wealth who does evil is not only to neglect the interests of the public, but is to neglect the interests of the man of means who acts honorably by his fellows. The power of the Nation must be exerted to stop crimes of cunning no less than crimes of violence. There can be no halt in the course we have deliberately elected to pursue, the policy of asserting the right of the Nation, so far as it has the power, to supervise and control the business use of wealth, especially in its corporate form. (At Indianapolis, Ind., May 30, 1907.) *Presidential Addresses and State Papers* VI, 1248.

PROPERTY RIGHTS AND HUMAN RIGHTS. I believe in property rights; I believe that normally the rights of property and humanity coincide; but sometimes they conflict, and where this is so I put human rights above property rights. *Outlook,* November 15, 1913, p. 595.

———————. I urge that in such cases where the courts construe the due process clause as if property rights, to the exclusion of human rights, had a first mortgage on the Constitution, the people may, after sober deliberation, vote, and finally determine whether the law which the court set aside shall be valid or not. By this method can be clearly and finally ascertained the preponderant opinion of the people which Justice Holmes makes the test of due process in the case of laws enacted in the exercise of the police power. The ordinary methods now in vogue of amending the Constitution have in actual practice proved wholly inadequate to secure justice in such cases with reasonable speed, and cause intolerable delay and injustice, and those who stand against the changes I propose are champions of wrong and injustice, and of tyranny by the wealthy and the strong over the weak and the helpless. (At Carnegie Hall, New York, March 20, 1912.) *Mem. Ed.* XIX, 205; *Nat. Ed.* XVII, 155.

———————. We recognize that property has its rights; but they are only incident to, they come second to, the rights of humanity. We hold that the resources of the earth were placed here for the use of man in the mass, that they are to be developed for the common welfare of all, and that they are not to be seized by a few for the purpose of oppression of the many or even with disregard of the rights of the many. Yet we earnestly believe and insist that our policy so far from being detrimental to property or to business will be for the good of property and of business. Our policy alone can permanently benefit property and business because our policy is to put both property and business in their proper relations with humanity. (At New York City, February 12, 1913.) *Mem. Ed.* XIX, 485; *Nat. Ed.* XVII, 359.

———————. My position as regards the moneyed interests can be put in a few words. In every civilized society property rights must be carefully safeguarded; ordinarily, and in the great majority of cases, human rights and property rights are fundamentally and in the long run identical; but when it clearly appears that there is a real conflict between them, human rights must have the upper hand, for property belongs to man and not man to property. (At the Sorbonne, Paris, April 23, 1910.) *Mem. Ed.* XV, 360; *Nat. Ed.* XIII, 515.

PROPERTY. *See also* BUSINESS; CAPITALIST; CORPORATIONS; FORTUNES; MATERIALIST; PROFITS; PUBLIC WELFARE; WEALTH.

PROSPERITY. It cannot be too often repeated that in this country, in the long run, we all of us tend to go up or go down together. If the average of well-being is high, it means that the average wage-worker, the average farmer, and the average business man are all alike well off. If the average shrinks, there is not one of these classes which will not feel the shrinkage. Of course, there are always some men who are not affected by good times, just as there are some men who are not affected by bad times. But speaking broadly, it is true that if prosperity comes all of us tend to share more or less therein, and that if adversity comes each of us, to a greater or less extent, feels the tension. Unfortunately, in this world the innocent frequently find themselves obliged to pay some of the penalty for the misdeeds of the guilty; and so if hard times come, whether they be due to our own fault or to our misfortune, whether they be due to some burst of speculative frenzy that has caused a portion of the business world to lose its head—a loss which no legislation can possibly supply—or whether they be due to any lack of wisdom in a portion of the world of labor—in each case the trouble once started is felt more or less in every walk of life. (At State Fair, Syracuse, N. Y., September 7, 1903.) *Mem. Ed.* XVIII, 58; *Nat. Ed.* XVI, 50.

———————. Wise laws and fearless and upright administration of the laws can give the opportunity for such prosperity as we see about us. But that is all that they can do. When the conditions have been created which make prosperity possible, then each individual man must achieve it for himself by his own energy and thrift and business intelligence. If when people wax fat they kick, as they have kicked since the days of Jeshurun, they will speedily destroy their own prosperity. If they go into wild speculation and lose their heads they have lost that which no laws can supply. If in a spirit of sullen envy they insist upon pulling down those who have profited most in the years of fatness, they will bury themselves in the crash of the common disaster. It is difficult to make our material condition better by the best laws, but it is easy enough to ruin it by bad laws. (At Providence, R. I., August 23, 1902.) *Mem. Ed.* XVIII, 73-74; *Nat. Ed.* XVI, 61-62.

PROSPERITY — BASIS OF. The cornerstones of our unexampled prosperity are, on the one hand, the production of raw material, and its manufacture and distribution on the other. (At semicentennial celebration, founding of Agricultural Colleges, Lansing, Mich., May 31, 1907.) *Mem. Ed.* XVIII, 180; *Nat. Ed.* XVI, 136.

─────────────. Prosperity can only be lasting if it is based on justice, and it cannot be based on justice unless the small man, the farmer, the mechanic, the wage-worker generally, the clerk on a salary, the small business man, the retail dealer, have their rights guaranteed. If these men have their rights guaranteed, then they will prosper, and the prosperity will extend to the big men. Fundamentally, our opponents who say they are for prosperity differ from us in wishing to see the prosperity come to the big man first and then drip down through to the little man. Now I am just as anxious to see the big man prosper as they are, but I do not believe that he can prosper in any really enduring manner unless under conditions which insure to the small men their fair chance. (At Chicago, March 27, 1912.) *Mem. Ed.* XIX, 225.

─────────────. Prosperity can never be created by law alone, although it is easy enough to destroy it by mischievous laws. If the hand of the Lord is heavy upon any country, if flood or drought comes, human wisdom is powerless to avert the calamity. Moreover, no law can guard us against the consequences of our own folly. The men who are idle or credulous, the men who seek gains not by genuine work with head or hand but by gambling in any form, are always a source of menace not only to themselves but to others. If the business world loses its head, it loses what legislation cannot supply. Fundamentally, the welfare of each citizen, and therefore the welfare of the aggregate of citizens which makes the nation, must rest upon individual thrift and energy, resolution, and intelligence. Nothing can take the place of this individual capacity; but wise legislation and honest and intelligent administration can give it the fullest scope, the largest opportunity to work to good effect. (First Annual Message, Washington, December 3, 1901.) *Mem. Ed.* XVII, 100; *Nat. Ed.* XV, 87.

PROSPERITY—CONDITIONS OF. We are in a period of change; we are fronting a great period of further change. Never was the need more imperative for men of vision who are also men of action. Disaster is ahead of us if we trust to the leadership of the men whose hearts are seared and whose eyes are blinded, who believe that we can find safety in dull timidity and dull inaction. The unrest cannot be quieted by the ingenious trickery of those who profess to advance by merely marking time. It cannot be quieted by demanding only the prosperity which is to come to those who have much, in such quantity that some will drip through to those who have little. There must be material prosperity; they are enemies of all of us who wantonly or unwisely interfere with it or disregard it; but it can only come in permanent shape if obtained in accordance with, and not against, the spirit of justice and righteousness. Clouds hover above the horizon throughout the civilized world. But here in America the fault is our own if the sky above us is not clear. We have a continent on which to work out our destiny. Our people, our men and women, are fit to face the mighty days. If we fail, the failure will be lamentable; for not only shall we fail for ourselves, but our failure will wreck the fond desires of all, throughout the world, who look toward us with the eager hope that here, in this great Republic, it shall be proved from ocean to ocean that the people can rule themselves, and thus ruling can give liberty and do justice both to themselves and to others. (At Louisville, Ky., April 3, 1912.) *Mem. Ed.* XIX, 251; *Nat. Ed.* XVII, 186.

─────────────. General prosperity is conditioned mainly upon private business prosperity. Such private prosperity, if obtained by swindling in any form, represents general detriment. But it is essential, in the common interest, not to damage legitimate private business by either misdirected or overrapid activity in securing, for the public at large or for the less fortunate among our fellows, benefits which ought to be secured but which can only be secured if the community as a whole is in a strong, healthy, and prosperous condition. It is essential to pass prosperity around; but it is mere common sense to recognize that unless it exists it cannot be passed around. The wageworkers must get their full share in the general well-being; but if there is no general well-being there will be no share of it for anybody. (*Metropolitan*, May 1917.) *Mem. Ed.* XXI, 98-99; *Nat. Ed.* XIX, 85.

PROSPERITY—DIVISION OF. There is no point in having prosperity unless there can be an equitable division of prosperity. But there can be no equitable division of prosperity until the prosperity is there to divide. All reformers with any wisdom will keep this fact steadily in mind, and will realize that it is their duty

[489]

in all legislation to work for the general prosperity of the community; and this in spite of the further fact that no good comes from the performance of this first duty unless some system of equity and justice is built upon the prosperity thus secured. (*Outlook,* November 18, 1914.) *Mem. Ed.* XIV, 222; *Nat. Ed.* XII, 239.

────────────. The only prosperity worth having is that which affects the mass of the people. We are bound to strive for the fair distribution of prosperity. But it behooves us to remember that there is no use in devising methods for the proper distribution of prosperity unless the prosperity is there to distribute. I hold it to be our duty to see that the wage-worker, the small producer, the ordinary consumer, shall get their fair share of the benefit of business prosperity. But it either is or ought to be evident to every one that business has to prosper before anybody can get any benefit from it. Therefore I hold that he is the real Progressive, that he is the genuine champion of the people, who endeavors to shape the policy alike of the nation and of the several States so as to encourage legitimate and honest business at the same time that he wars against all crookedness and injustice and unfairness and tyranny in the business world (for of course we can only get business put on a basis of permanent prosperity when the element of injustice is taken out of it). (Before Ohio Constitutional Convention, Columbus, February 21, 1912.) *Mem. Ed.* XIX, 169; *Nat. Ed.* XVII, 124.

────────────. Our purpose is to see that there is a proper division of prosperity. But there can be no division unless the prosperity is there to divide. One of the methods by which the prosperity will certainly be abolished is to draw the line against size and efficiency instead of against misconduct. Another way to destroy it is to impose burdens, however necessary and proper, without facing the fact that some one must pay for the burdens, and that if the investor cannot pay for them and at the same time get a reasonable return on his investment, then either the business will close or the public must share the burden with the investor. (*Outlook,* July 5, 1913.) *Mem. Ed.* XVIII, 122.

────────────. Unfortunately, those dealing with the subject [of material prosperity] have tended to divide into two camps, each as unwise as the other. One camp has fixed its eyes only on the need of prosperity, loudly announcing that our attention must be confined to securing it in bulk, and that the division must be left to take care of itself. This is merely the plan, already tested and found wanting, of giving prosperity to the big men on top, and trusting to their mercy to let something leak through to the mass of their countrymen below—which, in effect, means that there shall be no attempt to regulate the ferocious scramble in which greed and cunning reap the largest rewards. The other set has fixed its eyes purely on the injustices of distribution, omitting all consideration of the need of having something to distribute, and advocates action which, it is true, would abolish most of the inequalities of the distribution of prosperity, but only by the unfortunately simple process of abolishing the prosperity itself. This means merely that conditions are to be evened, not up, but down, so that all shall stand on a common level, where nobody has any prosperity at all. The task of the wise radical must be to refuse to be misled by either set of false advisers; he must both favor and promote the agencies that make for prosperity, and at the same time see to it that these agencies are so used as to be primarily of service to the average man. (Before Progressive National Convention, Chicago, August 6, 1912.) *Mem. Ed.* XIX, 380; *Nat. Ed.* XVII, 273.

PROSPERITY—EFFECTS OF. When people have become very prosperous they tend to become sluggishly indifferent to the continuation of the policies that brought about their prosperity. (At Union League, Phila., November 22, 1902.) *Mem. Ed.* XVIII, 481; *Nat. Ed.* XVI, 358.

PROSPERITY—PLACE OF. No country can long endure if its foundations are not laid deep in the material prosperity which comes from thrift, from business energy and enterprise, from hard, unsparing effort in the fields of industrial activity; but neither was any nation ever yet truly great if it relied upon material prosperity alone. (Before the Hamilton Club, Chicago, April 10, 1899.) *Mem. Ed.* XV, 272; *Nat. Ed.* XIII, 323.

────────────. Though material prosperity is indispensable, yet it cannot by itself atone for the lack of that higher and finer moral and spiritual excellence which ultimately counts for more than all else in the true life of a great nation. (Campaign speech, New York City, October 5, 1898.) *Mem. Ed.* XVI, 447; *Nat. Ed.* XIV, 295.

PROSPERITY. *See also* HARD TIMES; LEGISLATION; PANIC; PROFITS; PUBLIC WELFARE; TARIFF; THRIFT; WEALTH.

PROSTITUTION—ECONOMIC CAUSES OF. As for the wretched girls who follow the dreadful trade in question, a good deal can be done by a change in economic conditions. This ought to be done. When girls are paid wages inadequate to keep them from starvation, or to permit them to live decently, a certain proportion are forced by their economic misery into lives of vice. The employers and all others responsible for these conditions stand on a moral level not far above the white slavers themselves. But it is a mistake to suppose that either the correction of these economic conditions or the abolition of the white-slave trade will wholly correct the evil or will even reach the major part of it. The economic factor is very far from being the chief factor in inducing girls to go into this dreadful life. As with so many other problems, while there must be governmental action, there must also be strengthening of the average individual character in order to achieve the desired end. Even where economic conditions are bad, girls who are both strong and pure will remain unaffected by temptations to which girls of weak character or lax standards readily yield. Any man who knows the wide variation in the proportions of the different races and nationalities engaged in prostitution must come to the conclusion that it is out of the question to treat economic conditions as the sole conditions or even as the chief conditions that determine this question. (1913.) *Mem. Ed.* XXII, 237; *Nat. Ed.* XX, 203.

PROSTITUTION—REMEDIES FOR. I do not know of any method which will put a complete stop to the evil, but I do know certain things that ought to be done to minimize it. One of these is treating men and women on an exact equality for the same act. Another is the establishment of night courts and of special commissions to deal with this special class of cases. Another is that suggested by the Reverend Charles Stelzle, of the Labor Temple—to publish conspicuously the name of the owner of any property used for immoral purposes, after said owner had been notified of the use and has failed to prevent it. Another is to prosecute the keepers and backers of brothels, men and women, as relentlessly and punish them as severely as pickpockets and common thieves. They should never be fined; they should be imprisoned. As for the girls, the very young ones and first offenders should be put in the charge of probation officers or sent to reformatories, and the large percentage of feeble-minded girls and of incorrigible girls and women should be sent to institutions created for them. We would thus remove from this hideous commerce the articles of commerce. Moreover, the Federal Government must in ever-increasing measure proceed against the degraded promoters of this commercialism, for their activities are inter-State and the nation can often deal with them more effectively than the States; although, as public sentiment becomes aroused, nation, State, and municipality will all co-operate toward the same end of rooting out the traffic. But the prime need is to raise the level of individual morality; and moreover, to encourage early marriages, the single standard of sex morality, and a strict sense of reciprocal conjugal obligation. The women who preach late marriages are by just so much making it difficult to better the standard of chastity. (1913.) *Mem. Ed.* XXII, 235-236; *Nat. Ed.* XX, 202.

PROSTITUTION. See also WHITE SLAVE TRAFFIC.

PROTECTION. See RECIPROCITY; TARIFF.

PROTECTIVE COLORATION. See ANIMALS; BIRDS.

PROVINCIALISM. See INDEPENDENCE SPIRIT; NATIONALISM; NEW ENGLAND; SECTIONALISM; STATES' RIGHTS; WEST.

PUBLIC BUILDINGS. Whenever hereafter a public building is provided for and erected, it should be erected in accordance with a carefully thought out plan adopted long before; . . . it should be not only beautiful in itself, but fitting in its relations to the whole scheme of the public buildings, the parks, the drives of the District.

Working through municipal commissions, very great progress has already been made in rendering more beautiful our cities, from New York to San Francisco. An incredible amount remains to be done. But a beginning has been made, and now I most earnestly hope that in the National Capital a better beginning will be made than anywhere else, and that can be made only by utilizing to the fullest degree the thought and the disinterested effort of the architects, the artists, the men of art, who stand foremost in their professions here in the United States, and who ask no other reward than the reward of feeling that they have done their full part to make as beautiful as it should be the capital city of the great Republic. (At dinner of American Institute of Architects, Washington, D. C., January 11, 1905.) *Presidential Addresses and State Papers* III, 204.

——————. It is to our discredit as a nation that our governmental buildings should so frequently be monuments of sordid ugliness. Only too often the Government does less to advance the standards of architecture, and therefore of public taste, than has been done by many big private corporations. As instances of what can be done privately, witness the New York City railroad terminals and many of their stations, and the Harvey eating-houses and hotels in the Southwest. Always, when the Government has done something well, it has been by searching for or accepting expert leadership. In public buildings this means getting the better architects or artists to guide and represent the public taste. Congress, acting on its own initiative, is as unfit to prescribe conditions for the erection of public buildings as it would be to prescribe conditions for a general or an admiral, for a Grant or a Sheridan, a Farragut or a Dewey. It needs leadership in one case just as much as in the other; the function of Congress should be to try to secure the best and wisest leadership in all cases. (Letter to American Institute of Architects, read December 7, 1916.) *Proceedings of the Fiftieth Annual Convention of the American Institute of Architects, Minneapolis, Minn.*, p. 45.

PUBLIC BUILDINGS. See also ARCHITECTURE.

PUBLIC HEALTH. See HEALTH.

PUBLIC INTEREST. See PUBLIC OPINION.

PUBLIC LANDS—DISPOSITION OF. So far as they are available for agriculture, and to whatever extent they may be reclaimed under the national irrigation law, the remaining public lands should be held rigidly for the home-builder, the settler who lives on his land, and for no one else. In their actual use the desert-land law, the timber and stone law, and the commutation clause of the homestead law have been so perverted from the intention with which they were enacted as to permit the acquisition of large areas of the public domain for other than actual settlers and the consequent prevention of settlement. Moreover, the approaching exhaustion of the public ranges has of late led to much discussion as to the best manner of using these public lands in the West which are suitable chiefly or only for grazing. The sound and steady development of the West depends upon the building up of homes therein. (Second Annual Message, Washington, December 2, 1902.) *Mem. Ed.* XVII, 187-188; *Nat. Ed.* XV, 161-162.

——————. Our public lands, whose highest use is to supply homes for our people, have been and are still being taken in great quantities by large private owners, to whom home-making is at the very best but a secondary motive subordinate to the desire for profit. To allow the public lands to be worked by the tenants of rich men for the profit of the landlords, instead of by freeholders for the livelihood of their wives and children, is little less than a crime against our people and our institutions. The great central fact of the public-land situation, as the Public Lands Commission well said, is that the amount of public land patented by the government to individuals is increasing out of all proportion to the number of new homes. It is clear beyond peradventure that our natural resources have been and are still being abused, that continued abuse will destroy them, and that we have at last reached the forks of the road. (Before Deep Waterway Convention, Memphis, Tenn., October 4, 1907.) *Mem. Ed.* XVIII, 155; *Nat. Ed.* XVI, 118.

PUBLIC LANDS. See also CONSERVATION; HOMESTEAD LAW; NORTHWEST ORDINANCE; RECLAMATION.

PUBLIC LIFE. There is every reason why a man should have an honorable ambition to enter public life, and an honorable ambition to stay there when he is in; but he ought to make up his mind that he cares for it only as long as he can stay in it on his own terms, without sacrifice of his own principles; and if he does thus make up his mind he can really accomplish twice as much for the nation, and can reflect a hundredfold greater honor upon himself, in a short term of service, than can the man who grows gray in the public employment at the cost of sacrificing what he believes to be true and honest. (Before the Liberal Club, Buffalo, N. Y., January 26, 1893.) *Mem. Ed.* XV, 72; *Nat. Ed.* XIII, 289.

——————. Whenever men just like ourselves—possibly not much better, but probably not in the least worse—continually fail to give us the results we have a right to expect from their efforts, we may just as well make up our minds that the fault lies, not in their personalities, but in the conditions under which they work, and profit comes, not from denouncing them, but from seeing that the conditions are changed. *Outlook,* January 28, 1911, p. 236.

PUBLIC LIFE. See also CHARACTER; CITIZENSHIP; CIVIC DUTY; COLLEGE EDUCATION; CONSCIENCE; DEMOCRACY; EDUCATED MEN; POLITICS; ROOSEVELT'S POLITICAL CAREER.

PUBLIC MEN—CHARACTER OF.

A nation must be judged in part by the character of its public men, not merely by their ability but by their ideals and the measure in which they realize these ideals; by their attitude in private life, and much more by their attitude in public life, both as regards their conception of their duties toward their country and their conception of the duty of that country, embodied in its government, toward its own people and toward foreign nations.

While the private life of a public man is of secondary importance, it is certainly a mistake to assume that it is of no importance. Of course, excellence of private conduct—that is, domestic morality, punctuality in the payment of debts, being a good husband and father, being a good neighbor—do not, taken together, furnish adequate reason for reposing confidence in a man as a public servant. But lack of these qualities certainly does establish a presumption against any public man. One function of any great public leader should be to exert an influence upon the community at large, especially upon the young men of the community; and therefore it is idle to say that those interested in the perpetuity of good government should not take into account the fact of a public man's example being something to follow or to avoid, even in matters not connected with his direct public services. (*Outlook*, January 23, 1909.) *Mem. Ed.* XII, 419; *Nat. Ed.* XI, 183.

———. No man can be of any service to the State, no man can amount to anything from the standpoint of usefulness to the community at large, unless first and foremost he is a decent man in the close relations of life. No community can afford to think for one moment that great public service, that great material achievement, that ability shown in no matter how many different directions, will atone for the lack of a sound family life. (At Pacific Theological Seminary, Spring 1911.) *Mem. Ed.* XV, 593; *Nat. Ed.* XIII, 631.

PUBLIC OFFICE. See OFFICE.

PUBLIC OFFICIALS.

A man who stays long in our American political life, if he has in his soul the generous desire to do effective service for great causes, inevitably grows to regard himself merely as one of many instruments, all of which it may be necessary to use, one at one time, one at another, in achieving the triumph of those causes; and whenever the usefulness of any one has been exhausted, it is to be thrown aside. If such a man is wise, he will gladly do the thing that is next, when the time and the need come together, without asking what the future holds for him. Let the half-god play his part well and manfully, and then be content to draw aside when the god appears. Nor should he feel vain regrets that to another it is given to render greater services and reap a greater reward. Let it be enough for him that he too has served, and that by doing well he has prepared the way for the other man who can do better. (1913.) *Mem. Ed.* XXII, 111; *Nat. Ed.* XX, 95.

PUBLIC OFFICIALS — DISCRIMINATION BETWEEN.

Emphasis ... must be laid on the uprightness, on the decency, on the ability and willingness to serve the public, so far as the official is concerned, rather than upon the office which he holds. It is impossible adequately to honor the faithful public servant unless we discriminate in the sharpest possible fashion between him and the unfaithful public servant; and all sense of such discrimination, all sense of proportion, is equally lost, whether we confound the honest and the dishonest, the competent and the incompetent, in indiscriminate praise or in indiscriminate abuse. (*Outlook*, March 4, 1911.) *Mem. Ed.* XIX, 118; *Nat. Ed.* XVII, 81.

PUBLIC OFFICIALS—DUTY OF.

I should heartily despise the public servant who failed to do his duty because it might jeopardize his own future. (Letter of February 21, 1899.) *Mem. Ed.* XXIII, 138; Bishop I, 119.

PUBLIC OFFICIALS—INDEPENDENCE OF.

I hold that the judge should be independent, of course, and so should every executive or legislative officer. I have been accused of many things when I was an executive officer, but never of lack of independence. No public servant who is worth his salt should hesitate to stand by his conscience, and if necessary, to surrender his office rather than to yield his conscientious conviction in a case of any importance. But while that is his right and duty—while it was my right and duty—it is also our right and our duty to see that the man is responsible to us, to the people. (At New York City, October 20, 1911.) *Mem. Ed.* XVIII, 274; *Nat. Ed.* XVI, 206.

———. I hold that public servants are in very truth the servants and not the masters of the people, and that this is true not only of executive and legislative officers but of judicial officers as well. The judge should be independent, but so should every proper executive or legislative officer. *Outlook,* January 5, 1912, p. 48.

PUBLIC OFFICIALS—POWER OF. Public servants must be given ample power to enable them to do their work. Remember that. If you tie the hands of a public servant so that he cannot do ill, you tie his hands so that he cannot do well. Don't try for a moment to restrain the public man in office by shackling him. Leave his hands free. Give him the chance to do the job, and turn him out if he does not do the job well. (At Los Angeles, March 21, 1911.) *Mem. Ed.* XVIII, 604; *Nat. Ed.* XVI, 436.

PUBLIC OFFICIALS — RESPONSIBILITY OF. No man can get power without at the same time acquiring the duty of being held to a rigid accountability for his use of that power. I wish to see the people in absolute control, but when you, the people, assume that control remember that you cannot shirk the responsibility that comes with it. The sovereign in any country, and in any land, must be held accountable for the way in which he uses the vast power that is his, and in our case the sovereign is the people. The idea each of us must have first and foremost, all you individually and severally, and you collectively in company with us as fellow laborers, is duty. That is the important word for us, because the thought it symbolizes is the important thought for us to have ever in our hearts, in our minds. The man who is in danger of oppression from the sovereign can afford to think of his rights, first and foremost, but the man who is really sovereign, or the entity which is really sovereign, must think of its duties first. (At University of Wisconsin, Madison, April 15, 1911.) *Mem. Ed.* XV, 546; *Nat. Ed.* XIII, 593.

——————. The people have nothing whatever to fear from giving any public servant power so long as they retain their own power to hold him accountable for his use of the power they have delegated him. You will get best service where you elect only a few men, and where each man has his definite duties and responsibilities, and is obliged to work in the open, so that the people know who he is and what he is doing, and have the information that will enable them to hold him to account for his stewardship. (Before Ohio Constitutional Convention, Columbus, February 21, 1912.) *Mem. Ed.* XIX, 179; *Nat. Ed.* XVII, 133.

PUBLIC OFFICIALS — THE PEOPLE AND. If you always find bad public servants, look out for the public! We here—you my hearers and I—live in a government where we are the people and, in consequence, where we are not to be excused if the government goes wrong. There are many countries where the government can be very wrong indeed and where nevertheless it can be said that the people are fundamentally right, for they don't choose their public servants, they don't choose their government. On the contrary, we do choose our government, not temporarily but permanently, and in the long run our public servants must necessarily be what we choose to have them. They represent us; they must represent our self-restraint and sense of decency and common sense, or else our folly, our wickedness, or at least our supine indifference in letting others do the work of government for us. Not only should we have the right type of public servants, but we should remember that the wrong type discredits not only the man himself but each of us whose servant he is. Sometimes I hear our countrymen inveigh against politicians; I hear our countrymen abroad saying: "Oh, you mustn't judge us by our politicians." I always want to interrupt and answer: "You must judge us by our politicians." We pretend to be the masters—we, the people—and if we permit ourselves to be ill served, to be served by corrupt and incompetent and inefficient men, then on our own heads must the blame rest. (At Pacific Theological Seminary, Spring 1911.) *Mem. Ed.* XV, 618; *Nat. Ed.* XIII, 652.

PUBLIC OFFICIALS. *See also* Bribery; Bureaucracy; Corruption; Criticism; Honesty; Politicians; Recall; Representatives; Slander; Sovereignty.

PUBLIC OPINION. We shall never reach the proper standard in public service or in private conduct until we have a public opinion so aroused, so resolute, so intelligent, that it shall be understood that we are more bitter against the scoundrel who succeeds than against the scoundrel who fails. We ought to admire intelligence and ability; but only when the intelligence and ability are controlled and guided by the will to do right. (At Pacific Theological Seminary, Spring 1911.) *Mem. Ed.* XV, 624; *Nat. Ed.* XIII, 658.

PUBLIC OPINION—DEPENDENCE ON. The belief that public opinion or international public opinion, unbacked by force, had the slightest effect in restraining a powerful military nation in any course of action it chose to undertake . . . [has been] shown to be a pathetic fallacy. . . . It is the simple and literal truth that public opinion during the last eighteen months has not had the very smallest effect in mitigating any atrocities or preventing any wrong-doing by aggressive military powers, save to the exact degree that there was behind the public opinion actual strength which would be used if the provocation was sufficiently great. Public opinion has been absolutely useless as regards Belgium, as regards Armenia, as regards Poland. No man can assert the contrary with sincerity if he takes the trouble to examine the facts. (*Metropolitan,* February 1916.) *Mem. Ed.* XX, 282; *Nat. Ed.* XVIII, 242.

PUBLIC OPINION—FUNCTION OF. Our standard of public and private conduct will never be raised to the proper level until we make the scoundrel who succeeds feel the weight of a hostile public opinion even more strongly than the scoundrel who fails. (*Century,* June 1900.) *Mem. Ed.* XV, 379; *Nat. Ed.* XIII, 342.

———————. It is easy to say what we ought to do, but it is hard to do it; and yet no scheme can be devised which will save us from the need of doing just this hard work. Not merely must each of us strive to do his duty; in addition it is imperatively necessary also to establish a strong and intelligent public opinion which will require each to do his duty. (At Pan-American Exposition, Buffalo, May 20, 1901.) *Mem. Ed.* XV, 313; *Nat. Ed.* XIII, 447.

PUBLIC OPINION AND LAW. There must be the public opinion back of the laws or the laws themselves will be of no avail. (Seventh Annual Message, Washington, December 3, 1907.) *Mem. Ed.* XVII, 505; *Nat. Ed.* XV, 431.

———————. In addition to the law and its enforcement we must have the public opinion which frowns on the man who violates the spirit of the law even though he keeps within the letter. I cannot tell you any one way in which that feeling can be made to carry weight. I think it must find expression in a dozen different ways. . . . We should strive to create in the community the sense of proportion which will make us respect the decent man who does well, and condemn the man who does not act decently and who does wrong. (At Pacific Theological Seminary, Spring 1911.) *Mem. Ed.* XV, 586; *Nat. Ed.* XIII, 624.

PUBLIC OPINION AND PUBLIC INTEREST. I am not paying heed to public opinion; I am paying heed to the public interest; and if I can accomplish, not all that I desire, but a reasonable proportion of what I desire, by the end of my term (and in the four and a half years that have gone by I have succeeded in accomplishing such reasonable proportion) why, I am more than satisfied. (To Sereno S. Pratt, March 1, 1906.) *Mem. Ed.* XXIV, 11; Bishop II, 8.

PUBLIC SCHOOLS. I do not suppose there is anything quite as important to our government as the public-school system. We must have that properly conducted, and the one thing we must insist on in it is that those who administer it shall be honest and efficient. (Before Liberal Club, Buffalo, N. Y., September 10, 1895.) *Mem. Ed.* XVI, 283; *Nat. Ed.* XIV, 203.

———————. I doubt if there is anything that has reflected more credit upon the civilization of the American Republic in the past than our common-school system, and, my friends, that is just one of its dangers. The minute that people become too satisfied with what has been done by them in the past, they are in great danger of coming short in the present and in the future. (Before Iowa State Teachers' Association, Des Moines, November 4, 1910.) *Mem. Ed.* XVIII, 444; *Nat. Ed.* XVI, 331.

PUBLIC SCHOOLS AND AMERICANIZATION. Perhaps the best work of the public school has been in the direction of Americanizing immigrants, or rather the children of immigrants; and it would be almost impossible to overestimate the good it has accomplished in this direction. (1891.) *Mem. Ed.* IX, 383; *Nat. Ed.* X, 502.

PUBLIC SCHOOLS AND CITIZENSHIP. The public schools are the nurseries from which spring the future masters of the commonwealth; and, in making up the estimate of any State's real greatness, the efficiency of its public-school system and the extent to which it is successful in reaching all the children in the State count for a hundredfold more than railroads and manufactories, than shipping or farms, than anything which is symbolic of mere material prosperity, great though the importance of this mere material prosperity undoubtedly also is. (At Boston, Mass., November 1893.) *Mem. Ed.* XV, 32; *Nat. Ed.* XIII, 274.

PUBLIC SCHOOLS AND TOLERATION. To it [the public school] more than to any other among the many causes which, in our

American life, tell for religious toleration is due the impossibility of persecution of a particular creed. When in their earliest and most impressionable years Protestants, Catholics, and Jews go to the same schools, learn the same lessons, play the same games, and are forced, in the rough-and-ready democracy of boy life, to take each at his true worth, it is impossible later to make the disciples of one creed persecute those of another. From the evils of religious persecution America is safe. (*Century*, January 1900.) *Mem. Ed.* XV, 404; *Nat. Ed.* XIII, 355.

PUBLIC SCHOOLS. See also EDUCATION; SCHOOLS; TEACHERS.

PUBLIC SERVANTS. See PUBLIC OFFICIALS.

PUBLIC SERVICE. See CITIZENSHIP; CIVIC DUTY; DEMOCRACY; DUTY; EDUCATED MEN; GOVERNMENT; HONESTY; POLITICS.

PUBLIC WELFARE. Public welfare depends upon general public prosperity, and the reformer whose reforms interfere with the general prosperity will accomplish little. (*Outlook*, November 18, 1914.) *Mem. Ed.* XIV, 221; *Nat. Ed.* XII, 238.

PUBLIC WELFARE—PRIMACY OF. We are face to face with new conceptions of the relations of property to human welfare, chiefly because certain advocates of the rights of property as against the rights of men have been pushing their claims too far. The man who wrongly holds that every human right is secondary to his profit must now give way to the advocate of human welfare, who rightly maintains that every man holds his property subject to the general right of the community to regulate its use to whatever degree the public welfare may require it. (At Osawatomie, Kan., August 31, 1910.) *Mem. Ed.* XIX, 24; *Nat. Ed.* XVII, 17.

PUBLIC WELFARE. See also HEALTH; SOCIAL INSURANCE.

PUBLICITY. See CORPORATIONS; MUCKRAKING; PUBLIC OPINION; TRUSTS.

PULLMAN STRIKE. See ALTGELD, JOHN PETER.

PUNISHMENT. See CAPITAL PUNISHMENT; CRIME; INSANITY PLEA; LYNCHING.

PURE FOOD LAW. The enactment of a pure food law was a recognition of the fact that the public welfare outweighs the right to private gain, and that no man may poison the people for his private profit. (Message to Congress, January 22, 1909.) *Presidential Addresses and State Papers* VIII, 2098.

——————. By means of the pure food law the federal government has within two years been able to accomplish a great benefit to the public in the direction of protecting it from impure and misbranded foods and drugs. But it should be realized that the work thus begun must be unflinchingly carried forward in the interest both of the public and of the great body of food producers who are engaged in honest business. It is largely true in all cases, but particularly true in this case, that a broadly effective and successful enforcement of law depends upon the support of an aroused and intelligent public opinion. Much has already been done in stopping the traffic in unhealthy and adulterated foodstuffs, but there remains yet more to do and the progress which has been made must be safeguarded. (Letter dated February 3, 1909.) *Good Housekeeping*, April 1909, p. 431.

PURE FOOD. See also AGRICULTURE—DEPARTMENT OF; HEALTH, PUBLIC.

PURITANISM. Puritanism left if anything a more lasting impress upon America than upon England; the history of its rise, and especially of its fall, has quite as direct a bearing upon the development of New England as a province, and afterwards of the United States as a nation, as it has upon the development of latter-day Britain. (To H. C. Lodge, August 24, 1884.) Lodge *Letters* I, 8.

——————. To endeavor to shape the whole course of individual existence in accordance with the hidden or half-indulged law of perfect righteousness has to it a very lofty side; but if the endeavor is extended to include mankind at large, it has also a very dangerous side: so dangerous indeed that in practice the effort is apt to result in harm, unless it is undertaken in a spirit of the broadest charity and toleration; for the more sincere the men who make it, the more certain they are to treat, not only their own principles, but their own passions, prejudices, vanities, and jealousies, as representing the will, not of themselves, but of Heaven. The constant appeal to the Word of God in all trivial matters is, moreover, apt to breed hypocrisy of that sanctimonious kind which is peculiarly repellent, and which invariably invites reaction against all religious feeling and expression. (1900.) *Mem. Ed.* XIII, 320; *Nat. Ed.* X, 215.

———————. The influence of the Puritan has been most potent for strength and for virtue in our national life. But its somber austerity left one evil: the tendency to confuse pleasure and vice, a tendency which, in the end, is much more certain to encourage vice than to discourage pleasure.

Let every layman interested in church work battle against this tendency. Let him proceed on the assumption that innocent pleasure which does not interfere with things even more desirable is in itself a good; that this is as true of one day of the week as of another; and that one function of the church should be the encouragement of happiness in small things as well as in large. *Ladies' Home Journal,* October 1917, p. 119.

PURITANISM. See also PLEASURE.

PURITANS. The Puritan owed his extraordinary success in subduing this continent and making it the foundation for a social life of ordered liberty primarily to the fact that he combined in a very remarkable degree both the power of individual initiative, of individual self-help, and the power of acting in combination with his fellows; and that furthermore he joined to a high heart that shrewd common sense which saves a man from the besetting sins of the visionary and the doctrinaire. He was stout-hearted and hard-headed. He had lofty purposes, but he had practical good sense, too. He could hold his own in the rough workaday world without clamorous insistence upon being helped by others, and yet he could combine with others whenever it became necessary to do a job which could not be as well done by any one man individually.

These were the qualities which enabled him to do his work, and they are the very qualities which we must show in doing our work to-day. There is no use in our coming here to pay homage to the men who founded this nation unless we first of all come in the spirit of trying to do our work to-day as they did their work in the yesterdays that have vanished. The problems shift from generation to generation, but the spirit in which they must be approached, if they are to be successfully solved, remains ever the same. The Puritan tamed the wilderness, and built up a free government on the stump-dotted clearings amid the primeval forest. His descendants must try to shape the life of our complex industrial civilization by new devices, by new methods, so as to achieve in the end the same results of justice and fair dealing toward all. (At Pilgrim Memorial Monument, Provincetown, Mass., August 20, 1907.) *Mem. Ed.* XVIII, 93-94; *Nat. Ed.* XVI, 78-79.

PURITANS—DEBT TO. We cannot as a nation be too profoundly grateful for the fact that the Puritan has stamped his influence so deeply on our national life. We need have but scant patience with the men who now rail at the Puritan's faults. They were evident, of course, for it is a quality of strong natures that their failings, like their virtues, should stand out in bold relief; but there is nothing easier than to belittle the great men of the past by dwelling only on the points where they come short of the universally recognized standards of the present. Men must be judged with reference to the age in which they dwell, and the work they have to do. The Puritan's task was to conquer a continent; not merely to overrun it, but to settle it, to till it, to build upon it a high industrial and social life; and, while engaged in the rough work of taming the shaggy wilderness, at that very time also to lay deep the immovable foundations of our whole American system of civil, political, and religious liberty achieved through the orderly process of law. This was the work allotted to him to do; this is the work he did; and only a master spirit among men could have done it. (At Pilgrim Memorial Monument, Provincetown, Mass., August 20, 1907.) *Mem. Ed.* XVIII, 90-91; *Nat. Ed.* XVI, 76-77.

Q

QUACKS. See LUNATIC FRINGE; NATURE FAKERS; POLITICAL QUACKS.

QUARRELS. There are certain elementary facts to be grasped by this people before we can have any policy at all. The first fact is a thorough understanding of that hoary falsehood which declares that it takes two to make a quarrel. It did not take two nations to make the quarrel that resulted in Germany trampling Belgium into the mire. It is no more true that it takes two to make a quarrel in international matters than it is to make the same assertion about a highwayman who holds up a passer-by or a black-hander who kidnaps a child. The people who do not make quarrels, who are not offensive, who give no cause for anger, are those who ordinarily furnish the victims of highwaymen, black-handers, and white-slavers. (*Metropolitan,* February 1916.) *Mem. Ed.* XX, 279; *Nat. Ed.* XVIII, 239.

QUEENS. See ROYALTY.

[497]

R

RACE PRESERVATION. The prime factor in the preservation of a race is its power to attain a high degree of social efficiency. Love of order, ability to fight well and breed well, capacity to subordinate the interests of the individual to the interests of the community, these and similar rather humdrum qualities go to make up the sum of social efficiency. The race that has them is sure to overturn the race whose members have brilliant intellects, but who are cold and selfish and timid, who do not breed well or fight well, and who are not capable of disinterested love of the community. (*North American Review*, July 1895.) *Mem. Ed.* XIV, 127; *Nat. Ed.* XIII, 240.

——————. To increase greatly a race must be prolific, and there is no curse so great as the curse of barrenness, whether for a nation or an individual. When a people gets to a position even now occupied by the mass of the French and by sections of the New Englanders, where the death-rate surpasses the birth-rate, then that race is not only fated to extinction but it deserves extinction. When the capacity and desire for fatherhood and motherhood is lost the race goes down, and should go down; and we need to have the plainest kind of plain speaking addressed to those individuals who fear to bring children into the world. But while this is all true, it remains equally true that immoderate increase in no way furthers the development of a race, and does not always help its increase even in numbers. The English-speaking peoples during the past two centuries and a half have increased faster than any others, yet there have been many other peoples whose birth-rate during the same period has stood higher. (*North American Review*, July 1895.) *Mem. Ed.* XIV, 111; *Nat. Ed.* XIII, 226.

RACE RIOTS. See BROWNSVILLE RIOT; LYNCHING.

RACE SUICIDE. Even more important than ability to work, even more important than ability to fight at need, is it to remember that the chief of blessings for any nation is that it shall leave its seed to inherit the land. It was the crown of blessings in Biblical times; and it is the crown of blessings now. The greatest of all curses is the curse of sterility, and the severest of all condemnations should be that visited upon wilful sterility. The first essential in any civilization is that the man and woman shall be father and mother of healthy children, so that the race shall increase and not decrease. (At the Sorbonne, Paris, April 23, 1910.) *Mem. Ed.* XV, 357; *Nat. Ed.* XIII, 513.

——————. I have never preached the imposition of an excessive maternity on any woman. I have always said that every man worth calling such will feel a peculiar sense of chivalric tenderness toward his wife, the mother of his children. He must be unselfish and considerate with her. But, exactly as he must do his duty, so she must do her duty. I have said that it is self-evident that unless the average woman, capable of having children, has four, the race will not go forward; for this is necessary in order to offset the women who for proper reasons do not marry, or who, from no fault of their own, have no children, or only one or two, or whose children die before they grow up. I do not want to see us Americans forced to import our babies from abroad. I do not want to see the stock of people like yourself and like my family die out—and you do not either; and it will inevitably die out if the average man and the average woman are so selfish and so cold that they wish either no children, or just one or two children. (Letter of February 9, 1916.) *Mem. Ed.* XXI, 152-153; *Nat. Ed.* XIX, 149.

RACE SUICIDE. *See also* BIRTH CONTROL; EUGENICS.

RACIAL AND NATIONAL UNITY. Most of the great societies which have developed a high civilization and have played a dominant part in the world have been—and are—artificial; not merely in social structure, but in the sense of including totally different race types. A great nation rarely belongs to any one race, though its citizens generally have one essentially national speech. Yet the curious fact remains that these great artificial societies acquire such unity that in each one all the parts feel a subtle sympathy, and move or cease to move, go forward or go back, all together, in response to some stir or throbbing, very powerful, and yet not to be discerned by our senses.

National unity is far more apt than race unity to be a fact to reckon with; until indeed we come to race differences as fundamental as those which divide from one another the half-dozen great ethnic divisions of mankind, when they become so important that differences of nationality, speech, and creed sink into littleness. (At Oxford University, June 7, 1910.) *Mem. Ed.* XIV, 84; *Nat. Ed.* XII, 41.

RACIAL ANTAGONISMS. Doubtless in the long run most is to be hoped from the slow growth of a better feeling, a more real feeling of brotherhood among the nations, among the peoples. The experience of the United States shows that there is no real foundation in race for the bitter antagonism felt among Slavs and Germans, French and English. . . . It is idle to tell us that the Frenchman and the German, the Slav and the Englishman are irreconcilably hostile one to the other because of difference of race. From our own daily experiences we know the contrary. We know that good men and bad men are to be found in each race. We know that the differences between the races above named and many others are infinitesimal compared with the vital points of likeness. (New York *Times,* October 18, 1914.) *Mem. Ed.* XX, 61-62; *Nat. Ed.* XVIII, 52-53.

RACIAL DECAY. There is a certain softness of fibre in civilized nations which, if it were to prove progressive, might mean the development of a cultured and refined people quite unable to hold its own in those conflicts through which alone any great race can ultimately march to victory. . . . Most ominous of all, there has become evident, during the last two generations, a very pronounced tendency among the most highly civilized races, and among the most highly civilized portions of all races, to lose the power of multiplying, and even to decrease; so much so as to make the fears of the disciples of Malthus a century ago seem rather absurd to the dweller in France or New England to-day. (*Forum,* January 1897.) *Mem. Ed.* XIV, 135; *Nat. Ed.* XIII, 247.

RACIAL DECAY. *See also* CIVILIZATION; DECADENCE; FIGHTING VIRTUES; NATIONAL DECAY.

RACIAL DIFFERENCES. No hard-and-fast rule can be drawn as applying to all alien races, because they differ from one another far more widely than some of them differ from us. But there are one or two rules which must not be forgotten.

In the long run there can be no justification for one race managing or controlling another unless the management and control are exercised in the interest and for the benefit of that other race.

This is what our peoples have in the main done, and must continue in the future in even greater degree to do, in India, Egypt and the Philippines alike. In the next place, as regards every race, everywhere, at home or abroad, we cannot afford to deviate from the great rule of righteousness which bids us treat each man on his worth as a man. (At Oxford University, June 7, 1910.) *Mem. Ed.* XIV, 104; *Nat. Ed.* XII, 57-58.

RACIAL THEORIES. *See* CHAMBERLAIN, HOUSTON STEWART.

RADICALS. In peaceful times and places like the United States at the present day, they [radicals] merely join little extreme parties, and run small, separate tickets on election day, thereby giving aid, comfort, and amusement to the totally unregenerate. In times of great political convulsion, when the appeal to arms has been made, these harmless bodies may draft into their ranks—as the Fifth Monarchy men did—fierce and dangerous spirits, ever ready to smite down with any weapons the possible good, because it is not the impossible best. When this occurs they need to be narrowly watched.

There are many good people who find it difficult to keep in mind the obvious fact that, while extremists are sometimes men who are in advance of their age, more often they are men who are not in advance at all, but simply to one side or the other of a great movement, or even lagging behind it, or trying to pilot it in the wrong direction. (1900.) *Mem. Ed.* XIII, 368; *Nat. Ed.* X, 256-257.

―――――――. Fundamentally it is the radical liberal with whom I sympathize. He is at least working toward the end for which I think we should all of us strive; and when he adds sanity and moderation to courage and enthusiasm for high ideals he develops into the kind of statesman whom alone I can wholeheartedly support. (To Sir George Otto Trevelyan, October 1, 1911.) *Mem. Ed.* XXIV, 272; Bishop II, 233.

RADICALS. *See also* ANARCHISTS; BOLSHEVISTS; CONSERVATIVES; EXTREMISTS; INDUSTRIAL WORKERS OF THE WORLD; LINCOLN, ABRAHAM; LUNATIC FRINGE; ORDER; REACTIONARIES; REFORMERS.

RAILROAD CASUALTIES. The ever-increasing casualty list upon our railroads is a matter of grave public concern, and urgently calls for action by the Congress. In the matter of speed and comfort of railway travel our railroads give at least as good service as those of any other nation, and there is no reason why this service should not also be as safe as human ingenuity can make it. Many of our leading roads have been foremost in the adoption of the most approved safeguards for the protection of travellers and employees, yet the list of clearly avoidable accidents continues unduly large. The passage of a law requiring the adoption of a block-signal system has been proposed to the Congress. I earnestly concur in that recommendation, and would also point out to the Congress the urgent need of legislation in the interest of the public safety limiting the hours of labor for railroad employees in train service upon railroads engaged in interstate commerce, and providing that only trained and experienced persons be employed in positions of responsibility connected with the operation of trains. Of course nothing can ever prevent accidents caused by human weakness or misconduct; and there should be drastic punishment for any railroad employee, whether officer or man, who by issuance of wrong orders or by disobedience of orders causes disaster. (Fourth Annual Message, Washington, December 6, 1904.) *Mem. Ed.* XVII, 254-255; *Nat. Ed.* XV, 218-219.

RAILROAD PROBLEM, THE. Of course in the whole railway situation that confronts this country we have continually to keep in mind the three interests: the interest of the men whose money has permitted the building of the roads; the interests of the engineers, firemen, and other men, trainmen and so on, who actually run the roads; and, third, the interests of the general public. *Outlook,* June 8, 1912, p. 294.

─────────. By actual experience it has been found that it is unsafe to leave the wage-worker, the shipper, and the general public, and furthermore that it is unsafe to leave the small investor himself, at the mercy of the big men who manage railways. But on certain points the interests of the big man and the small investor are identical. On certain other points the interests of both of them are identical with those of the wage-worker. On all points the only way of securing permanent justice to each class is by giving permanent justice to all classes. The public can be well served, and the wage-workers can be well paid, only if the railway is successful, that is, if there is such a certainty of reasonable dividends as to make investors content, and therefore willing and desirous to invest in further developments and enterprises. (*Outlook,* July 5, 1913.) *Mem. Ed.* XVIII, 120.

RAILROAD RATE LAW. Two years ago the railroads were all clamoring against the passage of the rate law—an act of folly on their part and on the part of their friends and abettors which cannot be too harshly stigmatized. The one hope for the honest railroad man, for the honest investor, is in the extension and perfection of the system inaugurated by that law; in the absolute carrying out of the law at present and in its strengthening, if possible, at the next session of Congress so as to make it even more effective. (To Henry L. Higginson, March 28, 1907.) *Mem. Ed.* XXIV, 46; Bishop II, 39-40.

RAILROAD RATES—ADJUSTMENT OF. If governmental action places too heavy burdens on railways, it will be impossible for them to operate without doing injustice to somebody. Railways cannot pay proper wages and render proper service unless they make money. The investors must get a reasonable profit or they will not invest, and the public cannot be well served unless the investors are making reasonable profits. There is every reason why rates should not be too high, but they must be sufficiently high to allow the railways to pay good wages. (1913.) *Mem. Ed.* XXII, 569; *Nat. Ed.* XX, 489-490.

─────────. It is just as much the duty of the commission to permit rates to be raised when the raise is justifiable as to require them to be lowered if the lowering is justifiable. The commission is created precisely because this is the kind of work it can and ought to do, and the kind of work that no legislative body could with wisdom perform. The commission is no true servant of the public unless it unhesitatingly raises the rates when justice in the public interest requires such action, and unhesitatingly lowers the rates when this is the course which will ultimately best meet the public needs. (*Outlook,* July 5, 1913.) *Mem. Ed.* XVIII, 121.

─────────. There is much wise legislation necessary for the safety of the public, or—like workmen's compensation—necessary to the well-being of the employee, which nevertheless imposes such a burden on the road that the burden must be distributed between the general public and the corporation, or there will be no dividends. In such a case it may be the highest duty of the commission to raise rates; and the commission, when satisfied that the necessity exists, in order to do justice to the owners of the road, should no more hesitate to raise rates than under other circumstances to lower them. (1913.) *Mem. Ed.* XXII, 498; *Nat. Ed.* XX, 428.

RAILROAD RATES—REGULATION OF. While I am of the opinion that at present it would be undesirable, if it were not impracticable, finally to clothe the commission with general authority to fix railroad rates, I do believe that, as a fair security to shippers, the commission should be vested with the power, where a given rate has been challenged and after full hearing found to be unreasonable, to decide, subject to judicial review, what shall be a reasonable rate to take its place; the ruling of the commission to take effect immediately, and to obtain unless and until it is reversed by the court of review. The government must in increasing degree supervise and regulate the workings of the railways engaged in interstate commerce; and such increased supervision is the only alternative to an increase of the present evils on the one hand or a still more radical policy on the other. (Fourth Annual Message, Washington, December 6, 1904.) *Mem. Ed.* XVII, 263; *Nat. Ed.* XV, 226.

——————————. Those who complain of the management of the railways allege that established rates are not maintained; that rebates and similar devices are habitually resorted to; that these preferences are usually in favor of the large shipper; that they drive out of business the smaller competitor; that while many rates are too low, many others are excessive; and that gross preferences are made, affecting both localities and commodities. Upon the other hand, the railways assert that the law by its very terms tends to produce many of these illegal practices by depriving carriers of that right of concerted action which they claim is necessary to establish and maintain non-discriminating rates.

The act should be amended. The railway is a public servant. Its rates should be just to and open to all shippers alike. The government should see to it that within its jurisdiction this is so and should provide a speedy, inexpensive, and effective remedy to that end. (First Annual Message, Washington, December 3, 1901.) *Mem. Ed.* XVII, 117; *Nat. Ed.* XV, 101.

——————————. The immediate and most pressing need, so far as legislation is concerned, is the enactment into law of some scheme to secure to the agents of the government such supervision and regulation of the rates charged by the railroads of the country engaged in interstate traffic as shall summarily and effectively prevent the imposition of unjust or unreasonable rates. It must include putting a complete stop to rebates in every shape and form.

This power to regulate rates, like all similar powers over the business world, should be exercised with moderation, caution, and self-restraint; but it should exist, so that it can be effectively exercised when the need arises.

The first consideration to be kept in mind is that the power should be affirmative and should be given to some administrative body created by the Congress. If given to the present Interstate Commerce Commission, or to a reorganized Interstate Commerce Commission, such commission should be made unequivocally administrative. (Fifth Annual Message, Washington, December 5, 1905.) *Mem. Ed.* XVII, 321; *Nat. Ed.* XV, 275.

RAILROAD REBATES. Above all else, we must strive to keep the highways of commerce open to all on equal terms; and to do this it is necessary to put a complete stop to all rebates. Whether the shipper or the railroad is to blame makes no difference; the rebate must be stopped, the abuses of the private car and private terminal-track and side-track systems must be stopped. (Fourth Annual Message, Washington, December 6, 1904.) *Mem. Ed.* XVII, 262; *Nat. Ed.* XV, 225.

RAILROAD WAGES. If the reduction in wages [by the Louisville and Nashville Railway] is due to natural causes, the loss of business being such that the burden should be, and is, equitably distributed between capitalist and wage-worker, the public should know it. If it is caused by legislation, the public, and Congress, should know it; and if it is caused by misconduct in the past financial or other operations of any railroad, then everybody should know it, especially if the excuse of unfriendly legislation is advanced as a method of covering up past business misconduct by the railroad managers, or as a justification for failure to treat fairly the wage-earning employees of the company.

It is sincerely to be hoped, therefore, that any wage controversy that may arise between the railroads and their employees may find a peaceful solution through the methods of conciliation and arbitration already provided by Congress, which have proven so effective during the past year. To this end the Commission should be in a position to have available for any Board of Conciliation or Arbitration relevant data pertaining to such carriers as may become involved in industrial disputes. Should conciliation fail to effect a settlement and arbitration be rejected, accurate information should be available in order to develop a properly formed public opinion. (To Interstate Commerce Commission, February 18, 1908.) *Mem. Ed.* XXIV, 95; Bishop II, 81.

RAILROADS—CONTROL OF. It is because, in my judgment, public ownership of railroads is highly undesirable and would probably in this country entail far-reaching disaster, that I wish to see such supervision and regulation of them in the interest of the public as will make it evident that there is no need for public ownership. The opponents of government regulation dwell upon the difficulties to be encountered and the intricate and involved nature of the problem. Their contention is true. It is a complicated and delicate problem, and all kinds of difficulties are sure to arise in connection with any plan of solution, while no plan will bring all the benefits hoped for by its more optimistic adherents. Moreover, under any healthy plan the benefits will develop gradually and not rapidly. Finally, we must clearly understand that the public servants who are to do this peculiarly responsible and delicate work must themselves be of the highest type both as regards integrity and efficiency. They must be well paid, for otherwise able men cannot in the long run be secured; and they must possess a lofty probity which will revolt as quickly at the thought of pandering to any gust of popular prejudice against rich men as at the thought of anything even remotely resembling subserviency to rich men. But while I fully admit the difficulties in the way, I do not for a moment admit that these difficulties warrant us in stopping in our effort to secure a wise and just system. They should have no other effect than to spur us on to the exercise of the resolution, the even-handed justice, and the fertility of resource, which we like to think of as typically American, and which will in the end achieve good results in this as in other fields of activity. The task is a great one and underlies the task of dealing with the whole industrial problem. But the fact that it is a great problem does not warrant us in shrinking from the attempt to solve it. (Fifth Annual Message, Washington, December 5, 1905.) *Mem. Ed.* XVII, 328-329; *Nat. Ed.* XV, 281-282.

——————. There can be no swerving from the course that has thus been marked out in the legislation actually enacted and in the messages in which I have asked for further legislation. We best serve the interests of the honest railway men when we announce that we will follow out precisely this course. It is the course of real, of ultimate conservatism. There will be no halt in the forward movement toward a full development of this policy; and those who wish us to take a step backward or to stand still, if their wishes were realized, would find that they had incited an outbreak of the very radicalism they fear. (At Indianapolis, May 30, 1907.) *Mem. Ed.* XXIV, 70; Bishop II, 60.

——————. The present unsatisfactory condition in railroad affairs is due ninety-five per cent to the misconduct, the short-sightedness, and the folly of the railroad men themselves. Unquestionably there is loose demagogic attack upon them in some of the States, but not one particle of harm has come to them by Federal action; on the contrary, merely good. I wish very much that our laws could be strengthened, and I think that the worst thing that could be done for the railroads would be an announcement that for two or three years the Federal Government would keep its hands off of them. It would result in a tidal wave of violent State action against them throughout three-fourths of this country. I am astonished at the curious short-sightedness of the railroad people — a short-sightedness which, thanks to their own action, extends to would-be investors. Legislation such as I have proposed, or whatever legislation in the future I shall propose, will be in the interest of honest investors and to protect the public and the investors against dishonest action. (To Henry L. Higginson, February 11, 1907.) *Mem. Ed.* XXIV, 45; Bishop II, 38.

——————. In some such body as the Interstate Commerce Commission there must be lodged in effective shape the power to see that every shipper who uses the railroads and every man who owns or manages a railroad shall on the one hand be given justice and on the other hand be required to do justice. Justice—so far as it is humanly possible to give and to get justice—is the foundation of our Government. (At Union League Club, Philadelphia, January 30, 1905.) *Mem. Ed.* XXIII, 490; Bishop I, 427.

——————. The most vital need is in connection with the railroads. As to these, in my judgment there should now be either a national incorporation act or a law licensing railway companies to engage in interstate commerce upon certain conditions. The law should be so framed as to give to the Interstate Commerce Commission power to pass upon the future issue of securities, while ample means should be provided to enable the commission, whenever in its judgment it is necessary, to make a physical valuation of any railroad. As I stated in my message to the Congress a year ago, railroads should be given power to enter into agreements, subject to these agreements being made public in minute detail and to the consent of the Interstate Commerce Commission being first obtained. Until the National Government assumes proper control of interstate commerce, in the exercise of the authority it already possesses, it will be impossible either to give or to get from the railroads full justice. The railroads and all other great corporations will do well to recognize that this control must come; the only question is as to what governmental body can most wisely exercise it. The courts will determine the limits within which the Federal authority can exercise it, and there will still remain ample work within each State for the railway commission of that State. (Seventh Annual Message, Washington, December 3, 1907.) *Mem. Ed.* XVII, 487; *Nat. Ed.* XV, 415-416.

RAILROADS—GOVERNMENT OWNERSHIP OF. The railroads have been making a most active campaign against my rate-making proposition. They think they have it beaten. Personally I do not believe they have, and I think they are very short-sighted not to understand that to beat it means to increase the danger of the movement for the government ownership of railroads. (To H. C. Lodge, May 24, 1905.) *Mem. Ed.* XXIII, 492; Bishop I, 428.

————. To exercise a constantly increasing and constantly more efficient supervision and control over the great common carriers of the country prevents all necessity for seriously considering such a project as the government ownership of railroads—a policy which would be evil in its results from every standpoint. . . . The government ought not to conduct the business of the country; but it ought to regulate it so that it shall be conducted in the interest of the public. (At Harrisburg, Pa., October 4, 1906.) *Mem. Ed.* XVIII, 86-87; *Nat. Ed.* XVI, 73.

RAILROADS — INVESTIGATION OF. It would in my judgment be most undesirable for the ultimate good of the railways to interfere in any way with a full and fair investigation. However, I am certain that we have got to make up our minds that the railroads must not in the future do things that cannot bear the light. If trouble comes from having the light turned on, remember it is not really due to the light but the misconduct which it exposed.

I quite agree with you that there is danger in ill-directed agitation, and especially in agitation in the States; but the only way to meet it is by having the fullest and most thorough investigation by the national government, and in conferring upon the national government full power to act. The federal authorities, including the President, must state as clearly as possible that railroads which do well are to be encouraged and when they make a good showing it is to be emphasized; and that the people who invest will be given a chance of profit which alone will make them willing to invest, and which alone will make big men willing to undertake the job. (To Paul Morton, January 24, 1907.) *Mem. Ed.* XXIV, 42; Bishop II, 36.

RAILROADS. *See also* INDUSTRIAL COMMISSION; INTERSTATE COMMERCE.

RANCH LIFE. I do not believe there ever was any life more attractive to a vigorous young fellow than life on a cattle ranch in those days. It was a fine, healthy life, too; it taught a man self-reliance, hardihood, and the value of instant decision—in short, the virtues that ought to come from life in the open country. I enjoyed the life to the full. (1913.) *Mem. Ed.* XXII, 115; *Nat. Ed.* XX, 98.

————. It is the life of men who live in the open, who tend their herds on horseback, who go armed and ready to guard their lives by their own prowess, whose wants are very simple, and who call no man master. Ranching is an occupation like those of vigorous, primitive pastoral peoples, having little in common with the humdrum, workaday business world of the nineteenth century; and the free ranchman in his manner of life shows more kinship to an Arab sheik than to a sleek city merchant or tradesman. (1888.) *Mem. Ed.* IV, 367; *Nat. Ed.* I, 274.

————. Life on a cattle-ranch, on the great plains or among the foot-hills of the high mountains, has a peculiar attraction for those hardy, adventurous spirits who take most kindly to a vigorous out-of-door existence, and who are therefore most apt to care passionately for the chase of big game. The free ranchman lives in a wild, lonely country, and exactly as he breaks and tames his own horses and guards and tends his own branded herds, so he takes the keenest enjoyment in the chase, which is to him not merely the pleasantest of sports, but also a means of adding materially to his comforts, and often his only method of providing himself with fresh meat. (1893.) *Mem. Ed.* II, 19; *Nat. Ed.* II, 16-17.

──────────────. The charm of ranch life comes in its freedom and the vigorous open-air existence it forces a man to lead. Except when hunting in bad ground, the whole time away from the house is spent in the saddle, and there are so many ponies that a fresh one can always be had. (1885.) *Mem. Ed.* I, 15; *Nat. Ed.* I, 13.

──────────────. No ranchmen have time to make such extended trips as are made by some devotees of sport who are so fortunate as to have no every-day work to which to attend. Still, ranch life undoubtedly offers more chances to a man to get sport than is now the case with any other occupation in America, and those who follow it are apt to be men of game spirit, fond of excitement and adventure, who perforce lead an open-air life, who must needs ride well, for they are often in the saddle from sunrise to sunset, and who naturally take kindly to that noblest of weapons, the rifle. With such men hunting is one of the chief of pleasures; and they follow it eagerly when their work will allow them. (1885.) *Mem. Ed.* I, 29; *Nat. Ed.* I, 24.

──────────────. It was still the Wild West in those days, the far West, the West of Owen Wister's stories and Frederic Remington's drawings, the West of the Indian and the buffalo-hunter, the soldier and the cow-puncher. That land of the West has gone now, "gone, gone with lost Atlantis," gone to the isle of ghosts and of strange dead memories. It was a land of vast silent spaces, of lonely rivers, and of plains where the wild game stared at the passing horseman. It was a land of scattered ranches, of herds of long-horned cattle, and of reckless riders who unmoved looked in the eyes of life or of death. In that land we led a free and hardy life, with horse and with rifle. We worked under the scorching midsummer sun, when the wide plains shimmered and wavered in the heat; and we knew the freezing misery of riding night guard round the cattle in the late fall round-up. In the soft springtime the stars were glorious in our eyes each night before we fell asleep; and in the winter we rode through blinding blizzards, when the driven snow-dust burned our faces. There were monotonous days, as we guided the trail cattle or the beef herds, hour after hour, at the slowest of walks; and minutes or hours teeming with excitement as we stopped stampedes or swam the herds across rivers treacherous with quicksands or brimmed with running ice. We knew toil and hardship and hunger and thirst; and we saw men die violent deaths as they worked among the horses and cattle, or fought in evil feuds with one another; but we felt the beat of hardy life in our veins, and ours was the glory of work and the joy of living. (1913.) *Mem. Ed.* XXII, 112; *Nat. Ed.* XX, 96.

──────────────. I never became a good roper, nor more than an average rider, according to ranch standards. Of course a man on a ranch has to ride a good many bad horses, and is bound to encounter a certain number of accidents, and of these I had my share, at one time cracking a rib, and on another occasion the point of my shoulder.... When I had the opportunity I broke my own horses, doing it gently and gradually and spending much time over it, and choosing the horses that seemed gentle to begin with. With these horses I never had any difficulty. But frequently there was neither time nor opportunity to handle our mounts so elaborately. (1913.) *Mem Ed.* XXII, 127; *Nat. Ed.* XX, 109.

──────────────. There is so great a charm in absolute solitude, in the wild, lonely freedom of the great plains, that often I would make some excuse and go off entirely by myself.

Such rides had a fascination of their own. Hour after hour the wiry pony shuffled onward across the sea of short, matted grass. On every side the plains stretched seemingly limitless. Sometimes there would be no object to break the horizon; sometimes across a score of miles there would loom through the clear air the fantastic outlines of a chain of buttes, rising grim and barren. Occasionally there might be a slightly marked watercourse, every drop of moisture long dried; and usually there would not be as much as the smallest sage-brush anywhere in sight. As the sun rose higher and higher the shadows of horse and rider shortened, and the beams were reflected from the short, bleached blades until in the hot air all the landscape afar off seemed to dance and waver. (1905.) *Mem. Ed.* III, 146; *Nat. Ed.* II, 515.

RANCH LIFE. *See also* BAD LANDS; CHIMNEY BUTTE RANCH; ELKHORN RANCH.

RANCHING. A large number of young men from the cities and from the country districts of the East have recently taken to ranching. Many apparently think that this is a business needing no especial skill or training on the part of those who take it up. A greater mistake could not well be made. All over the plains there are now plenty of skilled cowhands—

men who have been all their lives in the saddle, and who know every trait of the cattle they have to guard, and every phase of the wild life of the wilderness. An outsider, to compete with these men, must not only be naturally well fitted for the life, but he must also spend at least two years in downright hard drudgery learning the business. A great many young fellows — including, by-the-way, quite a fair proportion of clergymen's sons—have an idea that the life of a ranchman, from its very hardships and risks, must have a certain romantic attraction to it. So it has; but it is wonderful how the romance evaporates for many of these same young fellows after a couple of months spent in a muddy dug-out, with no amusements whatever, and on a steady diet of rancid bacon, sodden biscuits, and alkali water. Hardships are romantic enough in the abstract, but in the concrete cold, hunger, wet, dirt, and fatigue are not only annoying, but are also very prosaic. The risks, too, are by no means imaginary. The tyro will be far from enjoying the vicious, half-broken horses that will certainly fall to his lot; and he will find it no joke in the bitter winter weather to make his daily rounds over a country whose main features may be entirely changed by the snow, and where getting lost may mean death, while the long, dreary winter nights will as often as not be passed in shivering discomfort, and at the best will be unutterably monotonous. To sit in the saddle all day is not such hard work as to wield axe, spade, or hammer for the same length of time; but it is real work, nevertheless, and for the months during which the different round-ups take place it is always very severe, as well as being often both tame and irksome.

To be able to follow the business at all, the man must be made of fairly stern stuff. He must be stout and hardy; he must be quick to learn, and have a fair share of dogged resolution; and he must rapidly accustom himself to habits of complete self-reliance. *Harper's Weekly*, January 2, 1886, p. 7.

RANCHING. *See also* CATTLE INDUSTRY.

REACTIONARIES. The reactionary is always willing to take a progressive attitude on any issue that is dead. (At New York City, February 12, 1913.) *Mem. Ed.* XIX, 486; *Nat. Ed.* XVII, 360.

———. A period of change is upon us. Our opponents, the men of reaction, ask us to stand still. But we could not stand still if we would; we must either go forward or go backward. Never was the need more imperative than now for men of vision who are also men of action. Disaster is ahead of us if we trust to the leadership of men whose souls are seared and whose eyes are blinded, men of cold heart and narrow mind, who believe we can find safety in dull timidity and dull inaction. The unrest cannot be quieted by ingenious trickery of those who profess to advance by merely marking time, or who seek to drown the cry for justice by loud and insincere clamor about issues that are false and issues that are dead. (At Chicago, June 17, 1912.) *Mem. Ed.* XIX, 314; *Nat. Ed.* XVII, 228.

———. These real masters of the reactionary forces have a tremendous personal interest in perpetuating the right of the boss in politics with as its necessary accompaniment, the safeguarding of privilege and the enlarging of the sphere of special interest. They are the men who stand back of the ordinary political leaders who are against us. They are the men who directly or indirectly control the majority of the great daily newspapers that are against us. Behind them comes the host of honest citizens who because the channels of their information are choked misunderstand our position and believe that in opposing us they are opposing disturbers of the peace. In addition these are the men who now, as in every age—are intellectually and temperamentally incapable of consenting to progress and who worship at the shrine of the sanctity of property even though that property be illicitly acquired and used to the detriment of the community. All of these honest men are sedulously taught by the big sinister men above them that revolution impends if we strike at even the most obvious injustice. They are taught to believe that change means destruction. They are wrong. The men who temperately and with self-restraint but with unflinching resolution and efficiency strike at injustice, right grievous wrong, and drive intrenched privilege from its sanctuary, are the men who prevent revolutions. (At Chicago, June 17, 1912.) *Mem. Ed.* XIX, 306; *Nat. Ed.* XVII, 222.

REACTIONARIES—FOLLY OF. I have always maintained that our worst revolutionaries to-day are those reactionaries who do not see and will not admit that there is any need for change. Such men seem to believe that the four and a half million Progressive voters, who in 1912 registered their solemn protest against our social and industrial injustices, are "anarchists," who are not willing to let ill enough alone. If these reactionaries had lived at an earlier time in our history, they would have advocated sedition laws, opposed free speech and free assembly, and voted against free schools, free access by settlers to the public lands, mechanics' lien laws, the prohibition of truck stores and the abolition of imprisonment for debt; and they are the men who today oppose minimum-wage laws, insurance of workmen against the ills of industrial life, and the reform of our legislators and our courts, which can alone render such measures possible. Some of these reactionaries are not bad men, but merely short-sighted and belated.

It is these reactionaries, however, who, by "standing pat" on industrial injustice, incite inevitably to industrial revolt, and it is only we who advocate political and industrial democracy who render possible the progress of our American industry on large constructive lines with a minimum of friction because with a maximum of justice. (1913.) *Mem. Ed.* XXII, 553-554; *Nat. Ed.* XX, 475-476.

——————. The reactionaries, the men whose only idea is to restore their power to the bourbons of wealth and politics, and obstinately to oppose all rational forward movements for the general betterment, would, if they had their way, bring to this country the ruin wrought by the régime of the Romanoffs in Russia. To withstand the sane movement for social and industrial justice is enormously to increase the likelihood that the movement will be turned into insane and sinister channels. And to oscillate between the sheer brutal greed of the haves and the sheer brutal greed of the have-nots means to plumb the depths of degradation. (1918.) *Mem. Ed.* XXI, 381; *Nat. Ed.* XIX, 345.

REACTIONARIES. *See also* CONSERVATIVES; EXTREMISTS; HISTORY; ORDER; PROGRESSIVE MOVEMENT; RADICALS; REFORMERS.

READING. I as emphatically object to nothing but heavy reading as I do to nothing but light reading—all that is indispensable being that the heavy and the light reading alike shall be both interesting and wholesome. (*Outlook*, April 30, 1910.) *Mem. Ed.* XIV, 467; *Nat. Ed.* XII, 340.

——————. I find reading a great comfort. People often say to me that they do not see how I find time for it, to which I answer them (much more truthfully than they believe) that to me it is a dissipation, which I have sometimes to try to avoid, instead of an irksome duty. Of course I have been so busy for the last ten years, so absorbed in political work, that I have simply given up reading any book that I do not find interesting. But there are a great many books which ordinarily pass for "dry" which to me possess much interest—notably history and anthropology; and these give me ease and relaxation that I can get in no other way, not even on horseback! (To Sir George Otto Trevelyan, May 28, 1904.) *Mem. Ed.* XXIV, 166; Bishop II, 142.

——————. I find it a great comfort to like all kinds of books, and to be able to get half an hour or an hour's complete rest and complete detachment from the fighting of the moment, by plunging into the genius and misdeeds of Marlborough, or the wicked perversity of James II, or the brilliant battle for human freedom fought by Fox—or in short, anything that Macaulay wrote or that you have written, or any one of the novels of Scott and of some of the novels of Thackeray and Dickens; or to turn to Hawthorne or Poe; or to Longfellow, who I think has been underestimated of late years, by the way. (To Sir George Otto Trevelyan, January 22, 1906.) *Mem. Ed.* XXIV, 184; Bishop II, 158.

——————. I have never followed any plan in reading which would apply to all persons under all circumstances; and indeed it seems to me that no plan can be laid down that will be generally applicable. If a man is not fond of books, to him reading of any kind will be drudgery. I most sincerely commiserate such a person, but I do not know how to help him. If a man or a woman is fond of books he or she will naturally seek the books that the mind and soul demand. Suggestions of a possibly helpful character can be made by outsiders, but only suggestions; and they will probably be helpful about in proportion to the outsider's knowledge of the mind and soul of the person to be helped. (1916.) *Mem. Ed.* IV, 187; *Nat. Ed.* III, 343.

READING—TASTES IN. A book must be interesting to the particular reader at that particular time. But there are tens of thousands of interesting books, and some of them are sealed to some men and some are sealed to others; and some stir the soul at some given point of a man's life and yet convey no message at other times. The reader, the booklover, must meet his own needs without paying too much attention to what his neighbors say those needs should be. He must not hypocritically pretend to like what he does not like. Yet at the same time he must avoid that most unpleasant of all the indications of puffed-up vanity which consists in treating mere individual, and perhaps unfortunate, idiosyncrasy as a matter of pride. (1913.) *Mem. Ed.* XXII, 379; *Nat. Ed.* XX, 325.

——————. The equation of personal taste is as powerful in reading as in eating; and within certain broad limits the matter is merely one of individual preference, having nothing to do with the quality either of the book or of the reader's mind. (1916.) *Mem. Ed.* IV, 188; *Nat. Ed.* III, 344.

READING. See also BOOKS; DRAMA; LITERATURE; POETRY.

REASON. Reason can deal effectively only with certain categories. True wisdom must necessarily refuse to allow reason to assume a sway outside of its limitations; and where experience plainly proves that the intellect has reasoned wrongly, then it is the part of wisdom to accept the teachings of experience, and bid reason be humble—just as under like conditions it would bid theology be humble. (*Outlook*, December 2, 1911.) *Mem. Ed.* XIV, 427; *Nat. Ed.* XII, 121.

REASON. See also INTELLIGENCE; RELIGION; SCIENCE.

REBATES. See RAILROAD RATES; TRUSTS.

REBELLION. See REVOLUTION.

RECALL. I believe the people should be provided with the means of recalling or unelecting important elective administrative officers, to be used only when there is a widespread and genuine public feeling for such a recall among the majority of the voters. I believe that there is scant necessity for using it in connection with short-term elective officers. *Outlook*, March 30, 1912, p. 721.

——————. As regards the recall, it is sometimes very useful, but it contains undoubted possibilities of mischief, and of course it is least necessary in the case of short-term elective officers. There is, however, unquestionably a very real argument to be made for it as regards officers elected or appointed for life. In the United States Government practically the only body to whom this applies is the judiciary. (*Outlook*, January 21, 1911.) *Mem. Ed.* XIX, 89; *Nat. Ed.* XVII, 56.

——————. As to the recall, I do not believe that there is any great necessity for it as regards short-term elective officers. On abstract grounds I was originally inclined to be hostile to it. I know of one case where it was actually used with mischievous results. On the other hand, in three cases in municipalities on the Pacific coast which have come to my knowledge it was used with excellent results. I believe it should be generally provided, but with such restrictions as will make it available only when there is a wide-spread and genuine public feeling among a majority of the voters. (Before Ohio Constitutional Convention, Columbus, February 21, 1912.) *Mem. Ed,* XIX, 182; *Nat. Ed.* XVII, 135.

——————. I believe that the prompt removal of unfaithful or incompetent public servants should be made easy and sure in whatever way experience shall show to be most expedient in any given class of cases. (At Osawatomie, Kan., August 31, 1910.) *Mem. Ed.* XIX, 28; *Nat. Ed.* XVII, 21.

——————. There is the recall of public officers—the principle that an officer chosen by the people who is unfaithful may be recalled by vote of the majority before he finishes his term. I will speak of the recall of judges in a moment—leave that aside—but as to the other officers, I have heard no argument advanced against the proposition, save that it will make the public officer timid and always currying favor with the mob. That argument means that you can fool all the people all the time, and is an avowal of disbelief in democracy. If it be true—and I believe it is not—it is less important than to stop those public officers from currying favor with the interests. Certain States may need the recall, others may not; where the term of elective office is short it may be quite needless; but there are occasions when it meets a real evil, and provides a needed check and balance against the special interests. (At Carnegie Hall, New York, March 20, 1912.) *Mem. Ed.* XIX, 202; *Nat. Ed.* XVII, 153.

RECALL. See also PROGRESSIVE PRINCIPLES; REPRESENTATIVE GOVERNMENT.

RECALL OF JUDGES. I believe that the evils which have led to the very widespread proposal to apply the recall to judges are very real. I see no reason why the people, if they are competent to elect judges, are not also competent to un-elect them. I think the judiciary should be made clearly to understand that they represent justice for the whole people. . . . In addition, I would have the appointive judges removable; and, in feeling our way to the proper solution I would try having this done by a majority vote of the two houses of the Legislature. . . . But this is merely my preference. . . . My prime concern is with the end, not the means. I wish to see good judges put on the bench and bad ones taken off it. Any system which in its actual workings accomplishes these two ends is a good system. I do not wish to use the recall if it is possible to avoid doing so; but I would far rather have recourse to the recall than continue the present system which provides an impeachment remedy that in practice never works, and provides no efficient way whatever for overruling judicial misconstruction of the Constitution. *Outlook,* March 30, 1912, p. 721.

──────────. The recall of judges [is] a measure which I do not wish to see adopted in any community unless it proves impossible in any other way to get the judges to do justice—and I will add that nothing will so tend to strengthen the movement for the recall as action like this of Messrs. Choate and Milburn, and their associates, in seeking to buttress special privilege in the courts and to make them the bulwark of injustice instead of justice. (At Philadelphia, April 10, 1912.) *Mem. Ed.* XIX, 261; *Nat. Ed.* XVII, 195.

──────────. The Progressive party in its attitude both toward the recall of judges and toward the right of the people to insist that they and not the judges are to have the ultimate say-so in making their own constitution, takes precisely the attitude of Abraham Lincoln when he said that "the people are the masters of both Congresses and the courts, not to destroy the Constitution, but to overthrow those who would destroy the Constitution." A case like that in Idaho shows the need of the power of popular recall of the judiciary, a need which I believe could probably be best met by having the judges appointed or elected for life, but subject on petition to recall by popular vote every two years—which system in its essentials would be like that which has actually, although not nominally, obtained in Vermont, except that it would substitute popular vote for legislative action.

This action would not, however, meet all the difficulties of the case. In this State, for instance, there have been many well-meaning judges who, in certain cases, usually affecting labor, have rendered decisions which were wholly improper, wholly reactionary, and fraught with the gravest injustice to those classes of the community standing most in need of justice. What is needed here is not the right to recall the judge, who in some one instance gives a mistaken and reactionary interpretation of the Constitution, but the right of the people themselves to express after due deliberation their definite judgment as to what the Constitution shall permit in the way of legislation for social and industrial justice. Always remember, friends, that I am not speaking of the judicial functions which can properly be called such. I am not speaking of the functions exercised by the judges in other great industrial countries such as France, Germany, or England. I am speaking of the purely political function exercised by the judge in our country, and only in our country, in annulling legislation. (At New York City, February 12, 1913.) *Mem. Ed.* XIX, 502-503, *Nat. Ed.* XVII, 373-374.

──────────. The administration of justice should be humanized. We believe that by some means quick and available to the people the incompetent or unjust judge should be removed from office. *Outlook,* November 15, 1913, p. 595.

──────────. The people, having framed the Constitution and the statutes . . . should choose the best judge that they can to carry out the provisions of the Constitution and the statutes; but if they decide that they want a Workmen's Compensation Act, they ought to expect the judge to administer such an act, and not to determine whether a Workmen's Compensation Act is good for them or not. It is none of the judge's business to say whether the people ought to wish to have such an Act; it is the people's business and only theirs. . . . If the judges endeavor to assert their view as opposed to the people's view, the people ought in legal fashion to tell them they are mistaken, and, if the judges persist, remove them and get judges who will administer the law based upon the theory of government which the people in the exercise of their sober and deliberate judgment have decided to be good. *Outlook,* March 30, 1912, p. 721.

──────────. If in any state the adoption of the recall was found to mean the subjection of the judge to the whim of the mob, then it would become the imperative duty of every good citizen, without regard to previous prejudices, to work for the alteration of the system. If, on the other hand, in any state the judiciary yields to improper influence on the part of special interests, or if the judges even, although honest men, show themselves so narrow-minded and so utterly out of sympathy with the industrial and social needs brought about by changed conditions that they seek to fetter the movement for progress and betterment, then the people are not to be excused if, in a servile spirit, they submit to such domination, and fail to take any measures necessary to secure their right to go forward along the path of economic and social justice and fair dealing. *Outlook,* June 24, 1911, p. 378.

RECALL OF JUDICIAL DECISIONS. Now as to the name which has been given by me to the doctrine. It was given by me in a number of arguments in which I was trying to show that what was needed was not to recall judges who gave wrong constitutional decisions, but to recall the decisions. I have myself regretted the continuous use of the term, but it is difficult to get a short term to explain just what we want to do. (To George V. Crocker, November 19, 1912.) *Mem. Ed.* XXIV, 409-410; Bishop II, 348.

——————. There is one kind of recall in which I very earnestly believe, and the immediate adoption of which I urge.

There are sound reasons for being cautious about the recall of a good judge who has rendered an unwise and improper decision. Every public servant, no matter how valuable—and not omitting Washington or Lincoln or Marshall—at times makes mistakes. Therefore we should be cautious about recalling the judge, and we should be cautious about interfering in any way with the judge in decisions which he makes in the ordinary course as between individuals. But when a judge decides a constitutional question, when he decides what the people as a whole can or cannot do, the people should have the right to recall that decision if they think it wrong. We should hold the judiciary in all respect; but it is both absurd and degrading to make a fetich of a judge or of any one else. (Before Ohio Constitutional Convention, Columbus, February 21, 1912.) *Mem. Ed.* XIX, 186; *Nat. Ed.* XVII, 138.

——————. My proposal is merely to secure to the people the right which the Supreme Court, speaking through Mr. Justice Holmes, in the Oklahoma Bank Cases, say they undoubtedly should possess. My proposal is that the people shall have the power to decide for themselves, in the last resort, what legislation is necessary in exercising the police powers, the general welfare powers, so as to give expression to the general morality, the general opinion, of the people. In England, Canada, and the other countries I have mentioned, no one dreams that the court has a right to express an opinion in such matters as against the will of the people shown by the action of the legislature. I do not propose to go as far as this. I do not propose to do in these matters what England, Canada, Australia, and France have always done, that is, make the legislature supreme over the courts in these cases. I merely propose to make legislature and court alike responsible to the sober and deliberate judgment of the people, who are masters of both legislature and courts. (At Philadelphia, April 10, 1912.) *Mem. Ed.* XIX, 260; *Nat. Ed.* XVII, 194.

——————. During the last forty years the beneficiaries of reaction have found in the courts their main allies; and this condition, so unfortunate for the courts, no less than for the people, has been due to our governmental failure to furnish methods by which an appeal can be taken directly to the people when, in any such case as the cases I have above enumerated, there is an issue between the court and the legislature. It is idle to profess devotion to our Progressive proposals for social and industrial betterment if at the same time there is opposition to the one additional proposal by which they can be made effective. It is useless to advocate the passing of laws for social justice if we permit these laws to be annulled with impunity by the courts, or by any one else, after they have been passed. (*Century,* October 1913.) *Mem. Ed.* XIX, 553; *Nat. Ed.* XVII, 408.

——————. We propose that, in any specific case where the courts declare unconstitutional a given law in the interest of social justice, the people themselves shall have the power to decide whether, notwithstanding such decision, the law in question shall become part of the law of the land. . . . We do intend that in these matters of lawmaking and Constitution-making the people shall be made supreme over the courts, not merely nominally and theoretically, but practically and as a matter of actual fact. Our proposal is that the court shall continue to have the right to declare a given law of the legislature unconstitutional; but that in such case the people shall have the right, by expeditious process, after taking time for deliberation, but without any improper or excessive delay, to say whether the legislature or the court shall be held best to have interpreted their wishes. We do not wish to take away the power of the courts to pass on the constitutionality of a law. But where they thus declare a law unconstitutional, we wish to give the people who made the Constitution, whose fathers died for it, who now live under it, and to whom it belongs, the right to say whether or not the law shall stand. We wish to make the people the supreme arbiters between their servants the court and the legislature when the court and the legislature differ as to the proper interpretation of the Constitution which the people made. We wish to give to the people the power finally to make their own Constitution, and to make it by declaring specifically what it is to be held to mean in any given case where the two servants of the people, the court and the legislature, disagree on some definite act in the interest of social and industrial justice. *Outlook,* November 15, 1913, pp. 595-596.

——————. So that no man may misunderstand me, let me recapitulate:

(1) I am not proposing anything in connection with the Supreme Court of the United States, or with the Federal Constitution.

(2) I am not proposing anything having any connection with ordinary suits, civil or criminal, as between individuals.

(3) I am not speaking of the recall of judges.

(4) I am proposing merely that in a certain class of cases involving police power, when a State court has set aside as unconstitutional a law passed by the legislature for the general welfare, the question of the validity of the law —which should depend, as Justice Holmes so well phrases it, upon the prevailing morality or preponderant opinion—be submitted for final determination to a vote of the people, taken after due time for consideration.

And I contend that the people, in the nature of things, must be better judges of what is the preponderant opinion than the courts, and that the courts should not be allowed to reverse the political philosophy of the people. My point is well illustrated by a recent decision of the Supreme Court, holding that the court would not take jurisdiction of a case involving the constitutionality of the initiative and referendum laws of Oregon. The ground of the decision was that such a question was not judicial in its nature, but should be left for determination to the other co-ordinate departments of the government. Is it not equally plain that the question whether a given social policy is for the public good is not of a judicial nature, but should be settled by the legislature, or in the final instance by the people themselves? (At Carnegie Hall, New York, March 20, 1912.) *Mem. Ed.* XIX, 205; *Nat. Ed.* XVII, 156.

——————. What the Supreme Court of the nation decides to be law binds both the national and the State courts and all the people within the boundaries of the nation. But the decision of a State court on a constitutional question should be subject to revision by the people of the State.

Again and again in the past justice has been scandalously obstructed by State courts declaring State laws in conflict with the Federal Constitution, although the Supreme Court of the nation had never so decided or had even decided in a contrary sense.

When the supreme court of the State declares a given statute unconstitutional, because in conflict with the State or the National Constitution, its opinion should be subject to revision by the people themselves. Such an opinion ought always to be treated with great respect by the people, and unquestionably in the majority of cases would be accepted and followed by them. But actual experience has shown the vital need of the people reserving to themselves the right to pass upon such opinion. If any considerable number of the people feel that the decision is in defiance of justice, they should be given the right by petition to bring before the voters at some subsequent election, special or otherwise, as might be decided, and after the fullest opportunity for deliberation and debate, the question whether or not the judges' interpretation of the Constitution is to be sustained. If it is sustained, well and good. If not, then the popular verdict is to be accepted as final, the decision is to be treated as reversed, and the construction of the Constitution definitely decided—subject only to action by the Supreme Court of the United States. (Before Ohio Constitutional Convention, Columbus, February 21, 1912.) *Mem. Ed.* XIX, 187; *Nat. Ed.* XVII, 139.

——————. If in any State the courts, in addition to doing justice in the ordinary cases between man and man, have striven to help and not hamper the people in their efforts to secure social and industrial justice in a far broader sense for the people as a whole, then in that community there may be no need for change, as regards them. But where, in any community, as in my own State of New York, for instance, the highest court of the State, because of its adherence to outworn, to dead and gone, systems of philosophy, and its lack of understanding of and sympathy with the living, the vital needs of those in the community whose needs are greatest, becomes a bulwark of privilege and the most effective of all means for preventing the people from working in efficient fashion for true justice; then I hold that the people must themselves be given the power, after due deliberation and in constitutional fashion, to have their judgment made efficient and their interpretation of the Constitution made binding upon their servants, the judges, no less than upon their servants the legislators and executives. (At Louisville, Ky., April 3, 1912.) *Mem. Ed.* XIX, 243; *Nat. Ed.* XVII, 179.

——————. If in any case the legislature has passed a law under the police power for the purpose of promoting social and industrial justice and the courts declare it in conflict with the fundamental law of the State, the constitution as laid down by the people, then I propose that after due deliberation—for a period which could not be for less than two years after the passage of the original law—the people shall themselves have the right to declare whether or not the proposed law is to be treated as constitutional. (At Philadelphia, April 10, 1912.) *Mem. Ed.* XIX, 261; *Nat. Ed.* XVII, 195.

RECALL OF JUDICIAL DECISIONS. *See also* CONSTITUTION; COURTS; JUDGES; JUDICIARY; LAW.

RECIPROCITY. Reciprocity must be treated as the handmaiden of protection. Our first duty is to see that the protection granted by the tariff in every case where it is needed is maintained, and that reciprocity be sought for so far as it can safely be done without injury to our home industries. Just how far this is must be determined according to the individual case, remembering always that every application of our tariff policy to meet our shifting national needs must be conditioned upon the cardinal fact that the duties must never be reduced below the point that will cover the difference between the labor cost here and abroad. . . .

Subject to this proviso of the proper protection necessary to our industrial well-being at home, the principle of reciprocity must command our hearty support. The phenomenal growth of our export trade emphasizes the urgency of the need for wider markets and for a liberal policy in dealing with foreign nations. Whatever is merely petty and vexatious in the way of trade restrictions should be avoided. The customers to whom we dispose of our surplus products in the long run, directly or indirectly, purchase those surplus products by giving us something in return. Their ability to purchase our products should as far as possible be secured by so arranging our tariff as to enable us to take from them those products which we can use without harm to our own industries and labor, or the use of which will be of marked benefit to us. (First Annual Message, Washington, December 3, 1901.) *Mem. Ed.* XVII, 112-113; *Nat. Ed.* XV, 97-98.

——————. There can be no reciprocity unless there is a substantial tariff; free trade and reciprocity are not compatible. We are on record as favoring arrangements for reciprocal trade relations with other countries, these arrangements to be on an equitable basis of benefit to both the contracting parties. The Republican party stands pledged to every wise and consistent method of increasing the foreign commerce of the country. (Letter accepting Republican nomination for President, September 12, 1904.) *Mem. Ed.* XVIII, 520; *Nat. Ed.* XVI, 390.

RECIPROCITY TREATIES. It is greatly to be desired that such treaties may be adopted. They can be used to widen our markets and to give a greater field for the activities of our producers on the one hand, and on the other hand to secure in practical shape the lowering of duties when they are no longer needed for protection among our own people, or when the minimum of damage done may be disregarded for the sake of the maximum of good accomplished. (Second Annual Message, Washington, December 2, 1902.) *Mem. Ed.* XVII, 168-169; *Nat. Ed.* XV, 145.

RECIPROCITY. *See also* TARIFF.

RECLAMATION. *See* CONSERVATION; INLAND WATERWAYS; IRRIGATION; PUBLIC LANDS.

RECLAMATION ACT. On June 17, 1902, the Reclamation Act was passed. It set aside the proceeds of the disposal of public lands for the purpose of reclaiming the waste areas of the arid West by irrigating lands otherwise worthless, and thus creating new homes upon the land. The money so appropriated was to be repaid to the government by the settlers, and to be used again as a revolving fund continuously available for the work.

The impatience of the Western people to see immediate results from the Reclamation Act was so great that red tape was disregarded, and the work was pushed forward at a rate previously unknown in government affairs. . . .

What the Reclamation Act has done for the country is by no means limited to its material accomplishment. This Act and the results flowing from it have helped powerfully to prove to the nation that it can handle its own resources and exercise direct and business-like control over them. The population which the Reclamation Act has brought into the arid West, while comparatively small when compared with that in the more closely inhabited East, has been a most effective contribution to the national life, for it has gone far to transform the social aspect of the West, making for the stability of the institutions upon which the welfare of the whole country rests: it has substituted actual home-makers, who have settled on the land with their families, for huge, migratory bands of sheep herded by the hired shepherds of absentee owners. (1913.) *Mem. Ed.* XXII, 450-452; *Nat. Ed.* XX, 387-389.

RECONSTRUCTION. The trouble I am having with the Southern question . . . emphasizes the infinite damage done in reconstruction days by the unregenerate arrogance and shortsightedness of the Southerners and the doctrinaire folly of radicals like Sumner and Thaddeus Stevens. (To James Ford Rhodes, November 29, 1904.) *Mem. Ed.* XXIII, 403; Bishop I, 350.

RECONSTRUCTION. *See also* CIVIL WAR.

RED CROSS. The Red Cross, and kindred organizations, have done admirable work for our soldiers during the summer just past. The Red Cross Society should be the right hand of the Medical Department of the army, in peace and war; for even the best medical department will always need volunteer aid in the case either of battles or of camp epidemics. In America the Red Cross should have a Federal organization, with, in every State, chapters which should be in close touch with the National Guard, attending the encampments and forming schools of instruction in military methods. (Annual Message as Governor, Albany, January 2, 1899.) *Mem. Ed.* XVII, 19; *Nat. Ed.* XV, 17.

REDWOODS. *See* TREES.

REED, THOMAS B. Speaker Reed has won his place in history as one of the great leaders of the great Republican party, as a man whose name is entitled to rank high among the first in her long roll-call of honor, as a man who has rendered a service to the nation which will be more and more appreciated as time goes on and its worth is fully understood, and as a man who has laid under a great debt all those all over the world who believe in responsible popular government. (Before Federal Club, New York City, March 6, 1891.) *Mem. Ed.* XVI, 198; *Nat. Ed.* XIV, 132-133.

——————. Speaker Reed rendered a great service to his party by his action as speaker of the Fifty-first Congress; and, by the fact of having rendered this service, placed himself at one leap among the foremost of the party leaders; but he rendered an even greater service to the American Republic. In order that a republic may exist there must be some form of representative government, and this representative government must include a legislature. If the practices to which Mr. Reed put a stop were allowed to become chronic, representative government would itself be an impossibility. Not for many years has there been a man in our public life to whom the American people owe as great a debt as they do to Speaker Thomas B. Reed. (*Forum,* December 1895.) *Mem. Ed.* XVI, 255; *Nat. Ed.* XIV, 180.

REED RULES. *See* DEBATE; FILIBUSTERING.

REFERENDUM. As regards both [the initiative and the referendum], I think that the anticipations of their adherents and the fears of their opponents are equally exaggerated. The value of each depends mainly upon the way it is applied and upon the extent and complexity of the governmental unit to which it is applied. Every one is agreed that there must be a popular referendum on such a fundamental matter as a constitutional change, and in New York State we already have what is really a referendum on various other propositions by which the State or one of its local subdivisions passes upon the propriety of action which implies the spending of money, permission to establish a trolley-line system, or something of the kind. . . . I believe that it would be a good thing to have the principle of the initiative and the referendum applied in most of our States, always provided that it be so safeguarded as to prevent its being used either wantonly or in a spirit of levity. . . . On any bill important enough to arouse genuine public interest there should be power for the people to insist upon the bill being referred to popular vote, so that the constituents may authoritatively determine whether or not their representatives have misrepresented them. (*Outlook,* January 21, 1911.) *Mem. Ed.* XIX, 89-90; *Nat. Ed.* XVII, 56-57.

———————. My proposal is for the exercise of the referendum by the people themselves in a certain class of decisions of constitutional questions in which the courts decide against the power of the people to do elementary justice. When men of trained intelligence call this "putting the axe to the tree of well-ordered freedom," it is quite impossible to reconcile their statements both with good faith and with even reasonably full knowledge of the facts. (At Philadelphia, April 10, 1912.) *Mem. Ed.* XIX, 258; *Nat. Ed.* XVII, 193.

———————. One of the prime reasons for the reckless legislation which we so often see in Congress and in State legislatures is the lack of responsibility of members, who believe they can safely pass any law demanded by a section of the people because the courts will declare it unconstitutional. Such a practice is destructive to self-respect in the legislator, it encourages ignorance and tyranny in the judge, and it is ruinous to the interests of the people. Our proposal is that when two of the agencies established by the Constitution for its own enforcement, the legislature and the courts, differ between themselves as to what the Constitution which created them, means, or what it is to be held to mean, then that the people themselves, the people who created the Constitution, who established, whom Abraham Lincoln said are masters of both court and legislature, shall step in and after due deliberation decide what the Constitution is or is not to permit. (At New York City, February 12, 1913.) *Mem. Ed.* XIX, 505; *Nat. Ed.* XVII, 376.

———————. The referendum is certain to be of great use in a particular class of cases which very much puzzle the average legislator —where a minority of his constituents, but a large and influential minority, may demand something concerning which there is grave doubt whether the majority does or does not sympathize with the demand. In such a case the minority is active and determined; the majority can be roused only if the question is directly before it. In other words, the majority does not count it for righteousness in a representative if he refuses to yield to a minority; while a minority, on the other hand, will not tolerate adverse action. In such cases the temptation to the ordinary legislator is very great to yield to the demand of the minority, as he fears its concrete and interested wrath much more than the tepid disapproval of the majority. In all such questions the referendum would offer much the wisest and most efficient and satisfactory solution. (*Outlook,* January 21, 1911.) *Mem. Ed.* XIX, 94; *Nat. Ed.* XVII, 60.

REFERENDUM. *See also* INITIATIVE; PROGRESSIVE PRINCIPLES; RECALL; REPRESENTATIVE GOVERNMENT.

REFORM. All reforms of first-class importance must look toward raising both men and women to a higher level, alike as regards the things of the body and as regards the things of the soul. (*Outlook,* February 3, 1912.) *Mem. Ed.* XVIII, 289; *Nat. Ed.* XVI, 219.

———————. The really valuable—the invaluable—reform is that which in actual practice works; and therefore the credit due is overwhelmingly greater as regards the men and women actually engaged in doing the job, than as regards the other men and women who merely agitate the subject or write about it— and a single study of a reform which is being applied is worth any number of uplift books which are evolved from the reformer's inner consciousness. Of course there must be agitation in order to get the reform started, and there must be some preliminary theoretical studies, and where the object is really worth while, the agitation sensible as well as zealous, and the studies capable of application, the early agitators and writers deserve well of the community. But under no circumstances do they deserve as well as do the men and women who in very fact make the machinery function to advantage, and who by constant test and trial and experiment eliminate faults and develop new and useful activities. (*Metropolitan,* May 1917.) *Mem. Ed.* XXI, 99; *Nat. Ed.* XIX, 86.

———————. No man ever permanently helped a reform by lying on behalf of the reform. Tell the truth about it; and then you can expect to be believed when you tell further truths. (At Pacific Theological Seminary, Spring 1911.) *Mem. Ed.* XV, 588; *Nat. Ed.* XIII, 626.

———————. It is almost equally dangerous either to blink evils and refuse to acknowledge their existence, or to strike at them in a spirit of ignorant revenge, thereby doing far more harm than is remedied. The need can be met only by careful study of conditions, and by action which while taken boldly and without hesitation is neither heedless nor reckless.

It is well to remember on the one hand that the adoption of what is reasonable in the demands of reformers is the surest way to prevent the adoption of what is unreasonable; and on the other hand that many of the worst and most dangerous laws which have been put upon statute-books have been put there by zealous reformers with excellent intentions. (Annual Message as Governor, Albany, January 3, 1900.) *Mem. Ed.* XVII, 47-48; *Nat. Ed.* XV, 41-42.

REFORM—NATURE OF. As we strive for reform we find that it is not at all merely the case of a long up-hill pull. On the contrary, there is almost as much of breeching work as of collar work; to depend only on traces means that there will soon be a runaway and an upset. The men of wealth who to-day are trying to prevent the regulation and control of their business in the interest of the public by the proper government authorities will not succeed, in my judgment, in checking the progress of the movement. But if they did succeed they would find that they had sown the wind and would surely reap the whirlwind, for they would ultimately provoke the violent excesses which accompany a reform coming by convulsion instead of by steady and natural growth. (At Washington, April 14, 1906.) *Mem. Ed.* XVIII, 580; *Nat. Ed.* XVI, 422.

REFORM—NEED OF. Heaven knows I appreciate the need of disinterestedness, of public spirit, of all that we associate with the name of reform; and it is because I do appreciate the need that I hate to see men in New York who ought to be forces on the right side, not only decline to go with decent men who are striving practicably for decency, but by their course alienate shrewd and sensible men from all reform movements. (To James C. Carter, March 19, 1900.) *Mem. Ed.* XXIII, 154; Bishop I, 133.

——————. At this moment we are passing through a period of great unrest—social, political, and industrial unrest. It is of the utmost importance for our future that this should prove to be not the unrest of mere rebelliousness against life, of mere dissatisfaction with the inevitable inequality of conditions, but the unrest of a resolute and eager ambition to secure the betterment of the individual and the nation. So far as this movement of agitation throughout the country takes the form of a fierce discontent with evil, of a determination to punish the authors of evil, whether in industry or politics, the feeling is to be heartily welcomed as a sign of healthy life. . . .

It is a prime necessity that if the present unrest is to result in permanent good the emotion shall be translated into action, and that the action shall be marked by honesty, sanity, and self-restraint.

There is mighty little good in a mere spasm of reform. The reform that counts is that which comes through steady, continuous growth; violent emotionalism leads to exhaustion. (At Washington, April 14, 1906.) *Mem. Ed.* XVIII, 576-577; *Nat. Ed.* XVI, 420-421.

REFORM—OPPONENTS OF. The wild preachers of unrest and discontent, the wild agitators against the entire existing order, the men who act crookedly, whether because of sinister design or from mere puzzle-headedness, the men who preach destruction without proposing any substitute for what they intend to destroy, or who propose a substitute which would be far worse than the existing evils—all these men are the most dangerous opponents of real reform. If they get their way they will lead the people into a deeper pit than any into which they could fall under the present system. If they fail to get their way they will still do incalculable harm by provoking the kind of reaction which, in its revolt against the senseless evil of their teaching, would enthrone more securely than ever the very evils which their misguided followers believe they are attacking. (At Washington, April 14, 1906.) *Mem. Ed.* XVIII, 580; *Nat. Ed.* XVI, 423.

REFORM AND REVOLUTION. [Men often] forget that constructive change offers the best method of avoiding destructive change; that reform is the antidote to revolution; and that social reform is not the precursor but the preventive of Socialism. (At Cairo, Ill., October 3, 1907.) *Mem. Ed.* XVIII, 19; *Nat. Ed.* XVI, 17.

——————. Distrust of radical innovation and preference for reform to revolution . . . gives to the English race its greatest strength.

This last attitude, the dislike of revolution, [is] entirely wholesome and praiseworthy. (1900.) *Mem. Ed.* XIII, 301; *Nat. Ed.* X, 199.

REFORM IN POLITICS. There are not a few reforms so important that it would be hard to speak of any as pre-eminently necessary; but at least it can be said that there is greater room for reform in our political life than almost anywhere else. There are shortcomings enough and to spare on all sides; but compared to the proper standard we fall farther below in politics than in almost any other branch of our life or labor. Moreover, political life is something in which every man, indeed every woman, should take an active and intelligent interest. There is no other reform for which the entire population should work, or indeed could work; but every man, worth being an American citizen at all, is bound, if he does his duty, to try to do his part in politics. (*Outlook*, December 21, 1895.) *Mem. Ed.* XV, 143; *Nat. Ed.* XIII, 299.

REFORM MOVEMENTS. Every leader of a great reform has to contend, on the one hand, with the open, avowed enemies of the reform, and, on the other hand, with its extreme advocates, who wish the impossible, and who join hands with their extreme opponents to defeat the rational friends of the reform. (*Churchman*, March 17, 1900.) *Mem. Ed.* XV, 394-395; *Nat. Ed.* XIII, 392.

————————. Every democratic movement or movement for social or industrial reform, must have its leaders and its martyrs, and unfortunately every such movement also develops a few fools and a few knaves, who give an alloy of base metal to the pure gold of the leadership and the martyrdom. (*Outlook*, January 10, 1914.) *Mem. Ed.* XIV, 180; *Nat. Ed.* XII, 209.

REFORM. *See also* Boss; Economic Reform; Election Reform; Hypocrisy; Lunatic Fringe; Machine; Muck-raking; Politics; Progressive Movement.

REFORMERS. Reformers . . . [lose] sight of the fact that a reform must be practicable in order to make it of value. . . .

It is just as necessary for the practical man to remember that his practical qualities are useless, or worse than useless, unless he joins with them that spirit of striving after better things which marks the reformer, as it is for this same reformer to remember that he cannot give effective expression to his desire for a higher life save by following rigidly practical ways. (1900.) *Mem. Ed.* XIII, 427; *Nat. Ed.* X, 307.

————————. The attitude of deifying mere efficiency, mere success, without regard to the moral qualities lying behind it, and the attitude of disregarding efficiency, disregarding practical results, are the Scylla and Charybdis between which every earnest reformer, every politician who desires to make the name of his profession a term of honor instead of shame, must steer. He must avoid both under penalty of wreckage, and it avails him nothing to have avoided one, if he founders on the other. People are apt to speak as if in political life, public life, it ought to be a mere case of striving upward—striving toward a high peak. The simile is inexact. Every man who is striving to do good public work is travelling along a ridge crest, with the gulf of failure on each side— the gulf of inefficiency on the one side, the gulf of unrighteousness on the other. All kinds of forces are continually playing on him, to shove him first into one gulf and then into the other; and even a wise and good man, unless he braces himself with uncommon firmness and foresight, as he is pushed this way and that, will find that his course becomes a pronounced zigzag instead of a straight line; and if it becomes too pronounced he is lost, no matter to which side the zigzag may take him. Nor is he lost only as regards his own career. What is far more serious, his power of doing useful service to the public is at an end. He may still, if a mere politician, have political place, or, if a make-believe reformer, retain that notoriety upon which his vanity feeds. But, in either case, his usefulness to the community has ceased. (*Century*, June 1900.) *Mem. Ed.* XV, 380-381; *Nat. Ed.* XIII, 343-344.

————————. There are certain qualities the reformer must have if he is to be a real reformer and not merely a faddist; for of course every reformer is in continual danger of slipping into the mass of well-meaning people who in their advocacy of the impracticable do more harm than good. He must possess high courage, disinterested desire to do good, and sane, wholesome common sense. These qualities he must have, and it is furthermore much to his benefit if he also possesses a sound sense of humor. (*McClure's*, March 1901.) *Mem. Ed.* XV, 210; *Nat. Ed.* XIII, 271.

————————. More and more I have grown to have a horror of the reformer who is half charlatan and half fanatic, and ruins his own cause by overstatement. (To Wister, July 20, 1901.) Owen Wister, *Roosevelt, The Story of a Friendship*. (Macmillan Co., N. Y., 1930), p. 83.

————————. The true reformer must ever work in the spirit, and with the purpose, of that greatest of all democratic reformers, Abraham Lincoln. Therefore he must make up his mind that like Abraham Lincoln he will be assailed on the one side by the reactionary, and on the other by that type of bubble reformer who is only anxious to go to extremes, and who always gets angry when he is asked what practical results he can show. . . .

Reformers, if they are to do well, must look both backward and forward; must be bold and yet must exercise prudence and caution in all they do. They must never fear to advance, and yet they must carefully plan how to advance, before they make the effort. They must carefully plan how and what they are to construct before they tear down what exists. Introduction to *The Wisconsin Idea* by Charles McCarthy. (Macmillan Co., N. Y., 1912), p. ix.

REFORMERS—ADVICE TO. An ardent young reformer is very apt to try to begin by reforming too much. He needs always to keep in mind that he has got to serve as a sergeant before he assumes the duties of commander-in-chief. It is right for him from the beginning to take a great interest in national, State, and municipal affairs, and to try to make himself felt in them if the occasion arises; but the best work must be done by the citizen working in his own ward or district. Let him associate himself with the men who think as he does, and who, like him, are sincerely devoted to the public good. Then let them try to make themselves felt in the choice of alderman, of councilman, of assemblyman. The politicians will be prompt to recognize (their power, and the people will recognize) it too, after a while. Let them organize and work, undaunted by any temporary defeat. If they fail at first, and if they fail again, let them merely make up their minds to redouble their efforts, and perhaps alter their methods; but let them keep on working. (*Forum,* July 1894.) *Mem. Ed.* XV, 47; *Nat. Ed.* XIII, 33.

——————. One seemingly very necessary caution to utter is, that a man who goes into politics should not expect to reform everything right off, with a jump. I know many excellent young men who, when awakened to the fact that they have neglected their political duties, feel an immediate impulse to form themselves into an organization which shall forthwith purify politics everywhere, national, State, and city alike; and I know of a man who having gone round once to a primary, and having, of course, been unable to accomplish anything in a place where he knew no one and could not combine with any one, returned saying it was quite useless for a good citizen to try to accomplish anything in such a manner. (Before the Liberal Club, Buffalo, N. Y., January 26, 1893.) *Mem. Ed.* XV, 68; *Nat. Ed.* XIII, 285.

REFORMERS — SHORTCOMINGS OF. Very early I learned through my reading of history, and I found through my association with reformers, that one of the prime difficulties was to get the man who wished reform within a nation also to pay heed to the needs of the nation from the international standpoint. Every little city or republic of antiquity was continually torn between factions which wished to do justice at home but were weak abroad, and other factions which secured justice abroad by the loss of personal liberty at home. So here at home I too often found that men who were ardent for social and industrial reform would be ignorant of the needs of this nation as a nation, would be ignorant of what the navy meant to the nation, of what it meant to the nation to have and to fortify and protect the Panama Canal, of what it meant to the nation to get from the other nations of mankind the respect which comes only to the just, and which is denied to the weaker nation far more quickly than it is denied to the stronger. (*Outlook,* October 12, 1912.) *Mem. Ed.* XIX, 438; *Nat. Ed.* XVII, 318.

——————. Reformers [often] . . . lack sanity, and it is very difficult to do decent reform work, or any other kind of work, if for sanity we substitute a condition of mere morbid hysteria. (To Sir George Otto Trevelyan, September 12, 1905.) *Mem. Ed.* XXIII, 482; Bishop I, 419.

REFORMERS AND REACTIONARIES. It is always a difficult thing to state a position which has two sides with such clearness as to bring it home to the hearers. In the world of politics it is easy to appeal to the unreasoning reactionary, and no less easy to appeal to the unreasoning advocate of change, but difficult to get the people to show for the cause of sanity and progress combined the zeal so easily aroused against sanity by one set of extremists and against progress by another set of extremists. *Outlook,* December 2, 1911, p. 823.

——————. I am always having to fight the silly reactionaries and the inert, fatuous creatures who will not think seriously; and on the other hand to try to exercise some control over the lunatic fringe among the reformers. (To Sir George Otto Trevelyan, March 19, 1913.) *Mem. Ed.* XXIV, 207; Bishop II, 177.

REFORMERS IN PROGRESSIVE PARTY. There is just one element of relief to me in the smash that came to the Progressive party. We did not have many practical men with us. Under such circumstances the reformers tended to go into sheer lunacy. I now can preach the doctrines of labor and capital just as I did when I was President, without being hampered by the well-meant extravagances of so many among my Progressive friends. (To Kermit Roosevelt, January 27, 1915.) *Mem. Ed.* XXIV, 421; Bishop II, 358.

REFORMERS. See also BEVERIDGE, ALBERT J.; CONSERVATIVES; HISTORY; INDEPENDENT; LaFOLLETTE, ROBERT M.; MACHINE; MUCK-RAKERS; MUGWUMPS; RADICALS; REACTIONARIES; RIIS, JACOB A.

REFUGEES. See BELGIAN REFUGEES.

RELIEF. See PHILANTHROPY.

RELIGION. No democracy can afford to overlook the vital importance of the ethical and spiritual, the truly religious, element in life; and in practice the average good man grows clearly to understand this, and to express the need in concrete form by saying that no community can make much headway if it does not contain both a church and a school. (1914.) *Mem. Ed.* VI, 56; *Nat. Ed.* V, 48.

———. The religious man who is most useful is not he whose sole care is to save his own soul, but the man whose religion bids him strive to advance decency and clean living and to make the world a better place for his fellows to live in. (At the Harvard Union, Cambridge, February 23, 1907.) *Mem. Ed.* XV, 490; *Nat. Ed.* XIII, 565.

———. I wonder if you recall one verse of Micah that I am very fond of—'to do justly and to love mercy and to walk humbly with thy God'—that to me is the essence of religion. To be just with all men, to be merciful to those to whom mercy should be shown, to realize that there are some things that must always remain a mystery to us, and when the time comes for us to enter the great blackness, to go smiling and unafraid.

That is my religion, my faith. To me it sums up all religion, it is all the creed I need. It seems simple and easy, but there is more in that verse than in the involved rituals and confessions of faith of many creeds we know.

To love justice, to be merciful, to appreciate that the great mysteries shall not be known to us, and so living, face the beyond confident and without fear—that is life.

That's too simple a creed for many of us, though. Perhaps it is as well and that through more involved paths and mazes of theology the majority should seek the same result. (Summer or fall 1916; reported by Leary.) *Talks with T. R.* From the diaries of John J. Leary, Jr. (Houghton Mifflin Co., Boston, 1920), pp. 65-66.

RELIGION AND MORALITY. While there is in modern times a decrease in emotional religion, there is an immense increase in practical morality. (*Forum*, January 1897.) *Mem. Ed.* XIV, 149; *Nat. Ed.* XIII, 259.

———. In this country we are long past the stage of regarding it as any part of the state's duty to enforce a particular religious dogma; and more and more the professors of the different creeds themselves are beginning tacitly to acknowledge that the prime worth of a creed is to be gauged by the standard of conduct it exacts among its followers toward their fellows.

The creed which each man in his heart believes to be essential to his own salvation is for him alone to determine; but we have a right to pass judgment upon his actions toward those about him. (*Century*, October 1900.) *Mem. Ed.* XV, 421; *Nat. Ed.* XIII, 369.

———. There is one test which we have a right to apply to the professors of all creeds—the test of conduct. More and more, people who possess either religious belief or aspiration after religious belief are growing to demand conduct as the ultimate test of the worth of the belief. (At Pacific Theological Seminary, Spring 1911.) *Mem. Ed.* XV, 613; *Nat. Ed.* XIII, 648.

RELIGION. See also BIBLE STUDY; CHRISTIANITY; FERVOR; MATERIALISM; MORALITY; REASON; SCIENCE; SPIRITUAL GROWTH.

RELIGIOUS DISCRIMINATION. The one thing upon which we must insist is ruling out questions of creed in our politics so long as the men for whom we vote are honest and in good faith Americans. (Before Liberal Club of Buffalo, N. Y., September 10, 1895.) *Mem. Ed.* XVI, 284; *Nat. Ed.* XIV, 203.

———. We maintain that it is an outrage, in voting for a man for any position, whether State or national, to take into account his religious faith, provided only he is a good American. When a secret society does what in some places the American Protective Associa-

RELIGIOUS DISCRIMINATION

tion seems to have done, and tries to proscribe Catholics both politically and socially, the members of such society show that they themselves are as utterly un-American, as alien to our school of political thought, as the worst immigrants who land on our shores. Their conduct is equally base and contemptible. (*Forum*, April 1894.) *Mem. Ed.* XV, 25; *Nat. Ed.* XIII, 21-22.

———————. The surest way in which you can make a movement to better our politics fail is to have that movement troubled with proscription for religious reasons. The two evils, I am almost inclined to say the two worst evils, of which I know in municipal politics, and in some other politics as well, are, on the one hand, to discriminate against a faithful and efficient public servant because of his creed, and on the other, to pardon and support an unfaithful and inefficient public servant because of his creed. (Before Liberal Club of Buffalo, N. Y., September 10, 1895.) *Mem. Ed.* XVI, 271; *Nat. Ed.* XIV, 192.

———————. If there is one thing for which we stand in this country, it is for complete religious freedom and for the right of every man to worship his Creator as his conscience dictates. It is an emphatic negation of this right to cross-examine a man on his religious views before being willing to support him for office. Is he a good man, and is he fit for the office? These are the only questions which there is a right to ask. . . . In my own Cabinet there are at present Catholic, Protestant and Jew—the Protestants being of various denominations. I am incapable of discriminating between them, or of judging any one of them save as to the way in which he performs his public duty. The rule of conduct applicable to Catholic, Protestant and Jew as regards lesser offices is just as applicable as regards the Presidency. (Letter of October 16, 1908.) Lodge *Letters* II, 325.

———————. The demand for a statement of a candidate's religious belief can have no meaning except that there may be discrimination for or against him because of that belief. Discrimination against the holder of one faith means retaliatory discrimination against men of other faiths. The inevitable result of entering upon such a practice would be an abandonment of our real freedom of conscience and a reversion to the dreadful conditions of religious dissension which in so many lands have proved fatal to true liberty, to true religion, and to all advance in civilization.

RELIGIOUS FREEDOM

To discriminate against a thoroughly upright citizen because he belongs to some particular church, or because, like Abraham Lincoln, he has not avowed his allegiance to any church, is an outrage against that liberty of conscience which is one of the foundations of American life. You are entitled to know whether a man seeking your suffrages is a man of clean and upright life, honorable in all of his dealings with his fellows, and fit by qualification and purpose to do well in the great office for which he is a candidate; but you are not entitled to know matters which lie purely between himself and his Maker. (To J. C. Martin, November 6, 1908.) *Mem. Ed.* XVIII, 53-54; *Nat. Ed.* XVI, 46.

RELIGIOUS DISCRIMINATION. *See also* ANTI-SEMITISM; JEWS; KNOW-NOTHING MOVEMENT.

RELIGIOUS FREEDOM. We must all strive to keep as our most precious heritage the liberty each to worship his God as to him seems best, and, as part of this liberty, freely either to exercise it or to surrender it, in a greater or less degree, each according to his own beliefs and convictions, without infringing on the beliefs and convictions of others. (*Outlook*, December 2, 1911.) *Mem. Ed.* XIV, 437; *Nat. Ed.* XII, 129.

———————. There must be absolute religious liberty, for tyranny and intolerance are as abhorrent in matters intellectual and spiritual as in matters political and material; and more and more we must all realize that conduct is of infinitely greater importance than dogma. (1914.) *Mem. Ed.* VI, 56; *Nat. Ed.* V, 48.

———————. There are in our own country individuals who sincerely believe that the Masons, or the Knights of Columbus, or the members of the Junior Order of American Mechanics, or the Catholic Church, or the Methodist Church or the Ethical Culture Society, represent what is all wrong. There are sincere men in the United States who by argument desire to convince their fellows belonging to any one of the bodies above mentioned (and to any one of many others) that they are mistaken, either when they go to church or when they do not go to church, when they "preach sermons of a fanatical type" or inveigh against "sermons of a fanatical type," when they put money in the plate to help support a church or when they refuse to support a church, when they join secret societies or sit on the mourners' bench or practise confession. According to our

[518]

ideas, all men have an absolute right to favor or oppose any of these practices. But, according to our ideas, no men have any right to endeavor to make the government either favor or oppose them. According to our ideas, we should emphatically disapprove of any action in any Spanish-American country which is designed to oppress either Catholics or Protestants, either Masons or anti-Masons, either Liberals or clericals, or to interfere with religious liberty, whether by intolerance exercised for or against any religious creed, or by people who do or do not believe in any religious creed. (New York *Times*, December 6, 1914.) *Mem. Ed.* XX, 402; *Nat. Ed.* XVIII, 344-345.

——————. One of the most important things to secure for [each man] . . . is the right to hold and to express the religious views that best meet his own soul needs. Any political movement directed against any body of our fellow citizens because of their religious creed is a grave offense against American principles and American institutions. It is a wicked thing either to support or to oppose a man because of the creed he professes. This applies to Jew and Gentile, to Catholic and Protestant, and to the man who would be regarded as unorthodox by all of them alike. Political movements directed against certain men because of their religious belief, and intended to prevent men of that creed from holding office, have never accomplished anything but harm. This was true in the days of the "Know-Nothing" and Native-American parties in the middle of the last century; and it is just as true today. Such a movement directly contravenes the spirit of the Constitution itself. (Before Knights of Columbus, New York City, October 12, 1915.) *Mem. Ed.* XX, 453; *Nat. Ed.* XVIII, 389.

RELIGIOUS ORGANIZATIONS. *See* CHURCH; EPISCOPAL CHURCH; JEWS; LUTHERAN CHURCH; METHODIST CHURCH; MORMONS; SUNDAY SCHOOL.

RELIGIOUS TEACHERS. The religious teachers of the community stand most honorably high. It is probable that no other class of our citizens do anything like the amount of disinterested labor for their fellow-men. To those who are associated with them at close quarters this statement will seem so obviously a truism as to rank among the platitudes. But there is a far from inconsiderable body of public opinion which, to judge by the speeches, writings, and jests in which it delights, has no conception of this state of things. If such people would but take the trouble to follow out the actual life of a hard-worked clergyman or priest, I think they would become a little ashamed of the tone of flippancy they are so prone to adopt when speaking about them. (*Century*, October 1900.) *Mem. Ed.* XV, 421; *Nat. Ed.* XIII, 369.

——————. That man is unfortunate who has not owed much, in teaching and in companionship, to hard-working priest or hard-working parson. In my own experience I recall priest after priest whose disinterested parish work has represented one continuous battle for civilization and humanity. . . . Surely the average man ought to sympathize with such work and help such workers; and he cannot do this if his attitude is merely that of an unsympathetic outsider. (1917.) *Mem. Ed.* XXI, 135-136; *Nat. Ed.* XIX, 135.

RELIGIOUS TEACHERS. *See also* JESUITS; MISSIONARIES; PIONEER PREACHERS.

RELIGIOUS TESTS. The Constitution explicitly forbids the requiring of any religious test as a qualification for holding office. To impose such a test by popular vote is as bad as to impose it by law. To vote either for or against a man because of his creed is to impose upon him a religious test and is a clear violation of the spirit of the Constitution. (Before Knights of Columbus, New York City, October 12, 1915.) *Mem. Ed.* XX, 454; *Nat. Ed.* XVIII, 389.

RELIGIOUS TOLERATION. Even yet there are advocates of religious intolerance, but they are mostly of the academic kind, and there is no chance for any political party of the least importance to try to put their doctrines into effect. More and more, at least here in the United States, Catholics and Protestants, Jews and Gentiles, are learning the grandest of all lessons—that they can best serve their God by serving their fellow men, and best serve their fellow men, not by wrangling among themselves, but by a generous rivalry in working for righteousness and against evil. (1900.) *Mem. Ed.* XIII, 322; *Nat. Ed.* X, 217.

——————. The more an American sees of other countries the more profound must be his feelings of gratitude that in his own land there is not merely complete toleration but the heartiest good-will and sympathy between sincere and honest men of different faith—good-will and sympathy so complete that in the inevitable daily relations of our American life

Catholics and Protestants meet together and work together without the thought of difference of creed being even present in their minds. This is a condition so vital to our National well-being that nothing should be permitted to jeopard it. (To Lyman Abbott, April 3, 1910.) *Mem. Ed.* XXIV, 233; *Bishop* II, 199.

———————. An American Catholic and an American Protestant of to-day, whatever the difference between their theologies, yet in their ways of looking at real life, at its relation to religions, and the relations of religion and the state, are infinitely more akin to one another than either is to the men of his religious faith who lived three centuries ago. We now admit, as a matter of course, that any man may, in religious matters, profess to be guided by authority or by reason, as suits him best; but that he must not interfere with similar freedom of belief in others; and that all men, whatever their religious beliefs, have exactly the same political rights and are to be held to the same responsibility for the way they exercise these rights. (1900.) *Mem. Ed.* XIII, 294; *Nat. Ed.* X, 193.

———————. When faith is very strong and belief very sincere, men must possess great wisdom, broad charity, and the ability to learn by experience, or else they will certainly try to make others live up to their own standards. This would be bad enough, even were the standards absolutely right; and it is necessarily worse in practice than in theory, inasmuch as mixed with the right there is invariably an element of what is wrong or foolish. The extreme exponents and apologists of any fervent creed can always justify themselves, in the realm of pure logic, for insisting that all the world shall be made to accept and act up to their standards, and that they must necessarily strive to bring this about, if they really believe what they profess to believe. Of course, in practice, the answer is that there are hundreds of different creeds, or shades of creeds, all of which are believed in with equal devoutness by their followers, and therefore in a workaday government it is necessary to insist that none shall interfere with any other. Where people are as far advanced in practical good sense and in true religious toleration as in the United States to-day, the great majority of each creed gradually grows to accept this position as axiomatic, and the smaller minority is kept in check without effort both by law and by public opinion. (1900.) *Mem. Ed.* XIII, 445; *Nat. Ed.* X, 323.

RELIGIOUS TOLERATION. *See also* TOLERANCE.

REMINGTON, FREDERIC. I regard Frederic Remington as one of the Americans who has done real work for this country, and we all owe him a debt of gratitude. He has been granted the very unusual gift of excelling in two entirely distinct types of artistic work; for his bronzes are as noteworthy as his pictures. He is, of course, one of the most typical American artists we have ever had, and he has portrayed a most characteristic and yet vanishing type of American life. The soldier, the cowboy and rancher, the Indian, the horses and the cattle of the plains, will live in his pictures and bronzes, I verily believe, for all time. Nor must we forget the excellent literary work he has done in such pieces as "Masi's Crooked Trail," with its peculiar insight into the character of the wildest Indians.

It is no small thing for the nation that such an artist and man of letters should arise to make permanent record of certain of the most interesting features of our national life. (To Arthur W. Little, July 17, 1907.) *Pearson's Magazine,* October 1907, pp. 392-393.

RENO, NEV. *See* DIVORCE.

RENUNCIATION. *See* ELECTION OF 1908.

REPRESENTATIVE GOVERNMENT. We rule ourselves, and we choose our representatives, not to rule us, but to manage the public business for us along the lines we have laid down and approved. (At St. Louis, Mo., March 28, 1912.) *Mem. Ed.* XIX, 238; *Nat. Ed.* XVII, 175.

———————. Unquestionably an ideal representative body is the best imaginable legislative body. Such a body, if composed of men of unusual courage, intelligence, sympathy, and high-mindedness, anxious to represent the people, and at the same time conscientious in their determination to do nothing that is wrong, would so act that there would never come the slightest demand for any change in the methods of enacting laws. Unfortunately, however, in actual practice, too many of our legislative bodies have not really been representative; and not a few of the ablest and most prominent men in public life have prided themselves on their ability to use parliamentary forms to defeat measures for which there was a great popular demand. Special interests which would be powerless in a general election may be all-powerful in a legislature if they enlist the services of a few skilful tacticians; and the result is the same whether these tacticians are unscrupulous and are hired by the special interests, or whether they are sincere men who honestly believe that the people desire what is wrong and should not be allowed to have it. (*Outlook*, January 21, 1911.) *Mem. Ed.* XIX, 92; *Nat. Ed.* XVII, 58.

───────────. We are a representative government—executives, legislators, judges; all public servants are representatives of the people. We are bound to represent the will of the people, but we are bound still more to obey our own consciences; and if ever there is any gust of popular feeling that demands what is wrong, what is unrighteous, then the true servant of the people, the man who truly serves the interest of the people, is that man who disregards the wish of the people to do evil. Let the representative represent the people so long as he conscientiously can; when he can no longer do so, let him do what his conscience dictates, and cheerfully accept the penalty of retirement to private life. (At Nashville, Tenn., October 22, 1907.) *Presidential Addresses and State Papers* VI, 1467.

REPRESENTATIVE GOVERNMENT — IMPROVEMENT OF. Beyond question the historian who in the future shall write a history of representative government through a legislative assembly will have to credit Speaker Reed and the Republican majority of the Fifty-first Congress with having achieved one of the greatest victories for the cause which has ever been achieved, which, moreover, was achieved at precisely the right time. (Before Federal Club, New York, March 6, 1891.) *Mem. Ed.* XVI, 193; *Nat. Ed.* XIV, 128.

───────────. I do not mean that we shall abandon representative government; on the contrary, I mean that we shall devise methods by which our government shall become really representative. To use such measures as the initiative, referendum, and recall indiscriminately and promiscuously on all kinds of occasions would undoubtedly cause disaster; but events have shown that at present our institutions are not representative—at any rate in many States, and sometimes in the nation—and that we cannot wisely afford to let this condition of things remain longer uncorrected. We have permitted the growing up of a breed of politicians who, sometimes for improper political purposes, sometimes as a means of serving the great special interests of privilege which stand behind them, twist so-called representative institutions into a means of thwarting instead of expressing the deliberate and well-thought-out judgment of the people as a whole. This cannot be permitted. (Before Progressive National Convention, Chicago, August 6, 1912.) *Mem. Ed.* XIX, 364; *Nat. Ed.* XVII, 259.

REPRESENTATIVE GOVERNMENT. *See also* DEMOCRACY; GOVERNMENT; INITIATIVE; LEGISLATURE; POPULAR RULE; RECALL; REFERENDUM; SELF-GOVERNMENT.

REPRESENTATIVES — CHARACTER OF. Each community has the kind of politicians that it deserves. Each community is represented with absolute fidelity by the men whom it chooses to have in public life. Those men represent its virtue or they represent its vice, or, what is more common, they represent its gross and culpable indifference; and gross and culpable indifference may, on some occasions, be worse than any wickedness. (Before Independent Club, Buffalo, N. Y., May 15, 1899.) *Mem. Ed.* XVI, 489; *Nat. Ed.* XIV, 328.

REPRESENTATIVES—DUTY OF. A public man is bound to represent his constituents, but he is no less bound to cease to represent them when, on a great moral question of right or wrong, he feels that they are taking the wrong side. Let him go out of politics rather than stay in at the cost of doing what his own conscience forbids him to do; and, while upholding that principle in theory, do not forget to uphold it in practice. (Before Independent Club, Buffalo, N. Y., May 15, 1899.) *Mem. Ed.* XVI, 486; *Nat. Ed.* XIV, 325.

───────────. It is all-essential to the continuance of our healthy national life that we should recognize this community of interest among our people. The welfare of each of us is dependent fundamentally upon the welfare of all of us, and therefore in public life that man is the best representative of each of us who seeks to do good to each by doing good to all; in other words, whose endeavor it is, not to represent any special class and promote merely that class's selfish interests, but to represent all true and honest men of all sections and all classes and to work for their interests by working for our common country. (At State Fair, Syracuse, N. Y., September 7, 1903.) *Mem. Ed.* XVIII, 58; *Nat. Ed.* XVI, 50.

───────────. Normally a representative should represent his constituents. If on any point of real importance he finds that he concientiously differs with them, he must, as a matter of course, follow his conscience, and thereby he may not only perform his highest duty, but also render the highest possible service to his constituents themselves. But in such case he should not try to achieve his purpose by tricking his constituents or by adroitly seeking at the same time to thwart their wishes in secret and yet apparently to act so as to retain their good-will. He should never put holding his office above keeping straight with his conscience, and if the measure as to which he differs with his constituents is of sufficient importance, he should be prepared to go out of office rather than surrender on a matter of vital principle. Normally, however, he must remember that the very meaning of the word representative is that the constituents shall be represented. It is his duty to try to lead them to accept his views, and it is their duty to give him as large a latitude as possible in matters of conscience, realizing that the more conscientious the representative is the better he will in general represent them; but if a real and vital split on a matter of principle occurs, as in the case of a man who believes in the gold standard but finds that his constituents believe in free silver, the representative's duty is neither to abandon his own belief nor to try to beat his constituents by a trick, but to fight fairly for his convictions and cheerfully accept defeat if he cannot convert his constituents. (*Outlook*, January 21, 1911.) *Mem. Ed.* XIX, 93; *Nat. Ed.* XVII, 59.

REPRESENTATIVES — THE PEOPLE AND THEIR. We need to make our political representatives more quickly and sensitively responsive to the people whose servants they are. More direct action by the people in their own affairs under proper safeguards is vitally necessary. The direct primary is a step in this direction, if it is associated with a corrupt-practices act effective to prevent the advantage of the man willing recklessly and unscrupulously to spend money over his more honest competitor. (At Osawatomie, Kan., August 31, 1910.) *Mem. Ed.* XIX, 28; *Nat. Ed.* XVII, 20.

——————. We choose our representatives for two purposes. In the first place, we choose them with the desire that, as experts, they shall study certain matters with which we, the people as a whole, cannot be intimately acquainted, and that as regards these matters they shall formulate a policy for our betterment. Even as regards such a policy, and the actions taken thereunder, we ourselves should have the right ultimately to vote our disapproval of it, if we feel such disapproval. But, in the next place, our representatives are chosen to carry out certain policies as to which we have definitely made up our minds, and here we expect them to represent us by doing what we have decided ought to be done. All I desire to do by securing more direct control of the governmental agents and agencies of the people is to give the people the chance to make their representatives really represent them whenever the government becomes misrepresentative instead of representative. (Before Progressive National Convention, Chicago, August 6, 1912.) *Mem. Ed.* XIX, 364-365, *Nat. Ed.* XVII, 260.

REPUBLICAN GOVERNMENT. Under no form of government is it so necessary thus to combine efficiency and morality, high principle and rough common sense, justice and the sturdiest physical and moral courage, as in a republic. It is absolutely impossible for a republic long to endure if it becomes either corrupt or cowardly; if its public men, no less than its private men, lose the indispensable virtue of honesty, if its leaders of thought become visionary doctrinaires, or if it shows a lack of courage in dealing with the many grave problems which it must surely face, both at home and abroad, as it strives to work out the destiny meet for a mighty nation. (Inaugural Address as Governor, Albany, January 2, 1899.) *Mem. Ed.* XVII, 4; *Nat. Ed.* XV. 4.

——————. We do not intend that this Republic shall ever fail as those republics of olden times failed, in which there finally came to be a government by classes, which resulted either in the poor plundering the rich or in the rich exploiting and in one form or another enslaving the poor; for either event means the destruction of free institutions and of individual liberty. (At Union League Club, Philadelphia, January 30, 1905.) *Mem. Ed.* XXIII, 491; Bishop I, 427.

REPUBLICAN GOVERNMENT. *See also* DEMOCRACY.

REPUBLICAN LEADERS. The trouble, as it looks to me, is that much of what has been called leadership in the Republican Party consists of leadership which has no following. Now I may be utterly mistaken, and I write with a full knowledge that I may thus be mistaken, but my impression is that even as strong and able a man as Aldrich, a man whom I have been obliged to oppose on many fundamental points, but whose good qualities I cordially recognize, has no real following whatever among the people at large, not even in his own state. Cannon has had a much greater personal following, but he also excites even more hostility. The trouble is that the Cannon-Aldrich type of leadership down at bottom represents not more than, say, ten per cent. of the rank and file of the party's voting strength. This ten per cent. or whatever it may be, includes the bulk of the big business men, the big professional politicians, the big lawyers who carry on their work in connection with the leaders of high finance, and of the political machine, their representatives among the great papers, and so forth and so forth. All this makes a body of exceedingly influential people, but if the great mass—the ninety per cent. of the party—the men who stand for it as their fathers stood for it in the days of Lincoln, get convinced that the ten per cent. are not leading them right, a revolt is sure to ensue. If politicians of sufficient ability lead that revolt, as in the Western States, they get control of the organization. (To H. C. Lodge, April 11, 1910.) Lodge *Letters* II, 370.

REPUBLICAN NATIONAL CONVENTION OF 1912. The platform of the Republican party is bad anyhow. Taken in connection with the action of the convention, it amounts to a declaration against actual rule by the people and a determination that the politicians or the beneficiaries of special privilege shall completely dominate the people in the future just as they are doing at this moment. The actions of Mr. Taft and his Administration and the actions of the Republican National Convention itself make any protestations of virtue on the part of the Barnes-Penrose-Guggenheim combination, which at the moment represents all that is efficient and real in the existing Republican party, of no consequence whatsoever. Any declaration of good intentions in the Republican platform on any subject is rendered worthless, first, by the fact that the present Administration has broken the most important pledges on which it was elected; and, second, by the fact that the national convention at Chicago, which nominated Mr. Taft, acted with such deliberate bad faith, such flagrant violation of every obligation of decency and honesty, as to make any and all of its promises not worth the paper on which they are written. A homily upon honesty by a pickpocket who still keeps the stolen goods does not tend toward edification. Not a promise made by any man who took part in, apologizes for, or benefited by the stealing of the Chicago Convention should receive a moment's consideration. (*Outlook,* July 27, 1912.) *Mem. Ed.* XIX, 349-350; *Nat. Ed.* XVII, 247.

————————. Some day the honest men and women who make up the rank and file of the Republican party will realize the full iniquity of which the men were guilty who in the Republican convention of June last by deliberate political theft wrenched the control of the party from the people, made it the party of reaction, and gave it into the absolute control of the bosses. These men preferred to see the party destroyed rather than see it made once more what it was in the days of Lincoln. Their purpose was at all costs to perpetuate the rule of privilege, political privilege and financial privilege, within the party. The men who took part in, profited by, or condoned and indorsed the theft of the Chicago Convention should never again be trusted by men who believe in honesty. Their action differed from the crime of the ordinary ballot-box stuffer or crooked election official, only as the action of the great corrupt financier who swindles on a gigantic scale just within the law differs from the crime of the poor wretch who steals because he is in want. The theft of the Chicago Convention can be defended only by the type of corporation lawyer whose business it is to advise big financiers how to violate the law in wholesale fashion with impunity. These big politicians, financiers, and corporation lawyers, and their hangers-on, such as the college presidents of the "little-brother-to-the-rich" type, asserted and perhaps believed that they were acting in the interests of conservatism. They most urgently need to learn that sitting on the safety-valve is not the right way to prevent revolutions. (At Chicago, December 10, 1912.) *Mem. Ed.* XIX, 473; *Nat. Ed.* XVII, 349.

REPUBLICAN PARTY — BOSSES IN. While they [the Republican bosses] do not like me, they dread you. You are the people that they dread. They dread the people themselves, and those bosses and the big special interests behind them made up their mind that they would rather see the Republican party wrecked than see it come under the control of the people themselves. So I am not dealing with the Republican party. There are only two ways you can vote this year. You can be progressive or reactionary. Whether you vote Republican or Democratic it does not make any difference, you are voting reactionary. (At Milwaukee, Wis., October 14, 1912.) *Mem. Ed.* XIX, 451; *Nat. Ed.* XVII, 328.

REPUBLICAN PARTY — CHALLENGE TO. I believe in the party to which we belong because I believe in the principles for which the Republican party stood in the days of

Abraham Lincoln; and furthermore, and especially because I believe in treating those principles not as dead but as living. We best show our loyalty to the memory of Lincoln, and the principles for which Lincoln stood, not by treating it and them from the standpoint of historic interest in what is dead, but by treating them as vital, as alive to-day, and by endeavoring to meet the problems of the present, the new problems of our day, in exactly the same spirit in which he and those associated with him met the new problems of their day. . . . We can deserve the confidence of the people, not by stating that our forefathers preserved the Union and freed the slaves, but by proving in deed, as well as in word, that we face the problem of dealing with political and business corruption, and of working for social and economic justice and for the betterment of the conditions of life and the uplifting of our people, with the same fervor and sincerity that Lincoln and his followers brought to the great tasks allotted to them in their day. I hold that we show ourselves the best servants of our party when with all our might we strive to make that party the best servant of the people as a whole. (Before New York Republican State Convention, Saratoga, September 27, 1910.) *Mem. Ed.* XIX, 33-34; *Nat. Ed.* XVII, 25.

REPUBLICAN PARTY—CONTROL OF.

It was very bitter for me to see the Republican Party, when I had put it back on the Abraham Lincoln basis, in three years turn over to a combination of big financiers and unscrupulous political bosses. (To Sir Henry Lucy, December 18, 1912.) *Mem. Ed.* XXIV, 409; Bishop II, 348.

——————. On a square issue of power between the Republican national committee and the Republican voters the committee has won, and has demonstrated that it can win again. The organization has frankly abandoned the pretense of making effective the will of the voters. Its leaders, from the President down, take especial pride in the fact that they have outwitted the majority and have controlled the convention against the will of the rank and file of the voters—the "rabble," as Mr. Taft's chairman, Mr. McKinley, termed them. If the American people are really fit for self-government, they will instantly take up the challenge which a knot of political conspirators have so insolently thrown down. Non-resistance to such treason against popular government would be almost as reprehensible as active participation therein. Both a great moral issue and a fundamental principle of self-government are involved in the action of the so-called Republican convention at Chicago; and we cannot submit to that action without being false both to the basic principles of American democracy and to that spirit of righteousness and honesty which must underlie every form of successful government. (*Outlook,* July 13, 1912.) *Mem. Ed.* XIX, 330; *Nat. Ed.* XVII, 242.

——————. The control of the Republican National Convention in June, 1912, in the interest of Mr. Taft was achieved by methods full of as corrupt menace to popular government as ballot-box stuffing or any species of fraud or violence at the polls. Yet it was condoned by multitudes of respectable men of wealth and respectable men of cultivation because in their hearts they regarded genuine control by what they called "the mob"—that is, the people—as an evil so great that compared with it corruption and fraud became meritorious. The Republican party of to-day has given absolute control of its destinies into the hands of a national committee composed of fifty-three irresponsible and on the whole obscure politicians. It has specifically provided that these men, who have no responsibility whatever to the public, can override the lawfully expressed will of the majority in any State primary. It has perpetuated a system of representation at national conventions which gives a third of the delegates to communities where there is no real Republican vote, where no delegation for or against any man really represents anything, and where, in consequence, the national committee can plausibly seat any delegates it chooses without exciting popular indignation. In sum, these fifty-three politicians have the absolute and unchallenged control of the national convention. They do not have to allow the rank and file of the party any representation in that convention whatever, and, as has been shown in actual practice, they surrender to them any control whatever, on the occasion when they deem it imperatively necessary, merely as a matter of expediency and favor, and not as a matter of right or principle. (*Century,* October 1913.) *Mem. Ed.* XIX, 538, *Nat. Ed.* XVII, 395.

REPUBLICAN PARTY—FAILURE OF.

The Republican party has proved false to its principles; and those principles have lived; and they have produced another party, the party of progress, which has grasped the banner of righteous liberty from the traitor hands that were trailing it in the dust. (At New

York City, February 12, 1913.) *Mem. Ed.* XIX, 488; *Nat. Ed.* XVII, 362.

REPUBLICAN PARTY—FUTURE OF.
We are only interested in the organization in so far as that organization gives us a free play to make the Republican party a constructive forward-moving party and we are only interested in the Republican party in so far as it is just that.

There is no use in trying to rally around the past. This war has buried the past. New issues are going to force themselves into American politics and those issues are going to require a party which believes in a strong centralized government that shall be strong for the purpose of construction and not for the purpose of checking the progress of things. The new issues which will require a strongly centralized government are going to revolve about:

Transportation; price-fixing; rigid public control if not ownership of mines, forests and waterways.

And if the Republican party takes the ground that the world must be the same old world, the Republican party is lost. (To Will H. Hays, May 15, 1918.) *Mem. Ed.* XXIV, 522; Bishop II, 446.

REPUBLICAN PARTY—POSITION OF.
I do not believe that it is wise or safe for us as a party to take refuge in mere negation and to say that there are no evils to be corrected. It seems to me that our attitude should be one of correcting the evils and thereby showing that, whereas the Populists, Socialists and others really do not correct the evils at all, or else only do so at the expense of producing others in aggravated form, on the contrary we Republicans hold the just balance and set ourselves as resolutely against improper corporate influence on the one hand as against demagogy and mob rule on the other. (To Senator T. C. Platt, Spring 1899.) *Mem. Ed.* XXIII, 146; Bishop I, 126.

————. We are sundered from the men who now control and manage the Republican party by the gulf of their actual practices and of the openly avowed or secretly held principles which rendered it necessary for them to resort to these practises. The rank and file of the Republicans, as was shown in the spring primaries of 1912, are with us; but they have no real power against the bosses, and the channels of information are so choked that they are kept in ignorance of what is really happening. The doctrines laid down by Mr. Taft as law professor at Yale give the theoretical justification for the practical action of Mr. Penrose and Mr. Smoot. . . . This acquiescence in wrong-doing as the necessary means of preventing popular action is not a new position. It was the position of many upright and well-meaning Tories who antagonized the Declaration of Independence and the movement which made us a nation. It was the position of a portion of the very useful Federalist party, which at the close of the eighteenth century insisted upon the vital need of national union and governmental efficiency, but which was exceedingly anxious to devise methods for making believe to give the people full power while really putting them under the control of a propertied political oligarchy. (*Century,* October 1913.) *Mem. Ed.* XIX, 537; *Nat. Ed.* XVII, 394.

————. In 1896, 1898, and 1900 the campaigns were waged on two great moral issues: (1) the imperative need of a sound and honest currency; (2) the need, after 1898, of meeting in manful and straightforward fashion the extraterritorial problems arising from the Spanish War. On these great moral issues the Republican party was right, and the men who were opposed to it, and who claimed to be the radicals, and their allies among the sentimentalists, were utterly and hopelessly wrong. This had, regrettably but perhaps inevitably, tended to throw the party into the hands not merely of the conservatives but of the reactionaries; of men who, sometimes for personal and improper reasons, but more often with entire sympathy and uprightness of purpose, distrusted anything that was progressive and dreaded radicalism. These men still from force of habit applauded what Lincoln had done in the way of radical dealing with the abuses of his day; but they did not apply the spirit in which Lincoln worked to the abuses of their own day. (1913.) *Mem. Ed.* XXII, 397-398; *Nat. Ed.* XX, 341.

REPUBLICAN PARTY — ROOSEVELT AND THE.
I am by inheritance and by education a Republican; whatever good I have been able to accomplish in public life has been accomplished through the Republican party; I have acted with it in the past, and wish to act with it in the future. (Interview, Boston *Herald,* July 20, 1884.) *Mem. Ed.* XVI, 72; *Nat. Ed.* XIV, 40.

————. I am well aware that a man with strong convictions is always apt to feel overintensely the difference between himself and others with slighter convictions, and throughout most of my political career I have been in the position of adhering to one side because, after a general balancing, in spite of my discontent with my own people, I was infinitely more discontented with the other side. But I do think we had the Republican Party in a shape that warranted the practical continuance of just what we were doing. To announce allegiance to what had been done, and to abandon the only methods by which it was possible to get it done, was not satisfactory from my standpoint. (To H. C. Lodge, April 11, 1910.) Lodge *Letters* II, 372.

──────────. Our own party leaders did not realize that I was able to hold the Republican party in power only because I insisted on a steady advance, and dragged them along with me. Now the advance has been stopped, and whether we blame the people on the one side, or the leaders on the other, the fact remains that we are in a very uncomfortable position. (To H. C. Lodge, May 5, 1910.) Lodge *Letters* II, 380.

──────────. I wish to do everything in my power to make the Republican party the party of sane, constructive radicalism, just as it was under Lincoln. If it is not that, then of course I have no place in it. And while I might very probably vote for its candidate as the least unattractive course open, I would not attempt any serious championship of it, or expect to have any share in guiding it. If the Romanoffs of our social and industrial world are kept at the head of our Government the result will be Bolshevism, and Bolshevism means disaster to liberty, writ large across the face of this continent. (To William Allen White, April 4, 1918.) *Mem. Ed.* XXIV, 518; Bishop II, 442.

REPUBLICAN PARTY AND THE DEMOCRATIC PARTY. We can say this much of the Republican party: it is the party that had in it Alexander Hamilton, of the older day; that had Webster and Clay; the great party which has produced a Lincoln, the party of Seward and of Chase; the party within whose ranks we now hold Schurz and Choate, and every other name almost that tends to make this city illustrious. I think we can say this much, Republicans have not always done well, but it will be an evil day when they do as badly as the Democrats. (At Republican mass-meeting, 21st Assembly Dist., N. Y., October 28, 1882.) *Mem. Ed.* XVI, 15; *Nat. Ed.* XIV, 13.

──────────. This difference in the attitude of the two parties is fundamental; it comes from their composition. Throughout the North the bulk of the honesty and intelligence of the community is to be found in the Republican ranks. If the Republicans take a false step it is usually because the politicians have tricked them into it; while if the Democrats make a good move it is almost always merely because the astute party leaders have been able for a short time to dragoon their dense-witted followers into the appearance of deference to decent public sentiment. (Before Young Republican Club, Brooklyn, N. Y., October 17, 1885.) *Mem. Ed.* XVI, 103; *Nat. Ed.* XIV, 63.

──────────. Neither the Republican nor the Democratic platform contains the slightest promise of approaching the great problems of to-day either with understanding or good faith; and yet never was there greater need in this nation than now of understanding and of action taken in good faith, on the part of the men and the organizations shaping our governmental policy. Moreover, our needs are such that there should be coherent action among those responsible for the conduct of national affairs and those responsible for the conduct of State affairs; because our aim should be the same in both State and nation; that is, to use the government as an efficient agency for the practical betterment of social and economic conditions throughout this land. There are other important things to be done, but this is the most important thing. It is preposterous to leave such a movement in the hands of men who have broken their promises as have the present heads of the Republican organization (not of the Republican voters, for they in no shape represent the rank and file of the Republican voters). These men by their deeds give the lie to their words. There is no health in them, and they cannot be trusted. But the Democratic party is just as little to be trusted. The Underwood-Fitzgerald combination in the House of Representatives has shown that it cannot safely be trusted to maintain the interests of this country abroad or to represent the interests of the plain people at home. . . . The Democratic platform not only shows an utter failure to understand either present conditions or the means of making these conditions better but also a reckless willingness to try to attract various sections of the electorate by making mutually incompatible promises which there is not the slightest intention of redeeming, and which, if redeemed, would result in sheer ruin. . . . At present both the old parties are controlled by professional politicians in the interests of the privileged classes, and apparently each has set up as its ideal of business and political development a government by financial despotism tempered by make-believe political assassination. Democrat and Republican alike, they represent government of the needy many by professional politicians in the interests of the rich few. This is class government, and class government of a peculiarly unwholesome kind. (Before Progressive National Convention, Chicago, August 6, 1912.) *Mem. Ed.* XIX, 361-362; *Nat. Ed.* XVII, 256-257.

REPUBLICAN PARTY. *See also* DEMOCRATIC PARTY; ELECTIONS; MUGWUMPS; POLITICAL PARTIES; PROGRESSIVE PARTY.

REPUTATION. *See* FAME; NATIONAL REPUTATION.

RESEARCH. *See* HISTORIANS; PRIMITIVE SOCIETY; SCHOLARSHIP; UNIVERSITY.

RESERVATIONS. *See* INDIAN POLICY.

RESERVOIRS. *See* WATER CONSERVATION.

RESPECT. *See* FELLOW-FEELING.

RESPONSIBLE GOVERNMENT. See PARLIAMENTARY GOVERNMENT.

RESPONSIBILITY. *See* AUTHORITY; DUTY; FOREIGN RELATIONS; FREEDOM; NATIONAL RESPONSIBILITY; POWER; SOVEREIGNTY; WEALTH.

REVOLUTIONARIES. The general continental European revolutionary attitude . . . in governmental matters is a revolt against order as well as against tyranny, and in domestic matters is a revolt against the ordinary decencies and moralities even more than against conventional hypocrisies and cruelties. (Letter of April 23, 1906.) *Mem. Ed.* XXIV, 16; Bishop II, 12.

REVOLUTIONARIES. *See also* ANARCHISTS; BOLSHEVISTS; GORKY, MAXIM; INDUSTRIAL WORKERS OF THE WORLD; ORDER; SOCIALISTS.

REVOLUTIONARY AND CIVIL WARS. The Revolutionary leaders can never be too highly praised; but taken in bulk the Americans of the last quarter of the eighteenth century do not compare to advantage with the Americans of the third quarter of the nineteenth. In our Civil War it was the people who pressed on the leaders, and won almost as much in spite of as because of them; but the leaders of the Revolution had to goad the rank and file into line. They were forced to contend not only with the active hostility of the Tories, but with the passive neutrality of the indifferent, and the selfishness, jealousy, and short-sightedness of the patriotic. Had the Americans of 1776 been united, and had they possessed the stubborn, unyielding tenacity and high devotion to an ideal shown by the North, or the heroic constancy and matchless valor shown by the South, in the Civil War, the British would have been driven off the continent before three years were over. (1888.) *Mem. Ed.* VIII, 313; *Nat. Ed.* VII, 270.

———. It has been so habitual among American writers to praise all the deeds, good, bad, and indifferent, of our Revolutionary ancestors, and to belittle and make light of what we have recently done, that most men seem not to know that the Union and Confederate troops in the Civil War fought far more stubbornly and skilfully than did their forefathers at the time of the Revolution. It is impossible to estimate too highly the devoted patriotism and statesmanship of the founders of our national life; and however high we rank Washington, I am confident that we err, if anything, in not ranking him high enough, for on the whole the world has never seen a man deserving to be placed above him; but we certainly have over-estimated the actual fighting qualities of the Revolutionary troops, and have never laid enough stress on the folly and jealousy with which the States behaved during the contest. In 1776, the Americans were still in the gristle; and the feats of arms they then performed do not bear comparison with what they did in the prime of their lusty youth, eighty or ninety years later. The continentals who had been long drilled by Washington and Greene were most excellent troops; but they never had a chance to show at their best, because they were always mixed in with a mass of poor soldiers, either militia or just-enlisted regulars. (1889.) *Mem. Ed.* XI, 169; *Nat. Ed.* VIII, 532-533.

REVOLUTIONARY WAR. In the Revolutionary War the Americans stood toward the British as the Protestant peoples stood toward the Catholic powers in the sixteenth century, as the Parliamentarians stood toward the Stuarts in the seventeenth, or as the upholders of the American Union stood toward the Confederate slaveholders in the nineteenth; that is, they warred victoriously for the right in a struggle whose outcome vitally affected the welfare of the whole human race. They settled, once for all, that thereafter the people of English stock should spread at will over the world's waste spaces, keeping all their old liberties and winning new ones; and they took the first and longest step in establishing the great principle that thenceforth those Europeans, who by their strength and daring founded new states abroad, should be deemed to have done so for their own profit as freemen, and not for the benefit of their more timid, lazy, or contented brethren who stayed behind. (1888.) *Mem. Ed.* VIII, 282; *Nat. Ed.* VII, 243-244.

REVOLUTIONARY WAR — FACTIONS DURING. It must be remembered that all through the Revolutionary War not only was there a minority actively favorable to the royal cause, but there was also a minority . . . that was but lukewarm in its devotion to the American side, and was kept even moderately patriotic almost as much by the excesses of the British troops and blunders of the British generals and ministers as by the valor of our own soldiers, or the skill of our own statesmen. We can now see clearly that the right of the matter was with the patriotic party; and it was a great thing for the whole English-speaking race that that section of it which was destined to be the most numerous and powerful should not be cramped and fettered by the peculiarly galling shackles of provincial dependency; but all this was not by any means so clear then as now, and some of our best citizens thought themselves in honor bound to take the opposite side—though of necessity those among our most high-minded men, who were also far-sighted enough to see the true nature of the struggle, went with the patriots. (1888.) *Mem. Ed.* VIII, 298; *Nat. Ed.* VII, 257.

———. Throughout the Revolutionary War our people hardly once pulled with a will together; although almost every locality in turn, on some one occasion, varied its lethargy by a spasm of terrible energy. Yet, again, it must be remembered that we were never more to be dreaded than when our last hope seemed gone; and if the people were unwilling to show the wisdom and self-sacrifice that would have insured success, they were equally determined under no circumstances whatever to acknowledge final defeat. (1888.) *Mem. Ed.* VIII, 333-334; *Nat. Ed.* VII, 288-289.

REVOLUTIONARY WAR. *See also* ANDRÉ, JOHN; ARNOLD, BENEDICT; COLONIES; DECLARATION OF INDEPENDENCE; FRENCH REVOLUTION; LAFAYETTE, MARQUIS DE; VALLEY FORGE; WASHINGTON, GEORGE; WAYNE, ANTHONY.

REVOLUTIONS. Healthy growth cannot normally come through revolution. A revolution is sometimes necessary, but if revolutions become habitual the country in which they take place is going down-hill. (*Churchman,* March 17, 1900.) *Mem. Ed.* XV, 395-396; *Nat. Ed.* XIII, 393.

———. Rebellion, revolution — the appeal to arms to redress grievances; these are measures that can only be justified in extreme cases. It is far better to suffer any moderate evil, or even a very serious evil, so long as there is a chance of its peaceable redress, than to plunge the country into civil war; and the men who head or instigate armed rebellions for which there is not the most ample justification must be held as one degree worse than any but the most evil tyrants. Between the Scylla of despotism and the Charybdis of anarchy there is but little to choose; and the pilot who throws the ship upon one is as blameworthy as he who throws it on the other. But a point may be reached where the people have to assert their rights, be the peril what it may. (1900.) *Mem. Ed.* XIII, 313; *Nat. Ed.* X, 209-210.

———. I do not believe in violent revolutions, but I do believe in steady and healthy growth in the right direction. (To Howells, August 28, 1906.) *Life in Letters of William Dean Howells,* ed. by Mildred Howells. (Doubleday, Doran & Co., Garden City, N. Y., 1928), II, p. 229.

REVOLUTIONS—COURSE OF. In every . . . Revolution some of the original adherents of the movement drop off at each stage, feeling that it has gone too far; and at every halt the extremists insist on further progress. As stage succeeds stage, these extremists become a constantly diminishing body, and the irritation and alarm of the growing remainder increase. If the movement is not checked at the right moment by the good sense and moderation of the people themselves, or if some master-spirit does not appear, the extremists carry it ever farther forward until it provokes the most violent reaction; and when the master-spirit does stop it, he has to guard against both the men who think it has gone too far and the men who think it has not gone far enough.

(1900.) *Mem. Ed.* XIII, 389; *Nat. Ed.* X, 274.

REVOLUTIONS—DANGERS OF. In great crises it may be necessary to overturn constitutions and disregard statutes, just as it may be necessary to establish a vigilance committee, or take refuge in lynch-law; but such a remedy is always dangerous, even when absolutely necessary; and the moment it becomes the habitual remedy, it is a proof that society is going backward. Of this retrogression the deeds of the strong man who sets himself above the law may be partly the cause and partly the consequence; but they are always the signs of decay. (1900.) *Mem. Ed.* XIII, 325; *Nat. Ed.* X, 220.

REVOLUTIONS—SUCCESS OF. Any revolutionary movement must be carried through by parties whose aims are so different, or whose feelings and interests are so divergent, that there is great difficulty in the victors coming to a working agreement to conserve the fruits of their victory. Not only the leaders, but more especially their followers—that is, the mass of the people—must possess great moderation and good sense for this to be possible. Otherwise, after much warfare of factions, some strong man, a Cromwell or a Napoleon, is forced or forces himself to the front and saves the factions from destroying one another by laying his iron hand on all. (1900.) *Mem. Ed.* XIII, 358; *Nat. Ed.* X, 248.

REVOLUTIONS. See also FRENCH REVOLUTION; HAITI; PANAMA REVOLUTION; PROGRESS; REFORM; REVOLUTIONARY WAR; SOCIAL REVOLUTION; SOUTH AMERICA.

REWARDS. It has been wisely said that the most valuable work done by any individual in a nation, from the standpoint of the nation itself, is apt to be, from that individual's own standpoint, non-remunerative work. The statesmen and soldiers who have really rendered most service to the country were not paid, and indeed, according to our theories, ought not to have been paid, in a way that represented any adequate material reward as compared, for instance, to the sums earned by the most successful business and professional men. Great scientists, great philosophers, great writers, must also get most of their reward from the actual doing of the deed itself; for any pay they receive, measured in money, is of necessity wholly inadequate compared to the worth of the service. (*Outlook,* December 9, 1911.) *Mem. Ed.* XIV, 554; *Nat. Ed.* XII, 413.

———. One of the principal needs in any civilization is to keep always open to certain men an opportunity for doing non-remunerative work, work which, from the very nature of things, will be totally unpaid, or paid in a manner altogether out of proportion to its value when accomplished. I think it would hardly be too much to say that the lives of those men whose work has been of the greatest value to this and every country have been in a material sense absurdly, ridiculously, underpaid. Since Milton received five pounds for one of the greatest epics ever written, the story has always been the same. The reward of the men who have left great names, whether as soldiers, statesmen, or in other walks, was almost always the work they did. The work which is on the whole best worth doing for any great people is work which from its very nature cannot pay for itself. The great mass of the body politic has got to understand this, or there will be a failure to provide opportunities for this non-remunerative work, the work which does not and cannot bring quick and profitable pecuniary returns to the doer of it. (Remarks at dedication, December 29, 1900.) *Opening of the Medical School.* (Cornell University, Ithaca, N. Y., 1901), p. 20.

REWARDS—ADJUSTMENT OF. While I think we live in a pretty good world, I do not think it is all the best possible world, and I hope we shall have an adjustment of rewards, even those of a pecuniary or material kind. Altogether there is much in the way of reward that comes to a certain type of financiers and too little comes to the student, to the scholar, to the teacher, to the man who represents the scholarly side, the side of thought. (At Clark University, Worcester, Mass., June 21, 1905.) *Mem. Ed.* XV, 579; *Nat. Ed.* XIII, 618.

REWARDS TO THE EXCEPTIONAL. In this country we rightly go upon the theory that it is more important to care for the welfare of the average man than to put a premium upon the exertions of the exceptional. But we must not forget that the establishment of such a premium for the exceptional, though of less importance, is nevertheless of very great importance. It is important even to the development of the average man, for the average of all of us is raised by the work of the great masters. (At Harvard University, Cambridge, June 28, 1905.) *Mem. Ed.* XVIII, 433; *Nat. Ed.* XVI, 322.

———. We do not want to produce a dead level of achievement and reward; we want to give the exceptional rewards, in the way of approbation or in whatever other fashion may be necessary, to the exceptional men, the Lincolns, Grants, Marshalls, Emersons, Longfellows, Edisons, Pearys, who each in his own line does some special service; but we wish so far as possible to prevent a reward being given that is altogether disproportionate to the services, and especially to prevent huge rewards coming where there is no service or indeed where the action rewarded is detrimental instead of beneficial to the public interest. (*Outlook*, January 21, 1911.) *Mem. Ed.* XIX, 97; *Nat. Ed.* XVII, 63.

REWARDS. See also OPPORTUNITY; SERVICE; SUCCESS.

RHETORIC. See ACTION; DEEDS; ORATORY.

RICHES. See FORTUNES; MILLIONAIRES; MONEY; PROPERTY; WEALTH.

RIDING. See HORSEBACK RIDING.

RIFLE VS. SHOT-GUN. To my mind, there is no comparison between sport with the rifle and sport with the shot-gun. The rifle is the freeman's weapon. The man who uses it well in the chase shows that he can at need use it also in war with human foes. I would no more compare the feat of one who bags his score of ducks or quail with that of him who fairly hunts down and slays a buck or bear than I would compare the skill necessary to drive a buggy with that required to ride a horse across country; or the dexterity acquired in handling a billiard cue with that shown by a skilful boxer or oarsman. The difference is not one of degree; it is one of kind.

I am far from decrying the shot-gun. It is always pleasant as a change from the rifle, and in the Eastern States it is almost the only firearm which we now have a chance to use. But out in the cattle country it is the rifle that is always carried by the ranchman who cares for sport. Large game is still that which is sought after, and most of the birds killed are either simply slaughtered for the pot, or else shot for the sake of variety while really after deer or antelope; though every now and then I have taken a day with the shot-gun after nothing else but prairie fowl. (1885.) *Mem. Ed.* I, 63; *Nat. Ed.* I, 52.

RIGHT AND MIGHT. There is just one way in which to meet the upholders of the doctrine that might makes right. To do so we must prove that right will make might, by backing right with might. (New York *Times*, Nov. 1, 1914.) *Mem. Ed.* XX, 80; *Nat. Ed.* XVIII, 69.

RIGHT AND MIGHT. See also FORCE.

RIGHT AND WRONG. Right is right and wrong is wrong, and it is a sign of weakness and not of generosity to confuse them. (To H. C. Lodge, October 8, 1913.) Lodge *Letters* II, 441.

———. My duty was to stand with every one while he was right, and to stand against him when he went wrong; and this I have tried to do as regards individuals and as regards groups of individuals. When a business man or labor leader, politician or reformer, is right, I support him; when he goes wrong, I leave him. (1913.) *Mem. Ed.* XXII, 182; *Nat. Ed.* XX, 156.

RIGHT AND WRONG. See also NEUTRALITY.

RIGHTEOUSNESS. We, the American people, believe, and ought to believe, in righteousness first, and in peace as the handmaid of righteousness. We abhor brutality and wrongdoing, whether exhibited by nations or by individuals. We hold that the same law of righteousness should obtain between nation and nation as between man and man. I, for one, would rather cut off my hand than see the United States adopt the attitude either of cringing before great and powerful nations who wish to wrong us, or of bullying small and weak nations who have done us no wrong. The American people desire to do justice and to act with frank generosity toward all the other nations of mankind; but I err greatly in my judgment of my countrymen if they are willing to submit to wrong and injustice. Again and again in the past they have shown, and rightly shown, that when the choice lay between righteousness and peace they chose righteousness, just exactly as they also chose righteousness when the choice lay between righteousness and war. (*Outlook*, September 9, 1911.) *Mem. Ed.* XVIII, 417; *Nat. Ed.* XVI, 311.

———. As yet the great civilized peoples, if they are to be true to themselves and to the cause of humanity and civilization, must keep ever in mind that in the last resort they must possess both the will and the power to resent wrong-doing from others.

The men who sanely believe in a lofty

morality preach righteousness; but they do not preach weakness, whether among private citizens or among nations. We believe that our ideals should be high, but not so high as to make it impossible measurably to realize them. We sincerely and earnestly believe in peace; but if peace and justice conflict, we scorn the man who would not stand for justice though the whole world came in arms against him. (At the Sorbonne, Paris, April 23, 1910.) *Mem. Ed.* XV, 375; *Nat. Ed.* XIII, 528.

―――――――――. It is noxious to work for a peace not based on righteousness, and useless to work for a peace based on righteousness unless we put force back of righteousness. At present this means that adequate preparedness against war offers to our nation its sole guaranty against wrong and aggression. (*Everybody's*, January 1915.) *Mem. Ed.* XX, 150; *Nat. Ed.* XVIII, 129.

―――――――――. The United States owes not only its greatness but its very existence to the fact that in the Civil War the men who controlled its destinies were the fighting men. The counsels of the ultrapacifists, the peace-at-any-price men of that day, if adopted, would have meant not only the death of the nation but an incalculable disaster to humanity. A righteous war may at any moment be essential to national welfare; and it is a lamentable fact that nations have sometimes profited greatly by war that was not righteous. Such evil profit will never be done away with until armed force is put behind righteousness. (*Everybody's*, January 1915.) *Mem. Ed.* XX, 155; *Nat. Ed.* XVIII, 133.

RIGHTEOUSNESS—PRIMACY OF. Peace is not the end. Righteousness is the end. . . . Righteousness is the end, and peace a means to the end, and sometimes it is not peace, but war which is the proper means to achieve the end. Righteousness should breed valor and strength. When it does breed them, it is triumphant; and when triumphant, it necessarily brings peace. But peace does not necessarily bring righteousness. (1916.) *Mem. Ed.* XX, 239; *Nat. Ed.* XVIII, 206.

―――――――――. We must ever bear in mind that the great end in view is righteousness, justice as between man and man, nation and nation, the chance to lead our lives on a somewhat higher level, with a broader spirit of brotherly good-will one for another. Peace is generally good in itself, but it is never the highest good unless it comes as the handmaid of righteousness; and it becomes a very evil thing if it serves merely as a mask for cowardice and sloth, or as an instrument to further the ends of despotism or anarchy. We despise and abhor the bully, the brawler, the oppressor, whether in private or public life; but we despise no less the coward and the voluptuary. No man is worth calling a man who will not fight rather than submit to infamy or see those that are dear to him suffer wrong. No nation deserves to exist if it permits itself to lose the stern and virile virtues; and this without regard to whether the loss is due to the growth of a heartless and all-absorbing commercialism, to prolonged indulgence in luxury and soft effortless ease, or to the deification of a warped and twisted sentimentality. (Before Nobel Prize Committee, Christiania, Norway, May 5, 1910.) *Mem. Ed.* XVIII, 411; *Nat. Ed.* XVI, 306.

―――――――――. We must insist on righteousness first and foremost. We must strive for peace always; but we must never hesitate to put righteousness above peace. In order to do this, we must put force back of righteousness, for, as the world now is, national righteousness without force back of it speedily becomes a matter of derision. To the doctrine that might makes right, it is utterly useless to oppose the doctrine of right unbacked by might. (New York *Times*, November 1, 1914.) *Mem. Ed.* XX, 77; *Nat. Ed.* XVIII, 66.

RIGHTEOUSNESS. *See also* CIVIC RIGHTEOUSNESS; NATIONAL GREATNESS; PACIFISM; PEACE; PREPAREDNESS; UNPREPAREDNESS; WAR.

RIGHTS—DEFENSE OF. We have in this country an equality of rights. It is the plain duty of every man to see that his rights are respected. That weak good nature which acquiesces in wrong-doing, whether from laziness, timidity, or indifference, is a very unwholesome quality. It should be second nature with every man to insist that he be given full justice. (*Atlantic Monthly*, August 1894.) *Mem. Ed.* XV, 50; *Nat. Ed.* XIII, 36.

―――――――――. For a man to stand up for his own rights, or especially for the rights of somebody else, means that he must have virile qualities: courage, foresight, willingness to face risk and undergo effort. It is much easier to be timid and lazy. The average man does not like to face death and endure hardship and labor. He can be roused to do so if a leader of the right type, a Washington or Lincoln, appeals to the higher qualities, including the stern qualities, of his soul. (1916.) *Mem. Ed.* XX, 238; *Nat. Ed.* XVIII, 205.

RIGHTS—PROTECTION OF. There must be equal rights for all, and special privileges for none; but we must remember that to achieve this ideal it is necessary to construe rights and privileges very differently from the way they were necessarily construed, by statesmen and people alike, a century ago. We must strive to achieve our ideal by an exercise of governmental power which the conditions did not render necessary a century ago, and of which our forefathers would have felt suspicious. This is no reflection on the wisdom of our forefathers; it is simply an acknowledgment that conditions have now changed. *Outlook,* September 3, 1910, p. 22.

——————. We are for the people's rights. Where these rights can best be obtained by exercise of the powers of the State, there we are for States' rights. Where they can best be obtained by the exercise of the powers of the National Government, there we are for national rights. We are not interested in this as an abstract doctrine; we are interested in it concretely. Wisconsin possesses advanced laws in the interest of labor. There are other States in this respect more backward, where wage-workers, and especially women and child wage-workers, are left at the mercy of greedy and unscrupulous capitalists. (*Century,* October 1913.) *Mem. Ed.* XIX, 543; *Nat. Ed.* XVII, 399.

RIGHTS, HUMAN. I believe in property rights, but I believe in them as adjuncts to, and not as substitutes for, human rights. I believe that normally the rights of property coincide with the rights of man: but where they do not, then the rights of man must be put above the rights of property. I believe in shaping the ends of government to protect property; but wherever the alternative must be faced, I am for man and not for property. *Outlook,* September 3, 1910, p. 28.

RIGHTS AND DUTIES. I have not the slightest sympathy with any movement which looks to excusing men and women for the non-performance of duty and fixes attention only on rights and not on duties. *Outlook,* August 27, 1910, p. 922.

——————. If there is any lesson, more essential than any other, for this country to learn, it is the lesson that the enjoyment of rights should be made conditional upon the performance of duty. For one failure in the history of our country which is due to the people not asserting their rights, there are hundreds due to their not performing their duties. (Preface to E. J. Scott and L. B. Stowe, *Booker T. Washington,* dated August 28, 1916.) *Mem. Ed.* XII, 549; *Nat. Ed.* XI, 274.

——————. No human being is entitled to any "right," any privilege, that is not correlated with the obligation to perform duty. (1917.) *Mem. Ed.* XXI, 9; *Nat. Ed.* XIX, 8.

——————. Both capitalists and wage-workers must understand that the performance of duties and the enjoyment of rights go hand in hand. Any shirking of obligation toward the nation, and toward the people that make up the nation, deprives the offenders of all moral right to the enjoyment of privileges of any kind. This applies alike to corporations and to labor-unions, to rich men and poor men, to big men and little men. (At Cooper Union, New York City, November 3, 1916.) *Mem. Ed.* XX, 518; *Nat. Ed.* XVIII, 444.

——————. The people should be greater than any one man, and the people cannot be greater unless the people think of duty more than of right, just as the individual man who rises has to think first of duty and then of his rights. They must think of rights as developed in duty rather than of only their individual rights. Unless the people, unless the sovereign, develop the capacity to think, each one, of what is due from him to his fellows and not of what is due from his fellow to him, unless they develop that capacity, this country, based as it is on popular government, cannot achieve the place that it must and will achieve. (At University of Wisconsin, Madison, April 15, 1911.) *Mem. Ed.* XV, 546; *Nat. Ed.* XIII, 593.

RIGHTS. See also DUTY; EQUALITY; FREEDOM; INTERNATIONAL DUTIES; NEUTRAL RIGHTS; PRIVILEGE; PROPERTY RIGHTS; WOMEN.

RIIS, JACOB A. Recently a man well qualified to pass judgment alluded to Mr. Jacob Riis as "the most useful citizen of New York." Those fellow-citizens of Mr. Riis who best know his work will be most apt to agree with this statement. The countless evils which lurk in the dark corners of our civic institutions, which stalk abroad in the slums, and have their permanent abode in the crowded tenement houses, have met in Mr. Riis the most formidable opponent ever encountered by them in New York City. Many earnest men and earnest women have been stirred to the depths by the want and misery and foul crime which are bred in the crowded blocks of tenement rookeries. These men and women have planned and worked, intelligently and resolutely, to overcome the evils. But to Mr. Riis was given, in addition to earnestness and zeal, the great gift of expression, the great gift of making others see what he saw and feel what he felt. His book, *How the Other Half Lives,* did really go a long way toward removing the ignorance in which one half of the world of New York dwelt concerning the life of the other half. Moreover, Mr. Riis possessed the further great advantage of having himself passed through not a few of the experiences of which he had to tell. . . . No rebuff, no seeming failure, has ever caused him to lose faith. The memory of his own trials never soured him. His keen sense of the sufferings of others never clouded his judgment, never led him into hysterical or sentimental excess, the pit into which not a few men are drawn by the very keenness of their sympathies; and which some other men avoid, not because they are wise, but because they are cold-hearted. He ever advocates mercy, but he ever recognizes the need of justice. The mob leader, the bomb-thrower, have no sympathy from him. No man has ever insisted more on the danger which comes to the community from the lawbreaker. He set himself to kill the living evil, and small is his kinship with the dreamers who seek the impossible, the men who talk of reconstituting the entire social order, but who do not work to lighten the burden of mankind by so much as a feather's weight. Every man who strives, be it ever so feebly, to do good according to the light that is in him, can count on the aid of Jacob Riis if the chance comes. (*McClure's,* March 1901.) Mem. Ed. XV, 209-211; Nat. Ed. XIII, 270-272.

——————. Jacob Riis was one of those men who by his writings contributed most to raising the standard of unselfishness, of disinterestedness, of sane and kindly good citizenship, in this country. But in addition to this he was one of the few great writers for clean and decent living and for upright conduct who was also a great doer. He never wrote sentences which he did not in good faith try to act whenever he could find the opportunity for action. He was emphatically a "doer of the word," and not either a mere hearer or a mere preacher. Moreover, he was one of those good men whose goodness was free from the least taint of priggishness or self-righteousness. He had a white soul; but he had the keenest sympathy for his brethren who stumbled and fell. He had the most flaming intensity of passion for righteousness, but he also had kindliness and a most humorously human way of looking at life and a sense of companionship with his fellows. He did not come to this country until he was almost a young man; but if I were asked to name a fellowman who came nearest to being the ideal American citizen, I should name Jacob Riis. (*Outlook,* June 6, 1914; used as Introduction.) Jacob A. Riis, *The Making of an American.* (Macmillan Co., N. Y., 1916), p. xv-xvi.

RIIS, JACOB A. *See also* CITY LIFE.

RIOTS—SUPPRESSION OF. If it comes to putting down a riot, make up your mind that the person with whom to feel sympathy is the law-abiding citizen, not the lawless. When people put themselves in opposition to law, start to put them down with a healthy desire to see that they get put down quick, and if any damage comes, let it come on them and not on the men who have refrained from violating the law. (Before Liberal Club, Buffalo, N. Y., September 10, 1895.) Mem. Ed. XVI, 275; Nat. Ed. XIV, 195.

RIOTS. *See also* BROWNSVILLE RIOT; LABOR DISPUTES; VIOLENCE.

RIVER IMPROVEMENT. *See* INLAND WATERWAYS; MISSISSIPPI RIVER.

ROADS—IMPORTANCE OF. No one thing can do more to offset the tendency toward an unhealthy growth from the country into the city than the making and keeping of good roads. They are needed for the sake of their effect upon the industrial conditions of the country districts; and I am almost tempted to say they are needed for the sake of social conditions in the country districts. (Before Nat. and Internat. Good Roads Convention, St. Louis, April 29, 1903.) Mem. Ed. XVIII, 616; Nat. Ed. XVI, 446.

ROADS. *See also* FARM LIFE.

ROBINSON, EDWIN ARLINGTON. It is rather curious that Mr. Robinson's volume [*The Children of the Night*] should not have attracted more attention. There is an undoubted touch of genius in the poems collected in this volume, and a curious simplicity and good faith, all of which qualities differentiate them sharply from ordinary collections of the kind. There is in them just a little of the light that never was on land or sea, and in such light the objects described often have nebulous outlines; but it is not always necessary in order to enjoy a poem that one should be able to translate it into terms of mathematical accuracy. Indeed, those who admire the coloring of Turner, those who like to read how—and to wonder why—Childe Roland to the Dark Tower came, do not wish always to have the ideas presented to them with cold, hard, definite outlines; and to a man with the poetic temperament it is inevitable that life should often appear clothed with a certain sad mysticism. In the present volume I am not sure that I understand "Luke Havergal"; but I am entirely sure that I like it. (*Outlook,* August 12, 1905.) *Mem. Ed.* XIV, 360-361; *Nat. Ed.* XII, 296-297.

ROMAN EMPIRE—FALL OF. Much of the fall of the Roman Republic we can account for. For one thing, I do not think historians have ever laid sufficient emphasis on the fact that the widening of the franchise in Italy and the provinces meant so little from the governmental standpoint because citizens could only vote in one city, Rome; I should hate at this day to see the United States governed by votes cast in the city of New York, even though Texas, Oregon, and Maine could in theory send their people thither to vote if they chose. But the reasons for the change in military and governmental ability under the empire between, say, the days of Hadrian and of Valens are hardly even to be guessed at. (To A. J. Balfour, March 5, 1908.) *Mem. Ed.* XXIV, 124; Bishop II, 107.

——————. There is nothing mysterious about Rome's dissolution at the time of the barbarian invasions; apart from the impoverishment and depopulation of the empire, its fall would be quite sufficiently explained by the mere fact that the average citizen had lost the fighting edge—an essential even under a despotism, and therefore far more essential in free, self-governing communities, such as those of the English-speaking peoples of to-day. (At Oxford University, June 7, 1910.) *Mem. Ed.* XIV, 87; *Nat. Ed.* XII, 43.

ROMAN EMPIRE. *See also* LATIN LITERATURE.

ROMANOFFS. *See* RUSSIA.

ROME. To you who know your Rome so well, . . . I need hardly say that the Eternal City offers the very sharpest contrasts between the extremes of radical modern progress, social, political, and religious, and the extremes of opposition to all such progress. At the time of my visit the Vatican represented the last; the free-thinking Jew mayor, a good fellow, and his Socialist backers in the Town Council, represented the first; and between them came the king and statesmen like his Jewish Prime Minister, and writers like that high and fine character Foggazaro, and ecclesiastics like some of the cardinals, as for instance Janssens, the head of the Benedictines. (To Sir George Otto Trevelyan, October 1, 1911.) *Mem. Ed.* XXIV, 227; Bishop II, 194.

ROME—ROOSEVELT'S VISIT TO. At Rome I had an elegant row, the details of which you have doubtless seen in the papers. The Pope imposed conditions upon my reception, requiring a pledge—secret or open—that I would not visit and speak to the Methodist Mission. Of course I declined absolutely to assent to any conditions whatever, and the reception did not take place. Then with a folly as incredible as that of the Vatican itself, the Methodist missionaries, whose game was perfectly simple because the Pope had played it for them, and who had nothing to do but sit quiet, promptly issued an address of exultation which can only be called scurrilous, and with equal promptness I cancelled the arrangements I had made for seeing them. Our clerical brother is capable of showing extraordinarily little sense when he gets into public affairs. The only satisfaction I had out of the affair, and it was a very great satisfaction, was that on the one hand I administered a needed lesson to the Vatican, and on the other hand I made it understood that I feared the most powerful Protestant Church just as little as I feared the Roman Catholics. If I were in politics, or intended to run for any public office, I should regard the incident as gravely compromising my usefulness as a candidate, but inasmuch as I have no idea that I shall ever again be a candidate for anything, I can take unalloyed satisfaction in having rendered what I regard as a small service to the cause of right-thinking in America. (To H. C. Lodge, April 6, 1910.) *Lodge Letters* II, 364.

ROOSEVELT — PRONUNCIATION OF. As for my name, it is pronounced as if it was spelled "Rosavelt." That is in three syllables. The first syllable as if it was "Rose." (To Rev.

[534]

William W. Moir, October 10, 1898.) Roosevelt Memorial Association Library.

ROOSEVELT, THEODORE. I am, if I am anything, an American. I am an American from the crown of my head to the soles of my feet. If I take office I will take it as a freeman, as an equal to my fellow freemen, to serve loyally, honestly, and conscientiously every citizen of this great Commonwealth. (At Cooper Union Hall, New York City, October 15, 1886.) *Mem. Ed.* XVI, 117; *Nat. Ed.* XIV, 74.

———. I am just an ordinary man without any special ability in any direction. In most things I am just above the average; in some of them a little under, rather than over. I am only an ordinary walker. I can't run. I am not a good swimmer, although I am a strong one. I probably ride better than I do anything else, but I am certainly not a remarkably good rider. I am not a good shot. My eyesight is not strong, and I have to get close to my game in order to make any shot at all. I never could be a good boxer, although I like to box and do keep at it, whenever I can. My eyesight prevents me from ever being a good tennis player, even if otherwise I could qualify.

So you see that from the physical point of view I am just an ordinary, or perhaps a little less than ordinary man. Now, take the things that I have done in public life or in private life either, for that matter. I am not a brilliant writer. I have written a great deal, but I always have to work and slave over everything I write. The things that I have done, in one office, or another, are all, with the possible exception of the Panama Canal, just such things as any ordinary man could have done. There is nothing brilliant or outstanding in my record, except, perhaps, this one thing. Whatever I think it is right for me to do, I do. I do the things that I believe ought to be done. And when I make up my mind to do a thing, I act. (January 1909; reported by Davis.) Oscar King Davis, *Released for Publication.* (Houghton Mifflin Co., Boston, 1925), pp. 131-132.

———. I am not in the least a hero, my dear fellow. I am a perfectly commonplace man and I know it; I am just a decent American citizen who tries to stand for what is decent in his own country and in other countries and who owes very much to you and to certain men like you who are not fellow countrymen of his. (To Sir George Otto Trevelyan, May 29, 1915.) *Mem. Ed.* XXIV, 211; Bishop II, 181.

ROOSEVELT, THEODORE. *See also* BOYHOOD; ROUGH RIDERS; SPANISH-AMERICAN WAR; SUNDAY SCHOOL; WHITE HOUSE.

ROOSEVELT AS A LEADER. I'm no orator, and in writing I'm afraid I'm not gifted at all, except perhaps that I have a good instinct and a liking for simplicity and directness. If I have anything at all resembling genius it is the gift for leadership. (To Julian Street.) *Mem. Ed.* IX, 213; *Nat. Ed.* X, 357.

———. I am already an old man, and the chances are very small that I will ever again grow into touch with the people of this country to the degree that will make me useful as a leader; and a man who has been a leader is very rarely useful as an adviser when the period of his leadership has passed. (To E. A. Van Valkenberg, September 5, 1916.) *Mem. Ed.* XXIV, 487; Bishop II, 414.

ROOSEVELT DIVISION, THE. If a war should occur while I am still physically fit, I should certainly try to raise a brigade, and if possible a division, of cavalry, mounted riflemen, such as those in my regiment ten years ago. (To John St. Loe Strachey, November 28, 1908.) *Mem. Ed.* XXIV, 146; Bishop II, 126.

———. If war came, I would certainly wish you in my division; but it would not be possible to say in advance in just what position I could use you; and moreover the Administration would be apt to try either not to employ me at the front or not to give me a free hand. (To Bacon, July 7, 1916.) James Brown Scott, *Robert Bacon. Life and Letters.* (Doubleday, Page & Co., Garden City, N. Y., 1923), p. 254.

———. My hope is, if we are drawn into this European war, to get Congress to authorize me to raise a Cavalry Division, which would consist of four cavalry brigades each of two regiments, and a brigade of Horse Artillery of two regiments, with a pioneer battalion or, better still, two pioneer battalions, and a field battalion of signal troops in addition to a supply train and a sanitary train. I would wish the ammunition train and the supply train to be both motor trains; and I would also like a regiment or battalion of machine guns; although I should want to consult you as to just the way in which this organization should be maintained, for of course the machine guns would be distributed among the troops. (To Captain Frank McCoy, July 10, 1916.) Major-General James G. Harbord, "Theodore Roosevelt and the Army." *Review of Reviews,* January 1924, p. 76.

—————————. In view of the fact that Germany is now actually engaged in war with us, I again earnestly ask permission to be allowed to raise a division for immediate service at the front. My purpose would be after some six weeks preliminary training here to take it direct to France for intensive training so that it could be sent to the front in the shortest possible time to whatever point was desired. I should of course ask no favors of any kind except that the division be put in the fighting line at the earliest possible moment. If the Department will allow me to assemble the division at Fort Sill, Oklahoma, and will give me what aid it can, and will furnish arms and supplies as it did for the early Plattsburg camps, I will raise the money to prepare the division until Congress can act, and we shall thereby gain a start of over a month in making ready. (To Secretary Newton D. Baker, March 19, 1917.) *Mem. Ed.* XXI, 200; *Nat. Ed.* XIX, 190.

—————————. If I were a younger man I would be entirely content to go in any position, as a second lieutenant, or as a private in the force. With my age I cannot do good service, however, unless as a general officer. I remember when I went to the Spanish War there was talk about rejecting me on account of my eyes; but, of course, even in the position I then went in, it was nonsense to reject me for any such reason. To the position which I now seek, of course, the physical examination does not apply, so long as I am fit to do the work, which I certainly can do—that is enlisting the best type of fighting men, and putting into them the spirit which will enable me to get the best possible results out of them in the actual fight. Hindenburg, was of course, a retired officer, who had been for years on the retired list, and who could not physically have passed an examination. I am not a Hindenburg; but I can raise and handle this division in a way that will do credit to the American people, and to you, and to the President. (To Secretary Newton D. Baker, April 12, 1917.) *Mem. Ed.* XXI, 203; *Nat. Ed.* XIX, 193.

—————————. I now ask permission to raise a division to consist of regiments like the regiment which I commanded in the Santiago campaign (and I can raise you an army corps on this basis). If I were young enough I should be willing to raise that division, and myself merely go as a second lieutenant in it. As it is, I believe I am best fitted to be the division commander in an expeditionary corps, under the chief of that corps; but if you desire to put me in a less position, and make me a brigade commander, I will at once raise the division, and can raise it without difficulty, if it is to be put under any man of the type of General Wood, General Pershing, or General Kuhn. (To Secretary Newton D. Baker, April 22, 1917.) *Mem. Ed.* XXI, 216; *Nat. Ed.* XIX, 204.

—————————. All I am asking is the chance to help make good the President's message of April 2d. If you don't know whether the governments of the Allies would like me to raise such a division, and take it abroad at the earliest possible moment, I wish you would ask those governments yourself their feeling in the matter. I know that they earnestly desire us to send our men to the fighting line; and I have been informed from the highest sources that they would like to have me in the fighting line. Of course, they will not desire to have me go, or the division go, unless the Administration expresses its willingness.

Let me repeat that if you permit me to raise a division, it will be composed of men who would not be reached in the bill you proposed to Congress, and who would otherwise not be utilized at all. I should, of course, like your authority to have about two Regular officers for every thousand men, and perhaps four of the Reserve Officers for every thousand men, and perhaps certain additional ones if you saw fit to grant them. But the subtraction of these men from the number of men available to train the force called out under your proposed bill would be inconsiderable, compared to the immense gain which would come from having such a division put into the fighting line at the earliest possible moment. (To Secretary Newton D. Baker, April 22, 1917.) *Mem. Ed.* XXI, 218; *Nat. Ed.* XIX, 206.

—————————. I wish respectfully to point out certain errors into which the President has been led in his announcement. He states that the purpose was to give me an "independent" command. In my last letter to the Secretary of War I respectfully stated that if I were given permission to raise an army corps of two divisions, to be put under the command of some General like Wood or Bell or Pershing or Barry or Kuhn, I desired for myself only the position of junior among the eight brigade commanders. My position would have been exactly the same as theirs, except that I would have ranked after and have been subordinate to the rest of them.

The President alludes to our proffered action as one that would have an effect "politically," but as not contributing to the "success of the war," and as representing a "policy of personal gratification or advantage." I wish respectfully but emphatically to deny that any political consideration whatever or any desire for personal gratification or advantage entered into our calculations. Our undivided purpose was to contribute effectively to the success of the war....

The President condemns our proposal on the ground that "undramatic" action is needed, action that is "practical and of scientific definiteness and precision." There was nothing dramatic in our proposal save as all proposals indicating eagerness or willingness to sacrifice life for an ideal are dramatic. It is true that our division would have contained the sons or grandsons of men who in the Civil War wore the blue or the gray; for instance, the sons or grandsons of Phil Sheridan, Fitzhugh Lee, Stonewall Jackson, James A. Garfield, Simon Bolivar Buckner, Adna R. Chaffee, Nathan Bedford Forest; but these men would have served either with commissions or in the ranks, precisely like the rest of us; and all alike would have been judged solely by the efficiency—including the "scientific definiteness"—with which they did their work and served the flag of their loyal devotion. (Statement to men who had volunteered for service in the division, May 21, 1917.) *Mem. Ed.* XXI, 235-237; *Nat. Ed.* XIX, 221, 222.

——————. I bitterly regret to say that my Government has refused to allow me to raise troops and take them to France. The reasons were not connected with patriotism, or with military efficiency, and so there is no use of my trying to get the decision altered. My four sons and one of my sons-in-law are now in the army that is being trained, and I hope that all five of them will not too long hence go to your country. (To Captain de Rochambeau, June 1, 1917.) *Mem. Ed.* XXIV, 503, Bishop II, 429.

ROOSEVELT'S CANDIDACY FOR MAYOR. I don't care what may be his politics, I don't care what may be his religion, I don't care what may be his color. I don't care who he is, so long as he is honest he shall be served by me. All I ask of him is that he discharge faithfully the duties of an American citizen, and I am his representative. If I am chosen I will have one ambition—which is lawful and honorable—to so comport myself as to earn the right to the respect and esteem of every citizen of the city of New York. I am the candidate for mayor nominated and indorsed by the citizens and the Republican party. If I am made mayor, I will be mayor of the city of New York. (At Cooper Union Hall, New York City, October 15, 1886.) *Mem. Ed.* XVI, 117; *Nat. Ed.* XIV, 74.

ROOSEVELT'S DRINKING. It happens that in the matter of drinking I am an extremely abstemious man; I suppose that no man not a total abstainer could well drink less than I do; and whiskey and brandy I practically never touch. The accusation that I ever have been addicted in the slightest degree to drinking to excess, or to drinking even wine—and liquor, as I say, I practically never touch—in any but the most moderate way, is not only the blackest falsehood but an utterly ridiculous falsehood; it does not represent any distortion or exaggeration; it has no slightest base in fact; it is simply malignant invention—just as sheer an invention as if they had said that at the age of five I had poisoned my grandmother or had been mixed up in the assassination of Lincoln by Wilkes Booth. One accusation would be exactly as infamous and exactly as ludicrous as the other. (Letter of February 25, 1909.) *Mem. Ed.* XXIV, 138; Bishop II, 118.

——————. I have never claimed to be a total abstainer, but I drink as little as most total abstainers, for I really doubt whether on an average, year in and year out, I drink more than is given for medicinal purposes to many people. I never touch whisky, and I have never drunk a cocktail or a highball in my life. I doubt whether I have drunk a dozen teaspoonfuls of brandy since I came back from Africa, and as far as I now recollect, in each case it was for medicinal purposes. In Africa during the eleven months I drank exactly seven ounces of brandy; this was under our doctor's direction in my first fever attack, and once when I was completely exhausted. My experience on these two occasions convinced me that tea was better than brandy, and during the last six months in Africa I took no brandy, even when sick, taking tea instead. (To F. C. Iglehart, May 12, 1912.) F. C. Iglehart, *King Alcohol Dethroned.* (The Christian Herald, N. Y., 1917), p. 209.

ROOSEVELT'S LIFE. As far as I am personally concerned, I am well ahead of the game, whatever happens. I have had an exceedingly good time; I have been exceedingly well treated

[537]

by the American people; and I have enjoyed the respect of those for whose respect I care most. (To William Allen White, November 26, 1907.) *Mem. Ed.* XXIV, 60; Bishop II, 51.

——————. I am still looking forward, and not back. I do not know any man who has had as happy a fifty years as I have had. I have had about as good a run for my money as any human being possibly could have; and whatever happens now I am ahead of the game. Besides, I hope still to be able to do some good work now and then; and I am looking forward to my African trip with just as much eagerness as if I were a boy; and when I come back there are lots of things in our social, industrial and political life in which I shall take an absorbed interest. I have never sympathized in the least with the kind of man who feels that because he has been fortunate enough to hold a big position he cannot be expected to enjoy himself afterward in a less prominent position. (To Frederic Remington, October 28, 1908.) *Mem. Ed.* XXIV, 142; Bishop II, 122.

ROOSEVELT'S OPPONENTS. It is to be expected as a matter of course that the corporation judge, the corporation senator and ex-senator, the big corporation attorney, the newspaper owned in or controlled from Wall Street will attack me. I should be very foolish if I expected anything else; I should be still more foolish if I were greatly disturbed over the attacks. If there is much depression, if we meet hard times, then a great number of honest and well-meaning people will gradually come to believe in the truth of these attacks, and I shall probably end my term of service as President under a more or less dark cloud of obloquy. If so, I shall be sorry, of course; but I shall neither regret what I have done nor alter my line of conduct in the least degree, nor yet be unduly cast down. (To William Allen White, November 26, 1907.) *Mem. Ed.* XXIV, 60; Bishop II, 51.

ROOSEVELT'S POLICIES. If I stand for anything it is for this kind of substantive achievement, and above all, for treating public affairs with courage, honesty and sanity; for keeping our Army and Navy up; for making it evident that as a nation we do not intend to inflict wrong or submit to wrong, and that we do intend to try to do justice within our own borders, and so far as it can be done by legislation, to favor the growth of intelligence and the diffusion of wealth in such a manner as will measurably avoid the extremes of swollen fortunes and grinding poverty. This represents the ideal toward which I am striving. I hope we can fairly realize it. (To Jacob Riis, June 26, 1906.) *Mem. Ed.* XXIV, 24; Bishop II, 19-20.

——————. I am as sure as man can be of anything that I have been following the course which the best interests of this country demand; and under such circumstances, if I had known that the obloquy were to be permanent I should still not have altered this course. But I do not believe that it will be permanent, because I do not believe that there can be a permanent deviation from the lines of policy along which I have worked—that is, if the Republic is to endure at all. If there is such permanent deviation I shall esteem the calamity so great that any thought of my own reputation in the matter will be entirely swallowed up. (To William Allen White, November 26, 1907.) *Mem. Ed.* XXIV, 60; Bishop II, 51.

ROOSEVELT'S POLITICAL CAREER. Really, though elected as an independent Republican, I hardly know what to call myself. As regards civil service, reform, tariff reform, local self-government, etc., I am quite in sympathy with Democratic principles; it is Democratic practice that I object to. Besides as I am neither of Celtic descent nor yet a liquor seller, I would be ostracized among our New York Democrats. I cannot join myself with the party that, at least in my city and State, contains the vast majority of the vicious and illiterate population. (To Joseph Henry Adams, November 20, 1882.) Walter F. McCaleb, *Theodore Roosevelt*. (Albert & Charles Boni, N. Y., 1931), p. 31.

——————. I have very little expectation of being able to keep on in politics; my success so far has only been won by absolute indifference to my future career; for I doubt if any one can realise the bitter and venomous hatred with which I am regarded by the very politicians who at Utica supported me, under dictation from masters who were influenced by political considerations that were national and not local in their scope. I realise very thoroughly the absolutely ephemeral nature of the hold I have upon the people, and the very real and positive hostility I have excited among the politicians. I will not stay in public life unless I can do so on my own terms; and my ideal, whether lived up to or not, is rather a high one. (To S. N. D. North, April 30, 1884.) G. W. Douglas, *The Many-Sided*

Roosevelt. (Dodd, Mead & Co., N. Y., 1907.), p. 42.

———————. Of course it may be that we have had our day; it is far more likely that this is true in my case than in yours, for I have no hold on the party managers in New York. Blaine's nomination meant to me pretty sure political death if I supported him; this I realized entirely, and went in with my eyes open. I have won again and again; finally chance placed me where I was sure to lose whatever I did; and I will balance the last against the first. I have stood a great deal; and now that the throw has been against me, I shall certainly not complain. I have not believed and do not believe that I shall ever be likely to come back into political life; we fought a good winning fight when our friends the Independents were backing us; and we have both of us, when circumstances turned them against us, fought the losing fight grimly out to the end. What we have been cannot be taken from us; what we are is due to the folly of others and to no fault of ours. (To H. C. Lodge, November 11, 1884.) Lodge *Letters* I, 26.

———————. As you know, I am a man of moderate means . . . and I should have to live very simply in Washington and could not entertain in any way as Mr. Hobart and Mr. Morton entertained. My children are all growing up and I find the burden of their education constantly heavier, so that I am by no means sure that I ought to go into public life at all, provided some remunerative work offered itself. The only reason I would like to go on is that as I have not been a money maker I feel rather in honor bound to leave my children the equivalent in a way of a substantial sum of actual achievement in politics or letters. Now, as Governor, I can achieve something, but as Vice-President I should achieve nothing. The more I look at it, the less I feel as if the Vice-Presidency offered anything to me that would warrant my taking it. (To T. C. Platt, February 1, 1900.) William R. Thayer, *Theodore Roosevelt.* (Houghton Mifflin Co., Boston, 1919), p. 144.

———————. To consider the Presidency in any way as a possibility would be foolish. American politics are kaleidoscopic, and long before the next five years are out, the kaleidoscope is certain to have been many times shaken and some new men to have turned up. The only thing for me to do is to do exactly as I have always done; and that is, when there is a chance of attempting a bit of work worth the trial, to attempt it. You got me the chance to be Civil Service Commissioner and Assistant Secretary of the Navy, and it was by your advice that I went into the police department. All three jobs were worth doing and I did them reasonably to my own satisfaction. Now the thing to decide at the moment is whether I shall try for the Governorship again, or accept the Vice Presidency, if offered. (To H. C. Lodge, February 2, 1900.) Lodge *Letters* I, 447.

———————. I do not expect to go any further in politics. Heaven knows there is no reason to expect that a man of so many and so loudly and not always wisely expressed convictions on so many different subjects should go so far! But I have had a first-class run for my money, and I honestly think I have accomplished a certain amount. (To Edward S. Martin, November 22, 1900.) *Mem. Ed.* XXIII, 162; Bishop I, 140.

———————. Every office I have held I have quite sincerely believed would be the last I should hold, the only exception being that during my first term as President I gradually grew to think it probable that I should be reelected. (To John St. Loe Strachey, February 12, 1906.) *Mem. Ed.* XXIV, 7; Bishop II, 5.

———————. I have been in active politics almost from the moment I left Harvard twenty-five years ago. I possessed a very moderate income. I could not have gone into politics at all if the expenses of election had at any time come anywhere near the salaries I have received in the different positions I have held; and except from these salaries, I of course never made a cent out of politics—I could no more do it than I could cheat at cards. I have always occupied working positions. I have seen New York State politics from the inside as a member of the legislature, and New York City politics from the inside as Police Commissioner. I have carried my ward and lost it; have been delegate to county and state and national conventions; have stumped year in and year out, and served on committees, before and after elections, which determined much of what the inside policy was to be. I have had on occasions to fight bosses and rings and machines; and have had to get along as best I could with bosses and rings and machines when the conditions were different. I have seen reform movements that failed and reform movements that succeeded and have taken part in both, and have also taken part in opposing fool reform movements which it would be a misfortune to have succeed. In particular, I have been so placed as to see very much of the inside of the administration of three Presidents in addition to my own—that is, of Harrison, Cleveland, and McKinley. (To George H. Lorimer, May 12, 1906.) *Mem. Ed.* XXIV, 16; Bishop II, 13.

———————. As soon as I left college I wanted to take an interest in political life; I wanted to find out how the work of governing was really done. Quite a number of nice people in New York, along Fifth Avenue, solemnly advised me not to join any of the regular political organizations, because I would find that they were composed only of "muckers," not of "gentlemen." The answer was easy: "Then they are the ones that govern; if it is the muckers that govern, I want to see if I cannot hold my own with them. I will join with them in governing you if you are too weak to govern yourselves." I intended to be one of the class that governs, not one of the class that is governed. So I joined the political club in my district. I joined it just as I joined the National Guard. If there came a time of civic disturbance in the community, or if we were invaded or were at war with any country, I did not intend to have to hire somebody else to do my shooting for me. I intended to do it myself; and in the same way I intended to do the governing myself, to do my part of it. I want to see you feel the same way. (At the Harvard Union, Cambridge, Mass., February 23, 1907.) *Mem. Ed.* XV, 488; *Nat. Ed.* XIII, 564.

———————. Neither the praise nor the blame makes one partical of difference in my career. I have worked hard; and now I have revelled in staying quietly here in my own home, with those for whom I care most in the world, and with my own books, and the things with which I have associations. Twenty years ago, even ten years ago, this would not have been so; I would have felt that it spelled failure to have me forced out of the contest while it was still my business to fight. But now I *have* fought. I am entirely ready to take up any task I ought to; but if no task comes, why I feel I have done enough to warrant my enjoying the rest without the haunting sense of having failed to strive my best while it was still the day of action. (To Lady Delamere, March 7, 1911.) Lord Charnwood, *Theodore Roosevelt*. (Atlantic Monthly Press, Boston, 1923), p. 220.

———————. Like most young men in politics, I went through various oscillations of feeling before I "found myself." At one period I became so impressed with the virtue of complete independence that I proceeded to act on each case purely as I personally viewed it, without paying any heed to the principles and prejudices of others. The result was that I speedily and deservedly lost all power of accomplishing anything at all; and I thereby learned the invaluable lesson that in the practical activities of life no man can render the highest service unless he can act in combination with his fellows, which means a certain amount of give-and-take between him and them. Again, I at one period began to believe that I had a future before me, and that it behooved me to be very far-sighted and scan each action carefully with a view to its possible effect on that future. This speedily made me useless to the public and an object of aversion to myself; and I then made up my mind that I would try not to think of the future at all, but would proceed on the assumption that each office I held would be the last I ever should hold, and that I would confine myself to trying to do my work as well as possible while I held that office. I found that for me personally this was the only way in which I could either enjoy myself or render good service to the country, and I never afterward deviated from this plan. (1913.) *Mem. Ed.* XXII, 103; *Nat. Ed.* XX, 88.

———————. It may be that after I left the Presidency I ought not to have tried to take any part in politics at all. But all the men of the highest type made the strongest kind of appeal to me not to desert them. There was no use of my talking about virtue in the abstract, unless I applied it to concrete cases; and I either had to do just as I did or else completely abandon all effort to say anything on any public question whatsoever. Perhaps I ought to have done this; but, if I had done so, it is quite possible that I should now be feeling that I had a little shirked my duty. (To Kermit Roosevelt, January 27, 1915.) *Mem. Ed.* XXIV, 421; Bishop II, 358.

ROOSEVELT'S POLITICAL CAREER. *See also* CIVIL SERVICE COMMISSIONER; GOVERNOR OF NEW YORK; NAVY, ASSISTANT SECRETARY OF THE; NEW YORK ASSEMBLY; POLICE COMMISSIONER; PRESIDENT; PROGRESSIVE PARTY; REPUBLICAN PARTY; ROOSEVELT'S CANDIDACY FOR MAYOR; VICE-PRESIDENCY.

ROOSEVELT'S POPULARITY. Just at the moment people are speaking altogether too well of me, which is enough to make any man feel uncomfortable; for if he has any sense he knows that the reaction is perfectly certain to come under such circumstances, and that then people will revenge themselves for feeling humiliated for having said too much on one side by saying too much on the other. (To Henry Cabot Lodge, September 15, 1905.) *Mem. Ed.* XXIII, 393; Bishop I, 342.

——————. I have felt a slightly contemptuous amusement over the discussion that has been going on for several months about my popularity or waning popularity or absence of popularity. I am not a college freshman nor that would-be popular fox-hunting hero in "Soapy Sponge," and therefore I am not concerned about my popularity save in exactly so far as it is an instrument which will help me to achieve my purposes. That is, in so far as my good repute among the people helps me to secure the passage of the rate bill, I value it. In so far as it fails to help me secure the adoption of the Santo Domingo treaty, I do not value it. A couple of years ago or thereabouts, a good many timid souls told me that by my action in Panama I had ruined my popularity and was no longer available as a candidate; to which I answered that while I much wished to be a candidate and hoped that I had not ruined my popularity, yet if it was necessary to ruin it in order to secure to the United States the chance to build the Panama Canal, I should not hesitate a half-second, and did not understand how any man could hesitate. (To Sereno S. Pratt, March 1, 1906.) *Mem. Ed.* XXIV, 10; Bishop II, 7.

——————. One more word about my "popularity." It certainly seems as if for the moment I were popular, but I know too much about popularity and above all, of the utter evanescence of a great and unwarranted popularity, to attach more than very slight weight to such manifestations as I see. . . . Now, a tremendous hip-hip-hurrah is very apt to leave people exhausted, and rather to invite reaction; and I attach more importance to the cold calculated malignance of the foes I have made than to the wild plaudits of men who at the moment speak well of me chiefly because they are discontented in a rather vague way with existing conditions, and are groping about for somebody whom they can strive to follow. (To H. C. Lodge, May 14, 1910.) Lodge *Letters* II, 382.

——————. As regards myself, I think that the American people feel a little tired of me, a feeling with which I cordially sympathize; for they cannot be expected as a whole to understand that my speeches and writings during the last six months have been due not in the least to a desire to speak and write, but to the fact that I could not avoid doing so without shirking what I regarded as my duty. Moreover I am certain that the American people would greatly resent any thought that I would want them to give me another job of any kind for my own sake. I shall never wittingly put myself in a position where they can believe this. I feel most strongly that I never again should take any public position unless it could be made perfectly clear that I was taking it not for my own sake, but because the people thought it would be to their advantage to have me do so. (To William Allen White, December 12, 1910.) *Mem. Ed.* XXIV, 363; Bishop II, 309.

ROOSEVELT'S POWER. They talk of my power: my power vanishes into thin air the instant that my fellow citizens who are straight and honest cease to believe that I represent them and fight for what is straight and honest; that is all the strength I have. (At Binghamton, N. Y., October 24, 1910.) *Mem. Ed.* XIX, 59; *Nat. Ed.* XVII, 39.

——————. I am not under the slightest delusion as to any power that during my political career I have at any time possessed. Whatever of power I at any time had, I obtained from the people. I could exercise it only so long as, and to the extent that, the people not merely believed in me, but heartily backed me up. Whatever I did as President I was able to do only because I had the backing of the people. When on any point I did not have that backing, when on any point I differed from the people, it mattered not whether I was right or whether I was wrong, my power vanished. (Before Progressive National Convention, Chicago, August 6, 1912.) *Mem. Ed.* XIX, 409; *Nat. Ed.* XVII, 297.

ROOSEVELT'S RECEPTION IN EUROPE. I have no time to tell you of the really extraordinary reception that has been given me here. I have been somewhat puzzled by it. The various sovereigns have vied with one another in entertaining us. When we reached Denmark we stayed at the Palace; we are staying at the Palace here in Christiania; and shall do the same in Stockholm and Berlin. The popular reception, however, has been even more remarkable. I drive through dense throngs of people cheering and calling, exactly as if I were President and visiting cities at home where there was great enthusiasm for me. As I say, I have been much puzzled by it. It is largely because, and perhaps almost exclusively because I am a former President of the American Republic, which stands to the average European as a queer attractive dream, being sometimes regarded as a golden Utopia partially realized, and sometimes as a field for wild adventure of a by no means necessarily moral type—in fact a kind of mixture of Bacon's Utopia and Raleigh's Spanish Main. In addition, there is, I think, a certain amount to be credited to me personally, as a man who has appealed to their imaginations, who is accepted by them as a leader, but as a leader whom they suppose to represent democracy, liberty, honesty and justice. The diplomats are perfectly paralyzed, both at the enormous popular demonstrations, and at our being asked to stay in the royal palaces, something hitherto unheard of in the case of any but actual sovereigns. It is all interesting, and at times amusing, but it is very fatiguing and irksome, and much though I dread having to get into the confusion of American politics again, I long inexpressibly to be back at Sagamore Hill, in my own house, with my own books, and among my own friends. (To H. C. Lodge, May 5, 1910.) Lodge *Letters* II, 381.

ROOSEVELT'S SUPPORTERS. It has been peculiarly pleasant to me to find that my supporters are to be found in the overwhelming majority among those whom Abraham Lincoln called the plain people. . . .

I am a college-bred man, belonging to a well-to-do family, so that, as I was more than contented to live simply, and was fortunate to marry a wife with the same tastes, I have not had to make my own livelihood; though I have always had to add to my private income by work of some kind. But the farmers, lumbermen, mechanics, ranchmen, miners, of the North, East, and West have felt that I was just as much in sympathy with them, just as devoted to their interests, and as proud of them and as representative of them, as if I had sprung from among their own ranks; and I certainly feel that I do understand them and believe in them and feel for them and try to represent them just as much as if I had from earliest childhood made each day's toil pay for that day's existence or achievement. How long this feeling toward me will last I cannot say. It was overwhelming at the time of the election last November, and I judge by the extraordinary turnout for the Inauguration it is overwhelming now. Inasmuch as the crest of the wave is invariably succeeded by the hollow, this means that there will be a reaction. But meanwhile I shall have accomplished something worth accomplishing, I hope. (To Sir George Otto Trevelyan, March 9, 1905.) *Mem. Ed.* XXIII, 420; Bishop I, 364-365.

———————. It is a peculiar gratification to me to have owed my election not to the politicians primarily, although of course I have done my best to get on with them; not to the financiers, although I have staunchly upheld the rights of property; but above all to Abraham Lincoln's "plain people"; to the folk who worked hard on farm, in shop, or on the railroads, or who owned little stores, little businesses which they managed themselves. I would literally, not figuratively, rather cut off my right hand than forfeit by any improper act of mine the trust and regard of these people. I may have to do something of which they will disapprove, because I deem it absolutely right and necessary; but most assuredly I shall endeavor not to merit their disapproval by any act inconsistent with the ideal they have formed with me. (To Owen Wister, November 19, 1904.) *Mem. Ed.* XXIII, 397; Bishop I, 345.

ROOT, ELIHU. [Root] was the man of my cabinet, the man on whom I most relied, to whom I owed most, the greatest Secretary of State we have ever had, as great a cabinet officer as we have ever had, save Alexander Hamilton alone. He is as sane and cool-headed as he is high-minded; he neither lets facts blind him to ideals, nor ideals to fact; he is the wisest and safest of advisers, and staunchly loyal alike to friends and causes—and all I say I mean, and it is said with full remembrance that on certain points he and I would hardly agree. (To Carnegie, February 18, 1910.) Burton J. Hendrick, *The Life of Andrew Carnegie*. (Doubleday, Doran & Co., Garden City, N. Y., 1932), II, 327.

———————. I have once had to accept your resignation as Secretary of War. Now I have to accept it as Secretary of State. On the former occasion you retired from a great office where you had done work which no other man could have done as well, and after a few months you came back to fill a still higher office. In this higher office you have again done work which no other man could have done as well. I do not suppose that this letter can be made public, for some foolish people would think I was speaking hyperbolically, whereas I am speaking what I believe to be the literal truth, when I say that in my judgment you will be regarded as the greatest and ablest man who has ever filled the position of Secretary of State.

You leave the office to go into the Senate. I do not see how you can possibly do better work in the Senate than you have done in the Cabinet, but I am sure you will do as good work. (To Root, January 26, 1909.) Philip C. Jessup, *Elihu Root.* (Dodd, Mead & Co., N. Y., 1938), II, 137.

——————. I would rather see Elihu Root in the White House than any other man now possible. I have told several men recently that I would walk on my hands and knees from the White House to the Capitol to see Root made President. But I know it cannot be done. He couldn't be elected. There is too much opposition to him on account of his corporation connections.

But the people don't know Root. I do. I knew him when I was Governor of New York, and I have known him here, very intimately, during the years he has been in my Cabinet. The very thing on account of which there is so much objection to him would make him an ideal President. He is a great lawyer. He has always given all that he had to his clients. He has great intelligence, wonderful industry, and complete fidelity to his clients.

What the people do not understand about him is that if he were President they would be his clients. He would be serving the Nation with absolute singleness of purpose, and with all that intelligence, industry, and fidelity. Nothing would be, or could be, paramount with him to the interests of his clients. I know that, for I have seen him repeatedly take that attitude as a Cabinet officer. (Late 1907-early 1908; reported by Davis.) Oscar King Davis, *Released for Publication.* (Houghton Mifflin Co., Boston, 1925), pp. 54-55.

ROOT, ELIHU, AS SECRETARY OF STATE. I wished Root as Secretary of State partly because I am extremely fond of him and prize his companionship as well as his advice, but primarily because I think that in all the country he is the best man for the position, and that no minister of foreign affairs in any other country at this moment in any way compares with him. Nobody can praise him too highly to suit me. (To Albert J. Beveridge, July 11, 1905.) *Mem. Ed.* XXIII, p. 427; Bishop I, 371.

ROOT, ELIHU, AS SECRETARY OF WAR. Just at the moment Mr. Root has been savagely attacked. Now Mr. Root, by himself and through Governor Taft and General Wood and other military and civilian assistants, has done work which I regard as making the United States always his debtor. He gave up the position of leader of the New York bar, with a practice which brought him over $100,000 a year, to come down here. . . . He has worked so as almost to wear himself out. . . . He has not one thought save how to benefit the public service, how to see that the Army is kept up to the highest standard, how to secure the faithful fulfillment of our obligations to Cuba, how to help bring peace and enlightenment and self-government in the Philippines. During these three years he has performed a mass of work such as has been performed by no other minister of any civilized nation during the same time, nor has any other minister in any government of any civilized nation had a task so important which at the same time he has fulfilled so well. Yet, in spite of this, he has been most cruelly attacked, usually without any basis at all, sometimes because an occasional subordinate has done wrong—or even, as with every other public man from Washington and Lincoln down, because an occasional mistake has been made under him in the Department itself. (Letter of June 17, 1902.) *Mem. Ed.* XXIII, p. 222; Bishop I, 193.

ROUGH RIDERS. The men who made up the bulk of the regiment, and gave it its peculiar character . . . came from the four Territories which yet remained within the boundaries of the United States; that is, from the lands that have been most recently won over to white civilization, and in which the conditions of life are nearest those that obtained on the frontier when there still was a frontier. They were a splendid set of men, these southwesterners—tall and sinewy, with resolute, weather-beaten faces, and eyes that looked a man straight in the face without flinching. They included in their ranks men of every occupation; but the three types were those of the cowboy, the hunter, and the mining prospector—the man who wandered hither and thither, killing game for a living, and spending his life in the quest for metal wealth.

In all the world there could be no better material for soldiers than that afforded by these grim hunters of the mountains, these wild rough riders of the plains. They were accustomed to handling wild and savage horses; they were accustomed to following the chase with the rifle, both for sport and as a means of livelihood. Varied though their occupations had been, almost all had, at one time or another, herded cattle and hunted big game. They were hardened to life in the open, and to shifting for themselves under adverse circumstances. They were used, for all their lawless freedom, to the rough discipline of the round-up and the mining company. Some of them came from the small frontier towns; but most were from the wilderness, having left their lonely hunters' cabins and shifting cow camps to seek new and more stirring adventures beyond the sea.

They had their natural leaders—the men who had shown they could master other men, and could more than hold their own in the eager driving life of the new settlements. (1899.) *Mem. Ed.* XIII, 13-14; *Nat. Ed.* XI, 11-12.

——————. After the battle of San Juan my men had really become veterans; they and I understood each other perfectly, and trusted each other implicitly; they knew I would share every hardship and danger with them, would do everything in my power to see that they were fed, and so far as might be, sheltered and spared; and in return I knew that they would endure every kind of hardship and fatigue without a murmur and face every danger with entire fearlessness. I felt utter confidence in them, and would have been more than willing to put them to any task which any crack regiment of the world, at home or abroad, could perform. They were natural fighters, men of great intelligence, great courage, great hardihood, and physical prowess; and I could draw on these qualities and upon their spirit of ready, soldierly obedience to make up for any deficiencies in the technic of the trade which they had temporarily adopted. It must be remembered that they were already good individual fighters, skilled in the use of the horse and the rifle, so that there was no need of putting them through the kind of training in which the ordinary raw recruit must spend his first year or two. (1899.) *Mem. Ed.* XIII, 137-138; *Nat. Ed.* XI, 116-117.

——————. The regiment was a wholly exceptional volunteer organization, and its career cannot be taken as in any way a justification for the belief that the average volunteer regiment approaches the average regular regiment in point of efficiency until it has had many months of active service. In the first place, though the regular regiments may differ markedly among themselves, yet the range of variation among them is nothing like so wide as that among volunteer regiments, where at first there is no common standard at all; the very best being, perhaps, up to the level of the regulars . . . while the very worst are no better than mobs, and the great bulk come in between. The average regular regiment is superior to the average volunteer regiment in the physique of the enlisted men, who have been very carefully selected, who have been trained to life in the open, and who know how to cook and take care of themselves generally.

Now, in all these respects, and in others like them, the Rough Riders were the equals of the regulars. They were hardy, self-reliant, accustomed to shift for themselves in the open under very adverse circumstances. The two all-important qualifications for a cavalryman are riding and shooting—the modern cavalryman being so often used dismounted, as an infantryman. The average recruit requires a couple of years before he becomes proficient in horsemanship and marksmanship; but my men were already good shots and first-class riders when they came into the regiment. The difference as regards officers and non-commissioned officers, between regulars and volunteers, is usually very great; but in my regiment (keeping in view the material we had to handle), it was easy to develop non-commissioned officers out of men who had been roundup foremen, ranch foremen, mining bosses, and the like. These men were intelligent and resolute; they knew they had a great deal to learn, and they set to work to learn it; while they were already accustomed to managing considerable interests, to obeying orders, and to taking care of others as well as themselves.

As for the officers, the great point in our favor was the anxiety they showed to learn from those among their number who, like Capron, had already served in the regular army; and the fact that we had chosen a regular army man as colonel. (1899.) *Mem. Ed.* XIII, 183-186; *Nat. Ed.* XI, 157-159.

——————. They have been worn down by the terrific strain of fighting, marching, digging in the trenches, during the tropical midsummer; they have been in the fore-front, all through, they never complained though half-fed and with clothes and shoes in tatters; but it is bitter to think of the wealth at home, which would be so gladly used in their behalf if only it could be so used. They are devoted to me, and I cannot get their condition out of my thoughts. If only you could see them in battle, or feeding these wretched refugee women and children, whose misery beggars description. (To Corinne Roosevelt Robinson, July 19, 1898.) C. R. Robinson, *My Brother Theodore Roosevelt*, 175.

——————. In a sense my regiment in its composition was a typical American regiment.

Its people came from the West chiefly, but some from the East, from the South chiefly, but some from the North, so that every section was represented in it. They varied in birthplace as in creed. . . . There were men in that regiment who themselves were born, or whose parents were born in England, Ireland, Germany, or Scandinavia, but there was not a man, no matter what his creed, what his birthplace, what his ancestry, who was not an American and nothing else. We had representatives of the real, original, native Americans, because we had no inconsiderable number who were in whole or in part of Indian blood. There was in the regiment but one kind of rivalry among those men, and but one would have been tolerated. That was the rivalry of each man to see if he could not do his duty a little better than any one else. Short would have been the shrift of any man who tried to introduce division along lines of section, or creed, or class. We had serving in the ranks men of inherited wealth and men who all their lives had earned each day's bread by that day's labor, and they stood on a footing of exact equality. It would not have been any more possible for a feeling of arrogance to exist on one side than for a feeling of rancor and envy to exist on the other. (At Santa Fe, New Mexico, May 5, 1903.) *Presidential Addresses and State Papers* I, 365-366.

—————. Now, for a bit of brag. My Rough Riders, hunters of the mountains and horsemen of the plains, could not, taken as a whole, have walked quite as well as Morgan's men, nor yet have starved as well, though they were good enough at both. But they rode without thought horses that Morgan's men would not have ventured so much as to try to get on, and I firmly believe that they were fully as formidable in battle. Mine was a volunteer regiment, and at least half of the officers at the outset were very bad, so that in a long campaign I should have had to make a complete change among them—a change that was already well begun when the regiment was disbanded. But as compared with any volunteer regiment of the Revolution, of the Civil War during a like short period of service—four months—I think its record stood well. It was raised, drilled—so far as it was drilled—armed and equipped, kept two weeks on transports, and put through two victorious aggressive (not defensive) fights, in which it lost over a third of its officers and nearly a fourth of its men, and this within sixty days. The men already knew how to ride, shoot, and live in the open; and they had the fighting edge. (To Sir George Otto Trevelyan, January 1, 1908.) *Mem. Ed.* XXIV, 197; Bishop II, 169.

ROUGH RIDERS — ROOSEVELT AND THE. In my regiment nine-tenths of the men were better horsemen than I was, and probably two-thirds of them better shots than I was, while on the average they were certainly hardier and more enduring. Yet after I had had them a very short while they all knew, and I knew too, that nobody else could command them as I could. (To Theodore Roosevelt, Jr., October 4, 1903.) *Mem. Ed.* XXI, 503; *Nat. Ed.* XIX, 446.

ROUGH RIDERS. *See also* CAPRON, ALLYN; O'NEILL, BUCKY; SPANISH-AMERICAN WAR.

ROUND-UP. Though there is much work and hardship, rough fare, monotony, and exposure connected with the round-up, yet there are few men who do not look forward to it and back to it with pleasure. The only fault to be found is that the hours of work are so long that one does not usually have enough time to sleep. The food, if rough, is good: beef, bread, pork, beans, coffee or tea, always canned tomatoes, and often rice, canned corn, or sauce made from dried apples. The men are good-humored, bold, and thoroughly interested in their business, continually vying with one another in the effort to see which can do the work best. It is superbly health-giving, and is full of excitement and adventure, calling for the exhibition of pluck, self-reliance, hardihood, and dashing horsemanship; and of all forms of physical labor the easiest and pleasantest is to sit in the saddle. (1888.) *Mem. Ed.* IV, 445; *Nat Ed.* I, 340.

ROYALTY. Before I had seen them I had realized in a vague way that a king's life nowadays must be a very limited life; but the realization was brought home to me very closely on this trip. I can understand a woman's liking to be queen fairly well (that is, if she is not an exceptional woman), for if, as is sometimes the case, as was the case for instance with both the Queen of Norway and the Crown Princess of Sweden, she has made a love-match, she has the ordinary happiness that comes to the happy woman with husband and children, and in addition the ceremonial and social part would be apt to appeal to her and to be taken seriously by her. (To Sir George Otto Trevelyan, October 1, 1911.) *Mem. Ed.* XXIV, 250; Bishop II, 213.

—————. I shall always bear testimony to the courtesy and good manners, and the obvious sense of responsibility and duty, of the various sovereigns I met. But of course, as was to be expected, they were like other human beings in that the average among them was not very high as regards intellect and force. Indeed the kind of driving force and energy needed to make a first-class President or Prime Minister, a great general or War Minister, would be singularly out of place in the ordinary constitutional monarch. Apparently what is needed in a constitutional king is that he shall be a kind of sublimated American Vice-President; plus being socially at the head of that part of his people which you have called "the free masons of fashion." The last function is very important; and the king's lack of political power, and his exalted social position, alike cut him off from all real comradeship with the men who really do the things that count; for comradeship must imply some equality, and from this standpoint the king is doubly barred from all that is most vital and interesting. Politically he can never rise to, and socially he can never descend to, the level of the really able men of the nation. I cannot imagine a more appallingly dreary life for a man of ambition and power. (To Sir George Otto Trevelyan, October 1, 1911.) *Mem Ed.* XXIV, 246; Bishop II, 211.

ROYALTY—ROOSEVELT AND. I thoroughly liked and respected almost all the various kings and queens I met; they struck me as serious people, with charming manners, devoted to their people and anxious to justify their own positions by the way they did their duty—it is no disparagement to their good intentions and disinterestedness to add that each sovereign was obviously conscious that he was looking a possible republic in the face, which was naturally an incentive to good conduct; I was very glad to have met them; and it was pleasant to see them for a short while; but longer intercourse, or renewed intercourse, would have been unnatural unless there had been, as there was not, some real intellectual interest, or other bond in common, and if there was any such, it happened not to develop itself. (To Sir George Otto Trevelyan, October 1, 1911.) *Mem. Ed.* XXIV, 238; Bishop II, 204.

ROYALTY—VISITS OF. We make a strong effort to prevent royalties coming here. Mr. Bacon will send you a circular issued by John Hay some years ago to our diplomatic and consular representatives, explaining this point. I am continually importuned to get over here, now Emperor William, now President Diaz, now King Edward, and now all sorts and kinds of princes. If one comes it makes a precedent which others are apt to follow, and you know as well as I do that with all these princes we are apt to have difficulties — sometimes because some demagogue thinks it will help him to say disagreeable things about them; sometimes because of the officious and rather snobbish action of the people who regard themselves as of high social position in desiring to entertain the princes; and sometimes from the simple fact that in a democratic government like ours it is very hard to arrange properly for the reception of members of royal houses. Of course you understand that I cannot make him a guest of the nation. Congress only can do that. (To Melville E. Stone, July 16, 1907.) *Mem. Ed.* XXIV, 81; Bishop II, 70.

ROYALTY. See also KINGS; PRESIDENCY.

RUGBY. See FOOTBALL.

RURAL FREE DELIVERY. See FARM LIFE.

RURAL LIFE. See AGRICULTURE; COUNTRY LIFE COMMISSION; FARM LIFE; ROADS.

RUSSIA—FUTURE OF. The destruction of Russia is not thinkable, but if it were, it would be a most frightful calamity. The Slavs are a young people, of limitless possibilities, who from various causes have not been able to develop as rapidly as the peoples of central and western Europe. They have grown in civilization until their further advance has become something greatly to be desired, because it will be a factor of immense importance in the welfare of the world. All that is necessary is for Russia to throw aside the spirit of absolutism developed in her during the centuries of Mongol dominion. She will then be found doing what no other race can do and what it is of peculiar advantage to the English-speaking peoples that she should do. (*New York Times,* October 11, 1914.) *Mem. Ed.* XX, 57; *Nat. Ed.* XVIII, 49.

——————. Russia's sufferings have been sore, but it is not possible to overestimate Russia's tremendous tenacity of purpose and power of endurance. Russia is mighty, and her future looms so vast that it is hardly possible to overstate it. The Russian people feel this to be their war. Russia's part in the world is great, and will be greater; it is well that she should stand valiantly and stubbornly for her own rights; and as a firm and ardent friend of the Russian people may I add that Russia will stand for her rights all the more effectively when she also stands for the rights of Finn and Pole and Jew; when she learns the lesson that we Americans must also learn—to grant every man his full rights, and to exact from each man the full performance of his duty. (1916.) *Mem. Ed.* XX, 257; *Nat. Ed.* XVIII, 222.

RUSSIA—TYRANNY IN. If Russia chooses to develop purely on her own line and to resist the growth of liberalism, then she may put off the day of reckoning; but she cannot ultimately avert it, and instead of occasionally having to go through what Kansas has gone through with the Populists, she will some time experience a red terror which will make the French Revolution pale. (To Sir Cecil Arthur Spring Rice, August 11, 1897.) *Mem. Ed.* XXIII, 94; Bishop I, 80.

―――――――. The most powerful indictment of the corrupt and inefficient tyranny of the Romanoffs, or rather of the Russian autocracy, is that it produced Bolshevism. Dreadful though it is that despotism should ruin men's bodies, it is worse that it should ruin men's souls. (*Metropolitan,* June 1918.) *Mem. Ed.* XXI, 386; *Nat. Ed.* XIX, 350.

―――――――. Before our eyes the unfortunate Russian nation furnishes an example on a gigantic scale of what to avoid in oscillating between extremes. The autocratic and bureaucratic despotism of the Romanoffs combined extreme tyranny with extreme inefficiency; and the Bolshevists have turned the revolution into a veritable Witches' Sabbath of anarchy, plunder, murder, utterly faithless treachery and inefficiency carried to the verge of complete disintegration. Each side sought salvation by formulas which were condemned alike by common sense and common morality; and even these formulas were by their actions belied.

I do not say these things from any desire to speak ill of the Russian people. (1918.) *Mem. Ed.* XXI, 378; *Nat. Ed.* XIX, 343.

RUSSIA. *See also* BOLSHEVISTS; WITTE, COUNT.

RUSSIA AND THE UNITED STATES. I have a strong liking and respect for them [the Russians], but unless they change in some marked way they contain the chance of menace to the higher life of the world. I knew they now disliked the United States; I did not know that they singled out me. In one way they are right. Our people have become suspicious of Russia and I personally share this view. Probably our interests are not at the moment so great as to make it possible for us to be drawn into war with them; I shall certainly not fight unless we have ample reasons, and unless I can show our people that we have such cause. Remote though the chance is, it does exist, if the Russians push us improperly and too evidently. "Peace, if possible; but in any event, Justice!" (To Spring Rice, February 2, 1904.) *The Letters and the Friendships of Sir Cecil Spring Rice.* (Houghton Mifflin Co., Boston, 1929), I, 377-378.

RUSSIAN GOVERNMENT — DISTRUST OF. I like the Russian people, but I abhor the Russian system of government and I cannot trust the word of those at the head. (To Sir George Otto Trevelyan, May 13, 1905.) *Mem. Ed.* XXIII, 438; Bishop I, 381.

―――――――. Of course, if the Rusisans go on as they have gone ever since I have been President—and so far as I can find out, ever since the Spanish War—they are hopeless creatures with whom to deal. They are utterly insincere and treacherous; they have no conception of truth, no willingness to look facts in the face, no regard for others of any sort or kind, no knowledge of their own strength or weakness; and they are helplessly unable to meet emergencies. (To Henry Cabot Lodge, June 5, 1905.) Lodge *Letters* II, 133-134.

RUSSO-JAPANESE WAR. I am entirely sincere in my purpose to keep this Government neutral in the war. And I am no less sincere in my hope that the area of the war will be as limited as possible, and that it will be brought to a close with as little loss to either combatant as is possible. But this country as a whole tends to sympathise with Russia; while the Jews are as violent in their anti-Russian feeling as the Irish in their pro-Russian feeling. I do not think that the country looks forward to, or concerns itself about, the immense possibilities which the war holds for the future. I suppose democracies will always be short-sighted about anything that is not brought roughly home to them. Still, when I feel exasperated by the limitations upon preparedness and forethought which are imposed by democratic conditions, I can comfort myself by the extraordinary example of these very limitations which the autocratic government of Russia has itself furnished in this crisis. (To Spring Rice, March 19, 1904.) *The Letters and Friendships of Sir Cecil Spring Rice.* (Houghton Mifflin Co., Boston, 1929), I, 397.

―――――――. It is now nearly four years since the close of the Russian-Japanese war. There were various factors that brought about Russia's defeat; but most important by all odds was her having divided her fleet between the

Baltic and the Pacific, and, furthermore, splitting up her Pacific fleet into three utterly unequal divisions. The entire Japanese force was always used to smash some fraction of the Russian force. The knaves and fools who advise the separation of our fleet nowadays and the honest, misguided creatures who think so little that they are misled by such advice, ought to take into account this striking lesson furnished by actual experience in a great war but four years ago. Keep the battle fleet either in one ocean or the other and have the armed cruisers always in trim, as they are now, so that they can be at once sent to join the battle fleet if the need should arise. (To William Howard Taft, March 3, 1909.) *Mem. Ed.* XXIV, 139; Bishop II, 120.

RUSSO-JAPANESE WAR—PEACE SETTLEMENT OF. During the past fortnight, and indeed for a considerable time before, I have been carrying on negotiations with both Russia and Japan, together with side negotiations with Germany, France and England, to try to get the present war stopped. With infinite labor and by the exercise of a good deal of tact and judgment—if I do say it myself—I have finally gotten the Japanese and Russians to agree to meet to discuss the terms of peace. Whether they will be able to come to an agreement or not I can't say. But it is worth while to have obtained the chance of peace, and the only possible way to get this chance was to secure such an agreement of the two powers that they would meet and discuss the terms direct. Of course Japan will want to ask more than she ought to ask, and Russia to give less than she ought to give. Perhaps both sides will prove impracticable. Perhaps one will. But there is the chance that they will prove sensible, and make a peace, which will really be for the interest of each as things are now. At any rate the experiment was worth trying. I have kept the secret very successfully, and my dealings with the Japanese in particular have been known to no one, so that the result is in the nature of a surprise. (To Kermit Roosevelt, June 11, 1905.) *Mem. Ed.* XXI, 545; *Nat. Ed.* XIX, 490.

——————. You know how urgently I advised the Russians to conclude peace. With equal firmness I advise Japan not to continue the war for the sake of war indemnity. Should she do so, I believe that there will occur a considerable reversal of public opinion against her. I do not believe that this public opinion could have a tangible effect. Nevertheless, it must not be altogether neglected. Moreover, I do not think that the Japanese people could attain its aims if it continued the war solely because of the question of an indemnity. I think that Russia will refuse to pay and that the common opinion of the civilized world will support her in her refusal to pay the enormous sum which is being demanded or anything like that sum. Of course, if Russia pays that sum, there is nothing else for me to say. But should she refuse to pay, you will see that, having waged war for another year, even if you succeeded in occupying Eastern Siberia, you would spend four or five hundred more millions in addition to those expended, you would shed an enormous quantity of blood, and even if you obtained Eastern Siberia, you would get something which you do not need, and Russia would be completely unable to pay you anything. At any rate, she would not be in a position to pay you enough to cover the surplus expended by you. Of course, my judgment may be erroneous in this case, but it is my conviction expressed in good faith, from the standpoint of Japan's interests as I understand them. Besides, I consider that all the interests of civilization and humanity forbid the continuation of the war for the sake of a large indemnity. (To Baron Kaneko, August 22, 1905.) *The Memoirs of Count Witte.* (Doubleday, Page & Co., Garden City, N. Y., 1921), pp. 156-157.

——————. It is enough to give any one a sense of sardonic amusement to see the way in which the people generally, not only in my own country, but elsewhere, gauge the work purely by the fact that it succeeded. If I had not brought about peace I should have been laughed at and condemned. Now I am overpraised. I am credited with being extremely long-headed, etc. As a matter of fact I took the position I finally did not of my own volition but because events so shaped themselves that I would have felt as if I was flinching from a plain duty if I had acted otherwise. (To Alice Roosevelt, September 2, 1905.) *Mem. Ed.* XXIII, 476; Bishop I, 415.

——————. My object . . . was not my own personal credit or even the advancement of this country, but the securing of peace. Peace was secured. Personally I believe that the credit of this country was greatly increased by it, and as far as I am personally affected I have received infinitely more praise for it than in my opinion I deserve, and I have not been very greatly concerned as to whether I was praised or blamed. . . . I acted at the time I did at the written request of Japan, and when Japan made the request I explained to the Japanese Government that in my judgment she would not get an indemnity, and she asked me to bring about the peace meeting with full knowledge of the fact that in my opinion she neither deserved nor would get an indemnity. . . .

I believe that Japan was partly influenced by proper motives of humanity and by the desire to have the respect of the nations as a whole, and that this feeling had its weight in influencing the Japanese statesmen who knew the facts to disregard the views held by the Tokio mob and which are substantially the views set forth by you.

But the main factor in influencing Japan was undoubtedly the fact that to go on with the war meant such an enormous loss, such an enormous cost to her, that she could not afford to incur it save from dire need. (To George Kennan, written October 15, 1905, but never sent.) Tyler Dennett, *Roosevelt and the Russo-Japanese War*. (Doubleday, Page & Co., Garden City, N. Y., 1925), pp. 282-284.

───────────. I have been blamed by both the Russians and Japanese for bringing the war in Manchuria to an end prematurely, when neither side had gained a decisive victory and neither was willing to quit. The Russians claimed that they were just getting into their stride, while the Japanese asserted that had the war continued a few months more they would have been able to obtain a huge indemnity. It will probably astonish you, then, to learn that I jammed through the Treaty of Portsmouth because I had been secretly implored by the Japanese government itself to intervene and bring about a cessation of hostilities on my own initiative. Rather a peculiar phrasing, wasn't it? The message from the Emperor, making this extraordinary request, was brought to the White House late one evening by the Japanese ambassador, who insisted on seeing me even when informed that I had retired for the night.

The truth was that the Japanese had to have peace. Their money was exhausted. So was their credit. The villages from one end of the country to the other had been so drained of men that the greatest difficulty was experienced in harvesting the rice crop. When I intervened, Japan was on the verge of collapse. She was bled white.

I don't believe that I could have concluded the Treaty of Portsmouth, however, without the help of George Meyer, our ambassador at St. Petersburg, who enjoyed the confidence of the Czar and had his ear. For the Russian diplomats lied to me right and left, while the officials who surrounded the Czar deliberately misrepresented to him everything I said and did. At length it became necessary for me to order Meyer to ignore the Russian Foreign Office and deliver my messages to the Czar himself in order that they might not be falsified or distorted. I could have won the Czar over to my way of thinking in ten minutes had I been able to sit down and talk things over with him. (In conversation with Mr. Powell aboard *Hamburg*, March, 1909.) E. Alexander Powell, *Yonder Lies Adventure!* (Macmillan Co., N. Y., 1932), pp. 313-314.

───────────. During the early part of the year 1905, the strain on the civilized world caused by the Russo-Japanese War became serious. The losses of life and treasure were frightful. From all sources of information at hand, I grew most strongly to believe that a further continuation of the struggle would be a very bad thing for Japan, and an even worse thing for Russia. Japan was already suffering terribly from the drain upon her men, and especially upon her resources, and had nothing further to gain from continuation of the struggle; its continuance meant to her more loss than gain, even if she were victorious. Russia, in spite of her gigantic strength, was, in my judgment, apt to lose even more than she had already lost if the struggle continued. . . .

If the war went on, I thought it, on the whole, likely that Russia would be driven west of Lake Baikal. But it was very far from certain. There is no certainty in such a war. Japan might have met defeat, and defeat to her would have spelled overwhelming disaster; and even if she had continued to win, what she thus won would have been of no value to her, and the cost in blood and money would have left her drained white. I believed, therefore, that the time had come when it was greatly to the interest of both combatants to have peace, and when therefore it was possible to get both to agree to peace. (1913.) *Mem. Ed.* XXII, 613; *Nat. Ed.* XX, 527.

S

SAGAMORE HILL. Sagamore Hill takes its name from the old Sagamore Mohannis, who, as chief of his little tribe, signed away his rights to the land two centuries and a half ago. The house stands right on the top of the hill, separated by fields and belts of woodland from all other houses, and looks out over the bay and the Sound. We see the sun go down beyond long reaches of land and of water. Many birds dwell in the trees round the house or in the pastures and the woods near by, and of course in winter gulls, loons, and wild fowl frequent the waters of the bay and the Sound. We love all the seasons; the snows and bare woods of winter; the rush of growing things and the blossom-spray of spring; the yellow grain, the ripening fruits and tasselled corn, and the deep, leafy shades that are heralded by "the green dance of summer"; and the sharp fall winds that tear the brilliant banners with which the trees greet the dying year. (1913.) *Mem. Ed.* XXII, 359-360; *Nat. Ed.* XX, 308-309.

――――――. After all, fond as I am of the White House and much though I have appreciated these years in it, there isn't any place in the world like home—like Sagamore Hill, where things are our own, with our own associations, and where it is real country. (To Ethel Roosevelt, June 11, 1906.) *Mem. Ed.* XXI, 556; *Nat. Ed.* XIX, 508.

SAGAMORE HILL. *See also* WHITE HOUSE.

SAGAS. *See* CELTIC LITERATURE.

SAINT-GAUDENS, AUGUSTUS. The work of a very great artist must be judged by the impression it makes not only upon other artists but also upon laymen.... His [Saint-Gaudens] genius had that lofty quality of insight which enables a man to see to the root of things, to discard all trappings that are not essential, and to grasp close at hand in the present the beauty and majesty which in most men's eyes are dimmed until distance has softened the harsh angles and blotted out the trivial and the unlovely. He had, furthermore, that peculiar kind of genius in which a soaring imagination is held in check by a self-mastery which eliminates all risk of the fantastic and the overstrained. He knew when to give the most complete rein to this imagination....

It is Saint-Gaudens' peculiar quality that, without abating one jot of the truthfulness of portrayal of the man's outside aspect, yet makes that outside aspect of little weight because of what is shown of the soul within. (At Augustus Saint-Gaudens Exhibition, Corcoran Art Gallery, Washington, December 15, 1908.) *Mem. Ed.* XII, 562, 564; *Nat. Ed.* XI, 285, 287.

SAINT-GAUDENS, AUGUSTUS. *See also* COINAGE.

SALOON—INFLUENCE OF THE. In New York the saloonkeepers have always stood high among professional politicians. Nearly two thirds of the political leaders of Tammany Hall have, at one time or another, been in the liquor business. The saloon is the natural club and meeting place for the ward heelers and leaders, and the bar-room politician is one of the most common and best recognized factors, in local political government. The saloonkeepers are always hand in glove with the professional politicians, and occupy toward them a position such as is not held by any other class of men. (*Atlantic Monthly*, September 1897.) *Mem. Ed.* XV, 164; *Nat. Ed.* XIII, 129.

SALOON. *See also* LIQUOR LAW.

SAMPSON-SCHLEY CONTROVERSY. I do not anticipate any good out of the belated action in the Sampson-Schley case. The trouble is that Sampson, originally absolutely right, had elaborately done the wrong thing again and again; and that their superiors have committed the fatal error of striking soft. It has just been one of the cases where the effort to weave in and out around the trouble has proved a failure. Either the President and Secretary ought to have stood by Schley straight out from the beginning, or if they shared the belief of ninety-five percent of the navy, including all the best officers, they should have hit him hard at the very beginning. In the course they have pursued they have elaborately combined all possible disadvantages. As regards the Board, Dewey, I suppose, will take the lead. The popular feeling is overwhelmingly for Schley, and I think that Dewey now cares very little for the navy people, or for the real interest of the navy. In consequence I thoroughly believe that he will yield to the popular clamor and to his feeling against the administration and whitewash Schley. Of course, he may be true to his old naval traditions, in which case he will be very severe upon him. But I do not regard the outlook as promising. (To H. C. Lodge, August 20, 1901.) Lodge *Letters* I, 497.

SANTO DOMINGO — ROOSEVELT'S POLICY IN. I have been hoping and praying for three months that the Santo Domingans would behave so that I would not have to act in any way. I want to do nothing but what a policeman has to do in Santo Domingo. As for annexing the island, I have about the same desire to annex it as a gorged boa-constrictor might have to swallow a porcupine wrong-end-to. Is that strong enough? I have asked some of our people to go there because, after having refused for three months to do anything, the attitude of the Santo Domingans has become one of half chaotic war toward us. If I possibly can I want to do nothing to them. If it is absolutely necessary to do something, then I want to do as little as possible. Their government has been bedevilling us to establish some kind of a protectorate over the islands, and take charge of their finances. We have been answering them that we could not possibly go into the subject now at all. (To Joseph Bucklin Bishop, February 23, 1904.) *Mem. Ed.* XXIII, 494; Bishop I, 431.

──────────. Under the course taken, stability and order and all the benefits of peace are at last coming to Santo Domingo, danger of foreign intervention has been suspended, and there is at last a prospect that all creditors will get justice, no more and no less. If the arrangement is terminated by the failure of the treaty chaos will follow; and if chaos follows, sooner or later this government may be involved in serious difficulties with foreign governments over the island, or else may be forced itself to intervene in the island in some unpleasant fashion. Under the proposed treaty the independence of the island is scrupulously respected, the danger of violation of the Monroe Doctrine by the intervention of foreign powers vanishes, and the interference of our government is minimized, so that we shall only act in conjunction with the Santo Domingo authorities to secure the proper administration of the customs, and therefore to secure the payment of just debts and to secure the Dominican Government against demands for unjust debts. The proposed method will give the people of Santo Domingo the same chance to move onward and upward which we have already given to the people of Cuba. It will be doubly to our discredit as a nation if we fail to take advantage of this chance; for it will be of damage to ourselves, and it will be of incalculable damage to Santo Domingo. Every consideration of wise policy, and, above all, every consideration of large generosity, bids us meet the request of Santo Domingo as we are now trying to meet it. (Fifth Annual Message, Washington, December 5, 1905.) *Mem. Ed.* XVII, 358; *Nat. Ed.* XV, 306.

──────────. In Santo Domingo I am trying to forestall the necessity for interference by us or by any foreign power. I was immensely amused when, at a professional peace meeting, the other day, they incidentally alluded to me as having made "war" on Santo Domingo. The war I have made literally consists in having loaned them a collector of customs, at their request. We now give them forty-five per cent of the customs to run the government, and the other fifty-five per cent is put up to pay those of their debts which are found to be righteous. This arrangement has gone on two years now, while the co-ordinate branch of the government discussed whether or not I had usurped power in the matter, and finally concluded I had not, and ratified the treaty. Of the fifty-five per cent we have been able to put two and a half millions toward paying their debts; and with the forty-five per cent that we collected for them they have received more money than they ever got when they collected one hundred per cent themselves; and the island has prospered as never before. (At the Harvard Union, Cambridge, February 23, 1907.) *Mem. Ed.* XV, 493; *Nat. Ed.* XIII, 568.

──────────. In Santo Domingo, after two years' delay I got the Senate to ratify the treaty I had made (and under which, incidentally, I had been acting for two years) and have now put the affairs of the island on a better basis than they have been for a century—indeed, I do not think it would be an overstatement to say on a better basis than they have ever been before. (To Sydney Brooks, December 28, 1908.) *Mem. Ed.* XXIV, 152; Bishop II, 130.

──────────. Perhaps my conception of the Monroe Doctrine, and of proper international relations between the strong and the weak powers, is best illustrated by what occurred in San Domingo. Revolutionary disturbance had brought San Domingo to such utter anarchy that her government was impotent, and all her creditors unpaid. Finally, I learned that no less than three Old-World powers intended to land troops and seize ports, so as to take control of the custom houses of San Domingo. If this had been done, San Domingo as a nation would have disappeared, and those Old-World powers would have been in practical possession of the island to-day. This I did not intend to permit; and I did not permit it. But I intended also to try to secure justice for their citizens as San Domingo by herself could neither do justice to others nor protect even her own national life. I made an arrangement with San Domingo by which one American civil official, and only one, was sent in to supervise the entire work of the customs. I notified the foreign powers that they must not seize San Domingo soil. I also notified the people themselves that in any revolution the custom-houses were not to be interfered with. The receipts were thus collected without interference. . . . The improper claims of the creditors were rejected. Their just claims were completely satisfied. Old-World nations were kept off the island, and a measure of peace, prosperity and

[551]

stability came to the island, such as she had never in her history previously enjoyed. (At Santiago, November 24, 1913.) *Souvenir of the visit of Colonel Mr. Theodore Roosevelt, ex-President of the United States of America, to Chile.* (Santiago de Chile, 1914), pp. 51-52.

SANTO DOMINGO. See also INTERVENTION; SENATE.

SAVAGE PEOPLES. See EXPANSION; IMPERIALISM; MISSIONARIES; PRIMITIVE SOCIETY; WARS OF CONQUEST.

SCHLEY, ADMIRAL. See SAMPSON-SCHLEY CONTROVERSY.

SCHOLARSHIP. Scholarship that consists in mere learning, but finds no expression in production, may be of interest and value to the individual, just as ability to shoot well at clay pigeons may be of interest and value to him, but it ranks no higher unless it finds expression in achievement. From the standpoint of the nation, and from the broader standpoint of mankind, scholarship is of worth chiefly when it is productive, when the scholar not merely receives or acquires, but gives.

Of course there is much production by scholarly men which is not, strictly speaking, scholarship; any more than the men themselves, despite their scholarly tastes and attributes, would claim to be scholars in the technical or purely erudite sense. (*Outlook,* January 13, 1912.) *Mem. Ed.* XIV, 340; *Nat. Ed.* XII, 85.

——————. The ideal for the graduate school and for those undergraduates who are to go into it must be the ideal of high scholarly production, which is to be distinguished in the sharpest fashion from the mere transmittal of ready-made knowledge without adding to it. If America is to contribute its full share to the progress not alone of knowledge, but of wisdom, then we must put ever-increasing emphasis on university work done along the lines of the graduate school. We can best help the growth of American scholarship by seeing that as a career it is put more on a level with the other careers open to our young men. The general opinion of the community is bound to have a very great effect even upon its most vigorous and independent minds. If in the public mind the career of the scholar is regarded as of insignificant value when compared with that of a glorified pawnbroker, then it will with difficulty be made attractive to the most vigorous and gifted of our American young men. Good teachers, excellent institutions, and libraries are all demanded in a graduate school worthy of the name. But there is an even more urgent demand for the right sort of student. No first-class science, no first-class literature or art, can ever be built up with second-class men. The scholarly career, the career of the man of letters, the man of arts, the man of science, must be made such as to attract those strong and virile youths who now feel that they can only turn to business, law, or politics. There is no one thing which will bring about this desired change, but there is one thing which will materially help in bringing it about, and that is to secure to scholars the chance of getting one of a few brilliant positions as prizes if they rise to the first rank in their chosen career. Every such brilliant position should have as an accompaniment an added salary, which shall help indicate how high the position really is; and it must be the efforts of the alumni which can alone secure such salaries for such positions. (At Harvard University, Cambridge, June 28, 1905.) *Mem. Ed.* XVIII, 431-432; *Nat. Ed.* XVI, 320-321.

SCHOLARSHIP. See also UNIVERSITY.

SCHOOL AND PARENT — RESPONSIBILITY OF. I wish to extend my profound sympathy to the teachers and instructors who are continually brought into contact with what I may call the cuckoo style of parent — the parent who believes that when he can once turn his child into school he shifts all responsibility from his own shoulders for the child's education, the parent who believes that he can buy for a certain sum—which he usually denounces as excessive—a deputy parent to do his work for him. (At Pacific Theological Seminary, Spring 1911.) *Mem. Ed.* XV, 600; *Nat. Ed.* XIII, 637.

SCHOOLING—PLACE OF. School education can never supplant or take the place of self-education, still less can it in any way take the place of those rugged and manly qualities which we group together under the name of character; but it can be of enormous use in supplementing both. (At University of Pennsylvania, Philadelphia, February 22, 1905.) *Mem. Ed.* XV, 347; *Nat. Ed.* XIII, 504.

SCHOOLS, PAROCHIAL. We could suffer no national calamity more far-reaching in its effects than would be implied in the abandonment of our system of non-sectarian common schools; and it is a very unfortunate thing for any man, or body of men, to be identified with opposition thereto. But it must be borne in mind that hostility to the public schools is not really a question of sects at all; it is merely an illustration of the survival or importation here of the utterly un-American and thoroughly old-world idea of the subordination of the layman to the priest. Not a few Protestant clergymen oppose our public schools on the one hand, and an ever-increasing number of Catholic laymen support them on the other. At my own home on Long Island, for instance, the chief opponent of the public schools is, not the Catholic priest, but the Episcopalian clergyman, and he reinforces his slender stock of tritely foolish arguments by liberal quotations from the work of a Presbyterian theologian. The fight is not one between creeds; it is an issue between intelligent American laymen of every faith on the one hand and ambitious, foolish or misguided supporters of a worn out system of clerical government on the other, these supporters including Episcopalians and Presbyterians as well as Catholics. Our public-school system is here to stay; it cannot be overturned; wherever hurt even, it is only at the much greater cost of the person hurting it. The boy brought up in the parochial school is not only less qualified to be a good American citizen, but he is also at a distinct disadvantage in the race of life, compared to the boy brought up in the public schools. *America,* April 14, 1888, p. 3.

——————. We should set our faces like a rock against any attempt to allow State aid to be given to any sectarian system of education; and on the other hand, we should set our faces like a rock against any attempt to exclude any set of men from their full and proper share in the government of the public schools because of their religion. (Speech at Boston, Mass., November 1893.) *Mem. Ed.* XV, 36; *Nat. Ed.* XIII, 278.

——————. We are against any division of the school fund, and against any appropriation of public money for sectarian purposes. We are against any recognition whatever by the State in any shape or form of State-aided parochial schools. But we are equally opposed to any discrimination against or for a man because of his creed. We demand that all citizens, Protestant and Catholic, Jew and Gentile, shall have fair treatment in every way; that all alike shall have their rights guaranteed them. The very reasons that make us unqualified in our opposition to State-aided sectarian schools make us equally bent that, in the management of our public schools, the adherents of each creed shall be given exact and equal justice, wholly without regard to their religious affiliations; that trustees, superintendents, teachers, scholars, all alike, shall be treated without any reference whatsoever to the creed they profess. (*Forum,* April 1894.) *Mem. Ed.* XV, 25; *Nat. Ed.* XIII, 21.

SCHOOLS. *See also* COLLEGE; EDUCATION; HOME; PLAYGROUNDS; PUBLIC SCHOOLS; SUNDAY SCHOOL; TEACHERS; UNIVERSITY.

SCHRANK, JOHN. *See* ASSASSINATION, ATTEMPTED.

SCHURZ, CARL. *See* MUGWUMPS.

SCIENCE—STUDY OF. There is a twofold warrant for encouragement by the State of science thus followed purely for the sake of science. In the first place, and I can not too emphatically state this, the knowledge justifies itself. The scientific student is justified if he studies science for serious purpose exactly as is true of the man of arts or the man of letters. Mere addition to the sum of the interesting knowledge of nature is in itself a good thing, exactly as the writing of a beautiful poem or the chiseling of a beautiful statue is in itself a good thing. Only a sordid people, and a blind people, can fail to recognize this fact. No civilization is a great civilization unless upon the foundation of utilitarian achievement is reared the superstructure of a higher life. . . .

In the next place, the greatest utilitarian discoveries have often resulted from scientific investigations which had no distinct utilitarian purpose. Our whole art of navigation arose from the studies of certain Greek mathematicians in Alexandria and Syracuse who had no idea that their studies in geometry and trigonometry would ever have a direct material value. It is impossible to tell at what point independent investigations into the workings of nature may prove to have an immediate and direct connection with the betterment of man's physical condition, as witness the studies of Pasteur.

Most of the men and women, indeed the immense majority of the men and women, who work for pure science can not aspire to the position of leadership, exactly as most business men can not expect to press into the front rank of captains of industry. Yet each of us can do work which is not only creditable and useful but which may at some time become literally indispensable in helping to discover some great law of nature or to draw some great conclusion from the present condition or from the former physical history, the geological or paleontological history of the world. (At Albany, N. Y., December 29, 1916.) "Opening of the State

Museum." *University of the State of New York Bulletin*, March 1, 1917, pp. 36-38.

——————————. The change in the status of the man of science during the last century has been immeasurable. A hundred years ago he was treated as an interesting virtuoso, a man who was capable of giving amusement, but with whom no practical man dealt with any idea of standing on a footing of equality. Now more and more the wisest men of affairs realize that the great chance for the advancement of the human race in material things lies in the close interrelationship of the man of practical affairs and the man of science, so that the man of practical affairs can give all possible effect to the discoveries of the most unforeseen and unexpected character now made by the man of science. (Before International Congress on Tuberculosis, Washington, D. C., October 12, 1908.) S. A. Knopf, *A History of the National Tuberculosis Association.* (New York, 1922), p. 281.

SCIENCE—TEACHING OF. I fully intended to make science my life-work. I did not, for the simple reason that at that time Harvard, and I suppose our other colleges, utterly ignored the possibilities of the faunal naturalist, the outdoor naturalist and observer of nature. They treated biology as purely a science of the laboratory and the microscope, a science whose adherents were to spend their time in the study of minute forms of marine life, or else in section-cutting and the study of the tissues of the higher organisms under the microscope. This attitude was, no doubt, in part due to the fact that in most colleges then there was a not always intelligent copying of what was done in the great German universities. The sound revolt against superficiality of study had been carried to an extreme; thoroughness in minutiae as the only end of study had been erected into a fetich. There was a total failure to understand the great variety of kinds of work that could be done by naturalists, including what could be done by outdoor naturalists. . . . In the entirely proper desire to be thorough and to avoid slipshod methods, the tendency was to treat as not serious, as unscientific, any kind of work that was not carried on with laborious minuteness in the laboratory. My taste was specialized in a totally different direction, and I had no more desire or ability to be a microscopist and section-cutter than to be a mathematician. Accordingly I abandoned all thought of becoming a scientist. (1913.) *Mem. Ed.* XXII, 30-31; *Nat. Ed.* XX, 26-27.

SCIENCE AND LITERATURE. Modern scientists, like modern historians and, above all, scientific and historical educators, should ever keep in mind that clearness of speech and writing is essential to clearness of thought and that a simple, clear, and if possible, vivid style is vital to the production of the best work in either science or history. Darwin and Huxley are classics, and they would not have been if they had not written good English. The thought is essential, but ability to give it clear expression is only less essential. Ability to write well, if the writer has nothing to write about, entitles him to mere derision. But the greatest thought is robbed of an immense proportion of its value if expressed in a mean or obscure manner. (1914.) *Mem. Ed.* VI, 335; *Nat. Ed.* V, 286.

——————————. I believe that as the field of science encroaches on the field of literature there should be a corresponding encroachment of literature upon science; and I hold that one of the great needs, which can only be met by very able men whose culture is broad enough to include literature as well as science, is the need of books for scientific laymen. We need a literature of science which shall be readable. (At Oxford University, June 7, 1910.) *Mem. Ed.* XIV, 68; *Nat. Ed.* XII, 28.

——————————. I believe that already science has owed more than it suspects to the unconscious literary power of some of its representatives. Scientific writers of note had grasped the fact of evolution long before Darwin and Huxley; and the theories advanced by these men to explain evolution were not much more unsatisfactory, as full explanations, than the theory of natural selection itself. Yet, where their predecessors had created hardly a ripple, Darwin and Huxley succeeded in effecting a complete revolution in the thought of the age, a revolution as great as that caused by the discovery of the truth about the solar system. I believe that the chief explanation of the difference was the very simple one that what Darwin and Huxley wrote was interesting to read. Every cultivated man soon had their volumes in his library, and they still keep their places on our book-shelves. But Lamarck and Cope are only to be found in the libraries of a few special students. If they had possessed a gift of expression akin to Darwin's, the doctrine of evolution would not in the popular mind have been confounded with the doctrine of natural selection and a juster estimate than at present would obtain as to the relative merits of the explanation of evolution championed by the different scientific schools. (Presidential Address, American Historical Association, Boston, December 27, 1912.) *Mem. Ed.* XIV, 9-10; *Nat. Ed.* XII, 8-9.

SCIENCE AND RELIGION. The claims of certain so-called scientific men as to "science overthrowing religion" are as baseless as the fears of certain sincerely religious men on the same subject. The establishment of the doctrine of evolution in our time offers no more justification for upsetting religious beliefs than the discovery of the facts concerning the solar system a few centuries ago. Any faith sufficiently robust to stand the—surely very slight—strain of admitting that the world is not flat and does move round the sun need have no apprehensions on the score of evolution, and the materialistic scientists who gleefully hail the discovery of the principle of evolution as establishing their dreary creed might with just as much propriety rest it upon the discovery of the principle of gravitation. Science and religion, and the relations between them, are affected by one only as they are affected by the other. (*Outlook,* December 2, 1911.) *Mem. Ed.* XIV, 424; *Nat. Ed.* XII, 118.

——————————. In the world of the intellect it is easy to take the position of the hard materialists who rail against religion, and easy also to take the position of those whose zeal for orthodoxy makes them distrust all action by men of independent mind in the search for scientific truth; but it is not so easy to make it understood that we both acknowledge our inestimable debt to the great masters of science, and yet are keenly alive to their errors and decline to surrender our judgment to theirs when they go wrong. It is imperative to realize how very grave their errors are, and how foolish we should be to abandon our adherence to the old ideals of duty toward God and man without better security than the more radical among the new prophets can offer us. (*Outlook,* December 2, 1911.) *Mem. Ed.* XIV, 430; *Nat. Ed.* XII, 123.

——————————. There are plenty of phenomena unquestionably proceeding from natural law which nevertheless have in them an element totally incomprehensible to, and probably totally incapable of comprehension by, our intelligence. All successful scientific discoveries have been anathematized by certain pietistic theologians, and exultantly screamed over by certain materialists as marking the end of religion. The discovery that the earth was round, the discovery that the world went round the sun, the discovery of enormous geological ages, the growth of appreciation of law in the natural world, the discovery of the law of gravitation, and recently the understanding of the law of evolution (which, incidentally, had been at least strongly suspected by thinkers as far apart as Aristotle and St. Augustine), were all in succession treated as mischievous heresies by certain champions of orthodoxy, and were also, with equal folly, accepted by certain sceptical materialists as overthrowing spiritual laws with which they had no more to do than the discovery of steam-power has to do with altruism. (*Outlook,* January 16, 1918.) *Mem. Ed.* XIV, 35; *Nat. Ed.* XII, 157.

SCIENCE. *See also* EDUCATION, LIBERAL; HISTORY; MATERIALISM, SCIENTIFIC; REASON; SUPERSTITION.

SCIENTIFIC ADVANCE. In the world of intellect, doubtless, the most marked features in the history of the past century have been the extraordinary advances in scientific knowledge and investigation, and in the position held by the men of science with reference to those engaged in other pursuits. I am not now speaking of applied science; of the science, for instance, which, having revolutionized transportation on the earth and the water, is now on the brink of carrying it into the air; of the science that finds its expression in such extraordinary achievements as the telephone and the telegraph; of the sciences which have so accelerated the velocity of movement in social and industrial conditions—for the changes in the mechanical appliances of ordinary life during the last three generations have been greater than in all the preceding generations since history dawned. I speak of the science which has no more direct bearing upon the affairs of our every-day life than literature or music, painting or sculpture, poetry or history. A hundred years ago the ordinary man of cultivation had to know something of these last subjects; but the probabilities were rather against his having any but the most superficial scientific knowledge. At present all this has changed, thanks to the interest taken in scientific discoveries, the large circulation of scientific books, and the rapidity with which ideas originating among students of the most advanced and abstruse sciences become, at least partially, domiciled in the popular mind. (At Oxford University, June 7, 1910.) *Mem. Ed.* XIV, 66-67; *Nat. Ed.* XII, 26-27.

SCOTCH-IRISH IN AMERICA. The backwoodsmen were American by birth and parentage, and of mixed race; but the dominant strain in their blood was that of the Presbyterian Irish — the Scotch-Irish, as they were often called. Full credit has been awarded the Roundhead and the Cavalier for their leadership in our history; nor have we been altogether blind to the deeds of the Hollander and the Huguenot; but it is doubtful if we have wholly realized the importance of the part played by that stern and virile people, the Irish whose preachers taught the creed of Knox and Calvin. These Irish representatives of the Covenanters were in the West almost what the Puritans were in the Northeast, and more than the Cavaliers were in the South. Mingled with the descendants of many other races, they nevertheless formed the kernel of the distinctively and intensely American stock who were the pioneers of our people in the march westward, and the vanguard of the army of fighting settlers, who, with axe and rifle, won their way from the Alleghanies to the Rio Grande and the Pacific. (1889.) *Mem. Ed.* X, 96-97; *Nat. Ed.* VIII, 84.

SCULPTURE. See PAINTING.

SEA POWER. See MAHAN, A. T.; NAVAL ARMAMENTS; NAVY.

SECESSION. See CIVIL WAR; SLAVERY; SOUTH.

SECRET SERVICE. The secret service men are a very small but very necessary thorn in the flesh. Of course they would not be the least use in preventing any assault upon my life. I do not believe there is any danger of such an assault, and if there were it would be simple nonsense to try to prevent it, for as Lincoln said, though it would be safer for a President to live in a cage, it would interfere with his business.

But it is only the secret service men who render life endurable, as you would realize if you saw the procession of carriages that pass through the place, the procession of people on foot who try to get into the place, not to speak of the multitude of cranks and others who are stopped in the village. (To H. C. Lodge, August 6, 1906.) Lodge *Letters* II, 224.

————. Such a body as the Secret Service, such a body of trained investigating agents, occupying a permanent position in the Government service, and separate from local investigating forces in different Departments, is an absolute necessity if the best work is to be done against criminals. It is by far the most efficient instrument possible to use against crime. Of course the more efficient an instrument is, the more dangerous it is if misused. To the argument that a force like this can be misused it is only necessary to answer that the condition of its usefulness if handled properly is that it shall be so efficient as to be dangerous if handled improperly. (Message to House of Representatives, January 4, 1909.) *Presidential Addresses and State Papers* VIII, 2038.

SECTARIAN INTOLERANCE. See ANTI-SEMITISM; BIGOTRY; RELIGIOUS DISCRIMINATION; TOLERANCE.

SECTARIAN SCHOOLS. See SCHOOLS, PAROCHIAL.

SECTIONALISM. I am an American first. To all true Americans sectional hatred and class hatred are equally abhorrent, and the most abhorrent of all is sectional hatred piled on class hatred. We know no North nor South, East nor West. (At Utica, N. Y., September 29, 1896.) *Mem. Ed.* XVI, 393.

SECTIONALISM — DECLINE OF. From the evils of sectional hostility we are, at any rate, far safer than we were. The war with Spain was the most absolutely righteous foreign war in which any nation has engaged during the nineteenth century, and not the least of its many good features was the unity it brought about between the sons of the men who wore the blue and of those who wore the gray. This necessarily meant the dying out of the old antipathy. Of course embers smolder here and there; but the country at large is growing more and more to take pride in the valor, the self-devotion, the loyalty to an ideal, displayed alike by the soldiers of both sides in the Civil War. We are all united now. We are all glad that the Union was restored, and are one in our loyalty to it; and hand in hand with this general recognition of the all-importance of preserving the Union has gone the recognition of the fact that at the outbreak of the Civil War men could not cut loose from the ingrained habits and traditions of generations, and that the man from the North and the man from the South each was loyal to his highest ideal of duty when he drew sword or shouldered rifle to fight to the death for what he believed to be right. (*Century*, January 1900.) *Mem. Ed.* XV, 405; *Nat. Ed.* XIII, 355-356.

SECTIONALISM. See also AMERICAN PEOPLE; AMERICANISM; CIVIL WAR; NATIONALISM; PROGRESSIVE PARTY—APPEAL OF.

SECTIONS. *See* EAST; NEW ENGLAND; NORTH; NORTHWEST; SOUTH; WEST.

SEDENTARY LIFE. *See* EXERCISE; OUTDOOR LIFE.

SELF-DETERMINATION. *See* FOURTEEN POINTS.

SELF-GOVERNMENT. The noblest of all forms of government is self-government; but it is also the most difficult. (Fifth Annual Message, Washington, December 5, 1905.) *Mem. Ed.* XVII, 337; *Nat. Ed.* XV, 288.

———. The art of successful self-government is not an easy art for people or for individuals. It comes to our people here as the inheritance of ages of effort. It can be thrown away; it can be unlearned very easily, and it surely will be unlearned if we forget the vital need not merely of preaching, but of practicing both sets of virtues—if we forget the vital need of having the average citizen not only a good man, but a man. (At banquet to Justice Harlan, Washington, D. C., December 9, 1902.) *Presidential Addresses and State Papers* I, 224.

———. It must not be forgotten that a great and patriotic leader may, if the people have any capacity for self-government whatever, help them upward along their hard path by his wise leadership, his wise yielding to even what he does not like, and his wise refusal to consider his own selfish interests. A people thoroughly unfit for self-government, as were the French at the end of the eighteenth century, are the natural prey of a conscienceless tyrant like Napoleon. A people like the Americans of the same generation can be led along the path of liberty and order by a Washington. The English people, in the middle of the seventeenth century, might have been helped to entire self-government by Cromwell, but were not sufficiently advanced politically to keep him from making himself their absolute master if he proved morally unequal to rising to the Washington level; though doubtless they would not have tolerated a man of the Napoleonic type. (1900.) *Mem. Ed.* XIII, 424; *Nat. Ed.* X, 305.

———. I do not believe that it is safe or wise to pretend that we have self-government and yet by indirect methods to try to rob ourselves of self-government. I believe that the only ultimate safety for our people is in self-control; not in control from the outside. I do not believe in snap judgments, I do not believe in permitting the determination of a moment to be transmuted into a permanent policy; but I do believe that the serious, sober, well thought-out judgment of the people must be given effect; I do believe that this people must ultimately control its own destinies, and cannot surrender the right of ultimate control to a judge any more than to a legislator or executive; . . . but the control must be there, the power must exist in the people to see to it that the judge, like the legislator and executive, becomes in the long run representative of and answerable to the well-thought-out judgment of the people as a whole. *Outlook*, January 6, 1912, p. 48.

SELF-GOVERNMENT — FITNESS FOR. Fitness [for self-government] is not a God-given, natural right, but comes to a race only through the slow growth of centuries, and then only to those races which possess an immense reserve fund of strength, common sense, and morality. (1900.) *Mem. Ed.* XIII, 358; *Nat. Ed.* X, 248.

———. In one sense of the word, self-government can never be bestowed by outsiders upon any people. It must be achieved by themselves. It means in this sense primarily self-control, self-restraint, and if those qualities do not exist—that is, if the people are unable to govern themselves—then, as there must be government somewhere, it has to come from outside. (At celebration of Methodist Episcopal Church, Washington, January 18, 1909.) *Mem. Ed.* XVIII, 348; *Nat. Ed.* XVI, 264.

———. If our people are really fit for self-government, then they will insist upon governing themselves. In all matters affecting the Nation as a whole this power of self-government should reside in a majority of the Nation as a whole; and upon this doctrine no one has insisted more strongly than I have insisted, for in such case "popular rights" becomes a meaningless phrase save as it is translated into national rights. *Outlook*, June 24, 1911, p. 379.

———. Self-government cannot be thrust upon nations from without. It must be developed from within. It cannot exist unless the people have a strong and sound character. . . . Only a very advanced people, a people of sound intelligence, and above all, of robust character is fit to govern itself. No gift of popular institutions will avail if the people who receive them do not possess certain great and masterful qualities; and above all the combination of two qualities—individual self-reliance and the power of combining for the common good. . . . The resolute insistence upon their own rights must go hand in hand with the ready acknowledgment of the rights of others. Above all there must be in the people the power of self-control. There must always be government, there must always be control, somewhere. If the individual cannot control himself, if he cannot govern himself, then the lack must be supplied from outside. Exactly the same thing is true of nations. Only those people who to self-reliance and self-confidence add also self-control can permanently embark on the difficult course of moulding their own destinies. *Outlook,* November 15, 1913, p. 589-90.

──────────. The absolute prerequisite for successful self-government in any people is the power of self-restraint which refuses to follow either the wild-eyed extremists of radicalism or the dull-eyed extremists of reaction. Either set of extremists will wreck the Nation just as certainly as the other. (September 12, 1918.) *Roosevelt in the Kansas City Star,* 213.

SELF-GOVERNMENT — RESPONSIBILITIES OF. You cannot give self-government to anybody. He has got to earn it for himself. You can give him the chance to obtain self-government, but he himself out of his own heart must do the governing. He must govern himself. That is what it means. That is what self-government means. . . . There must be control. There must be mastery, somewhere, and if there is no self-control and self-mastery, the control and the mastery will ultimately be imposed from without. (At University of Wisconsin, Madison, April 15, 1911.) *Mem. Ed.* XV, 548; *Nat. Ed.* XIII, 594.

──────────. It behooves us to remember that men can never escape being governed. Either they must govern themselves or they must submit to being governed by others. If from lawlessness or fickleness, from folly or self-indulgence, they refuse to govern themselves, then most assuredly in the end they will have to be governed from the outside. They can prevent the need of government from without only by showing that they possess the power of government from within. A sovereign cannot make excuses for his failures; a sovereign must accept the responsibility for the exercise of the power that inheres in him; and where, as is true in our Republic, the people are sovereign, then the people must show a sober understanding and a sane and steadfast purpose if they are to preserve that orderly liberty upon which as a foundation every republic must rest. (At Jamestown Exposition, April 26, 1907.) *Mem. Ed.* XII, 593; *Nat. Ed.* XI, 312.

──────────. When I say that I believe not only in the right of the people to rule, but in their duty to rule themselves and to refuse to submit to being ruled by others, I am not using a figure of speech, I am speaking of a vital issue which fundamentally affects our whole American life. I not merely admit but insist that in all government, and especially in popular government, there must be control; and, furthermore, that if control does not come from within it must come from without. Therefore it is essential that any people which engages in the difficult experiment of self-government should be able to practise self-control. There are peoples in the world which have proved by their lamentable experiences that they are not capable of this self-control; but I contend that the American people most emphatically are capable of it. I hold that in the long run, taken as a whole, our people can and will govern themselves a great deal better than any small set of men can govern them. (At St. Louis, Mo., March 28, 1912.) *Mem. Ed.* XIX, 234; *Nat. Ed.* XVII, 172.

SELF-GOVERNMENT AND TYRANNY. The truth is, that a strong nation can only be saved by itself, and not by a strong man, though it can be greatly aided and guided by a strong man. A weak nation may be doomed anyhow, or it may find its sole refuge in a despot; a nation struggling out of darkness may be able to take its first steps only by the help of a master hand, as was true of Russia, under Peter the Great; and if a nation, whether free or unfree, loses the capacity for self-government, loses the spirit of sobriety and of orderly liberty, then it has no cause to complain of tyranny; but a really great people, a people really capable of freedom and of doing mighty deeds in the world, must work out its own destiny, and must find men who will be its leaders—not its masters. (1900.) *Mem. Ed.* XIII, 458; *Nat. Ed.* X, 334.

SELF-GOVERNMENT. *See also* DEMOCRACY; GOVERNMENT; POPULAR RULE; REPRESENTATIVE GOVERNMENT; WASHINGTON, GEORGE.

SELF-HELP. The only effective way to help any man is to help him to help himself; and the worst lesson to teach him is that he can be permanently helped at the expense of some one else (At Oxford University, June 7, 1910.) *Mem. Ed.* XIV, 102; *Nat. Ed.* XII, 56.

SELF-HELP. *See also* BROTHERHOOD; CHARITY; PHILANTHROPY; SELF-RELIANCE.

SELF-MASTERY. No man can do good work in the world for himself, for those whom he loves who are dependent upon him, or for the State at large, unless he has the great virtue of self-mastery, unless he can control his passions and appetites, and force head and hand to work according to the dictates of conscience. This is so obvious that to many people it will seem too obvious to need repetition. But, though obvious enough in theory, it is continually forgotten in practice; and the political leaders who address, not each man individually, but men in a mass, often forget to inculcate it even in theory. (*Outlook,* March 25, 1911.) *Mem. Ed.* XIX, 145; *Nat. Ed.* XVII, 104.

SELF-MASTERY. *See also* CHARACTER; CONSCIENCE.

SELF-PRESERVATION. The law of self-preservation is the primary law for nations as for individuals. If a nation cannot protect itself under a democratic form of government, then it will either die or evolve a new form of government. (*Metropolitan,* November 1915.) *Mem. Ed.* XX, 387; *Nat. Ed.* XVIII, 331.

SELF-PRESERVATION. *See also* NATIONAL DEFENSE; PREPAREDNESS.

SELF-RELIANCE. The worst lesson that can be taught a man is to rely upon others and to whine over his sufferings. If an American is to amount to anything he must rely upon himself, and not upon the State; he must take pride in his own work, instead of sitting idle to envy the luck of others; he must face life with resolute courage, win victory if he can, and accept defeat if he must, without seeking to place on his fellow men a responsibility which is not theirs. . . . It is both foolish and wicked to teach the average man who is not well off that some wrong or injustice has been done him, and that he should hope for redress elsewhere than in his own industry, honesty, and intelligence. (*Review of Reviews,* January 1897.) *Mem. Ed.* XVI, 382, 383; *Nat. Ed.* XIII, 165, 166.

SELF-RELIANCE. *See also* SELF-HELP.

SELF-RESPECT. There are prices too dear to pay for success or to pay for retention in office, and one of those prices is the loss of self-respect. (Before Liberal Club, Buffalo, N. Y., September 10, 1895.) *Mem. Ed.* XVI, 275; *Nat. Ed.* XIV, 196.

SELF-RESPECT. *See also* NATIONAL SELF-RESPECT.

SELOUS, FREDERICK COURTENEY. No other hunter alive has had the experience of Selous; and, so far as I now recall, no hunter of anything like his experience has ever also possessed his gift of penetrating observation joined to his power of vivid and accurate narration. He has killed scores of lion and rhinoceros and hundreds of elephant and buffalo; and these four animals are the most dangerous of the world's big game, when hunted as they are hunted in Africa. To hear him tell of what he has seen and done is no less interesting to a naturalist than to a hunter. (1910.) *Mem. Ed.* V, 7-8; *Nat. Ed.* IV, 7.

——————. For a quarter of a century he was a leading figure among the hard-bit men who pushed ever northward the frontier of civilization. His life was one of hazard, hardship, and daring adventure, and was as full of romantic interest and excitement as that of a viking of the tenth century. He hunted the lion and the elephant, the buffalo and the rhinoceros. He knew the extremes of fatigue in following the heavy game, and of thirst when lost in the desert wilderness. . . .

But, in addition, he was a highly intelligent civilized man, with phenomenal powers of observation and of narration. There is no more foolish cant than to praise the man of action on the ground that he will not or cannot tell of his feats. Of course loquacious boastfulness renders any human being an intolerable nuisance. But, except among the very foremost . . . the men of action who can tell truthfully, and with power and charm, what they have seen and done add infinitely more to the sum of worthy achievement than do the inarticulate ones, whose deeds are often of value only to themselves. (*Outlook,* March 7, 1917.) *Mem. Ed.* XII, 570-571; *Nat. Ed.* XI, 292-293.

SENATE, THE. I do not much admire the Senate, because it is such a helpless body when efficient work for good is to be done. Two or three determined Senators seem able to hold up legislation, or at least good legislation, in an astonishing way; but the worst thing the Senate did this year—the failure to confirm the Santo Domingo treaty—was due to the fact that

[559]

the Democratic party as such went solidly against us, and this fact, coupled with the absence of certain Republican Senators, rendered us helpless to put through the treaty. The result has been that I am in a very awkward and unpleasant situation in endeavoring to keep foreign powers off Santo Domingo and also in trying to settle Venezuelan affairs. (To Joseph Bucklin Bishop, March 23, 1905.) *Mem. Ed.* XXIII, 497; Bishop I, 433.

───────────. It is a very powerful body with an illustrious history, and life is easy in it, the Senators not being harassed as are members of the lower House, who go through one campaign for their seats only to begin another. The *esprit de corps* in the Senate is strong, and the traditions they inherit come from the day when, in the first place, men duelled and were more considerate of one another's feelings, even in doing business; and when, in the second place, the theories of all doctrinaire statesmen were that the one thing that was needed in government was a system of checks, and that the whole danger to government came not from inefficiency but from tyranny. In consequence, the Senate has an immense capacity for resistance. There is no closure, and if a small body of men are sufficiently resolute they can prevent the passage of any measure until they are physically wearied out by debate. The Senators get to know one another intimately and tend all to stand together if they think any one of them is treated with discourtesy by the Executive.

I do not see that the Senate is any stronger relatively to the rest of the government than it was sixty or seventy years ago. Nor do I think that the Senate and the lower House taken together are any stronger with reference to the President than they were a century ago.

Some of the things the Senate does really work to increase the power of the Executive. They are able so effectually to hold up action when they are consulted, and are so slow about it, that they force a President who has any strength to such individual action as I took in both Panama and Santo Domingo. In neither case would a President a hundred years ago have ventured to act without previous assent by the Senate. (To John St. Loe Strachey, February 12, 1906.) *Mem. Ed.* XXIV, 7-8; Bishop II, 5-6.

SENATE, THE. See also CONGRESS; TREATIES.

SENATORIAL COURTESY. See APPOINTMENTS.

SENATORS—ELECTION OF. I think the people are just as competent to elect United States Senators directly as they are to elect Governors or representatives in Congress or State Legislatures. *Outlook,* March 30, 1912, p. 720.

───────────. If we choose senators by popular vote instead of through the legislatures, we shall not thereby have secured good representatives; we shall merely have given the people a better chance to get good representatives. If they choose bad men, unworthy men, whether their unworthiness take the form of corruption or demagogy, of truckling to special interests or of truckling to the mob, we shall have worked no improvement. There have been in the past plenty of unworthy governors and congressmen elected, just as there have been plenty of bad senators elected. (*Outlook,* January 21, 1911.) *Mem. Ed.* XIX, 98; *Nat. Ed.* XVII, 63.

───────────. I believe in the election of United States senators by direct vote. Just as actual experience convinced our people that Presidents should be elected (as they now are in practice, although not in theory) by direct vote of the people instead of by indirect vote through an untrammelled electoral college, so actual experience has convinced us that senators should be elected by direct vote of the people instead of indirectly through the various legislatures. (Before Ohio Constitutional Convention, Columbus, February 21, 1912.) *Mem. Ed.* XIX, 180; *Nat. Ed.* XVII, 133.

SEPARATISM. See INDEPENDENCE SPIRIT; SLAVERY; WEST.

SEQUOIAS. See TREES.

SERVICE. Those who have earned joy, but are rewarded only with sorrow, must learn the stern comfort dear to great souls, the comfort that springs from the knowledge taught in times of iron that the law of worthy living is not fulfilled by pleasure, but by service, and by sacrifice when only thereby can service be rendered. (*Metropolitan,* October 1918.) *Mem. Ed.* XXI, 264; *Nat. Ed.* XIX, 244.

SERVICE AND REWARD. It is simply common sense to recognize that there is the widest inequality of service, and that therefore there must be an equally wide inequality of reward, if our society is to rest upon the basis of justice and wisdom. Service is the true test by which a man's worth should be judged.

We are against privilege in any form: privilege to the capitalist who exploits the poor man, and privilege to the shiftless or vicious poor man who would rob his thrifty brother of what he has earned. Certain exceedingly valuable forms of service are rendered wholly without capital. On the other hand, there are exceedingly valuable forms of service which can be rendered only by means of great accumulations of capital, and not to recognize this fact would be to deprive our whole people of one of the great agencies for their betterment. The test of a man's worth to the community is the service he renders to it, and we cannot afford to make this test by material considerations alone. (*Outlook*, March 20, 1909.) *Mem. Ed.* XVIII, 562; *Nat. Ed.* XIX, 105.

SERVICE. *See also* DUTY; JOY OF LIVING; WORK.

SERVICE TEST. *See* EXPERIMENT.

SERVILITY. One form of servility consists in a slavish attitude—of the kind incompatible with self-respecting manliness—toward any person who is powerful by reason of his office or position. Servility may be shown by a public servant toward the profiteering head of a large corporation, or toward the anti-American head of a big labor organization. (1918.) *Mem. Ed.* XXI, 316; *Nat. Ed.* XIX, 289.

SEVIER, JOHN. For many years Sevier was the best Indian fighter on the border. He was far more successful than Clark, for instance, inflicting greater loss on his foes and suffering much less himself, though he never had anything like Clark's number of soldiers. His mere name was a word of dread to the Cherokees, the Chickamaugas, and the upper Creeks. His success was due to several causes. He wielded great influence over his own followers, whose love for and trust in "Chucky Jack" were absolutely unbounded; for he possessed in the highest degree the virtues most prized on the frontier. He was open-hearted and hospitable, with winning ways toward all, and combined a cool head with a dauntless heart; he loved a battle for its own sake, and was never so much at his ease as when under fire. (1889.) *Mem. Ed.* XI, 144; *Nat. Ed.* VIII, 510.

SEWALL, W. W. *See* WEST.

SEX INSTINCT. The atrophy of the healthy sexual instinct is in its effects equally destructive whether it be due to licentiousness, asceticism, coldness, or timidity; whether it be due to calculated self-indulgence, love of ease and comfort, or absorption in worldly success on the part of the man, or, on the part of the woman, to that kind of shrieking "feminism," the antithesis of all worth calling womanly, which gives fine names to shirking of duty, and to the fear of danger and discomfort, and actually exalts as praiseworthy the abandonment or subordination by women of the most sacred and vitally important of the functions of womanhood. It is not enough that a race shall be composed of good fighters, good workers, and good breeders; but, unless the qualities thus indicated are present in the race foundation, then the superstructure, however seemingly imposing, will topple. (1916.) *Mem. Ed.* IV, 233; *Nat. Ed.* III, 382.

SEX INSTINCT. *See also* BIRTH CONTROL; MARRIAGE.

SHAFTER, GENERAL W. R. *See* SPANISH-AMERICAN WAR.

SHEEP. No man can associate with sheep and retain his self-respect. Intellectually, a sheep is about on the lowest level of the brute creation; why the early Christians admired it, whether young or old, is to a good cattleman always a profound mystery. (1885.) *Mem. Ed.* I, 112; *Nat. Ed.* I, 93.

SHEEP—DOMESTICATION OF. No animal seems to have been more changed by domestication than the sheep. The timid, helpless, fleecy idiot of the folds, the most foolish of all tame animals, has hardly a trait in common with his self-reliant wild relative who combines the horns of a sheep with the hide of a deer, whose home is in the rocks and the mountains, and who is so abundantly able to take care of himself. Wild sheep are as good mountaineers as wild goats or as mountain-antelopes, and are to the full as wary and intelligent. (1888.) *Mem. Ed.* IV, 549-550; *Nat. Ed.* I, 430.

SHEEP, BIGHORN — HUNTING THE. The big-horn ranks highest among all the species of game that are killed by still-hunting, and its chase constitutes the noblest form of sport with the rifle, always excepting, of course, those kinds of hunting where the quarry is itself dangerous to attack. (1885.) *Mem. Ed.* I, 207; *Nat. Ed.* I, 173.

——————. Still-hunting the big-horn is always a toilsome and laborious task, and the very bitter weather during which we had been out had not lessened the difficulty of the work, though in the cold it was much less exhausting than it would have been to have hunted across the same ground in summer. No other kind of hunting does as much to bring out the good qualities, both moral and physical, of the sportsmen who follow it. If a man keeps at it, it is bound to make him both hardy and resolute; to strengthen his muscles and fill out his lungs. (1885.) *Mem. Ed.* I, 220; *Nat. Ed.* I, 183.

SHERIDAN, PHILIP H. His name will always stand high on the list of American worthies. Not only was he a great general, but he showed his greatness with that touch of originality which we call genius. Indeed this quality of brilliance has been in one sense a disadvantage to his reputation, for it has tended to overshadow his solid ability. We tend to think of him only as the dashing cavalry leader, whereas he was in reality not only that, but also a great commander. Of course, the fact in his career most readily recognized was his mastery in the necessarily modern art of handling masses of modern cavalry so as to give them the fullest possible effect, not only in the ordinary operations of cavalry which precede and follow a battle, but in the battle itself. But in addition he showed in the Civil War that he was a first-class army commander, both as a subordinate of Grant and when in independent command. . . . After the close of the great war, in a field where there was scant glory to be won by the general-in-chief, he rendered a signal service which has gone almost unnoticed; for in the tedious weary Indian wars on the great plains it was he who developed in thoroughgoing fashion the system of campaigning in winter, which, at the cost of bitter hardship and peril, finally broke down the banded strength of those formidable warriors, the horse Indians. (At unveiling of monument to Gen. Sheridan, Washington, D. C., November 25, 1908.) *Mem. Ed.* XII, 476-477; *Nat. Ed.* XI, 220-221.

SHERMAN ANTI-TRUST ACT — AMENDMENT OF. The antitrust law should not be repealed; but it should be made both more efficient and more in harmony with actual conditions. It should be so amended as to forbid only the kind of combination which does harm to the general public, such amendment to be accompanied by, or to be an incident of, a grant of supervisory power to the Government over these big concerns engaged in interstate commerce business. This should be accompanied by provision for the compulsory publication of accounts and the subjection of books and papers to the inspection of Government officials. (Seventh Annual Message, Washington, December 3, 1907.) *Mem. Ed.* XVII, 493; *Nat. Ed.* XV. 420.

——————. The attempt in this law to provide in sweeping terms against all combinations of whatever character, if technically in restraint of trade as such restraint has been defined by the courts, must necessarily be either futile or mischievous, and sometimes both. The present law makes some combinations illegal, although they may be useful to the country. On the other hand, as to some huge combinations which are both noxious and illegal, even if the action undertaken against them under the law by the Government is successful, the result may be to work but a minimum benefit to the public. Even though the combination be broken up and a small measure of reform thereby produced, the real good aimed at can not be obtained, for such real good can come only by a thorough and continuing supervision over the acts of the combination in all its parts, so as to prevent stock watering, improper forms of competition, and, in short, wrong-doing generally. The law should correct that portion of the Sherman act which prohibits all combinations of the character above described, whether they be reasonable or unreasonable; but this should be done only as part of a general scheme to provide for this effective and thorough-going supervision by the National Government of all the operations of the big interstate business concerns. (Message to Congress, January 31, 1908.) *Presidential Addresses and State Papers* VII, 1607-1608.

——————. I am advocating . . . amendments to the antitrust and interstate commerce laws in order to make legal proper combinations. But the very corporations that have been loudly insisting that those laws are bad, take not the slightest interest in their amendment. They do not want them changed and they do not care to have them removed from the statute-books, but they expect to have them administered crookedly. Of course, as far as I am concerned such expectation is vain. (To Colonel Henry L. Higginson, February 19, 1908.) *Mem. Ed.* XXIV, 96; Bishop II, 83.

——————. Merely to repeal the Sherman Law without putting anything in its place would do harm. It should at once be amended or superseded by a law which would in some shape permit and require the issuing of licenses by the Federal Government to corporations doing an interstate or international business. Corporations which did not take out such licenses or comply with the rules of the Government's administrative board would be subject to the Sherman Law. The others would be under government control and would be encouraged to coöperate and in every way to become prosperous and efficient, the Government guaranteeing by its supervision that the corporations' prosperity and efficiency were in the public interest. (January 8, 1918.) *Roosevelt in the Kansas City Star*, 86-87.

SHERMAN ANTI-TRUST ACT—ENFORCEMENT OF. When I came into office that law was dead; I took it up and for the first time had it enforced. We gained this much by the enforcement: we gained the establishment of the principle that the government was supreme over the great corporations; but that is almost the end of the good that came through our lawsuits. *Outlook*, September 21, 1912, p. 105.

──────────. When I took office the antitrust law was practically a dead letter and the interstate commerce law in as poor a condition. I had to revive both laws. I did. I enforced both. It will be easy enough to do now what I did then, but the reason that it is easy now is because I did it when it was hard.

Nobody was doing anything. I found speedily that the interstate commerce law by being made more perfect could be made a most useful instrument for helping solve some of our industrial problems. So with the antitrust law. I speedily found that almost the only positive good achieved by such a successful lawsuit as the Northern Securities suit, for instance, was in establishing the principle that the government was supreme over the big corporation, but that by itself that law did not accomplish any of the things that we ought to have accomplished; and so I began to fight for the amendment of the law along the lines of the interstate commerce law. (At Milwaukee, Wis., October 14, 1912.) *Mem. Ed.* XIX, 448; *Nat. Ed.* XVII, 326.

SHERMAN ANTI-TRUST ACT—INEFFECTIVENESS OF. As construed by the Supreme Court, the Anti-Trust Law accomplishes a certain amount of good, and it has been a good thing to obtain the decision that has been obtained against the Standard Oil Company. But as a means of effectually grappling on behalf of the whole people with the problem created by what are commonly called trusts—that is, of enormous combinations of corporate capital engaged in inter-State business—the Anti-Trust Law is radically and vitally defective, and any effort to strengthen it would be worse than futile, and would result only in prolonging the time during which the corporations will escape control of the kind demanded in the interests of the people. *Outlook*, June 3, 1911, p. 239.

──────────. Again and again while I was President, from 1902 to 1908, I pointed out that under the antitrust law alone it was neither possible to put a stop to business abuses nor possible to secure the highest efficiency in the service rendered by business to the general public. The antitrust law must be kept on our statute-books, and, as hereafter shown, must be rendered more effective in the cases where it is applied. But to treat the antitrust law as an adequate, or as by itself a wise, measure of relief and betterment is a sign not of progress, but of Toryism and reaction. It has been of benefit so far as it has implied the recognition of a real and great evil, and the at least sporadic application of the principle that all men alike must obey the law. But as a sole remedy, universally applicable, it has in actual practice completely broken down; as now applied it works more mischief than benefit. It represents the waste of effort—always damaging to a community—which arises from the attempt to meet new conditions by the application of out-worn remedies instead of fearlessly and in common-sense fashion facing the new conditions and devising the new remedies which alone can work effectively for good. (Before Progressive National Convention, Chicago, August 6, 1912.) *Mem. Ed.* XIX, 381; *Nat. Ed.* XVII, 274.

──────────. It is utterly hopeless to attempt to control the trusts merely by the antitrust law, or by any law the same in principle, no matter what the modifications may be in detail. In the first place, these great corporations cannot possibly be controlled merely by a succession of lawsuits. The administrative branch of the government must exercise such control. The preposterous failure of the Commerce Court has shown that only damage comes from the effort to substitute judicial for administrative control of great corporations. In the next place, a loosely drawn law which promises to do everything would reduce business to complete ruin if it were not also so drawn as to accomplish almost nothing. (Before Progressive National Convention, Chicago, August 6,

1912.) *Mem. Ed.* XIX, 386; *Nat. Ed.* XVII, 278.

———————. The Sherman Law, or so-called Anti-Trust Law, is just as mischievous in peace as in war. It represents an effort to meet a great evil in the wrong way. As long as corporations claimed complete immunity from government control, the first necessity was to establish the right of the Government to control them. This right and power of the Government was established by the Northern Securities suit, which prevented all the railroads of the country from being united under one corporation which defied government control. The suits against the Standard Oil and Tobacco trusts followed. The Supreme Court decreed that the trusts had been guilty of grave misconduct and should be dissolved, but not a particle of good followed their dissolution. It is evident that the Sherman Law, or so-called Anti-Trust Law, in no way meets the evils of the industrial world. To try to break up corporations because they are big and efficient is either ineffective or mischievous. What is needed is to exercise government control over them, so as to encourage their efficiency and prosperity, but to insure that the efficiency is used in the public interest and that the prosperity is properly passed around. (January 8, 1918.) *Roosevelt in the Kansas City Star*, 86.

SHERMAN ANTI-TRUST ACT—PROSECUTIONS UNDER. There is a grim irony in the effect that has been produced upon Wall Street by the complete breakdown of the prosecutions against various trusts, notably the Standard Oil and Tobacco Trusts, under the Sherman law. I have always insisted that while the Sherman law should be kept upon the books so as to be used wherever possible against monopolies, yet that it is by itself wholly unable to afford the relief demanded by the American people as against all the great corporations actually or potentially guilty of antisocial practices.

Wall Street was at first flurried by the decisions in the Oil and Tobacco Trust cases. But as regards the Sherman antitrust law Wall Street has now caught up with the Administration. The President has expressed his entire satisfaction with the antitrust law, and now that the result of the prosecutions under it has been to strengthen the Standard Oil and Tobacco Trusts, to increase the value of their stocks, and, at least in the case of the Standard Oil, to increase the price to the consumer, Wall Street is also showing, in practical fashion, its satisfaction with the workings of the law, by its antagonism to us who intend to establish a real control of big business, which shall not harm legitimate business, but which shall really, and not nominally, put a stop to the evil practices of evil combinations. (At Louisville, Ky., April 3, 1912.) *Mem. Ed.* XIX, 250; *Nat. Ed.* XVII, 185.

SHERMAN ANTI-TRUST ACT. *See also* BUSINESS; COMBINATIONS; CORPORATIONS; GOVERNMENT CONTROL; INDUSTRIAL COMMISSION; KNIGHT CASE; MONOPOLIES; NORTHERN SECURITIES CASE; STANDARD OIL COMPANY; TRUSTS.

SHIPPING. *See* MERCHANT MARINE.

SHORT BALLOT. *See* BALLOT.

SHOT-GUN. *See* RIFLE.

SICKNESS INSURANCE. *See* SOCIAL INSURANCE.

SILVER—FREE COINAGE OF. There is a certain difficulty in arguing the issue of this campaign, the question of free silver. It is always difficult to make elaborate argument about the eighth commandment. When a man quotes, "Thou shalt not steal," and another promptly replies by asking "Why not?" really the best answer is to repeat the commandment again. If a man cannot at first glance see that it is as immoral and vicious to repudiate debts as it is to steal, why, it becomes quite a hopeless task to try to convince him by the most elaborate arguments. (Before Commercial Travellers' Sound-Money League, New York City, September 11, 1896.) *Mem. Ed.* XVI, 384; *Nat. Ed.* XIV, 251.

———————. The policy of the free coinage of silver at a ratio of sixteen to one is a policy fraught with destruction to every home in the land. It means untold misery to the head of every household, and, above all, to the women and children of every home. When our opponents champion free silver at sixteen to one they are either insincere or sincere in their attitude. If insincere in their championship, they, of course, forfeit all right to belief or support on any ground. If sincere, then they are a menace to the welfare of the country. Whether they shout their sinister purpose or merely whisper it makes but little difference, save as it reflects their own honesty. (Letter accepting nomination for Vice-Presidency, September 15, 1900.) *Mem. Ed.* XVI, 548; *Nat. Ed.* XIV, 362.

[564]

SILVER AND BIMETALLISM. Some of the anti-free-silver men, the extreme gold men, are as unreasonable in their fanaticism as any representatives of the Rocky Mountain mine-owners. These men violently oppose any scheme looking toward international bimetallism, and, indeed, at times seem to object to it almost as much as to free silver. Such conduct is mere foolishness. The financial question is far too complicated to permit any persons to refuse to discuss any method which offers a reasonable hope of bettering the situation.

The question of the free coinage of silver is not complicated at all. Very many honest men honestly advocate free coinage; nevertheless, in its essence, the measure is one of partial repudiation, and is to be opposed because it would shake the country's credit, and would damage that reputation for honest dealing which should be as dear to a nation as to a private individual. But the question of bimetallism stands on an entirely different footing. Very many men of high repute as statesmen and as students of finance, both at home and abroad, believe that great good would come from an international agreement which would permit the use of both metals in the currency of the world. No one is prepared to say that such an agreement would do harm. There is grave doubt as to whether the agreement can be reached; but the end is of such importance as to justify an effort to attain it. The people who oppose the move are, as a rule, men whom the insane folly of the ultra-free-silver men has worked into a panic of folly only less acute. (*Century*, November 1895.) *Mem. Ed.* XVI, 343-344; *Nat. Ed.* XIV, 244-245.

SILVER ISSUE, THE. Many entirely honest and intelligent men have been misled by the silver talk, and have for the moment joined the ranks of the ignorant, the vicious and wrong-headed. These men of character and capacity are blinded by their own misfortunes, or their own needs, or else they have never fairly looked into the matter for themselves, being, like most men, whether in "gold" or "silver" communities, content to follow the opinion of those they are accustomed to trust. After full and fair inquiry these men, I am sure, whether they live in Maine, in Tennessee, or in Oregon, will come out on the side of honest money. The shiftless and vicious and the honest but hopelessly ignorant and puzzle-headed voters cannot be reached; but the average farmer, the average business man, the average workman—in short, the average American—will always stand up for honesty and decency when he can once satisfy himself as to the side on which they are to be found. (*Review of Reviews*, September 1896.) *Mem. Ed.* XVI, 371; *Nat. Ed.* XIII, 156.

————. The demand for free silver is largely not an expression of opinion, but is rather a demand for something which it is believed will punish the people who have the most thrift and the most intelligence. Yet history teaches us nothing more plainly than that if the hard-working and the thrifty be punished the ultimate loss falls most heavily on the poorer classes. Cheap money is in the end the dearest money for the working man. (Before Commercial Travellers' Sound-Money League, New York City, September 11, 1896.) *Mem. Ed.* XVI, 391; *Nat. Ed.* XIV, 257.

————. With the majority of the men who want cheap money the silver dollar is desired, not because of any abstruse theories about the benefits of bimetallism, but because it is the first step toward that money. . . . These men champion a silver dollar because it is cheaper than the gold dollar, just as they would champion a copper dollar rather than one of silver if copper would be made an issue at the moment. What they really want is irredeemable paper money. In other words these curious beings, who sometimes possess good hearts and sometimes not, but who always possess foggy brains, think that the money is of value precisely in the ratio of its being valueless. Gold and its equivalents possessing the greatest value, and forming, therefore, the currency of all the prosperous civilized communities, seem to them undesirable. They want money that is cheap; that is not so valuable. They like a silver dollar, as compared to a gold dollar, because it is worth only half as much; but they like a paper dollar even more because it is not worth anything. They seem to have a curious inverted idea that the minute we can get money that is not worth anything it will turn out to be able to purchase everything. (Before American Republican College League, Chicago, October 15, 1896.) *Mem. Ed.* XVI, 299-400; *Nat. Ed.* XIV, 263.

SILVER. *See also* CLEVELAND, GROVER; CURRENCY; ELECTION OF 1896; GOLD STANDARD; POPULISM.

SIMMS, WILLIAM GILMORE. Simms was much the most considerable of the Southern school of writers in the years before the war —for Poe belongs to no school and no section —and he was the most prolific novelist, essayist, and (Heaven save the mark!) poet this country has ever produced. Yet he is now completely forgotten. It is probable that most people, even among those who are fairly well read, do not so much as know the name of an author some of whose books, at least, are well worth a permanent place on our book-shelves.

Unfortunately, his faults were many and grave. His natural talents were great, but his education was very defective, and he lived in a society totally devoid of a creative literary atmosphere. He had no idea of such qualities as thoroughness, finish, and self-restraint. His style is hurried and slipshod; many of his passages are wooden or bombastic; and his petulant impatience of criticism forbade his gaining any profit by experience. At one time he was foolish enough to make ventures in the field of European romance, only to meet deserved and dismal failure. (*Atlantic Monthly,* June 1892.) *Mem. Ed.* XIV, 334, 335 & 337; *Nat. Ed.* XII, 287-289.

SIMPLIFIED SPELLING. See SPELLING REFORM.

"SISSY." See "MOLLYCODDLE."

SKYLARK. See OUSEL.

SLACKERS. See CONSCIENTIOUS OBJECTORS; DRAFT; MILITARY SERVICE; PACIFISTS; PROFITEERS.

SLANDER—PUNISHMENT OF. I hope in the end to see legislation which will punish the circulation of untruth, and above all of slanderous untruth, in a newspaper or magazine meant to be read by the public; which will punish such action as severely as we punish the introduction into commerce of adulterated food falsely described and meant to be eaten by the public.

At present men sufficiently wealthy to pay for slander and libel, and the other men wishing to earn a base livelihood by pandering to the taste of those who like to read slander and libel, can undoubtedly do an enormous quantity of damage to the upright public servant. But keep in mind that I am not concerned with him; I am speaking from the standpoint of the public. The enormous damage, the incredible damage, is done to the public, by completely misinforming them as to the character of the decent public servant, and also misinforming them as to the character of that man in public life who is an unworthy public servant. (At Pacific Theological Seminary, Spring 1911.) *Mem. Ed.* XV, 639; *Nat. Ed.* XIII, 670.

SLAVERY. Black slavery was such a grossly anachronistic and un-American form of evil, that it is difficult to discuss calmly the efforts to abolish it, and to remember that many of these efforts were calculated to do, and actually did, more harm than good. We are also very apt to forget that it was perfectly possible and reasonable for enlightened and virtuous men, who fully recognized it as an evil, yet to prefer its continuance to having it interfered with in a way that would produce even worse results. Black slavery in Hayti was characterized by worse abuse than ever was the case in the United States; yet, looking at the condition of that republic now, it may well be questioned whether it would not have been greatly to her benefit in the end to have had slavery continue a century or so longer—its ultimate extinction being certain—rather than to have had her attain freedom as she actually did, with the results that have flowed from her action. (1887.) *Mem. Ed.* VIII, 117; *Nat. Ed.* VII, 102.

——————. Slavery must of necessity exercise the most baleful influence upon any slave-holding people, and especially upon those members of the dominant caste who do not themselves own slaves. Moreover, the negro, unlike so many of the inferior races, does not dwindle away in the presence of the white man. He holds his own; indeed, under the conditions of American slavery he increased faster than the white, threatening to supplant him. He actually has supplanted him in certain of the West Indian Islands, where the sin of the white in enslaving the black has been visited upon the head of the wrong-doer by his victim with a dramatically terrible completeness of revenge. (1894.) *Mem. Ed.* XI, 260; *Nat. Ed.* IX, 44.

SLAVERY AND EXPANSION. The greed for the conquest of new lands which characterized the Western people had nothing whatever to do with the fact that some of them owned slaves. Long before there had been so much as the faintest foreshadowing of the importance which the slavery question was to assume, the West had been eagerly pressing on to territorial conquest, and had been chafing and fretting at the restraint put upon it, and at the limits set to its strivings by the treaties established with foreign powers. (1887.) *Mem. Ed.* VIII, 129; *Nat. Ed.* VII, 112.

SLAVERY AND FREEDOM. The attitude of slaveholders toward freedom in the abstract was grotesque in its lack of logic; but the attitude of many other classes of men, both abroad and at home, toward it was equally full of a grimly unconscious humor. The Southern planters, who loudly sympathized with Kossuth and the Hungarians, were entirely unconscious that their tyranny over their own black bondsmen made their attacks upon Austria's despotism absurd; and Germans, who were shocked at our holding the blacks in slavery, could not think of freedom in their own country without a shudder. On one night the Democrats of the Northern States would hold a mass-meeting to further the cause of Irish freedom, on the next night the same men would break up another meeting held to help along the freeing of the negroes; while the English aristocracy held up its hands in horror at American slavery and set its face like a flint against all efforts to do Ireland tardy and incomplete justice. (1887.) *Mem. Ed.* VIII, 204; *Nat. Ed.* VII, 176.

SLAVERY AND SEPARATISM. There had always been a strong separatist feeling in the South; but hitherto its manifestations had been local and sporadic, never affecting all the States at the same time; for it had never happened that the cause which called forth any particular manifestation was one bearing on the whole South alike. . . . But slavery was an interest common to the whole South. When it was felt to be in any way menaced, all Southerners came together for its protection; and, from the time of the rise of the Abolitionists onward, the separatist movement through the South began to identify itself with the maintenance of slavery, and gradually to develop greater and greater strength. Its growth was furthered and hastened by the actions of the more ambitious and unscrupulous of the Southern politicians, who saw that it offered a chance for them to push themselves forward, and who were perfectly willing to wreak almost irreparable harm to the nation if by so doing they could advance their own selfish interests. (1887.) *Mem. Ed.* VIII, 120-121; *Nat. Ed.* VII, 105.

SLAVERY IN THE WEST INDIES. No race ever so sacrificed the permanent welfare of the race to the profit of the individuals of two or three generations, no race ever for temporary ease and gain invited such nemesis of race destruction as the Northern white race—English, French, Dutch, and Danish—did by the introduction of black slavery in the West Indies. Whites can live and thrive in these lands; not only are the upper-class whites of creole origin in the islands a handsome, vigorous, and fertile people, but the same thing is true of the few spots where white yeoman farmers or fishermen have permanently established themselves, as is notably true of Saba, but also in small isolated localities which I came across elsewhere. The white did not die out because he could not live and work. He died out because for his ease and profit he wickedly introduced negro slaves whose descendants elbowed his descendants from the land—the process going on at practically the same rate of speed before and after slavery was abolished. (1917.) *Mem. Ed.* IV, 310; *Nat. Ed.* III, 446.

SLAVERY. See also ABOLITIONISTS; BENTON, T. H.; BROWN, JOHN; CIVIL WAR; HAITI; NEGRO; SOUTH.

SLUMS. See HOUSING; RIIS, JACOB A.

SOCIAL ABASEMENT. See LABOR; SERVICE; WORK.

SOCIAL AND INDUSTRIAL JUSTICE. Friends, our task as Americans is to strive for social and industrial justice, achieved through the genuine rule of the people. This is our end, our purpose. The methods for achieving the end are merely expedients, to be finally accepted or rejected, according as actual experience shows that they work well or ill. But in our hearts we must have this lofty purpose, and we must strive for it in all earnestness and sincerity, or our work will come to nothing. (At Carnegie Hall, New York, March 20, 1912.) *Mem. Ed.* XIX, 222; *Nat. Ed.* XVII, 170.

———. The leaders in the fight for industrial and social justice to-day should be the men to whom much has been given and from whom we have a right to expect in return much of honesty and of courage, much of disinterested and valorous effort for the common good. The multimillionaire who opposes us is the worst foe of his own children and children's children, and, little though he knows it, we are their benefactors when we strive to make this country one in which justice shall prevail; for it is they themselves who would in the end suffer most if in this country we permitted the average man gradually to grow to feel that fair play was denied him, that justice was denied to the many and privilege accorded to the few. (At Chicago, June 17, 1912.) *Mem. Ed.* XIX, 311; *Nat. Ed.* XVII, 225.

———————. Before I began to go with the cow-punchers, I had already, as the result of experience in the legislature at Albany, begun rather timidly to strive for social and industrial justice. But at that time my attitude was that of giving justice from above. It was the experience on the range that first taught me to try to get justice for all of us by working on the same level with the rest of my fellow citizens.

It was the conviction that there was much social and industrial injustice and the effort to secure social and industrial justice that first led me to taking so keen an interest in popular rule. (*Outlook,* October 12, 1912.) *Mem. Ed.* XIX, 435; *Nat. Ed.* XVII, 315.

———————. Life means change; where there is no change, death comes. We who fight [for] sanctity for the rights of the people, for industrial justice, and social reforms are also fighting for material well-being; for justice is the handmaiden of prosperity; and without justice there can be no lasting prosperity. We pledge ourselves not only to strive for prosperity but to bring it about; for it can only come on a basis of fair treatment for all; and on such a basis it shall come, if the people intrust power to us. (At Chicago, June 17, 1912.) *Mem. Ed.* XIX, 307; *Nat. Ed.* XVII, 222.

———————. We must strive to do away with the social and economic injustice that have come from failing to meet by proper legislation the changed conditions brought about by the gigantic growth of our gigantic industrialism. We of this State must make it our business to help in efficient fashion the country districts, to shape matters so as to encourage the growth of the farming communities, and to help give the people in these communities the advantages which have come in disproportionate measure to the city rather than to the country during the industrial growth of the last fifty years. We must guard the interests of the wage-worker, the man who works with his hands; we must safeguard the woman who toils, and see that the young child does not toil. We must see that, by far-reaching legislation, the workman who is crippled, and the family of the workman who is killed in industry, are compensated, so that the loss necessarily incident to certain industries shall be equitably and fairly distributed instead of being placed upon the shoulders of those least able to bear them. We must make it a matter of obligation by the State to see that the conditions under which working men and women do their work shall be safe and healthful. So far as by legislation it is possible, we must strive to give to the working man the power to achieve and maintain a high standard of living. Finally, and as a matter of course, we must do everything possible to promote and conserve the business prosperity of the whole country. (Before New York Republican State Convention, Saratoga, September 27, 1910.) *Mem. Ed.* XIX, 35; *Nat. Ed.* XVII, 27.

———————. The next fact to remember is that it is of no use talking about reform and social justice and equality of industrial opportunity inside of a nation, unless that nation can protect itself from outside attack. It is not worth while bothering about any social or industrial problem in the United States unless the United States is willing to train itself, to fit itself, so that it can be sure that its own people will have the say-so in the settlement of these problems, and not some nation of alien invaders and oppressors. (*Metropolitan,* February 1916.) *Mem. Ed.* XX, 279; *Nat. Ed.* XVIII, 240.

SOCIAL AND INDUSTRIAL JUSTICE. *See also* CAPITAL; COURTS; INDUSTRIAL JUSTICE; LABOR; PROGRESSIVE MOVEMENT; SQUARE DEAL.

SOCIAL CONDITIONS. I don't at all like the social conditions at present. The dull, purblind folly of very rich men, their greed and arrogance, and the way in which they have unduly prospered by the help of the ablest lawyers, and, too often, through the weakness and short-sightedness of the judges, or by their unfortunate possession of meticulous minds; these facts, and the corruption in business and politics, have tended to produce a very unhealthy condition of excitement and irritation in the popular mind, which shows itself in part in the enormous increase in the Socialistic propaganda. (To William H. Taft, March 15, 1906.) *Mem. Ed.* XXIV, 117; Bishop II, 100.

SOCIAL CONVENTIONS. I have not the slightest objections to conventions, no matter how pointless, when they do not interfere with one's comfort; but I do strongly object to them, when for no earthly reason, they do so interfere. As regards the table, I have had two life-long convictions. First, that when I wanted to eat a soft boiled egg, I wanted to eat it out of a cup, and not to peck at it inside its shell as if I was a magpie robbing a nest. Second, and vastly more important, that when I was eating a fish, especially if it was a smelt, or something of the kind, when there was no earthly reason why I should be forbidden a knife, and forced to make ineffective jabs at the fish with my fork, while it scattered free around the place. (To Anna Roosevelt Cowles, December 27, 1899.) Cowles *Letters*, 227.

SOCIAL INSURANCE. It is abnormal for any industry to throw back upon the community the human wreckage due to its wear and tear, and the hazards of sickness, accident, invalidism, involuntary unemployment, and old age should be provided for through insurance. This should be made a charge in whole or in part upon the industries, the employer, the employee, and perhaps the people at large to contribute severally in some degree. Wherever such standards are not met by given establishments, by given industries, are unprovided for by a legislature, or are balked by unenlightened courts, the workers are in jeopardy, the progressive employer is penalized, and the community pays a heavy cost in lessened efficiency and in misery. What Germany has done in the way of old-age pensions or insurance should be studied by us, and the system adapted to our uses, with whatever modifications are rendered necessary by our different ways of life and habits of thought. (Before Progressive National Convention, Chicago, August 6, 1912.) *Mem. Ed.* XIX, 376; *Nat. Ed.* XVII, 269.

SOCIAL INSURANCE. See also WORKMEN'S COMPENSATION.

SOCIAL LEGISLATION. Much the same kind of argument that is now advanced against the effort to regulate big corporations has been again and again advanced against the effort to secure proper employers' liability laws or proper factory laws with reference to women and children; much the same kind of argument was advanced but five years ago against the franchise-tax law enacted in this State while I was Governor.

Of course there is always the danger of abuse if legislation of this type is approached in a hysterical or sentimental spirit, or, above all, if it is approached in a spirit of envy and hatred toward men of wealth.

We must not try to go too fast, under penalty of finding that we may be going in the wrong direction; and, in any event, we ought always to proceed by evolution and not by revolution. The laws must be conceived and executed in a spirit of sanity and justice, and with exactly as much regard for the rights of the big man as for the rights of the little man —treating big man and little man exactly alike. (At Chautauqua, N. Y., August 11, 1905.) *Presidential Addresses and State Papers* IV, 455.

SOCIAL LEGISLATION. *See also* CHILD LABOR; DENMARK; LA FOLLETTE, R. M.; LABOR; PURE FOOD; SOCIAL AND INDUSTRIAL JUSTICE; WORKMEN'S COMPENSATION.

SOCIAL REVOLUTION—RESULTS OF. In the hideous welter of a social revolution it is the brutal, the reckless, and the criminal who prosper, not the hard-working, sober, and thrifty. Life is often hard enough at best; it is sometimes quite as hard for the rich as for the poor, and too often the good man, the honest and patriotic citizen, suffers many blows from fate, and sees some rascals and some idlers prosper undeservedly; but the surest way to increase his misery tenfold is for him to play into the hands of the scoundrelly demagogues, to abandon that stern morality without which no man and no nation can ever permanently succeed, and to seek a temporary relief for his own real or imaginary sufferings by plunging others into misery. (Before American Republican College League, Chicago, October 15, 1896.) *Mem. Ed.* XVI, 404; *Nat. Ed.* XIV, 267.

SOCIAL REVOLUTION. *See also* REVOLUTIONS.

SOCIAL WORK. Anyone who has a serious appreciation of the immensely complex problems of our present-day life, and of those kinds of benevolent effort which for lack of a better term we group under the name of philanthropy, must realize the infinite diversity there is in the field of social work. Each man can, of course, do best if he takes up that branch of work to which his tastes and his interests lead him, and the field is of such large size that there is more than ample room for every variety of workman. Of course there are certain attributes which must be possessed in common by all who want to do well. The worker must possess not only resolution, firmness of purpose, broad charity, and great-hearted sympathy, but he must also possess common-sense sanity, and a wholesome aversion alike to the merely sentimental and the merely spectacular. (*McClure's*, March 1901.) *Mem. Ed.* XV, 198; *Nat. Ed.* XIII, 261.

SOCIAL WORK. *See also* CHARITY; PHILANTHROPY; REFORM; RIIS, JACOB A.

SOCIALISM. Socialism . . . is blind to everything except the merely material side of life. It is not only indifferent, but at bottom hostile, to the intellectual, the religious, the domestic and moral life; it is a form of communism with no moral foundation, but essentially based on the immediate annihilation of personal ownership of capital, and, in the near future, the annihilation of the family, and ultimately the annihilation of civilization. (*Outlook,* March 20, 1909.) *Mem. Ed.* XVIII, 563; *Nat. Ed.* XIX, 106.

———. The Socialists are trying to construct a party based on class consciousness, and for one class only. Socialism may mean almost anything. A Socialist may be a man who in practice is a violent anarchist, and the greatest possible menace to this country, or he may merely be a radical reformer with whom most of the men who think as I do can work heartily as regards the major part of his programme. But we thoroughly repudiate his doctrine of class consciousness. The Progressives preach social consciousness as an antidote to class conciousness. We point out to the reactionaries who so bitterly opposed us that such social consciousness is the only effective antidote to the class consciousness of the Socialist. (Introduction dated September 12, 1913.) S. J. Duncan-Clark, *The Progressive Movement.* (Boston, 1913), p. xvi.

———. We ought to go with any man in the effort to bring about justice and the equality of opportunity, to turn the tool-user more and more into the tool-owner, to shift burdens so that they can be more equitably borne. The deadening effect on any race of the adoption of a logical and extreme socialistic system could not be overstated; it would spell sheer destruction; it would produce grosser wrong and outrage, fouler immorality, than any existing system. But this does not mean that we may not with great advantage adopt certain of the principles professed by some given set of men who happen to call themselves Socialists; to be afraid to do so would be to make a mark of weakness on our part. (At the Sorbonne, Paris, April 23, 1910.) *Mem. Ed.* XV, 366; *Nat. Ed.* XIII, 520.

———. It is to the last degree improbable that State socialism will ever be adopted in its extreme form, save in a few places. It exists, of course, to a certain extent wherever a police force and a fire department exist; and the sphere of the State's action may be vastly increased without in any way diminishing the happiness of either the many or the few. It is even conceivable that a combination of legislative enactments and natural forces may greatly reduce the inequalities of wealth without in any way diminishing the real power of enjoyment or power for good work of what are now the favored classes. In our own country the best work has always been produced by men who lived in castes or social circles where the standard of essential comfort was high; that is, where men were well clothed, well fed, well housed, and had plenty of books and the opportunity of using them; but where there was small room for extravagant luxury. (*Sewanee Review,* August 1894.) *Mem. Ed.* XIV, 253; *Nat. Ed.* XIII, 219-220.

———. On the social and domestic side doctrinaire Socialism would replace the family and home life by a glorified state free-lunch counter and state foundling asylum, deliberately enthroning self-indulgence as the ideal, with, on its darker side, the absolute abandonment of all morality as between man and woman; while in place of what Socialists call "wage slavery" there would be created a system which would necessitate either the prompt dying out of the community through sheer starvation, or an iron despotism over all workers, compared to which any slave system of the past would seem beneficent, because less utterly hopeless. (*Outlook,* March 20, 1909.) *Mem. Ed.* XVIII, 556; *Nat. Ed.* XIX, 100.

SOCIALISM—SPREAD OF. There has been during the last six or eight years a great growth of socialistic and radical spirit among the workingmen, and the leaders are obliged to play to this or lose their leadership. Then the idiotic folly of the high financiers and of their organs, such as the *Sun,* helps to aggravate the unrest. (To H. C. Lodge, October 2, 1906.) *Lodge Letters* II, 240.

SOCIALISM AND INDIVIDUALISM. It is true that the doctrines of communistic Socialism, if consistently followed, mean the ultimate annihilation of civilization. Yet the converse is also true. Ruin faces us if we decline steadily to try to reshape our whole civilization in accordance with the law of service, and if we permit ourselves to be misled by any empirical or academic consideration into refusing to exert the common power of the community where only collective action can do what individualism has left undone, or can remedy the wrongs done by an unrestricted and ill-regulated individualism. (*Outlook,* March

27, 1909.) *Mem. Ed.* XVIII, 563; *Nat. Ed.* XIX, 106.

——————. The goal is a long way off, but we are striving toward it; and the goal is not Socialism, but so much of Socialism as will best permit the building thereon of a sanely altruistic individualism, an individualism where self-respect is combined with a lively sense of consideration for and duty toward others, and where full recognition of the increased need of collective action goes hand in hand with a developed instead of an atrophied power of individual action. (*Century,* October 1913.) *Mem. Ed.* XIX, 536; *Nat. Ed.* XVII, 394.

SOCIALISM IN ITALY. What I saw of Italy made me feel that there was infinite need for radical action toward the betterment of social and industrial conditions; and this made me feel a very strong sympathy with some of the Socialistic aims, and a very profound distrust of most of the Socialistic methods. (To Sir George Otto Trevelyan, October 1, 1911.) *Mem. Ed.* XXIV, 235; Bishop II, 201.

SOCIALISM IN SWEDEN. I was saddened to see how Socialism had grown among the people, and in a very ugly form; for one of the Socialist tracts was an elaborate appeal to stop having children; the Socialists being so bitter in their class hatred as to welcome race destruction as a means of slaking it. Personally, as Sweden practically has not only free but almost democratic institutions, I could not understand the extreme bitterness of the Socialist attitude, and in view of what at that very moment the Russians were doing in Finland, I felt that any weakening of Sweden in Russia's face came pretty near being a crime against all real progress and civilization. (To Sir George Otto Trevelyan, October 1, 1911.) *Mem. Ed.* XXIV, 285; Bishop II, 244.

SOCIALISM. *See also* BOLSHEVISM; COLLECTIVISM; INDIVIDUALISM.

SOCIALISTS. Because of things I have done on behalf of justice to the working man, I have often been called a Socialist. Usually I have not taken the trouble even to notice the epithet. I am not afraid of names, and I am not one of those who fear to do what is right because some one else will confound me with partisans with whose principles I am not in accord. Moreover, I know that many American Socialists are high-minded and honorable citizens, who in reality are merely radical social reformers. They are oppressed by the brutalities and industrial injustices which we see everywhere about us. When I recall how often I have seen Socialists and ardent non-Socialists working side by side for some specific measure of social or industrial reform, and how I have found opposed to them on the side of privilege many shrill reactionaries who insist on calling all reformers Socialists, I refuse to be panic-stricken by having this title mistakenly applied to me.

None the less, without impugning their motives, I do disagree most emphatically with both the fundamental philosophy and the proposed remedies of the Marxian Socialists. (1913.) *Mem. Ed.* XXII, 551; *Nat. Ed.* XX, 474.

SOIL CONSERVATION. In any great country the prime physical asset—the physical asset more valuable than any other—is the fertility of the soil. All our industrial and commercial welfare, all our material development of every kind, depends in the last resort, upon our preserving and increasing the fertility of the soil. This, of course, means the conservation of the soil as the great natural resource; and equally, of course, it furthermore implies the development of country life, for there cannot be a permanent improvement of the soil if the life of those who live on it, and make their living out of it, is suffered to starve and languish, to become stunted and weazened and inferior to the type of life lived elsewhere. *Outlook,* August 27, 1910, p. 919.

SOLDIERLY QUALITIES. In a regiment the prime need is to have fighting men; the prime virtue is to be able and eager to fight with the utmost effectiveness. I have never believed that this was incompatible with other virtues. On the contrary, while there are of course exceptions, I believe that on the average the best fighting men are also the best citizens. I do not believe that a finer set of natural soldiers than the men of my regiment could have been found anywhere, and they were first-class citizens in civil life also. (1913.) *Mem. Ed.* XXII, 297; *Nat. Ed.* XX, 254.

SOLDIERLY QUALITIES — DEVELOPMENT OF. It is by no means necessary that we should have war to develop soldierly attributes and soldierly qualities; but if the peace we enjoy is of such a kind that it causes their loss, then it is far too dearly purchased, no matter what may be its attendant benefits. (Address as Assistant Secretary of the Navy, Naval War College, June 1897.) *Mem. Ed.* XV, 243; *Nat. Ed.* XIII, 185.

SOLDIERLY QUALITIES. See also FIGHTING EDGE; MANLY VIRTUES; MILITARY TRAINING; PACIFISTS.

SOLDIERS. A war is primarily won by soldiers; the work of the non-soldiers, however valuable, is merely accessory to the primary work of the fighting men. (*Metropolitan,* September, 1917.) Mem. Ed. XXI, 27; Nat. Ed. XIX, 23.

———. There is nothing sacrosanct in the trade of the soldier. It is a trade which can be learned without special difficulty by any man who is brave and intelligent, who realizes the necessity of obedience, and who is already gifted with physical hardihood and is accustomed to the use of the horse and of weapons, to enduring fatigue and exposure, and to acting on his own responsibility, taking care of himself in the open. (1900.) Mem. Ed. XIII, 333; Nat. Ed. X, 226.

SOLDIERS—DEBT TO. In a great war for the right the one great debt owed by the nation is that to the men who go to the front and pay with their bodies for the faith that is in them. At the front there are of course of necessity a few men who, from the nature of the case, are not in positions of great danger—as regards the staff and the high command, the burden of crushing responsibility borne by such men outweighs danger. But as a rule the men who do the great work for the nation are the men who, for a money payment infinitely less than what they would earn in civil life, face terrible risk and endure indescribable hardship and fatigue and misery at the front. (*Metropolitan,* November 1918.) Mem. Ed. XXI, 268; Nat. Ed. XIX, 248.

SOLDIERS — DISCRIMINATION AGAINST. To strive to discriminate against him in any way is literally an infamy; for it is in reality one of the most serious offenses which can be committed against the stability and greatness of our nation. If a hotel-keeper or the owner of a theatre or any other public resort attempts such discrimination, everything possible should be done by all good citizens to make the man attempting it feel the full weight of a just popular resentment, and if possible, legal proceedings should be taken against him. As for the commissioned officers, it both is and must be their pride alike to train the enlisted man how to do his duty and to see that the enlisted man who does his duty is held in honor and respect. (To William Howard Taft, February 3, 1906.) Mem. Ed. XXIV, 6; Bishop II, 4.

SOLDIERS, DISABLED—TRAINING OF. A peculiarly important branch of [our educational system] at the present time ought to be the training of the disabled and the crippled returning soldiers, so that they may become, not objects of charity, but self-supporting citizens. (*Metropolitan,* November 1918.) Mem. Ed. XXI, 280; Nat. Ed. XIX, 258.

SOLDIERS. See also ARMY; DRAFT; MILITARY SERVICE; MILITIA; VETERANS; VOLUNTEER SYSTEM.

SOUTH, THE. I fully believe in and appreciate not only the valor of the South, but its lofty devotion to the right as it saw the right; and yet I think that on every ground—that is, on the question of the Union, on the question of slavery, on the question of State rights—it was wrong with a folly that amounted to madness, and with a perversity that amounted to wickedness. (To James Ford Rhodes, November 29, 1904.) Mem. Ed. XXIII, 402; Bishop I, 349.

———. Great though the need of praise is which is due the South for the soldierly valor her sons displayed during the four years of war, I think that even greater praise is due to her for what her people have accomplished in the forty years of peace which followed. For forty years the South has made not merely a courageous, but at times a desperate struggle, as she has striven for moral and material well-being. Her success has been extraordinary, and all citizens of our common country should feel joy and pride in it; for any great deed done or any fine qualities shown by one group of Americans of necessity reflects credit upon all Americans. Only a heroic people could have battled successfully against the conditions with which the people of the South found themselves face to face at the end of the Civil War. (At Richmond, Va., October 18, 1905.) Mem. Ed. XVIII, 39; Nat. Ed. XVI, 33-34.

———. I have just finished a fortnight's trip in the Southern States, where I was received with the utmost enthusiasm. As far as I know I did not flinch from one of my principles; but I did do my best to show the Southern people not only that I was earnestly desirous of doing what was best for them, but that I felt a profound sympathy and admiration for them; and they met me half-way. This does not mean any political change at all in the South, and it means but a slight permanent change in the attitude of the Southerners; but I think it does mean this slight permanent change, and it marks one more step toward what I believe will some day come about—the complete reunion of the two sections. (To Sir George Otto Trevelyan, November 8, 1905.) *Mem. Ed.* XXIV, 181; Bishop II, 155.

SOUTH, THE. *See also* CIVIL WAR; CONFEDERATES; COPPERHEADS; LEE, R. E.; NEGRO; NORTH; NULLIFICATION; RECONSTRUCTION; SECTIONALISM; SLAVERY; TUSKEGEE INSTITUTE; WASHINGTON, BOOKER T.

SOUTH AMERICA. Portions of South America are now entering on a career of great social and industrial development. Much remains to be known, so far as the outside world is concerned, of the social and industrial condition in the long-settled interior regions. More remains to be done, in the way of pioneer exploring and of scientific work, in the great stretches of virgin wilderness. The only two other continents where such work, of like volume and value, remains to be done are Africa and Asia; and neither Africa nor Asia offers a more inviting field for the best kind of fieldworker in geographical exploration and in zoological, geological, and paleontological investigation. (1914.) *Mem. Ed.* VI, 328; *Nat. Ed.* V, 280.

————. When the white man reached South America he found the same weak and impoverished mammalian fauna that exists practically unchanged to-day. Elsewhere civilized man has been even more destructive than his very destructive uncivilized brothers of the magnificent mammalian life of the wilderness; for ages he has been rooting out the higher forms of beast life in Europe, Asia, and North Africa; and in our own day he has repeated the feat, on a very large scale, in the rest of Africa and in North America. But in South America, although he is in places responsible for the wanton slaughter of the most interesting and the largest, or the most beautiful, birds, his advent has meant a positive enrichment of the wild mammalian fauna. None of the native grass-eating mammals, the graminivores, approach in size and beauty the herds of wild or half-wild cattle and horses, or so add to the interest of the landscape. There is every reason why the good people of South America should waken, as we of North America, very late in the day, are beginning to waken, and as the peoples of northern Europe—not southern Europe—have already partially wakened, to the duty of preserving from impoverishment and extinction the wild life which is an asset of such interest and value in our several lands; but the case against civilized man in this matter is gruesomely heavy anyhow, when the plain truth is told, and it is harmed by exaggeration. (1914.) *Mem. Ed.* VI, 68; *Nat. Ed.* V, 58.

SOUTH AMERICA — EXPLORATION OF. There yet remains plenty of exploring work to be done in South America, as hard, as dangerous, and almost as important as any that has already been done. . . . The collecting naturalists who go into the wilds and do firstclass work encounter every kind of risk and undergo every kind of hardship and exertion. Explorers and naturalists of the right type have open to them in South America a field of extraordinary attraction and difficulty. But to excavate ruins that have already long been known, to visit out-of-the-way towns that date from colonial days, to traverse old, even if uncomfortable, routes of travel, or to ascend or descend highway rivers like the Amazon, the Paraguay, and the lower Orinoco—all of these exploits are well worth performing, but they in no sense represent exploration or adventure, and they do not entitle the performer, no matter how well he writes and no matter how much of real value he contributes to human knowledge, to compare himself in any way with the real wilderness wanderer, or to criticise the latter. (1914.) *Mem. Ed.* VI, 166; *Nat. Ed.* V, 142-143.

SOUTH AMERICA—TRADE WITH. We wish to open the countries of South America to our business, we wish to create a market for the products of our business men, the farmers, and wage-workers in South America. This cannot be done at all unless it is to the advantage of the various peoples of South America to have such products. It cannot be made a striking success unless the South Americans find that it is very much to *their* advantage to deal with us, and unless they so thrive and prosper that it will be greatly to *our* advantage to extend our dealings with them. In private life a man's only customers who are worth anything are those who can pay for what they get, and his best customers are those whose prosperity increases so that they can get a great deal; in other words it is self-evidently to the advantage of every business man to have a prosperous community with which to do business.

In just the same way it is to the advantage of us as a nation to see the nations with which we do business thrive, prosper, and enormously to increase their material well-being, and therefore their wish and their ability to enter into business relations with us. (At New York City, October 3, 1913.) *Mem. Ed.* XVIII, 394; *Nat. Ed.* XVI, 294-295.

SOUTH AMERICA. *See also* BRAZIL; COLOMBIA; GERMANY; INTERVENTION; LATIN AMERICA; MONROE DOCTRINE; PANAMA CANAL; VENEZUELA.

SOUTH AMERICAN WARS OF INDEPENDENCE. The Revolutionary War itself had certain points of similarity with the struggles of which men like Bolivar were the heroes; where the parallel totally fails is in what followed. There were features in which the campaigns of the Mexicans and South American insurgent leaders resembled at least the partisan warfare so often waged by American Revolutionary generals; but with the deeds of the great constructive statesmen of the United States there is nothing in the career of any Spanish-American community to compare. It was the power to build a solid and permanent Union, the power to construct a mighty nation out of the wreck of a crumbling confederacy, which drew a sharp line between the Americans of the North and the Spanish-speaking races of the South. . . .

The men who brought into being and preserved the Union have had no compeers in Southern America. The North American colonies wrested their independence from Great Britain as the colonies of South America wrested theirs from Spain; but whereas the United States grew with giant strides into a strong and orderly nation, Spanish America has remained split into a dozen turbulent states, and has become a by-word for anarchy and weakness. (1894.) *Mem. Ed.* XI, 318-319; *Nat. Ed.* IX, 95.

SOVEREIGNS. *See* KINGS; ROYALTY.

SOVEREIGNTY. There are few evils greater than an irresponsible sovereignty, where the final power is exercised by men who cannot be held accountable for its exercise. *Outlook,* November 15, 1913, p. 592.

SOVEREIGNTY. *See also* POWER.

SOVEREIGNTY, POPULAR. *See* CONSTITUTION; DEMOCRACY; GOVERNMENT; POPULAR RULE; SELF-GOVERNMENT.

SOVEREIGNTY, STATE. *See* STATES' RIGHTS.

SPAIN—DECAY OF. The expulsion of Moor and heretic, the loss of the anarchistic and much misused individual liberties of the provincial towns, the economic and social changes wrought by the inflow of American gold—all of them put together do not explain the military decadence of the Spaniard; do not explain why he grew so rigid that, at first on sea and then on land, he could not adapt himself to new tactics, and above all, what subtle transformation it was that came over the fighting edge of the soldiers themselves. For nearly a century and a half following the beginning of Gonsalvo's campaigns, the Spanish infantry showed itself superior in sheer fighting ability to any other infantry in Europe. Toward the end of the sixteenth century, neither the Hollanders, fighting with despair for their own firesides, nor the Scotch and English volunteers, actuated by love of fighting and zeal for their faith, were able on anything like equal terms to hold their own against the Spanish armies, who walked at will to and fro through the Netherlands, save where strong city walls or burst dikes held them at bay. Yet the Hollander, the Englishman, and the Scotchman were trained soldiers, and they were spurred by every hope and feeling which we ordinarily accept as making men formidable in fight. A century passed; and these same Spaniards had become contemptible creatures in war compared with the Dutch and Scotch, the English and French, whom they had once surpassed. Many partial explanations can be given for the change, but none that wholly or mainly explain it. (To A. J. Balfour, March 5, 1908.) *Mem. Ed.* XXIV, 122-123; Bishop II, 105-106.

SPAIN. *See also* FRENCH REVOLUTION.

SPANISH-AMERICAN WAR. I would regard a war with Spain from two viewpoints: First, the advisability on the ground both of humanity and self-interest of interfering on behalf of the Cubans, and of taking one more step toward the complete freeing of America from European domination; second, the benefit done to our people by giving them something to think of which isn't material gain, and especially the benefit done our military forces by trying both the Army and Navy in actual practise. I should be very sorry not to see us make the experiment of trying to land, and therefore to feed and clothe, an expeditionary force, if only for the sake of learning from our blunders. I should hope that the force would have some fighting to do. It would be a great lesson, and we would profit much by it. (To W. W. Kimball, November 19, 1897.)

Henry F. Pringle, *Theodore Roosevelt*. (Harcourt, Brace & Co., N. Y., 1931), p. 176.

──────────. War is a grim thing at best, but the war through which we have passed has left us not merely memories of glory won on land and sea, but an even more blessed heritage, the knowledge that it was waged from the highest motives, for the good of others as well as for our own national honor. Above all, we are thankful that it brought home to all of us the fact that the country was indeed one when serious danger confronted it. (Annual Message as Governor, Albany, January 2, 1899.) *Mem. Ed.* XVII, 5-6; *Nat. Ed.* XV, 5-6.

SPANISH-AMERICAN WAR—MISMANAGEMENT IN.
The mismanagement of the transportation, and hospital services has been beyond belief. The wounded lie in the mud on sodden blankets; some of my men went *forty-eight* hours without food after being sent to the hospital. The attendance has been bad; and above all, they have had no proper food and but little medicine. I have had to buy from my own pocket rice and oatmeal and condensed milk for my sick men and beans and cornmeal and sugar for the wornout hungry fighters who were still able to dig in the trenches. It is small wonder that of the 600 men with whom I landed, today over 300 are dead or in hospital from wounds and disease. Shafter's utter incapacity and the lack of transportation, that is, the utter lack of executive ability and head, both at Washington and here, are responsible for it all. Nothing but the splendid fighting capacity and uncomplaining endurance of the regular army (with which my regiment alone of the volunteer organization can be classed) carried us through.

The suffering has been hideous; and at least half of it was readily avoidable. There have been practically no supplies at the front save hardtack, bacon and coffee; and for men in high fever such fare is not good. (To Anna Roosevelt Cowles, July 19, 1898.) Cowles *Letters*, 218-219.

SPANISH-AMERICAN WAR—ORIGINS OF.
Our own direct interests were great, because of the Cuban tobacco and sugar, and especially because of Cuba's relations to the projected Isthmian canal. But even greater were our interests from the standpoint of humanity. Cuba was at our very doors. It was a dreadful thing for us to sit supinely and watch her death agony. It was our duty, even more from the standpoint of national honor than from the standpoint of national interest, to stop the devastation and destruction. Because of these considerations I favored war; and to-day, when in retrospect it is easier to see things clearly, there are few humane and honorable men who do not believe that the war was both just and necessary. (1913.) *Mem. Ed.* XXII, 251; *Nat. Ed.* XX, 215.

──────────. I believe it criminal for us to submit to the murder of our men, and to the butchery of Cuban women and children. The resources of diplomacy have been exhausted. This nation has erred on the side of overbearance. When you talk of this war being undertaken to satisfy the political greed of a parcel of politicians you show the most astounding ignorance of the conditions. The only effective forces against the war are the forces inspired by greed and fear, and the forces that tell in favor of war are the belief in national honor and common humanity. (To Henry Jackson, April 6, 1898.) *Mem. Ed.* XXIII, 105; Bishop I, 90.

SPANISH-AMERICAN WAR—RESULTS OF.
There was never a war in which so much was accomplished for humanity, at so small a cost of blood, as the war which resulted in the freeing of Cuba and the starting of the Philippines on the road toward self-government and civilization. (*Outlook*, June 4, 1910.) *Mem. Ed.* XIV, 190; *Nat. Ed.* XII, 219.

──────────. There was one peculiar reason for pleasure in the Spanish-American War, one reason above all others why our people should look back to it with pride and satisfaction, and that is the fact that it marked in very truth the complete reunion of our country. In that war there served in the ranks and in the positions of junior officers the sons of men who had worn the blue and the sons of men who had worn the gray; and they served under men who in their youth had begun their careers as soldiers, some of them in the army of Grant, some of them in the army of Lee. . . . In our own regiment there were at least as many sons of the ex-Confederates as sons of ex-Union soldiers, and they stood shoulder to shoulder, knit together by the closest of ties, and acknowledging with respect to one another only that generous jealousy each to try to be first to do all that in him lay for the honor and the interest of the flag that covered the reunited country. (At unveiling of monument, 1st U. S. Volunteer Cavalry, Arlington, Va., April 12, 1907.) *Mem. Ed.* XII, 626-627; *Nat. Ed.* XI, 340-341.

SPANISH-AMERICAN WAR — ROOSEVELT IN.
Of course I can't leave this position

until it is perfectly certain we are going to have a war, and that I can get down to it. I don't want to be in office during war, I want to be at the front; but I would rather be in this office than guarding a fort and no enemy within a thousand miles of me. Of course being here hampers me. If I were in New York City I think I could raise a regiment of volunteers in short order when the President told me to go ahead, but it is going to be difficult from here. (To General Whitney Tillinghast, March 10, 1898.) *Mem. Ed.* XXIII, 117; Bishop I, 101.

———————. I do not know that I shall be able to go to Cuba if there is a war. The army may not be employed at all, and even if it is employed it will consist chiefly of regular troops; and as regards the volunteers only a very small proportion can be taken from among the multitudes who are even now coming forward. Therefore it may be that I shall be unable to go, and shall have to stay here. In that case I shall do my duty here to the best of my ability, although I shall be eating out my heart. But if I am able to go I certainly shall. It is perfectly true that I shall be leaving one duty, but it will only be for the purpose of taking up another. I say quite sincerely that I shall not go for my own pleasure. On the contrary, if I should consult purely my own feelings I should earnestly hope that we would have peace. I like life very much. I have always led a joyous life. I like thought and I like action, and it will be very bitter to me to leave my wife and children; and while I think I could face death with dignity, I have no desire before my time has come to go out into the everlasting darkness. So I shall not go into a war with any undue exhilaration of spirits or in a frame of mind in any way approaching recklessness or levity. (To Dr. Sturgis Bigelow, March 29, 1898.) *Mem. Ed.* XXIII, 118; Bishop I, 102.

———————. If I went I shouldn't expect to win any military glory, or at the utmost to do more than feel I had respectably performed my duty; but I think I would be quite as useful in the Army as here, and it does not seem to me that it would be honorable for a man who has consistently advocated a warlike policy not to be willing himself to bear the brunt of carrying out that policy. I have a horror of the people who bark but don't bite. If I am ever to accomplish anything worth doing in politics, or ever have accomplished it, it is because I act up to what I preach, and it does not seem to me that I would have the right in a big crisis not to act up to what I preach. (To Douglas Robinson, April 2, 1898.) Corinne Roosevelt Robinson, *My Brother Theodore Roosevelt,* 162.

SPANISH-AMERICAN WAR — UNPREPAREDNESS FOR. I feel that I ought to bring to your attention the very serious consequences to the Government as a whole, and especially to the Navy Department — upon which would be visited the national indignation—for any check, no matter how little the Department was really responsible for the check —if we should drift into a war with Spain and suddenly find ourselves obliged to begin it without preparation, instead of having at least a month's warning, during which we could actively prepare to strike. Some preparation can and should be undertaken now on the mere chance of having to strike.

Certain things should be done at once if there is any reasonable chance of trouble with Spain during the next six months. For instance, the disposition of the fleet on foreign stations should be radically altered, and altered without delay. For the past six or eight months we have been sending small cruisers and gunboats off to various parts of the world with a total disregard of the fact that in the event of war this would be the worst possible policy to have pursued. . . . If we have war with Spain there will be immediate need for every gunboat and cruiser that we can possibly get together to blockade Cuba, threaten or take the less protected ports, and ferret out the scores of small Spanish cruisers and gunboats which form practically the entire Spanish naval force around the island. (To John D. Long, January 14, 1898.) *Mem. Ed.* XXIII, 98; Bishop I, 84.

SPANISH-AMERICAN WAR. *See also* CUBA; DEWEY, ADMIRAL; *Maine;* NAVY; ROUGH RIDERS; SAMPSON-SCHLEY CONTROVERSY; VETERANS.

"SPEAK SOFTLY." *See* BIG STICK.

SPECIAL INTERESTS. In this country at the moment our chief concern must be to deprive the special interests of the power to which they are not entitled and which they use for the corruption of our institutions and to our economic and social undoing. There are persons who contend that "special interests" is a vague and indeed a demagogic term, and incapable of definition. . . . Practically there is little difficulty in saying whether or not the average big concern is the beneficiary of special privilege. A special interest is one which has been given by law certain improper advantages as compared with the mass of our people, or which enjoys such advantages owing to the absence of needed laws. As regards certain great corporations, the facts are so patent—being often made so by confession or judicial proceeding—that no discussion of them is necessary. (*Outlook*, March 25, 1911.) *Mem. Ed.* XIX, 142; *Nat. Ed.* XVII, 101.

SPECIAL INTERESTS — CONTROL BY. One of the fundamental necessities in a representative government such as ours is to make certain that the men to whom the people delegate their power shall serve the people by whom they are elected, and not the special interests. (At Osawatomie, Kan., August 31, 1910.) *Mem. Ed.* XIX, 28; *Nat. Ed.* XVII, 21.

——————. Our government, National and State, must be freed from the sinister influence or control of special interests. Exactly as the special interests of cotton and slavery threatened our political integrity before the Civil War, so now the great special business interests too often control and corrupt the men and methods of government for their own profit. We must drive the special interests out of politics. That is one of our tasks to-day. Every special interest is entitled to justice—full, fair, and complete—and, now, mind you, if there were any attempt by mob-violence to plunder and work harm to the special interest, whatever it may be, that I most dislike, and the wealthy man, whomsoever he may be, for whom I have the greatest contempt, I would fight for him, and you would if you were worth your salt. He should have justice. For every special interest is entitled to justice, but not one is entitled to a vote in Congress, to a voice on the bench, or to representation in any public office. The Constitution guarantees protection to property, and we must make that promise good. But it does not give the right of suffrage to any corporation. (At Osawatomie, Kan., August 31, 1910.) *Mem. Ed.* XIX, 16; *Nat. Ed.* XVII, 10.

SPECIAL INTERESTS — INFLUENCE OF. It is as true as it is forgotten that the influence of any interest upon legislation and administration is strictly proportional to the extent to which the interest is organized—not, mark you, for political, but for business, purposes. *Outlook*, April 20, 1912, p. 855.

SPECIAL INTERESTS—PROGRAM OF. The representatives and beneficiaries of the special interests desire, not unnaturally, to escape all governmental control. What they prefer is that popular unrest should find its vent in mere debate, in unlimited discussion of an academic kind as to the sanctity of contract, full liberty of contract, and other kindred subjects. They feel the need of construing the Constitution with rigid narrowness when property rights are involved, and of carrying the "division of power" theory to such an extreme as to deprive every governmental agency of all real power and responsibility. They prefer the *status quo*, for they know that the mass of conflicting judicial decision has created just what they wish, a neutral ground where State and nation each merely exercises the power of maintaining that the other has none. I wish to contrast with this position of the special interests the spirit and purpose of Progressive Nationalism. Its advocates desire to secure to both State and nation, each within its own sphere, power to give the people complete control over the various forms of corporate activity, and power to permit the people to safeguard the vital interests of all citizens, of whatever class. (*Outlook*, January 14, 1911.) *Mem. Ed.* XIX, 84; *Nat. Ed.* XVII, 52.

SPECIAL INTERESTS—RULE BY. No free people can afford to submit to government by theft. If the will of the people is defeated by fraud, then the people do not rule. If those who are thus foisted on them represent the special interests instead of the people, then the interests and not the people rule. When the people are denied their only thoroughly efficient weapon, the direct primary, against this usurpation, as was done by the ruling in the California case, then under the system thus established the people cannot rule. (*Outlook*, July 13, 1912.) *Mem. Ed.* XIX, 329; *Nat. Ed.* XVII, 241.

SPECIAL INTERESTS. See also CORPORATIONS; GOVERNMENT; NEW NATIONALISM; PRIVILEGE; SELF-GOVERNMENT; TARIFF; WALL STREET; WEALTH.

SPECIAL LEGISLATION. See LEGISLATION.

SPECIALIZATION. Specialization is a good thing, but it may readily be carried too far; and after it has reached a certain point it is well to try to develop again, and on a larger scale, the man who has a special side, but who possesses broader instincts also, and who is able to combine the peculiar aptitudes of the specialist with the larger power that belongs to the man with a broad grasp of the general subject. (*Outlook*, September 16, 1911.) *Mem. Ed.* XIV, 500; *Nat. Ed.* XII, 368-369.

SPECIALIZATION. See also HISTORIANS; NATURALISTS.

SPECULATION. No legislation can by any possibility guarantee the business community against the results of speculative folly any more than it can guarantee an individual against the results of his extravagance. When an individual mortgages his house to buy an automobile he invites disaster; and when wealthy men, or men who pose as such, or are unscrupulously or foolishly eager to become such, indulge in reckless speculation—especially if it is accompanied by dishonesty—they jeopardize not only their own future but the future of all their innocent fellow citizens, for they expose the whole business community to panic and distress. (Seventh Annual Message, Washington, December 3, 1907.) *Mem. Ed.* XVII, 500; *Nat. Ed.* XV, 426.

SPECULATION. See also PROSPERITY.

SPECULATORS. The conscienceless stock speculator who acquires wealth by swindling his fellows, by debauching judges and corrupting legislatures, and who ends his days with the reputation of being among the richest men in America, exerts over the minds of the rising generation an influence worse than that of the average murderer or bandit, because his career is even more dazzling in its success, and even more dangerous in its effects upon the community. (*Forum*, February 1895.) *Mem. Ed.* XV, 7; *Nat. Ed.* XIII, 6.

SPECULATORS. See also FINANCIERS.

SPEECH—LIBERTY OF. See FREE SPEECH.

SPELLING REFORM. Most of the criticism of the proposed step is evidently made in entire ignorance of what the step is, no less than in entire ignorance of the very moderate and common-sense views as to the purposes to be achieved, which views are so excellently set forth in the circulars to which I have referred. There is not the slightest intention to do anything revolutionary or initiate any far-reaching policy.

The purpose simply is for the Government, instead of lagging behind popular sentiment, to advance abreast of it and at the same time abreast of the views of the ablest and most practical educators of our time as well as of the most profound scholars—men of the stamp of Professor Lounsbury and Professor Skeat.

If the slight changes in the spelling of the three hundred words proposed wholly or partially meet popular approval, then the changes will become permanent without any reference to what public officials or individual private citizens may feel; if they do not ultimately meet with popular approval they will be dropt, and that is all there is about it.

They represent nothing in the world but a very slight extension of the unconscious movement which has made agricultural implement makers and farmers write "plow" instead of "plough"; which has made most Americans write "honor" without the somewhat absurd, superfluous "u"; and which is even now making people write "program" without the "me"....

It is not an attack on the language of Shakespeare and Milton, because it is in some instances a going back to the forms they used, and in others merely the extension of changes which, as regards other words, have taken place since their time.

It is not an attempt to do anything far-reaching or sudden or violent; or indeed anything very great at all. It is merely an attempt to cast what slight weight can properly be cast on the side of the popular forces which are endeavoring to make our spelling a little less foolish and fantastic. (To Charles A. Stillings, Public Printer, August 27, 1906.) *Simplified Spelling.* (Government Printing Office, Washington, 1906), pp. 5-6.

————. I could not by fighting have kept the new spelling in, and it was evidently worse than useless to go into an undignified contest when I was beaten. Do you know that the one word as to which I thought the new spelling was wrong—thru—was more responsible than anything else for our discomfiture? But I am mighty glad I did the thing anyhow. In my own correspondence I shall continue using the new spelling. (To Brander Matthews, December 16, 1906.) *Mem. Ed.* XXIV, 39; Bishop II, 33.

"SPEND AND BE SPENT." See LEADERS—NEED FOR; LIFE.

SPIRITUAL DEVELOPMENT. It is more important that a people should be of full stature from the spiritual and moral standpoint than from the standpoint of culture, but the latter is very important also, and no National development that omits it can ever be really satisfactory. *Outlook,* September 23, 1911, p. 160.

SPIRITUAL DEVELOPMENT. See also CHARACTER; MORAL SENSE.

SPIRITUAL GROWTH. All our extraordinary material development, our wonderful industrial growth will go for nothing unless with that growth goes hand in hand the moral, the spiritual growth that will enable us to use aright the other as an instrument. (At Pacific Theological Seminary, Spring 1911.) *Mem. Ed.* XV, 575; *Nat. Ed.* XIII, 615.

SPIRITUAL TRAINING. We must direct every national resource, material and spiritual, to the task not of shirking difficulties, but of training our people to overcome difficulties. Our aim must be, not to make life easy and soft, not to soften soul and body, but to fit us in virile fashion to do a great work for all mankind. This great work can only be done by a mighty democracy, with those qualities of soul, guided by those qualities of mind, which will both make it refuse to do injustice to any other nation, and also enable it to hold its own against aggression by any other nation. (Before Knights of Columbus, New York City, October 12, 1915.) *Mem. Ed.* XX, 471; *Nat. Ed.* XVIII, 404.

SPOILS SYSTEM. There is in American public life no one other cause so fruitful of harm to the body politic as the spoils system. (*Scribner's,* August 1895.) *Mem. Ed.* XV, 195; *Nat. Ed.* XIII, 115.

————————. No cause is more potent in working the degradation of American political institutions than the spoils system, and by cutting it out root and branch we will do more to elevate the tone of our political life than we can do in any other conceivable way. (Before Boston Civil Service Reform Association, February 20, 1893.) *Mem. Ed.* XVI, 231; *Nat. Ed.* XIV, 159.

————————. It is one of the hardest tasks that decent citizens have to face, when they come into public life, to find themselves pitted against the brigades of trained mercenaries who are paid out of the public chest, into which these very citizens, who are trying to overthrow them, pay their own taxes; for you, the ordinary citizen, the average American, are taxed for the support of the very men against whom you have to work hardest if you want to obtain good government. You go through the average ward organization in any big city, or into any place where the spoils system prevails, and you find these mercenaries in possession. You find them at the crossroads in the country, when the fourth-class postmaster, as the time for the primaries comes around, marshals eight or ten people of the neighborhood whom he has been able to placate, or whom he has an interest in placating, because they will help him keep his two-hundred-and-fifty-dollar per year salary. And when you turn from him to the man who has a great local office, you find that he hires his "heelers" to support his faction, in a spirit as absolutely and professedly immoral as that in which the Hessian troops were hired by the British king a century ago. We want to do away, as far as we can, with the profound iniquities of such a system. (At memorial meeting for George William Curtis, New York, November 14, 1892.) *Mem. Ed.* XII, 490; *Nat. Ed.* XI, 233.

————————. The spoils theory of politics is that public office is so much plunder which the victorious political party is entitled to appropriate to the use of its adherents. Under this system the work of the government was often done well even in those days, when civil service reform was only an experiment, because the man running an office if himself an able and far-sighted man, knew that inefficiency in administration would be visited on his head in the long run, and therefore insisted upon most of his subordinates doing good work; and, moreover, the men appointed under the spoils system were necessarily men of a certain initiative and power, because those who lacked these qualities were not able to shoulder themselves to the front. Yet there were many flagrant instances of inefficiency, where a powerful chief quartered friend, adherent, or kinsman upon the government. (1913.) *Mem. Ed.* XXII, 155; *Nat. Ed.* XX, 133.

SPOILS SYSTEM—EVILS OF. I think that, of all people who are harmed by the spoils system, the poor suffer most. The rich man who wishes to corrupt a legislature, or the rich company which wishes to buy franchises from a board of aldermen and pay a big price for it, do not suffer so much as the poor from the results of the system. I dare say that in New York we see the system at its worst, but at its best it is thoroughly rotten, and a disgrace to every community enjoying the right of suffrage. (Before Civil Service Reform Association, Baltimore, February 23, 1889.) *Mem. Ed.* XVI, 149; *Nat. Ed.* XIV, 92.

————————. Moreover, great though the evil is that the spoils system works to the public service, this is but a minor affair. The chief curse comes in its effects upon our public life. . . . No one cause has been so potent in tending to degrade American political life as the spoils system. It puts a premium upon partisan activity with a view to a reward out of the public treasury and powerfully discourages good men from taking part in contests where they find themselves opposed by bands of drilled henchmen, kept together by what has been aptly styled the cohesive power of public plunder.

The plea sometimes advanced by honest but thick-headed beings that more efficient service can be secured if the subordinates and the heads of departments are of the same political faith is simply nonsense. *Congregationalist,* January 12, 1893, p. 53.

———————. No question of internal administration is so important to the United States as the question of civil-service reform, because the spoils system, which can only be supplanted through the agencies which have found expression in the act creating the Civil Service Commission, has been for seventy years the most potent of all the forces tending to bring about the degradation of our politics. No republic can permanently endure when its politics are corrupt and base; and the spoils system, the application in political life of the degrading doctrine that to the victor belong the spoils, produces corruption and degradation. . . . The spoils-monger and spoils-seeker invariably breed the bribe-taker and bribe-giver, the embezzler of public funds and the corrupter of voters. (*Scribner's,* August 1895.) *Mem. Ed.* XV, 176-177; *Nat. Ed.* XIII, 99.

———————. The necessarily haphazard nature of the employment, the need of obtaining and holding the office by service wholly unconnected with official duty, inevitably tended to lower the standard of public morality, alike among the office-holders and among the politicians who rendered party service with the hope of reward in office. Indeed, the doctrine that "To the victor belong the spoils," the cynical battle-cry of the spoils politician in America for the sixty years preceding my own entrance into public life, is so nakedly vicious that few right-thinking men of trained mind defend it. To appoint, promote, reduce, and expel from the public service, letter-carriers, stenographers, women typewriters, clerks, because of the politics of themselves or their friends, without regard to their own service, is, from the standpoint of the people at large, as foolish and degrading as it is wicked. (1913.) *Mem. Ed.* XXII, 156; *Nat. Ed.* XX, 134.

———————. One of the worst features of the old spoils system was the ruthless cruelty and brutality it so often bred in the treatment of faithful public servants without political influence. Life is hard enough and cruel enough at best, and this is as true of public service as of private service. Under no system will it be possible to do away with all favoritism and brutality and meanness and malice. But at least we can try to minimize the exhibition of these qualities. (1913.) *Mem. Ed.* XXII, 168; *Nat. Ed.* XX, 144.

SPOILS SYSTEM — OPERATION OF.
If a party victory meant that all offices already filled by the most competent members of the defeated party were to be thereafter filled by the most competent members of the victorious party, the system would still be absurd, but it would not be particularly baneful. In reality, however, this is not what the system of partisan appointments means at all. Wherever it is adopted it is inevitable that the degree of party service, or more often of service to some particular leader, and not merit, shall ultimately determine the appointment, even as among the different party candidates themselves. Once admit that it is proper to turn out an efficient Republican clerk in order to replace him by an efficient Democratic clerk, or *vice versa,* and the inevitable next step is to consider solely Republicanism or Democracy, and not efficiency, in making the appointment; while the equally inevitable third step is to consider only that peculiar species of Republicanism or Democracy which is implied in adroit and unscrupulous service rendered to the most influential local boss. (*Century,* February 1890.) *Mem. Ed.* XVI, 160; *Nat. Ed.* XIV, 100-101.

———————. A system which opens the public service to all men, of whatever rank in life, who prove themselves most worthy to enter it, and which retains them in office only so long as they serve the public with honesty, efficiency, and courtesy, is in its very essence democratic; whereas, on the contrary, the spoils system—which still obtains in most European kingdoms, and reaches its fullest development under the despotic government of Russia—is essentially undemocratic, in that it treats the public service not as the property of the whole people, to be administered solely in their interest, but as a bribery chest for the benefit of a few powerful individuals, or groups of individuals, who use it purely in the spirit of personal or political favoritism. It is among the most potent of the many forces which combine to produce the ward boss, the district heeler, the boodle alderman, and all their base and obscure kindred who in our great cities are ever striving to change the government from an honest democracy into a corrupt and ignorant oligarchy, wherein only the vile and the dishonest shall rule and hold office. (*Century*, February 1890.) *Mem. Ed.* XVI, 170; *Nat. Ed.* XIV, 109.

───────────. Under the spoils system a man is appointed to an ordinary clerical or ministerial position in the municipal, federal, or State government, not primarily because he is expected to be a good servant, but because he has rendered help to some big boss or the henchman of some big boss. His stay in office depends not upon how he performs service, but upon how he retains his influence in the party. This necessarily means that his attention to the interests of the public at large, even though real, is secondary to his devotion to his organization, or to the interest of the ward leader who put him in his place. So he and his fellows attend to politics, not once a year, not two or three times a year, like the average citizen, but every day in the year. It is the one thing that they talk of, for it is their bread and butter. They plan about it and they scheme about it. They do it because it is their business. I do not blame them in the least. I blame us, the people, for we ought to make it clear as a bell that the business of serving the people in one of the ordinary ministerial government positions, which have nothing to do with deciding the policy of the government, should have no necessary connection with the management of primaries, of caucuses, and of nominating conventions. (1913.) *Mem. Ed.* XXII, 159; *Nat. Ed.* XX, 136.

SPOILS SYSTEM. *See also* APPOINTMENTS; BOSS; BRIBERY; CIVIC DUTY; CIVIL SERVICE REFORM; CORRUPTION; HONESTY; JACKSON, ANDREW; MERIT SYSTEM; OFFICE; PATRONAGE; POLITICAL ASSESSMENTS; POLITICS.

SPORTS. Vigorous training of mind, body, and soul in manly sport is a first-class thing; to obtain rest and enjoyment by looking at other men practise an interesting sport is entirely proper; excessive indulgence in the latter type of amusement, however, with the consequent distortion of the perspective of life, is of course noxious; and enjoyment in looking on at a sport because it is cruel, or is dangerous to the lives of those taking part in it, is thoroughly vicious and demoralizing. *Outlook*, October 21, 1911, p. 409.

───────────. Granting that athletic sports do good, it remains to be considered what athletic sports are the best. The answer to this is obvious. They are those sports which call for the greatest exercise of fine moral qualities, such as resolution, courage, endurance, and capacity to hold one's own and to stand up under punishment. For this reason out-of-door sports are better than gymnastics and calisthenics. To be really beneficial the sport must be enjoyed by the participator. Much more health will be gained by the man who is not always thinking of his health than by the poor being who is forever wondering whether he has helped his stomach or his lungs, or developed this or that muscle. Laborious work in the gymnasium, directed towards the fulfilling of certain tests of skill or strength, is very good in its way; but the man who goes through it does not begin to get the good he would in a season's play with an eleven or a nine on the gridiron field or the diamond. The mere fact that the moral qualities are not needed in the one case, but are all the time called into play in the other, is sufficient to show the little worth of the calisthenic system of gymnastic development when compared with rough outdoor games. *Harper's Weekly*, December 23, 1893, p. 1236.

SPORTS — COMMERCIALISM IN. Commercialism though sometimes inevitable, is always an unhealthy element in any sport, and when it becomes the chief factor in continuing the sport's existence, it is time for that sport to be brought to an end. . . .

Neither in the case of automobiles nor in the case of flying machines should we permit the kind of commercialization of sport which means the coining of money out of that shameful and hysterical curiosity which is to be satisfied only by seeing men risk their lives, where the risking of the life is itself what really attracts the onlooker, and not the courage or address shown in a manly sport. *Outlook*, October 21, 1911, pp. 409-410.

SPORTS — PARTICIPATION IN. I went in for boxing and wrestling a good deal, and I really think that while this was partly because I liked them as sports, it was even more because I intended to be a middling decent fellow, and I did not intend that any one should laugh at me with impunity because I was decent. (To Edward S. Martin, November 26, 1900.) *Mem. Ed.* XXIII, 6; Bishop I, 3-4.

───────────. Always in our modern life, the life of a highly complex industrialism, there is a tendency to softening of fibre. This is true of our enjoyments; and it is no less true of very many of our business occupations. It is not true of such work as railroading, a purely modern development, nor yet of work like that of those who man the fishing fleets; but it is pre-eminently true of all occupations which cause men to lead sedentary lives in great cities. For these men it is especially necessary to provide hard and rough play. Of course, if such play is made a serious business, the result is very bad; but this does not in the least affect the fact that within proper limits the play itself is good. Vigorous athletic sports carried on in a sane spirit are healthy. The hardy out-of-door sports of the wilderness are even healthier. (1905.) *Mem. Ed.* III, 235; *Nat. Ed.* III, 59.

SPORTS—PLACE OF. Sport is a fine thing as a pastime, and indeed it is more than a mere pastime; but it is a very poor business if it is permitted to become the one serious occupation of life. . . .

I thoroughly believe in sport, but I think it is a great mistake if it is made anything like a profession, or carried on in a way that gives just cause for fault-finding and complaint among people whose objection is not really to the defects, but to the sport itself. (At Cambridge Union, Cambridge, Eng., May 26, 1910.) *Mem. Ed.* XV, 505-506; *Nat. Ed.* XIII, 573.

———————. If sport is made an end instead of a means, it is better to avoid it altogether. . . . Sportsmen . . . do run the risk of becoming a curse to themselves and to every one else, if they once get into the frame of mind which can look on the business of life as merely an interruption to sport. (1905.) *Mem. Ed.* III, 312; *Nat. Ed.* III, 123.

SPORTS—RISK IN. There are very few sports, indeed, where it does not exist. Under a proper system of rules it is doubtful whether football is as dangerous as mountaineering or as the better kinds of sport on horseback, such as riding across country and playing polo. No untrained boy or man unfit to take part in the game and unacquainted with the rules should be allowed to play. If he does he is liable to meet with fatal accidents, precisely as a man would be who, with no knowledge of horsemanship, mounted a spirited horse and tried to ride him over the fences. But after every precaution has been taken, then it is mere unmanliness to complain of occasional mishaps. Among my many friends who have played football I know of few who have met with serious, and none who have met with fatal, accidents; but more than one has been killed, and many have been injured, in riding to hounds, in polo, and in kindred pastimes. The sports especially dear to a vigorous and manly nation are always those in which there is a certain slight element of risk. Every effort should be made to minimize this risk, but it is mere unmanly folly to try to do away with the sport because the risk exists. *Harper's Weekly,* December 23, 1893, p. 1236.

SPORTS, COLLEGIATE. It is a bad thing for any college man to grow to regard sport as the serious business of life. It is a bad thing to permit sensationalism and hysteria to shape the development of our sports. And finally it is a much worse thing to permit college sport to become in any shape or way tainted by professionalism, or by so much as the slightest suspicion of money-making; and this is especially true if the professionalism is furtive, if the boy or man violates the spirit of the rule while striving to keep within the letter. . . . The college undergraduate who, in furtive fashion, becomes a semiprofessional is an unmitigated curse, and that not alone to university life and to the cause of amateur sport; for the college graduate ought in after-years to take the lead in putting the business morality of this country on a proper plane, and he cannot do it if in his own college career his code of conduct has been warped and twisted. Moreover, the spirit which puts so excessive a value upon his work as to produce this semiprofessional is itself unhealthy. . . . I think our effort should be to minimize rather than to increase that kind of love of athletics which manifests itself, not in joining in the athletic sports, but in crowding by tens of thousands to see other people indulge in them. It is a far better thing for our colleges to have the average student interested in some form of athletics than to have them all gather in a mass to see other people do their athletics for them. (At Harvard University, Cambridge, June 28, 1905.) *Mem. Ed.* XVIII, 437-438; *Nat. Ed.* XVI, 325-326.

SPORTS. *See also* ATHLETICS; BOXING; FOOTBALL; FOX-HUNTING; GYMNASTICS; HUNTING; JIU JITSU; MOUNTAIN CLIMBING; PLAYGROUNDS; PRIZE-FIGHTING.

SQUARE DEAL, THE. A square deal for every man! That is the only safe motto for the United States. (To Victor A. Olander, Illinois State Federation of Labor, July 17, 1917.) *Mem. Ed.* XXI, 176; *Mem. Ed.* XIX, 169.

———————. There must be ever present in our minds the fundamental truth that in a republic such as ours the only safety is to stand neither for nor against any man because he is rich or because he is poor, because he is engaged in one occupation or another, because he works with his brains or because he works with his hands. We must treat each man on his worth and merits as a man. We must see that each is given a square deal, because he is entitled to no more and should receive no less. (At State Fair, Syracuse, N. Y., September 7, 1903.) *Mem. Ed.* XVIII, 69; *Nat. Ed.* XVI, 59.

―――――――. When I say I believe in a square deal I do not mean, and probably nobody that speaks the truth can mean, that he believes it possible to give every man the best hand. If the cards do not come to any man, or if they do come, and he has not got the power to play them, that is his affair. All I mean is that there shall be no crookedness in the dealing. In other words, it is not in the power of any human being to devise legislation or administration by which each man shall achieve success and have happiness; it not only is not in the power of any man to do that, but if any man says that he can do it, distrust him as a quack. . . . All any of us can pretend to do is to come as near as our imperfect abilities will allow to securing through governmental agencies an equal opportunity for each man to show the stuff that is in him; and that must be done with no more intention of discrimination against the rich man than the poor man, or against the poor man than the rich man; with the intention of safeguarding every man, rich or poor, poor or rich, in his rights, and giving him as nearly as may be a fair chance to do what his powers permit him to do; always providing he does not wrong his neighbor. (At Dallas, Tex., April 5, 1905.) Daniel Henderson, *"Great-Heart." The Life Story of Theodore Roosevelt.* (New York, 1919), p. 180.

―――――――. When I say "square deal," I mean a square deal to every one; it is equally a violation of the policy of the square deal for a capitalist to protest against denunciation of a capitalist who is guilty of wrong-doing and for a labor leader to protest against the denunciation of a labor leader who has been guilty of wrong-doing. I stand for equal justice to both; and so far as in my power lies I shall uphold justice, whether the man accused of guilt has behind him the wealthiest corporations, the greatest aggregations of riches in the country, or whether he has behind him the most influential labor organizations in the country. (Letter of April 22, 1907.) *Mem. Ed.* XXII, 560; *Nat. Ed.* XX, 482.

―――――――. In the first place, my dear sir, I trust I need hardly assure you that I shall not "surrender" to the bankers, or to any one else, and there will be no "secret midnight conferences" with any big financier, or any one else. I have not seen Mr. Morgan, but I intend to see him soon, and he will call at the White House just as openly as Mr. Gompers did the other day, just as openly as he has called in the past, and just as openly as Mr. Gompers and his associates have more often called in the past. I know I have your hearty support in the proposition that the doors of the White House swing open with equal readiness to capitalist and wage-worker, to the head of a great corporation or a union, to the man who is neither―all shall have a fair hearing from me, and none shall exert any influence save that their case, openly stated and openly repeated, warrants. (To Thomas E. Watson, November 12, 1907.) *Mem. Ed.* XXIV, 56; Bishop II, 48.

―――――――. We must stand for the good citizen, because he is a good citizen, whether he be rich or whether he be poor, and we must mercilessly attack the man who does evil, wholly without regard to whether the evil is done in high or low places, whether it takes the form of homicidal violence among members of a federation of miners, or of unscrupulous craft and greed in the head of some great corporation. *Outlook,* June 19, 1909, p. 395.

―――――――. I stand for the square deal. But when I say that I am for the square deal, I mean not merely that I stand for fair play under the present rules of the game, but that I stand for having those rules changed so as to work for a more substantial equality of opportunity and of reward for equally good service. One word of warning which, I think, is hardly necessary in Kansas. When I say I want a square deal for the poor man, I do not mean that I want a square deal for the man who remains poor because he has not got the energy to work for himself. If a man who has had a chance will not make good, then he has got to quit. (At Osawatomie, Kan., August 31, 1910.) *Mem. Ed.* XIX, 16; *Nat. Ed.* XVII, 10.

SQUARE DEAL. *See also* BUSINESS; CAPITAL; INDUSTRIAL JUSTICE; LABOR; OPPORTUNITY; PROGRESSIVE MOVEMENT; SOCIAL AND INDUSTRIAL JUSTICE; TARIFF.

STABILITY. *See* ORDER.

STANDARD OIL COMPANY. If we had our way, there would be an administrative body to deal radically and thoroughly with such a case as that of the Standard Oil Company. We would make any split-up of the company that was necessary real and not nominal. We would step in in such a case as this where the value of the stock was going up in such enormous proportion and forbid any increase of the price of the product. We would examine thoroughly and searchingly the books of the company and put a stop to every type of rebate and to every practice which would result in the swindling either of investors or competitors or wage-workers or of the general public.

Our plan—the plan to which Mr. Archbold of the Standard Oil Trust so feelingly objects as "Abyssinian treatment"—would result in preventing any increase of cost to the consumer and in exercising the kind of radical control over the corporation itself, which would prevent the stock-gambling antics which result in enormous profits to those on the inside, to those who, in the parlance of the street, know that "there is a melon to be cut." (At San Francisco, September 14, 1912.) *Mem. Ed.* XIX, 425; *Nat. Ed.* XVII, 311.

——————. The Standard Oil Corporation and the railway company have both been found guilty by the courts of criminal misconduct; both have been sentenced to pay heavy fines; and each has issued and published broadcast these statements, asserting their innocence and denouncing as improper the action of the courts and juries in convicting them of guilt. These statements are very elaborate, very ingenious, and are untruthful in important particulars.

The amount of money the representatives of certain great moneyed interests are willing to spend can be gauged by their recent publication broadcast throughout the papers of this country, from the Atlantic to the Pacific, of huge advertisements attacking with envenomed bitterness the Administration's policy of warring against successful dishonesty, and by their circulation of pamphlets and books prepared with the same object while they likewise push the circulation of the writings and speeches of men who, whether because they are misled or because, seeing the light, they yet are willing to sin against the light, serve these their masters of great wealth to the cost of the plain people. The books and pamphlets, the controlled newspapers, the speeches by public or private men, to which I refer, are usually and especially in the interest of the Standard Oil Trust and of certain notorious railroad combinations, but they also defend other individuals and corporations of great wealth that have been guilty of wrong-doing. (Special message to Congress, January 31, 1908.) *Mem. Ed.* XXIV, 94; Bishop II, 80.

——————. The Standard Oil Company took the lead in opposing all this [anti-trust] legislation. This was natural, for it had been the worst offender in the amassing of enormous fortunes by improper methods of all kinds, at the expense of business rivals and of the public, including the corruption of public servants. If any man thinks this condemnation extreme, I refer him to the language officially used by the Supreme Court of the nation in its decision against the Standard Oil Company. Through their counsel, and by direct telegrams and letters to senators and congressmen from various heads of the Standard Oil organization, they did their best to kill the bill providing for the Bureau of Corporations. I got hold of one or two of these telegrams and letters, however, and promptly published them; and, as generally happens in such a case, the men who were all-powerful as long as they could work in secret and behind closed doors became powerless as soon as they were forced into the open. The bill went through without further difficulty. (1913.) *Mem. Ed.* XXII, 491; *Nat. Ed.* XX, 423.

STANDARD OIL COMPANY. *See also* Campaign Contributions; Northern Securities Case; Sherman Anti-Trust Act; Trusts.

STATE OWNERSHIP. *See* Government Ownership; Socialism.

STATES' RIGHTS. States' rights should be preserved when they mean the people's rights, but not when they mean the people's wrongs; not, for instance, when they are invoked to prevent the abolition of child labor, or to break the force of the laws which prohibit the importation of contract labor to this country; in short, not when they stand for wrong or oppression of any kind or for national weakness or impotence at home or abroad. (At the Harvard Union, Cambridge, February 23, 1907.) *Mem. Ed.* XV, 492; *Nat. Ed.* XIII, 567.

——————. To preserve the general welfare, to see to it that the rights of the public are protected, and the liberty of the individual secured and encouraged as long as consistent with this welfare, and curbed when it becomes inconsistent therewith, it is necessary to invoke the aid of the government. There are points in which this governmental aid can best be rendered by the States; that is, where the exercise of States' rights helps to secure popular rights, and as to these I believe in States' rights. But there are large classes of cases where only the authority of the National Government will secure the rights of the people, and where this is the case I am a convinced and a thoroughgoing believer in the rights of the National Government. (*Outlook,* September 10, 1910.) *Mem. Ed.* XVIII, 26; *Nat. Ed.* XVI, 24.

——————. Little permanent good can be done by any party which worships the States' rights fetich or which fails to regard the State, like the county or the municipality, as merely a convenient unit for local self-government, while in all national matters, of importance to the whole people, the nation is to be supreme over State, county, and town alike. (1913.) *Mem. Ed.* XXII, 397; *Nat. Ed.* XX, 341.

STATES' RIGHTS AND FOREIGN RELATIONS. Inasmuch as in the last resort, including that last of all resorts, war, the dealing of necessity had to be between the foreign power and the National Government, it was impossible to admit that the doctrine of State sovereignty could be invoked . . . . As soon as legislative or other action in any State affects a foreign nation, then the affair becomes one for the nation, and the State should deal with the foreign power purely through the nation. (1913.) *Mem. Ed.* XXII, 430; *Nat. Ed.* XX, 369.

STATES' RIGHTS AND NATIONAL RIGHTS. I am for the rights of the people. I am for popular rights and where they can best be obtained by the exercise of State rights I am a good States' rights man; and where they can best be obtained by the exercise of the power of the nation I am a nationalist. I believe in national rights. In other words, I treat national rights and States' rights as not in themselves ends, but as means to the end; as means to the end of securing better government and justice as between man and man. (Before Chamber of Commerce, New Haven, Conn., December 13, 1910.) *Mem. Ed.* XVIII, 109; *Nat. Ed.* XVI, 92.

——————. We are for both the rights of the nation and the rights of the States, because we are for the rights of the people; and where States' rights means popular rights, then we are for States' rights; and where the exercise of the national power is necessary in order to secure the rights of the people, then we are for national rights, because national rights then means popular rights. Above all, we feel that by legislative and judicial and executive action alike it should be made evident that there is no neutral ground over which neither State nor nation has real control, and in which wrong-doers of sufficient wealth to hire the most cunning legal counsel can dwell unmolested by either nation or State. (At Cleveland, O., November 5, 1910.) *Mem. Ed.* XIX, 69.

STATES' RIGHTS AND NATIONALISM. I cannot too often repeat that true Nationalism represents in its essence merely a demand for the people's rights, for the rights of the whole people. Therefore true Nationalism means championship of the rights of the States when insistence on their rights offers the best method of securing popular rights, and championship of the power of the Federal Government when the rights of all the people are involved, because then the rights of the people as a whole can be secured only by the action of the Federal Government. (*Outlook,* March 25, 1911.) *Mem. Ed.* XIX, 144; *Nat. Ed.* XVII, 102.

STATES' RIGHTS. See also NULLIFICATION.

STATESMANSHIP. The first requisite in the statesmanship that shall benefit mankind, so far as we are concerned, is that that statesmanship shall be thoroughly American. No American statesman who forgot to be first and foremost an American was ever yet able to do anything to benefit the world as a whole. The world moves upward as a whole by means of the people who make the different countries of the world move upward; the man who lifts America higher, by just so much makes higher the civilization of all mankind. (At dinner in honor of J. H. Choate, New York City, February 17, 1899.) *Mem. Ed.* XII, 539; *Nat. Ed.* XI, 266.

——————. No man ever really learned from books how to manage a governmental system. Books are admirable adjuncts, and the statesman who has carefully studied them is far more apt to do good work than if he had not; but if he has never done anything but study books he will not be a statesman at all. (*Atlantic Monthly,* August 1894.) *Mem. Ed.* XV, 57; *Nat. Ed.* XIII, 42.

——————. The blood-and-iron statesman of one nation finds in the milk-and-water statesman of another nation the man predestined through the ages to be his ally and his tool. (*Metropolitan*, August 1915.) *Mem. Ed.* XX, 360; *Nat. Ed.* XVIII, 309.

STATESMEN. The business of statesmen is to try constantly to keep international relations better, to do away with causes of friction, and secure as nearly ideal justice as actual conditions will permit. (To Baron Kentaro Kaneko, May 23, 1907.) Julian Street, *Mysterious Japan.* (Doubleday, Page & Co., Garden City, N. Y., 1921), p. 225.

───────────. It does not seem to me that it is fair to say that passionate earnestness and self-devotion, delicateness of conscience, and lofty aim are likely to prove a hindrance instead of a help to a statesman or a politician. Of course if he has no balance of common sense, then the man will go to pieces; but it will be because he is a fool, not because he has some of the qualities of a moral hero. Undoubtedly many great statesmen whose names are written in history in imperishable—though personally I think in rather unpleasant — character, have lacked these characteristics, yet there are other great men who certainly have possessed them. (To Sir George Otto Trevelyan, September 1905.) *Mem. Ed.* XXIV, 178; Bishop II, 152.

───────────. The first duty of a statesman is efficiently to work for the betterment of his country and for its good relations with the rest of the world. He must have high ideals, and in addition he must possess the practical sagacity and force that will enable him measurably to realize them. If he does not possess the high ideals, then the greater his ability the more dangerous he is and the more essential it is to hunt him out of public life. Sagacity, courage, all that makes for efficiency—these are of use only if the man's character is such that he will use them for good and not for evil. On the other hand, fine aspirations, no matter how good, are useless if a man lacks either strength and courage or else the practical good sense which will enable him to face facts as they actually are and to work with his fellows under existing conditions, instead of confining himself to complaints about the conditions, or to railing at the men because they are not other than he finds them. (*Outlook*, January 23, 1909.) *Mem. Ed.* XII, 420; *Nat. Ed.* XI, 183.

STATESMEN. See also LAWYERS; LEADERS; POLITICIANS.

STATUES. See MONUMENTS.

STEEL TRUST. See TENNESSEE COAL AND IRON COMPANY.

STEFFENS, LINCOLN. See CORRUPTION.

STERILITY. See BIRTH CONTROL; MARRIAGE; RACE SUICIDE; WOMEN.

STERNBERG, BARON SPECK VON. All that your Majesty says about poor Speck is simply warranted by the facts. He was not only a devoted German, but he had an intense feeling of devotion to you personally, a feeling shared to the full by the poor Baroness whom his death has left so lonely. He was also sincerely attached to America, and he played no small part in promoting the good-will between the two countries; which good-will, however, is due primarily to your Majesty's own actions during the past six years. (To Emperor William II, January 2, 1909.) *Mem. Ed.* XXIV, 337; Bishop II, 286.

───────────. Among the many other good men was a staunch friend, Baron Speck von Sternberg, afterward German ambassador at Washington during my presidency. He was a capital shot, rider, and walker, a devoted and most efficient servant of Germany, who had fought with distinction in the Franco-German War when barely more than a boy; he was the hero of the story of "the pig dog" in Archibald Forbes's volume of reminiscences. It was he who first talked over with me the raising of a regiment of horse riflemen from among the ranchmen and cowboys of the plains. When ambassador, the poor, gallant, tender-hearted fellow was dying of a slow and painful disease, so that he could not play with the rest of us, but the agony of his mortal illness never in the slightest degree interfered with his work. (1913.) *Mem. Ed.* XXII, 39; *Nat. Ed.* XX, 34.

STOCKHOLDERS. See CORPORATIONS; DIVIDENDS.

STOCK-WATERING. The issuing of valueless watered stock does not come in point of morality one whit above the issuing of counterfeit money. The issuing of valueless watered stock I regard as, if possible, an even worse moral offense than the issuing of counterfeit money; and yet you will find that unwise people, when I say this, will assert that I am attacking capital. I am defending capital when I attack watered capital; and while there is great difficulty in going back and correcting all the abuses of the past, yet we ought to make it absolutely impossible that in the future in this country of ours there can be the issuance of counterfeit stocks. *Outlook*, June 8, 1912, p. 295.

[586]

———————. When the stock is watered so that the innocent investors suffer, a grave wrong is indeed done to these innocent investors as well as to the public; but [certain] public men, lawyers, and editors, . . . do not under these circumstances express sympathy for the innocent; on the contrary they are the first to protest with frantic vehemence against our efforts by law to put a stop to over-capitalization and stock-watering. The apologists of successful dishonesty always declaim against any effort to punish or prevent it on the ground that such effort will "unsettle business." It is they who by their acts have unsettled business; and the very men raising this cry spend hundreds of thousands of dollars in securing, by speech, editorial, book or pamphlet, the defense by misstatement of what they have done; and yet when we correct their misstatements by telling the truth, they declaim against us for breaking silence, lest "values be unsettled!" They have hurt honest business men, honest working men, honest farmers; and now they clamor against the truth being told. (1913.) *Mem. Ed.* XXII, 518; *Nat. Ed.* XX, 446.

STRAUS, OSCAR S. I have had from Mr. Straus aid that I can not over-estimate, for which I can not too much express my gratitude, in so much of the diplomatic work that has arisen in this administration—aid by suggestion, aid by actual work in helping me to carry out the suggestions; and Mr. Straus was one of the two or three men who first set my mind, after I came in as President, in the direction of doing everything that could be done for the Hague Tribunal, as that seemed to be the best way to turn for arbitration. (At White House, January 1904.) Oscar S. Straus, *Under Four Administrations from Cleveland to Taft.* (Houghton Mifflin Co., Boston, 1922), p. 178.

STRAUS, OSCAR S. See also CABINET.

STRENGTH. See COURAGE; DECENCY; FIGHTING QUALITIES; MANLY VIRTUES; WEAKNESS.

STRENUOUS LIFE, THE. I preach to you, then, my countrymen, that our country calls not for the life of ease but for the life of strenuous endeavor. The twentieth century looms before us big with the fate of many nations. If we stand idly by, if we seek merely swollen, slothful ease and ignoble peace, if we shrink from the hard contests where men must win at hazard of their lives and at the risk of all they hold dear, then the bolder and stronger peoples will pass us by, and will win for themselves the domination of the world. Let us therefore boldly face the life of strife, resolute to do our duty well and manfully; resolute to uphold righteousness by deed and by word; resolute to be both honest and brave, to serve high ideals, yet to use practical methods. Above all, let us shrink from no strife, moral or physical, within or without the nation, provided we are certain that the strife is justified, for it is only through strife, through hard and dangerous endeavor, that we shall ultimately win the goal of true national greatness. (Before the Hamilton Club, Chicago, April 10, 1899.) *Mem. Ed.* XV, 281; *Nat. Ed.* XIII, 331.

———————. Nothing in this world is worth having or worth doing unless it means effort, pain, difficulty. No kind of life is worth leading if it is always an easy life. . . . I have never in my life envied a human being who led an easy life; I have envied a great many people who led difficult lives and led them well. (Before Iowa State Teachers' Association, Des Moines, November 4, 1910.) *Mem. Ed.* XVIII, 455; *Nat. Ed.* XVI, 340.

———————. I always believe in going hard at everything, whether it is Latin or mathematics, boxing or football, but at the same time I want to keep the sense of proportion. It is never worth while to absolutely exhaust one's self or to take big chances unless for an adequate object. (To Theodore Roosevelt, Jr., May 7, 1901.) *Mem. Ed.* XXI, 479; *Nat. Ed.* XIX, 424.

———————. We are face to face with our destiny and we must meet it with a high and resolute courage. For us is the life of action, of strenuous performance of duty; let us live in the harness, striving mightily; let us rather run the risk of wearing out than rusting out. (Campaign Speech, New York City, October 5, 1898.) *Mem. Ed.* XVI, 442; *Nat. Ed.* XIV, 291.

STRENUOUS LIFE, THE. *See also* DUTY; JOY OF LIVING; LIFE; MANLY VIRTUES; STRIFE; VIGOR; VIRTUES; WORK.

STRIFE—LAW OF. The law of worthy national life, like the law of worthy individual life, is, after all, fundamentally, the law of strife. It may be strife military, it may be strife civic; but certain it is that only through strife, through labor and painful effort, by grim energy and by resolute courage, we move on to better things. (At Republican Club Dinner,

New York City, February 13, 1899.) *Mem. Ed.* XVI, 475; *Nat. Ed.* XIV, 316.

STRIKE, PULLMAN. *See* ALTGELD, JOHN PETER.

STRIKES. A strike is a clumsy weapon for righting wrongs done to labor, and we should extend, so far as possible, the process of conciliation and arbitration as a substitute for strikes. Moreover, violence, disorder, and coercion, when committed in connection with strikes, should be as promptly and as sternly repressed as when committed in any other connection. But strikes themselves are, and should be, recognized to be entirely legal. (Message to Congress, March 25, 1908.) *Presidential Addresses and State Papers* VII, 1684.

STRIKES—MEDIATION OF. Where possible it is always better to mediate before the strike begins than to try to arbitrate when the fight is on and both sides have grown stubborn and bitter. (At Labor Day Picnic, Chicago, September 3, 1900.) *Mem. Ed.* XVI, 515; *Nat. Ed.* XIII, 486.

STRIKES—PUBLIC INTEREST IN. No man and no group of men may so exercise their rights as to deprive the nation of the things which are necessary and vital to the common life. A strike which ties up the coal supplies of a whole section is a strike invested with a public interest. (1913.) *Mem. Ed.* XXII, 540; *Nat. Ed.* XX, 464.

STRIKES IN WAR-TIME. The strike situation in the United States at this time is a scandal to the country as a whole and discreditable alike to employer and employee. Any employer who fails to recognize that human rights come first and that the friendly relationship between himself and those working for him should be one of partnership and comradeship in mutual help no less than self-help is recreant to his duty as an American citizen and it is to his interest, having in view the enormous destruction of life in the present war, to conserve, and to train to higher efficiency alike for his benefit and for its, the labor supply. In return any employee who acts along the lines publicly advocated by the men who profess to speak for the I. W. W. is not merely an open enemy of business but of this entire country and is out of place in our government. (Before Knights of Columbus, New York City, October 12, 1915.) *Mem. Ed.* XX, 462; *Nat. Ed.* XVIII, 397.

STRIKES. *See also* CAPITAL AND LABOR; COAL STRIKE; COLLECTIVE BARGAINING; INDUSTRIAL ARBITRATION; LABOR DISPUTES.

SUBMARINE WARFARE. The news this morning of the sinking of our three ships—*City of Memphis, Vigilancia,* and *Illinois*—with loss of American life, makes it imperative that every self-respecting American should speak out and demand that we hit hard and effectively. Words are wasted on Germany. What we need is effective and thoroughgoing action.

Seven weeks have passed since Germany renewed with the utmost ruthlessness her never wholly abandoned submarine war against neutrals and noncombatants. She then notified our Government of her intention. This notification was itself a declaration of war and should have been treated as such. During the seven weeks that have since elapsed she has steadily waged war upon us. It has been a war of murder upon us; she has killed American women and children as well as American men upon the high seas. She has sunk our ships, our ports have been put under blockade....

Seemingly her submarine warfare has failed and is less menacing now than it was seven weeks ago. We are profiting and shall profit by this failure. But we have done nothing to bring it about. It has been due solely to the efficiency of the British navy. We have done nothing to help ourselves. We have done nothing to secure our own safety or to vindicate our own honor. We have been content to shelter ourselves behind the fleet of a foreign power. (Published statement, March 19, 1917.) *Mem. Ed.* XXIV, 492-493; Bishop II, 419-420.

SUBMARINE WARFARE. *See also* CONTRABAND; GERMANY; *Lusitania;* WORLD WAR.

SUBMARINES. The events of this war have shown that submarines can play a tremendous part. We should develop our force of submarines and train the officers and crews who have charge of them to the highest pitch of efficiency—for they will be useless in time of war unless those aboard them have been trained in time of peace. These submarines, when used in connection with destroyers and with air-ships, can undoubtedly serve to minimize the danger of successful attack on our own shores. (New York *Times,* November 22, 1914.) *Mem. Ed.* XX, 128; *Nat. Ed.* XVIII, 110.

SUCCESS. To judge a man merely by success is an abhorrent wrong; and if the people at large habitually so judge men, if they grow to condone wickedness because the wicked man triumphs, they show their inability to understand that in the last analysis free institutions rest upon the character of citizenship, and that by such admiration of evil they prove themselves unfit for liberty. (At the Sorbonne, Paris, April 23, 1910.) *Mem. Ed.* XV, 363; *Nat. Ed.* XIII, 518.

———————. I think that any man who has had what is regarded in the world as a great success must realize that the element of chance has played a great part in it. Of course a man has to take advantage of his opportunities; but the opportunities have to come. If there is not the war, you don't get the great general; if there is not a great occasion, you don't get the great statesman; if Lincoln had lived in times of peace, no one would have known his name now. The great crisis must come, or no man has the chance to develop great qualities. . . .

Normally the man who makes the great success when the emergency arises is the man who would have made a fair success in any event. I believe that the man who is really happy in a great position—in what we call a career—is the man who would also be happy and regard his life as successful if he had never been thrown into that position. If a man lives a decent life and does his work fairly and squarely so that those dependent on him and attached to him are better for his having lived, then he is a success, and he deserves to feel that he has done his duty and he deserves to be treated by those who have had greater success as nevertheless having shown the fundamental qualities that entitle him to respect. (At the Cambridge Union, Cambridge, Eng., May 26, 1910.) *Mem. Ed.* XV, 508-509; *Nat. Ed.* XIII, 575-576.

———————. There are many forms of success, many forms of triumph. But there is no other success that in any shape or way approaches that which is open to most of the many, many men and women who have the right ideals. These are the men and women who see that it is the intimate and homely things that count most. They are the men and women who have the courage to strive for the happiness which comes only with labor and effort and self-sacrifice, and only to those whose joy in life springs in part from power of work and sense of duty (1913.) *Mem. Ed.* XXII, 394; *Nat. Ed.* XX, 338.

———————. There are two kinds of success, or rather two kinds of ability displayed in the achievement of success. There is, first, the success either in big things or small things which comes to the man who has in him the natural power to do what no one else can do, and what no amount of training, no perseverance or will-power, will enable any ordinary man to do. This success, of course, like every other kind of success, may be on a very big scale or on a small scale. The quality which the man possesses may be that which enables him to run a hundred yards in nine and three-fifths seconds, or to play ten separate games of chess at the same time blindfolded, or to add five columns of figures at once without effort, or to write the "Ode to a Grecian Urn," or to deliver the Gettysburg speech, or to show the ability of Frederick at Leuthen or Nelson at Trafalgar. No amount of training of body or mind would enable any good ordinary man to perform any one of these feats. Of course the proper performance of each implies much previous study or training, but in no one of them is success to be attained save by the altogether exceptional man who has in him the something additional which the ordinary man does not have.

This is the most striking kind of success, and it can be attained only by the man who has in him the quality which separates him in kind no less than in degree from his fellows. But much the commoner type of success in every walk of life and in every species of effort is that which comes to the man who differs from his fellows not by the kind of quality which he possesses but by the degree of development which he has given that quality. This kind of success is open to a large number of persons, if only they seriously determine to achieve it. It is the kind of success which is open to the average man of sound body and fair mind, who has no remarkable mental or physical attributes, but who gets just as much as possible in the way of work out of the aptitudes that he does possess. It is the only kind of success that is open to most of us. Yet some of the greatest successes in history have been those of this second class—when I call it second class I am not running it down in the least, I am merely pointing out that it differs in kind from the first class. To the average man it is probably more useful to study this second type of success than to study the first. From the study of the first he can learn inspiration, he can get uplift and lofty enthusiasm. From the study of the second he can, if he chooses, find out how to win a similar success himself.

I need hardly say that all the successes I have ever won have been of the second type. I never won anything without hard labor and the exercise of my best judgment and careful planning and working long in advance. Having been a rather sickly and awkward boy, I was as a young man at first both nervous and distrustful of my own prowess. I had to train myself painfully and laboriously not merely as regards my body but as regards my soul and spirit. (1913.) *Mem. Ed.* XXII, 62; *Nat. Ed.* XX, 54.

SUCCESS—ATTAINMENT OF. No great success can ever be won save by accepting the fact that, normally, sacrifice of some kind must come in winning the success. (At Occidental College, Los Angeles, Cal., March 22, 1911.) *Mem. Ed.* XV, 513; *Nat. Ed.* XIII, 580.

——————. It has always seemed to me that in life there are two ways of achieving success, or, for the matter of that, of achieving what is commonly called greatness. One is to do that which can only be done by the man of exceptional and extraordinary abilities. Of course this means that only one man can do it, and it is a very rare kind of success or of greatness. The other is to do that which many men could do, but which as a matter of fact none of them actually does. This is the ordinary kind of success or kind of greatness. Nobody but one of the world's rare geniuses could have written the Gettysburg speech, or the Second Inaugural, or met as Lincoln met the awful crises of the Civil War. (To Henry Beach Needham, July 19, 1905.) *Mem. Ed.* XXIII, 513; Bishop I, 446.

SUCCESS—STANDARDS OF. It is a bad thing for a nation to raise and to admire a false standard of success; and there can be no falser standard than that set by the deification of material well-being in and for itself. (At the Sorbonne, Paris, April 23, 1910.) *Mem. Ed.* XV, 360; *Nat. Ed.* XIII, 515.

——————. The acquisition of wealth is not in the least the only test of success. After a certain amount of wealth has been accumulated, the accumulation of more is of very little consequence indeed from the standpoint of success, as success should be understood both by the community and the individual. (*Outlook*, March 31, 1900.) *Mem. Ed.* XV, 498; *Nat. Ed.* XIII, 382.

SUCCESS AND FAILURE. No man can be guaranteed success. Men who are not prepared for labor and effort and rough living, for persistence and self-denial, are out of place in a new country; and foolish people who will probably fail anywhere are more certain to fail badly in a new country than anywhere else. During the whole period of the marvellous growth of the United States there has been a constant and uninterrupted stream of failure going side by side with the larger stream of success. (1916.) *Mem. Ed.* IV, 82; *Nat. Ed.* III, 253.

SUCCESS AND MORALITY. It is inexcusable in an honest people to deify mere success without regard to the qualities by which that success is achieved. Indeed there is a revolting injustice, intolerable to just minds, in punishing the weak scoundrel who fails, and bowing down to and making life easy for the far more dangerous scoundrel who succeeds. (At Northfield, Mass., September 1, 1902.) *Presidential Addresses and State Papers* I, 135.

——————. When we can create the public opinion which will mean that the average honest man turns away from the successful knave, one of the prime incentives for being a successful knave will have vanished. (At Pacific Theological Seminary, Spring 1911.) *Mem. Ed.* XV, 588; *Nat. Ed.* XIII, 626.

——————. If there is one tendency of the day which more than any other is unhealthy and undesirable, it is the tendency to deify mere "smartness," unaccompanied by a sense of moral accountability. We shall never make our Republic what it should be until as a people we thoroughly understand and put in practice the doctrine that success is abhorrent if attained by the sacrifice of the fundamental principles of morality. The successful man, whether in business or in politics, who has risen by conscienceless swindling of his neighbors, by deceit and chicanery, by unscrupulous boldness and unscrupulous cunning, stands toward society as a dangerous wild beast. The mean and cringing admiration which such a career commands among those who think crookedly or not at all makes this kind of success perhaps the most dangerous of all the influences that threaten our national life. (*Century*, June 1900.) *Mem. Ed.* XV, 378; *Nat. Ed.* XIII, 342.

——————. There are very different kinds of success. There is the success that brings with it the seared soul—the success which is achieved by wolfish greed and vulpine cunning —the success which makes honest men uneasy or indignant in its presence. Then there is the other kind of success—the success which comes as the reward of keen insight, of sagacity, of resolution, of address, combined with unflinching rectitude of behavior, public and private. The first kind of success may, in a sense—and a poor sense at that—benefit the individual, but it is always and necessarily a curse to the community; whereas the man who wins the second kind, as an incident of its winning becomes a beneficiary to the whole commonwealth. (At banquet of Chamber of Commerce of the State of New York, New York City, November 11, 1902.) *Presidential Addresses and State Papers* I, 200-201.

SUCCESS. *See also* CHARACTER; DEMOCRACY; FAMILY LIFE; MATERIALIST; REWARDS; WEALTH.

SUFFRAGE. In any purely native American community manhood suffrage works infinitely better than would any other system of government, and throughout our country at large, in spite of the large number of ignorant foreign-born or colored voters, it is probably preferable as it stands to any modification of it; but there is no more "natural right" why a white man over twenty-one should vote than there is why a negro woman under eighteen should not. "Civil rights" and "personal freedom" are not terms that necessarily imply the right to vote. (1887.) *Mem. Ed.* VIII, 180; *Nat. Ed.* VII, 156-157.

———. A vote is like a rifle: its usefulness depends upon the character of the user. The mere possession of the vote will no more benefit men and women not sufficiently developed to use it than the possession of rifles will turn untrained Egyptian fellaheen into soldiers. This is as true of woman as of man —and no more true. Universal suffrage in Hayti has not made the Haytians able to govern themselves in any true sense; and woman suffrage in Utah in no shape or way affected the problem of polygamy. I believe in suffrage for women in America, because I think they are fit for it. I believe for women, as for men, more in the duty of fitting one's self to do well and wisely with the ballot than in the naked right to cast the ballot. (1913.) *Mem. Ed.* XXII, 196; *Nat. Ed.* XX, 168.

———. Universal suffrage should be based on universal service in peace and war; those who refuse to render the one have no title to the enjoyment of the other. We stand for the democracy of service; we are against privilege, and therefore against the privilege which would escape service in war. (1917.) *Mem. Ed.* XXI, 9; *Nat. Ed.* XIX, 8.

SUFFRAGE. *See also* CIVIC DUTY; MILITARY SERVICE; NEGRO SUFFRAGE; VOTING; WOMAN SUFFRAGE.

SUGAR TRUST. *See* TRUSTS.

SUNDAY — OBSERVANCE OF. I never want to see the observance of our American Sunday changed. There is a great deal to condemn in it, possibly, from a foreign standpoint, and a great deal that is narrow, but I believe it is wholesome and strengthening. It is very hard not to be able to shoot, for instance, on Sundays, but then the majority of our people believe it is wrong and I certainly would be the last to try to change their opinions. If I were a private citizen I would possibly join you today in tennis, but were I to do so as President all the papers in the country would have something to say about it and the example might be harmful to many. I am afraid that I sometimes shock the sensibilities of our people, but I never want to do so in any matters pertaining to the morals or the religious prejudices of the people. (Recorded by Butt in letter of July 27, 1908.) *The Letters of Archie Butt. Personal Aide to President Roosevelt.* (Doubleday Page & Co., Garden City, N. Y., 1924), p. 77.

SUNDAY. *See also* CHURCH ATTENDANCE.

SUNDAY LIQUOR LAW. *See* LIQUOR LAW; POLICE COMMISSIONER.

SUNDAY SCHOOL TEACHING. There were many things I tried to do because [my father] did them, which I found afterward were not in my line. For instance, I taught Sunday-school all through college, but afterward gave it up, just as on experiment I could not do the charitable work which he had done. In doing my Sunday-school work I was very much struck by the fact that the other men who did it only possessed one side of his character. My ordinary companions in college would, I think, have had a tendency to look down upon me for doing Sunday-school work if I had not also been a corking boxer, a good runner, and a genial member of the Porcellian Club. (To Edward S. Martin, November 26, 1900.) *Mem. Ed.* XXIII, 6; Bishop I, 3.

———. I am really pleased that you are going to teach Sunday school. I think I told you that I taught it for seven years, most of the time in a mission class, my pupils being of a kind which furnished me plenty of vigorous excitement. (To Ethel Roosevelt, June 11,

1906.) *Mem. Ed.* XXI, 567; *Nat. Ed.* XIX, 509.

SUPERSTITION. There is superstition in science quite as much as there is superstition in theology, and it is all the more dangerous because those suffering from it are profoundly convinced that they are freeing themselves from all superstition. (*Outlook,* December 2, 1911.) *Mem. Ed.* XIV, 418; *Nat. Ed.* XII, 113.

SUPREME COURT. One of the most admirable features of our constitutional system is the high position which it gives to the judiciary. In no other country in the world have the judges possessed or exercised the enormous influence upon the constitutional and institutional growth of society that they have here exercised. This is particularly true of the national judiciary, and therefore of its head, the Supreme Court. It would be hard to overstate the debt due by the American people to the bench, national and State, and hardest of all to overestimate the debt due to the Supreme Court. (*Outlook,* March 4, 1911.) *Mem. Ed.* XIX, 116; *Nat. Ed.* XVII, 79-80.

———. We are now entering on a period when the vast and complex growth of modern industrialism renders it of vital interest to our people that the court should apply the old essential underlying principles of our government to the new and totally different conditions in such fashion that the spirit of the Constitution shall in very fact be preserved and not sacrificed to a narrow construction of the letter. Much of the future of this country depends upon the direction from which the judges of the Supreme Court approach the great Constitutional questions that they will have to decide. It is impossible to overestimate the services which may be rendered on this court by the judge who is really a far-sighted statesman, who has the modern type of mind, who is fully alive to the great governmental needs of the time and to the far-reaching importance which the decisions of the courts may have, and who in dealing with the problems that confront him never forgets that in addition to being a lawyer on the bench he is also an American citizen in a place of the highest responsibility who owes a great duty not only to the people of this country to-day, but to the people of this country to-morrow. (*Outlook,* November 5, 1910.) *Mem. Ed.* XII, 534; *Nat. Ed.* XI, 262.

———. Marshall performed a great and needed service, one of the greatest services any statesman ever performed, when in a period of national weakness he put the Supreme Court behind the national ideal. But such a practice as he inaugurated could be maintained permanently only if it was exercised with the greatest moderation. For over half a century it was thus exercised. But under the strain of what I must call class pressure—the pressure of the privileged classes—this power has during the last fifty years come to be exercised in utterly reckless fashion. The result has been in a lamentably large number of cases to make the courts the bulwarks of special privilege against justice. Against this misconception and perversion of our Constitution the organization of the Progressive party is the protest of the American people. (At New York City, February 12, 1913.) *Mem. Ed.* XIX, 504; *Nat. Ed.* XVII, 375.

SUPREME COURT — JUSTICES OF. In the ordinary and low sense which we attach to the words "partisan" and "politician," a judge of the Supreme Court should be neither. But in the higher sense, in the proper sense, he is not in my judgment fitted for the position unless he is a party man, a constructive statesman, constantly keeping in mind his adherence to the principles and policies under which this nation has been built up and in accordance with which it must go on; and keeping in mind also his relations with his fellow statesmen who in other branches of the government are striving in cooperation with him to advance the ends of government. (To H. C. Lodge, July 10, 1902.) Lodge *Letters* I, 518.

———. The judges of the Supreme Court of the land must be not only great jurists, but they must be great constructive statesmen. And the truth of what I say is illustrated by every study of American statesmanship, for in not one serious study of American political life will it be possible to omit the immense part played by the Supreme Court in the creation, not merely the modification, of the great policies through and by means of which the country has moved on to its present position. (At banquet to Justice Harlan, Washington, D. C., December 9, 1902.) *Presidential Addresses and State Papers* I, 221.

———. All sober and serious statesmen and publicists, and all leaders of the people, when they deal with the Supreme Court, should remember not only the incalculable service it rendered under Marshall, but the menace it was to the nation under Taney, and the way in which it then forced Abraham Lincoln and

[592]

all far-seeing patriots to antagonize it. There is no reason for supposing that Marshall and Taney differed in ability as lawyers or in sincerity and loftiness of private character. But one was a great, far-seeing statesman who builded for the future, the other was a man who clung to outworn theories, . . . and who in consequence worked for the detriment of the country as surely as if it had been his conscious purpose so to do. (*Outlook,* November 5, 1910.) *Mem. Ed.* XII, 534; *Nat. Ed.* XI, 261.

——————. Taney was probably as good a lawyer as Marshall; the abysmal difference between the two men came because one was a statesman and the other was not. We now need on the Supreme Court not better lawyers, but broad-minded, far-seeing statesmen, utterly out of sympathy with higgling technicalities. (To H. C. Lodge, April 11, 1910.) Lodge *Letters* II, 374.

——————. The office of chief justice is, under some circumstances, as great an office as that of President, and at all times comes second only to it in importance. And the man who fills that office is, like the President, the representative of all the people, and is entitled to their respect and support. (*Outlook,* March 4, 1911.) *Mem. Ed.* XIX, 117; *Nat. Ed.* XVII, 80.

SUPREME COURT—POWER OF. Under our form of government no other body of men occupy a position of such far-reaching importance as the justices of the Supreme Court. Neither the executive nor the legislative branch of the government, under ordinary conditions, does as much in shaping our Constitutional growth as the Supreme Court. This is not true of any other country. In every other country the judges, though they exercise a great and decisive influence in civil contests between individuals, have little or no power to shape the governmental course of development—that is, the course of national development, the course of affairs that affect the people not individually but as a whole. In our country, however, a number of causes which were not in evidence during the first decade after the establishment of the Constitution have combined to render the Supreme Court in many ways the most important governmental body in the land, and to give it a position which places it infinitely above any other court in the entire world. (*Outlook,* November 5, 1910.) *Mem. Ed.* XII, 531; *Nat. Ed.* XI, 259.

——————. It is contended that in these recent decisions the Supreme Court legislated; so it did; and it had to; because Congress had signally failed to do *its* duty by legislating. For the Supreme Court to nullify an act of the Legislature as unconstitutional except on the clearest ground is usurpation; to interpret such an act in an obviously wrong sense is usurpation; but where the legislative body persistently leaves open a field which it is absolutely imperative from the public standpoint to fill, then no possible blame attaches to the official or officials who step in because they have to, and who then do the needed work in the interest of the people. The blame in such cases lies with the body which has been derelict, and not with the body which reluctantly makes good the dereliction. *Outlook,* November 18, 1911, p. 653.

SUPREME COURT. See also CONSTITUTION; COURTS; DIVISION OF POWERS; JUDGES; JUDICIARY; LAW; LEGALISM; MARSHALL, JOHN; MOODY, W. H.; WILSON, JAMES.

SURVEYORS. See WESTERN EXPLORERS.

SURVIVAL OF SPECIES. See ANIMALS.

SWEATSHOPS. See LABOR CONDITIONS.

SWEDEN. See SOCIALISM.

SWITZERLAND. See MILITARY TRAINING; PREPAREDNESS.

SYMPATHY. See FELLOW-FEELING; FELLOWSHIP.

T

TABLE MANNERS. See SOCIAL CONVENTIONS.

TAFT, WILLIAM H. I think that of all men in the country Taft is the best fitted at this time to be President and to carry on the work upon which we have entered during the past six years. (To Lyman Abbott, May 29, 1908.) *Mem. Ed.* XXIV, 101; Bishop II, 86.

——————. To a flaming hatred of injustice, to a scorn of all that is base and mean, to a hearty sympathy with the oppressed, he unites entire disinterestedness, courage both moral and physical of the very highest type, and a kindly generosity of nature which makes him feel that all of his fellow-countrymen are in very truth his friends and brothers, that their interests are his, and that all his great qualities are to be spent with lavish freedom in their service. The honest man of means, the honest and law-abiding business man, can feel safe in his hands because of the very fact that the dishonest man of great wealth, the man who swindles or robs his fellows, would not so much as dare to defend his evil-doing in Mr. Taft's presence. The honest wage-worker, the honest laboring man, the honest farmer, the honest mechanic or small trader, or man of small means, can feel that in a peculiar sense Mr. Taft will be his representative because of the very fact that he has the same scorn for the demagogue that he has for the corruptionist, and that he would front threats of personal violence from a mob with the unquailing and lofty indifference with which he would front the bitter anger of the wealthiest and most powerful corporations. Broad though his sympathies are, there is in him not the slightest tinge of weakness. No consideration of personal interest, any more than of fear for his personal safety, could make him swerve a hair's breadth from the course which he regards as right and in the interest of the whole people. (To Conrad Kohrs, September 9, 1908.) *Presidential Addresses and State Papers* VII, 1783-1784.

───────────. You know, Archie, that I think he has the most lovable personality I have ever come in contact with. He is going to be greatly beloved as President. I almost envy a man possessing a personality like Taft's. People are always prepossessed by it. One loves him at first sight. He has nothing to overcome when he meets people. I realize that I have always got to overcome a little something before I get to the heart of people. (Recorded by Butt in letter of December 10, 1908.) *The Letters of Archie Butt. Personal Aide to President Roosevelt.* (Doubleday, Page & Co., Garden City, N. Y., 1924), p. 232-233.

───────────. Taft is utterly hopeless. I think he would be beaten if nominated, but in any event it would be a misfortune to have him in the Presidential chair for another term, for he has shown himself an entirely unfit President, and he merely discredits the Republican Party, and therefore discredits those of us who believe that, with the Democratic Party as it is now constituted, the Republican Party offers the only instrument through which to secure really sane, progressive government.

(To Joseph Bucklin Bishop, December 29, 1911.) *Mem. Ed.* XXIV, 367; Bishop II, 313.

───────────. Mr. Taft's position is the position that has been held from the beginning of our government, although not always so openly held, by a large number of reputable and honorable men who, down at bottom, distrust popular government, and, when they must accept it, accept it with reluctance, and hedge it around with every species of restriction and check and balance, so as to make the power of the people as limited and as ineffective as possible.

Mr. Taft fairly defines the issue when he says that our government is and should be a government of all the people by a representative part of the people. This is an excellent and moderate description of an oligarchy. It defines our government as a government of all the people by a few of the people. (At Carnegie Hall, New York City, March 20, 1912.) *Mem. Ed.* XIX, 208; *Nat. Ed.* XVII, 158.

───────────. Taft, second only to Wilson and Bryan, is the most distinguished exponent of what is worst in our political character at the present day as regards international affairs; and a universal peace league meeting which has him as its most prominent leader is found on the whole to do mischief and not good. (To Owen Wister, June 23, 1915.) *Mem. Ed.* XXIV, 453; Bishop II, 385.

───────────. I am awfully sorry, old man, but after faithful effort for a month to try to arrange matters on the basis you wanted I find that I shall have to bring you home and put you on the Supreme Court. I am very sorry. I have the greatest confidence in your judgment; but after all, old fellow, if you will permit me to say so, I am President and see the whole field. The responsibility for any error must ultimately come upon me, and therefore I cannot shirk this responsibility or in the last resort yield to anyone else's decision if my judgment is against it. . . . I am very sorry if what I am doing displeases you, but as I said, old man, this is one of the cases where the President, if he is fit for his position, must take the responsibility and put the men on whom he most relies in the particular positions in which he himself thinks they can render the greatest public good. (To Taft, January 6, 1903.) Henry F. Pringle, *The Life and Times of William Howard Taft.* (Farrar & Rinehart, N. Y., 1939), I, 244.

———————. You could do very much if you were on the bench; you could do very much if you were in active political life outside. I think you could do most as President, but you could do very much as Chief Justice, and you could do less, but still very much, as Associate Justice. Where you can fight best I cannot say, for you know what your soul turns to better than I can.

As I see the situation, it is this: There are strong arguments against your taking this justiceship. In the first place, my belief is that of all the men who have appeared so far you are the man who is most likely to receive the Republican nomination, and who is, I think, the best man to receive it. It is not a light thing to cast aside the chance of the Presidency, even though, of course, it is a chance, however, a good one. (To William H. Taft, March 15, 1906.) *Mem. Ed.* XXIV, 118; Bishop II, 101.

TAFT, WILLIAM H.—BELIEF IN. Taft will carry on the work substantially as I have carried it on. His policies, principles, purposes and ideals are the same as mine and he is a strong, forceful, efficient man, absolutely upright, absolutely disinterested and fearless. In leaving, I have the profound satisfaction of knowing that he will do all in his power to further every one of the great causes for which I have fought and that he will persevere in every one of the great governmental policies in which I most firmly believe. Therefore nothing whatever is lost by my having refused to run for a third term, and much is gained. (To Sir George Otto Trevelyan, November 6, 1908.) *Mem. Ed.* XXIV, 145; Bishop II, 124.

TAFT, WILLIAM H. — NOMINATION OF. Taft was nominated solely on my assurance to the Western people especially, but almost as much to the people of the East, that he would carry out my work unbroken; not (as he has done) merely working for somewhat the same objects in a totally different spirit, and with a totally different result, but exactly along my lines with all his heart and strength. Of course you know that among my heartiest supporters, especially in the West, and, curiously enough, also in the Eastern states like New York and New Jersey, there has been any amount of criticism of me because I got them to take a man on my word who they now find understood his own promise in a totally different sense from that in which both I and the men who acted on my word understood it. There is only a little harsh criticism either of my sincerity or of his, but there is a very widespread feeling that, quite unintentionally, I have deceived them, and that however much they may still believe in my professions when I say what I myself will do, they do not intend again to accept any statements of mine as to what anyone else will do. (To H. C. Lodge, April 11, 1910.) Lodge *Letters* II, 369.

TAFT ADMINISTRATION. The great interests . . . were responsible for the President's abandoning the Country Life and Conservation Commissions, which had cost the government nothing, and had rendered invaluable service to the country; and they also cordially approved the nomination of Mr. Ballinger to the position of secretary of the interior. For two years the Administration did everything in its power to undo the most valuable work that had been done in conservation, especially in securing to the people the right to regulate water-power franchise in the public interest. This effort became so flagrant, and the criticism so universal, that it was finally abandoned even by the Administration itself. As for the efforts to secure social justice in industrial matters, by securing child-labor legislation, for instance, the Administration simply abandoned them completely.

Alike in its action and in its inaction the conduct of the Administration during the last three years has been such as to merit the support and approval of Messrs. Aldrich, Gallinger, Penrose, Lorimer, Cox, Guggenheim, and the other gentlemen I have mentioned. I do not wonder that they support it; but I do not regard an administration which has merited and which receives such support as being entitled to call itself Progressive, no matter with what elasticity the word may be stretched. No men have been closer or more interested students of the career of President Taft than these men, no men better understand its real significance, no men better appreciate what the effect of the continuance of this Administration for another four years would mean. I believe that their judgment upon the Administration and upon what its continuance would mean to the people can be accepted; and I think that their judgment, as shown by the extreme recklessness of their actions in trying to secure the President's renomination, gives us an accurate gauge as to what the Administration merits from the people and what the action of the people should be. (At Louisville, Ky., April 3, 1912.) *Mem. Ed.* XIX, 247; *Nat. Ed.* XVII, 183.

TAFT AND ROOSEVELT. For a year after Taft took office, for a year and a quarter after he had been elected, I would not let myself think ill of anything he did. I finally had to admit that he had gone wrong on certain points; and I then also had to admit to myself that deep down underneath I had all along known he was wrong, on points as to which I had tried to deceive myself, by loudly proclaiming to myself, that he was right. I went out of the country and gave him the fullest possible chance to work out his own salvation. (To H. C. Lodge, May 5, 1910.) Lodge *Letters* II, 380.

——————. As far as my personal inclinations were concerned, my personal pleasure and comfort, I should infinitely have preferred to keep wholly out of politics. I need hardly say that I never made a speech or took an action save in response to the earnest and repeated requests of men many of whom I well knew, in spite of their anxiety to use me at the moment, were exceedingly anxious to limit that use before elections with the understanding that I should have no say afterward.

I have on every occasion this year praised everything I conscientiously could of both Taft and the Congress, and I have never said a word in condemnation of either, strongly though I have felt. Very possibly circumstances will be such that I shall support Taft for the Presidency next time; but this is not a point now necessary for decision, and if I do support him it will be under no illusion and simply as being the best thing that the conditions permit. (To Elihu Root, October 21, 1910.) *Mem. Ed.* XXIV, 359; Bishop II, 305.

——————. I faced a situation where there was no "best course," it was merely a choice between courses, all of them unsatisfactory. I think I took the only course that was right, and the only course that I could have taken without loss of self-respect. I told the exact truth as I saw it. I praised Taft for every action of his as to which I could conscientiously praise him. Where I could not praise him, or disapproved of what he had done, I kept silent. I was opposed by the lunatic Insurgents of all grades, receiving very lukewarm support, I am sorry to say, from those who were not contented with anything short of denunciation of Taft, and who have no conception of the difference in difficulty between tearing down and building up. On the other hand, the reactionaries, the representatives of the special interests and all those whom they control, literally went insane in their opposition.

(To Joseph Bucklin Bishop, November 21, 1910.) *Mem. Ed.* XXIV, 360; Bishop II, 306.

——————. The break in our relations was due to no one thing, but to the cumulative effect of many things—the abandonment of everything my Administration had stood for, and other things.

Taft changed greatly between the time he was elected and the time he took office.

The first friction came in the matter of his Cabinet. . . .

After he was elected he came to me and told me he wished to retain my Cabinet and would like to have me tell the members so. I realized at once that this was a rather delicate matter, believing he might and probably would change his mind later; that his wishes in November might not be his wishes in March; and I asked him if he really desired the message delivered. . . .

He agreed that he would wish new men in some posts, but he insisted that he wanted the others to stay, and on his definite insistence I delivered the message. More than that, those thus assured thanked Taft for the offer in my presence. . . .

By inauguration time, however, Mr. Taft had changed his mind, just as I had feared he would, and it made a great deal of feeling. Some had made very definite plans on the strength of his offer, renewing leases of houses and that sort of thing, and it was bad all around.

That was the first bit of friction—the beginning.

In office, his militancy evaporated and he at once set about undoing all my Administration had done. Conservation went by the board, Newell of the Reclamation Service had to quit, and things went from bad to worse. They had reached such a pass that, when I got to Rome on my way home from Africa, I found Gifford Pinchot awaiting me. He wanted me to attack Taft then and there. Others were in the same mood. . . .

Thus things went, one thing after another, until finally the Rural Welfare Commission, one of the best things we had, was abandoned. That was the last straw. The break came on that, but it was not because of that. It was because of the many things of which that was the capstone, the climax. (April 8, 1916; reported by Leary.) *Talks with T. R.* From the diaries of John J. Leary, Jr. (Houghton Mifflin Co., Boston, 1920), pp. 25-27.

TAFT AND THE PROGRESSIVES. Four years ago the Progressives supported Mr. Taft for President, and he was opposed by such representatives of special privilege as Mr. Penrose, of Pennsylvania, Mr. Aldrich, of Rhode Island, Mr. Gallinger, of New Hampshire, and Messrs. Lorimer, Cannon, and McKinley, of Illinois, and he was opposed by practically all the men of the stamp of Messrs. Guggenheim and Evans in Colorado, Mr. Cox in Ohio, and Mr. Patrick Calhoun, of San Francisco. These men were not Progressives then and they do not pretend to be Progressives now. But unlike the President, they know who is a Progressive and who is not. They know that he is not a Progressive. Their judgment in this matter is good. After three and a half years of association with and knowledge of the President, these and their fellows are now the President's chief supporters; and they and the men who feel and act as they do in business and in politics, give him the great bulk of his strength. The President says that he is a Progressive. These men know him well, and have studied his actions for three years, and they regard him as being precisely the kind of Progressive whom they approve; that is, as not a Progressive at all. (At Louisville, Ky., April 3, 1912.) *Mem. Ed.* XIX, 245; *Nat. Ed.* XVII, 181.

TAFT AS PRESIDENT. I have not asked Mr. Taft to retain a single man; no Cabinet officer, nobody in any position; in the cases of a very few small men in different States who had been devoted adherents of his for the nomination I have informed him of the fact, and I have given him full information about a number of men in office concerning whom he asked me, and as to one or two in response to questions of his, I have told him positions in which I thought they would do well or which I thought they would like. But I have volunteered no information and said nothing to him unless he has asked me to say it; except that as regards one representative at a foreign court whom I had appointed I told him certain facts which I felt I ought to, as they were not to the representative's credit. (Letter of January 31, 1909.) *Mem. Ed.* XXIV, 150; Bishop II, 128.

————————. I don't want you to think that I have the slightest feeling of personal chagrin about Taft. The Presidency of the United States, the success of the Republican Party, above all the welfare of the country—matters like these cannot possibly be considered from any standpoint but that of the broadest public interest. I am sincere when I say that I am not yet sure whether Taft could with wisdom have followed any course save the one he did. The qualities shown by a thoroughly able and trustworthy lieutenant are totally different, or at least may be totally different, from those needed by the leader, the commander. Very possibly if Taft had tried to work in my spirit, along my lines, he would have failed; that he has conscientiously tried to work for the objects I had in view, so far as he could approve them, I have no doubt. I wish, in my own mind, and to you, to give Taft the benefit of every doubt, and to think and say the very utmost that can be said and thought in his favor. Probably the only course open was not to do as he originally told me before the nomination he intended to do, and as he even sometimes said he intended to do between nomination and election, but to do as he actually has done. Moreover, it seems to me, there is at least a good chance that a reaction will come in his favor. Everyone believes him to be honest, and most believe him to be doing the best he knows how. I have noticed very little real personal abuse of him, or indeed attack upon him. Such being the case, it is entirely possible that there will be a revulsion of feeling in his favor, a revulsion of feeling which may put him all right not only as the head of the party but as able to make the party continue in control of the country. (To H. C. Lodge, April 11, 1910.) Lodge *Letters* II, 367.

TAFT, WILLIAM H. *See also* ELECTION OF 1908; ELECTION OF 1912.

TAMMANY HALL. Tammany Hall has contracts to give out and contracts to interfere with. Every man who has risen to prominence in Tammany Hall has risen by combining business and politics, and you all know that; even by combining the very worst kind of business with the very worst kind of politics; by combining a system of blackmail of those who cannot resist, with mutual payment and repayment of favors in connection with the great and the powerful. The bosses of Tammany Hall appeal to hope of reward and fear of punishment, and especially do they do that now when they have a certain element of Wall Street, the crooked element, as contrasted with the honest element of the business world, with them. (At Binghamton, N. Y., October 24, 1910.) *Mem. Ed.* XIX, 59; *Nat. Ed.* XVII, 39.

TAMMANY HALL AND THE IRISH. Tammany looked upon all races of mankind with a broad and genial tolerance, provided only that they came up (or rather down) to its standard. If a man had political influence behind him, he would be appointed, no matter whether he was a native American, a German, or a Jew, just as quickly as if he were an Irishman. The reason that the Irish so overwhelmingly predominated was because their race furnished the great mass of active political workers of the party. (*Munsey's,* June 1897.) *Mem. Ed.* XVI, 321-322; *Nat. Ed.* XIV, 227.

TAMMANY HALL. *See also* SALOON.

TANEY, ROGER B. *See* SUPREME COURT.

TARIFF, PROTECTIVE. Free-traders are apt to look at the tariff from a sentimental standpoint; but it is in reality purely a business matter, and should be decided solely on grounds of expediency. Political economists have pretty generally agreed that protection is vicious in theory and harmful in practice; but if the majority of the people in interest wish it, and it affects only themselves, there is no earthly reason why they should not be allowed to try the experiment to their hearts' content. The trouble is that it rarely does affect only themselves. (1887.) *Mem. Ed.* VIII, 51; *Nat. Ed.* VII, 44.

——————. I expect to say on the tariff simply that we believe in protection, but of course hold ourselves at liberty to revise any particular schedule when it is shown that that schedule is wrong and it is possible to revise it without interfering with other schedules; and that we will undertake a general revision of the tariff whenever it becomes evident to the American people as a whole that the damage thereby done will be offset by the advantage gained. (To H. C. Lodge, August 9, 1906.) Lodge *Letters* II, 225.

——————. I believe in a protective tariff, but I believe in it as a principle, approached from the standpoint of the interests of the whole people, and not as a bundle of preferences to be given to favored individuals. In my opinion, the American people favor the principle of a protective tariff, but they desire such a tariff to be established primarily in the interests of the wage-worker and the consumer. The chief opposition to our tariff at the present moment comes from the general conviction that certain interests have been improperly favored by over-protection. I agree with this view. The commercial and industrial experience of this country has demonstrated the wisdom of the protective policy, but it has also demonstrated that in the application of that policy certain clearly recognized abuses have developed. (Before Progressive National Convention, Chicago, August 6, 1912.) *Mem. Ed.* XIX, 393; *Nat. Ed.* XVII, 283.

——————. I believe that this country is fully committed to the principle of protection; but it is to protection as a principle; to protection primarily in the interest of the standard of living of the American working-man. I believe that when protection becomes, not a principle, but a privilege and a preference —or, rather, a jumble of privileges and preferences—then the American people disapprove of it. . . . What we want is what I have already said—a square deal in the tariff as in everything else; a square deal for the wage earner, a square deal for the employer, and a square deal for the general public. To obtain it, we must have a thoroughly efficient and well-equipped tariff commission. The tariff ought to be a material issue, and not a moral issue; but if, instead of a square deal, we get a crooked deal, then it becomes very emphatically a moral issue. *Outlook,* January 28, 1911, p. 237.

TARIFF, PROTECTIVE — CONSTITUTIONALITY OF. The Baltimore platform . . . first declares that protective duties are unconstitutional. If the Democratic party is sincere in this belief, then it is necessarily committed to a construction of the Constitution which would gravely impair the powers which the government has employed time and time again for industrial and social betterment. If it is unconstitutional to impose protective duties for the sake of helping wage-workers, then it is unconstitutional to lay an inheritance tax or an income tax for the purpose of equalizing burdens and securing a better distribution of wealth; then it is unconstitutional to collect a corporation tax levied with the incidental purpose of securing publicity regarding corporation and trust methods; then the State bank tax, imposed for the purpose of regulating the issuance of currency, was and still is unconstitutional; then it would be unconstitutional to enact any kind of workmen's insurance law that would levy a tax for the purpose of creating a fund out of which wage-earners would receive insurance; it would be unconstitutional to use the taxing power of the government in any form for the purpose of improving social conditions and promoting economic efficiency. There can be legitimate discussion as to the extent to which the principle of protection should be applied, and, in my judgment, it should be applied for totally different purposes than those for which it has been applied for the last three years. But it is quite impossible to declare the principle of protection itself as unconstitutional unless the Constitution is interpreted in a way that would at once reduce us to impotence in dealing with nine-tenths of the serious social and industrial problems which now confront us. Nor is this all. If the Democrats are sincere in what they say about protection, if they really believe it to be unconstitutional, it is out of the question for any protective duty to be left for more than a very short period on the statute-books. If the tariff is really to be made a tariff for revenue only, then every species of protection must be removed from the American farmer and the American laboring man no less than from the American manufacturer, and duties must be imposed on such articles as tea and coffee. (*Outlook,* July 27, 1912.) *Mem. Ed.* XIX, 351; *Nat. Ed.* XVII, 248.

TARIFF, PROTECTIVE — OPERATION OF. Whether a protective tariff is right or wrong may be open to question; but if it exists at all, it should work as simply and with as much certainty and exactitude as possible; if its interpretation varies, or if it is continually meddled with by Congress, great damage ensues. It is in reality of far less importance that a law should be ideally right than that it should be certain and steady in its workings. Even supposing that a high tariff is all wrong, it would work infinitely better for the country than would a series of changes between high and low duties. (1887.) *Mem. Ed.* VIII, 166; *Nat. Ed.* VII, 144.

TARIFF, PROTECTIVE—RESULTS OF. It is a matter of regret that the protective-tariff policy, which, during the last forty-odd years, has become part of the very fibre of the country, is not now accepted as definitely established. Surely we have a right to say that it has passed beyond the domain of theory, and a right to expect that not only its original advocates but those who at one time distrusted it on theoretic grounds should now acquiesce in the results that have been proved over and over again by actual experience. These forty-odd years have been the most prosperous years this Nation has ever seen; more prosperous years than any other nation has ever seen. Beyond question this prosperity could not have come if the American people had not possessed the necessary thrift, energy, and business intelligence to turn their vast material resources to account. But it is no less true that it is our economic policy as regards the tariff and finance which has enabled us as a nation to make such good use of the individual capacities of our citizens, and the natural resources of our country. Every class of our people is benefited by the protective tariff. (Letter accepting Republican nomination for President, September 12, 1904.) *Mem. Ed.* XVIII, 521; *Nat. Ed.* XVI, 391.

TARIFF AND TRUSTS. The only relation of the tariff to big corporations as a whole is that the tariff makes manufactures profitable, and the tariff remedy proposed would be in effect simply to make manufactures unprofitable. To remove the tariff as a punitive measure directed against trusts would inevitably result in ruin to the weaker competitors who are struggling against them. Our aim should be not by unwise tariff changes to give foreign products the advantage over domestic products, but by proper regulation to give domestic competition a fair chance; and this end cannot be reached by any tariff changes which would affect unfavorably all domestic competitors, good and bad alike. (Second Annual Message, Washington, December 2, 1902.) *Mem. Ed.* XVII, 167; *Nat. Ed.* XV, 144.

TARIFF AND WAGES. I can put my position on the tariff in a nutshell. I believe in such measure of protection as will equalize the cost of production here and abroad: that is, will equalize the cost of labor here and abroad. I believe in such supervision of the workings of the law as to make it certain that protection is given to the man we are most anxious to protect—the laboring man. *Outlook,* January 28, 1911, p. 236.

————. There is urgent need of nonpartisan expert examination into any tariff schedule which seems to increase the cost of living, and, unless the increase thus caused is more than countervailed by the benefit to the class of the community which actually receives the protection, it must of course mean that that particular duty must be reduced. The system of levying a tariff for the protection and encouragement of American industry so as to secure higher wages and better conditions of life for American laborers must never be perverted so as to operate for the impoverishment of those whom it was intended to benefit. But, in any event, the effect of the tariff on the cost of living is slight; any householder can satisfy himself of this fact by considering the increase in price of articles, like milk and eggs, where the influence of both the tariff and the trusts is negligible. No conditions have been shown which warrant us in believing that the abolition of the protective tariff as a whole would bring any substantial benefit to the consumer, while it would certainly cause unheard-of immediate disaster to all wage-workers, all business men, and all farmers, and in all probability would permanently lower the standard of living here. In order to show the utter futility of the belief that the abolition of the tariff and the establishment of free trade would remedy the condition complained of, all that is necessary is to look at the course of industrial events in England and in Germany during the last thirty years, the former under free trade, the latter under a protective system. During these thirty years it is a matter of common knowledge that Germany has forged ahead relatively to England, and this not only as regards the employers, but as regards the wage-earners—in short, as regards all members of the industrial classes. Doubtless, many causes have combined to produce this result; it is not to be ascribed to the tariff alone, but, on the other hand, it is evident that it could not have come about if a protective tariff were even a chief cause among many other causes of the high cost of living. (Before Progressive National Convention, Chicago, August 6, 1912.) *Mem. Ed.* XIX, 399-400; *Nat. Ed.* XVII, 289-290.

TARIFF COMMISSION. Events have shown that the methods hitherto obtaining for generations in tariff-making no longer produce satisfactory results, and that we must have a tariff commission of impartial, disinterested, independent experts, who shall report on each schedule by itself so that action can be taken on the schedule by itself without the inevitable log-rolling and general business disturbance which necessarily accompany any attempt at general tariff revision. *Outlook,* January 28, 1911, p. 146.

──────────. The time has come when all genuine Progressives should insist upon a thorough and radical change in the method of tariff-making.

The first step should be the creation of a permanent commission of non-partisan experts whose business shall be to study scientifically all phases of tariff-making and of tariff effects. This commission should be large enough to cover all the different and widely varying branches of American industry. It should have ample powers to enable it to secure exact and reliable information. It should have authority to examine closely all correlated subjects, such as the effect of any given duty on the consumers of the article on which the duty is levied; that is, it should directly consider the question as to what any duty costs the people in the price of living. It should examine into the wages and conditions of labor and life of the workmen in any industry so as to insure our refusing protection to any industry unless the showing as regards the share labor receives therefrom is satisfactory. This commission would be wholly different from the present unsatisfactory Tariff Board, which was created under a provision of law which failed to give it the powers indispensable if it was to do the work it should do. . . .

The reports of a permanent, expert, and non-partisan tariff commission would at once strike a most powerful blow against the chief iniquity of the old log-rolling method of tariff-making. One of the principal difficulties with the old method has been that it was impossible for the public generally, and especially for those members of Congress not directly connected with the committees handling a tariff bill, to secure anything like adequate and impartial information on the particular subjects under consideration.

The reports of such a tariff commission would at once correct this evil and furnish to the general public full, complete, and disinterested information on every subject treated in a tariff bill. With such reports it would no longer be possible to construct a tariff bill in secret or to jam it through either House of Congress without the fullest and most illuminating discussion. The path of the tariff "joker" would be rendered infinitely difficult. (Before Progressive National Convention, Chicago, August 6, 1912.) *Mem. Ed.* XIX, 394; *Nat. Ed.* XVII, 285.

TARIFF ISSUE. For years the tariff has been the red herring drawn across the trail of social reform alike by the free-traders and the protectionists, both of whom object to all real social and industrial reform. Today the tariff is the false scent designed to delay efficient steps for social and industrial progress along the lines indicated in the Progressive platform. This is precisely what is done by the ultra-protectionist on the other side, who endeavors to persuade us that the protective tariff by itself will solve all of our industrial problems. One contention is just as absurd as the other. But of all beliefs, both ludicrous and pathetic, there is none more ludicrous and pathetic than the belief that with the advent of the angel of free trade, clad in a garment of untaxed calico, the millennium will be brought about. Free trade would not in the slightest degree change the conditions that now call for the social and industrial reforms advocated by the Progressive party. *Saturday Evening Post,* October 26, 1912, p. 4.

───────────. The Republican proposal is a tariff for privilege; the Democratic proposal is a tariff for destruction; the Progressive proposal is a tariff for labor, a tariff which shall give to the American business man his fair show, both permitting and requiring him to pay the American laborer the wages necessary to keep up the standard of living in this country. (At San Francisco, September 14, 1912.) *Mem. Ed.* XIX, 428; *Nat. Ed.* XVII, 314.

───────────. As regard the tariff, both the Republicans and the Democrats propose to cling to the old, vicious methods of tariff-making, the Republicans continuing the policy of protection for special privilege and the Democrats proposing in one breath to introduce free trade and in the next asserting that they will work no disturbance of business—which is about like asserting an intention to burn down a house without causing any disturbance to the inmates or the furniture. We propose to reduce all excessive duties while maintaining the principle of protection through the action of a tariff commission like that which in actual practice has worked so admirably in Germany. (At Oyster Bay, N. Y., November 2, 1912.) *Mem. Ed.* XIX, 471; *Nat. Ed.* XVII, 347.

TARIFF ISSUE—DEMOCRATIC STAND ON. If the Democratic platform is sincere when it says that the legislation it advocates is not to injure any legitimate industry, then it is simply advocating what the Republican platform advocates, doubtless with equal insincerity, when that platform says that it wishes to reduce excessive rates, and, using the language which the Democratic platform a few days later copied, to do so "without injury to any American industry." If, on the other hand, it is true that our present system does make the rich richer and the poor poorer, and if it is unconstitutional to have anything except a revenue tariff, then it is out of the question to alter the situation except by legislation that will destroy the present industries. The two pledges made about the tariff in the Democratic platform are mutually exclusive. One can not be kept without repudiating the other. As a matter of fact, if the Democratic party came into power, it would doubtless break both pledges; it would not abolish all protective duties, but it would act with sufficient unwisdom about them to cause nation-wide disaster. (*Outlook,* July 27, 1912.) *Mem. Ed.* XIX, 353; *Nat. Ed.* XVII, 250.

───────────. The Democratic platform declares for a tariff for revenue only, asserting that a protective tariff is unconstitutional. To say that a protective tariff is unconstitutional, as the Democratic platform insists, is only excusable on a theory of the Constitution which would make it unconstitutional to legislate in any shape or way for the betterment of social and industrial conditions. The abolition of the protective tariff or the substitution for it of a tariff for revenue only, as proposed by the Democratic platform, would plunge this country into the most wide-spread industrial depression we have yet seen, and this depression would continue for an indefinite period. There is no hope from the standpoint of our people from action such as the Democrats propose. The one and only chance to secure stable and favorable business conditions in this country, while at the same time guaranteeing fair play to farmer, consumer, business man, and wage-worker, lies in the creation of such a commission as I herein advocate. Only by such a commission and only by such activities of the commission will it be possible for us to get a reasonably quick revision of the tariff schedule by schedule—revision which shall be downward and not upward, and at the same time secure a square deal not merely to the manufacturer, but to the wage-worker and to the general consumer. (Before Progressive National Convention, Chicago, August 6, 1912.) *Mem. Ed.* XIX, 396; *Nat. Ed.* XVII, 286.

TARIFF ISSUE—NATURE OF. Much the most serious argument advanced against a policy of high tariff is that it puts a premium upon the sacrifice of the general welfare to the selfish interests of particular individuals and particular businesses or localities, and the most forceful plea advanced for a policy of low tariff is that it does away with this scramble of greedy and conflicting interests. (*Century,* November 1895.) *Mem. Ed.* XVI, 338; *Nat. Ed.* XIV, 240.

───────────. The question of what tariff is best for our people is primarily one of expediency, to be determined not on abstract academic grounds, but in the light of experience. It is a matter of business; for fundamentally ours is a business people—manufacturers, merchants, farmers, wage-workers, professional men, all alike. Our experience as a people in the past has certainly not shown us that we could afford in this matter to follow those professional counsellors who have confined themselves to study in the closet; for the actual working of the tariff has emphatically contradicted their theories. (Letter accepting Republican nomination for President, September 12, 1904.) *Mem. Ed.* XVIII, 518; *Nat. Ed.* XVI, 389.

TARIFF REVISION. We should meet the tariff question. The Republican party, and the country at large as well, is definitely committed to the policy of protection; and, unquestionably, any reversal of that policy at present would do harm and produce widespread suffering. But for the Republican party to announce that the inequalities and anomalies in the present tariff must not be touched, and to announce that the high tariff is a fetich, something to which every other interest must yield, and to which every other issue must be subordinated, would be in my opinion a serious mistake. (Before Union League Club, New York City, January 11, 1888.) *Mem. Ed.* XVI, 130; *Nat. Ed.* XIV, 78.

——————. That whenever the need arises there should be a readjustment of the tariff schedules is undoubted; but such changes can with safety be made only by those whose devotion to the principle of a protective tariff is beyond question; for otherwise the changes would amount not to readjustment, but to repeal. The readjustment when made must maintain and not destroy the protective principle. To the farmer, the merchant, the manufacturer this is vital; but perhaps no other man is so much interested as the wage-worker in the maintenance of our present economic system both as regards the finances and the tariff. The standard of living of our wage-workers is higher than that of any other country, and it cannot so remain unless we have a protective tariff which shall always keep as a minimum a rate of duty sufficient to cover the difference between the labor cost here and abroad. (At Oyster Bay, N. Y., July 27, 1904, in response to notification of nomination.) *Mem. Ed.* XVIII, 492; *Nat. Ed.* XVI, 366-367.

——————. From time to time schedules must undoubtedly be rearranged and readjusted to meet the shifting needs of the country; but this can with safety be done only by those who are committed to the cause of the protective system. To uproot and destroy that system would be to insure the prostration of business, the closing of factories, the impoverishment of the farmer, the ruin of the capitalist, and the starvation of the wage-worker. (Letter accepting Republican nomination for President, September 12, 1904.) *Mem. Ed.* XVIII, 519; *Nat. Ed.* XVI, 389.

TARIFF REVISION — CONSIDERATIONS IN. I am by no means certain as yet what we can get the party as a whole to do— what position we can get it to take—and of course I do not want to take a position upon a matter of expediency (that is all the question of tariff revision is) until I can have some reasonable hope of bringing the party up to that position. It is possible that something, at least along the line of legislative reciprocity, may be done next winter. But I shall be scrupulously careful not to promise what I may not be able to perform. It is possible again that nothing can be done next winter, for of course the year before a Presidential election is a most unwise one in which to enter upon a general upsetting of the tariff, and in such case I am inclined to think that it may be well for us in our platform at the National Convention to state that in our judgment the time has come for going over the schedules and for, wherever necessary, revising them, and for reducing such as it may be found desirable to reduce; but that this revision must be made in accordance with the principles of the protective system, and by the friends of that system. Such a pledge we could keep, for we could set to work immediately after the election, if we were victorious, and with four years ahead of us we could do the work with very little chance of jarring business interests. (To H. C. Lodge, April 27, 1903.) *Lodge Letters* II, 7.

——————. Beveridge was out here and added very slightly to my troubles by announcing that in his judgment popular feeling was against "stand-patism" and in favor of an immediate revision of the tariff, and that as popular feeling was that way we ought at once to declare for it. I asked him to consider two facts: first, that we must under no circumstances promise what we do not intend to perform; and second, that as a corollary to the first, he ought seriously to consider whether there was any chance of revising the tariff before the Presidential election, whether he could get the Republicans to entertain the idea at all, and whether if they did entertain it, it would be possible to have a revision without inviting disaster to the Presidential election. He treated both these considerations as irrelevant. (To H. C. Lodge, September 27, 1906.) *Lodge Letters* II, 233.

——————. This country is definitely committed to the protective system and any effort to uproot it could not but cause widespread industrial disaster. In other words, the principle of the present tariff law could not with wisdom be changed. But in a country of such phenomenal growth as ours it is probably well that every dozen years or so the tariff laws should be carefully scrutinized so as to see that no excessive or improper benefits are conferred thereby, that proper revenue is provided, and that our foreign trade is encouraged. There must always be as a minimum a tariff which will not only allow for the collection of an ample revenue but which will at least make good the difference in cost of production here and abroad; that is, the difference in the labor cost here and abroad, for the well-being of the wage-worker must ever be a cardinal point of American policy. The question should be approached purely from a business standpoint; both the time and the manner of the change being such as to arouse the minimum of agitation and disturbance in the business world, and to give the least play for selfish and factional motives. The sole consideration should be to see that the sum total of changes represents the public good. (Seventh Annual Message, Washington, December 3, 1907.) *Mem. Ed.* XVII, 501-502; *Nat. Ed.* XV, 427-428.

TARIFF SCHEDULES — FRAMING OF. I am not at all sure that it was possible under the old methods to get any other result. I am very much afraid that the trouble was fundamental; in other words, that it is not possible, as Congress is actually constituted, to expect the tariff to be well handled *by representatives of localities*. I am beginning to believe in the truth of what Root continually said while he was in the Cabinet; that it was useless to hope to do good work on the tariff if we adhered to the way which Cannon, Payne, Dalzell, and even as able a man as Aldrich, declared to be the only way, and that a complete change, into the details of which I need not go, ought to have been made in the methods of achieving the result. Now this may not be the right impression at all. I shall read through your memorandum most carefully; but with my present information I should be excessively uncomfortable going on the stump and trying to defend the tariff and in addition, as an offhand judgment, I am inclined to doubt whether any good whatever would come from such a course. (To H. C. Lodge, April 6, 1910.) Lodge *Letters* II, 365-366.

———. There is a wide-spread belief among our people that, under the methods of making tariffs which have hitherto obtained, the special interests are too influential. Probably this is true of both the big special interests and the little special interests. These methods have put a premium on selfishness, and, naturally, the selfish big interests have gotten more than their smaller, though equally selfish, brothers. The duty of Congress is to provide a method by which the interest of the whole people shall be all that receives consideration. To this end there must be an expert tariff commission, wholly removed from the possibility of political pressure or of improper business influence. Such a commission can find the real difference between cost of production, which is mainly the difference of labor cost here and abroad. As fast as its recommendations are made, I believe in revising one schedule at a time. A general revision of the tariff almost inevitably leads to log-rolling and the subordination of the general public interest to local and special interests. (At Osawatomie, Kan., August 31, 1910.) *Mem. Ed.* XIX, 19; *Nat. Ed.* XVII, 13.

———. It is not merely the tariff that should be revised, but the method of tariff-making and of tariff administration. Wherever nowadays an industry is to be protected it should be on the theory that such protection will serve to keep up the wages and the standard of living of the wage-worker in that industry with full regard for the interest of the consumer. To accomplish this the tariff to be levied should as nearly as is scientifically possible approximate the differential between the cost of production at home and abroad. This differential is chiefly, if not wholly, in labor cost. No duty should be permitted to stand as regards any industry unless the workers receive their full share of the benefits of that duty. In other words, there is no warrant for protection unless a legitimate share of the benefits gets into the pay-envelope of the wage-worker.

The practice of undertaking a general revision of all the schedules at one time and of securing information as to conditions in the different industries and as to rates of duty desired chiefly from those engaged in the industries, who themselves benefit directly from the rates they propose, has been demonstrated to be not only iniquitous but futile. It has afforded opportunity for practically all of the abuses which have crept into our tariff-making and our tariff administration. The day of the log-rolling tariff must end. The progressive thought of the country has recognized this fact for several years. (Before Progressive National Convention, Chicago, August 6, 1912.) *Mem. Ed.* XIX, 393; *Nat. Ed.* XVII, 284.

TARIFF STABILITY. The country has acquiesced in the wisdom of the protective-tariff principle. It is exceedingly undesirable that this system should be destroyed or that there should be violent and radical changes therein. Our past experience shows that great prosperity in this country has always come under a protective-tariff; and that the country cannot prosper under fitful tariff changes at short intervals. Moreover, if the tariff laws as a whole work well, and if business has prospered under them and is prospering, it is better to endure for a time slight inconveniences and inequalities in some schedules than to upset business by too quick and too radical changes. It is most earnestly to be wished that we could treat the tariff from the standpoint solely of our business needs. (Second Annual Message, Washington, December 2, 1902.) *Mem. Ed.* XVII, 167; *Nat. Ed.* XV, 144.

―――――. What we really need in this country is to treat the tariff as a business proposition from the standpoint of the interests of the country as a whole, and not from the standpoint of the temporary needs of any political party. It surely ought not to be necessary to dwell upon the extreme unwisdom, from a business standpoint, from the standpoint of national prosperity, of violent and radical changes amounting to the direct upsetting of tariff policies at intervals of every few years. A nation like ours can adjust its business after a fashion to any kind of tariff. But neither our nation nor any other can stand the ruinous policy of readjusting its business to radical changes in the tariff at short intervals. This is more true now than ever it was before, for owing to the immense extent and variety of our products, the tariff schedules of to-day carry rates of duty on more than four thousand articles. Continual sweeping changes in such a tariff, touching so intimately the commercial interests of the nation which stands as one of the two or three greatest in the whole industrial world, can not but be disastrous. . . .

We need to devise some machinery by which, while persevering in the policy of a protective tariff, in which I think the nation as a whole has now generally acquiesced, we would be able to correct the irregularities and remove the incongruities produced by changing conditions, without destroying the whole structure. Such machinery would permit us to continue our definitely settled tariff policy, while providing for the changes in duties upon particular schedules which must inevitably and necessarily take place from time to time as matters of legislative and administrative detail. This would secure the needed stability of economic policy which is a prime factor in our industrial success, while doing away with any tendency to fossilization. (At Logansport, Ind., September 23, 1902.) *Presidential Addresses and State Papers* I, 191-193.

TARIFF. *See also* AGRICULTURE; FREE TRADE; RECIPROCITY.

TAXATION. The whole problem of taxation is now, as it has been at almost all times and in almost all places, one of extreme difficulty. It has become more and more evident in recent years that existing methods of taxation, which worked well enough in a simpler state of society, are not adequate to secure justice when applied to the conditions of our complex and highly specialized modern industrial development. At present the real-estate owner is certainly bearing an excessive proportion of the tax burden. Men who have made a special study of the theory of taxation and men who have had long experience in its practical application are alike in conflict among themselves as to the best general system. Absolute equality, absolute justice in matters of taxation will probably never be realized; but we can approximate it much more closely than at present. (Annual Message as Governor, Albany, January 3, 1900.) *Mem. Ed.* XVII, 39-40; *Nat. Ed.* XV, 35.

TAXATION. *See also* CORPORATIONS; FARM LAND; FRANCHISE TAX; INCOME TAX; INHERITANCE TAX; LIQUOR TAX; TARIFF; WEALTH.

TEACHERS. There is no profession in this country quite as important as the profession of teacher, ranging from the college president right down to the lowest-paid teacher in any one of our smallest country public schools. There is no other profession so important. But not the best teacher can wholly supply the want of what ought to be done in the home by the father and the mother. (At Pacific Theological Seminary, Spring, 1911.) *Mem. Ed.* XV, 601; *Nat. Ed.* XIII, 637.

TEACHERS—RESPONSIBILITY OF. No body of public servants, no body of individuals associated in private life, are better worth the admiration and respect of all who value citizenship at its true worth than the body composed of the teachers in the public schools throughout the length and breadth of this Union. They have to deal with citizenship in the raw, and turn it out something like a finished product. I think that all of us who also endeavor to deal with that citizenship in the raw in our own homes appreciate the burden and the responsibility. The training given in the public schools must, of course, be not merely a training in intellect, but a training in what counts for infinitely more than intellect—a training in character. And the chief factor in that training must be the personal equation of the teacher; the influence exerted, sometimes consciously, sometimes unconsciously, by the man or woman who stands in so peculiar a relation to the boys and girls under his or her care—a relation closer, more intricate, and more vital in its after-effects than any other relation save that of parent and child. Wherever a burden of that kind is laid, those who carry it necessarily carry a great responsibility. There can be no greater. Scant should be our patience with any man or woman doing a bit of work vitally worth doing, who does not approach it in the spirit of sincere love for the work and of desire to do it well for the work's sake. (At Philadelphia, Pa., November 22, 1902.) *Proceedings of the Dedication of the New Buildings of the Central High School.* (Board of Public Education, 1910), pp. 62-63.

——————. I wish to say a word of special acknowledgment to the teachers. There is no body of men and women in the country to whom more is owing than to that body of men and women upon whose efforts so much of the cleanliness and efficiency of our government twenty years hence depends; because on their training largely depends the kind of citizenship of the next generation. There is no duty as important as the duty of taking care that the boys and girls are so trained as to make the highest type of men and women in the future. It is a duty that cannot be shirked by the home. The fathers and mothers must remember that it is the duty that comes before everything else after the getting of mere subsistence. The first duty after the duty of self-support is the training of the children as they should be trained. That comes upon the fathers and mothers. They cannot put it off entirely upon the teachers; but much depends upon the teachers also, and the fact that they have done and are doing their duty so well entitles them in a peculiar degree to the gratitude of all Americans who understand the prime needs of the republic. (Remarks to school children, San Bernardino, Cal., May 7, 1903.) Theodore Roosevelt, *California Addresses.* (San Francisco, 1903), p. 11.

TEACHERS—SERVICE OF. It is not too much to say that the most characteristic work of the Republic is that done by the educators, for whatever our shortcomings as a Nation may be, we have at least firmly grasped the fact that we can not do our part in the difficult and all-important work of self-government, that we can not rule and govern ourselves, unless we approach the task with developed minds and trained characters. You teachers make the whole world your debtor. If you did not do your work well this Republic would not endure beyond the span of the generation. Moreover, as an incident to your avowed work, you render some well-nigh unbelievable services to the country. For instance, you render to the Republic the prime, the vital service of amalgamating into one homogeneous body the children alike of those who are born here and of those who come here from so many different lands abroad. You furnish a common training and common ideals for the children of all the mixed peoples who are here being fused into one nationality. It is in no small degree due to you and your efforts that we are one people instead of a group of jarring peoples. (Before National Educational Association, Ocean Grove, N. J., July 7, 1905.) *Presidential Addresses and State Papers* IV, 423.

——————. You men and women engaged in this great work are in the highest and truest sense the real servants of the Republic. You have a greater task to perform than any public man can perform. It rests with you to see that the boys are turned out manly, fearless, and yet tender; turned out so that they shall be ashamed to flinch from any man or to wrong any woman; ashamed to show weakness in the face of strength, or not to deal gently with weakness if shown in others; and to teach the girls equally that to them belong by right not only the virtues of tenderness and unselfishness, but the virtues of strength and courage; so that it shall be a disgrace to the man if he is only strong, but not gentle; and a disgrace to the girl if in addition to gentleness she does not have strength. . . .

I hold no other class of people in our community in quite the regard that I hold the American teacher who is moulding the American nation of to-morrow. (Before Iowa State Teachers' Association, Des Moines, November 4, 1910.) *Mem. Ed.* XVIII, 455-456; *Nat. Ed.* XVI, 340-341.

TEACHERS, WOMEN. Speaking generally, however, the women teachers—I mention these because they are more numerous than the men —who carry on their work in the poorer districts of the great cities form as high-principled and useful a body of citizens as is to be found in the entire community, and render an amount of service which can hardly be paralleled by that of any other equal number of men or women. (*Century*, October 1900.) *Mem. Ed.* XV, 430; *Nat. Ed.* XIII, 377.

TEACHERS. See also EDUCATION; PUBLIC SCHOOLS; RELIGIOUS TEACHERS; SCHOOLS.

TECHNICAL EDUCATION. See EDUCATION, INDUSTRIAL; TUSKEGEE INSTITUTE.

TELEPATHY. I am not in the least surprised about the mental telepathy; there is much in it and in kindred things which are real and which at present we do not understand. The only trouble is that it usually gets mixed up with all kinds of fakes. (To Ethel Roosevelt, June 17, 1906.) *Mem. Ed.* XXI, 566; *Nat. Ed.* XIX, 508.

TEMPERANCE. No one society can do more to help the wage worker than such a temperance society as that which I am now addressing. It is of incalculable consequence to the man himself that he should be sober and temperate, and it is of even more consequence to his wife and his children; for it is a hard and cruel fact that in this life of ours the sins of the man are often visited most heavily upon those whose welfare should be his one especial care.

For the drunkard, for the man who loses his job because he can not control or will not control his desire for liquor and for vicious pleasure, we have a feeling of anger and contempt mixed with our pity; but for his unfortunate wife and little ones we feel only pity, and that of the deepest and tenderest kind. (At Wilkes-Barre, Pa., August 10, 1905.) *Presidential Addresses and State Papers* IV, 434-435.

TEMPERANCE. See also LIQUOR; PROHIBITION.

TEN COMMANDMENTS. Our country will never be safe until the time comes when it will be an insult to any man in public place to think it necessary to say that he is honest. I urge you to have the widest toleration in matters of opinion, but to have no toleration at all when it comes to matters of the Ten Commandments and the Golden Rule. Those are fundamental, essential principles, which must live in the heart of every American citizen, and by which every man asking place or political power must be tested. (At Mount Pleasant Military Academy, Sing Sing, N. Y., June 3, 1899.) *Public Papers of Theodore Roosevelt, Governor, 1899.* (Albany, 1899), p. 331.

——————. No man is a good citizen unless he so acts as to show that he actually uses the Ten Commandments, and translates the Golden Rule into his life conduct—and I don't mean by this in exceptional cases under spectacular circumstances, but I mean applying the Ten Commandments and the Golden Rule in the ordinary affairs of every-day life. (To James E. West, July 20, 1911.) *Boy Scouts of America. The Official Handbook for Boys.* (New York, 1914), p. 390.

TENANT FARMERS. See FARMERS.

TENEMENTS. See HOUSING; LABOR CONDITIONS; RIIS, JACOB A.

TENNESSEE COAL AND IRON COMPANY. It was a matter of general knowledge and belief that they [various financial institutions] or the individuals prominent in them, held the securities of the Tennessee Coal and Iron Company, which securities had no market value, and were useless as a source of strength in the emergency. The Steel Corporation securities, on the contrary, were immediately marketable, their great value being known and admitted all over the world—as the event showed. The proposal of Messrs. Frick and Gary was that the Steel Corporation should at once acquire the Tennessee Coal and Iron Company, and thereby substitute, among the assets of the threatened institutions (which by the way, they did not name to me), securities of great and immediate value for securities which at the moment were of no value. It was necessary for me to decide on the instant, before the Stock Exchange opened, for the situation in New York was such that any hour might make all subsequent efforts to act utterly useless. From the best information at my disposal, I believed (what was actually the fact) that the addition of the Tennessee Coal and Iron property would only increase the proportion of the Steel Company's holdings by about four per cent., making them about sixty-two per cent. instead of about fifty-eight per cent. of the total value in the country; an addition which, by itself, in my judgment (concurred in, not only by the attorney-general but by every competent lawyer), worked no change in the legal status of the Steel Corporation....

The action was emphatically for the general good. It offered the only chance for arresting the panic, and it did arrest the panic. I answered Messrs. Frick and Gary . . . to the effect that I did not deem it my duty to interfere, that is, to forbid the action which more than anything else in actual fact saved the situation. The result justified my judgment. The panic was stopped, public confidence in the solvency of the threatened institution being at once restored. (1913.) *Mem. Ed.* XXII, 502; *Nat. Ed.* XX, 432.

TENNESSEE COAL AND IRON COMPANY. *See also* PANIC OF 1907.

TENURE OF OFFICE. *See* OFFICE.

TEXANS. *See* COWBOYS.

TEXAS—CONQUEST OF. The conquest of Texas should properly be classed with conquests like those of the Norse sea-rovers. The virtues and faults alike of the Texans were those of a barbaric age. They were restless, brave, and eager for adventure, excitement, and plunder; they were warlike, resolute, and enterprising; they had all the marks of a young and hardy race, flushed with the pride of strength and self-confidence. On the other hand they showed again and again the barbaric vices of boastfulness, ignorance, and cruelty; and they were utterly careless of the rights of others, looking upon the possessions of all weaker races as simply their natural prey. A band of settlers entering Texas was troubled by no greater scruples of conscience than, a thousand years before, a shipload of Knut's followers might have felt at landing in England; and when they were engaged in warfare with the Mexicans they could count with certainty upon assistance from their kinsfolk who had been left behind, and for the same reasons that had enabled Rolf's Norsemen on the seacoast of France to rely confidently on Scandinavian help in their quarrels with their Karling overlords. (1887.) *Mem. Ed.* VIII, 132-133; *Nat. Ed.* VII, 115.

THANKSGIVING DAY. When nearly three centuries ago the first settlers came to the country which has now become this great Republic, they fronted not only hardships and privation, but terrible risk to their lives. In those grim years the custom grew of setting apart one day in each year for a special service of thanksgiving to the Almighty for preserving the people through the changing seasons. The custom has now become national and hallowed by immemorial usage. We live in easier and more plentiful times than our forefathers, the men who with rugged strength faced the rugged days; and yet the dangers to national life are quite as great now as at any previous time in our history. It is eminently fitting that once a year our people should set apart a day for praise and thanksgiving to the Giver of Good, and, at the same time that they express their thankfulness for the abundant mercies received, should manfully acknowledge their shortcomings and pledge themselves solemnly and in good faith to strive to overcome them. During the past year we have been blessed with bountiful crops. Our business prosperity has been great. No other people has ever stood on as high a level of material well-being as ours now stands. We are not threatened by foes from without. The foes from whom we should pray to be delivered are our own passions, appetites, and follies; and against these there is always need that we should war. (Proclamation, November 2, 1905.) *Presidential Addresses and State Papers* VI, 1477-1478.

THAYER, ABBOTT H., and GERALD H. *See* ANIMALS—PROTECTIVE COLORATION OF.

THEATRE. *See* ABBEY THEATRE.

THEOLOGY. *See* REASON; RELIGION.

THEORISTS. *See* CROMWELL, O.; *Federalist, The;* PRACTICALITY.

THIRD TERM ISSUE. *See* PRESIDENCY.

THRIFT. Thrift and industry are indispensable virtues; but they are not all-sufficient. We must base our appeals for civic and national betterment on nobler grounds than those of mere business expediency. (*Forum*, February 1895.) *Mem. Ed.* XV, 13; *Nat. Ed.* XIII, 11.

THRIFT. *See also* WEALTH.

THRIFT STAMPS. *See* LIBERTY LOANS.

TOBACCO TRUST. *See* NORTHERN SECURITIES CASE; SHERMAN ANTI-TRUST ACT.

TOLERANCE. In a republic, to be successful we must learn to combine intensity of conviction with a broad tolerance of difference of conviction. Wide differences of opinion in matters of religious, political and social belief must exist if conscience and intellect alike are not to be stunted, if there is to be room for healthy growth. Bitter internecine hatreds, based on such differences, are signs, not of earnestness of belief, but of that fanaticism which, whether religious or antireligious, democratic or antidemocratic, is itself but a manifestation of the gloomy bigotry which has been the chief factor in the downfall of so many, many nations. (At the Sorbonne, Paris, April 23, 1910.) *Mem. Ed.* XV, 371; *Nat. Ed.* XIII, 524.

TOLERANCE. See also FERVOR; FREEDOM; LIBERTY; PUBLIC SCHOOLS; RELIGIOUS FREEDOM; RELIGIOUS TOLERATION.

TOLSTOY, COUNT. To minimize the chance of anything but wilful misunderstanding, let me repeat that Tolstoy is a great writer, a great novelist; that the unconscious influence of his novels is probably, on the whole, good, even disregarding their standing as works of art; that even as a professional moralist and philosophical adviser of mankind in religious matters he has some excellent theories and on some points develops a noble and elevating teaching; but that taken as a whole, and if generally diffused, his moral and philosophical teachings, so far as they had any influence at all, would have an influence for bad; partly because on certain points they teach downright immorality, but much more because they tend to be both foolish and fantastic, and if logically applied would mean the extinction of humanity in a generation. (*Outlook,* May 15, 1909.) *Mem. Ed.* XIV, 417; *Nat. Ed.* XII, 324.

TORPEDO BOATS. Boats so delicate, which to be handled effectively must be handled with great daring, necessarily run great risks, and their commanders must, of course, realize that a prerequisite to successfully handling them is the willingness to run such risks. That they will observe proper precautions is, of course, required, but it is more important that our officers should handle these boats with dash and daring than that the boats should be kept unscratched. There must be developed in the men who handle them that mixture of skill and daring which can only be attained if the boats are habitually used under circumstances which imply the risk of an accident. (Report to Secretary of the Navy, May 1897.) *Mem. Ed.* XXIII, 85; Bishop I, 73.

TRADE UNIONS. See LABOR UNIONS.

TRAINING CAMPS. Let us profit by our own experience of the last year. Our training-camps have been universities of applied Americanism. For every young man between the ages of eighteen and twenty to have six months in such a camp, which would include, of course, some field service, would be of incalculable benefit to him, and of like benefit to the nation. It would teach him self-reliance, self-respect, mutuality of respect between himself and others, the power to command and the power to obey; it would teach him habits of cleanliness and order and the power of coöperation, and above all, devotion to the flag, the ideal of country. It would make him a soldier immediately fit for defensive work, and readily to be turned into a soldier fit for offensive work if, as in the present war, offense prove the only method of real defense. Every such man, after his experience in the camp, would tend to be a better citizen and would tend to do his own work for himself and his family better and with more efficient result. His experience would help him in material matters and at the same time would teach him to put certain great spiritual ideals in the foremost place. (*Metropolitan,* November 1918.) *Mem. Ed.* XXI, 278; *Nat. Ed.* XIX, 256.

———————. Now, either these camps are justified or they are not. If we are utterly unprepared, then they are justified and required. Otherwise they are not, for of course they are only makeshifts, adopted because of the lack of proper governmental action. This improper failure of the government to act may be due either to the Administration leading the people wrong or to the people not permitting the Administration to lead it right. In my speech I was most careful to put the responsibility on the people, on the nation. As a matter of fact, I do not think that that is where it primarily belongs. I think it primarily rests on the shoulders of Mr. Wilson; but I agreed with the view you expressed, that the camp was not the place to say so.

However, if there is to be any speechmaking at all at the camp, then that speechmaking should be truthful and to the point. To support the great immediate need of national preparedness is of course by implication to condemn the Administration to whose supine action we owe our present utter unpreparedness. To condemn the folly and worse of those who favor this policy of supine action is of course to condemn the Administration. You say you approve of both. Then you approve of all that I have done. If it is not proper to say these things which should be said to all patriotic Americans, to such a camp, then in my judgment it is wholly improper to hold these camps at all, and the sooner they are abandoned the better. (To Henry S. Drinker, September 1, 1915.) *Mem. Ed.* XXIV, 465; Bishop II, 396.

TRAINING CAMPS. *See also* MILITARY TRAINING.

TRANSPORTATION. *See* INLAND WATERWAYS; RAILROADS.

TREASON. Moral treason is not necessarily legal treason, but it may be as dangerous, and from senators to school teachers, all public servants who deal in it should promptly be removed from office. (March 2, 1918.) *Roosevelt in the Kansas City Star,* 110.

TREASON. *See also* WAR.

TREATIES. Treaties must never be recklessly made; improper treaties should be repudiated long before the need for action under them arises; and all treaties not thus repudiated in advance should be scrupulously kept. (1915.) *Mem. Ed.* XX, xxiii; *Nat. Ed.* XVIII, xxii.

―――――――. No treaties, whether between civilized nations or not, can ever be regarded as binding in perpetuity; with changing conditions, circumstances may arise which render it not only expedient, but imperative and honorable, to abrogate them. (1894.) *Mem. Ed.* XI, 274; *Nat. Ed.* IX, 56.

TREATIES—ABROGATION OF. I do not admit the "dead hand" of the treaty-making power in the past. A treaty can always be honorably abrogated—though it must never be abrogated in dishonest fashion. (To John Hay, February 18, 1900.) *Mem. Ed.* XXIII, 169; Bishop I, 145.

―――――――. It is infinitely better to have a treaty under which the power to exercise a necessary right is explicitly retained rather than a treaty so drawn that recourse must be had to the extreme step of abrogating if it ever becomes necessary to exercise the right in question. (1913.) *Mem. Ed.* XXII, 432; *Nat. Ed.* XX, 371.

―――――――. One good purpose which would be served by the kind of international action I advocate is that of authoritatively deciding when treaties terminate or lapse. At present every treaty ought to contain provision for its abrogation; and at present the wrong done in disregarding a treaty may be one primarily of time and manner. Unquestionably it may become an imperative duty to abrogate a treaty. The Supreme Court of the United States set forth this right and duty in convincing manner when discussing our treaty with France during the administration of John Adams, and again a century later when discussing the Chinese treaty. The difficulty at present is that each case must be treated on its own merits; for in some cases it may be right and necessary for a nation to abrogate or denounce (not to violate) a treaty; and yet in other cases such abrogation may represent wrong-doing which should be suppressed by the armed strength of civilization. At present in cases where only two nations are concerned there is no substitute for such abrogation or violation of the treaty by one of them; for each of the two has to be judge in its own case. But the tribunal of a world league would offer the proper place to which to apply for the abrogation of treaties; and, with international force back of such a tribunal, the infraction of a treaty could be punished in whatever way the necessities of the case demanded. (New York *Times,* October 18, 1914.) *Mem. Ed.* XX, 65; *Nat. Ed.* XVIII, 56.

TREATIES—AMENDMENT OF. The Senate has, of course, the absolute right to reject or to amend in any way it sees fit any treaty laid before it, and it is clearly the duty of the Senate to take any step which, in the exercise of its best judgment, it deems to be for the interest of the nation. If, however, in the judgment of the President, a given amendment nullifies a proposed treaty, it seems to me that it is no less clearly his duty to refrain from endeavoring to secure a ratification, by the other contracting power or powers, of the amended treaty. (To Senator Shelby Cullom, February 10, 1905.) *Mem. Ed.* XXIII, 500; Bishop I, 436.

―――――――. I am exceedingly anxious to establish relations which will prevent the need of the incessant amendment of treaties. In my judgment incessant exercise of the right of amendment is as unwise as the excessive use of the veto power would be. It is eminently desirable that the State Department shall be in such close touch with the leaders and the Senate committee on foreign affairs that they shall be able to agree in substance in advance upon what shall be done in treaties, and we shall be spared—and that without regard to which side is at fault—the irritation and indeed the humiliation of starting to negotiate treaties, of committing ourselves to them in the eyes of foreign people, and then of failing to put them through; and what is even more important, prevent treaties which are important from the standpoint of national policy from getting into such shape that the one country or the other refuses to ratify them. I do not want to start anything the Senate won't approve. (To H. C. Lodge, July 18, 1905.) Lodge *Letters* II, 168-169.

TREATIES — FAILURE OF. In making treaties . . . there must be give and take; and yet too often a treaty will fail simply because our people permit a small section of their number to insist that it shall be all take and no give. (*Outlook,* April 1, 1911.) *Mem. Ed.* XIX, 152; *Nat. Ed.* XVII, 108.

TREATIES — OBSERVANCE OF. As a people there is no lesson we more need to learn than the lesson not in an outburst of emotionalism to make a treaty that ought not to be, and could not be, kept; and the further lesson that, when we do make a treaty, we must soberly live up to it as long as changed conditions do not warrant the serious step of denouncing it. (Before Progressive National Convention, Chicago, August 6, 1912.) *Mem. Ed.* XIX, 408; *Nat. Ed.* XVII, 296.

―――――――. It is eminently necessary that the United States should in good faith observe its treaties, and it is therefore eminently necessary not to pass treaties which it is absolutely certain will not be obeyed, and which themselves provoke disobedience to them. The height of folly, of course, is to pass treaties which will not be obeyed and the disregard of which may cause the gravest possible trouble, even war, and at the same time to refuse to prepare for war and to pass other foolish treaties calculated to lure our people into the belief that there will never be war. (*New York Times,* November 15, 1914.) *Mem. Ed.* XX, 120; *Nat. Ed.* XVIII, 103.

―――――――. We must seriously and in good faith, and once for all, abandon the wicked and foolish habit of treating words as all-sufficient by themselves, and as wholly irrelevant to deeds; and as an incident thereto we must from now on refuse to make treaties which cannot be, and which will not be, lived up to in time of strain. (*Metropolitan,* August 1915.) *Mem. Ed.* XX, 349; *Nat. Ed.* XVIII, 299.

―――――――. Let no man propose a treaty unless he has reduced it to concrete terms; has proposed it in these concrete terms to his fellows, and has determined whether, when thus made concrete, it ought to be and will be observed. (*Metropolitan,* August 1915.) *Mem. Ed.* XX, 352; *Nat. Ed.* XVIII, 302.

―――――――. The point I wish to make is, first, the extreme unwisdom and impropriety of making promises that cannot be kept, and second, the utter futility of expecting that in any save exceptional cases a strong power will keep a promise which it finds to its disadvantage, unless there is some way of putting force back of the demand that the treaty be observed.

America has no claim whatever to superior virtue in this matter. We have shown an appalling recklessness in making treaties, especially all-inclusive arbitration treaties and the like, which in time of stress would not and could not be observed. When such a treaty is not observed the blame really rests upon the unwise persons who made the treaty. Unfortunately, however, this apportionment of blame cannot be made by outsiders. All they can say is that the country concerned—and I speak of the United States—does not keep faith. The responsibility for breaking an improper promise really rests with those who make it; but the penalty is paid by the whole country. (*New York Times,* October 4, 1914.) *Mem. Ed.* XX, 38; *Nat. Ed.* XVIII, 33.

TREATIES—WORTH OF. It is imperative that we shall take the steps necessary in order, by our own strength and wisdom, to safeguard ourselves against such disaster as has occurred in Europe. Events have shown that peace treaties, arbitration treaties, neutrality treaties, Hague treaties, and the like as at present existing, offer not even the smallest protection against such disasters. The prime duty of the moment is therefore to keep Uncle Sam in such a position that by his own stout heart and ready hand he can defend the vital honor and vital interest of the American people. (*New York Times,* September 27, 1914.) *Mem. Ed.* XX, 4; *Nat. Ed.* XVIII, 4.

―――――――. The most obvious lesson taught by what has occurred is the utter worthlessness of treaties unless backed by force. It is evident that as things are now, all-inclusive arbitration treaties, neutrality treaties, treaties of alliance, and the like do not serve one particle of good in protecting a peaceful nation when some great military power deems its vital needs at stake, unless the rights of this peaceful nation are backed by force. The devastation of Belgium, the burning of Louvain, the holding of Brussels to heavy ransom, the killing of women and children, the wrecking of houses in Antwerp by bombs from air-ships have excited genuine sympathy among neutral nations. But no neutral nation has protested; and while unquestionably a neutral nation like the United States ought to have protested, yet the only certain way to make such a protest effective would be to put force back of it. Let our people remember that what has been done to Belgium would unquestionably be done to us by any great military power with which we were drawn into war, no matter how just our cause. Moreover, it would be done without any more protest on the part of neutral nations than we have ourselves made in the case of Belgium. (New York *Times,* September 27, 1914.) *Mem. Ed.* XX, 10; *Nat. Ed.* XVIII, 9.

———————. [A prime lesson of this war] is the utter inadequacy in times of great crises of existing peace and neutrality treaties, and of all treaties conceived in the spirit of the all-inclusive arbitration treaties recently adopted at Washington; and, in fact, of all treaties which do not put potential force behind the treaty, which do not create some kind of international police power to stand behind international sense of right as expressed in some competent tribunal. (New York *Times,* October 11, 1914.) *Mem. Ed.* XX, 51; *Nat. Ed.* XVIII, 43.

———————. Events have clearly demonstrated that in any serious crisis treaties unbacked by force are not worth the paper upon which they are written. Events have clearly shown that it is the idlest of folly to assert, and little short of treason against the nation for statesmen who should know better to pretend, that the salvation of any nation under existing world conditions can be trusted to treaties, to little bits of paper with names signed on them but without any efficient force behind them.... In every great crisis treaties have shown themselves not worth the paper they are written on, and the multitude of peace congresses that have been held have failed to secure even the slightest tangible result, as regards any contest in which the passions of great nations were fully aroused and their vital interests really concerned. In other words, each nation at present in any crisis of fundamental importance has to rely purely on its own power, its own strength, its own individual force. (New York *Times,* October 18, 1914.) *Mem. Ed.* XX, 60, 62; *Nat. Ed.* XVIII, 51, 53.

———————. We must recognize clearly the old common-law doctrine that a right without a remedy is void. We must firmly grasp the fact that measures should be taken to put force back of good faith in the observance of treaties. The worth of treaties depends purely upon the good faith with which they are executed; and it is mischievous folly to enter into treaties without providing for their execution and wicked folly to enter into them if they ought not be executed. (New York *Times,* November 8, 1914.) *Mem. Ed.* XX, 84; *Nat. Ed.* XVIII, 73.

TREATIES. *See also* ARBITRATION TREATIES; HAGUE TREATIES; PEACE TREATIES; PROMISES.

TREES—PRESERVATION OF. A grove of giant redwoods or sequoias should be kept just as we keep a great and beautiful cathedral. (1916.) *Mem. Ed.* IV, 227; *Nat. Ed.* III, 377.

———————. This is the first glimpse I have ever had of the big trees, and I wish to pay the highest tribute I can to the State of California, to those private citizens and associations of citizens who have co-operated with the State in preserving these wonderful trees for the whole nation, in preserving them in whatever part of the State they may be found. All of us ought to want to see nature preserved. Take a big tree whose architect has been the ages—anything that man does toward it may hurt it and can not help it. (At Big Tree Grove, Santa Cruz, Cal., May 11, 1903.) *Presidential Addresses and State Papers* I, 375.

TREES. *See also* ARBOR DAY; FOREST CONSERVATION.

TREES, TROPICAL. In the heat and moisture of the tropics the struggle for life among the forest trees and plants is far more intense than in the North. The trees stand close together, tall and straight, and most of them without branches, until a great height has been reached; for they are striving toward the sun, and to reach it they must devote all their energies to producing a stem which will thrust its crown of leaves out of the gloom below into the riotous sunlight which bathes the billowy green upper plane of the forest. A huge buttressed giant keeps all the neighboring trees dwarfed, until it falls and yields its place in the sunlight to the most instantly vigorous of the trees it formerly suppressed. Near the streams the forests are almost impassable, so thick is the tangle below; but away from the streams the walking is easier, because only a few bushes and small trees grow in the perpetual shade. To the newcomer one unending wonder is the mass of vines, the lianas or bush-ropes; everywhere they hang from

[611]

the summits of the trees, or twist round the trunks, or lace them together. A few kill the trees; most seem to do them no damage. Some are huge, twisted, knotted cables, dragging down the branches around which they are wrapped, and themselves serving as supports for lesser vines that twine around them. Others stretch up, up, as straight and slender as the shrouds of a ship, until they are lost overhead in the green ceiling of interlocked leaf and branch. Of most of the trees I did not know the names; but among the tallest were the mora, with huge flying buttresses, and the greenheart, with its white trunk. It was unending pleasure to walk through the towering forest. In the shade it was always cool even at midday. There was no wind. All sounds seemed faint and far away. Under the solemn archways of the trees it was dim and mysterious, like some great cathedral at dusk. (1917.) *Mem. Ed.* IV, 265; *Nat. Ed.* III, 409.

TREVELYAN'S *AMERICAN REVOLUTION*. I have now read through your last volume. It is a little difficult to say just what I feel about your history without subjecting you to the discomfort always felt by a fastidious man when he suspects he is overpraised. Yet I cannot refrain from expressing my sincere opinion that you have not only written the final history of our Revolution, but that you have done what is given to so very, very few men to do—that you have written one of the few histories which can deservedly be called great. I do not want to be misled by national feeling; and yet I cannot help believing that the American Revolution was one of the great historic events which will always stand forth in the story of mankind; and now we have been fortunate enough to see that rare combination of a great historic event treated by a great writer, a great student, a great historian. (To Sir George Otto Trevelyan, November 11, 1907.) *Mem. Ed.* XXIV, 191; Bishop II, 163.

TRIAL AND ERROR. *See* ACTION; EXPERIMENT.

TRIUMPHS. *See* FAILURES.

TROPICS. *See* NATURE.

TRUST LEGISLATION. The legislation [in regard to trusts] was moderate. It was characterized throughout by the idea that we were not attacking corporations, but endeavoring to provide for doing away with any evil in them; that we drew the line against misconduct, not against wealth; gladly recognizing the great good done by the capitalist who alone, or in conjunction with his fellows, does his work along proper and legitimate lines. (Third Annual Message, Washington, December 7, 1903.) *Mem. Ed.* XVII, 198; *Nat. Ed.* XV, 171.

―――――――. When new evils appear there is always at first difficulty in finding the proper remedy; and as the evils grow more complex, the remedies become increasingly difficult of application. There is no use whatever in seeking to apply a remedy blindly; yet this is just what has been done in reference to trusts.

Much of the legislation not only proposed but enacted against trusts is not one whit more intelligent than the mediaeval bull against the comet, and has not been one particle more effective. Yet there can and must be courageous and effective remedial legislation. (Annual Message as Governor, Albany, January 3, 1900.) *Mem. Ed.* XVII, 51; *Nat. Ed.* XV, 45.

TRUST PROBLEM. I have been in a great quandary over trusts. I do not know what attitude to take. I do not intend to play a demagogue. On the other hand, I do intend, so far as in me lies, to see that the rich man is held to the same accountability as the poor man, and when the rich man is rich enough to buy unscrupulous advice from very able lawyers; this is not always easy. (To Charles F. Scott, August 15, 1899.) *Mem. Ed.* XXIII, 148; Bishop I, 127.

―――――――. Beyond a question the great industrial combinations which we group in popular parlance under the name of trusts have produced great and serious evils. There is every reason why we should try to abate these evils and to make men of wealth, whether they act individually or collectively, bear their full share of the country's burdens and keep as scrupulously within the bounds of equity and morality as any of their neighbors. But wild and frantic denunciation does not do them the least harm and simply postpones the day when we can make them amenable to proper laws. Hasty legislation of a violent type is either wholly ineffective against the evil, or else crushes the evil at the expense of crushing even more of good. We need to approach the subject both with a firm resolution to abate the evils and in a spirit of hard common sense as we search for the means of abating them. One of the first things to obtain is publicity. We must be able by law to find out exactly what each corporation does and earns. This mere publicity itself will effect something toward remedying many evils. Moreover, it will give us a clearer idea as to what the remaining evils are, and will therefore enable us to shape our measures for attacking the latter with good prospects of success. Immoderate attack always invites reaction and often defeat. Moderation combined with resolution can alone secure results worth having. (At Grand Rapids, Mich., September 7, 1900.) *Mem. Ed.* XVI, 532-533; *Nat. Ed.* XIV, 348-349.

TRUST PROBLEM—SOLUTION OF. The question of the so-called trusts is but one of the questions we must meet in connection with our industrial system. There are many of them and they are serious; but they can and will be met. Time may be needed for making the solution perfect; but it is idle to tell this people that we have not the power to solve such a problem as that of exercising adequate supervision over the great industrial combinations of to-day. We have the power and we shall find out the way. We shall not act hastily or recklessly; but we have firmly made up our minds that a solution, and a right solution, shall be found, and found it will be. (At Union League, Philadelphia, November 22, 1902.) *Mem. Ed.* XVIII, 486; *Nat. Ed.* XVI, 362.

TRUST TRANSACTIONS — PUBLICITY FOR. Where a trust becomes a monopoly the State has an immediate right to interfere. Care should be taken not to stifle enterprise or disclose any facts of a business that are essentially private; but the State for the protection of the public should exercise the right to inspect, to examine thoroughly all the workings of great corporations just as is now done with banks; and wherever the interests of the public demand it, it should publish the results of its examination. Then, if there are inordinate profits, competition or public sentiment will give the public the benefit in lowered prices; and if not, the power of taxation remains. It is therefore evident that publicity is the one sure and adequate remedy which we can now invoke. There may be other remedies, but what these others are we can only find out by publicity, as the result of investigation. The first requisite is knowledge, full and complete. (Annual Message as Governor, Albany, January 3, 1900.) *Mem. Ed.* XVII, 54; *Nat. Ed.* XV, 47.

TRUSTS—ATTITUDE TOWARDS. More and more it seems to me that there will be a good deal of importance to the trust matter in the next campaign and I want to consult with men whom I trust as to what line of policy should be pursued. During the last few months I have been growing exceedingly alarmed at the growth of popular unrest and popular distrust on this question. It is largely aimless and baseless, but there is a very unpleasant side to this overrun trust development and what I fear is if we do not have some consistent policy to advocate then the multitudes will follow the crank who advocates an absurd policy, but who does advocate something. (To Kohlsaat, August 7, 1899.) H. H. Kohlsaat, *From McKinley to Harding.* (Charles Scribner's Sons, N. Y., 1923), p. 82.

————————. There is a wide-spread conviction in the minds of the American people that the great corporations known as trusts are in certain of their features and tendencies hurtful to the general welfare. This springs from no spirit of envy or uncharitableness, nor lack of pride in the great industrial achievements that have placed this country at the head of the nations struggling for commercial supremacy. It does not rest upon a lack of intelligent appreciation of the necessity of meeting changing and changed conditions of trade with new methods, nor upon ignorance of the fact that combination of capital in the effort to accomplish great things is necessary when the world's progress demands that great things be done. It is based upon sincere conviction that combination and concentration should be, not prohibited, but supervised and within reasonable limits controlled; and in my judgment this conviction is right. (First Annual Message, Washington, December 3, 1901.) *Mem. Ed.* XVII, 104; *Nat. Ed.* XV, 90.

TRUSTS—CONTROL OF. The large corporations, commonly called trusts, though organized in one State, always do business in many States, often doing very little business in the State where they are incorporated. There is utter lack of uniformity in the State laws about them; and as no State has any exclusive interest in or power over their acts, it has in practice proved impossible to get adequate regulation through State action. Therefore, in the interest of the whole people, the nation should, without interfering with the power of the States in the matter itself, also assume power of supervision and regulation over all corporations doing an inter-state business. This is especially true where the corporation derives a portion of its wealth from the existence of some monopolistic element or tendency in its business. There would be no hardship in such supervision; banks are subject to it, and in their case it is now accepted as a simple matter

[613]

of course. (First Annual Message, Washington, December 3, 1901.) *Mem. Ed.* XVII, 105-106; *Nat. Ed.* XV, 92.

——————. The great corporations which we have grown to speak of rather loosely as trusts are the creatures of the State, and the State not only has the right to control them, but it is in duty bound to control them wherever the need of such control is shown. There is clearly need of supervision—need to possess the power of regulation of these great corporations through the representatives of the public—wherever, as in our own country at the present time, business corporations become so very powerful alike for beneficent work and for work that is not always beneficent. It is idle to say that there is no need for such supervision. There is, and a sufficient warrant for it is to be found in any one of the admitted evils appertaining to them. (At Providence, R. I., August 23, 1902.) *Mem. Ed.* XVIII, 77-78; *Nat. Ed.* XVI, 64-65.

——————. So far as the great trusts are concerned, only the National Government can deal with them, for their economic power is achieved only by reason of their participation in inter-state commerce, and so only the Federal Government can effectively control them. (*Outlook,* March 25, 1911.) *Mem. Ed.* XIX, 144; *Nat. Ed.* XVII, 102.

——————. The worst of the big trusts have always endeavored to keep alive the feeling in favor of having the States themselves, and not the nation, attempt to do this work, because they know that in the long run such effort would be ineffective. There is no surer way to prevent all successful effort to deal with the trusts than to insist that they be dealt with by the States rather than by the nation, or to create a conflict between the States and the nation on the subject. The well-meaning ignorant man who advances such a proposition does as much damage as if he were hired by the trusts themselves, for he is playing the game of every big crooked corporation in the country. The only effective way in which to regulate the trusts is through the exercise of the collective power of our people as a whole through the governmental agencies established by the Constitution for this very purpose. Grave injustice is done by the Congress when it fails to give the National Government complete power in this matter; and still graver injustice by the Federal courts when they endeavor in any way to pare down the right of the people collectively to act in this matter as they deem wise; such conduct does itself tend to cause the creation of a twilight zone in which neither the nation nor the States have power. Fortunately, the Federal courts have more and more of recent years tended to adopt the true doctrine, which is that all these matters are to be settled by the people themselves, and that the conscience of the people, and not the preferences of any servants of the people, is to be the standard in deciding what action shall be taken by the people. (Before Progressive National Convention, Chicago, August 6, 1912.) *Mem. Ed.* XIX, 385; *Nat. Ed.* XVII, 277.

TRUSTS — DISSOLUTION OF. Not only should any huge corporation which has gained its position by unfair methods, and by interference with the rights of others, by demoralizing and corrupt practices, in short, by sheer baseness and wrong doing, be broken up, but it should be made the business of some administrative governmental body, by constant supervision, to see that it does not come together again, save under such strict control as shall insure the community against all repetition of the bad conduct—and it should never be permitted thus to assemble its parts as long as these parts are under the control of the original offenders, for actual experience has shown that these men are, from the standpoint of the people at large, unfit to be trusted with the power implied in the management of a large corporation. But nothing of importance is gained by breaking up a huge inter-State and international industrial organization *which has not offended otherwise than by its size,* into a number of small concerns without any attempt to regulate the way in which those concerns as a whole shall do business. *Outlook,* November 18, 1911, p. 654.

TRUSTS—GROWTH OF. In dealing with business, the Progressive party is the only party which has put forth a rational and comprehensive plan. We believe that the business world must change from a competitive to a co-operative basis. We absolutely repudiate the theory that any good whatever can come from confining ourselves solely to the effort to reproduce the dead-and-gone conditions of sixty years ago—conditions of uncontrolled competition between competitors most of whom were small and weak. The reason that the trusts have grown to such enormous size is to be found primarily in the fact that we relied upon the competitive principle and the absence of governmental interference to solve the problems of industry. Their growth is specifically and precisely due to the practice of the archaic doctrines advocated by President Wilson under the pleasingly delusive title of the "New Freedom."

We hold that all such efforts to reproduce dead-and-gone conditions are bound to result in failure or worse than failure. The breaking-up of the Standard Oil Trust, for example, has not produced the very smallest benefit. It has merely resulted in enormously increasing the already excessive profits of a small number of persons. (*Century*, October 1913.) *Mem. Ed.* XIX, 546-547; *Nat. Ed.* XVII, 402-403.

TRUSTS—ORIGINS OF. People have said that the tariff causes trusts. It does nothing of the sort. The Sugar Trust, for example, has not been harmed in the smallest degree by the removal of the tariff on sugar, although multitudes of small producers have been ruined. The Standard Oil Corporation was wholly unaffected by the tariff (and breaking it into small corporations under the Sherman law merely resulted in the oil costing more to the consumer, in the men on the inside making enormous fortunes, and in the reduction of the efficiency of the concern in international business). The unscientific lowering of the tariff has not harmed the trusts in the smallest degree save as an incident of harming the entire business world. People have said that governmental corruption has favored trusts, that they have been built up by rebates and the like. Unquestionably some trusts have been favored improperly by certain governmental bodies; and others have been built up by improper practices. But, speaking of the business world as a whole, these are not the prime causes and are hardly even considerable factors in the growth of big corporations. They are responsible for some of the evil that has accompanied the growth; and to suppress them there must be efficient governmental control. But the simple fact is that modern big corporations are due primarily to three causes; namely, steam transportation, the electric telegraph, and the telephone. No change in the tariff will stop the up-growth of big corporations. No moral reform in the world of business or the world of politics will stop it. But big corporations could be ended to-morrow by the abandonment of the railway, the telegraph, and the telephone. The trouble is that the price would be somewhat heavy! (1917.) *Mem. Ed.* XXI, 83; *Nat. Ed.* XIX, 71-72.

TRUSTS — REGULATION OF. I believe that monopolies, unjust discriminations, which prevent or cripple competition, fraudulent overcapitalization, and other evils in trust organizations and practices which injuriously affect interstate trade can be prevented under the power of the Congress to "regulate commerce with foreign nations and among the several States" through regulations and requirements operating directly upon such commerce, the instrumentalities thereof, and those engaged therein. (Second Annual Message, Washington, December 2, 1902.) *Mem. Ed.* XVII, 165; *Nat. Ed.* XV, 143.

TRUSTS—TREATMENT OF. During the past quarter of a century probably more mischief has been done, and is now being done, by our treatment of the trusts than by any other one phase of our governmental activity. (*Outlook*, November 18, 1914.) *Mem. Ed.* XIV, 219; *Nat. Ed.* XII, 236.

————————. I am not going to try to define with technical accuracy what ought to be meant when we speak of a trust. But if by trust we mean merely a big corporation, then I ask you to ponder the utter folly of the man who either in a spirit of rancor or in a spirit of folly says "destroy the trusts," without giving you an idea of what he means really to do. I will go with him if he says destroy the evil in the trusts, gladly. I will try to find out that evil, I will seek to apply remedies; . . . but if his policy, from whatever motive, whether hatred, fear, panic or just sheer ignorance, is to destroy the trusts in a way that will destroy all our property—no. Those men who advocate wild and foolish remedies which would be worse than the disease are doing all in their power to perpetuate the evils against which they nominally war, because, if we are brought face to face with the naked issue of either keeping or totally destroying a prosperity in which the majority share, but in which some share improperly, why, as sensible men, we must decide that it is a great deal better that some people should prosper too much than that no one should prosper enough. So that the man who advocates destroying the trusts by measures which would paralyze the industries of the country is at least a quack, and at worst an enemy to the Republic. (At Fitchburg, Mass., September 2, 1902.) *Presidential Addresses and State Papers* I, 139.

————————. In my judgment, the way for a democracy to deal with special interests . . . is plain. The Sugar Trust should be deprived of every particle of the tariff protection which it has abused. The same is, of course, true of the Standard Oil Company. . . . Furthermore, as regards these two great trusts, the Sugar Trust and the Standard Oil Trust, the Bureau of Corporations in the Department of the Interior should be given precisely such control as the Railway Commission now exercises over railways, precisely such control as is exercised by the German Government at this moment over potash—a control which shall be efficient and thoroughgoing in every department of the business. (*Outlook,* March 25, 1911.) *Mem. Ed.* XIX, 143; *Nat. Ed.* XVII, 102.

TRUSTS AND THE COST OF LIVING. It is . . . asserted that the trusts are responsible for the high cost of living. I have no question that, as regards certain trusts, this is true. . . . There will be no diminution in the cost of trust-made articles so long as our government attempts the impossible task of restoring the flintlock conditions of business sixty years ago by trusting only to a succession of lawsuits under the antitrust law—a method which it has been definitely shown usually results to the benefit of any big business concern which really ought to be dissolved, but which causes disturbance and distress to multitudes of smaller concerns. Trusts which increase production—unless they do it wastefully, as in certain forms of mining and lumbering—cannot permanently increase the cost of living; it is the trusts which limit production, or which, without limiting production, take advantage of the lack of government control, and eliminate competition by combining to control the market, that cause an increase in the cost of living. There should be established at once, as I have elsewhere said, under the National Government an interstate industrial commission, which should exercise full supervision over the big industrial concerns doing an interstate business into which an element of monopoly enters. Where these concerns deal with the necessaries of life the commission should not shrink, if the necessity is proved, of going to the extent of exercising regulatory control over the conditions that create or determine monopoly prices. (Before Progressive National Convention, Chicago, August 6, 1912.) *Mem. Ed.* XIX, 401; *Nat. Ed.* XVII, 290.

TRUSTS. *See also* BUSINESS; COMBINATIONS; CORPORATIONS; GOVERNMENT CONTROL; INDUSTRIAL COMMISSION; KNIGHT CASE; MONOPOLIES; NORTHERN SECURITIES CASE; SHERMAN ANTI-TRUST ACT; STANDARD OIL COMPANY; TARIFF; TENNESSEE COAL AND IRON COMPANY.

TRUTH. A half-truth is always simple, whereas the whole truth is very, very difficult. Unfortunately, a half-truth, if applied, may turn out to be the most dangerous type of falsehood. (New York *Times,* September 27, 1914.) *Mem. Ed.* XX, 4; *Nat. Ed.* XVIII, 4.

——————. If . . . [a man] does not tell the truth then nothing can be done with him in any way or shape. You can pardon most anything in a man who will tell the truth, because you know where that man is; you know what he means. If any one lies, if he has the habit of untruthfulness, you cannot deal with him, because there is nothing to depend on. You cannot tell what can be done with him or by his aid. Truth telling is a virtue upon which we should not only insist in the schools and at home, but in business and in politics just as much. (At Ventura, Cal., May 9, 1903.) Theodore Roosevelt, *California Addresses.* (San Francisco, 1903), p. 33.

——————. I would far rather speak words of boastful flattery; it is not pleasant to tell unpleasant truths. Probably it is personally more advantageous to utter high-sounding platitudes; but platitudes are not what this nation needs at this time. (1917.) *Mem. Ed.* XXI, 6; *Nat. Ed.* XIX, 6.

——————. Criticism should be both truthful and constructive. . . . Let us insist that the truth be told. The truth only harms weaklings. The American people wish the truth, and can stand the truth. (January 21, 1918.) *Roosevelt in the Kansas City Star,* 93.

——————. We need absolute honesty in public life; and we shall not get it until we remember that truth-telling must go hand in hand with it, and that it is quite as important not to tell an untruth about a decent man as it is to tell the truth about one who is not decent. (*Outlook,* May 12, 1900.) *Mem. Ed.* XV, 446; *Nat. Ed.* XIII, 390.

TRUTH—SEARCH FOR. We must all recognize the search for truth as an imperative duty; and we ought all of us likewise to recognize that this search for truth should be carried on, not only fearlessly, but also with reverence, with humility of spirit, and with full recognition of our own limitations both of the mind and the soul. We must stand equally against tyranny and against irreverence in all things of the spirit, with the firm conviction that we can all work together for a higher social and individual life if only, whatever form of creed we profess, we make the doing of duty and the love of our fellow men two of the prime articles in our universal faith. (*Outlook*, December 2, 1911.) *Mem. Ed.* XIV, 438; *Nat. Ed.* XII, 129.

TRUTH. *See also* CRITICISM; FALSEHOOD; HONESTY; LIARS; PARTISANSHIP.

TUBERCULOSIS. The importance of the crusade against tuberculosis, in the interest of which this Congress convenes, cannot be overestimated when it is realized that tuberculosis costs our country two hundred thousand lives a year, and the entire world over a million lives a year, besides constituting a most serious handicap to material progress, prosperity, and happiness, and being an enormous expense to society, most often in those walks of life where the burden is least bearable.

Science has demonstrated that this disease can be stamped out, but the rapidity and completeness with which this can be accomplished depend upon the promptness with which the new doctrine about tuberculosis can be inculcated into the minds of the people and engrafted upon our customs, habits, and laws. The presence in our midst of representatives of world-wide workers in this magnificent cause gives an unusual opportunity for accelerating the educational part of the process.

The modern crusade against tuberculosis brings hope and bright prospects of recovery to hundreds of thousands of victims of the disease, who under old teachings were abandoned to despair. The work of the Congress will bring the results of the latest studies and investigations before the profession at large and place in the hands of our physicians all the newest and most approved methods of treating the disease—a knowledge which will add many years of valuable life to our people and will thereby increase our public wealth and happiness. (Letter accepting presidency of International Congress on Tuberculosis, May 5, 1908.) S. A. Knopf, *A History of the National Tuberculosis Association*. (New York, 1922), pp. 143-144.

TUSKEGEE INSTITUTE. In view of the scarcity not only of common labor, but of skilled labor [in the South], it becomes doubly important to train every available man to be of the utmost use, by developing his intelligence, his skill, and his capacity for conscientious effort. Hence the work of the Tuskegee Normal and Industrial Institute is a matter of the highest practical importance to both the white man and the black man, and well worth the support of both races alike in the South and in the North. Your fifteen hundred students are not only being educated in head and heart, but also trained to industrial efficiency, for from the beginning Tuskegee has placed especial emphasis upon the training of men and women in agriculture, mechanics, and household duties. Training in these three fundamental directions does not embrace all that the negro, or any other race needs, but it does cover in a very large degree the field in which the negro can at present do most for himself and be most helpful to his white neighbors. Every black man who leaves this institute better able to do mechanical or industrial work adds by so much to the wealth of the whole community and benefits all people in the community. (At Tuskegee Institute, Tuskegee, Ala., October 24, 1905.) *Mem. Ed.* XVIII, 471; *Nat. Ed.* XVI, 351.

TYLER, JOHN. He has been called a mediocre man; but this is unwarranted flattery. He was a politician of monumental littleness. Owing to the nicely divided condition of parties, and to the sheer accident which threw him into a position of such prominence that it allowed him to hold the balance of power between them, he was enabled to turn politics completely topsyturvy; but his chief mental and moral attributes were peevishness, fretful obstinacy, inconsistency, incapacity to make up his own mind, and the ability to quibble indefinitely over the most microscopic and hairsplitting plays upon words, together with an inordinate vanity that so blinded him to all outside feeling as to make him really think that he stood a chance to be renominated for the presidency. (1887.) *Mem. Ed.* VIII, 177-178; *Nat. Ed.* VII, 154.

TYRANNY. *See* ANARCHY; BUREAUCRACY; CROMWELL, OLIVER; LIBERTY; MAJORITY; MINORITY; PRIVILEGE; REVOLUTION; RUSSIA; SELF-GOVERNMENT; WASHINGTON, GEORGE; WEALTH.

U

UGANDA. The problem set to the governing caste in Uganda is totally different from that which offers itself in British East Africa. The highlands of East Africa form a white man's country, and the prime need is to build up a large, healthy population of true white settlers, white home-makers, who shall take the land as an inheritance for their children's children.

Uganda can never be this kind of white man's country; and although planters and merchants of the right type can undoubtedly do well there—to the advantage of the country as well as of themselves—it must remain essentially a black man's country, and the chief task of the officials of the intrusive and masterful race must be to bring forward the natives, to train them, and above all to help them train themselves, so that they may advance in industry, in learning, in morality, in capacity for self-government—for it is idle to talk of "giving" a people self-government; the gift of the forms when the inward spirit is lacking, is mere folly; all that can be done is patiently to help a people acquire the necessary qualities — social, moral, intellectual, industrial, and lastly political—and meanwhile to exercise for their benefit, with justice, sympathy, and firmness, the governing ability which as yet they themselves lack. (1910.) *Mem. Ed.* V, 362; *Nat. Ed.* IV, 311-312.

UNEMPLOYMENT. We should consider practicable ways and try to develop long-time projects for the purpose of tackling the permanent industrial problem of unemployment in this country. . . .

Let me urge that we keep clear of the two besetting sins, hardness of the heart and softness of head. Just at the moment hardness of the heart, or at least callous and careless indifference to the dreadful misery around us, is the prime difficulty to be overcome; but when we come to long-time projects and permanent plans we must remember all the innumerable evils that flow from softness of head.

The municipality must of course take the lead in securing immediate relief measures. But the city government cannot do more than a certain amount. In addition, the decent citizens who have jobs, the decent citizens who have money, are bound to try in practical fashion to show their belief in the doctrine that each man and each woman must be in some sort the keeper of his or her less fortunate brothers and sisters. What we really need just at this moment is to be good neighbors to our neighbors who are badly off. . . .

I hope that the big industrial industries will look out for their working men, remembering that the chief need now is not for charity, but for work, and incidentally I hope that instead of cutting the rate of wages they will cut hours and employ as many men as possible on half time, rather than half that number on full time. (At New York City, January 26, 1915.) *Mem. Ed.* XVIII, 629-630; *Nat. Ed.* XVI, 457-458.

UNEMPLOYMENT. See also EMPLOYMENT BUREAUS.

UNEMPLOYMENT INSURANCE. See SOCIAL INSURANCE.

UNIONS. See LABOR UNIONS.

UNITY. See NATIONAL UNITY; RACIAL UNITY.

UNIVERSAL MILITARY SERVICE. See MILITARY SERVICE.

UNIVERSAL SUFFRAGE. See SUFFRAGE.

UNIVERSITY — FUNCTIONS OF A. A great university like this has two especial functions. The first is to produce a small number of scholars of the highest rank, a small number of men who, in science and literature, or in art, will do productive work of the first class. The second is to send out into the world a very large number of men who never could achieve, and who ought not to try to achieve, such a position in the field of scholarship, but whose energies are to be felt in every other form of activity; and who should go out from our doors with the balanced development of body, of mind, and above all of character, which shall fit them to do work both honorable and efficient. (At Harvard University, Cambridge, June 28, 1905.) *Mem. Ed.* XVIII, 431; *Nat. Ed.* XVI, 320.

———————. The work that our colleges can do is to fit their graduates to do service—to fit the bulk of them, the men who can not go in for the highest type of scholarship, to do the ordinary citizen's service for the country; and they can fit them to do this service only by training them in character. To train them in character means to train them not only to possess, as they must possess, the softer and gentler virtues, but also the virile powers of a race of vigorous men, the virtues of courage, of honesty—not merely the honesty that refrains from doing wrong, but the honesty that wars aggressively for the right—the virtues of courage, honesty, and, finally, hard common-sense. (At banquet in honor of Nicholas Murray Butler, April 19, 1902.) *Presidential Addresses and State Papers* I, 32-33.

———————. There is a twofold side to the work done in any institution of this kind. In the first place the institution is to turn out scholars and men proficient in the different technical branches for which it trains them. It should be the aim of every university which seeks to develop the liberal side of education to turn out men and women who will add to the sum of productive achievement in scholarship; who will not merely be content to work in the fields that have already been harrowed a thousand times by other workers, but who will strike out for themselves and try to do new work that counts; so in each technical school if the institution is worthy of standing in the front rank, it will turn out those who in that particular specialty stand at the head. But in addition to this merely technical work, to the turning out of the scholar, the professional man, the man or woman trained on some special line, each university worthy of the name must endeavor to turn out men and women in the fullest sense of the word, good citizens, men and women who will add by what they do to the sum of noble work in the whole community. (At University of Minnesota, Minneapolis, April 4, 1903.) *Presidential Addresses and State Papers* I, 293.

———————. My plea is that our great universities, while paying heed, as they ought, chiefly to vocational training, while paying heed, as they ought, chiefly to turning out men and women who will be of practical service in the life of the state, should also remember that our national life will be hopelessly one-sided and will come very far short of what the life of the Nation must be if it is to be a great Nation, unless we also steadfastly turn our attention to developing the kind of men who shall be masters in exceptional lines of work; unless in addition to the vocational training we have a cultural training which shall fit men to do the highest and best work in the fields of literary and artistic endeavor, and in the field of pure science—of abstract science, of science not pursued with any expectation of making it immediately remunerative. (Charter Day Address, Berkeley, Cal., March 23, 1911.) University of California *Chronicle*, April 1911, pp. 143-144.

UNIVERSITY. See also COLLEGE; EDUCATION, LIBERAL.

UNPREPAREDNESS. No nation can afford to rely upon utterly unprepared strength. Even the strongest man can with safety rejoice to run a race only on condition that he is in some kind of training to make the effort. If he lets his muscles become mere fat, he can rest assured that he will be beaten by any one who takes the trouble. The unwieldy possibility of strength would not save the United States any more than it saved China. Of course Americans are very different people from the Chinese; and I have altogether too firm a faith in my countrymen not to believe that ultimately they would make any antagonist regret having assailed them; but this might well be only after terrible disaster and bitter humiliation; only after repeated defeat in battles and campaigns, or, indeed, defeat in the first war itself. If our lack of preparation caused us such defeats, though we might subsequently redeem them, we could never wipe out their memory or undo the damage they did. *Gunton's Magazine*, January 1898, p. 2.

———————. If the attitude of this nation toward foreign affairs and military preparedness at the present day seems disheartening, a study of the first fifteen years of the nineteenth century will at any rate give us whatever comfort we can extract from the fact that our great-grandfathers were no less foolish than we are. (1916.) *Mem. Ed.* IV, 196; *Nat. Ed.* III, 351.

———————. The United States has never once in the course of its history suffered harm because of preparation for war, or because of entering into war. But we have suffered incalculable harm, again and again, from a foolish failure to prepare for war or from reluctance to fight when to fight was proper. (Address as Assistant Secretary of the Navy, Naval War College, June 1897.) *Mem. Ed.* XV, 246; *Nat. Ed.* XIII, 187.

———————. For eighteen months, with this world-cyclone before our eyes, we as a nation have sat supine without preparing in any shape or way. It is an actual fact that there has not been one soldier, one rifle, one gun, one boat, added to the American army or navy so far, because of anything that has occurred in this war, and not the slightest step has yet been taken looking toward the necessary preparedness. Such national short-sightedness, such national folly, is almost inconceivable. We have had ample warning to organize a scheme of defense. We have absolutely disregarded the warning, and the measures so far officially advocated are at best measures of half-preparedness, and as regards the large aspect of the question, are not even that. (*Metropolitan*, February 1916.) *Mem. Ed.* XX, 282; *Nat. Ed.* XVIII, 242.

UNPREPAREDNESS — DANGERS OF. The fatal weakness [in seventeenth century

Holland] was that so common in rich, peace-loving societies, where men hate to think of war as possible, and try to justify their own reluctance to face it either by high-sounding moral platitudes, or else by a philosophy of short-sighted materialism. The Dutch were very wealthy. They grew to believe that they could hire others to do their fighting for them on land; and on sea, where they did their own fighting, and fought very well, they refused in time of peace to make ready fleets so efficient as either to insure them against the peace being broken or else to give them the victory when war came. To be opulent and unarmed is to secure ease in the present at the almost certain cost of disaster in the future. (At Oxford University, June 7, 1910.) *Mem. Ed.* XIV, 88; *Nat. Ed.* XII, 44.

——————. The nation that waits until the crisis is upon it before taking measures for its own safety pays heavy toll in the blood of its best and its bravest and in bitter shame and humiliation. Small is the comfort it can then take from the memory of the times when the noisy and feeble folk in its own ranks cried "Peace, peace," without taking one practical step to secure peace.

We can never follow out a worthy national policy, we can never be of benefit to others or to ourselves, unless we keep steadily in view as our ideal that of the just man armed, the man who is fearless, self-reliant, ready, because he has prepared himself for possible contingencies; the man who is scornful alike of those who would advise him to do wrong and of those who would advise him tamely to suffer wrong. (New York *Times,* November 15, 1914.) *Mem. Ed.* XX, 114; *Nat. Ed.* XVIII, 98.

UNPREPAREDNESS — LESSONS OF. Compared with the neighboring Indians, they [the cliff-dwellers] had already made a long stride in cultural advance when the Spaniards arrived; but they were shrinking back before the advance of the more savage tribes. Their history should teach the lesson—taught by all history in thousands of cases, and now being taught before our eyes by the experience of China, but being taught to no purpose so far as concerns those ultra-peace advocates whose heads are even softer than their hearts—that the industrious race of advanced culture and peaceful ideals is lost unless it retains the power not merely for defensive but for offensive action, when itself menaced by vigorous and aggressive foes. (1916.) *Mem. Ed.* IV, 33; *Nat. Ed.* III, 212.

——————. [The operations on land during the war of 1812] teach nothing new; it is the old, old lesson, that a miserly economy in preparation may in the end involve a lavish outlay of men and money, which, after all, comes too late to offset more than partially the evils produced by the original short-sighted parsimony. . . . It was criminal folly for Jefferson and his follower, Madison, to neglect to give us a force either of regulars or of well-trained volunteers during the twelve years they had in which to prepare for the struggle that any one might see was inevitable. (1883.) *Mem. Ed.* VII, xxxi; *Nat. Ed.* VI, xxvii.

——————. In 1814 this nation was paying for its folly in having for fourteen years conducted its foreign policy, and refused to prepare for defense against possible foreign foes, in accordance with the views of the ultra-pacifists of that day. It behooves us now, in the presence of a world war even vaster and more terrible than the world war of the early nineteenth century, to beware of taking the advice of the equally foolish pacifists of our own day. To follow their advice at the present time might expose our democracy to far greater disaster than was brought upon it by its disregard of Washington's maxim, and its failure to secure peace by preparing against war, a hundred years ago. (1915.) *Mem. Ed.* XX, xx; *Nat. Ed.* XVIII, xx.

——————. Switzerland, at the time of the Napoleonic wars, was wholly unprepared for war. In spite of her mountains, her neighbors overran her at will. Great battles were fought on her soil, including one great battle between the French and the Russians; but the Swiss took no part in these battles. Their territory was practically annexed to the French Republic, and they were domineered over first by the Emperor Napoleon and then by his enemies. It was a bitter lesson, but the Swiss learned it. Since then they have gradually prepared for war as no other small state of Europe has done, and it is in consequence of this preparedness that none of the combatants has violated Swiss territory in the present struggle.

The briefest examination of the facts shows that unpreparedness for war tends to lead to immeasurable disaster, and that preparedness, while it does not certainly avert war any more than the fire department of a city certainly averts fire, yet tends very strongly to guarantee the nation against war and to secure success in war if it should unhappily arise.

(*Everybody's,* January 1915.) *Mem. Ed.* XX, 138; *Nat. Ed.* XVIII, 119.

UNPREPAREDNESS — RESPONSIBILITY FOR. Now the prime reason why we are at present unprepared, is that you, my dear Mr. President, and the men like you, from the highest motives, persist in making general statements in favor of preparedness in the abstract, and then utterly undoing everything you say by repudiation of these principles when applied in the concrete; and even, as now appears, by repudiation of abstract statements if, as in the present instance, the Administration shows sensitiveness when they are made. (To Henry S. Drinker, president of Lehigh University, September 1, 1915.) *Mem. Ed.* XXIV, 464; Bishop II, 395.

——————. Nine-tenths of wisdom is being wise in time. In this crisis we have been saved by the valor of others from paying a ruinous price for our folly. Let us now put ourselves in such shape that next time we shall be able to save ourselves, instead of helplessly asking some one who is stronger and braver to do the job for us. The first step toward the achievement of this end is clearly to understand the present situation. Seven months after Germany virtually declared war on us, five months after we reluctantly admitted that we were at war, we have a few tens of thousands of gallant infantry near the front, forming an almost inappreciable proportion of the large armies engaged; we have some hundreds of thousands of men who have just begun, or expect soon to begin, training. We have refused to standardize our ammunition by the ammunition of our allies. We are beginning to manufacture good artillery; . . . we have shaped an excellent plan for aircraft development; but as yet we have not a single big field gun or a single war aeroplane fit to match against the field-artillery and flying-machines of either our allies or our enemies. We are short of rifles, of tents, of clothing, of everything. We are actually building rifles of a new type which nevertheless will not take the standardized ammunition of either of our allies. And in the Official Journal of the Administration we are officially told on behalf of the Administration that this is a "happy confusion" and that we should feel "delight" because of our shameful unpreparedness. (*Metropolitan,* September 1917.) *Mem. Ed.* XXI, 23; *Nat. Ed.* XIX, 19-20.

UNPREPAREDNESS — RESULTS OF. A policy of unpreparedness and of tame submission to insult and aggression invites the kind of repeated insolence by foreign nations which in the end will drive our people into war. I advocate preparedness, and action (not merely words) on behalf of our honor and interest, because such preparedness and the readiness for such action are the surest guarantees of self-respecting peace. (*Metropolitan,* February 1916.) *Mem. Ed.* XX, 301; *Nat. Ed.* XVIII, 258.

——————. Our refusal to prepare in advance and our fatuous acceptance of rhetorical platitudes as a substitute for preparations have resulted in our present military impotence and profound and far-reaching economic derangement. The profound business distrust, the unrest of labor, the coal famine, the congestion of traffic, and the shutting down of industries at the time when it is most important that production should be speeded to the highest point, all are due primarily to the refusal to face facts during the first two years and a half of the World War and the seething welter of inefficiency and confusion in which the policy of watchful waiting finally plunged us. Nine-tenths of wisdom is being wise in time. All far-sighted patriots most earnestly hope that this Nation will learn the bitter lesson and that never again will we be caught so shamefully unprepared, spiritually, economically, and from the military standpoint as has been the case in the year that is now passing. (January 18, 1918.) *Roosevelt in the Kansas City Star,* 91.

——————. The policy of unpreparedness, of watchful waiting, has borne most evil fruit. For two and a half years before we drifted stern foremost into the war we were given such warning as never before in history was given a great nation. Yet we failed in the smallest degree to profit by the warning, and we drifted into war unarmed and helpless, without having taken the smallest step to harden our huge but soft and lazy strength. In consequence, although over a year has passed, we are still in a military sense impotent to render real aid to the allies or be a real menace to Germany. (Before Republican State Convention, Portland, Me., March 28, 1918.) *Mem. Ed.* XXIV, 517; Bishop II, 441.

UNPREPAREDNESS AND WAR. China has shown herself utterly impotent to defend her neutrality. Again and again she made this evident in the past. Order was not well kept at home and above all she was powerless to defend herself from outside attack. She has not prepared for war. She has kept utterly unprepared for war. Yet she has suffered more from war, in our own time, than any military power in the world during the same period. She has fulfilled exactly the conditions advocated by these well-meaning persons who for the last five months have been saying in speeches, editorials, articles for syndicates, and the like that the United States ought not to keep up battleships and ought not to trust to fortifications nor in any way to be ready or prepared to defend herself against hostile attack, but should endeavor to secure peace by being so inoffensive and helpless as not to arouse fear in others. (New York *Times,* October 4, 1914.) *Mem. Ed.* XX, 37; *Nat. Ed.* XVIII, 32.

─────────────. Affairs in the international world are at this time in analogous condition. There is no central police power, and not the least likelihood of its being created. Well-meaning enthusiasts have tried their hands to an almost unlimited extent in the way of devising all-inclusive arbitration treaties, neutrality treaties, disarmament proposals, and the like, with no force back of them, and the result has been stupendous and discreditable failure. Preparedness for war on the part of individual nations has sometimes but not always averted war. Unpreparedness for war, as in the case of China, Korea, and Luxembourg, has invariably invited smashing disaster, and sometimes complete conquest. Surely these conditions should teach a lesson that any man who runs may read unless his eyes have been blinded by folly or his heart weakened by cowardice. (New York *Times,* November 8, 1914.) *Mem. Ed.* XX, 83; *Nat. Ed.* XVIII, 72.

─────────────. The prime and all-important lesson to learn is that while preparedness will not guarantee a nation against war, unpreparedness eventually insures not merely war, but utter disaster. (*Metropolitan,* August 1915.) *Mem. Ed.* XX, 370; *Nat. Ed.* XVIII, 317.

─────────────. Unpreparedness has not the slightest effect in averting war. Its only effect is immensely to increase the likelihood of disgrace and disaster in war. The United States should immediately strengthen its navy and provide for its steady training in purely military functions; it should similarly strengthen the Regular Army and provide a reserve; and, furthermore, it should provide for all the young men of the nation military training of the kind practised by the free democracy of Switzerland. Switzerland is the least "militaristic" and most democratic of republics, and the best prepared against war. If we follow her example we will be carrying out the precepts of Washington. (1915.) *Mem. Ed.* XX, xxiv; *Nat. Ed.* XVIII, xxiii.

─────────────. Our unpreparedness did not "keep us out" of the war. Unpreparedness never does keep a nation out of war; it merely makes a nation incompetent to carry it on effectively. And preparedness does not "invite" war; on the contrary it usually averts war, and always renders the prepared nation able to act efficiently if war should, unhappily, come. (*Metropolitan,* September 1917.) *Mem. Ed.* XXI, 19; *Nat. Ed.* XIX, 17.

UNPREPAREDNESS. *See also* DEFENSE; MILITARY SERVICE; MILITARY TRAINING; NATIONAL DEFENSE; PACIFISM; PEACE; PREPAREDNESS; RIGHTEOUSNESS; SPANISH-AMERICAN WAR; WAR OF 1812; WEAKNESS; WORLD WAR.

UNSELFISHNESS. *See* NATIONAL UNSELFISHNESS.

URBANIZATION. Excessive urban development undoubtedly does constitute a real and great danger. All that can be said about it is that it is quite impossible to prophesy how long this growth will continue. Moreover, some of the evils, as far as they really exist, will cure themselves. If townspeople do, generation by generation, tend to become stunted and weak, then they will die out, and the problem they cause will not be permanent; while on the other hand, if the cities can be made healthy, both physically and morally, the objections to them must largely disappear. (*Sewanee Review,* August 1894.) *Mem. Ed.* XIV, 250; *Nat. Ed.* XIII, 217.

URBANIZATION. *See also* CITY.

URUGUAY. *See* MONROE DOCTRINE.

V

VALLEY FORGE. At Valley Forge Washington and his Continentals warred not against the foreign soldiery, but against themselves, against all the appeals of our nature that are most difficult to resist—against discouragement, discontent, the mean envies and jealousies, and heart-burnings sure to arise at any time in large bodies of men, but especially sure to arise when defeat and disaster have come to large bodies of men. Here the soldiers who carried our national flag had to suffer from cold, from privation, from hardship, knowing that their foes were well housed, knowing that things went easier for the others than it did for them. And they conquered, because they had in them the spirit that made them steadfast, not merely on an occasional great day, but day after day in the life of daily endeavor to do duty well....

The vital things for this nation to do is steadily to cultivate the quality which Washington and those under him so pre-eminently showed during the winter at Valley Forge—the quality of steady adherence to duty in the teeth of difficulty, in the teeth of discouragement, and even disaster, the quality that makes a man do what is straight and decent, not one day when a great crisis comes, but every day, day in and day out, until success comes at the end. (At Valley Forge, Pa., June 19, 1904.) *Mem. Ed.* XII, 616-617; *Nat. Ed.* XI, 332-333.

——————. The dreadful suffering of the American army in this winter camp was such that its memory has literally eaten its way into the hearts of our people, and it comes before our minds with a vividness that dims the remembrance of any other disaster. Washington's gaunt, half-starved Continentals, shoeless and ragged, shivered in their crazy huts, worn out by want and illness, and by the bitter cold; while the members of the Continental Congress not only failed to support them in the present, but even grudged them the poor gift of a promise of half-pay in the future. (1888.) *Mem. Ed.* VIII, 333; *Nat. Ed.* VII, 288.

VAN BUREN, MARTIN. Van Buren faithfully served the mammon of unrighteousness, both in his own State and, later on, at Washington; and he had his reward, for he was advanced to the highest offices in the gift of the nation. He had no reason to blame his own conduct for his final downfall; he got just as far along as he could possibly get; he succeeded because of, and not in spite of, his moral shortcomings; if he had always governed his actions by a high moral standard he would probably never have been heard of. Still, there is some comfort in reflecting that, exactly as he was made President for no virtue of his own, but simply on account of being Jackson's heir, so he was turned out of the office, not for personal failure, but because he was taken as scapegoat, and had the sins of his political fathers visited on his own head. (1887.) *Mem. Ed.* VIII, 139; *Nat. Ed.* VII, 121.

VENEZUELA BOUNDARY DISPUTE. I most earnestly hope that our people won't weaken in any way on the Venezuela matter. The antics of the bankers, brokers and anglomaniacs generally are humiliating to a degree; but the bulk of the American people will I think surely stand behind the man who boldly and without flinching takes the American view. (To H. C. Lodge, December 27, 1895.) *Lodge Letters* I, 204.

——————. Great Britain has a boundary dispute with Venezuela. She claims as her own a territory which Venezuela asserts to be hers, a territory which in point of size very nearly equals the Kingdom of Italy. Our government of course, cannot, if it wishes to remain true to the traditions of the Monroe Doctrine, submit to the acquisition by England of such an enormous tract of territory, and it must therefore find out whether the English claims are or are not well founded. It would, of course, be preposterous to lay down the rule that no European power should seize American territory which was not its own, and yet to permit the power itself to decide the question of the ownership of such territory. Great Britain refused to settle the question either by amicable agreement with Venezuela or by arbitration. All that remained for the United States, was to do what it actually did; that is, to try to find out the facts for itself, by its own commission. If the facts show England to be in the right, well and good. If they show England to be in the wrong, we most certainly ought not to permit her to profit, at Venezuela's expense, by her own wrongdoing....

It would be difficult to overestimate the good done in this country by the vigorous course already taken by the national executive and legislature in this matter. The lesson taught Lord Salisbury is one which will not soon be forgotten by English statesmen. His position is false, and is recognized as false by the best English statesmen and publicists. If he does not consent to arrange the matter with Venezuela, it will have to be arranged in some way by arbitration. In either case, the United States gains its point. The only possible danger of war comes from the action of the selfish and timid men on this side of the water, who clamorously strive to misrepresent American, and to mislead English, public opinion. If they succeed in persuading Lord Salisbury that the American people will back down if he presses them, they will do the greatest damage possible to both countries, for they will render war, at some time in the future, almost inevitable. (*Bachelor of Arts,* March 1896.) *Mem. Ed.* XV, 231-233; *Nat. Ed.* XIII, 174-175.

VENEZUELA DEBT DISPUTE. The Venezuelan question has very much changed my view as to the interpretation of the Monroe Doctrine with relation to public opinion here. Before the intervention I believed that the temporary landing of foreign troops in Venezuela would call forth no opposition here. I see that I was mistaken. Had the allies landed troops there, Congress and the people would have raised the most strenuous objection. I conclude from this, that a control of the finances of Venezuela through American and European financial institutions would be condemned by public opinion here. These wretched republics cause me a great deal of trouble. A second attempt of foreign powers, to collect their debts by force, would simply not be tolerated here. I often think that a sort of protectorate over South and Central America is the only way out. Personally I am absolutely against it, I would even be ready to sponsor a retrocession of New Mexico and Arizona. Foreign financial groups should make no efforts at the development of these ill-governed republics, if they lose their money, they should take the consequences. (In conversation with Speck von Sternberg, March 1903.) Dexter Perkins, *The Monroe Doctrine, 1867–1907.* (Johns Hopkins Press, Baltimore, 1937), p. 408.

——————. Trouble arose in connection with the Republic of Venezuela because of certain wrongs alleged to have been committed, and debts overdue, by this Republic to citizens of various foreign powers, notably England, Germany, and Italy. After failure to reach an agreement these powers began a blockade of the Venezuelan coast and condition of quasi-war ensued. The concern of our Government was of course not to interfere needlessly in any quarrel so far as it did not touch our interests or our honor, and not to take the attitude of protecting from coercion any power unless we were willing to espouse the quarrel of that power, but to keep an attitude of watchful vigilance and see that there was no infringement of the Monroe Doctrine—no acquirement of territorial rights by a European power at the expense of a weak sister republic—whether this acquisition might take the shape of an outright and avowed seizure of territory or of the exercise of control which would in effect be equivalent to such seizure. (At Chicago, Ill., April 2, 1903.) *Presidential Addresses and State Papers* I, 260-261.

VETERANS—DEBT TO. It is difficult to express the full measure of obligation under which this country is to the men who from '61 to '65 took up the most terrible and vitally necessary task which has ever fallen to the lot of any generation of men in the western hemisphere. Other men have rendered great service to the country, but the service you rendered was not merely great—it was incalculable. Other men by their lives or their deaths have kept unstained our honor, have wrought marvels for our interest, have led us forward to triumph, or warded off disaster from us; other men have marshaled our ranks upward across the stony slopes of greatness. But you did more, for you saved us from annihilation. We can feel proud of what others did only because of what you did. It was given to you, when the mighty days came, to do the mighty deeds, for which the days called, and if your deeds had been left undone, all that had been already accomplished would have turned into apples of Sodom under our teeth. (At Veterans' Reunion, Burlington, Vt., September 5, 1901.) *Mem. Ed.* XV, 536-537; *Nat. Ed.* XIII, 460-461.

——————. No other citizens deserve so well of the Republic as the veterans, the survivors of those who saved the Union. They did the one deed which if left undone would have meant that all else in our history went for nothing. But for their steadfast prowess in the greatest crisis of our history, all our annals would be meaningless, and our great experiment in popular freedom and self-government a gloomy failure. Moreover, they not only left us a united nation, but they left us also as a heritage the memory of the mighty deeds by which the nation has kept united. (First Annual Message, Washington, December 3, 1901.) *Mem. Ed.* XVII, 147; *Nat. Ed.* XV, 127.

——————. I know that no one will grudge my saying a special word of acknowledgment to the veterans of the Civil War. A man would indeed be but a poor American who could without a thrill witness the way in which, in city after city in the North as in the South, on every public occasion, the men who wore the blue and the men who wore the gray now march and stand shoulder to shoulder, giving tangible proof that we are all now in fact as well as in name a reunited people, a people infinitely richer because of the priceless memories left to all Americans by you men who fought in the great war. (At Richmond, Va.,

VETERANS

October 18, 1905.) *Mem. Ed.* XVIII, 37; *Nat. Ed.* XVI, 32.

VETERANS — PREFERENCE TO. The veteran of the Civil War should be legally guaranteed preference in appointment to, and in retention in, office; that is, he should be appointed to any vacancy when he can show his fitness to fill it, and he should not be removed without trial by the appointing officer, at which he can make his defense. There is no intention to condone corruption or pass over inefficiency in a veteran; but, if he is honest and efficient, he is entitled to preference. (Annual Message as Governor, Albany, January 2, 1899.) *Mem. Ed.* XVII, 23; *Nat. Ed.* XV, 20.

VETERANS. See also CONFEDERATES; GRAND ARMY OF THE REPUBLIC; SOLDIERS.

VICE. Vice in its cruder and more archaic forms shocks everybody; but there is very urgent need that public opinion should be just as severe in condemnation of the vice which hides itself behind class or professional loyalty, or which denies that it is vice if it can escape conviction in the courts. The public and the representatives of the public, the high officials, whether on the bench or in executive or legislative positions, need to remember that often the most dangerous criminals, so far as the life of the nation is concerned, are not those who commit the crimes known to and condemned by the popular conscience for centuries, but those who commit crimes only rendered possible by the complex conditions of our modern industrial life. (Seventh Annual Message, Washington, December 3, 1907.) *Mem. Ed.* XVII, 515; *Nat. Ed.* XV, 438-439.

VICE. See also BRIBERY; CORRUPTION; CRIME; HONESTY; PLEASURE; PROSTITUTION; WHITE SLAVE TRAFFIC.

VICE-PRESIDENCY. The Vice-President is an officer unique in his character and functions, or, to speak more properly, in his want of functions while he remains Vice-President, and in his possibility of at any moment ceasing to be a functionless official and becoming the head of the whole nation. There is no corresponding position in any constitutional government. Perhaps the nearest analogue is the heir apparent in a monarchy. Neither the French President nor the British prime minister has a substitute, ready at any moment to take his place, but exercising scarcely any authority until his place is taken. The history of such an office is interesting, and the personality of the incumbent for the time being may at any moment become of vast importance. (*Review of Reviews,* September 1896.) *Mem. Ed.* XVI, 351.

———. I can't help feeling more and more that the Vice-Presidency is not an office in which I could do anything and not an office in which a man still vigorous and not past middle life has much chance of doing anything. . . . As Vice-President I don't see there is anything I can do. I would be simply a presiding officer and that I should find a bore. (To Thomas C. Platt, February 1, 1900.) *Mem. Ed.* XXIII, 156; Bishop I, 134-135.

———. In the Vice Presidency I could do nothing. I am a comparatively young man and I like to work. I do not like to be a figurehead. It would not entertain me to preside in the Senate. I should be in a cold shiver of rage at inability to answer hounds like Pettigrew and the scarcely more admirable Mason and Hale. I could not *do* anything; and yet I would be seeing continually things that I would like to do, and very possibly would like to do differently from the way in which they were being done. Finally the personal element comes in. Though I am a little better off than the *Sun* correspondent believes, I have not sufficient means to run the social side of the Vice Presidency as it ought to be run. I should have to live very simply, and would always be in the position of "poor man at a frolic." I would not give a snap of my fingers for this if I went into the Cabinet or as a Senator, or was doing a real bit of work; but I should want to consider it when the office is in fact merely a show office. So, old man, I am going to declare decisively that I want to be Governor and do not want to be Vice President. Publicly I shall only say I don't want to be Vice P. (To H. C. Lodge, February 2, 1900.) *Lodge Letters* I, 448.

———. The more I have thought over it, the more I have felt that I would a great deal rather be anything, say professor of history, than Vice-President. (To Thomas C. Platt, February 7, 1900.) *Mem. Ed.* XXIII, 158; Bishop I, 136.

VICE - PRESIDENCY — NOMINATION FOR. I have found out one reason why Senator Platt wants me nominated for the Vice-Presidency. . . . The big monied men with whom he is in close touch and whose campaign contributions have certainly been no inconsiderable factor in his strength, have been pressing him very strongly to get me put in the Vice-

Presidency, so as to get me out of the State. It was the big insurance companies, possessing enormous wealth, that gave Payne his formidable strength, and they to a man want me out. The great corporations affected by the franchise tax have also been at the Senator. In fact, all the high monied interests that make campaign contributions of large size and feel that they should have favors in return, are extremely anxious to get me out of the State. I find that they have been at Platt for the last two or three months and he has finally begun to yield to them and to take their view. Outside of that the feeling here is very strong against my going. In fact, all of my friends in the State would feel that I was deserting them, and are simply unable to understand my considering it. (To Henry Cabot Lodge, February 3, 1900.) Lodge *Letters* I, 449.

———————. Let me point out that I am convinced that I can do most good to the national ticket by running as Governor of this State. There will be in New York a very curious feeling of resentment both against myself and against the party leaders if I run as Vice-President, and this will affect our vote I believe; whereas if I run as Governor I can strengthen the national ticket more than in any other way. I do not think we can afford to take liberties in this State. (To Marcus A. Hanna, April 3, 1900.) *Mem. Ed.* XXIII, 158; Bishop I, 136.

———————. There is unquestionably a strong desire to make me take the Vice-Presidency. Many corporations have served notice on the Republican leaders that they won't contribute if I am nominated for Governor, and that they will do their best to beat me. This is mainly on account of the franchise tax, but also on account of various other acts which I am bound to say I still regard as extremely creditable—as, to be frank, I do their whole opposition, if it comes to that. (To John Proctor Clarke, April 15, 1900.) *Mem. Ed.* XXIII, 160; Bishop I, 138.

———————. The Organization, pressed by the corporations, is still very anxious to have me nominated for the Vice-Presidency. It is however, entirely too late now for me to alter my position. I will not accept under any circumstances, and that is all there is about it. (To General F. V. Greene, June 12, 1900.) *Mem. Ed.* XXIII, 161; Bishop I, 138.

———————. Well, I now join the innumerable throng of New York's Vice-Presidential progeny in esse or posse. I should like to have stayed where there was real work; but I would be a fool not to appreciate and be deeply touched by the way I was nominated; and the one great thing at the next election is to re-elect the President, and if my candidacy helps toward that end, well and good. (To John Hay, June 25, 1900.) *Mem. Ed.* XXIII, 163; Bishop I, 140.

———————. The thing could not be helped. There were two entirely different forces at work. The first was the desire to get me out of New York, partly because the machine naturally prefers some one more pliable, but mainly because of the corporations' or rather the big speculative corporations' unhealthy attitude toward me. This desire was absolutely unoperative as regards results, for I stood Mr. Platt and the machine on their heads when the trial of strength came and forced the entire New York delegation to declare for some one else. It was the feeling of the great bulk of the Republicans that I would strengthen the National ticket and they wanted me on it at all hazards. Mr. Hanna was quite as much opposed to my going on as Mr. Platt was to my staying off, but both were absolutely and utterly powerless. While of course I should have preferred to stay where there was more work, I would be both ungrateful and a fool not to be deeply touched by the way in which I was nominated. (To Anna Roosevelt Cowles, June 25, 1900.) Cowles *Letters*, 245.

———————. Every real friend of mine will consistently speak of me as exactly what I am—the man chosen because it is believed he will add strength to a cause which, however, is already infinitely stronger than any strength of his—a man absolutely and entirely, in the second place, whom it is grossly absurd and unjust to speak of in any other capacity. This is the attitude which must be assumed in the most emphatic way. (To George H. Lyman, June 27, 1900.) *Mem. Ed.* XXIII, 162; Bishop I, 139.

———————. The nomination came to me at Philadelphia simply because the bulk of the enormous majority of the delegates were bent upon having me whether I wished it or not, and all the more because Senator Hanna objected to it. Senator Platt wished me nominated and, as you saw, I absolutely upset him and stood the New York machine on its head, forcing them without one exception to stand against me and support another candidate. When I did this I supposed that it completely dissipated the possibility of my nomination. The effect was just the opposite. The delegates who had already been saying that they would not have Senator Hanna dictate whom they should or should not nominate, now merely said: "So Roosevelt has stood Platt on his head, has he? Well, that settles it. We might not wish him placed on the ticket by Platt, but now we have got to have him anyway." (To Lyman Abbott, June 27, 1900.) *Mem. Ed.* XXIII, 161; Bishop I, 138-139.

VICE-PRESIDENCY. *See also* ELECTION OF 1900; ROOSEVELT'S POLITICAL CAREER.

VICE-PRESIDENT—ROOSEVELT AS. I have really enjoyed presiding over the Senate for the week the extra session lasted. I shall get fearfully tired in the future no doubt and of course I should like a more active position. (To Cecil Arthur Spring-Rice, March 16, 1901.) *Mem. Ed.* XXIII, 170; Bishop I, 147.

——————. Just a line in reference to my studying law. . . . Could I go into an office in New York—say Evarts & Choate—or study in New York or here in Oyster Bay, so as to get admitted to the bar before the end of my term as Vice-President? (To John Proctor Clarke, March 29, 1901.) *Mem. Ed.* XXIII, 170-171; Bishop I, 147.

VICTOR EMMANUEL. I thoroughly enjoyed meeting the King and Queen here, and their children. They are as nice a family as I have come across anywhere, thoroughly good citizens in every way, very cultivated, very intelligent, very simple and upright and straightforward. I should greatly like to have them as neighbors, and the King would make a first-class United States Senator, or Cabinet Minister, and, with a little change, a first-class President! (To H. C. Lodge, April 6, 1900.) *Lodge Letters* II, 365.

——————. He is the strongest man in Europe, that is my opinion. He is a stronger man than the German Emperor, but whether George will grow stronger than them all remains as yet to be seen. The Italian King has greater insight than any man I met on a throne. Unfortunately, he lacks confidence in himself. He is undersized, and it is always uppermost in his mind. If he is standing he wants to sit down at once so that his height will not be so apparent, and when he sits he always chooses a high chair and his little feet hardly touch the floor. If I were in his place, I would not care a hang about my height. (Recorded by Butt in letter of June 30, 1910.) *Taft and Roosevelt, The Intimate Letters of Archie Butt.* (Doubleday, Doran & Co., Garden City, N. Y., 1930), I, 424.

VIERECK, GEORGE SYLVESTER. *See* GERMAN-AMERICANS.

"VIGILANT WATCHING." *See* "WATCHFUL WAITING."

VIGILANTES. The regulators of backwoods society corresponded exactly to the vigilantes of the Western border to-day. In many of the cases of lynch-law which have come to my knowledge the effect has been healthy for the community; but sometimes great injustice is done. Generally, the vigilantes, by a series of summary executions, do really good work; but I have rarely known them fail, among the men whom they killed for good reason, to also kill one or two either by mistake or to gratify private malice. (1889.) *Mem. Ed.* X, 122; *Nat. Ed.* VIII, 107.

VIGOR. I have mentioned all these experiences, and I could mention scores of others, because out of them grew my philosophy—perhaps they were in part caused by my philosophy—of bodily vigor as a method of getting that vigor of soul without which vigor of the body counts for nothing. The dweller in cities has less chance than the dweller in the country to keep his body sound and vigorous. But he can do so, if only he will take the trouble. Any young lawyer, shopkeeper, or clerk, or shop-assistant can keep himself in good condition if he tries. (1913.) *Mem. Ed.* XXII, 59; *Nat. Ed.* XX, 52.

VIGOR. *See also* OUTDOOR LIFE; STRENUOUS LIFE.

VILLA, PANCHO. In March last, Villa made a raid into American territory. He was a bandit leader whose career of successful infamy had been greatly aided by Mr. Wilson's favor and backing. He was at the head of Mexican soldiers, whose arms and ammunition had been supplied to them in consequence of Mr. Wilson's reversing Mr. Taft's policy and lifting the embargo against arms and munitions into Mexico. They attacked Columbus, New Mexico, and killed a number of civilians and a number of United States troops. On the next day the President issued an announcement that adequate forces would be sent in pursuit of Villa "with the single object of capturing him." On April 8th the announcement was made from

[627]

the White House that the troops would remain in Mexico until Villa was captured. It was furthermore announced in the press despatches from Washington that he was to be taken "dead or alive." Fine words! Only—they meant nothing. He is not dead. He has not been taken alive. (At Lewiston, Me., August 31, 1916.) Theodore Roosevelt, *Americanism and Preparedness.* (New York, 1917), p. 11.

VILLA, PANCHO. *See also* MEXICO.

VIOLENCE. Lawless violence inevitably breeds lawless violence in return, and the first duty of the government is relentlessly to put a stop to the violence and then to deal firmly and wisely with all the conditions that led up to the violence. (To Victor A. Olander, Illinois State Federation of Labor, July 17, 1917.) *Mem. Ed.* XXI, 177; *Nat. Ed.* XIX, 170.

———. There is no worse enemy of the wage-worker than the man who condones mob violence in any shape or who preaches class hatred; and surely the slightest acquaintance with our industrial history should teach even the most short-sighted that the times of most suffering for our people as a whole, the times when business is stagnant, and capital suffers from shrinkage and gets no return from its investments, are exactly the times of hardship, and want, and grim disaster among the poor. If all the existing instrumentalities of wealth could be abolished, the first and severest suffering would come among those of us who are least well off at present. The wage-worker is well off only when the rest of the country is well off; and he can best contribute to this general well-being by showing sanity and a firm purpose to do justice to others. (At State Fair, Syracuse, N. Y., September 7, 1903.) *Mem. Ed.* XVIII, 65; *Nat. Ed.* XVI, 55.

VIOLENCE. *See also* LABOR DISPUTES; REVOLUTION; RIOTS; WAR.

VIRTUE. One thing I believe that we are realizing more and more, and that is the valuelessness of mere virtue that does not take a tangible and efficient shape. I do not give the snap of my finger for a very good man who possesses that peculiar kind of goodness that benefits only himself, in his own home. I think we all understand more and more that the virtue that is worth having is the virtue that can sustain the rough shock of actual living; the virtue that can achieve practical results, that finds expression in actual life. (At New York State Bar Association Banquet, January 18, 1899.) *Mem. Ed.* XVI, 468; *Nat. Ed.* XIV, 309.

VIRTUES, THE ESSENTIAL. There is much less need of genius or of any special brilliancy in the administration of our government than there is need of such homely virtues and qualities as common sense, honesty, and courage. (Inaugural Address as Governor, Albany, January 2, 1899.) *Mem. Ed.* XVII, 3; *Nat. Ed.* XV, 3.

———. There are many qualities which we need alike in private citizen and in public man, but three above all—three for the lack of which no brilliancy and no genius can atone—and those three are courage, honesty, and common sense. (At Antietam, Md., September 17, 1903.) *Mem. Ed.* XII, 623; *Nat. Ed.* XI, 338.

VIRTUES, THE HOMELY. We, the men of to-day and of the future, need many qualities if we are to do our work well. We need, first of all and most important of all, the qualities which stand at the base of individual, of family life, the fundamental and essential qualities—the homely, every-day, all-important virtues. If the average man will not work, if he has not in him the will and the power to be a good husband and father; if the average woman is not a good housewife, a good mother of many healthy children, then the state will topple, will go down, no matter what may be its brilliance of artistic development or material achievement. But these homely qualities are not enough. There must, in addition, be that power of organization, that power of working in common for a common end. (At University of Berlin, May 12, 1910.) *Mem. Ed.* XIV, 282; *Nat. Ed.* XII, 82.

VIRTUES, THE VIRILE. Beauty, refinement, grace, are excellent qualities in a man, as in a nation, but they come second, and very far second, to the great virile virtues, the virtues of courage, energy, and daring; the virtues which beseem a masterful race—a race fit to fell forests, to build roads, to found commonwealths, to conquer continents, to overthrow armed enemies! *Harper's Weekly*, December 21, 1895, p. 1216.

———. No abundance of the milder virtues will save a nation that has lost the virile qualities; and, on the other hand, no admiration of strength must make us deviate from the laws of righteousness. (*Outlook*, September 23,

1914.) *Mem. Ed.* XX, 31; *Nat. Ed.* XVIII, 26.

VIRTUES. See also CHARACTER; COMMON SENSE; COURAGE; FIGHTING VIRTUES; HEROIC VIRTUES; HONESTY; INTELLECTUAL ACUTENESS; MANLY VIRTUES; MORAL SENSE; PIONEER VIRTUES.

VOCATIONAL EDUCATION. See EDUCATION, INDUSTRIAL.

VOLUNTEER SYSTEM. The much-praised "volunteer" system means nothing but encouraging brave men to do double duty and incur double risk in order that cowards and shirks and mere money-getters may sit at home in a safety bought by the lives of better men. (*Metropolitan*, November 1915.) *Mem. Ed.* XX, 390; *Nat. Ed.* XVIII, 334.

———. The vice of the volunteer system lies chiefly, not in the men who do volunteer, but in the men who don't. A chief, although not the only, merit in the obligatory system lies in its securing preparedness in advance. By our folly in not adopting the obligatory system as soon as this war broke out, we have forfeited this prime benefit of preparedness. You now propose to use its belated adoption as an excuse for depriving us of the benefits of the volunteer system. This is a very grave blunder. The only right course under existing conditions is to combine the two systems. My proposal is to use the volunteer system so that we can at once avail ourselves of the services of men who would otherwise be exempt, and to use the obligatory as the permanent system as to make all serve who ought to serve. You propose to use the belated adoption of the obligatory system as a reason for refusing the services of half the men of the nation who are most fit to serve, who are most eager to serve, and whose services can be utilized at once. (To Secretary Newton D. Baker, April 22, 1917.) *Mem. Ed.* XXI, 209; *Nat. Ed.* XIX, 198.

VOLUNTEER SYSTEM. See also DRAFT; MILITARY SERVICE; MILITARY TRAINING; ROOSEVELT DIVISION; ROUGH RIDERS; SOLDIERS.

VOTING AS A DUTY. It is not only your right to vote, but it is your duty if you are indeed freemen and American citizens. I want to see every man vote. I would rather have you come to the polls even if you voted against me than have you shirk your duty. (At Richland, N. Y., October 29, 1898.) *Mem. Ed.* XVI, 463.

———. Under our form of government voting is not merely a right but a duty, and, moreover, a fundamental and necessary duty if a man is to be a good citizen. (Seventh Annual Message, Washington, December 3, 1907.) *Mem. Ed.* XVII, 540; *Nat. Ed.* XV, 460.

VOTING. See also CIVIC DUTY; MILITARY SERVICE; NEGRO SUFFRAGE; POLITICS; SUFFRAGE; WOMAN SUFFRAGE.

W

WAGES. We believe in the principle of a living wage. We hold that it is ruinous for all our people if some of our people are forced to subsist on a wage such that body and soul alike are stunted. (*Century*, October 1913.) *Mem. Ed.* XIX, 543; *Nat. Ed.* XVII, 400.

———. We shall sedulously safeguard the rights of property and protect it from all injustice. But we hold with Lincoln that labor deserves higher consideration than capital. Therefore we hold that labor has a right to the means of life—that there must be a living wage. *Outlook*, September 28, 1912, p. 160.

———. The corporation or individual capitalist paying a starvation wage to an employee, and especially to a woman employee, is guilty of iniquity, and is an enemy of morality, of religion and of the State. Let us as a people face the fact that there must be a living wage for every employee; and that the employer who does not give it is a bad citizen. *Outlook*, July 15, 1911, p. 570.

WAGES. See also DIVIDENDS; LABOR; TARIFF; WORKERS.

WALL STREET. It is difficult for me to understand why there should be this belief in Wall Street that I am a wild-eyed revolutionist. I cannot condone wrong, but I certainly do not intend to do aught save what is beneficial to the man of means who acts squarely and fairly. (To Jacob Schiff, March 28, 1907.) *Mem. Ed.* XXIV, 48; Bishop II, 41.

———. The big Wall Street financiers of the type of which I am speaking, the men who are our embittered opponents to-

[629]

night, own railroads, oil, mines, whatever it may be, and also own newspapers and magazines, and have owned legislatures, governors, and judges. Now our warfare, fundamentally, is to break up the alliance between crooked business and crooked politics. We would be the very first to insist that the corporation should have the rights to which it is entitled; it must have its rights. But it is not entitled to a vote and it is not entitled to own any man in public life. The richest man in the world is entitled to every right that the poor man has, but to no more. Now, I will fight for the rights of the richest man in the country just as quick as I will for the rights of the poorest man, provided they are the same rights. (At Elmira, N. Y., October 14, 1910.) *Mem. Ed.* XIX, 42; *Nat. Ed.* XVII, 33.

WALL STREET. *See also* BUSINESS, BIG; CORPORATIONS; FINANCIERS; "MALEFACTORS OF GREAT WEALTH"; MONEYED MEN; PRIVILEGE; SPECIAL INTERESTS; SPECULATORS; WEALTH.

WAPITI. The wapiti is the largest and stateliest deer in the world. A full-grown bull is as big as a steer. The antlers are the most magnificent trophies yielded by any game animal of America, save the giant Alaskan moose. When full grown they are normally of twelve tines; frequently the tines are more numerous, but the increase in their number has no necessary accompaniment in increase in the size of the antlers. The length, massiveness, roughness, spread, and symmetry of the antlers must all be taken into account in rating the value of a head. Antlers over fifty inches in length are large; if over sixty, they are gigantic. (1905.) *Mem. Ed.* III, 237; *Nat. Ed.* III, 61.

WAPITI—HABITAT OF THE. The wapiti, like the bison, and even more than the whitetail deer, can thrive in widely varying surroundings. It is at home among the high mountains, in the deep forests, and on the treeless, level plains. It is rather omnivorous in its tastes, browsing and grazing on all kinds of trees, shrubs, and grasses. These traits and its hardihood make it comparatively easy to perpetuate in big parks and forest preserves in a semiwild condition; and it has thrived in such preserves and parks in many of the Eastern States. As it does not by preference dwell in such tangled forests as are the delight of the moose and the whitetail deer, it vanishes much quicker than either when settlers appear in the land. In the mountains and foothills its habitat is much the same as that of the mule-deer, the two animals being often found in the immediate neighborhood of each other. In such places the superior size and value of the wapiti put it at a disadvantage in the keen struggle for life, and when the rifle-bearing hunter appears upon the scene, it is killed out long before its smaller kinsman. (1905.) *Mem. Ed.* III, 241; *Nat. Ed.* III, 65.

WAPITI—HUNTING THE. No chase is more fascinating than that of the wapiti. In the old days, when the mighty-antlered beasts were found upon the open plains, they could be followed upon horseback, with or without hounds. Nowadays, when they dwell in the mountains, they are to be killed only by the rifle-bearing still-hunter. Needless butchery of any kind of animal is repulsive, but in the case of the wapiti it is little short of criminal. He is the grandest of the deer kind throughout the world, and he has already vanished from most of the places where he once dwelt in his pride. Every true sportsman should feel it incumbent upon him to do all in his power to preserve so noble a beast of the chase from extinction. (1905.) *Mem. Ed.* III, 251; *Nat. Ed.* III, 72.

WAR. It must ever be kept in mind that war is not merely justifiable, but imperative, upon honorable men, upon an honorable nation, where peace can only be obtained by the sacrifice of conscientious conviction or of national welfare. . . . A just war is in the long run far better for a nation's soul than the most prosperous peace obtained by acquiescence in wrong or injustice. (Sixth Annual Message, Washington, December 3, 1906.) *Mem. Ed.* XVII, 472; *Nat. Ed.* XV, 402.

——————. I abhor violence and bloodshed. I believe that war should never be resorted to when, or so long as, it is honorably possible to avoid it. I respect all men and women who from high motives and with sanity and self-respect do all they can to avert war. I advocate preparation for war in order to avert war; and I should never advocate war unless it were the only alternative to dishonor. (1913.) *Mem. Ed.* XXII, 248; *Nat. Ed.* XX, 212.

——————. Nothing is gained by debate on non-debatable subjects. No intelligent man desires war. But neither can any intelligent man who is willing to think fail to realize that we live in a great and free country only because our forefathers were willing to wage war rather than accept the peace that spells destruction. No nation can permanently retain any "social values" worth having unless it develops the warlike strength necessary for its own defense. (American Sociological Society, *Papers*, 1915.) *Mem. Ed.* XX, 276; *Nat. Ed.* XVIII, 237.

──────────. The man who fears death more than dishonor, more than failure to perform duty, is a poor citizen; and the nation that regards war as the worst of all evils and the avoidance of war as the highest good is a wretched and contemptible nation, and it is well that it should vanish from the face of the earth. (*Metropolitan*, August 1915.) *Mem. Ed.* XX, 369; *Nat. Ed.* XVIII, 316.

──────────. I do not believe that the firm assertion of our rights means war, but, in any event, it is well to remember there are things worse than war. (Statement to the press, May 11, 1915.) *Mem. Ed.* XX, 444; *Nat. Ed.* XVIII, 381.

──────────. Our rule should be the same for the nation as for the individual. Do not get into a fight if you can possibly avoid it. If you get in, see it through. Don't hit if it is honorably possible to avoid hitting, but never hit soft. Don't hit at all if you can help it; don't hit a man if you can possibly avoid it; but if you do hit him, put him to sleep. (Before National Press Club, Washington, January 24, 1918.) *Mem. Ed.* XXIV, 513; Bishop II, 437.

──────────. All wise and good women and all wise and good men abhor war. Washington and Lincoln abhorred war. But no man or woman is either wise or good unless he or she abhors some things even more than war, exactly as Washington and Lincoln abhorred them. (April 12, 1918.) *Roosevelt in the Kansas City Star*, 134.

WAR—DEFINITION OF. The first thing to do is to make these citizens understand that war and militarism are terms whose values depend wholly upon the sense in which they are used. The second thing is to make them understand that there is a real analogy between the use of force in international and the use of force in intranational or civil matters; although of course this analogy must not be pushed too far.

In the first place, we are dealing with a matter of definition. A war can be defined as violence between nations, as the use of force between nations. It is analogous to violence between individuals within a nation—using violence in a large sense as equivalent to the use of force. When this fact is clearly grasped, the average citizen will be spared the mental confusion he now suffers because he thinks of war as *in itself* wrong. War, like peace, is properly a means to an end—righteousness.... Whether war is right or wrong depends purely upon the purpose for which, and the spirit in which, it is waged. Here the analogy with what takes place in civil life is perfect. The exertion of force or violence by which one man masters another may be illustrated by the case of a black-hander who kidnaps a child, knocking down the nurse or guardian; and it may also be illustrated by the case of the policeman who by force arrests the black-hander or white-slaver or whoever it is and takes his victim away from him. (American Sociological Society, *Papers*, 1915.) *Mem. Ed.* XX, 268-269; *Nat. Ed.* XVIII, 230-231.

WAR — INDUSTRY DURING. Business men, professional men, and wage-workers alike must understand that there should be no question of their enjoying any rights whatsoever unless in the fullest way they recognize and live up to the duties that go with those rights. This is just as true of the corporation as of the trade-union, and if either corporation or trade-union fails heartily to acknowledge this truth, then its activities are necessarily antisocial and detrimental to the welfare of the body politic as a whole. In war-time, when the welfare of the nation is at stake, it should be accepted as axiomatic that the employer is to make no profit out of the war save that which is necessary to the efficient running of the business and to the living expenses of himself and family, and that the wage-worker is to treat his wage from exactly the same standpoint and is to see to it that the labor organization to which he belongs is, in all its activities, subordinated to the service of the nation. (Before Knights of Columbus, New York City, October 12, 1915.) *Mem. Ed.* XX, 462; *Nat. Ed.* XVIII, 396.

WAR—OPPOSITION DURING. It may be the highest duty to oppose a war before it is brought on, but once the country is at war, the man who fails to support it with all possible heartiness comes perilously near being a traitor, and his conduct can only be justified on grounds which in time of peace would justify a revolution. (1900.) *Mem. Ed.* XIII, 406; *Nat. Ed.* X, 288.

WAR—ORIGINS OF. An unmanly desire to avoid a quarrel is often the surest way to precipitate one; and utter unreadiness to fight is even surer....

If in the future we have war, it will almost certainly come because of some action, or lack of action, on our part in the way of refusing to accept responsibilities at the proper time, or failing to prepare for war when war does not threaten. An ignoble peace is even worse than an unsuccessful war; but an unsuccessful war would leave behind it a legacy of bitter memories which would hurt our national development for a generation to come. It is true that no nation could actually conquer us, owing to our isolated position; but we would be seriously harmed, even materially, by disasters that stopped far short of conquest; and in these matters, which are far more important than things material, we could readily be damaged beyond repair. (Address as Assistant Secretary of the Navy, Naval War College, June 1897.) *Mem. Ed.* XV, 256-257; *Nat. Ed.* XIII, 196-197.

——————. The real chance of war for this nation comes only if we combine a policy which disregards the interests or feelings of others, with a policy of helplessness to hold our own if our right to do as we wish is challenged. If, on the other hand, we are ready in very fact to hold our own, the chance becomes infinitesimal that we will be called upon to do so. (At Naval War College, Newport, R. I., July 22, 1908.) *Mem. Ed.* XVIII, 334; *Nat. Ed.* XVI, 253.

——————. The questions which sometimes involve nations in war are far more difficult and complex than any questions that affect merely individuals. Almost every great nation has inherited certain questions, either with other nations or with sections of its own people, which it is quite impossible, in the present state of civilization, to decide as matters between private individuals can be decided. . . .

There are big and powerful nations which habitually commit, either upon other nations or upon sections of their own people, wrongs so outrageous as to justify even the most peaceful persons in going to war. There are also weak nations so utterly incompetent either to protect the rights of foreigners against their own citizens, or to protect their own citizens against foreigners, that it becomes a matter of sheer duty for some outside power to interfere in connection with them. As yet in neither case is there any efficient method of getting international action; and if joint action by several powers is secured, the result is usually considerably worse than if only one power interfered. (1913.) *Mem. Ed.* XXII, 605; *Nat. Ed.* XX, 520.

WAR—POSSIBILITY OF. One of the difficulties in dealing with foreign affairs is the queer tendency of many people to treat desire on our part to have an adequate navy and coast fortifications as equivalent to the statement that we believe there will be a war, and as justifying offensive war talk. Most certainly we see at times offensive, and therefore utterly improper, talk of war with some entirely friendly nation, now Germany, now England, now Japan. No one can regret such talk more than I do, and it is almost never indulged in by men who would themselves respond to the call to arms if war should unhappily come. A man who is of the type apt to be useful in war is usually of too serious a nature to talk with levity or brutality of war, or in such fashion as to provoke war. My hearty reprobation of this type of offensive agitation does not interfere in the least with my belief, in the first place, that war is unlikely with any power, and in the next place that we can render it still more unlikely, as well as guarantee ourselves against possible humiliation and disaster, by the exercise of moderate forethought and preparation. (*Outlook,* April 1, 1911.) *Mem. Ed.* XIX, 157; *Nat. Ed.* XVII, 113.

WAR—RESULTS OF. Where such results flow from battles as flowed from Bannockburn and Yorktown, centuries must pass before the wound not only scars over but becomes completely forgotten, and the memory becomes a bond of union and not a cause of division. It is our business to shorten the time as much as possible. (To Sir George Otto Trevelyan, January 1, 1908.) *Mem. Ed.* XXIV, 199; Bishop II, 170.

WAR, MODERN — ORGANIZATION FOR. Modern war makes terrible demands upon those who fight. To an infinitely greater degree than ever before the outcome depends upon long preparation in advance, and upon the skilful and unified use of the nation's entire social and industrial no less than military power. The work of the general staff is infinitely more important than any work of the kind in times past. The actual machinery of battle is so vast, delicate and complicated that years are needed to complete it. At all points we see the immense need of thorough organization and machinery ready far in advance of the day of trial. But this does not mean that there is any less need than before of those qualities of endurance and hardihood, of daring and resolution, which in their sum make up the stern and enduring valor which has been and ever will be the mark of mighty victorious armies. (To Henry Bordeaux, June 27,

1918.) *Mem. Ed.* XXIV, 526; Bishop II, 449.

WAR, RIGHTEOUS. We know that in itself war is neither moral nor immoral, that the test of the righteousness of war is the object and purpose for which it is waged. Therefore, it is worth while for our people seriously to consider the problems ahead of them; and the first problem is the problem of preparedness. (*Metropolitan*, August 1915.) *Mem. Ed.* XX, 369; *Nat. Ed.* XVIII, 317.

——————. If the people have not vision, they shall surely perish. No man has a right to live who has not in his soul the power to die nobly for a great cause. Let abhorrence be for those who wage wanton or wicked wars, who with ruthless violence oppress the upright and the unoffending. Pay all honor to the preachers of peace who put righteousness above peace. But shame on the creatures who would teach our people that it is anything but base to be unready and unable to defend right, even at need by the sternest of all tests, the test of righteous war, war waged by a high-couraged people with souls attuned to the demands of a lofty ideal. (*Metropolitan*, January 1916.) *Mem. Ed.* XX, 323; *Nat. Ed.* XVIII, 277.

WAR, UNJUST. War is a dreadful thing, and unjust war is a crime against humanity. But it is such a crime because it is unjust, not because it is war. The choice must ever be in favor of righteousness, and this whether the alternative be peace or whether the alternative be war. . . . Every honorable effort should always be made to avoid war, just as every honorable effort should always be made by the individual in private life to keep out of a brawl, to keep out of trouble; but no self-respecting individual, no self-respecting nation, can or ought to submit to wrong. (At the Sorbonne, Paris, April 23, 1910.) *Mem. Ed.* XV, 357; *Nat. Ed.* XIII, 513.

——————. Wanton or unjust war is an abhorrent evil. But there are even worse evils. (1916.) *Mem. Ed.* XX, 261; *Nat. Ed.* XVIII, 224.

——————. I abhor unjust war, and I deplore that the need even for just war should ever occur. I believe we should set our faces like flint against any policy of aggression by this country on the rights of any other country. (New York *Times*, November 15, 1914.) *Mem. Ed.* XX, 103; *Nat. Ed.* XVIII, 89.

WAR AND PEACE. We are not to be excused if we do not make a resolute and intelligent effort to devise some scheme which will minimize the chance for a recurrence of such horror in the future and which will at least limit and alleviate it if it should occur. In other words, it is our duty to try to devise some efficient plan for securing the peace of righteousness throughout the world.

That any plan will surely and automatically bring peace we cannot promise. Nevertheless, I think a plan can be devised which will render it far more difficult than at present to plunge us into a world war and far more easy than at present to find workable and practical substitutes even for ordinary war. In order to do this, however, it is necessary that we shall fearlessly look facts in the face. We cannot devise methods for securing peace which will actually work unless we are in good faith willing to face the fact that the present all-inclusive arbitration treaties, peace conferences, and the like, upon which our well-meaning pacifists have pinned so much hope, have proved utterly worthless under serious strain. We must face this fact and clearly understand the reason for it before we can advance an adequate remedy. (New York *Times*, September 27, 1914.) *Mem. Ed.* XX, 5; *Nat. Ed.* XVIII, 4-5.

——————. The really essential things for men to remember, therefore, in connection with war are, first, that neither war nor peace is immoral in itself, and, secondly, that in order to preserve the "social values" it is absolutely essential to prevent the dominance in our country of the one form of militarism which is surely and completely fatal—that is, the military dominion of an alien enemy. (American Sociological Society, *Papers*, 1915.) *Mem. Ed.* XX, 272; *Nat. Ed.* XVIII, 234.

——————. The only proper rule is never to fight at all if you can honorably avoid it, but never under any circumstances to fight in a half-hearted way. When peace comes it must be the peace of complete victory. (*Metropolitan*, September 1917.) *Mem. Ed.* XXI, 33; *Nat. Ed.* XIX, 28.

WAR AND PEACE — MEN OF. Popular sentiment is just when it selects as popular heroes the men who have led in the struggle against malice domestic or foreign levy. No triumph of peace is quite so great as the supreme triumphs of war. . . . It is true that no nation can be really great unless it is great in peace; in industry, integrity, honesty. Skilled intelligence in civic affairs and industrial enterprises alike; the special ability of the artist, the man of letters, the man of science, and the man of business; the rigid determination to wrong no man, and to stand for righteousness— all these are necessary in a great nation. But it is also necessary that the nation should have physical no less than moral courage. . . .

We of the United States have passed most of our few years of national life in peace. We honor the architects of our wonderful material prosperity; we appreciate the necessity of thrift, energy, and business enterprise, and we know that even these are of no avail without the civic and social virtues. But we feel, after all, that the men who have dared greatly in war, or the work which is akin to war, are those who deserve best of the country. (Address as Assistant Secretary of the Navy, Naval War College, June 1897.) *Mem. Ed.* XV, 243-245; *Nat. Ed.* XIII, 185-186.

WAR AND PEACE — VICTORIES OF. The victories of peace are great, but the victories of war are greater. No merchant, no banker, no railroad magnate, no inventor of improved industrial processes, can do for any nation what can be done for it by its great fighting men. No triumph of peace can equal the armed triumph over malice domestic or foreign levy. No qualities called out by a purely peaceful life stand on a level with those stern and virile virtues which move the men of stout heart and strong hand who uphold the honor of their flag in battle. It is better for a nation to produce one Grant or one Farragut than a thousand shrewd manufacturers or successful speculators. (*Bookman*, June 1897.) *Mem. Ed.* XIV, 330; *Nat. Ed.* XII, 283.

WAR. *See also* ARBITRATION; DEFENSE; FORCE; INTERNATIONAL DISPUTES; LEAGUE FOR PEACE; LEAGUE OF NATIONS; MILITARISM; MILITARY TRAINING; NATIONAL DEFENSE; PACIFISM; PEACE; PREPAREDNESS; RIGHTEOUSNESS; SOLDIERS; TREASON; UNPREPAREDNESS.

WAR OF 1812. The war had a dual aspect. It was partly a contest between the two branches of the English race, and partly a last attempt on the part of the Indian tribes to check the advance of the most rapidly growing one of these same two branches; and this last portion of the struggle, though attracting comparatively little attention, was really much the most far-reaching in its effect upon history. The triumph of the British would have distinctly meant the giving a new lease of life to the Indian nationalities, the hemming in, for a time, of the United States, and the stoppage, perhaps for many years, of the march of English civilization across the continent. (1882.) *Mem. Ed.* VII, 425-426; *Nat. Ed.* VI, 374-375.

————————. The war cannot ever be fairly understood by any one who does not bear in mind that the combatants were men of the same stock, who far more nearly resembled each other than either resembled any other nation. I honestly believe that the American sailor offered rather better material for a man-of-war's man than the British, because the freer institutions of his country (as compared with the Britain of the drunken Prince Regent and his dotard father—a very different land from the present free England) and the peculiar exigencies of his life tended to make him more intelligent and self-reliant; but the difference, when there was any, was very small. . . . The advantage consisted in the fact that our average commander was equal to the best, and higher than the average, of the opposing captains; and this held good throughout the various grades of the officers. The American officers knew they had redoubtable foes to contend with, and made every preparation accordingly. Owing their rank to their own exertions, trained by practical experience, and with large liberty of action, they made every effort to have their crews in the most perfect state of skill and discipline. (1882.) *Mem. Ed.* VII, 417-418; *Nat. Ed.* VI, 367-368.

————————. It was highly to the credit of the United States that her frigates were of better make and armament than any others; it always speaks well for a nation's energy and capacity that any of her implements of warfare are of a superior kind. This is a perfectly legitimate reason for pride. . . .

Thus, it must be remembered that two things contributed to our victories. One was the excellent make and armament of our ships; the other was the skilful seamanship, excellent discipline, and superb gunnery of the men who were in them. British writers are apt only to speak of the first, and Americans only of the last, whereas both should be taken into consideration. (1882.) *Mem. Ed.* VII, 56-57; *Nat. Ed.* VI, 50-51.

WAR OF 1812—ORIGINS OF. Wide differences in the views of the two nations produced endless difficulties. To escape the press-gang, or for other reasons, many British seamen took service under the American flag; and if they were demanded back, it is not likely that they or their American shipmates had much hesitation in swearing either that they were not British at all, or else that they had been naturalized as Americans. Equally probable is it that the American blockade-runners were guilty of a great deal of fraud and more or less thinly veiled perjury. But the wrongs done by the Americans were insignificant compared with those they received. Any innocent merchant vessel was liable to seizure at any moment; and when overhauled by a British cruiser short of men was sure to be stripped of most of her crew. The British officers were themselves the judges as to whether a seaman should be pronounced a native of America or of Britain, and there was no appeal from their judgment. If a captain lacked his full complement there was little doubt as to the view he would take of any man's nationality. The wrongs inflicted on our seafaring countrymen by their impressment into foreign ships formed the main cause of the war. (1882.) *Mem. Ed.* VII, 4-5; *Nat. Ed.* VI, 4.

WAR OF 1812—RESULTS OF. In the West the war was only the closing act of the struggle that for many years had been waged by the hardy and restless pioneers of our race, as with rifle and axe they carved out the mighty empire that we their children inherit; it was but the final effort with which they wrested from the Indian lords of the soil the wide and fair domain that now forms the heart of our great Republic. It was the breaking down of the last barrier that stayed the flood of our civilization; it settled, once and forever, that henceforth the law, the tongue, and the blood of the land should be neither Indian, nor yet French, but English. The few French of the West were fighting against a race that was to leave as little trace of them as of the doomed Indian peoples with whom they made common cause. The presence of the British mercenaries did not alter the character of the contest; it merely served to show the bitter and narrow hatred with which the Mother-Island regarded her greater daughter, predestined as the latter was to be queen of the lands that lay beyond the Atlantic. (1883.) *Mem. Ed.* VII, xxxvi; *Nat. Ed.* VI, xxxi-xxxii.

WAR OF 1812 — UNPREPAREDNESS FOR. The administration thus drifted into a war which it had neither the wisdom to avoid nor the forethought to prepare for. In view of the fact that the war was their own, it is impossible to condemn sufficiently strongly the incredible folly of the Democrats in having all along refused to build a navy or provide any other adequate means of defense. In accordance with their curiously foolish theories, they persisted in relying on that weakest of all weak reeds, the militia, who promptly ran away every time they faced a foe in the open. (1888.) *Mem. Ed.* VIII, 532; *Nat. Ed.* VII, 460.

WAR OF 1812. *See also* JACKSON, ANDREW; MORRIS, GOUVERNEUR; UNPREPAREDNESS.

WARS. *See* BOER WAR; CIVIL WAR; REVOLUTIONARY WAR; RUSSO-JAPANESE WAR; SPANISH-AMERICAN WAR; WAR OF 1812; WORLD WAR.

WARS, AMERICAN. Wars are, of course, as a rule to be avoided; but they are far better than certain kinds of peace. Every war in which we have been engaged, except the one with Mexico, has been justifiable in its origin; and each one, without any exception whatever, has left us better off, taking both moral and material considerations into account, than we should have been if we had not waged it. (1887.) *Mem. Ed.* VIII, 214; *Nat. Ed.* VII, 185.

WARS OF CONQUEST. Many good persons seem prone to speak of all wars of conquest as necessarily evil. This is, of course, a short-sighted view. In its after-effects a conquest may be fraught either with evil or with good for mankind, according to the comparative worth of the conquering and conquered peoples. It is useless to try to generalize about conquests simply as such in the abstract; each case or set of cases must be judged by itself. The world would have halted had it not been for the Teutonic conquests in alien lands; but the victories of Moslem over Christian have always proved a curse in the end. Nothing but sheer evil has come from the victories of Turk and Tartar. This is true generally of the victories of barbarians of low racial characteristics over gentler, more moral, and more refined peoples, even though these people have, to their shame and discredit, lost the vigorous fighting virtues. Yet it remains no less true that the world would probably have gone forward very little, indeed would probably not have gone forward at all, had it not been for the displacement or submersion of savage and barbaric peoples as a consequence of the armed settlement in strange lands of the races who hold in their hands the fate of the years. Every such submersion or displacement of an inferior race, every such armed settlement or conquest by a superior race, means the infliction and suffering of hideous woe and misery. It is a sad and dreadful thing that there should be of necessity such throes of agony; and yet they are the birth-pangs of a new and vigorous people. That they are in truth birth-pangs does not lessen the grim and hopeless woe of the race supplanted; of the race outworn or overthrown. The wrongs done and suffered cannot be blinked. Neither can they be allowed to hide the results to mankind of what has been achieved. (1894.) *Mem. Ed.* XI, 389; *Nat. Ed.* IX, 155.

WARS OF CONQUEST. *See also* EXPANSION; IMPERIALISM; MONGOL INVASIONS.

WARSHIPS. *See* BATTLESHIPS; NAVAL ARMAMENTS; SUBMARINES; TORPEDO BOATS.

WASHINGTON, BOOKER T. Booker Washington owed his wonderful success, his wonderful achievement, to the combination of many rare qualities. It was not to any one quality alone that he owed success and achievement, it was to many. He understood, for example, and preached the gospel of efficiency, the gospel of work, and he realized that this is as necessary for the white man as it is for the black man; that for almost all of us there must be a foundation of manual efficiency, of the efficiency that is industrial, or else there cannot be any superstructure of mere efficiency built upon it. Men have got to learn to do the primary useful things before they can do the things that are secondarily useful, and the average man in the community must have the efficiency that shows itself in the work of the mechanic in the city, or the work of the farmer in the country, else the community cannot be on a healthy basis. . . .

Also, he had that quality, that essential quality in every teacher . . . which will teach the boy and the girl that the real happiness of life is to be found, not in shirking difficulties, but in overcoming them; not in striving to lead a life which shall so far as possible avoid effort and labor and hardship, but a life which shall face difficulty and win over it, be it ever so hard, by labor very intelligently entered into and resolutely persevered in. He never sought to make you believe that you were going to have easy times ahead of you. There are only a few people who do what he did in life, and they are always the happiest and they are really the most useful. (At memorial service for B. T. Washington, Tuskegee Institute, December 12, 1915.) *The Southern Workman*, January 1916, pp. 12-13.

————————. It is not hyperbole to say that Booker T. Washington was a great American. For twenty years before his death he had been the most useful, as well as the most distinguished, member of his race in the world, and one of the most useful, as well as one of the most distinguished, of American citizens of any race.

Eminent though his services were to the people of his own color, the white men of our Republic were almost as much indebted to him, both directly and indirectly. They were indebted to him directly, because of the work he did on behalf of industrial education for the negro, thus giving impetus to the work for the industrial education of the white man, which is, at least, as necessary; and, moreover, every successful effort to turn the thoughts of the natural leaders of the negro race into the fields of business endeavor, of agricultural effort, of every species of success in private life, is not only to their advantage, but to the advantage of the white man, as tending to remove the friction and trouble that inevitably come through the South at this time in any negro district where the negroes turn for their advancement primarily to political life.

The indirect indebtedness of the white race to Booker T. Washington is due to the simple fact that here in America we are all in the end going up or down together; and therefore, in the long run, the man who makes a substantial contribution toward uplifting any part of the community has helped to uplift all of the community. (Preface to E. J. Scott and L. B. Stowe, *Booker T. Washington;* August 28, 1916.) *Mem. Ed.* XII, 548; *Nat. Ed.* XI, 273.

————————. As nearly as any man I have ever met, Booker T. Washington lived up to Micah's verse, "What more doth the Lord require of thee than to do Justice and love Mercy and walk humbly with thy God." He did justice to every man. He did justice to those to whom it was a hard thing to do justice. He showed mercy; and this meant that he showed mercy not only to the poor, and to those beneath him, but that he showed mercy by an understanding of the shortcomings of those who failed to do him justice, and failed to do his race justice. He always understood and acted upon the belief that the black man could not rise if he so acted as to incur the enmity and hatred of the white man. . . .

He was never led away, as the educated negro so often is led away, into the pursuit of fantastic visions; into the drawing up of plans fit only for a world of two dimensions. He kept his high ideals, always; but he never forgot for a moment that he was living in an actual world of three dimensions, in a world of unpleasant facts, where those unpleasant facts have to be faced; and he made the best possible out of a bad situation from which there was no ideal best to be obtained. . . .

To a very extraordinary degree he combined humility and dignity; and I think that the explanation of this extraordinary degree of success in a very difficult combination was due to the fact that at the bottom his humility was really the outward expression, not of a servile attitude toward any man, but of the spiritual fact that in very truth he walked humbly with his God. (Preface to E. J. Scott and L. B. Stowe, *Booker T. Washington;* August 28, 1916.) *Mem. Ed.* XII, 550; *Nat. Ed.* XI, 274-275.

——————. The Booker T. Washington incident was to me so much a matter of course that I regarded its sole importance as consisting in the view it gave one of the continued existence of that combination of Bourbon intellect and intolerant truculence of spirit, through much of the South, which brought on the Civil War. If these creatures had any sense they would understand that they can't bluff me. They can't even make me abandon my policy of appointing decent men to office in their own localities. (To H. C. Lodge, October 28, 1901.) Lodge *Letters* I, 510.

——————. When I asked Booker T. Washington to dinner I did not devote very much thought to the matter one way or the other. I respect him greatly and believe in the work he has done. I have consulted so much with him it seemed to me that it was natural to ask him to dinner to talk over this work, and the very fact that I felt a moment's qualm on inviting him because of his color made me ashamed of myself and made me hasten to send the invitation. I did not think of its bearing one way or the other, either on my own future or on any thing else. As things have turned out, I am very glad that I asked him, for the clamor aroused by the act makes me feel as if the act was necessary. (To Albion W. Tourgee, November 8, 1901.) *Mem. Ed.* XXIII, 192; Bishop I, 166.

WASHINGTON, BOOKER T. *See also* TUSKEGEE INSTITUTE.

WASHINGTON, GEORGE. I believe Washington was, not even excepting Lincoln, the very greatest man of modern times; and a great general, of the Fabian order, too, but on the battle field I doubt if he equalled any one of half a dozen of the Union and Rebel chiefs who fought in the great Civil War. (To H. C. Lodge, August 24, 1884.) Lodge *Letters* I, 9.

——————. After the American Revolution Washington's greatness of character, sound common sense, and entirely disinterested patriotism, made him a bulwark both against anarchy and against despotism coming in the name of a safeguard against anarchy; and the people were fit for self-government, adding to their fierce jealousy of tyranny a reluctant and by no means whole-hearted, but genuine, admission that it could be averted only by coming to an agreement among themselves. Washington would not let his officers try to make him Dictator, nor allow the Continental army to march against the weak Congress which distrusted it, was ungrateful to it, and refused to provide for it. Unlike Cromwell, he saw that the safety of the people lay in working out their own salvation, even though they showed much wrong-headedness and blindness, not merely to morality, but to their own interests; and, in the long run, the people justified this trust. (1900.) *Mem. Ed.* XIII, 359-360; *Nat. Ed.* X, 249-250.

——————. No American should ever forget Washington's insistence upon the absolute necessity of preserving the Union; his appeals to our people that they should cherish the American nationality as something indestructible from within and as separating us in clear-cut manner from all other nations; his stern refusal to yield to the tyranny of either an individual or a mob, and his demand that we seek both liberty and order as indispensable to the life of a democratic republic; and his unwearied persistence in preaching the great truth that military preparedness is essential to our self-respect and usefulness, and that the only way to prepare for war is to prepare in time of peace. (1917.) *Mem. Ed.* XXI, 57; *Nat. Ed.* XIX, 49.

WASHINGTON, GEORGE. *See also* CROMWELL, OLIVER; JEFFERSON, THOMAS; REVOLUTIONARY WAR; VALLEY FORGE.

WASHINGTON AND LINCOLN. I regard the memories of Washington and Lincoln as priceless heritages for our people, just because they are the memories of strong men, of men who cannot be accused of weakness or timidity, of men who I believe were quite as strong, for instance, as Cromwell or Bismarck, and very much stronger than the Louis-Napoleon type who, nevertheless, led careers marked by disinterestedness just as much as by strength; who, like Timoleon and Hampden, in very deed, and not as a mere matter of oratory or fine writing, sought just the public good, the good of the people as a whole, as the first of all considerations. (To Sir George Otto Trevelyan, June 19, 1908.) *Mem. Ed.* XXIV, 109; Bishop II, 93.

──────────. It is the peculiar good fortune of the United States that in its two greatest citizens, Washington and Lincoln, it has developed men whose ideals were lofty, not only as regards their conduct toward their fellow citizens within the borders of their own land, but also as to the way in which their country should behave in dealing with other countries. These men were the greatest of their type, the type of Timoleon and Hampden, and it is no small honor to America that this, the highest, type of statesmanship should have here received its highest development. . . . Both Washington and Lincoln were devoted Americans, devoted patriots. Each was willing to pour out the blood of the bravest and best in the land for a high and worthy cause, and each was a practical man, as far removed as possible from the sentimentalist and the doctrinaire. But each lived his life in accordance with a high ideal of right which forbade him to wrong his neighbor, and which when he became head of the state forbade him to inflict international wrong, as it forbade him to inflict private wrong. Each left to his countrymen as a priceless heritage the ennobling memory of a life which achieved great success through rendering far greater service, of a life lived in practical fashion for the achievement of lofty ideals, of a life lived in accordance with a standard of duty which forbade maltreatment of one man by another, which forbade maltreatment by one nation of another. (*Outlook,* January 23, 1909.) *Mem. Ed.* XII, 420-421; *Nat. Ed.* XI, 184-185.

──────────. As a people we are indeed beyond measure fortunate in the characters of the two greatest of our public men, Washington and Lincoln. Widely though they differed in externals, the Virginia landed gentleman and the Kentucky backwoodsman, they were alike in essentials, they were alike in the great qualities which made each able to render service to his nation and to all mankind such as no other man of his generation could or did render. Each had lofty ideals, but each in striving to attain these lofty ideals was guided by the soundest common sense. Each possessed inflexible courage in adversity, and a soul wholly unspoiled by prosperity. Each possessed all the gentler virtues commonly exhibited by good men who lack rugged strength of character. Each possessed also all the strong qualities commonly exhibited by those towering masters of mankind who have too often shown themselves devoid of so much as the understanding of the words by which we signify the qualities of duty, of mercy, of devotion to the right, of lofty disinterestedness in battling for the good of others. There have been other men as great and other men as good; but in all the history of mankind there are no other two great men as good as these, no other two good men as great. (Address at Hodgenville, Ky., February 12, 1909.) *Mem. Ed.* XII, 452; *Nat. Ed.* XI, 211.

WASHINGTON AND LINCOLN—SERVICE OF. Washington and Lincoln set the standard of conduct for the public servants of this people. They showed how men of the strongest type could also possess all the disinterested, all the unselfish, devotion to duty and to the interests of their fellow countrymen that we have a right to expect, but can only hope to see in the very highest type of public servant. At however great a distance, I have been anxious to follow in their footsteps, and anxious that, however great the difference in degree, my service to the Nation should be approximately the same *in kind* as theirs. (To Sir George Otto Trevelyan, November 6, 1908.) *Mem. Ed.* XXIV, 145; Bishop II, 125.

WASHINGTON AND LINCOLN — TEACHINGS OF. Lip-loyalty to Washington and Lincoln costs nothing and is worth just exactly what it costs. What counts is the application of their principles to the conditions of to-day. Whoever is too proud to fight, whoever believes that there are times when it is not well to arouse the spirit of patriotism, whoever demands peace without victory, whoever regards the demand for ample preparedness as hysterical, whoever attacks conscription and the draft or fails to uphold universal, obligatory military service, is false to the teachings and lives of Washington and Lincoln. Whoever seeks office, or upholds a candidate for office, on the ground that he "kept us out of war," without regard to whether the honor and vital interests of the nation and of mankind demand the war, is treacherous to the principles of Washington and Lincoln; *they* did not "keep us out of war," and they never sought or accepted office on a platform which they cynically repudiated when once they had secured office. (1917.) *Mem. Ed.* XXI, 56; *Nat. Ed.* XIX, 48.

WASHINGTON AS HUNTER. The greatest of Americans, Washington, was very fond of hunting, both with rifle and fowling-piece, and especially with horse, horn and hound. Essentially the representative of all that is best in our national life, standing high as a general, high as a statesman, and highest of all as a man, he could never have been what he was had he not taken delight in feats of hardihood, of daring, and of bodily prowess. He was strongly drawn to those field-sports which demand in their follower the exercise of the manly virtues—courage, endurance, physical address. As a young man, clad in the distinctive garb of the backwoodsman, the fringed and tasselled hunting-shirt, he led the life of a frontier surveyor; and like his fellow adventurers in wilderness exploration and Indian campaigning, he was often forced to trust to the long rifle for keeping his party in food. When at his home at Mount Vernon he hunted from simple delight in the sport. (1893.) *Mem. Ed.* II, 421-422; *Nat. Ed.* II, 361.

WASHINGTON'S BIRTHPLACE. On Sunday Mother and I spent about four hours ashore, taking our lunch and walking up to the monument which marks where the house stood in which Washington was born. It is a simple shaft. Every vestige of the house is destroyed, but a curious and rather pathetic thing is that, although it must be a hundred years since the place was deserted, there are still multitudes of flowers which must have come from those in the old garden. There are iris and narcissus and a little blue flower, with a neat, prim, clean smell that makes one feel as if it ought to be put with lavender into chests of fresh old linen. The narcissus in particular was growing around everywhere, together with real wild flowers like the painted columbine and star of Bethlehem. It was a lovely spot on a headland overlooking a broad inlet from the Potomac. There was also the old graveyard or grave plot in which were the gravestones of Washington's father and mother and grandmother, all pretty nearly ruined. (Kermit Roosevelt, April 30, 1906.) *Mem. Ed.* XXI, 563; *Nat. Ed.* XIX, 506.

WATAUGA SETTLEMENT. The Watauga folk were the first Americans who, as a separate body, moved into the wilderness to hew out dwellings for themselves and their children, trusting only to their own shrewd heads, stout hearts, and strong arms, unhelped and unhampered by the power nominally their sovereign. They built up a commonwealth which had many successors; they showed that the frontiersmen could do their work unassisted; for they not only proved that they were made of stuff stern enough to hold its own against outside pressure of any sort, but they also made it evident that having won the land they were competent to govern both it and themselves. They were the first to do what the whole nation has since done. . . .

The Watauga settlers outlined in advance the nation's work. They tamed the rugged and shaggy wilderness, they bid defiance to outside foes, and they successfully solved the difficult problem of self-government. (1889.) *Mem. Ed.* X, 178-179; *Nat. Ed.* VIII, 157-158.

"WATCHFUL WAITING." The policy of watchful waiting, a policy popular among governmental chiefs of a certain type ever since the days of Ethelred the Unready and for thousands of years anterior to that not wholly fortunate ruler, has failed, as of course it always does fail in the presence of serious difficulty and of a resolute and ruthless foe. We have tried every possible expedient save only the application of wisdom and resolution. (*Metropolitan,* November 1915.) *Mem. Ed.* XX, 374; *Nat. Ed.* XVIII, 320.

——————. On August 27th, 1913, President Wilson said with marked oratorical effect: "We shall vigilantly watch the fortunes of those Americans who cannot get away from Mexico." "Vigilant watching" — "watchful waiting" — the phrase matters nothing; for there never is any deed to back it up. Three years have passed since the date of this oration; three years of incessant elocution on the part of Mr. Wilson; three years of repeated invocations to humanity and peace by Mr. Wilson; and Mr. Wilson still continues to "vigilantly watch the fortunes of those Americans who cannot get away." There are not many of them left now. Hundreds have been killed, and Mr. Wilson has watched their fortunes as disinterestedly as if they had been rats pursued by terriers. This administration has displayed no more feeling of responsibility for the American women who have been raped, and for the American men, women and children who have been killed in Mexico, than a farmer shows for the rats killed by his dogs when the hay is taken from a barn. And now the American people are asked to sanction this policy in the name of peace, righteousness and humanity. (At Lewiston, Me., August 31, 1916.) Theodore Roosevelt,

Americanism and Preparedness. (New York, 1917), pp. 15-16.

"WATCHFUL WAITING." See also MEXICO; UNPREPAREDNESS.

WATER CONSERVATION. The forests alone cannot . . . fully regulate and conserve the waters of the arid region. Great storage works are necessary to equalize the flow of streams and to save the flood waters. Their construction has been conclusively shown to be an undertaking too vast for private effort. Nor can it be best accomplished by the individual States acting alone. Far-reaching interstate problems are involved; and the resources of single States would often be inadequate. It is properly a national function, at least in some of its features. It is as right for the National Government to make the streams and rivers of the arid region useful by engineering works for water storage as to make useful the rivers and harbors of the humid region by engineering works of another kind. The storing of the floods in reservoirs at the headwaters of our rivers is but an enlargement of our present policy of river control, under which levees are built on the lower reaches of the same streams.

The government should construct and maintain these reservoirs as it does other public works. Where their purpose is to regulate the flow of streams, the water should be turned freely into the channels in the dry season to take the same course under the same laws as the natural flow. (First Annual Message, Washington, December 3, 1901.) *Mem. Ed.* XVII, 121-122; *Nat. Ed.* XV, 105.

WATER CONSERVATION. See also CONSERVATION; FLOOD PREVENTION; INLAND WATERWAYS.

WATER POWER. Running water pays no heed to State lines. Every important river system of our country includes more than one State in its area. The Nation, and the Nation alone, can act with full effect in this matter. Water power will play an enormous part in the future of industrialism. The people should not surrender it in fee to any individual or corporation, but merely rent it for a time on terms amply favorable to the users, but on terms which will safeguard the public; while the fact that the lease is only for a period of years will permit the public to take account of changing conditions. *Outlook*, January 28, 1911, p. 146.

————. All the remaining water power in our country should be retained in full by the people, and should be developed and used so as to pay a good, fair profit to the developers, but with the prime aim of keeping the ultimate ownership in the people and making its beneficial use by the people the first consideration. *Outlook*, April 20, 1912, p. 853.

————. The public should not alienate its fee in the water-power which will be of incalculable consequence as a source of power in the immediate future. The nation and the States within their several spheres should by immediate legislation keep the fee of the water-power, leasing its use only for a reasonable length of time on terms that will secure the interests of the public. (Before Progressive National Convention, Chicago, August 6, 1912.) *Mem. Ed.* XIX, 405; *Nat. Ed.* XVII, 293.

WATER POWER. See also ELECTRIC POWER.

WATERED STOCK. See STOCK-WATERING.

WATERWAYS. See INLAND WATERWAYS; MISSISSIPPI RIVER.

WAYNE, ANTHONY. One of the heroic figures of the Revolution was Anthony Wayne, major-general of the Continental line. With the exception of Washington, and perhaps Greene, he was the best general the Americans developed in the contest; and without exception he showed himself to be the hardest fighter produced on either side. He belongs, as regards this latter characteristic, with the men like Winfield Scott, Phil Kearney, Hancock, and Forrest, who revelled in the danger and the actual shock of arms. Indeed, his eager love of battle, and splendid disregard of peril, have made many writers forget his really great qualities as a general. Soldiers are always prompt to recognize the prime virtue of physical courage, and Wayne's followers christened their daring commander "Mad Anthony," in loving allusion to his reckless bravery. It is perfectly true that Wayne had this courage, and that he was a born fighter; otherwise, he never would have been a great commander. A man who lacks the fondness for fighting, the eager desire to punish his adversary, and the willingness to suffer punishment in return, may be a great organizer, like McClellan, but can never become a great general or win great victories. There are, however, plenty of men, who, though they possess these fine manly traits, yet lack the head to command an army;

but Wayne had not only the heart and the hand but the head likewise. No man could dare as greatly as he did without incurring the risk of an occasional check; but he was an able and bold tactician, a vigilant and cautious leader, well fitted to bear the terrible burden of responsibility which rests upon a commander-in-chief. (1895.) *Mem. Ed.* IX, 45-46; *Nat. Ed.* X, 40-41.

WEAKNESS. Weakness invites contempt. Weakness combined with bluster invites both contempt and aggression. Self-respecting strength that respects the rights of others is the only quality that secures respect from others. If, in our foreign policy, we are weak, if we use lofty words at the same time that we commit mean or unworthy actions, and above all, if we fail to protect our own rights, we shall not secure the good-will of any one, and we shall incur the contempt of other nations; and contempt of that kind is easily turned into active international violence. (At Kansas City, Mo., May 30, 1916.) *The Progressive Party; Its Record from January to July 1916.* (Progressive National Committee, 1916), p. 57.

WEAKNESS—DANGERS OF. A weakling who fears to stand up manfully for the right may work as much mischief as any strong-armed wrong-doer. (*Metropolitan*, March 1915.) *Mem. Ed.* XX, 432; *Nat. Ed.* XVIII, 370.

——————. Criminals always attack the helpless if possible. In exactly similar fashion aggressive and militarist nations attack weak nations where it is possible. Weakness always invites attack. Preparedness usually, but not always, averts it. (*Metropolitan*, February 1916.) *Mem. Ed.* XX, 279; *Nat. Ed.* XVIII, 240.

WEAKNESS AND STRENGTH. It is not enough to be well-meaning and kindly, but weak; neither is it enough to be strong, unless morality and decency go hand in hand with strength. (At State Fair, Syracuse, N. Y., September 7, 1903.) *Mem. Ed.* XVIII, 69; *Nat. Ed.* XVI, 59.

WEAKNESS AND WICKEDNESS. We ought not to tolerate wrong. It is a sign of weakness to do so, and in its ultimate effects weakness is often quite as bad as wickedness. But in putting a stop to the wrong we should, so far as possible, avoid getting into an attitude of vindictive hatred toward the wrong-doer. (At Jamestown Exposition, Virginia, June 10, 1907.) *Mem. Ed.* XVIII, 236; *Nat. Ed.* XVI, 174.

WEAKNESS. *See also* COURAGE; MANLY VIRTUES; "MOLLYCODDLE"; PREPAREDNESS.

WEALTH. I am simply unable to understand the value placed by so many people upon great wealth. I very thoroughly understand the need of sufficient means to enable the man or woman to be comfortable; I also entirely understand the pleasure of having enough more than this to add certain luxuries, and above all, that greatest of all luxuries, the escape from the need of considering at every turn whether it is possible to spend a dollar or two extra; but when the last limit has been reached, then increase in wealth means but little, certainly as compared with all kinds of other things. In consequence, I am simply unable to make myself take the attitude of respect toward the very wealthy men which such an enormous multitude of people evidently really feel. I am delighted to show any courtesy to Pierpont Morgan or Andrew Carnegie or James J. Hill, but as for regarding any one of them as, for instance, I regard Professor Bury, or Peary, the Arctic explorer, or Admiral Evans, or Rhodes, the historian, or Selous, the big-game hunter (to mention at random guests who have been at the White House not long ago)—why, I could not force myself to do it even if I wanted to, which I do not. (To Sir Cecil Arthur Spring-Rice, April 11, 1908.) *Mem. Ed.* XXIV, 128; Bishop II, 110.

——————. Wealthy men who use their wealth aright are a great power for good in the community, and help to upbuild that material national prosperity which must underlie national greatness; but if this were the only kind of success, the nation would be indeed poorly off. (*Outlook*, March 31, 1900.) *Mem. Ed.* XV, 498; *Nat. Ed.* XIII, 383.

——————. There are plenty of ugly things about wealth and its possessors in the present age, and I suppose there have been in all ages. There are many rich people who so utterly lack patriotism, or show such sordid and selfish traits of character, or lead such mean and vacuous lives, that all right-minded men must look upon them with angry contempt; but, on the whole, the thrifty are apt to be better citizens than the thriftless; and the worst capitalist cannot harm laboring men as they are harmed by demagogues. (*Review* of *Reviews,* January 1897.) *Mem. Ed.* XVI, 376; *Nat. Ed.* XIII, 160.

WEALTH—ABUSE OF. Our sternest effort should be exerted against the man of wealth and power who gets the wealth by harming others and uses the power without regard to the general welfare. (1918.) *Mem. Ed.* XXI, 385; *Nat. Ed.* XIX, 349.

——————. A great fortune if used wrongly is a menace to the community. A man of great wealth who does not use that wealth decently is, in a peculiar sense, a menace to the community, and so is the man who does not use his intellect aright. Each talent—the talent for making money, the talent for showing intellect at the bar, or in any other way—if unaccompanied by character, makes the possessor a menace to the community. But such a fact no more warrants us in attacking wealth than it does in attacking intellect. Every man of power, by the very fact of that power, is capable of doing damage to his neighbors; but we cannot afford to discourage the development of such men merely because it is possible they may use their power for wrong ends. If we did so we should leave our history a blank, for we should have no great statesmen, soldiers, merchants, no great men of arts, of letters, of science. Doubtless on the average the most useful citizen to the community as a whole is the man to whom has been granted what the Psalmist asked for—neither poverty nor riches. But the great captain of industry, the man of wealth, who, alone or in combination with his fellows, drives through our great business enterprises, is a factor without whom the civilization that we see roundabout us here could not have been built up. Good, not harm, normally comes from the upbuilding of such wealth. Probably the greatest harm done by vast wealth is the harm that we of moderate means do ourselves when we let the vices of envy and hatred enter deep into our own natures. (At Providence, R. I., August 23, 1902.) *Mem. Ed.* XVIII, 76; *Nat. Ed.* XVI, 64.

——————. Much of the outcry against wealth, against the men who acquire wealth, and against the means by which it is acquired, is blind, unreasoning, and unjust; but in too many cases it has a basis in real abuses; and we must remember that every act of misconduct which affords any justification for this clamor is not only bad because of the wrong done, but also because the justification thus given inevitably strengthens movements which are in reality profoundly antisocial and anticivic. (Annual Message as Governor, Albany, January 3, 1900.) *Mem. Ed.* XVII, 42; *Nat. Ed.* XV, 37.

——————. The outcry against stopping dishonest practices among the very wealthy is precisely similar to the outcry raised against every effort for cleanliness and decency in city government because, forsooth, it will "hurt business." . . . It is meet and fit that the apologists for corrupt wealth should oppose every effort to relieve weak and helpless people from crushing misfortune brought upon them by injury in the business from which they gain a bare livelihood and their employers fortunes. (To Charles J. Bonaparte, January 2, 1908.) *Mem. Ed.* XXII, 520, 521; *Nat. Ed.* XX, 447, 448.

WEALTH — ACCUMULATION OF. The man who, having far surpassed the limit of providing for the wants, both of body and mind, of himself and of those depending upon him, then piles up a great fortune, for the acquisition or retention of which he returns no corresponding benefit to the nation as a whole, should himself be made to feel that, so far from being a desirable, he is an unworthy, citizen of the community; that he is to be neither admired nor envied; that his right-thinking fellow countrymen put him low in the scale of citizenship, and leave him to be consoled by the admiration of those whose level of purpose is even lower than his own. (At the Sorbonne, Paris, April 23, 1910.) *Mem. Ed.* XV, 360; *Nat. Ed.* XIII, 515.

——————. The mere acquisition of wealth in and by itself, beyond a certain point, speaks very little indeed for the man compared with success in most other lines of endeavor. . . . It is a great epic feat to drive a railroad across a continent; it is a great epic feat to build up a business worth building. For the man who performs that feat I have a genuine regard. For the man who makes a great fortune as an incident to rendering a great service I have nothing but admiration—although unfortunately the men who are entitled to our regard, and a little more—to our admiration—for the feats that they have thus done, have too often forfeited all right to that regard and admiration and more than forfeited it by the course that they have afterward, or coincidently, pursued in regard to money-making or in other matters. (At Pacific Theological Seminary, Spring 1911.) *Mem. Ed.* XV, 585; *Nat. Ed.* XIII, 623.

WEALTH — ACQUISITION OF. The chicanery and the dishonest, even though not technically illegal, methods through which some great fortunes have been made, are scandals to our civilization. The man who by swindling or wrong-doing acquires great wealth for himself at the expense of his fellow, stands as low morally as any predatory mediaeval nobleman, and is a more dangerous member of society. Any law, and any method of construing the law which will enable the community to punish him, either by taking away his wealth or by imprisonment, should be welcomed. (Annual Message as Governor, Albany, January 3, 1900.) *Mem. Ed.* XVII, 52; *Nat. Ed.* XV, 45.

WEALTH—CONTROL OF. There is no one problem that is so difficult to deal with as the problem of how to do justice to wealth, either in the hands of the individual or the corporation, on the one hand, or, on the other, how to see that that wealth in return is used for the benefit of the whole community. The tendency, as is natural, is for men to range themselves in two extreme camps, each taking a position that, in the long run, would be almost equally fatal to the community. We have, on the one hand, the ignorant declaimer against all men of means; the man who paints his fellows who are well off as being, because of that very fact, the foes of the community as a whole, and, on the other, we find him, who, whether honestly or dishonestly, permits his fear of improper interference with property to take the form of shrinking from and avoiding all proper interference with it, who fears to take any attitude which any of his friends, any of those with whom he associates, may denounce as being an attitude hostile to men of means. (Before Independent Club, Buffalo, N. Y., May 15, 1899.) *Mem. Ed.* XVI, 486; *Nat. Ed.* XIV, 325.

————————. There may be better schemes of taxation than those at present employed; it may be wise to devise inheritance taxes, and to impose regulations on the kinds of business which can be carried on only under the especial protection of the State; and where there is a real abuse by wealth it needs to be, and in this country generally has been, promptly done away with; but the first lesson to teach the poor man is that, as a whole, the wealth in the community is distinctly beneficial to him; that he is better off in the long run because other men are well off; and that the surest way to destroy what measure of prosperity he may have is to paralyze industry and the well-being of those men who have achieved success. (*Review of Reviews,* January 1897.) *Mem. Ed.* XVI, 376; *Nat. Ed.* XIII, 161.

————————. The point to be aimed at is the protection of the individual against wrong, not the attempt to limit and hamper the acquisition and output of wealth. (Annual Message as Governor, Albany, January 3, 1900.) *Mem. Ed.* XVII, 47; *Nat. Ed.* XV, 41.

————————. We have no quarrel with the individuals, whether public men, lawyers or editors. . . . These men derive their sole power from the great, sinister offenders who stand behind them. They are but puppets who move as the strings are pulled by those who control the enormous masses of corporate wealth which if itself left uncontrolled threatens dire evil to the Republic. It is not the puppets, but the strong, cunning men and the mighty forces working for evil behind, and to a certain extent through, the puppets, with whom we have to deal. We seek to control law-defying wealth, in the first place to prevent its doing evil, and in the next place to avoid the vindictive and dreadful radicalism which if left uncontrolled it is certain in the end to arouse. . . . We stand with equal stoutness for the rights of the man of wealth and for the rights of the wage-workers; just as much so for one as for the other. We seek to stop wrong-doing; and we desire to punish the wrong-doer only so far as is necessary in order to achieve this end. We are the stanch upholders of every honest man, whether business man or wage-worker. (To Charles J. Bonaparte, January 2, 1908.) *Mem. Ed.* XXII, 523-524; *Nat. Ed.* XX, 450.

————————. Those men of enormous wealth who bitterly oppose every species of effective control, by the people through their governmental agents over the business use of that wealth are, I verily believe, most shortsighted as to their own ultimate interests. They should welcome such effort, they should welcome every effort to make them observe and to assist them in observing the law, so that their activities shall be helpful and not harmful to the American people. Most surely if the wise and moderate control we advocate does not come, then some day these men or their descendants will have to face the chance of some movement of really dangerous and drastic character being directed against them. The very wealthy men who oppose this action illustrate the undoubted truth that some of the men who have the money touch, some of the men who can amass enormous fortunes, possess an ability as specialized and non-indicative of other forms of ability as the ability to play chess exceptionally well, or to add up four columns of figures at once. The men of wealth of this type are not only hostile to the interests of the country but hostile to their own interests; their great business ability is unaccompanied by even the slightest ability to read the signs of the times or understand the temper of the American people. (At Louisville, Ky., April 3, 1912.) *Mem. Ed.* XIX, 249; *Nat. Ed.* XVII, 184.

WEALTH — HOSTILITY TOWARDS. If demagogues or ignorant enthusiasts who are misled by demagogues, could succeed in destroying wealth, they would, of course, simply work the ruin of the entire community, and, first of all, of the unfortunates for whom they profess to feel an especial interest. But the very existence of unreasoning hostility to wealth should make us all the more careful in seeing that wealth does nothing to justify such hostility. We are the true friends of the men of means; we are the true friends of the lawful corporate interests, which do good work for the community, when we insist that the men of means and the great corporations shall pay their full share of taxes and have their full share of the public burdens. If this is done, then, sooner or later, will follow public recognition of the fact that it is done; and when there is no legitimate basis for discontent the American public is sure, sooner or later, to cease feeling discontent. (To New York Legislature, May 22, 1899.) *Mem. Ed.* XXIII, 143; Bishop I, 122-123.

WEALTH—POWER OF. Neither this people nor any other free people will permanently tolerate the use of the vast power conferred by vast wealth, and especially by wealth in its corporate form, without lodging somewhere in the Government the still higher power of seeing that this power, in addition to being used in the interest of the individual or individuals possessing it, is also used for and not against the interests of the people as a whole. (At Union League Club, Philadelphia, January 30, 1905.) *Mem. Ed.* XXIII, 490; Bishop I, 427.

——————. The absence of effective State, and, especially, national, restraint upon unfair money-getting has tended to create a small class of enormously wealthy and economically powerful men, whose chief object is to hold and increase their power. The prime need is to change the conditions which enable these men to accumulate power which it is not for the general welfare that they should hold or exercise. We grudge no man a fortune which represents his own power and sagacity, when exercised with entire regard to the welfare of his fellows. . . . We grudge no man a fortune in civil life if it is honorably obtained and well used. It is not even enough that it should have been gained without doing damage to the community. We should permit it to be gained only so long as the gaining represents benefit to the community. This, I know, implies a policy of a far more active governmental interference with social and economic conditions in this country than we have yet had, but I think we have got to face the fact that such an increase in governmental control is now necessary. (At Osawatomie, Kan., August 31, 1910.) *Mem. Ed.* XIX, 20; *Nat. Ed.* XVII, 13.

WEALTH — RESPONSIBILITY OF. To whom much has been given, from him much is rightfully expected, and a heavy burden of responsibility rests upon the man of means to justify by his actions the social conditions which have rendered it possible for him or his forefathers to accumulate and to keep the property he enjoys. He is not to be excused if he does not render full measure of service to the State and to the community at large. There are many ways in which this service can be rendered—in art, in literature, in philanthropy, as a statesman, as a soldier—but in some way he is in honor bound to render it, so that benefit may accrue to his brethren who have been less favored by fortune than he has been. In short, he must work, and work not only for himself, but for others. If he does not work, he fails not only in his duty to the rest of the community, but he fails signally in his duty to himself. (At Labor Day Picnic, Chicago, September 3, 1900.) *Mem. Ed.* XVI, 516; *Nat. Ed.* XIII, 487.

——————. It is practically impossible to keep a great fortune so that it shall be neutral. Its possessor will use it either for good or for evil. The individual man of wealth must be either a benefit to the commonweal or the reverse. All honor to the man who is on the watch to take advantage of every opportunity to do good with his money. If he fails to take advantage of the chance when offered, a heavy weight of responsibility lies upon him. In some way or other every man can serve the civilization in which he lives, and not the

[644]

least of the opportunities open to every man of wealth is that of furnishing the tools and the field for the great non-remunerative work which marks so much of the world's real progress. (Remarks at dedication, December 29, 1900.) *Opening of the Medical School.* (Cornell University, Ithaca, N. Y., 1901), pp. 21-22.

———. Our men of vast wealth do not fully realize that great responsibility must always go hand in hand with great privileges. (To King Edward VII, February 12, 1908.) *Mem. Ed.* XXIV, 318; Bishop II, 269.

WEALTH — TAXATION OF. No man should receive a dollar unless that dollar has been fairly earned. Every dollar received should represent a dollar's worth of service rendered —not gambling in stocks, but service rendered. The really big fortune, the swollen fortune, by the mere fact of its size acquires qualities which differentiate it in kind as well as in degree from what is possessed by men of relatively small means. Therefore, I believe in a graduated income tax on big fortunes, and in another tax which is far more easily collected and far more effective—a graduated inheritance tax on big fortunes, properly safeguarded against evasion and increasing rapidly in amount with the size of the estate. (At Osawatomie, Kan., August 31, 1910.) *Mem. Ed.* XIX, 20; *Nat. Ed.* XVII, 14.

WEALTH—TYRANNY OF. Of all forms of tyranny the least attractive and the most vulgar is the tyranny of mere wealth, the tyranny of a plutocracy. (1913.) *Mem. Ed.* XXII, 484; *Nat. Ed.* XX, 416.

WEALTH. *See also* CAPITALISTS; FORTUNES; GOVERNMENT, AMERICAN; INCOME TAX; INHERITANCE TAX; "MALEFACTORS OF GREAT WEALTH"; MATERIALIST; MILLIONAIRES; MONEYED MEN; NATIONAL GREATNESS; POPULAR RULE; PRIVILEGE; PROPERTY; SPECIAL INTERESTS; SUCCESS; WALL STREET; WORK.

WEASEL WORDS. Bill Sewall at that time had two brothers. Sam was a deacon. Dave was NOT a deacon. It was from Dave that I heard an expression which ever after remained in my mind. He was speaking of a local personage of shifty character who was very adroit in using fair-sounding words which completely nullified the meaning of other fair-sounding words which preceded them. "His words weasel the meaning of the words in front of them," said Dave, "just like a weasel when he sucks the meat out of an egg and leaves nothing but the shell;" and I always remembered "weasel words" as applicable to certain forms of oratory, especially political oratory, which I do not admire. ("My Debt to Maine," dated March 20, 1918). *Maine, My State.* (Maine Writers Research Club, 1919), pp. 19-20.

———. The Baltimore [Democratic] platform offers perhaps as good an example as any platform of the last thirty years of what has become a typical vice of American politics—the avoidance of saying anything real on real issues, and the announcement of radical policies with much sound and fury, and at the same time with a cautious accompaniment of weasel phrases each of which sucks the meat out of the preceding statement. (*Outlook*, July 27, 1912.) *Mem. Ed.* XIX, 350; *Nat. Ed.* XVII, 248.

———. One of our defects as a nation is a tendency to use what have been called "weasel words." When a weasel sucks eggs the meat is sucked out of the egg. If you use a "weasel word" after another there is nothing left of the other. (At St. Louis, May 31, 1916.) *Mem. Ed.* XXIV, 483; Bishop II, 411.

WELFARE. *See* PUBLIC WELFARE.

WEST — IMPORTANCE OF THE. Using the word "West" in the old sense, as meaning the country west of the Alleghanies, it is, of course, perfectly obvious that it is the West which will shape the destinies of this nation. The great group of wealthy and powerful States about the upper Mississippi, the Ohio, the Missouri, and their tributaries, will have far more weight than any other section in deciding the fate of the Republic in the centuries that are opening. This is not in the least to be regretted by the East, for the simple and excellent reason that the interests of the West and the East are one. The West will shape our destinies because she will have more people and a greater territory, and because the whole development of the Western country is such as to make it peculiarly the exponent of all that is most vigorously and characteristically American in our national life. (*Century*, January 1900.) *Mem. Ed.* XV, 405; *Nat. Ed.* XIII, 356.

WEST — SEPARATISM IN THE. Evil though the separatist movements were, they were at times imperfectly justified by the spirit of sectional distrust and bitterness rife in portions of the country which, at the moment, were themselves loyal to the Union. This was especially true of the early separatist movements in the West. Unfortunately, the attitude toward the Westerners of certain portions of the population in the older States, and especially in the northeastern States, was one of unreasoning jealousy and suspicion; and though this mental attitude rarely crystallized into hostile deeds, its very existence, and the knowledge that it did exist, embittered the men of the West. (1894.) *Mem. Ed.* XI, 320; *Nat. Ed.* IX, 96.

WEST—SUCCESS IN THE. Now a little plain talk, though I think it unnecessary, for I know you too well. If you are afraid of hard work and privation, don't come out west. If you expect to make a fortune in a year or two, don't come west. If you will give up under temporary discouragements, don't come out west. If, on the other hand, you are willing to work hard, especially the first year; if you realize that for a couple of years you cannot expect to make much more than you are now making; if you also know at the end of that time you will be in the receipt of about a thousand dollars for the third year, with an unlimited field ahead of you and a future as bright as you yourself choose to make it, then come. (To Sewall, July 6, 1884.) William W. Sewall, *Bill Sewall's Story of T. R.* (Harper & Bros., N. Y., 1919), pp. 13-14.

─────────. The man most apt to succeed in the West is he who knows a trade well or who is a skillful craftsman with his hands. An energetic, thrifty, hard-working young fellow who is a good carpenter or blacksmith will always find an opening, and if he labors as hard as he did in the East, will get along much faster. Of course I am not now speaking of such exceptional success as falls to the lot of a few of the men who go West, but of the chances opening themselves to the average man who possesses both push and honesty. It is always possible that a man may make a fortune by speculating in town lots, by striking pay gravel in mining, by having an unusual chance in cattle or sheep; but such instances as these stand on the same plane with the fortunes made in Wall Street. An exceptionally able speculator always runs a chance of making a fortune, West or East, and in both places he also runs at least a hundred chances of losing everything he has in the world. Men forget this, however; and those who, if they stayed at home, would esteem themselves fortunate if they were able to earn a competence, become discontented in the West if they do not rapidly acquire great wealth. *Harper's Weekly,* January 2, 1886, p. 7.

WEST, THE. See also BENTON, T. H.; BOONE, DANIEL; CANADIAN NORTHWEST; CATTLEMAN; CLARK, GEORGE ROGERS; COWBOYS; EXPANSION; EXPLORERS; FRONTIER; FRONTIERSMEN; HOMESTEAD LAW; HUNTERS; INDIVIDUALISM; JESUITS; LOUISIANA PURCHASE; MANIFEST DESTINY; METHODIST CHURCH; MILITIA; NEW ENGLAND; NORTHWEST; PIONEER; SCOTCH-IRISH; SEVIER, JOHN; SLAVERY; TEXAS; VIGILANTES; WAR OF 1812; WATAUGA SETTLEMENT; WESTERN; WESTWARD; WISTER, OWEN.

WEST INDIES. The events of the last four years have shown us that the West Indies and the Isthmus must in the future occupy a far larger place in our national policy than in the past. This is proved by the negotiations for the purchase of the Danish Islands, the acquisition of Porto Rico, the preparation for building an Isthmian Canal, and, finally, by the changed relations which these years have produced between us and Cuba. (At Charleston Exposition, S. C., April 9, 1902.) *Mem. Ed.* XVIII, 34-35; *Nat. Ed.* XVI, 29.

WEST INDIES. See also CUBA; HAITI; MARTINIQUE; MONROE DOCTRINE; PORTO RICO; SANTO DOMINGO; SLAVERY.

WEST POINT. Not merely has West Point contributed a greater number of the men who stand highest on the nation's honor-roll, but I think beyond question that, taken as a whole, the average graduate of West Point, during this hundred years, has given a greater sum of service to the country through his life than has the average graduate of any other institution in this broad land. Now, gentlemen, that is not surprising. It is what we had a right to expect from this military university, founded by the nation. It is what we had a right to expect, but I am glad that the expectation has been made good. And of all the institutions in this country, none is more absolutely American, none, in the proper sense of the word, more absolutely democratic than this.

Here we care nothing for the boy's birthplace, nor his creed, nor his social standing; here we care nothing save for his worth as he is able to show it. Here you represent with almost mathematical exactness all the country geographically. You are drawn from every walk of life by a method of choice made to insure, and which in the great majority of cases does insure, that heed shall be paid to nothing save the boy's aptitude for the profession into which he seeks entrance. Here you come together as representatives of America in a higher and more peculiar sense than can possibly be true of any other institution in the land, save your sister college that makes similar preparation for the service of the country on the seas. (At Centennial Celebration, U. S. Military Academy, West Point, June 11, 1902.) *Mem. Ed.* XVIII, 303-304; *Nat. Ed.* XVI, 227-228.

WEST POINT AND ANNAPOLIS. West Point and Annapolis already turn out excellent officers. We do not need to have these schools made more scholastic. On the contrary we should never lose sight of the fact that the aim of each school is to turn out a man who shall be above everything else a fighting man. In the army in particular it is not necessary that either the cavalry or infantry officer should have special mathematical ability. Probably in both schools the best part of the education is the high standard of character and of professional morale which it confers. (Sixth Annual Message, Washington, December 3, 1906.) *Mem. Ed.* XVII, 476; *Nat. Ed.* XV, 406.

WEST POINT. *See also* ARMY OFFICERS; WESTWARD MOVEMENT.

WESTERN EXPLORERS. The hunters were the pioneers; but close behind them came another set of explorers quite as hardy and resolute. These were the surveyors. The men of chain and compass played a part in the exploration of the West scarcely inferior to that of the heroes of axe and rifle. Often, indeed, the parts were combined; Boone himself was a surveyor. Vast tracts of Western land were continually being allotted either to actual settlers or as bounties to soldiers who had served against the French and Indians. These had to be explored and mapped, and as there was much risk as well as reward in the task it naturally proved attractive to all adventurous young men who had some education, a good deal of ambition, and not too much fortune. A great number of young men of good families, like Washington and Clark, went into the business. (1889.) *Mem. Ed.* X, 144; *Nat. Ed.* VIII, 127.

WESTERN SETTLEMENT. The method of settlement of these States of the Mississippi valley had nothing whatever in common with the way in which California and the Australian colonies were suddenly filled up by the promiscuous overflow of a civilized population, which had practically no fear of any resistance from the stunted and scanty native races. It was far more closely akin to the tribe movements of the Germanic peoples in time past; to that movement, for example, by which the Juttish and Low Dutch sea-thieves on the Coast of Britain worked their way inland at the cost of the Cymric Celts. The early settlers of the territory lying immediately west of the Alleghanies were all of the same kind; they were in search of homes, not of riches, and their actions were planned accordingly, except in so far as they were influenced by mere restless love of adventure and excitement. (1887.) *Mem. Ed.* VIII, 5-6; *Nat. Ed.* VII, 5.

——————. The Americans began their work of Western conquest as a separate and individual people, at the moment when they sprang into national life. It has been their great work ever since. All other questions, save those of the preservation of the Union itself and of the emancipation of the blacks, have been of subordinate importance when compared with the great question of how rapidly and how completely they were to subjugate that part of their continent lying between the eastern mountains and the Pacific. (1889.) *Mem. Ed.* X, 21; *Nat. Ed.* VIII, 18.

——————. The West was neither discovered, won, nor settled by any single man. No keen-eyed statesman planned the movement, nor was it carried out by any great military leader; it was the work of a whole people, of whom each man was impelled mainly by sheer love of adventure; it was the outcome of the ceaseless strivings of all the dauntless, restless backwoods folk to win homes for their descendants and to each penetrate deeper than his neighbors into the remote forest hunting-grounds where the perilous pleasures of the chase and of war could be best enjoyed. We owe the conquest of the West to all the backwoodsmen, not to any solitary individual among them; where all alike were strong and daring there was no chance for any single man to rise to unquestioned pre-eminence. (1889.) *Mem. Ed.* X, 136; *Nat. Ed.* VIII, 120.

WESTERN TERRITORY — STRUGGLE FOR. It is difficult to exaggerate the importance of the treaties and wars by means of which we finally gave definite bounds to our territory beyond the Mississippi. Contemporary political writers and students, of the lesser sort, are always painfully deficient in the sense of historic perspective; and to such the struggles for the possession of the unknown and dimly outlined Western wastes seemed of small consequence compared to similar European contests for territorial aggrandizement. Yet, in reality, when we look at the far-reaching nature of the results, the questions as to what kingdom should receive the fealty of Holstein or Lorraine, of Savoy or the Dobrudscha, seem of absolutely trivial importance compared to the infinitely more momentous ones as to the future race settlement and national ownership of the then lonely and unpeopled lands of Texas, California, and Oregon. (1887.) *Mem. Ed.* VIII, 195; *Nat. Ed.* VII, 169.

WESTWARD MOVEMENT. The whole character of the westward movement, the methods of warfare, of settlement and government, were determined by the extreme and defiant individualism of the backwoodsmen, their inborn independence and self-reliance, and their intensely democratic spirit. The West was won and settled by a number of groups of men, all acting independently of one another, but with a common object, and at about the same time. There was no one controlling spirit; it was essentially the movement of a whole free people, not of a single master-mind. There were strong and able leaders, who showed themselves fearless soldiers and just law-givers, undaunted by danger, resolute to persevere in the teeth of disaster; but even these leaders are most deeply interesting because they stand foremost among a host of others like them. (1889.) *Mem. Ed.* XI, 224; *Nat. Ed.* IX, 12.

—————. On the vital question of the West and its territorial expansion the Jeffersonian party was, on the whole, emphatically right, and its opponents, the Federalists, emphatically wrong. The Jeffersonians believed in the acquisition of territory in the West, and the Federalists did not. The Jeffersonians believed that the Westerners should be allowed to govern themselves precisely as other citizens of the United States did, and should be given their full share in the management of national affairs. Too many Federalists failed to see that these positions were the only proper ones to take. In consequence, notwithstanding all their manifold shortcomings, the Jeffersonians, and not the Federalists, were those to whom the West owed most. (1896.) *Mem. Ed.* XII, 279; *Nat. Ed.* IX, 434-435.

—————. [The] marvellously rapid westward extension of our people across the continent would have been impossible had it not been for the quiet, faithful, uncomplaining, often heroic, and almost always absolutely unnoticed service rendered by the regular army. Abreast of the first hardy pioneers, whether miners or cattlemen, appeared the West Point officer and his little company of trained soldiers; and the more regular settlers never made their appearance until, in campaign after campaign, always very wearing and harassing, and often very bloody in character, the scarred and tattered troops had decisively overthrown the Indian lords of the land. Save for the presence of the regular army a large portion of the territory inclosed within the limits of the flourishing States of the great plains and the Rockies would still be in the possession of hostile Indians, and the work of settlement in the West could not have reached its present point. (*Atlantic Monthly,* February 1892.) *Mem. Ed.* XIV, 295-296; *Nat. Ed.* XII, 254-255.

WESTERN; WESTWARD. *See also* CROSS REFERENCES UNDER WEST, THE.

WHARTON, EDITH. *See* BELGIAN REFUGEES.

WHIG PARTY. The principles of the Whigs were hazily outlined at the best, and the party was never a very creditable organization; indeed, throughout its career, it could be most easily defined as the opposition to the Democracy. It was a free constructionist party, believing in giving liberal interpretation to the doctrines of the Constitution; otherwise, its principles were purely economic, as it favored a high tariff, internal improvements, a bank, and kindred schemes; and its leaders, however they might quarrel among themselves, agreed thoroughly in their devout hatred of Jackson and all his works. (1887.) *Mem. Ed.* VIII, 177; *Nat. Ed.* VII, 153-154.

WHITE, HENRY. The most useful man in the entire diplomatic service, during my Presidency and for many years before, was Harry White; and I say this having in mind the high quality of work done by such admirable ambassadors and ministers as Bacon, Meyer, Straus, O'Brien, Rockhill, and Egan, to name only a few among many. When I left the Presidency, White was ambassador to France; shortly afterwards he was removed by Mr. Taft, for reasons unconnected with the good of the service. (July 1913.) Allan Nevins,

Henry White. Thirty Years of American Diplomacy. (Harper & Bros., N. Y., 1930), p. 305.

WHITE, HORACE. See Mugwumps.

WHITE HOUSE. The White House is the property of the nation, and so far as is compatible with living therein it should be kept as it originally was, for the same reasons that we keep Mount Vernon as it originally was. The stately simplicity of its architecture is an expression of the character of the period in which it was built, and is in accord with the purposes it was designed to serve. It is a good thing to preserve such buildings as historic monuments which keep alive our sense of continuity with the nation's past. (Second Annual Message, Washington, December 2, 1902.) *Mem. Ed.* XVII, 194-195; *Nat. Ed.* XV, 167-168.

──────────. I don't think that any family has ever enjoyed the White House more than we have. I was thinking about it just this morning when Mother and I took breakfast on the portico and afterwards walked about the lovely grounds and looked at the stately historic old house. It is a wonderful privilege to have been here and to have been given the chance to do this work, and I should regard myself as having a small and mean mind if in the event of defeat I felt soured at not having had more instead of being thankful for having had so much. (To Kermit Roosevelt, June 21, 1904.) *Mem. Ed.* XXI, 528; *Nat. Ed.* XIX, 474.

──────────. We were all of us, I am almost ashamed to say, rather blue at getting back in the White House, simply because we missed Sagamore Hill so much. But it is very beautiful and we feel very ungrateful at having even a passing fit of blueness, and we are enjoying it to the full now. (To Theodore Roosevelt, Jr., October 2, 1905.) *Mem. Ed.* XXI, 548; *Nat. Ed.* XIX, 492.

WHITE SLAVE TRAFFIC. As regards the white-slave traffic, the men engaged in it, and the women too, are far worse criminals than any ordinary murderers can be. For them there is need of such a law as that recently adopted in England through the efforts of Arthur Lee, M.P., a law which includes whipping for the male offenders. There are brutes so low, so infamous, so degraded and bestial in their cruelty and brutality, that the only way to get at them is through their skins. Sentimentality on behalf of such men is really almost as unhealthy and wicked as the criminality of the men themselves. My experience is that there should be no toleration of any "tenderloin" or "red light" district, and that, above all, there should be the most relentless war on commercialized vice. The men who profit and make their living by the depravity and the awful misery of other human beings stand far below any ordinary criminals, and no measures taken against them can be too severe. (1913.) *Mem. Ed.* XXII, 236; *Nat. Ed.* XX, 203.

WHITE SLAVE TRAFFIC. See also Prostitution.

WHITMAN, WALT. Of all the poets of the nineteenth century, Walt Whitman was the only one who dared use the Bowery—that is, use anything that was striking and vividly typical of the humanity around him—as Dante used the ordinary humanity of his day; and even Whitman was not quite natural in doing so, for he always felt that he was defying the conventions and prejudices of his neighbors, and his self-consciousness made him a little defiant. . . . Whitman wrote of homely things and every-day men, and of their greatness, but his art was not equal to his power and his purpose; and, even as it was, he, the poet, by set intention, of the democracy, is not known to the people as widely as he should be known; and it is only the few—the men like Edward FitzGerald, John Burroughs, and W. E. Henley—who prize him as he ought to be prized. (*Outlook*, August 26, 1911.) *Mem. Ed.* XIV, 439-440; *Nat. Ed.* XII, 98-99.

WICKEDNESS. See Vice; Weakness.

WILD LIFE—DESTRUCTION OF. It is deeply discreditable to the people of any country calling itself civilized that as regards many of the grandest or most beautiful or most interesting forms of wild life once to be found in the land we should now be limited to describing, usually in the driest of dry books, the physical characteristics which when living they possessed, and the melancholy date at which they ceased to live. (*Outlook*, January 20, 1915.) *Mem. Ed.* XIV, 566; *Nat. Ed.* XII, 424.

WILD LIFE—PRESERVATION OF. In a civilized and cultivated country wild animals only continue to exist at all when preserved by sportsmen. The excellent people who protest against all hunting, and consider sportsmen as enemies of wild life, are ignorant of the fact that in reality the genuine sportsman is by all odds the most important factor in keeping the larger and more valuable wild creatures from total extermination. Of course, if wild animals were allowed to breed unchecked, they would, in an incredibly short space of time, render any country uninhabitable by man—a fact which ought to be a matter of elementary knowledge in any community where the average intelligence is above that of certain portions of Hindoostan. Equally, of course, in a purely utilitarian community, all wild animals are exterminated out of hand. In order to preserve the wild life of the wilderness at all, some middle ground must be found between brutal and senseless slaughter and the unhealthy sentimentalism which would just as surely defeat its own end by bringing about the eventual total extinction of the game. It is impossible to preserve the larger wild animals in regions thoroughly fit for agriculture; and it is perhaps too much to hope that the larger carnivora can be preserved for merely aesthetic reasons. But throughout our country there are large regions entirely unsuited for agriculture, where, if the people only have foresight, they can, through the power of the State, keep the game in perpetuity. (1905.) *Mem. Ed.* III, 252; *Nat. Ed.* III, 73-74.

—————————. Every believer in manliness and therefore in manly sport, and every lover of nature, every man who appreciates the majesty and beauty of the wilderness and of wild life, should strike hands with the far-sighted men who wish to preserve our material resources, in the effort to keep our forests and our game beasts, game-birds, and game-fish—indeed, all the living creatures of prairie and woodland and seashore—from wanton destruction.

Above all, we should realize that the effort toward this end is essentially a democratic movement. It is entirely in our power as a nation to preserve large tracts of wilderness, which are valueless for agricultural purposes and unfit for settlement, as playgrounds for rich and poor alike, and to preserve the game so that it shall continue to exist for the benefit of all lovers of nature, and to give reasonable opportunities for the exercise of the skill of the hunter, whether he is or is not a man of means. But this end can only be achieved by wise laws and by a resolute enforcement of the laws. Lack of such legislation and administration will result in harm to all of us, but most of all in harm to the nature-lover who does not possess vast wealth. (1905.) *Mem. Ed.* III, 267-268; *Nat. Ed.* III, 86-87.

—————————. All civilized governments are now realizing that it is their duty here and there to preserve, unharmed, tracts of wild nature, with thereon the wild things the destruction of which means the destruction of half the charm of wild nature. The English Government has made a large game reserve of much of the region on the way to Nairobi, stretching far to the south, and one mile to the north, of the track. The reserve swarms with game; it would be of little value except as a reserve; and the attraction it now offers to travellers renders it an asset of real consequence to the whole colony. The wise people of Maine, in our own country, have discovered that intelligent game preservation, carried out in good faith, and in a spirit of common sense as far removed from mushy sentimentality as from brutality, results in adding one more to the State's natural resources of value. (1910.) *Mem. Ed.* V, 12-13; *Nat. Ed.* IV, 11.

—————————. The civilized people of to-day look back with horror at their mediaeval ancestors who wantonly destroyed great works of art, or sat slothfully by while they were destroyed. We have passed that stage. We treasure pictures and sculptures. We regard Attic temples and Roman triumphal arches and Gothic cathedrals as of priceless value. But we are, as a whole, still in that low state of civilization where we do not understand that it is also vandalism wantonly to destroy or to permit the destruction of what is beautiful in nature, whether it be a cliff, a forest, or a species of mammal or bird. Here in the United States we turn our rivers and streams into sewers and dumping-grounds, we pollute the air, we destroy forests, and exterminate fishes, birds and mammals—not to speak of vulgarizing charming landscapes with hideous advertisements. But at last it looks as if our people were awakening. (*Outlook*, January 25, 1913.) *Mem. Ed.* XIV, 561-562; *Nat. Ed.* XII, 419-420.

—————————. I hope that the efforts of the Audubon societies and kindred organizations will gradually make themselves felt until it becomes a point of honor not only with the American man, but with the American small boy, to shield and protect all forms of harmless wild life. True sportsmen should take the lead in such a movement, for if there is to be any shooting there must be something to shoot;

the prime necessity is to keep, and not kill out, even the birds which in legitimate numbers may be shot. (1913.) *Mem. Ed.* XXII, 365; *Nat. Ed.* XX, 314.

WILD LIFE. See also AUDUBON SOCIETIES; BIRDS; CONSERVATION; GAME; HUNTING; YELLOWSTONE PARK.

WILDERNESS, THE AFRICAN. There are no words that can tell the hidden spirit of the wilderness, that can reveal its mystery, its melancholy, and its charm. There is delight in the hardy life of the open, in long rides rifle in hand, in the thrill of the fight with dangerous game. Apart from this, yet mingled with it, is the strong attraction of the silent places, of the large tropic moons, and the splendor of the new stars; where the wanderer sees the awful glory of sunrise and sunset in the wide waste spaces of the earth, unworn of man, and changed only by the slow change of the ages through time everlasting. (1910.) *Mem. Ed.* V, xxvii; *Nat. Ed.* IV, xxiv-xxv.

WILDERNESS, THE AMERICAN. The differences in plant life and animal life, no less than in the physical features of the land, are sufficiently marked to give the American wilderness a character distinctly its own. Some of the most characteristic of the woodland animals, some of those which have most vividly impressed themselves on the imagination of the hunters and pioneer settlers, are the very ones which have no Old World representatives. The wild turkey is in every way the king of American game-birds. Among the small beasts the coon and the possum are those which have left the deepest traces in the humbler lore of the frontier; exactly as the cougar—usually under the name of panther or mountain lion—is a favorite figure in the wilder hunting tales. Nowhere else is there anything to match the wealth of the eastern hardwood forests, in number, variety and beauty of trees; nowhere else is it possible to find conifers approaching in size the giant redwoods and sequoias of the Pacific slope. Nature here is generally on a larger scale than in the Old World home of our race. The lakes are like inland seas, the rivers like arms of the sea. Among stupendous mountain chains there are valleys and canyons of fathomless depth and incredible beauty and majesty. There are tropical swamps, and sad, frozen marshes; deserts and Death Valleys, weird and evil, and the strange wonderland of the Wyoming geyser region. The waterfalls are rivers rushing over precipices; the prairies seem without limit, and the forest never-ending. (1893.) *Mem. Ed.* II, 6-7; *Nat. Ed.* II, 5-6.

WILDERNESS LIFE. All life in the wilderness is so pleasant that the temptation is to consider each particular variety, while one is enjoying it, as better than any other. A canoe trip through the great forests, a trip with a pack-train among the mountains, a trip on snow-shoes through the silent, mysterious fairy-land of the woods in winter—each has its peculiar charm. To some men the sunny monotony of the great plains is wearisome; personally there are few things I have enjoyed more than journeying over them where the game was at all plentiful. (1905.) *Mem. Ed.* III, 144-145; *Nat. Ed.* II, 514.

WILDERNESS. See also ADVENTURE; GRAND CANYON; HUNTING; NATURE; OUTDOOR LIFE.

WILLIAM II. I wish the Kaiser well. I should never dream of counting on his friendship for this country. He respects us because he thinks that for a sufficient object and on our own terms we would fight, and that we have a pretty good navy with which to fight. . . . I get exasperated with the Kaiser because of his sudden vagaries like this Morocco policy, or like his speech about the yellow peril the other day—a speech worthy of any fool congressman; and I cannot, of course, follow or take too seriously a man whose policy is one of such violent and often wholly irrational zigzags. . . . If the Kaiser ever causes trouble, it will be from jumpiness and not because of long-thought out and deliberate purpose. In other words he is much more apt to be an exasperating and unpleasant than a dangerous neighbour. (To Spring-Rice, May 13, 1905.) *The Letters and Friendships of Sir Cecil Spring-Rice.* (Houghton Mifflin Co., Boston, 1929), I, 470-471.

―――――――. My chief interest at Berlin was in the Emperor himself. He is an able and powerful man. . . . Moreover, he is entirely modest about the many things which he thoroughly knows, such as the industrial and military conditions and needs of Germany. But he lacks all sense of humor when he comes to discuss the things that he does not know, and which he pride himself upon knowing, such as matters artistic and scientific. (To Sir George Otto Trevelyan, October 1, 1911.) *Mem. Ed.* XXIV, 294-295; Bishop II, 251-252.

―――――――. It is very possible that the same spirit which makes the Emperor like to

[651]

hector small kings also makes him dictatorial in his family. In public affairs, experience has taught him as far as his own people are concerned that he must be very careful in going too far in making believe that he is an all-powerful monarch by divine right, and I think he likes to relieve himself by acting the part where it is safer. In international affairs he at times acts as a bully, and moreover as a bully who bluffs and then backs down; I would not regard him nor Germany as a pleasant national neighbor. Yet again and again, and I think sincerely for the moment at least, he dwelt to me on his desire to see England, Germany and the United States act together in all matters of world policy. (To Sir George Otto Trevelyan, October 1, 1911.) *Mem. Ed.* XXIV, 302; Bishop II, 258.

—————————. To paint the Kaiser as a devil, merely bent on gratifying a wicked thirst for bloodshed, is an absurdity, and worse than an absurdity. I believe that history will declare the Kaiser acted in conformity with the feelings of the German people and as he sincerely believed the interests of his people demanded; and, as so often before in his personal and family life, he and his family have given honorable proof that they possess the qualities that are characteristic of the German people. Every one of his sons went to the war, not nominally, but to face every danger and hardship. Two of his sons hastily married the girls to whom they were betrothed and immediately afterward left for the front. (New York *Times,* October 11, 1914.) *Mem. Ed.* XX, 53; *Nat. Ed.* XVIII, 45.

WILLIAM II—POWER OF. William is no longer the German people. He is not as big a man in Germany . . . as he is out of Germany. I must say that on the whole I was disappointed with him. I found him vain as a peacock. He would rather ride at the head of a procession than govern an empire. That is what has contributed mostly to his downfall, for he certainly has had a downfall. (Recorded by Butt in letter of June 30, 1910.) *Taft and Roosevelt. The Intimate Letters of Archie Butt.* (Doubleday, Doran & Co., Garden City, N. Y., 1930), I, 421.

—————————. I was not a little surprised to find that the Emperor was by no means as great a character in Berlin as outsiders supposed him to be, and that both the men highest in politics and the Administration and the people at large, took evident pleasure in having him understand that he was not supreme, and that he must yield to the will of the Nation on any point as to which the Nation had decided views. (To Sir George Otto Trevelyan, October 1, 1911.) *Mem. Ed.* XXIV, 291; Bishop II, 249.

WILLIAM II AND ROOSEVELT. It always amuses me to find that the English think that I am under the influence of the Kaiser. The heavy-witted creatures do not understand that nothing would persuade me to follow the lead of or enter into close alliance with a man who is so jumpy, so little capable of continuity of action, and therefore, so little capable of being loyal to his friends or steadfastly hostile to an enemy. Undoubtedly with Russia weakened Germany feels it can be fairly insolent within the borders of Europe. I intend to do my best to keep on good terms with Germany, as with all other nations, and so far as I can to keep them on good terms with one another; and I shall be friendly to the Kaiser as I am friendly to every one. But as for his having any special influence with me, the thought is absurd. (To H. C. Lodge, May 15, 1905.) Lodge *Letters* II, 123.

—————————. My course with him during the last five years has been uniform. I admire him, respect him, and like him. I think him a big man, and on the whole a good man; but I think his international and indeed his personal attitude one of intense egoism. I have always been most polite with him, have done my best to avoid our taking any attitude which could possibly give him legitimate offense, and have endeavored to show him that I was sincerely friendly to him and to Germany. Moreover, where I have forced him to give way I have been sedulously anxious to build a bridge of gold for him, and to give him the satisfaction of feeling that his dignity and reputation in the face of the world were safe. In other words, where I have had to take part of the kernel from him, I have been anxious that he should have all the shell possible, and have that shell painted any way he wished. At the same time I have had to speak with express emphasis to him on more than one occasion; and on one occasion (that of Venezuela) have had to make a display of force and to convince him definitely that I would use the force if necessary. (To Henry White, August 14, 1906.) *Mem. Ed.* XXIV, 319; Bishop II, 270.

—————————. In the fundamentals of domestic morality, and as regards all that side of religion which is moral, we agreed heartily;

[652]

but there is a good deal of dogmatic theology which to him means much and to me is entirely meaningless; and on the other hand, as is inevitable with a man brought up in the school of Frederick the Great and Bismarck —in contrast to any one whose heroes are men like Timoleon, John Hampden, Washington, and Lincoln—there were many points in international morality where he and I were completely asunder. But at least we agreed in a cordial dislike of shams and of pretense, and therefore in a cordial dislike of the kind of washy movement for international peace with which Carnegie's name has become so closely associated. (To Sir George Otto Trevelyan, October 1, 1911.) *Mem. Ed.* XXIV, 295; Bishop II, 252.

WILLIAM II. *See also* ALGECIRAS CONFERENCE; GERMANY.

WILSON, JAMES. I cannot do better than base my theory of governmental action upon the words and deeds of one of Pennsylvania's greatest sons, Justice James Wilson. Wilson's career has been singularly overlooked for many years, but I believe that more and more it is now being adequately appreciated; and I congratulate your State upon the fact that Wilson's body is to be taken away from where it now rests and brought back to lie, as it should, in Pennsylvania soil. He was a signer of the Declaration of Independence. He was one of the men who saw that the Revolution, in which he had served as a soldier, would be utterly fruitless unless it was followed by a close and permanent union of the States; and in the Constitutional Convention, and in securing the adoption of the Constitution and expounding what it meant, he rendered services even greater than he rendered as a member of the Continental Congress, which declared our independence; for it was the success of the makers and preservers of the Union which justified our independence.

He believed in the people with the faith of Abraham Lincoln; and coupled with his faith in the people he had what most of the men who in this generation believed in the people did not have; that is, the courage to recognize the fact that faith in the people amounted to nothing unless the representatives of the people assembled together in the National Government were given full and complete power to work on behalf of the people. He developed even before Marshall the doctrine (absolutely essential not merely to the efficiency but to the existence of this nation) that an inherent power rested in the nation, outside of the enumerated powers conferred upon it by the Constitution, in all cases where the object involved was beyond the power of the several States and was a power ordinarily exercised by sovereign nations. (At Harrisburg, Pa., October 4, 1906.) *Mem. Ed.* XVIII, 82-83; *Nat. Ed.* XVI, 69-70.

WILSON, WOODROW. Wilson, although still the strongest man the Democrats could nominate, is much weaker than he was. He has given a good many people a feeling that he is very ambitious and not entirely sincere, and his demand for the Carnegie pension created an unpleasant impression. (Letter of December 23, 1911.) Harold Howland, *Theodore Roosevelt and His Times.* (New Haven, 1921), p. 208.

——————. Wilson was from their standpoint the best man that they could have nominated. I do not regard him as a man of great intensity of principle or conviction, or of much reality of sympathy with our cause. He is an adroit man, a good speaker and writer, with a certain amount of ability of just the kind requisite to his party under present conditions. He showed his adroitness during the campaign, and he may well be able to show similar adroitness during the next four years in the Presidency, and with the same result. In the campaign he talked ardent but diffuse progressiveness. He championed concretely a number of minor things for which we stand, and he trusted to the fact that the Bourbon Democrats, especially the Bourbon Democrats of the South, but also those of the North, would feel that they had to stand by him because their only hope is in the Democratic Party. He may do the same thing successfully as President. (To Hiram W. Johnson, January 28, 1913.) *Mem. Ed.* XXIV, 412; Bishop II, 351.

——————. Nothing is more sickening than the continual praise of Wilson's English, of Wilson's style. He is a true logothete, a real sophist; and he firmly believes, and has had no inconsiderable effect in making our people believe, that elocution is an admirable substitute for and improvement on action. (To Owen Wister, June 23, 1915.) *Mem. Ed.* XXIV, 454; Bishop II, 386.

——————. Wilson is a very adroit and able (but not forceful) hypocrite; and the Republican leaders have neither courage nor convictions and therefore can do little against him. (To Anna Roosevelt Cowles, February 3, 1916.) Cowles *Letters,* 306.

[653]

———————. President Wilson, however amiable his intentions, has rendered to this people the most evil service that can be rendered to a great democracy by its chosen leader. He has dulled the national conscience and relaxed the spring of lofty, national motives by teaching our people to accept high sounding words as the offset and atonement for shabby deeds and to use words which mean nothing in order to draw all meaning from those which have a meaning. It will be no easy task to arouse the austere self-respect which has been lulled to slumber by those means. (Telegram to W. P. Jackson, June 8, 1916.) *The Progressive Party; Its Record from January to July 1916*. (Progressive National Committee, 1916), p. 88.

———————. Mr. Wilson has been tried and found wanting. His party because of its devotion to the outworn theory of State rights, and because of its reliance upon purely sectional support, stands against that spirit of farsighted nationalism which is essential if we are to deal adequately with our gravest social and industrial problems.

Mr. Wilson and his party have in actual practice lamentably failed to safeguard the interest and honor of the United States. They have brought us to impotence abroad and to division and weakness at home. They have accustomed us to see the highest and most responsible offices of government filled by incompetent men, appointed only for reasons of partisan politics. They have dulled the moral sense of the people. They have taught us that peace, the peace of cowardice and dishonor and indifference to the welfare of others, is to be put above righteousness, above the stern and unflinching performance of duty, whether the duty is pleasant or unpleasant. (To Progressive National Committee, June 22, 1916.) *Mem. Ed*. XIX, 575; *Nat. Ed*. XVII, 423.

———————. He is so purely a demagogue that if the people were really aroused and resolute—as they were in '98—he would give them leadership in the direction they demanded, even tho to do so stirred with fear his cold and timid heart. But his extreme adroitness in appealing to all that is basest in the hearts of our people has made him able for the time being to drug the soul of the nation into a coma. He is responsible for Germany's brutal wrong doing to us; he is responsible for the existence of the very peace party which he brings forward as an excuse when told that he ought to act boldly. (To H. C. Lodge, February 28, 1917.) Lodge *Letters* II, 498.

———————. Wilson dislikes courage and patriotism and resents ardor and fervor. He is pursuing with much ingenuity the course best calculated to put a premium on tepid indifference and to discourage the qualities in our boys and young men which above all others ought to be encouraged. (To Anna Roosevelt Cowles, April 26, 1917.) Cowles *Letters*, 311.

———————. Wilson feels tepidly hostile to Germany, but he feels a far more active hostility toward Wood and myself. His sole purpose is to serve his own selfish ends. No doubt he would do something that was useful to the country, if he were sure it would help him; but his inveterate habit is not to do the thing that is useful, but by lofty phrases and sentences to make believe that he is doing it, so as to persuade good puzzleheaded people that he is doing it. (To Wister, May 10, 1917.) Owen Wister, *Roosevelt, The Story of a Friendship*. (Macmillan Co., N. Y., 1930), p. 365.

———————. Wilson is profiting to the full by his two great powers; that of puzzling ordinary men who are well-meaning but not wise; and that of appealing to the basest element in every man, wise or unwise. He has profited immensely by his entire devotion to his own interest. He is neither for nor against Democracy or reaction, Germany or the Allies, radicalism or conservatism, socialism or high finance; he is for himself, and for or against any man or any cause exactly as it suits his own interest. We should have beaten him last year if it had not been for the smallness of soul of the Republican leaders. Now I suppose he will appear as the "great idealist of the war for Democracy." (To H. C. Lodge, May 26, 1917.) Lodge *Letters* II, 526.

———————. He is a conscienceless rhetorician and he will always get the well-meaning, foolish creatures who are misled by names. At present anything he says about the World League is in the domain of empty and windy eloquence. The important point will be reached when he has to make definite the things for which he stands. (Letter of December 28, 1918.) *Roosevelt in the Kansas City Star*, xlvii.

———————. This is a grumble from a faithful *Tribune* reader, over an editorial in Sunday's *Tribune*. For Heaven's sake never allude to Wilson as an idealist or militaire or altruist. He is a doctrinaire when he can be so with safety to his personal ambition, and he is always utterly and coldly selfish. He hasn't a touch of idealism in him. His advocacy of the League of Nations no more represents idealism on his part than his advocacy of peace without victory, or his statement that we had no concern with the origin or cause of the European war, or with his profoundly unethical refusal for two and a half years to express a particle of sympathy for poor Belgium. His supporters are cheered when we tell about him being a misguided idealist. He is not. He is a silly doctrinaire at times and an utterly selfish and cold-blooded politician always. (To Ogden Reid, January 1, 1919.) *Mem. Ed.* XXIV, 550; Bishop II, 470.

WILSON, WOODROW—CRITICISM OF. I do not like to bother the men who are at the helm, and I kept silent as long as I thought there was any chance that Wilson was really developing a worthy policy. I came to the conclusion that he had no policy whatever; that what he did was mischievous; and that the bulk of my fellow citizens were inclined to support him in his actions. Therefore, it seemed to me well that some man should speak to them frankly and as only one of their own countrymen should speak to them. I do not believe I have spoken intemperately; but I have put the emphasis with all clearness where I thought it ought to be put. If this country is going to take the position of China, then I at least desire that the bulk of the citizens shall understand what they are doing, and I also wish it understood that I will not be a party to the transaction. (To Rudyard Kipling, January 16, 1915.) *Mem. Ed.* XXIV, 438; Bishop II, 373.

──────────. I have been assailed because I have criticised Mr. Wilson. I have not said one thing of him that was not absolutely accurate and truthful. I have not said one thing of him which I did not deem it necessary to say because of the vital interests of this Republic. I have criticised him because I believe he has dragged in the dust what was most sacred in our past, and has jeopardized the most vital hopes of our future. I have never spoken of him as strongly as Abraham Lincoln in his day spoke of Buchanan and Pierce when they were Presidents of the United States. I spoke of him at all, only because I have felt that in this great world crisis he has played a more evil part than Buchanan and Pierce ever played in the years that led up to and saw the opening of the Civil War. I criticise him now because he has adroitly and cleverly and with sinister ability appealed to all that is weakest and most unworthy in the American character; and also because he has adroitly and cleverly and with sinister ability sought to mislead many men and women who are neither weak nor unworthy, but who have been misled by a shadow dance of words. He has made our statesmanship a thing of empty elocution. He has covered his fear of standing for the right behind a veil of rhetorical phrases. He has wrapped the true heart of the nation in a spangled shroud of rhetoric. He has kept the eyes of the people dazzled so that they know not what is real and what is false, so that they turn, bewildered, unable to discern the difference between the glitter that veneers evil and the stark realities of courage and honesty, of truth and strength. In the face of the world he has covered this nation's face with shame as with a garment. (At Cooper Union, New York City, November 3, 1916.) *Mem. Ed.* XX, 520; *Nat. Ed.* XVIII, 447.

WILSON, WOODROW — SUPPORT OF. No man can support Mr. Wilson without being false to the ideals of national duty and international humanity. No one can support Mr. Wilson without opposing the larger Americanism, the true Americanism. No man can support Mr. Wilson and at the same time be really in favor of thoroughgoing preparedness against war. No man can support Mr. Wilson without at the same time supporting a policy of criminal inefficiency as regards the United States navy, of short-sighted inadequacy as regards the army, of abandonment of the duty owed by the United States to weak and well-behaved nations, and of failure to insist on our just rights when we are ourselves maltreated by powerful and unscrupulous nations. (1916.) *Mem. Ed.* XX, 249; *Nat. Ed.* XVIII, 214.

WILSON ADMINISTRATION. The present Administration, during its three years of life, had been guilty of shortcomings more signal than those of any Administration since the days of Buchanan. From the standpoint of national honor and interest, it stood on an even lower level than the Administration of Buchanan.

No Administration in our history had done more to relax the spring of the national will and to deaden the national conscience. (To Progressive National Committee, June 22, 1916.) *Mem. Ed.* XIX, 567; *Nat. Ed.* XVII, 416-417.

WILSON AND BRYAN. Wilson and Bryan are the very worst men we have ever had in their positions. It would not hurt them to say publicly what is nevertheless historically true, namely, that they are worse than Jefferson and

Madison. I really believe that I would rather have Murphy, Penrose or Barnes as the standard-bearer of this nation in the face of international wrong-doing. (To H. C. Lodge, December 8, 1914.) Lodge *Letters* II, 450.

——————————. The antics between Wilson and Bryan have given me a certain saturnine pleasure. Of course, I entirely agree that on the point at issue, as set forth by Bryan, Wilson was right. But it is only possible to support Wilson in refusing to arbitrate the case as Bryan demanded by taking the ground that he has committed literally an infamy in negotiating the thirty all-inclusive arbitration treaties or commission treaties. If it was right to pass those treaties, it is right now, and not only right but necessary, to grant Germany's request and have a Commission of Inquiry to last for one year in accordance with the terms of the treaties. (To H. C. Lodge, June 15, 1915.) Lodge *Letters* II, 459.

WILSON AND LINCOLN. I am sick at heart about Wilson, and therefore about the American people. The only thing to say in defense of the people is that a bad colonel always makes a bad regiment. If, the day after the firing on Sumter, Lincoln had stated that he was too proud to fight and if he had then carried on a four-months' correspondence with Jefferson Davis, well written from the rhetorical standpoint but without a deed to back any word, and if Seward had resigned because these notes were too stiff, by midsummer of '61 the northerners as a whole would have said that Greeley was quite right and they would let the erring sisters go. Yet even then I think somebody would have roused them in the end. I have done everything I can to rouse them. I have the skeleton of a division already outlined, with acceptances from my Chief of Staff, my brigade commanders, colonels, etc. (To Frederick Palmer, August 28, 1915.) *Mem. Ed.* XXIV, 466; Bishop II, 396.

WILSON'S FOREIGN POLICY. It is folly to pay heed to any of the promises in the platform on which he now stands in view of the fact that almost every important promise contained in the platform on which he stood four years ago has since been broken. We owe all of our present trouble with the professional German-American element in the United States to Mr. Wilson's timid and vacillating course during the last two years. The defenders of Mr. Wilson have alleged in excuse for him that he confronted a difficult situation.

As regards Mexico, the situation which Mr. Wilson confronted was nothing like as difficult as that which President McKinley confronted in connection with Cuba and the Philippines at the time of the Spanish War.

Under the actual circumstances we could with only a minimum of risk have protested on behalf of Belgium, a small, well-behaved nation, when she was exposed to the last extremity of outrage by the brutal violation of her neutral rights, this violation being itself a violation of The Hague conventions to which we were a signatory power.

As regards the foreign situation generally during the great war, the fact of the existence of the war made it far easier and safer for Mr. Wilson to assert our rights than if he had had to deal with some single strong power which was at the time unhampered by war.

During the last twenty years questions have arisen with powers of the first rank, such as England, Japan, and Germany, each of which has necessitated far greater courage, resolution, and judgment on the part of the President dealing with it than President Wilson need have shown in order to put a complete stop to the continually repeated murder of American men, women, and children on the high seas by German submarines — the *Lusitania* being merely the worst of many such cases. The same feebleness that was shown by President Wilson in dealing with Germany abroad was also shown by him in dealing with the organized German outrages within our own land, and, finally, in dealing with the organized German-American vote. The continued existence of the German-American menace at home is directly due to Mr. Wilson's course of action during the last two years. (To Progressive National Committee, June 22, 1916.) *Mem. Ed.* XIX, 572; *Nat. Ed.* XVII, 421.

——————————. As good Americans, you ought unqualifiedly to condemn at least 99 per cent of that policy. His first note, "the strict accountability note," would have been excellent if he had lived up to it, but as he has for two years failed to live up to it, it becomes infamous. We then had two years of note-writing, of tame submission to brutal wrong-doing, and of utter failure to prepare. Then he broke relations. This was excellent, but only if he meant to follow it up; it amounts to nothing whatever by itself. Seven weeks have gone by, and he has done not one thing. He is himself responsible for the growth of the pacifist and pro-German party in Congress. He never asked for any real action, and the little action he did ask for was asked for so late that he must have known perfectly well any small group of Senators could prevent its being taken. Congress has been summoned to meet in April. By that time, either submarine warfare against England will have succeeded, in which case what Mr. Wilson does is of no earthly consequence, or, what is far more probable, it will have failed, in which case he will have put us in the ignoble position of sheltering ourselves behind the British Navy until all danger is past. Indeed, he has already put us in such a position. (To John J. Richeson, March 21, 1917.) *Mem. Ed.* XXIV, 494; Bishop II, 421.

WILSON'S PARTISANSHIP. The simple truth is that never in our history has any other administration during a great war played politics of the narrowest personal and partisan type as President Wilson has done; and one of the features of this effort has been the careful and studied effort to mislead and misinform the public through information sedulously and copiously furnished them by government officials. An even worse feature has been the largely successful effort to break down freedom of speech and the freedom of the press by government action. Much of this action has been taken under the guise of attacking disloyalty; but it has represented action, not against those who were disloyal to the nation, but against those who disagreed with or criticised the President for failure in the performance of duty to the nation. The action of the government against real traitors, and against German spies and agents, has been singularly weak and ineffective. The chief of the Secret Service said that there were a quarter of a million German spies in this country. Senator Overman put the number at a larger figure; but not one has been shot or hung, and relatively few have been interfered with in any way. The real vigor of the Administration has been directed against honest critics who have endeavored to force it to speed up the war and to act with prompt efficiency against Germany. (1918.) *Mem. Ed.* XXI, 323; *Nat. Ed.* XIX, 295.

————. When this war broke out I, and all those who believed as I did, cast all thought of politics aside and put ourselves unreservedly at the service of the President. Of course if Mr. Wilson had really meant to disregard politics he would at once have constructed a coalition, non-partisan Cabinet, calling the best men of the nation to the highest and most important offices under him, without regard to politics. He did nothing of the kind. In the positions most vital to the conduct of the war, and in the positions now most important in connection with negotiating peace, he retained or appointed men without the slightest fitness for the performance of the tasks, whose sole recommendation was a supple eagerness to serve Mr. Wilson personally and to serve Mr. Wilson's party insofar as such serving benefited Mr. Wilson. . . .

Mr. Wilson applies the most rigid party test. He explicitly repudiates loyalty to the war as a test. He demands the success of the Democratic party, and asks the defeat of all pro-war men if they have been anti-Administration. He asks for the defeat of pro-war Republicans. He does not ask for the defeat of anti-war Democrats. On the contrary, he supports such men if, although anti-war, they are pro-Administration.

He does not ask for loyalty to the nation. He asks only for support of himself. There is not the slightest suggestion that he disapproves of disloyalty to the nation. I do not doubt that he feels some disapproval of such disloyalty; but apparently this feeling on his part is so tepid that it slips from his mind when he contemplates what he regards as the far greater sin of failure in adherence to himself. (At Carnegie Hall, New York City, October 28, 1918.) *Mem. Ed.* XXI, 432-433; *Nat. Ed.* XIX, 390-391.

WILSON'S WAR MESSAGE. The President's message [of April 2] is a great state paper which will rank in history with the great state papers of which Americans in future years will be proud. It now rests with the people of the country to see that we put in practice the policy that the President has outlined and that we strike as hard, as soon, and as efficiently as possible in aggressive war against the government of Germany. (Statement to the press, April 2, 1917.) *Mem. Ed.* XXIV, 496; Bishop II, 423.

WILSON, WOODROW. *See also* DEMOCRATIC PARTY; ELECTION OF 1912; ELECTION OF 1916; FOREIGN POLICY; FOURTEEN POINTS; HAGUE CONVENTIONS; HUGHES, CHARLES E.; LEAGUE FOR PEACE; LEAGUE OF NATIONS; LESE MAJESTY; *Lusitania;* MEXICO; NATIONAL OBLIGATIONS; NEUTRALITY; NEW FREEDOM; PEACE; PREPAREDNESS; PRESIDENT; PROGRESSIVE PARTY; ROOSEVELT DIVISION; TARIFF; TRUSTS; "WATCHFUL WAITING"; WORLD WAR.

WISCONSIN. *See* LA FOLLETTE, ROBERT M.

WISTER, OWEN. I really think you have done for the plainsmen and mountainmen, the soldiers, frontiersmen and Indians what nobody else but Bret Harte and Kipling could have

———————. Mr. Owen Wister's stories ... turned a new page in our literature, and, indeed, may almost be said to have turned a new page in that form of contemporary historical writing which consists in the vivid portrayal, once for all, of types that should be commemorated. Many men before him have seen and felt the wonder of that phase of Western life which is now closing, but Mr. Wister makes us see what he has seen and interprets for us what he has heard. His short sketches are so many cantos in the great epic of life on the border of the vanishing wilderness. He shows us heroic figures and a heroic life; not heroes and the heroic life as they are conceived by the cloistered intellect, but rough and strong and native, the good and evil alike challenging the eye. To read his writings is like walking on a windy upland in fall, when the hard weather braces body and mind. There is a certain school of American writers that loves to deal, not with the great problems of American existence and with the infinite picturesqueness of our life as it has been and is being led here on our own continent, where we stumble and blunder, and still, on the whole, go forward, but with the life of those Americans who cannot swim in troubled waters, and go to live as idlers in Europe. What pale, anaemic figures they are, these creations of the émigré novelists, when put side by side with the men, the grim stalwart men, who stride through Mr. Wister's pages!

It is this note of manliness which is dominant through the writings of Mr. Wister. *Harpers' Weekly*, December 21, 1895, p. 1216.

WITTE, COUNT. I suppose Witte is the best man that Russia could have at the head of her affairs at present, and probably too good a man for the grand dukes to be willing to stand him. He interested me. I cannot say that I liked him, for I thought his bragging and bluster not only foolish but shockingly vulgar when compared with the gentlemanly self-respecting self-restraint of the Japanese. Moreover, he struck me as a very selfish man, totally without high ideals. He calmly mentioned to me, for instance, that it was Russia's interest to keep Turkey in power in the Balkan Peninsula; that he believed that Turkey would last a long time, because it would be a very bad thing for Russia to have the Bulgarians, for instance, substituted for the Turks, for the very reason that they might give a wholesome, reputable government and thereby build up a great Slav State to the South. He added cynically that such a consummation might be good for sentimental reasons, but that sentiment did not count in practical politics. (To Sir George Otto Trevelyan, September 12, 1905.) *Mem. Ed.* XXIII, 480-481; Bishop I, 418.

WOMAN SUFFRAGE. Personally I believe in woman's suffrage, but I am not an enthusiastic advocate of it, because I do not regard it as a very important matter. I am unable to see that there has been any special improvement in the position of women in those states in the West that have adopted woman's suffrage, as compared with those states adjoining them that have not adopted it. I do not think that giving the women suffrage will produce any marked improvement in the condition of women. I do not believe that it will produce any of the evils feared, and I am very certain that when women as a whole take any special interest in the matter they will have suffrage if they desire it.

But at present I think most of them are lukewarm; I find some actively for it, and some actively against it. I am, for the reasons above given, rather what you would regard as lukewarm or tepid in my support of it because, while I believe in it, I do not regard it as of very much importance. (To Lyman Abbott, November 10, 1908.) *The Remonstrance*, January 1909, p. 3.

———————. It seemed to me that no man was worth his salt who did not think very deeply of woman's rights; and that no woman was worth her salt who did not think more of her duties than of her rights. Now, personally I am rather tepidly in favor of woman's suffrage. When the opportunity came I have always supported it. But I have studied the condition of women in those States where they have the suffrage and in the adjacent States where they do not have it; and, after such study I have never been able to take as great interest in the question as in many other questions because it has always seemed to me so infinitely less important than so many other questions affecting women. I do not think that the harm that its opponents fear will come from it, but I do not think that more than a fraction of the good that its advocates anticipate will come from it. In consequence, while I favor it, yet, as I said, I favor it tepidly, because I am infinitely more interested in other things. (At

——————. As for woman suffrage, I have never said very much about it, and always to the same effect, that I tepidly favored its application wherever it was shown to be desired by the majority of the women themselves, but that I did not regard it as a reform of much consequence, nothing like as important as any number of others, for I thought it would do only the tiniest fraction of the good that is anticipated—although I do not think it will do any of the harm that is anticipated. (To Anna Roosevelt Cowles, June 29, 1911.) Cowles *Letters*, 292.

——————. I believe in woman's suffrage wherever the women want it. Where they do not want it, the suffrage should not be forced upon them. I think that it would be well to let the women themselves, and only the women, vote at some special election as to whether they do or do not wish the vote as a permanent possession. In other words, this is peculiarly a case for the referendum to those most directly affected—that is, the women themselves. (*Outlook*, February 3, 1912.) *Mem. Ed.* XVIII, 276; *Nat. Ed.* XVI, 208.

——————. Personally I feel that it is exactly as much a "right" of women as of men to vote. But the important point with both men and women is to treat the exercise of the suffrage as a duty, which, in the long run, must be well performed to be of the slightest value. I always favored woman's suffrage, but only tepidly, until my association with women like Jane Addams and Frances Kellor, who desired it as one means of enabling them to render better and more efficient service, changed me into a zealous instead of a lukewarm adherent of the cause—in spite of the fact that a few of the best women of the same type, women like Mary Antin, did not favor the movement. (1913.) *Mem. Ed.* XXII, 196; *Nat. Ed.* XX, 167.

——————. It is the men who insist upon women doing their full duty, who insist that the primary duty of the woman is in the home, who also have a right to insist that she is just as much entitled to the suffrage as is the man. We believe in equality of right, not in identity of functions. The woman must bear and rear the children, as her first duty to the state; and the man's first duty is to take care of her and the children. In neither case is it the exclusive duty. In neither case does it exclude the performance of other duties. The right to vote no more implies that a woman will neglect her home than that a man will neglect his business. Indeed, as regards one of the greatest and most useful of all professions, that of surgery and medicine, it is probably true that the average doctor's wife has more time for the performance of political duties than the average doctor himself. (*Metropolitan*, May 1916.) *Mem. Ed.* XXI, 148; *Nat. Ed.* XIX, 145.

WOMEN—CAREERS FOR. I believe that man and woman should stand on an equality of right, but I do not believe that equality of right means identity of function; and I am more and more convinced that the great field, the indispensable field, for the usefulness of woman is as the mother of the family. It is her work in the household, in the home, her work in bearing and rearing the children, which is more important than any mans' work, and it is that work which should be normally the woman's special work, just as normally the man's work should be that of the breadwinner, the supporter of the home, and if necessary the soldier who will fight for the home. There are exceptions as regards both man and woman; but the full and perfect life, the life of highest happiness and of highest usefulness to the State, is the life of the man and the woman who are husband and wife, who live in the partnership of love and duty, the one earning enough to keep the home, the other managing the home and the children. (To Mrs. Harriet Taylor Upton, November 10, 1908.) *Mem. Ed.* XXIV, 148; Bishop II, 127.

——————. Women should have free access to every field of labor which they care to enter, and when their work is as valuable as that of a man it should be paid as highly. Yet normally for the man and the woman whose welfare is more important than the welfare of any other human beings, the woman must remain the housemother, the homekeeper, and the man must remain the breadwinner, the provider for the wife who bears his children and for the children she brings into the world. No other work is as valuable or as exacting for either man or woman; it must always, in every healthy society, be for both man and woman the prime work, the most important work; normally all other work is of secondary importance, and must come as an addition to, not a substitute for, this primary work. The partnership should be one of equal rights, one of love, of self-respect and unselfishness, above all a partnership for the performance of the most vitally important of all duties. The performance of duty, and not an indulgence in vapid ease and vapid pleasure, is all that makes life worth while. (1913.) *Mem. Ed.* XXII, 195; *Nat. Ed.* XX, 167.

———————. Let any woman who says that she prefers a career to marriage understand that she is preferring the less to the greater. The prime benefactors of humanity are the man and woman who leave to the next generation boys and girls who will turn out good and useful men and women. I honor the good man, I honor the good woman still more. I believe that the woman should have open to her everything that is open to man, every profession, every opportunity; and, furthermore, I believe with all my heart that no other woman and no man will ever have a career approaching in dignity, in usefulness to the whole community, in fine self-sacrifice and devotion, the career of the good mother who brings into the world and rears and trains as they should be reared and trained many healthy children. (*Outlook*, January 3, 1914.) *Mem. Ed.* XIV, 178; *Nat. Ed.* XII, 206.

———————. It is entirely right that any woman should be allowed to make any career for herself of which she is capable, whether or not it is a career followed by a man. She has the same right to be a lawyer, a doctor, a farmer, or a storekeeper that the man has to be a poet, an explorer, a politician, or a painter. There are women whose peculiar circumstances or whose peculiar attributes render it advisable that they should follow one of the professions named, just as there are men who can do most good to their fellows by following one of the careers above indicated for men. More than this. It is indispensable that such careers shall be open to women and that certain women shall follow them, if the women of a country, and therefore if the country itself, expect any development. In just the same way, it is indispensable that some men shall be explorers, artists, sculptors, literary men, politicians, if the country is to have its full life. Some of the best farmers are women, just as some of the best exploring work and scientific work has been done by women. There is a real need for a certain number of women doctors and women lawyers. Whether a writer or a painter or a singer is a man or a woman makes not the slightest difference, provided that the work he or she does is good. (*Metropolitan*, May 1916.) *Mem. Ed.* XXI, 143; *Nat. Ed.* XIX, 141.

WOMEN—POSITION OF. To talk of a wife or mother as an "economic parasite" is the veriest nonsense. If she is worth her salt, she is a full partner; and the man is not worth his salt unless he acknowledges this fact and welcomes it. And the more each partner loves and respects the other, the more anxious each is to share the other's burden, the less either will feel like encouraging the other to shirk any duty that ought to be faced. The duties are mutual and reciprocal. (*Outlook*, January 3, 1914.) *Mem. Ed.* XIV, 177; *Nat. Ed.* XII, 205.

———————. Of all species of silliness the silliest is the assertion sometimes made that the woman whose primary lifework is taking care of her home and children is somehow a "parasite woman." It is such a ridiculous inversion of the truth that it ought not to be necessary even to allude to it. (*Metropolitan*, May 1916.) *Mem. Ed.* XXI, 142; *Nat. Ed.* XIX, 140.

WOMEN — RIGHTS OF. I believe in woman's rights. I believe even more earnestly in the performance of duty by both men and women; for unless the average man and the average woman live lives of duty, not only our democracy but civilization itself will perish. I heartily believe in equality of rights as between man and woman, but also in full and emphatic recognition of the fact that normally there cannot be identity of function. Indeed, there must normally be complete dissimilarity of function between them, and the effort to ignore this patent fact is silly. (*Outlook*, February 3, 1912.) *Mem. Ed.* XVIII, 276; *Nat. Ed.* XVI, 208.

———————. Working women have the same need to combine for protection that working men have; the ballot is as necessary for one class as for the other; we do not believe that with the two sexes there is identity of function; but we do believe that there should be equality of right; and therefore we favor woman suffrage. Surely, if women could vote, they would strengthen the hands of those who are endeavoring to deal in efficient fashion with evils such as the white-slave traffic; evils which can in part be dealt with nationally, but which in large part can be reached only by determined local action, such as insisting on the wide-spread publication of the names of the owners, the landlords, of houses used for immoral purposes. (Before Progressive National Convention, Chicago, August 6, 1912.) *Mem. Ed.* XIX, 376; *Nat. Ed.* XVII, 269.

———. The relationship of man and woman is the fundamental relationship that stands at the base of the whole social structure. Much can be done by law toward putting women on a footing of complete and entire equal rights with man—including the right to vote, the right to hold and use property, and the right to enter any profession she desires on the same terms as a man. Yet when this has been done it will amount to little unless on the one hand the man himself realizes his duty to the woman, and unless on the other hand the woman realizes that she has no claim to rights unless she performs the duties that go with those rights and that alone justify her in appealing to them. A cruel, selfish, or licentious man is an abhorrent member of the community; but, after all, his actions are no worse in the long run than those of the woman who is content to be a parasite on others, who is cold, selfish, caring for nothing but frivolous pleasure and ignoble ease. The law of worthy effort, the law of service for a worthy end, without regard to whether it brings pleasure or pain, is the only right law of life, whether for man or for woman. The man must not be selfish; nor, if the woman is wise, will she let the man grow selfish, and this not only for her own sake but for his. (1913.) *Mem. Ed.* XXII, 193; *Nat. Ed.* XX, 165.

WOMEN IN INDUSTRY. As regards women, there should be strict regulation as to the number of hours they are allowed to be employed and as to the conditions of their work, both as regards cleanliness and surroundings. As yet no way has been devised by which the government can directly deal with the cases in which the wages paid are insufficient to sustain life under the conditions demanded by the woman's self-respect. I am well aware that this is a question fraught with the greatest difficulties, but it is imperative for us to face the fact that we are making a failure of our democratic experiment just to the extent that there exist large classes of people, and especially large classes of women, who work under conditions and for salaries such that they cannot retain their self-respect. No adequate remedy has yet been proposed. In all probability a great many remedies would have to be concurrently tried and adopted. But nothing is gained by blinking the fact that remedies are imperatively needed. (*Outlook*, February 4, 1911.) *Mem. Ed.* XIX, 105; *Nat. Ed.* XVII, 70.

WOMEN IN POLITICS. Now for the statement that women have no proper share in a political convention, and that men ought to be able to regulate their own politics and meet all needs without direct assistance from the women. That man knows little of our political, social and industrial needs as a nation who does not know that in political conventions the politics that ought to be "regulated" are the politics that affect women precisely as much as they affect men; and he must be unfortunate in his life of acquaintances if he does not know women whose advice and counsel are pre-eminently worth having in regard to the matters affecting our welfare which it is of most consequence to have dealt with by political conventions. . . . The Progressive Party is the one party which since the war has dealt with real issues; and these real issues affect women precisely as much as men. The women who bear children and attend to their own homes have precisely the same right to speak in politics that their husbands have who are the fathers of their children and who work to keep up their homes. It is these women who bear children and attend to their own homes, and these men, their husbands, who work for their wives and children and homes, whom the Progressive Party is endeavoring to represent and in whose interest the Progressive Party proposes that the governmental policy of this nation shall hereafter be shaped. Such being the case, it is eminently wise that the women should share in the political conventions, and that they should join with the men in regulating the politics, which are in no proper sense only "the politics of the men," . . . because they are of as vital concern to the women as to the men. *Mr. Roosevelt's Speech on Suffrage, delivered at St. Johnsbury, Vt., August 30, 1912*, pp. 2-3.

WOMEN IN PUBLIC AFFAIRS. Women have the vote in this State. They should be given it at once in the nation at large. And in the councils of this State, and in the councils of our party, women should be admitted to their share of the direction on an exact equality with the men, and wherever it is wisely possible their judgment and directive power should be utilized in association with men rather than separately. (Before Republican State Convention, Saratoga Springs, N. Y., July 18, 1918.) *Mem. Ed.* XXI, 400; *Nat. Ed.* XIX, 363.

WOMEN. See also BIRTH CONTROL; CHILDREN; FAMILY; HOME; HOWE, JULIA WARD; HUSBANDS; MARRIAGE; MOTHER; PROSTITUTION; TEACHERS; WHITE SLAVE TRAFFIC.

WOOD, LEONARD. I only met him after I entered the navy department, but we soon found that we had kindred tastes and kindred principles. . . . Like so many of the gallant fighters with whom it was later my good fortune to serve, he combined, in a very high degree, the qualities of entire manliness with entire uprightness and cleanliness of character. It was a pleasure to deal with a man of high ideals, who scorned everything mean and base, and who also possessed those robust and hardy qualities of body and mind, for the lack of which no merely negative virtue can ever atone. He was by nature a soldier of the highest type, and, like most natural soldiers, he was, of course, born with a keen longing for adventure; and, though an excellent doctor, what he really desired was the chance to lead men in some kind of hazard. To every possibility of such adventure he paid quick attention. (1899.) *Mem. Ed.* XIII, 4; *Nat. Ed.* XI, 4.

───────. The successful administrator of a tropic colony must ordinarily be a man of boundless energy and endurance; and there were probably very few men in the army at Santiago, whether among the officers or in the ranks, who could match General Wood in either respect. No soldier could outwalk him, could live with more indifference on hard and scanty fare, could endure hardship better, or do better without sleep; no officer ever showed more ceaseless energy in providing for his soldiers, in reconnoitering, in overseeing personally all the countless details of life in camp, in patrolling the trenches at night, in seeing by personal inspection that the outposts were doing their duty, in attending personally to all the thousand and one things to which a commander should attend, and to which only those commanders of marked and exceptional mental and bodily vigor are able to attend. (*Outlook,* January 7, 1899.) *Mem. Ed.* XII, 521; *Nat. Ed.* XI, 250.

───────. One of the most important items of the work done by our Government in Cuba was the work of hygiene, the work of cleaning and disinfecting the cities so as to minimize the chance for yellow fever, so as to do away with as many as possible of the conditions that told for disease. This country has never had done for it better work, that is, work that reflected more honor upon the country, or for humanity at large, than the work done for it in Cuba. And the man who above all others was responsible for doing that work so well was a member of your profession, who when the call to arms came himself went as a soldier to the field—the present Major-General Leonard Wood. Leonard Wood did in Cuba just the kind of work that, for instance, Lord Cromer has done in Egypt. We have not been able to reward Wood in anything like the proportion in which services such as his would have been rewarded in any other country of the first rank; and there have been no meaner and more unpleasant manifestations in all our public history than the feelings of envy and jealousy manifested toward Wood. And the foul assaults and attacks made upon him, gentlemen, were largely because they grudged the fact that this admirable military officer should have been a doctor. (Before Long Island Medical Society, Oyster Bay, N. Y., July 12, 1905.) *Presidential Addresses and State Papers* IV, 432-433.

───────. The part played by the United States in Cuba has been one of the most honorable ever played by any nation in dealing with a weaker power, one of the most satisfactory in all respects; and to General Wood more than to any other one man is due the credit of starting this work and conducting it to a successful conclusion during the earliest and most difficult years. . . . General Wood of course incurred the violent hatred of many dishonest schemers and unscrupulous adventurers, and of a few more or less well-meaning persons who were misled by these schemers and adventurers; but it is astounding to any one acquainted with the facts to realize, not merely what he accomplished, but how he succeeded in gaining the good-will of the enormous majority of the men whose good-will could be won only in honorable fashion. Spaniards and Cubans, Christian Filipinos and Moros, Catholic ecclesiastics and Protestant missionaries—in each case the great majority of those whose opinion was best worth having—grew to regard General Wood as their special champion and ablest friend, as the man who more than any others understood and sympathized with their peculiar needs and was anxious and able to render them the help they most needed. (*Outlook,* July 30, 1910.) *Mem. Ed.* XII, 528; *Nat. Ed.* XI, 256.

WOOD, LEONARD. *See also* CUBA; GREY, SIR EDWARD.

WORDS. *See* ACTION; BOASTING; CRITICISM; DEEDS; ORATORY; PRACTICALITY; WEASEL WORDS.

WORK. We hold work not as a curse but as a blessing, and we regard the idler with scornful pity. It would be in the highest degree undesirable that we should all work in the same way or at the same things, and for the sake of the real greatness of the nation we should in the fullest and most cordial way recognize the fact that some of the most needed work must, from its very nature, be unremunerative in a material sense. Each man must choose so far as the conditions will allow him the path to which he is bidden by his own peculiar powers and inclinations. But if he is a man he must in some way or shape do a man's work. (At Colorado Springs, Col., August 2, 1901.) *Mem. Ed.* XV, 325; *Nat. Ed.* XIII, 457.

——————. The work is what counts, and if a man does his work well and it is worth doing, then it matters but little in which line that work is done; the man is a good American citizen. If he does his work in slipshod fashion, then no matter what kind of work it is, he is a poor American citizen. (Before Brotherhood of Locomotive Firemen, Chattanooga, Tenn., September 8, 1902.) *Mem. Ed.* XVIII, 202; *Nat. Ed.* XVI, 153.

——————. Doubtless most of you remember the distinction drawn between the two kinds of work—the work done for the sake of the fee, and the work done for the sake of the work itself. The man or woman in public or private life who ever works for the sake of the reward that comes outside of the work will in the long run do poor work. The man or woman who does work worth doing is the man or woman who lives, who breathes that work; with whom it is ever-present in his or her soul; whose ambition is to do it well and to feel rewarded by the thought of having done it well. That man, that woman, puts the whole country under an obligation. As a body all those connected with the education of our people are entitled to the highest praise from all lovers of their country, because as a body they are devoting heart and soul to the welfare of those under them. (At Philadelphia, Pa., November 22, 1902.) *Proceedings of the Dedication of the New Buildings of the Central High School.* (Board of Public Education, 1910), p. 63.

——————. Work [is] the quality which makes a man ashamed not to be able to pull his own weight, not to be able to do for himself as well as for others without being beholden to any one for what he is doing. No man is happy if he does not work. Of all miserable creatures the idler, in whatever rank of society, is in the long run the most miserable. If a man does not work, if he has not in him not merely the capacity for work but the desire for work, then nothing can be done with him. He is out of place in our community. We have in our scheme of government no room for the man who does not wish to pay his way through life by what he does for himself and for the community. If he has leisure which makes it unnecessary for him to devote his time to earning his daily bread, then all the more he is bound to work just as hard in some way that will make the community the better off for his existence. If he fails in that, he fails to justify his existence. Work, the capacity for work, is absolutely necessary; and no man's life is full, no man can be said to live in the true sense of the word, if he does not work. (At Topeka, Kan., May 1, 1903.) *Presidential Addresses and State Papers* I, 355-356.

——————. No individual ever became great and no individual ever led a really worthy life, unless he or she possessed within himself or herself the power, if need be, for effort long sustained, at the cost of discomfort, of pain, and hardship; and the power to face risk, to face danger and difficulty and even disaster, rather than not achieve a worthy end. (At Occidental College, Los Angeles, March 22, 1911.) *Mem. Ed.* XV, 513; *Nat. Ed.* XIII, 580.

——————. We Progressives are trying to represent what we know to be the highest ideals and the deepest and most intimate convictions of the plain men and women, of the good men and women, who work for the home and within the home.

Our people work hard and faithfully. They do not wish to shirk their work. They must feel pride in the work for the work's sake. But there must be bread for the work. There must be a time for play when the men and women are young. When they grow old there must be the certainty of rest under conditions free from the haunting terror of utter poverty. We believe that no life is worth anything unless it is a life of labor and effort and endeavor. We believe in the joy that comes with work, for he who labors best is really happiest. We must shape conditions so that no one can own the spirit of the man who loves his task and gives the best there is in him to that task, and it matters not whether this man reaps and sows and wrests his livelihood from the rugged reluctance of the soil or whether with hand or brain he plays his part in the tremendous industrial activities of our great cities. We are striving to meet the needs of all these men, and to meet them in such fashion that all alike shall feel bound together in the bond of a common brotherhood, where each works hard for himself and for those dearest to him, and yet feels that he must also think of his brother's rights because he is in very truth that brother's keeper. (At Madison Square Garden, New York City, October 30, 1912.) *Mem. Ed.* XIX, 462; *Nat. Ed.* XVII, 339.

WORK—DIGNITY OF. Under the old system [in Russia] the men whose boots the porter blacked looked down on him for blacking them. Are we entirely free from this attitude in America? Until we are we may as well make up our minds that to just that extent we are providing for the growth of Bolshevism here. No man has a right to ask or accept any service unless under changed conditions he would feel that he could keep his entire self-respect while rendering it. Service which carries with it the slightest implication of social abasement should not be rendered. (*Metropolitan*, March 1918.) *Mem. Ed.* XXI, 373; *Nat. Ed.* XIX, 338.

WORK. *See also* EFFORT; IDLERS; LEISURE; NATIONAL INHERITANCE; PLEASURE; REWARD; STRENUOUS LIFE; WEALTH.

WORKERS. The prosperity of the wage-earning class is more important to the state than the prosperity of any other class in the community, for it numbers within its ranks two-thirds of the people of the community. The fact that modern society rests upon the wage-earner, whereas ancient society rested upon the slave, is of such transcendent importance as to forbid any exact comparison between the two, save by way of contrast. (*Forum*, January 1897.) *Mem. Ed.* XIV, 149; *Nat. Ed.* XIII, 259.

──────────. Gradually I hope to see the wage-worker become in a real sense a partner in the enterprise in which he works; and to achieve this end he must develop the power of self-control, the power of recognizing the rights of others no less than insisting upon his own; he must develop common sense; and that strength of character which cannot be conferred from without, and the lack of which renders everything else of no avail. (*Metropolitan*, November 1918.) *Mem. Ed.* XXI, 274; *Nat. Ed.* XIX, 253.

──────────. In the long run the one vital factor in the permanent prosperity of the country is the high individual character of the average American worker, the average American citizen, no matter whether his work be mental or manual, whether he be farmer or wage-worker, business man or professional man. (Fifth Annual Message, Washington, December 5, 1905.) *Mem. Ed.* XVII, 315; *Nat. Ed.* XV, 270.

WORKERS—INTERESTS OF. It would be idle to deny that wage-earners have certain different economic interests from, let us say, manufacturers or importers, just as farmers have different interests from sailors, and fishermen from bankers. There is no reason why any of these economic groups should not consult their group interests by any legitimate means and with due regard to the common, overlying interests of all. I do not even deny that the majority of wage-earners, because they have less property and less industrial security than others and because they do not own the machinery with which they work (as does the farmer), are perhaps in greater need of acting together than are other groups in the community. But I do insist (and I believe that the great majority of wage-earners take the same view) that employers and employees have overwhelming interests in common, both as partners in industry and as citizens of the Republic, and that where these interests are apart they can be adjusted by so altering our laws and their interpretation as to secure to all members of the community social and industrial justice. (1913.) *Mem. Ed.* XXII, 553; *Nat. Ed.* XX, 475.

WORKERS—NEEDS OF. We wish to get for the workers, among other things, permanency of employment, pensions which will permit them to face old age with a feeling of dignity and security, insurance against accidents and disease, proper working and living conditions, reasonable leisure—all these as tending toward enabling the worker to get for himself interest and joy in life, and on condition that he prove his fitness for partnership, for the enjoyment of rights, by the way in which he in his turn performs his duties and heartily and nobly recognizes his obligation to others. Now, of course, it ought to be accepted as an axiomatic truth that none of these things can be obtained from an unprosperous business; that if profits are not existent, all talk of sharing them becomes idle. (1917.) *Mem. Ed.* XXI, 88; *Nat. Ed.* XIX, 76.

WORKERS—REWARDS FOR. The toiler, the manual laborer, has received less than justice, and he must be protected, both by law, by custom, and by the exercise of his right to increase his wage; and yet to decrease the quantity and quality of his work will work only evil. There must be a far greater need of respect and reward for the hand worker than we

[664]

now give him, if our society is to be put on a sound basis; and this respect and reward cannot be given him unless he is as ambitious to do the best possible work as is the highest type of brain worker, whether doctor or writer or artist. (1913.) *Mem. Ed.* XXII, 192; *Nat. Ed.* XX, 164.

WORKERS — TREATMENT OF. Everything possible should be done to secure the wage-workers fair treatment. There should be an increased wage for the worker of increased productiveness. Everything possible should be done against the capitalist who strives, not to reward special efficiency, but to use it as an excuse for reducing the reward of moderate efficiency. The capitalist is an unworthy citizen who pays the efficient man no more than he has been content to pay the average man, and nevertheless reduces the wage of the average man; and effort should be made by the government to check and punish him. When labor-saving machinery is introduced, special care should be taken—by the government if necessary—to see that the wage-worker gets his share of the benefit, and that it is not all absorbed by the employer or capitalist. (1913.) *Mem. Ed.* XXII, 554; *Nat. Ed.* XX, 476.

WORKERS — WELFARE OF. The well-being of the wage-worker is a prime consideration of our entire policy of economic legislation. (First Annual Message, Washington, December 3, 1901.) *Mem. Ed.* XVII, 112; *Nat. Ed.* XV, 97.

——————. It is humiliating to think that until very recently we had done nothing whatever to regulate such an industry as that of the manufacture of poisonous matches, and that even yet we have to struggle against that attitude of mind which has shown itself among those judges who have decided against workmen's compensation laws on the ground that they interfere with liberty of contract. The railway employees on any railway doing interstate business can be guaranteed their rights only by the action of the Federal Government, and no greater wrong can be committed against labor than the wrong committed by those who, on the bench or in the legislatures, seek to prevent the Federal Government from having full power in this matter. The Federal Government should pass drastic compensation laws as regards its own employees, and as regards all wage-workers employed in connection with interstate commerce. But as regards labor the field of action is wider for the State governments than for the Federal Government. The legislators in the several States should see to the abolition of the sweat-shop system everywhere; they should secure to the laboring man release from employment for one day in seven; they should secure far-reaching and thoroughgoing workmen's compensation acts, and acts providing for the sanitary inspection of factory, workshop, mine, and home; they should provide suitable and plentiful playgrounds for children in all the cities; they should rigidly supervise the conditions of tenement-house life, should pass and enforce rigid anti-child-labor laws and laws limiting women's labor. (*Outlook*, February 4, 1911.) *Mem. Ed.* XIX, 107; *Nat. Ed.* XVII, 71.

WORKERS. See also CAPITAL; COLLECTIVE BARGAINING; EMPLOYER; EMPLOYMENT; GOVERNMENT EMPLOYEES; INDUSTRIAL ARBITRATION; LABOR; SOCIAL INSURANCE; SOCIALISM; SQUARE DEAL; STRIKES; UNEMPLOYMENT; VIOLENCE; WAGES.

WORKMEN'S COMPENSATION. Workmen should receive certain and definite compensation for all accidents in industry irrespective of negligence. The employer is the agent of the public and on his own responsibility and for his own profit he serves the public. When he starts in motion agencies which create risks for others, he should take all the ordinary and extraordinary risks involved; and the risk he thus at the moment assumes will ultimately be assumed, as it ought to be, by the general public. Only in this way can the shock of the accident be diffused, instead of falling upon the man or woman least able to bear it, as is now the case. The community at large should share the burdens as well as the benefits of industry. (Seventh Annual Message, Washington, December 3, 1907.) *Mem. Ed.* XVII, 509; *Nat. Ed.* XV, 434.

——————. Our present system, or rather no system, works dreadful wrong, and is of benefit to only one class of people—the lawyers. When a workman is injured what he needs is not an expensive and doubtful lawsuit, but the certainty of relief through immediate administrative action. The number of accidents which result in the death or crippling of wage-workers, in the Union at large, is simply appalling; in a very few years it runs up a total far in excess of the aggregate of the dead and wounded in any modern war. No academic theory about "freedom of contract" or "constitutional liberty to contract" should be permitted to interfere with this and similar movements. (Eighth Annual Message, Washington, December 8, 1908.) *Mem. Ed.* XVII, 589-590; *Nat. Ed.* XV, 501-502.

WORKMEN'S COMPENSATION ACT—CONSTITUTIONALITY OF. A typical case [of the triumph of legalism over justice] was the decision rendered but a few months ago by the court of appeals of my own State, the State of New York, declaring unconstitutional the Workmen's Compensation Act. In their decision the judges admitted the wrong and the suffering caused by the practices against which the law was aimed. They admitted that other civilized nations had abolished these wrongs and practices. But they took the ground that the Constitution of the United States, instead of being an instrument to secure justice, had been ingeniously devised absolutely to prevent justice. They insisted that the clause in the Constitution which forbade the taking of property without due process of law forbade the effort which had been made in the law to distribute among all the partners in an enterprise the effects of the injuries to life or limb of a wage-worker. In other words, they insisted that the Constitution had permanently cursed our people with impotence to right wrong, and had perpetuated a cruel iniquity; for cruel iniquity is not too harsh a term to use in describing the law which, in the event of such an accident, binds the whole burden of crippling disaster on the shoulders least able to bear it—the shoulders of the crippled man himself, or of the dead man's helpless wife and children. (Before Ohio Constitutional Convention, Columbus, February 21, 1912.) *Mem. Ed.* XIX, 191; *Nat. Ed.* XVII, 143.

WORKMEN'S COMPENSATION LAWS—NEED FOR. We should have in the national law-books and on the statute-books of every State . . . a far-reaching and thoroughgoing compensation act by which there should be paid automatically a certain specified sum to any man who is crippled in any industry such as railroading and to the kinsfolk of any man who loses his life therein. It should not be left to lawsuits. Lawsuits are objectionable on three different grounds. In the first place, there is always a chance that an excessive amount of damages may be recovered—more than the railroad ought to pay. In the next place, there is always a chance that no damages will be recovered, and, therefore, the man on whose behalf the suit is brought will get nothing; and, finally, the only person certain to benefit from the suit is the lawyer, who is the only person who ought not to have any interest in it. (At Freeport, Ill., September 8, 1910.) *Mem. Ed.* XVIII, 209-210; *Nat. Ed.* XVI, 159-160.

————————. In nation and State alike there should be far-reaching and comprehensive legislation to guarantee safe and healthy conditions for the workmen while at work. In both these regards the workman should not be left to fight for his own interests, and should be explicitly forbidden from making contracts which would imperil these interests. His protection in the place where he works, and his right to compensation if injured, should be guaranteed by the laws of the land. If one of the machines owned by an employer is damaged, the employer has to pay for the damage; and if the man who runs it is hurt, it is just as much the duty of the employer to compensate him as it is to repair the machine. In each case those who use the product will in the end, and quite properly, pay for the damage. (*Outlook*, February 4, 1911.) *Mem. Ed.* XIX, 106; *Nat. Ed.* XVII, 70.

WORKMEN'S COMPENSATION LAWS—PURPOSE OF. When laws like workmen's compensation laws and the like are passed, it must always be kept in mind by the legislature that the purpose is to distribute over the whole community a burden that should not be borne only by those least able to bear it—that is, by the injured man or the widow and orphans of the dead man. (1913.) *Mem. Ed.* XXII, 570; *Nat. Ed.* XX, 490.

WORLD COURT. See INTERNATIONAL COURT.

WORLD LEAGUE. See LEAGUE FOR PEACE; LEAGUE OF NATIONS.

WORLD WAR. It is idle to say that this is not a people's war. The intensity of conviction in the righteousness of their several causes shown by the several peoples is a prime factor for consideration, if we are to take efficient means to try to prevent a repetition of this incredible world tragedy. . . . To each of these peoples the war seems a crusade against threatening wrong, and each man fervently believes in the justice of his cause. Moreover, each combatant fights with that terrible determination to destroy the opponent which springs from fear. It is not the fear which any one of these powers has inspired that offers the difficult problem. It is the fear which each of them genuinely feels. Russia believes that a quarter of the Slav people will be trodden under the heel of the Germans, unless she succeeds. France and England believe that their very existence depends on the destruction of the German menace. Germany believes that unless she can so cripple, and, if possible, destroy her western foes, as to make them harmless in the future, she will be unable hereafter to protect herself against the mighty Slav people on her eastern boundary and will be reduced to a condition of international impotence. Some of her leaders are doubtless influenced by worse motives; but the motives above given are, I believe, those that influence the great mass of Germans, and these are in their essence merely the motives of patriotism, of devotion to one's people and one's native land. (New York *Times,* October 11, 1914.) *Mem. Ed.* XX, 54, 56; *Nat. Ed.* XVIII, 46, 48.

———————. This year we are in the presence of a crisis in the history of the world. In the terrible whirlwind of war all the great nations of the world, save the United States and Italy, are facing the supreme test of their history. All of the pleasant and alluring but futile theories of the pacifists, all the theories enunciated in the peace congresses of the past twenty years, have vanished at the first sound of the drumming guns. The work of all The Hague conventions, and all the arbitration treaties, neutrality treaties, and peace treaties of the last twenty years has been swept before the gusts of war like withered leaves before a November storm. In this great crisis the stern and actual facts have shown that the fate of each nation depends not in the least upon any elevated international aspirations to which it has given expression in speech or treaty, but on practical preparation, on intensity of patriotism, on grim endurance, and on the possession of the fighting edge. (New York *Times,* November 29, 1914.) *Mem. Ed.* XX, 214; *Nat. Ed.* XVIII, 183.

———————. This war is the greatest the world has ever seen. The vast size of the armies, the tremendous slaughter, the loftiness of the heroism shown and the hideous horror of the brutalities committed, the valor of the fighting men and the extraordinary ingenuity of those who have designed and built the fighting machines, the burning patriotism of the peoples who defend their hearthstones and the far-reaching complexity of the plans of the leaders—all are on a scale so huge that nothing in past history can be compared with them.

The issues at stake are elemental. The free peoples of the world have banded together against tyrannous militarism and government by caste. It is not too much to say that the outcome will largely determine, for daring and liberty-loving souls, whether or not life is worth living. A Prussianized world would be as intolerable as a world ruled over by Attila or by Timur the Lame. (Preface dated May 1, 1917.) Mrs. Humphry Ward, *Towards the Goal.* (Scribner's, N. Y., 1917), pp. vii-viii.

———————. At the outbreak of the war our people were stunned, blinded, terrified by the extent of the world disaster. Those among our leaders who were greedy, those who were selfish and ease-loving, those who were timid, and those who were merely short-sighted, all joined to blindfold the eyes and dull the conscience of the people so that it might neither see iniquity nor gird its loins for the inevitable struggle. The moral sense of our people was drugged into stupor by the men in high places who taught us that we had no concern with the causes of this war, that all the combatants were fighting for the same things, that it was our duty to be neutral between right and wrong, that we should look with tepid indifference on the murder of our unarmed men, women, and children, that we ought to be too proud to fight for our just rights, that our proper aim should be to secure peace without victory for the right. (1917.) *Mem. Ed.* XXI, 3; *Nat. Ed.* XIX, 3.

———————. In this great war for righteousness, we Americans have a tremendous task ahead of us. I believe the American people are entirely willing to make any sacrifice, and to render any service, and I believe that they should be explicitly shown how great the service is they are called upon to render, how great the need is that they should unflinchingly face any sacrifice that is made. (*Metropolitan,* September 1917.) *Mem. Ed.* XXI, 32; *Nat. Ed.* XIX, 27.

———————. This is the people's war. It is not the President's war. It is not Congress's war. It is America's war. We are in honor bound in conducting it to stand by every official who does well, and against every official who fails to do well. Any other attitude is servile and unworthy of an American freeman. (*Metropolitan,* January 1918.) *Mem. Ed.* XXI, 282; *Nat. Ed.* XIX, 260.

WORLD WAR—AMERICAN RESPONSIBILITY DURING. All of the terrible iniquities of the past year and a half, including this crowning iniquity of the wholesale slaughter of the Armenians, can be traced directly to the initial wrong committed on Belgium by her

[667]

'invasion and subjugation; and the criminal responsibility of Germany must be shared by the neutral powers, headed by the United States, for their failure to protest when this initial wrong was committed. In the case of the United States additional responsibility rests upon it because its lack of influence for justice and peace during the last sixteen months has been largely due to the course of timid and unworthy abandonment of duty which it has followed for nearly five years as regards Mexico. (To Samuel T. Dutton, Chairman of Committee on Armenian Outrages, November 24, 1915.) *Mem. Ed.* XX, 447; *Nat. Ed.* XVIII, 384.

WORLD WAR — AMERICAN RIGHTS DURING. Submission to an initial wrong means that all protests against subsequent and lesser wrongs are hypocritical and ineffective. Had we protested, in such fashion that our protest was effective, against what was done in Belgium by Germany, and against the sinking of the *Lusitania* by Germany, we could have (and in such case we ought to have) protested against all subsequent and minor infractions of international law and morals, including those which interfered with our commerce or with any other neutral rights. But failure to protest against the first and worst offenses of the strongest wrong-doer made it contemptible, and an act of bad faith, to protest against subsequent and smaller misdeeds; and failure to act (not merely speak or write notes) when our women and children were murdered made protests against interference with American business profits both offensive and ludicrous. (1916.) *Mem. Ed.* XX, 239; *Nat. Ed.* XVIII, 206.

WORLD WAR—AMERICA'S DUTY IN. A deputation of Belgians has arrived in this country to invoke our assistance in the time of their dreadful need. What action our Government can or will take I know not. It has been announced that no action can be taken that will interfere with our entire neutrality. It is certainly eminently desirable that we should remain entirely neutral, and nothing but urgent need would warrant breaking our neutrality and taking sides one way or the other. Our first duty is to hold ourselves ready to do whatever the changing circumstances demand in order to protect our own interests in the present and in the future; although, for my own part, I desire to add to this statement the proviso that under no circumstances must we do anything dishonorable, especially towards unoffending weaker nations. Neutrality may be of prime necessity in order to preserve our own interest, to maintain peace in so much of the world as is not affected by the war, and to conserve our influence for helping toward the re-establishment of general peace when the time comes; for if any outside Power is able at such time to be the medium for bringing peace, it is more likely to be the United States than any other. But we pay the penalty of this action on behalf of peace for ourselves, and possibly for others in the future, by forfeiting our right to do anything on behalf of peace for the Belgians in the present. We can maintain our neutrality only by refusal to do anything to aid unoffending weak powers which are dragged into the gulf of bloodshed and misery through no fault of their own. Of course it would be folly to jump into the gulf ourselves to no good purpose; and very probably nothing that we could have done would have helped Belgium. We have not the smallest responsibility for what has befallen her, and I am sure that the sympathy of this country for the suffering of the men, women, and children of Belgium is very real. Nevertheless, this sympathy is compatible with full acknowledgment of the unwisdom of our uttering a single word of official protest unless we are prepared to make that protest effective; and only the clearest and most urgent National duty would ever justify us in deviating from our rule of neutrality and non-interference. *Outlook,* September 23, 1914, p. 173.

————————. I have been in a very difficult position. I am in opposition to the Administration, and to say how I myself would have acted, when I am not in power and when the action I would have taken is the reverse of that which the present Administration takes, would do harm and not good. This is especially so because the bulk of our people do not understand foreign politics and have no idea about any impending military danger. When I was President, I really succeeded in educating them to a fairly good understanding of these matters, and I believe that if I had been President at the outset of this war they would have acquiesced in my taking the stand I most assuredly would have taken as the head of a signatory nation of the Hague Treaties in reference to the violation of Belgium neutrality. But, of course, I should not have taken such a stand if I had not been prepared to back it up to the end, no matter what course it necessitated; and it would be utterly silly to advocate the Administration taking such a position unless I knew that the Administration would proceed to back up its position. In my articles I spoke very plainly, but I believe with proper reserve and courtesy. (To Sir Edward Grey, October 3, 1914.) *Twenty-Five Years*, by Viscount Grey of Fallodon. (Hodder & Stoughton, London, 1925), II, 139-140.

——————. As a nation, during the past eighteen months we have refused to prepare to defend our own rights by our own strength. We have also refused to say one word against international wrong-doing of the most dreadful character. We have refused to carry out the promises we made in The Hague conventions. We have been guilty of all these mean sins of omission, we are officially told, in the hope that the Administration may secure the empty honor of being a go-between when the belligerents decide to make peace. The actions of the Administration have tended to create such conditions that the "peace" shall be in the interest of the wrong-doer, and at the expense of his helpless victim. It is not right that this nation should be asked thus to shirk its duty to itself and to others in order to secure such a worthless function for any person whatsoever. Our plain duty was to stand against wrong, to help in stamping out the wrong, to help in protecting the innocent who had been wronged. This duty we have ignobly shirked. (*Metropolitan*, October 1915.) *Mem. Ed.* XX, 330; *Nat. Ed.* XVIII, 284.

——————. In this crisis I hold that we have signally failed in our duty to Belgium and Armenia, and in our duty to ourselves. In this crisis I hold that the Allies are standing for the principles to which Abraham Lincoln said this country was dedicated; and the rulers of Germany have, in practical fashion, shown this to be the case by conducting a campaign against Americans on the ocean, which has resulted in the wholesale murder of American men, women, and children, and by conducting within our own borders a campaign of the bomb and the torch against American industries. They have carried on war against our people; for wholesale and repeated killing is war—even though the killing takes the shape of assassination of non-combatants, instead of battle against armed men. (1916.) *Mem. Ed.* XX, 255; *Nat. Ed.* XVIII, 220.

——————. Our country has shirked its clear duty. One outspoken and straightforward declaration by this government against the dreadful iniquities perpetrated in Belgium, Armenia, and Servia would have been worth to humanity a thousand times as much as all that the professional pacifists have done in the past fifty years. (*Metropolitan*, January 1916.) *Mem. Ed.* XX, 306; *Nat. Ed.* XVIII, 262.

——————. We Americans are not, and must not permit ourselves to become, swayed by question of material gain in this war. We must think primarily of our duties. We must keep our minds fixed on what we owe to others, and what we owe to ourselves. We owe a service to humanity. Our sons and brothers at the front pay this service in blood. The rest of us must pay it in money. (September 17, 1918.) *Roosevelt in the Kansas City Star*, 217.

WORLD WAR — AMERICA'S PART IN. For the sake of our own souls, for the sake of the memories of the great Americans of the past, we must show that we do not intend to make this merely a dollar war. Let us pay with our bodies for our souls' desire. Let us, without one hour's unnecessary delay, put the American flag at the battle-front in this great world war for Democracy and civilization, and for the reign of Justice and fair-dealing among the nations of mankind. (To Senator George E. Chamberlain, Spring 1917.) C. R. Robinson, *My Brother Theodore Roosevelt*, 326.

——————. Along many lines of preparation the work here is now going fairly fast— not much of a eulogy when we are in the ninth month of the war. But there cannot be much speed when military efficiency is subordinated to selfish personal politics, the gratification of malice, and sheer wooden-headed folly. (Letter of October 14, 1917.) Theodore Roosevelt, Jr., *Average Americans*. (G. P. Putnam's Sons, N. Y., 1919), p. viii.

——————. America played in the closing months of the war a gallant part, but not in any way the leading part, and she played this part only by acting in strictest agreement with our Allies and under the joint high command. She should take precisely the same attitude at the Peace Conference. We have lost in this war about two hundred and thirty-six thousand men killed and wounded. England and France have lost about seven million. Italy and Belgium and the other Allies have doubtless lost three million more. Of the terrible sacrifice which has enabled the Allies to win the victory, America has contributed just about two per cent. At the end, I personally believe that our intervention was decisive because the combatants were so equally matched and were so weakened by the terrible strain that our money and our enthusiasm and the million fighting men whom we got to the front, even

[669]

although armed substantially with nothing but French field-cannon, tanks, machine-guns, and airplanes, was decisive in the scale. But we could render this decisive aid only because for four years the Allies, in keeping Germany from conquering their own countries, had incidentally kept her from conquering ours. (*Kansas City Star*, November 26, 1918.) *Mem. Ed.* XXI, 442; *Nat. Ed.* XIX, 398.

WORLD WAR—AMERICA'S PURPOSE IN. We are fighting this war for others. But we are also, and primarily, fighting it for ourselves. We wish to safeguard to all civilized nations which themselves do justice to others, the right to enjoy their independence, and therefore to enjoy whatever governmental system they desire. But rightly and properly our first concern is for our own country. Our own welfare is at stake. Our own interests are vitally concerned. We are fighting for the honor of America and for our permanent place among the self-governing nations of mankind. We are fighting for our homes, our freedom, our independence, our self-respect and well-being. We are fighting for our dearest rights, and to avert measureless disaster in the future from the land in which our children's children are to dwell when we are dead. (1917.) *Mem. Ed.* XXI, 5; *Nat. Ed.* XIX, 4.

──────────. We fight for our own rights. We fight for the rights of mankind. This great struggle is fundamentally a struggle for the fundamentals of civilization and democracy. The future of the free institutions of the world is at stake. The free people who govern themselves are lined up against the governments which deny freedom to their people. Our cause is the cause of humanity. But we also have bitter wrongs of our own which it is our duty to redress. Our women and children and unarmed men, going about their peaceful business, have been murdered on the high seas, not once, but again and again and again. With brutal insolence, after having for well nigh two years persevered in this policy, Germany has announced that she will continue it, at our expense and at the expense of other neutrals, more ruthlessly than ever. . . .

I ask that we send a fighting force over to the fighting line at the earliest possible moment, and I ask it in the name of our children and our children's children, so that they may hold their heads high over the memory of what this nation did in the world's great crisis. I ask it for reasons of national morality no less than for our material self-interest. I ask it for the sake of our self-respect, our self-esteem. *Speech by Theodore Roosevelt, Stock Yards Pavilion, Chicago, April 28, 1917.* (National Security League, N. Y., 1917), pp. 5-6.

──────────. We are fighting for humanity; but we are also, and primarily, fighting for our own vital interests. Our army in France will fight for France and Belgium; but most of all it will be fighting for America. Until we make the world safe for America (and incidentally until we make democracy safe in America), it is empty rhetoric to talk of making the world safe for democracy; and no one of these objects can be obtained merely by high-sounding words, or by anything else save by the exercise of hard, grim, common sense in advance preparation, and then by unflinching courage in the use of the hardened strength which has thus been prepared. (*Metropolitan*, September 1917.) *Mem. Ed.* XXI, 22; *Nat. Ed.* XIX, 19.

WORLD WAR — CAUSES OF. Looking back at the real and ultimate causes rather than at the temporary occasions of the war, what has occurred is due primarily to the intense fear felt by each nation for other nations and to the anger born of that fear. Doubtless in certain elements, notably certain militaristic elements, of the population other motives have been at work; but I believe that the people of each country, in backing the government of that country, in the present war have been influenced mainly by a genuine patriotism and a genuine fear of what might happen to their beloved land in the event of aggression by other nations. (New York *Times*, October 18, 1914.) *Mem. Ed.* XX, 60; *Nat. Ed.* XVIII, 51.

WORLD WAR — CONSEQUENCES OF. Unless all history is valueless as a guide, we are going, sooner or later, to have to pay for the enormous destructions of capital in this war. We cannot hope to evade some period of depression. How severe that will be depends largely upon ourselves. We cannot avoid it, but we can make it less severe than it otherwise might be. In this labor and capital must work together—must realize that their problems are alike, and that unless the employer is prosperous, the employee cannot be. Equally so, unless the employee is treated fairly, the employer and the community cannot be prosperous. The partners in the enterprise must realize their responsibilities to each other and act accordingly. (Fall 1917; reported by Leary.) *Talks with T. R. From the diaries of John J. Leary, Jr.* (Houghton Mifflin Co., Boston, 1920), p. 154.

WORLD WAR—ENTRANCE INTO. We did not go to war to make democracy safe, and we did go to war because we had a special grievance. We went to war, because, after two years, during which, with utter contempt of our protests, she had habitually and continually murdered our noncombatant men, women, and children on the high seas, Germany formally announced that she intended to pursue this course more ruthlessly and vigorously than ever. This was the special grievance because of which we went to war, and it was far more than an empty justification for going to war. As you know, my own belief is that we should have acted immediately after the sinking of the *Lusitania*. (At Johnstown, Pa., September 30, 1917.) *Mem. Ed.* XXIV, 511; Bishop II, 436.

WORLD WAR — INTERVENTION IN. The first thing I would like to do . . . would be to interfere in the world war on the side of justice and honesty, by exactly such a league [of neutrals] as you mention. I do not believe in neutrality between right and wrong. I believe in justice. (To Baron Rosen, August 7, 1915.) *Mem. Ed.* XXIV, 461; Bishop II, 392.

——————. The storm that is raging in Europe at this moment is terrible and evil; but it is also grand and noble. Untried men who live at ease will do well to remember that there is a certain sublimity even in Milton's defeated archangel, but none whatever in the spirits who kept neutral, who remained at peace, and dared side neither with hell nor with heaven. They will also do well to remember that when heroes have battled together, and have wrought good and evil, and when the time has come out of the contest to get all the good possible and to prevent as far as possible the evil from being made permanent, they will not be influenced much by the theory that soft and shortsighted outsiders have put themselves in better condition to stop war abroad by making themselves defenseless at home. (New York *Times*, November 29, 1914.) *Mem. Ed.* XX, 216; *Nat. Ed.* XVIII, 185.

WORLD WAR — PARTICIPATION IN. France and England have been fighting the battle of this nation as certainly as they have been fighting for themselves. Every consideration of honor, of self-respect, of self-interest, and self-preservation demand that we Americans throw our full force into this war immediately, without reservation, with entire loyalty to our allies, and with the stern and steadfast determination to fight the war through to a victorious finish. Moreover, we should act at once. We have to atone for three years of folly and indecision.

We are a nation of a hundred millions of people, richer in wealth and resources than any other on the earth. Yet we were so utterly unprepared that although Germany declared war on us seven months ago we are still merely getting ready our strength, we still owe our safety exclusively to the fleets and armies of our hard-pressed and war-worn allies, to whose help we nominally came. (1917.) *Mem. Ed.* XXI, 5; *Nat. Ed.* XIX, 5.

——————. I am certain that as rapidly as possible the various units should be transferred to France for intensive training; that as soon as possible an American force, under the American flag, should be established on the fighting line, should be steadily fed with new men to keep its members to the required point, and steadily reinforced by other units, so that it would be playing a continually more important part in the fighting. It is an ignoble thing for us not to put our men into the fighting line at the earliest possible moment. Such failure will excite derision and may have a very evil effect upon our national future. (To Newton D. Baker, April 22, 1917.) *Mem. Ed.* XXI, 214; *Nat. Ed.* XIX, 202.

——————. In my judgment, the way to render help to the Allies is primarily to wake America to its own shortcomings as regards its own effort, to enlighten it as to the need of making that effort quickly and formidably felt; or in other words, to struggle as hard as possible to increase our weight in the war. It would be a far more difficult thing for me to get our country speeded to action by knowledge of England's effort than to get it speeded to action by knowledge of its own shortcomings and duties. (To Sir Arthur Lee, February 21, 1918.) *Mem. Ed.* XXIV, 514; Bishop II, 439.

WORLD WAR—PEACE SETTLEMENT OF. There are multitudes of professional pacifists in the United States, and of well-meaning but ill-informed persons who sympathize with them from ignorance. There are not a few astute persons, bankers of foreign birth, and others, who wish to take sinister advantage of the folly of these persons, in the interest of Germany. All of these men clamor for immediate peace. They wish the United States to take action for immediate peace or for a truce, under conditions designed to leave Belgium with her wrongs unredressed and in the possession of Germany. They strive to bring about a peace which would contain within itself the elements

[671]

of frightful future disaster, by making no effective provision to prevent the repetition of such wrong-doing as has been inflicted upon Belgium. All of the men advocating such action, including the professional pacifists, the big business men largely of foreign birth, and the well-meaning but feeble-minded creatures among their allies, and including especially all those who from sheer timidity or weakness shrink from duty, occupy a thoroughly base and improper position. (*Independent,* January 4, 1915.) *Mem. Ed.* XX, 183; *Nat. Ed.* XVIII, 157.

───────────. If the United States enters . . . a congress with nothing but a record of comfortable neutrality or tame acquiescence in violated Hague conventions, plus an array of vague treaties with no relation to actual facts, it will be allowed to fill the position of international drum-major and of nothing more; and even this position it will be allowed to fill only so long as it suits the convenience of the men who have done the actual fighting. The warring nations will settle the issues in accordance with their own strength and position. Under such conditions we shall be treated as we deserve to be treated, as a nation of people who mean well feebly, whose words are not backed by deeds, who like to prattle about both their own strength and their own righteousness, but who are unwilling to run the risks without which righteousness cannot be effectively served, and who are also unwilling to undergo the toil of intelligent and hard-working preparation without which strength when tested proves weakness. (New York *Times,* November 29, 1914.) *Mem. Ed.* XX, 202; *Nat. Ed.* XVIII, 173.

───────────. Peace in Europe will be made by the warring nations. They and they alone will in fact determine the terms of settlement. The United States may be used as a convenient means of getting together; but that is all. If the nations of Europe desire peace and our assistance in securing it, it will be because they have fought as long as they will or can. It will not be because they regard us as having set a spiritual example to them by sitting idle, uttering cheap platitudes, and picking up their trade, while they have poured out their blood like water in support of the ideals in which, with all their hearts and souls, they believe. For us to assume superior virtue in the face of the war-worn nations of the Old World will not make us more acceptable as mediators among them. Such self-consciousness on our part will not impress the nations who have sacrificed and are sacrificing all that is dearest to them in the world, for the things that they believe to be the noblest in the world. (New York *Times,* November 29, 1914.) *Mem. Ed.* XX, 215; *Nat. Ed.* XVIII, 185.

───────────. What is needed at this time is not the compounding of felony by the discussion of terms with the felons, but the concentration and speedy development of our whole strength so as to overwhelm Germany in battle and to dictate to her the peace of unconditional surrender. . . . Our present business is to fight, and to continue fighting until Germany is brought to her knees. Our next business will be to help guarantee the peace of justice for the world at large, and to set in order the affairs of our own household. (1918.) *Mem. Ed.* XXI, 256, 257; *Nat. Ed.* XIX, 238, 239.

───────────. The one absolute essential for our people is to insist that this war be seen through at no matter what cost, until it is crowned with the peace of overwhelming victory for the right.

There are foolish persons who still say we ought to make peace now, a negotiated peace, and then be good friends with Germany. These persons with all the lessons of the last four years fresh in their minds still cling pathetically to the belief that if only we will show that we are harmless Germany will begin to love us. (*Metropolitan,* January 1918.) *Mem. Ed.* XXI, 284; *Nat. Ed.* XIX, 261.

───────────. We must win the war as speedily as possible. But we must set ourselves to fight it through no matter how long it takes, with the resolute determination to accept no peace until, no matter at what cost, we win the peace of overwhelming victory. The peace that we win must guarantee full reparation for the awful cost of life and treasure which the Prussianized Germany of the Hohenzollerns has inflicted on the entire world; and this reparation must take the form of action that will render it impossible for Germany to repeat her colossal wrong-doing. (Lafayette Day exercises, New York City, September 6, 1918.) *Mem. Ed.* XXI, 408; *Nat. Ed.* XIX, 370.

───────────. When the American people speak for unconditional surrender, it means that Germany must accept whatever terms the United States and its Allies think necessary in order to right the dreadful wrongs that have been committed and to safeguard the world for at least a generation to come from another attempt by Germany to secure world dominion. Unconditional surrender is the reverse of a negotiated peace. The interchange of notes, which has been going on between our government and the governments of Germany and Austria during the last three weeks, means, of course, if persisted in, a negotiated peace. It is the abandonment of force and the substitution of negotiation. This fact should be clearly and truthfully stated by our leaders, so that the American people may decide with their eyes open which course they will follow. (Kansas City *Star*, October 26, 1918.) *Mem. Ed.* XXI, 418; *Nat. Ed.* XIX, 378.

──────────. It is our business to act with our Allies and to show an undivided front with them against any move of our late enemies. I am no Utopian. I understand entirely that there can be shifting alliances, I understand entirely that twenty years hence or thirty years hence we don't know what combination we may have to face, and for this reason I wish to see us preparing our own strength in advance and trust to nothing but our own strength for our own self-defense as our permanent policy. But in the present war we have won only by standing shoulder to shoulder with our Allies and presenting an undivided front to the enemy. It is our business to show the same loyalty and good faith at the Peace Conference. Let it be clearly understood that the American people absolutely stand behind France, England, Italy, Belgium, and the other Allies at the Peace Conference, just as she has stood with them during the last eighteen months of war. Let every difference of opinion be settled among the Allies themselves and then let them impose their common will on the nations responsible for the hideous disaster which has almost wrecked mankind. (Kansas City *Star*, November 26, 1918.) *Mem. Ed.* XXI, 442; *Nat. Ed.* XIX, 399.

WORLD WAR. *See also* AMERICANS, HYPHENATED; AVIATION; BAKER, NEWTON D.; BELGIUM; CONSCIENTIOUS OBJECTORS; CONTRABAND; DEMOCRACY; DRAFT; ENGLAND; FOURTEEN POINTS; FRANCE; GERMANY; HAGUE CONVENTIONS; JAPAN; LEAGUE OF NATIONS; LIBERTY LOANS; *Lusitania;* MILITARISM; MILITARY SERVICE; MUNITIONS; NEUTRAL RIGHTS; NEUTRALITY; PACIFISM; PEACE; PERSHING, JOHN J.; PREPAREDNESS; PROFITEERS; ROOSEVELT DIVISION; RUSSIA; SUBMARINE WARFARE; TREATIES; UNPREPAREDNESS; VOLUNTEER SYSTEM; WILLIAM II; WILSON, WOODROW.

WRESTLING. *See* JIU JITSU.

Y

YELLOW JOURNALISM. *See* JOURNALISM; MUCK-RAKING; PRESS.

"YELLOW PERIL." I have just your feeling about the Japanese Nation. As for their having a yellow skin, if we go back two thousand years we will find that to the Greek and Roman the most dreaded and yet in a sense the most despised barbarian was the white-skinned, blue-eyed and red- or yellow-haired barbarian of the North—the men from whom you and I in a large part derive our blood. It would not seem possible to the Greek and Roman of that day that the northern barbarian should ever become part of the civilized world—his equal in civilization. (To D. B. Schneder, June 19, 1905.) Tyler Dennett, *Roosevelt and the Russo-Japanese War.* (Doubleday, Page & Co., Garden City, N. Y., 1925), p. 159.

"YELLOW PERIL." *See also* JAPAN.

YELLOWSTONE PARK. It is of the utmost importance that the Park shall be kept in its present form as a great forestry preserve and a National pleasure ground, the like of which is not to be found on any other continent than ours; and all public-spirited Americans should join with "Forest and Stream" in the effort to prevent the greed of a little group of speculators, careless of everything save their own selfish interests, from doing the damage they threaten to the whole people of the United States, by wrecking the Yellowstone National Park. So far from having this Park cut down it should be extended, and legislation adopted which would enable the military authorities who now have charge of it to administer it solely in the interests of the whole public, and to punish in the most rigorous way people who trespass upon it. The Yellowstone Park is a park for the people and the representatives of the people should see that it is molested in no way. (To editor of *Forest and Stream,* December 5, 1892.) Robert Underwood Johnson, *Remembered Yesterdays.* (Little, Brown & Co., Boston, 1923), p. 309.

──────────. The Yellowstone Park is something absolutely unique in the world, so far as I know. Nowhere else in any civilized country is there to be found such a tract of veritable wonderland made accessible to all visitors, where at the same time not only the scenery of the wilderness, but the wild creatures of the Park are scrupulously preserved;

[673]

the only change being that these same wild creatures have been so carefully protected as to show a literally astounding tameness. The creation and preservation of such a great natural playground in the interest of our people as a whole is a credit to the nation.... This Park was created, and is now administered, for the benefit and enjoyment of the people. The government must continue to appropriate for it especially in the direction of completing and perfecting an excellent system of driveways. But already its beauties can be seen with great comfort in a short space of time and at an astoundingly small cost, and with the sense on the part of every visitor that it is in part his property, that it is the property of Uncle Sam and therefore of all of us. The only way that the people as a whole can secure to themselves and their children the enjoyment in perpetuity of what the Yellowstone Park has to give is by assuming the ownership in the name of the nation and by jealously safeguarding and preserving the scenery, the forests, and the wild creatures. (At laying of cornerstone of Gateway to Yellowstone Park, Gardiner, Montana, April 24, 1903.) *Presidential Addresses and State Papers* I, 324-325.

YELLOWSTONE PARK. *See also* FOREST RESERVES.

YOUNG MEN'S CHRISTIAN ASSOCIATIONS. The Young Men's Christian Associations and the Young Women's Christian Associations, which have now spread over all the country, are invaluable because they can reach every one. I am certainly a beneficiary myself, having not infrequently used them as clubs or reading-rooms when I was in some city in which I had but little or no personal acquaintance.

In part they develop the good qualities of those who join them; in part they do what is even more valuable, that is, simply give opportunity for the men or women to develop the qualities themselves. In most cases they provide reading-rooms and gymnasiums, and therefore furnish a means for a man or woman to pass his or her leisure hours in profit or amusement as seems best. The average individual will not spend the hours in which he is not working in doing something that is unpleasant, and absolutely the only way permanently to draw average men or women from occupations and amusements that are unhealthy for soul or body is to furnish an alternative which they will accept. (*Century*, October 1900.) *Mem. Ed.* XV, 428; *Nat. Ed.* XIII, 375.

——————. Your organization recognizes the vital need of brotherhood, the most vital of all our needs here in this great republic. The existence of a Young Men's or Young Women's Christian Association is certain proof that some people at least recognize in practical shape the identity of aspiration and interest, both in things material and in things higher, which with us must be widespread through the masses of our people if our national life is to attain full development. (Before Young Men's Christian Association, New York City, December 30, 1900.) *Mem. Ed.* XV, 527-528; *Nat. Ed.* XIII, 492.

YOUTH. *See* BOYHOOD, ROOSEVELT'S; BOYS; CHARACTER; CHILD LABOR; CHILDREN; EDUCATION; JUVENILE COURTS; PLAYGROUNDS; PUBLIC SCHOOLS.

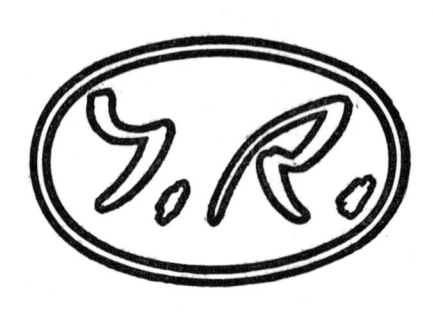

ROOSEVELT MEMORIAL ASSOCIATION

THE ROOSEVELT MEMORIAL ASSOCIATION was founded in March 1919 and received a federal charter a year later. The aims of the Association are as follows:

I—The establishment of a suitable and adequate memorial in the District of Columbia;

II—The acquisition, development and maintenance of a park in the town of Oyster Bay, New York;

III—The establishment and endowment of an incorporated society to promote the development and application of the ideals of Theodore Roosevelt.

I. Memorial in Washington

The memorial in Washington, to this son of the North and the South, is a ninety-acre wooded island in the Potomac, situated almost equally distant from the Lincoln Memorial and the Lee Mansion at Arlington. Theodore Roosevelt Island, formerly known as Analostan Island, is a wild yet accessible playground such as the great lover of the outdoor world would have cherished. The Association has presented the area to the United States government which has cleared and developed it under the direction of the distinguished landscape architect, Mr. Frederick Law Olmsted, acting for the Roosevelt Association, and will open it to the public in the near future.

II. Park at Oyster Bay

In fulfillment of the *Second Aim* of the Association, 35 acres of land were purchased in the town of Oyster Bay. A memorial park, designed by the noted landscape architect, Mr. Charles N. Lowrie, was completed and dedicated May 30, 1928. The walks, playgrounds, shrubbery, trees, flower beds, and band-stand contribute to make this a civic center of beauty and practical value to the community which Theodore Roosevelt called home, where he lived as a boy, where he found deep and sure peace as a statesman, and now rests in the simplicity of true greatness.

III. Perpetuation of Theodore Roosevelt's Ideals

To realize the *Third Aim*—the development and application of the ideals of Theodore Roosevelt—the Association has been active in a wide field.

1. Roosevelt House

The ideal background for this undertaking was supplied when the Woman's Roosevelt Memorial Association purchased, restored and furnished Theodore Roosevelt's birthplace at 28 East 20th Street, New York City, and invited the Roosevelt Memorial Association to share these premises. Roosevelt House is a national museum as well as a natural gathering-place for his admirers. It contains an auditorium in which an important part of the educational work of both Associations is carried on. More than 20,000 visitors, who annually come to Roosevelt House, catch inspiration there for public spirited citizenship and sound patriotism.

2. New York City Schools

Into this setting of Theodore Roosevelt's childhood home, enriched with trophies and records of his adventurous life, the Woman's Roosevelt Memorial Association annually brings over 8,000 school children from the New York City schools. In the restored rooms and the Museums and through the motion pictures they are brought into close touch—and many of them perhaps the only close touch—with the home and the life of a great American. The Association annually presents bronze medallions for character, exceptional scholarship or service to the school, in approximately 800 grade and high schools in the New York public school system.

3. Research Library and Museum

A research library, containing 10,000 books and pamphlets, 2,500 cartoons, countless clippings and 5,000 photographs, has been collected and is maintained in the same building, under the direction of a trained librarian. A private study is available for visiting scholars, and an information service is maintained.

The Association has gathered priceless memorabilia of Mr. Roosevelt, which are exhibited at Roosevelt House and in the American Museum of Natural History.

Micro-film copies of all letters by Theodore Roosevelt in the collection in the Manuscripts Division of the Library of Congress—a total of over 50,000 items—have recently been acquired by the Association and are available to scholars under the same conditions as the Roosevelt Collection in the Library of Congress.

4. Motion Picture Library

At Roosevelt House has been assembled the Roosevelt Motion Picture Library, the first biographical motion picture library in the world. Thousands of feet of negative and positive film relating to Mr. Roosevelt's career and photographed on four continents has been collected and assembled in the following productions:

T. R. Himself	The River of Doubt
Roosevelt, the Great Scout	Return from Europe
Roosevelt, Friend of the Birds	Roosevelt at Home
The Roosevelt Dam	Roosevelt in the Great War
The Panama Canal	President Roosevelt

These productions, dealing with the principal phases of Theodore Roosevelt's life, dramatize vividly the breadth of his interests and the vigor of his personality; and are available, free of charge, for use in schools.

5. The Theodore Roosevelt Medals

The Association annually awards from one to three medals for distinguished public service. These awards are made in fields especially associated with Theodore Roosevelt's life and work. These fields are:

Administration of public office; development of public and international law; promotion of industrial peace; conservation of natural resources; promotion of social justice; the study of natural history; promotion of outdoor life; promotion of the national defense; American literature; leadership of youth and the development of American character; expression of the pioneer virtues; distinguished public service by a private citizen.

The medals have been presented, since the awards were established in 1923, to the following:

LOUISA LEE SCHUYLER	CHARLES EVANS HUGHES	WILLIAM ALLEN WHITE
HENRY FAIRFIELD OSBORN	FRANK M. CHAPMAN	WILLIAM HALLOCK PARK
LEONARD WOOD	CHARLES A. LINDBERGH	HELEN KELLER
GIFFORD PINCHOT	HERBERT PUTNAM	ANNE SULLIVAN MACY
GEORGE BIRD GRINNELL	OWEN WISTER	JAMES HARDY DILLARD
MARTHA BERRY	OWEN D. YOUNG	CARTER GLASS
OLIVER WENDELL HOLMES	RICHARD EVELYN BYRD	ROBERT MOSES
CHARLES WILLIAM ELIOT	WILLIAM GREEN	GEO. WASHINGTON CARVER
ELIHU ROOT	HASTINGS HORNELL HART	FRANK R. MCCOY
DANIEL CARTER BEARD	HAMLIN GARLAND	CARL SANDBURG
WILLIAM SOWDEN SIMS	BENJAMIN NATHAN CARDOZO	GRENVILLE CLARK
ALBERT J. BEVERIDGE	C. HART MERRIAM	HOMER FOLKS
JOHN BASSETT MOORE	ROBERT ANDREWS MILLIKAN	CHESTER H. ROWELL
HERBERT HOOVER	STEPHEN VINCENT BENÉT	
JOHN J. PERSHING	SAMUEL A. SEABURY	

6. National Re-Dedication

The Association gave the initiative and provided the initial funds for the launching of the National Re-Dedication movement, aimed to help Americans "to understand what liberty means and what it takes to keep it." The movement, which aroused warm public interest and brought together representatives of twenty leading national organizations, including the Boy Scouts of America, the American Federation of Labor, the Federal Council of Churches, the National Conference of Christians and Jews, the Camp Fire Girls, the National Council of Women, the Jewish Welfare Board and the Workers Education Bureau, culminated, on December 15th, 1938, the 147th anniversary of the ratification of the Bill of Rights, in extensive observances throughout the country, among them a national broadcast of exceptional brilliance and power, in which the leading figures of the motion picture world took part.

7. Publications

A list of works published is printed in the front of this volume. In addition, the Association, recognizing the importance of developing in young Americans an understanding of American life and political institutions, and recognizing also that the adolescent mind is reached most effectively through the imagination, has initiated a series of one-act historical plays called "America in Action," for use in schools without payment of royalty. The plays are being written by professional playwrights and published by the Dramatists Play Service, a non-profit affiliate of the Authors League of America.

The following plays have been published:

Haven of The Spirit, by Merrill Denison. About Roger Williams and religious tolerance.
Ship Forever Sailing, by Stanley Young. About the Mayflower Pact.
We'd Never Be Happy Otherwise, by E. P. Conkle. On Elijah Lovejoy and the freedom of the press.
Seeing The Elephant, by Dan Totheroh. Showing the courage of the Forty-Niners.
Enter Women, by Olivia Howard Dunbar. Showing the courageous founders of the principles of women's rights.
Fires at Valley Forge, by Harold Harper. Washington shows American youth how it can win liberty.
A Salute to the Fourth, by Elizabeth McFadden. On race tolerance and patriotism.
Franklin and the King, by Paul Green. On the American attitude toward liberty.

Among others in preparation are:
Young Hickory, by Stanley Young.
The United States vs. Susan B. Anthony, by Merrill Denison.
The Three Royal Rs, by Mary Thurman Pyle.
The Declaration and Thomas Jefferson, by Melvin Levy.
Common Sense, by Ridgely Torrence.

A definitive edition of *The Letters of Theodore Roosevelt,* under the editorship of Herbert Ronald Ferleger, is now in preparation. This collection, which will run to about ten volumes, will include the best letters written over a period of fifty years by one of America's great letter-writers. A nation-wide search for letters, beyond the collection now at Roosevelt House in microfilm form, is now in progress. The collected edition of the letters promises to be one of the major historical projects of this decade. The first volume will be ready for publication late in 1942 and the others will follow shortly thereafter.

ROOSEVELT MEMORIAL ASSOCIATION
ROOSEVELT HOUSE
28 East 20th Street   New York City

Officers

Honorary Vice President
HIRAM W. JOHNSON

President
JAMES R. GARFIELD

Vice-Presidents
FRANK R. MCCOY   WILL H. HAYS

Treasurer
ALBERT H. WIGGIN

Secretary and Director
HERMANN HAGEDORN

Assistant Secretary
GISELA WESTHOFF

Board of Trustees

HORACE ALBRIGHT
HENRY J. ALLEN
JOSEPH W. ALSOP
JOSEPH W. ALSOP, JR.
JOHN F. BERMINGHAM
WALTER F. BROWN
WILLIAM M. CHADBOURNE
GRENVILLE CLARK
MRS. THOMAS L. CLARKE
WILLIAM H. COWLES
W. J. CRAWFORD, JR.
R. J. CUDDIHY
FREDERICK M. DAVENPORT
F. TRUBEE DAVISON
ARTHUR FLEMMING
HENRY P. FLETCHER
W. CAMERON FORBES
JAMES A. GARFIELD
JAMES R. GARFIELD
DAVID M. GOODRICH
ULYSSES S. GRANT, 3D.
LLOYD C. GRISCOM
ARTHUR GUITERMAN
HERMANN HAGEDORN
CHAUNCEY J. HAMLIN
JAMES G. HARBORD
WILLIAM HARD
ALBERT BUSHNELL HART
WILL H. HAYS
DAVID HINSHAW
FRANK J. HOGAN
MRS. SARAH C. W. HOPPIN
HIRAM W. JOHNSON
MRS. HARRY ORLAND KING
PAUL H. KING
FRANK KNOX

CHRISTOPHER LA FARGE
MRS. GRANT LA FARGE
JOHN J. LEARY, JR.
LUCIUS N. LITTAUER
EARLE LOOKER
FRANK R. MCCOY
CHARLES MERZ
GUY MURCHIE
TRUMAN H. NEWBERRY
WALTER H. NEWTON
ACOSTA NICHOLS
JOHN C. O'LAUGHLIN
MRS. JAMES RUSSELL PARSONS
GEORGE W. PERKINS
GIFFORD PINCHOT
HAROLD T. PULSIFER
RAYMOND ROBINS
CHESTER H. ROWELL
GEORGE RUBLEE
JOHN M. SCHIFF
ALBERT SHAW
MRS. ALBERT G. SIMMS
HOWARD C. SMITH
ALBERT A. SPRAGUE
PHILIP B. STEWART
HENRY L. STIMSON
MARSHALL STIMSON
HENRY L. STODDARD
ROGER W. STRAUS
JULIAN STREET
MARK SULLIVAN
MRS. WILLIAM BOYCE THOMPSON
RICHARD WELLING
WILLIAM ALLEN WHITE
ALBERT H. WIGGIN
JOHN G. WINANT